HUMAN RESOURCE MANAGEMENT IN CANADA
THIRD EDITION

HUMAN RESOURCE MANAGEMENT IN CANADA
THIRD EDITION

Thomas H. Stone
Oklahoma State University

Noah M. Meltz
University of Toronto

DRYDEN

A Division of Holt, Rinehart and Winston of Canada, Limited

Toronto Montreal Orlando Fort Worth San Diego
Philadelphia London Sydney Tokyo

Copyright © 1993
Holt, Rinehart and Winston of Canada, Limited
All rights reserved

No part of this publication may be reproduced or transmitted in any form or by any means, electronic or mechanical, including photocopy, recording, or any information storage and retrieval system, without permission in writing from the publisher.

Requests for permission to make copies of any part of the work should be mailed to: Permissions, College Division, Holt, Rinehart and Winston of Canada, Limited, 55 Horner Avenue, Toronto, Ontario M8Z 4X6.

Every reasonable effort has been made to acquire permission for copyright material used in this text, and to acknowledge all such indebtedness accurately. Any errors and omissions called to the publisher's attention will be corrected in future printings.

Canadian Cataloguing in Publication Data
Stone, Thomas H.
   Human resource management in Canada

3rd ed.
First ed. published under title: Personnel management in Canada.
Includes index.
ISBN 0-03-922797-9

1. Personnel management. 2. Personnel management – Canada. I. Meltz, Noah M. II. Title. III. Title: Personnel management in Canada.

HF5549.S76 1993   658.3   C92-093323-8

Editorial Director: Scott Duncan
Acquisitions Editor: Donna Muirhead
Developmental Editor: Cheryl Teelucksingh
Editorial Assistant: Tracey Syvret
Director of Publishing Services: Jean Lancee
Editorial Manager: Marcel Chiera
Editorial Co-ordinator: Semareh Al-Hillal
Production Manager: Sue-Ann Becker
Production Co-ordinator: Denise Wake
Copy Editor: Lenore d'Anjou
Permissions Editor: Claudia Kutchukian
Cover and Interior Design: Dave Peters
Typesetting and Assembly: Compeer Typographic Services Limited
Printing and Binding: John Deyell Company Limited

Cover Art: *Currency*, by Ritchie Donaghue. Used with permission.

∞ This book was printed in Canada on acid-free paper.

1 2 3 4 5   97 96 95 94 93

This edition is dedicated to
Lena Meltz
and to
Thomas B. Stone and Minnie E. Stone

PREFACE

Human resource management (HRM) has become a strategic function for both private and public organizations in the 1990s. This enhanced role for HRM has arisen from positive and negative developments. The positive developments include the growing recognition that the effective management of human resources is perhaps the most significant way organizations can gain an international competitive advantage. At the same time, a more highly educated work force is demanding more recognition and involvement in the workplace. Employees want to be treated better, and research shows that better treatment pays off. Organizations that view their employees as strategic resources tend to be more effective in their other activities. The challenge for organizations in the 1990s is to balance considerations of efficiency with those of fair treatment of employees.

The negative reasons for the enhanced role of human resource management relate to the deep recession of the early 1990s. The recession has been accompanied by a major restructuring: massive plant closures and layoffs as well as major restructuring within organizations. These developments have required strategic human resource planning to take a long-term view of what is best for an organization and what this means for employees.

Changes in government legislation have long had an important impact on the human resource function, and they continue to do so. Perhaps the most significant changes in the early 1990s have been the spread of employment equity and pay equity programs as well as the increasing liberalization of worker compensation programs.

All of these developments combine to create new expectations for the role of human resource management. Those in the field have begun to integrate more strategic decision making into the practice of HRM, and it is on these new directions that the third edition of *Human Resource Management in Canada* focusses.

A number of significant changes have been made to this edition. They include:

1. The concept of strategic human resource management has been introduced into the performance of HRM functions. The concept not only receives separate recognition but is also used to provide an overview of how all of the HRM functions can be linked together. From recruitment to compensation, strategic HRM considerations have to be taken into account.
2. The material has been updated to include both changes in employment legislation and the results of effective practice. The findings from recent research are presented as well.

3. A new feature, HRM in Action, has been added. Every chapter has at least one of these feature boxes, which are a way of highlighting special developments in each of the HRM functions.
4. In response to users' and reviewers' suggestions, the order of the career planning and the performance appraisal chapters has been reversed. This better positioning permits training to flow into career planning and performance appraisal into compensation.
5. Review questions and suggestions for further reading are presented at the end of every chapter.
6. A video package is available to accompany the textbook. The package includes one video for each of the five parts of the book. These integrated videos illustrate the issues managers and human resource professionals face in the performance of their job: how to deal with sexual harassment in the workplace, recruiting, training, pay equity, and assisting employees in balancing work with family responsibilities.
7. In addition to the substantive changes in the text and the accompanying material, this edition features a completely new design intended to make the text more readable and highlight the major developments in each HRM function.

The Plan of the Book

The textbook contains five parts, which follow the flow of the normal sequence of the human resource management functions in any organization. The first part is concerned with the HRM context. It includes strategic decisions that every organization has to make, given the supply of various types of workers and the laws and regulations that govern how employees must be treated.

The second part presents the steps necessary to identify the number and type of employees who have to be recruited or released in response to changes in demand, and how this may be done. Part Three is concerned with the development of employees, those recently hired and those who have been with the organization for a long time. Employee development includes orientation, training and development, career planning, and performance appraisal.

Part Four focusses on employee maintenance—that is, the fair treatment of employees in their ongoing relationships. The major components of employee maintenance are compensation, benefits, health and safety, and labour relations. The final part looks ahead at the issues that will face human resource management in the future.

A Word to the Instructor

This textbook is designed to be used in a modular way. An instructor can either present the HRM functions in the sequence we have adopted or arrange another order that seems appropriate. For example, some instructors may prefer to combine the details on HRM considerations (part of Chapter 1) with the summing-up presented in Chapter 16. An instructor using the textbook for a one-term course may assign only selected chapters and depend on the overview of all of the functions provided by the introductory chapter. We have tried to make the material flexible so it can be adapted for varying needs and approaches.

We are excited about this third edition because it contains new features and much new material while retaining the essential material and approach that have contributed to the success of the earlier editions. We have endeavoured to incorporate the suggestions of both the users of past editions and the reviewers of this edition. We welcome your comments and advice.

A WORD TO THE STUDENT

More than 70 000 people in Canada are employed as human resource managers or officers. The main aspects of their jobs and what they are attempting to achieve are described in this textbook. Clearly, we can not capture every detail and all the variations in practice across Canada, especially given the differences in employment legislation from province to province. We want you to understand, however, what is involved in human resource management and how this function has become central in organizations. We welcome your comments and suggestions.

ACKNOWLEDGEMENTS

The third edition of *Human Resource Management in Canada* has been enriched by the comments and suggestions of many colleagues, reviewers, and students. The reviewers for this edition deserve thanks for their many insightful comments and suggestions. They were

Andrew Weber	*Carleton University*
Terry Hercus	*University of Manitoba*
Joseph Rose	*McMaster University*
Peggy Miller	*John Abbott College*
Andrew Templer	*University of Windsor*
Ed Roach	*Algonquin College*
Barrie Gibbs	*Simon Fraser University*
Doug Bicknell	*University of Saskatchewan*
Normand Fortier	*University of Ottawa*
John Holzman	*Algonquin College*
Anne Harper	*Humber College*
Ian Sakinofsky	*Ryerson Polytechnical Institute*
Murray Lapp	*Pay Equity Commission*

Special thanks to Ed Roach and John Holzman, who prepared the video cases and video teaching notes, and to Lydia Dragunas, who contributed to the instructor's manual.

We would like to acknowledge the skill and effort of all the staff in the College Division at HBJ-Holt Canada for their contribution to the book. Thanks to Scott Duncan for his input, and to Donna Muirhead for reminding us of the "big picture" when we got bogged down in the details of revising this new edition. Many thanks also to Cheryl Teelucksingh for her guidance and hard work in developing the manuscript, and her patience and valuable advice in general; and to Semareh Al-Hillal, who expertly incorporated the revisions and dealt with many last-minute changes, oversaw the copy editing and proofreading, and put in long hours to see this complex project through to completion. Lenore d'Anjou was the copy editor for the first edition of the textbook and we are pleased that she rejoined us for this edition and made excellent suggestions, as always. We also appreciate the assistance of the following: Peter Dungan, University of Toronto; Ross Finlay, Human Resources Professionals Association of Ontario; Tom Fournier, Bureau of Labour Information, Labour Canada; Stephen Gibson, Pay Equity Trends Inc.; Ian Macredi, Statistics Canada; Wayne Roth, Employment and Immigration Canada; and Neil Walker, Profit Sharing of Canada.

Professor Stone wishes to extend special thanks to Carolyn Mangum and Wanxiang Jiang, the graduate students who assisted with the research for this edition. Maurene Langston also deserves thanks for typing the manuscript.

Professor Meltz would like to thank the staff of the Jean and Dorothy Newman Industrial Relations Library, Centre for Industrial Relations, University of Toronto. In particular, he would like to thank Bruce Pearce, who provided so much valuable assistance and insight. Elizabeth Perry of the Centre's library was extremely helpful, as were Vicki Darlington, Monica Hypher, and Hilary Shelton. The Centre's other staff members, the Director, Professor Morley Gunderson; his assistant, Deborah Campbell; the Acting Director, Professor Frank Reid; and Carolynn Alton and Joan Ng all helped to complete the invaluable role of the Centre. Special thanks also go to Professor Meltz's secretary at Woodsworth College, University of Toronto, Ms. Eva Hollander. The many pressures on the Principal of the College were eased considerably by the able and enthusiastic assistance of Ms. Hollander.

Since every endeavour is a family event, Professor Meltz wants to cite the support of his wife, Rochelle, and his children, David, Jonathan, Toba, and Hillel. His son David assisted in several important ways. First, he helped to check and update some of the material. Second, he conducted a complete review of the entire manuscript and made many valuable suggestions for revisions. Third, David, along with Michael Hattin, prepared a 43-page update to accompany the second edition as a bridge before the completion of the third edition. It was David's idea that there be an update to accompany the second edition. Professor Stone thanks his father, Thomas B. Stone, who contributed both material and ideas for the text's cases. He also wishes to thank his wife, Lana, for her contributions to earlier editions and for the many hours spent proofreading and correcting galleys for this edition.

Professor Meltz dedicated the first edition to both his parents. The second edition was dedicated to the memory of his father, Jack Henry Meltz, who had just passed away. This third edition is dedicated to his mother, Lena Meltz, for her perseverance in all tasks. Professor Stone is dedicating this edition to his parents, Thomas B. Stone and Minnie E. Stone.

All Statistics Canada information was provided through the co-operation of Statistics Canada. Readers wishing further information may obtain copies of related publications by mail from Publications Sales, Statistics Canada, Ottawa, Ontario K1A 0T6, by phone at 1-613-951-7277 or national toll-free 1-800-267-6677. You may also fax your order by dialling 1-613-951-1584.

A NOTE FROM THE PUBLISHER

Thank you for selecting *Human Resource Management in Canada*, Third Edition by Thomas H. Stone and Noah M. Meltz. The authors and publisher have devoted considerable time to the careful development of this book. We appreciate your recognition of this effort and accomplishment.

We want to hear what you think about *Human Resource Management in Canada*. Please take a few minutes to fill in the stamped reply card at the back of the book. Your comments and suggestions will be valuable to us as we prepare new editions and other books.

Brief Contents

PART ONE THE HUMAN RESOURCE MANAGEMENT CONTEXT   1

    CHAPTER 1 HUMAN RESOURCE MANAGEMENT:
                   A NEW STRATEGIC FUNCTION   2
    CHAPTER 2 THE HUMAN ASSET   39
    CHAPTER 3 THE LEGAL ENVIRONMENT   91

PART TWO PLANNING AND STAFFING   131

    CHAPTER 4 HUMAN RESOURCE PLANNING   132
    CHAPTER 5 JOB ANALYSIS   184
    CHAPTER 6 RECRUITING: ATTRACTING APPLICANTS   234
    CHAPTER 7 SELECTION   279

PART THREE EMPLOYEE DEVELOPMENT   343

    CHAPTER 8 ORIENTATION   344
    CHAPTER 9 TRAINING AND DEVELOPMENT   372
    CHAPTER 10 CAREER PLANNING   435
    CHAPTER 11 PERFORMANCE APPRAISAL   476

PART FOUR EMPLOYEE MAINTENANCE   537

    CHAPTER 12 COMPENSATION   538
    CHAPTER 13 BENEFITS   613
    CHAPTER 14 EMPLOYEE HEALTH AND SAFETY   657
    CHAPTER 15 LABOUR RELATIONS   709

**PART FIVE ISSUES AND CHALLENGES IN
             HUMAN RESOURCE MANAGEMENT**   771

    CHAPTER 16 THE FUTURE OF HUMAN RESOURCE MANAGEMENT   772

INDEX   793

CONTENTS

PART ONE THE HUMAN RESOURCE MANAGEMENT CONTEXT — 1

CHAPTER 1
HUMAN RESOURCE MANAGEMENT: A NEW STRATEGIC FUNCTION — 2
- HUMAN RESOURCE MANAGEMENT AS A STRATEGIC FUNCTION — 3
- FIVE MAJOR AREAS OF HRM RESPONSIBILITY — 6
- HRM FUNCTIONS — 7
- HRM IN ACTION ▸ TO BE EFFECTIVE, MANAGERS MUST LISTEN TO THEIR EMPLOYEES — 11
- ASSIGNMENT OF HRM RESPONSIBILITIES — 16
- THE HRM PROFESSION — 17
- THE CONTEXT OF CHANGE AFFECTING HRM — 22
- MAJOR ISSUES HR MANAGERS WILL FACE IN THE 1990s — 27
- HRM IN ACTION ▸ STRATEGIC PLANNING AND COMPETITIVENESS — 28
- REVIEW QUESTIONS — 31
- CASE 1.1 ▸ LABATT'S MANAGERS REORGANIZE FROM WITHIN — 31
- CASE 1.2 ▸ GAMMA COMPANY: A FAILURE OF HR PLANNING AND CONSULTATION — 34
- NOTES — 36
- SUGGESTIONS FOR FURTHER READING — 38

CHAPTER 2
THE HUMAN ASSET — 39
- THE LABOUR FORCE — 40
- HRM IN ACTION ▸ DEMOGRAPHICS AND LABOUR COSTS — 49
- INDIVIDUAL BEHAVIOUR AND JOB PERFORMANCE — 55
- OLDER EMPLOYEES: A VALUABLE RESOURCE — 74
- SUMMARY — 78
- REVIEW QUESTIONS — 79
- PROJECT IDEAS — 79
- CASE 2.1 ▸ TRENDS IN EMPLOYEE ATTITUDES: DIFFERENCES BETWEEN CANADIAN AND AMERICAN WORKERS — 80
- CASE 2.2 ▸ CHALLENGE AT RED MAPLE FOODS — 83
- NOTES — 86
- SUGGESTIONS FOR FURTHER READING — 90

CHAPTER 3
THE LEGAL ENVIRONMENT — 91
- LEGISLATION AND JURISDICTION — 93
- HUMAN RIGHTS: CONCEPTS AND PROHIBITIONS — 96

HRM IN ACTION ▸ How Employers Can Avoid Liability for Workplace Harassment	101
Affirmative Action and Employment Equity	108
Employment Standards Legislation	112
Summary	119
Review Questions	119
Project Ideas	120
Case 3.1 ▸ National's Job Equity Starts at the Top	121
Case 3.2 ▸ Management and Complaints of Sexual Harassment	122
Notes	125
Suggestions for Further Reading	128
Video Case ▸ Sexual Harassment in the Workplace	129

Part Two   Planning and Staffing   131

Chapter 4
Human Resource Planning	132
The Need for Human Resource Planning	134
Purposes of Human Resource Planning	135
Relation to Other HRM Functions	137
HRM IN ACTION ▸ Unplanned Cutbacks Can Be Like Fad Diets	140
The Human Resource Planning Process	141
Projecting Human Resource Supply	143
Forecasting Future Human Resource Needs	149
Comparing Forecast Needs with Projections of Supply	156
Planning Policies and Programs	158
Evaluating Human Resource Planning Effectiveness	169
The HRM Audit	170
Summary	172
Review Questions	173
Project Ideas	173
Case 4.1 ▸ Ontario Hydro's Corporate Planning Process	174
Case 4.2 ▸ Evaluating HR Departments	176
Notes	178
Suggestions for Further Reading	182

Chapter 5
Job Analysis	184
Job Analysis: A Definition	185
Job-Related Definitions	186
Relation to Other HRM Functions	189
Responsibilities for Job Analysis	194
HRM IN ACTION ▸ Job Analysis and Expert Systems	195
Methods of Job Analysis	196

JOB ANALYSIS PROBLEMS AND ISSUES	210
SUMMARY	214
REVIEW QUESTIONS	214
PROJECT IDEAS	215
CASE 5.1 ▸ JOB TASK INVENTORY: A TOOL FOR ORGANIZATIONAL CHANGE?	215
CASE 5.2 ▸ JOB ANALYSIS AT ST. JUDE'S HOSPITAL: AVOIDING GENDER BIAS	223
NOTES	231
SUGGESTIONS FOR FURTHER READING	233

CHAPTER 6
RECRUITING: ATTRACTING APPLICANTS	**234**
THE ROLE OF RECRUITING	236
RECRUITING ACTIVITIES	240
FACTORS AFFECTING THE APPLICANT-ATTRACTION PROCESS	242
HRM IN ACTION ▸ RCMP MAKES PROGRESS IN MINORITY RECRUITING	249
RECRUITING METHODS AND SOURCES	251
EVALUATING THE RECRUITING EFFORT	264
SUMMARY	268
REVIEW QUESTIONS	269
PROJECT IDEAS	269
CASE 6.1 ▸ RECRUITING AT NOVATEL COMMUNICATIONS	271
CASE 6.2 ▸ EXPANSION AT QUINAN STORES	273
NOTES	275
SUGGESTIONS FOR FURTHER READING	278

CHAPTER 7
SELECTION	**279**
SELECTION: DEFINITION AND PROCESS	281
RELATION TO OTHER HRM FUNCTIONS	284
THE ROLE OF SELECTION IN ORGANIZATIONAL EFFECTIVENESS	286
VALIDATING PREDICTORS	289
SELECTION INSTRUMENTS AND PROCEDURES	298
HRM IN ACTION ▸ SELECTING TEAM MEMBERS AT HONDA AND MAZDA	302
SELECTION OF MANAGERIAL TALENT	321
THE UTILITY OF SELECTION	323
SUMMARY	326
REVIEW QUESTIONS	326
PROJECT IDEAS	327
CASE 7.1 ▸ DISPUTED SELECTION AT SUNNYBROOK	328
CASE 7.2 ▸ FLYER INDUSTRIES: BUILDING A BETTER BUS	329
APPENDIX 7A ▸ ESTIMATING UTILITY GAINS OF A PREDICTOR	331
NOTES	333
SUGGESTIONS FOR FURTHER READING	337

VIDEO CASE ▸ PATAGONIA	**338**

Part Three Employee Development 343

Chapter 8
Orientation 344
- Orientation: A Definition 346
- Relation to Other HRM Functions 346
- How Orientation Contributes to Organizational Effectiveness 347
- Orientation and the Socialization Process 349
- HRM in Action ▸ Realistic Job Previews: Uppers and Downers 358
- Orientation Programs and Procedures 359
- Orientation in Practice 362
- Evaluation of Orientation Programs 363
- Summary 364
- Review Questions 364
- Project Ideas 364
  - Case 8.1 ▸ The Eight-Week Orientation Program 365
  - Case 8.2 ▸ Firefighting Dropouts 368
- Notes 369
- Suggestions for Further Reading 371

Chapter 9
Training and Development 372
- The Growth of Training and Development 374
- The Role of T&D in Organizational Strategy and Effectiveness 377
- Relation to Other HRM Functions 380
- Responsibilities for Training and Development 382
- Determining Training and Development Needs 383
- Specifying Training Objectives 387
- Choosing a Training Program 388
- Training and Development Methods and Aids 400
- HRM in Action ▸ Beyond Interactive Video: Virtual Reality 406
- Implementing the Training Program 413
- Training Programs in Practice 414
- Evaluating the Training Program 419
- Summary 422
- Review Questions 422
- Project Ideas 423
  - Case 9.1 ▸ Training and Development at Deli-Delite 424
  - Case 9.2 ▸ Organization of Training for Northern Telecom Teams 428
- Notes 430
- Suggestions for Further Reading 434

Chapter 10
Career Planning 435
- Reasons for Career Planning 436
- Relation to Other HRM Functions 440

WHAT PEOPLE WANT FROM THEIR CAREERS	442
ELEMENTS OF CAREER PLANNING PROGRAMS	445
CAREER PLANNING PROGRAMS	452
CEIC AIDS FOR CAREER PLANNING	454
FACILITATING CAREER PLANNING AND DEVELOPMENT	455
CAREER PLANNING ISSUES	461
HRM IN ACTION ▸ ACCOMMODATING A CHANGING WORK FORCE	462
SUMMARY	465
REVIEW QUESTIONS	465
PROJECT IDEAS	466
CASE 10.1 ▸ TUITION AID AND TURNOVER AT WESTFELD CONSTRUCTION	466
CASE 10.2 ▸ WORK AND FAMILY ISSUES	468
NOTES	471
SUGGESTIONS FOR FURTHER READING	475

CHAPTER 11
PERFORMANCE APPRAISAL — 476

PERFORMANCE APPRAISAL: A DEFINITION	477
THE PURPOSES OF PERFORMANCE APPRAISAL	478
RELATION TO OTHER HRM FUNCTIONS	481
RESPONSIBILITIES FOR PERFORMANCE APPRAISAL	482
DESIGNING AN APPRAISAL SYSTEM	482
GENERAL REQUIREMENTS OF PERFORMANCE APPRAISAL SYSTEMS	484
PERFORMANCE APPRAISAL METHODS	486
HRM IN ACTION ▸ PARTNERSHIP APPRAISAL	498
A PERFORMANCE APPRAISAL SYSTEM: CORNING, INC.	506
IMPLEMENTING AN APPRAISAL SYSTEM	509
THE APPRAISAL INTERVIEW	513
COLLECTING AND STORING APPRAISAL DATA	520
SUMMARY	521
REVIEW QUESTIONS	522
PROJECT IDEAS	522
CASE 11.1 ▸ PERFORMANCE REVIEW AT BERGHOFF'S	523
CASE 11.2 ▸ PERFORMANCE MONITORING AT BELL CANADA	525
NOTES	527
SUGGESTIONS FOR FURTHER READING	532
VIDEO CASE ▸ ALL IN A DAY'S WORK	533

PART FOUR EMPLOYEE MAINTENANCE — 537

CHAPTER 12
COMPENSATION — 538

COMPENSATION: A DEFINITION	539
COMPENSATION AND ORGANIZATIONAL EFFECTIVENESS	539

COMPENSATION RESPONSIBILITIES	542
RELATION TO OTHER HRM FUNCTIONS	542
MAJOR LAWS AFFECTING COMPENSATION	545
PAY SURVEYS	546
HRM IN ACTION ▸ PAYING BY SKILL	548
JOB EVALUATION SYSTEMS	554
PRICING THE PAY STRUCTURE: ASSIGNING PAY TO JOBS	564
USING PAY TO MOTIVATE EMPLOYEES	570
CONTROLLING COMPENSATION COSTS	580
PAY EQUITY	583
HRM IN ACTION ▸ PAY EQUITY AT THE ROYAL BANK	591
COMPENSATION ISSUES AND INNOVATIONS	594
SUMMARY	597
REVIEW QUESTIONS	597
PROJECT IDEAS	598
CASE 12.1 ▸ PAY EQUITY AT *THE OTTAWA CITIZEN*	599
CASE 12.2 ▸ SALARY PROGRESSION AT SHELL CANADA'S SARNIA CHEMICAL PLANT	605
NOTES	608
SUGGESTIONS FOR FURTHER READING	612

CHAPTER 13
BENEFITS — 613

GROWTH OF EMPLOYEE BENEFITS	614
HOW BENEFITS CONTRIBUTE TO ORGANIZATIONAL EFFECTIVENESS	616
RELATION TO OTHER HRM FUNCTIONS	619
BENEFITS AND THE HRM PROFESSIONAL	621
CATEGORIES OF BENEFITS AND TYPES OF PROTECTION	623
UNIVERSAL BENEFITS	624
MANDATORY BENEFITS	627
DISCRETIONARY BENEFITS FOR EMPLOYEE PROTECTION	632
HOLIDAY AND VACATION PAY	637
EMPLOYEE SERVICE BENEFITS	639
CAFETERIA BENEFITS: AN INDIVIDUALIZED APPROACH	640
HRM IN ACTION ▸ THE EVOLUTIONARY WAY TO FLEXIBLE BENEFITS	641
CONTROLLING BENEFIT COSTS	645
ISSUES IN THE BENEFITS AREA	645
SUMMARY	648
REVIEW QUESTIONS	648
PROJECT IDEAS	649
CASE 13.1 ▸ INDEXED PENSIONS AT INCO	650
CASE 13.2 ▸ ENHANCING PRODUCTIVITY THROUGH ON-SITE CHILD CARE	651
NOTES	652
SUGGESTIONS FOR FURTHER READING	656

Chapter 14
Employee Health and Safety — 657
- Organizational Benefits of a Safe and Healthy Workplace — 658
- Relation to Other HRM Functions — 660
- Health and Safety Responsibilities — 665
- The Ontario Occupational Health and Safety Act — 666
- Workers' Compensation — 675
- Ensuring a Safe and Healthy Workplace — 677
- Special Health Problems — 686
- HRM in Action ▸ Should Compensation Benefits Be Paid for Work Stress? — 691
- HRM in Action ▸ Drug Testing at Imperial Oil — 696
- Summary — 699
- Review Questions — 699
- Project Ideas — 700
  - Case 14.1 ▸ Employee Fitness at Canada Life — 700
  - Case 14.2 ▸ A Workplace Policy for AIDS — 702
- Notes — 703
- Suggestions for Further Reading — 707

Chapter 15
Labour Relations — 709
- Unions: A Definition — 710
- Labour Relations and Public Policy — 711
- Labour Relations and Organizational Effectiveness — 717
- Relation to Other HRM Functions — 718
- Responsibilities for Labour Relations — 720
- Labour Union Goals — 722
- Labour Unions: Structure — 723
- The Transition from Employee Relations to Labour Relations — 727
- HRM in Action ▸ CAW Gains Voluntary Recognition from Team-Based CAMI Plant — 736
- Collective Bargaining — 740
- The Grievance Procedure — 743
- Dissatisfaction among Union Members — 746
- Improving Labour Relations — 747
- HRM in Action ▸ Employee Involvement at Inmont — 752
- Summary — 754
- Review Questions — 755
- Project Ideas — 755
  - Case 15.1 ▸ Unions Unite Forces against Northern Telecom — 756
  - Case 15.2 ▸ Meeting Employee Needs for Flexibility — 759
- Notes — 761
- Suggestions for Further Reading — 765

Video Case ▸ An Even Break — 767

PART FIVE   ISSUES AND CHALLENGES IN HUMAN RESOURCE MANAGEMENT   771

CHAPTER 16
THE FUTURE OF HUMAN RESOURCE MANAGEMENT   772
- HUMAN RESOURCE MANAGEMENT AS A STRATEGIC FUNCTION   772
- HRM IN ACTION ▸ KeepRite Gains from Co-operation   775
- WHAT LIES AHEAD?   779
- SUMMARY   785
- REVIEW QUESTIONS   785
- PROJECT IDEAS   786
- NOTES   786
- SUGGESTIONS FOR FURTHER READING   787

VIDEO CASE ▸ QUAD GRAPHICS, INC.   788

INDEX   793

ORGANIZATIONAL GOALS AND OBJECTIVES AND STRATEGIC PLANNING
Survival and growth
Productivity
Profits
Service

JOB ANALYSIS
Provides planners with jobs' requirements for human resources

STRATEGIC HUMAN RESOURCE ANALYSIS
Uses HRM expertise and experience to assist in developing organizational objectives and to propose alternatives to obtain these objectives

HUMAN RESOURCE PLANNING
Specifies number and kind of employees needed

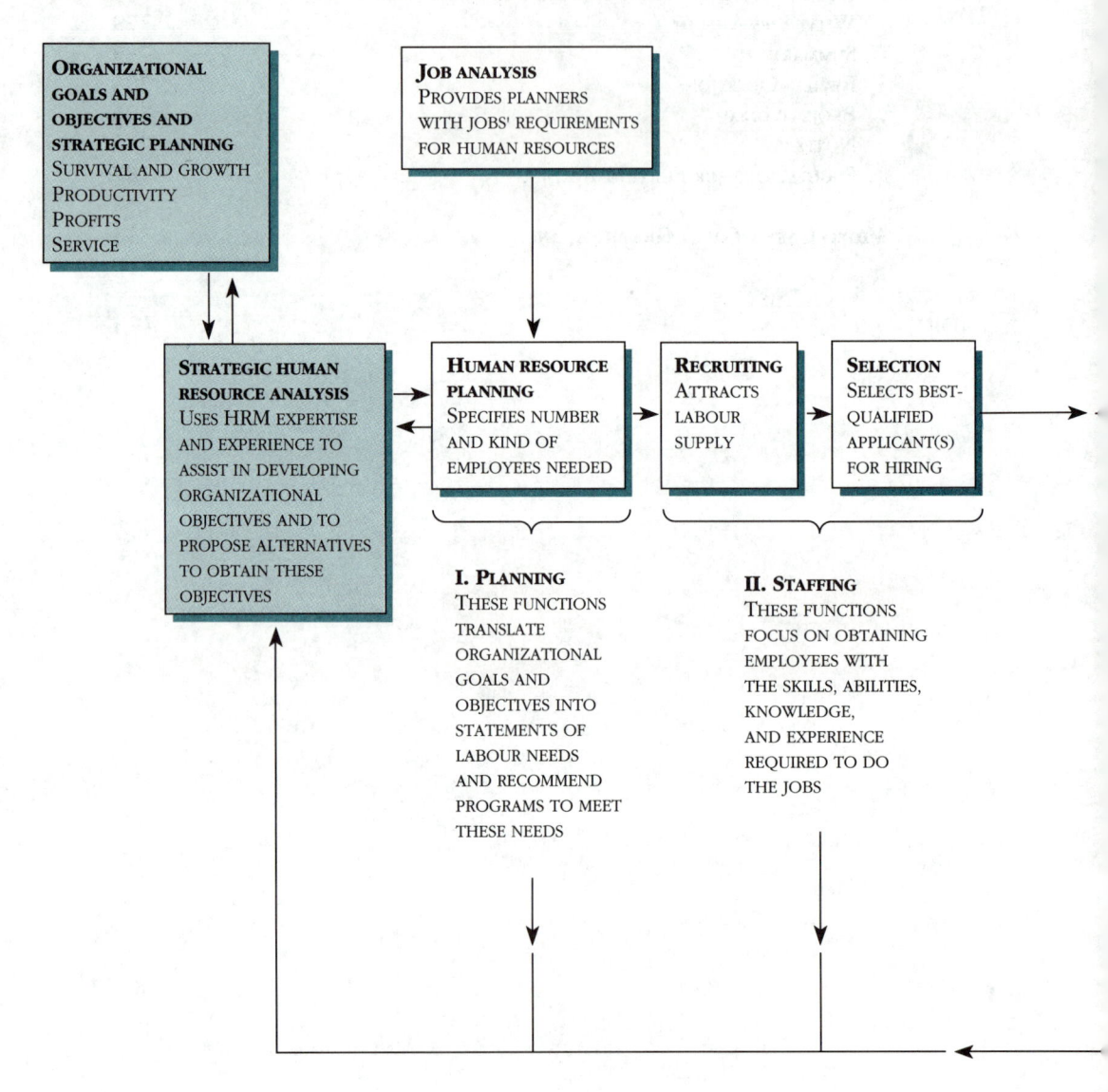

RECRUITING
Attracts labour supply

SELECTION
Selects best-qualified applicant(s) for hiring

I. PLANNING
These functions translate organizational goals and objectives into statements of labour needs and recommend programs to meet these needs

II. STAFFING
These functions focus on obtaining employees with the skills, abilities, knowledge, and experience required to do the jobs

Input from major areas of HRM responsibility

PART ONE

THE HUMAN RESOURCE MANAGEMENT CONTEXT

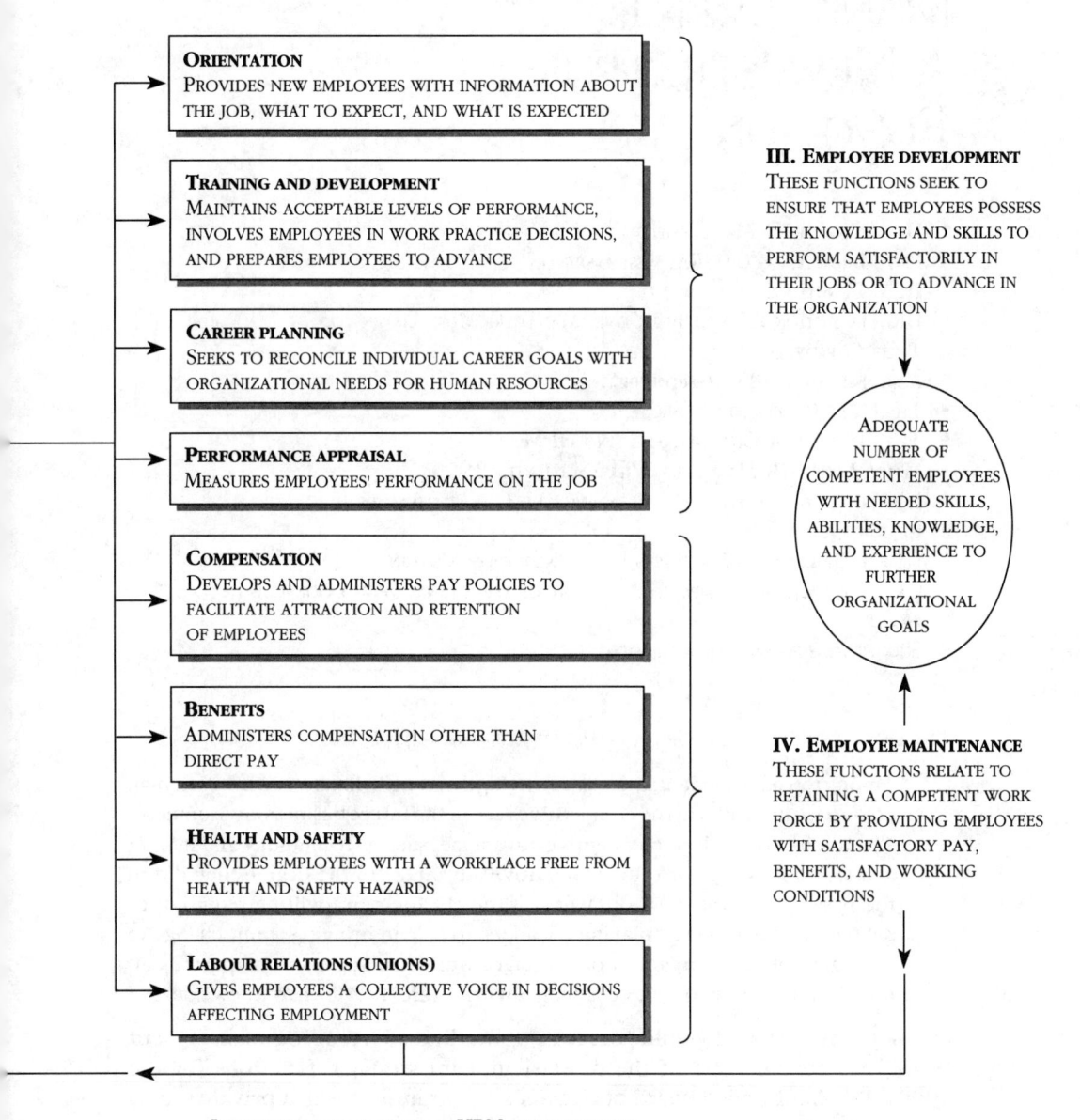

ORIENTATION
Provides new employees with information about the job, what to expect, and what is expected

TRAINING AND DEVELOPMENT
Maintains acceptable levels of performance, involves employees in work practice decisions, and prepares employees to advance

CAREER PLANNING
Seeks to reconcile individual career goals with organizational needs for human resources

PERFORMANCE APPRAISAL
Measures employees' performance on the job

III. EMPLOYEE DEVELOPMENT
These functions seek to ensure that employees possess the knowledge and skills to perform satisfactorily in their jobs or to advance in the organization

COMPENSATION
Develops and administers pay policies to facilitate attraction and retention of employees

BENEFITS
Administers compensation other than direct pay

HEALTH AND SAFETY
Provides employees with a workplace free from health and safety hazards

LABOUR RELATIONS (UNIONS)
Gives employees a collective voice in decisions affecting employment

Adequate number of competent employees with needed skills, abilities, knowledge, and experience to further organizational goals

IV. EMPLOYEE MAINTENANCE
These functions relate to retaining a competent work force by providing employees with satisfactory pay, benefits, and working conditions

Input from major areas of HRM responsibility

CHAPTER 1

HUMAN RESOURCE MANAGEMENT: A NEW STRATEGIC FUNCTION

- HUMAN RESOURCE MANAGEMENT AS A STRATEGIC FUNCTION
- FIVE MAJOR AREAS OF HRM RESPONSIBILITY
- HRM FUNCTIONS
- HRM IN ACTION ▸ TO BE EFFECTIVE, MANAGERS MUST LISTEN TO THEIR EMPLOYEES
- ASSIGNMENT OF HRM RESPONSIBILITIES
- THE HRM PROFESSION
- THE CONTEXT OF CHANGE AFFECTING HRM
- MAJOR ISSUES HR MANAGERS WILL FACE IN THE 1990s
- HRM IN ACTION ▸ STRATEGIC PLANNING AND COMPETITIVENESS
- REVIEW QUESTIONS
- CASE 1.1 ▸ LABATT'S MANAGERS REORGANIZE FROM WITHIN
- CASE 1.2 ▸ GAMMA COMPANY: A FAILURE OF HR PLANNING AND CONSULTATION
- NOTES
- SUGGESTIONS FOR FURTHER READING

THE CONFERENCE BOARD OF CANADA REPORTED in May 1989:

> Among top management, there is a growing awareness that it is the firm's human resources that will win the competitive race in the future business environment. The traditional tools of competitive advantage, such as technology and market access, no longer afford the competitive advantage to the degree they did in the past. . . . In this environment . . . the HR function [will be required] to become a change agent, playing a leadership role in bringing about change in management style, organizational design, work structures and corporate culture. Meeting these complex challenges will require HRM to chart a new course.[1]

For both private and public organizations, human resource management (HRM) has become one of the most significant strategic functions for the 1990s. The Conference Board of Canada's report indicates that private sector firms can no longer count on basic technology to give them an edge because it can now be copied by competitors more quickly than ever. Therefore, firms are increasingly coming to rely on the ability to attract, retain, and motivate employees with drive, talent, and skills as the key to success in a competitive environment. Developing that ability is one aspect of the human resource management function in organizations.

This HRM task is clearly crucial for private sector organizations, and there is a growing awareness of its importance in public organizations. Although government departments, universities, hospitals, and the like have no formal profit motive, pressure is intensifying on all public sector organizations to provide services at reduced costs. Since costs in the public sector are primarily wages and salaries, HRM clearly has a strategic task in the public as well as the private sector.

What this strategic role is, how it has changed, and how it can be enhanced is the subject of this book. In exploring these topics, the text gives the student an understanding of human resource management and of the diverse functions of HRM professionals in helping organizations manage their most important resource — people. Specifically, the book describes methods and approaches HRM professionals use to acquire, develop, retain, and motivate the human resources needed in today's highly competitive environment. The forces of global competition—made stronger by the 1989 Canada–U.S. Free Trade Agreement and perhaps soon to be made even more so by a Mexico–U.S.–Canada trade agreement — of increased legislative pressure, and of changes in labour force demography demand that HRM professionals anticipate and initiate programs and practices that lead to optimal utilization of human resources. They must work both as developers of corporate strategies and as partners with line managers. This book, therefore, presents the most effective HRM methods and approaches and describes the current practices of many of the more progressive organizations. Because excellent human resource management is essential for organizational success, it is suggested that HRM concepts, methods, and issues be studied by all business students, regardless of major or specialty.

HUMAN RESOURCE MANAGEMENT AS A STRATEGIC FUNCTION

The expeditious use of scarce and valued resources, including human resources, is called *organizational effectiveness*, and every organization strives to achieve it. Yet organizational effectiveness has a variety of components. Arnold and Feldman list eight: profitability, growth, resource acquisition, adaptability, innovation, productivity, customer and client satisfaction, and employee satisfaction and commitment.[2] Senior management decides which components of organizational effectiveness are to be stressed in the firm's overall strategic goals and objectives.

Human resource managers in modern organizations participate in senior management decision making, determining the mix of organizational effectiveness components; they also put in place policies and programs to attain the agreed-on strategic goals and objectives.

Thus, HRM combines those practices traditionally associated with personnel administration and involvement in strategic decision making at the highest levels of an organization. The traditional practices are those of planning, developing, and administering policies and programs designed to make the best use of the organization's human resources. The strategic function involves not only analyzing and weighing the human resource implications of strategic decisions (such as entry into new product lines, mergers, and plant closures) but also making strategic decisions based on human resource analysis. For example, in the process of deciding whether to embark on a new product line in the next decade, the organization assesses its existing and potential human resources to determine whether the line could be cost-competitive. Assessment of the human resource implications of the change might also lead to suggestions for modifications in the product line to make better use of special skills in the organization's work force.

This emphasis on the strategic function of human resource management is both enlarging its role and making its practitioners ever more vital to the organization. Georgiades describes the change in the HRM function as equivalent to a shift in focus "from throwing lifebelts to drowning men to walking upstream and finding out who is throwing them off the bridge and why."[3] The HRM function is becoming proactive rather than reactive.

The Development of HRM

The shift to a strategic approach in HRM is a new development. Traditionally, personnel management was purely a staff function, with duties delegated by line management. World War I and industrial psychology contributed to the growth and stature of HRM insofar as both led to the creation of group-administered, paper-and-pencil intelligence and ability tests. Such tests enabled personnel professionals to increase organizational effectiveness quickly and inexpensively by screening out less qualified job applicants.

The growth of unions in the years before World War II created a need for expertise in bargaining and administering labour contracts. While this need contributed to the growth and importance of the HRM field, labour relations represented a reactive and often adversarial function, rather than a proactive, co-operative one. The World War II period brought rapid improvements in the training and development area. Larger and more progressive companies saw training and development as an additional means of increasing organizational effectiveness.

In the 1960s and 1970s, HRM received a further boost with the renewed growth of trade unions, particularly among public sector employees in government, education, and health.[4] The increased unionization meant the recruitment of staff trained in industrial relations to counsel management prior to collective bargaining, to conduct the bargaining, and to administer the collective agreements (contracts) with the unions. The negotiations were more difficult in this period because of the sharp increase in the number of strikes and in the work time lost during them. (Canada became one of the world's leaders in overall time lost per employee.[5] A part of this increase is attributable to the growth of unions, especially in the public sector, and to the fact that employers were unaccustomed to the new kinds of demands being made on the human resource management functions.)

In the early 1980s Canada experienced the deepest recession since the Great Depression. The watchword of organizations became *downsizing*, a euphemism for laying people off. Employment in manufacturing in Canada fell 15 percent from the beginning of the recession in mid-1981 to its official end in December 1982.[6] For human resource (HR) managers, the unenviable task was to administer the layoffs yet maintain productivity and morale and attempt to preserve the organization's skill levels sufficiently to meet the subsequent economic upturn.

By the mid-1980s, the pressures on HR managers came from the growth of employment standards provisions, human rights and employment equity policies, and pay equity legislation. In addition, both management and unions were increasingly recognizing the importance of training.[7]

Then came the recession of the early 1990s, whose effects on the economy and on the HRM function differed from those of the 1981–82 recession. The earlier downturn had spread across Canada; the new hard times had a relatively greater impact on central Canada, particularly Ontario, where the number of plant closings rose to record highs and the unemployment rate, which had been the lowest in Canada, skyrocketed. The situation was also difficult vis-à-vis Canada's largest trading partner, the United States, itself gripped by recession. High interest rates enhanced the value of the Canadian dollar in terms of the U.S. dollar. The free trade agreement appears to have had negative effects on many branch plants. For human resource managers, the task was often administering not just layoffs but plant closings and major consolidations. In the public sector, many provinces imposed zero or low wage rate increases. Job security became a major issue there as well as in the private sector. And simultaneously, the issue of Canada's ability to compete internationally was raising questions about the skills and wage levels of the country's work force.

The combination of competitive pressures, changes in employment standards and human rights legislation, demographic changes associated with an aging population, and a more highly educated work force has resulted in HRM's becoming a strategic function in the 1990s. The increase in the political power of trade unions has led to greater emphasis being placed on the HRM role in giving advice on the implications of policies, particularly those related to changes in labour legislation.[8] The Conference Board of Canada reports that the most important issue HRM executives identified for the 1988–93 period is linking human resource planning to the strategic business plan. This issue is of top importance because the survey shows that 84 percent of HRM executives are full contributing members in their organization's strategic planning process and participate in senior management planning meetings. Seventy-six percent of senior human resource managers reported to the chief executive officer in 1988, and 12 percent to the corporate vice-president. More than three-quarters of the HR managers responding to the Conference Board survey said that the human resource function wielded greater influence within their organization in 1988 than it had five years earlier.[9]

OTHER CHANGES

Students should be aware of three additional developments in the HRM field in recent years. First, there is a trend away from performing the mechanical functions that used to be identified as personnel components, such as handling payroll and benefits. Some firms are transferring these functions to separate units within the finance department or even contracting them out.[10]

Second, as a result of the recession of the early 1990s, which produced a return to basics and cost-effectiveness as an HRM concern, there is a growing emphasis on measuring the costs and benefits of alternative HRM policies and programs. Despite the difficulty of fully determining the financial benefits of all human resource programs, the active participation of HR managers in strategic planning increasingly means assuming responsibility for the measurable "bottom-line" impact of what they do.

Third, the HRM field is becoming increasingly professionalized. Practitioners in Ontario have created a professional designation, Certified Human Resources Professional (CHRP), and in the process of doing so, changed the name of their association from the Personnel Association of Ontario to the Human Resources Professionals Association of Ontario. (The objectives of this association are presented later in this chapter.) Whether HRM professionals in other provinces follow with similar legislation remains to be seen. Nevertheless, the largest group of HRM professionals in Canada now has a certified professional designation and a mechanism for people to acquire it.

FIVE MAJOR AREAS OF HRM RESPONSIBILITY

The major areas of responsibility in human resource management are (1) strategic analysis, (2) planning, (3) staffing, (4) employee development, and (5) employee maintenance. These five areas and their related HRM functions have the common objective of ensuring that the organization's goals and objectives are consistent with what its human resources can attain and that these goals can be furthered by the staffing, development, and maintenance of its employees.

Figure 1.1 shows a model of these responsibilities and functions. Although each function has been assigned to a particular area of HRM responsibility, some functions serve a purpose in more than one of the five. For example, performance appraisal measures employees' performance for development purposes as well as for salary administration (a part of the employee maintenance responsibility). The compensation function facilitates retention of employees and also attracts potential employees to the organization (a part of the staffing responsibility). While the figure presents a logical schema for listing HRM functions according to major areas of responsibility, it is only one of a number of ways that they might be organized.

The starting point for the model is the organizational goals and objectives specified by top management. Strategic human resource analysis is a part both of determining these goals and objectives and of developing the overall strategy to attain them. This strategy is derived from general HRM expertise as well as the organization's performance experience in the other four areas of responsibility.

Planning functions, including human resource planning and job analysis, translate strategy into statements of labour needs (number and types of employees needed). Designing and recommending programs to meet these needs is also part of planning.

The third area, staffing, includes the recruiting and selection functions. It requires a strategy for attracting employees with the requisite skills, abilities, knowledge, and experience to do the job.

Employee development is the fourth major area of HRM responsibility. After workers have been hired (and often after they have been on the job for a fair amount of time), activities in this area seek to ensure that they possess the knowledge and skills to perform their jobs satisfactorily. Also important here are concern with individuals' career plans and the company's efforts to prepare some employees for positions of more responsibility within the organization. Included in the employee development area are the HRM functions of orientation; training and development, including employee involvement; performance appraisal; and career planning.

The maintenance of human resources — retaining an optimal number of competent employees — is the fifth major area of HRM responsibility. Employee maintenance refers to providing employees with adequate pay and benefits for their labour; with good, safe working conditions; and with other desirable aspects of employment, such as a voice in decisions affecting human resource policies. Accordingly, HRM functions of major importance to employee maintenance are compensation, benefits, health and safety, and labour relations.

HRM FUNCTIONS

Individual HRM functions are summarized in Figure 1.1 and described briefly in this section.

STRATEGIC HUMAN RESOURCE ANALYSIS

Strategic human resource analysis has two major aspects: (1) participating with other senior managers in formulating the organization's strategic goals

FIGURE 1.1
The Role of Human Resource Management

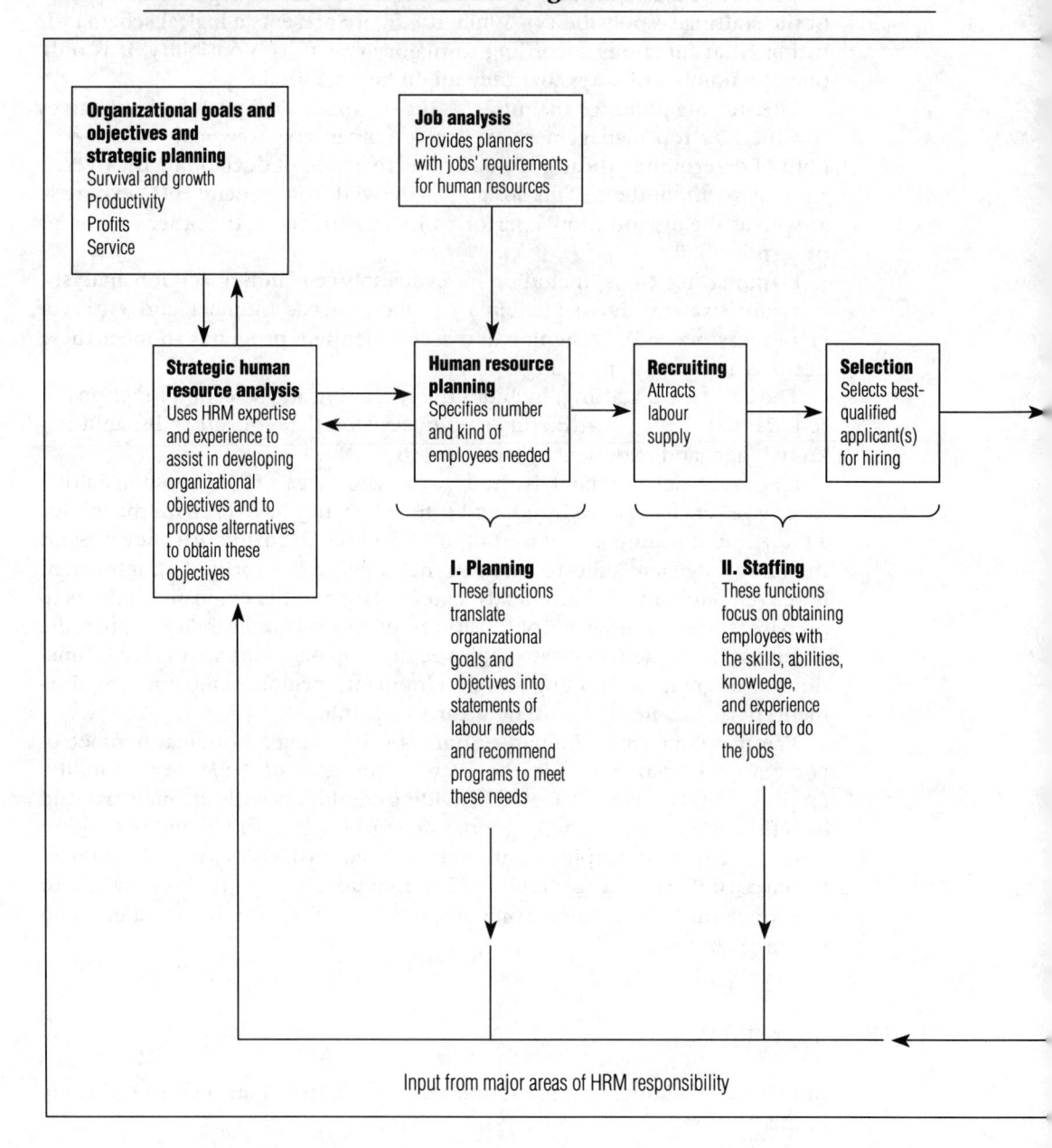

Organizational goals and objectives and strategic planning
Survival and growth
Productivity
Profits
Service

Job analysis
Provides planners with jobs' requirements for human resources

Strategic human resource analysis
Uses HRM expertise and experience to assist in developing organizational objectives and to propose alternatives to obtain these objectives

Human resource planning
Specifies number and kind of employees needed

Recruiting
Attracts labour supply

Selection
Selects best-qualified applicant(s) for hiring

I. Planning
These functions translate organizational goals and objectives into statements of labour needs and recommend programs to meet these needs

II. Staffing
These functions focus on obtaining employees with the skills, abilities, knowledge, and experience required to do the jobs

Input from major areas of HRM responsibility

Orientation
Provides new employees with information about the job, what to expect, and what is expected

Training and development
Maintains acceptable levels of performance, involves employees in work practice decisions, and prepares employees to advance

Career planning
Seeks to reconcile individual career goals with organizational needs for human resources

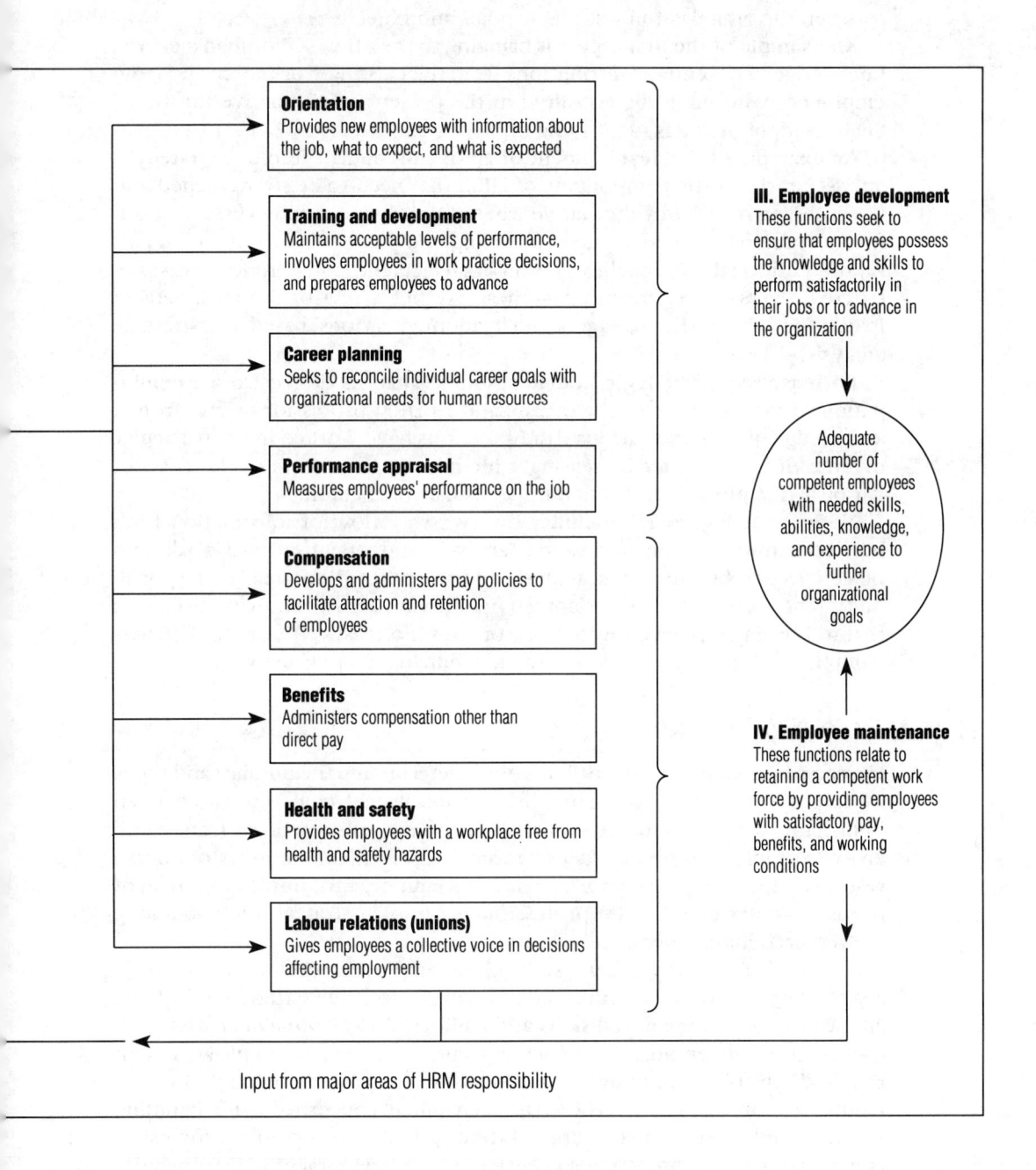

Performance appraisal
Measures employees' performance on the job

III. Employee development
These functions seek to ensure that employees possess the knowledge and skills to perform satisfactorily in their jobs or to advance in the organization

Compensation
Develops and administers pay policies to facilitate attraction and retention of employees

Benefits
Administers compensation other than direct pay

Health and safety
Provides employees with a workplace free from health and safety hazards

Labour relations (unions)
Gives employees a collective voice in decisions affecting employment

IV. Employee maintenance
These functions relate to retaining a competent work force by providing employees with satisfactory pay, benefits, and working conditions

Adequate number of competent employees with needed skills, abilities, knowledge, and experience to further organizational goals

Input from major areas of HRM responsibility

and objectives; and (2) developing and supervising a human resource strategy to attain the organization's strategic goals and objectives.

An example of the first aspect is bringing to the other senior managers the knowledge of potential contributions from the existing work force and from employees who might be recruited in the present or alternative locations. Such an input includes identifying untapped abilities.

An example of the development of an overall human resource strategy is an assessment of the components of HRM that need to be strengthened and the costs and benefits of alternative ways of doing so. Training versus recruitment, recruitment versus subcontracting, employee involvement versus more traditional approaches, union–management co-operation versus a strictly adversarial relationship — these are but a few of the innumerable issues for which HR managers must adopt positions based on strategic analysis.

Both aspects of strategic human resource analysis derive from a combination of the expertise of the organization's HRM professionals and from a knowledge of how the various HRM functions have worked in the particular organization. The latter increasingly includes an awareness of the costs of various HRM policies and programs as well as the benefits.

Notice that Figure 1.1 includes the two-way flow of information both between strategic human resource analysis and organizational goals and objectives and between that analysis and the other HRM areas of responsibility. The second flow is designated by outward arrows showing decisions that follow an employee through the organization, as well as inward arrows from the various stages back to strategic human resource analysis.

HUMAN RESOURCE PLANNING

Human resource planning (HRP) involves determining the number and types of employees needed to accomplish organizational goals. Research is an important part of this function because planning requires the collection and analysis of information in order to forecast the available supplies of human resources and to predict future needs. Once an organization's employment needs are determined, HRM professionals can plan strategies for obtaining the required human resources.

Two basic HRP strategies are staffing and employee development. A *staffing strategy* involves recruiting and selecting from either external or internal applicants with the required skills and abilities. A *development strategy*, on the other hand, emphasizes providing current and new employees with required job skills and knowledge through extensive training and development programs. Recently, HRP has been much concerned with handling surplus employees, as many organizations have been forced to downsize. Human resource planning is also central to the development of employment equity and pay equity programs.

HRM IN ACTION

TO BE EFFECTIVE, MANAGERS MUST LISTEN TO THEIR EMPLOYEES

A recent survey of employees' attitudes demonstrates that management is a two-way process: managers must not only do a good job in strategic planning but must also listen to what employees think. WorkCanada, the survey of 2400 workers conducted in the spring of 1991 by the benefits consulting firm Wyatt Company, found that a clear majority of employees "are generally satisfied with the content of their jobs, their pay and benefits, the way their work is organized and the teamwork where they work." Two-thirds felt they were paid fairly compared to other workers, and over half believed their pay was competitive. Unionized workers were even more positive, with a 65 percent approval rate for their pay compared with 57 percent for nonunion employees.

On the negative side, few of the workers were pleased with the supervision they received or with their companies' management or decision making. Only 45 percent felt "that the organization rewards managers for being effective 'people managers.'" Only 41 percent of employees said that supervisors were effective at solving "people problems." There was also frustration with how well employees perceive they are being treated by management.

Managers perceive themselves differently. "Seven out of ten [managers] said they treat employees with respect and dignity, and that they show a genuine interest in the well-being of employees." Eighty-two percent of employees approved of the way their companies communicate key issues and 68 percent felt they understood the steps being taken to reach these goals. On the other hand, employees said they "want to be asked what they think on key work-related issues.... They want to participate."

A specific example of the need for managers to listen more effectively relates to performance reviews. While most employees thought it was fair for their companies to conduct performance reviews, few were happy with the way the review was handled. Less than four out of ten felt that the reviews helped them to improve their job performance.

Source: Adapted from George Brett, "Canadians Satisfied with Their Jobs, but Down on Bosses, Survey Finds," *The Toronto Star*, September 19, 1991. Used with permission—The Toronto Star Syndicate.

Job Analysis

Job analysis is the process of describing the nature of a job and specifying the human requirements (skills, experience, training, and so on) needed to perform it. The end product of the process is the job description, which spells out work duties and activities of employees. Job descriptions are a vital source of information to employers, managers, and HRM professionals because job content has a great influence on human resource programs and practices relating to recruiting, selection, training, performance appraisal, career planning, compensation, and labour relations. Job analysis is also an important component of pay equity and employment equity programs.

Recruiting

Recruiting is the process of attracting qualified applicants to fill job vacancies. It includes both external recruiting, attracting applicants from outside the organization, and internal recruiting, attracting applicants from among current employees. Recruiting messages list the skills, abilities, knowledge, and experience required for certain jobs. (The requirements are determined through the process of job analysis, while the pay for the positions is based on the organization's compensation policy.)

Selection

The most qualified applicant or applicants are selected from among the pool of applicants generated by the recruiting process. With respect to selection, HRM professionals are involved in developing and administering selection methods that enable the organization to decide which applicants to choose and which to reject for given jobs.

Orientation

Orientation is the first step in helping an employee adjust to the new job and employer. Typically, HRM professionals plan and administer programs to acquaint new employees with particular aspects of their jobs, including pay and benefit programs, work hours, and company rules and expectations. The orientation function has recently taken on new dimensions in Canada because of the increasingly multicultural nature of the work force.

Training and Development

Training and development give employees the skills and knowledge to perform effectively in their jobs. In addition to providing training for new or inexperienced employees, organizations often train experienced employees whose jobs are undergoing change or becoming obsolete. Large organizations often have development programs that prepare employees for higher-level responsibilities. Training and development programs are a way of ensuring that employees are capable of performing their jobs at acceptable levels. Increasingly, too, organizations are involving employees in work-practice decisions.

Performance Appraisal

Performance appraisal involves monitoring employees' performance to ensure that it is at acceptable levels. Although the actual appraisal is the responsibility of supervisors and managers, HRM professionals are usually responsible for developing and administering appraisal systems. Besides providing a basis for pay, promotion, and disciplinary action, performance appraisal provides information essential for employee development, since knowledge of results (feedback) is necessary to motivate and guide improvements in performance.

Career Planning

Career planning has gained recent prominence in HRM for two reasons. First, employees want to grow in their jobs and advance in their careers. Second, government legislation relating to employment equity (affirmative action) puts pressure on organizations to promote people within four target groups: women, people with disabilities, visible minorities, and aboriginals. Thus, HRM professionals engage in career-planning and employment equity activities that involve assessing individual employees' potential for growth and advancement in the organization and planning for job experience and other development opportunities to encourage their growth and promotions. In some organizations, HRM professionals chart career paths showing how an employee can logically progress from one job to another within the organization. They also help people in employment equity target groups to advance.

Compensation

Human resource professionals seek to provide a rational method for determining how much employees should be paid for performing certain jobs. Pay is obviously related to the maintenance of human resources; employees must earn a living, and they may seek alternative employment if the organization's pay levels are inadequate. However, the compensation function also affects the planning, staffing, and employee development concerns of HRM professionals. Since compensation is a major cost to many organizations, it is a major consideration in HRP. For example, an organization may find it less costly to maintain an employee development strategy than to rely on external staffing for higher-level positions in the organization. Compensation affects staffing in that people are generally attracted to employers who offer relatively high levels of pay in exchange for work provided. It is related to employee development in that pay can supply an important incentive for motivating employees to higher levels of job performance and to higher-paying jobs in the organization.

Developing a compensation strategy may require not only keeping up with competition in the local labour market but also formulating an approach to collective bargaining with the union or unions that represent the organization's employees. In addition, compensation policy can be affected by employment standards legislation and by legislation governing pay equity.

BENEFITS

Benefits are employee compensation other than direct pay for work provided. Thus, the HRM function of administering employee benefits shares many characteristics of the compensation function, including involving items that are important in collective bargaining with unions. Benefits include both legally required items (such as the employer's contributions to the Canada (or Quebec) Pension Plan, workers' compensation, health insurance plans in some provinces, and unemployment insurance) and benefits offered at an employer's discretion (including pensions; "sick days"; dental and extended health care plans; and employee services, such as cafeteria discounts and parking privileges). The cost of benefits has risen to the point of becoming a major consideration in human resource planning. Benefits are primarily related to the maintenance area, however, since they provide for many basic employee needs.

HEALTH AND SAFETY

Before passage of Saskatchewan's Occupational Health and Safety Act of 1972, health and safety programs were usually found only in hazardous industries, such as mining and construction. Now, however, legislation in many jurisdictions requires employers to have labour–management committees to enforce health and safety rules. Ensuring compliance with health and safety rules is a major HRM responsibility, as are the development and enforcement of safety rules and regulations and the creation and administration of health and safety programs.

LABOUR RELATIONS

The term *labour relations* refers to an employer's interactions with employees who are represented by a trade union. The HRM responsibility for labour relations includes negotiating a collective agreement, administering it, and resolving disputes and grievances pertaining to it. In unionized organizations, management must consult the union on employee-involvement programs relating to work practices. Since many aspects of labour relations directly concern employees' welfare, it is a major function of the maintenance area.

In fact, the collective agreement affects all major areas of HRM responsibility in unionized organizations. (Approximately 40 percent of Canadian employees are covered by collective agreements.)

EMPLOYEE RECORDS

The oldest and most basic HRM function, one that crosscuts each of the major areas of responsibility, is employee record keeping. This function involves recording, maintaining, and retrieving employee-related information for a variety of purposes, including compliance with government regulations. Many of the records that must be kept are set out in Employment Standards acts. Records that must be maintained include application forms; health and medical records; employment histories (jobs held, promotions, transfers, layoffs); seniority lists detailing length of time in present job, department, and/or organization; earnings and hours of work; absences, turnover, and tardiness; and deductions, living allowances, and vacation pay. Increasingly, information for purposes of employment equity is required for members of the four target groups.

Complete and up-to-date employee records are essential for most HRM functions. Fortunately for HRM professionals, the recent availability of inexpensive personal computers and HR software has made data storage, manipulation, and retrieval much easier and less time-consuming than ever before. This situation, in turn, has provided the basis for the specialized but growing area of human resource information systems.

OTHER FUNCTIONS AND CHANGING EMPHASES

The HRM functions just listed are the major ones carried out in most organizations. Depending upon individual organizational needs and stage of growth, HRM staff may engage in other activities. For example, given the substantial layoffs of the early 1990s, some conduct outplacement programs to help terminated employees find new jobs. In other cases, HRM professionals are involved in a variety of organizational change programs, ranging from improving the quality of working life to assisting with a merger or a takeover by another company.

It is likely that the relative importance of the various HRM functions changes over the life cycle of an organization and that the specific focus of each HRM function changes over time. In a new organization, recruiting, selection, and compensation are keys for acquiring talented managerial, professional, and technical personnel. At the growth stage, recruiting and selection emphasize obtaining an adequate supply of qualified employees, and internal recruiting is important. Compensation policies become more formalized during this time, and internal equity (the perceived fairness of the pay structure) receives greater emphasis than does external market competitiveness. Training and development also become more important during the growth stage. As the organization matures and declines, recruiting and selection diminish in importance, compensation emphasizes cost control, and retraining of older employees becomes an important aspect of training. While labour relations remains important over time, its emphasis changes from one of keeping peace at the growth stage to controlling costs (while also keeping peace) at the maturity stage. During decline, issues of productivity and job security dominate labour relations.[11]

ASSIGNMENT OF HRM RESPONSIBILITIES

Assignment of responsibility for HRM varies from one organization to another and may be affected by the size, goals, philosophy, and structure of the firm. Even the smallest of organizations engages in the basic HRM functions of hiring, training, providing compensation and benefits, and record keeping.

Small firms may divide HRM functions among several people, ranging from clerical workers to the head of the organization. A company that expands to several hundred workers usually assigns one employee to HRM on a full-time basis. A major advantage of having one HR manager is that it eases co-ordination of human resource policies, eliminating the redundancies and inconsistencies that occur when several people handle the various functions.

With increasing growth and/or profitability of an organization, however, more people are required to handle the HRM function, and the HRM department must expand. Such departments tend to branch out into specialized areas. For example, compensation and benefits specialists, training and development specialists, or labour relations specialists may become a part of the HRM department. If health and safety is a major concern, an industrial nurse or safety specialist may be added.

The HRM professional may not handle all of the responsibilities for every group of employees. For example, the recruiting of academic staff in a university is normally handled by professors in the particular departments, rather than by HRM professionals. The latter are involved only to assist with orientation of new employees and to ensure that no human rights codes or union agreements are violated.

Basically, HRM professionals are considered staff rather than line employees since they provide specialized, technical, and professional advice to production or operations (line) managers and administer policies and programs affecting human resources.

Line managers have direct responsibility for a production unit, such as an assembly line. Staff personnel do not have direct responsibility, but their role is to assist, for example, by preparing the pay cheques and advising on benefit packages.

Take, for example, the common situation in which HRM professionals are consulted about the problem of absenteeism in an organization. In dealing with such an issue, HRM staffers engage in research to determine the nature and extent of the problem, to examine and evaluate alternative solutions, and to make recommendations to management. If management approves a suggested program, HRM professionals are likely to be assigned responsibility for developing and administering it. In the case of absenteeism, they might develop a program to reward employees with an extra day's pay and special recognition for each three-month period of perfect attendance. In addition, a policy could be adopted whereby employees who exceed a certain number of absences within a given period may be terminated. In administering absenteeism policies and programs, HRM professionals would keep attendance records, compile lists of employees with perfect records, schedule recognition ceremonies for these employees, publicize the policy on excessive absenteeism, and enforce it by terminating employees whose absences have exceeded the predetermined limit.[12]

There is a trend, however, toward viewing the relationship between the HRM function and line management as one of partnership in which HRM's role is consultative — that is, HRM is there to help solve the organization's major problems. The resulting concept is one of hyphenated accountability; line managers are primarily responsible to their superiors, but they also have to take into consideration the advice of the HRM unit, so they are also partly responsible to that unit as well.

Except within their own department, human resources managers have no managerial authority other than that delegated to them by top management, and this may vary from one organization to another. Generally, HRM professionals are likely to exercise greater authority and responsibility when human resources are valued highly in the organization and when HRM staff are respected by top management. The trend, however, is for increased responsibilities for all HRM professionals.

THE HRM PROFESSION

GROWTH OF THE PROFESSION

The past few decades have seen an enormous growth in the number of HRM professionals. According to a Conference Board of Canada survey, the median ratio of HRM professionals to employees in 1988 was 8.7 per 1000, with smaller firms (fewer than 2500 employees) above the average and very large ones (more than 10 000 employees) below it. The ratios also varied with the particular industry and the degree of unionization. Service and knowledge-based industries had the highest ratios of HRM professionals, which the Conference Board study attributes to the combination of development needs, highly skilled and educated employees requiring more HRM activities, and attention to positive employee relations in an effort to avoid unionization. Unionized firms had lower ratios than nonunionized firms.[13]

Figure 1.2 contains historical information from the Canadian census and projections for future job opportunities prepared by Employment and Immigration Canada. The figure includes two categories of HRM professionals — human resource and industrial relations managers and human resource and related officers — and statistics on personnel clerks.

There was a remarkable sixfold increase in human resource and industrial relations managers between 1971 and 1981 (from 4055 to 26 025) and a smaller but above-average growth between 1981 and 1989 (to 34 837). Projections indicate that numbers of human resource managers will increase at more than three times the rate for the labour force as a whole, to 42 537, by 1995. Numbers of human resource and related officers have been increasing, but at a slower rate. By 1995, it is estimated that there will be 40 468 of them, some 2000 fewer jobs than in the managerial category.

It is possible that some of the increase in "managers" includes individuals who would have been identified as "officers" in 1971. (The *Canadian Classification and Dictionary of Occupations* [*CCDO*][14] is designed to prevent such inflation in titles, but some erosion may have occurred.) Whatever the precise division between managers and officers, the fact remains that a large number of people are employed in various capacities in the HRM field, and, on balance, the group is growing at an above-average rate. The only declining component is personnel clerks, whose numbers decreased between 1981 and 1989. The rapid expansion in the use of computers may have reduced the number of people in this occupation since many of its functions include record keeping and searching records. (A related occupation, that of payroll clerk, is included with bookkeepers and accounting clerks, who have also decreased in number, although by not nearly as many.) The Canadian Occupational Projection System (COPS) anticipates a very small increase between 1989 and 1995 in the number of jobs for personnel clerks.[15]

THE NATURE OF JOBS IN THE HRM FIELD

One need only look at classified ads to see the diversity of HRM positions. Some of these jobs are very specialized; others are more generalized and include responsibility for most or all HRM functions. Most HRM jobs are generalist positions simply because most employers in Canada have fewer than 100 employees. Such positions offer the best opportunities to be a jack-of-all-trades in the profession.

Jobs in HRM range from personnel clerk to vice-president of human resources and can be classified into four major types:

1. Support jobs: word processing operators, data entry clerks, and receptionists.
2. Technical and professional jobs: functional specialists in such areas as labour relations, compensation, and training.

FIGURE 1.2
Growth of the HRM Profession in Canada

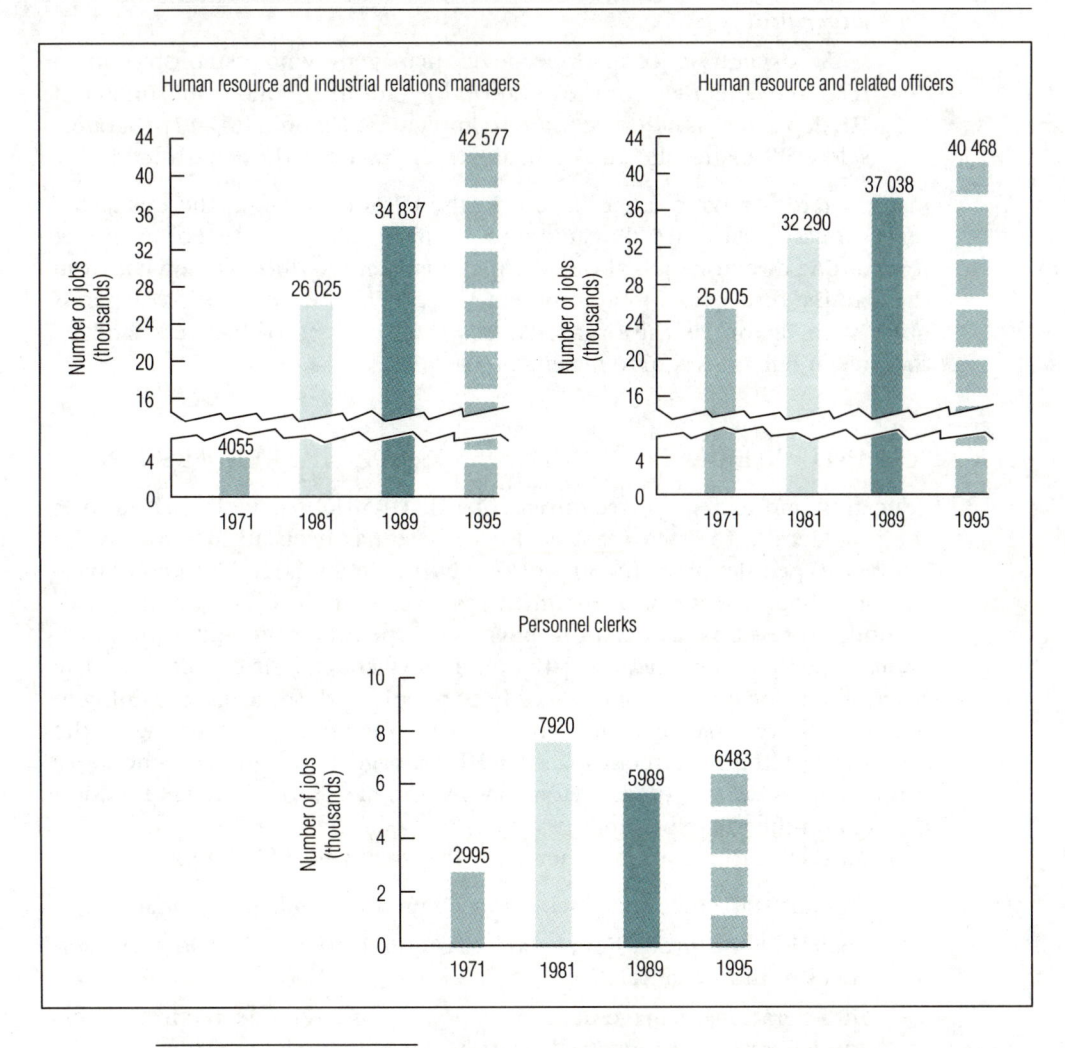

Human resource and industrial relations managers

Year	Number of jobs (thousands)
1971	4 055
1981	26 025
1989	34 837
1995	42 577

Human resource and related officers

Year	Number of jobs (thousands)
1971	25 005
1981	32 290
1989	37 038
1995	40 468

Personnel clerks

Year	Number of jobs (thousands)
1971	2 995
1981	7 920
1989	5 989
1995	6 483

Source: Compiled from 1971 and 1981: Statistics Canada, *Occupational Trends in Canada: 1961–1986*, Census of Canada 1986, cat. no. 93–151; 1989 and 1995: Employment and Immigration Canada, *Job Futures: An Occupational Outlook to 1995, Volume 1: Occupational Outlooks*, 1990 ed., prepared by the Canadian Occupational Projection System (COPS) (Toronto: Nelson Canada, 1990), and special tabulations prepared by Employment and Immigration Canada. Reproduced with the permission of the Minister of Supply and Services Canada, 1992. Please note that *Job Futures* uses the formal designation "Personnel and Industrial Relations Management Occupations," but the grouping has been referred to here as "Human Resource and Industrial Relations Managers" to reflect the more current designation.

3. HR operations management jobs: HR generalists who handle most or all of the HRM functions in a small organization or in the plant of a larger firm.
4. HRM executive jobs: Upper-level managers who establish human resource objectives for the organization, authorize the establishment of HR departments, allocate funds to implement HR policies and programs, select HR managers, and co-ordinate the work of HR departments.[16]

Just as there is a wide range of jobs in the HRM profession, there is also a range of responsibilities allocated under a particular job title. For example, the training director's job at one company is likely to differ somewhat from the training director's job at another. The precise job description depends upon such factors as the organization's size, its type of business, and its theories of human resource management.

EDUCATION AND EXPERIENCE REQUIREMENTS FOR HRM PROFESSIONALS

Education and experience requirements for HRM jobs have increased over the past decade for two reasons. First, there has been an increase in the number of people interested in working in the field who have taken university or college courses in the human resource or industrial relations field. Second, professional associations have developed their own education programs, usually in conjunction with community colleges or universities. The result is a major increase in the supply of people with some basic training in human resource management. This increase in supply is occurring at the same time as the retirement of older HR managers and officers who were former supervisors or functional managers and had learned the HR function through on-the-job experience.

Typical educational requirements for the four types of HRM jobs are:

1. Support staff: secondary school or community college diploma.
2. Technical and professional staff: master's degree or PhD in social sciences or industrial relations.
3. HR operations management: bachelor's or master's degree in business administration or industrial relations, or a diploma in business.
4. HRM executives: master's degree in business administration or industrial relations.[17]

Employers frequently prefer job applicants with experience in their particular industry. For example, HRM professionals with experience in public sector organizations such as municipal or provincial governments usually do not take jobs in the private sector. Even within the private sector, employers usually prefer applicants with experience in the same industry. Examples of major industry groups include banking, insurance, manufacturing, and retail and finance.

Secretaries and clerks working in the HRM area usually have a secondary school certificate or community college diploma. Most other HRM jobs require a bachelor's degree in commerce, psychology, sociology, economics, labour–management relations, or industrial relations. Frequently, students ask how one gets a job in HRM when so many ads require experience. There are several ways. One is a co-op program, in which an undergraduate alternately attends university and works for a company. Some organizations offer internships in HRM, and some students also gain experience by working part-time in HRM jobs.

Professional Organizations

Most professions have organizations that promote educational and professional standards among their members. These professional associations also serve as communication channels for information regarding federal and provincial legislation and court decisions affecting the profession.

An HRM professional may hold membership in more than one professional association, usually depending on his or her area of specialization and/or professional training. For example, a director of training and development who has a graduate degree in psychology and works in Winnipeg might be a member of the Human Resource Management Association of Manitoba, the Manitoba Society for Training and Development, the Canadian Psychological Association (CPA), and the American Psychological Association (APA).

A major change in the role of professional organizations occurred in 1990 when the Ontario Legislature passed Bill 70, An Act Respecting the Human Resources Professionals Association of Ontario (HRPAO). It authorized the HRPAO, which replaced the Personnel Association of Ontario, to grant its members the exclusive use of the designation Certified Human Resources Professional (CHRP).

As described in the act, the objectives of the HRPAO include:

- To establish and encourage the acceptance and maintenance of uniform province-wide standards of knowledge, experience and ethics for all persons engaged in the field of human resources management;
- To promote and further the education and improve the competence of persons engaged in human resource management by granting registration and membership to persons who meet the standards of the Association;
- To hold examinations and prescribe tests of competency deemed appropriate to qualify membership in and certification by the Association;
- To maintain discipline among members of the Association.[18]

The HRPAO is Canada's largest HR professional association, with 6500 members in 1991. It not only co-ordinates the CHRP accreditation and related education programs but combines 27 local associations, which provide their members with many services, including regular seminars and annual conventions.

Associations representing general HR interests also exist in Quebec, British Columbia, Alberta, Saskatchewan, Manitoba, and the Maritimes. Meetings are taking place among these associations to determine whether national standards can be established.

Whether or not national standards are established, these organizations play an important role in maintaining high standards among HRM professionals. They keep members abreast of changes and innovations and also serve as a communication network, a source of identity, and a means of influence for many members.

THE CONTEXT OF CHANGE AFFECTING HRM

Human resource management takes place within a context of change. Four major areas of change affecting HRM are the business climate, technology, government legislation, and labour force characteristics.

BUSINESS CLIMATE

At the outset of the 1990s, the business climate was buffeted by a combination of factors that produced a record high level of bankruptcies, declining employment, and rising unemployment. The factors that initially had such a negative effect on the Canadian economy included high interest rates, a high exchange rate for the Canadian dollar vis-à-vis the U.S. dollar, the introduction of the Canada–U.S. Free Trade Agreement (FTA), and the slowdown in the U.S. economy.

The auto industry, so important to Canada's (particularly Ontario's) economy, is an interesting example. The industry provides direct and indirect employment to almost one million Canadian workers and accounts for one-quarter of Canada's exports and imports. In the 1980s, it performed better than its counterpart in the United States in terms of output and jobs,[19] but in the early 1990s excess capacity in the industry together with the economic slowdown across North America brought major layoffs in the Canadian plants of the big three auto manufacturers (General Motors, Ford, and Chrysler).[20] On the other hand, the Asian transplant firms (Honda, Toyota, and Suzuki) have been expanding their production and employment. How this crucial sector of the economy will be affected by the Mexico–U.S. free trade agreement and its incorporation into the Canada–U.S. FTA is something that is being observed very closely.

For HR managers, the continuing restructuring of the North American economy will have a major impact on competition, and thereby on such functions as recruiting, retraining, compensation, benefits, and layoffs.

TECHNOLOGY

A fundamental adjustment in our view of technology and change has to take place in the 1990s. Technological advance must be seen not in isolation but rather as integrally—in fact, synergistically—bound up with the training and preparation of the work force. As the authors of *Two Steps Forward: Human Resource Management in a High-Tech World* observe:

> Global economic and technological realities have changed. Pure technological advantage is a fleeting, transitory phenomenon. . . . There is growing evidence that without more flexible, collaborative organizational designs supported by innovative reward structures even the most technologically sophisticated processes and products may not prosper.[21]

The role of the HR manager is not simply to react to technological change but rather to equip people for coping with adjustments to technological change and to develop and implement approaches that will ensure the best use of the new technologies' potential. Thus, technological change must be viewed not as a threat but as an opportunity to harness new developments both for the effectiveness of the organization and for the welfare and future of individual employees.

Exhibit 1.1 presents examples of specific HRM practices that should be considered when technology has advanced. (For an example of what can go wrong, see Case 1.2 at the end of this chapter.) There have also been some public efforts to provide adjustments to technological change. The Canadian Steel Trade and Employment Congress (CSTEC), a joint effort of the United Steel Workers and Canada's major steel companies in Canada, has provided adjustment mechanisms for laid-off steel workers, setting an example of joint planning to facilitate the adjustment of workers to technological and other changes affecting production while helping firms to improve their potential to be competitive.

GOVERNMENT LEGISLATION

Government legislation is another area of change affecting employment and the practice of human resource management. Of continuing importance are provincial and federal laws passed since the 1970s relating to human rights, such as employment equity, employment standards (discussed in Chapter 3), pay equity for women (discussed in Chapter 12), and occupational health and safety (discussed in Chapter 14). Such laws and others have a profound effect upon the HRM profession in terms of responsibilities and activities. In a recent survey, one-third of senior human resource executives in Canada ranked employment equity and pay equity as crucial in achieving business and human resource objectives.[22] The cost considerations of these initiatives have important implications for HRM as well.

EXHIBIT 1.1
Human Resource Management in a High-Tech World

In a recent examination of the keys to successful innovation, the Economic Council of Canada identified human resource management practices that were far from ideal or even desirable. They included such situations as the following: the innovation design was purely technical, and no attention had been paid to its implications for job content; workers found out about technological change only when the new equipment arrived at the plant door; so-called joint decision making actually involved management simply telling workers what it was going to do; fundamental disagreements between the parties were left unresolved; and union-free operations were part of planning for high-tech production. These are not the sorts of practices that will lead to successful change; in fact, taken together, they would almost certainly lead to disaster. Indeed, these examples were noted by the Economic Council in its descriptions of innovation *failures*.

The following are the challenges that organizations and their workers face in making technology work for them:

- Featuring advance planning of both the technical and social aspects of change.
- Developing job designs that incorporate human discretion, responsibility, and skill.
- Retraining so that existing employees will be part of the future.
- Adapting technologies to expand opportunities for the disabled.
- Sharing the added prosperity brought about by technological change.
- Committing themselves to the concept of "involvement" in which all stakeholders have the opportunity to influence the innovation process.

In many respects, approaches such as these run against the traditional ways of doing things in Canadian industry. Yet, they must become a fundamental part of the hardware and software in the high-technology economy.

Source: Adapted from Gordon Betcherman, Keith Newton, and Joanne Godin, eds., *Two Steps Forward: Human Resource Management in a High-Tech World*, Economic Council of Canada (Ottawa: Supply and Services Canada, 1990), p. 2. Reproduced with the permission of the Chairman of the Economic Council of Canada, 1992.

The difficulties of this aspect of the HRM function are enhanced in Canada by the variety of laws affecting employment in the different provinces and in those industries operating under federal government jurisdiction (such as transportation and communication). In the United States, an estimated 90 percent of all employees fall under federal jurisdiction. In Canada, however, the federal government is responsible for fewer than 10 percent of all employees. Ten different sets of provincial regulations (plus those of the two territories) cover 90 percent of all the country's employees. Companies with employees in two or more provinces have to take account of variations in labour relations laws and other legislation.

The various provincial and federal laws are administered by many different boards, commissions, agencies, departments, and ministries. The HRM professional must learn what records have to be maintained or presented to these various bodies. In addition, numerous posters must be displayed in employment areas to acquaint employees with their rights and responsibilities. Again, usually HRM officials are ultimately responsible for informing employees of these matters.

In addition to legislation setting the ground rules for HRM, federal and provincial governments have passed special legislation for labour–management relations in the public sector. Approximately one-quarter of the work force is in government employment, education, health, firefighting, and the police.

THE LABOUR FORCE

A fourth area of change affecting organizations and human resource management is the labour force itself. The next chapter is devoted to people both in the context of the labour force and on an individual basis, but some major demographic and value changes must be mentioned here. A well-known demographic fact regarding the Canadian population is that the education level is higher than it has ever been. There is, however, concern that the quality of education has declined. An even more serious concern is the disparity between the skills people learn in school and the jobs available. The resulting situation is ironic — unemployment is high, but many employers have jobs they cannot fill.[23] Some of these jobs require specialized training, such as machining and computer technology, while others are relatively unskilled, such as restaurant help and gardening. Many unemployed people are not trained for specialized jobs, but their education has raised their expectations so much that they will not accept menial jobs at low rates of pay. Therefore, some people who are able to work find themselves standing in unemployment lines.

A second demographic characteristic of the Canadian labour force of the 1990s is that the average age of employees is higher than at any time in recent history. The major cause is the "baby bust" that began in the mid-1960s. This period saw the lowest birth rate since the Great Depression. As a result, there are fewer young people entering the labour force today.[24] Simultaneous with the reduction of new entrants into the labour force has been the continued exit of older workers (age 55 and older). Factors that have decreased the number of older workers include the introduction of the Canada and Quebec pension plans, changes in unemployment insurance regulations that have reduced benefits available to older workers, the existence of mandatory retirement at age 65 in many provinces, and the availability of workers' compensation for some people permanently unable to work. From 1966 to 1978, the labour force participation rate of men age 55 and over fell from 57.5 to 47.1 percent.[25] By 1990, the participation rate of this group was down to 37.4 percent.[26] The main groups of older men who continue to work are those who are self-employed and those who are highly educated: "for the poorly-educated and therefore less well-paid, government transfer income may compare favourably with potential employment income."[27] Workers also tend to withdraw from jobs that are too physically demanding. Although workers are leaving the labour force earlier, the effect of changes in technology in eliminating jobs is that today's workers are likely to experience two or more different careers during the span of their work life. The burden of preparing — training and developing — employees for such "second careers" falls upon the business community and government.

Perhaps one of the most significant changes in the past quarter century is the increased proportion of women in the labour force. The road to women's entrance into the work force and into nontraditional jobs has been paved with governmental legislation, technology, changed attitudes toward the family, and recently declining real incomes, which have caused more women to seek work. The effects of equality of the sexes in the workplace are far-reaching and have presented many problems for organizations and society as well. Although there has been some move toward equality of pay and job opportunities for women, the 1984 Abella Commission concluded that there was systemic discrimination in the form of workplace barriers that could be eliminated only through legislation designed to foster employment equity.[28] This commission led to the introduction of federal legislation concerning employment equity. The province of Ontario is planning to introduce similar legislation, and many municipalities and organizations have employment equity programs. Demographers expect that by the mid-1990s, as our society ages and many workers retire, there will be shortages of properly educated and skilled labour. Wasting valuable human resources through human resource practices that are biased according to sex, age, race, ethnic origin, or religion is not only morally unacceptable but harmful to the economy.

Another area of change in the labour force involves values and attitudes. Arnold Deutsch, author of *The Human Resource Revolution: Communicate or Litigate*, describes these elements of change as "new attitudes in the work place adapted from those developed outside; rising expectations for a more rewarding, more human working experience, and a greater 'democratization' of the working world in response to the tides of change."[29] Increasingly, workers want a voice in decisions affecting their jobs and their employment. No longer content to "check their brains at the door," many workers want to contribute ideas for improving production, reducing costs, and making the workplace safer. Realizing the potential value of employee inputs, some organizations have introduced labour–management consultation on production and financial results and other forms of employee participation and involvement in work-related decisions, such as quality of working life (QWL) programs.[30] Forty-seven percent of collective agreements in Canada in 1991 had a provision for a labour–management committee and 11 percent had some form of QWL.[31] Kumar's earlier survey of personnel managers identifies changing work ethics and employee values as the most significant new demand on the HRM function.[32]

To summarize, in the past quarter century and continuing into the present, changes in the business climate, including globalization and international competition; technology; government legislation; and the labour force itself have presented challenges for the business community and society in general. HRM executives and professionals have been actively involved in meeting these challenges, and their role will likely continue to increase in importance.

MAJOR ISSUES HR MANAGERS WILL FACE IN THE 1990S

In a 1988 survey, HR executives were asked to indicate the issues they thought would be the most important in the next five years. The seventeen they identified are presented in Figure 1.3 (see page 30). A majority of the respondents cited four of them: linking human resource planning to the strategic business plan (76 percent); leadership within the organization (64 percent); productivity improvements (59 percent); and quality of services and products (52 percent).[33]

Linking HR planning to the strategic business plan is essential to avoid a misdirected business thrust arising from human resources that are insufficient or inadequately trained. HR managers are increasingly considered change agents who link line management with the organizational thrust. The key is the extent of employee co-operation, which, in turn, is viewed as requiring HR leadership in employee involvement and recognition. Examples of such leadership and union co-operation occurred during the severe recession at the beginning of the 1990s in segments of the construction industry, the steel industry, and the auto parts industry. At Hamilton Wire Products Ltd., the management opened its books to the steelworkers' union to prove that hard times were having a significant impact on the small firm. Many firms and unions also agreed to take part in an unemployment-insurance–assisted work sharing program.[34] HR managers not only determine what programs would be suitable in the particular organizational context but also participate in the implementation and the evaluation of those programs.

Productivity improvements increasingly require moving away from traditionally structured work to greater employee involvement, a broadening of the scope of responsibilities, and a change from individual to group or team bases for production. The HR manager is the essential link in determining the appropriate forms of employee involvement for enhancing productivity.

HRM IN ACTION

STRATEGIC PLANNING AND COMPETITIVENESS

In the fall of 1991 Harvard University Business School professor Michael Porter completed a $1 million study entitled *Canada at the Crossroads*, which followed the model of his 1990 book *The Competitive Advantage of Nations*. The report deals with what is needed to improve Canada's competitiveness. Porter's prescription is addressed to companies, to governments, and to unions, but the most compelling recommendations are those directed to business. A summary of the advice to all three groups is set out below. Half of the recommendations to companies, seven of the ten to governments, and all of those to labour relate to the HR function.

SUMMARY OF *CANADA AT THE CROSSROADS*

TO COMPANIES:

- Make sure you understand the competitive environment for your product and your Canadian home base.
- Compete on the basis of innovation, not cost alone. Invest in innovative production processes to raise productivity and shift to more highly processed, differentiated products.
- Concentrate on product lines, market segments and businesses that give you a lasting competitive advantage.
- Spend more money on employee training.
- Establish closer ties with universities and colleges. Take part in co-op programs.
- Help to finance university research to ensure that more of it is commercially relevant.
- Strengthen your Canadian suppliers and try to sell to the most demanding buyers of your product in Canada.
- Treat labour as a partner, not an adversary. Be less authoritarian.
- Base compensation for all employees, including management, on both individual and company performance.
- Develop global strategies that go beyond North America, using both exports and foreign investment to penetrate foreign markets.
- Subsidiaries of foreign companies should try to carve out a role as the North American or global headquarters for a particular product line or segment of their parents' business.
- Stop looking to governments for assistance like subsidies, artificial cost structures, lax regulations and government procurement. Instead, pres-

sure governments for high-quality infrastructure and support for research and development centres and training programs.

TO GOVERNMENTS:

- Provide more training for the unemployed and promote private sector training.
- Set high national educational standards.
- Put more emphasis on practical curriculums and science skills.
- Expand apprenticeship programs.
- Realign university financing toward programs directly linked to competitiveness.
- Improve the co-ordination of government R&D programs to reduce duplication.
- Change government policies and financing mechanisms to encourage universities to specialize more.
- Restructure government procurement by abandoning "make-to-blueprint" design specifications in favour of more challenging specifications based on performance.
- Adopt more stringent regulatory standards that force companies to improve products in ways that are eventually demanded by world markets.
- Redesign social programs to ensure that they do not undermine incentives, upgrading and productivity growth.

TO LABOUR:

- Recognize that efforts to increase productivity, upgrade skills and allow shifts into more sophisticated jobs are the best guarantee of good wages in the long term.
- Help companies identify and remove obstacles to productivity gains by pressing for job enhancement and flexibility and supporting advancement based on training and merit.
- Set as a central objective the broadening and increasing of workers' skills.
- Take a more collaborative approach to labour-management relations by encouraging a greater exchange of information and participating in company planning.

Source: John Geddes and Alan Toulin, "Key Report Slams Canada's Managers," *The Financial Post*, October 21, 1991; and Harvey Enchin, "Canada Urged to Stop Living Off Fat of the Land," *The Globe and Mail*, October 25, 1991. Reprinted with the permission of the publishers. For the complete study, see Michael Porter, *Canada at the Crossroads* (Ottawa: Business Council on National Issues, 1991).

FIGURE 1.3
Major Issues Confronting Human Resource Management in the Next Five Years ($n = 94$)

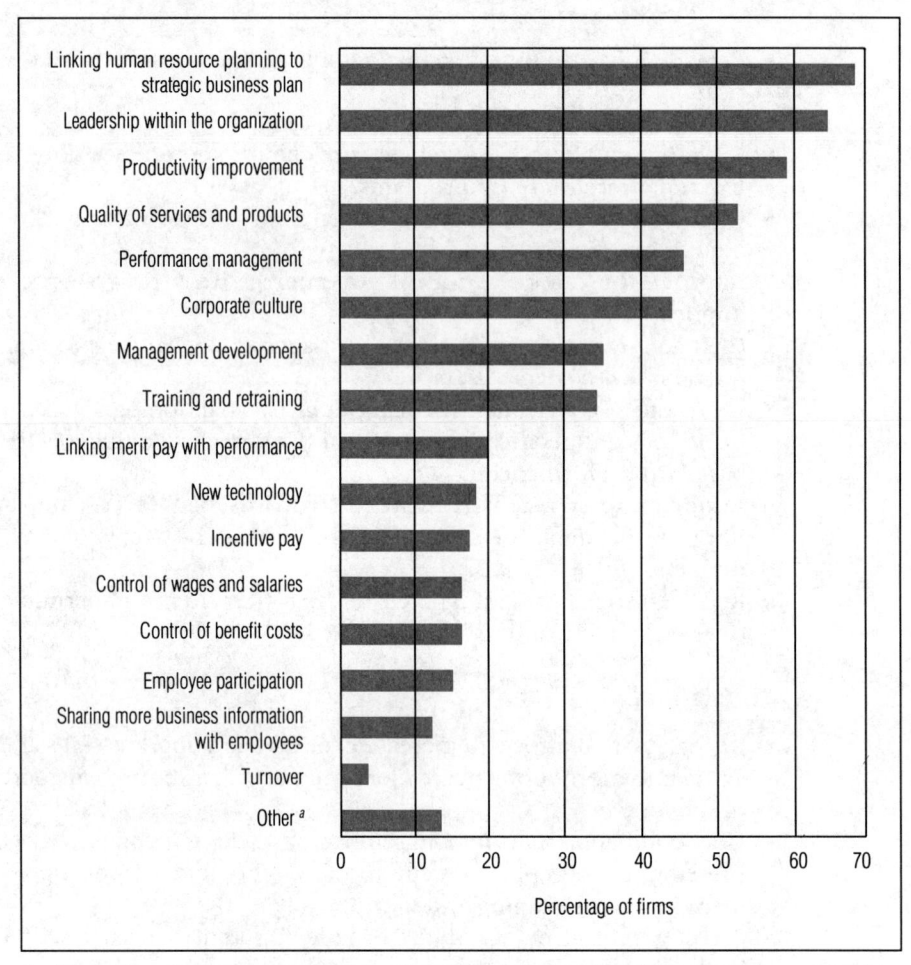

Issue	Percentage of firms
Linking human resource planning to strategic business plan	~68
Leadership within the organization	~64
Productivity improvement	~58
Quality of services and products	~52
Performance management	~45
Corporate culture	~43
Management development	~35
Training and retraining	~33
Linking merit pay with performance	~20
New technology	~18
Incentive pay	~17
Control of wages and salaries	~16
Control of benefit costs	~16
Employee participation	~15
Sharing more business information with employees	~12
Turnover	~4
Other [a]	~13

[a] The other issues most often mentioned related to legislation and human rights, succession planning, career plateauing, and changes in the labour force.

Source: P.P. Benimadhu, *Human Resource Management: Charting a New Course* (Ottawa: The Conference Board of Canada, May 1989), p. 15. Reprinted with the permission of The Conference Board of Canada.

Finally, the increasingly competitive environment requires greater attention to the quality of services and products, which, in turn, requires HR executives to build quality into the organization's culture and operations by designing incentives and involvement programs to reward quality. Globalization and increasing international competition also put pressure on an organization in general and human resource managers in particular to run cost-effective operations while maintaining and enhancing the quality of products and services.

REVIEW QUESTIONS

1. Explain the relationship between the increasing extent and complexity of government legislation regulating employer–employee relations and the growth of the human resource management field.

2. Outline the five major areas of HRM responsibility. Discuss the one you think will be the most important in the 1990s. In your answer, include reasons for your choice.

3. Discuss how and why the globalization of the production of goods and, to some extent, the provision of services puts pressure on human resource managers to be more cost-effective while maintaining quality.

4. Some people say, "There is no difference between human resource management and personnel management except for the change in name." Discuss whether or not you agree with this statement and why. Support your views with specific evidence.

▸▸▸ CASES

CASE 1.1 ▸ LABATT'S MANAGERS REORGANIZE FROM WITHIN

Employees arriving at a day-long strategy meeting of Labatt Breweries of Canada's senior staff last month were shown their new organization chart. Most of the boxes were empty.

As part of a reorganization, the company plans to cut its salaried staff by 7 per cent, letting about 100 people go. But rather than design the new organization in the corner office, top company officials want to involve employees.

So, directors—Labatt's third level of executives—were being asked to tell their bosses where their interests lay: which of the empty boxes they might be interested in occupying.

Reports that the company had asked staff members to resign and re-apply for their jobs were incorrect, said Jim Ranson, director of employee development.

"Nobody was asked to resign. All we said was that we were adopting a new strategy and that for it to work would require some restructuring, so we said all jobs and all incumbents are under review."

But what it did mean for some people was that others might get a look at their jobs. Going in, no one knew how many of the people in the room would end up leaving the company as part of the cuts, how many would change jobs and how many would stay in their present positions.

The meeting opened with a description of the company's new vision and strategy by president John Morgan, who took over last fall shortly after Labatt was knocked out of the No. 1 position among Canadian breweries by the merger of rival Molson Breweries of Canada Ltd. with Carling O'Keefe Breweries of Canada Ltd.

Labatt, a division of John Labatt Ltd. of London, Ont., had hoped to be able to take customers away from Molson because of upheaval during the merger. Instead, Montreal-based Molson announced last week it had increased its market share in the brewing business.

Labatt's new vision involves nationalizing the development of strategy in Toronto and then getting provincial teams to execute those strategies, Mr. Ranson said.

David Barbour, Labatt's executive vice-president of marketing, has been quoted as saying a changing business environment has required the company to think in a more global sense and to act more quickly.

Staffers were told some would see their jobs on the new chart and some would not, but just because their current job had disappeared did not mean there was no place for them in the organization, explained Don Tyler of Mainstream Access Corp., a consultant working with Labatt on the changes.

After the managers attending the meeting were given the organization chart, the vice-presidents described how their part of the new organization would work, Mr. Ranson said. Everyone attending was given detailed descriptions of the new jobs, including their general purpose, reporting structure, and what characteristics or background were needed for people to be considered serious candidates.

Following a lunch break, the company described services it would offer to anyone who was displaced. As well as financial support, these included programs to help people identify their strengths and understand their impact on co-workers, superiors, subordinates and clients.

Arrangements were made for the managers to talk with their current boss. The boss's job during that meeting was to make it clear to each manager whether the company wanted them in that job or whether they should consider moving. It also gave the employees a chance to state their wishes and career objectives as well as any restrictions he or she faced, for example, in moving.

The bosses had one of three messages to give, Mr. Tyler said:

- "You are doing a wonderful job where you are and we want to keep you there."
- "You are doing all right, but we are not sure where you want to be in the organization."
- "In this new organization, I'm not sure you are the right person for the job. I have to be honest, you are at risk."

After this round, directors were encouraged to do "career interest interviews" with any other vice-president, exploring areas they were interested in working in.

These went on late into the night and continued the next morning, said Eldon Elgie, Labatt's director of compensation and benefits. New jobs available included provincial general manager positions, which the company had not had for several years.

As a result of this, job offers were made Jan. 18. They had to be accepted by Jan. 23.

"You need to make these decisions and execute them as soon as possible so nobody is left hanging," Mr. Elgie said, "but the need to involve people adds time."

People who were "out" in that first round of musical chairs are now being offered the programs to help them define their career direction. Not necessarily all of them will leave the company. Some may have been offered jobs that they turned down because they meant a move to another location.

Labatt's program is similar to one Mr. Tyler designed for Ontario Hydro, where he worked until recently.

Some of the differences in the program reflect different corporate cultures, he said.

Ontario Hydro promised there would be another job somewhere in the organization for anyone who wanted one, though it might mean a change of location or accepting a less senior position. About 85 per cent of those whose jobs had disappeared chose to stay.

Labatt is not making that kind of promise. "At Labatt's, it is not a new message to be unsure where you stand," Mr. Tyler observes.

Last week, the newly appointed directors and provincial general managers continued the redesign in their departments. They had to defend their plans in a discussion with peers. Once the structures were confirmed, they, too, invited their employees for the career interest interviews. By the end of this month, Labatt hopes to have the new organization in place.

Source: M. Gibb-Clark, "Reorganization by the People," *The Globe and Mail*, February 11, 1991. Reprinted with the permission of *The Globe and Mail*.

Tasks and Questions

1. How do you think the involvement of the managers in the redesign of the organization will further the corporate goals in the changing business environment of Labatt Breweries?

2. List the advantages and disadvantages of having the managers design the organization structure at their level as compared with the more traditional approach of having it designed by top company officials, particularly the vice-president of human resources.

3. Labatt intends to have the managers invite their employees for the career interest interviews to continue the redesign process within each department. Present your views on whether or not the lower-level employees will support the new reorganization approach to the same extent as the managers. Keep in mind that about 100 people will be let go in the process of reorganization.

4. How can HR managers avoid the taint of becoming known as the corporate downsizers?

CASE 1.2 ▸ Gamma Company: A Failure of HR Planning and Consultation

The Gamma Heavy Machinery Company manufactures electrical and transportation equipment. It is a Crown corporation employing approximately 1600 workers, who are represented by a very strong union. The company was one of the first manufacturing firms in Canada to adopt a CAD/CAM system, and did so on the recommendation of a consultant's feasibility study. Technicians and draftsmen were to be the main users of the system for their design work, and all draftsroom personnel were to be trained to use the system. Engineers were also to be given access to the system to do analyses.

The system's implementation was overseen by the company's Engineering Department, but no proper administrative structure was set up, and no one was officially designated in charge. In addition, the company did not set up a user advisory committee and, most importantly, did not develop an implementation plan and training program.

The consultants who had recommended the use of a CAD/CAM system had also recommended that two shifts should be used on each of the four work stations set up in the initial installation phase for the system to prove cost-effective. But the company's directors were convinced that the unionized technicians and draftsmen would never agree to work shifts and did not bother to consult them. When the system was installed, however, the unionized draftsmen and technicians immediately volunteered to work shifts and even to come in at night if necessary in order to learn how to use the system. They realized that CAD/CAM was still not in widespread use at that time, and that this represented an excellent opportunity for them to learn how to use a technology of the future. They never got that chance.

The young engineers who found it easier to learn how to use the system because of their backgrounds eagerly started to use it and, in fact, began to monopolize it. The draftsmen had little opportunity to receive the necessary training and so many of them abandoned hope of ever becoming CAD/CAM technicians. A gulf was created between engineers and draftsmen. Without training and access by technicians and draftsmen, the system did not prove productive in the draftsroom and was ignored completely by many unionized employees.

As engineers found the system more productive than did the technicians and draftsmen, the engineering directors began to hire young engineers who cost less money than unionized technicians and draftsmen. As a result, the number of technicians and draftsmen began to decline.

As is often the case when a large computer system is installed, there were some major software problems; the lack of communication in reporting these faults to the supplier turned out to be a serious problem. In light of the poor results and lack of improved productivity in the draftsroom, some administrators concluded that the wrong system had been acquired, and that the system manufacturer was doing nothing to help them.

Without a clear company policy on the training for and use of the CAD/CAM system, the people who were supposed to be its main users were effectively muscled out of the way by employees in the Engineering Department who were used to working with technology and who could see the benefits of the system for their work. With no one designated in charge of the system's implementation, the problems that ensued for the draftsroom personnel were allowed to worsen, until the workers disregarded the system, and management doubted its value.

It was only after three and a half years that the Gamma Heavy Machinery Company's administrators took a serious look at the problems and gradually instituted corrective measures to make the system productive.

Without clear line responsibility for the implementation of the CAD/CAM system at Gamma, the system was not used for its original purpose, was not used to capacity, and threatened the jobs of technicians and draftsmen.

Gamma's managers' lack of communication with the union, the system's intended users, and the manufacturer, and the lack of communication between the engineers and the draftsmen and technicians led to a series of problems that were entirely avoidable. The lack of appropriate planning for training and system selection meant that the system was blamed for problems related to the company's own mismanagement.

Source: Gordon Betcherman, Keith Newton, and Joanne Godin, eds., *Two Steps Forward: Human Resource Management in a High-Tech World*, Economic Council of Canada (Ottawa: Supply and Services Canada, 1990), pp. 49–50. Reprinted with the permission of the Chairman of the Economic Council of Canada, 1992.

Tasks and Questions

1. Summarize the major failures in Gamma's planning and implementation of the CAD/CAM system.

2. Outline what roles should have been assigned to the HR manager and the HR staff with respect to the CAD/CAM system.

3. Discuss how the lack of communication between the engineers and the technicians could have been avoided.

Notes

1. P.P. Benimadhu, *Human Resource Management: Charting a New Course* (Ottawa: The Conference Board of Canada, May 1989), p. vii. Reprinted with the permission of The Conference Board of Canada.

2. H.J. Arnold and D.C. Feldman, *Organizational Behaviour* (Toronto: McGraw-Hill, 1986), p. 10.

3. Nick Georgiades, "A Strategic Future for Personnel?" *Personnel Management*, February 1990, p. 44.

4. N.M. Meltz, "Labor Movements in Canada and the United States," in T.A. Kochan, ed., *Challenges and Choices Facing American Labor* (Cambridge, Mass.: MIT Press, 1985), pp. 315–34; N.M. Meltz, "Interstate vs. Interprovincial Differences in Union Density," *Industrial Relations*, vol. 28, no. 2 (Spring 1989), pp. 142–58; and G.N. Chaison and J.B. Rose, "Continental Divide: The Direction and Fate of North American Unions," in D. Sockell, D. Lewin, and D. Lipsky, eds., *Advances in Industrial and Labor Relations*, vol. 5 (Greenwich, Conn.: JAI Press, 1991), pp. 169–205.

5. R.J. Adams, "Industrial Relations Systems: Canada in Comparative Perspective", in John C. Anderson, Morley Gunderson, and Allen Ponak, eds., *Union–Management Relations in Canada*, 2nd ed. (Don Mills, Ont.: Addison-Wesley, 1989), p. 454.

6. Statistics Canada, *Historical Labour Force Statistics 1990*, cat. no. 71–201, p. 176, seasonally adjusted series. Reproduced with the permission of the Minister of Supply and Services Canada, 1992.

7. Canadian Labour Market and Productivity Centre, Task Force on the Labour Force Development Strategy, *Report* (Ottawa: CLMPC, 1989); and Economic Council of Canada, *Twenty-seventh Annual Review* (Ottawa, 1990).

8. Virginia Galt, "Labour Gaining Political Clout," *The Globe and Mail*, March 4, 1992.

9. Benimadhu, *Human Resource Management*, pp. 1–13. Used with the permission of The Conference Board of Canada.

10. Benimadhu, *Human Resource Management*, pp. 1–13. Used with the permission of The Conference Board of Canada.

11. T.A. Kochan and T.A. Baroci, *Human Resource Management and Industrial Relations* (Boston: Little, Brown, 1985), pp. 104–9.

12. See A. Mikalachki and J. Gandz, *Managing Absenteeism* (London, Ont.: Research and Publication Division, School of Business, University of Western Ontario, 1982).

13. Benimadhu, *Human Resource Management*, pp. 21–23. Used with the permission of The Conference Board of Canada.

14. Manpower and Immigration Canada, *Canadian Classification and Dictionary of Occupations* (Ottawa: Information Canada, 1971). Reproduced with the permission of the Minister of Supply and Services Canada, 1992. Additional definitions and recent changes in the *CCDO* are in Employment and Immigration Canada, *Canadian Classification and Dictionary of Occupations, Guide*, 9th ed. (Ottawa: Supply and Services Canada, 1989).

15. Employment and Immigration Canada, *Job Futures: An Occupational Outlook to 1995, Volume 1: Occupational Outlooks*, 1990 ed., prepared by the Canadian Occupational Projection System (COPS) (Toronto: Nelson Canada, 1990). See pp. 16–17 and 36–37 for an outline of the job environment, educational background and skills, nature of supply, market conditions and job prospects, and earnings for personnel and industrial relations management occupations and personnel and related officers.

16. Adapted from Employment and Immigration Canada, *National Occupational Classification (NOC)*, March 1990, first draft for discussion purposes (Ottawa, 1990), pp. 50–51.

17. Terry Hercus, "Professional Education in Industrial Relations and Human Resource Management: A Canadian Perspective," *Proceedings of the 18th Annual Meeting of the Canadian Industrial Relations Association*, Halifax, vol. 2 (May 1981), pp. 434–54.

18. Bill Pr 70, An Act Respecting the Human Resources Professionals Association of Ontario (HRPAO), 1990. © Reproduced with permission from the Queen's Printer for Ontario.

19. M. Cote, "The Canadian Auto Industry, 1978–1986," *Perspectives on Labour and Income*, vol. 1, no. 2 (Autumn 1989), pp. 7–18; P. Kumar and N.M. Meltz, "Industrial Relations in the Canadian Automobile Industry," in Richard P. Chaykowski and Anil Verma, eds., *Industrial Relations in Canadian Industry* (Toronto: Dryden, 1992), pp. 39–86.

20. H. Enchin. "Domestic Car Sales Skid," *The Globe and Mail*, January 5, 1991; Kumar and Meltz, "Industrial Relations in the Canadian Automobile Industry."

21. Gordon Betcherman, Keith Newton, and Joanne Godin, eds., *Two Steps Forward: Human Resource Management in a High-Tech World*, Economic Council of Canada (Ottawa: Supply and Services Canada, 1990), p. 1. Reproduced with the permission of the Chairman of the Economic Council of Canada, 1992.

22. Benimadhu, *Human Resource Management*, p. 20. Used with the permission of The Conference Board of Canada.

23. "The Changing Nature of the Canadian Labour Market: The Increased Importance of Education and Training," *Quarterly Labour Market and Productivity Review*, Winter 1988, pp. 17–23. In a subsequent report, the Canadian Labour Market and Productivity Centre (CLMPC) surveyed 822 high-tech firms and found that 55 percent were facing difficulties recruiting and retaining profes-

sional, scientific, and technical staff, while 34 percent had similar difficulties with respect to skilled trades. See CLMPC, *High-Tech Sector: A Growing Source of Skilled Jobs* (Ottawa, June 1990), p. 10.

24. B.T. Wigdor and D.K. Foot, *The Over-Forty Society: Issues for Canada's Aging Population* (Toronto: Lorimer, 1988).
25. Statistics Canada, "The Declining Labour Force Participation Rate of Men Age 55 and Over: An Examination of Possible Causes," *The Labour Force: October 1980*, cat. no. 71-001. Reproduced with the permission of the Minister of Supply and Services Canada, 1992.
26. Statistics Canada, *Labour Force Annual Averages 1990*, cat. no. 71-220, p. 13-2. Reproduced with the permission of the Minister of Supply and Services Canada, 1992.
27. Statistics Canada, *The Labour Force: October 1980*, p. 79. Reproduced with the permission of the Minister of Supply and Services Canada, 1992.
28. Canada, *Report of the Commission on Equality in Employment*, Judge Rosalie Silberman Abella, Chair (Ottawa: Supply and Services Canada, 1984).
29. A. Deutsch, *The Human Resource Revolution: Communicate or Litigate* (New York: McGraw-Hill, 1979), p. 56. Reproduced with the permission of McGraw-Hill, Inc.
30. A. Verma and M. Thompson, "Managerial Strategies in Canada and the U.S. in the 1980s," *Proceedings of the Forty-First Annual Meeting, Industrial Relations Research Association* (Madison, Wisc., 1989), pp. 257-64.
31. Bureau of Labour Information, *Provisions in Collective Agreements* (Ottawa: Labour Canada, October 22, 1991), special tabulation.
32. P. Kumar, *Professionalism in the Canadian PAIR Function: Report of a Survey* (Kingston, Ont.: Industrial Relations Centre, Queen's University, 1980).
33. Benimadhu, *Human Resource Management*, pp. 15-20. Used with the permission of The Conference Board of Canada.
34. Leslie Papp, "Bridging the Gap: Labor, Management Find Innovative Ways to Keep Peace in Tough Times," *The Toronto Star*, March 7, 1992.

SUGGESTIONS FOR FURTHER READING

- Roger Cooke and Michael Armstrong. "The Search for Strategic HRM." *Personnel Management*, December 1990, pp. 31-33.
- Nick Georgiades. "A Strategic Future for Personnel?" *Personnel Management*, February 1990, pp. 43-45.
- Michael Porter. *Canada at the Crossroads*. Ottawa: Business Council on National Issues, 1991.
- Randall Schuler. "Repositioning the Human Resource Function: Transformation or Demise?" *Academy of Management Executive*, vol. 4, no. 3 (1990), pp. 49-60.
- James W. Walker. "Human Resource Roles for the '90s." *Human Resource Planning*, vol. 12, no. 1 (1989), pp. 55-61.

CHAPTER 2

THE HUMAN ASSET

- THE LABOUR FORCE
- HRM IN ACTION ▸ DEMOGRAPHICS AND LABOUR COSTS
- INDIVIDUAL BEHAVIOUR AND JOB PERFORMANCE
- OLDER EMPLOYEES: A VALUABLE RESOURCE
- SUMMARY
- REVIEW QUESTIONS
- PROJECT IDEAS
- CASE 2.1 ▸ TRENDS IN EMPLOYEE ATTITUDES: DIFFERENCES BETWEEN CANADIAN AND AMERICAN WORKERS
- CASE 2.2 ▸ CHALLENGE AT RED MAPLE FOODS
- NOTES
- SUGGESTIONS FOR FURTHER READING

AN ECONOMIC COUNCIL OF CANADA CASEBOOK ENTITLED *Two Steps Forward: Human Resource Management in a High-Tech World* tells an interesting story about the Ford Motor Company's Essex Engine plant.

In 1986, product line changes and the resulting changes in jobs led to workers' complaints about jobs which were "too tight" or "not tight enough." Management's response was typically, "That's the way it is." In 1989, when line changes led to problems in job content or processes, management's response [was] likely to be, "If it's too tight, we'll change it—for an honest day's work."

There have also been changes in personnel, management, and the union since 1986. With a plant manager who has worked in every part of the engine business and who insists on a clear vision of the plant's goals, the emphasis in hiring new managers is on finding people who will fit into Essex Engine's approaches to union–management relations and quality. Assignments for managers and supervisors are decided on the basis of people skills, not just technical skills. And management continues to work on developing the relationships in the plant.

Historically, there has never been a high number of grievances at Essex Engine. And today, with an increased emphasis on solving problems on the shop floor, the industrial relations manager becomes involved with union complaints only infrequently. The union says that the manager's willingness to listen has made a big difference at Essex Engine, and that the "guys in Windsor give it their best." The manager responds by saying that there is a "very strong work ethic" in Windsor.

... Whereas in 1986 the Council researchers heard all about the lessons management had learned from their visit to Japanese auto plants, in 1989 we learned that the Japanese auto makers now visit the Essex Engine plant.[1]

In 1989, Essex Engine became the first Ford plant to win the prestigious Q1 award from Ford.

This example demonstrates the potential of people to be their company's greatest asset. The degree to which that potential is reached depends largely on the way an organization manages and deploys its people. This chapter discusses human resources from both a general and a specific perspective. From a general perspective, we look at the labour force, especially its characteristics, its trends, and common indices used to describe it. From a specific perspective, we examine employee behaviour and performance on an individual level.

Both economic and psychological perspectives are important in planning and administering many human resource policies and practices. For example, research has shown that economic indicators such as the number of people in the labour force and the unemployment rate are related to turnover rates.[2] When the unemployment rate is low and job opportunities exist, it is easier for employees to find alternative employment than when the unemployment rate is high. Thus, employers often find it necessary to adjust pay and benefits upwards and to make other human resource policy changes in order to retain current employees and to attract new ones. A recent model of employee turnover includes economic factors, level of job satisfaction (a psychological factor), and human resource policies and practices.[3] Knowledge of general economic information and specific psychological theory and research is essential if HRM professionals are to help the organization achieve its goals.

This chapter discusses the labour force, and then examines employee behaviour and the psychological aspects of work behaviour.

The Labour Force

HRM professionals must be able to understand and interpret labour force statistics that reflect demographic changes in the population. Some large employers, such as General Motors, have hired demographers to help HRM professionals plan.[4] Labour force statistics provide planners and policy makers with information regarding the number of people employed and unemployed, turnover rates, and the types of industries experiencing growth or decline.

Knowledge of labour force characteristics, trends, and local labour market conditions is particularly useful for the HRM functions of human resource planning, recruiting, and compensation. For example, the fact that the birth rate in Canada has been declining and the mortality rate has been stable for several years means that the demand for an employer's product may not be as great in the future as it has been in the past, unless net immigration continues at least at the level of the past two decades, that is, at 0.4 percent of the population per year. The Economic Council of Canada's recent statement, "New Faces in the Crowd," calls for a gradual increase in annual net immigration to 0.8 percent of the population by the year 2015.[5] Employment and Immigration Canada has proposed a greater immediate increase to attain almost the same level by 1995.[6] Both agencies see increased immigration as a means to offset the aging of the work force and the reduction in the proportion of younger workers resulting from the sharp decline in the Canadian birth rate. Whichever scenario is adopted, the rate of increase of new entrants to the labour force will be smaller than it was in the early 1970s, when the labour force grew at an annual average rate of 3.4 percent. (The comparable figure at the end of the 1980s was 2.0 percent.)

This trend may demand a major change in human resource planning programs—perhaps less emphasis on recruiting and selection and more on training and development.

Trends and changes in the numbers of people employed in various industries and jobs also affect the planning and administration of many HRM programs. For example, when the unemployment rate is very low, employers have to expend more effort on recruiting; selection standards may have to be lowered in order to fill vacancies, and compensation raised both to attract new employees and to retain current ones. When the unemployment rate is high the reverse generally occurs, except that compensation may be adjusted only moderately to reflect the rate of inflation.

These are only a few examples of the importance to HRM professionals of monitoring various labour statistics and trends so that human resource policies and practices can be modified to meet changes in the supply of and demand for labour.

The major source of labour force data is Statistics Canada, which regularly conducts a number of pertinent surveys and analyzes and publishes the results. *The Labour Force* (catalogue number 71-001), its monthly survey of 62 000 representative households across the country, provides the most complete picture available of the employed and unemployed in Canada. Exhibit 2.1 shows the types of information collected in it, the size and nature of the survey sample, and the definitions it uses. Another Statistics Canada survey, ***Employment Earnings and Hours*** (catalogue number 72-002), is based on establishment—that is, employer—information; it collects monthly data on the numbers of people employed, hours worked, and average pay or earnings by province and industry. A new quarterly publication from Statistics Canada, *Perspectives on Labour and Income* (catalogue number 75-001E), presents articles analyzing developments in the Canadian work force as well as a summary of key statistics. An overview of regular labour market and employee compensation publications is contained in *Labour Research Resource Manual*, published by the Canadian Labour Market and Productivity Centre in 1990.

EXHIBIT 2.1
Statistics Canada's Definitions of Labour Force Terms

The statistics contained in this report [*The Labour Force*] are based on information obtained through a sample survey of households. Interviews are carried out in about 62 000 representative households across the country, involving some 115 000 respondents.

The Labour Force Survey, started in November 1945, was taken at quarterly intervals until November 1952. Since then it has been carried out monthly. Beginning in January 1976, following more than 3 years of development, substantial revisions to the labour force survey were introduced. Details of these changes are available on request from the Labour Force Survey Sub-Division, Statistics Canada, Ottawa, K1A 0T6.

The sample used in the surveys of the labour force has been designed to represent all persons in the population 15 years of age and over residing in Canada, with the exception of the following: residents of the Yukon and Northwest Territories, persons living on Indian reserves, full-time members of the armed forces and people living in institutions.

Data collection is carried out during the week following the reference week. Statistics Canada interviewers contact each of the dwellings in the sample through personal and/or telephone interviews to obtain the information needed to produce the labour force data. . . . Each interviewer contacts approximately 65 designated dwellings (the individual assignment size varies by type of area) and conducts a personal interview in all dwellings where interviews are being conducted for the first time. In most areas, provided the respondent agrees, subsequent interviews may be conducted by telephone, an interview technique which has been shown to have no discernible impact on the data and which offers significant savings in time and cost.

DEFINITIONS AND EXPLANATIONS

Labour Force
The labour force is composed of those members of the civilian non-institutional population 15 years of age and over who, during the reference week, were employed or unemployed.

Employed
Employed persons are those who, during the reference week:
a. did any work at all
b. had a job but were not at work due to:
- own illness or disability
- personal or family responsibilities
- bad weather
- labour dispute
- vacation
- other reason not specified above (excluding persons on layoff and persons whose job attachment was to a job to start at a definite date in the future).

EXHIBIT 2.1 *(continued)*

Unemployed

Unemployed persons are those who, during the reference week:
a. were without work, had actively looked for work in the past four weeks (ending with reference week), and were available for work;
b. had not actively looked for work in the past four weeks but had been on layoff and were available for work;
c. had not actively looked for work in the past four weeks but had a new job to start in four weeks or less from reference week, and were available for work.

Not in the Labour Force

Those persons in the civilian non-institutional population 15 years of age and over who, during the reference week, were neither employed nor unemployed.

Unemployment Rate

The unemployment rate represents the number of unemployed persons expressed as a per cent of the labour force. The unemployment rate for a particular group (age, sex, marital status, etc.) is the number unemployed in that group expressed as a per cent of the labour force for that group.

Participation Rate

The participation rate represents the labour force expressed as a percentage of the population 15 years of age and over. The participation rate for a particular group (age, sex, marital status, etc.) is the labour force in that group expressed as a percentage of the population for that group.

Employment/Population Ratio

The employment/population ratio represents the number of persons employed expressed as a percentage of the population 15 years of age and over. The employment/population ratio for a particular group (age, sex, marital status, etc.) is the number employed in that group expressed as a percentage of the population for that group.

Source: Statistics Canada, *The Labour Force*, cat. no. 71–001, December 1990, C-3. Reproduced with the permission of the Minister of Supply and Services Canada, 1992.

Some Labour Force Terminology

It is important to use exact definitions in order to permit correct interpretation of statistics and to ensure the consistency of data over time. When changes in definitions are deemed necessary, they almost inevitably affect results. For example, the 1975 revision of Statistics Canada's monthly household survey enlarged the size of the sample and excluded 14-year-olds from its definition of potential members of the labour force; it also substituted a direct form of questioning for an indirect one. (The old survey had asked "What did this person do mostly last week?" The revised version has "Last week, did . . . do any work at a job or business?") These changes in themselves made the survey produce a higher unemployment rate for females (8.1 percent) than for males (6.2 percent), whereas the old version would have produced the reverse (6.4 percent versus 7.4 percent).[7]

Participation Rate

An index commonly used to describe the labour force is the *participation rate*, which is broadly defined as the percentage of persons eligible for the labour force who actually are in it. An "eligible" person is any person age 15 or older who is not institutionalized and who is not living on an Indian reserve. It is important to realize that being "in the labour force" is not a synonym for being employed. A person is considered to be *in the labour force* if he or she is employed or is unemployed but actively seeking employment. When we say the female participation rate reached 58.4 percent in 1990, we are saying that almost three-fifths of the noninstitutionalized women age 15 and older (those "eligible") were actually in the labour force. Some were employed; others were unemployed but seeking work.

Discouraged Workers

A related concept is what economists term *discouraged workers*: people who want work and yet are not job hunting because they believe suitable employment is not available. The Labour Force Survey identifies persons who looked for work in the previous six months but who have stopped searching. In addition, each March, Statistics Canada adds to the Labour Force Survey a supplement called the Survey of Job Opportunities (SJO). It counts all those people expressing a desire for work and available for work, irrespective of their past job-search activity.

Data from the SJO show that the number of discouraged workers moves with the economic cycle: it is high when unemployment is high and low in a boom period. In March 1983, in the wake of the 1981–82 recession, the number of discouraged workers reached 197 000. By 1989, after a prolonged economic growth, the number was down to 70 000.

Discouraged workers tend to be older people (over age 45) and young people (ages 15 to 24). They are concentrated in the Atlantic provinces and Quebec, and the numbers are almost equally divided between men and women. In March 1989, if discouraged workers had been counted as unemployed, the unemployment rate would have been 9.1 percent instead of the recorded 8.6. In March 1983, discouraged workers would have added 1.4 percentage points to the employment rate.[8] The number of discouraged workers, like the number of long-term unemployed, rose significantly during the recession of the early 1990s.

Projections

Nobody can say exactly how the labour force will change in a decade or five years or even six months. Yet many kinds of industrial and government planning require the best possible estimates of how many and what kinds of people will be working—or available for work—at specific times and places in the future. Accordingly, researchers regularly make forecasts about the labour force. Like all economic forecasting, the subject is enormously complicated, but one method is to take trends that occurred in the recent past and *project* them into the future by assuming that the same changes will continue. For example, aside from possible immigrants, we know how many people in Canada will be 15 to 24 years of age in the year 2000. One way to project their rate of participation in the labour force is to assume that the net change from 1990 to 2000 will be the same as the net change from 1980 to 1990. This simplifying assumption provides one of a number of alternative ways of coming up with future scenarios for the labour force.

GENERAL TRENDS AND CHARACTERISTICS OF THE LABOUR FORCE

General Participation Rates

The recent overall trend is toward increased participation in the labour force. This means that a higher proportion of the population is entering the labour force today than in the past. As illustrated in Figure 2.1, and detailed in Table 2.1, the proportion of the eligible population that was either employed or

TABLE 2.1
Labour Force Participation Rates in Canada by Age Group and Sex

	TOTAL M & F Combined	M	F	AGES 15–24 M	F	AGES 25–54 M	F	AGES 55+ M	F
1966	57.3	79.8	35.4	64.1	48.4	96.5	36.9	56.7	18.0
1970	57.8	77.8	38.3	62.5	49.5	95.3	41.9	54.9	18.5
1980	64.1	78.4	50.4	71.8	62.6	94.8	60.1	46.6	18.4
1990	67.0	75.9	58.4	71.1	66.6	93.3	75.6	37.5	17.5
2000	68.1	74.1	62.5	69.0	65.0	92.5	84.6	35.8	19.8
2005	67.2	72.2	62.6	69.0	65.0	92.0	86.7	35.0	22.0
2010	66.2	70.8	62.0	69.0	65.0	92.0	87.5	35.0	24.5
2015	64.9	69.2	60.9	69.0	65.0	92.0	87.5	35.0	27.0

Source: Compiled from Statistics Canada, *Historical Labour Force Statistics 1990*, cat. no. 71-201. Reproduced with the permission of the Minister of Supply and Services Canada, 1992; and Peter Dungan, Steven Murphy, and Thomas Wilson, *National Projections through 2015*, Policy and Economic Analysis Program, Policy Study 92–1 (Toronto: Institute for Policy Analysis, University of Toronto, April 1992), and special tabulations. Reproduced with the permission of the Institute for Policy Analysis.

seeking work remained relatively stable, at about 55 percent, in the 1950s and 1960s. Since the early 1970s, however, there has been a small but significant increase in the participation rate, indicating that, as the eligible population has grown, the size of the labour force has grown more than proportionately. In 1990, the Canadian labour force had 13.7 million people. This represented a 67 percent participation rate, up from 64 percent in 1980

FIGURE 2.1
Actual and Projected Labour Force Participation Rates in Canada

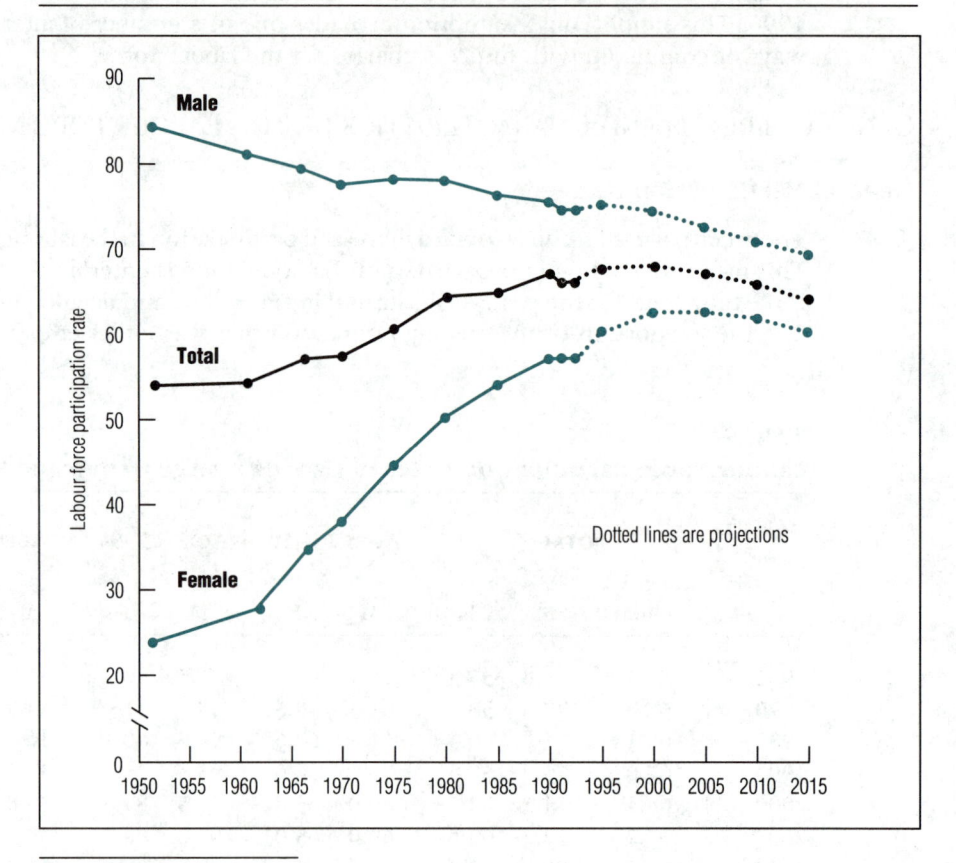

Source: Compiled from 1951 and 1961: Census data; 1966 to 1990: Canada, Department of Finance, *Quarterly Economic Review*, June 1991; 1991: Statistics Canada, *Labour Force Annual Averages 1991*, cat. no. 71-220, February 1992; 1992 to 2015: Peter Dungan, Steven Murphy, and Thomas Wilson, *National Projections through 2015*, Policy and Economic Analysis Program, Policy Study No. 92-1 (Toronto: Institute for Policy Analysis, University of Toronto, April 1992), Table 6, and special tabulations. Data used with permission.

and from almost 58 percent in 1970. Due to the recession, the participation rate in 1991 was slightly below the 67 percent rate in 1990. Projections to 1995 and 2000 suggest that the combined participation rate will continue to increase as in the 1980s but at a slower rate than in the 1970s. The participation rate is projected to start declining at the beginning of the next century and is expected to decrease to 64.9 percent by 2015, which is just above the level of 1980. This will occur in the absence of major changes in immigration, unless there is an increase in the participation rate of older males.

Female Participation Rates

Changes in participation rates among certain groups of the population have been more dramatic than among others. In fact, as illustrated in Figure 2.1, the increase in the overall participation rate resulted from a steady surge in the proportion of women who entered the labour force. The breakdowns in Table 2.1 show that 38.3 percent of Canadian women were either working or looking for work in 1970; the figure in 1990 had grown by more than half, to 58.4 percent. By contrast, the participation rate of males in 1990 was lower than that of 1970.

Further examination of the table reveals that the participation rate for women has increased most in the 25-to-54 age group. These have traditionally been regarded as the childbearing and childrearing years. Now many women in this age group are not having children, and many others are working mothers.

Many factors combine to explain the trend toward women's increased participation in the labour force. These causes include cultural values involving work and the family; changed attitudes toward family size; more labour- and time-saving devices in the home; the rising cost of living; and, most important, the huge increase in jobs that already had high proportions of female employees, such as the teaching and nursing professions, and clerical and personal service work.

The trend toward increased female participation has prompted and will continue to prompt changes in human resource policies and practices. In particular, the increasing employment of mothers means that employers must adapt and change some human resource policies, such as working hours and health care programs. For example, the Unemployment Insurance (UI) Act now provides women who are absent from work because of pregnancy a maximum of fifteen weeks of benefits that amount to 60 percent of the average weekly insurable earnings. In addition, ten weeks of parental benefits are available to natural or adoptive parents (for either parent or to be shared) as weeks of sickness benefits. However, in a trend initiated by the Canadian Union of Postal Workers following a strike in 1981, many collective agreements now include additions to UI benefits for maternity leave. The CUPW agreement provides for 93 percent of pay for seventeen weeks.

Male Participation Rates

The trend in male participation rates has been downwards, from 79.8 percent in the civilian labour force in 1966 to 75.9 percent in 1990. As shown in Figure 2.1, this decline was not steady during the 40-year period; rather, the rate rose and fell with economic cycles. The deep recession of the early 1990s produced a marked decrease of almost two percentage points.

This downward trend is age-related, concentrated in the younger and older groups (ages 24 and under and 55 and over). The fall-off for male youths, which reversed itself, particularly among teenagers, by 1980, reflected society's increased urbanization and industrialization, which required workers to obtain considerable training. It was a result of the increased accessibility of higher education and a desire by increasingly educated parents to keep their children in school longer.[9] The downward trend for the older group resulted from a number of factors, such as early retirement policies and improved pensions. Thus, we see that economic conditions, social values, and employment policies, such as pensions, all affect the participation rate.

The projections in Table 2.1 indicate a continuation of the decline among older men, an expectation reflecting retirement policies and expanded pension coverage. On the other hand, given the increasing proportion of 45- to 54-year-olds in this group and the effects of reduced real incomes, these rates may be underestimated. Forecasters differ in their projections for the participation rate of male youths; Table 2.1 provides one forecast.

Age Trends

The median age of the working population is increasing and is expected to continue to do so for some decades. The cause is the postwar "baby boomers," who reached working age in the late 1960s and 1970s, plus the subsequent fall in the birth rate. Unless the participation rate increases drastically and unexpectedly, the proportion of youths (15 to 24 years) in the labour force will decline from less than one-fifth in 1990 to a low point of 16.2 percent in 2021.[10] The baby boomers will be the dominant age group in the labour force until they begin to retire in the early part of the twenty-first century. The competition for jobs among them is expected to be intense.

The effects of an aging population on the labour force are further discussed at the end of this chapter, along with some thoughts on the roles of older workers.

Overall Growth

As a result of a combination of these and other trends, the economy's total supply of labour is expected to grow at about 1.5 percent per annum between 1990 and 2000, down from 3.2 percent during the 1970s (which was the fastest growth rate of any of the industrialized countries) and 1.8 percent per

HRM IN ACTION

DEMOGRAPHICS AND LABOUR COSTS

The aging of Canada's working population means that ways must be found to allow some people to continue working past 65 without the company incurring too many costs or liabilities in the process. There may be ways of accomplishing this goal. The key is that while most workers would like to retire early, many are also looking for part-time work or a different sort of work after retirement. With the anticipated shortage of skilled younger workers many companies may be prepared to retain older workers and their expertise.

An American insurance company allows retired employees to work up to 960 hours a year without reductions in their pension income. Because of the increasing costs of health care, companies are likely to favour "wellness programs," such as workplace fitness, and programs to assist employees with drug, alcohol, or personal problems. At the same time, companies may begin looking at putting caps on the daily hospital charges they will cover. Older employees may also need different dental coverages, less frequent checkups but more coverage for periodontal (gum) treatment. All of these considerations suggest that human resource professionals have to be very conscious of the demographic (age and gender) composition of their workforce and of the available supply of labour.

Source: Adapted from Margot Gibb-Clark, "Aging Work Force Poses Challenges," *The Globe and Mail*, November 8, 1991. Used with the permission of *The Globe and Mail*.

---

annum during the 1980s. Two-thirds of the increase will come from population growth; increased participation will add the rest.[11]

Provincial Differences

Interprovincial migration patterns can also affect overall labour force growth since participation rates differ by province, with the highest rates in the West, particularly Alberta, and lowest in the East, particularly Newfoundland, as shown in Table 2.2. The major factors underlying the differences are the age structure of the population and the demand for labour. Provinces with relatively low unemployment rates tend to have relatively high participation rates and vice versa. For example, in 1990, Ontario had the lowest

TABLE 2.2
Employment/Population Ratio, Labour Force Participation, and Labour Force by Province

	CAN.	NFLD.	PEI	NS	NB	QUE.	ONT.	MAN.	SASK.	ALTA.	BC
Employment/Population ratio											
1990	61.5	46.4	56.2	55.6	52.5	57.8	65.0	62.7	62.1	67.1	60.6
Labour force participation (%)											
1990	67.0	56.0	66.0	62.1	59.8	64.3	69.4	67.6	66.8	72.1	66.0
Labour force											
1990 (000s)	13 681	242	65	424	331	3 399	5 268	544	483	1 324	1 601
2000											
Projected no., 000s	15 849	283	67	457	363	3 899	6 165	586	509	1 561	1 958
Projected % increase	15.8	16.9	3.1	7.8	9.7	14.7	17.0	7.7	5.4	17.9	22.3

Source: Compiled from Statistics Canada, *Historical Labour Force Statistics 1990*, cat. 71-201; and Employment and Immigration Canada, *Job Futures: An Occupational Outlook to 1995, Volume 1: Occupational Outlooks*, 1990 ed., prepared by the Canadian Occupational Projection System (COPS) (Toronto, Nelson Canada, 1990). Reproduced with the permission of the Minister of Supply and Services Canada, 1992.

unemployment rate (6.3 percent) and the second-highest participation rate (69.4 percent), while Newfoundland had the highest unemployment rate (17.1 percent) and the lowest participation rate (56.0 percent). The projected growth rate in Table 2.2 shows low population and labour force growth in Prince Edward Island, Alberta, and Saskatchewan. The latter two are the result of significant net out-migration. For Alberta this represents a reversal of earlier projections made before the drop in world oil prices in the mid-1980s, which sharply reduced investment in oil projects and led to a substantial rise in unemployment. Only Ontario stands out as having substantially above average labour force growth. However, the recession of the early 1990s hit Ontario harder than any other province in Canada and this may affect future labour force growth.

Part-Time Workers

Another trend in the labour force has been the growth in the number of part-time employees. Statistics Canada defines a *part-time employee* as one who works fewer than 30 hours per week. The number of employees working part-time on a voluntary basis has grown steadily in recent years, except during the severe recession of the early 1980s. The rate of increase of part-time workers has been more than twice the rate of increase in full-timers over the past decade.

Involuntary part-time—part-time employment accepted by workers who would prefer full-time work but cannot find it—is also rising. In 1981, 18 percent of part-timers were involuntary. The figure was 28.5 percent two years later, when the overall unemployment rate had risen by more than half. It declined to 22.2 percent in 1989, after unemployment had decreased to the 1981 level, but rose to 26.8 percent in January 1992.[12]

A variant of part-time work that is in some ways involuntary is also on the rise. *Work sharing* involves the agreement of all employees in a unit to work part-time rather than having some of them laid off. Between 1977 and 1979, the federal government experimented with using unemployment insurance (UI) funds to assist work sharing. Although the experiment resulted in greater-than-expected costs, both employees and plant officials were enthusiastic about it. Union leaders opposed it, however, because they thought it would deflect efforts to fight the recession. And employer associations were concerned that the shorter work weeks would become a permanent feature and lead to increased labour costs.[13] Nevertheless, in the face of sharp increases in unemployment, the UI-assisted program was reintroduced in fall 1981 and expanded the following spring. By the summer of 1982, an estimated 150 000 Canadian workers were engaged in work sharing,[14] and by the end of 1982, 8780 firms and more than 200 000 employees were participating. With the economic recovery of the mid-1980s, work sharing declined sharply. The onset of the recession of the early 1990s, however, brought renewed interest in it.[15]

Of course, many organizations hire part-time employees not to mitigate the effects of recession but to solve particular problems, such as scheduling. In the past, part-time employees derived no benefits, but now that part-time employment is more common and is accepted by both management and unions, an increasing number of these employees receive benefits in proportion to their hours worked. In briefs presented to the 1982 Commission of Inquiry into Part-Time Work, the majority of employer associations reported, however, that part-time workers are not paid fringe benefits other than mandated benefits, such as those for the Canada (or Quebec) Pension Plan, unemployment insurance, and holiday pay. Employers who did pay benefits tended to be in the public sector, such as health care facilities and municipal governments. Private employers in some industries, such as insurance, also reported that they paid benefits to regular part-time workers.[16]

Most legislated benefits, such as holiday and vacation pay, are prorated for part-timers by the number of hours worked.

In Canada, part-timers are concentrated in the retail trade and in service industries.[17] Employers with concentrated periods of activity find it advantageous to use part-timers, especially for relatively low-paying work, because they do not have to pay the full range of benefits for part-time employees. It has been estimated that prorating all fringe benefits for part-time employees would increase straight-line labour costs by an average of 9.1 percent.[18]

Clearly, the part-time labour force has become an established part of our economy and labour force. Part-time employment will in all likelihood continue to grow for several reasons: (1) the entrance to the labour force of a rising proportion of women, many of whom will assume part-time positions; (2) continued growth in the service industries, which employ more than 50 percent of all part-timers;[19] and (3) the difficulty for single-income families to increase their standard of living.

Minorities

Although Canada is a country of minorities and ethnic groups, from a labour market perspective the most disadvantaged are the Native people, particularly Indians. Those living on reserves are excluded from labour force statistics, a method of data gathering that lowers the measured rate of Native unemployment but does not reduce the severity of the problem. Statistics from the 1986 census indicate that even with a lower participation rate than the total population, the unemployment rate of aboriginal peoples was more than two in ten (22.7 percent), twice the national average of one in ten (10.3 percent). In contrast, the unemployment rate among visible minorities in 1986 was only a fraction above the national average (10.8 percent versus 10.3 percent), and the participation rate was higher than the national average. These data indicate the continuing relevance of the findings of an earlier federal task force report that called for special training programs; wage subsidies to encourage employment; intensive counselling; and employment support services, such as child care, transportation, and adjustment assistance.[20]

The 1984 Abella Commission identified the need for programs of employment equity to remove discrimination against women, Native people, people with disabilities, and visible minorities. A key element in these programs is government intervention through law to remove what the commission termed "systemic discrimination" against these groups.[21]

In April 1986, the federal government passed Bill C-62, An Act Respecting Employment Equity. Bill C-62 contains two federal programs: the Legislated Employment Equity Program and the Federal Contractors Program. The Legislated Program applies to Crown corporations and to federally regulated employers (primarily the banking, transportation, and communications industries) with two or more employees. Employers are required to submit annual reports that show the representation of members of the four designated groups in specific salary ranges, occupational groups, hirings, promotions, and terminations. Employers who fail to report may be fined up to $50 000. The Federal Contractors Program requires that federal government suppliers of goods and services with 100 or more employees that are bidding on government contracts worth $200 000 or more commit themselves to comply with employment equity as a condition of their bid. If there is not a satisfactory commitment to employment equity, a bid can be declared invalid.

Suppliers who make employment equity commitments and are awarded contracts are subject to on-site reviews.

Industry Employment Projections

Chapter 1 introduced the concept of redundancy planning, explaining that technological and market changes are causing sizable changes in the demand for employees in various industries. Some industries are growing and are seeking more qualified employees, while others are declining and laying off workers. Knowing which industries will experience growth and which will experience decline is very useful to human resource planners. This is especially true since the "baby boomers" are now in the labour force, and there will be fewer new workers because of the "baby bust" of the past two and a half decades. The implication is that growth industries must develop programs to recruit, hire, and train experienced employees from declining industries.

As reflected in Table 2.3, employment growth between 1980 and 1990 was confined to construction and the service industries, in particular community, business, and personal services and finance, insurance, and real estate. There were declines in manufacturing, agriculture, and other primary industries. (It should be noted, however, that the lack of employment growth in manufacturing and other goods sectors was partly a reflection of the greater growth of productivity — output per person hours — there than in services. The share of total output from manufacturing did not decline between 1980 and 1990, even though its share of employment fell from 19.7 to 15.9 percent.)

The projections to the year 2000 suggest a continuation of these trends, with the service sector growing faster than the goods-producing sector, though more moderately than in the past. The most significant change expected in the goods sector is fairly strong growth in the construction industry, initially because of pent-up demand for housing following limited construction in the recession at the beginning of the 1990s. The service-producing industries will still experience above-average growth, but it will be confined to the community, business, and personal service sectors, reflecting continued demand for health care from an aging population and to the finance, insurance, and real-estate group, reflecting the continuing importance of financial services. The growth of health care, however, may be tempered by provincial and federal budget restrictions.

Manufacturing as a whole is projected to have little growth. The industry experienced a major decline in employment during the 1981–82 recession and an even larger decline during the recession of the early 1990s. Some sectors will, however, show interesting variations. For example, the telecommunication products and aerospace industries are expected to grow rapidly in keeping with the upsurge in technology-based output. On the other hand, the growth of the automotive industry will be below average as a result of

TABLE 2.3
Past and Projected Employment and Employment Growth in Canada by Industry Sector, 1980–2000

	EMPLOYMENT			CHANGE	
	1980	1990	2000	1980–1990	1990–2000
	thousands			*percent*	
Goods-producing industries	3 514	3 489	3 916	9.9	12.2
Agriculture	479	428	434	−10.6	1.4
Other primary	300	283	315	−5.7	11.3
Manufacturing	2 111	2 001	2 266	−5.2	13.2
Construction	624	778	901	24.7	15.8
Service-producing industries	7 194	9 083	10 673	26.3	17.5
Transportation, communications, and utilities	906	951	1 064	5.0	11.9
Trade	1 837	2 247	2 420	22.3	7.7
Finance, insurance and real estate	611	755	908	23.6	20.3
Community, business, and personal service	3 096	4 299	5 411	38.9	25.9
Public administration	744	831	870	11.7	4.7
Total, all industries	10 708	12 572	14 587	17.4	16.0

Source: Compiled from Statistics Canada, *Historical Labour Force Statistics 1990*, cat. no. 71-201; and Employment and Immigration Canada, *Job Futures: An Occupational Outlook to 1995, Volume 1: Occupational Outlooks*, 1990 ed., prepared by the Canadian Occupational Projection System (COPS) (Toronto: Nelson Canada, 1990). Reproduced with the permission of the Minister of Supply and Services Canada, 1992.

long-run structural adjustments related to the development of fuel-efficient vehicles and the effects on demand of slower population growth. The major changes in the patterns of employment growth and the severe recessions of the early 1980s and early 1990s have focussed attention on job security. A 1990 Gallup poll indicated that 69 percent of Canadians are very concerned about unemployment.[22] The effect of changes in technology points up the continuing importance of education and training beyond the secondary school level, as well as the need for human resource planning in the economy.

CONCLUSION

This section has presented labour force statistics and trends, plus the terminology needed to interpret labour force data. Knowledge of labour force data is especially useful to the planning and staffing areas of HRM responsibility. We now turn from this more macro focus to a closer inspection of the individual worker and of how behaviour and performance can be explained and directed. This knowledge is especially useful in formulating and administering effective HRM policies for employee development and maintenance.

Individual Behaviour and Job Performance

HRM professionals are required to know a great deal about human behaviour because they are responsible for developing and administering most of the organizational policies, programs, and rules that affect employee work behaviour. *Work behaviour* is simply what people do at work. It includes activities directed toward accomplishment of work-related tasks, as well as nonessential activities such as coffee breaks with co-workers and twiddling one's thumbs. Some kinds of behaviour, such as attendance, promptness, compliance with rules, and producing high-quality work, are desirable to employers, but others, such as high absenteeism, tardiness, chatting too much, and theft, are undesirable. Most human resource policies and programs are aimed at encouraging desired work behaviour and discouraging undesirable behaviour.

Employers are primarily interested in two major aspects of employee behaviour: job performance and job satisfaction. High levels of performance and satisfaction contribute to the achievement of organizational goals and objectives. This section discusses performance and job satisfaction, as well as ways to encourage appropriate and desired behaviour.

A Model of Performance and Satisfaction

Figure 2.2 is adapted only slightly from the Porter and Lawler model of job performance and satisfaction. This model portrays the relationship between two factors, or variables, important to organizational effectiveness — performance and job satisfaction. Though the Porter–Lawler model does not include all the factors related to performance and satisfaction, it does identify some of the major ones. Thus, the model can be used as a framework for discussion of factors affecting employee behaviour and how they relate to various HRM functions. Additionally, components of the model will be discussed here.

Before examining the model in detail, it is helpful to have a brief overview. Performance is the result of an employee's work. It is determined by three factors: (1) abilities, skills, and knowledge; (2) effort; and (3) role perceptions (what an employee is expected to do on the job). Performance leads to both extrinsic rewards, such as pay, promotion, privileges, and recognition, and intrinsic rewards, such as feelings of accomplishment and self-worth. Rewards received for performance result in certain levels of job satisfaction.

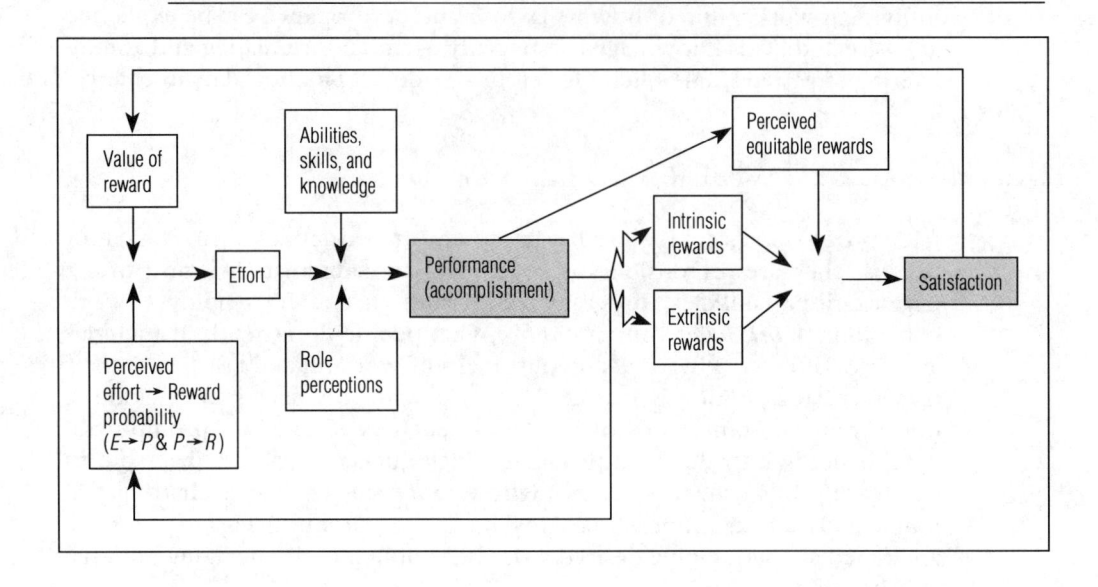

FIGURE 2.2
Porter and Lawler's Model of Job Performance and Satisfaction

Source: Adapted from Lyman W. Porter and E.E. Lawler III, *Managerial Attitudes and Performance* (Homewood, Ill.: Richard D. Irwin and Dorsey Press, 1968), p. 165. Reprinted with the permission of the publisher.

Level of satisfaction is determined by employee perception of the fairness of those rewards. If, for example, an employee perceives a reward to be quite generous, the level of satisfaction is higher than if the reward is perceived as negligible or is not valued. Job satisfaction, in turn, affects the effort an employee will put into future performance. Generally, more effort is expended by someone who is satisfied with the rewards received for previous performance. Level of effort expended is also influenced by the value an employee attaches to a reward based on performance, and the employee's perception of his or her efforts leading to a given reward (perceived effort–reward probability).

There are many aspects of job performance, including quantity and quality of production, and speed of performance. A basic goal of human resource management is to ensure that employees perform at a level acceptable to the organization.

Abilities, Skills, and Knowledge

Abilities, skills, and knowledge are work-related physical and mental characteristics of each employee. An *ability* is a person's competence to perform a particular kind of observable behaviour. People have a large number of abilities—verbal ability, mathematical ability, athletic ability, to name a few. Abilities are present in varying amounts in each individual. These differing levels of ability within an individual are referred to as *intra-individual differences*. There are also differences in ability levels among individuals, which are referred to as *inter-individual differences*. For example, people differ in their ability to bench-press weight. Figure 2.3 shows two hypothetical distributions of the amount of weight bench-pressed by a random sample of 140 men and 140 women. (Amount bench-pressed is a measure of upper body strength.) The average, or mean, weight pressed by men in the sample is 132.0 kilograms, compared to approximately 81.5 kilograms for women. The shaded area in the figure represents the amount of overlap between men and women in the sample. *Overlap* means simply that a certain number of the members of one group have ability levels equal to or greater than some members of the other group. In this example, 21 percent of the women can bench-press more weight than 21 percent of the men (30 women can press 112.5 kilograms or more; 30 men can press less than 100 kilograms). It is important for HRM professionals to acknowledge the existence of overlap between groups such as men and women, whites and visible minorities, and so on and not to make categorical decisions about people based on group

FIGURE 2.3
Hypothetical Distribution of Weight Bench-Pressed by a Random Sample of 140 Men and 140 Women

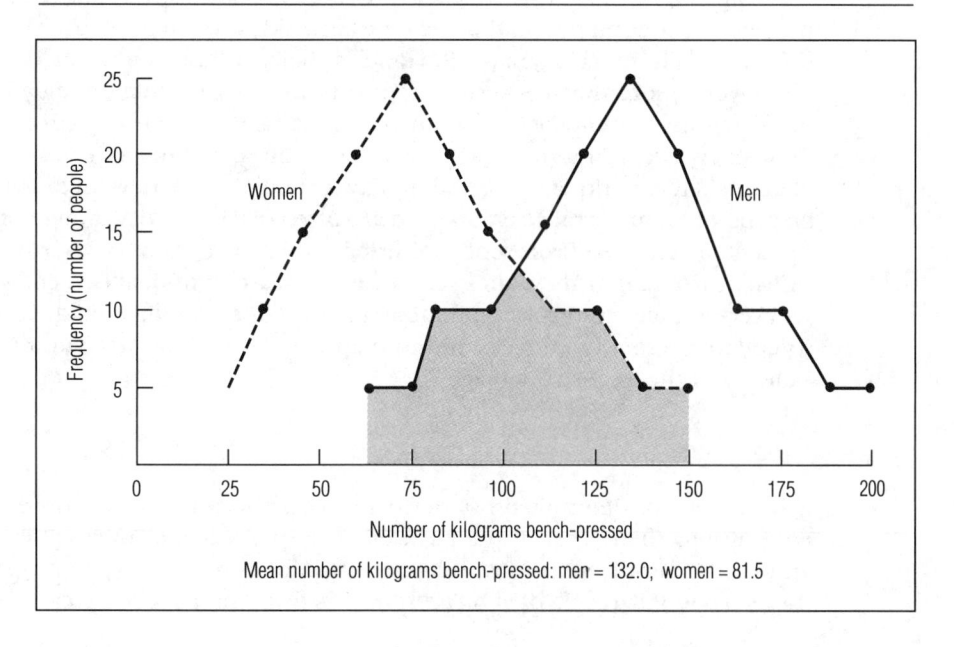

membership. Because of the phenomenon of overlap, such decisions are discriminatory and wasteful of human resources.

Skills are specific, developed abilities. Skills of interest to organizations include leadership and other interpersonal skills and psychomotor or motor skills, among others. Research has identified eleven types of motor skills, including speed of arm movement, arm–hand steadiness, and wrist–finger speed.[23] Finally, in addition to abilities and skills, employees must have specific knowledge or information to perform their jobs.

Abilities, skills, and knowledge are obviously essential to performance. HRM professionals are responsible for attracting and maintaining employees with the abilities, skills, and knowledge to perform their jobs adequately. The HRM functions of recruiting, selection, and training and development are especially related to the abilities, skills, and knowledge of employees. They are also associated with human resource planning (HRP) and job analysis in that HRM professionals must understand what a job entails in order to specify its human requirements. Further, through HRP and job analysis activities, managers and HRM professionals may decide to design or redesign jobs so that relatively low levels of abilities, skills, and knowledge are necessary for successful performance. Or jobs may be enlarged or enriched, possibly with the addition of new responsibilities, to recruit employees of higher calibre. Though employers may incur lower pay and benefits costs for relatively simple jobs, evidence shows that such jobs lead to employee dissatisfaction, absenteeism, and turnover.[24]

Unfortunately, recent evidence shows that many employees (and job applicants) in both Canada and the United States lack basic skills, a situation that is giving employers severe problems. One Canadian study estimates that 24 percent of the adult population lack the basic skills to use printed and written information to function on the job (and in society).[25] In a survey of 1328 U.S. employers, more than 63 percent report knowingly or unknowingly having hired employees who lacked minimal basic skills.[26] The consequences of this deficiency, according to the survey, are that these employees can't adapt to changes in the workplace necessitated by technology and new methods, can't be promoted, make more errors, and are often discharged. Although only 30 percent of surveyed firms report offering training programs to improve basic skills, nearly half of these do so because of a scarcity of qualified entry-level workers. Other reasons for conducting basic skills training include the need to update present employees and to help employees who have limited proficiency in the English language.[27]

Effort

A second major determinant of performance is the amount of effort employees put into their jobs. In the past, effort at work meant physical exertion and sweat, but, in most jobs today, effort implies mental exertion. *Effort* is the behavioural result of *motivation*, which is the psychological force or energy a person uses to satisfy his or her goals and needs. The level of effort an employee exerts on a job is determined by the satisfaction received from previous performance and rewards, by the value of the reward offered for a given level of performance, and by the perceived effort–reward probability.

Previous performance and rewards affect level of effort through job satisfaction. For example, if an employee is satisfied with the fairness of rewards such as pay, praise from the boss, and personal feelings of having done a good job, then he or she is likely to exert the same or greater amount of effort again. On the other hand, a dissatisfied employee is likely to exert only enough effort to keep his or her job. One should keep in mind, however, that individuals differ in their responses to dissatisfaction with rewards. Dissatisfaction may motivate some to work harder the next time to achieve the desired rewards.

Employee perceptions of the fairness or unfairness of rewards may be explained by equity theory.[28] *Equity theory* postulates that people compare their inputs (abilities, effort, experience, and education) and their outcomes (pay, promotions, and other rewards) with the inputs and outcomes of other people. The amount of a person's inputs in relation to his or her outcomes is referred to as the *ratio of exchange*. If an employee believes that his or her ratio of exchange is equal to that of another "comparison" employee, the situation is perceived as equitable. A perceived imbalance (say, a person with similar education and experience receiving more pay) is likely to produce feelings of inequity and dissatisfaction. Table 2.4 illustrates an equitable and an inequitable ratio of exchange.

Since equity theory involves subjective perceptions, feelings of inequity can be resolved in a number of ways. Perhaps the simplest way is for the individual to choose a different person for comparison. Another is to reduce inputs—most notably, the amount of effort—in order to make the ratio of exchange more equitable. In order to minimize perceived inequities, HRM professionals must try to maintain consistent and fair policies of pay, promotion, discipline, and other actions that affect an employee's pay, benefits, and working conditions.

TABLE 2.4
Equitable and Inequitable Ratios of Exchange

EMPLOYEE		COMPARISON EMPLOYEE		RESULT
$\dfrac{\text{Input (abilities, effort)}}{\text{Outcomes (pay, other rewards)}}$	=	$\dfrac{\text{Input (abilities, effort)}}{\text{Outcomes (pay, other rewards)}}$	→	Perceived equity
$\dfrac{\text{Input (abilities, effort)}}{\text{Outcomes (pay, other rewards)}}$	≠	$\dfrac{\text{Input (abilities, effort)}}{\text{Outcomes (pay, other rewards)}}$	→	Perceived inequity

The second factor determining amount of effort put forth on the job is value of the rewards offered. Rewards serve as incentives when they are desirable to employees. Most people are willing to work harder to obtain rewards they really want, such as a large pay raise or two weeks' paid vacation in Florida, than for rewards that have little value to them, such as a small raise or a minor promotion. But employers cannot always predict whether an employee will value a particular reward since there is a wide range of individual differences in employees' needs and desires. For a look at one incentive program, see Exhibit 2.2.

The third factor affecting an employee's level of effort is belief or expectancy about the probability of receiving a reward. According to *expectancy*

EXHIBIT 2.2
Businesses and Schools Use Expectancy Theory to Motivate High School Students

For most high school students seeking admission to a college or university, the incentive value of good grades is clear and accepted. For those planning to get a job after high school, however, the connection between good grades and a good job is often lacking. John Bishop of Cornell University argues that the reason is that businesses rarely look at the high school records of students entering the labour market. In California, Texas, Florida, and Washington, schools and businesses are working on programs to change this situation to one more like that of Japan, where the schools work much more closely with businesses, and students are motivated to work hard because the best ones are rewarded with the best jobs.

The American Business Conference has begun a program called Worklink, a computerized system that maintains high school, test, and work records to provide potential employers with better information for hiring high school graduates. Additionally, some schools are adding information about attendance, punctuality, ability to work in groups, and other factors indicative of the basic and interpersonal skills required by many employers. In Texas, a task force including Tandy, Pier I Imports, and American Airlines is communicating requirements and skills for entry-level jobs to schools. The schools, in turn, are reviewing their courses to ensure that the required skills are covered.

The essence of these programs is to establish closer ties between schools and businesses so that students will realize that good grades and work habits will lead to the valued extrinsic reward—a good job. Programs such as this may be the answer to the problem of lack of basic skills, which so many employers complain of in high school graduates.

Source: Based on K.H. Bacon, "Businesses Link High School Grades to Jobs," *The Wall Street Journal*, May 8, 1990. Used by permission of *The Wall Street Journal* ©1990 Dow Jones & Company, Inc. All rights reserved worldwide.

theory, employees exert extra effort when they believe (1) that they can achieve certain performance levels, and (2) that they will receive the rewards attached to certain performance levels. Less effort is expended if employees believe that they do not possess the abilities, skills, or knowledge necessary to perform at certain levels or that performance will not result in desired rewards. An employee's belief that he or she can achieve a certain performance level by exerting some amount of effort is called the *effort → performance*, or *E → P, relationship*. The belief that a certain performance level will earn one an expected reward or rewards is called the *performance → reward*, or *P → R, relationship*. Employers have more control over the *P → R* relationship because they can choose to administer rewards fairly and consistently, thus raising employees' expectancies that performance will result in certain rewards.

The failure of managers and HRM professionals to maintain consistency between employee performance and rewards can lead to low job satisfaction, low levels of job performance, low levels of trust in management, and high rates of absenteeism and turnover. For example, imagine how frustrated and angry you would be if you worked very hard to meet a deadline on your job, and the $500 bonus your boss promised you was not given. You would be tempted to put forth less effort on a future assignment even if you were again promised a bonus of $500. Your previous experience would have caused you to lower your expectation of receiving the promised reward in exchange for your performance.

Role Perceptions

Role perceptions are an employee's understanding of what he or she should do on the job. Even highly motivated employees with all the necessary abilities, skills, and knowledge to perform well may contribute nothing or actually hinder organizational effectiveness if they do not have a clear and correct understanding of what to do on the job. The primary responsibility for clear role perceptions lies with each employee's immediate supervisor. However, several HRM functions also contribute to clear role perceptions. Chapter 8 discusses orientation, in which new employees begin the socialization process and learn what is expected of them. Employees also learn what is expected of them through their job descriptions. Finally, they receive periodic clarification and modification of what their bosses expect from them in performance appraisal interviews, which also provide opportunities to set specific goals for employees.

Closely related to expectancy theory is the theory of goal setting. *Goal setting* is the process of establishing a work-related goal for one or more employees. The basic principles of goal-setting theory are stated in Exhibit 2.3. Typical goal-setting methods involve establishing specific, quantitative goals for each employee based upon past performance. Research at the Weyerhaeuser Corporation in the United States has shown that hundreds of

EXHIBIT 2.3
Goal-Setting Theory and Principles

The use of goal theory is one of the most powerful and effective means of influencing human motivation and performance known to social scientists. Pinder, in a review of the major theories of work motivation, concludes that goal-setting theory "probably holds more promise as an applied motivational tool for managers than does any other approach."[a]

The theory's principles, which have been supported in numerous laboratory and field studies, are:

1. There is a positive, linear relationship between goal difficulty and performance up to the point of an employee's maximum ability. This relationship exists because hard goals, assuming they are accepted, lead to greater effort and persistence than easy ones.
2. Specific, difficult goals result in significantly higher performance than "do your best" or no goals.
3. Goal setting has positive effects on both performance and satisfaction regardless of whether goals are set by others or participatively.
4. Feedback must be given employees for goal setting to be effective. Feedback facilitates adjustment of effort or approach to a task.
5. Monetary incentives enhance the effectiveness of goal setting.
6. Goal setting is effective across all education levels, ages, and countries and for both men and women.

[a] C.C. Pinder, *Work Motivation* (Glenview, Ill.: Scott, Foresman, 1984), p. 169.

Source: Based on E.A. Locke and G.P. Latham, *A Theory of Goal Setting and Task Performance* (Englewood Cliffs, NJ: Prentice-Hall ©1990).

thousands of dollars can be saved by using a procedure of assigning specific, quantitative goals to employees.[29] Goal setting has also proved very useful in improving the effectiveness of training programs.[30]

Summary of Job Performance

The Porter and Lawler model shows three direct determinants of performance: (1) abilities, skills, and knowledge; (2) effort; and (3) role perceptions. Of the three, abilities are the most basic determinant since employees deficient in them cannot perform at an acceptable level. A major way in which HRM professionals can contribute to organizational effectiveness is by ensuring that employees have the required abilities, skills, and knowledge. This is accomplished through the HRM functions of (1) job analysis, which identifies required abilities, skills, and knowledge; (2) recruiting, selection, and placement, which seek, select, and place people in jobs that match their abilities; and (3) training and development and career planning, which provide programs and job experiences to develop and maintain employee qualifications for current and future jobs.

The second major determinant of performance is the amount of effort exerted on the job. Though jobs vary in the degree to which different levels of effort affect performance, all require some amount of effort (for example, the effort involved in coming to work). Therefore, acceptable job performance requires some minimal level of both abilities and effort, and higher levels of job performance result from additional effort, higher levels of abilities, skills, knowledge, or both. As discussed earlier, level of effort depends upon many factors under the organization's control, including the performance appraisal process, compensation and benefits policies and practices, and supervisors' behaviour toward employees. Though none of these factors is directly controlled by HRM professionals, they have a substantial influence on them through development and administration of appraisal and compensation programs. Further, supervisors' behaviour can be influenced by training and development programs designed by HRM professionals.

Effort can also be affected by the employee's work group at the job. Research has shown that co-workers often have more influence over employee behaviour than do the organization's policies and rewards.[31] (Of course, level of effort may also be affected by factors not related to work, such as family problems, illness, and fatigue.) Recent research reveals that teaming two skill-deficient employees, one reading at a fourth-grade level and another at a fifth-grade level, lets the two handle material written at the eighth-grade level.[32] In other words, small work groups can help employers overcome basic skill deficiencies in their work force.[33]

A significant determinant of job performance that is under employer control is role perceptions. Role perceptions are crucial because they guide or direct an employee's work behaviour. Even low-ability employees can perform acceptably if they have a clear understanding of what they should do, while highly talented and motivated employees may contribute little to organizational effectiveness if their role perceptions are ambiguous. Organizations communicate role perceptions to employees through job descriptions, orientation programs, and performance appraisals.

Organization Rewards

Figure 2.2 identifies two types of rewards: intrinsic and extrinsic. *Intrinsic rewards* are positive outcomes of job performance that employees either receive directly from the job or give themselves. Through work experience, employees learn when they have done a good job, and they reward themselves with feelings of a job well done. *Extrinsic rewards* are those provided by the organization, such as praise from the boss, pay increases, promotions, or some other form of recognition. The relationship between job performance and intrinsic rewards is more reliable and direct than the relationship between performance and extrinsic rewards since the latter depends upon the organization's performance monitoring and appraisal system, which can have a number of shortcomings.

Intrinsic rewards are developed from the extrinsic rewards employees receive from their supervisors and their peers. When an employee first begins a new job, he or she often does not know what constitutes acceptable job performance. Feedback from supervisors and co-workers, along with the employee's past experience, provides this information. From feedback, praise, and other extrinsic rewards, employees learn what constitutes good and poor performance, and they can then provide intrinsic rewards to themselves. This process is called *internalization*. Employees' experience with extrinsic rewards also provides them with expectations about the fairness of rewards for various levels of job performance. These expectations are indicated in the diagram by the arrow from performance to perceived equitable rewards.

Ideally, employers would design performance appraisal and compensation systems that would administer rewards on a contingent basis. That is, the amount of money or other rewards received would depend upon the amount and/or quality of an employee's work. Although that approach is often not practical, some organizations have found ways to make innovative uses of extrinsic rewards, such as performance feedback and praise. In the early 1970s, for example, Emery Air Freight obtained substantial increases in job performance and profits by using behaviour modification programs based upon reinforcement principles.[34]

Though contingency or performance-based reward systems are far from universal, competitive pressures have led a growing number of employers to try these methods. A mid-1980s survey of 1600 private sector businesses in Canada and the United States found that nearly 40 percent had implemented some form of performance-based reward system, including lump-sum bonuses (cash paid at the end of the year in recognition of employee performance); small-group incentives (pay offered to work teams for accomplishment of specific work goals); gain sharing (extra pay given to employees for achieving specific levels of efficiency and cost savings); and pay for knowledge (employees earn more when they acquire more job-related knowledge).[35] Another study by the Conference Board of Canada found growing use of various performance-based pay plans, including stock purchase (employees can purchase company shares at a discount) and gain-sharing plans.[36] Advocates argue that this approach makes even the lowest-level employees feel and behave as if they have a real stake in the organization's success. Profit sharing motivates employees to work harder because they receive a share of the company's profits.

Except for stock purchase and profit-sharing plans, all these extrinsic rewards programs have several major components in common: specification of standards of performance, careful monitoring of performance by both supervisors and employees, and frequent feedback and rewards based upon level of performance. Thus, they have the effect of clarifying role perceptions and specifying the performance → reward relationship.

Performance-based reward systems are still relatively rare among unionized employers. The 1991 Labour Canada data on collective agreements indicate that only 1 percent of agreements contained a profit-sharing, production bonus, or group incentive plan, but slightly more than 5 percent had a piece-rate incentive plan.[37]

Job Satisfaction

Job satisfaction is an attitude of employees regarding aspects of their work. Porter and Lawler's model focusses on satisfaction with rewards that come directly from the job itself—for example, pride in a job well done, feelings of self-worth, praise, recognition, pay, and promotions. In a broader sense, job satisfaction also includes employees' attitudes toward elements in the work environment—for example, satisfaction with company policies, with the boss, with co-workers, and with such physical characteristics of the work environment as lighting, noise, and safety.

Employers have long been interested in job satisfaction. The major reason for their interest has been the long-held, but incorrect, belief that happy workers are productive workers. Years of research have shown that there is a very small relationship between performance and satisfaction and very little evidence that highly satisfied employees are highly productive employees.[38] Currently, a well-accepted relationship between satisfaction and performance is that portrayed in the Porter and Lawler model: namely, that satisfaction with rewards is one of several factors affecting the amount of effort expended on the job. Employers' interest in job satisfaction is justified, however, for other reasons; research has shown that job satisfaction is negatively related to absenteeism and voluntary turnover (resignation), both of which represent considerable cost to employers.[39]

Job satisfaction is a useful indicator of the condition and effectiveness of many organizational policies and practices. Information about employees' attitudes and feelings can be used to identify problems and to help design changes to resolve sources of discontent. There is evidence that attitude surveys can predict whether employees will engage in and support unionization activities in nonunionized organizations.[40] Specifically, employees who are dissatisfied with various aspects of their jobs are more likely to vote in favour of a union.[41] Other evidence suggests that efforts to increase job satisfaction can be very beneficial to organizations. A study of U.S. bank tellers found that even a moderate increase in job satisfaction resulted in an annual savings to the bank of more than $125 000 through reductions in absences, turnover, and tellers' cash shortages.[42] Thus, employees may exert more effort and be more productive if they are satisfied with the rewards they receive.

HRM professionals are frequently responsible for measuring job satisfaction among employees. It is possible to measure overall job satisfaction, but most measurement is of its facets or components. One commonly used tool is the Job Description Index (JDI), which measures five facets of satisfaction: with the work itself, with pay, with co-workers, with promotions, and with supervision.[43] The JDI consists of a list of adjectives or descriptive statements about each of the five components. Items relating to the work itself, for example, include "fascinating," "satisfying," "tiresome," and "endless." The employee responds to each adjective, indicating whether it describes a particular aspect of the job. Research has shown that the five facets of the JDI are independent of one another, and that the results are highly reliable or stable over a moderate length of time.[44] Overall job satisfaction is highest when employees are satisfied with all five components in the JDI. Besides providing an overall measure of job satisfaction, the JDI is useful because it can identify specific areas contributing to satisfaction or dissatisfaction.

In measuring job satisfaction, HRM professionals must consider the advantages and disadvantages of using standard measures versus constructing their own. An advantage of using a standard measure such as the JDI is that an employer can compare the satisfaction level of his or her employees with the results gathered by other employers using the same instrument. In some cases, however, employers need to measure employees' attitudes and degree of satisfaction regarding various policies, issues, or problems unique to their organizations. One solution for those who would also like to be able to compare their data with those of other employers is to use both a standardized measure of job satisfaction and a questionnaire covering areas of particular interest.

Employers who use any questionnaires or attitude surveys to measure job satisfaction should be prepared to respond to employees' views. If employers fail to do so, employees are likely to be more dissatisfied than before, since attitude surveys create the expectation that management is responsive to needs and ready to change.

Employers need not rely entirely on attitude surveys or satisfaction questionnaires to measure satisfaction. Various kinds of employee behaviour, including absenteeism and voluntary turnover, also provide indicators of job satisfaction. In unionized organizations, large numbers of grievances and strikes indicate employees' dissatisfaction. Low levels of job satisfaction *may* be reflected in substandard quantity and quality of job performance, and sabotage of equipment or products is a clear indication. A final source of information is exit interviews with employees who are leaving the organization. However, employees who have quit may not be completely candid about why they are leaving, since they may foresee needing a reference from the employer.

Encouraging Appropriate and Desired Behaviour

Organizations seek to encourage appropriate and desired work behaviour in order to facilitate organizational effectiveness. Appropriate and desired behaviour is encouraged by clearly communicating rules and expectations to employees, providing honest and constructive feedback on performance, and offering a variety of rewards and incentives. Surveys conducted by Hay Management Consultants of Canada revealed that high-performing companies differed from low-performing companies in several important ways. In high-performing companies, all employees felt better informed, information was viewed as more credible, and employees felt more freedom to take risks and to develop themselves.[45]

Though positive approaches to managing employees are preferable, all employers must have disciplinary policies and rules for employees who exhibit inappropriate or undesirable behaviour. Disciplinary sanctions let employees know that certain behaviours will not be tolerated and must be corrected in order to avoid the consequences. Under systems of progressive discipline, the consequences of rule violations become more severe as offences are repeated. For example, a first violation usually brings only an instructive counselling session to ensure that the employee knows the rules and the consequences of failure to comply. A second violation typically results in a written reprimand, which becomes part of the employee's personnel file. Penalties for subsequent violations include suspension without pay, final warnings, and ultimately, dismissal. Exhibit 2.4 presents behaviours that result in progressive discipline under a union contract in one large manufacturing plant. Exhibit 2.5 spells out rule violations that are grounds for immediate dismissal.

HRM professionals often monitor employee behaviour and recommend policies and programs to achieve desired results. For example, they are usually responsible for developing progressive discipline systems and for overseeing such systems to ensure they are administered fairly. Inconsistent administration of discipline threatens job satisfaction and often leads to charges of discrimination.

Two kinds of employee behaviour that are of major concern to employers are absenteeism and voluntary turnover (resignation).

Absenteeism

Absenteeism costs organizations millions of dollars annually in lost production, sick leave, and replacement personnel.[46] Though it is tempting to assume absenteeism is caused by low job satisfaction and, indeed, many studies support this conclusion, research indicates multiple causes of absences.[47] One model of employee absence (or attendance) argues that five factors affect employees' motivation to come to work.[48] They are: (1) work-related attitudes (including job satisfaction); (2) economic and labour market

EXHIBIT 2.4
Rule Violations Subject to Progressive Discipline

1. Smoking in restricted areas.
2. Refusal to comply with a proper request or demand from the employee's supervisor.
3. Ringing, altering, defacing, or tampering with the time card of another employee.
4. Using slugs in or tampering with the plant vending machines.
5. Threatening, intimidating, coercing, or interfering with fellow employees on company premises at any time.
6. Disregard of safety rules or practices.
7. Use of profane, vulgar, or threatening language directed to either a fellow employee or a supervisor.
8. Leaving the work area or department during working hours or being present in another department's work area without authorization from the employee's supervisor or department manager.
9. Gambling, or the promotion thereof, in any form on the company's premises.
10. Excessive absenteeism or tardiness.
11. Failure to use designated entrance or exits.
12. Failure to report tardiness immediately.
13. Leaving work area to ring out prior to quitting bell or prior to being properly relieved.
14. Stopping work to commence clean-up prior to the sounding of the clean-up bell.
15. Failure to observe parking regulations.
16. Failure to work overtime when required unless such failure is due to circumstances that are substantiated to be beyond the control of the employee or due to the employee's illness or injury or the required attendance at a critical illness of a family member.
17. Discarding refuse or litter on the floor or company premises.
18. Failure to maintain job performance and quality standards.
19. Indulging in horseplay, scuffling, water fights, and similar acts on company premises.
20. Fighting on company premises that results in an injury to an employee.
21. Participating in the first 24 hours of any unauthorized strike, slowdown, work stoppage, boycott, picketing or similar interruption or interference with company operations.
22. Determination (after investigation) that sexual harassment has occurred.

Source: Taken from an employee handbook of a unionized auto parts manufacturer. Used with permission.

EXHIBIT 2.5
Rule Violations That Are Grounds for Immediate Dismissal

1. Possession of firearms or other concealed weapons inside the company building.
2. Theft or appropriation of property of employees or of outside individuals or organizations servicing the company.
3. The unauthorized taking, removal, or disclosure of company reports, blueprints, records, confidential information, or company correspondence or communication of any nature.
4. The unauthorized alteration or falsification of personnel records, payroll records, time cards, or production records.
5. Reporting for work while under the influence of any type of intoxicating beverage and/or narcotics, or the possession or consumption of intoxicating beverages or narcotics on company premises, other than narcotics being taken under medical prescription.
6. Indecent or immoral conduct on company property.
7. Wilful slowdown, work stoppage, or walkout.
8. Flagrant abuse or destruction of company tools, machines, materials, and equipment or the property of other employees.
9. Sleeping on duty.
10. Carelessness or negligence in performing work duties that results in a substantial monetary loss to the company either in the form of lost production time or for labour and material costs to repair broken machinery, tools, and equipment.
11. Failure to notify the company of pregnancy as soon as the employee knows of this condition.

Source: Taken from an employee handbook of a unionized auto parts manufacturer. Used with permission.

---

factors (absenteeism is typically lower in poor economic times); (3) organizational policies and rules regarding absenteeism; (4) personal factors such as health, family size, and poor previous attendance; and (5) absence culture and work group norms (absenteeism is acceptable behaviour in some work groups and not in others). An employee's actual attendance is influenced by two factors: attendance motivation and the perceived ability to attend work. That is, an employee may enjoy the job, may not want to let co-workers down, and may be trying for a perfect-attendance award, but if a child is ill, he or she may believe it impossible to be at work that day.

Although organizations have some measure of control over attendance motivation, they have little control over inability to attend. Employers have used a wide variety of methods to reduce absenteeism. The approaches range from attempts to make work more satisfying and attractive to the imposition of discipline and punishment for excessive absenteeism. An example of the positive approach is quality of working life (QWL) programs, in which employees meet with a manager in small, problem-solving groups. Ford's five Windsor plants experienced a marked drop in absenteeism after implementation of what that company called Employee Involvement programs.[49] A successful approach to absence reduction was recently developed by two Canadian researchers, Gary Latham and Colette Frayne.[50] They used self-efficacy training in which employees of a government agency were taught how to set and monitor goals for their own job attendance and to reinforce themselves for good attendance. A year after the training, the group of employees who had received training had better attendance than an untrained group.

Some organizations have no mechanism for controlling absenteeism, but others have formal absence-control programs. Formal programs typically combine careful monitoring of attendance with systems of progressive discipline. Exhibit 2.6 provides excerpts from one manufacturing company's absence-control program for hourly workers. Note that, in this particular case, supervisors have primary responsibility for absence control but HRM professionals assist by maintaining records and reports and by defining who is excessively absent. Note also that this program emphasizes "day-to-day" attention to absence as a means of avoiding absenteeism and possible disciplinary action.

Another way employers and HRM professionals encourage good attendance is by tying attendance to rewards. For example, attendance can be made a factor in pay and promotion decisions, and rewards can be denied to those who are excessively absent. Some companies have special attendance incentive programs. One such program awards employees a full day's extra pay for each quarter of perfect attendance. An employee who has a full year's perfect attendance gets special recognition at the annual company banquet. According to the company's human resources manager, the company hasn't had an absence problem in years.

Turnover

Turnover occurs in organizations when employees exit because of termination of their employment. When employment is terminated by the employee, as in the case of quitting, turnover is said to be *voluntary*. Turnover is *involuntary* when initiated by the employer, as in the case of layoff or dismissal.

Turnover is both an individual and an organizational phenomenon. At an organizational level, companies sometimes calculate employee turnover rates

EXHIBIT 2.6
Excerpts from the Absence-Control Program of a Personal Products Manufacturer

RESPONSIBILITY FOR ABSENCE CONTROL

1. The primary responsibility for control of absenteeism must, of necessity, rest with the supervisor. A part of the supervisor's job is to see that everyone in the department is working and that excessive absenteeism is controlled. The individual supervisor is closest to the problem and most affected by it. It is he or she who suffers most when department personnel are absent.

2. Secondary responsibility for attendance lies with the department manager because he or she is responsible for production in the department. If people are absent, schedules cannot be met.

3. Further responsibility lies with the production manager. It is his or her responsibility to see that adequate absence control is maintained and consistent throughout the plant.

4. It is the responsibility of the human resources department to assist the supervisor, department manager, and production manager in maintaining absence records and reports and in determining whether a particular employee has a record of excessive absenteeism.

PROGRESSIVE DISCIPLINE SYSTEM FOR EXCESSIVE ABSENTEEISM

1. First excessive absence interview. You (the supervisor) should interview the employee privately, listen to reasons for absence, and make sure it's known you're trying to help. Never reprimand an employee in front of other people. Never become belligerent or offensive and don't apologize for discipline. Be fair but firm. If, after your discussion, you feel the employee is entitled to discipline, then formally complete a reprimand form. If, after the interview, you feel a reprimand form is not necessary, then fill out a corrective interview report and send a copy to the Human Resources Office. Indicate on either form that further attendance problems may result in further and more serious discipline action up to and including disciplinary layoff or discharge.

2. Second excessive absence interview. The time interval between the first and second offense will, to a certain extent, influence how serious this step should be. The same procedure should be followed in counselling the individual as outlined in step one. Either of the following disciplinary actions may be taken:
    a. Another interview and warning of written reprimand.
    b. A formal written reprimand. If this step is chosen, it should be made clear to the employee that if attendance doesn't improve substantially, the next step will be suspension from work (without pay) for periods varying from one to five days.

EXHIBIT 2.6 *(continued)*

3. Third excessive absence interview. The employee should be counselled and a decision made based on the past record of the employee and seriousness of the present offence. Time interval between offences will be taken into account. Any of the following actions may be taken:
   a. Issue another formal written reprimand notice.
   b. Issue a one-day suspension from work (without pay).
   c. Issue a more lengthy suspension from work for up to five days' time off without pay.

4. Fourth excessive absence interview. Time interval will again be a factor. Any of the disciplinary actions taken previously may be repeated for less serious violators, but this step may also include discharge of serious offenders. Before any suspension from work or discharge action is taken, it must be reviewed by the personnel manager.

Note: Many supervisors assume that there's no need to talk to an employee about his or her attendance until the record becomes unsatisfactory. Not so! Supervisors should review an employee's attendance record each time an absence occurs. Without day-to-day attention to absence, a disciplinary problem may mature — one that possibly could have been prevented. This practice not only helps the supervisor clarify the reason for absence but also lets the employee know that the company is concerned about his or her losing time. The prospect of having to give a face-to-face explanation for each day missed can also discourage not-so-conscientious employees from taking the unnecessary time off.

Source: Taken from a policy manual of a unionized personal products manufacturing plant. Used with permission.

---

for use in human resource planning. By measuring rates of exit among various types of workers, planners can project future internal supply and address specific labour needs. Turnover rates may also be calculated in order to assess the degree to which turnover is a problem in the organization. HRM professionals typically conduct exit interviews with departing employees in order to determine causes of turnover in the organization.

Organizations try to control turnover because it is expensive. There are costs associated with recruiting, selecting, and training replacement personnel, and costs associated with turnover's disruptive effects on production. High levels of turnover also result in more paperwork for HRM professionals. Turnover requires people processing from entry (recruiting, selecting, orienting, training) to exit (exit interviews and the computation and curtailment of benefits).

Though turnover is generally thought of in negative terms, it can have a number of benefits, among them performance gains (if poor performers are replaced by better workers), cost savings (if new hires are paid less than departing employees), and increased opportunity for upward mobility (if turnover occurs at higher levels in the organization). Finally, turnover can be used to facilitate organizational change requiring reallocation of human resources. Units and departments of decreasing importance can be allowed to shrink by attrition, while new personnel, if any, are assigned to areas of growing importance.

An important and practical question is, how is performance related to voluntary turnover? One suggestion is a U-shaped relationship: low performers leave because of the actual or perceived threat of firing,[51] and high performers may also leave because they see numerous and better employment opportunities elsewhere. The turnover of poor performers has been labelled functional turnover and the turnover of high performers dysfunctional. A recent meta-analysis (a method of aggregating results of multiple studies) of 52 studies supported the U-shape explanation.[52] Generally, poorer performers are more likely to leave when alternative employment opportunities exist and when pay and rewards are based on performance. This means that having human resource management policies that reward employees for high performance will help organizations retain high performers while eliminating poor ones.

Voluntary turnover is more likely to occur when levels of employment are high. It is also more likely among young workers, blue-collar workers, workers with short tenure, workers with low job satisfaction, and workers with low organizational commitment. Turnover tends to be higher in low-paying jobs, jobs that are routine and repetitive, and jobs that are low in autonomy and responsibility. It tends to be less likely in organizations with good communication systems, concerned and caring supervisors, employee participation in decision making, and opportunities for upward mobility.[53]

The Absenteeism–Turnover Relationship

So far, we have discussed several work outcomes — performance, job satisfaction, absenteeism, and turnover — that are vital to managers. The relationship between absenteeism and turnover is particularly important since there is evidence that employees who are excessively absent are more likely to turn over.[54] A meta-analysis of 17 studies found a fairly strong relationship ($r = 0.40$) between individual employees' absence level and their subsequent leaving of the organization.[55] This finding suggests that employers can use absenteeism as an indicator of potential turnover. Depending upon the performance level of an excessively absent employee, management may wish to counsel and try to retain the individual.

What leads employees to decide to quit? How do employees make the decision to quit or stay? A number of turnover models have been proposed in the past several decades, though few have received strong research support.[56] One of the most recent models providing a good explanation of turnover is that of Hom and Griffeth.[57] Their model, a revision of Mobley's theory,[58] begins with job dissatisfaction, which creates thoughts of quitting. Consideration of quitting leads to employees' evaluating the various costs and benefits of both quitting and staying. Those employees who find attractive other jobs and perceive low turnover costs will quit if they judge the alternative position superior to their present job. Of course, some employees quit without having another job, and others stay because no superior alternative job was found. Research has not been able to determine, however, whether the decision to seek another job occurs before, at the same time as, or even after the decision to quit. From the HR manager's perspective, these findings, combined with those of the absenteeism–turnover relationship, suggest two types of interventions: (1) take note of increases in an employee's absence rate; and (2) talk with the individual about sources of dissatisfaction and about the positive aspects of the current job and the employer.

Turnover can also be reduced by human resource policies and programs that encourage employee retention. For example, retention is encouraged by competitive pay policies, promote-from-within policies, and policies that give employees a voice in work-related decisions. Recently, however, it is not unusual for organizations to seek to increase turnover. This can be done by withholding rewards and offering incentives to leave, such as early retirement programs.

OLDER EMPLOYEES: A VALUABLE RESOURCE

For more than a decade, demographers have forecast an increase in the average age of the populations of Canada, the United States, and most industrialized nations.[59] In 1990, more than half the Canadian population was over age 30 and the over-65 population had doubled since 1970. The average age of the U.S. work force is predicted to move from 32 in 1989 to nearly 40 by 2000. Causes of this phenomenon include reductions in the fertility rate and increases in life expectancy. For nearly two decades following World War II, the fertility rate was high, producing the "baby boom." By the mid-1960s, however, the fertility rate had declined dramatically; the result was the "baby bust." Meanwhile advances in medical and health sciences led to an eleven-year increase in life expectancy, from 63 for a person born in 1940 to 74 for someone born in 1980.

What are the effects of these changes on the population? For the United States, demographers find that the proportion of the population age 65 or older will increase from 11 percent in 1980 to 13 percent in 2010 and will peak at about 20 percent in 2030. Approximately 10 percent of the Canadian population was 65 years of age or older in 1990 and this is expected to grow to 25 percent by 2031. Of course, the forecasts for the future may be wrong. They assume a continuation of recent fertility and life expectancy trends, and although life expectancy is unlikely to change greatly, fertility rates can change dramatically. Nevertheless, two points are clear: there are many more older people today than ever before, and their proportion of the total population is likely to increase for some time.

Why should HR managers be concerned about the growing number of older people? First, the number of new entrants to the labour force has declined since the baby-bust generation is substantially smaller in absolute numbers than the baby-boom generation. Second, if present retirement trends among men continue, many of the male baby boomers will have retired by the early part of the twenty-first century. (The participation rate for males age 55 and older declined from approximately 57 percent of those eligible in 1966 to only 38 percent in 1990, although the rate for women over the same period increased slightly.) Thus, employers may face labour shortages. In fact, they have already occurred in some urban areas, particularly for jobs traditionally filled by young people such as those in the fast food industry. A third concern is that a large retired population will be difficult to support if the working population is comparatively small.

One obvious solution to this situation is to utilize a greater proportion of older workers. You may recall seeing McDonald's television ads showing older employees working with the fast food industry's traditionally young employees. Whether or not older employees will be a solution to labour shortages depends upon retirement-age legislation, employer pension programs, and attitudes of older workers toward work versus retirement. Despite relatively recent legislation in some provinces ending mandatory retirement for most occupations, the trend toward early retirement among males continues. According to the 1989 Canadian General Social Survey, nearly two-thirds of their national sample opposed mandatory retirement, though opinion differences across provinces were large. Why then do employees retire early?

The survey provides some explanation for why employees retire early. It found that over one-quarter of retired respondents retired because they reached mandatory retirement age, while one-quarter retired for health reasons. The largest category was "other reasons," and among these the most common were personal choice and family responsibilities (cited primarily by women). Early retirement incentives were cited by only 6 percent of retirees as their reason for retirement. The vast majority (63 percent) of Canadian retirees retired before age 65, 17 percent at 65, and 16 percent after 65. Among all respondents to the survey, over one-third favoured mandatory retirement. Of those favouring mandatory retirement, those with employer-sponsored pensions were more supportive than those without such pensions. However, support for mandatory retirement weakened as income and education levels rose.[60] In contrast, Parnes's research shows that in the United States, retirement is generally a voluntary decision. Over the past two decades, it is estimated that fewer than 5 percent of retirements in the United

States resulted from mandatory retirement rules and approximately 10 percent from layoffs and plant closings. Poor health may account for 15 to 20 percent. Parnes estimates that at least 65 to 70 percent of retirement is voluntary, though he points out the retirement decision is complex and research is difficult.[61] It should be noted that differences between the Canadian and U.S. data are attributable more to the methodology used in the research than to actual differences between the two countries.

In summary, employees retire for a number of reasons and, though the research is inconsistent, the major reasons appear to be: (1) the desire to retire and the financial ability to do so; (2) poor health of either themselves or a close relative; and (3) either mandatory retirement or employer-encouraged early retirement.

In view of the demographic trends, should employers encourage older employees to retire? Early retirements offer employers both advantages and disadvantages. They may reduce labour costs since they often open up opportunities to younger employers, who tend to be paid less than senior ones. Yet older employees may have knowledge and expertise that are difficult to replace, retirement may be painful for some employees, and poorly administered early retirement programs may lead to lawsuits. Perhaps employers are justified in replacing older workers with younger ones if there is evidence that younger workers are superior in some important ways.

Test your knowledge and beliefs about older persons by taking the quiz in Exhibit 2.7. Don't read any further before you complete it. (Your instructor can provide you with the answers.)

What are some of the characteristics of older workers? Recall from the discussion of individual differences that there is always substantial overlap in the distribution of abilities or traits of different groups. For example, though I am a pretty good runner in my age group, many 60-year-olds and probably some 70-year-olds can beat me in a ten-kilometre race. A review of 25 studies found that age typically accounts for no more than 10 percent of the variance in measures of job behaviour.[62] The same study found that older workers tend to have fewer absences, lower turnover, lower illness and accident rates, and higher job satisfaction and work values. A meta-analysis of 96 studies found no relationship between age and performance.[63] Though it is true that the senses of touch, hearing, and sight, as well as physical strength, tend to decline with age, older workers compensate with high levels of experience and reliability. Finally, a recent survey of 400 HR managers, commissioned by the American Association of Retired Persons (AARP), rated workers over age 55 highly on numerous factors such as loyalty, practical knowledge, reliability in a crisis, and emotional stability.[64] Lower ratings were given on educational background, physical agility, and feeling comfortable with new technologies. Given the importance of new technologies, the last finding indicates a potential problem area. There is, however, evidence that older employees can learn new material.

EXHIBIT 2.7
The Facts on Aging Quiz

Mark the statements T for true, F for false, or ? for don't know.

_____ 1. The majority of old people (age 65+) are senile.
_____ 2. The five senses (sight, hearing, taste, touch, and smell) all tend to weaken in old age.
_____ 3. The majority of old people have no interest in, or capacity for, sexual relations.
_____ 4. Lung vital capacity tends to decline in old age.
_____ 5. The majority of old people feel miserable most of the time.
_____ 6. Physical strength tends to decline in old age.
_____ 7. At least one-tenth of the aged are living in long-term institutions (such as nursing homes, mental hospitals, homes for the aged, etc.).
_____ 8. Aged drivers have fewer accidents per driver than those under age 65.
_____ 9. Older workers usually cannot work as effectively as younger workers.
_____ 10. Over three-fourths of the aged are healthy enough to carry out their normal activities.
_____ 11. The majority of old people are unable to adapt to change.
_____ 12. Old people usually take longer to learn something new.
_____ 13. It is almost impossible for the average old person to learn something new.
_____ 14. Older people tend to react slower than younger people.
_____ 15. In general, old people tend to be pretty much alike.
_____ 16. The majority of old people say they are seldom bored.
_____ 17. The majority of old people are socially isolated.
_____ 18. Older workers have fewer accidents than younger workers.
_____ 19. Over 15 percent of the population are now age 65 or older.
_____ 20. The majority of medical practitioners tend to give low priority to the aged.
_____ 21. The majority of old people have incomes below the poverty line.
_____ 22. The majority of old people are working or would like to have some kind of work to do (including housework and volunteer work).
_____ 23. Old people tend to become more religious as they age.
_____ 24. The majority of old people say they are seldom irritated or angry.
_____ 25. The health and economic status of old people will be about the same or worse in the year 2000 (compared to younger people).

Source: Erdman B. Palmore, *The Facts on Aging Quiz* (New York: Springer, 1988), pp. 3–5. © Used by permission of Springer Publishing Company, Inc., New York 10012.

Do older employees want to continue working? According to a Gallup poll in the late 1980s, nearly three-quarters of the surveyed workers age 55 and older preferred to continue working.[65] Older and better-educated employees are less interested in retirement than the younger and less educated. More than half would continue working if they could stay in the same job on either a full- or a part-time basis. Yet, for many employees, continuing to work offers no financial incentive because of the terms of their pension plans and old age security rates. If employers want to retain older workers, they must develop policies and programs with positive incentives.

With a little luck, you and many of your friends will be able to choose when to retire. When do you feel you would like to retire? Do you know anyone who has recently retired? Is he or she happy? To what extent did employer policies and practices affect the retirement decision?

❑❑❑❑❑

SUMMARY

This chapter has provided an overview of the "people environment" in which HRM professionals work to further organizational goals and objectives. The human asset was examined from the general perspective of the labour force at large and from a specific perspective focussing on individual behaviour, performance, and job satisfaction.

The labour force section of this chapter defined important terms and discussed major trends occurring in the Canadian labour force. Although a particular employer may not experience exactly the same trends and changes as are occurring nationally or even provincially, local labour markets can be analyzed using similar concepts. Knowledge and analysis of labour market conditions and trends are essential to effective recruiting and to retention of an adequate supply of qualified employees.

The second part of this chapter examined determinants of employee job performance and satisfaction, as well as ways to encourage appropriate and desired behaviour. High levels of performance and satisfaction are essential to organizational effectiveness and survival. The Porter and Lawler model of performance and satisfaction was used to explain the relationship of these two variables to each other and to other variables that affect them. Various HRM functions were discussed in terms of components of the Porter and Lawler model. The section included discussions of progressive discipline systems and two kinds of employee behaviour of major interest to organizations: absenteeism and turnover. The final part of this chapter examined the potential of older persons as a valuable human resource.

Review Questions

1. Recent years have seen a major change in the composition of the Canadian work force. An increase in the female participation rate and a decrease in the male participation rate have left the overall participation rate somewhat higher than it was a decade ago. What difference does the male–female composition of the work force make to human resource professionals? Discuss.

2. Explain how the local rate of unemployment affects human resource management in particular establishments.

Project Ideas

1. In 1979, two economists, Butz and Ward, proposed a theory that the fertility rate (number of births per 1000 women) increases in recessionary times and decreases in economically good times. The rationale is that "it costs a woman more to take off to have children" in good economic times than in bad.

    This theory runs counter to prior experience; the fertility rate declined during the Depression and rose during the prosperous 1960s. Discuss (in class or in a short paper) why the Butz and Ward theory might be accurate today but inaccurate for earlier years. Also, specify what factors in the economy might affect the link between economic conditions and fertility rates. How does this theory, assuming it has some validity, affect the supply of employees to organizations?

2. Business consultants often hear a problem employee described in terms of a "personality conflict" or "personality problem." The client says, "I've tried everything with Sandy and nothing seems to work." Such personality problems are usually "resolved" in one of two ways—the organization tolerates a person who is, at least sometimes, an ineffective employee, or the boss finally musters the courage to terminate the individual.

    Try to recall one or two "problem personalities" you have known or worked with. Exactly why were they regarded as problems? What did others do to try to change them? What do you think should have been done?

3. Discuss the Porter and Lawler model of job performance and satisfaction in terms of your personal work experience. Try to recall an example of how each element in the model (abilities, skills, knowledge; effort; role perceptions; and job satisfaction) affected your job performance or

work behaviour. How was the level of effort you expended influenced by the value you assigned to the reward and by your perceived probability of receiving that reward? Were you pleased or displeased with the rewards you received for performance? What factors determined whether or not you perceived a reward as equitable or inequitable? Did satisfaction with previous rewards affect your subsequent performance? Be specific in your examples and with respect to the Porter and Lawler model.

▶▶▶ CASES

CASE 2.1 ▶ TRENDS IN EMPLOYEE ATTITUDES: DIFFERENCES BETWEEN CANADIAN AND AMERICAN WORKERS

Canada and the United States both advocate what has been called the North American way of managing people, and they share an affinity that flows from geographical proximity, strong cultural bonds, and partnership in the free trade agreement and the rush to globalization of trade. Thus, it should come as no surprise that Canadian and U.S. workers share several perceptions about human resource issues. As a 1988 study puts it:

> No significant differences are observed, for example, in their view on supervision, management credibility or general work force capabilities. . . . Most important, our surveys demonstrate no substantial differences between Canadians and Americans in the basic levels of satisfaction they derive from their work. Workers in both countries are generally satisfied with their jobs and with their companies as places to work. Similarly, employees in Canadian and U.S. companies held comparable views on their own job security.[66]

Despite similarities of views about human resource practices and employee attitudes toward work, differences in perception do exist. These differences in perceptions between Canadian and U.S. employees fall into four categories:

1. Level of cohesiveness within the company.
    a. Fewer than half of all employees in either country rate any aspect of "organizational integration" favourably.
    b. Canadians are more positive than Americans about the quality of management–employee relations, co-operation between departments, and top-management contact with employees.

2. Perceived level of job stress.
   a. The day-to-day work environment is generally felt to be more stressful in U.S. companies than in Canadian firms.
   b. The majority of U.S. respondents feel their companies are growing too fast.
   c. A smaller percentage of U.S. employees than Canadian employees feel their work is well planned — a view that is likely fuelling concerns about the adequacy of staffing levels needed to get work done.
   d. U.S. employees are greatly concerned about the quality of equipment and the safety of work areas. Canadian employees perceive their workplaces to be more orderly and, above all, much safer.
   e. A larger proportion of Canadian employees than U.S. employees feel that their supervisors insist on high standards of quality.
   f. More Canadian employees than U.S. employees claim to be satisfied with their pay.
   g. In general, employees in high-stress organizations have difficulty perceiving firm links between their own efforts or performance and their wages.
3. Organizational investment in individual development.
   a. A smaller percentage of Canadian employees than U.S. employees believe their skills and abilities are being used on the job. U.S. employees see more of an opportunity to learn new skills and are more likely to perceive that their companies offer opportunity for individual growth and development.
   b. U.S. employers seem to be doing a somewhat better job than Canadian employers of informing their employees about job openings and training them for better jobs as they become available.
   c. Canadian workers feel more uncertain and unprepared by their organizations for future growth.
   d. The U.S. experience in managing more dynamic and demanding work environments has apparently led to greater success in both tapping human potential today and developing it for the future.
4. Company and identity.
   a. Americans are more confident than Canadians about the ability of their companies to compete in the marketplace. The former also see a stronger pattern of improved quality in their companies' products and services.
   b. Though Canadian employees report more stable environments and higher supervisory expectations for quality, in the final analysis they are more likely to feel they have lost more ground than are U.S. workers.

  c. U.S. employees express a stronger sense of pride in their companies than do Canadian workers.

A second study by the same authors deals exclusively with Canadian employees. It, like the first study, shows signs of diminishing employee commitment. According to this study:

> The changes required by business are best accomplished with the co-operation and understanding of employees. But, at a time when the management of human resources is most critical to the success of organizations, many employers appear to be losing the battle for the hearts and minds of their employees.
>
> Analysis of ten-year trend data in employee attitudes between 1977 and 1987 shows that there has been a significant decline in how employees rate their "company as a place to work compared to other companies." The most dramatic drop has been among middle managers and professionals. Their views of the organization are now converging with those of hourly employees, who have traditionally been the most pessimistic of all employee groups. Although the data for clerical employees have levelled over the last four years, this group expressed much higher satisfaction in 1977.[67]

The employee perceptions this Canadian study uncovered fell into three groups:

1. Limits on opportunity.
    a. A perceived decline in promotional opportunities accounts for some of the increased dissatisfaction of employees.
    b. Fewer than 40 percent of employees believe in their organization's ability to reward them with promotions, compared with 70 percent a decade ago. The proportion of professionals, clerical employees, and hourly workers who perceive their opportunities to be very good has never reached 40 percent.
    c. Whereas blue-collar workers have traditionally been the most affected by downsizing and cyclical layoffs, the recent changes in many organizations have also threatened the job security of managers.

2. Lack of information.
    a. Employees at all levels feel less informed about what is going on in their organizations than they have in the past.
    b. What kind of information do employees want? They want to know how the business is run. They want to know the basis upon which business decisions are made. They want honest and full information about where the company is headed. And they want to know where they stand and how to improve their performance.

3. Direction from the top.
   a. The lack of information among employees within the organization is parallelled, in large part, by senior managers' uncertainty about corporate direction. In 1986, only 36 percent of senior managers claimed that their organizations had a clear strategic direction; the comparable figure for top executives was 70 percent—a gap of 34 percent. When communication fails so high in the organization, it is not surprising that employees feel uninformed about what is going on.
   b. The most recent data suggest that employees are being isolated by their organizations. Seventy-six percent of employees say that their companies demand high levels of performance, yet fewer than 50 percent claim that they receive the support they need from management to carry out their responsibilities.

These trend data on employee attitudes suggest that without a fundamental reassessment of management practices, we will continue to witness an increase in disgruntled professionals, alienation of middle managers, and erosion of commitment among hourly and clerical employees.

Source: Adapted from R.J. Grey and G.C. Johnson, "Differences between Canadian and American Workers," *Canadian Business Review*, Winter 1988, pp. 20–23; and G.C. Johnson and R.J. Grey, "Signs of Diminishing Employee Commitment," *Canadian Business Review*, Spring 1988, pp. 20–23. Used with the permission of *Canadian Business Review*, The Conference Board of Canada.

TASKS AND QUESTIONS

1. Consider the various attitudes expressed in the two studies. Identify the HRM functions related to these attitudes and briefly explain how they are related.

2. Judging from these two studies, what policies and practices could be implemented in Canadian organizations to improve some of the negative attitudes?

CASE 2.2 ▶ CHALLENGE AT RED MAPLE FOODS

Jean Hylck, vice-president of human resources at Red Maple Foods, sat looking out his window, which faced the plant parking lot, but he didn't really see the employees hurrying to catch buses or drive home. He was, instead, reflecting upon that afternoon's meeting with Sally Crutchfield, the CEO; Jacques Auberge, the comptroller; Cynthia Gray, the director of marketing; and Will Kalinga, the production manager. The meeting covered a number of areas, including the effects of the Canada–U.S. Free Trade Agreement on Red Maple's sales, sales forecasts for both the next year and the next five years, Cynthia's plans for regaining lost market share, Jacques's concern that the company must become more cost-efficient to return to profitability, and Will's report on the progress of automating more of the company's production operations. Jean appreciated being included in this strategic planning session; the policy of his previous employer was simply to tell him what was expected of human resources after such meetings. The other officers seemed genuinely concerned as he discussed how the company was going to handle training employees to efficiently operate the new automated equipment, as well as employees' concerns regarding the ability of the company to face the competitive challenges of the 1990s. Jean presented a demographic analysis of the current work force, noting that more than 60 percent of the employees were over 50 years of age and some of them had less than a Grade 8 education. Sally wanted to know if this could cause problems with maximizing the return on the investment they were making in the new equipment. Both Jacques and, to a lesser degree, Will suggested they encourage older employees to retire through use of an early retirement plan and simply hire younger workers, who they believed would be better able to cope with the new technology. This approach was the one often taken in the past, but Jean felt it had a number of disadvantages. Sally asked him to prepare a brief report on the pros and cons of the early retirement approach versus his recommended retraining approach.

Another issue Cynthia had brought up at the meeting was the quality of Red Maple's products. She presented survey and customer complaint data showing that some of Red Maple's ice cream cartons had product smeared on the sides and lid, labels on other products were sometimes loose or misaligned, and there were a few instances of contaminated product — dirt, insect parts, or packaging material found in Red Maple's products. The officers discussed whether the cause of these problems was poor quality control by employees, the equipment, or a combination of the two. Jean suggested that these problems in quality may indicate morale problems among the employees. Will felt the new equipment would solve many of these problems. Jean noted that absences had increased since Will told the supervisors to place more emphasis on efficiency and cost reduction. Will stated that he had done this in response to Jacques's earlier concern regarding the profitability of Red Maple.

As Jean reflected upon the discussion at the meeting, he regretted not also mentioning results of his recent though small sample employee attitude survey that found some dissatisfaction with pay. Many Red Maple employees were, however, earning more than many workers in comparable jobs in the area. He wondered if most of the dissatisfaction about pay came from women or men. Red Maple employed more women than most manufacturing companies, and Jean felt that his job evaluation plan, though a little old, was fair.

As Jean packed up some work to take home, he recalled two articles he had read a while ago that might be useful in preparing his recommendations to Sally and the other officers. The two articles highlighted the following points:

1. Canada has lagged behind many other nations in introduction of new forms of technology such as process automation, which includes computer-aided manufacturing, computer-controlled machines, and statistical process control — many of the innovations Red Maple was now installing. Unlike Red Maple, the Canadian companies that have been leaders in this area have been either large or foreign-owned.

2. Innovation must be on two fronts, namely, technology and people. Therefore, change should occur in how work is organized, how employees are used, and how decisions are made in order to make the best use of new technology and to remain competitive.

3. Retraining is an essential part of the innovative process.

4. A study of high- and low-performing companies found striking differences in the attitudes of employees. First, employees of high-performing companies had very favourable attitudes toward their employer, while employees of poor-performing companies had much less favourable attitudes. Second, satisfaction with pay was usually higher in high-performing companies than in low-performing companies despite little actual differences in pay. Third, employees of high-performing firms rated the overall quality of decisions made by management as higher than did those in lower-performing organizations.

5. The high-performing companies had three distinguishing characteristics: (a) communication — employees feel they are kept well informed about the business, and employees at different levels hold similar views; (b) performance management — employees at all levels are expected to meet high levels of performance; and (c) freedom to develop — employees are given freedom to solve problems and take remedial actions in solving job problems.

Jean felt that Red Maple was at a crucial point in its history and that the company must change not only its technology but its way of organizing and utilizing its human resources. The problems Red Maple now faces are not unlike those of many other Canadian employers, and the solutions involve a strategic perspective on both technology and human resources. Jean knew that his recommendations must show how factors such as absenteeism; demographics; and employee knowledge, skills, and attitudes are related to the overall goal of the survival and competitiveness of the company.

Source: Adapted from K. Newton and G. Betcherman, "Innovating on Two Fronts," *Canadian Business Review*, Autumn 1987, pp. 18–21; and G. Johnson and R. Grey, "Employee Motivation in High Performance Companies," *Canadian Business Review*, Autumn 1988, pp. 25–28. Used with the permission of *Canadian Business Review*, The Conference Board of Canada.

TASKS AND QUESTIONS

1. Assume you are Jean Hylck. Outline the major points you would make in your report to Sally Crutchfield. Be sure to mention all factors related to the decision on whether to use retraining or early retirement to meet the human resource needs of the new equipment.

2. Discuss how human resource policies can affect an organization's ability to be competitive.

NOTES

1. Gordon Betcherman, Keith Newton, and Joanne Godin, eds., *Two Steps Forward: Human Resource Management in a High-Tech World*, Economic Council of Canada (Ottawa: Supply and Services Canada, 1990), pp. 15–19. Reprinted with the permission of the Chairman of the Economic Council of Canada, 1992.

2. S.F. Kaliski, *Labour Turnover in Canada: A Survey of Literature and Data* (Ottawa: Labour Canada, 1981).

3. J.E. Gardener, *Stabilizing the Workforce: A Complete Guide to Controlling Turnover* (New York: Quorum Books, 1986).

4. J.C. Hyatt, "People Watchers: Demographers Finally Come into Their Own in Firms, Government," *Wall Street Journal*, July 19, 1978.

5. Economic Council of Canada, *Au Courant*, vol. 2, no. 3 (1991), pp. 4–11.

6. Economic Council of Canada, *Au Courant*, p. 5; and Susan Delacourt, "Immigration Gate Opens Wider," *The Globe and Mail*, October 26, 1990.

7. Statistics Canada, *Comparison of the 1975 Labour Force Survey Estimates Derived from the Former and Revised Surveys* (Ottawa, 1976). Reproduced with the permission of the Minister of Supply and Services Canada, 1992.

8. E.B. Akyeampong, "Discouraged Workers," *Perspectives on Labour and Income*, Statistics Canada, cat. no. 75-001E, Autumn 1989, pp. 64–69. Reproduced with the permission of the Minister of Supply and Services Canada, 1992.

9. Sylvia Ostry and Mahmood A. Zaidi, *Labour Economics in Canada*, 3rd ed. (Toronto: Macmillan, 1979), p. 35.

10. David K. Foot, *Canada's Population Outlook, Demographic Futures and Economic Challenges* (Ottawa: Canadian Institute for Economic Policy, 1982).

11. Foot, *Canada's Population Outlook*, p. v.; and Statistics Canada, *Labour Force Annual Averages 1990*, cat. no. 71-220, A-14, Table 1. Reproduced with the permission of the Minister of Supply and Services Canada.

12. Statistics Canada, *Labour Force Annual Averages 1981–1988*, cat. no. 71-529, Occasional, 1989; and Statistics Canada, *The Labour Force*, cat. no. 71-001, December 1989 and 1991, January 1992. Reproduced with the permission of the Minister of Supply and Services Canada, 1992.

13. N.M. Meltz and F. Reid, "Reducing the Impact of Unemployment through Worksharing: Some Industrial Relations Considerations," *Journal of Industrial Relations*, vol. 25 (June 1983), pp. 152–60.

14. See N.M. Meltz, F. Reid, and G.S. Swartz, *Sharing the Work: An Analysis of the Issues in Worksharing and Job Sharing* (Toronto: University of Toronto Press, 1981); and Carol Goar, "Work-Sharing: A Success No One Really Expected," *The Toronto Star*, March 27, 1982.

15. A. Freeman, "Ottawa Doubles UI Work-Sharing Money," *The Globe and Mail*, September 19, 1990; see also Leslie Papp, "Bridging the Gap, Labor Management Find Innovative Ways to Keep Peace in Tough Times" *The Toronto Star*, March 7, 1992.

16. Joan Wallace, *Part-Time Work in Canada*, Report of the Commission of Inquiry into Part-Time Work, Department of Labour Canada (Ottawa: Supply and Services Canada, 1983). Reproduced with the permission of the Minister of Supply and Services Canada, 1992.

17. Statistics Canada, *The Labour Force*, cat. no. 71-001, December 1990. Reproduced with the permission of the Minister of Supply and Services Canada, 1992. Part-timers made up 26 percent of all employees in trade and 25 percent of all employees in community, business, and personal service. These two categories represented more than three-quarters of all part-time workers.

18. Frank Reid and Gerald S. Swartz, *Prorating Fringe Benefits for Part-Time Employees in Canada* (Toronto: Centre for Industrial Relations, University of Toronto, 1982), p. 1.

19. Gordon Robertson, *Part-Time Work in Ontario: 1966 to 1976* (Toronto: Research Branch, Ontario Ministry of Labour, 1976); and Statistics Canada, *The Labour Force*, cat. no. 71-001, April 1977; and Statistics Canada, *Labour Force Annual*, cat. no. 71-220, August 1990. Reproduced with the permission of the Minister of Supply and Services Canada, 1992.

20. Canada, Employment and Immigration Commission, Employment Equity, 1986 Census of Canada, unpublished data. The participation rates in 1986 were 66.5 percent total, 60.3 percent for aboriginal peoples, and 72.1 percent for visible minorities; see also Canada, Employment and Immigration Commission, *Labour Market Development in the 1980's* [The Dodge Report] (Hull, Que.: Supply and Services Canada, 1981).

21. Canada, *Report of the Commission on Equality in Employment*, Judge Rosalie Silberman Abella, chair (Ottawa: Supply and Services Canada, 1984).

22. Reported in "60% Pick Economy as Top Concern," *The Toronto Star*, January 14, 1991.

23. E.A. Fleishman, "Human Abilities and the Acquisition of Skill," in E.A. Bilodeau, ed., *Acquisition of Skill* (New York: Academic Press, 1966), pp. 147–67.

24. J.R. Hackman, "Work Design," in J.L. Suttle and J.R. Hackman, *Improving Life at Work* (Santa Monica, Calif.: Goodyear, 1977), pp. 96–162.

25. B. Des Lauriers, "Functional Illiteracy in Canadian Business," *Canadian Business Review*, Winter 1989, pp. 36–41.

26. SHRM/CCH Survey, "Workplace Literacy/Basic Skills," June 26, 1990.

27. SHRM/CCH Survey.

28. J.S. Adams, "Inequity in Social Exchange," in L. Berkowitz, ed., *Advances in Experimental Social Psychology*, vol. 2 (New York: Academic Press, 1965), pp. 267–300.

29. G.P. Latham and J.J. Baldes, "The 'Practical Significance' of Locke's Theory of Goal Setting," *Journal of Applied Psychology*, February 1975, pp. 122–24.

30. G.P. Latham and S.B. Kinne III, "Improving Job Performance through Training in Goal Setting," *Journal of Applied Psychology*, April 1974, pp. 187–91.

31. F.J. Roethlisberger and W. Dickson, *Management and the Worker* (Cambridge, Mass.: Harvard University Press, 1939).

32. Society for Human Resource Management, *Issues in HR*, January 1991, p. 4.

33. J.L. McAdams, "Performance-Based Reward Systems," *Canadian Business Review*, Spring 1988, pp. 17–19.

34. W.C. Hamner and E.P. Hamner, "Behavior Modification on the Bottom Line," *Organizational Dynamics*, no. 4 (1976), pp. 3–21.

35. P.L. Booth, "Employee Involvement and Corporate Performance," *Canadian Business Review*, Spring 1988, pp. 14–16.

36. Conference Board of Canada, *Paying for Performance: The Growing Use of Incentives and Bonus Plans* (Ottawa, 1987).

37. Labour Canada, *Provisions in Collective Agreements* (Ottawa: Bureau of Labour Information, October 22, 1991).

38. V.H. Vroom, *Work and Motivation* (New York: Wiley, 1964); and M.T. Iaffaldano and P.M. Muchinsky "Job Satisfaction and Job Performance: A Meta-Analysis," *Psychological Bulletin*, March 1985, pp. 251–73.

39. S.L. McShane, "Job Satisfaction and Absenteeism: A Meta-Analytic Re-Examination," *Canadian Journal of Administrative Sciences*, vol. 1, no. 1 (1984), pp. 61–77; R.D. Hackett and R.M. Guion, "A Reevaluation of the Absenteeism–Job Satisfaction Relationship," *Organizational Behavior and Human Decision Processes*, June 1985, pp. 340–81; W.H. Mobley, R.W. Griffeth, H.H. Hand, and B.M. Meglino, "Review and Conceptual Analysis of the Employee Turnover Process," *Psychological Bulletin*, vol. 86 (1979), pp. 493–522; and G. Robertson and J. Humphreys, *Labour Turnover and Absenteeism in Selected Industries: Northwestern Ontario and Ontario* (Toronto: Ontario Ministry of Labour, 1979).

40. W.C. Hamner and F.J. Smith, "Work Attitudes as Predictors of Unionization Activity," *Journal of Applied Psychology*, August 1978, pp. 415–21.

41. J.G. Getman, S.B. Goldberg, and J.B. Herman, *Union Representation Elections: Law and Reality* (New York: Russell Sage Foundation, 1976).

42. P.H. Mirvis and E.E. Lawler III, "Measuring the Financial Impact of Employee Attitudes," *Journal of Applied Psychology*, no. 1 (1977), pp. 1–8.

43. P.C. Smith, L.M. Kendall, and C.L. Hulin, *The Measurement of Satisfaction in Work and Retirement* (Chicago: Rand NcNally, 1969).

44. B. Schneider and H.P. Dachler, "A Note on the Stability of the Job Description Index," *Journal of Applied Psychology*, October 1978, pp. 650–53.

45. G.C. Johnson and R.J. Grey, "Employee Motivation in High-Performing Companies," *Canadian Business Review*, Autumn 1988, pp. 26–29.

46. J. Gandz and A. Mikalachki, "Absenteeism: Costs, Causes, and Cures," *The Business Quarterly*, Spring 1980, pp. 22–30; and "Measuring Absenteeism," *Relations Industrielles/Industrial Relations*, vol. 34, no. 3 (1979), pp. 516–48.

47. See McShane, "Job Satisfaction and Absenteeism"; Hackett and Guion, "A Reevaluation"; and D. Farrell and C.L. Stamm, "Meta-Analysis of the Correlates of Employee Absence," *Human Relations*, vol. 41 (1988), pp. 211–27.

48. R.M. Steers and S.R. Rhodes, "Knowledge and Speculation about Absenteeism," in P.S. Goodman and R.S. Atkin, eds., *Absenteeism* (San Francisco: Jossey-Bass, 1984), pp. 229–75.

49. Daniel Stoffman, "Blue-Collar Turnaround Artists," *Canadian Business*, February 1984, p. 41.

50. G.P. Latham and C.A. Frayne, "Self-Management Training for Increasing Job Attendance: A Follow-Up and Replication," *Journal of Applied Psychology*, vol. 74, no. 3 (1989), pp. 411–16.

51. E.F. Jackofsky, "Turnover and Job Performance: An Integrated Process Model," *Academy of Management Review*, vol. 9 (1984), pp. 74–83.

52. C.R. Williams and L.P. Livingstone, "A Second Look at the Relationship between Performance and Voluntary Turnover," *Academy of Management Journal*, in press.

53. James L. Price, *The Study of Turnover* (Ames, Ia.: Iowa State University Press, 1977).

54. J.G. Rosse and C.L. Hulin, "Adaptation to Work: An Analysis of Employee Health, Withdrawal and Change," *Organizational Behavior and Human Decision Processes*, vol. 36 (1985), pp. 324–47; J.G. Rosse, "Relations among Lateness, Absence, and Turnover: Is There a Progression of Withdrawal?" *Human Relations*, vol. 41 (1988), pp. 517–31; A. Mitra, G.D. Jenkins, and W. Gupta, "A Meta-Analytic Review of the Relationship between Absence and Turnover," *Southern Management Association Proceedings*, 1990, pp. 166–68.

55. Mitra, Jenkins, and Gupta, "A Meta-Analytic Review," pp. 166–68.

56. W.H. Mobley, *Employee Turnover: Causes, Consequences, and Control* (Reading, Mass.: Addison-Wesley, 1982).

57. P.W. Hom and R.W. Griffeth, "Structural Equations Modeling Test of a Turnover Theory: Cross-Sectional and Longitudinal Analysis," *Journal of Applied Psychology*, in press.

58. W.H. Mobley, "Intermediate Linkages in the Relationship between Job Satisfaction and Employee Turnover," *Journal of Applied Psychology*, vol. 62 (1977), pp. 237–40.

59. This section was based upon material from M.E. Borus, H.S. Parnes, S.H. Sandell, and B. Seidman, eds., *The Older Worker* (Madison, Wisc.: Industrial Relations Research Association, 1988); American Association of Retired Persons, *The Aging Work Force* (Washington, DC, 1990); G.M. McEvoy and W.F. Cascio,

"Cumulative Evidence of the Relationship between Employee Age and Job Performance," *Journal of Applied Psychology*, vol. 74 (1989), pp. 11–17; S.R. Rhodes, "Age-Related Differences in Work Attitudes and Behavior: A Review and Conceptual Analysis," *Psychological Bulletin*, vol. 93 (1983), pp. 328–67; G.S. Lowe, "Retirement Attitudes, Plans and Behaviour," *Perspectives*, Autumn 1991, pp. 8–17; and E.B. Harvey, "Trends in the Canadian Labour Force," *CVA/ACFP Journal*, vol. 25, no. 4 (1990), pp. 17–18.

60. Lowe, "Retirement Attitudes, Plans, and Behaviour," pp. 9–11.
61. H.S. Parnes, "The Retirement Decision," in Borus, Parnes, Sandell, and Seidman, eds., *The Older Worker*, pp. 115–50.
62. Rhodes, "Age-Related Differences in Work Attitudes and Behaviour."
63. McEvoy and Cascio, "Cumulative Evidence."
64. American Association of Retired Persons, *The Aging Work Force* (Washington, DC, 1990).
65. *Working Age*, Jan/Feb 1988.
66. R.J. Grey and G.C. Johnson, "Differences between Canadian and American Workers," *Canadian Business Review*, Winter 1989, p. 22.
67. G.C. Johnson and R.J. Grey, "Signs of Diminishing Employee Commitment," *Canadian Business Review*, Spring 1988, p. 23.

SUGGESTIONS FOR FURTHER READING

☐ Employment and Immigration Canada. *Job Futures: An Occupational Outlook to 1995, Volume 1: Occupational Outlooks* and *Volume 2: Experience of Recent Graduates*. 1990 ed. Prepared by the Canadian Occupational Projection System (COPS). Toronto: Nelson Canada, 1990.

☐ Statistics Canada. *Perspectives on Labour and Incomes*, cat. no. 75-001E. A quarterly magazine with articles on developments in the Canadian work force.

CHAPTER 3

THE LEGAL ENVIRONMENT

- LEGISLATION AND JURISDICTION
- HUMAN RIGHTS: CONCEPTS AND PROHIBITIONS
- HRM IN ACTION ▸ HOW EMPLOYERS CAN AVOID LIABILITY FOR WORKPLACE HARASSMENT
- AFFIRMATIVE ACTION AND EMPLOYMENT EQUITY
- EMPLOYMENT STANDARDS LEGISLATION
- SUMMARY
- REVIEW QUESTIONS
- PROJECT IDEAS
- CASE 3.1 ▸ NATIONAL'S JOB EQUITY STARTS AT THE TOP
- CASE 3.2 ▸ MANAGEMENT AND COMPLAINTS OF SEXUAL HARASSMENT
- NOTES
- SUGGESTIONS FOR FURTHER READING

THE ENVIRONMENT IN WHICH HRM professionals work to acquire, develop, and maintain a qualified work force — the human assets of an organization — is governed by a complete network of laws and regulations. For example:

1. No employer in Canada may discriminate, in hiring or in terms and conditions of employment, on the basis of race, religion, ethnic or national origin, colour, mental disability, physical disability, sex, or marital status.

2. Most jurisdictions prohibit discrimination on the basis of age, but the meaning of "age" varies; it is 45 to 65 in British Columbia, 19 and over in New Brunswick, unqualified in Manitoba and the federal jurisdiction, and so on.

3. All jurisdictions have minimum wage provisions, but the rates change frequently and vary among provinces. Some provinces exempt certain types or classes of workers or set lower rates for them.

4. All Canadian employers are prohibited from paying men and women differently. Three distinct approaches to avoiding discrimination are used: equal pay for equal work, equal pay for work of equal value, and pay equity. Not only do the various jurisdictions follow different

approaches, but some apply different approaches to different groups of employees. For example, Nova Scotia requires pay equity for public sector employees and equal pay for equal (substantially the same) work for private sector employees.

5. Various aspects of work time—maximum hours per day and per week, rest days, annual vacations and holidays — are legislated. So are the conditions under which minors may be employed. The details vary considerably from jurisdiction to jurisdiction.

6. Employers are required to give notice to individual workers and to groups of workers whose employment is to be terminated. The amount of notice may differ not only with the jurisdiction but with the number of employees being laid off. Moreover, there is the question of severance pay. The federal jurisdiction requires severance pay for individuals and groups of workers, but Ontario requires it only when groups of workers are laid off and when employees are terminated by an employer with a payroll of $2.5 million or more.

7. A healthy and safe workplace must be provided for employees. Health and safety rules vary across jurisdictions and also among different kinds of industries.

8. Employers must abide by regulations on union–management relations, including the process of unionization and collective bargaining. Each jurisdiction has its own laws in this area.

9. Employers, as well as employees, are required to make contributions to the unemployment insurance (UI) fund and to the Canada (or Quebec) Pension Plan (C/QPP).

10. Employers are required to pay into workers' compensation programs; the rates depend on the type of industry, as well as the jurisdiction.

These laws and regulations represent only a sampling of the legislation that affects administration of HRM functions and activities of HRM professionals.

To a great extent, government regulations shape human resource policies and pose constraints on HRM practices. Compliance with the law requires that certain procedures be performed in certain ways and not in others. For example, human rights acts prohibit recruiting for jobs in such a way as to lead to potential discrimination. Advertisements and application forms cannot refer to such things as race, religion, or sex.

Government regulation also creates considerable paperwork because it requires maintaining specific records. Even if a company's policies and practices are in compliance with the law, the employer must have data available and be ready to invest time and money answering any charges of discrimination or failure to meet required employment standards. And a multitude of forms must be filed relating to the C/QPP, unemployment insurance, and so on.

Plaintive remarks about government regulation can probably be heard among HRM professionals in every industrialized country today. Canada, however, has a special problem because its labour-related laws are set by thirteen different jurisdictions — all ten provinces, both territories, and the federal government. In fact, Canadian employment law is often called a legal jungle because of the resulting differences in regulations. Firms operating in more than one jurisdiction are subject to different regulations, and these differences show up whenever an employee is transferred from one province to another. For example, in Ontario an employee must receive two weeks of vacation pay after one year of employment, but in Saskatchewan it is three weeks. If an employee is transferred after one year of employment in Ontario, does he or she receive two weeks or three weeks of vacation? (The answer is two weeks until a full year has been completed in Saskatchewan.)

Rather than attempt to cover the full range of employment-related legislation in Canada, this chapter concentrates on the laws that guarantee what are termed human rights and on those that establish standards for many aspects of the employment relationship. Both types of laws are subject to almost constant change, both from the enactment of new regulations and from court or board decisions on the interpretation of existing regulations. The wise HRM professional keeps up-to-date on legislation and interpretation pertinent to his or her area. (Chapter 12 discusses the application of pay equity legislation in Ontario, which has the most far-reaching of the equal pay provisions. Other legislation applying specifically to benefits, health and safety, and labour relations is discussed in Chapters 13, 14, and 15.)

LEGISLATION AND JURISDICTION

Canada's present labour laws evolved under the Constitution Act, 1867 (formerly known as the British North America Act) under which both the Parliament of Canada and the provincial legislatures have the power to enact labour laws. Judicial interpretation of sections 91 and 92 has given major jurisdiction to the provinces, with federal authority limited to a narrow field. In practice, federal labour and employment laws now cover less than 10 percent of the Canadian labour force: those people who work for interprovincial and international railways; highway transport; telephone, telegraph, and cable systems; pipelines; ferries, tunnels, bridges, and shipping; radio and television broadcasting (including cablevision); air transport and airports; banks; grain elevators; flour and feed mills; and certain Crown corporations.

Each of the ten provinces and two territories has separate human rights and labour standards laws and separate commissions (and courts) to enforce them. An establishment is deemed to be under only one jurisdiction; in cases of uncertainty as to what that jurisdiction is, legal counsels within the pertinent commissions decide the issue. However, a firm with several establishments may operate in a number of different provinces. Table 3.1 lists selected legislation relating to human rights and employment standards in Canada.

Given thirteen jurisdictions, the variation in laws is great, not to mention the differences in regulations and interpretations. Keeping informed is important to HRM professionals, particularly those who work for organizations which have plants or offices in several provinces.

Added to this already complex situation is the federal Constitution Act, 1982, which contains the Canadian Charter of Rights and Freedoms. The Charter's section on equality rights is designed to provide individuals protection against discrimination. However, section 15(2) permits affirmative action that has as its object "the amelioration of conditions of disadvantaged individuals or groups including those that are disadvantaged because of race, national or ethnic origin, colour, religion, sex, age or mental or physical disability."[1] The provincial legislatures have the right to opt out of some of the equality rights clauses, and some of the laws are being tested in the courts by some provinces and by groups and individuals. Two cases in point are the issues of mandatory retirement and discrimination arising from bona fide work rules.

In 1991 the Supreme Court of Canada held that mandatory retirement at age 65 is a reasonable limit on the right set out in section 15 of the Charter of Rights and Freedoms to be protected from discrimination because of age. The case concerned universities in British Columbia and Ontario. The majority of the Supreme Court concluded that the objectives of the governments in limiting protection against age discrimination to those age 45 to 65 and 18 to 65 respectively, allowing mandatory retirement policies to exist for those 65 and over, were pressing and substantial. The governments' objectives were to preserve the integrity of pension plans and to foster the prospects of younger workers.[2]

A related case concerned whether a mandatory retirement policy was justified as a bona fide occupational requirement. A Saskatoon firefighter was forced to retire at age 60, as provided by the collective agreement. The fire department argued that it had not contravened the Saskatchewan Human Rights Code because the Code permitted discrimination where there "is a reasonable occupational qualification and requirement for the position of employment." According to a Board of Inquiry, the reasonable occupational requirement was to engage in actual firefighting, and the ability to perform a firefighter's task decreases with age and there is no reliable method of determining how an individual firefighter would cope in an emergency situation, therefore it was unnecessary to individually test each firefighter at retirement age. The Supreme Court of Canada accepted the Board's conclusion and agreed that the employer was acting reasonably and had not contravened the Saskatchewan Human Rights Code's prohibition against discrimination between the ages of 18 and 65. The Court indicated, however, that employers will not be able to successfully present a bona fide occupational requirement defence unless they can establish why it was not possible to deal with employees on an individual basis.[3]

TABLE 3.1
Selected Legislation Relating to Human Rights and Employment Standards in Canada, 1990

JURISDICTION	HUMAN RIGHTS	EMPLOYMENT STANDARDS
Federal	Canadian Human Rights Act, Equal Wages Guidelines	Canada Labour Code, Fair Wages and Hours of Labour Act, Holidays Act, Wages Liability Act
Alberta	Individual's Rights Protection Act	Employment Standards Code
British Columbia	Human Rights Act	Employment Standards Act, Public Construction Fair Wages Act
Manitoba	Human Rights Act, Pay Equity Act	Employment Standards Act, Construction Industry Wages Act, Vacations with Pay Act, Wages Recovery Act
New Brunswick	Human Rights Act, Pay Equity Act	Employment Standards Act
Newfoundland	Human Rights Code	Labour Standards Act
Nova Scotia	Human Rights Act, Pay Equity Act	Labour Standards Code
Ontario	Human Rights Code, Pay Equity Act	Employment Standards Act, One Day's Rest in Seven Act
Prince Edward Island	Human Rights Act, Pay Equity Act	Labour Act, Minimum Age of Employment Act
Quebec	Charter of Human Rights and Freedoms	Labour Standards Act, National Holiday Act
Saskatchewan	Human Rights Code	Labour Standards Act, Wages Recovery Act
Northwest Territories	Fair Practices Act	Labour Standards Act, Wages Recovery Act
Yukon	Human Rights Act	Employment Standards Act

Source: Compiled from Labour Canada, *Employment Standards Legislation in Canada*, 1991 ed. (Hull, Que.: Supply and Services Canada, 1991). Used with the permission of the Minister of Supply and Services Canada, 1992; Peter Barnacle, *The Current Industrial Relations Scene in Canada: Labour Legislation and Public Policy Reference Tables, 1989* (Kingston, Ont.: Industrial Relations Centre, Queen's University, 1989). Used with the permission of the Industrial Relations Centre.

Since changes are continually occurring in the interpretation of the Charter as it applies to human rights and employment standards, HRM professionals should remain alert to developments.[4]

We will first examine the area of human rights and then turn to a discussion of employment standards.

HUMAN RIGHTS: CONCEPTS AND PROHIBITIONS

Human rights legislation is intended, in the words of the Canadian Human Rights Act, to give effect to the principle that "every individual should have an equal opportunity with other individuals to make for himself or herself the life that he or she is able and wishes to have consistent with his or her duties and obligations as a member of society."[5] Insofar as employment is concerned, the purpose of human rights legislation is to prevent people from being treated differently — that is, discriminated against — because of their race, ethnicity, religion, sex, marital status, and so on when it comes to decisions about hiring, pay, and promotion. Rather, these decisions should be made on the basis of individual qualifications.

In the workplace, *discrimination* means, in the words of a recent Canadian Human Rights Commission pamphlet, "making an unlawful distinction between certain individuals and others based on a characteristic that has nothing to do with the job or the service involved."[6]

The Abella Commission identified the fundamental issue of systemic discrimination. *Systemic discrimination* identifies discrimination in the workplace in terms of the impact of employment practices on the employment opportunities of designated group members. The impact of, rather than the intention behind, behaviour or employment practices is what defines systemic discrimination.[7] The federal government's Employment Equity Act of 1986 is designed to address systemic discrimination as it affects women, visible minorities, Native people, and people with disabilities.

A related concept in human rights in employment is indirect discrimination. *Indirect discrimination* occurs in the workplace when an employer has no malice or intention to discriminate but acts in such a way as to deny employment or advancement on grounds that are, in fact, discriminatory. For example, a department store required all employees to work Friday evenings and Saturdays on a rotation basis. Consequently, it terminated the employment of an employee who was a Seventh Day Adventist; she had refused to work on Friday evenings and Saturdays because her religion required strict observance of the Sabbath from sundown Friday to sundown Saturday. The Supreme Court of Canada, in a unanimous judgement (the *O'Malley* decision), found that the woman had been discriminated against because of creed. The Court held that it is not necessary to prove that discrimination was intentional to find that a violation of human rights legislation has occurred; an employment rule, neutral on its face and honestly made, can have discriminatory effects. Therefore, it is the *result* or the *effect* of an act that is important in determining whether discrimination has occurred.

The Court also held that, where an employment rule has a discriminatory effect, an employer has a duty to take reasonable steps to accommodate the employee unless accommodation creates an undue hardship for the employer. In this case, the employment rule that all employees had to rotate working Friday evenings and Saturdays had a discriminatory effect because of the woman's religion. The employer did not show that accommodating the employee would have created an undue hardship. The Court found that the onus of proving that accommodation will result in undue hardship is on the employer, since the information is in the employer's possession and the employee is not likely to be able to prove that there is no undue hardship. In the *O'Malley* case, the firm was ordered to pay compensation for wages lost due to discrimination.[8]

A 1990 decision by the Supreme Court of Canada reiterated that the onus is on the employer to accommodate the religious obligations of an employee up to the point of undue hardship. Speaking for the majority, Madame Justice Wilson said:

> I emphasize once again that there is nothing in the evidence to suggest that Monday absences of the complainant [the employee] would have become routine or that the general attendance record of the complainant was a subject of concern. The ability of the respondent [the employer] to accommodate the complainant on this occasion [Easter Monday] was, on the evidence, obvious and, to my mind, incontrovertible.[9]

The possibility of such "innocent" discrimination means HRM professionals and their employees must be increasingly careful about their advertising, interviewing, and employment practices. To protect themselves from challenge, Harish Jain, an expert at McMaster University, suggests: (1) establishing entry and training requirements that are truly prerequisite to the performance of a job, and (2) conducting structured interviews in which applicants are asked only questions of direct relevance to the job.[10]

An increasingly recognized type of human rights violation is sexual harassment at work. Sexual harassment includes situations in which submission to or rejection of an unsolicited sexual advance is used as a basis for employment or advancement. It also includes situations in which physical or verbal conduct that emphasizes the sex or sexual orientation of the individual creates a hostile or offensive working environment. (see Case 3.2 at the end of the chapter). Sexual harassment can also include ogling. For example, a University of Toronto professor was banned from the university's swimming pool for five years after the school's sexual harassment review board upheld a complaint from a student that the professor persistently swam behind her, leered at her through his mask, and used his flippers to catch up with her.[11] Based on a survey of 2000 people in 1983, the Canadian Human Rights Commission found that 1.2 million women and 300 000 men believed they had been sexually harassed at work. A study by Professors Jain and P. Andiappan found that unions, like employers, often ignore or resist action on the issue of sexual harassment.[12] At the same time, many unions, especially those with large numbers of female members, are writing clauses into collective agreements that specifically deal with sexual harassment and commit the employer to a work environment free of this problem. These same unions have undertaken programs to educate their members about the demeaning and offensive nature of sexual harassment and how to deal with it. Human rights commissions and arbitrators have equated sexual harassment with discrimination, and the labour codes of Newfoundland, New Brunswick, Ontario, Quebec, Yukon, and the federal government specifically prohibit it. In addition, the Quebec Workers' Compensation Board has ruled that sexual harassment that leads to extreme stress, depression, and physical symptoms is an appropriate cause for compensation as a work-related injury.[13] Though sexual harassment has not yet been established as a health and safety matter for Ontario employers, a 1988 settlement of a case of alleged sexual harassment at Stelco may lead to such a result.[14]

Some employers try to circumvent anti-discrimination laws by hiring through private employment agencies that will follow requests to screen out applicants from visible minorities and specified religious and ethnic groups. In 1988, the Canadian Recruiters Guild released a study that suggested discrimination was rampant among professional job recruiters. All of the recruiters who responded to the survey said they had received discriminatory requests and 94 percent admitted they had complied with them. Two developments may be on the horizon to reduce this form of silent discrimination, at least in Ontario. First, a committee of staffing consultants has been working with the government to draft amendments to the province's Employment Agencies Act that would establish regular audits of agencies' hiring practices and require job consultants to be trained in human rights and labour laws.[15] The second development that could reduce silent discrimination is the Ontario government's plan to introduce an employment equity program for the public and private sectors. Such a plan could include job targets and establish agencies that would examine employers' payrolls and their success in recruiting women, members of visible minorities, people with disabilities, and aboriginal Canadians.

PROHIBITIONS

Every province, territory, and the federal government has a human rights act or code (see Table 3.1). These acts usually prohibit discrimination in occupancy and property sales, public accommodations, publications, signs, and contracts, as well as in employment and employment-related areas. The discussion here, however, deals only with the aspects that relate to employment practices.

All jurisdictions in Canada have enacted prohibitions against discrimination in employment practices. The wording varies from one jurisdiction to another, but all say that an employer is prohibited from various types of discrimination in hiring, as well as in the terms and conditions of employment and matters relating to promotion and transfer. In most cases, the term "employer" includes not only individual employers but also employers' organizations, employment agencies, and others who act on behalf of employers; the legislation usually also covers unions, employee associations, and professional associations. Labour relations acts, provincial and federal, also forbid discrimination by employers and unions (see Chapter 15).

Each of Canada's thirteen jurisdictions forbids a slightly different set of discriminatory acts. Moreover, since enforcement and interpretation are the preserves of commissions and courts within each jurisdiction, there are considerable differences in actual practice.

Table 3.2 summarizes the grounds on which each jurisdiction's human rights act specifically prohibits discrimination in 1991. Some grounds are common to all the acts: race, colour, national or ethnic origin (phrased as "ancestry" by some provinces), physical disability, marital status, age, and sex. Many jurisdictions also specify discrimination because of religion, political beliefs, or mental disability. A few add other grounds, varying from having a pardoned criminal conviction to social origin, to sexual orientation.

A common prohibition is discrimination because of age, although, as the table shows, there is much variety in the ages to which it applies. Notice that the Manitoba, Quebec, PEI, NWT, and federal acts leave the prohibition unqualified, although, in practice, these jurisdictions' minimum-age-of-employment rules and school-leaving ages set some bottom limits.

The types of discrimination listed in Table 3.2 should not be regarded as all that is prohibited in any jurisdiction. Human rights laws and their interpretation undergo frequent change, especially with the judicial interpretation of the Charter of Rights. Manitoba and British Columbia have *reasonable cause clauses*, which require that employers be able to show that their actions in regard to hiring, promotion, and termination are based on reasonable, job-related requirements, not on discriminatory causes. Moreover, since the commissions and courts now accept the argument of indirect or systemic discrimination, some common practices and preconceptions have come under scrutiny. For example, commissions have ruled against height and weight requirements for a police constable and for a labourer.

All the jurisdictions' acts provide for some exceptions to the prohibitions, but here, too, there are differences. Most jurisdictions make exceptions where there is a bona fide qualification for employment or for an occupation. A *bona fide qualification* is one that is absolutely necessary to the performance of a job. For example, the Supreme Court of Canada has ruled that wearing a hard hat is a bona fide occupational requirement and that there is therefore no duty to accommodate members of the Sikh religion who are required to wear a turban and no other head covering. Although the Court

TABLE 3.2
Prohibited Grounds of Discrimination in Employment in Canada

Jurisdiction	Fed.	Alta.	BC	Man.	NB	Nfld.	NS	Ont.	PEI	Que.	Sask.	NWT	Yukon
Dependence on alcohol/drug	•												
Race	•	•	•	•	•	•	•	•	•	•	•	•	•
National/ethnic origin	•			•	•	•	•	•	•	•	•	•	•
Colour	•	•	•	•	•	•	•	•	•	•	•	•	•
Nationality/ citizenship				•				•			•		
Religion	•	•	•	•	•	•	•	•	•	•	•	•	•
Age	•	•	•	•	•	•	•	•	•	•	•	•	•
Sex[a]	•	•	•	•	•	•	•	•	•	•	•	•	•
Pregnancy/ childbirth[b]	•	•						•		•			•
Marital status	•	•	•	•	•	•	•	•	•	•	•	•	•
Criminal conviction	•		•					•				•	
Mental disability	•	•	•	•	•	•	•	•	•	•	•	•	•
Physical disability	•	•	•	•	•	•	•	•	•	•	•	•	•
Ancestry		•	•		•			•			•	•	•
Political beliefs			•	•	•	•			•	•	•		•
Family status	•			•				•			•		•
Sexual orientation			•	•				•		•			•
Harassment[c]	•			•	•			•		•			•
Civil status										•			
Language										•			
Source of income				•			•						
Social origin							•						
Social conditions										•			
Creed		•		•				•	•	•	•	•	•
Place of residence												•	
Place of origin		•		•	•				•			•	•
Pardoned offence	•										•	•	
Assignment, attachment, or seizure of play										•			

[a] Alberta uses the term gender rather than sex.

[b] In Alberta, Ontario, Manitoba, and the Yukon, discrimination on the basis of pregnancy is included in discrimination on the basis of sex.

[c] Harassment is banned on all proscribed grounds of discrimination except in New Brunswick, where it refers only to sexual harassment.

Source: Reproduced with permission from *The Canadian Master Labour Guide*, 7th ed., published by and copyright CCH Canadian Limited, Don Mills, Ont., 1992, p. 265.

HRM IN ACTION

HOW EMPLOYERS CAN AVOID LIABILITY FOR WORKPLACE HARASSMENT

Firms can deal with sexual harassment in two ways: they can either have a policy in place before any problems arise, or they can be dragged into the issue after an employee complains. It is important to have a policy in place since employers may, in some cases, be held responsible for harassment by members of their staff.

In 1990 Levac Supply Limited was held responsible for the actions of an employee who harassed Carol Shaw for 14 years with a stream of derogatory remarks about her size and the fact that she was not home with her children. She had complained to her employer but, according to evidence given to a board of enquiry, the employer decided the problem was a personality conflict between the two employees, not harassment. The board's chairman ruled that the employer should have recognized the behaviour as harassment. Levac was found jointly responsible with the person who had actually done the harassing and Ms. Shaw was awarded a total of $48 273, one of Canada's larger awards for sexual harassment. The payment, primarily in the form of a pension Ms. Shaw lost by quitting, was divided among the company, its owner and the employee who harassed her.

Even though the Ontario Human Rights Code excludes companies from vicarious liability in the case of sexual harassment, the chairman of the board said that exclusion might not be consistent with current social values.

How can employees avoid being entangled with human rights complaints about workplace harassment? First, have a policy in place to deal with workplace harassment. Start with the principles of the appropriate human rights code, and then indicate to managers and staff how the code has been interpreted in actual cases and the penalties provided. Second, indicate clearly how to file a complaint with the company and what to expect when this has been done. Maintain confidentiality as much as possible.

Third, never assume a harassment complaint is frivolous. Take notes immediately. Find out who was involved, what happened, when and where, as well as whether there were witnesses. Fourth, meet with the witnesses and prepare statements. Meet privately with the person being accused, assuring him or her of confidentiality. Review the evidence and get clarification if necessary. Get legal counsel to review the material. Fifth, consider taking steps to resolve the problem, such as changing reporting

> lines or work locations. Finally, if harassment did occur, impose formal discipline on the basis of a previously publicized policy up to and including termination.
>
> Employees should be involved in developing the harassment policy and a program to deal with harassment. Such a program might be tied to employment equity where staff are trained to be sensitive to the needs of other cultures to avoid racial as well as sexual harassment. The majority of sexual harassment claims are filed by women, particularly women on low incomes or in non-traditional jobs. A well-planned and well-communicated policy on harassment can reduce both the incidence of and the employer's liability for such occurrences.
>
> Source: Adapted from Margot Gibb-Clark, "Harassment Cases Can Also Hurt Employers," *The Globe and Mail*, September 16, 1991. Used with the permission of *The Globe and Mail*.

repeated its finding from the *O'Malley* case, that it is not necessary to show an intention to discriminate in order for there to be a violation of human rights legislation, the hard hat rule was allowed because it was a bona fide occupational requirement for the job in question.[16]

Another common exception to the prohibitions relates to age and the operation of a bona fide insurance or pension plan. Some pension plans have a minimum time period for contributions before retirement.

In addition to regulating hiring, promotion, and termination, human rights acts prohibit discrimination in connection with application forms, advertisements, and enquiries about employment. In general, the areas of specific prohibition are the same as those for hiring and advancement.

The question sometimes arises as to whether there is reverse discrimination in affirmative action programs designed to promote the hiring of people from disadvantaged groups. As already noted, however, the Charter of Rights and Freedoms says such programs are legal. So do legislation in most jurisdictions and the Canadian Human Rights Commission. As a result, Canadian employers are largely protected from charges of reverse discrimination.[17]

Table 3.3 gives the Canadian Human Rights Commission's guide to screening and selection in employment. The guide's extensiveness is an indication of the care with which employers and HRM professionals must seek job-related information so as not to open themselves to challenges of discrimination. Each province also provides its own guidelines for questions that are appropriate or inappropriate on application forms or in employment interviews. These guidelines can be obtained by contacting the appropriate provincial human rights commission.[18]

TABLE 3.3
A Guide to Screening and Selection in Employment

Subject	Avoid Asking	Preferred Question	Comment
Name	About name change—whether it was changed by court order, marriage, or other reason Maiden name Christian name		Details needed for a reference or to check on previously held jobs or on educational credentials can be requested after selection
Address	For addresses outside Canada	Place and duration of current or recent addresses	
Age	For birth certificates, baptismal records, or about age in general Age or birthdate	If applicant has reached age (minimum or maximum) for work as defined by law	If precise age is required for benefits plans or other legitimate purposes, it can be determined after selection
Sex	Mr./Mrs./Miss/Ms Males or females to fill in different or coded applications If male or female on applications About pregnancy, childbirth, or child care arrangements; if birth control is used; or about child bearing plans	 If applicant can meet the attendance requirement or minimum service commitment	Any applicants can be addressed during interviews or in correspondence without using courtesy titles such as Mr./Mrs./Miss
Marital status	Whether applicant is single, married, divorced, engaged, separated, widowed, or living common-law		If transfer or travel is part of the job, the applicant can be asked if this would cause a problem

TABLE 3.3 (continued)

Subject	Avoid asking	Preferred question	Comment
Marital status *(continued)*	Whether an applicant's spouse is subject to transfer About spouse's employment	If there are any known circumstances that might prevent completion of, for example, a minimum service commitment	Information on dependents needed for benefits can be determined after selection
Family status	Number of children or dependents About arrangements for child care	If the applicant would be able to work the hours required and, if applicable, whether he or she would be able to work overtime	Contacts for emergencies and/or details on dependents can be determined after selection
National or ethnic origin	About birthplace, nationality of ancestors, spouse, or other relatives Whether born in Canada If naturalized or landed immigrant For proof of citizenship	If applicant is legally entitled to work in Canada (those who are so entitled must be citizens, landed immigrants, or holders of valid work permits)	Documentation of eligibility to work (papers, visas, etc.) can be requested after selection
Military service	About military service in other countries	Inquiry about Canadian military service, where employment preference is given to veterans by law	
Language	Mother tongue Where language skills obtained	If applicant understands, reads, writes, or speaks languages required	Testing or scoring applicants for language proficiency is not permitted

TABLE 3.3 *(continued)*

Subject	Avoid Asking	Preferred Question	Comment
Language *(continued)*		for job (in the federal jurisdiction and in Ontario, applicants can be asked if they meet the definition of francophone)	unless fluency is job-related or, in the case of the federal and Ontario governments, where francophones are one of the designated groups for employment equity purposes
Race or colour	Anything that would indicate race or colour, including colour of eyes, skin, or hair		Information required for security clearances or similar purposes can be obtained after selection
Photographs	For photo to be attached to application or sent to interviewer before interview		Photos for security passes or company files can be taken after selection
Religion	About religious affiliation, church membership, frequency of church attendance		Employers must reasonably accommodate religious needs of workers
	If applicant will work on a specific religious holiday	After explaining the required work shifts, whether such a schedule would pose problems for applicant	
	For references from clergy or religious leader		

TABLE 3.3 (continued)

Subject	Avoid asking	Preferred question	Comment
Height and weight			No inquiry unless there is evidence that these are bona fide occupational requirements
Disability	For listing of all disabilities, limitations, or health problems Whether applicant drinks or uses drugs Whether applicant has ever received psychiatric care or been hospitalized for emotional problems Whether applicant drinks, uses drugs, has AIDS, or is HIV positive	If applicant has any condition that could affect ability to do the job If applicant has any condition that should be considered in selection	A disability is relevant to job ability only if it (1) threatens the safety or property of others; or (2) prevents the applicant from safe and adequate job performance even if reasonable efforts are made to accommodate the disability
Medical information	If currently under physician's care Name of family doctor If receiving counselling or therapy		Medical exams should preferably be conducted after selection and only if employee's condition is related to the job duties; offers of employment can be made conditional on successful completion of a medical exam

TABLE 3.3 *(continued)*

Subject	Avoid asking	Preferred question	Comment
Affiliations	For list of club or organizational memberships	Membership in professional associations or occupational groups, if a job requirement	Applicants can decline to list any affiliation that might indicate a prohibited ground
Pardoned conviction	Whether an applicant has ever been convicted If an applicant has ever been arrested Does applicant have a criminal record	If applicant is eligible for bonding, if that is a job requirement	Inquiries about criminal record convictions—even those that have been pardoned—are discouraged unless related to job duties
References			The same restrictions that apply to questions asked of applicants apply when asking for employment references

Source: Canadian Human Rights Commission (Ottawa: Supply and Services Canada, June 1990). Reprinted with the permission of the Canadian Human Rights Commission. For a similar guide for each of the provinces, see "Do Your Job Application Forms Meet Human Resource Requirements?" *The Employment Law Report*, vol. 11, no. 10/11 (October/November 1990), pp. 83–100.

ENFORCEMENT

Each jurisdiction's human rights provisions are enforced through a human rights commission.[19] All the acts use a complaint process whereby any person who believes he or she has been discriminated against files a complaint; the commission then investigates and takes action if it finds the complaint justified. In Alberta, Nova Scotia, Ontario, Manitoba, and the federal jurisdiction, the commission may itself initiate complaints.

Individuals who launch complaints are legally protected against reprisals. For example, the Human Rights Code of British Columbia states:

> No person shall evict, discharge, suspend, expel, intimidate, coerce, impose any pecuniary or other penalty upon, or otherwise discriminate against, any person because that person complains, gives evidence, or otherwise assists in respect of the initiation of a complaint or other proceeding under the act.[20]

In all jurisdictions except Quebec, the commission can make orders requiring compliance that it is an offence to violate. Most provinces also provide for appeal to the provincial supreme court. Orders of a federal human rights tribunal may be made on order of the Federal Court of Canada and are enforceable in the same manner as an order of that court.

Human rights commissions attempt, however, to settle complaints by conciliation and persuasion. Harish Jain, quoted in Goneau, explains:

> The bulk of a typical human rights commission's workload consists of cases that do not go before a board of inquiry. The data on conciliation cases and cases under investigation are confidential. A board of inquiry is used only when all efforts at settlement fail.[21]

AFFIRMATIVE ACTION AND EMPLOYMENT EQUITY

Three closely related concepts dealing with human rights in employment are affirmative action, employment equity, and equal employment opportunity. *Affirmative action* refers to measures designed to compensate for the effects of discrimination, such as special training and recruitment programs for women and visible minorities aimed at improving their employment opportunities.[22]

The goal of *employment equity* policies is for employers to have a representation in their internal workforce that is comparable to that which exists in the externally available labour market. These policies deal with fairness in the various dimensions of the employment relationship, such as recruiting, hiring, training, promotion, and dismissals. In Canada, employment equity policies are applied to four target groups: women, visible minorities, aboriginal peoples, and persons with disabilities.[23] The government of Ontario includes a fifth target group, francophones, in the employment equity policies applied to provincial government employees, and the federal government also has in place a program to increase the number of francophones in the civil service, particularly in more senior positions. A record is kept of the number of anglophones and francophones in each department, and attempts are made to maintain appropriate numbers.

The term *equal employment opportunity* (EEO) indicates fair access to all available jobs for all persons. On occasion, the term is used as a synonym for affirmative action, but in strict usage EEO does not require the establishment of plans to increase the employment of women, members of visible minorities, or people with disabilities. Some employers, particularly those in the public sector, include on their letterheads and in recruitment advertising the statement that they are equal employment opportunity employers.

Reverse discrimination is a term used to denote discrimination against an individual who belongs to a group that has historically been privileged.[24] "The connotation is that past discrimination is now justifying compensatory demands being made upon those in more privileged positions."[25] Reverse discrimination is usually associated with the establishment of fixed quotas that demand compliance. In Canada, most affirmative action and employment equity programs have not involved quotas but rather goals and timetables.[26]

Affirmative action is voluntary in Canada, and in recent years, both the public and the private sector have seen a number of voluntary programs, most of them aimed at the employment of women. A 1985 study reported that 52 employers out of 190 had affirmative action programs.[27] For example, in 1991 Loblaws instituted a plan to increase the numbers of women, visible minority groups, and people with disabilities on its National Grocers staff (see Case 3.1).[28] In 1984, Ontario Hydro established an affirmative action department to emphasize the hiring and promotion of women. The percentage of women in executive positions grew from under 1.5 percent in 1984 to over 7 percent in 1990. Women in managerial and professional positions now make up nearly 12.5 percent of the Hydro work force, compared with 6.8 percent in 1984.[29] Canadian National Rail has also had a long-standing interest in equal employment opportunity for women. CN's experience is described in Exhibit 3.1.

Because programs such as the above used to be the exception rather than the rule, the federal government established the Employment Equity Act of 1986, which applies to the federal jurisdiction, including the federal civil service. The Quebec and Ontario civil services are also covered by legislation with employment equity provisions, and the Ontario government is proposing to introduce a comprehensive employment equity act.

The Employment Equity Act is intended to correct the conditions of disadvantage in employment experienced by women, aboriginal peoples, people with disabilities, and people who, because of their race or colour, are in a visible minority in Canada. Though the act does not set specific quotas, its reporting procedures are designed to monitor and thereby encourage increased employment among the disadvantaged groups.

Since June 1988, every employer under federal jurisdiction with 100 employees or more has had to submit to the Minister of Employment and Immigration, an annual report with statistics on the number of persons in designated groups by location of employment; occupational distribution; salary ranges; and number hired, promoted, and terminated. This information is available for public inspection. Failure to comply with the reporting requirements can result in a fine of as much as $50 000.

EXHIBIT 3.1
Equal Opportunity at Canadian National Rail

Equal employment opportunity for women has been a concern of Canadian National Rail (CN) for over a decade. Many of CN's entry-level, blue-collar jobs have traditionally been held by men. In the late 1970s, CN decided to encourage women to apply for some of these positions, including brakeman, yardman, signal helper, and coach cleaner. CN contacted Action Travail des Femmes of Montreal (ATC), an organization that helps place women in nontraditional jobs. Soon ATC began sending referrals to CN.

But CN did not hire many of ATC's clients, leading seven of the women to charge CN with discrimination in hiring. ATC itself charged CN with systematic discrimination against women in nontraditional jobs. Clients' complaints were settled, mostly in their favour, by the Canadian Human Rights Commission. ATC's charge of systematic discrimination was investigated and upheld in 1984 by a tribunal appointed by the Commission.

The tribunal instructed CN to change its discriminatory policies, including one policy that required strength tests for female applicants but not for males. The tribunal also imposed a hiring quota on CN: 25 percent of its new hires for blue-collar jobs must be women. The quota would stand until CN's blue-collar work force totalled 13 percent women, the nation-wide average for women employed in blue-collar jobs. At the time of the ruling, fewer than 1 percent of blue-collar jobs in CN's St. Lawrence region were held by women.

In late 1984, CN announced its Employment Equity Program, designed to remove barriers to equal opportunity for women in every division of the company. Each division was to develop a three-to-five year plan, targeting goals and specifying procedures to achieve them. Some divisions found they needed new methods of recruiting; others needed ways to identify qualified candidates for promotion from within. Some divisions saw a need for retraining in order to make women eligible for promotion.

In July 1985, a Federal Court of Appeal struck down the 25-percent hiring quota imposed on CN, saying it was beyond the authority of the tribunal. According to Judge Hugessen, "The text [of the law] requires that the order look to the avoidance of future evil. It does not allow restitution for past wrongs." Other parts of the tribunal's ruling were allowed to stand.

In 1987, however, the Supreme Court of Canada ruled that the Canadian Human Rights Tribunal did have the power to order the Canadian National Railway company in 1984 to increase to 13 percent the proportion of women working in nontraditional occupations in its St. Lawrence region.

Source: Based on Louise Piche, "Employment Equity: On Track at CN," *Canadian Business Review*, Summer 1985, pp. 19–22. Used with the permission of *Canadian Business Review*, The Conference Board of Canada; "Court Rejects Quota for CN Jobs," *The Globe and Mail*, July 19, 1985; and Harish C. Jain, "Affirmative Action/Employment Equity Programs in Canada: Issues and Policies," *Labor Law Journal*, vol. 41, no. 8 (August 1990), pp. 487–92. Used with permission.

In addition, employers are required to prepare an annual equity plan with goals and timetables, and to retain it for a period of at least three years. Unlike the annual report, the equity plan does not have to be submitted to the government, and there is no penalty for failure to prepare or implement it. The act requires employers to consult with designated employee representatives (or with bargaining agents if the employees are unionized) for assistance in identifying and eliminating employment barriers against designated persons.[30] Such consultation can also help ease problems in unionized organizations, in which disadvantaged persons are often relatively newly hired and thus lack seniority and are the most vulnerable to layoffs.[31]

The federal Employment Equity Act also sets rules for federal contractors who employ 100 or more workers and bid on federal government contracts for goods or services worth $200 000 or more. Contractors must sign a certificate of commitment to design and carry out an employment equity program that will identify and remove artificial barriers to the selection, hiring, and training of persons from the four designated groups.

Employment and Immigration Canada (EIC) has a number of handbooks to assist employers in complying with the Employment Equity Act and the Federal Contractors Program.[32] There are also privately prepared employee guides to employment equity.[33] All sizable Canadian cities have EIC employment equity offices that can provide information and advice.

The federal government is not the only government in Canada with such programs. Quebec has a contractors' program, and the Quebec Human Rights Commission can recommend an affirmative action program (as can the Saskatchewan and federal commissions). The Manitoba and Ontario public services have adopted affirmative action programs, and so have the municipalities of Regina, Saskatoon, Toronto, Winnipeg, and Vancouver.

Despite all the publicity, actual experience to date suggests that the federal employment equity program makes only modest demands on firms to show their good intentions because it does not involve specific goals or enforceable timetables.[34] Whether there will be public pressure to tighten the federal legislation to make goals enforceable remains to be seen.

The Ontario government is moving in that direction. After consulting with business, it has drafted employment equity legislation, and it has already appointed an employment equity commissioner.

Some firms in Ontario and elsewhere are not waiting to be pressed by government legislation but are introducing their own programs. For example, National Grocers, with 27 000 employees in such grocery chains as Zehrs, Loblaws, and Fortinos, has already developed an employment equity program (Case 3.1, at the end of the chapter, discusses one aspect of it). It includes advertising jobs in ethnic newspapers, rather than only in *The Globe and Mail* and *The Toronto Star*, as was done formerly. National Grocers president David Williams says that, in addition to seeking to fight social and moral injustices, the firm has good business reasons for trying to attract and promote more people from minority groups. About 85 percent of new entrants to the job market in Canada are expected to come from these groups in the

1990s; having people from a number of different cultures on staff should help to bring the stores closer to their customer base, Williams observes.[35]

Ways in which employers can proceed to establish employment equity programs were recently set out in a comprehensive volume entitled *Information Systems for Employment Equity: An Employer Guide*.[36] It includes discussions about gathering target group information, taking an employment equity census and analysing the results, establishing goals and timetable action plans, and setting strategies for achieving change. There is also consideration of adapting personnel data systems to employment equity and integrating human resource planning and management. Another aid for employers is Employment and Immigration Canada's guide to the federal Employment Equity Act; it sets out employers' obligations, the key concepts in employment equity, and the basic requirements for conforming with the act.[37]

EMPLOYMENT STANDARDS LEGISLATION

Employment standards legislation, also called labour standards legislation, covers a wide and continually changing range of subjects affecting the relationship between employers and employees. From the perspective of the HRM professional, the main provisions of employment are those dealing with the statutory school-leaving age; the minimum age for employment; minimum wages; equal pay; hours of work; rest days, vacations and holidays; termination of employment; maternity and parental leave; and the recovery of unpaid wages.

In employment standards, as in human rights, Canada has thirteen jurisdictions. As might be expected, regulations vary widely from one jurisdiction to another, but all are concerned with providing standards of protection for employees. Table 3.1 at the beginning of this chapter lists the pertinent laws in the country's thirteen jurisdictions. This section is an overview of their major provisions, as of January 1, 1991, unless otherwise indicated. A complete summary of these provisions can be found in the latest issue of Labour Canada's publication *Employment Standards Legislation in Canada*.[38] The details are best examined in the various acts themselves or in the publications of CCH (Commerce Clearing House) Canadian Limited.

HRM professionals should remember that the agencies charged with administering employment standards are interested in voluntary compliance. Their staff members are generally helpful when asked about the rules.

STATUTORY SCHOOL-LEAVING AGE

All the provinces and territories forbid the employment of a child of school age during school hours, unless he or she is excused for some reason provided in the relevant school attendance act. School-leaving age is 16 in all jurisdictions except Newfoundland and the Northwest Territories, where it is 15. Exemptions are provided for a variety of circumstances. In five provinces (Manitoba, New Brunswick, Newfoundland, Nova Scotia, and Quebec), a child may be exempted temporarily from school attendance, on the application of a parent or guardian, if his or her services are required for employment or farm or home duties. Alberta and Saskatchewan have provisions for work experience programs.

MINIMUM AGE FOR EMPLOYMENT

The desire to establish minimum ages for employment was a goal of trade unions and social reformers in the nineteenth century. Developments were slow: factory legislation developed cautiously from the 1880s, caught between the more generous impulses of the age and the employers' firm grip on legislatures and party finances. By 1888, children were banned from smaller factories in Ontario, and shopkeepers could not employ boys under age 14 or girls under age 16 for more than 12 hours a day or 74 hours a week. Quebec and Nova Scotia, then eventually the other provinces, followed this humanitarian lead at a cautious distance. Enforcement in all provinces lagged even more. At the turn of the century, Ontario critics noted that while Toronto employed three inspectors merely to uncover liquor offences, the entire province employed only three inspectors to enforce its Factory Act.[39]

Today the minimum age for employment varies so greatly, by province and by type of work, that employers and HRM professionals are well advised to investigate the regulations for each specific situation they face. For example, in most jurisdictions, a person must be age 18 to work below ground in mines, but in Alberta it is 17 and in Nova Scotia it is 16 for metal mines but 18½ for coal mines. Above ground, the standard minimum age is 16, as it is in factories, but a few jurisdictions permit certain kinds of work at age 15 and forbid others, particularly heavy kinds and those with considerable inherent danger, until age 18. For example, a person under age 21 cannot be employed to drive a vehicle containing more that 2000 kilograms of explosives if the employer is in the federal jurisdiction.

Many jurisdictions permit younger youths to work outside school hours or on vacations in shops, hotels, and restaurants and in such occupations as messenger, newspaper vendor, and shoe shiner. Many acts prohibit young people's working at night. For example, Alberta forbids the employment of persons under age 15 between 9:00 P.M. and 6:00 A.M., while those between ages 15 and 18 can work from 9:00 P.M. to midnight on retail premises selling food or beverages only if there is constant supervision.

MINIMUM WAGE RATES

All jurisdictions set minimum wage rates, but, in addition to interprovincial differences, there are often special provisions for particular kinds of workers. And the rates are frequently adjusted upward.

Generally, minimum wage provisions cover almost all workers—excepting only most farm labourers and, in some jurisdictions, domestic workers. A lower minimum rate is usually set for young workers, student trainees, and people with disabilities and, in some provinces, for employees who serve alcoholic beverages (Ontario) or usually receive gratuities (Quebec) and for domestic workers (British Columbia, Newfoundland, Ontario, Quebec).

The interprovincial differences in minimum rates can be sizable. As of January 1, 1991, there was an almost $2.00 difference between the country's highest minimum wage rate ($5.97 per hour, in the Yukon) and its lowest ($4.00 per hour, in the federal jurisdiction). Five provinces required $5.00 per hour. Since the minimum wage rates change at different intervals in each province, the HRM professional should keep a table with the relevant rates and the dates of change, which can normally be obtained from the local employment standards branch of the department or ministry of labour.

EQUAL PAY FOR MEN AND WOMEN

The idea of pay equity for men and women goes back to the founding of the International Labour Organization (ILO) in 1919, when it set out that men and women should receive equal remuneration for work of equal value.[40] This principle of equal remuneration was adopted at an ILO convention in 1951 and was ratified by Canada in 1972. It was not until the late 1980s, however, that a majority of jurisdictions required equal pay for work of equal value.[41] Until then, most legislation required the payment of equal pay for the same or similar work.

By 1990, Canadian jurisdictions used three approaches to equal pay legislation: equal pay for equal work, equal pay for work of equal value, and pay equity. The three evolved in that order, and there are substantial differences in what they focus on and how they work.

Equal pay for equal work involves comparing the wages paid to female and male employees who perform the same or similar work and whose jobs require similar skill, effort, or responsibility. Comparisons are usually of similar work in the same establishment. Equal pay for equal work legislation applies throughout Alberta, British Columbia, Newfoundland, Ontario, Saskatchewan, and the Northwest Territories and to the private sectors of Manitoba, New Brunswick, Nova Scotia, Prince Edward Island, and the Yukon.

Equal pay for work of equal value (also termed *comparable worth*) allows a comparison of male and female jobs of a quite different nature to determine whether they have the same intrinsic value. Jobs are compared using specific job evaluation techniques to measure a composite of the skill, effort, responsibility, and working conditions required to perform the duties. In other words, the requirement is the comparison of dissimilar jobs in terms of their value to the employer. Equal value legislation exists in Quebec, the public sector (including municipalities) of the Yukon, and in the federal jurisdiction.

This approach involves the use of job analysis to apply the criterion prescribed by the act to each job function. Though this approach is more comprehensive than that of equal pay for equal work, it involves a reactive approach since the legislation relies on complaints being made before the provisions are applied.

The most proactive equal remuneration legislation is based on *pay equity*, which provides specific targets and deadlines and uses the collective bargaining process to get the parties involved in agreeing on the choice or the development of a job evaluation system and on the exact allocation of pay adjustments to be made. (If there is no collective agreement in place, the employer determines the job evaluation system and the exact allocation of pay adjustments and indicates this to the administrative body. An employee can appeal the employer's proposal.)

Pay equity was introduced in 1985 in Manitoba with compliance compulsory only in the public sector. In 1988, it was introduced in Ontario to begin to take effect in 1990 in the public and private sectors. Pay equity provisions also apply to the public sectors in New Brunswick, Nova Scotia, and Prince Edward Island.

Notice that in addition to contrasting with each other, all three approaches are aimed at achieving pay equity, in contrast to employment equity. Employment equity legislation is intended to reduce the occupational segregation that comes from the concentration of women in lower-paying jobs in sales, service, clerical, and health-related fields. Equal pay legislation is intended to remove wage discrimination.

Both kinds of discrimination exist and interact with each other and with other forms of societal restrictions. A 1985 Ontario green paper on pay equity found a female-to-male full-time earnings ratio of 62 percent, implying a gap of 38 percentage points. The gap was attributed to differences in hours worked (16 points); occupational segregation (10–15 points); experience, education, and unionization (5–10 points); and wage discrimination (5 points).[42] These figures suggest that although employment equity and pay equity programs can help to reduce male–female wage differences, other approaches should be considered to deal with the gaps arising from differences in experience, education, and unionization as well as hours. HR managers should be aware of the increased public pressure and legislation intended to reduce the wage gap and look to long-run policies that can draw on the potential of the female work force, as well as of other designated employment equity groups, to enhance the effectiveness of the organization by being proactive rather than reactive. The concept, method of application, and implications of equal pay provisions are discussed further in Chapter 12.[43]

HOURS OF WORK

Hours-of-work provisions relate both to the maximum number of hours of work permitted per day and per week and to the number of hours per day or week after which an overtime rate must be paid. Eight hours of work per day and 40 hours per week are the most common standards (the federal jurisdiction, British Columbia, Manitoba, Newfoundland [employees in retail stores only], Saskatchewan, the Northwest Territories, and the Yukon), but there are other combinations: Alberta, 8 and 44; Ontario, a standard 44-hour week with maximum of 8 and 48. Nova Scotia and Prince Edward Island have only a standard work week of 48, and Quebec has 44 hours.

The accepted rate for overtime is one and a half times the regular rate, but it comes into effect at different points in different jurisdictions and even after a different number of hours in the same province for different industries. For example, in Alberta overtime generally begins after 8 hours in a day and 44 in a week, but for ambulance drivers and cab drivers it starts after 10 hours in a day or 60 hours in a week. There are so many variations in the different jurisdictions that HRM professionals must consult the relevant employment standards branch.

They are also well advised to peruse the provisions themselves. Every jurisdiction permits exceptions to the general rules to allow for differences in production periods, seasonal variations, and customary standards and also provides for changes to accommodate special problems. (A common feature is the possibility of averaging hours over a number of weeks.) Familiarity with the regulations may suggest grounds on which the regulatory body may grant exemptions. It can also alert HRM officials to any need to obtain a permit beyond a stated maximum.

Weekly Rest Days

In general, employment standards legislation requires one full day of rest per week, often on Sunday whenever possible. Provincial legislation and municipal by-laws have become increasingly permissive, however, as more and more jurisdictions attempt reasonable accommodation of people on the grounds of freedom of conscience or religion. The result is a lack of uniformity among jurisdictions with regard to the weekly day of rest. In most, municipalities have the power to regulate, in one way or another, Sunday hours at commercial establishments. In Alberta, municipalities may pass bylaws, under certain conditions, to permit the carrying on of any commercial activity after 1:30 P.M. on Sunday. Similar powers, but with no time limitation, exist in British Columbia, New Brunswick, Newfoundland, and Ontario. Ontario requires that employees in retail business establishments that are open on Sunday be entitled to refuse Sunday work.

Because legislation is changing in this field, students are cautioned to consult the relevant employment standards officials to determine the most recent requirements for a weekly day of rest. Students should also note that a work week is not necessarily from Monday to Friday, but rather a period of seven consecutive days whose first and last days are defined by the employer.

Annual Vacations with Pay

Every jurisdiction except Saskatchewan requires two weeks of vacation with pay after one year of employment; in Saskatchewan, the figure is three weeks after one year. Six labour laws increase the amount of vacation to three weeks after a stated number of years of service with the same employer. In Saskatchewan, four weeks are required after ten years.

The usual rate for vacation pay begins at 4 percent of annual earnings (again, Saskatchewan is more generous, with $3/52$ annual earnings) and rises (in five jurisdictions to 6 percent of annual earnings) as an employee becomes entitled to more vacation (in Saskatchewan, it becomes $4/52$ annual earnings). Pay must be given one to fourteen days before the vacation begins, depending on the jurisdiction.

Holidays

The number of paid general holidays provided each year varies from five in Newfoundland and Prince Edward Island to nine in Alberta, British Columbia, Saskatchewan, the Northwest Territories, the Yukon, and the federal jurisdiction. Manitoba, Ontario, and Quebec have eight days of general holidays, the difference for the first two being the absence of a provincial or territorial day such as Alberta Family Day, British Columbia Day, Saskatchewan Day, and Discovery Day (Yukon). Newfoundland includes Memorial Day, while in Quebec employees can take either Dollard Day or Victoria Day but are not entitled to Boxing Day.

In most jurisdictions, employers must provide regular pay for a general holiday plus one and a half times the regular rate or another day off with pay for holidays worked. Newfoundland requires twice the regular pay, one full day's paid holiday within 30 days, or the addition of one full paid day to the annual vacation. Quebec requires regular pay plus indemnity equal to wages for a regular day of work plus one day off to be taken within three weeks before or after a holiday worked.

Most labour standards laws make special provisions for holiday work in continuous operations and selected industries such as construction.

Termination of Employment

In all jurisdictions an employer must give notice to most workers whose employment is to be terminated. The length of notice required depends on the number of persons involved and their length of employment, and varies from jurisdiction to jurisdiction. In the case of individual workers, it varies from one or two weeks after one month of employment to eight weeks after eight years. Many jurisdictions require longer notice for the layoff or termination of an entire group of employees; it may be eight, twelve, or sixteen weeks, depending on the number involved. In Manitoba, eighteen weeks' notice must be given for groups of more than 300 employees, and the Minister of Labour may require the establishment of a joint employer–employee (or trade union) committee to develop an adjustment program. New Brunswick requires six weeks' notice for ten or more employees if they represent at least 25 percent of the employer's work force.

Federally, severance pay is provided for employees with twelve months' service or more. Ontario has provisions for severance pay in the case of group terminations of 50 or more employees in a six-month period (one week's regular salary for each year of employment for employees with at least five years' service, to a maximum of 26 weeks' salary).

PARENTAL LEAVE

The term *parental leave* is used in two ways: (1) as the general term for several kinds of leave related to the birth or adoption of a child (maternity leave, paternity leave, adoption leave); and (2) as the specific term for leave (generally, to either parent) consecutive with or closely following maternity leave in the case of a newborn or as adoption leave in the case of adoption.

All jurisdictions provide maternity leave and job security for women before and after childbirth. They are protected from dismissal because of pregnancy and are entitled to reinstatement after maternity leave without loss of seniority or benefits. Employers must give them *maternity leave* (without pay), usually of seventeen to eighteen weeks after one year's service.

Paternity and adoption leave are provided in all jurisdictions except British Columbia, the Northwest Territories, and the Yukon. The federal jurisdiction provides for 24 weeks of child care leave, in addition to maternity leave, for either parent, whether natural or adoptive. Manitoba makes available a paternity leave of six weeks or an adoption leave of a maximum of seventeen weeks. New Brunswick allows an adoption leave of up to seventeen weeks for one adopting parent and of up to seven consecutive calendar days for the other. In Quebec, an employee may be absent from work (without pay) for two days at the birth or adoption of a child. Ontario provides for eighteen weeks of unpaid parental leave per parent, natural or adoptive, and Saskatchewan provides for a maximum of six weeks of unpaid paternity leave in addition to eighteen weeks of unpaid maternity leave.

Legislated parental leaves are unpaid, but unemployment insurance (UI) provides some money for many workers on such leave. Women who are eligible for UI benefits can receive them for up to fifteen weeks of maternity leave. In addition, ten weeks of parental benefits are available to natural or adoptive parents—either the mother or the father, or shared between them as they deem appropriate—and fifteen weeks of sickness benefits.

THE RECOVERY OF UNPAID WAGES

The various labour standards acts provide mechanisms for the prompt recovery of unpaid wages, including salaries, pay, commission, and any compensation for labour or personal services. Inspectors or labour standards officers are usually empowered to inquire into or investigate situations in which there is reason to believe that the law has been violated. They first endeavour to arrive at an amicable settlement with the parties. If they cannot, they are empowered to order the transgressors to "cease and desist" and to order that compensation be made to the victims.

Under the Canada Labour Code, an employer who does not provide minimum standards is liable not only for the arrears of wages and other minimum amounts but also to a fine ranging up to $10 000 or to imprisonment for a term not exceeding one year or both. More severe sanctions exist for failure to observe the required notice-of-termination provisions.[44]

SUMMARY

This chapter has discussed the concepts of human rights and employment standards. It has presented the major provisions of the laws in Canada's thirteen jurisdictions and suggested the need for the HRM professional to obtain detailed, current information on the areas relevant to his or her work in particular jurisdictions. In addition, the HRM professional can obtain a good overview of the regulations that apply across Canada by obtaining the annual Labour Canada publication *Employment Standards Legislation in Canada*. The impact of these laws will be felt throughout the rest of this book.

REVIEW QUESTIONS

1. Define and distinguish among systemic discrimination, indirect discrimination, and silent discrimination. Discuss the remedies that are provided to deal with each type of discrimination.

2. Describe the *O'Malley* case and discuss its implications for HR managers.

3. Saskatchewan prohibits discrimination based on age for employees 18 to 65 years old. What protection, if any, does a 66-year-old employee have in that province? Discuss the pros and cons limiting the range of ages protected from discrimination.

4. Discuss how HR managers can balance the seemingly opposed responsibilities of meeting strategic human resource goals of organizational efficiency on the one hand and employment equity goals on the other hand.

5. There is a patchwork of employment standards legislation across Canada. Explain how HR managers can use a knowledge of the different legislative requirements to better attain the goals of the organization.

PROJECT IDEAS

1. In an article entitled "Employment Equity as a Trojan Horse" (*The Globe and Mail*, March 22, 1991), Professor Jack Roberts of the Faculty of Law, University of Western Ontario, argues:

   > People see themselves as individuals, entitled to be judged on their own merits. Holding them back because they are the wrong colour or sex fosters resentment—deep resentment. Affirmative action blindly ignored this fundamental truth about human nature. Whites were routinely held back while blacks and other "disadvantaged" minorities were preferred. . . . If the Ontario government concludes that there must be a remedy for past discrimination, it should consider monetary reparations.

   Consider the arguments for and against employment equity, compared with monetary reparations, as a remedy for past discrimination in employment.

2. Obtain information from the nearest municipal, provincial, or federal government office, or corporation that has an employment equity program. Describe the program and assess its impact not only on persons in the designated groups but on the entire organization. Discuss the long-term employment implications of the program.

3. Contact the nearest provincial human rights commission or employment standards office and obtain material on the human rights or employment standards act in your jurisdiction. (The offices are listed in the government section of your telephone book.) Select one or two areas of discrimination or employment standards violations and obtain examples that have been reported in local newspapers. Prepare a short written description of the prohibited practices and discuss the role of the organization's human resources department in preventing repetition. How do these violations affect the organizations?

▶▶▶ CASES

CASE 3.1 ▶ NATIONAL'S JOB EQUITY STARTS AT THE TOP

Gord Brandt's voice is hoarse. He is half way through a series of fifteen four-hour workshops to explain National Grocers Co. Ltd.'s new employment equity policy to its senior managers.

As National's human resources director, he is going through the same experience that company president David Williams met when he sold the policy to vice-presidents.

"I get two major responses," Mr. Brandt said. "They deny that any form of discrimination even occurs. And they worry about reverse discrimination. It comes up all the time. More opportunities for these minority groups mean less for the white males. So the white male decision makers feel threatened."

But he stresses the company is not going to set up quotas for hiring women, aboriginals, visible minorities and people with disabilities.

"This company has always been founded on the merit principle," he said, "and that must remain so. But if we get candidates of equal opportunity, we may be inclined to go toward the one from these groups."

For the moment he is not saying that the company *will* choose the minority candidate. "I don't want to make those statements right away, though we will move in that direction. Maybe in six months, managers will say it's the right thing to do."

The seminars are part of a process of getting line management on side, because, Mr. Brandt said, job equity won't work without their support.

National intends to prepare a detailed study of its employee profile and by April or May prepare five-year goals for how many of each of the target groups it hopes to have on staff. At the same time, it is doing a general employee attitude survey.

To prepare the five-year goals, the company will use a model including projections of expected retirement and turnover rates as well as of employment growth. The model was created by Tom Mathers, a principal of Omnibus Consulting Inc., a Toronto-based company specializing in employment equity.

"I don't have the right to fire someone to open up a job," Mr. Williams said. "This has to be done through attrition and opportunities."

He believes growth of the 27 000-person organization will help create these opportunities and observes that he would hate to be trying such a plan in an industry that is downsizing.

For now, the equity plan will apply to National's roughly 2000 non-union employees. In two weeks, Mr. Brandt will begin discussing equity with union leaders who represent about 25 000 National workers in Ontario.

But he said head office wants to lead by example and the program might never have gotten off the ground if it had to begin with so many people.

One change, already being implemented, is posting of all non-union job openings, up to the vice-president level.

[Mr. Williams] hopes to see members of the target groups rise through the organization by what he describes as "overinvesting" in training for them. This will be done through the company's internal management school in Toronto, which emphasizes people skills over technical training. That is the only way to change the employee profile, he said.

"My feeling is that the gap between today and where we should be is the lack of skills or development opportunities those target groups have been given in the past. Whether it was stereotyping roles or systemic discrimination or pure prejudice, they weren't allowed an opportunity to develop their skills."

As part of the plan, he wants staff to feel free to talk about discrimination and stereotyping. He also wants Mr. Brandt and the human resources group to challenge the company if they think it is not living up to the new policies.

He knows that managing the expectations of the target groups may be difficult. "I don't want to say that tomorrow 50 percent of all the senior positions in the organization will be filled by women. That's not the reality. The reality is that we are changing. The time frame must be longer than anyone including me wants."

Source: Margot Gibb-Clark, "National's Job Equity Starts at the Top," *The Globe and Mail*, February 4, 1991. Reprinted with the permission of *The Globe and Mail*.

TASKS AND QUESTIONS

1. Discuss the distinction between setting up quotas for hiring persons belonging to identifiable groups and promoting persons from such groups when their merit is equal to that of persons from nonminority groups.

2. Discuss the advantages and disadvantages of beginning an employment equity program with a relatively small group of nonunion employees rather than a large group unionized or not.

3. Consider how you would make the case to senior management for the introduction of an employment equity program.

CASE 3.2 ▶ MANAGEMENT AND COMPLAINTS OF SEXUAL HARASSMENT

A Toronto company admits a female employee suffered appalling sexual harassment. But its personnel manager said she is partly at fault because she has an outgoing personality, got along well with co-workers and jogged during her lunch hour.

As a result of what she described as an intolerable working environment, Jean MacNairn has quit her $27 500-a-year job at the head office of Woolco department stores and is trying to reach a severance settlement.

Those responsible for the harassment, and managers who ignored complaints for eight months, have been reprimanded.

But MacNairn—married for eleven years, with two young children—says that's not enough compensation for being unfairly blamed for the months of obscene, lewd language and gestures.

The company's attitude has been outrageous, says her lawyer, Howard Levitt. In eleven years of practising law, "I've never seen a company blaming a woman for bringing on sexual harassment simply for being friendly."

And Alan Shefman, a spokesman for the Ontario Human Rights Commission, said the case is a typical example of blaming victims of sexual harassment and rape. "Very often, the first strategy is to blame the woman." . . .

MacNairn says two male employees used obscene language and gestures in her presence from the time she began working in Woolco's North York computer network operations room last April.

She had returned to the work force after taking two and a half years off to care for her children. During her nine months at Woolco, she received two raises, and no complaints about her work.

The men, usually alone with MacNairn in a small computer room, talked graphically about their sexual exploits.

"I'm quite tolerant . . . but the language was atrocious; not just the occasional word but every second sentence," she said in an interview at her home. "I said I didn't want to hear it, but they didn't stop."

And when she asked them for advice about using computer equipment, the usual response was an obscenity, she said.

Complaints to supervisors had no effect.

Early last fall, Woolco brought in a management consultant to assess working conditions, and MacNairn noted the offensive language in a written report.

A week later, she again complained to her manager. He said: "You have to try and get along," she recalls.

The obscene language continued and, in November, one of the men stripped down to his underwear in the computer room. On another occasion, in early December, he made a lewd gesture and suggestion.

MacNairn talked to friends about the problem and was put in touch with Levitt, who specializes in workplace issues.

In a . . . letter to Mac Lakhani, personnel manager for Woolco's parent, F.W. Woolworth Co. Ltd., Levitt complained about the "abusive treatment and sexual harassment," as well as "management's failure to do anything to stop this conduct and, in fact, continue to condone it."

Two weeks later, MacNairn said, management "took me to task" for being outgoing as well as for jogging during the unpaid lunch hour and changing into running clothes in the women's washroom.

. . . Lakhani wrote to Levitt that he had investigated the "alleged abusive treatment" by one of the male employees, and "we are appalled by this behavior." But he noted, the inquiry "revealed a few additional facts" that suggest MacNairn was partly to blame for the harassment.

"Ever since Jean joined us, she has demonstrated a very outgoing personality and appears to get along extremely well with her fellow employees," the letter states. "In talking to Jean, she admits in retrospect that this outward personality and the type of behavior that she exhibited could, in fact, have contributed to the poor behavior of others around her. . . . While [the man] was wrong in what he said, Jean, in fact, may have unknowingly set the stage for this behavior."

Lakhani wrote that the problem had been settled to MacNairn's satisfaction and "she assures me that she will be more cautious in her action, so incidents of this nature do not occur again."

"It appears because I am not a saint I should have to tolerate abuse," MacNairn said. "I'm very outgoing and friendly, but I'm not sexy or sleazy and I'm sure not on the hustle for guys. . . . I'm above reproach as far as I'm concerned. I'm trying to set a good example for my children."

After Levitt's letter, MacNairn started getting the cold shoulder at work. "Management didn't speak to me unless I spoke to them first," she said.

One of the men has now left Woolco. And recently, senior company officials got involved. The second man has been severely reprimanded and moved to a different area, Joe Riordan, vice-president of human resources, said. . . .

Lakhani and other managers who didn't act on the complaint have been told "that is not what we expect of our management. We don't believe any aspect of her conduct justified what had happened," Riordan said.

But MacNairn says the action came only after she hired Levitt and there was a threat of publicity. "I didn't want to take it this far, but nobody did anything until I got a lawyer involved. The point I'm trying to make is that I know there are a lot of women in the working environment having the same kinds of problems and not doing anything because they're afraid of losing their jobs."

Source: Peter Gorrie, "Victim of Harassment Told She Shares the Blame," *The Toronto Star*, January 23, 1991. Reprinted with permission—The Toronto Star Syndicate.

TASKS AND QUESTIONS

1. List some possible explanations for management's lack of response to the allegations of sexual harassment until a lawyer was brought in to complain.

2. How should the personnel manager have dealt with the situation and the employees involved, including Ms. MacNairn?

3. Assume you are the personnel manager at Woolco. Explain why putting part of the blame for harassment on the victim would make it easier or harder for you to introduce a successful program of sexual harassment prevention. Include the employees' perspective in your answer.

NOTES

1. Canadian Charter of Rights and Freedoms. Reproduced with the permission of the Queen's Printer for Canada, 1992.

2. "Mandatory Retirement Upheld by Supreme Court of Canada" (1991), 13 Canadian Human Rights Reporter i–ii; *Connell v. University of British Columbia* (1991), 91 Canadian Labour Law Cases 17001 (Supreme Court of Canada); *McKinney v. University of Guelph* (1991), 91 Canadian Labour Law Cases 17004 (Supreme Court of Canada).

3. "Mandatory Retirement," *Employment Law Report*, vol. 12, no. 11 (November 1991), pp. 101–2; *City of Saskatoon v. Saskatchewan Human Rights Commission* (1990), 90 Canadian Labour Law Cases 17001 (Supreme Court of Canada).

4. For ongoing developments in legislation and practice in this field, see *The Current Industrial Relations Scene in Canada* (Kingston, Ont.: Industrial Relations Centre, Queen's University, annual); *The Employment Law Report* (Toronto: Concord Publishing, monthly); and *Human Rights Forum* (formerly *Dossier*; Ottawa: Canadian Human Rights Commission, occasional). In addition, some aspects of human rights and employment standards are discussed in connection with labour–management grievance arbitration cases. See *Canadian Industrial Relations and Personnel Developments* (Don Mills, Ont.: CCH Canadian, weekly); *Labour Arbitration News* (Toronto: LAN Publications, monthly); CLV Reports (Toronto: Canada Labour Views Company, weekly); D.J.M. Brown and D.M. Beatty, *Canadian Labour Arbitration*, 3rd ed. (Agincourt, Ont.: Canada Law Book 1990); and *The Canadian Labour Law Reporter* (Don Mills, Ont., semimonthly). See also John G. Kelly, *Human Resource Management and the Human Rights Process* (Don Mills, Ont.: CCH Canadian, 1985).

5. Canadian Human Rights Commission, *The Canadian Human Rights Act: A Guide* (Ottawa, March 1984), p. 1.

6. Canadian Human Rights Commission, *Guide to Your Rights*, pamphlet series (Ottawa, n.d.).

7. Canada, *Report of the Commission on Equality in Employment*, Judge Rosalie Silberman Abella, chair (Ottawa: Supply and Services Canada, 1984), p. 193.

8. *Ontario Human Rights Commission and Theresa O'Malley (Vincent) v. Simpsons-Sears Limited* (1985), 7 Canadian Human Rights Reporter (Supreme Court of Canada), p. D/3109.

9. *Alberta Human Rights Commission v. Central Alberta Dairy Pool* (1990), 86 Canadian Labour Law Cases 17002 (Supreme Court of Canada). Reproduced with the permission of the Minister of Supply and Services Canada, 1992.
10. Cited in Marilyn Goneau, "Discrimination Is Still Part of the Workplace," *The Financial Post*, November 21, 1981.
11. "U of T Professor Banned from Pool for Ogling Woman," *The Toronto Star*, March 3, 1989.
12. Harish Jain and P. Andiappan, "Sexual Harassment in Employment in Canada: Issues and Policies," *Relations Industrielles/Industrial Relations*, vol. 41, no. 4 (1986), pp. 758–76.
13. Wilfred List, "Sexual Harassment: It's Spreading but Is the Boss Liable?" *The Globe and Mail*, March 16, 1987.
14. *Bonita Clark v. Steel Company of Canada (Stelco)*, a decision of the Ontario Labour Relations Board, September 12, 1988. Discussed in Ann Rauhala, "Sex Harassment Suit Settled but Job Health Issue Issue Remains," *The Globe and Mail*, September 13, 1988.
15. Jane Armstrong, "Job-Seekers Facing Silent Discrimination," *The Toronto Star*, February 17, 1991.
16. *K.S. Bhinder and the Canadian Human Rights Commission v. The Canadian National Railway Company* (1985), 86 Canadian Labour Law Cases 17003 (Supreme Court of Canada).
17. Harish C. Jain, "Affirmative Action/Employment Equity Programs in Canada: Issues and Policies," *Labour Law Journal*, vol. 41, no. 8 (August 1990), pp. 487–92.
18. For a compilation of provincial hiring guidelines, see "Do Your Job Application Forms Meet Human Rights Requirements?" *Employment Law Report*, vol. 11, no. 10/11 (October/November 1990).
19. For details of the enforcement procedure for each jurisdiction, see Labour Canada, *Human Rights in Canada* (Ottawa: Supply and Services Canada, 1975), p. 22.
20. Labour Canada, *Human Rights in Canada*, p. 39.
21. Quoted in Goneau, "Discrimination Is Still Part of the Workplace." Reprinted with permission.
22. J. Sack and I. Poskanzer, *Labour Law Terms: A Dictionary of Canadian Labour Law* (Toronto: Lancaster House, 1984), p. 23.
23. Canada, *Report of the Commission on Equality in Employment*.
24. Sack and Poskanzer, *Labour Law Terms*, p. 133.
25. John G. Kelly, *Equal Opportunity Management: Understanding Affirmative Action and Employment Equity* (Toronto: CCH Canadian, 1986), p. 47. For further discussion of the pros and cons of employment equity programs see: Harish C. Jain and Peter J. Sloane, *Equal Employment Issues: Race and Sex Discrimination in the United States, Canada, and Britain* (New York: Praeger,

1981); and W.E. Block and M.A. Walker, eds., *Discrimination, Affirmative Action, and Equal Opportunity: An Economic and Social Perspective* (Vancouver: The Fraser Institute, 1982).

26. Kelly, p. 48.

27. Harish C. Jain and Rick D. Hackett, "Measuring Employment Equity in Canada: Public Policy and a Survey," *Canadian Public Policy*, vol. 15, no. 2 (1989), pp. 189–204.

28. Margot Gibb-Clark, "Grocer Strives for Job Equity," *The Globe and Mail*, February 4, 1991.

29. Robert C. Franklin, "Promoting Equity at Hydro," *Canadian Business Review*, vol. 18, no. 2 (Summer 1991), pp. 26–27.

30. Jain, "Affirmative Action/Employment Equity."

31. Canadian Human Rights Commission, "Equity Issues Troublesome for Unions," *Dossier* (May 1986), extra 86–83.

32. See, for example, Employment and Immigration Canada, *Employment Equity: A Guide for Employers*, WH-3-596 (Ottawa, n.d.); *Employer's Handbook: Reporting on Employment Equity*, WH-3-628W (February 1987); *Employment Equity: Federal Contractors Program—Questions and Answers* (Ottawa: Supply and Services Canada, 1987); and *Employment Equity Act, Regulations and Schedules* (Ottawa: Supply and Services Canada, 1987).

33. See, for example, Edward B. Harvey, *Information Systems for Employment Equity: An Employer's Guide* (Toronto: CCH Canadian, 1990).

34. W.S. Tarnoposky, "Discrimination and Affirmative Action," in Harish C. Jain and D. Carroll, ed., *Race and Sex Equality in the Workplace: A Challenge and an Opportunity* (Ottawa: Labour Canada, 1980), pp. 72–98.

35. Gibb-Clark, "Grocer Strives for Job Equity."

36. Harvey, *Information Systems for Employment Equity*.

37. Employment and Immigration Canada, *Employment Equity*.

38. Labour Canada, *Employment Standards Legislation in Canada* (Ottawa: Supply and Services Canada, annual).

39. Desmond Morton, *Working People: An Illustrated History of the Canadian Labour Movement* (Toronto, Summerhill Press, 1990), p. 84.

40. L. Neiman, *Wage Discrimination and Women Workers: The Move Towards Equal Pay for Work of Equal Value* (Ottawa: Women's Bureau, Labour Canada, 1984), p. 5.

41. Labour Canada, *Employment Standards Legislation in Canada*, 1991 ed. (Ottawa: Supply and Services Canada, 1991), p. 46.

42. M. Gunderson and W.C. Riddell, *Labour Market Economics: Theory, Evidence and Policy in Canada*, 2nd ed. (Toronto: McGraw-Hill Ryerson, 1988), p. 455.

43. For some recent analysis and guides to implementing pay equity, see Nan Weiner and Morley Gunderson, *Pay Equity: Issues, Options and Experiences* (Ottawa:

Supply and Services Canada, 1990); and David W. Conklin and Paul Bergman, *Pay Equity in Ontario: A Manager's Guide* (Halifax: The Institute for Research on Public Policy and The National Centre for Management Research and Development, The University of Western Ontario, London, Ontario, 1990).

44. Labour Canada, *Employment Standards Legislation in Canada*, 1991 ed.

SUGGESTIONS FOR FURTHER READING

- Canada. *Report of the Commission on Equality in Employment*, Judge Rosalie Silberman Abella, chair. Ottawa: Supply and Services Canada, 1984.
- Employment and Immigration Canada. *Employment Equity: A Guide for Employers*. Ottawa, n.d. See also, *Employment Equity: Federal Contractors Programs — Questions and Answers*. Ottawa: Supply and Services Canada, 1987. *Employment Equity Act, Regulations and Schedules*. Ottawa: Supply and Services Canada, 1987. *Employers Handbook: Reporting on Employment Equity*. Ottawa, February 1987.
- *The Employment Law Report*. Concord Publishing, Toronto: monthly. See also note 4 for other regular publications on legislation and developments in the field.
- Edward B. Harvey. *Information Systems for Employment Equity: An Employer's Guide*. Toronto: CCH Canadian, 1990.
- *Human Rights Forum* (Canadian Human Rights Commission, Ottawa). Occasional.
- Harish C. Jain and Rick D. Hackett, "Measuring Employment Equity in Canada: Public Policy and a Survey." *Canadian Public Policy*, vol. 15 (1990).
- Labour Canada. *Employment Standards Legislation in Canada*. Annual.
- Nan Weiner and Morley Gunderson. *Pay Equity: Issues, Options, and Experiences*. Ottawa: Supply and Services Canada, 1990.

video CASE

SEXUAL HARASSMENT IN THE WORKPLACE

The Canadian Labour Code defines sexual harassment as any unwanted comments, suggestions, physical contact, or subtle acts that emphasize the sex or sexual orientation of the individual, thus creating a hostile or offensive working environment.

In most organizations, sexual harassment is a social problem. Victims of sexual harassment number in the thousands, and although both men and women can be victims, most are women.

There are many situations in the workplace where women face sexual harassment. Women working in traditionally male-dominated fields often encounter sexist attitudes that question their ability to do the job. These situations can undermine the confidence of female workers, regardless of their actual ability to perform the job. Other situations may involve male co-workers who jokingly look for opportunities to embarrass female colleagues with pornography or profane language. These situations cause female co-workers unnecessary stress and embarrassment. Sexual harassment also includes situations where acceptance of unsolicited sexual advances is considered a prerequisite for employment or advancement.

People who encounter sexual harassment in the workplace need to be aware that reporting the situation to someone who can take the necessary action to stop the harassment — that is, a supervisor, an HR manager, or a sexual harassment officer — is better than either ignoring the problem or leaving the job.

Many employers are implementing sexual harassment policies to ensure that employees know what steps to follow in the event of sexual harassment. Petro-Canada is one Canadian company that has implemented such a policy. Petro-Canada's sexual harassment policy is both an attempt to address the problem and an effort to heighten the awareness of it in the workplace. Establishing a grievance procedure and maintaining complainant anonymity are two of the issues that a sexual harassment policy should address.

An effective sexual harassment policy can result in increased productivity and contribute to the well-being of every employee.

Source: Based on "Sexual Harassment in the Workplace," video segment used with the permission of the Women's Bureau, Labour Canada.

DISCUSSION QUESTIONS

1. Why is it in the best interest of an organization to develop a policy on sexual harassment? Include in your explanation rejoinders to arguments that may be advanced against having such a policy.
2. Why do we often assume that victims of sexual harassment are female?
3. What actions should be taken to eliminate sexual harassment in the workplace?

ORGANIZATIONAL GOALS AND OBJECTIVES AND STRATEGIC PLANNING
SURVIVAL AND GROWTH
PRODUCTIVITY
PROFITS
SERVICE

JOB ANALYSIS
PROVIDES PLANNERS WITH JOBS' REQUIREMENTS FOR HUMAN RESOURCES

STRATEGIC HUMAN RESOURCE ANALYSIS
USES HRM EXPERTISE AND EXPERIENCE TO ASSIST IN DEVELOPING ORGANIZATIONAL OBJECTIVES AND TO PROPOSE ALTERNATIVES TO OBTAIN THESE OBJECTIVES

HUMAN RESOURCE PLANNING
SPECIFIES NUMBER AND KIND OF EMPLOYEES NEEDED

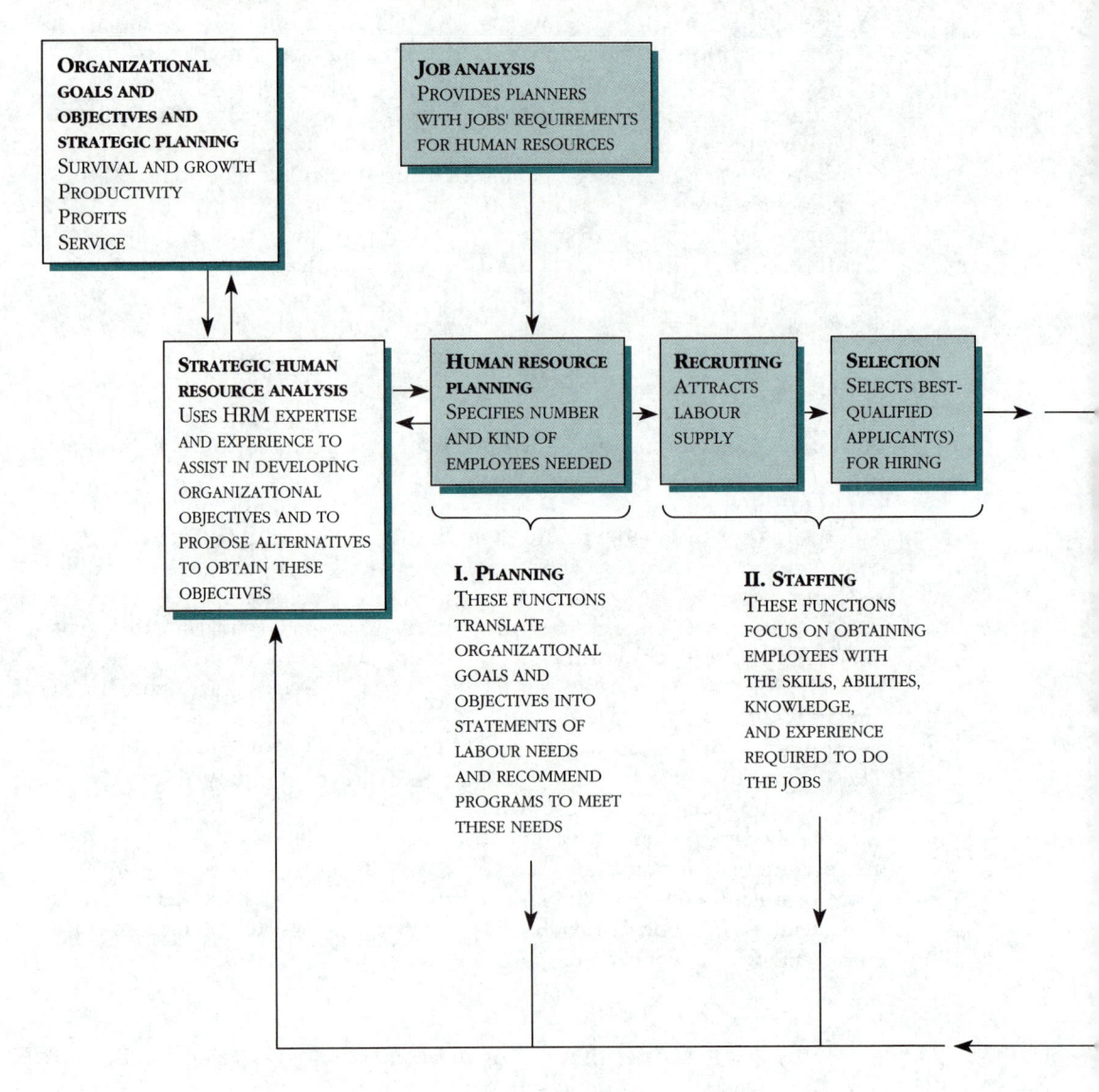

RECRUITING
ATTRACTS LABOUR SUPPLY

SELECTION
SELECTS BEST-QUALIFIED APPLICANT(S) FOR HIRING

I. PLANNING
THESE FUNCTIONS TRANSLATE ORGANIZATIONAL GOALS AND OBJECTIVES INTO STATEMENTS OF LABOUR NEEDS AND RECOMMEND PROGRAMS TO MEET THESE NEEDS

II. STAFFING
THESE FUNCTIONS FOCUS ON OBTAINING EMPLOYEES WITH THE SKILLS, ABILITIES, KNOWLEDGE, AND EXPERIENCE REQUIRED TO DO THE JOBS

INPUT FROM MAJOR AREAS OF HRM RESPONSIBILITY

PART TWO

PLANNING AND STAFFING

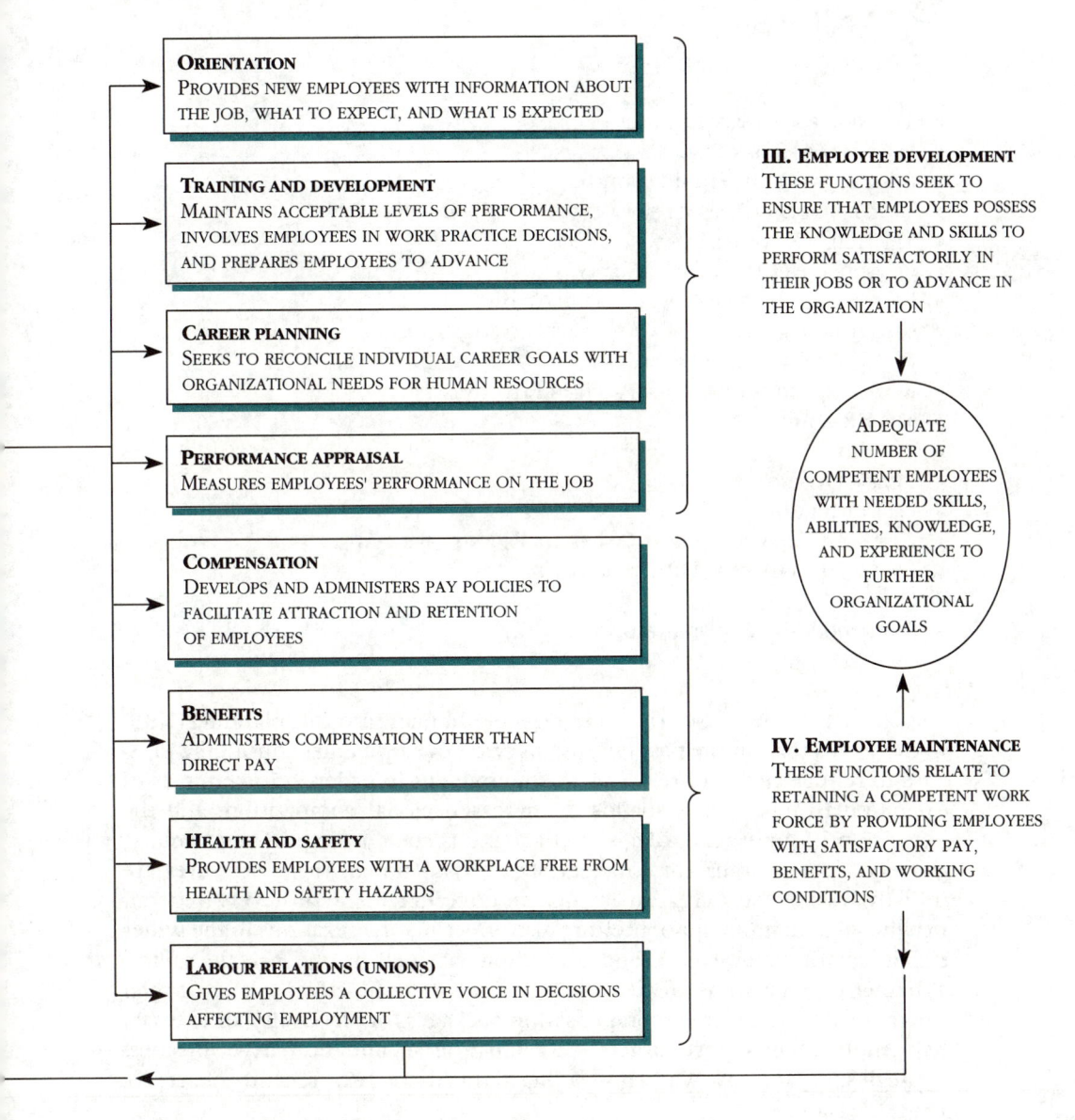

ORIENTATION
Provides new employees with information about the job, what to expect, and what is expected

TRAINING AND DEVELOPMENT
Maintains acceptable levels of performance, involves employees in work practice decisions, and prepares employees to advance

CAREER PLANNING
Seeks to reconcile individual career goals with organizational needs for human resources

PERFORMANCE APPRAISAL
Measures employees' performance on the job

COMPENSATION
Develops and administers pay policies to facilitate attraction and retention of employees

BENEFITS
Administers compensation other than direct pay

HEALTH AND SAFETY
Provides employees with a workplace free from health and safety hazards

LABOUR RELATIONS (UNIONS)
Gives employees a collective voice in decisions affecting employment

III. EMPLOYEE DEVELOPMENT
These functions seek to ensure that employees possess the knowledge and skills to perform satisfactorily in their jobs or to advance in the organization

Adequate number of competent employees with needed skills, abilities, knowledge, and experience to further organizational goals

IV. EMPLOYEE MAINTENANCE
These functions relate to retaining a competent work force by providing employees with satisfactory pay, benefits, and working conditions

Input from major areas of HRM responsibility

CHAPTER 4

HUMAN RESOURCE PLANNING

- THE NEED FOR HUMAN RESOURCE PLANNING
- PURPOSES OF HUMAN RESOURCE PLANNING
- RELATION TO OTHER HRM FUNCTIONS
- HRM IN ACTION ▸ UNPLANNED CUTBACKS CAN BE LIKE FAD DIETS
- THE HUMAN RESOURCE PLANNING PROCESS
- PROJECTING HUMAN RESOURCE SUPPLY
- FORECASTING FUTURE HUMAN RESOURCE NEEDS
- COMPARING FORECAST NEEDS WITH PROJECTIONS OF SUPPLY
- PLANNING POLICIES AND PROGRAMS
- EVALUATING HUMAN RESOURCE PLANNING EFFECTIVENESS
- THE HRM AUDIT
- SUMMARY
- REVIEW QUESTIONS
- PROJECT IDEAS
- CASE 4.1 ▸ ONTARIO HYDRO'S CORPORATE PLANNING PROCESS
- CASE 4.2 ▸ EVALUATING HR DEPARTMENTS
- NOTES
- SUGGESTIONS FOR FURTHER READING

ORGANIZATIONS ARE BEING FORCED to do more human resource planning (HRP) in the 1990s than in the past because of two developments: continuing pressure to reduce staff and restructure employment in order to lower costs of operation to meet the demands of increased global competition, and the expansion of government-legislated programs such as employment equity, pay equity, and other employment standards. Though these pressures are initially having their greatest impact on governments at all levels (federal, provincial, and municipal), they are also affecting organizations in the wider public sector (health care and education) as well as the private sector. Whether organizations are attempting to enhance the effectiveness of their operations, to adjust their compensation packages for pay equity, or to establish employment equity targets, HRP must be an integral part of business strategies. As James W. Walker, a leading authority on HRP, recently observed, HR professionals

> are becoming more directly involved in business activities — company downsizing, delayering, strategy implementation, and reorganization — and they are

changing human resource systems and practices to respond to changing business demands.[1]

Such an approach has been adopted at Noma Industries, whose success is attributed by the senior vice-president of human resources, Claude Saillant, to decentralization and an unwavering focus on its people.[2] One aspect of this increased activity is *delayering*, the flattening of an organization by reducing the number of levels between the top and the bottom. Management guru Peter Drucker observes that "the best example of a large and successful information-based organization has no middle management at all."[3] In addition to offering input into these types of reorganization, HRP is being used to address the impacts of change through the adoption of "simpler, shorter-range planning; a focus on issues; focused data analysis; and emphasis on action planning."[4]

Consistent with Walker's suggested approach of shorter-range planning and a focus on issues, the Ontario public service (OPS) has developed a strategic human resource plan that has two primary objectives: revitalizing the work force and reshaping the workplace. Revitalization includes increasing the representation of each designated employment equity group to target percentages by 1993 and developing comprehensive staffing strategies that include target percentages for external hiring and interministry and intraministry transfers. Reshaping the workplace for the Ontario public service includes reviewing organizational structures for effective delivery of programs and services; identifying and eliminating systemic barriers in the workplace through an employment systems review process; and increasing flexibility and responsiveness by promoting union–management initiatives, employee participation in work design, and employee involvement in decision making.[5]

A crucial component of this proposed HR plan is developing estimates of the demand for labour, based on likely openings within the OPS's various occupational groups and the supply of labour in terms of both expertise and employment equity representation. The OPS plan sets out objectives of employment equity representation for 33 occupational groups in 1993; the goals are expressed as percentages of the whole and compared with the actual situation in 1989 and 1990. Five groups are designated: aboriginal people, people with disabilities, francophones, racial minorities, and women. In the senior executive category, the target is to increase the proportion of women from 19.4 percent in 1990 to 27.1 percent in 1993 and of aboriginals from 0.0 to 1.1 percent. In the labour relations category, the objective is to raise the proportion of women from 25.9 percent in 1990 to 29.6 percent in 1993 (no corporate goal is yet specified in this category for aboriginal people).[6]

The HRP process involves not simply recommending how to achieve objectives but also ongoing analysis to determine which objectives are attainable and which should undergo adjustments. For example, HR professionals have to determine whether expected openings in the OPS will be sufficient to change the proportions of people from the various designated groups and whether there will be enough people from the designated groups qualified to fill the positions.

Whether the purpose is to attempt to attain occupational group objectives, as in the case of the OPS, or to assist in downsizing and reorganizing to respond to changing business demands, the HRP function will increasingly be an integral part of business activities and activities in the public sector.

THE NEED FOR HUMAN RESOURCE PLANNING

Planning future human resource needs is difficult, especially for jobs held by executives, professionals, skilled and technical workers, and tradespersons, that is, jobs that require lengthy training or the acquisition of considerable relevant experience. The challenges the Ontario public service is facing demonstrate the need for human resource planning (HRP) since a substantial number of the positions affected by the employment equity targets require long lead times for education and training. HRP is also necessary even for giant organizations such as IBM. In spite of its long-standing policy of protecting jobs, IBM in the United States eliminated 30 000 jobs between 1986 and 1990 through early retirements, voluntary layoffs, and attrition. In the fall of 1991, IBM announced that it wanted to reduce its work force worldwide by 20 000 to 30 000, but wanted "to do it on a selective basis," according to William J. Milton, an IBM analyst at Brown Brothers Harriman & Co. The senior management asked managers "to tighten the standards—in effect to raise the bar."[7] Canada's share of the downsizing was put at 2000 positions to be achieved through attrition and early retirement severance packages.[8] HRP provides information and alternative approaches for organizations such as IBM that want to downsize without having direct layoffs.

Human resource planning (HRP) is the process of forecasting human resource needs of an organization so that steps can be taken to ensure that those needs are met. This means avoiding both shortages and surpluses of labour. Until the mid- to late 1970s, organizational use of HRP was quite limited except for succession planning for executive positions. Rowland and Summers, in an in-depth 1980 study of six corporations' planning and staffing activities during the 1970s, found that succession planning was the only type of human resource planning the corporations undertook extensively.[9] A survey of Canadian firms taken the same year, however, documents the somewhat greater development of human resource planning in Canada (sometimes then called manpower planning). Of the 147 companies studied, 145 had some form of HRP, especially for the short term (one to two years into the future) in relation to operations plans. Larger companies—those with 1000 employees or more—tended to do more specific and longer-term planning.[10] HRP was encouraged in Canada by Employment and Immigration Canada's requirement that firms provide evidence of human resource plans before they could recruit overseas. The Ontario Manpower Commission also actively encouraged human resource planning.

Undoubtedly, concern over the shortage of certain skills in the late 1970s was a spur to human resource planning in organizations.[11] Factors such as rapid technological change also help explain the increase. Moreover, the process itself can be revealing to an organization that engages in it. Rowland and Summers observed that what some doubters considered important was

> not HRP (including forecasting) as a technique, but rather as a process of analysis and revision for the ultimate goal of innovative option generation by top and line management as well as staff.[12]

The process of analysis helps organizations to meet the challenges of rapidly changing technology. The introduction of new equipment, products, and processes invariably results in changes in jobs and in an organization's job structure. Existing jobs may have to change to include new equipment, new tasks, or new ways of doing familiar tasks. Some jobs, such as service station attendant, bank teller, and draftsman, may become obsolete or significantly reduced in the numbers required with advancing technology. Others may be eliminated because of decreased product demand. Human resource planners foresee such scenarios and recommend strategies for reducing excess supply.

In addition to changing the nature of some jobs and forcing the elimination of others, technological changes create a demand for specialized workers to fill new jobs. The high demand resulting from technological advances usually creates labour shortages because schools and training institutions cannot educate the new labour supply as quickly as it is needed. The time lag involved in training present employees in new skills and/or recruiting new workers with specialized skills means that planning to meet the requirements of future jobs is essential if organizations are to survive and remain competitive.

Thus, without effective HRP, organizations experiencing fluctuations in the demand for their products and the effects of rapid technological change will find themselves with a shortage of skilled employees. This was the case in Canada with general shortages of skilled workers in the mid-1950s, mid-1960s, late 1970s, and late 1980s.

Technological change and economic cycles are not the only kinds of change that create a need for HRP. Legislation can also cause a large, sudden demand for specialized workers. For example, the introduction of pay equity legislation in Ontario in 1987 caused an increase in the demand for job analysts.

PURPOSES OF HUMAN RESOURCE PLANNING

Human resource planning serves many organizational and managerial purposes.[13] Two major ones are: (1) to aid in setting organizational goals and objectives, including considerations of employment equity; and (2) to examine the effects of alternative human resource policies and programs and recommend implementation of the alternative that contributes most to organizational effectiveness.

Setting Goals and Objectives

Organizational goals and objectives specify where an organization wants to be at some future point in time. Typically, top management sets goals in terms of profitability, survival and growth, and production and/or service levels. Given the increasing social (and often legislated) demand for employment equity, many employers are also specifying goals for increasing participation of minorities in their work force.

Some examples of organizational goals are:

1. To increase company profits by 10 percent in the next fiscal year (profitability).
2. To close 25 retail outlets in the Prairies in the next four years (downsizing).
3. To bottle 10 percent more diet cola in the next year (production level).
4. To guarantee one-day delivery of all first-class mail within the province by 1995 (service level).
5. To increase the proportion of women in executive positions by 7 percentage points in the next three years (employment equity).

Human resource planners determine the implications various goals have for human resources and report their findings to management and business planners. For example, they investigate what policies must be put in place to deal with the layoffs, transfers, and severance pay arrangements resulting from closing 25 retail outlets or how many additional employees must be hired in order to bottle 10 percent more cola in the next year. Human resource planners help management and business planners in evaluating whether given goals can be met.

Consider the case of an electronics firm whose management is exploring the production of a new piece of equipment within the year. After analyzing the human resource requirements for producing this item, human resource planners might provide management with evidence that this goal would be impossible to meet within the next year, very costly within the next two years, but cost-efficient within four years. Given this information, management may want to plan to achieve the goal within a four-year time span.

Examining the Effects of Alternative Human Resource Policies and Programs

Organizational effectiveness was defined in Chapter 1 as making the most expeditious use of an organization's resources. Human resource planners must consider the long- and short-term costs and benefits of each alternative planning strategy in order to arrive at the one that maximizes organizational effectiveness. For example, if a new piece of equipment is introduced, is it in the best interests of the organization to hire new employees who know how to use the equipment or to invest time and money in training present employees in its use? If an employer faces a decline in demand for a product, will a number of workers have to be laid off, or can the organization retain them, perhaps transferring some of them to new job assignments and expecting attrition to take care of the remainder?

Alternative HRP policies and programs can be evaluated in several ways. One is computer simulations, which quantify and manipulate practices and human resource movement through an organization, enabling planners to examine the effects of changing or implementing various policies and practices. They are a valuable tool in planning human resource strategies.

Another way is to examine the effects of alternative scenarios. With the availability of computerized human resource information systems, many employers are likely to consider alternative human resource policies and programs by making forecasts and projections of employees, costs, and benefits. HRP benefits management to the extent that human resource alternatives are considered when strategic decisions are made.

Relation to Other HRM Functions

HRP is the most strategic and potentially proactive of all human resource management functions simply because it involves planning. As organizational goals and objectives are developed in the strategic and HRP process, human resource policies and programs are evaluated in terms of how they may contribute to goal attainment. Thus, HRP serves as the co-ordinating and integrating link to all other HRM functions, and each of the functions is in some way related to HRP. Specific relationships between HRP and other HRM functions are described in Figure 4.1.

Notice that the figure explicitly divides the general HRP function into two components: strategic human resource analysis and specific human resource planning. We drew it that way so as to highlight the differing types of decision-making processes involved in each component.

Strategic human resource analysis (SHRA) is the policy-making component that links the development of organizational goals and objectives with the carrying out of the HRM functions. SHRA is the responsibility of the vice-president of human resources or the most senior HR person in an organization. This function requires an overview of the entire HRM process and inputs from all areas of HRM with a particularly strong input from the human resource planners.[14] In contrast, HRP, which is the responsibility of a manager of HRP or HRP professionals, involves specifying the number and type of employees needed to meet future job requirements and organizational goals and objectives. This function relies on technical HRP expertise and provides

FIGURE 4.1
Human Resource Planning: Relation to Other HRM Functions

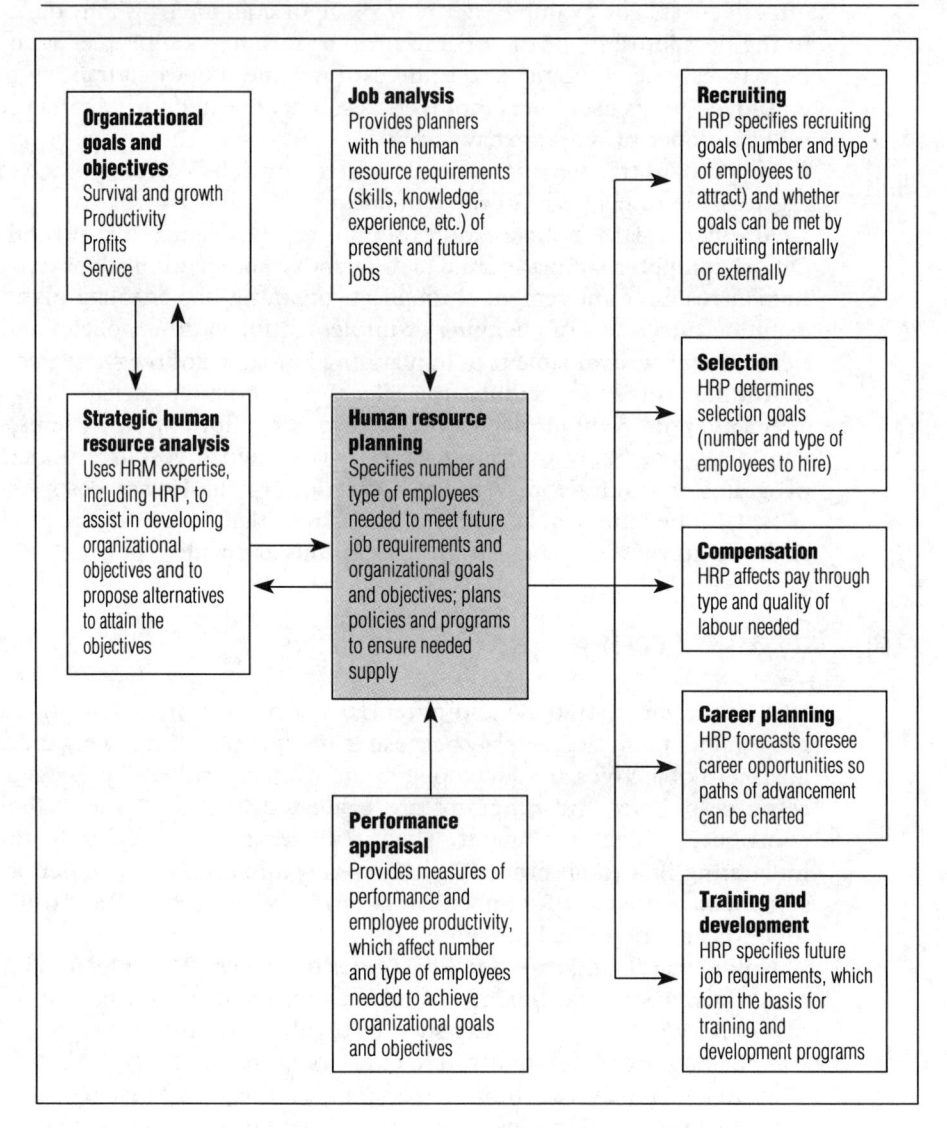

Organizational goals and objectives
Survival and growth
Productivity
Profits
Service

Job analysis
Provides planners with the human resource requirements (skills, knowledge, experience, etc.) of present and future jobs

Recruiting
HRP specifies recruiting goals (number and type of employees to attract) and whether goals can be met by recruiting internally or externally

Strategic human resource analysis
Uses HRM expertise, including HRP, to assist in developing organizational objectives and to propose alternatives to attain the objectives

Human resource planning
Specifies number and type of employees needed to meet future job requirements and organizational goals and objectives; plans policies and programs to ensure needed supply

Selection
HRP determines selection goals (number and type of employees to hire)

Compensation
HRP affects pay through type and quality of labour needed

Performance appraisal
Provides measures of performance and employee productivity, which affect number and type of employees needed to achieve organizational goals and objectives

Career planning
HRP forecasts foresee career opportunities so paths of advancement can be charted

Training and development
HRP specifies future job requirements, which form the basis for training and development programs

an essential input into SHRA. The specific HRP function also relates to a number of other HRM responsibilities.

The HRM functions of job analysis and performance appraisal provide important inputs to the human resource planning process. By analyzing the content of jobs, planners can evaluate the human resource requirements of present and future jobs. Performance appraisal systems provide measures of employee performance. It is important for planners to know performance levels of present employees so that they can forecast the number and kinds of personnel needed to achieve certain goals.

Human resource planning specifies recruiting goals — the number and kinds of employees to attract to positions in an organization. Planning also provides a database for determining if recruiting goals can be met from within the organization or whether external recruiting will be necessary. If recruiting needs can be met internally, present employees will have to be attracted to the new positions, and some retraining and development may be required. HRM professionals can make employees aware of new positions and advancement opportunities through career planning activities. Forecasts of human resource needs also serve as a basis for training and development programs designed to prepare employees to meet future job requirements.

If recruiting needs cannot be met internally, even with training and development, external recruiting is required. Compensation is a key factor here; pay must be competitive in order to attract individuals (who may be happily employed elsewhere). The number and type of workers needed and whether that kind of labour is in short or abundant supply affect the dollar amount an organization must pay in order to attract, hire, and retain the required employees. However, care has to be taken, especially in larger organizations, in changing pay levels in one job category because doing so can alter the existing pay structure and create discontent and requests for pay adjustments. HRP also has a direct relation to the selection function in that planning determines selection goals.

Human resource planning sometimes determines that there are too many workers in a certain job category. In this case, steps must be taken to reduce or redistribute supply.

Until recently, human resource planning in organizations was done by HRM generalists or other HRM professionals who had responsibility for training and development or recruitment and staffing. Since the mid- to late 1970s, the rise in importance of human resource planning has caused many organizations to establish full-time positions and support staff to handle the HRP function. The following job description for a manager of human resources planning provides insights into the responsibilities of this HRM specialist.

> MANAGER, HUMAN RESOURCES PLANNING
> Contributes to the corporation by analyzing and recommending policies and procedures and developing systems and models which contribute to the effective hiring, development, and utilization of human resources. Analyzes and recommends revisions to policies, regulations and procedures (e.g., candidate search and selection, performance evaluation, career pathing, promotions, and transfers). Develops and applies systems and models for human resource planning, including forecasting future requirements, defining logical career paths, inventorying human resources and projecting future time periods, identifying future hiring needs by skill type, level, and location, identifying future voids and imbalances, and performing analyses of human resource situations to identify opportunities for improvement.[15]

HRM IN ACTION

UNPLANNED CUTBACKS CAN BE LIKE FAD DIETS

Many organizations restructured and downsized in the late 1980s and early 1990s. This process is painful and disruptive; a survey by the consulting firm Wyatt Company indicates that it may also be unproductive. The key element for a successful downsizing appears to be conducting a systematic examination of what the company does and how it does it. Ideally, only after the work is redesigned more efficiently should the staff be looked at. The operating cost—not the headcount of employees—is the most crucial variable. The objective should be to become more efficient, not just to cut people.

Wyatt's survey of 1005 companies employing more than 4 million people showed that fewer than half of those that restructured to cut costs were able to meet their expense-reduction target, and only a third improved profitability to their satisfaction. Many companies were forced into successive rounds of downsizing because the difficulties proved more intractable than expected. Of the 86 percent of companies that downsized, only 42 percent took steps to eliminate low-value work.

What is worse, the survey revealed the tendency for firms to follow layoffs by adding back even more staff when good times returned. After AT&T cut 100 000 from its payroll in the mid-1980s, there was pressure to add staff. AT&T spokesman Burke Stinson says, "It's ironic to see that managers will hire back people who actually do the work in order for full-time people to attend meetings." Of the surveyed companies, 83 percent ended up replacing some of the people they dismissed. Twenty-five percent of the companies replaced more than one in ten of those who had left. Consultant Robert Gunn likens the cuts to fad diets: "They work instantaneously, but you didn't really change your eating habits. You just stopped eating." In Canada the federal bureaucracy was cut by 2 percent in 1979/80 and 2.4 percent in 1980/81; it rose by as much as 1.3 percent in the next five years, only to be cut again at the end of the 1980s.

Layoffs and restructuring have a severe adverse impact on the morale of remaining employees, says John Parkington of Wyatt. Fifty-eight percent of the surveyed companies that downsized said employee morale was hurt, and 37 percent said employee retention became more difficult. In addition, 80 percent said that when they offered employees early retirement options, they lost good performers.

CHAPTER 4 HUMAN RESOURCE PLANNING 141

> IBM Canada is one firm that is hoping to avoid the fad diet effect. In paring 2000 positions in 1992, it restructured, bringing more employees into contact with customers to make the firm's hardware stand out from that of its rivals. Time will tell whether IBM's planning for cutbacks paid off.
>
> Source: Based on Amanda Bennett, "Downsizing Doesn't Necessarily Bring an Upswing in Corporate Profitability," *The Wall Street Journal*, June 6, 1991. Used with the permission of *The Wall Street Journal*, © 1991 Dow Jones & Company, Inc. All rights reserved worldwide; John Kohut, "Critics See Hidden Costs in Cutting Bureaucracy," *The Globe and Mail*, March 27, 1989; and Carolyn Leitch, "IBM Canada to Slash 2,000 Jobs," *The Globe and Mail*, November 29, 1991. Used with the permission of *The Globe and Mail*.

THE HUMAN RESOURCE PLANNING PROCESS

The human resource planning process has five steps:
1. Project future human resource supply.
2. Forecast future human resource needs.
3. Compare forecast needs with projected supply.
4. Plan policies and programs to meet human resource needs.
5. Evaluate human resource planning effectiveness.

Basically, the process involves comparing projections of available supply with forecasts of human resource needs in order to determine net employee requirements for some future point(s) in time. Net requirements may reflect either shortages or surpluses of certain types of labour. When shortages and surpluses are identified, planners can suggest alternative approaches to ensure that supply conforms to demand.[16]

Figure 4.2 diagrams these five steps. (It also illustrates the interrelationships with SHRA.)

Step 1 of the process is projecting an organization's future human resource supply—estimating the number and kinds of employees expected to compose its work force at some future time. Projections are based on careful assessment of an organization's current work force and also on patterns of employee movement through the organization over time. These patterns are an important consideration in making projections because the composition of the work force can be expected to change over time through promotions, transfers, and terminations. It is important to note that these projections of supply relate only to the internal supply of human resources.

FIGURE 4.2
The Human Resource Planning Process

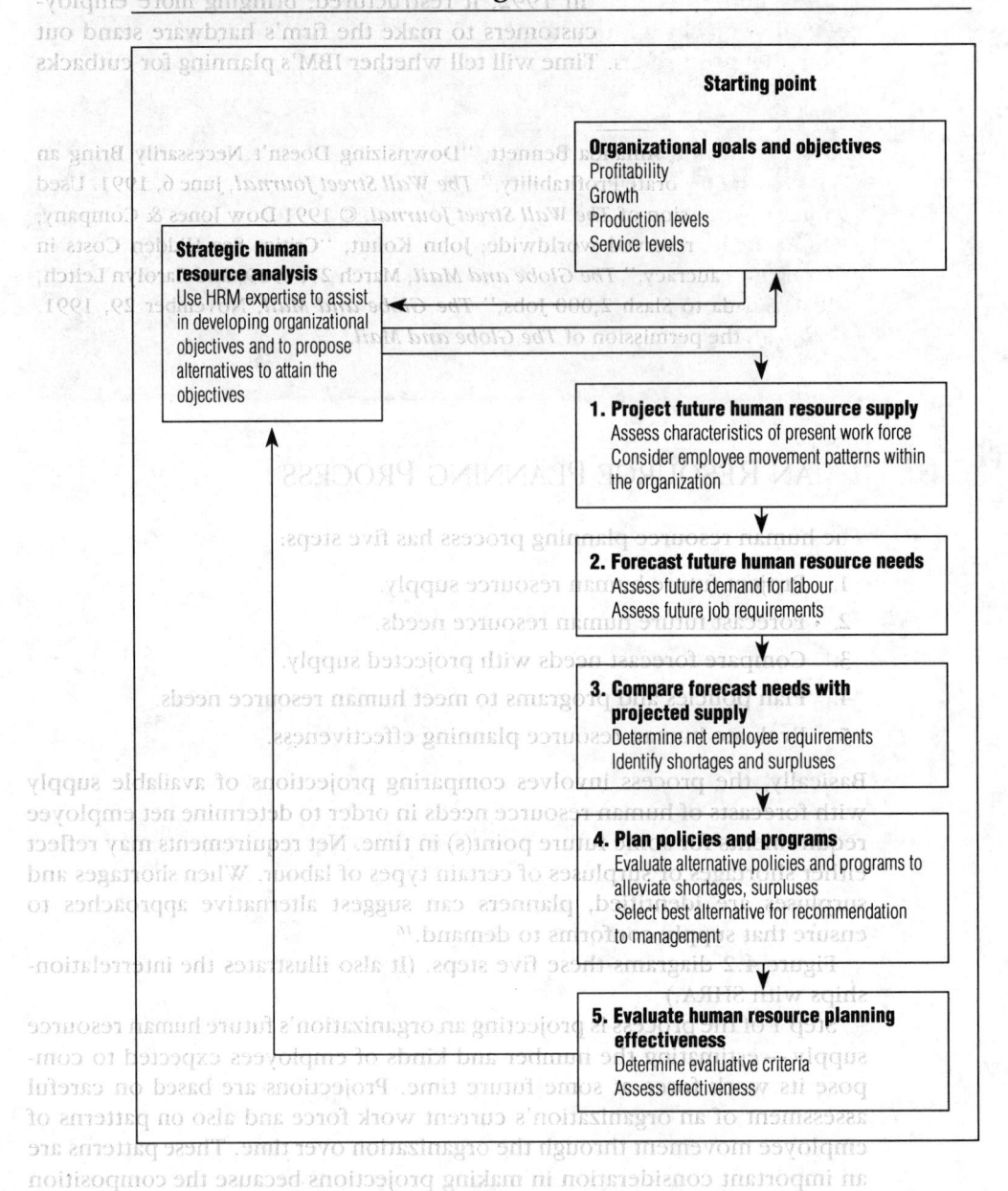

Starting point

Organizational goals and objectives
- Profitability
- Growth
- Production levels
- Service levels

Strategic human resource analysis
Use HRM expertise to assist in developing organizational objectives and to propose alternatives to attain the objectives

1. Project future human resource supply
- Assess characteristics of present work force
- Consider employee movement patterns within the organization

2. Forecast future human resource needs
- Assess future demand for labour
- Assess future job requirements

3. Compare forecast needs with projected supply
- Determine net employee requirements
- Identify shortages and surpluses

4. Plan policies and programs
- Evaluate alternative policies and programs to alleviate shortages, surpluses
- Select best alternative for recommendation to management

5. Evaluate human resource planning effectiveness
- Determine evaluative criteria
- Assess effectiveness

Step 2 is to forecast human resource needs based on forecasts of demand for the organization's goods or services. Future needs for human resources —and the kind of employee skills that will be needed—are also determined by the nature of future jobs and their requirements.

Step 3 of the process compares forecast needs for human resources with projections of internal supply to determine net employee requirements. Such comparisons should be made for each job in an organization as well as for the organization as a whole. Once net needs for human resources have been established, planners can evaluate alternative policies and programs for alleviating shortages or reducing surpluses and then select the best strategy for recommendation to management (Step 4).

Finally, an organization's human resource planning effort should be evaluated in order to determine its usefulness to the organization (Step 5). To make this assessment, planners must first determine the criteria for evaluation.

Projecting Human Resource Supply

Projections are estimates of the number and kinds of employees that can be expected to constitute an organization's work force at some future time. Projections are based on careful assessment of an organization's *current* supply, plus consideration of employee movement through the organization over time. Exhibit 4.1 displays some forms used to assist in projecting supply.

Assessing Current Supply

Data on current human resource supply are obtained from inventories of workers' characteristics and skills. These data are collected and stored in a human resource information system (HRIS). Exhibit 4.2 lists some of the kinds of information usually collected and stored in an HRIS. The categories generally include: (1) personal data; (2) work history data; (3) training and development history and career plans; (4) skills inventory data for current jobs; and (5) aggregate data, such as total number of employees and their age distribution. Most employers already have HRISs to collect and store some of the information necessary for human resource planning. For example, most employers maintain personal and work history data for payroll purposes. However, the data requirements of HRISs for human resource planning purposes are more comprehensive than for other purposes. Because planners seek to estimate availability of future skills, information on currently available skills is required. But skills change over time because of training and development programs and employee job changes within the organization. Thus, in projecting the nature of future supply, HRISs must also collect and store information on assessments of employee potential and promotability, employee career objectives, and training programs taken.

The Employment Equity Act of 1986 greatly increases the value of an HRIS to most large employers. Whether or not an employer uses an HRIS for HRP purposes, the reporting requirements of this act dictate that employment, pay, and employee mobility data must be available for various race, ethnic, and sex categories of employees.

EXHIBIT 4.1
Forms for Assisting in Projecting Supply

Current work force		
Which occupations do you currently employ?	How many workers do you employ?	
	▲ You can record current employment and employee movements on Schedule 4. If you have many employees approaching retirement, you can examine current age distribution using Schedule 5.	

▲ Your current work force will probably change over the planning period as you lose people to retirement, transfers, death, etc.

You can estimate or project these losses using Schedule 6 or project them in greater detail using Schedule 7.

Current work force available over planning period					
How many of your current work force in each occupation will remain in each of the next five years					
1st yr	2nd yr	3rd yr	4th yr	5th yr	
					Transfer for matching

Source: Adapted from Ontario Manpower Commission, *Human Resources Planning Manual* (Toronto: Ontario Ministry of Labour, and Ontario Regional Office, Employment and Immigration Canada, 1982). © Used with the permission of the Queen's Printer for Ontario and the Minister of Supply and Services Canada, 1992.

EXHIBIT 4.2
Typical Data for a Human Resource Information System

A. Personal data
   1. Name
   2. Sex
   3. Date of birth
   4. Marital status
   5. Physical disabilities, if any
   6. Education

B. Work history data
   1. Date of hire
   2. Initial job
   3. Starting pay
   4. Second job, date of job change, and pay
   5. Third and later jobs, if any; dates of job change and pay
   6. Current job and organizational unit or department and current pay
   7. Performance appraisal data—past and most recent

C. Training and development history and career plans
   1. Company-sponsored training programs completed in the last five years
   2. Other training, development, or educational programs completed
   3. Employee career objectives
   4. Assessment of employee potential and promotability

D. Skills inventory data (quantitative description of the skills, abilities, knowledge, and experience necessary to perform the job, as determined by job analysis)

E. Aggregate data
   1. Total number of employees
   2. Number of employees in each job and class of jobs
   3. Sex of employees in each job and class of jobs
   4. Age distribution of employees in each job and job class
   5. Listing of current vacant positions

Affirmative action regulations in the United States led to the development and growth of computerized HRISs that were useful both for meeting reporting requirements and for assessing labour supply. Employment-related data for categories of employees are used as the basis for determining underrepresentation of women and other minorities and as the basis for affirmative action goals. The description of the current work force provided by the HRIS may be combined with information about human resource flows to attain employment equity goals and timetables.

Skills Inventories

A major requirement of an HRIS is information about the skills available among current employees. A *job skills inventory* includes information about each employee's skills, abilities, knowledge, and experience. This information can be obtained from several sources, including job analysis, performance appraisal data, and educational and training program completion records.

Ideally, a skills inventory would be a major component of a computerized HRIS and would use a standardized coding system for jobs, skills, knowledge, and experience such as that found in the new National Occupational Classification or in the older but still-used *Canadian Classification and Dictionary of Occupations*. Such a system could be used not only in HRP, but also in deciding employee transfers, promotions, and layoffs.

Analysis of Human Resource Flows

Although projections of future human resource supply are based on assessment of current supply, projections that assume the same employees will be available in one, three, or five years invariably prove incorrect. Methods of projecting human resource supply must take into account patterns of employee movement into, through, and out of organizations. Such movement patterns are referred to as *human resource flows*.

Human resource flows logically begin with newly hired employees who "flow" into the organization at an entry-level job. Entry-level jobs, in most organizations, are the lowest-level jobs in the company. They must, therefore, be filled from the external work force. (Exceptions occur with specializations or in fields such as publishing, where an entry-level editorial position could be filled internally or externally and would be considered a promotion for a clerical or secretarial worker.) From this point, employees can: (1) stay *in* the same job; (2) move *across* to another, but not a higher-level job (transfer or lateral move); (3) move *up* to a higher-level job (promotion); or (4) move *out* of the organization through voluntary termination (resignation), involuntary termination (layoff, dismissal), or retirement. Downward flows are also available to employees who are not in entry-level jobs. Moving from a higher-level to a lower-level job in an organization is known as *demotion*. Although few would choose it as an alternative, some individuals tolerate demotion, at least temporarily, during recessionary periods or for personal reasons.

There are two general methods for projecting labour supply based on information about human resource flows. The first relies on estimates of supervisors and managers as to the number of employees entering and leaving various positions in their unit, including the number changing jobs within the unit. By adding up these estimates, planners can project the organization's internal labour supply. The second general method involves use of stochastic models.

Stochastic Models

The mathematical term "stochastic" is used to describe the process of employee movement, or flow, from one job in an organization to another. An example of a simple stochastic model is the transition matrix. A *transition matrix* is a rectangular display that portrays percentages of employees in certain jobs or positions at Time 1 and Time 2. It is important that Time 1 and Time 2 be far enough apart to allow some changes but not so far apart as to allow multiple changes for individual employees (both demotion and exit, for example). Table 4.1 is a hypothetical matrix for executives and managers in the Ontario public service.

As can be seen from the matrix, 90 percent of the 40 deputy ministers (A) at Time 1 remained at Time 2, and 10 percent left between Time 1 and Time 2. Of the 100 assistant deputy ministers (B) at Time 1, 80 percent remained in that job at Time 2 while 2 percent had moved up to the rank of deputy minister (A); 18 percent of them left between Time 1 and Time 2.

Transition matrices are useful for a variety of analytical purposes, such as tracking career paths and exit rates. In human resource planning, those matrices are used as the basis for projections of future supply in a process known

TABLE 4.1
Hypothetical Transition Matrix for Executives and Managers in the Ontario Public Service

Classification	Time 1 Number	Time 2 A	B	C	D	Exit	Total
				percent			
Executives							
A. Deputy ministers	40	90				10	**100**
B. Assistant deputy ministers	100	2	80			18	**100**
Managers							
C. Senior managers	300			5	75	20	**100**
D. Specialized supervisors	700				10	65	25	**100**

as Markov analysis or network flow analysis. *Markov analysis* bases estimates (probabilities) of future movement on actual flow data described in transition matrices. To see how this is done, let us use the matrix in Table 4.1 to project the future supply of executives and managers in the Ontario public service.

To make projections for the forecast period, we begin with the number of positions that will open up in the three top levels as a result of officials' leaving the public service or moving to higher positions and the number of executives and senior managers who will remain with the government.

Four deputy minister positions will open up because of deputies' leaving (40 × 0.10). Of these openings, two will be filled by assistant deputy ministers who are promoted to deputy (100 × 0.02) and two from outside. If we assume that the number of assistant deputy positions remains unchanged, twenty of them will open up, two because of promotions (100 × 0.02) and eighteen because of persons leaving the public service (100 × 0.18). Of these twenty, fifteen will be filled by the promotion of senior managers (300 × 0.05) and five by recruiting outside.

In summary, this analysis of flows of executives and senior managers shows that 99 positions will open up as a result of persons' leaving the Ontario public service or being promoted, of which 87 will be filled from within by promotions and 12 by hiring from outside. (Of the 87, some will probably be promotions within a ministry and some will be the result of interministry transfers.) Of the total of 440 persons in the top three levels of the Ontario public service, the gross turnover rate (persons who leave or change positions) will be 22.5 percent (99 ÷ 440), while 77.5 percent, or 341 persons, will remain in their positions.

Stochastic models can be very useful for projecting supply in situations of little change. For example, their projections can be quite accurate if future policies and organizational conditions are similar to what they were when the model was developed. An early example of the use of a stochastic model projected managerial turnover, promotions, and transfers in a large manufacturing firm. The model enabled management to project the availability of managers over a five-year period, thus identifying shortages.[17]

Stochastic models cannot, however, be used as effectively to project future supply if there will be changes that affect supply. For example, if a plant changes location, stochastic models of flow data from the previous location are not a sound base for projecting supply in the new location. Yet even in cases in which stochastic models cannot be used to project supply effectively, they can be helpful in providing planners with an understanding of human resource flows. Stochastic models of flows before and after certain changes can aid in an understanding of the effects of such changes in terms of employee movement through an organization. For example, an increase in the number of persons recruited from outside the public service could have the effect of reducing flow within the public service. Stochastic models are often used in computer simulations of human resource systems to examine effects of such changes in human resource policies.

Forecasting Future Human Resource Needs

Organizational goals and objectives serve as a starting point for forecasting future human resource needs. The demand for labour is derived from the demand for an organization's goods and services, as well as from the relationship between labour inputs and the output of goods and services. If the input/output ratio and other factors are held constant, increased demand for goods and services leads to an increased demand for labour; inversely, decreased demand for goods and services generally results in a decreased demand for labour.

Exhibit 4.3 is a form designed by federal and Ontario provincial employment agencies to assist employers in the process of planning for human resources. Note that in this early step, human resource requirements are tied to business plans.

Forecasts of the demand for human resources can be short-range, mid-range, or long-range, depending on how far into the future goals are set. Short-range planning looks at the coming year, the main concern being to meet an organization's immediate staffing needs. Emphasis is usually on budgeting and on recruiting programs. Mid-range forecasts focus on goals one to five years away. Long-range planning efforts are usually directed at organizational goals five or more years in the future; they reflect organizational philosophy concerning the direction of the firm and its responses to environmental change. Obviously, long-range forecasts for human resource needs are the most difficult of the three to make because they are based on predictions of conditions in the distant future. J.W. Walker draws an analogy between forecasting human resource needs and weather forecasting:

> Somewhat like weather forecasting, the assessment of changing environmental conditions is a difficult and uncertain task in human resource planning. We may survey the clouds, the winds, and weather conditions prevailing elsewhere as we develop forecasts of conditions to come. But we cannot always predict the future weather accurately and we certainly cannot change it. Nevertheless, the information is vital in our efforts to anticipate and prepare for it.[18]

Six different methods, or approaches, can be used to forecast future human resource needs. Some are more appropriate to short-range forecasting, while others are designed for long-range planning. The methods include (1) planning for the status quo, (2) rules of thumb, (3) unit forecasting, (4) the Delphi method, (5) scenarios, and (6) computer simulation.

Planning for the Status Quo

The simplest approach to forecasting human resource needs is to assume that the current supply and mix of employees will be adequate for the forecast period and that staff ratios will remain constant. In this case, planning simply

EXHIBIT 4.3
Tying Human Resource Requirements to Business Plans

Your future requirements for production/customer service personnel will be influenced by such business planning factors as change in output volume, change in product/service mix, and introduction of new processes and equipment. So, you will need to set down your business plans before you look at your human resource requirements. The forms below will help you.

Production/customer service: present

What products or customer services do you currently sell?	What are your sales of each? ($ 000s or units)		Summarize the types of occupations of workers you need for your production/service	How many workers in each are needed?
		▶ You can examine the relationship between individual products/customer services and their current employment requirements using Schedule 1.		

Planned/projected

What products or customer services do you plan to sell in the next 5 years?	What sales levels do you plan to reach ($ 000s or units)						Summarize the types of occupations you will require for the planned production/service	How many workers in each occupation will you require?				
	1st yr	2nd yr	3rd yr	4th yr	5th yr	▶ You can project manpower requirements by occupation for individual products/customer services using Schedule 2. For multi-year planning, complete a separate schedule for each year of the planning period.		1st yr	2nd yr	3rd yr	4th yr	5th yr

Transfer requirements for each occupation for matching against available internal supply.

Source: Ontario Manpower Commission, *Human Resources Planning Manual* (Toronto: Ontario Ministry of Labour, and Ontario Regional Office, Employment and Immigration Canada, 1982). © Reproduced with the permission of the Queen's Printer for Ontario and the Minister of Supply and Services Canada, 1992.

involves taking steps to replace any employees who either are promoted or leave the firm.

An example of planning for the status quo is *management succession planning*, which seeks to ensure that there is at least one qualified manager to replace any higher-level manager in the organization. Management succession planning is quite common. In a survey of HRP practice in 137 companies, Greer, Jackson, and Fiorito found that succession planning or replacement charts were the most widely reported HRP technique used by companies to forecast supply.[19]

In a large organization, particularly one with a business strategy of promotion from within, "succession planning becomes very important to the future development of the employees."[20] At the Toronto-Dominion Bank, for example, human resource planners first determine the business and strategic needs of each division (including considerations of employment equity), then consider the training and development of individuals, and then identify those employees who are considered key resources within each of the divisions. These employees are then encouraged to develop a career plan and eventually to participate in the training available. The planners place the key resources employees either in the succession planning category of being able to fill a vacancy immediately or in a one- to five-year plan for persons needing training and development.

Almost every organization needs succession planning. Other planning for the status quo is often adequate in the short run for organizations that experience little change in demand for their products and whose technologies remain relatively stable. An example of an organization that could use this approach successfully is a retail business in an area experiencing little population growth. Even this simple approach to forecasting of future needs should, however, begin with a complete description and analysis of current staffing requirements, to ensure that present needs are being adequately met by the current number and mix of employees.

Rules of Thumb

Some organizations use rules of thumb as a basis for forecasting changing human resource needs. For example, one firm has successfully used one production supervisor for every twelve production employees in the past and firmly believes this 1/12 staffing ratio is optimal. Thus, if it forecasts demand for 144 additional production employees, it plans to create positions for 12 new production supervisors.

Another rule of thumb based on previous experience is that one person can produce, say, 2000 units of output per day. Using this guideline, an organization that wants to produce an additional 10 000 units per day will need an additional five employees to accomplish its goal.

Because rules of thumb assume that past relationships between number of employees and outputs can be applied to future conditions, they are most useful in work environments that remain relatively stable. If conditions change, past formulas for success may not apply.

Rules of thumb can also be based on various indicators, or *predictor variables*, that have proved in the past to bear a relationship to what is being forecast. For example, a manufacturer may have a rule of thumb that annual sales of a product will reach $1 million if sales in the first two months equal $100 000 or more. In this case "the first two months of sales" is a predictor of a certain level of forecast product demand. Using this rule of thumb for forecast demand, production can be scheduled and human resource needs determined.

A more formal, quantitative version of rules of thumb combines several predictor variables into a multiple regression equation. This equation assigns weights to the different predictor variables. One large firm successfully used multiple regression equations, based on quarterly data, to forecast human resource requirements in different departments.[21]

Greer, Jackson, and Fiorito found that 27.3 percent of the 137 companies they surveyed used rules of thumb to forecast the supply of human resources and 37.9 percent used them to forecast demand.[22]

UNIT FORECASTING

The *unit forecasting approach* simply requires supervisors and managers to estimate their human resource needs for the next year or forecast period. The unit forecasts are then added for a total forecast. This approach is often referred to as a "bottom-up" approach to forecasting because judgements are made by lower-level management and simply added together at a higher organizational level. This method is usually used for making short-range forecasts.

The unit forecasting approach can be highly structured or very informal. An informal method has each supervisor or manager submit a statement of the number of new employees needed to fill all jobs in which vacancies are expected or additional employees needed. A more structured version requires managers to respond to a questionnaire about the nature of future jobs and their requirements, the number of expected vacancies in each job category, and expectations as to whether job vacancies can be filled internally via training, promotion, or transfer or whether additional personnel must be recruited externally. A sample questionnaire for unit forecasting is given in Exhibit 4.4. This sample questionnaire is not detailed, but it does provide examples of the types of questions that supervisors and managers could be asked in order to forecast human resource needs. Note that many of the questions emphasize information about future job requirements. This is because changes in job requirements often entail corresponding changes in employee skills, knowledge, and interests. (For example, if a restaurant intro-

EXHIBIT 4.4
Unit Forecasting Questionnaire

1. List any jobs that have changed since the last forecasting period and any that will change in the next forecasting period.
2. List any jobs that have been added or eliminated in the last forecasting period and any that will be added or eliminated in the next forecasting period.
3. Identify the job requirements (skills, knowledge, etc.) for each job listed in items 1 and 2 above.
4. List expected vacancies for each job category for the next forecasting period.
5. For each job vacancy, note whether the vacancy can be filled with present employees or whether additional employees will have to be hired.
6. If vacancy can be filled with present employees, note whether training will be required. Specify nature of training needs.
7. What percentage of employees are performing their jobs up to standard?
8. How many employees in the next forecasting period will require training to perform their jobs satisfactorily?
9. How many employees will be absent in the next forecasting period because of disability, educational, or other leaves?
10. How much overtime was needed in the last forecasting period, and how much will be needed in the next forecasting period? What was the cost of compensation for the overtime?

duces Caesar salad prepared at tableside, the job requirements for waiter and waitress must change to include skill at and interest in preparing Caesar salad at tableside.) Questionnaire results can be analyzed by top management or human resource planners and used as a basis for forecasting the needs of divisions and the organization as a whole.

THE DELPHI METHOD

The unit forecasting method seeks opinions from lower-level management regarding short-range staffing needs. The Delphi method, in contrast, relies on expert opinion in making long-range forecasts.

"Where is the organization going?" is a key question in long-range planning. Top management must address this question periodically in deciding whether the organization should continue producing the same goods or services it has in the past or should add, delete, or modify them. Decisions of this type require expert judgement based upon analysis of forecast changes in technology, the economy, and the legal and social environments.

The Delphi method provides one method of obtaining consensus regarding factors affecting an organization's future directions and human resource needs. It involves obtaining independent judgements from a panel of experts, usually through a questionnaire or interview, on a particular issue or question affecting the nature and magnitude of demand for an organization's products or services. The five steps in the Delphi method are:

1. An issue, question, or problem is identified.
2. A small group or panel of ten or fewer experts is identified.
3. Independent judgements about the issue are obtained from each expert through a questionnaire or structured interview.
4. An intermediary or facilitator collects, analyzes, and feeds back information from the first questionnaire or interview to each expert.
5. Steps 3 and 4 are repeated until there is a consensus on the issue or problem.

The Delphi method avoids face-to-face encounters between the experts so as to prevent such factors as social interaction, personality, and other psychological biases from affecting the judgement process. Because the panel members never interact, the role of intermediary or facilitator is very important in summarizing and feeding back information to each member. One study of the Delphi method found it to be more accurate and useful than a regression model for forecasting human resource needs.[23] A recent, much larger than usual use of the Delphi method was in a study in which 140 panel members examined the impact of technological change on human resources in health care in Canada.[24]

Scenarios

Scenarios are descriptive scenes that allow planners to consider combinations of several factors in order to forecast human resource needs for each set of circumstances. For example, one scenario might assume that environmental conditions in the next three years will include a recession, the entrance of a new competitor into the company's major market, and technological advances requiring some modifications in the production process. An alternative scenario for the same three-year period might include the entrance of a new competing firm and technological changes requiring some modifications but no recession. A third scenario for the same time span might describe a situation in which there is no recession, no competing firm, and only minor technological advances. Using this method, forecasts can be made for meeting the human resource needs of each set of circumstances portrayed.

The scenario approach is useful in making mid- to long-range forecasts of needs. At some point, however, top management must choose one scenario as the one most likely to occur so that human resource policies and programs can be implemented to ensure needs are being met. An advantage of the scenario method is that it compels planners to consider and plan specifically for more than one contingency. Thus, an alternative is available if the chosen scenario does not prove to be a true representation of conditions as they unfold over time.

COMPUTER SIMULATION

Use of computer simulation models is one of the most sophisticated methods of forecasting human resource needs. A *computer simulation* is a mathematical representation of major organizational processes, policies, and human resource movement through an organization. Computer simulations usually include the kinds of assumptions found in scenarios. Additional factors included might be minimum and maximum number of employees in each job, minimum lengths of time in jobs before promotion can occur, average rates of hiring for new employees, turnover and termination data, and data concerning costs and productivity rates. Many of the factors represented in a computer simulation of an organization are particularly useful for projecting the future supply of labour, but such models can also be very useful for both forecasting future human resource needs and evaluating alternative human resource policies.

Regression analysis is useful in computer simulations if forecasts of requirements and/or supplies are based on extrapolating past relationships among a number of variables, independent and dependent, that together explain a large portion of the preceeding trends. Regression analysis is most suited to conditions of stability or at least a predictable direction of change. A recent study, which suggests possible avenues for future HRP computer simulations, used demand models to forecast an electrical utility's required staffing levels in total and for professionals (the largest category of employees) and managers. The total staffing level was estimated as a function of the outside services budget, sales revenues, and assets (the net value of physical plant). The level for professionals was estimated as a function of outside services budget, net operating revenue, and assets, while the level for managers was estimated as a function of the number of professionals. Each regression equation had high coefficients of determination, suggesting a stable and predictable relationship that could be extrapolated into the future.[25]

Computer simulations are useful in forecasting human resource needs because they can provide infinitely detailed scenarios. Thus, needs for human resources can be pinpointed for any combination of organizational and environmental variables and for a variety of HR goals. In the example that opened this chapter, planners in the Ontario public service could use computer simulations to examine the impact of varying employment equity targets and job openings assumptions to plan future human resource training and development programs. Greer, Jackson, and Fiorito found that 12.1 percent of firms used computer simulations to forecast supply of human resources and 18.2 percent used it to forecast demand.[26]

Use of Forecasting in Organizations

A review of the literature on forecasting reports greater use of sophisticated techniques in organizations in stable and somewhat complex environments. Large organizations also tend to use more sophisticated techniques.[27] A model by Stone and Fiorito suggests that technique use can be explained by decision makers' perceptions of environmental uncertainty. When uncertainty is moderately low, as in the case of stable and somewhat complex environments, forecasting is both necessary and feasible, resulting in greater use of sophisticated techniques. Less use is made of sophisticated techniques in more dynamic, uncertain environments because forecasting is less feasible in situations of greater change. Techniques are used least frequently in simple and stable environments where there is simply less need for forecasting.[28]

These hypotheses from the Stone and Fiorito models are supported by the empirical findings of Greer, Jackson, and Fiorito, who report widespread use of simple forecasting techniques in recent years' dynamic environment, swinging between growth and recession. Though the concern for the long term has increased and HRP is receiving more attention, there has been a shift to planning techniques more appropriate for relatively short horizons. HRP is being associated more strongly with systematic management development and career development. There is also a trend toward greater involvement of line managers in the HRP function.[29] At the same time, organizations seem to be moving away from the more sophisticated forecasting techniques of Markov analysis.[30] These last two observations are supported by a statement by D. Quinn Mills: "Companies that do the best job of people planning . . . [do it by] keeping the process as informal as possible and leaving the responsibility in the hands of line officers."[31]

A final comment on forecasts: Even the most careful use of the most appropriate method cannot guarantee an accurate forecast of the future. Yet even an inaccurate forecast can prove useful to an organization. If a forecast of environmental and demand changes results in anticipation and planning for human resource shortages and surpluses, it has served a purpose.

Comparing Forecast Needs with Projections of Supply

The third major step in the process of human resource planning is comparing forecast needs with projections of internal supply. By subtracting projected supply from forecast needs, planners can determine an organization's net employee requirements for a future point in time. Exhibit 4.5 is a form to help planners determine surpluses and shortages in each occupation for the next five years.

For an example, let us return to the hypothetical situation of the Ontario public service (OPS). Table 4.2 sets out the net requirements for executives

EXHIBIT 4.5
Form for Determining Surpluses and Shortages

Matching and action planning																
List occupations required and employed	Human resources available internally over the next five years					Human resources required over the next five years					Will you have a surplus or a shortage in each occupation? (subtract requirements from supply)				
	1st yr	2nd yr	3rd yr	4th yr	5th yr	1st yr	2nd yr	3rd yr	4th yr	5th yr	1st yr	2nd yr	3rd yr	4th yr	5th yr

Source: Ontario Manpower Commission, *Human Resources Planning Manual* (Toronto: Ontario Ministry of Labour, and Ontario Regional Office, Employment and Immigration Canada, 1982). © Reproduced with the permission of the Queen's Printer for Ontario and the Minister of Supply and Services Canada, 1992.

TABLE 4.2
Net Forecasted Need and Targeted Source of Supply of Executives and Managers in the Ontario Public Service: A Hypothetical Simulation

	NET FORECASTED NEED	TARGETED SOURCE OF SUPPLY Within OPS	Outside OPS
Executives			
Deputy ministers	4	2	2
Assistant deputy ministers	20	15	5
Managers			
Senior managers	75	70	5
Subtotal	99	87	12
Specialized supervisors	245	237	8
Total	**344**	**324**	**20**

and senior managers and the anticipated sources of supply for each position. The table assumes that no shortages or surpluses exist—that is, that the OPS has personnel sufficiently qualified to be promoted to the higher ranks or knows it can recruit such workers from outside. It may well be, however, that difficulty may be encountered when it comes to the specialized supervisors (who have the highest turnover rate in the executive and managerial category). Sufficient numbers may be hard to recruit within or outside the OPS. Given the existing salary structure, the OPS may have to find alternative means of meeting the forecast: either training programs within the public service or a revision in the salary structure to reflect the labour market for the specialized resources.

A comparison of the skills of specialized supervisors with the skills of other managerial positions for which no recruiting difficulty is anticipated could be useful for subsequent rounds of HRP. By anticipating future needs and the possibility of transferring people after appropriate training, HR planners may be able to reduce time lags in filling specialized positions in the future.

PLANNING POLICIES AND PROGRAMS

After determining net employee requirements, planners generate and evaluate alternative human resource policies and programs designed to handle the anticipated shortages and surpluses. They present their considerations to management, along with their recommendations on policies and programs. Exhibit 4.6 is a form to help planners perform this step.

EXHIBIT 4.6
Form for Planning Alternative Solutions

If you project mismatches in any occupation, you can start planning training and development activites.

How many people each year will you train or upgrade for each occupation?						How many people each year will you hire externally for each occupation?						How many people each year will you promote or transfer into each occupation?				
1st yr	2nd yr	3rd yr	4th yr	5th yr	1st yr	2nd yr	3rd yr	4th yr	5th yr	1st yr	2nd yr	3rd yr	4th yr	5th yr

Source: Ontario Manpower Commission, *Human Resources Planning Manual* (Toronto: Ontario Ministry of Labour, and Ontario Regional Office, Employment and Immigration Canada, 1982). © Reproduced with the permission of the Queen's Printer for Ontario and the Minister of Supply and Services Canada, 1992.

Planning for Anticipated Shortages

Anticipated labour shortages can be met in several ways. The organization can

1. Transfer employees to jobs in which shortages exist.
2. Train employees to move up to jobs in which shortages exist.
3. Have employees work overtime.
4. Increase employee productivity.
5. Hire part-time employees.
6. Hire temporary full-time employees.
7. Hire permanent full-time employees.
8. Subcontract work to other firms.
9. Forgo increases in production.
10. Install equipment to perform some of the tasks that would have been done by workers (capital substitution).

Basically, these options represent variations on three approaches: the organization can try to use its present employees better (Options 1 to 4); it can hire additional workers (Options 5 to 7); or it can seek to lower its requirements for labour (Options 8 to 10).

Utilizing Present Employees

Making better use of present employees is a very common response to a labour shortage. Simply transferring employees within the organization is, of course, not always possible. The firm may not have a surplus of workers in other jobs, or the individuals who could be transferred may not have the job skills required for the area of shortage. Overtime or training may be the more appropriate response, with the choice depending on the lead time available and the amount of training involved. In 1979, the Economic Council of Canada conducted the Human Resources Survey, a broad-based survey of employers' human resource problems and practices. Approximately half the respondents had experienced "hiring difficulties" during the previous two years; as shown in Table 4.3, 58.1 percent responded with vocational training and 37.1 with the use of overtime.[32] Similarly, a detailed study of the shortage of tool and die makers, who are highly skilled workers, found that overtime was employers' most common response; some firms also increased the number of apprentices they were training.[33] Similar responses were observed during the skills shortage experienced in 1989.[34]

Another way of countering a labour shortage with existing employees is to increase productivity. *Productivity* refers simply to the amount of product or service provided by a specific number of employees in a given unit of time. The higher the level of productivity, the fewer employees are needed

TABLE 4.3
Specific Responses to Shortage Situations 1977–1979 (*n* = 1573)

	PERCENTAGE OF ALL SITUATIONS
Training personnel	58.1
Overtime	37.1
Searching outside region	35.2
Lowering qualifications	26.9
Improving wages and benefits	23.4
Curtailing production	17.2
Subcontracting	15.7
Searching outside Canada	10.6
Capital substitution	2.5

Note: Total exceeds 100 percent because of multiple responses.

Source: Gordon Betcherman, *Meeting Skill Requirements: Report of the Human Resources Survey* (Ottawa: Economic Council of Canada, 1982), p. 33. Reproduced with the permission of the chairman of the Economic Council of Canada, 1992.

to produce a given level of output. For example, ten highly productive computer programmers may be able to do the job of fifteen less productive ones. Employee productivity can be increased in a number of ways, including

1. Offering monetary incentives, such as pay increases or bonuses, for higher productivity or performance levels.
2. Improving employees' job skills so that they can produce more or produce the same amount in less time or at a lower cost to the organization.
3. Redesigning work processes and methods (for example, using autonomous work groups, multi-skilling, and job rotation, which will be discussed in Chapter 15) so that greater outputs are achieved. (Workers often have valuable contributions to make in this regard.)
4. Using more efficient equipment so that greater outputs are achieved.

Hiring Outside the Organization

Organizations can also plan to meet anticipated labour shortages by hiring new employees. If the need appears to be permanent, new positions may be created. In other circumstances, obtaining part-time or temporary workers may be more appropriate. For example, when a shortage of nurses developed in the late 1980s, many hospitals responded by hiring part-time and/or temporary nurses from agencies.[35]

Whether the strategy is to take on part-timers or full-timers, whether to hire temporary or permanent employees, it is at this point that the state of the external labour market becomes important to the HRP process. The extent to which an organization can rely on external sources of supply depends in large part on the general state of the labour market and on the state of the market for that particular kind of labour in that particular locality.

There is a complex relationship between human resource planning at the firm level and national labour projections. National, or macro, projections attempt to project overall demand–supply situations, while an individual firm may anticipate a shortage of workers with a particular skill. The degree of success the employer can expect in recruiting workers with that skill will depend on composite developments in the relevant labour market. If there is a general excess supply, the firm should have no trouble recruiting in the external (outside of the firm) labour market. If everyone else is looking for workers with the same skill at the same time, individual employers will have difficulty recruiting the people they need.

Because national projections deal with the whole economy, their occupational categories may sometimes be broader than the categories an individual firm would use. Nevertheless, Employment and Immigration Canada's Canadian Occupational Projection System (COPS) model, which is used to project demand and supply, contains approximately 500 occupations based on the four-digit listings of the *Canadian Classification and Dictionary of Occupations (CCDO)*.[36]

These projections include estimates of changes in requirements based on projections of output and attrition through retirements and deaths, along with projections of sources of supply from training and educational institutions and immigration. An attempt is also made to estimate interoccupational transfers. The result is a system that provides projections of the general demand–supply situation in a range of occupations for Canada and the provinces. The larger the geographic area and employment base, the more specific the details. (Regional offices of Employment and Immigration Canada are the appropriate points of contact for details on the availability of specific data and the costs of obtaining them.)

Even with access to macro human resources projections, the particular organization has to do some analysis in order to understand how its recruiting could be affected by macro labour market developments. For example, even in a shortage situation, a firm that pays well or has many opportunities for promotion will have much less difficulty recruiting workers than one that pays poorly or offers limited opportunities.[37] By the same token, even in a time of high unemployment (surplus of workers), a firm with very poor wages and working conditions may have trouble finding people who are prepared to work there. HRM professionals, therefore, have to interpret broad labour market developments and projections in the light of the specific wage, working conditions, and size of the firm. A small, high-paying firm with good working conditions in a large labour market should have little trouble recruiting high-quality workers, whatever the situation in the labour market. The opposite is true of poor-paying organizations. Any quantitative analysis by

HRM professionals should be strongly supplemented by qualitative supply outlooks from provincial labour departments or the regional offices of Employment and Immigration Canada.

A study of the accuracy of Canadian macro human resource projections in the 1960s and 1970s concluded that, in general, the estimates were reasonably close to what actually occurred.[38] The results of three national occupational projections were examined.[39] In all three cases, a majority of the major occupation groups were within ±10 percent of the actual employment, while for detailed occupations a third were within ±10 percent of the actual and almost a half were within ±20 percent. A study of U.S. projections also found that results were fairly close to the actual.[40] The conclusion is that these models can provide useful information for assessing future labour market developments.

When planners are able to foresee shortages for certain types of labour, they must develop strategies to obtain the necessary human resources. In general, when labour is scarce, organizations must recruit aggressively and offer potential employees attractive inducements. Aggressive recruitment often consists of looking for candidates in another locality, even outside the country, where the shortage may not exist. For example, the Human Resources Survey found that 35.2 percent of firms that encountered shortages searched for workers in other regions and 10.6 percent looked to import labour (see Table 4.3).[41]

Inducements can be in the form of high levels of pay, generous benefits packages, or good opportunities for career advancement. Such inducements can be highly effective in recruiting. For example, in the early 1970s, Canada had a shortage of nurses. In 1974–75, the salaries of nurses increased by 50 percent and the shortage disappeared.[42] The late 1980s' shortage of nurses was likely ended by the major wage increases several provinces gave unionized hospital nurses in 1990 and 1991 and the closure of hospital beds due to budgetary restraints.

Alternative recruiting policies and programs are discussed in Chapter 6.

Other Responses

As we have seen, organizations can respond to labour shortages by adjusting their labour supplies from within or without. Three other approaches are possible: subcontracting work to other firms; forgoing increases in production; and substituting capital for labour by mechanizing jobs that have been performed by hand. Subcontracting may be a viable alternative if the labour shortage is expected to be of short duration, if the firm believes it is more important to fill orders than to delay them, or if specialized skills are available outside at cheaper cost. If the costs of recruiting are too high or the shortage is too severe, it may be necessary to forgo increasing production. For example, in the late 1970s some tool and die firms simply closed their order books since they were already booked several years in advance. In the 1980s some hospitals said that operations were postponed because of the shortage of nurses. Capital substitution is usually expensive and can be justified as an answer to a labour shortage only if the shortage looks to be of long duration. However, many organizations are turning to capital substitution in order to streamline operations and become more competitive.

PLANNING FOR ANTICIPATED SURPLUSES

In the 1960s and 1970s, planners focussed mainly on avoiding costly shortages of scarce and valued labour. In the early 1980s and the early 1990s, introduction of new technologies and reduced demand for products forced many organizations to "downsize," or reduce the size of their work force. For example, General Motors laid off workers and closed plants as part of its corporate shrinkage.[43] Thus, excess supply emerged as a growing concern of human resource planners.[44] Nearly one-quarter of employers surveyed in one study reported using human resource forecasting in order to avoid layoffs.[45]

There are a number of strategies for dealing with labour surpluses. The organization can

1. Close plants.
2. Lay off some workers permanently.
3. Give incentives for early retirement.
4. Let the work force shrink via attrition.
5. Retrain and transfer workers.
6. Shut down plants (or parts of them) temporarily.
7. Lay off workers temporarily.
8. Reduce the work week.
9. Use work sharing.
10. Cut or freeze pay and/or benefits.

These strategies represent three basic ways of dealing with surpluses. Strategies 1 to 4 require permanent work force reductions; Strategy 5 redistributes supply to areas of demand; and Strategies 6 to 10 favour retention of surplus workers with accompanying cost-saving measures.

Permanent Reductions

Drastic measures, such as plant closures and permanent layoffs, are rarely chosen lightly, yet they affect tens of thousands of Canadian workers annually and increased dramatically in the recessions of 1981–82 and the early 1990s. Such measures are usually taken in response to reductions in product demand that make continued operation impractical or impossible. Although planning seeks to avoid drastic solutions, sometimes they cannot be avoided. Planning does make it possible, however, for management to give workers advance notice of closure or layoffs. Research has shown that advance notice reduces the negative impact of layoffs on employees.[46] And as discussed in Chapter 3, many provinces required advance notice for group layoffs.

Two more attractive alternatives are letting the work force shrink by attrition and offering incentives for early retirement. Letting the work force shrink by attrition is a gradual process, requiring advance planning. It is not an emergency response but rather a method of avoiding problems of oversupply, especially in certain areas, by curtailing hiring, promotion, and transfer into jobs in which surpluses are expected (see Case 4.1).

Providing incentives for early retirement is a fairly recent solution to labour surplus problems. Early retirement programs offer incentives such as bonuses and full retirement benefits "for a limited time only" to those nearing retirement who chose to exit at the company's convenience. This is often referred to as a window of opportunity. One problem with early retirement programs is that they are offered across the board to all employees who have reached a certain predetermined age, length of service, or combination of the two. The result is sometimes the loss of employees the company would like to retain. Early retirement programs may also be quite costly. However, they are viewed by many as a humane alternative to layoffs. International Business Machines (IBM), Imperial Oil, Ontario Hydro, Air Canada, and Sears are examples of companies that have at one time or another offered incentives for early retirement.

Redistribution of Workers

Redistribution of workers is a possibility if surpluses exist in some areas but not others. This option requires advance planning since displaced workers must often acquire new skills in order to be useful in areas of increased demand. Unfortunately, programs of retraining and transfer are rare. One company that adopted this approach is IBM, using a combination of human resource planning, training, and transfer to achieve a balance among units in its work force. Where surpluses existed, qualified and interested employees were trained in new capacities and equipped for second careers in the company. Successful program participants included obsolete assemblers who became clerical workers, engineers who worked as computer programmers, and technicians who transferred to customer service.[47] Although IBM Canada is currently using attrition and early retirement severance packages to reduce employment, the company still maintains a policy of redistributing employees, as demonstrated by its recent efforts to retrain and shift employees from administrative positions to customer support.[48]

Cost-Saving Measures

Cost-saving measures include temporary shutdown, temporary layoffs, reduced work weeks, work-sharing programs, and cuts or freezes in pay. Under a reduced work week, employees work fewer hours and receive reduced pay. Under work-sharing programs, employees work reduced hours and receive unemployment insurance (UI) benefits for hours not worked. Canada experimented with a program of work sharing between 1977 and 1979, and then reintroduced it in 1981 in the face of a substantial increase in unemployment. Demand for the work-sharing program increased again in the recession of the early 1990s.[49] The program permits workers to draw UI for part of the week without losing entitlement to future UI benefits. For example, instead of laying off, say, a fifth of its staff, a firm reduces the work week for all employees in a unit from five to four days, and the workers receive UI benefits for the fifth day.[50] Local managers and employees like the program, but employer associations and union federations have reservations; the former fear a demand for permanent reduction in the work week, and union officials see the program as reducing government efforts to counter recession.[51] (Human resource managers can obtain information on the UI-assisted work-sharing program from the local Canada Employment Centre.) Some unions and companies have negotiated provisions for work sharing, but the number is very small. In 1991, only 2 percent of collective agreements in Canada included a clause either applying work sharing or agreeing to discuss work sharing.[52]

During the recession of the early 1990s, pay freezes and even pay cuts occurred in both the public and the private sector. The most visible example of a pay freeze was the one imposed on federal government employees in the fall of 1991. In 1992, employees of Algoma Steel agreed to take a pay cut as part of a plan negotiated by the firm and the United Steelworkers of America that will see Algoma become a worker-owned company.[53]

EVALUATING THE ALTERNATIVES

After generating alternative approaches to solving anticipated labour shortages or surpluses, HR planners must evaluate the alternatives and select the best for recommendation to management. Many considerations affect choice of a planning strategy; three basic ones are: (1) size of the anticipated shortages or surpluses; (2) expected duration of the change in demand for human resources; and (3) amount of lead time before shortages or surpluses occur.

The size of a shortage or surplus affects the choice of a planning strategy. Small shortages can usually be handled by transferring employees in from other jobs, by attention to methods of improving employee productivity (including introduction of more efficient equipment and use of short training programs), by making heavy use of overtime, and by hiring temporary employees. Large shortages, on the other hand, usually require employers to use external sources of permanent labour, since internal supplies are usually inadequate to meet the demand. Small surpluses can usually be managed by transferring employees, by reducing work hours, and by curtailing hiring or promotion in that area. In the case of large surpluses in one area and shortages in another, it may be cost-effective for an organization to train surplus employees to assume the responsibilities of jobs in which there are shortages. Temporary and permanent layoffs are more appropriate when surpluses are great than when they are small.

Another factor affecting choice of a planning strategy is the expected duration of the change in demand. If the change is only temporary, temporary solutions often suffice. Many seasonal businesses, for example, must plan for wide variation in both duration and magnitude of demand. Toy manufacturers, seed companies, and gift-wrap manufacturers, for example, experience such variation regularly. In fact, its very predictability aids HRP.

Labour shortages of short duration can be handled by hiring additional, usually temporary, employees. Forecasts of long shortages, on the other hand, require consideration and implementation of many human resource policies and programs, including recruiting, hiring, and training. The costs associated with these programs can be large, especially if they involve skilled or professional workers. Short-duration surpluses are usually met with temporary layoffs or plant shutdowns, but in cases that involve skilled and professional workers, the potential cost of eventual replacement may be greater than the cost of maintaining surplus people. Employers may thus retain skilled workers during short-duration surpluses, rather than risk their finding other employment while they are laid off. Medium-duration surpluses are sometimes handled by temporary adoption of a three- or four-day work week. Long-duration surpluses invariably require the termination of employees and/or the heavy use of shrinkage by attrition and incentives for early retirement.

Regardless of the magnitude or duration of shortages and surpluses, they can almost certainly be handled more effectively if an organization has sufficient lead time to prepare for them. Surprise changes in the supply–demand equation for labour are costly to both employer and employee. Without ample lead time, an organization has a limited number of responses available. Surprises can usually be avoided by constant, careful monitoring of the economic, legislative, technological, and cultural environments.

Human resource planners can make a major contribution to organizational effectiveness and profitability by providing managers with alternative strategies for solving labour-supply problems. Planners should provide management with information on each alternative concerning

1. Its financial and human costs and benefits.
2. Its effects on other organizational components, such as units not directly affected by the labour problem.
3. The length of time required to execute it.
4. Its probable effectiveness in reducing the shortage or surplus.

There are three mathematically sophisticated methods useful in evaluating alternative human resource programs and in determining optimal combinations of human resources, money, and time. These methods are linear programming, goal programming, and computer simulation.

Linear Programming

Linear programming is a mathematical technique that provides an optimal solution for reaching a quantitative goal, such as minimizing total labour costs within a number of conditions or constraints. Linear programming begins with the selection of a goal or variable, such as labour costs, training time, or some other quantifiable factor. Next, planners select the major factors or constraints that affect and determine the goal to be optimized. For example, university administrators could use linear programming to determine the minimum cost of handling an undergraduate enrolment of 1500 within the constraints of certain maximum class sizes and numbers of instructors in various ranks. A linear programming solution would specify the values of each constraint necessary to handle the given enrolment at minimal (optimal) cost. Linear programming also provides planners with information on which constraints have some slack and which don't.

This method eliminates unfeasible solutions. If, for example, constraints of a maximum class size of 30 and a maximum faculty of 50 result in an unfeasible solution, additional linear programs could be run using different constraints to reach a feasible solution. The use of linear programming is limited by the necessity of specifying the goal and all constraints in quantitative terms.

Goal Programming

Goal programming is a more sophisticated and realistic version of linear programming that includes stochastic models and permits specification of multiple goals. Multiple goals such as increasing profits by 10 percent, maintaining current quality levels, *and* hiring bilingual salespeople are typical of the realities managers face.

Goal programming is a method of finding optimal solutions for a number of goals in combination. For example, the Ontario public service may want to reach its employment equity targets while

1. Increasing the proportion of the less-than-25-years age group to 10 percent of all staff.
2. Maintaining the proportion of the 25-to-34-years age group at 26 percent of all staff.
3. Having an external hiring rate of 30 percent.

Of course, any one of these goals may be more important than another. Goal programming can provide a solution that takes such priorities into account.

Goal programming was developed by the Office of Civilian Personnel in the U.S. Navy. Because of its complexity and associated costs, its use has been limited to large organizations, primarily the military and other government organizations.

Computer Simulation

Computer simulation was discussed earlier as a method of forecasting human resource needs. It can also be used to examine the effects of alternative policies and programs to reduce forecast shortages and surpluses. By considering each alternative in relation to the simulated human resource system, it provides an assessment of the probable effects of a policy or program on various components of the system or the system as a whole. These data form the basis for comparing one alternative with another in order to determine which can best serve an organization's purposes. The use of computers is now an integral part of human resource information systems. Two recent examples of detailed discussions on the use of computers are set out in works by Kavanagh, Guental, and Tannenbaum, and Forrer and Leibowitz.[54]

EVALUATING HUMAN RESOURCE PLANNING EFFECTIVENESS

Organizations should evaluate their human resource planning efforts to determine their effectiveness in helping to achieve organizational goals and objectives.[55] Evaluating in terms of costs and benefits is difficult. The costs are fairly clear, but the benefits are more intangible and difficult to measure.

For this reason, the benefits of human resource planning are often expressed not in positive terms but as the avoidance of costly problems, such as labour shortages, which can result in lost sales or other lost business opportunities. There are also benefits associated with avoiding oversupply. Surpluses can result in an organization's paying excessive wages and benefits and in boredom and low morale among employees who have little opportunity to be productive.

Evaluating the effectiveness of HRP is sometimes difficult since what is in the best interests of an employer may not be in the best interests of employees or the community. For example, a strategy of downsizing through layoffs and early retirement may benefit the company but demoralize many employees. Laid-off workers may argue that HRP has been ineffective in their organization, yet the layoff strategy may have resulted in greater profitability and higher prices of the company's shares. The HRP process may be regarded as successful if HRM staff have been able to alert and work with top management regarding likely labour shortages and surpluses. The fact that forecasting occurs, that potential shortages and surpluses are identified, and that alternative approaches are examined — these are all signs of an effective HRM function.

Since HRP seeks to forecast human resource needs, an obvious measure of its effectiveness is how well human resource needs are anticipated and met. One measure of the effective anticipation of human resource needs is the number of job vacancies in an organization and how long they remain vacant. Large numbers of jobs standing vacant for long periods of time indicate an organization's failure to plan effectively for its human resource needs.

The effectiveness of human resource planning can also be evaluated according to the purposes stated at the beginning of this chapter. Pertinent questions include the following:

1. How useful is human resource planning in setting organizational goals and objectives?
2. Does the planning process provide management with the information it needs to make sound decisions affecting policies and programs?
3. Is management willing to consider inputs from the planning process in setting organizational goals and in making policy and planning decisions? It is difficult for any planning process to achieve its aims without the co-operation and blessing of management.

THE HRM AUDIT

The *HRM* or *personnel audit* is a comprehensive examination of the effectiveness of all aspects of personnel and industrial relations in an organization.[56] It serves as a control function evaluating effectiveness of the human resource area.

An HRM auditing model focusses on HRM practices at three levels within an organization:

1. Strategic-level HRM. An audit at this level analyzes, from top management's perspective, how effectively HRM functions are being integrated into the overall strategic plan of the organization.
2. Managerial-level HRM. An audit at this level analyzes, from both the line managers' and the HR department manager's perspective, how effectively HRM functions are being managed and performed within departments and units.
3. Operational-level HRM. An audit at this level analyzes, from the human resource specialists' perspective, how effectively HRM functions are being performed throughout the entire organization.[57]

Organizations may conduct periodic HRM audits for several reasons. First, since labour costs are a large, if not the largest, component of total product or service costs, it is logical that management should utilize some control over the human resource area. Second, HRM staff may use personnel audit data to justify the existence and budgets of their staff and programs.[58] A third valuable function of the audit is that it provides, like other control mechanisms, valuable feedback from employees and line managers. This feedback may be used to modify and improve various HRM programs and policies to make more efficient use of human resources. Audits may also uncover problems such as unqualified HRM staff, lack of understanding of or compliance with human resource policies by line managers, and low levels of employee satisfaction with various policies and programs. Excessive absenteeism, turnover, or difficulty hiring adequate numbers of qualified employees may, for example, indicate needed changes in compensation, recruiting methods, and perhaps supervisor training. Thus, the HRM audit serves as an information-gathering process and as the basis for changes in policy and practice.

An HRM audit may utilize many types of data collected from many sources.[59] Some of the more common data used are the ratio of HRM staff to employees, changes in number of employees over several time periods, turnover, absenteeism, compensation and benefit costs, number of grievances filed, and number of workplace injuries. Additional sources of audit data that are sometimes used include surveys of employee attitudes toward various HRM programs and policies and managerial perceptions of HRM programs and their results. Some types of data, such as absences, must be continually collected, while others, such as surveys, are collected only periodically. There are, of course, many other sources of data that may be useful for HRM audit purposes. Some audit procedures include a descriptive component in which the major activities of the HRM unit are identified and compared with policies and procedures for internal consistency.

A study of an insurance company and a hospital provides insights into typical audit findings.[60] At the insurance company, the presence of an acting manager of human resources, instead of a permanent one, caused the HR staff to feel a lack of power and direction; operating managers also felt that the situation reduced the effectiveness of the HR unit. They also felt that the lack of an in-house training program hindered performance and that the performance rating form was ineffective and needed updating. Managers in the hospital, on the other hand, felt their HR department was too authoritarian and controlling and should serve in an advisory role. The audit of the hospital also revealed that recruiting and hiring policies needed to be centrally co-ordinated, rather than left to individual departments, and job descriptions, career counselling, exit interviews, and turnover statistics needed to be improved.

A study of 26 independent plants of a large electronics manufacturer examined the relationship between 37 personnel audit measures, executive perceptions, and magnitude of personnel budget on a per-capita basis.[61] This study found that the 37 audit measures resulted in nine factors representing the major HRM functions plus one factor related to managerial behaviour and a second to policies and procedures. High levels of employee satisfaction with personnel units were associated with high scores on the staffing and compensation aspects of the audit. The importance of staffing and compensation in this company is apparent from this finding. The results indicated that the magnitude of the personnel budget per capita is positively related to three factors: (1) net profits per capita, (2) employee satisfaction with personnel, and (3) executives' perception of the overall contribution of personnel to achievement of organizational goals. This finding suggests a relationship between effectiveness of the HRM area and profitability. There is, therefore, some evidence that the HRM audit is useful for describing and evaluating HRM functions, as well as being related to executive perceptions of personnel.

Though the benefits of conducting periodic HRM audits appear to outweigh their costs, few employers conduct thorough audits on a regular basis. A survey of 300 human resource professionals found that only 32 percent of those responding evaluate the HR department at least annually; 29 percent seldom or never conduct such an evaluation. The report on the survey concluded that human resource departments are not being evaluated to the proper degree, they are not making use of all the information available to them, and too many rely on too informal a process of having their own people pass judgement on the quality of what the department is doing. The survey also found that more frequent evaluation appears to facilitate the adoption of more rigorous, financially oriented evaluation techniques and to break down the perceived obstacles to evaluation (see Case 4.2).[62]

Some employers may evaluate various programs and policies only when there are indications of problems such as high turnover, high labour costs, or low quality or quantity of output. The more systematic HRM audit offers benefits to both HRM and operating managers.

SUMMARY

This chapter dealt with one of the most significant HRM functions, human resource planning. Economic, technological, and legislative changes are leading more employers to seek professionals with human resource planning skills. The growing importance of skilled labour is further increasing the use of human resource planning in top management decisions. As human resource planning grows in importance and usage, methods of forecasting, projection, and simulation are being refined.

Human resource planning is an important development for the HRM profession since it requires a systematic and goal-oriented approach to all major HRM functions, from recruiting to training and development, to compensation. It links human resources to organizational goals and leads to a systematic evaluation of the effectiveness of all human resource programs. Finally, it requires managers and HRM professionals to consider human resource programs as interrelated, rather than as separate and distinct. Considering the relative costs and benefits of a policy of hiring experienced, trained employees, as opposed to hiring inexperienced employees and training them, is an example of an approach to a planning problem that recognizes the interrelatedness of the separate HRM functions.

Review Questions

1. Some people claim "it is a waste of time and resources for an organization to undertake human resource planning because the plans may be obsolete by the time they are completed." Discuss this statement. Include in your answer the benefits gained from the HRP process even when the underlying assumptions have to be altered.

2. a. Explain the reason why projecting human resource supply is the first step in the HRP process.
   b. Discuss the role of HRP in influencing organizational objectives.

3. Outline the criteria used to determine the best approach to forecasting human resource needs in a particular organization. Indicate the commonly used methods of demand forecasting.

4. Explain what is meant by an HRM audit, and discuss how it can benefit an organization, particularly one that is either downsizing or regrouping.

Project Ideas

1. Locate a manager or an HRM professional in an organization engaged in human resource planning. Interview this individual on the nature of the planning effort, and relate the details in a written report. Find out what type of human resource planning is done (short-, medium-, or long-range) and how often. Do forecasts make subjective estimates, or are quantitative models used? What kind of human resource information system does the organization have and how is it used in making forecasts? Who in the organization is involved in human resource planning, and how do the planning efforts affect other human resource functions in the organization? If a number of students in the class conduct such interviews, oral reports can be given, demonstrating a range of real-world planning activities.

2. Construct a hypothetical city and forecast its need for parking meter collectors. (In other words, create a hypothetical situation on which to base forecasts of the need for parking meter collectors.) Give such descriptive details as population, proportion of the population that drives to work, number of parking meters, and so on. Be specific and include in your description of the city as many pieces of information as you can think of that could affect your forecast of the need for meter collectors. After describing your hypothetical city, forecast its need for parking meter collectors. Describe the rationale(s) behind your forecast. Did you use any rules of thumb or other forecasting methods?

3. Develop a simple transition matrix for a small group or organization. Categorize people according to their position in the organization (for example, "first year," "second year," "retiree," and so on). Record each person's position at the present time, and then, several months later, record each person's position again. Record, in a table such as the one shown here, how many people have remained in the same position or category and how many have moved to each of the other possible categories. If there is much movement between categories, suggest possible causes. (The purpose of this exercise is to give you a better understanding of the operation of flow factors.)

PROJECT 4.1
Transition Matrix

NUMBER OF PERSONS IN POSITION OR CATEGORY FOR TIME 1	NUMBER OF PERSONS IN POSITION OR CATEGORY FOR TIME 2				
	Pos. 1	Pos. 2	Pos. 3	Pos. 4	Pos. 5
Pos. 1					
Pos. 2					
Pos. 3					
Pos. 4					
Pos. 5					

▶▶▶ CASES

CASE 4.1 ▶ ONTARIO HYDRO'S CORPORATE PLANNING PROCESS

At the beginning of the 1980s, Ontario Hydro, one of the world's largest publicly owned utilities, had 30 000 employees. By the end of the decade, it had 25 000 employees and had declared redundant 2000 jobs, many of them in middle management.

The company's formalized, integrated corporate planning process was not established until the early 1980s. Before the 1970s, corporate planning at Ontario Hydro was characterized by fragmentation, and planning centred mainly around the design, development, and construction of facilities. Rarely was a thought given to a plan's human resource implications; rather, it was assumed that the necessary human support systems would be available, and they were, for the most part, in the predictable environment of the 1950s and 1960s. These were times when growth was steady and demand for the company's product could easily be forecast.

In the 1970s, the company's environment became less predictable, increasing its need for planning. The demand for energy decreased, and it became more difficult to find capital for purposes of expansion. Certain types of labour were also harder to find; for example, engineers were in short supply because of growth in the energy industry. (This situation reversed itself, however, after the recession of the early 1980s, when engineers were once again plentiful.) Other forces contributing to the uncertain environment of the 1970s were increased government intervention and changing employee attitudes toward work.

In the mid-1970s, Ontario Hydro separated its planning and administrative functions from operations in order to consolidate the planning function, which is co-ordinated by the Planning and Administrative Group. Three planning processes evolved and are now in use:

1. Corporate strategic planning, which is intended to provide a corporate vision to guide the next twenty years.
2. Corporate reference planning, a medium-term, ten-year time frame that translates the strategic plan into a committed facilities plan.
3. Work program planning and budgeting, which covers the short-term (one to three years) and provides specific work plans and resource approvals for the next twelve months.

HRP is an integral part of each planning process; in fact, policy dictates that human resource requirements be forecast as a part of other forecasts. Policy also dictates that "managers at all levels shall engage in human resource planning as an integrated and supporting part of work program planning."

During strategic planning, the human resource implications of alternative strategies are considered, and long-range forecasts of human resource requirements are prepared. In corporate reference planning, alternative plans are assessed as to whether their human resource implications are manageable. Such assessment requires close monitoring of the internal work force, as well as external monitoring of labour market trends. To monitor the internal work force, Ontario Hydro has developed a variety of analytical tools and systems that allow it to monitor work force demographics, staff flows, and employee capabilities.

Ontario Hydro's scenario for the 1990s is one of slow growth and environmental uncertainty. In order to adapt, the company must increase productivity while decreasing the size of its work force. To do this, Hydro has set up an elaborate process to help displaced employees find other jobs within the company. The process includes career assessment, training in interviewing skills, and advice on how to network within the company to find work. Bob Franklin, president and chairman of Hydro, decided to redeploy staff to areas where there was a need and allow attrition to reduce the overall size of the staff. Franklin reports that he has been criticized for choosing to redeploy instead of firing staff.

Source: Based on Margot Gibb-Clark, "'Redeploying' the Key Strategy in Ontario Hydro Job Reduction," *The Globe and Mail*, May 10, 1989. Used with the permission of *The Globe and Mail*; and J.C. Rush and L.C. Borne, "Human Resources Planning Contributions to Corporate Planning at Ontario Hydro," *Human Resource Planning*, vol. 6, no. 4 (1983), pp. 193–205. Used with the permission of *Human Resource Planning*.

TASKS AND QUESTIONS

1. What factors contributed to the need for corporate planning at Ontario Hydro? Discuss how each may affect the need for planning.

2. Ontario Hydro saw little need for human resource planning before the 1970s. Why? What benefits, if any, are to be gained by using human resource planning in a fairly predictable environment?

3. What do you think of Ontario Hydro's policy requiring strategic planners to consider the human resource requirements of plans? What are some advantages and disadvantages of such a policy?

4. What do you think of Ontario Hydro's strategy for downsizing? Discuss the pros and cons. Under what circumstances might Hydro's top management consider changing the strategy?

CASE 4.2 ▸ EVALUATING HR DEPARTMENTS

Attempts to find out the extent to which human resource departments are evaluated have tended to be qualitative, relying, for example, on case studies that are out of date.

Because of the inconsistency in existing information, researchers at Iowa State University developed a survey to study how organizations evaluate the effectiveness of their HR departments. The survey gathered data on the frequency with which organizations evaluated the effectiveness of their human resource departments, the specific measures of effectiveness used, and the obstacles to evaluation.

Questionnaires were sent to 300 human resource professionals randomly selected from companies listed in the 1988 edition of *A Directory of Those Who Manage the Leading 1000 Listed U.S. Companies*. Of the 300 questionnaires sent, 74 were returned, for a response rate of more than 24 percent.

The first issue addressed in the questionnaire was how often companies evaluate the effectiveness of their human resource departments. The results indicated inconsistency in these evaluations: Thirty-two percent of the responding organizations evaluate the HR department at least annually, but a nearly equal number—29 percent—seldom or never conduct such an evaluation. The average responses of the 66 firms that do conduct evaluations indicate more frequent reliance on judgmental processes and qualitative measures than on quantitative and scientifically proven evaluation techniques.

The survey also revealed that the evaluation of a human resource department is most likely to be conducted by someone in HR. Outside consultants or auditors are seldom brought in to perform the evaluation function. Organizations tend to evaluate their HR departments' effectiveness informally. That is, they rely on their own people to pass judgement on the quality of what the department is doing.

The biggest perceived obstacle to evaluating HR department effectiveness is the problem of conducting a scientific evaluation. This corresponds with the finding that outside academic consultants are seldom used to conduct evaluations and that techniques which foster scientific inquiry, such as control groups, are seldom used. Contrary to traditional research on evaluation, lack of top management support, the misuse of evaluation results and the anxiety associated with being evaluated pose few evaluation problems for these respondents.

Respondents of firms with an HR mission statement reported significantly more frequent evaluations of their HR departments than did those in firms without a mission statement. However, there were very few differences in how they actually carried out those evaluations.

Firms with an HR mission statement reported more frequent use of HR records, work analyses, and pre- and post-course evaluations than did firms without such mission statements, but no differences were found in the frequency with which other evaluation techniques are used.

The use of more quantitative techniques for evaluation was more evident in those firms that evaluate their HR departments more often. Specifically, firms that evaluate HR more often reported using analysis of results compared to standards, budget analysis, pre- and post-course evaluations, analysis of HR records, ROI, cost/benefit ratios, human resource accounting techniques and the use of formulas to a greater degree than did respondents in firms that conduct HR evaluations infrequently.

The implications of the results are clear. Human resource departments are not being evaluated to the proper degree. Indeed, one might argue that human resource professionals are not adequately making the case for the value of their departments to the organization because they are not making use of all the information available to them.

Moreover, results indicate that the process is far too informal. While this is not surprising, it does raise the question of why more formal methods are not used, particularly by HR professionals in the leading 1000 companies.

The obstacles most often cited by researchers and practitioners as impediments to evaluation—lack of adequately defined objectives, fear of evaluation, and lack of top management support—are not perceived as problematic in practice.

Finally, the results of this survey show that the process of evaluation itself creates an upward spiral. More frequent evaluation appears to facilitate the adoption of more rigorous, financially oriented evaluation techniques and to break down the perceived obstacles to evaluation.

Source: Margaret E. Cashman, and James C. McElroy, "Evaluating the HR Function," *HRMagazine*, vol. 36, no. 1 (January 1991), pp. 70–73. Reprinted with the permission of *HRMagazine* (formerly *Personnel Administrator*), published by the Society for Human Resource Management, Alexandria, Va.

TASKS AND QUESTIONS

1. Why do organizations often use someone in the HR department to evaluate the department rather than someone outside who could be more impartial?

2. What connection can you see between having a mission statement and the frequency of evaluation of HR departments?

3. What connection can you see between the frequency of evaluation of HR departments and the use of more quantitative evaluation techniques?

4. Discuss the following statement:

   Human resource departments are not adequately making the case for the value of their department to the organization because they are not making use of all the information available to them.

NOTES

1. James W. Walker, "Human Resource Roles for the '90s," *Human Resource Planning*, vol. 12, no. 1 (1989), pp. 55–61.

2. Tricia McCallum, "One of Noma's Brightest Lights, High Profile and High-Powered, Claude Saillant Is an HR Maverick," *Human Resources Professional*, December 1989, pp. 8–13.

3. Peter E. Drucker, "The Coming of the New Organization," *Harvard Business Review*, January–February 1988, p. 48.

4. James W. Walker, "Human Resource Planning, 1990s Style," *Human Resource Planning*, vol. 13, no. 4 (1990), pp. 229–40.

5. Ontario, Human Resources Secretariat, *Strategies for Renewal: Strategic Human Resource Planning in the Ontario Public Service 1991–1992* (Toronto, 1990); and Ontario, Human Resources Secretariat, *Strategies for Renewal: Stra-*

tegic *Human Resources Planning in the Ontario Public Service, Progress Report 1990* (Toronto, March 31, 1991), pp. 22–23.

6. Ontario, Human Resources Secretariat, *Strategies for Renewal: Human Resource Planning in the Ontario Public Service 1991–1992*, pp. 22–23.

7. Daniel de Vise, "IBM's New Policy Targets Unproductive Workers," *The Toronto Star*, October 14, 1991.

8. Carolyn Leitch, "IBM Canada to Slash 2,000 Jobs," *The Globe and Mail*, November 29, 1991.

9. Kendrith M. Rowland and Scott L. Summers, "Human Resource Planning: A Second Look," *Personnel Administrator*, December 1981, p. 78.

10. R.J. Clifford and Associates, *Survey of Manpower Planning Practices in Canada* (Ottawa: Employment and Immigration Canada, 1981).

11. Gordon Betcherman, *Meeting Skill Requirements: Report of the Human Resources Survey* (Ottawa: Economic Council of Canada, 1982).

12. Rowland and Summers, "Human Resource Planning," p. 79. Reprinted with the permission of *HRMagazine* (formerly *Personnel Administrator*), published by the Society for Human Resource Management, Alexandria, Va.

13. For articles on related subjects, see L. Moore and L. Charach, eds., *Manpower Planning for Canadians: An Anthology*, 2nd ed. (Vancouver: The Institute of Industrial Relations, University of British Columbia, 1979); and Walker, "Human Resource Planning, 1990s Style."

14. See Lee Dyer, "Linking Human Resource and Business Strategies," *Human Resource Planning*, vol. 7, no. 2 (1984), pp. 79–84; Dave Ulrich, "Strategic Human Resource Planning: Why and How?" *Human Resource Planning*, vol. 10, no. 1 (1987), pp. 37–56; and Lee Dyer, ed., *Human Resource Management, Evolving Roles and Responsibilities*, American Society for Personnel Administration (ASPA) Bureau of National Affairs (BNA) series (Washington, DC: Bureau of National Affairs, 1988).

15. J.W. Walker and M.N. Wolfe, "Patterns in Human Resource Planning Practices," *Human Resource Planning*, vol. 1, no. 4 (1978), p. 199. Reprinted with permission.

16. See Ontario Manpower Commission, *Human Resource Planning: An Introduction* (Toronto: Ontario Ministry of Labour, 1985).

17. V.H. Vroom and K.R. MacCrimmon, "Toward a Stochastic Model of Management Careers," *Administrative Science Quarterly*, vol. 13, no. 1 (June 1968), pp. 26–46.

18. J.W. Walker, *Human Resource Planning* (New York: McGraw-Hill, 1980), p. 24. Reproduced with the permission of McGraw-Hill, Inc.

19. Charles R. Greer, Dana L. Jackson, and Jack Fiorito, "Adopting Human Resource Planning in a Changing Business Environment," *Human Resource Management*, vol. 28, no. 1 (Spring 1989), p. 110.

20. Mark Ellsworth, "Focus on Succession Planning: Can It Exist in an Employment Equity Environment?" *Human Resource Professional*, August 1990, pp. 20–23.

21. Albert B. Drui, "The Use of Regression Equations to Predict Manpower Requirements," in Moore and Charach, eds., *Manpower Planning for Canadians*, pp. 393–403.
22. Greer, Jackson, and Fiorito, "Adopting Human Resource Planning," p. 110.
23. G. Milkovich, A.J. Annoni, and T.A. Mahoney. "The Use of Delphi Procedures in Manpower Forecasting," *Management Science*, vol. 19, no. 4 (1972), pp. 381–88.
24. *The Impact of Technological Change on Human Resources in Health Care*, prepared by the Canadian Hospital Association for Employment and Immigration Canada, Canadian Occupational Projection System (Ottawa, 1990).
25. Robert H. Meehan and S. Basheer Ahmed, "Forecasting Human Resources Requirements: A Demand Model," *Human Resources Planning*, vol. 13, no. 4 (1990), pp. 297–307.
26. Greer, Jackson, and Fiorito, "Adopting Human Resource Planning," p. 110.
27. Thomas H. Stone and Jack Fiorito, "A Perceived Uncertainty Model of Human Resource Forecasting Technique Use," *Academy of Management Review*, vol. 11, no. 3 (July 1986), pp. 635–42.
28. Stone and Fiorito, "A Perceived Uncertainty Model."
29. Walker, "Human Resource Planning, 1990s Style."
30. Greer, Jackson, and Fiorito, "Adopting Human Resource Planning," pp. 116–17.
31. D. Quinn Mills, "Planning with People in Mind." *Harvard Business Review*, vol. 63, no. 4 (1985), pp. 97–105.
32. Betcherman, *Meeting Skill Requirements*, p. 33.
33. Noah M. Meltz, *Economic Analysis of Labour Shortages: The Case of Tool and Die Makers in Ontario* (Toronto: Ontario Economic Council, 1982), pp. 32–35.
34. Gregor Robinson, "The Skills Shortage and What to Do About It," *Challenges*, vol. 2, no. 1 (Winter 1989), pp. 8–13.
35. Noah M. Meltz with Jill Marzeti, *The Shortage of Registered Nurses: An Analysis in a Labour Market Context* (Toronto: Registered Nurses' Association of Ontario, 1988).
36. Employment and Immigration Canada, *Job Futures: An Occupational Outlook to 1995, Volume 1: Occupational Outlooks*, 1990 ed., prepared by the Canadian Occupational Projection System (COPS) (Toronto: Nelson Canada, 1990); Manpower and Immigration Canada, *Canadian Classification and Dictionary of Occupations* (Ottawa: Information Canada, 1971). Additional definitions and recent changes in the *CCDO* are in Employment and Immigration Canada, *Canadian Classification and Dictionary of Occupations, Guide*, 9th ed. (Ottawa: Supply and Services Canada, 1989).
37. Noah M. Meltz and John H. Blakely, *Linking Firms' and Macro Human Resource Planning* (Toronto: Ontario Manpower Commission, Ontario Ministry of Labour, 1984).

38. David K. Foot and Noah M. Meltz, "An Ex Post Evaluation of Canadian Occupational Projections, 1961–1981," *Relations Industrielles*, vol. 47, no. 2 (1992), pp. 268–78; and *Canadian Occupational Projections: An Analysis of the Economic Determinants 1961–1981* (Hull, Que.: Employment and Immigration Canada, 1987).

39. The three projections examined were N.M. Meltz and G.P. Penz, *Canada's Manpower Requirements in 1970*, Department of Manpower and Immigration (Ottawa: Queen's Printer, 1968); B. Ahamad, *A Projection of Manpower Requirements by Occupation in 1975, Canada and Its Regions*, Department of Manpower and Immigration (Ottawa: Queen's Printer, 1969); and Canadian Occupational Forecasting Program, *Forecasts of Occupational Demand to 1982*, Department of Manpower and Immigration (Ottawa: Information Canada, 1975).

40. R.B. Freeman, "An Empirical Analysis of the Fixed Coefficient, 'Manpower Requirements' Model, 1960–1970," *The Journal of Human Resources*, vol. 15, no. 2 (Winter 1980), pp. 176–99.

41. Betcherman, *Meeting Skill Requirements*, p. 33.

42. David Stager and Noah M. Meltz, "Manpower Planning in the Professions," *The Canadian Journal of Higher Education*, vol. 7, no. 3 (1977), p. 79.

43. Jacquie McNish, "Corporate Dinosaurs Leaving Some Fossils Behind," *The Globe and Mail*, December 23, 1991.

44. In spite of the labour surpluses in the early 1990s, some projections based on demographic trends forecast labour shortages in the late 1990s, especially for workers less than 25 years of age. See David K. Foot, *Population Aging and the Canadian Labour Force*, discussion paper on the demographic review (Ottawa: Institute for Research on Public Policy, January 1987).

45. C.R. Greer and D. Armstrong, "Human Resource Forecasting and Planning: A State-of-the-Art Investigation," *Human Resource Planning*, vol. 3, no. 2 (1980), pp. 67–78.

46. J.P. Gordus, P. Jarley, and L.A. Ferman, *Plant Closings and Economic Dislocation* (Kalamazoo, Mich.: W.E. Upjohn Institute, 1981), pp. 124–26.

47. Beverly Jacobson, *Young Programs for Older Workers* (New York: Van Nostrand Reinhold, 1980), p. 12.

48. Leitch, "IBM Canada to Slash 2,000 Jobs."

49. A. Freeman, "Ottawa Doubles UI Work-Sharing Money," *The Globe and Mail*, September 19, 1990; and Leslie Papp, "Bridging the Gap, Labor, Management Find Innovative Ways to Keep Peace in Tough Times," *The Toronto Star*, March 7, 1992.

50. N.M. Meltz, F. Reid, and G.S. Swartz, *Sharing the Work: An Analysis of the Issues in Worksharing and Job Sharing* (Toronto: University of Toronto Press, 1981).

51. Noah M. Meltz and Frank Reid, "Reducing the Impact of Unemployment Through Worksharing: Some Industrial Relations Considerations," *Journal of Industrial Relations*, vol. 25 (June 1983), pp. 152–60.

52. Labour Canada, *Provisions in Collective Agreements*, special tabulation (Ottawa: Bureau of Labour Information, October 22, 1991).

53. Virginia Galt, "Algoma Workers Take Pay Cut to Own Mill," *The Globe and Mail*, April 16, 1992.

54. Michael J. Kavanagh, Hal G. Guental, and Scott I. Tannenbaum, *Human Resource Information Systems: Development and Application* (Boston: PWS-Kent, 1990); and Stephen E. Forrer and Zandy B. Leibowitz, eds., *Using Computers in Human Resources* (San Francisco: Josey-Bass, 1991). See specifically Chapters 8 and 9 of Kavanagh, Guental, and Tannenbaum; and Meryl Reis Louis, "Using Computers to Support Strategic Management of Human Resources," in Forrer and Leibowitz, pp. 54–81.

55. See Annie S. Tsui and Luis R. Gomez-Mejia, "Evaluating Human Resource Effectiveness," in Dyer, ed., *Human Resource Management, Evolving Roles and Responsibilities*, pp. 187–227.

56. See George E. Biles and Randall S. Schuler, *Audit Handbook of Human Resource Management Practices* (Alexandria, Va.: American Society for Personnel Administration, 1986).

57. George E. Biles, "Auditing HRM Practices," *Personnel Administrator*, vol. 31, no. 12 (December 1986), pp. 89–93. Used with the permission of *HRMagazine* (formerly *Personnel Administrator*), published by the Society for Human Resource Management, Alexandria, Va.

58. D.E. Dimick and V.V. Murray, "Correlates of Substantive Policy Decisions in Organizations: The Case of Human Resource Management," *Academy of Management Journal*, vol. 21 (1978), pp. 611–23.

59. For a discussion of the factors that influence the size of an organization's human resources staff, see James W. Walker, "How Large Should the HR Staff Be?" *Personnel*, October 1988, pp. 36–42.

60. T. Hercus and D. Oades, "The Human Resource Audit: An Instrument for Change," *Human Resource Planning*, vol. 5, no. 1 (1982), pp. 43–49.

61. L.R. Gomez-Mejia, "Dimensions and Correlates of the Personnel Audit as an Organizational Assessment Tool," *Personnel Psychology*, vol. 38, no. 2, pp. 293–308.

62. Margaret E. Cashman and James C. McElroy, "Evaluating the HR Function," *HRMagazine*, vol. 36, no. 1 (January 1991), pp. 69–73.

Suggestions for Further Reading

- George E. Biles and Randall S. Schuler. *Audit Handbook of Human Resource Management Practices*. Alexandria, Va.: American Society for Personnel Administration, 1986.
- E.H. Burack, *Creative Human Resource Planning and Application: A Strategic Approach*. Englewood Cliffs, NJ: Prentice-Hall, 1988.

- Lee Dyer, ed. *Human Resource Management, Evolving Roles and Responsibilities*. American Society for Personnel Administration (ASPA)/Bureau of National Affairs (BNA) series. Washington, DC: Bureau of National Affairs, 1988.
- Employment and Immigration Canada. *Job Futures: An Occupational Outlook to 1995, Volume 1: Occupational Outlooks* and *Volume 2: Experience of Recent Graduates*. 1990 ed. Prepared by the Canadian Occupational Projection System (COPS). Toronto: Nelson Canada, 1990.
- Charles R. Greer, Dana L. Jackson, and Jack Fiorito. "Adapting Human Resource Planning in a Changing Business Environment." *Human Resource Management*, vol. 28, no. 1 (Spring 1989), pp. 105–23.
- Ontario Human Resources Secretariat. *Strategies for Renewal: Strategic Human Resource Planning in the Ontario Public Service 1991–1992*. Toronto, 1990; and *Strategies for Renewal: Strategic Human Resources Planning in the Ontario Public Service, Progress Report 1990*, Toronto, March 31, 1991.
- W.J. Rothwell and H.C. Kazanas. *Strategic Human Resources Planning and Management*. Englewood Cliffs, NJ: Prentice-Hall, 1988.
- James W. Walker. "Human Resource Planning, 1990s Style." *Human Resources Planning*, vol. 13, no. 4 (1990), pp. 229–40.

CHAPTER 5

JOB ANALYSIS

- JOB ANALYSIS: A DEFINITION
- JOB-RELATED DEFINITIONS
- RELATION TO OTHER HRM FUNCTIONS
- RESPONSIBILITIES FOR JOB ANALYSIS
- HRM IN ACTION ▶ JOB ANALYSIS AND EXPERT SYSTEMS
- METHODS OF JOB ANALYSIS
- JOB ANALYSIS PROBLEMS AND ISSUES
- SUMMARY
- REVIEW QUESTIONS
- PROJECT IDEAS
- CASE 5.1 ▶ JOB TASK INVENTORY: A TOOL FOR ORGANIZATIONAL CHANGE?
- CASE 5.2 ▶ JOB ANALYSIS AT ST. JUDE'S HOSPITAL: AVOIDING GENDER BIAS
- NOTES
- SUGGESTIONS FOR FURTHER READING

HAROLD MULDRIDGE WAS RECENTLY APPOINTED human resources director of Waterford, a municipality with a population of 250 000. When Muldridge took the job, the chief executive officer told him to examine employee selection and performance appraisal procedures, which did not seem to be as effective as they should be. Muldridge was given the authority to hire several assistants to help with this endeavour, but the nature of their jobs was left largely up to him. Before Muldridge could make any progress on the selection and appraisal systems, several other problems were brought to his attention. An aspiring clerk in the records department wanted to know about opportunities for advancement, and Muldridge had little information to provide. The municipal vehicle-repair mechanics complained that they were underpaid for their work, and Muldridge could not say otherwise. Funds were obtained for a program to train drivers in the transport of people with physical disabilities in special vans, but the content of the training program remained unspecified. By this time, it was obvious to Muldridge that Waterford needed job analysis, which is basic to addressing all of the problems he was encountering and others in an organization.

The rumble of forklifts moving cases of fresh vegetables past her office window at Central Foods reminded Filiz Tasmack it was time to go home. Though she hadn't finished everything on her "to do" list, reading the file of information from the Ontario Pay Equity Commission had been put off long enough.

As she closed the file, the young human resource manager admitted to herself that she had been surprised to learn that her small, 130-employee wholesale food company would have to post a pay equity plan by January 1, 1991, and, if necessary, make some wage adjustments by the next year. Additionally, she had not realized it might be necessary to gather more information about the company's jobs and employee qualifications. How, for example, could the company meet the requirement that female-dominated job classes (those with women in at least 60 percent of the positions) be compared with male-dominated job classes (at least 70 percent men)? Though most of the warehouse employees and truck drivers were male and most of the office staff female, there were some of the opposite sex in each place. The brochure defined a job class as "those positions in an establishment that have similar duties and responsibilities and require similar qualifications, are filled by similar recruiting procedures and have the same compensation schedule, salary grade or range of salary rates."[1]

Filiz was concerned about how she would determine job classes. She doubted that the brief job descriptions she had been using primarily for job titles and recruiting would be adequate to compare job classes on the four factors — skill, effort, responsibility, and working conditions — required by the act. After considering the legal requirements, she concluded that she would have to use a method of job analysis yielding information on duties and responsibilities as well as employee qualifications. She decided her next step was to do some reading to find out which job analysis methods might work for Central Foods.

The challenges both Muldridge and Tasmack face illustrate the cornerstone role of job analysis in human resource functions. Additionally, the experience at Central Foods suggests that Ontario's Pay Equity Act has, at least in that province, led to more job analyses than ever. In this chapter, you will learn what job analysis is, the variety of job analysis methods, and how organizations use job analysis information. Additionally, we will explore the role of job analysis in teamwork and expert systems, along with other issues.

JOB ANALYSIS: A DEFINITION

Although job analysis may seem a new and unfamiliar topic, its results are seen every day in the Help Wanted columns of most newspapers. Job descriptions are an end product of job analysis; want ads represent miniature job descriptions.

Job analysis is the process of determining the nature or content of a job by collecting and organizing relevant information. A complete job analysis contains information about the following five factors, plus anything else deemed appropriate to describe fully the nature of the job:

1. Work products — what the job seeks to accomplish.
2. Necessary worker activities or behaviour required by the job.

3. Equipment used.
4. Factors in the work environment.
5. Personal characteristics required to do the job, such as typing speed, physical strength, or interest in working with children. The personal requirements of a job are referred to as job specifications. *Job specifications* are the human requirements deemed necessary for minimally acceptable performance on the job. They can include skills, abilities, level of education, experience, interests, personality traits, or physical characteristics.

The ad in Exhibit 5.1 contains all of these factors except Factor 3, equipment used.

Job analysis also includes organizing and summarizing information into job descriptions. A complete job description contains job title plus information relating to each factor already mentioned. Exhibit 5.2 is an example of a job description for a word-processing operator in a municipal government. Note that it includes an overall description of the job, a listing of specific duties associated with the job, and a section on job specifications, including the requirements for education; experience; and specific, task-related knowledge and abilities. Note also that the overall description states the conditions under which work will be performed ("close supervision") and the level of performance expected ("an acceptable level"). "Other duties as assigned" is a catchall phrase designed to give the employer some flexibility in the kinds of work that may be assigned to the word-processing operator.

JOB-RELATED DEFINITIONS

The work of an organization is divided into individual responsibilities that are structured in the form of jobs. A *job* is a set of duties or responsibilities whose completion serves to further organizational objectives. Jobs that are similar in their duties, activities, and personal requirements and that can be found in different organizations at different times are classified into *occupations*. Employment and Immigration Canada's *Canadian Classification and Dictionary of Occupations (CCDO)* lists more than 30 000 job titles.[2] It groups almost 7700 occupations (many have more than one job title) into progressively broader categories, using a seven-digit code rather like a library's book-classification system. At the top of the inverted pyramid are 23 major groups, such as social sciences and related fields, medicine and health, and sales.

There is a difference between a job and a position, although the two terms are often used interchangeably. Most jobs in an organization usually have more than one position. For example, banks have several positions for the job of bank teller, and most grocery stores have a number of positions for

EXHIBIT 5.1
A Familiar Result of Job Analysis

Suncor Inc. is one of Canada's most diversified oil and gas companies. We are a progressive organization, providing outstanding opportunities for career challenge in an environment where quality, excellence and teamwork go hand-in-hand. We currently have a vacancy for:

Manager - Insurance

Reporting directly to the Treasurer, you will be responsible for managing and developing our insurance programme to protect the corporation's integrity against a variety of risks. This challenging mandate encompasses the mining of oil sands, shipment of chemicals, oil and gas production, refining, real estate and construction projects.

Enthusiastic and energetic, you are AIIC accredited and fully experienced with risk analysis in a multi-divisional environment. Your credentials include extensive practical experience with both property and casualty insurance, and computer literacy. You must be a well organized self-starter with strong interpersonal skills and the ability to work without supervision.

We offer a competitive salary and benefits package. If you are interested in this excellent opportunity, please forward your resume, including salary expectations, to: Corporate Human Resources, Suncor Inc., 36 York Mills Road, North York, Ontario M2P 2C5.

In accordance with our Employment Equity Policy, Suncor Inc. encourages applications from qualified women, men, visible minorities, aboriginal peoples, and persons with disabilities.

Suncor inc.

An Equal Opportunity Employer

Source: Suncor Inc. Reprinted with permission.

EXHIBIT 5.2
A Typical Job Description

CLERK/WORD PROCESSOR OPERATOR IN A MUNICIPAL GOVERNMENT
Under close supervision, to perform a variety of clerical duties at an acceptable level of performance and other duties as assigned.

TYPICAL DUTIES

1. Inputs letters and other material from rough drafts or dictation devices; posts and updates information on various types of records and maintains files.

2. Answers enquiries from employees and the public about routine and established procedures and policies or refers to the appropriate individual or office.

3. Assists in preparing and checking forms, records, applications, and other materials for completeness and conformity with established procedures; makes routine follow-up to secure additional required information.

4. Composes routine correspondence; prepares departmental payroll records; orders departmental or divisional supplies.

5. Computes and extends figures that may involve several arithmetical processes.

6. Collects fees, prepares invoices, and verifies unusual entries.

7. Operates standard office equipment, including computers, adding machines, and calculators.

JOB SPECIFICATIONS
Education and experience: any combination equivalent to completion of secondary school and one year clerical and word processing experience.
Knowledge and abilities: knowledge of office procedures and practices; ability to meet the public effectively; ability to keyboard from clear copy at the rate of 55 words per minute; ability to do clerical work involving a limited use of independent judgement requiring speed and accuracy; ability to make arithmetical computations.

---

the job of grocery checker. Workers in similar positions in an organization have very similar or the same duties and responsibilities because they are performing the same job. Thus, an organization may have 70 positions filled by 70 employees, but only 12 different jobs.

A job, or a position for a job, consists of a set of *duties*, or work-related responsibilities. Completion of duties requires certain behaviour specific to the task at hand. For example, the duties of a university professor usually include teaching courses, counselling students, conducting research, and rendering service to the university.

In order to complete the duties of a job, the holder of the position must accomplish a number of tasks. A *task* is a specific work activity carried out to achieve a specific purpose. Tasks related to the duty of teaching courses include writing course outlines, preparing and giving lectures, and grading papers and examinations. The smallest unit used in most job analyses is an *element*, defined as a particular aspect of a particular task. Removing paper from one's desk drawer is an element related to the task of preparing a lecture or writing a course outline. Most job analysis methods and job descriptions do not specify job elements. Such detail is necessary only for describing jobs that are highly repetitive and manual, such as assembly-line jobs, and jobs in which pay is determined by the number of units produced (piecework). Elements are also used in engineering methods of job analysis, such as time-and-motion studies and micro-motion analysis.

RELATION TO OTHER HRM FUNCTIONS

Experts in industrial psychology argue that "job analysis information can affect every aspect of an organization," and they view job analysis as the "foundation upon which an organization's human resources are built."[3] The importance of this process can best be understood by examining job analysis in relation to other HRM functions. The relationships are summarized in Figure 5.1.

HUMAN RESOURCE PLANNING

As discussed in the previous chapter, job analysis plays a crucial role in human resource planning by providing information on the nature of a job and the skills required to do it. In assessing the needs of an organization, human resource planners use job analysis data to compare the skills required for particular jobs with the actual skills of employees in the organization (as determined by skills inventories). If employees' actual skills do not match the required skills of present jobs, organizations can take several actions to reduce the discrepancy. First, they can recruit, select, and hire persons with those skills that have been determined to be lacking or in short supply. Second, current employees can be trained to increase their present skill levels or to acquire new skills. Third, jobs can be redesigned, with or without the addition of more automated equipment, so that the skills required more closely match those available to the organization. A fourth alternative, useful in some cases, is to contract the work to groups or individuals outside the organization.

Human resource planners and management rely heavily on job analysis in carrying out organizational change and development programs. For example,

FIGURE 5.1
Job Analysis: Relation to Other HRM Functions

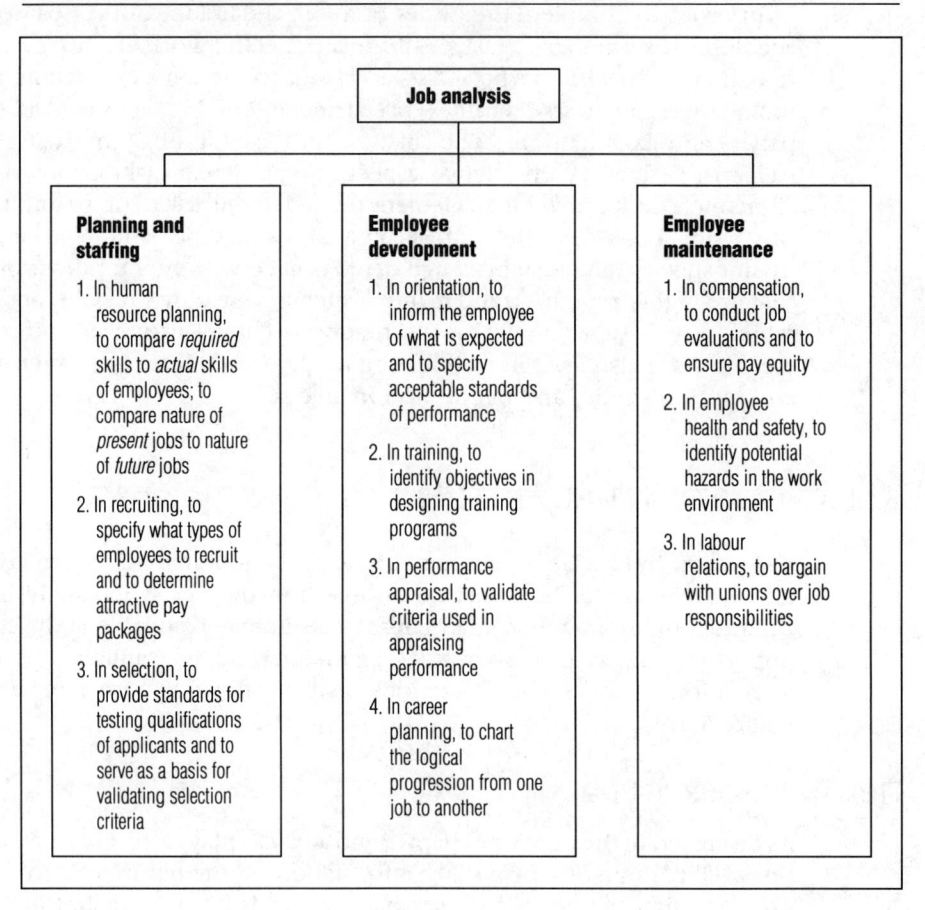

Job analysis

Planning and staffing

1. In human resource planning, to compare *required* skills to *actual* skills of employees; to compare nature of *present* jobs to nature of *future* jobs
2. In recruiting, to specify what types of employees to recruit and to determine attractive pay packages
3. In selection, to provide standards for testing qualifications of applicants and to serve as a basis for validating selection criteria

Employee development

1. In orientation, to inform the employee of what is expected and to specify acceptable standards of performance
2. In training, to identify objectives in designing training programs
3. In performance appraisal, to validate criteria used in appraising performance
4. In career planning, to chart the logical progression from one job to another

Employee maintenance

1. In compensation, to conduct job evaluations and to ensure pay equity
2. In employee health and safety, to identify potential hazards in the work environment
3. In labour relations, to bargain with unions over job responsibilities

---

the quality of working life (QWL) movement and, more recently, downsizing have led to the enlargement and enrichment of jobs. In this case, job analysis information is used to redesign jobs so that they contain a greater variety of tasks (enlargement) and/or require higher levels of autonomy and responsibility (enrichment). Redesign is, therefore, a major part of management's strategic plan for restructuring the organization. As such, it often creates a need for training, development of new career paths, adjustments in pay, and changes in labour agreements.

In any case, analyzing the nature of present jobs is an initial step in planning how jobs must change to meet future needs of the organization. Human resource planning requires a job analysis method that collects comparable data on a wide variety of jobs. These data are necessary to compare similarities and differences among jobs, and to ensure pay equity.

RECRUITING

Analyzing jobs helps define what types of employees to recruit—what skills, abilities, knowledge, and experience are needed to do the job. In the example at the beginning of the chapter, if Harold Muldridge had had job descriptions for the assistants he was authorized to hire, he would have had a much clearer idea of what job-related characteristics to look for in the persons recruited to fill these positions.

In order to recruit employees successfully, an organization must offer pay that is equitable and competitive with that of other organizations. One can determine the range of pay (the "going rate") for a particular job by comparing its description with those of similar jobs in the labour market. This type of information would have been useful to Muldridge in demonstrating to the vehicle-repair mechanics that they were not being underpaid in relation to similar mechanics working for other organizations. Another use of job descriptions in recruiting is in composing advertisements for job vacancies. For recruiting purposes, a job analysis method must provide information on the personal qualifications necessary to perform a job's tasks.

SELECTION

In selection, job specifications provide standards for testing the qualifications of applicants to perform successfully in a given position. For example, if job specifications require that a word-processing operator type 55 words per minute, then 55 words per minute serves as one standard of performance against which an applicant will be measured. Different job specifications require that different selection methods be used for testing applicants' qualifications.

The criteria used for selection must be job-related; that is, they must test the applicant on behaviour and skills necessary to the job and not on characteristics irrelevant to acceptable performance. It is important to note, however, that a job analysis method for selection purposes must provide detailed and complete information on the personal qualifications for jobs.

ORIENTATION

In orientation, the job description is used to convey to employees information regarding required duties and acceptable standards of performance. The job description tells the new employee what is expected. For example, the word-processing operator described in Exhibit 5.2 knows that he or she is expected to perform the duties listed in the job description and also to exhibit "knowledge of office procedures and practices; ability to meet the public effectively; ability to type from clear copy at the rate of 55 words per minute; ability to do clerical work involving a limited use of independent judgement requiring speed and accuracy; and ability to make arithmetical computations." Any one (or all) of these jobs specifications could serve as a criterion against which to measure an employee's performance once the job has been undertaken.

TRAINING AND DEVELOPMENT

Job specifications serve as training objectives in training and development programs. As an example, consider again the case of human resource director Harold Muldridge. He had received funds for a program to train bus drivers in the transport of people who are elderly or have physical disabilities, but the content of the training program was unspecified. A clear job description for bus drivers transporting these special populations would have enabled Muldridge to identify objectives for his training program. For example, the job specifications might have read:

> Interest in helping people with physical disabilities; ability to operate specially equipped vans; a knowledge of disabling conditions and how each affects transport; familiarity with special devices used by people with disabilities, such as wheelchairs, walkers, seeing-eye dogs.

Based on these job specifications, the objectives of the human resource director's training program would be to impart the necessary knowledge and training to drivers so that they could demonstrate mastery of the required job behaviours. Such activities would include (1) training drivers in the operation of specially equipped vans; (2) informing drivers of disabling conditions and how each affects transport; and (3) familiarizing drivers with special devices used by people with disabilities. The effectiveness of the training program could then be assessed by determining how successfully drivers were able to meet the stated job specifications after training. For training purposes, job analysis methods must specify necessary job behaviours and the standards of performance employees must achieve.

PERFORMANCE APPRAISAL

It has already been pointed out that job specifications can serve as criteria against which to appraise an employee's performance. The criteria used to appraise performance must be related to job content and not to extraneous factors. For example, driver performance would be a valid criterion for appraising the performance of van drivers transporting people with disabilities. Job analysis provides information necessary for selecting appraisal criteria.

CAREER PLANNING

Many of today's employees expect to pursue interesting and challenging careers. A *career* is a sequence of positions or jobs held by one person over a relatively long time, usually ten or more years. Comparison of job descriptions for different-level jobs in an organization can be used to chart the logical progression of an employee from one job to another. If Muldridge had had access to data of this type, he could have told the aspiring clerk in the records department that he or she could expect to be promoted to Clerk II after two years of service and eventually to Supervisor of Records when the position became vacant. To be useful for career planning, a job analysis method must provide comparable data on jobs so that the similarities and differences between jobs at different levels are evident.

COMPENSATION

Job analysis is undertaken most often for purposes of job evaluation. *Job evaluation* is the process of assigning relative value to jobs within an organization. Job evaluation provides a rationale for paying a Secretary II $125 more per month than a Secretary I, and a Computer Programmer $160 more per month than a Secretary II. It is difficult to conduct a good job evaluation without access to recent and complete job descriptions. Over a span of time, jobs may change so that one job's pay relative to another's becomes inequitable. This fact, plus employee and/or union complaints of unfair pay, can indicate the need for reevaluation of certain jobs. The passage of pay equity legislation has led many employers to conduct job analyses, prepare job descriptions, and do job evaluations.

Job analysis methods for purposes of job evaluation must enable comparison of jobs on certain compensable factors. *Compensable factors* are those that an organization chooses to use as a basis for differentiating between pay levels — for example, responsibility, effort, and skill levels.

EMPLOYEE HEALTH AND SAFETY

In some jobs, the nature of the tasks, working conditions, or equipment used can be hazardous to an employee's health and safety. Complete and accurate job descriptions document potential hazards so that steps can be taken to protect the employee. Identification of potential hazards allows safety engineers to design protective equipment. HRM professionals and safety specialists can enact and enforce safety rules for employees' protection, and safety programs can be developed.

LABOUR RELATIONS — UNIONS

In labour relations, job descriptions are used in bargaining with trade unions over pay, working conditions, and the ways in which certain jobs are done.[4] In order to gain control over the working environment of their members, unions normally prefer job descriptions to be very narrow and closely defined, whereas management usually wants them to be more flexible. When job descriptions are narrow, management must renegotiate collective agreements when even very small changes occur. For example, with a closely defined job description, the addition of a new piece of equipment could force renegotiation of an agreement if use of the equipment became an employee's responsibility. Human resource officers frequently retain reasonable flexibility and control over job content even with a collective agreement by including the clause "and other assigned duties" at the end of a job description.

Responsibilities for Job Analysis

The responsibilities of HRM professionals for job analysis can be divided into two major categories: conducting analyses and using job analysis information. Responsibility for conducting a job analysis includes: (1) choosing an appropriate method; (2) conducting the analysis; and (3) preparing job descriptions.

Choosing an appropriate method of job analysis involves consideration of how data will be used. As we have seen, various uses of job analysis data require the collection of different kinds of information. For example, information required for the purpose of job evaluation (assigning relative value to jobs in an organization) is quite different from that required by safety staff and engineers. The former require only enough information about working conditions to be able to categorize them according to a number of factors, while the latter need enough detail about working conditions and work-related hazards to design equipment and methods to alleviate unhealthy or unsafe conditions. Determining how data will be used is an important consideration in choosing a job analysis method because certain methods are more appropriate for some purposes than for others.

In implementing a method of job analysis, it is important that HRM professionals gain the co-operation of managers, of supervisors, of unions, and, often, of employees. These groups can provide valuable inputs into the process of job analysis, or they can provide unwelcome resistance. In many cases, the HRM professional serves as trainer, adviser, and co-ordinator for job analyses carried out by supervisors and employees. This is particularly true when a questionnaire is used and data are collected from many employees of a large organization. In this case, the HRM professional is involved in developing the questionnaire as well as in all planning, training, and administrative activities associated with the analysis. For example, supervisors must be trained to review their subordinates' questionnaires for omissions or exaggerations of duties, responsibilities, or required skills, and other errors. If disputes arise between supervisor and subordinates, the HRM professional must resolve them equitably while pursuing descriptions that are accurate and complete.

After job analysis data have been collected, job descriptions must be prepared. This involves classifying and summarizing data according to specific duties, task-related behaviour, personal requirements, and other descriptive characteristics of jobs.

HRM IN ACTION

JOB ANALYSIS AND EXPERT SYSTEMS

Innovations in automation and information processing are having substantial impact on the nature of work. Developments such as computer-aided design and laser scanners, for example, have changed the jobs of both engineers and sales clerks. During the 1990s, the work of many skilled, technical, and professional employees will be changed through use of expert systems and artificial intelligence (computer programs that use concepts, methods, and symbols to solve problems). An expert system "achieves competence in performing a specialized task by reasoning with a body of knowledge about the task and the task domain," in the words of Feigenbaum, McCorduck, and Nii, authors of a book about the use of such systems.

Conversion to an expert system at Northrop, for example, reduced the time to translate engineering drawings into plans for manufacturing aircraft parts from several days to fifteen minutes and also increased reliability. The British National Health Care Service developed an expert system to evaluate the quality of medical care, thereby reducing the task to nine minutes on an IBM-PC from two hours using six human experts. Digital computer company developed a system that reduced the task of system configuration from three hours to fifteen minutes. Beyond offering the obvious order-of-magnitude increases in productivity and cost savings, expert systems can preserve the expertise of scarce senior employees; allow experts to work on more important, nonroutine problems; reduce training time of knowledge employees (experienced employees who have acquired special knowledge); and facilitate teamwork.

Job analysis can play a crucial role in the development of expert systems by providing systematic methods for extracting information for such systems from expert employees. For example, in-depth interviewing and detailed observation are useful for this purpose.

For jobs that are using expert systems, the question of how pay is affected arises. To what extent is the knowledge attributable to the incumbent or to the computer? Job analysis, for purposes of job evaluation, must wrestle with this question.

Source: Adapted from *The Rise of the Expert Company* by Edward Feigenbaum, Pamela McCorduck, and Penny H. Nii. Copyright © 1988 by Edward Feigenbaum, Penny H. Nii, and Pamela McCorduck. Used by permission of Times Books, a division of Random House, Inc.

The HRM specialist responsible for conducting job analysis is the *occupational analyst*, also called the *job analyst*. Large organizations often employ full-time occupational analysts; smaller organizations may hire them as consultants. The *Canadian Classification and Dictionary of Occupations* provides a description of an occupational analyst (see Exhibit 5.3), which demonstrates the range and variety of activities required in the process of job analysis.

Not all job analyses, however, are conducted by occupational analysts. In fact, the responsibility is often assumed by other HRM professionals or supervisors trained in the use of job analysis methods.

METHODS OF JOB ANALYSIS

Job analysis methods can be classified into four basic types: (1) observation methods; (2) interview techniques; (3) combined observation/interview approaches; and (4) questionnaires, including job inventories or checklists. Table 5.1 compares the methods on a number of dimensions and can be used as a reference throughout the following discussion.

OBSERVATION METHODS

Observation of work activities and worker behaviour is a type of job analysis that can be used independently or in combination with other types. Three methods of job analysis based on observation are: (1) direct observation; (2) work methods analysis, including time-and-motion study and micro-motion analysis; and (3) the critical incident technique. Though they employ the same basic technique, these methods differ in terms of who does the observing, what is observed, and how it is observed.

Direct Observation

This method makes use of recorded observations of employees in the performance of their duties. The observer either takes general notes or works from a form that has structured categories for comment. Everything is observed: what the worker accomplishes, what equipment is used, what the work environment is like, and any other factors relevant to the job. For simple, repetitive jobs, one or two hours of direct observation may suffice for an adequate description. More complex and diverse jobs require multiple and often extended observations to achieve the same result. This is why direct observation is used primarily to describe manual, short-cycle jobs (such as that of a machine operator) or in combination with other methods of job analysis. It is especially useful for identifying the health and safety hazards of particular jobs.

EXHIBIT 5.3
A Job Description from the *CCDO*

1174-122 OCCUPATIONAL ANALYST

Analyzes and synthesizes job data to provide occupational information for personnel, administrative, information and other services of private, public or governmental organizations:

Consults with management to determine type, scope and purpose of analysis required. Searches for background information on nature of organization and its activities, and studies relevant data. Initiates job study of touring establishment, obtains or prepares charts showing broad functions of each department, and lists job titles used within establishment. Observes and studies jobs performed, and interviews workers, supervisors and managerial personnel to ascertain nature of work performed, worker characteristics required and other relevant factors. Writes detailed job definitions to describe work performed and other significant data, such as educational requirements, training time, environmental conditions, physical activities, and skills and abilities required for satisfactory job performance. Makes comparative analyses of job descriptions and specifications to determine employment activities that are common to a number of similar jobs. Writes occupational descriptions by combining and synthesizing groups of similar jobs. Prepares, from documentation services, drafts of occupational descriptions for validation by experts in the field of work or for verification through visits, observation and interview, and writes finished manuscript.

May prepare occupational classification systems, career information booklets, interviewing aids for employment officers and manpower counsellors, job evaluation reports and other aids to industrial, governmental and other organizations in activities; such as, personnel administration, manpower research and planning, training, placement, occupational information and vocational guidance. May specialize in a particular activity and be designated accordingly; for example,

Job Analyst
Job Evaluator
Occupational Analyst, Classification System
Occupational Monograph Specialist
Position Classifier
Salary Analyst

Source: Manpower and Immigration Canada, *Canadian Classification and Dictionary of Occupations, 1971*, vol. 1 (Ottawa: Information Canada, 1971), p. 36. Reprinted with the permission of the Occupational and Career Information Branch, Employment and Immigration Canada, and the Minister of Supply and Services Canada, 1992.

TABLE 5.1
Comparing Job Analysis Methods

METHOD	MAJOR USER	WHAT METHOD INVOLVES	MAJOR HUMAN RESOURCE USES	MAJOR ADVANTAGE(S)	MAJOR DISADVANTAGE(S)
Direct observation	Job analyst	Observation; recording	Health and safety; part of other methods	Can provide reasonably complete picture of manual, repetitive jobs	Limited to manual, repetitive jobs; mental process and worker qualifications cannot be observed
Work methods analysis	Industrial engineer	Observation; recording (stopwatch or video camera)	Compensation; health and safety; training	Serves as data base for setting performance standards	Limited to manual, repetitive jobs; same as above
Critical incident technique	Supervisor or manager	Judgement; observation; recording	Performance appraisal	Captures nonroutine, unusual behaviour	Lengthy data collection process; translation into job descriptions is difficult
Interviewing	Job analyst	Interviewing; recording	Job descriptions; training; with other methods	Can provide in-depth information	Time-consuming process
Functional job analysis (FJA)	Job analyst	Observation; interviewing; judgement; recording	Job descriptions; recruiting; selection; HRP	Widely applicable; useful job classification system	Requires analyst trained in FJA
VERJAS	Manager; HRM professional	Observation; interviewing; recording; judgement	Job descriptions; performance appraisal; compensation; recruiting; selection	Multipurpose method	Time-consuming
Job inventories and checklists	Job occupant	Judgement (rating)	HRP; selection; training	Data collection is fast; data for different jobs are easily compared	Time-consuming to construct the inventory
PAQ	Job analyst; supervisor; job occupant	Judgement (rating)	HRP; compensation; selection; training	Rapid results; ease of job comparisons	Does not provide a written description of job or duties

Direct observation is typically part of most job analyses because it is of value for the analyst to have some understanding of both the basic nature of the work and the context in which it is performed. However, direct observation methods have certain natural limitations. First, they cannot capture the mental aspects of jobs, such as decision making or planning, since mental processes are not observable. Second, observation methods can provide little information relating to personal requirements for various jobs because this kind of information is also not readily observable. Thus, observation methods provide little information on which to base job specifications.

Work Methods Analysis

A sophisticated observation method, work methods analysis is used by industrial engineers to describe manual repetitive production jobs, such as factory or assembly-line jobs. Two types of work methods analysis are time-and-motion study and micro-motion analysis. In time-and-motion studies, an industrial engineer observes and records each activity of a worker, using a stopwatch to note the time it takes to perform each separate element of the job. Micro-motion analysis uses video equipment to record workers' activities; the tapes are analyzed to discover acceptable ways of accomplishing tasks and to set standards on how long certain tasks should take. Such data are especially useful for developing training programs and setting pay rates.

Critical Incident Technique

The critical incident technique involves observing and recording examples of particularly effective or ineffective behaviour.[5] It can be used for all jobs but is most advantageous for more complex, less routine ones. Behaviour is judged "effective" or "ineffective" in terms of the results it produces. For example, if a shoe salesperson comments on the size of a customer's feet and he or she leaves the store in a huff, the salesperson's behaviour could be judged ineffective. The critical incident method requires a supervisor or other person familiar with a job to record, in an ongoing log, information relating to behaviour observed to be either particularly effective or ineffective. Over time, this process results in a growing description of a job.

The following information should be recorded for each critical incident: (1) what led up to the incident and the situation in which it occurred; (2) exactly what the employee did that was particularly effective or ineffective; (3) the perceived consequences or results of the behaviour; and (4) a judgement as to the degree of control the employee had over the results his or her behaviour produced (to what degree the employee should be held responsible for what resulted).

The critical incident method differs from direct observation and work methods analysis in that observations are not recorded as behaviour occurs, but only *after* it has been judged particularly effective or ineffective in terms of results produced. This means that a person using the critical incident method must describe behaviour in retrospect, rather than as the activity unfolds. Accurate recording of past observations is more difficult than recording behaviour as it occurs.

This method has the advantage of being able to capture both routine and nonroutine aspects of behaviour. However, describing a job adequately requires a very lengthy process of incident collection. Further, since incidents can be quite dissimilar, classifying the data into usable job descriptions can be difficult. The fact that this method of job analysis focusses on employee behaviour and is able to capture dynamic aspects of jobs that other methods might miss makes it especially useful for the development of performance-appraisal instruments that seek to evaluate employees according to acceptable or unacceptable job behaviours.

INTERVIEW TECHNIQUES

Interview techniques involve discussions between job analysts (or other interviewers) and job occupants or experts. Employees may be interviewed singly or in groups. Job analysis data from individual and group interviews with employees are often supplemented by information from supervisors of the employees whose jobs are analyzed. Job analysis interviews can also be held with a small panel of experts, such as supervisors or long-time employees who are very familiar with the job. Interviews of this type are called *technical conferences*. The end product of a technical conference is a job description that reflects a consensus of the experts' thinking.[6]

Interviews can be unstructured, with questions and areas of discussion unspecified, or they can be more highly structured, with each point for discussion spelled out. Using a structured format increases the likelihood that all aspects of a job will be covered in an interview; it also enables the collection of comparable data from all persons interviewed, making information classification easier.

One problem with this technique is that it can be very time-consuming if many employees must be interviewed. Another problem is that interviews —like some methods of observation—may create suspicion among workers. This is especially true of job analysis conducted to assign relative monetary values to jobs (as in job evaluation). Workers who feel that the analysis may affect their pay or status are often motivated to distort information about the job, most likely inflating their importance. For this reason, gaining the co-operation of workers can be important in achieving accurate job analysis results. In short, interview techniques can be time-consuming and therefore costly, but when properly used they can provide reasonably complete data for use in preparing job descriptions. They can also be used effectively to identify training needs of employees.

Interviews are a basic part of most job analyses, particularly in smaller organizations. When information must be gathered from many employees fairly quickly, interviews of a few employees and supervisors are often used to supplement information gathered from questionnaires.

COMBINED OBSERVATION/INTERVIEW APPROACHES

Observation and interview techniques are often used in combination as components of more sophisticated job analysis methods. Two methods that combine both techniques are functional job analysis and VERJAS (Versatile Job Analysis System).

Functional Job Analysis

Functional job analysis (FJA) is a comprehensive method developed by the Training and Employment Service of the U.S. Department of Labor. An analyst using this method observes, interviews, and records information on a structured job analysis "schedule" that uses very precise terminology. The analyst provides a job summary and a description of tasks for each job analyzed. He or she also assigns "work-performed ratings" and ratings of "worker traits."

Work-performed ratings specify the nature of the relationship a worker has to data, people, and things (DPT). Three separate eight-point scales are used in assigning a DPT rating. Scale items are descriptive terms, indicating increased levels of complexity, with higher numbers indicating less complex relationships to data, people, and things. Worker-trait ratings are assessments of personal characteristics needed for satisfactory performance of the job.

Analysts using FJA must be well-trained in order to write precise job descriptions and make accurate ratings. They should also be trained in observation and interview techniques.

Because of its descriptive summary and listing of job duties, FJA is especially useful to the recruiting and selection functions. It is also very useful for job evaluations, human resource planning, and career planning because it is applicable to a variety of jobs and provides a quantitative way to compare job similarities and differences.

The *Canadian Classification and Dictionary of Occupations* uses a variation of FJA to classify and describe jobs. For each specific occupation or job, the *CCDO* provides an occupational code number, occupational title, industry designation, coded job characteristics, a statement of job duties, and related occupational titles. An example is the *CCDO*'s statement of job duties for an Occupational Analyst, presented in Exhibit 5.3.

The *CCDO*'s coded job characteristics refer to educational and training requirements, physical demands, and worker functions in relation to data, people, and things (DPT). Educational requirements are measured by the General Educational Development scale (GED), a six-point scale that focusses on levels of reasoning and mathematical and language development. The *CCDO* assigns Occupational Analyst a GED rating of 5, the second-highest level, representing the need to apply principles of logical and scientific thinking, to interpret an extensive variety of technical instructions, and to deal with abstract and concrete variables. Training requirements are indicated by a Specific Vocational Preparation (SVP) rating from 1 (short demonstration only) to 9 (more than ten years). Occupational Analyst has an SVP rating of 7 (more than two years up to and including four years).

Physical demands of the job are coded according to environmental conditions (EC) and physical activities (PA). Physical activities include both physical requirements (how heavy the work is) and worker capacities (kind of physical activity required). According to the EC and PA codes, the work of an Occupational Analyst is located inside (EC I) and is sedentary, involving talking and hearing (PA S56).

The *CCDO* codes worker functions, as in FJA, by assessing the relationships of job activities to data, people, and things. Occupational Analyst has a DPT rating of 068, indicating that the occupation requires a high level of synthesizing (0), some speaking to people (6), and no significant relationship to things (8). The *CCDO*'s assessment of the job's required worker traits and career possibilities is shown in Exhibit 5.4.

EXHIBIT 5.4
Occupational Qualification Requirements for Occupational Analyst (*CCDO* Code 1174–122)

APTITUDES AND CAPACITIES

Personnel and Related Officers require:

—Learning ability to understand and apply the principles of personnel administration in such fields as employment, counselling, occupational and salary analysis, labour relations and student financial-aid programs.

—Verbal ability to communicate effectively with people at all levels of education and training and from a wide variety of occupational backgrounds, and to present information lucidly, both orally and in writing.

—Numerical ability to prepare financial and material estimates and reports.

—Clerical perception to review reports, collective-bargaining agreements, contracts, personnel records and other written material.

TRAINING AND ENTRY REQUIREMENTS

Personnel and Related Officers usually require:

—A bachelor's degree with a major in psychology, sociology or business administration.

—A minimum of two years' on-the-job experience.

—Completion of specialized courses provided by universities, community colleges or employers in personnel administration, labour relations, or job and occupational analysis.

ADVANCEMENT AND TRANSFER POSSIBILITIES

Advancement

Advancement for individuals with sufficient experience and managerial potential may be to 1136–110 *Industrial-Relations Manager* or 1136–114 *Personnel Manager*, while others with

EXHIBIT 5.4 *(continued)*

leadership qualities and supervisory potential may advance to the supervisory occupations in this chapter.

Transfer

Transfers may occur to other occupations in this chapter. Those who have a bachelor's degree in the social sciences or business administration may transfer to occupations in psychology, sociology or business administration, and those with appropriate qualifications and certification may transfer to occupations in teaching, occupational guidance or counselling.

Clues for relating persons to occupational requirements

Personnel and Related Officers require significant interests in, and dispositions for work involving the following:

Interests

— Activities involving business contact with people.
— Activities concerned with people and communication of ideas.
— Activities resulting in prestige or esteem of others by acting as an arbiter in labour–management disputes, or as a counsellor assisting job seekers or employees to solve their problems.

Temperaments

— Dealing with people in actual job duties beyond giving and receiving instructions.
— The evaluation of information against sensory or judgmental criteria by resolving staff problems, such as employee performance, absenteeism and grievances by interviewing employees and supervisors and recommending or initiating remedial action based on experience or precedent.
— The evaluation of information against measurable or verifiable criteria.
— Influencing people in their opinions, attitudes or judgments about ideas or things.
— The direction, control and planning of an entire activity or the activities of others.
— A variety of duties often characterized by frequent change.

OTHER CLUES

— Tact, discretion, integrity with others, and the ability to establish rapport.

Source: Manpower and Immigration Canada, *Canadian Classification and Dictionary of Occupations*, vol. 2 (Ottawa: Information Canada, 1971), pp. 15–16. Reprinted with the permission of the Occupational and Career Information Branch, Employment and Immigration Canada and the Minister of Supply and Services Canada, 1992. Additional definitions and recent changes in the *CCDO* are in Employment and Immigration Canada, *Canadian Classification and Dictionary of Occupations, Guide*, 9th ed. (Ottawa: Supply and Services Canada, 1989).

Both the FJA and the *CCDO* method offer organizations a systematic approach to analyzing and classifying jobs and job characteristics. The generality of the methods means that they may be used for most jobs. However, since both require trained analysts, they are most likely to benefit large employers.

VERJAS

Versatile Job Analysis System (VERJAS) is a relatively new method of job analysis that combines observation and interview techniques, as well as other job analysis procedures. The originators of the system describe it as "a job analysis melting pot in both origin and use."[7]

VERJAS is administered by managers or human resource staff assigned to study jobs. The method includes five basic steps, which are set out as follows by the authors of the method:

1. Write an overview of the job describing the purpose for which the job exists and the primary duties involved in accomplishing that purpose. This step provides job description information.

2. Describe the action, purpose, and result of each task involved in carrying out job duties, and then identify the training mode and rate its relative importance. This step provides a description of specific expected job behaviour, which is useful in identifying worker competencies, developing performance standards, and defending personnel practices as job related.

3. Describe the context of the job; its scope, effect, and environment. This step assures documentation of information needed to determine the value of a job.

4. Identify basic worker competencies needed for minimum acceptable performance of job tasks. This step is essential for determining employee specifications that are used in recruiting.

5. Identify the special worker competencies that make for successful job performance. This step is useful in developing selection criteria and identifying training needs.[8]

The VERJAS system provides job analysts with forms and instructions for completing each of these steps.

VERJAS provides information pertinent to most organizational uses of job analysis, though it does little to facilitate comparison of job similarities and differences. The system is also limited to description and analysis of existing jobs, since these are the starting point for VERJAS's analysis. Though the VERJAS method is fairly new and little research has examined it, the method is simple and basic enough to be carried out in most organizations.

QUESTIONNAIRES

Some questionnaires can be filled out by employees; others require job analysts for a group of employees. Questionnaires vary in the degree to which they are structured. Some ask open-ended questions that seek unspecified answers; for example:

1. Describe the duties of your job.
2. Describe your daily routine.
3. What skills do you feel are essential to the performance of your duties?

A questionnaire gains structure by specifying response alternatives. For example, if Item 1 were structured, it might read:

Check whether or not your duties include the following:

typing letters	___ Yes	___ No
taking dictation	___ Yes	___ No
filing correspondence	___ Yes	___ No
answering telephone	___ Yes	___ No

Questionnaires are often used to gather job analysis information when input from a large number of employees is desired and when speed and cost are major considerations. Questionnaires are relatively inexpensive to administer, and they permit data to be collected in a very short time. However, developing a questionnaire takes time and some degree of familiarity with the job in question. Time, effort, and expertise are also required to code and analyze information after it has been collected, although structured response categories make coding and analyzing easier.

Questionnaires can be used by most organizations for most kinds of jobs, assuming employees can understand the instrument. That means the reading ability of employees may limit the use of some questionnaires. (For example, the Position Analysis Questionnaire described later requires university-level reading ability.)[9] Generally, however, reading level is not a great problem since questionnaires are most commonly used for white-collar, professional, and managerial jobs. Pay equity legislation also requires attention to avoiding gender bias in questionnaires. For example, language must be neutral and equitable, and distribution and analysis of questionnaires must avoid gender bias.[10]

If an organization chooses to use a questionnaire for job analysis purposes, an HRM professional must either develop one for use in his or her particular organization or use one of the professionally developed, structured questionnaires discussed here.

Job Inventories or Checklists

Job inventories or checklists are structured questionnaires that require a respondent to check or rate behaviour and/or worker characteristics necessary to a particular job or occupation. Job inventories can be either task-oriented (job-oriented) or qualifications-oriented (worker-oriented), but most include both task and qualifications components. Exhibit 5.5 is an example of a task-oriented job checklist. Qualifications-oriented checklists ask respondents to check or rate knowledge, skills, abilities, or other worker characteristics presumed to be relevant to the performance of a particular job.

The U.S Air Force developed the job inventory method of job analysis in the 1960s, and it was first applied to military operative jobs, semiskilled and skilled, and some officers' jobs. In recent years, the job inventory approach has been used successfully to describe a broad range of jobs, from clerical, sales, and engineering occupations to managerial positions and professional jobs.[11] Because job inventories provide detailed information about particular worker behaviour and required qualifications, they are especially useful in selection and training, which require specific information in these areas. Comparison of detailed information from job inventories is also very useful to human resource planners who need to know the content of and specific qualifications for jobs.

Job inventories, by definition, tend to be specific to particular jobs or occupations, since they rate specific task behaviour or job qualifications. One disadvantage of this fact is that a specific inventory must be constructed for each job or occupation. The construction process involves the collection of job-related information from "subject matter experts," who know the job in depth, as well as development of a preliminary job inventory. The preliminary version is given to a sample of job occupants to determine the appropriateness of items to be included in the final inventory. Any task-related behaviour that has been omitted can be added at this time. An analysis of results is used in constructing the final task inventory. Job inventories have all the advantages of highly structured questionnaires, including comparability of collected data and ease of administration.

Position Analysis Questionnaire (PAQ)

The PAQ is a highly structured questionnaire, similar in design to a job inventory but different in scope. It was designed by Ernest J. McCormick and associates of Purdue University for analyzing blue-collar and nonmanagerial jobs in terms of a number of job elements. Earlier in this chapter we defined an element as a particular aspect of a particular task. McCormick uses the term more broadly to describe "some general work activity, work condition, or job characteristic."[12] The PAQ has 194 items, and 187 of them represent job elements related to six major divisions: (1) information inputs; (2) mental

EXHIBIT 5.5
A Task-Oriented Job Checklist

	THIS IS A PART OF MY JOB	TIME SPENT					IMPORTANCE					LEARNING TIME					
		MUCH LESS TIME Than Other Activities	LESS TIME Than Other Activities	ABOUT THE SAME Amount of Time as Other Activities	MORE TIME Than Other Activities	MUCH MORE TIME Than Other Activities	UNIMPORTANT	Minor Importance	IMPORTANT	Very Important	CRUCIAL	1 Day or Less	2 or 3 Days	4 or 5 Days	Up to a Month	1–3 Months	More than 3 Months
		1	2	3	4	5	1	2	3	4	5	1	2	3	4	5	6
153. Plan special sales promotions and see that they are carried out according to plan.																	
154. Keep track of and follow up on the activities of subordinates.																	
155. Transcribe from dictating machine records or tapes.																	
156. Schedule dates or times for appointments, meetings, etc. or delivery, pick-up, and repair of merchandise by checking with those involved for time and place.																	
157. Perform routine preventive mechanical maintenance on machines or equipment.																	
158. Look up, search for, or locate information in readily available sources such as files, parts lists, records, manuals, tables, catalogs, etc.																	
159. Set objectives for a department or unit of the company.		1	2	3	4	5	1	2	3	4	5	1	2	3	4	5	6

Source: M.D. Dunnette, L.H. Hough, and R.L. Rosse, "Task and Job Taxonomies as a Basis for Identifying Labor Supply Sources and Evaluating Employment Qualifications," *Human Resource Planning*, vol. 2, no. 1 (1979). Copyright © by The Human Resource Planning Society, 1979. All rights reserved. Reprinted with permission.

processes; (3) work output; (4) relationships with other persons; (5) job context; and (6) other characteristics. Exhibit 5.6 presents these major divisions along with examples of job elements relating to each. Divisions 1 to 3 are analogous to running a computer program. In order to perform a job, a

EXHIBIT 5.6
Job Elements from the Position Analysis Questionnaire

1. Information input (where and how the worker gets the information used in performing the job)
   a. written materials
   b. behaviours
   c. touch
   d. estimating speed of moving objects

2. Mental processes (reasoning, decision making, planning, and information processing activities involved in performing the job)
   a. reasoning in problem solving
   b. analyzing information or data
   c. using mathematics

3. Work output (physical activities the worker performs and the tools or devices used)
   a. precision tools
   b. foot-operated controls
   c. assembling/disassembling
   d. finger manipulation

4. Relationships with other persons (relationships with other persons required in performing the job)
   a. entertaining
   b. coordinates activities
   c. supervision received

5. Job context (physical and social contexts in which the work is performed)
   a. indoor temperature
   b. noise intensity
   c. frustrating situations

6. Other job characteristics (activities, conditions, or characteristics, other than those described above, relevant to the job)
   a. specific uniform/apparel
   b. irregular hours
   c. working under distractions
   d. travel

Note: The PAQ breaks down job elements into more specific questionnaire items.

Source: Compiled from Ernest J. McCormick, P.R. Jeanneret, and R.C. Mecham, *Position Analysis Questionnaire* (West Lafayette, Ind.: Purdue University Press, 1969). © 1969 Purdue Research Foundation. Used with permission.

computer must receive information from one or more sources (information input); it must then process this information in order to produce work outputs. Similarly, an employee must receive information (information input), process it (mental processes), and act upon it in order to achieve certain results (work output). Division 4 focusses on the kinds of interpersonal relationships required by the job. The work situation or environment is measured by items in Division 5. Division 6 includes a variety of items related to work schedules, apparel worn on the job, job responsibilities, and job demands. Seven additional items at the end of PAQ relate to the method of pay and the amount of pay employees receive. To analyze a job using PAQ, a job analyst, supervisor, or trained employee determines whether each item applies to the job being analyzed and, if so, the degree to which it applies.

An analyst familiar with the PAQ can complete it in less than an hour. Though supervisors and employees can also use the PAQ, they should be trained to use it properly. A PAQ manual is available for instructional purposes, and a technical manual provides information on the questionnaire's development, procedures for use, and potential applications.[13]

The PAQ has many advantages. It can be applied to a wide range of jobs; its results can be obtained rapidly and compared to substantial existing data and research findings. Such data are especially useful to the career planning function in which jobs at different levels are compared in terms of job specifications. Such comparison allows planners to chart logical paths of progression between jobs. A further advantage is the many computerized data analysis packages available to PAQ users, including wage survey and job evaluation, performance appraisal, and training and selection.[14]

One disadvantage of the PAQ is that it does not result in a descriptive summary of a job or a listing of duties and tasks related to it. Rather, this questionnaire profiles a job in terms of the degree to which certain job elements are present. Another disadvantage is that it may not distinguish between very similar jobs since it is designed to be generally applicable across jobs. Reliability may also be a problem if users were not properly trained.

Finally, the PAQ's high reading level precludes its use in some circumstances. That problem may be overcome, however, by a recent job analysis questionnaire, the Job Element Inventory (JEI).[15] Since the JEI yields results similar to the PAQ but has only a tenth-grade reading level, it may prove valuable where the PAQ cannot be used.

Recent Questionnaire Methods

A number of new methods of job analysis have been developed since the early 1980s. Most are questionnaires (VERJAS is the outstanding exception), and most were developed to meet a particular need or handle a deficiency in existing methods. Only three examples will be discussed here.

The Job Component Inventory (JCI) was developed by several British psychologists to meet their country's needs.[16] The JCI is a 400-item questionnaire that provides a profile of both the job and the employee. Some of the areas in which it has been used are assessment of skill proficiency, design and evaluation of training materials, and career education, guidance, and placement. One unusual use is in redesigning jobs for employees with disabilities. The reading level is appropriate for most incumbents, and there is evidence of acceptable levels of agreement between incumbents and supervisors.

A second recent method is the Multi-method Job Design Questionnaire (MJDQ),[17] a 48-item questionnaire developed to aid in the design of jobs. Studies of both blue-collar and white-collar employees using analysts and incumbents show good inter-rater reliability. The originator, M.A. Campion, has drawn some interesting conclusions regarding job design. He argues that a motivational approach to job design that "strives to produce jobs that are stimulating and mentally demanding . . . may have the unintended consequence of increasing training times and creating staffing difficulties."[18] On the other hand, work designed according to mechanistic or perceptual/motor approaches that emphasize task specialization and information processing requirements may not allow employees job satisfaction.

A third recently developed method is Levine's Combination Job Analysis Method (C-JAM),[19] designed to provide information on both job and worker attributes. The C-JAM is similar to a mixture of job inventory and the PAQ. The development of the C-JAM for a set of jobs is time-consuming since "subject matter" (job) experts must describe and rate tasks on difficulty, criticality, and time spent, as well as knowledge, skills, ability, and other required worker characteristics. The advantage of the C-JAM is that it can serve many organizational needs for job analysis information. A shorter, less time-consuming version of the C-JAM called the Brief Job Analysis Method is available.

Job Analysis Problems and Issues

Reliability and Validity

Since many human resource methods and procedures use data from job analysis, it is important that these data be as reliable and valid as possible. Ideally, an employer would collect comprehensive job analysis information using multiple methods and create the database necessary for a wide array of human resource methods and procedures. One study of nine organizations with comprehensive computerized human resource systems found the process required several years and more than $1 million.[20]

Of course, maximizing reliability and validity must be weighed against costs, time constraints, and the intended uses of job analysis information. As suggested earlier, the intended use of job analysis information is the major factor in choice of method.

Reliability

Most research examining the reliability of job analysis methods has been done using either the PAQ or other structured methods. A recent review found inter-rater reliability was lower than test–retest reliability.[21] In other words, the level of agreement between different job analysts' ratings of the same jobs seems to differ more than when the same analyst rates the job at two points in time. One reason for the low to moderate level of inter-rater reliability is differences between raters. Although research has shown that some job analysts are more accurate raters than others, education is the only variable tested that shows significant correlation—better-educated analysts are more accurate.[22] A second possible explanation for differences between analysts is that the same job may be described differently by different people. The following analogy between a picture and job analysis is illustrative:

> Pictures differ in degree of clarity, the "trueness" of their representation of reality. They also differ in point of view. A picture taken from one angle may present quite a different view than one taken at a different angle. So it is with job analysis. One can interview two or three incumbents (i.e., job occupants) and their supervisor and find substantial differences in their descriptions of the job. Perhaps the discovery of differing viewpoints about the nature of a job is more the exception than the rule. However, their existence serves as a warning to the analyst to seek out more than one viewpoint for "photographing" the job. With enough pictures one can finally figure out what one is looking at.[23]

The reliability of job analysis can be maximized by (1) thoroughly training those conducting analyses in use of the method; (2) providing analysts with detailed job information rather than brief descriptions;[24] and (3) using more structured methods rather than less structured ones.

Validity

The validity of a job analysis method depends upon the purpose of the analysis. In theory, a job analysis can be regarded as valid to the extent it gives as complete and accurate a picture of jobs as is necessary for the specified purpose. In reality, researchers have found it difficult to demonstrate the completeness or accuracy of job analysis methods. From a practical standpoint, one should be aware of factors that can cause an incomplete or inaccurate picture of a job. An important example of such a factor is gender bias. Pay equity legislation has emphasized the importance of removing this threat to validity.

M.D. Dunnette has identified three factors that make it difficult to obtain a complete job description. He refers to them as (1) "time-determined changes"; (2) "employee-determined changes"; and (3) "situation-determined changes."[25]

Time-determined changes are of two types. The first involves job-related duties or tasks that are performed only occasionally or at widely spaced times. A deficient analysis may be descriptive of a job at a specific time, but not at another. To be complete and representative, a job analysis method should lead to a description of a job at all points in time. This can be accomplished by sampling job behaviour across time, using methods such as critical incidents or observation.

The second type of time-determined change relates to the effect of employees' varying experience levels. The same job may look quite different when performed by an inexperienced employee and by an experienced one. Experienced employees may also have additional tasks and responsibilities, but even if they do not, their greater competence may alter one's impression of a job. Therefore, a job analysis method must include questioning job occupants at different levels of experience in order to obtain a true picture of a job's duties and task-related activities.

The second factor identified by Dunnette is employee-determined changes. A job may be difficult to describe because different employees in it may perform somewhat different tasks, depending on their individual skills, experience, and interests. Thus, the same job may *appear* different by virtue of the person in the position. A complete description can be obtained by sampling an adequate number of employees.

The third factor that Dunnette cites is situation-determined changes, meaning that job content may change as a result of physical or human forces operating in the work environment. These changes can be caused by emergencies; noise levels; job pressures; or actions of the boss, the work group, or previous job occupants. An example comes from a manufacturing plant that experienced a series of bomb threats. When the threats first began, the plant had no formal plan for handling them. Several times, the manager evacuated most of the employees and asked supervisors to search the plant for a bomb. Finally, someone from outside the plant facetiously suggested to the human resource manager that he include as a part of the supervisor's job description "periodically searches for bombs in the plant." Situation-determined changes are, by their nature, very difficult to anticipate, but Dunnette suggests that various "aspects in the job setting that could potentially alter job content" be identified and described.[26]

Another factor resulting in job description differences is human judgement. Human judgement is needed to reach conclusions based on observation, to assign the ratings required by the FJA, PAQ, and C-JAM, and to determine job specifications. Even when job-related behaviour and tasks are completely described, judgement is required to assign minimal levels of education, experience, skills, and ability. Consequently, job descriptions vary according to different judgements concerning specifications. One study of 58 pairs of managers and subordinates from three organizations found that 85 percent of the pairs agreed on half or more of the job duties of the subordinate, but only 64 percent agreed on half or more of the job specifications.[27] More recent research has examined convergence among different types of raters such as incumbents, supervisors, and analysts on methods such as the PAQ and JCI. Generally, the results are similar to those of inter-rater reliability: agreement is moderate ($r = 0.47$ to 0.72).[28]

JOB ANALYSIS: A CONSTRAINT VERSUS A VALUABLE TOOL

The challenge for managers is to use job analysis to further organizational goals, particularly those of survival and competitiveness. In today's turbulent business environment, job analysis can be a valuable tool. Yet it can also become a constraint. For example, Ontario's Pay Equity Act could lead to its being a constraint in some organizations. An Ontario government survey found that only 5 percent of employers with 100 or fewer employees had human resource managers and only 25 percent had formal job descriptions.[29] In the rush to meet the deadlines stipulated in the act, there is a risk that hastily executed job analyses, perhaps performed by consultants who don't fully understand the organization, may result in inaccurate and/or overly specific job descriptions. Additionally, job analyses performed in order to carry out job evaluations necessary for the act are likely to focus on the content of specific jobs, rather than on job behaviours or skills, knowledge, and abilities. In many small companies, employees may perform a wide range of tasks and/or work, and pay may be based upon skills, knowledge, and abilities. A hastily done job analysis could push such an organization toward a more traditional approach to structuring jobs, constraining its flexibility. Clearly, pay equity is a desirable goal, but achieving it should not constrain an employer's categories of work and jobs.

CHALLENGING USES OF JOB ANALYSIS

Job analysis can be a valuable tool for coping with many HRM challenges, such as downsizing, promoting teamwork, employing disabled people, and coping with technological innovations. For example, as many employers reduced the size of their work forces in the 1980s and continue to do so in the 1990s, fewer people must often do the same or more work. Job analysis methods, such as job inventories, may be used to compare both related tasks across jobs and worker qualifications. Such comparisons can facilitate both combining jobs and assigning capable employees to them. Comparison of specific job requirements with worker qualifications can be used to identify training needs in the restructured organization.

The movement toward teamwork, a form of work organization in which responsibility for performance of large portions of a manufacturing or service process is shared by a small group of workers, has created the need to broaden and redefine jobs and their requisite skills. Many Canadian firms are moving toward team organization in order to increase their flexibility in responding to changing business circumstances. For example, in the forestry industry, jobs such as millwright, welder, and oiler have been combined to create the broader job of general sawmill mechanic.[30] As narrow jobs are combined into broader categories, it becomes more important to determine the knowledge, skills, and abilities necessary for successful team members. Unions have been conceding such reductions in the number of job classifications in return for greater job security or higher wage increases.[31] In a few cases, job classes have been almost completely eliminated in favour of payment based on the acquisition of skills. An example of payment for skill is the collective agreement between the Energy and Chemical Workers Union and Shell Canada's chemical plant in Sarnia, Ontario.[32]

As skilled labour shortages increase and pressure to employ people with disabilities grows, employers must be able to determine whether individuals with specific disabilities could successfully perform various jobs and what parts of jobs could be modified to accommodate them. Detailed job analysis information, such as that provided by the JCI or VERJAS, is necessary to determine required job modifications.

Summary

Job analysis serves a variety of purposes in an organization. HRM responsibilities for job analysis range from conducting job analyses to using job analysis information in most of the other human resource functions. For purposes of discussion, job analysis methods have been divided into four basic types: (1) observation methods, including direct observation, work methods analysis, and the critical incident technique; (2) interview techniques; (3) combined observation and interview approaches, such as functional job analysis and VERJAS; and (4) questionnaires, including job inventories or checklists, and the PAQ. Care must be taken in selecting a method of job analysis because some methods are more suitable for some job analysis purposes than for others. Problems of reliability can be minimized by training analysts, providing detailed job descriptions, and using structured analysis methods. Valid job analyses depend upon using methods appropriate to organizational needs, maximizing reliability, and adequate samples. Finally, job analysis has important roles in meeting new management challenges and opportunities, such as pay equity, downsizing, teamwork, and expert systems.

Review Questions

1. For what HRM functions would information on job specifications be more useful than information on tasks and duties? Briefly explain why.

2. Discuss HRM situations in which various questionnaire methods of job analysis might be used. What are the advantages and disadvantages of questionnaires in these situations?

3. This chapter, like most of the others in the book, has presented job analysis information as very basic and necessary for many HRM functions. Is job analysis adequately reliable and valid to serve as the cornerstone of HRM? Discuss the evidence.

PROJECT IDEAS

1. Obtain several job descriptions from local businesses, hospitals, or service organizations. Discuss them in terms of completeness. To what extent do they provide information regarding work products, worker activities, equipment used, job context, and job specifications? Try to find out what job analysis methods were used to collect the information in the descriptions and how long ago it was collected. Prepare a brief written or oral report discussing the descriptions, the job analysis process(es) employed, and any ideas you have for improving the descriptions.

2. Pick a common job, such as bus driver, sales clerk, or bank teller, and use any one of the job analysis methods to describe it. After preparing your job description, look up the job in the *Canadian Classification and Dictionary of Occupations* and find its description. Compare the two descriptions. Discuss any discrepancies and why they exist.

3. Prepare job specifications for the occupational analyst position described in this chapter. Try to relate each personal requirement to one or more of the activities listed for the job. If the entire class does this project, resulting specifications can be compared.

▶▶▶ CASES

CASE 5.1 ▶ JOB TASK INVENTORY: A TOOL FOR ORGANIZATIONAL CHANGE?

Jim Engler, HR manager at a small electrical parts manufacturing plant, sat at his desk reflecting upon the presentation he had just made to division and company officers. The presentation reviewed results of the company's innovative new job analysis system, through which Engler hoped to increase the efficiency of the production process, improve product quality, and more fully utilize employee potential.

Engler calls his new system the Job Task Inventory (JTI). Like other task and skills inventories, the JTI identifies specific competencies for jobs. It also identifies the steps involved in performing each competency, as well as the knowledge and personal qualities required and the equipment and tools used in the job.

Employee involvement is key to JTI development: panels of "experts" consisting of experienced workers from within the company identify both necessary job competencies and criteria for successful job performance. A management committee reviews and edits the panel's work prior to JTI approval. Once approved, the JTI serves as a job description.

From the description, a general training manual is developed that specifies the competencies and training steps employees must master to be certified for a job. The JTI process also has a mechanism for documenting improvements and changes in jobs. As you can see, the JTI approach goes beyond mere job analysis in that training programs, performance appraisal, and compensation are all tied to JTI results.

Thinking back to his presentation, Jim was justifiably proud. His JTI approach had resulted in the enlargement and enrichment of fifteen assembly machine operator jobs at the plant. With enlargement came the elimination of several more narrowly defined jobs, namely, production planner, set-up mechanic, and quality control inspector. Further, employees performing the new assembly machine operator jobs were happy with the challenge of their added responsibilities.

To illustrate the magnitude of some of these job changes to management, Engler handed out old job descriptions of two of the eliminated jobs, plus the new description for the assembly machine operator job. They are set out below.

OLD JOB DESCRIPTION 1

TITLE: QUALITY CONTROL INSPECTOR

GENERAL DESCRIPTION:
Performs routine inspection checks of the manufacturing process and provides feedback (verbal and written communication) in regard to product quality. May also assist in mechanical repair and provide feedback as to machine performance.

KNOWLEDGE AND SKILLS:
Must have the aptitude to interpret detailed blueprints and understand geometric tolerances. Must be proficient in the use of gauges, microscope, comparitors, and vertical indicators. Must possess decision-making capabilities in determining the acceptance or rejection of component parts and finished goods. Must be able to perform simple mechanical adjustments.

JOB RESPONSIBILITIES:
I. Inspection
   A. Checks parts on an hourly basis by visual, dimensional, and/or functional testing methods. These testing methods are incorporated into every stage of the assembly process.
      1. Parts-process stages
         a. loading pins
         b. capping
         c. welding
         d. crimping
         e. misc.
      2. Cable-process stages
         a. cutting
         b. notching
         c. grinding
         d. crimping
         e. testing (electrical, for continuity and shorts)
         f. components
      3. Misc. assembly
      4. Packing of all components and assemblies
   B. Ensures that the correct parts are being used and are properly assembled per the product print, workmanship standards, and inspection instructions.
   C. Maintains records of work performed and results of inspection.
   D. Makes decisions in regard to acceptability of product.

II. Other Duties
   A. Performs first articles on all assemblies and maintains records of results. The first article is done with each successive revision change.
   B. Reviews Manufacturing Process Cards for correct process sequence and assembly criteria. Also establishes requirements to build a quality product.
   C. Determines need for workmanship standards and develops the basic layout.
   D. Keeps files updated (blueprints, instructions, and process cards) to latest revision level.
   E. Assists production in correcting discrepant products and processes.
   F. Performs Capability Studies (process, equipment) as directed.
   G. May assist production in maintenance and mechanical repair of equipment.
   H. Reviews all incoming material for correct parts; reviews all outgoing material for appropriate packing methods, correct labelling, specified quantity, etc.
   I. Assists in training new personnel in all aspects of quality. May assist in production process training.
   J. May assume role of production supervisor when latter is absent; must therefore learn all phases of production:
      1. Staging work in process
      2. Setting up work stations
      3. Overseeing clerical functions
      4. Supervising production personnel

K. Learns other inspection jobs and is able to substitute for absent personnel if required:
   1. Receiving, returned goods
   2. Stamping, molding
   3. Assembly
   4. Plating

OLD JOB DESCRIPTION 2

TITLE: SET-UP MECHANIC A

GENERAL DESCRIPTION:
Installs, repairs, rebuilds, and maintains machinery and mechanical equipment used in production and related services.

KNOWLEDGE AND SKILLS:
Must possess the analytical abilities necessary to perform the responsibilities of the position. Requires a broad knowledge of mechanics, machine design, and matching methods and techniques.

JOB RESPONSIBILITIES:
   I. Analyze and Repair
      A. Diagnoses machine malfunctions and operating difficulties accurately.
      B. Performs temporary and permanent adjustments necessary to keep machines in production.

   II. Rebuilding
      A. Rebuilds machines and overhauls troublesome components and attachments. This involves dismantling and inspecting the parts and then rebuilding or replacing them.

   III. Skilled Operations
      A. Fits and aligns bearings, shafts, and spindles.
      B. Adjusts timing and limit mechanisms.
      C. Installs new and relocates existing machines and equipment. This involves dismantling, erecting, levelling, fitting, and aligning equipment.
      D. Sets up and operates machine tools to make parts.
      E. Improvises machine set-ups and tooling with unusual operations.

   IV. Co-operation
      A. Works closely with supervisors, toolmakers, engineering personnel, and maintenance staff with regard to planning methods and repair procedures.
      B. Co-ordinates machine repair functions with supervision, toolroom, and maintenance functions to ensure timely repair of parts or machines and to limit downtime.

   V. Quality
      A. Conducts visual inspection and dimensional checks of parts and submits checks to Quality Control (QC) for approval.

B. Performs random checks for QC and makes adjustments when necessary.
C. Makes and records hourly QC checks and records in QC record book as regularly as possible.

VI. Safety
A. Makes regular checks of machine safeties to ensure they are in proper order.
B. Reports any hazard in the work area or corrects it immediately.

VII. Preventative Maintenance
A. Performs daily, weekly, or monthly lubrication requirements.
B. Checks and changes oil when necessary.
C. Maintains records pertinent to preventative maintenance.
D. Checks for damaged oil lines, worn or frayed electrical cords, wires, outlets, and switches. Also reports loose or broken guards and worn machine parts.
E. Fills out work requests for any preventative maintenance listed above.

VIII. Housekeeping
A. Cleans machines.
B. Sweeps floors.
C. Stacks materials in neat piles.
D. Performs other duties required in maintaining a neat and orderly work area.

IX. Other Responsibilities
A. Performs additional duties assigned by the Shift Supervisor when all work is completed in this position's designated work area or when assistance is needed in another area.
B. Plots and graphs $\bar{X}$ and R bar charts and interprets them.
C. Makes quality decisions that are advantageous to plant operations.

NEW JOB DESCRIPTION

TITLE: ASSEMBLY MACHINE OPERATOR

Competency	Steps to Perform Competency	Knowledge	Safety
A. Inspect Finished Product	1. Obtain sample parts from machine	Know how many parts to gather Know when to gather sample Know from what machine to gather sample Know where to get sample Know part numbers and lot number	Know safest place to retrieve sample

Competency	Steps to Perform Competency	Knowledge	Safety
	2. Perform visual inspection (if O.K., proceed with final inspection; if not, refer to problem solving)	Know what a normal part looks like Know how to do problem solving	
B. Strive toward and Communicate Continual Improvement	1. Identify a repetitive problem or situation	Know frequency of problem Know what constitutes a problem Know if you are part of the problem	
	2. Identify potential solutions and discuss quality issues and concerns with other departments	Know potential causes of problem Know how to be tactful Know how to describe problem	Make certain the solution is a safe one
C. Learn to Operate the Machines Correctly	1. Identify and acquire the necessary resources (manuals, people, etc.) to operate machine adequately	Know location of resources (people, log book, tech manuals, etc.)	
	2. Observe machine in operation	Know to watch and listen Know to observe machines, safety features, panel, etc., and quality parts	Follow general safety rules
	3. Evaluate performance (self and machine)	Know how to review machine performance Know how to review personal performance Know when to apply discipline	

Competency	Steps to Perform Competency	Knowledge	Safety
D. Perform Change-overs and Synchronize Production Equipment	1. Prepare machine for change-over	Know to clean bowls and machine rails, belts Know to stop machine in the "proper position" for change-over	Use emergency stop to avoid injury and shut off air if needed
	2. Synchronize and adjust adjacent machines	Know speed of master machine to control speed of related machines and equipment to match (i.e., feeder bowls, belts, tube loader)	Replace all guards, etc.; make certain all safety devices work and are switched on
E. Repair Machines	1. Develop a repair plan	Know consequences of plan Know how to use tools Know how machine operates Know plan will vary by category of problem	
	2. Perform quality check on product	Know quality parameters Know all updated revisions and specs Know how to gauge parts Know how to use all measuring equipment Know documentation procedures	
F. Solve Problems	1. Select the solution that has the highest probability of success and develop a repair plan	Know machine histories Know to discuss solution with appropriate people if needed Know to listen well and ask Know to remain open minded	

Competency	Steps to Perform Competency	Knowledge	Safety
G. Train Others	1. Evaluate the trainee's progress	Know how to judge the quality of the trainee's performance Know to be fair and honest Know what is expected of the trainee Know to evaluate trainee's safety awareness Know how to evaluate whether trainee is progressing or not	
H. Monitor Machine Process	1. Examine air pressure	Know where guages are located Know proper poundage and setting	Wear safety glasses
I. Adjust Machine Process	1. Adjust/replace belts when needed	Know location of belts Know how to identify worn belts Know proper tension Know correct tools to use	

Source: Based on personal communication between Jim Engler and the author, 1992. Used with permission.

TASKS AND QUESTIONS

1. Compare the eliminated positions with the assembly machine operator job. What job responsibilities of the eliminated positions are now part of the machine operator job?
2. Why should production be more efficient, quality be higher, and employees be more satisfied with the new assembly operator job?
3. What kinds of problems might this new system create for management or for those in other jobs?
4. What might be the implications for other HRM functions of using the JTI system?

CASE 5.2 ▸ JOB ANALYSIS AT ST. JUDE'S HOSPITAL: AVOIDING GENDER BIAS

Rohit Sharda, job analyst at St. Jude's Hospital, had just had a meeting with his boss, Sylvie Jardot. Jardot was concerned about both recent pay equity legislation and complaints from several female employees regarding the classification and pay of their jobs compared with some of the predominantly male jobs. Sharda's task was to investigate this situation and make recommendations to Jardot.

Sharda recalled hearing about pay equity but had thought that St. Jude's job descriptions and job evaluation system were fair and equitable, as he had worked with a professional management consulting company just a few years earlier to install the system. He decided to contact the Ontario Pay Equity Commission to see what information they could provide. After a short while, a package of information arrived from the commission. Sharda read the information with considerable interest and learned some surprising things about the job analysis process, job descriptions, and job evaluation.

In preparation for the meeting to discuss his recommendations with Jardot, Sharda highlighted excerpts of the important points on collecting and reporting job information from the commission's *How to Do Pay Equity Job Comparisons*. Those excerpts are given in the following sections.

COLLECTING JOB INFORMATION

Job information is usually collected in one of two ways: a self-administered questionnaire or an interview. Sometimes both methods are used to gain more detailed information on specific jobs.

There are other ways of collecting job information, such as observation (sometimes called a "desk audit"), or reviewing old job descriptions. But no matter what collection method is used, the process and the results must be free of gender bias.

There are ready-made questionnaires available; however, the Pay Equity Office does not endorse any specific type. Questionnaires developed by others should be examined for gender bias. Many ready-made questionnaires were devised before pay equity legislation was introduced and before gender bias became a serious concern. Using a single questionnaire to collect information on all jobs will facilitate standardized information.

If using the interview method, the interviewers should possess basic interviewing skills and know when to ask additional questions. Again, a good set of interview questions is essential to find out the job's content and ensure no gender bias.

The Questionnaire Method

When you design a questionnaire, ask only enough questions to acquire information on the skill, effort, responsibility and working conditions that the job involves. Too many questions can discourage people from responding.

Make sure all the questions are clear and will invite complete information. Decide if it is best to use open or closed questions, or a combination.

An open question does not provide potential answers, but simply asks the person to describe something in his or her own words. For example, "What kinds of situations make your job stressful?" is an open-ended question.

To ensure that the full range of female jobs will be reported, include examples. For instance, with the question "Describe your general responsibilities," examples could include activities with clients, patients, budgets, children, customers, and so on. It is also important to bear in mind that women may be more likely to omit facets of their jobs when they are asked to reply to open-ended questions. Including examples will help to offset this tendency. For instance, rather than asking people "What kind of equipment do you use in performing your job?," a listing of equipment could be given. A closed question, on the other hand, limits the possible responses: "What amount of time do you spend at the word processor—

20%? 40%? 60%? 80%? 100%?"

Make sure that the unbiased information needed to establish pay equity is collected.

When asking about skill, for example, remember human relations, communication and other activities found in female jobs. When asking about effort, remember that repeated lifting of children, patients, and supplies and repeated bending deserve recognition. Responsibility for clients and customers should be considered, along with responsibility for budget and staff. Working conditions in an office can expose workers to stale air and continual low-grade noise. Working in a hospital or a nursing home can expose the staff to disease, harassment and dirt, even though it is a clean environment in comparison with, for example, furnace room work.

Develop questions that probe—"how" and "why"—what the job really involves, and ask them in a way that invites truthful answers. As workers may be uncomfortable about describing their working conditions, ask them to rate them, or provide a list and request that they check off any items that apply.

Beware of biased language and questions. This is a hazard in collecting job information, as well as in recording it. A question may be leading, or produce a biased result. For example:

Please check the work aids you use:
- ❏ Typewriter
- ❏ Computer
- ❏ Power Tools (please describe)
- ❏ Floor Polisher

For a secretarial position, this form of question leaves out the word processor, the telephone, the calculator, the fax machine, the photocopier, etc. *The question is biased.*

Leading or biased questions can skew results. Consider this example: "Describe your responsibilities for staff and budgets." What about the responsibilities of a childcare worker for children?

The Interview Method

The Interviewer   To prepare interview questions, follow the same guidelines outlined earlier for the self-administered questionnaire. The interviewer should have a reasonable degree of familiarity with gender bias issues.

The interviewer and the worker should prepare for the interview. The interviewer should arrange the appointment well in advance, and should also arrange for a quiet place at the worksite to hold the interview. The interviewer should review the questions prior to the interview, and should prepare a list of job duties in advance.

In conducting the interview, the interviewer should be exact about the questions asked and should record responses precisely. The interviewer should probe to get more detailed information: for example, "How is that done?" "Tell me more about . . . ," etc.

Sensitivity to gender bias is as critical here as it is in preparing job questionnaires. The interviewer should be alert to cultural backgrounds; to gender discrimination in language; and to some women's tendencies to under-report what is involved in their jobs (while at the same time not overcompensating for this possibility).

A secretary may describe one of the job's duties as "arranging meetings," for instance. But by asking the secretary to explain what that entails, you may discover that it requires booking meeting rooms, hiring caterers, setting up the chairs, and moving and operating audio-visual equipment. It could also involve late hours, last-minute changes to agendas, and other stressful conditions.

You can collect job information from every member of a job class, or from a good sample. To address gender bias, you may consider surveying or interviewing more workers in female job classes than in male job classes.

Before sending out the questionnaire, review the questions with people familiar with the jobs. See if any of the questions are unclear, incomplete, or have the potential to produce biased results for female jobs.

Include clear instructions for the questionnaire's respondents. Outline the reasons for collecting this information, and make sure people understand that it is the job that is being looked at, not the person. Make sure, too, that the method for distributing the questionnaire and returning it guarantees maximum participation. The questionnaire should reach its audience promptly, and you should be able to retrieve it equally efficiently. If necessary, hold follow-up sessions to discuss the questionnaire and its results.

Developing a Job Information Statement

Defining the Statement

A job information statement summarizes the responsibilities, requirements and working conditions of a specific job based on the information collected in the job analysis process. It ranges from a list of tasks and duties to a formal job description.

This information statement can then be used as the basis for comparing and evaluating jobs.

A job information statement could include:
- the purpose of the job;
- the tasks and duties to be performed and the effort required;
- the supervision given and received;
- the work environment and the hazards encountered;
- the tools and work aids used to perform the duties.

From a job information statement, the skill, effort, responsibilities and working conditions for every job in the organization can be determined.

Like job analysis, the job information statement does not describe the skill, background or qualifications of the person doing the job, only the job itself.

Making the distinction between *jobs* and the *people* in the jobs is the hardest part of the process.

Recording Job Information

There is no single "correct" way to record job information. But these basic steps can make the process simple and straightforward. Both organizations with recorded job information and those without can follow them. Remember, however, to use the same approach and format for all jobs.

STEP 1: Review the results of job analysis. Make sure that information is collected in a fair way, and that complete, unbiased information is available on both female and male jobs.

STEP 2: Identify the job. It is helpful to have identifying information for each job so that titles, names of supervisors and other facts (for example, the date that information was collected) are clearly shown.

STEP 3: State the job's purpose. This can be a summary of the duties, outlining in general terms what the job contributes to the organization.

Examples

Title:	Payroll Clerk
Summary:	Processes payroll information into computer system and verifies paycheques.

Title: Estimator
Summary: Develops accurate, complete estimates for each project, and provides information and technical support to sales staff.

In each case, the summary provides the reader with a sense of the job's framework.

STEP 4: Check for inaccurate or sexist job titles.   This is a good opportunity to review the titles of the jobs in the organization. Check for inflated, biased or misleading titles, such as "Executive Assistant" for a male job, and "Administrative Assistant" for the female equivalent. (If the duties are identical, the same titles should be used for both.) Another example: "Charwoman" or "Cleaner" for the female job, and "Custodian" for the male job, though both may have identical duties in cleaning a building.

STEP 5: Identify the major and minor duties for each job.   Job duties are usually listed in descending order from the most to the least important. Duties can be defined as "major" or "minor."

Major duties are those which reflect the primary purpose of a job. Looking at the job summary and title can help determine the major duties. A major duty in a dietary job in a nursing home could be "preparing meal trays," for example.

Minor duties are those that are performed in support of the major duties, or those that are not necessarily related to the major purpose of the position. A minor duty in a dietary job, for instance, could be "cleaning up."

STEP 6: Rank the duties in frequency and importance.   When it is difficult to choose which duties are major or minor, duties can be ranked in terms of frequency and importance. Frequency refers to the amount of time spent doing a particular duty, and how often it is done. Importance refers to the relative value of a particular duty to the job and to the organization.

But this approach can lead to problems if frequency is the only way duties are ranked. In many jobs, relatively little time is spent doing very important duties. For instance, a childcare worker may spend 10 per cent of the time dealing with hard-to-handle children, which is an important part of the job. Traditional job evaluation has often contributed to the undervaluation of female jobs by considering only the amount of time spent on a duty, rather than the skills required, and the value of those skills to the organization.

STEP 7: Make sure others understand what the work involves.   Not everyone has the same understanding of job titles and duties. Provide enough detail so that there is no doubt of the skills and effort required in a job.

Which of the following descriptions gives you a complete idea of what is involved in the job?

Acts as receptionist **or** Greets visitors, determines the nature of their visits and directs them.

Performs accounting duties **or** Posts daily transactions to general ledger, balances accounts and contacts clients to resolve discrepancies.

In the past, many jobs have not been described in detail, and the incomplete, generalized way of looking at these job duties has led to undervaluing of their required skills, effort and responsibilities in addition to working conditions.

STEP 8: List the work aids used to perform the work. The job information should provide an accurate impression of the type of equipment that is operated to perform the duties of the job. The equipment used relates directly to the skill, effort, responsibilities and working conditions of each job.

STEP 9: Include the job requirements/job specifications. The job requirements (or job specifications) can be listed at the end of the job information statement. These are descriptions of the job in terms of the skill, effort, responsibility and working conditions involved. The job specifications give the reader additional information on the content of the job, and its impact on the organization.

Writing It Up: A Checklist

The purpose of a job information statement is to provide the reader with a clear understanding of what is done, why it is done and how it is done.

The following guidelines will help you to prepare clear, bias-free job information statements:

1. Make sure that both women's and men's work activities are described accurately, using simple, straightforward, precise and bias-free language.
2. Explain technical terms.
3. Start each duty statement with a verb in the third person, present tense.
4. Include enough detail about the job.
5. Review the content.

Sharda felt the material from the Pay Equity Commission was very informative and would be a great help to him in avoiding gender bias in St. Jude's job descriptions. Indeed, he felt the material provided some excellent guidelines for conducting job analyses. He decided to see how much he had learned by reviewing the two job information statements that follow. Job Information Statement 1 is an example of a biased job description and it is not in accordance with the Pay Equity Commission's guidelines. The problems with Job Information Statement 1 are noted in square brackets.

Your assignment is as follows: Using Job Information Statement 1 as an example, review Job Information Statement 2 and note any problems or biases you see in it. Your instructor can provide you with the problems and biases identified by the Pay Equity Commission.

JOB INFORMATION STATEMENT 1:
A BAD EXAMPLE

ABC Company: Retail Division

Job Title: Storesman [*man* is a sexist title]

Employee: Freddy Samson [do not need incumbent's name]

Summary: Reporting to the Warehouse Manager, receives and stores incoming shipments from suppliers, and maintains complex inventory records. [*Complex* is a value-loaded adjective—more description is needed to understand what exactly is involved.]

Duties

1. Receives incoming shipments; unloads trucks using forklifts and tow motors, and moves items to appropriate storage areas.

2. Verifies delivery slips against invoices, and liaises with suppliers to resolve discrepancies. Must be tactful, but firm. [Use *contacts* in place of *liaises with*. *Must be tactful* ... describes the person, not the job. Try "the job involves handling disagreements which may arise, etc. ..."]

3. Updates complex inventory records daily and co-ordinates their dispatch to clerk for processing. [What makes them complex? Use *forwards* in place of *co-ordinates*.]

4. Retrieves, packs and prepares items for delivery to retail stores. May involve his lifting up to 20 kg. [*May* ... — is it part of the job or not? *His* is not neutral.]

Job Specifications

Skill: Ability to operate very valuable, complex equipment and perform statistical calculations. Excellent human relations skills essential. Must be a high school graduate with three years' progressively responsible experience. [*Very valuable* ... — is it a forklift? Are *statistical calculations* arithmetic only? *Excellent human relations skills* is exaggerated.]

Effort: Heavy physical effort may be required. Frequent lifting demanded. [*Heavy* ... —how heavy? *May* ... —is it or isn't it? *Frequent* ... —how often? hourly, daily?]

Responsibility: Responsible for valuable equipment and shipment of goods. Errors costly to company if orders misplaced or delayed. [*Valuable* is misleading.]

Working Conditions: Lifting and moving heavy items can be hazardous. Some exposure to cold in winter, but most work performed in well-lit warehouse. [*Lifting* ... —double-counted, since also listed under "Effort."]

JOB INFORMATION STATEMENT 2: TEST YOURSELF

Job Title: Junior Admitting Co-ordinator

Summary: To assist the Admitting Supervisor in administering procedures and policies.

Duties

1. Responsible for ordering office supplies.
2. Assumes the responsibilities of the supervisor in his absence.
3. Provides the orientation of new admitting staff in liaison with the supervisor.
4. Assists other staff and clarifies procedures as required.
5. Assists in the implementation and enforcement of hospital procedures and policies.
6. Reviews daily admissions with respect to accuracy and discusses same with other staff.
7. Types and checks admission documentation and notes any information to be audited. Files in numerical order, as required.
8. Responsible for the proper function of all departmental equipment. Deals with repairmen when appropriate.

Requirements

- neat appearance
- good communication skills
- good health and grooming habits
- typing of minimum 50 w.p.m.
- ability to read, write and speak English
- second-language skills useful
- Grade 13 diploma

Source: Excerpts and job information statements are taken from Ontario, Pay Equity Commission, *How to Do Pay Equity Job Comparisons* (Toronto, March 1989), pp. 9–18. Used with permission.

NOTES

1. Ontario, Pay Equity Commission, *Questions and Answers—Pay Equity in the Workplace* (Toronto, March 1988), p. 6.

2. Manpower and Immigration Canada, *Canadian Classification and Dictionary of Occupations* (Ottawa: Information Canada, 1971). Additional definitions and recent changes in the *CCDO* are in Employment and Immigration Canada, *Canadian Classification and Dictionary of Occupations, Guide*, 9th ed. (Ottawa: Supply and Services Canada, 1989).

3. P.E. Spector, M.T. Brannick, and M.D. Coovert, "Job Analysis," in C.L. Cooper and I. Robertson, eds., *International Review of Industrial and Organizational Psychology* (Toronto: John Wiley, 1989), p. 281.

4. In the *Scarborough Firefighters* case (1979), the Ontario Supreme Court held that job descriptions can be the subject of negotiation. *Labour Law News*, vol. 5, no. 9 (September 1979).

5. J.C. Flanagan, "The Critical Incident Technique," *Psychological Bulletin*, vol. 51 (1954), pp. 28–35.

6. Ernest J. McCormick, *Job Analysis: Methods and Applications* (New York: AMACOM, 1979).

7. Stephen E. Bemis, Ann Holt Belenky, and Dee Ann Soder, *Job Analysis: An Effective Management Tool* (Washington, DC: Bureau of National Affairs, 1983), p. 11.

8. Bemis, Belenky, and Soder, *Job Analysis*, pp. 62–63.

9. R.A. Ash and S.L. Edgell, "A Note on the Readability of the Position Analysis Questionnaire (PAQ)," *Journal of Applied Psychology*, vol. 60 (1975), pp. 765–66.

10. Ontario, Pay Equity Commission, *How to Do Pay Equity Job Comparisons* (Toronto: March 1989).

11. S. Gael, "Development of Job Task Inventories and Their Use in Job Analysis Research," *JSAS Catalog of Selected Documents in Psychology*, vol. 7, no. 1 (1977), ms. 1445; and L.H. Hough, *Professional Activities Description Questionnaire* (Minneapolis, Minn.: Personnel Decisions Research Institute, 1979).

12. Ernest J. McCormick, P.R. Jeanneret, and R.C. Mecham, *Position Analysis Questionnaire* (West Lafayette, Ind.: Purdue University Press, 1969).

13. Ernest J. McCormick, P.R. Jeanneret, and R.C. Mecham, *PAQ: Job Analysis Manual* (Logan, Utah: PAQ Services Inc., 1977).

14. McCormick, Jeanneret, and Mecham, *PAQ*.

15. R.J. Harvey, M.D. Hakel, L. Friedman, and E.T. Cornelius, "Dimensionality of the Job Element Inventory: A Simplified Worker-Oriented Job Analysis Questionnaire," *Journal of Applied Psychology*, vol. 73 (1988), pp. 639–46.

16. M.H. Banks, P.R. Jackson, E.M. Stafford, and P.B. Warr, "The Job Components Inventory and the Analysis of Jobs Requiring Limited Skill," *Personnel Psychology*, vol. 36 (1983), pp. 57–66.

17. M.A. Campion, "Interdisciplinary Approaches to Job Design: A Constructive Replication with Extensions," *Journal of Applied Psychology*, vol. 73 (1988), pp. 467–481; and M.A. Campion and P.W. Thayer, "Development and Field Evaluation of an Interdisciplinary Measure of Job Design," *Journal of Applied Psychology*, vol. 70 (1985), pp. 29–43.

18. Campion, "Interdisciplinary Approaches to Job Design," p. 477.

19. E.L. Levine, *Everything You Always Wanted to Know about Job Analysis* (Tampa, Fla.: Mariner Publishing, 1983).

20. E.L. Levine, F. Sistrunk, K. McNutt, and S. Gael, "Review and Evaluation of Job Analysis Systems at Selected Organizations," a symposium conducted at the Annual Meeting of the Southeastern Industrial and Organizational Psychological Association, Orlando, Fla., 1986.

21. Spector, Brannick, and Coovert, "Job Analysis."

22. E.T. Cornelius and K.S. Lyness, "A Comparison of Holistic and Decomposed Judgment Strategies in Job Analyses by Job Incumbents," *Journal of Applied Psychology*, vol. 65 (1980), pp. 155–63.

23. G.M. Drauden and N.G. Peterson, *A Domain Sampling Approach to Job Analysis* (St. Paul, Minn.: Test Validation Center, State of Minnesota Department of Employee Relations, 1974).

24. R.J. Harvey and S.R. Lozada-Larsen, "Influence of Amount of Job Descriptive Information on Job Analysis Rating Accuracy," *Journal of Applied Psychology* vol. 73 (1988), pp. 457–61.

25. M.D. Dunnette, *Personnel Selection and Placement* (Belmont, Calif.: Wadsworth, 1986).

26. Dunnette, *Personnel Selection and Placement*.

27. N.R.F. Maier, L.R. Hoffman, J.J. Hoover, and W.H. Read, *Superior-Subordinate Communication in Management*, research study 52 (New York: American Management Association, 1961).

28. J.E. Smith and M.D. Hakel, "Convergence among Data Sources, Response Bias, and Reliability and Validity of a Structured Job Analysis Questionnaire," *Personnel Psychology*, vol. 32 (1979), pp. 677–92.

29. S. McKay, "Getting Even," *Canadian Business*, May 1988, pp. 48–54.

30. L.T. Pinfield and J.S. Atkinson, "The Flexible Firm," *Canadian Business Review*, Winter 1988, pp. 17–19.

31. Wilfred List, "Making Work Rules Flexible—New Pressure Facing Unions," *The Globe and Mail*, December 30, 1985; and Casey French, "Unions at Port Waler Agree to Be Flexible," *The Globe and Mail*, December 24, 1986.

32. Collective Agreement between Shell Canada (Sarnia Chemical Plant) and the Energy and Chemical Workers' Union (Local 800), February 1, 1990, to January 31, 1992.

SUGGESTIONS FOR FURTHER READING

☐ S.E. Bemis, A.H. Belenky, and D.A. Soder. *Job Analysis: An Effective Management Tool*. Washington, DC: Bureau of National Affairs, 1983.
☐ S. Gael. *The Job Analysis Handbook*. New York: Wiley, 1988.
☐ E.L. Levine. *Everything You Always Wanted to Know about Job Analysis*. Tampa, Fla.: Mariner Publishing, 1983.
☐ E.J. McCormick. *Job Analysis and Applications*. New York: AMACOM, 1979.
☐ P.E. Spector, M.T. Brannick, and M.D. Coovert. "Job Analysis." In G.L. Cooper and I. Robertson, eds., *International Review of Industrial and Organizational Psychology*. Toronto: John Wiley, 1989, pp. 281–329.

CHAPTER 6

RECRUITING: ATTRACTING APPLICANTS

- THE ROLE OF RECRUITING
- RECRUITING ACTIVITIES
- FACTORS AFFECTING THE APPLICANT-ATTRACTION PROCESS
- HRM IN ACTION ▸ RCMP MAKES PROGRESS IN MINORITY RECRUITING
- RECRUITING METHODS AND SOURCES
- EVALUATING THE RECRUITING EFFORT
- SUMMARY
- REVIEW QUESTIONS
- PROJECT IDEAS
- CASE 6.1 ▸ RECRUITING AT NOVATEL COMMUNICATIONS
- CASE 6.2 ▸ EXPANSION AT QUINAN STORES
- NOTES
- SUGGESTIONS FOR FURTHER READING

THE SUN HAD JUST BEGUN TO DRIVE AWAY the shadows of the pre-dawn darkness in early January 1988 as Garth Burlingham, recruiting manager for NovAtel Communications, boarded a 747 bound for Singapore. As he reached his seat, he was relieved to find Lin Chou, director of one of NovAtel's special projects groups, already sitting in the seat beside his. Garth remarked to Lin that he would be glad to escape Calgary's unusually cold winter for the next ten days. Lin agreed and added that he would enjoy the trip more if they didn't have to work so hard while they were there. Garth, who had made many trips to Singapore as well as Hong Kong and Europe since 1986, reassured Lin, saying the work wouldn't be too hard since it would mainly be talking with electrical engineers about what it was like to work for NovAtel and live in Calgary. Lin asked, with a poorly concealed grin, what he should say if someone asked how cold it got in Calgary? Though Garth could tell the question was only half serious, he replied with little trace of humour, saying that nearly 50 engineers from the Far East were enjoying the challenge of NovAtel and the beauty of Calgary. Burlingham smiled as he added, "You need a little cold weather to have some of the best skiing in the world. And if they don't like skiing, tell them the largest-in-the-world indoor mall is only two and a half hours away, in Edmonton."

As Garth settled back in his seat, he recalled the words of his firm's chief executive officer, Del Lippert: "We don't have a shortage of opportunities, we have a shortage of people."[1]

Despite unemployment rates hovering near 10 percent or higher, NovAtel Communications, a Calgary-based manufacturer of cellular phones, like many other high-technology firms in North America, was desperately seeking trained employees capable of helping Canadian companies successfully compete in global markets. Though Garth wished he did not have to leave Canada to find people with the knowledge, training, and experience that NovAtel required, the schools in Canada and the United States were simply not producing the quality and number of people needed. Ironically, NovAtel was founded in 1983 as a joint venture between Alberta Government Telephones and Nova Corporation in part to provide jobs for Alberta's electronics and computer engineers who were leaving the province to find employment.

Burlingham's human resource strategy of attracting highly skilled and experienced engineers was not unlike NovAtel's business strategy, which was to "buy technology created by other people's research and fine-tune it, with a view to perfecting the manufacturing process."[2] As it turned out, both business and HRM strategies proved highly effective over the next few years.

NovAtel grew quickly, despite a rapidly changing, globally competitive market. By early 1991, it had approximately 1800 employees, with 350 hired in 1990 and 338 in 1989. Gains were experienced in productivity and labour efficiency as well. In 1990, NovAtel shipped approximately 500 000 cellular phones from state-of-the-art plants in Calgary and Lethbridge. The highly automated Calgary plant used robots to assemble circuit boards and a just-in-time inventory system to minimize storage costs. Labour costs were reduced from 50 to 15 percent per unit, matching those of Japan or South Korea.

The difficulties of attracting qualified and motivated labour are not limited to Canada's high-technology firms. Businesses as varied as Canadian Pacific Hotels, Radio Shack, Coles bookstores, and McDonald's Restaurants have experienced great difficulties hiring and keeping good employees. The consequences of these shortages go beyond having to go around the world to hire qualified employees. For example, Radio Shack in Halifax had to send repair work to Montreal because of a lack of electronics technicians; Coles had to use employees from existing stores to open two new ones in Toronto; and McDonald's offered employees bonuses of up to $500 for recruiting a friend. The situation is unlikely to improve as the proportion of young people entering the labour market will continue to decline through the 1990s, more people are retiring earlier, the growth in new female labour force entrants appears to have peaked, and net immigration is not sufficient to meet demand. Additionally, as suggested by NovAtel's difficulties, far too many Canadians come to the job market with inadequate basic skills in reading and math.

As many as 41 percent of companies find that workers' deficiencies in basic skills are causing errors and other production problems.[3] Obviously, the problem is not a lack of applicants — the Toyota plant in Cambridge, Ontario, screened thousands of applicants to hire 800; the Mazda plant in Flat Rock, Michigan, hired 3500 out of 96 500.[4] The problems and shortcomings of the Canadian education system — which includes only 72 percent of 17-year-olds, compared with 94 percent in Japan, 89 percent in Germany, and 87 percent in the United States[5] — have led to many of the recruiting problems employers face today. Some of Canada's major employers such as IBM Canada, Northern Telecom, Imperial Oil, and Cargill Ltd. are very concerned about the shortage of qualified applicants.[6] At Imperial, for example, the need for linkage with the schools has been so clearly recognized that the manager of academic affairs, who has traditionally been responsible for the company's national recruiting strategy, is also now responsible for developing and implementing a strategy for relations with Canada's education system.[7]

As you begin learning about the recruiting process, consider the assumption underlying the entire recruiting function: that qualified or at least trainable applicants *can* be found either outside or within the organization without unreasonable costs or delays. The experiences of NovAtel and many other Canadian employers suggest that recruiting activities must include not only reaping but sowing human resources.

This chapter discusses *recruiting*, the process of attracting applicants with certain skills, abilities, and other personal characteristics to job vacancies in an organization. Specifically, recruiting includes developing a plan and preparing a message, choosing recruiting sources and methods, and evaluating the effort. From a broad perspective, the attraction process includes both the inducements and the nature of the applicant pools as well as recruiting activities. This distinction, made in a recent model of applicant-attraction strategies, points to the importance of both money and other benefits as well as the recruiting process.[8] With affirmative action in the United States and the possibility of employment equity being legislated in the provinces, recruitment challenges will include attracting qualified members of designated groups and promoting them.

The chapter begins with a discussion of the role of recruiting, recruiting activities, and five factors affecting recruiting. It then turns to an examination of more than a dozen different recruiting methods and sources. A final section describes some of the ways recruiting efforts are evaluated.

THE ROLE OF RECRUITING

Recruiting includes both attracting applicants from the outside — *external recruiting* — and seeking applicants from within the organization — *internal recruiting*. Though most of this chapter examines external recruiting methods, such as newspaper ads and the use of sources such as colleges and union hiring halls, internal methods such as job posting are also included. Regardless of the type of recruiting, the goal is the same — to attract a set of qualified applicants for job vacancies — and the approach is the same — to get the message describing the job to appropriate applicant populations. One of the major differences between internal and external recruiting is in the size and nature of applicant pools. Obviously, potential applicant pools are smaller for internal recruiting, but the organization has more control over and knowledge of applicants' training, development, and work experiences. The forces of employment equity, labour shortages, and competitive pressures are increasing the importance of internal recruiting as well as training and development. One can also easily argue that external recruiting is becoming more similar to internal recruiting in that employers are being forced to take a more active role in developing good applicant pools outside the boundaries of their own organizations.

THE CHANGING ROLE OF RECRUITING

Over the years, the basic role of recruiting—attracting applicants with certain skills, abilities, and personal characteristics to job vacancies in the organization—has changed little. But the nature of vacancies, the nature of applicants, and the nature of how they are attracted have changed from what they were in the recent past. For example, changes in the population and labour force have affected the characteristics of applicants. Chapter 2 discussed the increasing ethnic diversity of the Canadian work force as well as the aging of the population. In the past, many companies have considered members of minority groups and female applicants for some jobs but not others. For example, women and members of minority groups have tended to be underrepresented in upper management positions.

In the economy of the 1990s, such preferences are likely to lead to both legal and competitive problems. Employers cannot afford to ignore any group of potentially valuable applicants lest they fail to use all resources available to enhance their position as competitors in the global economy. Neither can they risk legal challenges of failing to offer employment equity. (Some companies have already made progress in this respect. Warner-Lambert Canada, which began an affirmative action program in 1975, is an example of a company that has both hired and promoted women and members of minority groups. In 1990, women held 43 percent of the firm's nearly 1600 positions, including 44 percent of supervisory positions, compared to 18 percent in 1975, and 9 of the 52 senior management positions, compared with 8 in 1975.[9])

Meanwhile, jobs and organizations have changed because of economic and competitive pressures as well as technological advances such as those in communications and computers. The effect has been both the elimination of many repetitive, lesser-skilled jobs and an increase in the knowledge and skills required to perform many of the new and restructured jobs. With such job changes, progressive employers have flattened their organizational structures and shortened career paths in their efforts to remain internationally competitive. Jobs in organizations of the 1990s will increasingly require the ability to change and to learn new skills. They will also require the ability to work closely with others, often in teams. Companies such as Corning, IBM, Xerox, General Electric, Ford, Kodak, Toyota, and Procter and Gamble already operate some teamwork plants.

What does all this change mean for recruiting? The role of recruiting has become more vital to the success of the organization than ever before. It is also more difficult than ever.

Adding to the challenge of recruiting is the fact that organizations' HRM professionals are doing less of the job while others, such as temporary employment agencies and in some cases line managers and even employees, act as recruiters. Since the recession and subsequent downsizing of the early and mid-1980s, most employers have been cautious about adding new employees. One increasingly popular approach is to have both a "core" labour force—"regular" or "permanent" employees—and a temporary or "flex" labour force of employees who are utilized as needed. Some companies recruit both core and temporary workers, but many use employment agencies for recruiting temporaries. Thus, the recruiting function may be subcontracted, in part, to one or more agencies, which also often hire and even train people. In other words, some degree of control over the recruiting and hiring process is delegated to the temporary-employment agency (though the employer can usually refuse to use a particular temporary employee). HRM professionals' responsibilities in this case are to select a temporary-help agency carefully and to ensure that it continues to provide acceptable service.

The advent of leaner and more participative organizations also creates a less direct but more consultative and advisory role for HRM professionals in recruitment. As more employers use semi-autonomous work groups and teamwork, at least some of the recruiting function is carried out by line managers and employees — an ironic change because most recruiting and hiring were done by supervisors or low-level managers long ago, before HRM departments were ever established. These are but some of the factors leading to changes in recruiting. Can you think of others?

The Importance of Recruiting

The role of recruiting in the staffing process cannot be overestimated. As Figure 6.1 shows, recruiting precedes selection but is in reality the start of the staffing process. Well-written recruiting messages both attract those applicants who have the desired basic qualifications and discourage people without those qualifications from applying. Effective recruitment must yield many more applicants than will be hired because the organization can hire better workers when the selection process screens many people rather than a few. The reason lies in the normal distribution curve: if abilities and knowledge are normally distributed, one is more likely to find and hire highly qualified applicants by looking at a large rather than a small sample. (This point is discussed further in Chapter 7.) Figure 6.1 also shows that human resource planning provides information about the quantity, knowledge, skill, and ability levels of needed employees and about when they are needed. From previous chapters, it should be clear that HRM goals are intimately related to strategic business objectives and constraints. For example, recruiting goals become much more challenging as organizations downsize; move to a more team-based style; and strive to hire and promote more women, minorities, and people with disabilities.

Specific worker requirements are determined via job analysis, which also provides recruiters with job descriptions for use in recruiting messages. Recruiting is facilitated by competitive pay and attractive benefits, which are determined in compensation and benefits functions. The recruiting function is closely tied to selection, as both are parts of the employment process. Those recruited form a selection pool from which the best-qualified applicant(s) are offered jobs.

FIGURE 6.1
Recruiting: Relation to Other HRM Functions

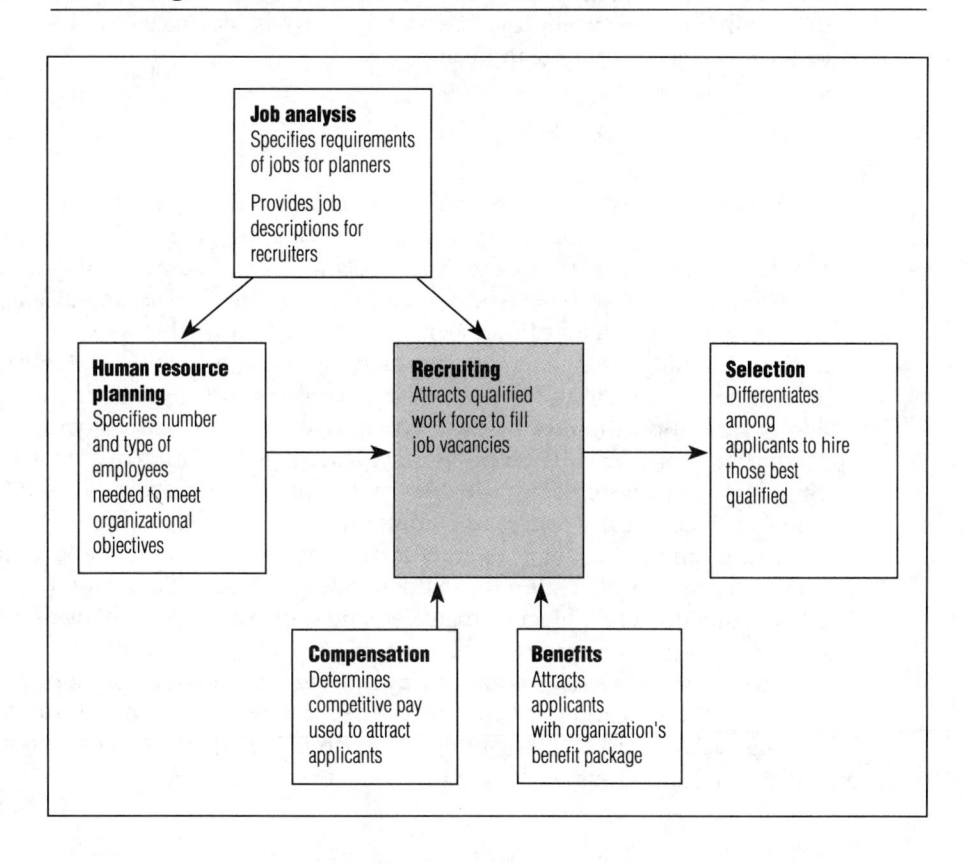

Recruiting Activities

Though the HRM professional of the 1990s has the same responsibilities for the planning, execution, and evaluation of recruiting as recruiters of the past, the diversity and complexity of these activities have changed. Additionally, actual recruitment activities may be carried out by employment agencies and/or line managers.

The variety of recruiting activities may be categorized into three areas: (1) development of a recruiting plan; (2) preparation of recruiting messages and implementation of the plan; and (3) evaluation of the results. As already suggested, recruiting activities must be planned even farther in advance of actual need than in the past, and some of these activities include investing time and money to cultivate both new and old sources of potential applicants. For example, a recruiting plan aimed at hiring 50 university-graduate chemists and engineers, 30 percent of whom are women or members of minority groups, should target first or second year high school students. Indeed, the very early high school years are the time to begin cultivating the skilled blue- and white-collar employees who are already in short supply. The old plan of simply contacting school placement offices and interviewing graduating students will leave many employers with the choice of leaving vacancies unfilled or hiring poorly qualified applicants.

Recruiting Plans

A recruiting plan is simply an extension of the strategic business and human resource planning goals stating how and when anticipated vacancies will be filled. Of course, not all vacancies can be anticipated; some employees quit, are fired, die, and so on. Also, not all anticipated vacancies actually occur; for example, growth may be slower than forecast. Nevertheless, every organization should be doing some recruitment planning, though one doubts that all will do so, even in the 1990s. Though labour shortages and employment equity legislation should cause more employers to more carefully plan their recruiting efforts, smaller employers are less likely to plan than are the larger employers and those using valuable "gold-collar" employees — the professional and technical workers in communications and electronics.

In addition to specifying the methods to be used and a timetable of activities, a recruiting plan should include a budget. The budget is prepared by HRM professionals, subject to management approval or prior consideration. Preparing a budget requires actual cost information plus estimates of running time for advertisements, required travel, long-distance telephone calls, and length of the recruiting effort, among others. Because of the difficulty of making such estimates, many budget-preparers base expected costs on information from previous recruiting efforts.

Recruiting Messages

The heart of a recruiting program is its message, but that message must be tailored to the target applicant group. Thus, messages may have to emphasize different features of the job or the employer, depending on the target group. For example, to attract parents with child-care responsibilities, and students, many fast food restaurants advertise flexible working hours. For many jobs in many parts of Canada, the message should be written or spoken in the mother language of the target group. Use of a language other than English or French helps employment equity and affirmative action recruiting; moreover, it is likely to be particularly effective, especially when combined with use of media and recruiting methods familiar to the target group.

Effective recruiting messages contain the following:

1. Job or position title.
2. A brief but clear description of job duties.
3. A statement of skills, abilities, knowledge, and experiences required to do the job.
4. Working conditions (for example, location, hours, days, level of supervision, level of pay, nature of benefits).
5. When and where to apply.
6. How to apply (for example, send a résumé, come in and fill out an application, phone for an interview, apply at a Canadian Employment Centre).

External recruiting messages should also include the organization's name and a brief statement of the nature of the business. Some employers choose to omit the organization's name, often because the company is either not well known or has a negative public image. Most employers also include an employment equity statement in their recruiting messages. Except for information about the employer, messages for both internal and external recruiting should contain the same parts.

In developing recruiting messages, care must be taken not to portray the job or the employer too favourably. Overselling the job or employer can lead to dissatisfaction and turnover in the long run if the reality of the job fails to meet initial expectations. Overselling is often a temptation since recruiters are competing against one another for talented and sometimes scarce labour.

Evaluating the Effort

After the recruiting effort is completed, it should be evaluated. Doing so involves collecting information on the costs and effectiveness of the various recruiting methods and sources used. This information should be stored for use in developing future plans.

It is also advisable to monitor the effectiveness of recruiting sources and methods while recruiting is under way. Doing so enables new methods and sources to be tried in case of poor results from earlier approaches.

Factors Affecting the Applicant-Attraction Process

There are a number of factors that affect the nature of the recruiting process. In this section, we will discuss five such factors: (1) organizational characteristics; (2) the type of labour to be recruited; (3) labour market conditions; (4) legal requirements; and (5) cost and time constraints.

Organizational Characteristics

Analysts have identified a number of characteristics that affect the attraction process.[10] First, an organization's culture and values affect how recruiting is done as well as the type of applicant pools tapped and the nature of monetary and nonmonetary inducements. Employers seek applicants who have not only the necessary skills, abilities, and experience but also values congruent with those of the organization's culture. In *The Vital Difference*, Harmon and Jacobs tell of a taxi driver who claimed to be able to pick which of his job-seeking riders would be hired for a job at Delta Airlines. The authors argue that successful companies have a distinct personality and "look for people with personalities like their own."[11]

Organizations tap different sources and use different methods, depending on whether they favour internal or external recruiting. Currently, the preferred policy in most organizations is internal recruiting. Policies of internal recruiting afford employees desired opportunities for growth and advancement. Large organizations are more likely than small ones to have internal recruiting policies because large organizations have greater pools of employees from which to choose in filling job vacancies. Organizations that choose policies of internal recruiting also tend to spend relatively large amounts on training and development programs to help employees move up. Of course, organizations with internal policies still must rely on external recruiting to fill entry-level positions. External recruiting may also be necessary if a sudden unexpected demand for a company's product or service creates a need for more labour at all levels of ability and experience.

A third organizational characteristic is ability to pay. This factor affects primarily the level of pay and benefits offered, but it may also affect the types of labour pools and the recruiting methods used by an employer. Obviously, a more profitable company is better able to offer high pay and excellent benefits than one that is barely breaking even. Research shows that inducements such as higher pay, more desirable benefits, better promotion opportunities, and other job-related factors are more important than the recruiting process itself for both attracting applicants and influencing their job acceptance decisions.[12] Perhaps one of the best examples of the effectiveness of inducements is the U.S. Army's experience that higher salaries, recruitment bonuses, and educational incentives led to both more and higher-ability applicants.[13] The more profitable firm is also more likely than a less profitable one to have a better-planned recruiting effort and better-trained recruiters.

Another characteristic that affects the attraction process is the business strategy pursued by an organization. Schuler and Jackson argue that different business strategies, such as cost reduction and innovation, have very different implications for various HRM functions, including recruiting.[14] Since an innovation strategy calls for highly competent employees who are flexible and can work both independently and with teams, a firm that uses such a strategy is likely to attract applicants with inducements such as high pay and challenging working conditions, and its recruiters are likely to be people with education and work experience similar to those of the desired applicants, rather than someone from the HR department.

Finally, an organization's stage of growth may also affect recruiting. For example, when an organization is in its growth stage, external rather than internal recruiting is generally more common, but this tendency may reverse as growth levels off. It is likely that recruiting messages for a rapidly expanding employer will emphasize growth and promotion opportunities, while messages for a mature employer may point to job security and excellent salary and benefits.

TYPE OF LABOUR

Recruiting goals are specified in terms of the number of workers and the type of labour needed. The type of labour needed affects the choice of a recruitment source and method, the scope of the applicant search, and the ultimate costs of recruiting. Each type of labour has its own market, which must be tapped in order to gain applicants. Some sources are better than others for tapping certain markets. For example, technical and trade schools are a good source for skilled entry-level workers; colleges and universities are a better source for professional and managerial employees. Generally, markets are smaller for labour types that are highly specialized or that require higher levels of education and experience. Jobs requiring these skills are more difficult and costly to fill; hence, the search for qualified applicants must be broader in scope. Since certain methods are better suited to extensive search than others, the type of labour to be recruited affects the choice of a recruiting method. For example, a recruiting effort to attract female executives must be broad in scope and may even require the services of a costly executive-search firm because of the scarcity of women executives. On the other hand, a recruiting goal of attracting 25 individuals to stuff envelopes could probably be met by simply placing an inexpensive advertisement in a local newspaper.

In a real sense, the growth of employment equity and affirmative action programs has led employers to add sex, age, race, and ethnic origin as well as physical disability to the characteristics of labour they seek. The implications of employment equity for recruiting are greater than for any other HRM function. Perhaps one of the major consequences is that the recruiting effort must be more comprehensive and better planned than in previous years. To meet the goals required by most employment equity and affirmative action plans, employers must first have fairly accurate forecasts of where, when, and for what types of labour they are likely to have vacancies. Planning for and anticipating vacancies is always a first rule of effective recruiting; when employment equity goals must be met, the importance increases for many reasons.

For example, in today's competitive economy, most employers are seeking the talented, well-educated employee, not the high school dropout. Efforts to recruit Canadian-educated members of visible minorities who meet these standards must begin well before graduation time. Examples of the type of activities useful in attracting applicants from minority groups include: (1) becoming involved with the special organizations representing each group; (2) establishing an early identification program through summer internships or co-op programs; (3) establishing a positive image of the company in the minority community by using guest-lecturer programs and other forms of media to let people know about its work, its opportunities, and its commitment to hiring and advancing members of minorities; (4) designating specific people as minority recruiters, preferably individuals from an appropriate minority with some experience with the company; and (5) establishing contact with a number of colleges and universities known to have minority group students in the relevant knowledge and skill areas.[15] These activities are aimed at college and university students, but similar programs could be established with high schools and trade schools.

The key elements appear to be making early contact with potential applicants and helping them by providing the real goal of getting a job and, in some cases, financial aid. Additionally, the employer must develop the reputation as a good place for visible minorities, aboriginals, people with disabilities, and women to work. Employers who entice members of these groups with promises of fairness and promotion opportunities and then fail to deliver will find their future employment equity recruiting efforts much more difficult.

LABOUR MARKET CONDITIONS

Labour market conditions exert a strong influence on recruiting. Labour markets are local, regional, national, or international, depending on the geographical area in which the forces of supply and demand operate for a particular labour type.

The boundaries of a local labour market are defined by the distance workers are willing to commute to jobs. If they are willing to commute 50 kilometres, the labour market has a 50-kilometre radius, and communities outside that circle are not within an employer's local labour market. For example, although Toronto and Oshawa are less than 50 kilometres apart, many people are not willing to commute from one city to the other to work. Therefore, Toronto's local labour market does not include Oshawa and vice versa. Factors that have little direct connection with jobs may, however, alter the boundaries of a local labour market. For example, the high cost of housing in Toronto and the availability of commuter trains and a network of limited-access highways have led many medium- to high-income workers to be willing to commute more than 50 kilometres.

Recruiting for jobs that require less highly skilled labour (such as clerical, sales, and service occupations) can usually be done in local labour markets, while regional markets function for jobs requiring more highly skilled labour (for example, water pollution specialists, computer programmers, and registered nurses). Professionals and executives are generally recruited from national markets, while engineers and various scientific specialists (such as astronomers, physicists, and chemists) enjoy international markets. Again, these rules of thumb can change with various factors. For example, as we have seen, shortages of even low-skilled workers have led to recruiting far beyond local labour markets in many cases.

One challenge of recruiting in national and international markets (and in regional markets that lack the infrastructure for long-distance commuting with ease) is that of inducing workers to relocate. For many people, an organization's location seems to be an important factor in considering a job change. Relocation costs can also be a factor. To increase labour mobility, some organizations pay moving expenses and even subsidize the purchase of homes. For example, when NovAtel Communications found it was unable to attract the experienced electronics engineers in the North American labour market, it expanded its search to the Far East and Europe despite the added cost. And it induced a generally positive response toward relocation in Calgary.

When the supply of a certain type of labour cannot meet the demand, shortages result and the labour market is called *tight*. A labour market is *loose* if the labour supply is abundant. When unemployment is relatively high, external recruiting for many types of labour is faster and less expensive than when unemployment is low. Of course, the general level of employment may have little effect on the specific type of labour an organization needs to recruit. For example, high unemployment in the Western provinces caused by low oil and grain prices would likely have little effect on the ease with which hospitals are able to recruit surgeons and radiologists. A shortage in a certain type of labour drives up the price of that labour and forces organizations to broaden their geographical areas of search for applicants. Table 6.1 shows the effect of various market conditions on the scope of a recruiting

TABLE 6.1

Effect of Labour Market Conditions on Recruiting Efforts for a Data-Entry Operator

CONDITION OF LABOUR MARKET	SCOPE OF EFFORT	TYPE OF EFFORT	COST OF RECRUITING
Tight (shortages exist)	Regional	Use private employment agency	High
Intermediate (supply not abundant, but no shortages exist)	Local–regional	Visit vocational schools with secretarial programs	Average
Loose (abundant supply)	Local	Place ads in local newspaper and list vacancies with Canada (Quebec) Employment Centres	Low

effort, the type of effort, and the cost of recruiting. Tight markets require broader search efforts. In the late 1970s, the shortage of skilled workers in Canada led 35 percent of employers with shortages to search for workers outside their region and 11 percent to search outside the country.[16] Since the late 1980s, unemployment has increased in most provinces. While this has made recruiting easier for some jobs, many employers find hiring good people still to be a very difficult task.[17] Conditions for many types of workers in the 1990s will be as tight if not worse because of skill deficiencies in the labour supply. Of course, reducing turnover, particularly in industries such as fast food and restaurants, and improving training would reduce the need to recruit new workers.

When organizations experience difficulty recruiting particular types of labour, they often tap new sources such as the secondary labour force, moonlighters, and temporary workers. Members of the *secondary labour force* are usually people who have elected not to seek conventional employment. They are typically students, people with disabilities, or retired persons. Since they often do not seek out employment, organizations must use somewhat unusual recruiting methods to reach them. One grocery store chain sends recruiters from store to store in a van that has become a mobile recruitment centre. Other stores use public address systems to inform customers of vacancies or stuff job notices into their shopping bags.[18] Some McDonald's restaurants in Canada have used placemats to deliver a sales pitch about working for McDonald's and an employment application. To attract workers in the secondary labour force, employers may need to offer special inducements such as part-time employment, higher pay, subsidized day care, flexible working hours, or the opportunity to work at home. According to one study, members of the secondary labour force make excellent part-time employees.[19]

Another source of labour that is tapped when shortages exist is *moonlighters*—individuals who hold more than one full- or part-time job. According to Statistics Canada's labour force survey of 1990, 4.8 percent of all employees held two or more jobs.[20] Periods of inflation seem to cause more moonlighting as people try to keep up with increased costs.

Temporary workers are being used increasingly to meet employee shortages, especially when demand for labour is forecast to be short-term. Temporary workers tend to be clerical or lower-level blue-collar workers, although some sales and professional positions may also be filled by temporaries. Temporary employees can serve an important role in recruiting in two ways. First, a temporary worker can fill in while the process continues to find a permanent employee. Second, excellent permanent employees can be recruited from temporary help in some situations. An organization can benefit from the use of temporaries because its total labour costs are lower than they would be if permanent labour was used for all needs. Temporaries work only when needed, they typically require no training, and their benefits are paid by the temporary agency that leases them.

This section has discussed how market conditions can affect recruiting plans. Labour market conditions affect the scope of a recruiting effort, the source and method used, and the going rate of pay necessary to attract applicants to a job. Information regarding supply of particular types of labour in local markets can be obtained through Canada and Quebec Employment Centres and through HRM officers' associations, such as the Human Resources Professionals Association of Ontario, the International Personnel Management Association, and other local affiliates and HRM groups. Information on regional and national labour market conditions is available through regional offices of Employment and Immigration Canada, industry associations, and newsletters and journals of union and professional associations. Information about labour force characteristics, unemployment, and turnover can be found in Statistics Canada publications such as *Employment Earnings and Hours* (catalogue number 72-002), *The Labour Force* (catalogue number 71-001), *Perspectives on Labour and Incomes* (catalogue number 75-001E), and *Labour Force Annual Averages* (catalogue number 71-220). *The Financial Post*, the *Report on Business*, and the *Financial Times of Canada* are also good sources of information on labour market changes.

Legal Requirements

Recruiting plans and messages are also affected by legal prohibitions and requirements. For example, human rights legislation requires that recruiting messages express no preference for a particular sex; age; or racial, ethnic, or religious group. Such references are prohibited unless membership in one of these groups is a bona fide occupational qualification for the job (as further discussed later in this chapter).

Legislation especially affects the recruiting plans and goals of employers under federal jurisdiction with 100 or more employees. These employers must structure their recruiting plans and methods to attract qualified applicants of a special target population: women, Native people, visible minorities, and people with disabilities. There is no one method of affirmative action recruiting, but reaching a special population requires getting a recruiting message to the "right place," one of maximum exposure to the target group. As already noted, doing so often requires the use of nontraditional methods of recruiting, such as notices on bulletin boards of ethnic community centres and development of long-term relationships with organizations of the appropriate target population. (See the HRM in Action box on the next page for an example of recruiting among Natives and visible minority groups.)

Cost and Time Constraints

Cost and time constraints place obvious limitations on recruiting efforts. For example, an organization with very little money budgeted for recruiting does not even consider hiring a graphic artist to design attractive recruiting materials. Rather than spend money to advertise openings, an organization with few cash resources for external recruiting often uses a system in which potential applicants are referred to the organization by present employees. Such organizations may also make use of Canada Employment Centres, which refer applicants at no cost.

More recruiting options are open to organizations with larger recruiting budgets. Such organizations can afford to advertise more widely, perhaps in a newspaper with national circulation, and to recruit actively by visiting universities and colleges, even in other parts of the country. Table 6.2 compares recruiting methods according to cost and time factors. The most expensive methods are university and college recruiting and the use of executive-search firms, which charge a fee for recruiting executives and managerial-level employees. Advertising can also be very expensive, depending upon the type of media used (radio, television, or newspaper), where it appears (in a publication with limited versus national circulation), and the length of time it runs.

Cost constraints can cause problems for organizations if relatively inexpensive methods prove unsuccessful. An example of the problems that can result is given by a manager of a medium-sized company that had several

HRM IN ACTION

RCMP MAKES PROGRESS IN MINORITY RECRUITING

Have you ever noticed that most police officers you see or meet are white? In most parts of Canada, the proportion of non-white to white police officers is less than in the population. For example, though the Metro Toronto force has one of the highest percentages of visible minorities, only 4 percent of the force are minorities compared with 17 percent of the population.

In an early attempt to remedy the situation, the RCMP created 145 special Native constable positions in the 1970s. However, a stigma came to be attached to these positions, as Native constables were given less training, fewer responsibilities, and lower pay than other officers. Recognizing the deficiencies of the earlier plan, the RCMP drew up a reform program in 1989 that called for phasing out the special constable positions and developing a new minority recruitment plan.

As part of this new approach to recruiting, Norman Inkester, Commissioner of the RCMP, established a six-person special recruiting force. Its mission was to stimulate interest among a population that had formerly shown little interest in police work. Toward this end, the force decided (in what might be called "traditional Mountie style") to single out individuals successful in other fields and persuade them to consider joining the force. This very individualized and intensive approach is most unusual, particularly when compared to the more typical approach of using videotapes, speeches, and brochures in high schools and with other groups of young people. In less than three years, the special recruiting force had doubled the number of minorities and increased the number of aboriginals, Indians, and Métis. While the total is still a smaller proportion than in Toronto's police force, the approach appears to be working. Perhaps changes in RCMP rules, such as allowing turbans and allowing Natives to wear their hair in the traditional braids, have also facilitated recruiting.

In a related approach to recruiting minorities, the government-financed Winnipeg Core Area Initiative provides pre-training for those seeking police and correctional officer jobs. These programs are directed toward upgrading both academic and physical ability levels. This program has also been successful in placing its graduates.

Source: Based on "RCMP Making Headway in Minority Hiring," *The Globe and Mail*, April 22, 1990. Used with the permission of *The Globe and Mail*.

TABLE 6.2
Cost and Time Variations of Recruiting Methods

Method	Approximate Cost Relative to Other Methods	Approximate Time Involved Relative to Other Methods
Posting and bidding	Low	Short
Skill inventories	Low	Short
Employee referral	Low	Short–medium
Walk-ins	Low	Short
Union hiring halls	Low	Varies with market conditions
Recruitment advertising	Varies with type of ad and market conditions	Varies with market conditions
Special events	Average	Short
Vocational, technical, and trade school recruiting	Average–high	Medium–long
University and college recruiting	High	Long
Professional meetings	Average–high	Medium–long
Canada (and Quebec) Employment Centres	Low	Varies with market conditions
Private employment agencies	Average–high	Medium
Executive search firms	High	Medium

executive positions to fill. Management ruled out using an executive search firm as too costly and decided instead to place advertisements in several newspapers across the country. Three months of advertising attracted no qualified applicants for the positions. The company finally contacted an executive-search firm that was able to supply qualified applicants within a few weeks. In this case, the recruiting method deemed less costly turned out to be a waste of money, and the "costly" method turned out to be very cost-effective.

Time constraints can also limit choice of a recruiting method. Organizations experiencing a sudden increase in demand for goods and services have little time to engage in such efforts as school recruiting. Rather, they must meet the demand for new labour as quickly as possible. Table 6.2 shows that time involved for many recruiting methods varies according to market conditions. When labour markets are tight, it generally takes longer for recruiting efforts to be successful.

An example of the effect of time constraints on a recruiting effort is provided by a human resource manager of an auto parts manufacturing firm. Faced with a sudden demand for the company's product, the company manager informed the HR manager on Friday afternoon that 40 new employees were needed by Monday! Since it was too late to advertise in the local newspaper, the human resource manager searched through a number of applications on file and also requested that the local Canada Employment Centre refer any suitable applicants in a hurry.

Good human resource planning can both reduce recruiting costs and make the process more efficient. Advance knowledge of needs for certain labour types allows organizations to plan less costly and more efficient strategies for obtaining needed personnel, particularly when the labour market is tight.

RECRUITING METHODS AND SOURCES

Recruiting methods and sources fall into two basic categories: those used for internal recruiting and those used for external recruiting.

INTERNAL METHODS

Many vacancies above the entry level are filled by employees who have been identified as next in line for promotion. Other vacancies require that promotable candidates be identified. Two methods used to attract and identify current workers for higher-level positions are posting and bidding and skill inventories.

Posting and Bidding

Posting and bidding is a common method of recruiting from within an organization's work force. It involves posting a notice of a job vacancy on company bulletin boards; employees have a specified length of time (usually a week) to "bid" for the vacancy. When employees bid for posted job vacancies, they fill out vacancy bid request forms. Bidding is analogous to making formal application for a job.

Several guidelines can be suggested for the posting and bidding method. First, all permanent job openings and transfers should be posted for at least one week prior to external recruiting. Second, both job descriptions and specifications should be clearly defined. Third, all applicants should receive feedback on the status of their applications and any actions that result.

The system of posting job vacancies and allowing employees to bid for them has traditionally been used for blue-collar union jobs. In fact, posting and bidding is usually required for jobs covered by collective agreements with trade unions. Under these agreements, a posted job is awarded to the qualified bidder who has the most seniority.

The posting and bidding method has recently increased in popularity. Common now in government, its use in private industry is also increasing. Posting and bidding is a good way of stimulating employee career development. It provides a vehicle for enabling women, members of minority groups, aboriginals, people with disabilities, and bilingual employees to move up in an organization and can thus play an important role in employment equity and affirmative action programs. Another advantage is that it is not costly or time-consuming.

Use of Skill Inventories

Another approach to internal recruiting is the use of skill inventory information on the present work force. An employer using this method searches through skill inventories to identify employees who are qualified for vacant jobs. They are then contacted and asked whether they want to apply. This method can be used in conjunction with posting and bidding to ensure that job vacancies come to the attention of all qualified employees.

An advantage of this method is that it affords a thorough search for possible applicants within an organization. If skill inventory information is readily available, the method is not costly or time-consuming. Skill inventory data are often a part of the human resource information systems (HRISs) that were discussed in Chapter 4.

EXTERNAL METHODS

External recruiting goes outside the organization's boundaries to attract applicants. It can take many forms; the most common are discussed in this section.

Employee Referral

The employee referral method involves informing present employees of job vacancies and asking them to recommend or refer applicants to the organization. Some organizations offer small cash rewards to employees for referring qualified applicants. For example, in early 1991, McDonald's Restaurants offered bonuses of up to $500 for each successful referral, and at Sun Life bonuses ranged from $100 to $1000, depending on the level of job being filled.[21] This sort of incentive is most often used when the market for certain labour is very tight.

The employee referral method is a popular one in many industries because it is neither costly nor time-consuming and it often yields good results. For example, research has shown that employees recruited by this method tend to have lower turnover than workers recruited by other methods.[22]

One disadvantage of employee referral is that it can perpetuate existing sex and ethnic distributions in organizations. People tend to know, associate with, and refer others like themselves. In the United States, courts have several times ruled as discriminatory specific recruiting efforts based on employee referrals. On the other hand, the employee referral method can be used constructively to achieve objectives such as affirmative action by asking for referrals from women and members of specific language groups or visible ethnic minorities.

Walk-Ins

People who come to an organization seeking employment without referral and without organizational encouragement are called *walk-ins*. Though they have not actually been recruited, walk-ins do provide a very inexpensive source of job applicants for an organization. They are a common source of lower-skilled, blue-collar, and clerical labour in a local labour market.

Walk-ins are most prevalent when unemployment in a local area is high and when demand for labour is low. In times of high unemployment, employers may wish to discourage walk-ins with signs saying "not accepting applications at this time." In the labour markets of the 1990s, walk-ins are unlikely to be a very productive source of qualified applicants. Touche Ross, a management consulting firm, suggests retailers not encourage walk-ins through "help wanted" signs in the window.[23]

Union Hiring Halls

Union hiring halls are very specialized placement agencies restricted to members of a particular union and to employers of a particular industry. The longshoremen and some construction unions, for example, commonly require employers to recruit first from their hiring halls. Employers submit their requisitions for new employees to the halls, which then forward job applicants to the employer. Under this method, unions become the primary recruiters for certain types of labour.

Recruitment Advertising

Recruitment advertising includes newspaper advertising; advertising or announcements in university and college placement bulletins and professional newsletters and journals; and ads on radio, television, and billboards. Some large companies have job lines with taped messages concerning job vacancies. A job seeker simply phones in to see what is available.

All the methods of advertising share a common purpose: to convey information to potential job applicants. Besides providing information on the nature of the job and employee qualifications, recruitment ads often seek to "sell" potential applicants on the advantages of the organization or the attractiveness of the job. Ads directed to applicants in national markets may mention location as a selling point. For instance, a company in a small community might stress the freedom from smog and rush-hour traffic jams.

It is important that recruiting messages convey honest information to applicants about the job and what it is like to work for the organization. Honest messages facilitate good matches between employees and organizations by allowing applicants to self-select out if they feel poorly suited to the job or work environment. Mismatches based on faulty information can be costly to employers, as they lead more often than not to employee dissatisfaction and turnover. An example of a newspaper recruitment ad is given in Exhibit 6.1.

V.M. Evans provides a number of suggestions about recruitment advertising.[24] Arguing that good ads should "reward the reader" and that information is the key ingredient, he points to four market segments that recruitment ads should influence. The first and major segment is the group of potential applicants that constitutes the "qualified response" the ad seeks to attract. A second segment is the 70 to 75 percent of readers who are already employed, even if only a small percentage of them are actively seeking other employment. Evans provides data showing that ads help build organizational images that determine where people seek jobs when they are actively searching. The third segment is the organization's own employees, who view advertising as a source of information about their company. Ads also provide a source of information for the fourth segment: customers, potential customers, investors, investment analysts, government officials, and others. Evans's article places the role of recruitment advertising in a very important position, not only for recruiting but for the creation and maintenance of an organization's image for virtually all interested parties. This means that ads must be carefully prepared with all relevant segments or audiences in mind, remembering that the major function is to generate applications from qualified applicants.

Recruitment ads should be carefully prepared for another reason: they must not indicate a preference for persons of a particular sex, marital status, religion, or ethnic group. Recruitment ads that do indicate a preference are discriminatory under human rights legislation. Even recruitment ads that seek to increase the number of women, minorities, aboriginals, and people with disabilities in an organization must not indicate any worker preference; they should, however, state that the company is committed to employment equity.

As we saw in Chapter 3, an ad *can* indicate a preference for a member of a particular sex, religion, or ethnic group if the preferred worker characteristic is a bona fide occupational qualification for the job. This situation exists when only a person of a particular sex, religion, or ethnic group can perform the job. For example, advertising for a nun could indicate a preference for a Catholic woman, since being a Catholic woman is essential for the sisterhood. Similarly, a sex preference could be indicated for the jobs of sperm donor and wet nurse.[25] Bona fide occupational qualifications are very narrowly defined, and very few jobs have them. Recruitment ads must also not discriminate on the basis of age, although, as we saw in Chapter 3, "age" for the purposes of nondiscrimination varies among the provinces.

EXHIBIT 6.1
Newspaper Recruitment Ad

NovAtel Communications Ltd. is seeking

PRODUCTION

OPERATORS

NovAtel Communications, a world leader in production of state-of-the-art cellular equipment, has vacancies in the Advanced Manufacturing Department. Operators will be responsible for ensuring continuous production in an electronic manufacturing environment.

Successful candidates must have a minimum Grade 12 education. Electronic assembly experience is highly desirable. Please submit your resume, quoting competition #9150CH, by September 8, 1989, to:

> Human Resources Department
> NovAtel Communications Ltd.
> 1020—64th Avenue N.E.
> CALGARY, Alberta
> T2E 7V8

Source: Adapted from an advertisement appearing in the *Calgary Herald*, September 1, 1989. Reprinted with the permission of NovAtel Communications Ltd.

Recruitment advertising has the advantage of being able to reach any type of labour in any labour market both easily and quickly. Large organizations can use company and/or union publications to advertise job vacancies in internal recruiting efforts. Local, regional, and national markets can be reached by placing ads in appropriate publications. Ads for professional and managerial employees can be placed in professional journals, newsletters, and similar publications. The key to effective recruitment advertising is to place the right ad in the right place at the right time. This requires a knowledge of labour market conditions and what audience an ad will reach. For example, Northern Telecom Canada pursues a strategic approach that involves identifying, segmenting, and communicating to a particular audience — on-campus college and university students. Specifically, this approach, which differs from their mainstream recruitment advertising, includes: (1) addressing a single audience that has been identified as most appropriate for the company's goals; (2) writing advertising from a student's perspective; (3) communicating with students, using their own language; and (4) providing specific information that will assist them in evaluating job and employer choices.[26] A Florida hospital used this kind of knowledge to recruit nurses in Montreal in 1978. When the province of Quebec first required all nurses to pass French-language examinations in order to be licensed, 40 percent failed. Capitalizing on the situation, the hospital ran recruiting ads on one of Montreal's English-language television stations and received a "torrent of applications." More recently, NovAtel took advantage of large layoffs at McDonnel-Douglas in Ft. Worth, Texas, and advertised for engineers and technicians.

The costs of advertising vary. Local newspaper and radio ads are relatively inexpensive, but ads in larger newspapers and national publications can be costly. A 1989 newspaper article stated that a one-day ad in a newspaper can cost $5000 or more.[27] Television advertising is most expensive, but one ad can reach a large number of people. Though many companies may want and need advertising for employment equity purposes, using a professional search firm may be more cost-effective if the potential applicant pool is small.

Special Recruiting Events

Special recruiting events, such as job fairs and open houses, are another external recruiting method. Job fairs are events in which many different employers gather at one location to interview applicants for jobs. Open houses are another kind of special event in which one employer hosts a get-together for job seekers. A more recent variation is the information seminar. Information seminars are sponsored by one or more employers and usually present information related to searching for a job or information on updating occupational skills. One innovative employer that had been seeking information systems professionals sponsored a seminar on recent technological changes in the field. The seminar attracted many professionals interested in staying current in their field and the employer made contact with a number of excellent job candidates.[28]

Special recruiting events are best suited to recruiting in the local labour market. They have the advantage of being able to get in-depth information to large numbers of potential applicants in a short time.

Vocational, Technical, and Trade School Recruiting

Vocational, technical, and trade schools are major sources of semi-skilled and skilled labour in various fields including mechanics, refrigeration, electronics, and data processing. To recruit recent graduates of these schools, recruiters usually send leaflets and brochures and other information about the company to the school, encouraging interested students to apply. Recruiters may also visit the school to talk with potential applicants.

Some Canadian jurisdictions offer a considerable number of training programs for the skilled trades and low-level management at the community colleges. These highly trained graduates are often particularly valuable workers, and recruiting for them may reach the extent described in the next section for university and college students in academic and professional programs. Recruiting at vocational, technical, and trade schools usually takes place in the local labour market; but for highly skilled labour, especially in the community colleges, it may extend to the regional market.

University and College Recruiting

Universities and colleges provide a major source of highly educated labour, including most professionals and managerial trainees. One way of recruiting on campuses is to have managers or other company representatives visit classrooms and lecture the students. Another way is to seek out promising students and visit the campuses to talk with them and other interested students. Large companies and the federal government hire recruiters for the sole purpose of recruiting on campuses.

The selection of schools to visit depends on several factors, the first of which is the type of job to be filled. If, for example, an organization needs water pollution control specialists, recruiters must visit schools with programs in environmental studies. Very few schools have such programs, so this will narrow the search. The size of the firm is another factor. A large organization is likely to send recruiters to many good schools throughout Canada, while a small one usually recruits mainly from schools in its region.

A third factor affecting the choice of schools is information from past recruiting efforts. An organization will probably cease its recruiting efforts at a university or college that has never provided a satisfactory recruit. (Of course, sometimes a firm recruits at a university simply because a member of upper management is an alumnus.)

University and college recruiting is a very specialized method consisting of five steps:

1. *Cultivating students.* Earlier in this chapter, we pointed out that all North America faced shortages of technically and scientifically trained labour. Like members of minority groups, high school, college, and university students need to be told of various employment opportunities. More students must be encouraged not only to pursue math and science programs but to work hard. A number of studies have found that the high academic performance and test scores of Asian Americans is the result not of superior intelligence but simply of the fact that they work harder.[29] Organizational representatives need to visit schools and talk with counsellors, teachers, and students. Firms must also be prepared to offer scholarships, summer internships, and co-operative education programs as inducements for students. Without this first step of cultivating human resources, there may not be enough of the well-trained graduates needed to keep Canada's employers competitive in the global economy.

2. *Attracting students.* A firm must attract students so that they will submit their résumés and sign up for interviews with the organization's recruiter. University and college placement offices can play a supportive role by distributing a company's recruiting materials and publicizing recruiter visits. Recruiting, however, involves more than simply visiting a campus and waiting to see who shows up for an interview. Often before the scheduled visit, recruiters scour student résumé books (available through placement offices), searching for particularly promising candidates. Students identified in this manner are contacted by letter or telephone and actively encouraged to meet with the recruiter when he or she is on campus. Says one prominent recruiter: "You can only talk to twelve or fourteen people a day, so you want to get the right people on your schedule."[30] University and college recruiters also seek to establish and maintain contacts with faculty members who can alert them to qualified applicants or channel a student's interest to a particular company.

   One study of why applicants choose their first employers suggests that recruiters should emphasize promotion opportunities, benefits, jobs that utilize a wide range of an employee's skills, pay, and job challenge.[31] For applicants seeking their second or a subsequent job, pay becomes the dominant feature. While it is clear that recruiting brochures, videos, and other materials can emphasize a broad utilization of skills, promotion opportunities, and challenge, neither the organization nor the job should be oversold. Recruiting efforts should, therefore, be used to develop a positive but accurate image of the employer. Representatives can participate in career days programs, increasing a company's exposure through informal contacts with students. Organizations can sponsor campus activities or even fund buildings or parts of buildings. Perhaps one of the better activities an organization can sponsor is a co-operative (co-op) education program, internship, or summer job. Such programs allow both student and employer to gauge the true degree of employer–employee fit. Co-op programs are quite popular. According to the Canadian Association for Co-operative Education, more than 40 000 students from approximately 80 post-secondary schools are participating in co-op programs with 5000 employers.[32]

3. *Interviewing students.* An effective recruiting interview serves as an information exchange between recruiter and student. The student wants to learn more about the organization, and the recruiter wants to learn more about the student. The recruiter generally seeks information about the student's background and career goals. The student's appearance (neat? attentive? interested? personable?) is also important to a recruiter's decision about pursuing him or her further.

   Trained interviewers are very important in university and college recruiting. A poor interviewer can damage an organization's image and discourage applicants. A student who has had a bad interview experience is likely to discuss it with other students, and future recruiting efforts at the school may be affected. Even if an organization is not interested in a particular student, a good recruiter must be courteous and attempt to give a favourable image of the organization. In addition, recruiters need training on the types of questions they can and cannot ask in an interview because of human rights legislation.

4. *Inviting students for site visits.* Using information from student résumés and recruiting interviews, a recruiter pre-screens potential applicants and decides which to invite to the organization for a site visit. This decision is made by the recruiter, sometimes independently and sometimes in consultation with other managers.

5. *Conducting site visits.* Site visits are almost always paid for by the organization and serve partly to "sell" the candidate and partly to further assess his or her abilities and usefulness to the organization. The latter purpose is really part of the selection process. Candidates who meet an organization's selection criteria will receive job offers.

ACCIS — The Graduate Workforce Professionals is an organization that enables employers who are involved in recruiting, as well as university placement centres, to exchange information on recruiting issues. The organization's annual publication for students, *Career Options*, contains articles to assist in job searches, recruiting procedures, job hunting in a recession, and so on.

University and college recruiting is a lengthy process that requires human resource planning. Requests for interview time and space must be made well in advance of actual recruiting visits, often six to twelve months in advance for schools whose graduates are in great demand. Thus, an organization must have some estimates or forecasts of the number and kinds of positions it will need to fill a year or more later.

Recruiting costs are high because they involve paying for travel, food, and lodging for both recruiters on campuses and candidates invited for site visits. Large firms may have the additional expense of salaries for full- or part-time recruiters. Other expenses associated with university and college recruiting are materials and advertising costs.

Recruiting at Professional Meetings

Professional associations, such as the Association of Professional Engineers of the Province of Ontario and the Human Resources Professionals Association of Ontario (HRPAO), are major sources of experienced or recently graduated professionals. Recruiting highly educated professionals, especially PhDs, is similar to university recruiting, but it is usually more informal and often done by professionals themselves rather than by recruiters from human resource departments.

Most professional associations have national, regional, and sometimes international meetings at which recruiting or placement centres function. These centres provide a mechanism for putting potential applicants and representatives of an organization in contact with one another. Résumés of potential applicants are available in one area of the placement centre, and job openings are listed in books in another area. Thus, an organization can use the placement centre to locate potential applicants, and would-be applicants can use it to locate potential employers. Job seekers and organization representatives can leave messages for each other at the centre. Tables are provided for informal discussions, and contacts are made that sometimes result in individuals' being invited for site visits to certain organizations. Besides providing a meeting place for job seekers and employers, professional associations publish job openings in professional journals and placement bulletins.

Professional association meetings provide recruiters with a large pool of qualified applicants, by virtue of membership in the group. That is, because they belong to the professional association, applicants are to some degree pre-selected according to professional qualifications. Professional meetings are an inexpensive way of making contact with potential applicants if organization representatives already plan to attend the meeting for other reasons. However, completing the recruiting process requires site visits to the organization, which can be costly.

Public Employment Agencies

An organization can choose to delegate the responsibility for searching for applicants to an employment agency. The most extensive public system in Canada is that of Employment and Immigration Canada, which operates 470 regular Canada Employment Centres (CECs), along with itinerant services to

187 remote or isolated communities. It also provides services through more than 100 CECs on university and community college campuses. Between April and August, the Canada Employment and Immigration Commission operates more than 400 CECs for students.[33] The province of Quebec has its own provincially run employment centres, as well as CECs.

CECs provide employers with a selection and job referral service. Job seekers are instructed in the development of personal job-search plans and are provided with leads to employment opportunities that have not been listed by employers. Employment counsellors may also attempt to interest prospective employers in job-seeking clients. In addition, CECs process unemployment insurance applications and administer employment programs subsidized by the federal government.

Canada (and Quebec) Employment Centres are virtually no-cost and can be of great service to an organization in both the recruiting and the selection function. Increasing use of automated equipment in selected CECs is making the service more efficient. Most CECs have Job Information Centres, where workers can make occupational and job choices from available lists, get assistance from a referring officer, and get information about job vacancies and employment conditions. In addition, there is a computerized, country-wide job bank. Local CECs can list job vacancies on behalf of employer clients and can also look for vacancies in the job bank on behalf of worker clients. During 1989–90, more than 2 million clients were referred for regular employment, using the National Employment Services System (NESS).[34] This computerized job bank also provides useful information on employment equity, such as the number of placements of aboriginals, people with disabilities, members of visible minorities, and women.

Some people unjustly assume that only applicants of low quality are available through the government agencies. Actually, many employers today recruit exclusively through CECs for certain types of labour. Because of the full range of services they offer at no cost, CECs and Quebec centres can be a most economical recruiting method for organizations, especially those too small to employ a personnel staff or recruiting specialist. In times of high unemployment, the centres are especially useful for helping employers screen very large numbers of job applicants.

Private Employment Agencies

Private employment agencies often flourish in labour markets where CECs are ineffective and in other markets as well. Private employment agencies usually handle all types of labour except for lower-skilled labour such as factory workers.

The primary difference between public and private employment agencies is that most private agencies are profit-oriented businesses that require a fee for services rendered. In most cases, these fees are paid by employers. Most provinces have legislation regulating these fees. Alberta, British Columbia,

Manitoba, Nova Scotia, and Saskatchewan prohibit their being charged to job seekers, and Ontario does the same for most classes of agencies.

A potential problem with private agencies is the possibility of violating employment equity legislation. In late 1991, two Toronto-based employment agencies were accused of racial and sex discrimination against job applicants. The two agencies reached a three-year employment equity settlement with the Ontario Human Rights Commission.[35] Investigations of these agencies and others found evidence of acceptance of orders from employers to refer only white applicants and evidence of maintenance of race, colour, sex, and age data on applicants.

Some private employment agencies are nonprofit organizations. An example is the Technical Service Council, an industry-sponsored employment service specializing in professional and technical personnel.

Many agencies serve the local market, but some are nation-wide, offering computerized job and applicant information. Since many firms specialize in one or two types of labour (for example, temporary clerical, computer operators, supervisory personnel), it may be necessary for an employer to use several different private employment agencies.

Private employment agencies are a good source of professional, technical, and managerial employees and all kinds of experienced employees. The fees they charge vary, but if an organization does not have the time or human resources to conduct an extensive search, even an expensive private employment agency can be cost-beneficial.

Executive-Search Firms

Executive-search firms, frequently called "headhunters," are a type of private employment agency specializing in experienced managerial and executive-level labour. Many specialize in recruiting certain types of executive talent.

In the late 1970s, with experienced managers and executives in short supply, there was a growth in executive-search firms. The recession of the early 1980s reduced the demand and forced many search firms to resort to layoffs and other cost-cutting techniques. Other firms began to specialize in finding jobs for executives who had been terminated. This service is called *outplacement*. The labour market of the 1990s is likely to be a mixture of that seen in the previous two decades; that is, managers with a proven track record for running profitable, efficient, high-quality units will be in great demand, but competitive pressures and downsizing will lead to continued terminations. So both headhunting and outplacement will be needed.

Executive-search firms operate in various ways. Some simply maintain files of résumés sent in by executives who are seeking other employment. When contacted by a client organization, such a firm searches its store of résumés to provide names of potential applicants. Other search firms recruit more aggressively, discreetly contacting executives and encouraging them to consider changing their organizational affiliations.

All fees for executive-search efforts are paid by the client organization, and they are high, usually a fixed rate amounting to 25 to 30 percent of an executive's first year's pay. The amount of a fee often depends on the geographical extent of the search. Payment of a fee is not usually contingent on the executive-search firm's finding a candidate; if no candidate is found, the client organization is charged a portion of the full fee.[36]

Selecting an executive-search firm can be difficult. Choosing the wrong firm for an organization's needs can be costly in terms of money and time spent. The better executive-search firms belong to the Institute of Certified Management Consultants. As in any industry, there are some very good firms and some rather poor ones. An employer should require a search firm to provide references and a list of client organizations.

Temporary Employment Agencies

While use of temporary employment agencies has been common for many years, downsizing and efforts of many employers to keep a lean work force have led to an increase in their use. This enables employers to maintain a core group of regular employees and when the need arises, temporary employees serve as a buffer work force. One of the disadvantages to this core and buffer type of work force is that the temporary employees do not always know the employer and their quality may be unknown and variable. Some employers have overcome these disadvantages by setting up in-house temporary employment agencies. One of the largest and best-known programs is that of Aetna Life and Casualty Company. Their pool is mostly for clerical work, though some guards, mailroom staff, cafeteria staff, and even some professionals such as accountants are included. Temporary employees tend to be retirees, students, mothers with young children, and people between jobs. These employees are screened and trained extensively and are familiar with Aetna's way of doing business. Advocates of in-house temporary agencies claim the advantages of flexibility and quality. Like regular "temps," some in-house "temps" are hired as regular employees.[37]

Newer Recruiting Methods

The electronic age of computers, telecommunications, fibre optics, and video tapes and disks has created an incredible variety of new possibilities for recruiting. For example, instead of sending brochures to schools, colleges, and universities and even potential applicants, employers can send recruiting messages on video tapes or disks. Large employers' job lines can be set to have callers use push-button phones to access recorded descriptions of job vacancies. Some employers use one or more cable TV channels to advertise vacancies. Employers seeking applicants with some minimal degree of computer literacy can advertise in easily retrievable computer files and use electronic mail (E mail) to send recruiting messages to a selected group of computer users. (In early 1991, one of the authors of this book recruited a PhD student through E mail.) Internal recruiting is benefiting from better and less expensive computers and software developments that make skills inventories and HRISs easier to use.[38]

Development-oriented approaches to recruiting are also growing in popularity because of current and forecast shortages of skilled labour of various types. For example, scholarships may induce students to enter a particular occupation. Internships may both serve as an inducement and provide students and employer the opportunity to try one another out. Though scholarships, internships, and visits to schools are not new methods, the labour market of the 1990s will make them a more important part of recruiting.

SUMMARY OF METHODS AND SOURCES

The recruiting methods and sources just described represent a wide variety of choices for HRM professionals. As we have seen, different methods have different advantages, and depending on recruiting goals, some methods are preferable to others. The key considerations in choosing a method are the type of labour and type of market a method usually reaches. Depending upon the method or source chosen, recruiters are engaged in activities ranging from simply taking applications from walk-ins to soliciting applicants by visiting community agencies and appropriate schools.

Table 6.3 summarizes and compares the recruiting methods and sources discussed in this section.

EVALUATING THE RECRUITING EFFORT

Developing a recruiting plan and preparing a budget require some knowledge of the cost and relative effectiveness of the various recruiting methods. One of the best sources of this knowledge is data collected by an organization from past recruiting efforts. HRM professionals have a responsibility to collect information on the recruiting methods used so methods can be evaluated and compared in terms of their cost-effectiveness. These data should be maintained and used in making future recruiting decisions.

A measure of a method's cost-effectiveness takes into account how much a method costs *and* how effective it is in meeting recruiting goals. Effectiveness refers to both yield ratios and time required. The *yield ratio* expresses the typical number of applicants needed to go from one recruiting step to the next. For example, if it takes 1000 résumés to yield 250 invitations for an interview, the yield ratio for this first step is 4/1. Yield ratios can be calculated for each step: (1) résumé to invitation; (2) invitation to interview; (3) interviews to offer; and (4) offers to acceptances. Obviously, a very efficient recruiting process is one with a low yield ratio—most applicants move from one step to the next. The quality of hires is more likely, however, to be maximized by high yield ratios, particularly at the early steps.

TABLE 6.3
Summary of Recruiting Methods and Sources

METHOD	TYPE OF LABOUR	LABOUR MARKET	RECRUITER ACTIVITY	ADVANTAGE	DISADVANTAGE
Posting and bidding	Any level above entry level but below professional and managerial level	Internal	Post notice of vacancy and accept bid	Employee development	Cannot reach external market
Skill inventories	Any level above entry level	Internal	Search files	Employee development	None
Employee referral	Any type	External, mostly local	Inform employees of vacancies and request referrals	Access to women and linguistic and ethnic minorities	Can perpetuate existing characteristics of the work force
Walk-ins	Lesser-skilled labour	Local	Take applications	Free	Greatest supply when demand is lowest
Union hiring halls	Members of certain unions	Local	Send requisition to union hiring hall	Compliance with collective agreement	Limits choice of employer
Recruitment advertising	Any type	Any market	Prepare and run ad	Can easily and quickly reach all markets	Can be costly
Special events	Any, except professional and managerial level	Local	Plan, advertise, and hold function	Can get in-depth information to large groups in a short time	None
Vocational, technical, and trade school recruiting	Semi-skilled and skilled labour	Local, perhaps regional	Cultivate developmental relationships such as internships, co-op programs, and scholarship programs; visit and interview students	Large pool of types of labour that are often much needed	Sometimes time-consuming for higher-level recruits
University and college recruiting	Professional and managerial trainees	Regional and national	Cultivate developmental relationships such as internships, co-op programs, and scholarship programs; visit and interview students	Large pool of qualified applicants	Costly, time-consuming

TABLE 6.3 (continued)

METHOD	TYPE OF LABOUR	LABOUR MARKET	RECRUITER ACTIVITY	ADVANTAGE	DISADVANTAGE
Professional meetings	Professionals	Regional, national, international	Hold informal discussions with job seekers	Large pool of pre-selected applicants	Can be costly
Canada (and Quebec) Employment Centres	Lesser-skilled labour	Local, access to regional, national, and international	Contact agency to refer applicants	Free; on-line computer system	Limited access to skilled and professional labour
Private employment agencies	Any, except lesser-skilled labour	Local, with regional and national networks	Contact agency to refer applicants	Delegation of search responsibility	Costly for higher-level recruits
Executive-search firms	Experienced executives	National	Contact agency to refer applicants	Access to executives	Expensive

Effectiveness is also evaluated in terms of time to hire and how soon the employee is on the job. The relative importance to an employer of cost versus time depends upon many factors, including the importance of the vacancy and the employer's financial resources. In an ideal world, an organization would have yield ratios and time and cost data available on all possible recruiting methods and could then choose those methods that best meet its current needs and constraints. The real world rarely offers the HRM professional such a range of information on past recruiting, but every bit helps.

Data from previous recruiting efforts cannot, however, present a completely accurate picture of present recruiting costs and effectiveness. Costs change with time, and methods that prove effective at one time may not prove effective at others because of changed market conditions. A method that was successful when market conditions were loose should not be presumed to be effective when they are tight.

Many indices can be used to evaluate effectiveness of a recruiting method. Some of these are given in Exhibit 6.2. Methods can be evaluated and compared according to the number of applicants attracted, the number of applicants attracted in a certain time period, and/or the cost of recruiting per applicant attracted. For example, if a newspaper ad costs $2000 and attracts 25 applicants, the cost per applicant is $80. This can be compared with the cost per applicant for another method, perhaps an open house that costs

EXHIBIT 6.2
Indices for Evaluating Recruiting Efforts

1. Number of applicants attracted per method
2. Number of applicants attracted by length of time
3. Costs per applicant attracted
4. Ratio of qualified to unqualified applicants attracted
5. Time from start to hiring of applicant
6. Total recruiting cost per employee hired
7. Yield ratio of applicants to interviews
8. Yield ratio of those interviewed who receive invitations to visit
9. Yield ratio of those invited who accept offers to visit

$5000 and attracts 50 applicants at a cost of $100 apiece. Another way to evaluate a method is to calculate the ratio of qualified to unqualified applicants attracted. If two methods draw the same number of applicants but one draws mostly unqualified applicants, the method that attracts the larger proportion of qualified applicants is the more effective.

Because recruiting efforts can be evaluated in so many ways, an initial step in evaluation has to be determining the criteria to be used. The choice of criteria depends to a large extent on whether an organization places more emphasis on cost reduction or on minimizing recruiting time.

No matter what indices are used in evaluation, some recruiting methods seem more effective than others. A major question is why. Schwab suggests that some methods, such as employee referral, provide better and more realistic information about jobs. An alternative possibility is that there are qualitative differences in the applicant pools tapped by the different methods. If differences in effectiveness result from differences in the information conveyed, attempts could be made to put more complete and accurate information into the least costly methods. If, on the other hand, differences in effectiveness result from qualitative differences in applicant populations, the most qualified population should be identified and used as the major recruiting source. Schwab also suggests that research into method effectiveness should take into account the interaction between recruiting methods and the labour market. It may be that the quality of applicants reached by different methods changes as the state of the labour market varies.[39]

A number of studies have found that informal recruiting methods, such as employee referrals, yield employees who stay longer than those attracted by more formal sources, such as newspaper ads and employment agencies.[40] Most of this research, however, suffers from several problems. One is that data were gathered only on employees who were hired, not on applicants. It is very likely that the applicants not hired differ in important ways from those hired. A recent study of nurses collected data from both applicants who were hired and those who were not; it concluded that although some recruiting methods tended to yield nurses who had less tendency to turnover and higher-rated job performance at the end of a year, these differences could be explained by differences in education, experience, and information about the employer.[41] The practical implications are that employers should select and use recruiting sources and methods on the basis of pre-hire outcomes, such as time, cost, and yield ratios, not on post-hire outcomes, such as performance and turnover. The recruiting process should not be credited or blamed for post-hire behaviour. Hiring decisions should be based strictly upon assessment of applicants' skills, abilities, and knowledge, not on how they were attracted to the employer.

SUMMARY

Recruiting has become a more challenging HRM function because of (1) the legislative pressures of employment equity and affirmative action; (2) shortages of skilled labour created by both demographic shifts and deficiencies in education; and (3) the trend toward jobs requiring broader and higher-level skills in organizations with flatter structures. As a result, the process of attracting applicants requires increased planning so that applicant pools can be developed or cultivated. Additionally, existing methods of recruiting have been modified, and new methods using computers and telecommunications are being created.

All recruiting involves the activities of developing a plan, preparing recruiting messages and implementing the plan, and evaluating the activities. The nature of the activities is affected by five factors: (1) organizational characteristics; (2) type of labour; (3) labour market conditions; (4) legal requirements; and (5) cost and time constraints.

Review Questions

1. Discuss the reasons recruiting can be described as a function that now includes the sowing or cultivation of human resources, rather than only the reaping of traditional recruiting activities.

2. Some people argue that employment equity legislation and affirmative action affect recruiting more than any other HRM function. Give several reasons why you agree or disagree with this statement.

3. Which recruiting methods seem likely to become less useful and efficient as the 1990s unfold? Which existing methods are likely to receive greater use? Describe new and innovative approaches to recruiting—some that you know of and some that you can imagine.

Project Ideas

1. Most employers do relatively little hiring during recessions and other economic downturns. There are, however, those such as Professor Bob Greer of Texas Christian University who advocate countercyclical hiring (CCH). Professor Greer believes that even during downsizing, companies need to protect certain core competencies in areas such as marketing or production. They should therefore hire, retain, and develop employees who are critical for the organization's survival. Some of the factors that lead employers to utilize CCH are:

   a. A strong belief that HRP is important as a means of avoiding shortages of critical human resources.
   b. A linkage between HRP and companies' strategic planning process.
   c. A belief that higher-quality applicants are more available during downturns than at other times.
   d. The view that age distributions are an important consideration, particularly for companies with promotion-from-within policies.
   e. Favourable views toward employee development and career planning.
   f. More-profitable companies will be more able and therefore more likely to use CCH.[42]

   What do you think of Greer's arguments? What factors would lead an employer not to try CCH? What advantages would an employer practising CCH have in terms of recruiting?

2. Discuss several recruitment experiences you have had. What methods were used to recruit you? Were they successful? For example, what recruiting methods attracted your interest to certain jobs? Describe the application procedures you encountered and the results. If you have ever used the services of a Canada Employment Centre or a private employment agency, discuss what was involved. What kinds of information did you have to supply? Were you interviewed? What kinds of questions did you have to answer? Were you successfully placed in a job? If you have ever used the services of a university or college placement office, describe your experiences with it.

3. Visit a Canada Employment Centre. Call in advance for an interview with the director of placement, and prepare a list of questions to ask. Summarize your findings in a short report. Examples of questions: (a) How many employers use the centre to recruit applicants each year (or month)? (b) Does the number of employers using the CEC vary over time? If so, why? (c) How does the agency place applicants? (d) Does the agency place all levels of labour skills and experience or only certain types? (e) How are computers used to help match applicants to jobs? and (f) What percentage of job applicants who register with the office are placed through the office?

4. Interview an employer regarding his or her company's recruiting program. Who is responsible for recruiting? What do the recruiters do? Are they trained? If so, how? What recruiting methods and sources are used? Is the effectiveness of recruiting methods evaluated? On what criteria? How are recruiting budgets determined? How far in advance of actual need is recruiting done? Answers to these and similar questions should form the basis of a short report. If several students conduct interviews with a number of employers, the recruiting efforts can be compared.

5. Have the class role-play recruiting interviews. Divide the students into three sections: job applicants, interviewers, and observers. The group of job applicants should be students nearing graduation. They should prepare résumés. The second group—the interviewers—should meet, perhaps with the instructor, to generate a list of questions to ask applicants. Depending on the time available, applicants can be interviewed by more than one interviewer. Interviewers should always get a copy of the applicant's résumé at least ten to fifteen minutes before the interview, in order to have some background information on the applicant. The group of observers should observe and take notes on how the interviewer and the applicant respond to each other's questions. After the role-playing, the observers should comment about how the interview was handled and how the applicant presented him- or herself. Role-playing may take place simultaneously by arranging chairs in

groups of three in the classroom (each group would have an interviewer, an applicant, and an observer). Since recruiting interviews should be a vehicle for the exchange of information, it would be advantageous for interviewers to pretend to represent a specific company or organization. This would enable applicants to ask questions about the company and encourage two-way communication.

▶▶▶ CASES

CASE 6.1 ▶ RECRUITING AT NOVATEL COMMUNICATIONS

The recruiting challenges faced by NovAtel Communications, a Calgary-based high-tech manufacturer of cellular phones, were briefly described at the beginning of this chapter. This case more closely examines how Garth Burlingham, NovAtel's recruiting manager, sought the talent vital to the organization's growth and survival between 1986 and 1990.

When we left Garth and Lin, they were on their way to Singapore. What had they done prior to that trip, and what did they do when they arrived? NovAtel began making recruiting trips to Singapore, Hong Kong, and sometimes Europe in 1986. In a short time, Burlingham developed a multistep process that proved very successful in attracting and hiring the experienced electronics and manufacturing engineers NovAtel needed.

Step 1 was to place ads in local newspapers describing the job, the company, and its location. The ads were in English since virtually all the well-educated, target population read that language. Applicants were asked to send their résumés and evidence of their work to Burlingham. One early mistake was to run an ad announcing a time and location at which any interested applicants could apply; the result was an overflow crowd of applicants. (Perhaps one of the most attractive aspects of going to work for NovAtel was the opportunity to become a Canadian landed immigrant in less than a year.)

In Step 2, Burlingham and relevant operations managers screened the résumés for the right mix of education and experience. Each ad yielded 160 to 200 résumés, and screening them was difficult and time-consuming since many applicants were very well qualified. A number of promising applicants were then contacted and invited to attend a briefing in their home country.

Step 3 included both that informational briefing and applicant interviews. These sessions, usually held at a conveniently located hotel, were conducted by Garth and one or more senior vice-presidents. Though one might argue that people such as Chris Groves, the vice-president for computer-integrated design and manufacturing, should have been in Calgary tending to business, the fact that he made a number of trips to Hong Kong and Singapore indicates the importance NovAtel's top management gave to recruiting. The involvement of high-level operations managers in the recruiting process had a very positive effect on applicants. In many cases, they could talk with and ask questions of the person who would be their boss. The briefing began with a presentation that included slides and videos of both NovAtel and Calgary. Afterwards, Garth, the operations managers, and usually a relocation counsellor answered questions. At this point, individual applicants were interviewed. Following the interviews, Garth and the other managers met and discussed the applicants and tentatively decided to whom jobs should be offered.

In Step 4, the recruiting team attempted to do reference checks on the applicants they had selected. Reference checks in Asian countries are usually less valuable than in North America, however, because expression of extreme opinions, either positive or negative, runs counter to Asian cultural norms. Thus, the checks usually served only to verify applicants' work experience and rarely provided additional information about the quality of their work.

By Step 5, the recruiting team was reasonably certain about those to whom they wanted to extend an offer. Still, phone calls were made and faxes sent to bosses and key co-workers back in Calgary to provide information learned in the interview or reference check and to seek their input to the job-offer decision.

In Step 6, the selected applicants were called back to the interview site for job-offer interviews. The primary purpose of these interviews was to sell the applicants on the job, NovAtel, Calgary, and Canada. This selling was necessary since those selected were experienced engineers who could easily have obtained four or five job offers. Most had families and homes, and almost all had many questions about matters such as the education system, taxes, selling and purchasing a home, and, of course, the immigration process. There was little demand for dual-career assistance (assisting a spouse in locating employment) among Far Eastern hires, although it was common among Europeans. The job of selling Canada and living in North America was made easier by the fact that most of those offered jobs had previously visited Canada and/or the United States.

The time between the acceptance of a job offer and the day the new employee began work was usually about nine to twelve months but could be as much as two years.

During the four years between 1986 and 1990, NovAtel screened approximately 3200 résumés from Singapore and Hong Kong, made 16 trips to Singapore, interviewed well over 300 applicants, and hired 50 engineers, two of them women. Of the 50, only one has returned to his home country. It is also noteworthy that the average quality of applicants who submitted résumés was much higher than was typical in North America.

Despite NovAtel's international recruiting program, the firm hired about a fifth of its engineers through co-op work-term programs with four schools in western Canada — the University of Alberta, the University of British Columbia, Simon Fraser University, and the University of Victoria—and one Ontario school known for its engineering programs — the University of Waterloo. Burlingham also used interview trips to these schools as a way to help teach operating managers how to interview. Each year NovAtel hired a total of approximately 80 co-op students in 4 co-op work-term programs of either four or eight months each. Eight to nine times as many students applied. Approximately a quarter of the work-term students were offered permanent jobs, and acceptance of offers was high. Generally, NovAtel was pleased with the co-op program.

Recruiting for clerical, assembly, and other jobs that did not require post-secondary degrees was primarily through walk-ins. NovAtel had a large applicant pool in both Calgary and Lethbridge because of its strong image as a highly desirable employer.

After growing rapidly for four years, NovAtel imposed a hiring freeze in 1991. It did, however, continue a search process for an engineer who had knowledge and experience in a special type of gas computer chip. The search process had identified seven people with the necessary knowledge. The recruiting task remaining was to convince one of these seven to leave the current employer and join NovAtel.

TASKS AND QUESTIONS

1. Explain why NovAtel used the methods it did to recruit various types of labour. Was NovAtel's situation unusual compared to that of other employers?

2. Review NovAtel's recruiting methods. Comment on the strengths of its recruiting efforts and on how they might have been modified or improved.

3. Turn back to the NovAtel ad from the *Calgary Herald* (Exhibit 6.1, page 255). Comment on the information and the organization of the ad. Compare what is in the ad with the text's suggestions for ads.

CASE 6.2 ▸ EXPANSION AT QUINAN STORES

Business has been good at Quinan Stores in Saint John, New Brunswick, and management has decided to expand its downtown store to include a bakery and deli, a cosmetics department, and a sporting goods department. No

Quinan store has ever had a bakery and deli, but several suburban outlets have very small cosmetics and sporting goods departments. Quinan stores have a reputation for high-quality merchandise and personal attention to customers. Employees in the new departments will be expected to meet Quinan's high standards of performance.

Management has estimated that the expansion, scheduled to open in nine months, will require 21 new employees. The bakery and deli will require two bakers, two butchers, two sales clerks, and one manager. The cosmetics department will need seven sales clerks and one manager; the sporting goods department, five sales clerks and one manager. The estimates were based on expected levels of customer demand for the new products and services and on the level of service the store wants to maintain (clerk-to-customer ratio).

Although Quinan tries to promote from within whenever possible for supervisory and managerial-level positions, the uniqueness of the new departments makes it unlikely that qualified applicants can be found internally for these positions.

Michael Robbins has worked as a human resource specialist for Quinan Stores for the past two years. His responsibilities have included recruiting, but never on such a grand scale. Robbins has his work cut out for him now; his boss, Vice-President of Human Resources Hilda Tjoveld, has asked him to prepare a recruiting plan and budget for staffing the expansion.

Robbins begins by gathering data on Quinan's previous recruiting efforts (see Tables 1 and 2). Data are available on the methods used to recruit sales clerks, supervisors and managers, but not bakers and butchers. The data pertain to average cost per applicant, average cost per hire, average time to hire, and average employee tenure. Cost per hire includes costs associated with processing applications, interviewing applicants, and selecting candidates for hire.

TABLE 1
Recruiting Data for Sales Clerks, Quinan Stores, 1985–1986

RECRUITING METHOD	AVERAGE COST PER APPLICANT	AVERAGE COST PER HIRE	AVERAGE TIME TO HIRE (WEEKS)	AVERAGE TENURE (MOS.)
Telegraph-Journal newspaper ad	$20	$840	3	20
Evening Times-Globe newspaper ad	$15	$900	3	22
Canada Employment Centre	0	$500[a]	4	14

[a] Although the CEC will pre-screen applicants, Quinan expects to interview four to six candidates for each position.

TABLE 2
Recruiting Data for Supervisors and Department Managers, Quinan Stores, 1985–1986

RECRUITING METHOD	AVERAGE COST PER APPLICANT	AVERAGE COST PER HIRE	AVERAGE TIME TO HIRE (WEEKS)	AVERAGE TENURE (MOS.)
Canada Employment Centre	0	$900[a]	8	18
Acme Employment Agency (private)	0	$2100 (10% of annual salary for position filled)	5	23
Kilgore Placement (private)	0	$2100 (10% of annual salary for position filled)	3	19

[a] Although the CEC will pre-screen applicants, Quinan expects to interview four to six candidates for each position.

TASKS AND QUESTIONS

1. Assume you are Robbins and prepare a recruiting plan and budget for the needed personnel at Quinan's. What method or methods will you use for recruiting each type of labour? What are your cost and time estimates? In developing your plan, feel free to suggest methods other than those used in the past, but be sure to justify your plan in terms of effectiveness criteria or other concerns.

2. After you have prepared your plan, assume a scenario in which labour market conditions are tighter than in the years for which recruiting data are available. How might tighter market conditions alter your recruiting plan?

NOTES

1. D. Stoffman, "How Canadians Can Compete," *Report on Business Magazine*, July 1990, p. 47.
2. D. Stoffman, "The Ring of Success," *Report on Business Magazine*, July 1990, pp. 49–53.
3. R. Maynard, "Getting Good Help," *Report on Business Magazine*, June 1990, pp. 40–48.
4. J.J. Fucini and S. Fucini, *Working for the Japanese* (New York: The Free Press, 1990).

5. Stoffman, "How Canadians Can Compete," p. 47.

6. "Case Studies: Business Involvement in Education," *Canadian Business Review*, Autumn 1990, pp. 24–25; A.K. Ross, "IBM Canada's Involvement in Education," *Canadian Business Review*, Autumn 1990, pp. 21–23; and B. Peterson, "Imperial Oil: Concern, Commitment, Contribution," *Canadian Business Review*, Autumn 1990, pp. 15–16.

7. Peterson, "Imperial Oil," pp. 15–16.

8. S.L. Rynes and A.E. Barber, "Applicant Attraction Strategies: An Organizational Perspective," *Academy of Management Review*, vol. 15, no. 2 (1990), pp. 286–310.

9. C. Davies, "Strategy Session 1990," *Canadian Business*, January 1990, pp. 47–55.

10. See, for example, Rynes and Barber, "Applicant Attraction Strategies."

11. F.G. Harmon and G. Jacobs, *The Vital Difference* (New York: AMACOM, 1985), p. 137.

12. G.N. Powell, "Effect of Job Attributes and Recruiting Practices on Applicant Decisions: A Comparison," *Personnel Psychology*, vol. 37 (1984), pp. 721–32; and S.L. Rynes and H.E. Miller, "Recruiter and Job Influences on Candidates for Employment," *Journal of Applied Psychology*, vol. 68 (1983), pp. 147–54.

13. H. Lakhani, "The Effect of Pay and Retention Bonuses on Quit Rates in the U.S. Army," *Industrial and Labor Relations Review*, vol. 41 (1988), pp. 430–38; and M.B. Tannen, "Is the Army College Fund Meeting Its Objectives?" *Industrial and Labor Relations Review*, vol. 41, (1987), pp. 50–62.

14. R.S. Schuler, and S.E. Jackson, "Linking Competitive Strategies with Human Resource Management Practices," *Academy of Management Executive*, vol. 1 (1987), pp. 207–20.

15. W.G. Shackelford, "Developing an Effective Minority Recruitment Program," *Journal of Staffing and Recruitment*, vol. 1, no. 2 (1989), pp. 10–14.

16. Gordon Betcherman, *Meeting Skill Requirements: Report of the Human Resources Survey* (Ottawa: Economic Council of Canada, 1982), p. 33.

17. Maynard, "Getting Good Help," pp. 40–48.

18. K. Kidd, " 'Help Wanted' Signs No Way to Hire: Touche Ross," *The Globe and Mail*, November 9, 1989.

19. M.J. Gannon, "A Profile of the Temporary Help Industry and Its Workers," *Monthly Labor Review*, vol. 97 (1974), pp. 44–49.

20. Statistics Canada, *Labour Force Annual Averages 1990*, cat. no. 71–220.

21. *Canadian HR Reporter*, vol. 4 (1991), p. 16.

22. Donald P. Schwab, "Organizational Recruiting and the Decision to Participate," in K. Rowland and G. Ferris, eds., *Personnel Management: New Perspectives* (Boston: Allyn and Bacon, 1982), pp. 103–28.

23. Kidd " 'Help Wanted' Signs."
24. V.M. Evans, "Recruitment Advertising in the '80's," *The Personnel Administrator*, vol. 23 (1978), pp. 21–25, 30.
25. R.D. Arvey and R.H. Faley, *Fairness in Selecting Employees*, 2nd ed. (Reading, Mass.: Addison-Wesley, 1988), p. 58.
26. M. Stoiko and C. Davenport, "Focus on Recruitment," *Human Resources Professional* (September 1989), pp. 32–34.
27. M. Gibb-Clark, "Recruiting Companies Taking a Hard Look at Cost of Advertising," *The Globe and Mail*, May 8, 1989.
28. C.D. Fyock, "Expanding the Talent Search: 19 Ways to Recruit Top Talent," *HR Magazine*, vol. 36, no. 7 (1991), pp. 32–35.
29. F. Butterfield, "Why They Excel," *Parade Magazine*, January 21, 1990, pp. 4–6.
30. B. Wysocki, Jr., "Chasing Collegians," *Wall Street Journal*, March 27, 1979.
31. E.D. Beway, "What Employees Look For in First and Subsequent Employers," *Personnel*, vol. 63, no. 4 (1986), pp. 49–54.
32. A. Castle, "Baiting the Hook for Campus Recruiting," *Canadian HR Reporter*, vol. 4 (1991), p. 9.
33. Employment and Immigration Canada, *Annual Report 1989–1990* (Ottawa: Supply and Services, 1990), p. 13. Reproduced with the permission of the Minister of Supply and Services Canada, 1992.
34. Employment and Immigration Canada, *Annual Report 1989–1990*, p. 18.
35. M. Gibb-Clark, "Placement Agencies Settle on Equity," *The Globe and Mail*, October 31, 1991.
36. Personal communication with a partner at Peat Marwick Stevenson Kellogg, August 1992.
37. S. Bergsman, "Setting Up a Temporary Shop," *HR Magazine*, vol. 35, no. 2 (1990), pp. 46–48.
38. S.F. Forrer and Z.B. Leibowitz, *Using Computers in Human Resources* (San Francisco: Jossey-Bass, 1991).
39. Schwab, "Organizational Recruiting," pp. 113–14.
40. J.P. Wanous and A. Colella, "Organizational Entry Research: Current Status and Future Directions," in G.R. Ferris and K.M. Rowland, eds., *Organizational Entry* (Greenwich, Conn.: JAI Press, 1990), pp. 253-314.
41. C.R. Williams, C. Labig, and T.H. Stone, "Employee Recruiting Sources and Post-Hire Outcomes: A Test of the Differential and Applicant Population Difference Hypotheses," *Journal of Applied Psychology*, forthcoming.
42. For more information, see C.R. Greer and T.C. Ireland, "Organizational and Financial Correlates of a Contrarian Human Resource Investment Strategy," *Academy of Management Journal*, forthcoming.

Suggestions for Further Reading

- D. Arthur. *Recruiting, Interviewing, Selecting and Orienting New Employees*. New York: AMACOM, 1986.
- J.A. Breaugh. *Recruitment: Science and Practice*. Boston: PWS-Kent, 1992.
- R.H. Hawk. *The Recruitment Function*. New York: American Management Association, 1967.
- D.P. Schwab, S.L. Rynes, and R.J. Aldag. "Theories and Research on Job Search and Choice." In G.R. Ferris and K.M. Rowland, eds., *Organizational Entry*. Greenwich, Conn.: JAI Press, 1990, pp. 1–38.

CHAPTER 7

SELECTION

- SELECTION: DEFINITION AND PROCESS
- RELATION TO OTHER HRM FUNCTIONS
- THE ROLE OF SELECTION IN ORGANIZATIONAL EFFECTIVENESS
- VALIDATING PREDICTORS
- SELECTION INSTRUMENTS AND PROCEDURES
- HRM IN ACTION ▶ SELECTING TEAM MEMBERS AT HONDA AND MAZDA
- SELECTION OF MANAGERIAL TALENT
- THE UTILITY OF SELECTION
- SUMMARY
- REVIEW QUESTIONS
- PROJECT IDEAS
- CASE 7.1 ▶ DISPUTED SELECTION AT SUNNYBROOK
- CASE 7.2 ▶ FLYER INDUSTRIES: BUILDING A BETTER BUS
- APPENDIX 7A ▶ ESTIMATING UTILITY GAINS OF A PREDICTOR
- NOTES
- SUGGESTIONS FOR FURTHER READING

JOHN ALLEN, THE HR MANAGER FOR the new Toyota plant in Georgetown, Kentucky, faced a formidable task in 1987. He had to hire a work force of 3000 from more than 60 000 applicants. The task was made even more challenging since Toyota was committed to using team-style management that demanded employees with a "unique combination of qualities: the flexibility, diligence and perseverance to help their teams to succeed and assure a commitment to 'kaizen' [which means 'continuous improvement' in Japanese]."[1] Mr. Allen was assisted in the hiring process by the Kentucky Employment Office and a consulting firm in Pittsburgh. Actually, 54 of the first team members hired were trained as assessors and helped with the selection process. In the first twelve months, more than 60 000 applicants were assessed and those who were accepted spent, on average, fifteen weeks in the process. The selection process was considerably more thorough and time-consuming than that used by most employers, but management felt the effort was necessary to create a world-class competitive organization.

The Georgetown plant, like the one in Cambridge, Ontario, and a few other Canadian and U.S. automobile plants, operates using the team style of management that requires employees, or team members as they are often called, to perform more than the typical, limited-scope production job of most manufacturing firms. Team members must also possess more than basic skills and an above-average level of motivation. One of the major differences is teamwork, which is defined as "active participation in, and facilitation of, team effectiveness; taking actions that demonstrate consideration for the feelings and needs of others; being aware of the effect of one's behaviors on others."[2] For the organization, the value of teamwork is that workers cooperate with one another, particularly in solving problems.

Determining who among the many applicants had the necessary teamwork abilities was one of the most time-consuming parts of the multistage selection process. Of course, not all applicants made it to this stage, which takes place at the Interpersonal Assessment Centre. Some applicants dropped out of the process after seeing a video that provided a good realistic job preview of what working at Georgetown would entail. Many more were excluded on the basis of their scores on the General Aptitude Test Battery, a measure of cognitive ability, psychomotor skills, and ability to learn, a key part of team-style organizations. The Interpersonal Assessment involved group discussions and problem solving on issues related to productivity, work safety, tardiness, or difficulties with a co-worker. Applicants also took part in a small-manufacturing exercise in which they worked as a group to assemble small sets of pipes or other small objects requiring manual dexterity and quality. One object of this exercise was to see how people work together as a group and how well they are able to make improvements in both productivity and the quality of their product. A set of team members, as well as the HR staff, had been trained by the consulting organization to help run and score the exercises. Not all managers felt completely comfortable at first with team members' involvement in the selection process, but most became strong advocates of it in time. In some team-style organizations, applicants who reach the later stages of the screening process critique it and suggest modifications—another type of "kaizen" exercise.

The multifaceted selection process also included assessment interviews. These interviews were different from those done in most organizations in that they focussed on specific behaviours that had been identified by a thorough job analysis as being critical to success as a team member. Additional assessment centres for team-leader candidates included an in-basket to measure ability to prioritize and delegate, an employee development exercise focussing on counselling and training abilities, and a work scheduling exercise. Applicants for maintenance jobs participated in additional assessments intended to evaluate technical knowledge and skills.

While the Toyota HR staff has good reason to feel proud of their team's accomplishments, they may wonder, in the spirit of "kaizen," if there are ways to improve their selection process. Could, perhaps, some part of the process be eliminated or made more efficient without sacrificing either the excellent results or employment equity? Of course, improving the selection process may prove difficult since its base rate of success is higher than that for the traditional hiring procedures used in most manufacturing firms. On the other hand, the cost per team member selected can range from $400 to

$2000, according to the firm that helped develop this system and others much like it. It is estimated that for every dollar invested in the selection process, there is a return of over $100 in improvements in quality and productivity.[3] The results have been excellent—the first shift reached full production within eight months of startup; turnover is less than 5 percent compared with the typical 20 for startup facilities; and absenteeism is far below the industry average, at only 2 percent. These results are even more impressive when one remembers that the Georgetown plant is the largest under one roof and makes the Camry, which is known for its quality. (The Cambridge plant produces Corollas.)

The selection process described here is typical of those used by a number of team-style organizations, including Cami in Ingersoll, Ontario; Subaru-Isuzu in Indiana; and Mazda in Flat Rock, Michigan. Of course, the procedures vary and some differences are discussed later in this chapter. This chapter explores the role of the selection process in achieving organizational objectives and describes basic selection concepts and theory as well as selection methods.

SELECTION: DEFINITION AND PROCESS

Selection is the process of differentiating among applicants in order to identify (and hire) those with a greater likelihood of success in a job. Although some selection devices are also useful within an organization for promotion or transfer, this chapter focusses on selecting applicants from outside the organization.

The most accurate differentiations would result if an employer could try each applicant in a job for a given length of time and observe the results. Time and costs generally make this approach impractical, although it is becoming more feasible as more employers move to a system of using a core work force plus a buffer force of temporaries from employment agencies. In the absence of "job tryouts," organizations do the next best thing: they collect information about an applicant that can be used to predict the likelihood of his or her success in a particular job. This information is collected by a sequential selection process that serves to narrow the pool of applicants by eliminating less desirable ones at each stage along the way.

The selection process employs a variety of instruments and screening devices to narrow the selection pool. Each applicant must successfully negotiate a number of hurdles in order to stay in the running for a particular job vacancy. Or, an applicant may self-select out at any stage in the process. Typical hurdles include the preliminary interview, the application form, the employment interview, tests, reference and background checks, a physical examination, a final interview with the boss, and a hiring decision. The selection process is portrayed in Figure 7.1.

FIGURE 7.1
The Selection Process

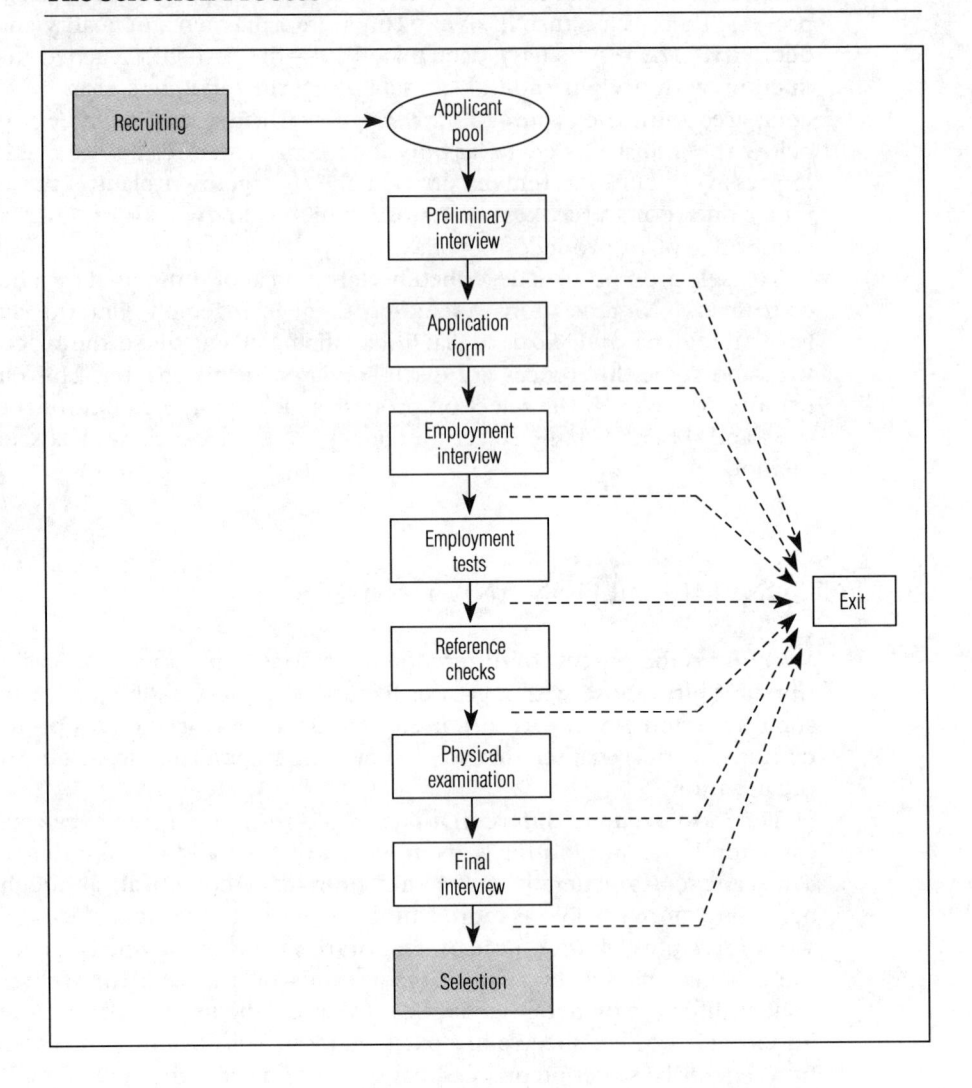

```
Recruiting → Applicant pool
                ↓
         Preliminary interview ----→ Exit
                ↓
         Application form ----→ Exit
                ↓
         Employment interview ----→ Exit
                ↓
         Employment tests ----→ Exit
                ↓
         Reference checks ----→ Exit
                ↓
         Physical examination ----→ Exit
                ↓
         Final interview ----→ Exit
                ↓
         Selection
```

The selection process proceeds sequentially from collecting relatively general information about an applicant to collecting more specific in-depth information. For example, application blanks solicit a broad range of information; the employment interview offers an opportunity to probe more deeply. Employment tests provide even more detailed information about an applicant's skills, knowledge, and abilities. Generally, the later steps in the selection process tend to be more expensive than the earlier ones.

As we have seen, the selection process actually begins with recruiting. Because recruiting messages seek a response from qualified individuals, applicants are to some extent pre-selected by the time they become a part of the selection pool.

Screening by the organization often begins with a preliminary interview — a brief exchange of information between a receptionist or secretary and the job applicant. The receptionist usually answers basic questions about job details, such as work hours, pay, and so on. The applicant is usually given an application form to complete. To ensure that discrimination does not occur at this point, receptionists should be trained to accept applications from everyone regardless of sex, race, ethnicity, or physical appearance.

Completing an application form is the second step in the selection process. Typical application forms request information on the applicant's home address, last employer, prior work experience, names and addresses of references, and so on. When this step has been completed, an HRM professional examines the application form. Less-qualified applicants are eliminated at this point, while the more-qualified continue to the next hurdle: the employment interview.

The employment interview is a face-to-face meeting between an applicant and an interviewer, usually an HRM professional from the organization. It provides an opportunity to pursue information from the application form and to obtain any other information relevant to the applicant's ability to do the job. Assessments of the applicant's appearance, ability to use the language of work, and interpersonal skills may be made during the interview. Applicants who are not eliminated at this stage may be required to take certain tests, depending on the nature of the job.

HRM professionals use a variety of tests for selection purposes. Ability tests measure an applicant's "current competence to perform an observable behavior or a behavior resulting in an observable product."[4] Aptitude tests measure potential or undeveloped abilities. Personality tests and interest inventories seek to determine whether an applicant's personality and/or interests are compatible with job requirements. Language tests may be appropriate in certain situations.

If an applicant is still in the running after testing, reference and background checks may be made. Such checks ensure that an applicant has not been misrepresented and that the information he or she has provided is true. Following this, an applicant may be asked to submit to a physical examination. Applicants who survive the screening process to this point are referred to management for final interviews.

In the final interview, an applicant meets with the person who will be his or her boss. The supervisor usually interviews several applicants. In this interview, both applicant and interviewer explore compatibility and mutual interests. At this stage of the selection process, only the best-qualified applicants remain, and the "chemistry" between superior and subordinate may well determine whether an applicant receives a job offer. In team-style organizations, team members, rather than a boss, may be conducting interviews to decide whether an applicant would fit their team. A survey of more than 500 organizations with work teams found that 89 percent of them involve team members in the selection process.[5]

In actuality, many organizations do not use all the possible steps of the selection process. Most use an application form and an employment interview, but tests and physical examinations are usually used only for certain types of jobs. Testing is generally not required for relatively simple jobs that are easily learned, such as many jobs in the fast food industry, or for higher-level professional jobs, such as lawyer, professor, and engineer. Problems of illiteracy and a lack of basic skills in the labour market may, however, lead to more testing of basic skills in the 1990s. Physical exams tend to be required for relatively strenuous jobs, such as police officer and firefighter, and for jobs involving public safety, such as bus driver and pilot. Reference checks are more likely to be used for jobs requiring responsibility for money, equipment, or the public safety. Organizations that use the entire process tend to be large companies and federal, provincial, and municipal governments. Specific instruments used in the selection process are discussed later in the chapter.

RELATION TO OTHER HRM FUNCTIONS

Selection is related most closely to the HRM functions of recruiting, human resource planning, job analysis, performance appraisal, orientation, and training and development. These relationships are described in the following subsections and depicted in Figure 7.2.

Recruiting

Recruiting can be viewed as a preliminary part of the selection process, and its effectiveness has implications for the selection function. If recruiting does not attract more applicants than an organization needs to hire, the selection function has a limited usefulness. As more applicants are recruited and participate in the selection process, the probability of hiring a successful applicant increases.

Human Resource Planning

Recruiting and selection together represent a major human resource planning strategy for acquiring the qualified labour necessary to achieve organizational goals and objectives. The HRP function specifies the number and type of employees needed. Recruiting and selection are hampered if time constraints reduce the chances of attracting a sufficiently large selection pool. Since

FIGURE 7.2
Selection: Relation to Other HRM Functions

```
                          ┌─────────────────┐
                          │ Job analysis    │
                          │ Through job     │
                          │ descriptions    │
                          │ and specifications,│
                          │ forms basis for │
                          │ selection       │
                          │ methods         │
                          └────────┬────────┘
                                   ▼
┌──────────────┐   ┌──────────────┐   ┌──────────────┐   ┌──────────────┐
│Human resource│   │ Recruiting   │   │ Selection    │   │ Orientation  │
│ planning     │   │ Attracts     │   │ Differentiates│  │ Familiarizes │
│ Specifies    │──▶│ applicants to│──▶│ among        │──▶│ employee     │
│ number       │   │ fill job     │   │ applicants to│   │ with new job │
│ and type of  │   │ vacancies in │   │ identify and │   │ and integrates│
│ employees    │   │ an organization│ │ hire those best│ │ him or her into│
│ needed       │   │              │   │ qualified    │   │ the organization│
└──────────────┘   └──────────────┘   └──────▲───────┘   └──────────────┘
                                             │                  ▲
                          ┌─────────────────┐│                  │
                          │ Performance     ││                  │
                          │ appraisal       ├┘          ┌──────────────┐
                          │ Measures        │           │ Training and │
                          │ employee's      │           │ development  │
                          │ performance     │           │ Needs        │
                          │ in the job and  │           │ revealed by  │
                          │ provides criterion│         │ selection    │
                          │ measures of job │           │ information  │
                          │ success         │           └──────────────┘
                          └─────────────────┘
```

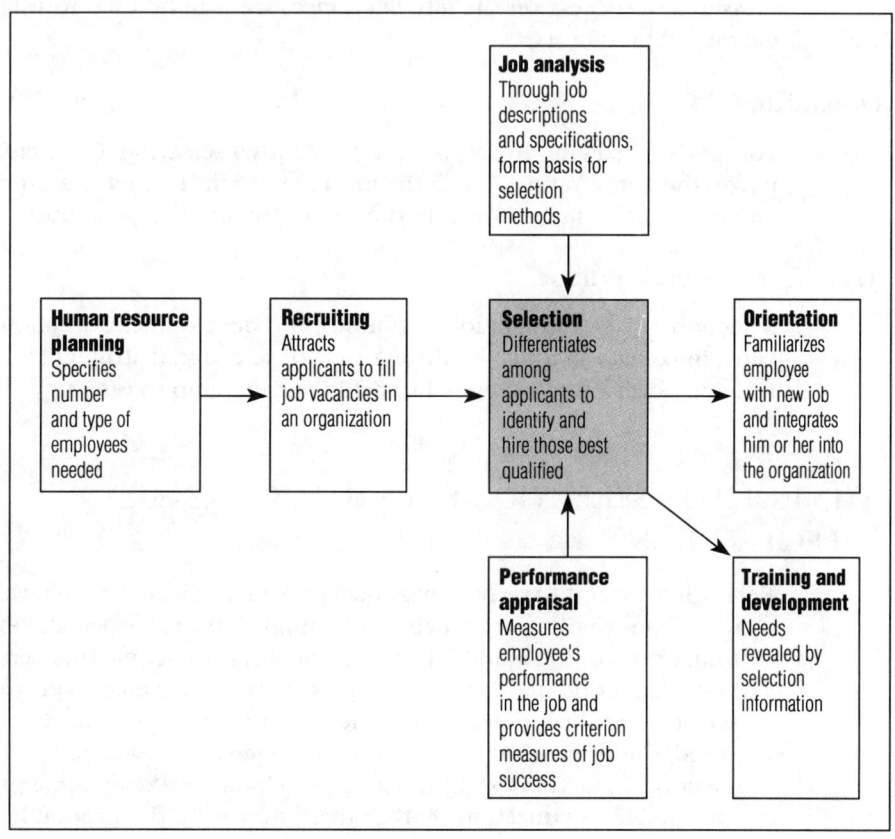

recruitment and selection can take several days to many months to complete, advance forecasting of specific employment needs is essential. If the planned numbers and types of employees are not available, adjustments may have to be made in the mix of occupations or in the amount and types of production.

Job Analysis

Job analysis is basic to the selection function. Job descriptions and specifications dictate the kinds of predictors of success appropriate for each job. For example, predictors for a word-processing job might include the results of a job-sample keyboarding and/or filing test or a clerical ability test. With the growing legal importance of employment equity, employers must be ready to demonstrate the job relevance of their hiring methods.

Performance Appraisal

Performance appraisal data provide the selection function with criterion measures of success on the job. Such measures can be used to establish the validity of predictors.

Orientation

For newly hired employees, orientation follows selection. Orientation familiarizes the new employee with the job and with the company's expectations. Orientation also helps integrate the employee into the organization.

Training and Development

Selection also has inputs to the training and development function. Specifically, information collected through use of selection instruments reveals the training needs of both newly hired and current employees.

THE ROLE OF SELECTION IN ORGANIZATIONAL EFFECTIVENESS

Recruiting attracts to an organization a pool of applicants who have the basic qualifications to fill job vacancies. If all applicants performed all jobs equally well, an organization could fill its vacancies on a first-come-first-served basis. The fact that individual differences do exist means that employers can benefit by selecting applicants with higher levels of job-related abilities, skills, and knowledge and those whose interests and needs are better suited to the job.

Selection is part of a staffing strategy to build and maintain a productive and profitable organization. Rather than increasing the productivity of the organization's existing labour force, selection regulates the quantity and quality of incoming human resources. It contributes to organizational effectiveness by helping to ensure high base rates of success for jobs.

The *base rate of success* for a job is the percentage of individuals who reach an acceptable level of performance in the job within a reasonable length of time. The base rate of success for Toyota's team member process is probably in the very high range of 80 to 90 percent, or 0.8–0.9. Definitions of "success" vary, of course, but generally a successful employee is one who consistently performs the tasks required by the job at or above a minimally acceptable level. An employee is judged unsuccessful if he or she repeatedly fails to perform important elements of the job at such a level. The organization retains successful employees, if possible. Less successful workers are candidates for training, transfer, demotion, or termination.

HRM professionals continually strive to improve base rates of success for jobs. One way they do this is by devising, testing, and using new and better predictors of actual work behaviour and on-the-job success. Another way is to apply existing selection procedures more vigorously — for example, by raising hiring standards to employ more highly qualified workers. Successful efforts to "beat the base rate" (to improve the percentage of successful employees in jobs) contribute to organizational effectiveness in two ways. First, they result in a higher-quality work force. Second, they reduce the costs associated with errors in selection (because fewer employees are unsuccessful).

IMPROVING QUALITY OF THE WORK FORCE

Improvements in base rates of success for jobs reflect improvements in quality of the work force, since a greater proportion of employees are performing successfully. Recall from Chapter 2 that individuals have a substantial range of differences in abilities. A selection policy that hires people who meet only minimum qualifications typically results in hiring employees from the lower part of the distribution of abilities. Research shows that the use of minimum-qualifications hiring procedures can lead to productivity declines that are almost as great as those that result from abandoning selection procedures.[6] One reason is that no true dichotomy exists between qualified and unqualified applicants. In most cases, the relationship between ability test scores and job performance is linear.[7] Thus, the optimal use of selection procedures requires rank-ordering candidates from highest to lowest and hiring from the top down. (Employers pursuing employment equity can also use this approach to maximize the quality of new hires.[8] They simply rank-order each category of applicants—the majority and the targeted groups—and hire from the top down the desired number from each group.)

There are great financial advantages to hiring employees with higher levels of ability since they can increase levels of performance and productivity in an organization. As we suggested in the Toyota example, they can also help reduce training costs and the cost of turnover incurred when performance is unacceptable.

High-ability employees are most beneficial to an organization when placed in jobs in which they can make maximum use of their special skills. Talents are wasted if an employee is placed in a position that does not require their use. Deciding which job an employee should be assigned to in an organization is referred to as *placement*. Placement is a part of the selection function but does not always occur since organizations usually consider applicants only for the specific job they are applying for. Thus, applicants are to a great extent pre-placed by virtue of making an application for a specific job. Both employer and applicant benefit, however, if an applicant is considered for a number of jobs in the organization and, if hired, placed in the one best suited to his or her abilities and the organization's needs. For example, an employee with a high degree of manual dexterity can be more useful to an organization in a job on an assembly line on which workers perform at their own pace than in one on an assembly line with a controlled speed.

288   PART 2   PLANNING AND STAFFING

Of course, unless they are motivated to do so, even high-ability employees may not produce more than do their co-workers of lesser ability. For this reason, many employers offer monetary incentives for superior performance by paying employees on the basis of the quantity and/or quality of their output. Even if employers must pay more for high output, high-performing employees are a better investment for an organization. Because their productivity levels are higher than those of low or average performers, fewer high-performing employees are needed to complete the work. Through the selection process, high-performing employees can be identified and hired, thus saving an employer money.

REDUCING THE COSTS OF ERRORS IN SELECTION

Table 7.1 shows the four possible outcomes of a selection decision. Two of these—the true positive ("high hit") and the true negative ("low hit")—are correct decisions. The other two outcomes represent errors. In the "false positive error," the selector predicts success for the applicant in the job and makes the decision to hire, but failure results. In the "false negative error," an applicant who would have succeeded is rejected because the selection process predicts failure. Each of these selection errors is costly to an organization. But the costs of hiring an employee who fails to perform at a minimally acceptable level are usually greater than the costs of failing to hire an individual who would have succeeded. One should recognize that although the decision to hire or not hire an applicant is dichotomous, the line between failure and success is not actually dichotomous. That is, some false positives

TABLE 7.1
Outcomes of the Selection Decision

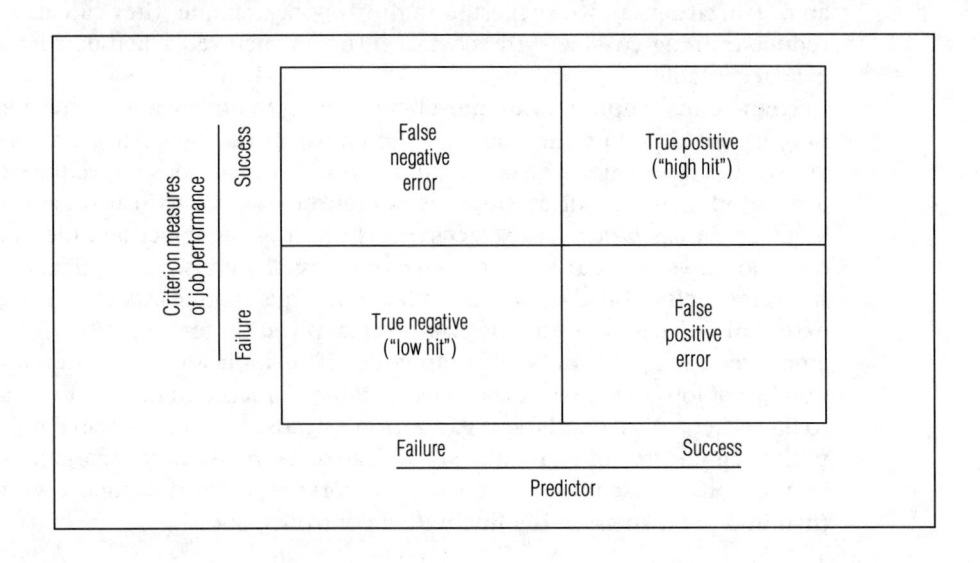

	Predictor: Failure	Predictor: Success
Criterion: Success	False negative error	True positive ("high hit")
Criterion: Failure	True negative ("low hit")	False positive error

may be less costly to an employer than others, and there will be a range of performance among high hits.

The False Positive Error

A false positive error — a faulty prediction of success that results in a hire — incurs three types of costs for the organization. The first are those incurred while the person is employed — the results of production or profit losses, damaged public relations or company reputation, accidents resulting from ineptitude or negligence, absenteeism, and so on. More costs are associated with training, transferring, or terminating the employee; they can include severance pay and the costs of any grievance proceedings resulting from a decision to terminate. Finally, there are the costs of replacing the unsuccessful employee, which include the costs of recruiting, selecting, and training a replacement. Generally, the more important the job, the greater the costs of a selection error. For example, the failure of a human resources director is potentially more detrimental (and therefore more costly) to an organization than is the failure of a janitor. Furthermore, replacement costs for the HR director would be greater.

The False Negative Error

In a false negative error, an applicant who would have succeeded is rejected because failure was predicted. Most false negative selection errors go unnoticed, unless the applicant happens to complain to the human rights commission or be hired after all for some other reason. Costs associated with this type of error are difficult to estimate.

One situation in which the impact of both false positive and false negative selection errors can be detected and measured is professional sports, such as football and hockey. Coaches and scouts analyze game films, statistics, scouting reports, and other data and decide whether they wish to draft a particular player. If they do draft an individual and performance fails to meet expectations, a false positive selection error has occurred. Suppose, however, a team decides against drafting a player but another team chooses the same individual. If that player subsequently turns out to be a star, the first team's rejection may represent a false negative selection error.

Although most organizations are unable to spot such errors, much less assess their costs, they do exist. But they can be minimized by using valid selection methods and procedures.

VALIDATING PREDICTORS

The selection function is an important one — and a difficult one — for HRM professionals. In addition to making selection decisions about people based on certain predictors of actual work behaviour, HRM professionals must determine those predictors, define "job success," and demonstrate, through a complex process known as validation, that predictors are related to measures of work behaviour for each job.

If predictors are invalid, decisions based on them are no more accurate than decisions based on a toss of a coin. *Validity* is the degree to which a measure accurately predicts job performance. Selection instruments are valid to the extent that predictors measure or are significantly related to work behaviour, job products, or outcomes. The process of demonstrating that a predictor is significantly related to a measure of work behaviour, job products, or outcomes is *validation*.

Validation is required to ensure that predictors do, in fact, make useful discriminations among applicants on the basis of their likely success in a job. Through the validation process, relatively accurate predictors can be found. Valid predictors enable employers to hire employees who have a relatively high likelihood of success and to avoid hiring those who would in all probability fail. Validation must also be done to ensure that predictors are job-related — that they measure characteristics directly related to job behaviour and/or job outcomes — and are not sexually, culturally, or linguistically biased.

THE VALIDATION PROCESS

The validation process examines the nature of the relationship between a predictor and a criterion measure of successful performance on a job. A *predictor* is any piece of information that can be used to screen applicants. Predictors include information from application blanks (education level, experience, and so on) and reference checks; scores on tests of skill, ability, or aptitude; data from interest and personality inventories; and interviewer ratings of an applicant.

Criterion measures are any measures of work behaviour, job products, or outcomes that have value to an employer. As already noted, job success is difficult to define; it is an abstract concept that means different things to different employers. Even for the same job, two employers may define success differently. For example, one manufacturer of valve springs defines it as production of 8500 valve springs per day, no more than two days absent per month, and a scrap rate of less than 5 percent. Another manufacturer sees it as production of 7500 valve springs per day and no more than one day absent per month. Note that the second employer does not include scrap rate as a criterion.

Since success is a concept that can include countless aspects of work behaviour and job products, employers must decide which aspects are most crucial to success for a particular job. These aspects may then serve as criterion measures of success for a job.

HRM professionals validate predictors of success using some of the following criteria: quantity of output (number of characters input, forms filed, valve springs produced); quality of output (number of errors, amount of scrap);

supervisors' ratings of job performance; length of time on the job (tenure); number of absences (absenteeism); and degree of success in training programs.

Correlation Coefficients

For a predictor to be useful, the validation process must demonstrate that a significant statistical relationship exists between it and a criterion measure of successful job performance. The most common index of the degree of relationship between two measures or variables, such as a predictor and a criterion measure, is the *correlation coefficient*, symbolized by r. Correlation coefficients vary from -1.0 to $+1.0$. (In practice, the plus sign is usually omitted from positive correlation coefficients.) A negative correlation coefficient indicates an inverse relationship between the variables: when the value of one goes up, the value of the other goes down. An example of an inverse relationship is that between labour costs and labour supply. Generally, as the supply of a particular type of labour decreases, the hiring wage for that labour goes up. A positive correlation coefficient indicates a relationship in which the values of both variables go up or down together. An example of a positive relationship is that between labour costs and the skill levels of employees. Generally, increased labour costs are associated with increased skill levels since wage rates are higher for more skilled workers. Stronger statistical relationships are indicated by larger values of r. Regardless of the size of a correlation coefficient, one may not infer a causal relationship between the two variables.

The significance of a statistical relationship refers to the degree of confidence one can place in it. That is, what are the chances that a correlation coefficient or some other index of the strength of a relationship could have occurred by chance or luck? The statistical significance of a statistical relationship depends on two factors: the magnitude of the relationship and the sample size from which the relationship was calculated. A correlation of small magnitude (such as 0.15) may be statistically significant if it was obtained from a very large sample. On the other hand, a correlation of 0.40 may not be significant if it was obtained from a small sample.

The significance of a statistical relationship is indicated by a small letter p and a two- or three-digit number. The U.S. *Uniform Guidelines on Employee Selection Procedures* specifies that predictor-criterion relationships should be $p = 0.05$ or less.[9] A p value of 0.05 means that the statistical relationship between two variables would occur by chance only five out of a hundred times. The smaller the p value, the more confident one can be that a correlation does not occur by chance.

Correlation coefficients can be used for two different purposes in the validation process. The first is to establish a relationship between the predictor and the criterion, which is expressed in terms of a correlation coefficient known as a *validity coefficient*. The second use of correlation coefficients is to demonstrate the consistency or reliability of the predictor and/or the criterion. This type of correlation coefficient is called a *reliability coefficient*. Keep in mind that although correlation coefficients are sometimes referred to as validity or reliability coefficients, this phrasing merely expresses a particular use of the correlation coefficient. In reality, the validity or reliability of a test or any other measure cannot be reduced to a single number. The validity of a particular test, for example, typically requires examination of the relationship between scores on that test and a variety of other non-test behaviours.

Validity Coefficients

A validity coefficient expresses the degree of relationship between a predictor and a criterion measure. For example, the validity coefficient between scores on a perceptual speed and accuracy test (predictor) and the average number of beer bottles packed per day (criterion measure) is 0.60 ($r = 0.60$).[10] Thus, the validity of the test for predicting the average number of beer bottles packed is 0.60. This positive relationship is shown in a scatter diagram or plot in Figure 7.3. Each dot in the diagram represents one employee's test score in relation to number of bottles packed. As shown by the scatter plot, employees with high test scores tend to have higher levels of output, while employees with lower scores tend to have lower levels. But the relationship is not perfect. Some employees have high test scores but low levels of output (see the lower right corner of diagram). If there were a perfect correlation between test scores and work outputs, the dots would fall in a straight line. (Though this example is simplistic and dated — most beer producers have automated the packing process — the task and the necessary skills are easily understood. Of course, many of us have more experience removing beer bottles from cases than packing them.)

Data show that validity coefficients usually vary between 0.30 and 0.60.[11] Therefore, the speed and accuracy test used in this example is a very good predictor. However, even a predictor with a validity of 0.30 is more useful in making a selection decision than a simple toss of a coin.

It is difficult to use either a correlation coefficient or a scatter diagram for making selection decisions. For this reason, predictor-criterion relationships are often described in expectancy tables. Table 7.2 shows an expectancy table constructed from the data in the scatter diagram in Figure 7.3. A minimum criterion of 6500 bottles per day was chosen. The expectancy table simply shows the probability, or odds, of individuals with particular test scores packing 6500 or more bottles per day. These probabilities were obtained by calculating the percentage of employees at each test score who packed an average of at least 6500 bottles per day. For example, a test score of 26 to 30 predicts an 89 percent probability — eight out of nine people with such a score, on average, will pack 6500 or more bottles per day. Expectancy tables should be developed using large samples of applicants and employees to ensure reliability of the probabilities.

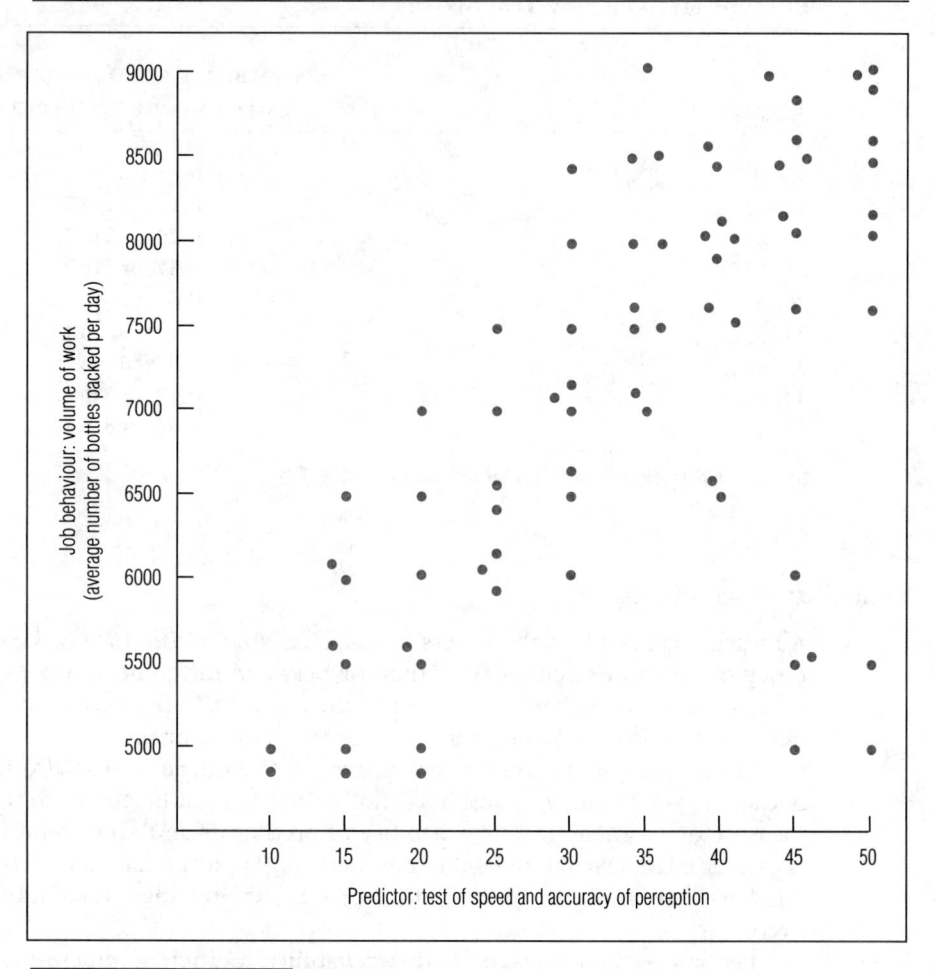

FIGURE 7.3
Relationship between Test Scores and Job Behaviour ($r = 0.60$)

[Scatter plot with x-axis "Predictor: test of speed and accuracy of perception" ranging from 10 to 50, and y-axis "Job behaviour: volume of work (average number of bottles packed per day)" ranging from 5000 to 9000.]

Source: Adapted from M.D. Dunnette, *Personnel Selection and Placement*. Copyright © 1966 by Wadsworth Publishing Company, Inc. Used with the permission of the author.

Expectancy tables provide an easy and understandable way to describe statistical relationships between a predictor and a criterion measure. They also easily portray nonlinear and curvilinear relations. For example, note that Figure 7.3 has a slight tendency toward a curvilinear relationship as some employees with very high test scores do not pack bottles at the "standard rate" of 6500 per day. Relationships of this type can occur when people with very high levels of ability are not motivated to perform well on the job.

TABLE 7.2

Expectancy Table: Job Behaviour Given Various Speed and Perceptual Accuracy Test Scores

TEST SCORES	PROBABILITY AND ODDS OF PACKING 6500 OR MORE BOTTLES PER DAY
≤ 10	0
11–15	0.14, or 1 in 7
16–20	0.29, or 2 in 7
21–25	0.57, or 4 in 7
26–30	0.89, or 8 in 9
31–35	1.0, or 10 in 10
36–40	1.0, or 10 in 10
41–45	0.67, or 8 in 12
46–50	0.80, or 8 in 10

Source: Compiled from the data used in Figure 7.3.

Reliability Coefficients

A measure cannot be valid unless it is also reliable. *Reliability* is the consistency of a measure, either over time or between different measures of the same concept or behaviour. A metre stick is a reliable measure of height because it yields the same result for a person at two or more points in time (assuming that the person has not grown in the interim). It is also reliable because it yields the same result as another measure of height, such as a tape measure or a yardstick. The reliability of predictors and criterion measures is expressed in terms of reliability coefficients. Typical reliability coefficients fall between 0.70 and 0.90, with 0.80 indicating high reliability for a predictor.

There are several ways to obtain a reliability coefficient for a test or other predictor. Each method measures sources of unreliability: stability across time, internal consistency at one point in time, or both. The test–retest, or stability, estimate measures sources of unreliability resulting from changes in the person and in the measurement situation over time. In this case, a high reliability coefficient indicates that people's responses to a predictor at one time are very similar to their responses to the same predictor at another time. This method usually uses relatively short time intervals of several weeks.

A second type of reliability estimate is the internal comparison. Of the many types of internal comparison or consistency estimates in use, one of the better ones is the odd–even method. To obtain a reliability coefficient using this method, one correlates the odd- and the even-numbered items of a single predictor (test) given to a group at *one* point in time. A high estimate of internal consistency means that responses to the odd-numbered items are very similar to those for the even-numbered items. Thus, the items are highly consistent with one another, and the reliability is high. This method of reliability estimation is commonly used since it is easily and quickly done. However, it provides no information about stability across time.

The best reliability estimate is the equivalent-form method. This method requires two separate tests or predictors designed to measure the same ability, skill, or other characteristic. The two are given to the *same* group of people at two *different* times. If they have a high reliability coefficient, people respond very similarly to them despite the time lapse and the use of different tests. For example, suppose your instructor wants to estimate the reliability of the midterm examination. Using the equivalent-form method, he or she could prepare two exams covering exactly the same material and give them to the class several weeks apart. A high correlation between the two sets of scores would indicate both stability and internal consistency reliability; a low coefficient could indicate either low internal consistency or low stability over time. To determine the source of unreliability in this case would require an internal consistency estimate treating both midterms as one test.

MAJOR TYPES OF VALIDATION

Three major types of validation are used to validate predictors. According to the U.S. *Uniform Guidelines on Employee Selection Procedures*, these types reflect different approaches to investigating the job-relatedness of selection procedures and may be interrelated in practice. They are: (1) criterion-related validity; (2) construct validity; and (3) content validity. In criterion-related validity, a selection procedure is justified by a statistical relationship between scores on the test or other selection procedure and measures of job performance. Construct validity involves identifying the psychological trait (the construct) that underlies successful performance on the job and then devising a selection procedure to measure the presence and degree of the construct. An example would be a test of leadership ability. In content validity, a selection procedure is justified by showing that it representatively samples significant parts of the job, such as a keyboarding test for a word-processing operator.[12]

Criterion-Related Validity

A predictor has *criterion-related validity* if a statistically significant relationship can be demonstrated between it and some measure of work behaviour or performance. Examples of performance measures are production rates, error rates, tardiness, absences, length of service, and supervisors' ratings. Suppose a department store uses one year of sales experience as a predictor for its sales personnel. To validate this predictor, the employer would have to demonstrate that a statistically significant relationship exists between one year of sales experience and some measure of work behaviour or job products, perhaps number of sales and/or a low percentage of errors in ringing up purchases.

Figure 7.4 illustrates how the three types of validity are demonstrated for a clerk/word-processing operator job. In each case, the process begins with job analysis, which determines major job activities and critical work behaviour on which to base selection procedures and to determine criterion meas-

FIGURE 7.4
Three Kinds of Validity

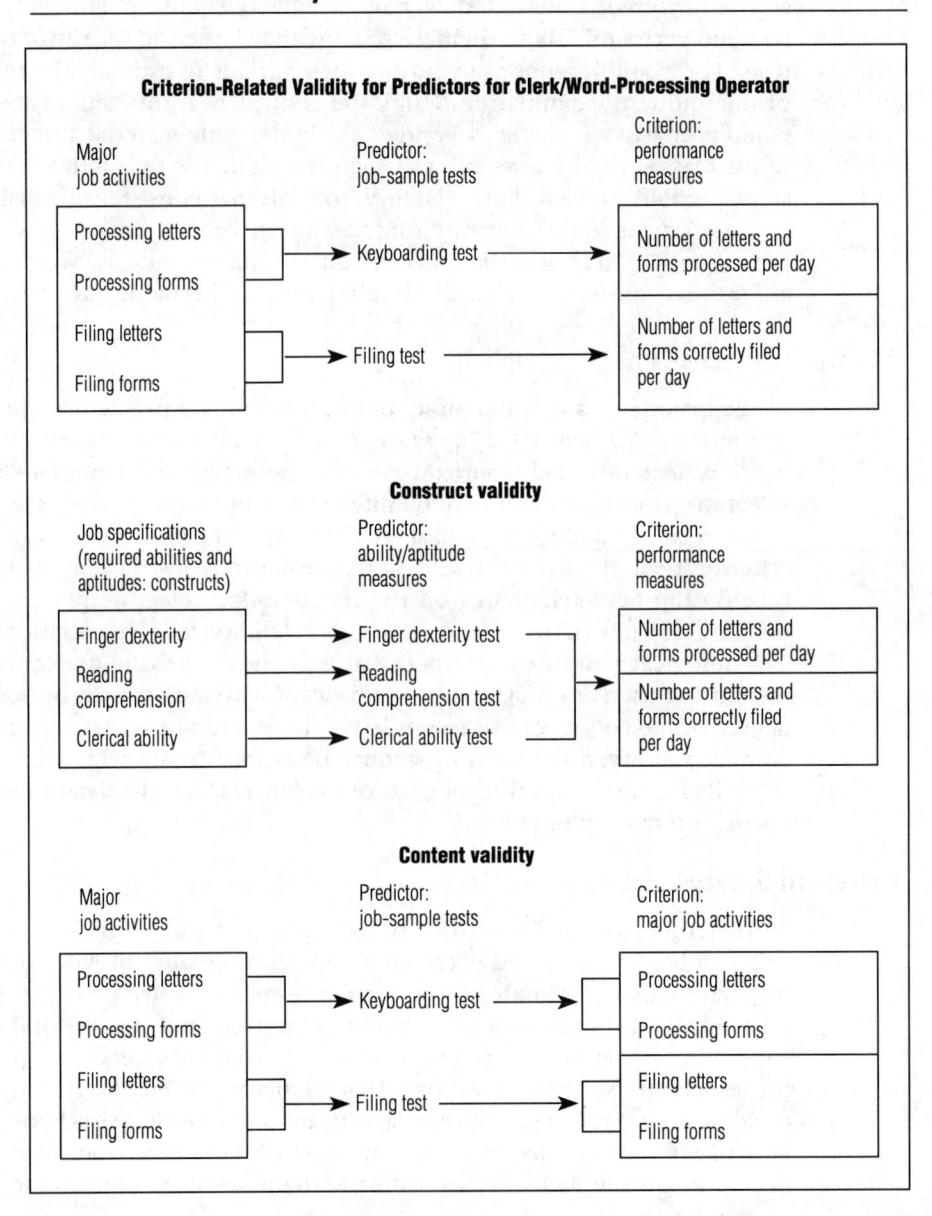

Criterion-Related Validity for Predictors for Clerk/Word-Processing Operator

Major job activities	Predictor: job-sample tests	Criterion: performance measures
Processing letters Processing forms	Keyboarding test	Number of letters and forms processed per day
Filing letters Filing forms	Filing test	Number of letters and forms correctly filed per day

Construct validity

Job specifications (required abilities and aptitudes: constructs)	Predictor: ability/aptitude measures	Criterion: performance measures
Finger dexterity Reading comprehension Clerical ability	Finger dexterity test Reading comprehension test Clerical ability test	Number of letters and forms processed per day Number of letters and forms correctly filed per day

Content validity

Major job activities	Predictor: job-sample tests	Criterion: major job activities
Processing letters Processing forms Filing letters Filing forms	Keyboarding test Filing test	Processing letters Processing forms Filing letters Filing forms

ures. The criterion measures chosen are the number of letters and forms processed per day and the number of letters and forms correctly filed per day — measures of quantity and quality of job outputs. In criterion-related validity, keyboarding and filing tests are used as predictors. A statistically significant relationship must be demonstrated between the scores on these tests and the criterion measures of job performance.

There are two general types of criterion-related validity: concurrent and predictive. Both involve the same basic steps: (1) job analysis; (2) selecting potentially useful predictors; (3) administering predictors; (4) examining the statistical relationships between predictors and criterion measures; and (5) cross-validating using a different sample. The two validation strategies differ within the third step: administering the predictors. In *concurrent* validity, potential predictors are administered to current employees; in *predictive* validity, they are given to job applicants. The concurrent method produces results faster than the predictive method since measures of job performance are already available for current employees. Though concurrent validity is used more often than predictive validity, examining for it can easily yield relationships between predictors and performance criteria that are biased and difficult to interpret; differences between job applicants and experienced employees (for example, age, experience) often make it difficult to generalize from the predictor-criterion relationships observed for current employees to those of job applicants.

Criterion-related validity has been very popular in the past, but recent research has shown that the sample size necessary to demonstrate it is larger than had previously been thought, from approximately 200 to 300.[13] Another problem is that criterion measures of performance must themselves be validated to ensure that they accurately measure aspects of work behaviour rather than factors unrelated to the job.

Construct Validity

Rather than using direct tests or similar instruments to predict job success, some selection methods seek to measure the degree to which an applicant possesses psychological traits called *constructs*, including intelligence, leadership ability, verbal ability, mechanical ability, and manual dexterity. Constructs deemed necessary for the successful performance of jobs are inferred from job behaviour and activities as summarized in job descriptions. They are the job specifications part of job descriptions. Figure 7.4 shows the construct validation process for the clerk/word-processing operator job already discussed. From the major activities of processing and filing letters and forms, analysts have inferred the necessity of three constructs: finger dexterity, reading comprehension, and clerical ability. These constructs can be tested by a finger dexterity test, a reading comprehension test, and a clerical ability test. When the tests are properly validated, the scores can be used to predict actual work behaviour or performance, measured in this case by the number of letters and forms processed per day and the number of letters and forms correctly filed per day.

Construct validity requires demonstrating that a statistically significant relationship exists between a selection procedure or test and the job construct it seeks to measure. For example, does a reading comprehension test reliably measure how well people can read and understand what they read? In order to demonstrate construct validity here, one needs data showing that high scorers on the test actually read and understand more difficult material than do low scorers on the test. The same type of relationship between test scores and actual non-test behaviour is necessary to demonstrate construct validity for any psychological construct. Fortunately for HRM managers, construct validation is usually done by research psychologists working for test development companies or for large companies or universities.

Besides demonstrated statistically significant relationships between constructs and tests to measure them, construct validity requires that there be (1) a demonstrated relationship between a predictor and a criterion measure, and (2) a demonstrated relationship between criterion measures and work behaviour or job products.

Content Validity

A selection procedure has *content validity* if it representatively samples significant parts of a job, such as a filing test for a file clerk or a test of cash register operation for a grocery checker. Selection tests that approximate significant aspects of a job are called *job-sample tests*. They require applicants to perform certain aspects of a job's major activities, thus demonstrating competence at tasks that are an actual and important part of the job. Significant aspects of a job are determined through job analysis and set forth in job descriptions. To increase content validity, job-sample tests should approximate aspects of the job as closely as possible.

SELECTION INSTRUMENTS AND PROCEDURES

HRM professionals are responsible for choosing, using, and sometimes developing selection instruments and procedures. It is important that these be administered in a *standardized* way. This means that selection instruments must be administered to every applicant in the same way and under the same conditions. Results must also be interpreted in the same way for all applicants. Without standardization of selection procedures, decisions are unreliable and reduce the validity of the selection process. HRM professionals should keep records of the selection process, since proof of standardization can become useful if the organization's hiring practices are challenged on human rights grounds. This section discusses a number of selection instruments including application blanks, employment interviews, tests, background and reference checks, and physical examinations.

Application Forms

Application forms are a means of collecting written information about an applicant's education, work, and other experiences, past and present. Almost all organizations ask applicants to complete an application form of some type. Typical forms request information about an applicant's home address, last employer, previous work experience, education, and other information pertinent to employment, such as the names and addresses of references. Skill in the other official language may be requested if the job is a bilingual one. As we pointed out in Chapter 3, employers are somewhat limited by law as to the kinds of information they may seek through application forms (see Tables 3.2 and 3.3).

Application forms are used in a variety of ways. One common use is to screen out applicants who do not meet minimum hiring standards. Some individuals who do not meet these standards can be spotted before receiving an application, but those who are not can be identified and eliminated by the information on their forms.

The application form also serves as a guide for the employment interview. Since it usually provides much general information about an applicant but not much in-depth detail, it may suggest the need for an interviewer to question or for the applicant to enlarge upon some areas. For example, an employer may want to investigate more fully the reasons for leaving a previous job.

Weighted Application Blank

Application forms may also serve to collect information on predictors of work behaviour and/or work performance. When used in this way, they are usually called weighted application blanks. A *weighted application blank (WAB)* is an application form in which weights or scores are assigned to different answers to each question. For example, two years of secondary school receives a certain score and four years another. Scores are determined by analyzing the relationship between the responses to items and measures of job performance (such as absences, productivity, and turnover).

One scoring method for WABs and for biographical inventory blanks (the latter are detailed in the next subsection) is the *horizontal percent method*. This method weights items according to the percentage of people who are successful on the job for each response category. For example, suppose 60 people answer yes to Item 1 in Exhibit 7.1. Forty-five of the 60 are high-performing workers and 15 are low performers. Thus, a yes response receives a weight of 75, since 45 is 75 percent of 60.

EXHIBIT 7.1
Sample Items for a Biographical Inventory Bank

1. Have you found your life to date to be pleasant and satisfying?

2. Check each of the following from which you have ever suffered.
    a. allergies
    b. asthma
    c. high blood pressure
    d. ulcers
    e. headaches
    f. gastrointestinal upsets
    g. arthritis

3. What was your length of service in your most recent full-time job?
    a. less than 6 months
    b. 6 months to 1 year
    c. 1 to 2 years
    d. 2 to 5 years
    e. more than 5 years
    f. no previous full-time job

4. When are you most likely to have a headache?
    a. when I strain my eyes
    b. when I don't eat on schedule
    c. when I am under tension
    d. January first
    e. never have headaches

5. Over the past five years, *how much* have you enjoyed each of the following? (Use continuum 1 to 4 below.)
    a. loafing or watching TV
    b. reading
    c. constructive hobbies
    d. home improvement
    e. outdoor recreation
    f. music, art, or dramatics, etc.
        1. very much
        2. some
        3. very little
        4. not at all

Source: W.A. Owens, "Background Data," in M.D. Dunnette, ed., *Handbook of Industrial and Organizational Psychology* (New York: Wiley, 1983), p. 613. Reprinted with the permission of M.D. Dunnette.

By adding up an applicant's score on a WAB, some measure of job performance can be predicted. Since WAB development requires a large number of workers (at least several hundred), this method is limited to large employers or smaller ones with high rates of turnover.

WABs have been used successfully to screen applicants according to their propensity for quitting. A WAB for this purpose is developed by comparing biographical data for a group of quitters against biographical data for a matched group of remainers. Items that discriminate between stayers and quitters are then weighted according to how well they differentiate between the two groups. Once developed, the WAB is administered to applicants, scored, and used to predict each applicant's quit or stay propensity. A large insurance company developed a WAB to reduce turnover among female clerical employees. Items that differentiated among employees who stayed less than one year versus those who stayed longer included education, tenure on previous job, previous salary, and length of time at present address. Use of the WAB scoring system increased the percentage of those who stayed more than a year to 72 percent from 48 percent.[14] Despite the fact that half of the employees were visible minorities, the WAB was not discriminatory. Care must be taken in developing WABs since items that are good predictors of short- versus long-tenure employees may create employment equity problems. For example, area of residence is likely to adversely affect members of certain racial or ethnic groups.

Research has shown that WABs are very useful for predicting length of tenure in an organization, job performance, and work interests. Personal data of the type collected in WABs are also useful for predicting managerial success.[15] "A review of 58 studies using biographical data as a predictor was found to have an average validity of 0.35 across a variety of job-related criteria and occupations.[16]

Biographical Inventory Blank

A *biographical inventory blank (BIB)* is an application form very much like a WAB, but its format is more structured. BIBs often use a multiple-choice or true–false format; unlike WABs, they sometimes include questions about present behaviour. Sample items from a BIB are shown in Exhibit 7.1.

Both WABs and BIBs can be very useful methods of predicting future behaviour from past behaviour. Care must be taken, however, to assure their validity and legal defensibility. Since the weighting and validation of biographical items has traditionally been purely empirical, such questions as "Do you own a red car?" may be positively weighted for a sales position. The job relevance of such a question is not likely to be obvious to either an applicant or an employment equity investigator. A much better approach is to derive hypotheses about the nature of job success from comprehensive job analysis and seek items that are related to these hypotheses.[17] This approach is superior to the purely empirical scoring approach because the relationship between items and measures of job behaviour will be more understandable and defensible.

HRM IN ACTION

SELECTING TEAM MEMBERS AT HONDA AND MAZDA

Many of the Hondas, Mazdas, Toyotas, Suzukis, Nissans, Subarus, and Geo Prizms you see on the streets were built in North American automobile plants. Many of these plants use a team style of management in which a group of six to ten employees co-ordinates its own work assignments and schedules. The hiring process at all of these plants is more rigorous than that of most plants of the Big Three auto manufacturers in North America. Mazda's approach is similar to that of other Japanese auto makers, but Honda's is distinctive. We will compare and contrast Mazda's approach with Honda's.

More than a year after mailing in a Mazda application clipped from a Detroit newspaper, Steve Ross had survived an arduous selection process to become one of the firm's first group of 400 hourly workers or "team members." Ross, like many who were hired, had no previous auto industry experience, but he had sixteen years' experience as a skilled tradesman. The screening process he survived had five separate steps:

1. The application form from the newspaper.

2. A battery of written tests that measured abilities such as basic literacy, including math and reading comprehension, and spatial ability. Since team members were to serve as their own quality inspectors, applicants were given a test in which they had to select the flawed light bulb from a set of six pictures of bulbs. Tests similar to this one are given to applicants at many Canadian plants, such as the Toyota site in Cambridge, Ontario.

3. A personal interview conducted by a man and a woman, one of whom was a representative of the trade union representing workers at the plant (the United Automobile Workers). Many of the questions concerned previous work, attitudes toward working in teams (including helping other team members who are having problems), and attitudes toward unions.

4. A group problem-solving assessment. Working in teams of varying sizes, applicants tackled a set of problem-solving exercises. One focussed on their ability to contribute to a consensus decision. For this exercise, applicants were asked to come up with a reward system that ranked achievements such as a perfect safety record and no absences. The raters, who watched from each end of a long table,

made notes about how the consensus was reached and graded applicants on how they listened as well as on how they expressed their ideas. A second exercise measured how effective applicants were at "Kaizen projects." (*Kaizen* is a Japanese word for the process of constant improvement.) Each group of applicants was given toy blocks and told to assemble an air-boat; the team then worked together to develop ways to build the boat faster. It was not uncommon for groups to "Kaizen" their assembly process to cut the boat-making time in half. A third exercise emphasized the ability to handle interpersonal problems. In one situation the group was asked how to improve the attitude of a worker who was rude and unpleasant toward others but was a reliable, high-performing worker.

5. A four-hour simulated work exercise, held at Mazda's training centre. Specific activities included assembling a dome light, installing it in a car, and manoeuvring a large drill around an engine. As in other exercises, Mazda assessors timed each task and made notes on factors such as orientation toward quality. This final hurdle measured applicants' endurance and physical co-ordination.

At each of the five steps, some applicants were eliminated. It is also important to note that the steps were separated from one another by several weeks. Many applicants had to make several trips from as far away as West Virginia since Mazda had not limited its recruiting to Michigan.

Even successful applicants sometimes wondered why the Mazda selection process probed them in such depth for auto assembly work. Mazda managers repeatedly stated, both to applicants and the public, that Mazda workers are given more responsibility and freedom than Big Three employees and that their participation in teams necessitates learning a variety of jobs and being able to contribute to Kaizen projects.

Honda also tries to hire bright, flexible people who are willing to work in teams and contribute to Kaizen projects. It differs from Mazda and most other Japanese auto manufacturers by relying on three separate interviews for selection, rather than on extensive testing and exercises. Of course, Honda carefully examines applications and résumés and checks on previous work history, particularly in terms of absences and high turnover. The nature of the previous work, however, is not considered nearly as important as attitudes about work. In fact, Honda, even more than Mazda, prefers people without previous manufacturing experience. Honda has, for example, hired a former pig farmer, a divorcee with four small children, and a vocational school teacher.

Unlike other Japanese auto manufacturers in North America, Honda insists on a local work force. Thus, when it began hiring for its Marysville, Ohio, plant in 1982, it established a hiring radius of 48 kilometres. This effectively excluded the city of Columbus, which was 56 kilometres away, and led to a U.S. work force that was less than 3 percent black. Since the plant opened, Honda has paid more than $6 million to settle employment discrimination suits.

Honda's first interview is often done with as many as five applicants (in an attempt to reduce the many hours of interviewing required). Applicants who are called back for the second as well as the third interview are interviewed individually by two managers. The third interview is longer than the first two, often lasting several hours. Typical questions asked of Honda applicants include

1. Do you service your own car?
2. Why do you want to work for Honda?
3. What would you do if you could not keep up with your job on the assembly line?
4. What would you do if a very experienced employee on the line kept passing bad parts to you?
5. What are your most creative areas?
6. In your opinion, what are the strengths and weaknesses of teamwork in the workplace?
7. How do you feel about working 50 hours a week?

Applicants appear to regard working for a Japanese auto maker as highly desirable. Honda, Mazda, and others enjoy selection ratios of 1/100 or even lower. While such large numbers of applicants may be partially due to the economically turbulent '80s, it is likely that applicants see a style of management they like.

Source: Mazda: adapted from *Working for the Japanese: Inside Mazda's American Auto Plant* by Joseph J. Fucini and Suzy Fucini. Copyright © 1990 by Joseph J. Fucini and Suzy Fucini. Used with the permission of The Free Press, a Division of Macmillan, Inc.; Honda: adapted from the book *Honda* by Robert L. Shook © 1988. Used by permission of the publisher, Prentice-Hall Press/A division of Simon & Schuster, New York.

Employment Interviews

The sequential selection process contains three types of interviews: the initial interview, the employment interview, and the final interview with the person who will be the employee's immediate superior. The most comprehensive of the three and the one of most concern to HRM professionals is the employment interview.

The *employment interview* is a face-to-face conversation between an applicant and an employer's representative, usually an HRM professional for the organization or an interviewer for an agency, public or private, that refers suitable applicants to an employer. On occasion, a representative of the operating department concerned may also be present. The interview is a vehicle for the exchange of information between the applicant and the interviewer regarding the former's suitability for and interest in a job the employer seeks to fill. Information provided in the application for employment can be probed more deeply in the interview, and other information relevant to an applicant's qualifications can be elicited. Since interviews can be flexible, any missing pieces of information about an applicant can be collected at this time. The employment interview also provides an interviewer with a sample of an applicant's behaviour in a one-to-one interaction situation. Following an interview, the interviewer usually formalizes his or her judgement of an applicant into an overall assessment of suitability for the job.

Management's main concern in the employment interview is to find a good match between candidate abilities and the demands of the job. Another type of match to consider is that between a candidate's needs and what the organization has to offer in the way of need fulfilment. It has been suggested that a mismatch between needs and job reinforcers (rewards) leads to low satisfaction and quits, while a mismatch between abilities and job demands leads to low performance and dismissal.[18] HRM professionals should consider both types of match in assessing job applicants. Honest information conveyed in employment interviews serves to reduce turnover by allowing applicants to self-select out if they think their needs won't be met.

A number of factors are believed to affect both the interview itself and interview outcomes. Figure 7.5 categorizes these factors into those associated with the interviewer, the applicant, and the situation. Although most of the variables listed in the figure have been investigated, little evidence has been collected to show how these factors are related.

Interview Problems and Rater Errors

Despite its problems, the selection interview continues to be used by the vast majority of employers, and most consider interviews to be a very important part of the selection process.[19] Additionally, despite nearly half a century of research and hundreds of studies, researchers continue to examine and improve the process. A review of early research found that reliability is good both for internal consistency and for the same interviewer rating applicants twice (test–retest), but low when different interviewers rate the same candidate (inter-rater reliability).[20] Low inter-rater reliability and relatively low validity are attributable to the unstructured and subjective trait-based nature of the typical employment interview. Recent research has found that more structured formats, such as that often used in panel interviews involving multiple interviewers, can produce both reliable and valid results, particularly when combined with questions generated from thorough job analyses.[21]

FIGURE 7.5
Factors Affecting Employment Interviews and Their Outcomes

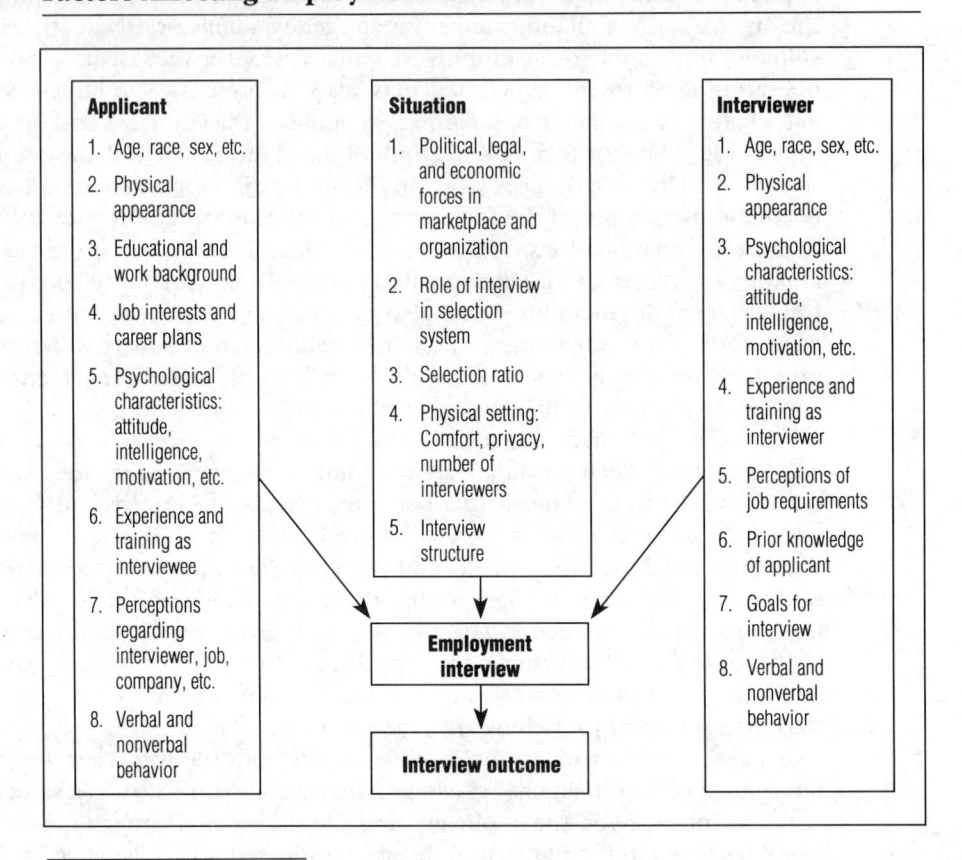

Applicant
1. Age, race, sex, etc.
2. Physical appearance
3. Educational and work background
4. Job interests and career plans
5. Psychological characteristics: attitude, intelligence, motivation, etc.
6. Experience and training as interviewee
7. Perceptions regarding interviewer, job, company, etc.
8. Verbal and nonverbal behavior

Situation
1. Political, legal, and economic forces in marketplace and organization
2. Role of interview in selection system
3. Selection ratio
4. Physical setting: Comfort, privacy, number of interviewers
5. Interview structure

Interviewer
1. Age, race, sex, etc.
2. Physical appearance
3. Psychological characteristics: attitude, intelligence, motivation, etc.
4. Experience and training as interviewer
5. Perceptions of job requirements
6. Prior knowledge of applicant
7. Goals for interview
8. Verbal and nonverbal behavior

→ **Employment interview** → **Interview outcome**

Source: R.D. Arvey and J.E. Campion, "The Employment Interview: A Summary and Review of Recent Research," *Personnel Psychology*, vol. 35 (1982), pp. 281–322. Copyright © 1982. Reprinted with the permission of *Personnel Psychology*.

Robert Dipboye has described the interview process as one in which "interviewers alternate between diagnostic, confirmatory, and disconfirmatory processes in assessing applicants."[22] (Confirmatory processes are those that incline the interviewer toward hiring; disconfirmatory processes are those that work toward screening out the applicant.) Dipboye argues that interviewers can reliably and validly assess applicants and not fall prey to the classic errors described below. The conditions under which this is most likely to occur are: (a) when the interviewer has good information on both the job and the applicant; (b) when the interviewer has time to make a good decision; and (c) when an accurate decision is important. On the other hand, he contends, in actual interview situations, there may be inadequate information and time pressures. In such cases, either confirmatory or disconfirmatory pressures may prevail. If, for example, the interviewer has strong positive feelings about a candidate, and is under pressure to make a quick decision that he or she is not likely to be held accountable for, Dipboye says there will be a confirmatory bias. When either confirmatory or disconfirmatory pressures are present, it is likely that the classic rating errors of hasty judgements, central tendency, leniency, strictness, halo error, contrast effects, stereotyping, and personal bias will occur.

Many common rating errors can be considered deviations from a normal or bell-shaped distribution. For example, the *error of central tendency* occurs when most applicants are rated as average though one would expect many to be rated as above or below average. In *leniency* and *strictness errors*, most applicants are given either uniformly high or uniformly low ratings, rather than being more widely dispersed. This type of dispersion error creates problems because the small differences between applicants renders discrimination between them nearly impossible. Additionally, strictness can lead to rejection of acceptable applicants (false negatives), while leniency may result in hiring poor performers (false positives).

With *halo error*, an applicant is seen as generally good or bad because one rated characteristic overshadows all others in the interviewer's mind. *Contrast errors* occur when an average applicant is rated higher than deserved because he or she is interviewed after several poor applicants or lower than deserved following several good ones. *Stereotyping* is the tendency to compare applicants with a stereotype of the ideal applicant; stereotypes of ideal applicants vary from one interviewer to another and may be unrelated to actual job requirements. These errors can be avoided or at least minimized by the methods and approaches discussed in the following subsection.

Improving Employment Interviews

The value of the employment interview as a selection instrument can be increased by following common-sense guidelines. One expert suggests:

1. A structured interview guide containing questions for applicants should be used to increase reliability.

2. An interviewer should be given complete job descriptions and job specifications for each job being interviewed for. This tends to reduce interviewer bias because actual requirements are spelled out in detail.

3. An interviewer should be trained in interviewing and know how to avoid errors such as talking too much and making hasty judgements.

4. An interviewer should be trained to deal with all applicants, regardless of their level of qualifications, since the interview is also a public relations vehicle.

5. An interviewer should receive special instructions on how to avoid discrimination and complaints of discrimination.[23]

A suggested interview plan is given in Exhibit 7.2.

Interviewers should receive feedback on the validity of their decisions on each applicant. Though it is not possible to provide performance feedback on applicants who were not hired, interviewers should be told which of the applicants they referred to management were hired and how well these people perform on the job. If interviewers use an interview guide and keep records of their decisions, they should be able to learn from their past decisions. Edwin Ghiselli, a famous industrial psychologist, used this approach while acting as a consultant to a brokerage firm. From data collected over a long period of time, he was able to predict with a high degree of accuracy whether a stockbroker would remain with the firm for a period of at least three years.[24] Since the interview is more valid for behaviours that are observable during it, such as verbal and interpersonal skills, it should be used to predict these things, rather than job performance as a whole.

A relatively new interviewing technique called the *behaviour description interview*, or *targeted interviewing*, has potential for significantly improving the employment interview. Using a structured format, the interviewer asks questions concerning certain aspects of an applicant's past behaviour. These aspects are selected because of their relevance to effective and ineffective on-the-job performance.[25]

As an example of how the method works, let us consider the job of a bank teller. Empirical research has uncovered five behaviour dimensions that distinguish between good and poor performance for this job. These dimensions relate to pleasantness versus rudeness to customers; co-operativeness versus dissension with peers; making good use of time versus wasting time; checking for errors versus making mistakes; and reporting problems versus hiding problems from the supervisor. Interview questions relate to each of these five dimensions. For example, with respect to the customer relations dimension, an applicant is asked: "Tell me about the nicest compliment you received when serving a customer. What did the customer want? Do you remember what you said at the time?" Another question on this same dimension is: "Tell me about the most irritating customer you have had to deal with. When did this happen? What did the person do that was irritating? What did you say in response?"[26] Note that the behaviour dimensions have both positive and negative aspects and that questions probe in a very detailed manner into specific instances of previous work behaviour.

Recent research has shown that behaviour description interviewing produces inter-rater reliabilities and validities significantly higher than other interview methods.[27] In fact, Janz, a professor at the University of Calgary, believes that behaviour description interviewing can be as reliable and valid as testing if interviewers are properly trained. He also reports that applicants are more satisfied with the interview because they feel it is fair and very relevant to the job.

EXHIBIT 7.2
Interview Plan

1. Greeting and statement of the purpose of the interview. Tell applicant you will be taking notes during the interview.

2. Yes–no questions about unchangeable aspects of the job. If the applicant cannot meet these requirements (i.e., can't do shift work if required), then terminate the interview at this point.

3. Questions designed to fill in the gaps in an application blank.

4. Interviewer describes the organization and the job, using organization chart, job description, etc.

5. Structural oral questions (ask and record answers). Do not make judgements at this time —just gather information
   a. Work history. (What special aspects of your work experience have prepared you for this job? Why are you leaving your present job? etc.)
   b. Education and training. (How does your education prepare you for this job? What additional training would you like if you get this job? etc.)
   c. Career goals. (What kind of a job do you see yourself holding five years from now? How does this job fit into your own career plan? etc.)
   d. Performance on your last job. (Everyone has strengths and weaknesses; what are your strengths? what are your weaknesses? How did your last superior evaluate your performance? etc.)
   e. Absenteeism, sick leave, tardiness record.
   f. Convictions and credit rating (if appropriate and permissible under jurisdiction's human rights legislation).
   g. Salary and benefits. (What kind of benefits do you think are important? What salary would you like to make? etc.)

6. Ask applicant if he or she has any questions, comments, or additions.

7. Tell applicant what happens next. (We have two more interviewees; then we'll decide and let you know within a week. Can we call you at home? etc.)

8. Close interview. Never offer the job at this point.

9. Review notes, make ratings on scales provided, and document your scale ratings. Beware of bias (halo error, contrast and similarity error, etc.) when rating.

Source: Adapted from E.L. Levine, *The Joy of Interviewing* (Tempe, Ariz.: Personnel Services Organization, 1976). Used with the permission of the author.

Interviewing and Human Rights Concerns

HRM professionals must be careful in interviewing to avoid questions that may breach the jurisdiction's human rights provisions against discrimination on the grounds of race, creed, colour, age, sex, marital status, nationality, ancestry, or place of origin. For example, the Ontario Human Rights Commission's guidelines for questions on application forms and during interviews include:

1. An interviewee cannot be asked for a birth or baptismal certificate; place of birth; place of birth of parents, grandparents, or spouse; or any information regarding national origin. After hiring, a person may be asked for a birth certificate.

2. A photograph cannot be requested during interviews but may be requested after hiring.

3. Elementary school name and location cannot be asked; neither can the nationality, racial, or religious affiliation of a school.

4. Interviewees cannot be asked about their willingness to work on any particular religious holiday. After hiring, a person may be asked when leave of absence might be required for the observance of religious holidays.

5. Employers can ask whether a person is legally entitled to work in Canada. After hiring, an employer may ask for documentary proof of eligibility to work in Canada. Eligibility means being a Canadian citizen, a landed immigrant, or a holder of a valid work permit.

6. Greater latitude is allowed in interview questions than on application forms, provided that such questions are related to genuine and reasonable job qualifications. For example, while questions regarding mental or physical health cannot appear on an application form, the applicant's ability to perform a particular job or task may be discussed in the interview.[28]

Existing research evidence suggests that interviews have often worked against hiring of the elderly, people with disabilities, and especially women.[29] For this reason, interviewers should be particularly careful in interviewing persons from these groups. For example, a female applicant should be addressed by her name, rather than as "dear." The don'ts include flirting, patronizing, and joking. Some jurisdictions, including Ontario, permit enquiries about marital status, but others do not, and none allows it to be used to discriminate.

Other details of what human rights laws permit and forbid in the selection process vary among Canada's thirteen jurisdictions. HRM professionals must know the regulations in the jurisdictions in which they work and keep up-to-date on changes and new interpretations.

The Role of the Interview

As a screening device and selection instrument, the interview appears to be experiencing a resurgence in importance. Despite decades of research by industrial psychologists demonstrating its low reliability and validity, both researchers and practitioners continue to study and improve the interviewing process. For example, interviewing plays a very important role in the selection process of many team-based organizations. The screening process at Honda, Toyota, and Mazda reflects this emphasis. Given the continued use and growing importance of interviewing, efforts must be made to ensure that interviews are both job-relevant and nondiscriminatory.

TESTS

Tests are a useful selection device for many jobs. Many organizations commonly use ability tests and aptitude tests; personality and interest measures are used less frequently because they are often not clearly related to the job and because results can be faked. Interest inventories and personality tests are most often used in selecting managerial candidates.

There are many different types of tests, but all share several features. All psychological tests have a set of standardized stimuli (test items), are administered in a standardized way, and are evaluated in a standardized manner.

Tests of Abilities, Aptitudes, and Skills

The three types of employment test commonly used for assessing abilities, aptitudes, and skills are cognitive ability tests, psychomotor tests, and job-sample tests. All three have minimum scores, called cutoff scores, for the purpose of screening applicants. Cutoff scores can be raised or lowered, depending on the number of applicants. If there are a lot of applicants for only a few positions, the cutoff score can be raised, thereby increasing the odds of hiring well-qualified employees.

Cognitive ability tests are used to measure a wide variety of abilities, aptitudes, and skills, including verbal and quantitative ability, mechanical comprehension, spatial ability, inductive and deductive reasoning, and memory. General intelligence tests are cognitive ability tests. Most cognitive ability tests are paper-and-pencil tests. Two cognitive ability tests that might be used for assessing the mechanical aptitude of an applicant for the job of auto mechanic are the Revised Minnesota Paper Form Board Test and the Bennett Test of Mechanical Comprehension. The former measures the ability to perceive geometric shapes in relation to one another; the latter uses pictures to examine knowledge of mechanical facts and principles.

HR managers at many Canadian plants might wonder if selection procedures such as the General Aptitude Test Battery (GATB) would work as well in Canada as in the Toyota plant at Georgetown, Kentucky. Additionally, would this cognitive ability test be as valid for different and more technical jobs, such as maintenance, and for those with greater responsibility, such as team leader?

Canadian HR managers should feel confident that, in the case of cognitive ability measures, there is considerable evidence for their validity across organizations. Differences between the United States and Canada should have no effect on the validity of measures such as the GATB. Such tests are also useful predictors for a variety of jobs, including maintenance personnel and team leaders, as well as for team members. Until the late 1970s, psychologists contended that validity for a test was both job-specific and organization-specific because research had shown tests to be valid for some jobs but not others in the same organization. But in the late 1970s, Schmidt, Hunter, and others conducted a series of validation studies using samples much larger than those used in previous studies. In one such study, validities for seven cognitive ability tests were examined for five clerical job families using data from 370 000 clerical workers. All seven tests were found to be highly valid for all five job families.[30] Other studies have confirmed that the most frequently used cognitive ability tests are valid for all jobs and job families.[31] The term *validity generalization* is used to describe the fact that a test has validity across jobs and organizations. There is, however, evidence that the validities of tests and other predictors such as grades tend to decline over time.[32]

Research has also shown that cognitive ability tests that are valid for predicting success in training programs are also valid for predicting job performance.[33] Thus, when Toyota properly uses a cognitive ability test to select people for its training program, it will also be selecting people who will do well on the job.

Psychomotor tests are another common type of employment test. These tests measure how accurately or rapidly a person can move his or her hands, fingers, feet, or entire body. They also measure co-ordination between body parts, such as eye–hand co-ordination or eye–hand–foot co-ordination. Psychomotor tests are most useful for jobs requiring skilled physical activities. Cognitive ability tests and psychomotor tests may be used to select both experienced and inexperienced persons into jobs or training programs.

Job-sample tests are another type of employment test. As described earlier in this chapter, job-sample tests require applicants to demonstrate specific job duties or constructs such as mechanical ability. For example, applicants for a mechanic's job could be asked to locate and fix a number of things wrong with a car or truck. Applicants for the job of interviewer might be asked to interview a client. Organizations can develop their own job-sample tests with the assistance of a qualified HRM professional.

Job-sample tests have received considerable support from various sources. A review of research using them found they generally had higher validities than paper-and-pencil tests.[34] One researcher found job-sample tests superior to the paper-and-pencil Mechanical Comprehension Test in a sample of maintenance mechanics.[35] Job-sample tests, if properly constructed, have high levels of content validity. They are also less likely to cause difficulties for people with low levels of reading ability than are paper-and-pencil tests. Job-sample tests are most useful for hiring experienced, trained applicants, rather than low-skill or trainee workers.

Closely related to job-sample tests are *job-simulation exercises* that place an applicant in a simulated but realistic situation to see how well he or she can cope. An example is Merrill Lynch's account-executive simulation exercise, in which a *Wall Street Journal* reporter participated. He re-creates the simulated situation for readers:

> My "in" basket is brimming with memos and unanswered letters. My desk calendar shows that conflicting appointments haven't been taken care of, and a client may pop in at any moment. Ignoring it all, I call a local industrialist who, I have been told, may be willing to buy some stock.
>
> "You've got to be kidding," he screams when I make my pitch. "Based on your recommendation, my brother lost $97 000 on a $100 000 investment, and now he is going to sue you."
>
> Who me?
>
> Well, sort of. Welcome to the Merrill Lynch account-executive simulation exercise, or, as dubbed by some, the Merrill Lynch stress test. It's a nail-biting three hours filled with alternating despair and satisfaction that leaves many longing for the good old days of calculus finals. Still, whether you leave in frustration or imbued with self-confidence, this exercise can't help but get you keyed up.[36]

Simulations make up a large part of the selection process at Toyota. For example, several simulations for team member positions take up to eight hours and there are others for team- and group-leader positions. A problem-solving simulation presents applicants with a description of a production or service problem. The applicant asks questions of a resource person and then makes a set of decisions. The resource person may question applicants regarding the reasoning and rationale for their decision. A second type of simulation is one in which applicants work together as a team to assemble some small object, such as a basket or toy boat. Candidates are evaluated on how well they make planning decisions, allocate resources, and co-operate with one another. A third type of simulation, the leaderless group discussion, has been used in managerial assessment centres for more than half a century. Small groups of applicants are given several problem situations such as worker safety, absenteeism, quality, and interpersonal conflicts among team members. While candidates are working, evaluators rate them on factors such as communication skills, listening skills, and leadership.[37]

Job simulations are proving useful as selection instruments for professional and managerial jobs. If properly developed, they are high in both content and criterion-related validity. Applicants are also more likely to accept such tests than they are paper-and-pencil tests because job-simulation tests, like job-sample tests, have face validity. A test is said to have *face validity* when it appears to applicants to be a good, fair test of a required ability or skill.

Language Tests

Language tests may be appropriate for bilingual jobs or other jobs that involve verbal skills in a language that is not the applicant's mother tongue—import–export work, tour guiding, order taking, sales, some government jobs, and so on. Language tests are a form of skills and ability test and, like other such tests, may be of the pencil-and-paper or job-sample variety. In deciding which sort to administer, HRM professionals should consider whether the job requires mostly written or spoken communication.

Personality Tests

People often believe that certain jobs require particular personalities or temperaments. For example, an accountant may be thought of as conservative, meticulous, and quiet, while a used-car salesman may be pictured as aggressive, flashy, and smooth-talking. Though it is probably true that some kinds of people often occupy certain jobs, there is little evidence that people must have a specific personality type to be successful at a particular type of job. It is more common that the job itself shapes the job holder's behaviour, and people create stereotypes of others according to their job behaviour.

Nonetheless, two general types of personality test are sometimes used in selection decisions. These are self-report personality tests and projective techniques. These personality measures have been used most often in the selection of candidates for managerial positions; they are also common in assessment centres, which are a popular method of identifying potential managerial talent.

Self-report personality tests have sets of questions or statements designed to describe and measure aspects of a person's personality. Examples of self-report personality measures frequently used in managerial selection are the Guilford–Zimmerman Temperament Survey and the California Personality Inventory. Some problems with such tests are that some applicants may not view them as job-relevant and others may see them as an invasion of privacy. Most tests of this type must be scored and interpreted by a trained psychologist or test specialist. Toyota and several other employers pursuing a team-style organization use a self-report inventory called the Job Fit Inventory. This inventory measures how well an applicant's motivation matches that required in a team-style environment. The inventory asks applicants the extent to which they agree with statements such as "Managers and employees can solve problems by talking to each other" and "Asking people to switch jobs keeps them from improving their work skills."[38]

Projective techniques require those taking the test to respond to ambiguous stimuli, rather than to questions or statements as in self-report measures. Examples of projective techniques are the Thematic Apperception Test (TAT), the Rorschach Inkblot Test, and the Miner Sentence Completion Scale. The TAT consists of a set of pictures to which the applicant responds by writing a brief story. Presumably, the story reveals something about the respondent's needs or motives. The Rorschach is a series of inkblots that the person being tested must identify as objects. The objects a person sees in the inkblots supposedly reveal something about his or her personality. There is little evidence that either the TAT or the Rorschach Inkblot Test is useful for selection purposes. The Miner Sentence Completion Scale is one of the very few tests specifically designed for managerial selection. Miner has presented data supporting the usefulness of his scale in predicting various criteria such as promotion rate, managerial level, and performance ratings.[39]

One study supporting the usefulness of personality measures, particularly projective ones, is a report on the assessment centres used by American Telephone and Telegraph (AT&T). The results of this study show that the projective assessment of motivational variables such as achievement motivation, self-confidence, and willingness to assume leadership showed low but positive correlations (0.11 to 0.30) with seven- to nine-year salary progress for a group of 200 AT&T managers.[40] This study suggests that if projective personality measures are used by trained psychologists to assess factors clearly relevant to management, they can make modest contributions to the selection process. The cost of this approach, however, is relatively high compared with alternative predictors, such as biographical data from application blanks and interviews.

Personality measures are not likely to be useful selection instruments for a number of reasons. First, it is difficult to demonstrate that personality characteristics are job-relevant. Job specifications usually focus on the skills and abilities needed for a job rather than on personality traits. Personality measures are designed to measure specific personality constructs, not the typical behaviour patterns associated with a job. Second, personality tests are generally less reliable than ability tests. A demonstration of low ability may allow an interviewer to conclude with certainty that the applicant could not perform a job, but one can almost never reach such a conclusion from a low score on a personality measure.

Interest Inventories

Since interest inventories have no correct answers, they are not truly tests. Rather, they consist of a series of questions or statements designed to elicit indications of interests and preferences. For example, they may ask the respondent to agree or disagree with a statement such as "I really enjoy taking things apart to see how they work."

When scored, such inventories provide information about how similar the respondent's interests are to those of successful people in various occupations. Examples of interest inventories are the Strong Vocational Interest Blank and the Kuder Preference Record. These interest inventories, especially the former, have demonstrated the ability to predict tenure in an occupation over periods of twenty or more years. However, their ability to predict success according to organizational criteria is limited. One review of the validities of selection methods found a mean validity of only 0.10 between interest measures and various measures of job performance.[41]

One problem with interest inventories is that they are easy for the respondent to fake. For example, a person applying for the job of summer camp director would be sure to indicate an interest in working outdoors with young people and in administering activities. For this reason, interest inventories are rarely used in selection, but they are often used for job placement and career counselling. As organizations increase their commitment to placement, counselling, and development, rather than selection, there will be an increased use of interest inventories.

Selecting and Evaluating Tests

Examination of job descriptions and specifications serves to direct HRM professionals' choice of tests to those most appropriate for certain job types. Once test possibilities have been identified, each test's manual should be examined and validation information sought in the *Mental Measurements Yearbook*.[42]

The major source of information for a new test is the test manual. It should be well documented and cover (1) the purpose of the test, (2) how the test was developed, (3) test reliability, (4) validation evidence, (5) normative data, (6) specific information on scoring the test, and (7) guidelines for interpreting test scores. A test that does not supply this information in its manual is not likely to be a good predictor. A test with an excellent manual that is favourably reviewed in the *Mental Measurements Yearbook* is an excellent candidate as a predictor. Finally, the best tests are likely to be those that have had the most validation studies done with large samples and those with relatively high validities.

New Canadian HRM professionals are often surprised to discover that virtually all tests used in this country come from the United States. Even Canadians who develop tests tend to publish them for the larger American market. For example, James Battle's Culture-Free Self-Esteem Inventory was originally developed in Alberta as the Canadian Self-Esteem Inventory. This situation troubles some Canadian experts because it means that the measures have been validated in the United States for a somewhat different population.

The idea that validities of tests differ significantly from one group to another is referred to as *differential validity*. Research in the United States in the late 1970s examined this hypothesis with regard to race (black versus white) and culture (Hispanic versus American). These studies found that cognitive ability tests were equally valid across races and cultures and that differences found in earlier studies were attributable to small sample sizes.[43] Thus, when large samples are used or when adjustments are made for sampling error, it is quite likely that a test valid in the United States is equally valid for similar jobs in Canada.

BACKGROUND AND REFERENCE CHECKS

Many employers request the names, addresses, and telephone numbers of references for the purpose of verifying information and, perhaps, gaining additional background information on an applicant. Although references are requested on the application form, they are usually not checked until an applicant has successfully reached the fourth or fifth stage of a sequential selection process. When the labour market is very tight, organizations sometimes hire applicants before checking references.

One study of nearly 600 Canadian employers found that 69 percent required letters of reference for new hires. Employers regarded them as more important for hiring white-collar, professional employees (83.5 percent) than for other groups. More than half the sample required at least two letters of reference, and more than 30 percent stated they gave considerable weight to references.[44] While some employers fear the threat of a lawsuit in giving much beyond basic facts of employment history, one legal expert argues that if the reference is honest and factual, there is little to fear. However, getting written permission from former employees before providing references to other employers is advised.[45]

Reference checks are a good idea judging by several U.S. studies documenting the use of phony credentials. "Operation Dipscam," a mid-1980s investigation by the Federal Bureau of Investigations (FBI), reported that one of every 200 Americans possesses fraudulent credentials that often are used for gaining employment. Among U.S. federal employees, about 200 hold phony academic or medical degrees. The report also stated that one-third of employed Americans were hired on the basis of credentials that were altered in some way.[46] A second study found that one in ten applicants for executive positions lied about his or her academic degrees. This study also found that only 32 percent of surveyed employers always checked academic claims. Claims were checked "hardly ever" by 27 percent of employers, "occasionally" by 24 percent, and "frequently" by 17 percent.[47]

Most employers who request references either ask for written letters of reference or make telephone reference checks. Many organizations require several letters of reference, even though such letters may have no real selection function. Some research shows that individually typed letters produce a better response than do form letters.[48] Many authors suggest that telephone reference checks provide the best combination of accuracy and low cost. Using the telephone to obtain a reference has the advantage of soliciting immediate, relatively candid comments, and attitudes can sometimes be inferred from hesitancies and inflections in speech. An employer is often reluctant to put into writing negative information about a previous employee. Also, letters of reference may be written by a secretary or assistant, rather than by the person who signs them. The field investigation—requesting a reference in a personal visit—is perhaps better than the telephone reference, but is far more expensive.

Validities between letters of reference and job performance are typically very low (0.08 to 0.14).[49] Low validities are likely the result of the lack of standardization of letters and the fact that the applicant often selects the letter writer. References from previous supervisors are more useful for predicting job success of applicants than are letters from friends, neighbours, or co-workers. A previous supervisor has observed the work of a subordinate and usually knows why he or she left the job. Of course, a previous supervisor may not be objective about the applicant or may not have known the individual well. Therefore, it is a good practice to request information about the relationship between an applicant and a previous supervisor or any other reference. A study by Knouse reports that human resource directors have a more positive impression of an applicant when letters of reference are well-written with specific examples and when the letter writer is well acquainted with the applicant.[50]

The validity of letters of recommendation is maximized when

1. The nature and degree of relationship between the candidate and the rater are known.
2. The rater is provided with a description of the job for which the candidate is being considered.
3. The letter provides specific examples of the applicant's performance.
4. Information regarding groups or individuals to which the applicant is compared is provided.[51]

Physical Examinations and Health Questionnaires

Many organizations gather information about an applicant's health and physical abilities through physical examinations. For some jobs, physical exams are required by law. Because of their expense, physical exams are usually given near the end of a sequential selection process. Thus, organizations require physical exams only for those applicants who have not been rejected by prior, less expensive selection procedures.

One of the primary purposes of a physical examination is to ensure that an applicant is physically able or fit to perform the job for which he or she is applying. For example, police and firefighters are often required to carry heavy objects, run, and perform other strenuous activities. While job-sample tests can be used to determine if an applicant can do the necessary physical activities, medical personnel should record heart rate and blood pressure to measure the effects of the activity on the person.

Organizations can also use physical exams to place employees in jobs most appropriate to their physical abilities and in which they are least likely to be injured. On the basis of physical characteristics, such as height, weight, and musculature, employees can be classified according to the type of work they are able to do (light work only, heavy work, and so on). By such classification, organizations reduce the odds of injury or accident.

There is relatively little evidence on the reliability or validity of physical exams for predicting job performance. One publication presenting a number of studies on U.S. pilots found that different doctors did not always agree on physical problems and that the validity of physical exams for predicting accident reduction and other criteria was low.[52]

J.B. Miner and M.G. Miner suggest that having applicants fill out a health questionnaire is a viable substitute for giving them physical examinations.[53] Specifically, the authors recommend using the Cornell Medical Index — Health Questionnaire, which contains 195 yes–no items covering present physical conditions and medical history. Despite evidence that people tend to hide some health problems, the questionnaire results correlate highly with actual physical examination acceptances and rejections. Health questionnaires can also be used in conjunction with physical exams to shorten them and direct an examining physician's attention toward specific problem areas.

Physical exams and fitness programs are a good idea for employees who have been on the job for a number of years. Indeed, a U.S. Department of Justice survey suggests that physical exams and fitness programs may be more important for experienced officers than for officer applicants. The report cites back trouble and heart conditions as major causes of early retirement and limited-duty assignments. Unfortunately, periodic physical exams and fitness programs for current employees are quite uncommon. Of 302 police departments in the survey, for example, only 43 had any form of fitness program and only 30 had a weight-control program.[54]

Drug Testing

A fairly recent purpose of physical exams is to screen applicants for drug use, which contributes to accidents, absenteeism, low productivity, and costly employee errors. Surveys show that use of marijuana and cocaine occurs on the job as well as outside the workplace.[55] It is no wonder, then, that a growing number of employers in Canada include drug testing as part of their selection procedures. A 1985 survey found that 25 percent of Fortune 500 companies screened applicants for drug use that year, and an additional 20 percent expected to begin testing in 1986.[56] The test most often used for drug screening is a urinanalysis test called EMIT (Enzyme Multiplied Immunoassay Test). This test is 97 percent accurate under the best of conditions, but unfortunately, errors in a number of laboratories have rendered test results suspect. For this reason, any positive test results should be confirmed by a second urinanalysis test.

There is very little evidence that drug testing leads to higher job performance or even fewer accidents. The U.S. Postal Service, however, studied the absenteeism and turnover of nearly 5500 hired applicants from whom urine samples had been obtained. Supervisors were not told results of the tests, and test results did not affect the hiring decision. After periods of six months or as much as a year, hired applicants who had tested positive were absent

41 percent more often and were 38 percent more likely to be fired than those who had tested negative; there was no difference in voluntary turnover between the two groups.[57] Though many contend drug testing is an invasion of privacy and it is not always accurate, there is clearly a need for it in jobs involving public safety such as airline pilot.

A related issue is AIDS (Acquired Immune Deficiency Syndrome) testing. A blood test can determine if a person is HIV positive. Presence of the HIV virus usually leads to AIDS, though a person may be HIV positive and not have AIDS symptoms for some time. HIV-positive applicants are a serious concern to all employers because of the substantial medical costs involved in treating people with AIDS. For health care industry employers, there are additional concerns and risks, mainly that an employee may infect patients. At present, employers may not legally screen applicants for the HIV virus, though there is pressure for such screening, particularly in the health care industry. A progressive policy regarding people with AIDS is one that treats the disease much like any other life-threatening illness. Specifically, if people with AIDS can perform their jobs satisfactorily and their illness does not threaten their safety or that of co-workers or clients, they should be treated the same as any other employee. The employer may have to make some accommodation to an employee with AIDS such as transferring him or her to a job in which the risk of transmission of the disease is minimized or making working hours more flexible. Since 1985, the Ontario Human Rights Commission has recognized AIDS as an illness, and has classified it as a handicap. Thus, people with AIDS are afforded equal treatment in employment and must be afforded reasonable accommodation in performing the essential requirements of their jobs. The AIDS issue for employers, at this time, is concentrated more in the areas of controlling health care costs, training and educating employees as to the nature of AIDS, and reducing the irrational fears of many people.

JOB TRYOUTS

A somewhat nontraditional method of selection has been made more possible and common by the growth in numbers of temporary employees. The recessions of the 1980s and early 1990s have led to great caution among many employers in hiring core employees. Employers have instead tried to keep the number of relatively permanent core employees to a bare minimum and to rely on temporary and part-time, "flexible," ones. Such flexible employees are often obtained from temporary employment agencies. Employers, in effect, rent an employee's services for a limited amount of time. Temporary employees are actually employees of the temporary help agency that hires and pays them and, in some cases, provides them with some training. Traditionally, only lower-skilled and clerical workers were obtained from temporary help agencies, but today, a wide variety of skilled, technical, professional, and even managerial employees may be found at temporary agencies. Many employers use flexible employees as an applicant pool and sometimes hire them for their core work force. This situation has many positive features for both the employer and the temporary employee. First, it approximates the perfect predictor insofar as it places the applicant in the actual job situation for some time. The applicant gets to know what it would be like to work for this employer in terms of the work itself, management, and co-workers. The employer gets to know the skills, abilities, knowledge, and typical work habits of the temporary employee. Perhaps the best part is that if neither the employer nor the temporary employee wishes to make the arrangement more permanent, the employer has incurred no cost beyond paying for work they wanted done, and the employee usually still has a job with the temporary agency. Thus, both employer and temporary employee can have a job tryout with very low costs that result from selection errors. Additionally, information available about a temporary employee's work behaviour is much more valid and reliable than comparable information gathered via any traditional selection method.

SELECTION OF MANAGERIAL TALENT

Selecting managers is almost always more complex, difficult, and expensive than selecting nonsupervisory employees. Most managerial jobs have greater variety and complexity than lower-level jobs, and very few are identical. The intricacy is suggested by the fact that one of the most complex but potentially useful models of managerial roles is a *four*-dimensional model; it includes: (1) functions, such as administration, persuasive communication, and influence and control; (2) roles, including innovator, evaluator, and director; (3) targets, including peers, subordinates, and external parties; and (4) style, such as objectivity, risk taking, and energy level.[58] Another model contains 21 competencies, such as developing others, logical thought, efficiency orientation, diagnostic use of concepts, and managing group processes.[59]

The multifaceted complexity of managerial jobs makes prediction of success difficult but important. Managerial jobs often have low base rates of success, and the potential costs of failure are high. Fortunately, managerial positions usually have many applicants, permitting an organization to benefit from a large applicant pool.

More than other jobs, managerial positions tend to be filled from within an organization via promotion. However, external recruiting and selection are also common.

The methods and instruments used to select managers include many of those already discussed, as well as others such as assessment centres. For example, the résumé often serves the same initial screening role for managerial applicants as does the application blank for other jobs. Similarly, interviews are invariably used for managerial candidates. Interviews can be focussed on specific behaviour dimensions identified by job analysis, just as in behaviour description interviews. Cognitive ability tests have been found to predict success to some degree for higher levels of management. Evidence from several studies also shows that personality measures alone (the Guilford–Zimmerman Temperament Survey) and in combination with cognitive ability tests have successfully predicted managerial success.[60] Projective personality measures, including the Miner Sentence Completion Scale and the Thematic Apperception Test, have also proved useful. Personality measures can add to the ability to predict managerial success, especially when candidates have already been screened in terms of cognitive abilities. Biographical data, especially work history information, can be useful in selecting managers and first-line supervisors because past behaviour is a good predictor of future behaviour when the managerial job is similar to past jobs or experiences.[61]

A fairly recent development is a paper-and-pencil assessment of management potential that focusses on tacit knowledge, which is defined as information gained through work and organizational experience that is typically not verbally stated.[62] The measure of tacit knowledge is a set of twelve work-related situations with as many as twenty possible responses to each. The situations and responses were obtained from interviews with experienced, successful managers. Though this method is new, preliminary results indicate it has promise.

A popular approach to managerial selection in recent years has been the assessment centre. An *assessment centre* is a collection of methods for the purpose of assessing the managerial potential of applicants or current employees. These methods include interviews, job samples or simulations, business games and exercises, and sometimes projective and self-report personality measures. Assessment centres are usually held for one to three days and are run by experienced managers. Candidates at assessment centres are often already employed by the sponsoring organization, usually as supervisors or members of lower management. Managers serving as assessors are usually trained by the industrial-personnel psychologists who organize and supervise the centres.

The assessment centre is popular in both Canada and the United States. Perhaps one of the major reasons for its success is that it has relatively good predictive validity. A meta-analysis of 50 assessment centre studies found an average corrected correlation of 0.37 between assessment centre results and several criteria of managerial performance, such as job performance ratings and career advancement.[63] It is not surprising that assessment centres are often better at predicting managerial success than are other methods; they include a number of different methods, and a group judgement is made by managers.

Assessment centres are not without problems, however. Despite their relatively good predictive validity, research has been unable to show adequately their content validity, and construct validity has not been demonstrated.[64]

THE UTILITY OF SELECTION

Selection procedures must be examined periodically to determine their usefulness to an organization. From an employer's perspective, the utility, or overall usefulness, of a selection procedure is the bottom line. Management's primary goal is to minimize labour costs while maximizing productivity. The concept of utility permits examination of the role of selection in achieving this goal.

One definition of *utility* calls it

> the overall usefulness of a personnel selection or placement procedure. The concept encompasses both the accuracy and the importance of personnel decisions. Moreover, utility implies a concern with costs—costs related to setting up and implementing personnel selection procedures and costs associated with errors in the decisions made.[65]

The utility of a predictor or selection instrument depends on four factors: (1) the accuracy or validity of the predictor; (2) the selection ratio; (3) the base rate of success; and (4) the costs and benefits of selection decisions.

Generally, the utility of a selection method is higher when it results in a higher base rate of success for a job. Base rates of success increase when higher validity predictors and lower selection ratios are used. *Selection ratio* is the number of applicants hired as a proportion of the total number of applicants for a job:

$$\text{Selection ratio} = \frac{\text{Number of applicants hired}}{\text{Number of job applicants}}$$

If an organization hires five sales representatives from a pool of 25 applicants, the selection ratio for the job is 0.2 (20 percent). If, on the other hand, the organization attracts only seven applicants for its five positions, the selection ratio is much higher—0.7 (70 percent). When selection ratios are high, selection methods have limited usefulness because most of those who apply will have to be hired, regardless of predictions of success or failure. If selection ratios are very high, hiring standards may have to be lowered to meet human resource needs. For example, if only five applicants are attracted to the sales representative positions, all five may have to be hired, even though some are only minimally qualified. In this case, selection information could be used to place the new employees in training programs to increase their competencies for certain work behaviour. The selection function increases in importance when the selection ratio is low enough for meaningful differentiations to be made among job applicants. However, since there are costs associated with processing applicants, very low selection ratios may not be cost-effective for an organization in some situations. Toyota, and most other team-style organizations, enjoy very low selection ratios of approximately 0.05, or 20 to 1. Despite a high average cost per applicant, the resulting high performance and long tenure justify the cost.

If a base rate is already quite high, it is difficult to find a predictor that can increase it. In this case, the utility of a predictor is low since there is little room for improvement. Base rates of success for jobs tend to be high for jobs that are easy and low for those that are complex. Selection is less useful for easy jobs because there is less need to differentiate among applicants if almost any of them can perform successfully. When job requirements are more complex, a smaller proportion of applicants will be able to do the job successfully, and selection becomes more important. Because defining success is more difficult for complex jobs, it is also more difficult to develop effective selection procedures for them.

Finally, the concept of utility includes cost considerations, particularly those relating to selection decisions. Both actual and potential costs and benefits of such decisions may be examined. Actual costs include those for all applicants, such as recruiting and selection process costs, and costs for newly hired employees, such as orientation and training costs, wages, and benefits. Potential costs are those associated with selection errors. Potential benefits come primarily from hiring applicants who exhibit high levels of job performance. The more important a job is to organizational effectiveness, the greater the importance of selection. Selection errors are far more costly for important jobs than for jobs of lesser importance. One measure of a job's value to an organization is the standard deviation of job performance in dollars (SD_y).

The SD_y of job performance is a measure of the potential range, or variation, of the dollar value of job performance. For some jobs, differences in performance extremes (excellent to incompetent) have little effect in terms of dollar value to an organization. For example, variability in performance for a keyboard operator is relatively insignificant compared to the effects of performance variability for a marketing manager. The utility of a predictor rises with the SD_y of a job because the potential costs of placing an unsuccessful person in a high SD_y job are much higher than the costs of placing an unsuccessful person in a low SD_y job. Of course, the potential benefits of a successful placement in a high SD_y job are higher than those in a low SD_y job.

Schmidt and his colleagues developed a method for estimating SD_y that uses supervisory estimates of employee output.[66] This method requires supervisors to estimate the value to the organization of a poor, average, and high performer in a given job. Based on 29 studies using this method of estimating SD_y, the authors conclude that SD_y is equal to approximately 40 percent of annual pay for a job.[67] For example, SD_y for a job with an annual salary of $50 000 is $20 000. Another method of estimating SD_y is the Cascio-Ramos method.[68] This method is more complex than Schmidt's and typically yields lower estimates.

Because the SD_y of jobs differs, low validity predictors often have greater utility to an organization than high validity predictors. For example, an informed employer might gladly pay $5000 to have each managerial candidate evaluated in an assessment centre whose results have a 0.25 correlation with managerial success. The organization could compensate for the low validity by using a low selection ratio (for example, assessing ten or more candidates and accepting the top person). On the other hand, the same employer might be reluctant to pay even $250 per applicant for a test whose results correlated 0.51 with success at a word-processing operator job. In this case, utility of the selection method is considerably lower since the job is less important to the organization and qualified applicants can easily be found.

The four factors affecting utility interact and must be considered together. Generally, utility is higher for jobs with a low base rate of success and a high SD_y. However, if recruiting provides very few applicants and a very high percentage of them must be hired, the utility of even a high validity predictor is low. On the other hand, the utility of a relatively low validity predictor is high if the rate is low and the SD_y is high. In the latter case, the utility of the low validity predictor could be increased by using a low selection ratio. The validity of the predictor is, of course, important, since the higher the validity, the more accurate the selection decisions.

Recall that the Toyota staff was interested in knowing what would be the effect of changing one or more components of their team-member selection process. That is, if the GATB or one of the simulations were dropped or replaced by a different test or simulation, for example, what would be the utility of such a change? Until the late 1970s, there were no methods available to estimate utility of a selection method, though the concept of utility had been available for some time. In the late 1970s, Schmidt, Hunter, and others developed a formula for estimating the increase in dollar value of job performance resulting from use of a new or additional predictor.[69] The formula is a decision aid to HRM professionals who must choose and evaluate alternative selection instruments. (For a discussion of the Schmidt et al. formula and its application at an airline, see Appendix 7A at the end of this chapter.)

In the mid-1980s, a Canadian study investigated the utility of testing for clerical/administrative groups in the Canadian Forces.[70] This study included all the previously discussed factors affecting utility as well as the time value of money (net present value) and other financial factors related to testing and its benefits. The results of this study revealed an average annual utility of more than $51 million for clerical/administrative personnel. This very large sum was based upon an average tenure of 18 years, an SD_y of $10 680, a validity of 0.52, a selection ratio of 0.33, and a testing and implementation cost of $608.60 per selectee. Among other things, this study illustrates that the utility of cognitive ability tests can be surprisingly large even for fairly low-level jobs.

Summary

Selection is one of management's most valuable means of increasing organizational effectiveness. Recent research estimating the utility to organizations of using predictors with good validity and hiring from the top down show large financial gains. The principle of validity generalization suggests that, at least for cognitive ability tests, employers can confidently use these predictors for most jobs without the expense of conducting their own validity studies.

Even with these recent selection advances, HRM professionals must still play an important role in developing and implementing an effective selection system. The key to selection is the use of valid predictors of job success. Criterion-related validity, construct validity, and content validity are three approaches to ensuring a significant relationship between a predictor of job success used in selection and job performance.

The selection process itself is a progressive screening of applicants, usually by some combination of application blanks, employment interviews, tests, and background and reference checks. Physical examinations and language tests may also be used when appropriate.

Application blanks are used for coarse screening and for guides to employment interviews; weighted application blanks and biographical inventory blanks also gather information for prediction. The employment interview presents opportunities for exchange of honest information but also leaves room for several kinds of rater errors. It can be improved by training interviewers and using structured guides that focus on job requirements. Progressive employers using team-based management rely heavily on interviews to help determine candidates who best fit that environment.

Many kinds of tests exist. Pencil-and-paper tests and job-sample tests, which screen for skills, abilities, and aptitudes, are generally more clearly related to job content than are personality tests or interest inventories. All selection methods must be used in a way that avoids discrimination on any grounds prohibited within the jurisdiction. The selection of managers requires special care; cognitive ability tests, personality tests, and biographical data are often used, and assessment centres are increasingly common.

Review Questions

1. Discuss how the selection process is affected by:
    a. A shortage of well-qualified, skilled applicants.
    b. The trend toward team-style management of work groups.
    c. The need to meet employment equity and affirmative action goals.

2. The interview has been and will continue to be an important screening and selection tool. Discuss recent improvements in interviewing. How can interviews be made both more valid and better able to withstand employment equity challenges?

3. Explain the concept of utility. Is utility a practical concept? How might utility be used to budget and justify implementation of drug testing or some other addition to the selection process?

Project Ideas

1. One source of discrimination and waste of human resources comes from job specifications (minimum ability, experience, and/or education standards) that are higher than necessary for adequate job performance. One way of studying this situation is to examine job descriptions and compare them with job specifications. Specifications are often stated in recruitment advertising. Talk with a human resource officer of a local organization and ask how the organization arrives at the job specifications used for various jobs. Approach the interview in an unbiased way and you will learn. Perhaps you could ask the human resource officer to show you several job descriptions and explain how the job specifications were derived. Write a short report on your interview.

2. Developing employment tests is a thriving industry. Through the library or with the help of your instructor, obtain sales brochures from several test publishers. Also obtain a copy of an employment test and its manual. Compare the brochure's description with the test and the manual. What type of information does the manual provide? Are detailed instructions given for both administration and scoring of the test? Are there test norms? Are reliability and validity studies reported? Were any of the studies done by researchers not associated with the test publisher? Personnel officers must be careful consumers in terms of purchasing tests and other selection-related methods.

3. Obtain job descriptions for at least two jobs, preferably a simple, common one, such as bus driver, and a more complex one, such as bank teller or personnel assistant. Develop job specifications and a selection procedure for each. Discuss why you chose each selection method and what specific information you will get from it. What cut-off scores or standards would you recommend for each method? What changes in the selection process would you make if the labour market became tighter?

▶ ▶ ▶ CASES

CASE 7.1 ▶ DISPUTED SELECTION AT SUNNYBROOK

Marty Souchek, head of personnel at Sunnybrook Hospital, was not at all pleased with a labour arbitration ruling requiring him to initiate a new selection procedure for the position of charge nurse in one of the hospital's operating theatres. The charge nurse position had been filled several months before with the promotion of operating room (OR) nurse Jodi Jacobsen. However, another applicant for the position, OR nurse Grace Chacko, had promptly filed a grievance. Chacko, who had seniority, contended that Sunnybrook improperly applied the provisions of article 10.07 of the collective agreement between the hospital and the Ontario Nurses' Association. This article stated:

> In cases of promotion or transfer (other than appointments to positions outside the bargaining unit), the following factors shall be considered by the hospital:
> a. skill, ability, experience, and qualifications;
> b. seniority.
> Where the factors in (a) are equal, seniority shall govern.

Chacko's grievance led to an arbitration hearing in which the nurses' union representing Chacko argued that she should have been awarded the promotion since she had seniority and was equal to Jacobsen in skill, ability, experience, and qualifications. The hospital, on the other hand, argued that article 10.07 had been properly applied and that the union had failed to show that Chacko was Jacobsen's equal.

After hearing evidence in the case, arbitrators concluded that there was a defect in Sunnybrook's selection procedure that could have affected its outcome. They ordered a new selection procedure to determine who rightfully deserved the position.

Souchek studied his notes. Before initiating any new selection procedure, he wanted to know what went wrong with the hospital's first attempt to fill the charge nurse position.

Notice of the opening had been posted with the following stated job specifications: "Demonstrated administrative ability, excellent interpersonal relationships, and above average technical skills." Four persons applied for the position, including Ms. Jacobsen and Ms. Chacko. Each filed a standard Sunnybrook Hospital application form and supporting statements with the personnel office. Each applicant received a brief preliminary interview with the personnel assistant, and then each was interviewed by the head nurse, Grace Miller.

Grace Miller testified at the hearing that she judged Ms. Jacobsen superior to Ms. Chacko in all categories of administrative skill, including ability to articulate and communicate, ability to judge situations, ability to problem-solve, ability to make decisions, and capacity to self-initiate. However, evidence presented by the union revealed little factual base for many of Miller's conclusions. For example, Miller had reached her assessment of Chacko's ability to articulate and communicate, at least in part, by comparing cover letters submitted with application forms. In fact, cover letters were not even required, and Miller had never suggested to Chacko that her letter would be used in evaluating her candidacy.

Miller also based her opinion of Chacko's ability to articulate and communicate on Chacko's responses to interview questions. However, evidence presented by the union showed that Miller never asked Chacko to elaborate or expand upon her answers beyond a simple "I think I can do it." There was also evidence presented that the atmosphere of the interview might have been affected by a negative relationship which had existed for some time between Chacko and the head nurse. On the other hand, Miller and Jacobsen enjoyed a positive relationship.

Finally, evidence was presented that cast doubt on Jacobsen's technical ability in the operating theatre in question, namely ophthalmology. Specifically, Jacobsen was observed on several occasions using the wrong instruments or equipment for the task at hand.

Source: Based on C.G. Simmons, K.P. Swan, and D.D. Carter, eds., *Labour Arbitration Cases*, 3rd series, vol. 2 (Aurora, Ont.: Canada Law Book, 1982), pp. 283–96. Used with the permission of the publisher.

TASKS AND QUESTIONS

1. Put yourself in Souchek's shoes and identify deficiencies in the first selection procedure for the charge nurse position.

2. How could the selection procedure have been improved?

3. What ingredients would you include in a new selection procedure in order to determine which candidate to promote?

4. Using this case as an example, discuss the benefits of a careful application of selection criteria in the case of promotions. Are there also any costs?

CASE 7.2 ▸ FLYER INDUSTRIES: BUILDING A BETTER BUS

When Kenneth Clark took over as chief executive officer (CEO) of Flyer Industries Ltd. in late 1983, he inherited a $32.5 million deficit and a busload of problems. It seems Clark's predecessor was more interested in selling the company's product, buses, than he was in quality control. In fact, the 53-year-old company had never had a research and development lab or an emphasis on quality control. Buses simply rolled off the assembly line with no prior testing of their structure or design. Because production often began with incomplete drawings and untested designs, problems surfaced on the assembly line causing delays and last-minute modifications. It was common practice to order spare parts on short notice at a price far exceeding what it would have cost Flyer to manufacture them itself. The company employed no industrial engineers to help streamline production and no cost-accounting procedures to determine the cost of building a bus. (When a cost was later determined, it was discovered that Flyer had lost $17 500 on every bus it sold in 1983.)

Flyer's engineers and assembly-line workers informed management of problems on the line, but management turned a deaf ear. The company's board of directors never got wind of problems at the plant because they relied on optimistic verbal reports given to them by management.

Despite the rosy picture painted by management, it was difficult to ignore complaints from buyers of the buses. Vancouver, which purchased 245 Flyer trolleys in 1983, complained of doors that slammed shut on passengers, poorly positioned hand grips, and door frames that impeded driver visibility. Further, the buses' electrical systems produced sparks and short-circuited during the winter months. Another city complained of problems with the buses' cooling system. The trolleys overheated and stalled at temperatures of more than 26°C. Other purchasers noted problems with rust, structural cracks, breaking windshield wipers, and faulty axle bolts.

Low morale and discontent characterized Flyer's work force of 450 manufacturing personnel and several hundred others. Absenteeism averaged 7 percent in 1983 and was as high as 32 percent in some departments. Labour–management relations were unhealthy; between 1973 and 1983, the company lost $100 000 in arbitration rulings. Turnover was also high. In 1983 alone, 40 employees either resigned or were forced out of their jobs. Many of those who left were experienced employees, some in middle management positions. During the twelve years before Clark was appointed CEO, workers operated under several management teams and six different CEOs. According to Clark, "Different CEOs came in with specific skills in such areas as manufacturing, engineering, or marketing. They attacked the company with similarly single-minded devotion, leaving the rest of the company to flounder."[71]

Although Flyer claimed to have a promotion ladder, workers saw little chance of moving up. For one thing, the company offered no formal training to upgrade their skills. For another, the few promotions that did occur seemed to defy logic. One employee appointed vice-president of engineering, for example, had no engineering degree. And a purchasing agent moved up to an executive vice-presidency after only two years with the company. There were no job descriptions to guide or constrain Flyer's hiring and promotion practices, and as many as ten different evaluation systems existed to assess employee performance.

Source: Adapted from A. Nikoruk, "Winging It," *Canadian Business* (November 1984), pp. 84–94. Used with the permission of *Canadian Business*.

TASKS AND QUESTIONS

1. What do you believe to be management's most serious mistakes or errors in judgement? How could these mistakes have been avoided?

2. Clark and others have blamed Flyer's problems on unqualified personnel (including management) and lack of technical expertise. What evidence do you find that such might be the case? Do you agree with Clark's assessment? Why or why not?

3. If you were serving as Clark's human resources consultant, what strategies would you suggest to ensure Flyer a better qualified work force now and in the future?

4. Clark devised a three-step salvage operation for Flyer. Decide on a salvage plan of your own and justify each step.

APPENDIX 7A ▸ ESTIMATING UTILITY GAINS OF A PREDICTOR

The Schmidt et al. utility formula[72] is analogous to capital budgeting models in finance, which are used to choose among alternative capital investments.
  The formula is

$$\Delta \bar{u} = (\Delta r_{xy})\, \text{SD}_y\, \bar{Z}_x,$$

where $\Delta \bar{u}$ is the increase in dollar value of output per person hired per year; Δr_{xy} is the difference in validity between the original predictor(s) and the new predictor; SD_y represents performance variability in dollars and is estimated at 40 percent of annual pay for the job; and $\bar{Z}_x$ is the average test score of employees hired expressed in standard score form. Selection procedure scores are standardized by transforming them to a mean of zero and a standard deviation of one. This allows test scores to be interpreted as points on a normal distribution. The value of $\bar{Z}_x$ is determined from the percentage of applicants hired (selection ratio) assuming a top-down hiring procedure. Table 7A.1 is a conversion table for estimating $\bar{Z}_x$ from the selection ratio.
  Note that in this formula for estimating utility, SD_y replaces the base rate of success concept. The reason is that the formula estimates value to the organization of employees hired, and SD_y reflects job performance gains resulting from higher-ability employees. The base rate concept, while con-

TABLE 7A.1
Estimating the Value of $\bar{Z}_x$

Test scores are typically normally distributed in job applicant populations. In a normal distribution, the test cut-off score (minimum acceptable score) and the average (standardized) score of those selected can be computed from the selection ratio. Here are some representative values.

SELECTION RATIOS	CUT-OFF SCORE	AVERAGE TEST SCORE OF THOSE SELECTED ($\bar{Z}_x$)
100%	No lower bound	0.00
90	−1.28	0.20
80	−0.84	0.35
70	−0.51	0.50
60	−0.25	0.64
50	0.00	0.80
40	0.25	0.97
30	0.51	1.17
20	0.84	1.40
10	1.28	1.76
5	1.64	2.08

Source: F.L. Schmidt, University of Iowa, class handout (selection principles class), 1992. Used with permission.

ceptually useful, makes no differentiations among successful employees. Thus, utility is higher when validity of the new predictor is greater than that for the previous predictor (reflected in a high Δr_{xy}), when the dollar variability of job performance (SD_y) is large, and when higher-scoring applicants are hired (higher $\bar{Z}_x$ values). This method of estimating utility assumes only that all applicants who are offered jobs are hired, that applicants are hired from the top down, and that the pool of applicants is a random sample from the population of applicants. Other versions of Schmidt's utility formula subtract the cost of selection methods, but these are usually negligible compared to performance gains.

Using this formula, let us estimate the utility of adding a cognitive ability test to the current set of hiring procedures used by a major airline for its customer service representative jobs. The cognitive ability test has, according to the company selling it, a validity of 0.30 for a variety of jobs. The cost of the test is $20 per applicant. Now assume that validity of existing methods at the airline (the interview and application form) together is 0.15. The difference between predictors is 0.15, which is Δr_{xy} in the formula. Assume also that average salary for service representatives is $30 000. Forty percent of this amount is $12 000, or SD_y. Finally, assume the selection ratio for these jobs is 70 percent. According to the table in Exhibit 7A.1, $\overline{Z}_x$ can be estimated at 0.50.

Inserting these values into the utility formula we find that

$$\Delta \overline{u} = (0.15)(12\ 000)(0.5) = \$900$$

Recall that this $900 is the gain in utility for only one employee per year. To obtain utility of the cognitive ability test at the airline, this $900 figure must be multiplied by the number of service representatives hired each year (50) and by their average length of tenure (4.0 years). Thus, the airline will save $45 000 per year, minus the cost of testing, or approximately $174 220 over four years. Further gains could be realized by lowering the selection ratio, though doing so would probably require additional recruiting and testing costs to obtain applicants who meeting the higher test cutoff score. If a selection ratio of 30 percent were used, for example, the value of $\overline{Z}_x$ would increase to 1.17 and the gain per hire per year would become $2106.

Gains from the addition of even a moderately valid predictor are substantial, particularly when a lower selection ratio is used. Although we have not subtracted the cost of testing, it is typically a very small proportion of the gain in utility, particularly when low selection ratios are used.

NOTES

1. C. Cosentino, J. Allen, and R.S. Wellins, "Choosing the Right People," *HR Magazine*, vol. 35, no. 3 (1990), p. 67.
2. R.S. Wellins, W.C. Byham, and J.M. Wilson, *Empowered Teams* (San Francisco: Jossey-Bass, 1991), p. 146.
3. Wellins, Byham, and Wilson, *Empowered Teams*, p. 157.
4. U.S. Equal Employment Opportunity Commission, *Uniform Guidelines on Employment Selection Procedures*, F.R. 42, no. 251 (December 30, 1977), 65542–52.
5. Wellins, Byham, and Wilson, *Empowered Teams*, p. 155.
6. M.J. Mack, F.L. Schmidt, and J.E. Hunter, *Estimating the Productivity Costs in Dollars of Minimum Selection Test Cutoff Scores* (Washington, DC: U.S. Office of Personnel Management, 1981).
7. American Psychological Association, Division of Industrial and Organizational Psychology, *Principles for the Validation and Use of Personnel Selection Procedures*, 2nd ed. (Berkeley, Calif., 1980).
8. F.L. Schmidt and J.E. Hunter, "Employment Testing: Old Theories and New Research Findings," *American Psychologist*, vol. 36 (1981), pp. 1128–37; and J.E. Hunter and R.F. Hunter, "Validity and Utility of Alternative Predictors of Job Performance," *Psychological Bulletin*, vol. 96 (1984), pp. 72–98.
9. U.S. Equal Employment Opportunity Commission, *Uniform Guidelines*, 65548.

10. M.D. Dunnette, *Personnel Selection and Placement* (Belmont, Calif.: Wadsworth Publishing, 1966).

11. Edwin E. Ghiselli, *The Validity of Occupational Aptitude Tests* (New York: Wiley, 1966).

12. U.S. Equal Employment Opportunity Commission, *Uniform Guidelines*.

13. F.L. Schmidt and J.E. Hunter, "The Future of Criterion-Related Validity," *Personnel Psychology*, vol. 33, no. 1 (1980), pp. 41–60.

14. W.F. Cascio, "Turnover, Biographical Data, and Fair Employment Practice," *Journal of Applied Psychology*, vol. 61, no. 5 (1976), pp. 576–80.

15. W.A. Owens, "Background Data," in M.D. Dunnette, ed., *Handbook of Industrial and Organizational Psychology* (Chicago: Rand McNally College Publishing, 1976); and G.S. Shaffer, V. Saunders, and W.A. Owens, "Additional Evidence for the Accuracy of Biographical Data: Long-Term Retest and Observer Ratings," *Personnel Psychology*, vol. 39 (1986), pp. 791–809.

16. R.R. Reilly and G.T. Chao, "Validity and Fairness of Some Alternative Employee Selection Procedures," *Personnel Psychology*, vol. 35 (1982), pp. 1–62.

17. L.A. Pace and L.F. Schoenfeldt, "Legal Concerns in the Use of Weighted Applications," *Personnel Psychology*, vol. 30 (1977), pp. 159–66; and E.D. Pulakos, W.C. Borman, and L.M. Hough, "Test Validation for Scientific Understanding: Two Demonstrations of an Approach to Studying Predictor-Criterion Linkages," *Personnel Psychology*, vol. 41 (1988), pp. 703–16.

18. John P. Wanous, *Organization Entry: Recruitment, Selection, and Socialization of Newcomers* (Reading, Mass.: Addison-Wesley, 1980), pp. 10–16.

19. Bureau of National Affairs, *Recruiting and Selection Procedures, Personnel Policies Forum Survey No. 146* (Washington, DC: Bureau of National Affairs, May 1988); and P.L. Blocklyn, "Employment Recruitment Practices," *Personnel*, vol. 65 (1988), pp. 63–65.

20. L. Ulrich and D. Trumbo, "The Selection Interview Since 1949," *Psychological Bulletin*, vol. 63 (1965), pp. 100–16.

21. W.H. Wiesner and S.F. Cronshaw, "The Moderating Impact of Interview Format and Degree of Structure on Interview Validity," *Journal of Occupational Psychology*, vol. 61 (1988), pp. 275–90; and P.M. Wright, P.A. Lichtenfels, and E.D. Pursell, "The Structured Interview: Additional Studies and a Meta-analysis," *Journal of Occupational Psychology*, vol. 50 (1989), pp. 191–99; and R.D. Arvey and J.E. Campion, "The Employment Interview: A Summary and Review of Recent Research," *Personnel Psychology*, vol. 35 (1982), pp. 281–322.

22. R.L. Dipboye, *Selection Interviews: Process Perspectives* (Cincinnati: South-Western, 1992), p. 242.

23. N. Schmitt, "Social and Situational Determinants of Interview Decisions: Implications for the Employment Interview," *Personnel Psychology*, vol. 29 (1976), pp. 79–101.

24. Edwin E. Ghiselli, "The Validity of a Personnel Interview," *Personnel Psychology*, vol. 19 (1966), pp. 389–95.

25. Tom Janz, Lowell Hellervik, and David C. Gilmore, *Behavior Description Interviewing* (Boston: Allyn and Bacon, 1986), pp. 31–42.
26. Janz, Hellervik, and Gilmore, *Behavior Description Interviewing*, pp. 122–23.
27. G.P. Latham, L.M. Saari, E.D. Purcell, and M.A. Campion, "The Situational Interview," *Journal of Applied Psychology*, vol. 65 (1980), pp. 422–27; and J.T. Janz, "Initial Comparisons of Patterned Behaviour Description Interviews vs. Unstructured Interviews," *Journal of Applied Psychology*, vol. 67 (1982), pp. 577–80.
28. Ontario Human Rights Commission, *Human Rights in Employment: A Guide for Employers, Employees and Employment Agencies* (Toronto, 1981).
29. R.D. Arvey, *Fairness in Selecting Employees* (Reading, Mass.: Addison-Wesley, 1979).
30. F.L. Schmidt, J.E. Hunter, and K. Pearlman, "Task Differences and Validity of Aptitude Tests in Selection: A Red Herring," *Journal of Applied Psychology*, vol. 66 (1981), pp. 166–85.
31. F.L. Schmidt and J.E. Hunter, "Employment Testing: Old Theories and New Research Findings," *American Psychologist*, vol. 36, no. 10 (October 1981), pp. 1128–37.
32. C.L. Hulin, R.A. Henry, and S.L. Noon, "Adding a Dimension: Time as a Factor in the Generalizability of Predictive Relationships," *Psychological Bulletin*, vol. 107 (1990), pp. 328–40.
33. K. Pearlman, F.L. Schmidt, and J.E. Hunter, "Validity Generalization Results for Tests Used to Predict Training Success and Job Proficiency in Clerical Occupations," *Journal of Applied Psychology*, vol. 65 (1980), pp. 373–406.
34. J.J. Asher and J.A. Sciarrino, "Realistic Work Sample Tests: A Review," *Personnel Psychology*, vol. 27 (1974), pp. 519–34; and Hunter and Hunter, "Validity and Utility of Alternative Predictors."
35. J.E. Campion, "Work Sampling for Personnel Selection," *Journal of Applied Psychology*, vol. 56 (1972), pp. 40–44.
36. L. Rout, "Going for Broker: Our Man Takes Part in Stock-Selling Test," *The Wall Street Journal*, April 4, 1979. Reprinted with the permission of *The Wall Street Journal*, Dow Jones & Company, Inc. All Rights Reserved Worldwide.
37. Wellins, Byham, and Wilson, *Empowered Teams*, pp. 148–49.
38. Wellins, Byham, and Wilson, *Empowered Teams*, pp. 150–51.
39. J.B. Miner, *Motivation to Manage* (Atlanta: Organizational Measurement Systems Press, 1977); and J.B. Miner, "The Miner Sentence Completion Scale: A Reappraisal," *Academy of Management Journal*, vol. 21 (1978), pp. 283–94.
40. D.L. Grant, W. Katkovsky, and D.W. Bray, "Contributions of Projective Techniques to Assessment of Management Potential," *Journal of Applied Psychology*, vol. 51 (1967), pp. 226–31.
41. Hunter and Hunter, "Validity and Utility of Alternative Predictors."
42. O.K. Buros, *The Ninth Mental Measurements Yearbook*, vol. 2 (Highland Park, N.J.: Gryphon Press, 1989).

43. Schmidt and Hunter, "Employment Testing."
44. H. Das and M. Das, "But He Had Excellent References," *The Human Resource*, June/July 1988, pp. 15–16.
45. P. Gorrie, "Lawsuit-Shy Companies Grow Wary of Providing Employee References," *The Toronto Star*, June 11, 1990.
46. "Phony Academic Degrees Held by Federal Workers," *Iowa City (Iowa) Press Citizen*, March 10, 1986.
47. "False Credentials," *Wall Street Journal*, July 3, 1985.
48. A.N. Nash and S.J. Carrol, Jr., "A Hard Look at the Reference Check: Its Modest Worth Can Be Improved," *Business Horizons*, October 1970, pp. 43–49.
49. R.R. Reilly and G.T. Chao, "Validity and Fairness of Some Alternative Employee Selection Procedures," *Personnel Psychology*, vol. 35 (1982), pp. 1–62.
50. S.B. Knouse, "The Letter of Recommendation: Specificity and Favourability of Information," *Personnel Psychology*, vol. 36 (1983), pp. 331–41.
51. S.B. Knouse, "An Attribution Theory Approach to the Letter of Recommendation," *International Journal of Management*, vol. 19 (1987), pp. 411–21.
52. R.A. McFarland, *Human Factors in Air Transportation* (New York: McGraw-Hill, 1953).
53. J.B. Miner and M.G. Miner, *Personnel and Industrial Relations*, 3rd ed. (New York: Macmillan, 1977).
54. M. Diamond and C.S. Feldman, "Not All the Finest Are the Fittest," *Austin American-Statesman*, Parade section, April 15, 1979.
55. "More Firms Require Employee Drug Tests," *Wall Street Journal*, August 8, 1985.
56. "Battling the Enemy Within," *Time Magazine*, March 17, 1986, pp. 52–61.
57. D. Wessel, "Evidence Is Skimpy That Drug Testing Works, but Employers Embrace Practice," *Wall Street Journal*, September 7, 1989.
58. J.A. Steger, G. Manners, A. Berstein, and R. May, "The Three Dimensions of the R&D Manager's Job," *Research Management*, vol. 18 (1975), pp. 32–37.
59. R.E. Boyatzia, *The Competent Manager: A Model for Effective Performance* (New York: Wiley, 1982).
60. G. Grimsley and H.F. Jarret, "The Relation of Past Managerial Achievement to Test Measures Obtained in the Employment Situation: Methodology and Results —II," *Personnel Psychology*, vol. 28 (1975), pp. 215–31; G. Grimsley and H.F. Jarret, "The Relation of Managerial Achievement to Test Measures Obtained in the Employment Situation: Methodology and Results," *Personnel Psychology*, vol. 26 (1973), pp. 31–48; and V.J. Bentz, "The Sears Experience in the Investigation, Description, and Prediction of Executive Behavior," in F.R. Wickert and D.E. McFarland, eds., *Measuring Executive Effectiveness* (New York: Appleton-Century-Crofts, 1967), pp. 147–207.
61. A.K. Korman, "The Prediction of Managerial Performance: A Review," *Personnel Psychology*, vol. 21 (1969), pp. 295–322; and H. Laurent, *The Validation of Aids for the Identification of Management Potential* (Standard Oil of New Jersey, 1962).

62. R.K. Wagner and R.J. Sternberg, "Practical Intelligence in Real-World Pursuits: The Role of Tacit Knowledge," *Journal of Personality and Social Psychology*, vol. 49 (1985), pp. 436–58.
63. B.B. Gauglar, D.B. Rosenthal, G.C. Thornton III, and C. Bentson, "Meta-Analysis of Assessment Center Validity," *Journal of Applied Psychology*, vol. 72 (1987), pp. 493–511.
64. G.F. Dreher and P.R. Sackett, "Some Problems with the Applicability of Content Validity to Assessment Centers," *Academy of Management Review*, vol. 6 (1981), pp. 551–60; and P.R. Sackett and G.F. Dreher, "Constructs and Assessment Center Dimensions: Some Troubling Findings," *Journal of Applied Psychology*, vol. 67 (1982), pp. 401–10.
65. Dunnette, *Personnel Selection and Placement*, p. 174. Reprinted with permission.
66. F.L. Schmidt, J.E. Hunter, R.C. McKenzie, and T.W. Muldrow, "Impact of Valid Selection Procedures on Work-Force Productivity," *Journal of Applied Psychology*, vol. 64 (1979), pp. 609–26.
67. F.L. Schmidt, J.E. Hunter, and K. Pearlman, "Assessing the Economic Impact of Personnel Programs on Workforce Productivity," *Personnel Psychology*, vol. 35 (1982), pp. 333–47.
68. W.F. Cascio, *Costing Human Resources: The Financial Impact of Behavior in Organizations*, 3rd ed. (Boston: Kent Publishing, 1991).
69. Schmidt et al., "Impact of Valid Selection Procedures."
70. Steven F. Cronshaw, "The Utility of Employment Testing for Clerical/Administrative Trades in the Canadian Military," *Canadian Journal of Administrative Sciences*, vol. 3 (December 1986), pp. 376–85.
71. A. Nikiforuk, "Winging It," *Canadian Business*, November 1984, pp. 85–94.
72. Schmidt et al., "Impact of Valid Selection Procedures"; and Schmidt and Hunter, "Employment Testing."

SUGGESTIONS FOR FURTHER READING

☐ R.D. Arvey and R.H. Faley. *Fairness in Selecting Employees*. 2nd ed. Reading, Mass.: Addison-Wesley, 1988.

☐ O.K. Buros. *The Ninth Mental Measurements Yearbook*. Vol. 2. Highland Park, NJ: Gryphon Press, 1989.

☐ R.L. Dipboye. *Selection Interviews: Process Perspectives*. Cincinnati: South-Western, 1992.

☐ R.D. Gatewood and H.S. Feild, *Human Resource Selection*. 2nd ed. Chicago: Dryden Press, 1990.

☐ T. Janz, L. Hellervik, and D.C. Gilmore. *Behavior Description Interviewing*. Boston: Allyn and Bacon, 1986.

☐ B. Schneider and N. Schmitt. *Staffing Organizations*. 2nd ed. Glenview, Fla.: Scott, Foresman 1986.

video CASE

PATAGONIA

Yvon Chouinard founded Chouinard Equipment in 1957 to market a small line of rock climbing equipment he manufactured in his backyard using an $800 forging die. He sold the products from the back of his van. During the early days, Chouinard made ends meet by working as a private detective for Howard Hughes.

In 1965, eight years after making his first prototypes, Chouinard opened a retail store to market his products in a small tin building behind a slaughterhouse in Ventura, California. Today the company's headquarters stands on that same site, and the original store has grown into a division of five stores under a holding company named Lost Arrow, Inc. Lost Arrow includes the corporation's retail arm, Great Pacific Iron Works; Patagonia, the clothing division; and Chouinard Equipment, the mountaineering equipment firm. It generated estimated sales revenues in 1989 of $76 million. The company has remained in private hands, despite numerous purchase offers.

Chouinard's values and his unique leadership style and business approach have played strong roles in shaping the culture of Patagonia. "You don't have to be in the Rotary Club or lunch with bankers to be a success," he says. "You take risks, use common sense and you make good products." He has been labeled an "anti-marketer" and an effortless success, but such labels deceive. Chouinard has ingrained in his employees a focus on producing the finest quality outdoor gear available.

Employees must understand and share the Patagonia mission because the company's owner is not present to direct activities for seven months of the year. Though Chouinard spends some of this time in business travel, he spends most of it having fun. The business's location in Ventura near one of the finest surfing beaches in California is no accident. Chouinard actively participates in 20 sports, including fly fishing, kayaking, alpine skiing, sailing, and surfing. Several personal business goals guide his activities:

1. Make money
2. Give money away
3. Be creative
4. Maintain pride
5. No hassles
6. "Pfun"

Chouinard realizes that someone has to manage Patagonia, he just doesn't want to be the one to do it. He works to duck the day-to-day burden by delegating authority. He has developed systems to make this leadership style work.

First, the firm hires the right people. Each of Lost Arrow's approximately 400 employees is hired with one basic question in mind, "Would I want to have dinner with this person?" If not, the candidate probably wouldn't fit in at Patagonia. Chouinard says, "We try to get the most intelligent people we can . . . but in the end, you really end up with fairly average people. The secret is to try to get average people to do above average work." He tries to accomplish this by giving each employee a sense of responsibility, keeping the direct result of the work visible, and showcasing its effect on the rest of the organization.

Another product of Chouinard's leadership approach is the 5–15 report, completed each week by virtually every Patagonia employee. This report must, by definition, take no longer than 15 minutes to prepare, and no more than 5 minutes to read. It focuses on three things: a summary of the employee's accomplishments for the week, an evaluation of the department's morale, and a single idea for improving the company, either within the employee's department, or company-wide.

Completed 5–15s travel up the organization chart to supervisors and managers, who likewise compile and pass along their own 5–15s. The sequence stops at the top with Chouinard, who receives approximately two dozen reports from Ventura each week, wherever in the world he happens to be, indicating the climates at all levels of Patagonia. The reports may signal the need for job redesign or expansion of responsibilities to remedy revealed boredom or undermotivation. Department managers sometimes share ideas from 5–15s. In addition, the reports foster creativity, employee participation in decision making, and enhanced communication.

Yvon Chouinard takes a long-term view of his company. He wants employees to view it as their company, too, to be happy and fulfilled. He estimates that each time an employee leaves the company, it costs him an average of $50 000 to find and train a replacement. To avoid this, he pays careful attention to benefits. For example, he offers flextime scheduling, recognizes outstanding performance via a formal recognition program, and allows employees to use vacation time in one-hour increments to surf or attend a kindergarten graduation ceremony, for example.

Besides offering its employers all the standard benefits, and then some, Patagonia maintains above average compensation levels ranging from $6 an hour to $50 000 to $60 000 annually for middle managers. "You get out of benefits what you put into them," says Chouinard. The company also subsidizes employees' wilderness adventures and sells them clothing at 10 percent below wholesale cost.

Of the many benefits, one of the most important is the excellent on-premise child care facility, Great Pacific Child Development Center. This center further emphasizes Patagonia's family-like concern for its employees, helping to integrate children's daily activities with their parents' workplace into an everyday environment, relieving anxiety and frustration for both. This also brings work satisfaction and productivity increases, creating a total and mutual benefit. Each staff member at the center meets or exceeds all qualifications required by the State of California, and the center maintains a staff–child ratio that allows individualized care and an enhanced learning environment for the children.

Patagonia also provides an excellent cafeteria facility for its employees that specializes in healthful and nutritious foods. Rather than going out to lunch at a cost of an hour and a half or so of work time, most employees dine in the cafeteria or take their meals back to their offices.

Source: Excerpt from *Organizational Behavior*, Second Edition, by Robert P. Vecchio, copyright © 1991 by The Dryden Press. Reprinted with the permission of the publisher.

DISCUSSION QUESTIONS

1. What types of managers did Chouinard target for recruitment?

2. What types of rewards does Chouinard use to enhance employee performance? What evidence can you give to prove that these rewards are effective?

3. In terms of group dynamics, why might someone want to work at Patagonia?

4. What are the advantages of the "5–15" report used by Chouinard?

5. Account for the low turnover rate of employees at Patagonia.

ORGANIZATIONAL GOALS AND OBJECTIVES AND STRATEGIC PLANNING
Survival and growth
Productivity
Profits
Service

JOB ANALYSIS
Provides planners with jobs' requirements for human resources

STRATEGIC HUMAN RESOURCE ANALYSIS
Uses HRM expertise and experience to assist in developing organizational objectives and to propose alternatives to obtain these objectives

HUMAN RESOURCE PLANNING
Specifies number and kind of employees needed

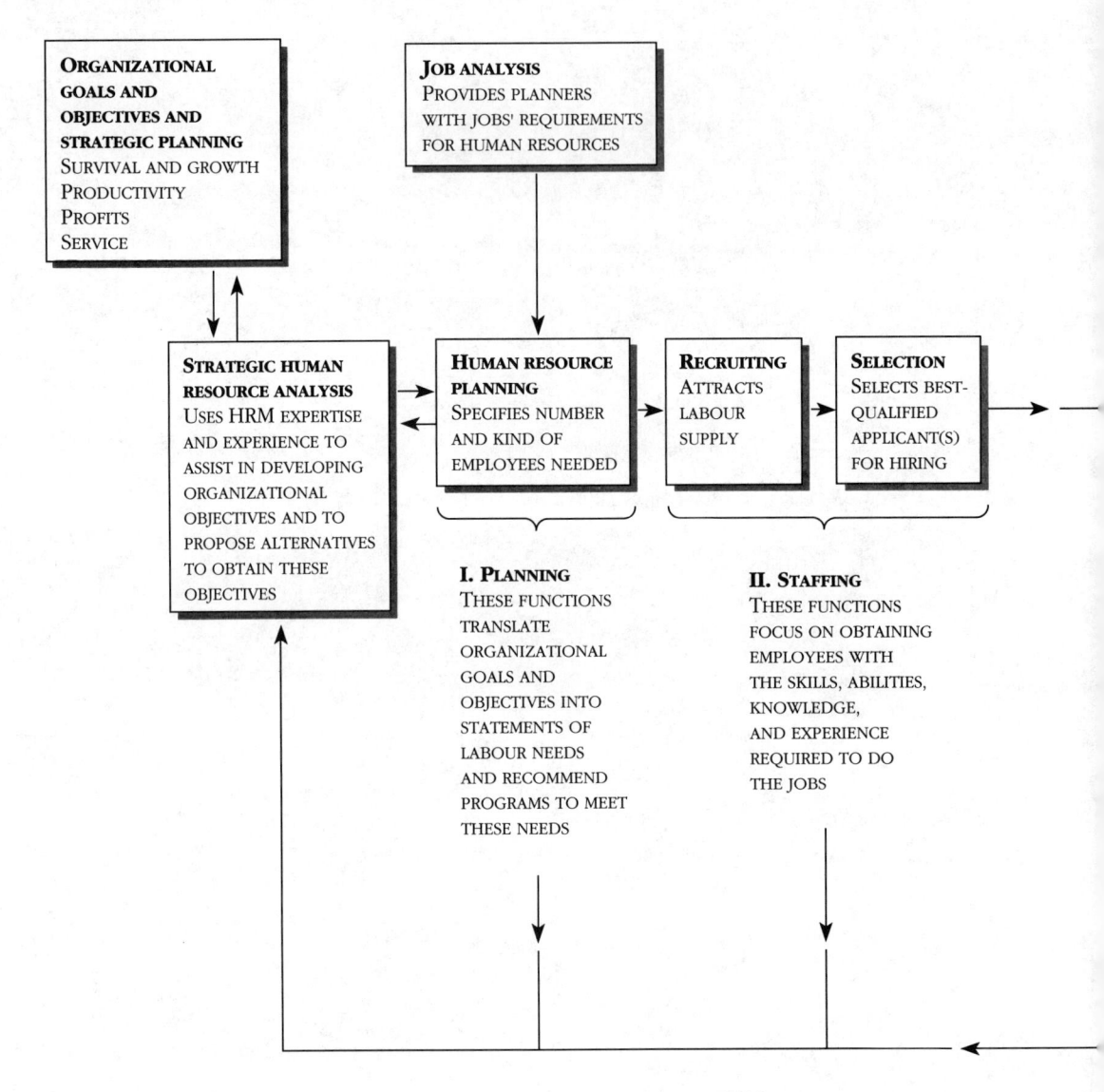

RECRUITING
Attracts labour supply

SELECTION
Selects best-qualified applicant(s) for hiring

I. Planning
These functions translate organizational goals and objectives into statements of labour needs and recommend programs to meet these needs

II. Staffing
These functions focus on obtaining employees with the skills, abilities, knowledge, and experience required to do the jobs

Input from major areas of HRM responsibility

PART THREE

EMPLOYEE DEVELOPMENT

ORIENTATION
Provides new employees with information about the job, what to expect, and what is expected

TRAINING AND DEVELOPMENT
Maintains acceptable levels of performance, involves employees in work practice decisions, and prepares employees to advance

CAREER PLANNING
Seeks to reconcile individual career goals with organizational needs for human resources

PERFORMANCE APPRAISAL
Measures employees' performance on the job

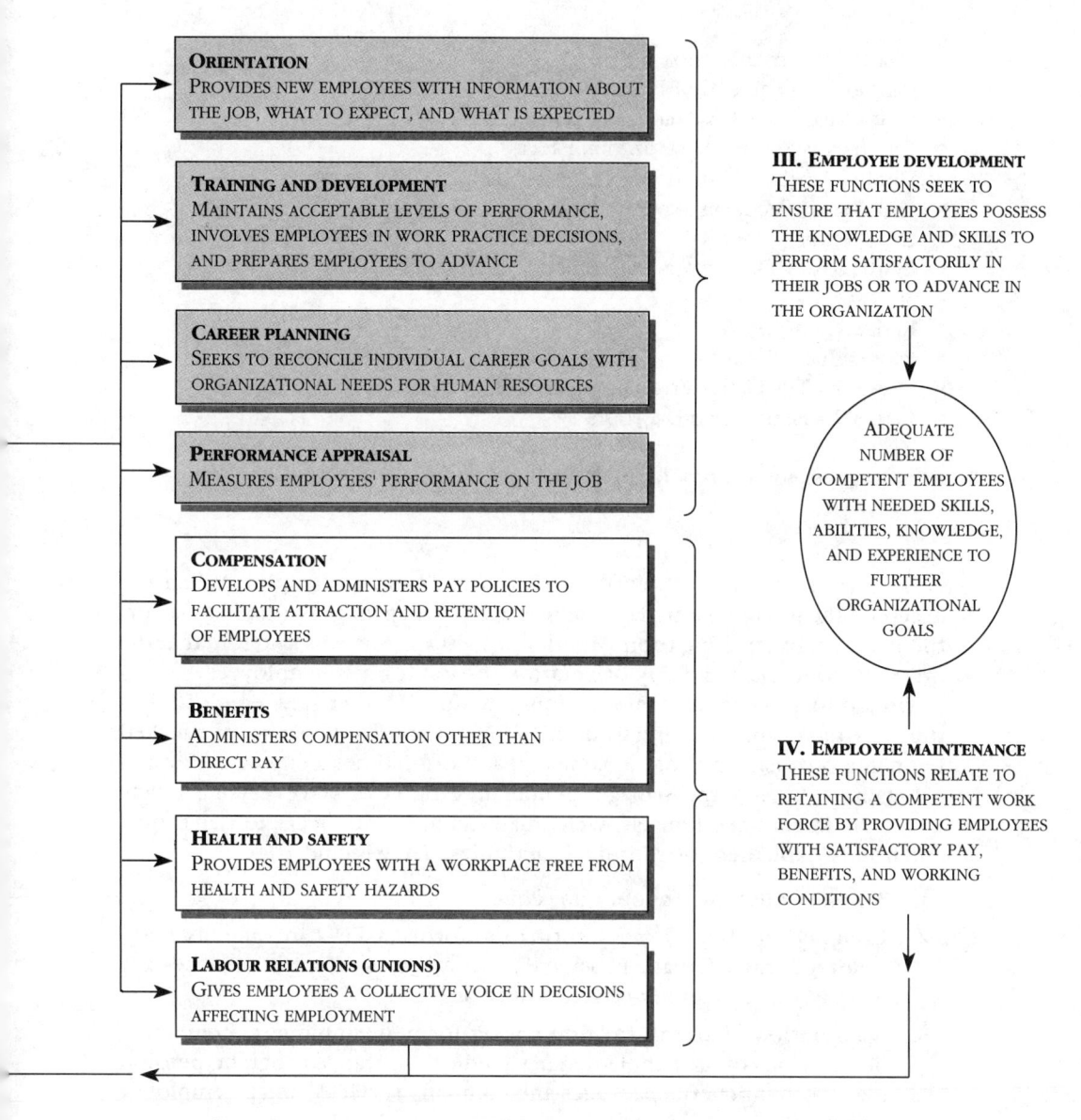

COMPENSATION
Develops and administers pay policies to facilitate attraction and retention of employees

BENEFITS
Administers compensation other than direct pay

HEALTH AND SAFETY
Provides employees with a workplace free from health and safety hazards

LABOUR RELATIONS (UNIONS)
Gives employees a collective voice in decisions affecting employment

III. EMPLOYEE DEVELOPMENT
These functions seek to ensure that employees possess the knowledge and skills to perform satisfactorily in their jobs or to advance in the organization

Adequate number of competent employees with needed skills, abilities, knowledge, and experience to further organizational goals

IV. EMPLOYEE MAINTENANCE
These functions relate to retaining a competent work force by providing employees with satisfactory pay, benefits, and working conditions

Input from major areas of HRM responsibility

CHAPTER 8

ORIENTATION

- ORIENTATION: A DEFINITION
- RELATION TO OTHER HRM FUNCTIONS
- HOW ORIENTATION CONTRIBUTES TO ORGANIZATIONAL EFFECTIVENESS
- ORIENTATION AND THE SOCIALIZATION PROCESS
- HRM IN ACTION ▸ REALISTIC JOB PREVIEWS: UPPERS AND DOWNERS
- ORIENTATION PROGRAMS AND PROCEDURES
- ORIENTATION IN PRACTICE
- EVALUATION OF ORIENTATION PROGRAMS
- SUMMARY
- REVIEW QUESTIONS
- PROJECT IDEAS
- CASE 8.1 ▸ THE EIGHT-WEEK ORIENTATION PROGRAM
- CASE 8.2 ▸ FIREFIGHTING DROPOUTS
- NOTES
- SUGGESTIONS FOR FURTHER READING

JANE SIMPSON IS A NEW SHIPPING CLERK AT CanTèque Electronics. When she accepted the job last Thursday, she was given a map and instructed to report to the company meeting room Monday at 7:30 A.M. She was also told that the meeting would be a half-day orientation session for new employees.

On Monday morning, Simpson found about 25 other new employees in the meeting room. Someone from the human resources department checked her name on a list, gave her a name tag, and offered her a cup of coffee and a doughnut. At 7:45, the manager of human resources asked everyone to take a seat. He introduced himself, welcomed the new employees to CanTèque, and briefly explained the morning's activities. They included

1. A 25-minute movie about CanTèque.
2. Completion of employee information forms: a TD-1 income tax withholding form, a Canada Pension Plan form, other information necessary for payroll, and family-related information.
3. Distribution of an information packet for new employees, containing descriptions of the supplementary medical insurance program, pension plans, other benefits packages and company services, and an employee handbook.
4. A slide-show presentation detailing employee benefits.

5. A 20-minute coffee break.
6. A plant tour.
7. Instructions on policy matters: how to report absence, where to park, etc.
8. A question and answer period.
9. Completion of a form evaluating the orientation program.

By lunch time Simpson was enthusiastic about her employer, but she also felt that she had been given a tremendous amount of information to digest in a very short time. She wondered which parts of it she needed to know right away. She was also somewhat anxious about her new job responsibilities.

After lunch, Simpson was introduced to her supervisor and several of her new co-workers. After some small talk, the supervisor began telling Simpson about her job. Orientation was over and job training had begun.

CanTèque's orientation program is typical of many organizational orientations. Though it gave Jane Simpson and other new employees a great deal of information about their new employer, it provided few insights about actually working for CanTèque and adapting to the organization's culture.

The experience of Jane Simpson stands in sharp contrast to that of Bill Constantino, a group leader at the Toyota-Georgetown plant. His comments on the process that he underwent follow:

> I was part of the first group that went through the selection process. I have to tell you, at times I wondered if it would ever end!
>
> But a funny thing happened along the way. I noticed how there were fewer and fewer people as I went through the process. I began to feel a real sense of accomplishment. I recognized that Toyota was taking its work force seriously, that the company was going to end up with high-caliber, motivated people . . . that if I was hired I'd be part of a group "beyond the ordinary."
>
> Some of the process was downright fun. I got to know many of the other applicants. Over time we developed a real sense of camaraderie. And I enjoyed many of the simulations, especially the ones that were "hands on." They taught me a lot about myself and gave me a clear sense of what the company was looking for.
>
> What impressed me the most about the process was its fairness. Everywhere you looked, the treatment was equal. Everyone experienced the same challenge.
>
> I'm glad I persisted. Now I'm working with a group of people who really participate and engage in creative action. Without question, the quality of our people is unmatched.[1]

Obviously, Toyota and CanTèque have very different approaches to selecting and orienting their new employees. Companies such as Toyota, Cami (the GM-Suzuki plant in Ingersoll, Ontario), Honda, Mazda, and a number of other team-style organizations carry out an extensive orientation during the hiring process, not after it, as is traditionally done. These extensive orientation programs convey a very explicit set of expectations to new members. Employers using such systems believe they pay off in terms of high levels of employee commitment and low turnover. Such systems are still fairly new and it is too early to tell how they will do in the long run. This chapter describes the orientation function, its purposes, and its role in organizational effectiveness.

ORIENTATION: A DEFINITION

Orientation is the process of introducing new employees to the organization, its philosophy, policies, rules, and procedures. It marks the beginning of *socialization*, the process by which an employee is indoctrinated to understand and accept the organization's culture—its norms, values, and ways of doing things.

Socialization is a period of adjustment in which new employees learn what is expected in terms of appropriate behaviour and acceptable performance. They also come to know what they can expect from the organization in return for their efforts. These things are learned not only through formal orientation programs but also via informal exchanges with co-workers and observation of supervisors and others who may serve as role models for the employee. Pascale and others argue that the socialization process continues well beyond orientation and is affected by other HRM functions such as training, performance appraisal, and compensation.[2] Indeed, as described in the chapters on recruiting and selection, many progressive employers, such as Honda and Toyota, realize the importance of hiring employees who are likely to fit the organization's culture. These employers use techniques such as realistic job previews, extensive interviews, and even some training that provides anticipatory socialization.

Though the formal orientation period is only a part of the socialization process, it is an important period since instilling values and norms to new hires is vital to managing an organization's culture. Many recent management books argue that an organization's culture is crucial to its level of effectiveness and profitability, and its ability to achieve goals such as high-quality products and services.[3]

RELATION TO OTHER HRM FUNCTIONS

The relationship of orientation to other HRM functions is shown in Figure 8.1. In most organizations, some form of orientation follows the selection and hiring of new employees. Orientation provides new hires with basic information about working conditions, policies, procedures, pay, and benefits and introduces management and co-workers. Information conveyed

FIGURE 8.1
Orientation: Relation to Other HRM Functions

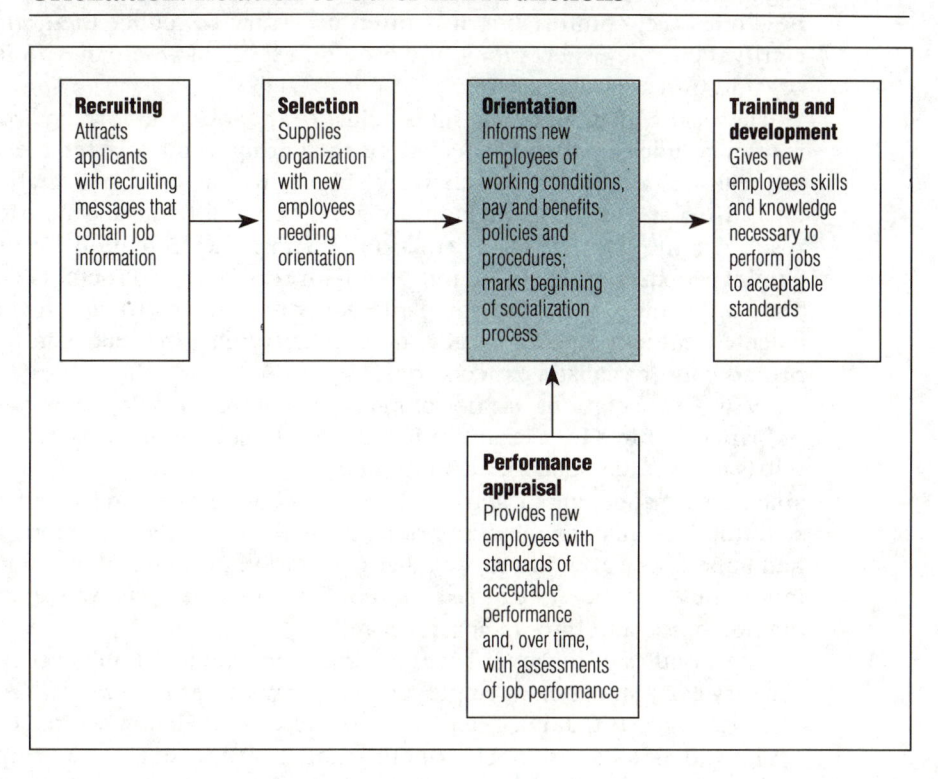

```
┌─────────────┐   ┌─────────────┐   ┌─────────────┐   ┌─────────────┐
│ Recruiting  │   │ Selection   │   │ Orientation │   │ Training and│
│ Attracts    │   │ Supplies    │   │ Informs new │   │ development │
│ applicants  │──▶│ organization│──▶│ employees of│──▶│ Gives new   │
│ with        │   │ with new    │   │ working     │   │ employees   │
│ recruiting  │   │ employees   │   │ conditions, │   │ skills and  │
│ messages    │   │ needing     │   │ pay and     │   │ knowledge   │
│ that contain│   │ orientation │   │ benefits,   │   │ necessary to│
│ job         │   │             │   │ policies and│   │ perform jobs│
│ information │   │             │   │ procedures; │   │ to          │
│             │   │             │   │ marks       │   │ acceptable  │
│             │   │             │   │ beginning of│   │ standards   │
│             │   │             │   │ socialization│  │             │
│             │   │             │   │ process     │   │             │
└─────────────┘   └─────────────┘   └─────────────┘   └─────────────┘
                                           ▲
                                    ┌─────────────┐
                                    │ Performance │
                                    │ appraisal   │
                                    │ Provides new│
                                    │ employees   │
                                    │ with        │
                                    │ standards of│
                                    │ acceptable  │
                                    │ performance │
                                    │ and, over   │
                                    │ time, with  │
                                    │ assessments │
                                    │ of job      │
                                    │ performance │
                                    └─────────────┘
```

during orientation may also correct false impressions created by recruiting messages and selection interviews.

Note that performance appraisal provides inputs to the orientation function in that new employees are informed of acceptable levels of performance and, over time, provided with assessments of job performance. This is an important aspect of socialization, for most employees want to know what is required for successful job performance.

For most jobs, some amount of training follows orientation. Orientation provides new employees with general information about the job and organization; training provides them with the specific knowledge and skills necessary to perform the job.

How Orientation Contributes to Organizational Effectiveness

Orientation contributes to organizational effectiveness by facilitating the socialization process so that new hires become integrated into the organization as soon as possible. The sooner new hires feel comfortable in the organization, the sooner they can be productive workers. In order to make new hires feel comfortable, it is often necessary to reduce their anxieties, clarify their role expectations, and provide a sense of where they fit into the organization as a whole.

The ease with which new hires adjust to the job and work environment is often a function of the expectations they bring to the job. If expectations are realistic, adjustment is relatively simple. If, however, expectations are unrealistic or unreasonable, adjustment is more difficult and quitting may result. In the latter case, orientation can facilitate retention by bringing employee expectations more into line with reality. IBM, Procter & Gamble, Toyota, Corning, and other companies known for their strong, achievement-oriented cultures purposely give new hires trying experiences in order to promote more realistic expectations.[4]

Even if expectations are not unrealistic or unreasonable, orientation can prepare new hires for the almost inevitable ambiguities and frustrations they will face, including uncertainties about the boss's expectations, about acceptable performance, about getting along with co-workers, and about dealing with the fact that the job may not be as interesting or autonomous as they had hoped. Research has shown that orientation programs that reduce anxiety of new employees can reduce training time and costs, waste and production costs, and rates of absenteeism.[5]

Many studies of turnover have found a large number of quits occurring in the very early stages of an employee's career with an organization.[6] A recent estimate suggests that between 50 and 60 percent of all newly hired employees leave their jobs within seven months and that the average cost of replacing these employees is $6000 per person.[7] Early termination is costly to employers, given the costs of recruiting, selecting, and training replacements. Corning, Inc. estimated in the early 1980s that it cost $30 000 to $40 000 per person to hire and train an optical designer, a CAD/CAM engineer, a systems programmer, or a technical salesperson.[8] Early termination of employees with high SD_y and those with skills that are in short supply can cost employers even more. Orientation programs can contribute to organizational effectiveness by helping to reduce turnover among new employees. Corning credited a 69 percent reduction in turnover in the first two years of employment to the introduction of a new orientation system, which is described later in this chapter.[9]

Researchers and many practitioners have argued that the major value of orientation to organizational effectiveness is its ability to refine the degree of "fit" between an individual's needs and those of the organization. A recent study of several groups, including managers, MBA graduates, and accountants, examined this question, using the Organizational Culture Profile, which measures the person–organization fit. Results from this study showed that the better the fit between the needs of 171 newly hired accountants and the realities of the organization, the lower the turnover. The authors concluded:

For an individual to be satisfied and attached to an organization, the person may need both task competency and a value system congruent with the central values of the organization. As for the organization, it needs to select people who fit a given situation, which is likely to include some combination of task and cultural requirements. Failure to fit on either dimension may reduce employees' satisfaction and commitment and increase the likelihood of their leaving.[10]

This study is one of many that make a strong case for a thorough orientation, like some of the examples mentioned in this chapter.

Even if orientation is successful in smoothing the way for new hires, some turnover will result, because of mismatches or poor fit between employees and organizations. If a mismatch has occurred, it is to everyone's benefit that this fact be discovered at the earliest opportunity. Organizations can save substantial training costs and individuals can avoid "spinning their wheels" at jobs for which they are unsuited. Orientations that provide realistic job previews (RJPs) contribute to organizational effectiveness by permitting early detection of mismatches. Information on mismatches, as well as on successful matches, should be communicated to those responsible for selection so that it may be used to reduce the possibility of future mismatches.

Finally, documentation of the information given to new hires during orientation sessions can provide the organization with protection from later legal action and costly litigation. New hires often sign lists recording their attendance at orientation sessions, and they may sign forms indicating that they understand company rules and various benefit options. Thus, if an employee is later disciplined for a rule violation, he or she cannot claim to have never been informed of the rule. Likewise, if an employee claims that he or she was not informed of a certain benefit option, the company can show otherwise.

ORIENTATION AND THE SOCIALIZATION PROCESS

Orientation marks the beginning of socialization and may be used to prepare employees for some of the ambiguities and frustrations they are likely to experience. The following descriptive model of the socialization process views such ambiguities and frustrations as tasks, or learning experiences, that a new employee must master in order to become an accepted member of the organization.

SCHEIN'S SOCIALIZATION MODEL

Schein's three-stage socialization model describes the steps in preparing for a job and entering an organization. The three stages are (1) entry, (2) socialization, and (3) mutual acceptance.[11] The model is illustrated in Figure 8.2.

FIGURE 8.2
Schein's Socialization Model

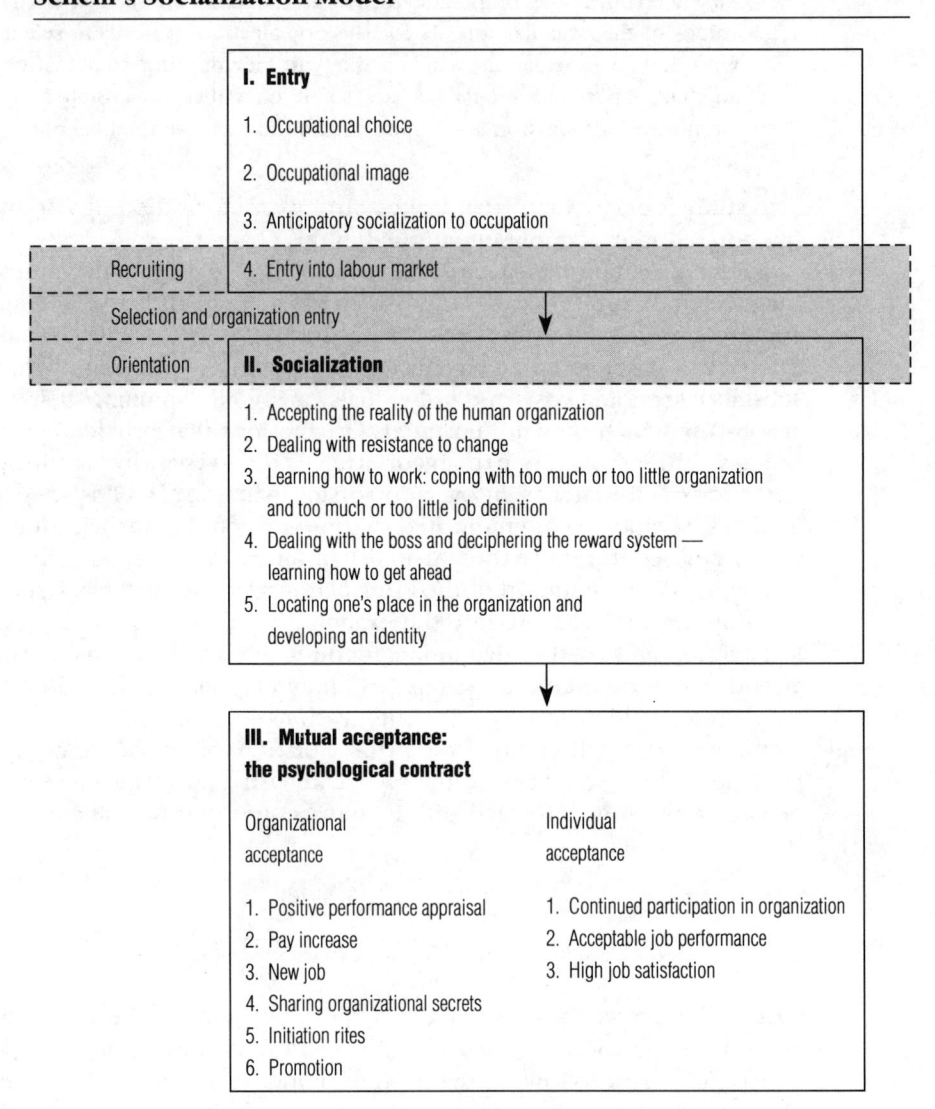

I. Entry
1. Occupational choice
2. Occupational image
3. Anticipatory socialization to occupation
4. Entry into labour market

Recruiting
Selection and organization entry
Orientation

II. Socialization
1. Accepting the reality of the human organization
2. Dealing with resistance to change
3. Learning how to work: coping with too much or too little organization and too much or too little job definition
4. Dealing with the boss and deciphering the reward system — learning how to get ahead
5. Locating one's place in the organization and developing an identity

III. Mutual acceptance: the psychological contract

Organizational acceptance
1. Positive performance appraisal
2. Pay increase
3. New job
4. Sharing organizational secrets
5. Initiation rites
6. Promotion

Individual acceptance
1. Continued participation in organization
2. Acceptable job performance
3. High job satisfaction

Source: Based on Edgar Schein, *Career Dynamics: Matching Individual and Organizational Needs*. © 1978 by Addison-Wesley Publishing Company, Reading, Mass. Used with the permission of the publisher.

Entry Stage

An individual selects an occupation and prepares to enter it by obtaining appropriate education and training. During this period, Schein states, people develop an idealistic image of what it is like to work in a particular occupation. Such images are usually unrealistic, emphasizing the positive aspects of the work and ignoring its negative features. Also during this period, the individual develops attitudes and values that he or she regards as appropriate for succeeding in the chosen occupation. This process is called *anticipatory socialization*.

The final part of the entry stage is looking for the first job. At this point, the potential employee begins to make contact with various employers through the recruiting process. This part of the entry stage often presents problems for both employer and applicant. Schein argues that both tend to emphasize their most favourable aspects and hide their negative elements, resulting in the development of unrealistic expectations. These distortions of reality prevent both interviewer and applicant from determining if a good fit exists between the worker and the organization. Recruiting materials often oversell the organization; the result is disillusioned and dissatisfied employees. Many problems of this sort can be avoided by realistic analyses of an organization's jobs and its promotion and compensation policies and practices and by making appropriate changes in recruiting and selection methods. Once new employees report to work, orientation can serve to align their expectations with the actualities of working for the particular employer.

Socialization Stage

Organizational socialization begins when the new employee begins work. From the employee's point of view, socialization is a process of "breaking in and joining up, of learning the ropes, of figuring out how to get along and how to make it."[12] From the organization's point of view, it is a process of "induction, basic training, and socialization of the individual to the major norms and values of the organization."[13] If the organization conducts an orientation program, it takes place at this point and helps to further the employee's socialization.

As an individual begins his or her first "real" job, there is invariably the experience of reality shock: discovering that it is very different from expectations.[14] Orientation can reduce this gap by better preparing new employees for what they will experience in their first months of employment. For an example of reality shock on Wall Street, see Exhibit 8.1.

Schein presents five tasks to be mastered in this stage: (1) accepting the reality of the human organization; (2) dealing with resistance to change; (3) learning how to work: coping with too much or too little organization and too much or too little job definition; (4) dealing with the boss and deciphering the reward system; and (5) locating one's place in the organization and developing an identity.

The first task of Schein's socialization stage is accepting *the reality of the human organization*. Schein's research revealed that a large part of the reality shock of organizational entry came from the fact that new employees expected near-perfection on the part of organizations and the people in them. The reality to be accepted in this early stage of the socialization process is

EXHIBIT 8.1
Reality Shock on Wall Street

When Elaine Ide Wood was hired into the mergers and acquisitions department at Morgan Stanley & Co., Inc., a few years back, she was on top of the world. "I felt tremendous," says Ms. Wood, a Harvard Business School graduate. "It was the ultimate in a high-powered, fast-learning job on Wall Street, and to me, Wall Street was the heartbeat of business."

But after less than two months of analyzing takeover deals, she quit, distressed by the seemingly endless workload. "I want to work 50 hours a week. Sixty hours is fine, and 70 or 80 is okay when there's a project. But working 90 or 100 hours a week just isn't the way I wanted to live my life," she says. Today she's marketing manager for an industrial-robot company.

The appeal of life in Wall Street's fast lane is strong. Lured by the expectations of high salaries, prestige, and excitement, top business and law school graduates queue up for jobs at big investment banking and law firms.

The attractions are obvious. Salaries at big Wall Street law firms start at about $50 000. At big securities firms it isn't unusual to find people in their early 30s making $100 000 or more. The rash of mergers and acquisitions, with tales of "poison pills," "white knights," and "shark repellant," adds an aura of glamour to the field.

But chasing just a piece of that glamour can be tiresome. One 32-year-old lawyer says that working on a famous and controversial securities default case means ploughing through "hundreds of thousands of documents" to piece together events "in a given department in a given period of time. It's monotonous."

Even the excitement of handling big sums can wear off with time. One 27-year-old was proud to be helping manage a $7 billion money market fund. But after a while he tired of checking rates, making phone calls, and reinvesting maturing securities. "Whether it was $1 million or $100 million, the procedure was still the same," he says. He quit when he decided that "except for the tension, a baboon could do what I was doing."

The pressure rarely lets up. "The attitude is 'it's fine you made a million dollars yesterday, but what have you done for me today,' " says a vice president at Salomon Brothers Inc. "It can be fatiguing. If you haven't booked your business for the day, you can't relax." People become preoccupied with their work to the exclusion of all else, he adds. "It's hard to measure yourself in any but the starkest terms: How many millions of dollars have you raised?" he says. "It's a very narrow world."

Source: Amanda Bennett, "Some Business Grads Learn to Hate Their Glamorous Wall Street Jobs," *The Wall Street Journal*, December 18, 1985. Reprinted by permission of *The Wall Street Journal* © 1985 Dow Jones & Company, Inc. All Rights Reserved Worldwide.

that organizations are not perfect and that a major source of this imperfection is, in fact, the people in the organization. Schein quotes new employees saying, after their first year of employment:

> People are a nuisance. . . .
>
> The number of unproductive people there are in corporations is astounding.
>
> All the problems I encounter boil down to communication and human relations.[15]

The second task of the socialization process is *dealing with resistance to change*. New employees, especially recent graduates of education or training programs, enter their first jobs filled with ideas and knowledge that they are eager to use in solving organizational problems. They expect their employers to be equally eager to have them use their newly acquired knowledge and skills. More often, however, new employees are given relatively routine, unchallenging jobs and told that their ideas and solutions to problems are impractical. Such experiences prove frustrating to many new employees.

The third experience in organizational socialization is *learning how to work*: coping with too much or too little organization and too much or too little job definition. New employees generally expect a reasonable amount of definition and clarity about what they should do in their jobs, as well as a certain amount of feedback on their performance. Schein's research shows that these expectations often go unmet. Frequently, new employees must carve out their own jobs and learn both what to do and how to do it largely on their own. One new employee expressed this frustration as

> Not knowing whom to ask or what to ask; not knowing what the ball park is . . . the problem of not knowing what it is you need to know.[16]

Of course, some new employees experience the opposite problem: a very tightly defined job with no flexibility for individual abilities and needs. New employees must often learn how to judge their own performance, since feedback from the boss is often inadequate. Again, these organizational realities are particularly frustrating because they are not what the new employee expected.

A fourth task in the socialization process is *dealing with the boss*. Research has shown that the first boss is the most important person in determining a new employee's degree of career success.[17] The boss usually has control over many work opportunities and provides many of the rewards and punishments a new employee receives. A related need of new employees is *deciphering the reward system*. In many organizations, written criteria for promotion or advancement do not provide a realistic description of what it actually takes to get ahead in the organization. Schein found considerable ambiguity among new employees on this point. Some felt "it's whom you know that counts," while others believed "it's who knows you." Some felt advancement depends upon "high visibility, getting along well, being important to the boss," while others said that "you get ahead by having the ability and working hard."[18] Very few orientation programs provide information of this type, but it is clear that new employees want and need it in order to direct their energies accordingly.

The final task in the socialization process is *locating one's place in the organization and developing an identity*. An organization, like any other group, has a status hierarchy in which some people have more power, influence, or prestige than others. Although newcomers invariably lack the status associated with experience in the organization, both old and new employees must learn how much influence and status should be afforded new members. Some organizations, such as Procter & Gamble, give newly hired graduates of colleges and universities kindergarten-like tasks, such as colouring a map of sales territories. Other organizations may demand twelve- to fourteen-hour workdays. Such bootcamp-like experiences are designed to generate feelings of humility and induce doubt about one's own values and beliefs, therefore increasing receptivity to the organization's values and norms.[19]

Mutual Acceptance Stage

The third major stage of Schein's socialization model is mutual acceptance. From the time an applicant first makes contact with a prospective employer to the end of the socialization process, some ambiguity, caution, and lack of trust exist between the individual and the organization. The major reason is that neither has complete information about the other's abilities or resources, motives, values, and needs. When the mutual acceptance stage is complete, the new employee and the organization have negotiated a psychological contract indicating their mutual acceptance and trust.

Schein describes this *psychological contract* as a set of expectations held by the employee and the employer regarding pay, rights, privileges, and obligations of the employee to the organization.[20] Certain work behaviour and levels of input into the job and the organization are expected from the employee, and certain outcomes (pay, benefits, rewards, privileges) are expected by the employee for his or her efforts. During socialization—and even during the application process—the individual is negotiating a psychological contract with the organization. The process is rarely as formal as negotiations between labour and management when a collective agreement is being worked out. Rather, a psychological contract is negotiated over time through interactions between the new employee and other organization members, particularly the boss and co-workers. Organization members communicate to newcomers the behaviour that is expected of all organization members. Underlying this expected behaviour, or *norms*, are *values*, defined as general attitudes and concepts regarding appropriate behaviour that organization members feel are important. An organization has rules, regulations, and procedures designed to ensure that members behave in ways consistent with its norms and values. For example, it may uphold a value of fairness. A corresponding norm of employee behaviour is "a fair day's work for a fair day's pay." The organization could enforce this norm through formal rules specifying standards of production and by informal work-group standards. Values and norms such as this are often major components of an employee's psychological contract.

New employees are eager to learn how hard they must work to satisfy their boss, get a raise, and perhaps earn a promotion. In some cases, co-workers communicate levels of work norms that are different — usually lower — than those the boss promotes. In these cases, separate psychological contracts are negotiated with the boss and with co-workers. For example, a psychological contract with the boss might include a higher-than-average level of production in exchange for a good pay raise and his or her approval. The contract with co-workers, on the other hand, might include an average level of production in exchange for their acceptance. Clearly, the two psychological contracts may conflict. If they do, which one the new employee chooses as pre-eminent depends on his or her needs and values.

The psychological contract requires a sense of fairness or equity in the employer–employee relationship in terms of what each gives and receives. An employee may or may not feel that the amount or quality of work expected by the boss is fair in terms of what the organization is willing to provide in pay, benefits, and other rewards. However, to achieve mutual acceptance, both employer and employee must feel that the ratio of exchange is fair. The psychological contract for this exchange, negotiated during the socialization process, defines what employer and employee expect of each other in the future. Violation of the contract by either party is likely to lead to voluntary or involuntary termination.

New employees are also eager to receive from their boss or other organization members signs of their acceptance into the organization. Schein lists six events as signs of an organization's acceptance of a new employee:

1. A positive first performance appraisal.
2. A pay increase.
3. A new job assignment.
4. Sharing of organizational secrets, such as how others evaluate the new employee and how the organization "really" works.
5. "Initiation rites," such as a party.
6. A promotion.[21]

Although each of these events signals organizational acceptance, promotion carries the most weight.

Socialization is a gradual process that can require several years' work in an organization. Therefore, even the most ambitious and effective orientation program cannot be expected to socialize the new employee completely.

Social Orientation: The Texas Instruments Experiment

It has been suggested that orientation should help reduce employees' anxieties about a new job and a new organization. A study on orientation conducted at Texas Instruments in the mid-1960s has become a classic because there have been very few, if any, other experiments on the subject.[22] Texas Instruments felt that its new female assemblers were anxious about whether they could be successful on the job. Experienced employees did not make the situation any easier; they subjected the newcomers to hazing, which made them even more anxious. Texas Instruments decided to try a different type of orientation, a social orientation designed to reduce anxiety, increase new employees' performance, and reduce turnover, which was high in the first few months of employment.

A control group of new employees was given the traditional two-hour orientation; a test group received that program plus an additional six hours of social orientation. The latter focussed on four major areas.

1. Employees were assured that their chances of succeeding on the job were good. Data were presented demonstrating that 99 percent of employees reached production standards. The point was made many times during the orientation period that everyone in the group would be successful.

2. New employees were warned about the hazing they would receive; they were told to take it in good humour and not let it bother them.

3. Employees were told to take the initiative in communicating with their supervisors. It was stressed that they should raise problems or questions even if they appeared stupid or silly and even if the supervisor was busy.

4. New employees were encouraged to get to know the boss. Just as students ask other students about what type of person a professor is, employees like to know something about their boss. The Texas Instruments experiment provided new employees with a short personality sketch of each supervisor, including hobbies, interests, and managerial style.

Texas Instruments reported very positive results from the orientation. Training time in the experimental group was reduced by 50 percent, training costs by 66 percent, waste by 80 percent, product costs by 15 to 30 percent, and tardiness and absenteeism by 50 percent.[23] More recent reports indicate that management at Texas Instruments credits social orientation for a 40 percent drop in early career turnover since the program began.[24] Texas Instruments' orientation seminars are now distributed worldwide in seven different languages. They also served as a model for Corning, Inc.'s orientation system, which is described later in the chapter.

REALISTIC JOB PREVIEWS: THEIR APPLICATION TO ORIENTATION

One technique for reducing reality shock is *realistic job previews (RJPs)*, which communicate to an applicant or new employee what it will actually be like to work for a company and perform a certain job. The idea of providing job applicants or new hires with information about what their jobs will *really* be like has existed since the mid-1950s, when a researcher mailed booklets describing actual job experiences of insurance agents to agent applicants.[25] Not until the 1970s, however, did J.P. Wanous popularize the concept of realistic job previews.[26]

RJPs can be developed in a number of ways. The most common is to interview current employees, asking them to relate actual experiences (good and bad) and state their attitudes toward the job. Another is to film or videotape employees at work and ask them for comments. The information provided in a well-done RJP is not all positive; employees are encouraged to describe some of their problems and frustrations. This information is presented to applicants or new employees verbally or in films, videotapes, or booklets.

Research shows that RJPs lower job expectations without completely "turning off" applicants to jobs.[27] Specifically, results of meta-analysis found that RJPs are modestly correlated with job satisfaction ($r = 0.05$) and job survival ($r = 0.06$).[28] Most RJP research has been done on low-level service industry jobs, and it is possible that the approach may be more effective for more complex jobs.[29] The reason is that applicants may already have fairly accurate information about low-level service jobs but know less about more complex jobs. A recent innovation in RJPs is to provide "enhanced" previews, which serve to raise expectations, rather than the usual "reduction" previews. A study of U.S. Army recruits found that some had expectations that were worse than reality, and that providing them with a combination of enhanced and reduced job previews produced the best results.[30]

McShane and Baal relate the following RJP story told them by representatives of a machinery distribution company in British Columbia:

> Recruits from the Lower Mainland and other areas of British Columbia had for some time been shown a film of the company's operations on the north coast. Since the film was shot on one of the few sunny days in the northern raintown community, the new hires looked forward to the beautiful scenery, recreation, and work—all in sunny weather. When they were stationed in raintown, however, the chilling and unexpected realities of the dreary weather were too much for many, with the result that turnover was very high. This, in turn, cost the firm dearly in lower productivity and high recruiting/selection expenses.
>
> Following the literature on realistic job previews, the company replaced the unrealistic film on raintown with a more realistic one which was taken on a rainy day. The result has been a dramatic reduction in turnover with corresponding higher productivity and lower personnel costs. In fact, employees who have been shown the new film claim that the weather is not nearly so bad as they had originally expected because there is the occasional sunny day.[31]

HRM IN ACTION

REALISTIC JOB PREVIEWS: UPPERS AND DOWNERS

Traditional realistic job previews (RJPs) are designed to reduce the overly optimistic expectations often created by the recruiting process. But what about the unrealistically pessimistic views held by many applicants and new hires? Can RJPs help to modify these?

An interesting survey of 533 male and female U.S. Army trainees addressed this question. It compared the effects of both a reduction ("downer") RJP and an enhancement ("upper") RJP given at the beginning of basic training. The logic behind using both a reduction and an enhancement preview is that while there are overly optimistic expectations that need to be brought down to reality, there are also overly pessimistic expectations about Army life that need to be modified in an upward direction. Two video previews of approximately 25 minutes in length, one enhancement and one reduction, were produced from surveys and interviews of soldiers in basic training. The enhancement preview presented events and activities whose difficulty is frequently overestimated. Such activities included: living and training conditions; firing live ammunition; amount of free time; and the standards for completing basic training. The reduction preview emphasized emotional aspects of basic training, specifically five adjustment problems to Army life that new trainees usually don't expect. Some of these problems are: homesickness; living and working with a group of "strangers"; worrying about not being able to meet physical requirements; and anxiety about talking with the sergeant about problems. The preview also covered approaches to dealing with these problems.

The study gave the reduction preview to one group, the enhancement preview to another, both to a third group, and no preview to a fourth control group. Perceptual and attitudinal measures were collected before the previews, immediately after, and five weeks following the previews. Additionally, turnover data were collected. (Even though subjects were in the Army, they seemed to know ways to get an honourable discharge if they wanted one.)

The results indicated that turnover was, as predicted by the authors, lowest for the group that received both previews. One particularly interesting aspect of the results is that previews were more effective at reducing turnover for the more intelligent trainees (measured by the Armed Forces Qualification Tests) and those who were more committed to the Army from the outset (measured by a commitment questionnaire).

The greater effectiveness for more intelligent trainees was attributed to their greater understanding of or attention to the material in the previews. While turnover was lower for all highly committed trainees who received any of the previews, the reverse was true for those who received no preview. That is, in the control group, turnover was higher among the more highly committed than among those who were less committed. The authors explain this apparent inconsistency by arguing that those who are most committed to an organization, before learning the "truth" about it, may be the most disillusioned and the most likely to leave. Finally, the perception that the organization could be trusted and was honest was highest for trainees receiving both previews. Additionally, the five-week post-RJP measures indicated that the trainees who had both RJPs saw the Army as more caring, felt more committed to the Army, and were more satisfied with their jobs.

This study, though carried out on Army trainees, provides valuable suggestions both for how to do RJPs and for how they might be used.

Source: Adapted from B.M. Meglino, A.S. DeNisi, S.A. Youngblood, and K.J. Williams, "Effects of Realistic Job Previews: A Comparison Using an Enhancement and a Reduction Preview," *Journal of Applied Psychology*, vol. 73 (1988), pp. 259–66. Used with the permission of the publisher.

From a cost-benefit standpoint, it is advantageous for employers to provide applicants with realistic job previews as early in the employment process as possible. If applicants have a realistic perception of the jobs they are applying for, they are in a better position to determine if they would be a good match. An organization can save selection, hiring, and start-up costs if an applicant discovers early in the process that a poor match exists. RJPs need not be used exclusively *before* hiring, however; using them afterwards, as part of the orientation process, provides benefits as well.

ORIENTATION PROGRAMS AND PROCEDURES

Most organizations have some type of orientation procedure. One survey of 196 North American organizations found that 86 percent offered some type of orientation. In more than half the organizations, these included formal orientation sessions.[32]

FORMAL ORIENTATION SESSIONS

Formal orientation sessions are developed and conducted by HRM departments and tend to last one to four hours. Like CanTèque's program, they generally include presentations by HRM professionals, audio-visual presentations, distribution of written materials, and company tours. Almost all formal orientation sessions cover the following topics:

1. Employee benefits.
2. Services for employees.
3. Company products or services.
4. Company rules and regulations.
5. Company organization.
6. Training and promotion.
7. Company history.

It is interesting that most organizations have the same formal orientation session for all employees, regardless of job level.[33]

There is considerable variation among employers regarding the frequency of formal orientation sessions. According to one survey, almost equal numbers conduct sessions "as needed," "weekly," and "bimonthly or monthly." More than half hold orientation on an employee's first day at work. Typically, fewer than 30 new employees attend a formal orientation session, with more than half the surveyed organizations reporting attendance in groups of no more than 15.[34]

INFORMAL ORIENTATION PROCEDURES

Informal orientation procedures are used by organizations that do not have formal sessions. Responsibility for orientation in this case is shared by the HRM department and an employee's immediate supervisor. New employees are often instructed to report to the HRM department for an explanation of company policies before being referred to the supervisor for an on-the-job briefing about specific work procedures. HRM professionals generally provide the new hire with written materials such as insurance and benefit brochures, employee handbooks, copies of rules and regulations, and company newspapers and magazines. These sessions tend to be brief, according to the survey already mentioned — one hour or less in nearly half the surveyed organizations.[35]

Organizations with informal orientation procedures often rely on checklists of topics to be discussed with the new employee. Checklists, used by the HRM department, the supervisor, or both, serve to document the new employee's having been informed of company policies, rules, and benefit options. One small manufacturing company provides its supervisors with the following instructions for using a detailed checklist:

> All supervisors will review with each new employee the general guidelines of performance, expected duties, and the supervisor's own personal philosophy during the first few days of employment. Preferably, the checklist should be

completed the first day, and under no circumstances more than five days from the date of hire. The employee will sign the form after it has been discussed and give it to the supervisor for inclusion in his/her personnel folder.[36]

Other informal orientation procedures include giving special orientation instruction to supervisors, briefing present employees before the arrival of a new employee, and choosing present employees as "buddies" for the new employee.

COMBINING FORMAL AND INFORMAL PROCEDURES

Many organizations combine formal and informal procedures in their orientation programs. Typically, such programs provide a formal orientation session in conjunction with more informal, on-the-job orientation by supervisors. A sophisticated combined approach is used at Corning, Inc.[37] Corning's orientation system is a long-term, nine-stage program that combines formal sessions and seminars with on-the-job orientation by supervisors. Corning's system is unlike many combined approaches in that its on-the-job orientation is highly formalized.

Orientation at Corning begins prior to employment with distribution of orientation materials and pre-arrival contacts. The first day's orientation activities are not unlike those of other organizations, including reading of an employee workbook, taking a tour of the building, and meeting co-workers. But unlike procedures at many organizations, including CanTèque, orientation at Corning does not end after Day 1. In fact, the entire first week of a new hire's employment is spent getting to know the supervisor, co-workers, the job, and the organization. Workbook questions guide the employee's learning. During this time also, employee and supervisor work together to set performance goals for the coming six months. Regular assignments begin in the second week of employment, and in the third and fourth weeks, the new hire attends a community seminar and an employee benefits seminar. During the second through fifth month of employment, the new hire attends six more seminars on a variety of work-related topics, again answering questions in the workbook. Answers to workbook questions are reviewed with the supervisor. During this period, biweekly progress reviews are held with the supervisor. In the sixth month, workbook answers are completed and performance goals are reviewed with the supervisor. Phase I orientation is over and the new hire is awarded a certificate of completion. Phase II orientation begins and continues through the fifteenth month of employment.

Corning's program uses many techniques to help socialize new employees, including interviews, seminars, and workbooks. Information is provided intermittently, rather than in one big chunk, facilitating learning by reducing information overload. New hires at Corning receive frequent periodic feedback from supervisors so they can measure their progress and learn what is valued in the organization. Because ultimate responsibility for orienting employees lies with the supervisor, all supervisors attend a three-hour training workshop on orientation.

Despite the fact that the Corning program is now over a decade old, it is a model for other programs. More recently, as Corning began to hire more mid-career employees, the company recognized the need to address the needs of this group and is modifying its program. The success of the program has been demonstrated by the results of a five-year tracking of employees who used the program and those who did not. Users of the program had a 25 to 35 percent higher retention rate than non-users, which translates into an excellent return on the investment the company makes in the program.[38]

ORIENTATION IN PRACTICE

Research on orientation practices in organizations is extremely limited, but a mid-1980s study by McShane and Baal documented socialization practices on Canada's west coast.[39] The study focussed on 85 of BC's largest public and private corporations, employing a total of 200 000 employees in the province and 600 000 across Canada. Thirty of the organizations had no orientation program; new hires simply reported for work, were documented by the personnel or HRM department, and started their jobs immediately. Twenty-three of the companies had what the authors described as a "basic" orientation program, though twelve of these were "marginal." Basic orientation programs included components such as company brochures, information about wages and benefits, an explanation of the job, an overview of the company and the new hire's place, assignment of a buddy to smooth the way, a formal performance review, and the practice of ongoing feedback. Thirty-two companies had "advanced" orientation programs. These included basic ingredients plus others, such as use of various media, tours, representation of top management, continuation into the work week, and program evaluation by new hires.

Orientation programs were more likely in firms with large numbers of employees and high corporate sales. They were least likely in the manufacturing, processing, product transportation, mining, forestry, and energy industries. Advanced programs were most prevalent in wholesale and retail and in both the public and the private service sectors, including government, hospitals, educational institutions, finance, insurance, communications, and people transportation.

Of the 55 companies in the study with formal programs, 87 percent offered orientation to all employees. Most began it on the first day of employment or within the first two weeks. Sixty percent said they conducted orientation "all at once," in one big session ranging from one hour (10 percent) to four hours (39 percent) to one day (16 percent). Slightly more than one-third said orientation lasted two to five days (14 percent) or one week or more (22 percent). Two-thirds of the programs included follow-up sessions a month or more later to demonstrate interest in the new employee and to elicit concerns and opinions.

It is not clear how many of these programs served to reduce the anxieties of new employees. Only a few of the companies used any type of RJP or tried to clarify expectations in some form of psychological contract. It is clear, however, that much information was conveyed to new hires regarding the organization and their place in it. As Corning and others have found, orientation is an excellent vehicle for communicating corporate culture.[40] Several common corporate themes emerged during orientation in the BC companies. These included the values of teamwork, a pioneering spirit, an emphasis on people, and an emphasis on the customer.[41]

Most orientation programs in the BC companies were established by HRM professionals, who also had responsibility for conducting them. Although HRM professionals co-ordinated programs and provided information about the company, supervisors tended to be responsible for introducing new employees to the job and new department. Current employees played a role in orientation too, though this was found to vary with the job and with whether the company had a formal orientation program. Where no formal program existed, current employees often showed new hires around. Teaming a new hire with an experienced employee was often used to orient employees in the retail sector. The importance of support and guidance from experienced employees was confirmed by the results of a study of the socialization experiences of MBAs.[42] Specifically, supportiveness and guidance from experienced employees were found to be more influential than formal orientation practices in psychological acceptance of the new job and adjustment to the organization.

EVALUATION OF ORIENTATION PROGRAMS

We have seen that HRM professionals are responsible for developing and conducting orientation programs, including preparing and presenting orientation materials. (HRM professionals may also train or instruct supervisors for their role in orientation, but this is considered a training function.) Orientation programs should be evaluated to determine whether they are accomplishing their stated objectives, and this is also a responsibility of HRM professionals. In order to evaluate their programs, many organizations solicit feedback from new hires at the end of orientation sessions. Seventy percent of the BC organizations with formal orientation programs did this either informally or via a questionnaire.[43] Follow-up sessions may offer a better opportunity to elicit feedback from new hires about program effectiveness. By this time they have been on the job for a month or more and have a better perspective from which to judge a program's strengths and weaknesses. Opinions can also be elicited in exit interviews. This source is especially useful in cases of early termination.

Program effectiveness can also be measured against such criteria as training time and turnover rates. For example, Corning measured results of its orientation system by comparing quit rates of two groups of 1981–82 hires: those who attended the orientation seminars and those who did not.[44]

SUMMARY

This chapter has focussed on orientation and how it can serve organizational effectiveness by helping to facilitate socialization of new employees. Effective orientation programs help to reduce anxieties, clarify expectations, and give new employees an overall sense of the organization, its culture, and where they fit in. Although most organizations use some type of orientation procedures, including formal orientation sessions, it is likely that many organizations scratch only the tip of the socialization iceberg. Since the early Texas Instruments example of the benefits of an orientation program that fits newcomers' needs, there have been more examples of successful programs, such as the one at Corning, Inc. There is growing evidence from team-style organizations, like Toyota, that time and effort spent to ensure a good fit between individual needs and the organization's culture can pay off in the form of higher employee commitment, improved quality and productivity, and lower turnover.

REVIEW QUESTIONS

1. Why is orientation important to both employees and employers? Given the importance of orientation, discuss why many employers spend little time or effort on it.

2. Based upon the material and ideas in this chapter, outline the components of an ideal orientation.

3. Discuss the relationship between recruiting/selection and orientation. As recruiting and selection become more in-depth processes, will the need for the acculturation portions of orientation be reduced? How might the state of the labour market affect orientation?

PROJECT IDEAS

1. Recall when you became a new member of an organization or group. What type of orientation did you receive? How long did it last? What

types of experiences did you have during this time? How did you feel about them? How did you know when you were an "accepted member"? Could your orientation and socialization period have been improved? How? Be prepared to discuss your experiences with other class members.

2. Contact two or three organizations and obtain copies of their employee handbooks. (If handbooks are not available, obtain copies of company rules and policies.) What kinds of information are conveyed in the handbooks? What types of employee behaviour are regulated by company rules and policies? Discuss these questions in a written report, comparing the organizations in terms of their philosophies, policies, rules, and procedures.

3. Interview an employer about his or her organization's orientation program. Obtain a description of its nature and goals. Does the employer regard the program as successful? Do formal procedures exist for evaluating it? Include with your report any written materials available about the program.

▶▶▶ CASES

CASE 8.1 ▶ THE EIGHT-WEEK ORIENTATION PROGRAM

Jan Wilklow was delighted to be one of about 200 new employees hired by an international manufacturer of personal products. The hiring process had been long and difficult, involving more than 30 hours of interviews, exercises, an assessment centre, and even three weeks of three class meetings per week. Now, she, along with fifteen other new hires, was about to begin an eight-week orientation — an acculturation process, as the company called it.

As Jan studied the detailed eight-week schedule she had been given, several aspects of it caught her attention. First, every session — each of the 40 scheduled — was to begin with discussion of a safety issue. Indeed, Jan learned later that the emphasis upon safety would not end with orientation; some safety issue was covered at every team meeting, which was held before the start of each work shift.

The second aspect of the schedule that struck Jan as unusual was that most of the sessions were to be held at a nearby technical school, rather than at the plant location. She also noted that the schedule included a variety of unusual activities — including a series titled "Visions of Transformation" — as well as numerous blocks labelled "math" and "participative leadership." The eight-week agenda confirmed what Jan had come to believe early in the hiring process: that this new facility was really something special. She had never heard of a company's spending so much time and effort on hiring and orientation for production workers. And she knew that the orientation period was to be followed by an additional fifteen weeks of on-the-job training.

The first week confirmed Jan's perception of the emphasis placed on safety. Nearly 60 percent of the group's time was devoted to this subject area. For example, they discussed what to do about a company in which people kept getting hurt in work-related accidents. At first, the newcomers suggested drawing up a set of rules and imposing penalties for violation. The leader pointed out, however, that this approach conflicted with the team approach used at the facility. The group then talked about and set standards of expected safety behaviour. Each person was given a pocket-sized manual of safety information, but it contained few real rules, and those it did include were requirements of the Ontario Health and Safety Act.

Another acculturation topic made it clear to the group that racism, sexism, and "classism" did not fit with the team culture of the facility.

An activity that seemed unusual, though typical of the team activities during acculturation, was discussion and critique of the company's hiring process. Jan felt that though management and the HR staff were genuinely interested in the group's feedback and proposals for modification, the primary objective of the exercise was to give everyone experience in using the team approach to discussing and presenting solutions to a process they had all experienced.

Another example of this approach involved coffee at the training facility. At first, the training staff provided coffee, but after a few days the new hires were told they had to arrange among themselves both to provide coffee and to clean up the pot and cups. The group decided to take turns coming in early to start the pot and to be sure coffee, sugar, and cups were on hand. This plan worked for a short while; then someone failed to clean up, and the next day someone else overslept. These failures caused some dissension in the group. The program leaders suggested that their handling of the coffee problem would be a small example of how they must learn to work together to ensure consistent, high-quality performance. The incident also served to point out that the group trusted each person not to fail. The theme of developing group trust continued throughout the eight weeks and was the focal point of a one-day, outdoor "ropes" or obstacle course in the final week.

Other activities during the first week included a discussion of team meetings and their purpose; presentation of the quality philosophy; a plant tour; the issuance of uniforms, safety shoes, and safety glasses; modules on listening; and information about the company, its products, and the facility.

Except for one day given over to first aid and CPR, the second week focussed almost entirely on participative leadership, with emphasis on problem solving and decision making as a group member. The third week was somewhat more diverse; topics included Edward Deming's fourteen points of quality; sexual harassment; child care and the firm's employee assistance program; more health and safety issues, such as back and hand injuries, hearing protection, and hazard communication; more group exercises on team work, success, and normative decision making; and information about how the company's product was made. The teams also worked on *Kaizen*, learning how to work together to make improvements in the performance of various tasks.

The fourth week continued team training, but two days were spent on mathematics and half a day on visiting a major vendor to the plant. Also during the fourth week, to Jan's delight, was a four-hour mini-orientation for the families of the new team members. The visitors were given a brief tour and then an explanation of the plant's philosophy and goals, as well as the company's benefits and how the rotating shifts worked.

The fifth week emphasized reading blueprints, math (to be sure the employees could use statistical process controls), and measurements. Like the third and fourth weeks, it ended with a Friday-afternoon team meeting. The sixth week was devoted to learning more math, the principles of electricity, and general maintenance. It too ended with a team meeting. The work-oriented focus continued in the seventh week with three days of analytical trouble-shooting training and two days on using hand and power tools. The eighth and final week covered lubrication of equipment, the one-day ropes course, job safety analysis, a videotape on the psychology of winning, and a module on working to resolve issues.

"Visions of Transformation" turned out to be a series of tapes, exercises, lectures, and discussions aimed at changing employees' attitudes and values. The company sought to replace the attitudes and values formed by previous work experiences to ones of safety, trust, teamwork, and quality.

At the end of the eight weeks, Jan felt she had learned a tremendous amount about the work she would be doing and also about herself and how to work with others. She was greatly impressed with how much the company valued her and all the team members. She was ready and eager to start the fifteen-week on-the-job training.

Source: This program is used by a leading North American personal products manufacturer.

TASKS AND QUESTIONS

1. What are the major goals of and areas covered in this orientation program? Given that this company is a major player in a highly competitive product market, do you feel this type of program is appropriate?

2. After describing the eight-week orientation program to an HR manager from an auto parts company, the HR manager for the company in the case was told, "You must be nuts to pay people and not get any production from them for eight weeks." Do you agree with the auto parts HR manager? What are your predictions for absenteeism, turnover, and

productivity of the facility in its first year of operation? What is the basis for these predictions?

3. Should or can all employers use an orientation program of this magnitude? Why or why not?

CASE 8.2 ▸ FIREFIGHTING DROPOUTS

One hundred firefighters are employed by the fire department of River Falls, which has three stations in the city of nearly 70 000. The department's record is good: its inspection and prevention program has reduced fire hazards substantially, and it has received commendation from the mayor for promptness of response to emergencies and for firefighting effectiveness. Morale and esprit de corps run high among River Falls' firefighters; they are a proud, cohesive bunch who often socialize with one another in their off-duty hours.

Applicants for the fire department's few annual openings must score well on a battery of firefighting knowledge tests, rigorous physical and agility tests, and an interview by a board of city officials, including the fire chief and one experienced firefighter. Applicants are hired on a six-month probationary basis; their performance is rated after one, three, and six months by the lieutenant and captain of their station. New firefighters undergo rigorous training but receive only a short orientation, including a tour of fire department facilities and a discussion of daily schedules.

The human resources director of River Falls, Roger Cameron, has noticed that 15 to 20 percent of newly hired firefighters do not survive the probationary period. Cameron, who has been at River Falls a little more than two years, first noticed this phenomenon six months ago when he interviewed Georgio Candino, a firefighter who quit after two and half months. As a job applicant, Candino had performed well on both ability and physical tests and had good interview ratings. Candino didn't have much to say at the time of his exit interview, except to suggest that he had not been well accepted by the other firefighters.

This incident made Cameron curious. He checked personnel records for the previous five years and found six additional quits and two dismissals of firefighters within the probationary period. Records also showed a number of complaints regarding tricks played on new firefighters, such as salted orange juice, boots lined with sludge, and fake assignments. For example, it was common practice to tell recruits they were being sent to fight a fire, when actually they were being sent to help a cat out of a tree. The department generally ignored such complaints, viewing the pranks as a natural part of the initiation process.

Cameron noticed that most such complaints were filed by firefighters who quit or were dismissed during the probationary period. Although many of the tricks were harmless attempts to humiliate or "test" new recruits, some were potentially hazardous to a firefighter's safety. For example, Candino had once had the middle finger cut off one of his safety gloves. Another time, a firefighter reached for his hat only to find it had been used as a bedpan.

Where matters of safety were concerned, the department generally took notice; more than once in the past it had posted a cautionary warning that disciplinary action would be taken against the offender if health and safety were compromised. No discipline was ever initiated, however, because the department was unable to identify the responsible party; no one would admit to pulling the pranks, and group norms made squealing unthinkable.

Cameron realizes that hazing is a common part of initiating new members of organizations and groups, but he wonders if something should be done about it in the fire department.

TASKS AND QUESTIONS

1. What key questions might Cameron seek answers to in order to determine whether something should be done about hazing in the fire department?

2. Assume you are Cameron. Weigh the pros and cons of hazing new firefighters. Why might experienced firefighters want to haze recruits?

3. What actions might Cameron take to control hazing or minimize its effect on new firefighters?

4. What effects might rules regulating hazing have on new firefighters? on experienced firefighters? on the fire department as a whole?

NOTES

1. C. Cosentino, J. Allen, and R. Wellins, "Choosing the Right People," *HRMagazine*, vol. 35, no. 3 (March 1991), p. 70. Reprinted with the permission of *HRMagazine* (formerly *Personnel Administrator*), published by the Society for Human Resource Management, Alexandria, Va.

2. R. Pascale, "Fitting New Employees into the Company Culture," *Fortune*, May 28, 1984, pp. 28–43.

3. See D. Ulrich and D. Lake, *Organizational Capability* (New York: John Wiley and Sons, 1990); J.P. Kotter, *A Force for Change: How Leadership Differs from Management* (New York: The Free Press, 1990); B.B. Tregoe, J.W. Zimmerman, R.A. Smith, and P.M. Tobia, *Vision in Action* (New York: Simon and Schuster, 1989); and M. Beer, R.A. Eisenstat, and B. Spector, *The Critical Path to Corporate Renewal* (Boston: Harvard Business School Press, 1990).

4. Pascale, "Fitting New Employees into the Company Culture."

5. E.R. Gommersall and M.S. Myers, "Breakthrough in On-the-job Training," *Harvard Business Review*, vol. 44 (July–August 1966), pp. 62–71.

6. J. Price and C. Mueller, *Absenteeism and Turnover of Hospital Employees* (Greenwich, Conn.: JAI Press, 1986).
7. Z.B. Leibowitz, N.K. Schlossberg, and J.E. Shore, "Stopping the Revolving Door," *Training and Development Journal*, vol. 45, no. 2 (1991), pp. 43–50.
8. E.J. McGarrell, Jr., "An Orientation System That Builds Productivity," *Personnel*, November–December 1983, pp. 32–41; and Leibowitz, Schlossberg, and Shore, "Stopping the Revolving Door," pp. 47–49.
9. McGarrell, Jr., "An Orientation System."
10. C.A. O'Reilly III, J. Chatman, and D.F. Caldwell, "People and Organizational Culture: A Profile Comparison Approach to Assessing Person–Organization Fit," *Academy of Management Journal*, vol. 34, no. 3 (1991), p. 511.
11. E.H. Schein, *Career Dynamics: Matching Individual and Organizational Needs* (Reading, Mass.: Addison-Wesley, 1978).
12. J. Van Maanen, "Breaking In: A Consideration of Organizational Socialization," in R. Dubin, ed., *Handbook of Work, Organization, and Society* (Chicago: Rand-McNally, 1975).
13. Schein, *Career Dynamics*, p. 81.
14. E.C. Hughes, *Men and Their Work* (Glencoe, Ill.: Free Press, 1958).
15. Schein, *Career Dynamics*, pp. 94–95. © 1978 by Addison-Wesley Publishing Company, Reading, Mass. Reprinted with the permission of the publisher.
16. Schein, *Career Dynamics*, p. 97.
17. D.W. Bray, R.J. Campbell, and D.L. Grant, *Formative Years in Business* (New York: Wiley, 1974); and D. Berlew and D.T. Hall, "The Socialization of Managers," *Administrative Science Quarterly*, vol. 11 (1966), pp. 207–23.
18. Schein, *Career Dynamics*, p. 99.
19. Pascale, "Fitting New Employees into the Company Culture."
20. Schein, *Career Dynamics*, p. 99.
21. Schein, *Career Dynamics*, p. 99.
22. Gommersall and Myers, "Breakthrough in On-the-Job Training."
23. Gommersall and Myers, "Breakthrough in On-the-Job Training."
24. McGarrell, Jr., "An Orientation System."
25. J. Weitz, "Job Expectancy and Survival," *Journal of Applied Psychology*, vol. 40 (1956), pp. 245–47.
26. J.P. Wanous, "Effects of a Realistic Job Preview on Job Acceptance, Job Attitudes, and Job Survival," *Journal of Applied Psychology*, vol. 58 (1973), pp. 327–32; and "Organizational Entry: Newcomers Moving from Outside to Inside," *Psychological Bulletin*, vol. 84 (1977), pp. 601–18.
27. Wanous, "Organizational Entry"; and J.P. Wanous, *Organization Entry: Recruitment, Selection, and Socialization of Newcomers* (Reading, Mass.: Addison-Wesley, 1980).

28. S.L. Premack and J.P. Wanous, "A Meta-analysis of Realistic Job Preview Experiments," *Journal of Applied Psychology*, vol. 70 (1985), pp. 706–19.
29. G.M. McEvoy and W.F. Cascio, "Strategies for Reducing Employee Turnover: A Meta-analysis," *Journal of Applied Psychology*, vol. 70 (1985), pp. 342–53.
30. B.M. Meglino, A.S. DeNisi, S.A. Youngblood, and K.J. Williams, "Effects of Realistic Job Previews: A Comparison Using an 'Enhancement' and a 'Reduction' Preview," *Journal of Applied Psychology*, vol. 73 (1988), pp. 259–66.
31. S.L. McShane and T. Baal, *Employee Socialization Practices on Canada's West Coast: A Management Report* (Burnaby, BC: Simon Fraser University, December 1984). Reprinted with permission.
32. [U.S.] Bureau of National Affairs, "ASPA-BNA Survey No. 32 Employee Orientation Programs," *Bulletin to Management*, August 25, 1977.
33. [U.S.] Bureau of National Affairs, "Employee Orientation Programs"; and McShane and Baal, *Employee Socialization Practices*.
34. [U.S.] Bureau of National Affairs, "Employee Orientation Programs."
35. [U.S.] Bureau of National Affairs, "Employee Orientation Programs."
36. [U.S.] Bureau of National Affairs, "Employee Orientation Programs."
37. McGarrell, Jr., "An Orientation System."
38. Leibowitz, Schlossberg, and Shore, "Stopping the Revolving Door," p. 49.
39. McShane and Baal, *Employee Socialization Practices*.
40. McGarrell, Jr., "An Orientation System."
41. McShane and Baal, *Employee Socialization Practices*.
42. G.R. Jones, "Socialization Tactics, Self-Efficacy, and Newcomers' Adjustments to Organizations," *Academy of Management Journal*, vol. 29 (1986), pp. 262–79.
43. Jones, "Socialization Tactics."
44. McGarrell, Jr., "An Orientation System."

SUGGESTIONS FOR FURTHER READING

☐ D. Arthur. *Recruiting, Interviewing, Selecting and Orienting New Employees*. New York: AMACOM, 1986.

☐ C.D. Fisher. "Organizational Socialization: An Integrative Review." In K.M. Rowland and G.R. Ferris, eds., *Research in Personnel and Human Resource Management*, vol. 4. Greenwich, Conn.: JAI Press, 1986.

☐ J.P. Wanous and A. Colella. "Organizational Entry Research: Current Status and Future Directions." In G.R. Ferris and K.M. Rowland, eds., *Organizational Entry*. Greenwich, Conn.: JAI Press, 1990.

CHAPTER 9

TRAINING AND DEVELOPMENT

- THE GROWTH OF TRAINING AND DEVELOPMENT
- THE ROLE OF T&D IN ORGANIZATIONAL STRATEGY AND EFFECTIVENESS
- RELATION TO OTHER HRM FUNCTIONS
- RESPONSIBILITIES FOR TRAINING AND DEVELOPMENT
- DETERMINING TRAINING AND DEVELOPMENT NEEDS
- SPECIFYING TRAINING OBJECTIVES
- CHOOSING A TRAINING PROGRAM
- TRAINING AND DEVELOPMENT METHODS AND AIDS
- HRM IN ACTION ▸ BEYOND INTERACTIVE VIDEO: VIRTUAL REALITY
- IMPLEMENTING THE TRAINING PROGRAM
- TRAINING PROGRAMS IN PRACTICE
- EVALUATING THE TRAINING PROGRAM
- SUMMARY
- REVIEW QUESTIONS
- PROJECT IDEAS
- CASE 9.1 ▸ TRAINING AND DEVELOPMENT AT DELI-DELITE
- CASE 9.2 ▸ ORGANIZATION OF TRAINING FOR NORTHERN TELECOM TEAMS
- NOTES
- SUGGESTIONS FOR FURTHER READING

"WE TOOK TWO RELATIVELY OLDER PULP MILLS, upgraded them and married them to an ultra-modern paper machine. Now look at this facility, it's world-class. The pulp mill has a future, the area has a future, and there's a lot of people learning new technology and they're doing it well."[1] The Repap Enterprises executive vice-president was referring to the summer 1986 start-up of a new coated-paper mill and the updating of two old pulp mills in the Miramichi Valley of northeastern New Brunswick. From an organizational strategy perspective, the acquisition and updating of the older pulp mills enabled Repap to complete a "backwards" integration into producing the raw materials needed to manufacture coated paper.

While the high-tech production and control equipment was being installed, Repap was conducting a massive training program. Almost every job in the three-mill operation required retraining. Unlike many firms that do major plant remodelling and build new facilities, Repap had made a commitment to give priority to the existing work force. This commitment was especially challenging since many of the pulp mill employees were older, poorly educated workers, and some had literacy problems. Jobs at the new mill were attractive since the classifications and wages would be high. Not surprisingly, most of the 400 current employees applied for the approximately 100 paper mill jobs.

Since much of the equipment and technology was being custom-tailored for Miramichi, there was considerable ambiguity about the content of jobs and who would occupy them. This uncertainty, of course, made it difficult to specify the content and design of the training programs. By early 1986, however, the classification system had been finalized, and the content of jobs and specification of who would hold them were resolved.

The traditional approach to training for a new or modernized facility is a top-down approach in which vendors, engineers, and plant supervisors train operators, generally teaching them only what they need to know to do a particular job. Repap Miramichi rejected this approach in favour of a train-the-trainer method, which would develop a substantial core of workers with superior technical expertise as well as strong employee involvement. A set of sixteen trainers for operators and twelve for maintenance was selected. Actually, nearly 80 employees ended up receiving trainer training courses, and this approach was later adopted at a Repap Wisconsin plant to improve the skills of experienced paper workers.

Trainer training involved two major areas: preparing the course materials, and learning training and communication techniques. Neither task was easy because the trainers, having come from pulp mills, had no papermaking experience. The courses were created with material from the mills' managers, personnel from Repap's Wisconsin plant, vendor manuals (some of which were in Portuguese, since much of the equipment had been made in Brazil), and engineering material. Trainers were given sessions covering teaching techniques, job analysis, blueprint reading, and manual writing. Working with them were members of a training materials production crew comprising a technical writer, a graphic artist, word-processing operators, and video technicians. Some material was videotaped both to supplement live presentations and for later use.

The pulp mill employees selected as trainers learned their teaching skills by giving lessons to each other. The result was cross-training (learning about tasks and jobs other than your own), an outcome consistent with the company's commitment to multiple skills. Employees were to be trained for both their own position and the next two higher jobs. This approach facilitated everyone's understanding of the operation and created a more versatile and promotable work force.[2]

What does this short case tell us about training and development in the 1990s? At least six points can be made. First, training and development activities are a vitally important part of Repap's business strategy. Without well-trained, motivated employees, the backwards integration strategy would not prove cost-effective. A second and related point is that training is crucial both to bringing about change in organizations and to operating a truly world-class manufacturing facility.

Third, Repap's management philosophy of commitment to its current work force led to the extensive training program, rather than layoffs and hiring new workers. A fourth and related point is that Repap's commitment was strong enough to meet the challenges of a poorly educated, older work force, some of whom were illiterate. Progressive employers are realizing that the loyalty, commitment, and good will of both employees and the community that are created by modernizing old plants and retraining older employees can outweigh the short-run savings of plant shutdowns and relocation. A fifth point is reflected in Repap's choice of the train-the-trainer approach. This participative approach is typical of progressive employers who realize that the key to high productivity, high quality, and innovation is a highly trained and motivated work force.

Finally, this case suggests the distinction between training and development. *Training* can be defined as any organizationally planned effort to change the behaviour or attitudes of employees to facilitate meeting job performance standards. Repap went beyond training in having production employees serve as trainers and giving employees both cross-training and training for higher-level jobs. Training for a future job is *development*. It has been described as a long-term process, a broadening and stretching experience that can create generalists and facilitates strategic thinking, thus serving the interests of both the organization and the employee.[3] Development helps an employer to have the flexible and innovative work force necessary to compete in a global economy. At the same time, an employee with an array of knowledge and skills is less likely to be unemployed than one who knows only one job.

This chapter examines both macro- and micro-level aspects of training. It begins by discussing the growth of training and development (T&D), the role T&D plays in organizational strategy and effectiveness, and how it relates to other HRM functions. The chapter then turns to more micro-level issues, such as who is responsible for training, identifying training needs, choosing training methods, and implementing and evaluating programs.

THE GROWTH OF TRAINING AND DEVELOPMENT

Training and development is growing as an HRM function and has become an industry itself. Virtually all employers conduct some form of training, with informal, on-the-job training being the most common. Large employers, particularly those in high-tech and/or very competitive industries, spend at least 2 to 5 percent of payroll each year on T&D. One source estimates that U.S. employers spend $210 billion annually for training.[4] IBM, which probably spends more on training than any other company, had expenditures of more than $1.5 billion in 1990.[5] A recent Conference Board of Canada study of 444 medium- to large-sized firms found T&D expenditures were $450 per employee, with larger and high return-on-investment (ROI) firms spending even more. The five firms with the largest T&D budgets, which ranged from 1.8 to 7.2 percent of payroll, included Royal Bank, IBM, BC Telephone, BC Hydro, and Xerox Canada. In addition, the Board study found that T&D budgets grew in the late 1980s and are growing faster than T&D budgets in the U.S.[6] Canadian federal government programs spent $945.2 million in 1987/88.[7] Another demonstration of the growth and importance of training was the 1979 founding of the Canadian Society for Training and Development; it grew out of earlier established societies in British Columbia, Alberta, Manitoba, Ontario, and Atlantic Canada.

What are the factors that have contributed to the growth of T&D? Will these and/or additional factors continue and further the growth of the area?

The first factor is the role T&D plays in attaining the organization's strategic goals. Not every organization recognizes this potential. As one study puts the matter:

> All too often training and development are the caboose on the corporate train. Training discussions occur after an important capital or process decision is made. . . . Training professionals have a legitimate place at the table when strategic issues are discussed.[8]

Elsewhere, we have discussed the turbulent conditions faced by many businesses in the 1980s. Their strategies for survival have included downsizing, improvement of quality and productivity, innovation, and upgraded customer service. Inevitably, these strategies demand that both employees and managers think and behave in new ways. T&D plays a tremendously large role in assuring the successful implementation of business strategy. (Naturally, other HRM functions, such as staffing, compensation, and performance appraisal, are also important.) T&D, in addition to providing the knowledge and skill needed for organizational change, is often used to communicate and to sell people on the need for change.

A second factor leading to T&D's growth is the attitudes of management toward human resources. From roots in Abraham Maslow's self-actualization theory to current notions of empowerment and team-style management, progressive managers have come to realize the enormous potential of a highly educated, trained, and motivated work force. At Honda, for example, top executives believe that "all learning stems from values." From adherence to a set of values, trust between the company and employees is established. Honda spokespeople explain:

> Values and trust establish the preconditions that encourage individuals to think, experiment, and improve. It follows that learning organizations share, above all else, an abiding commitment to people and a faith in the human capacity to find a better way.[9]

Many other companies are also taking an empowerment approach to their employees. Such an approach means that managers view human resources as a valued resource that can yield excellent returns *if* they invest in their employees and allow them to think and improve.

Meanwhile, a third factor is operating: technological change is destroying and creating new jobs at an astonishing rate. As we saw in the case of Repap, modernization is radically changing old jobs, and employees must learn new skills and knowledge. When jobs changed radically in the past, many employers simply laid off older, "redundant" employees and hired new, usually younger workers. This wasteful approach to human resources may have been possible in previous decades, but the demographics of the 1990s make it much more difficult.

The changing demographics of the labour force are a fourth factor contributing to the importance of training and development. As we discussed in Chapter 2, the growth rate of the labour force has declined by nearly half since the 1960s. The result is labour shortages for many kinds of work, particularly for skilled and professional jobs. Additionally, the education and skills of many seeking employment are often inadequate. Employers, therefore, are now engaging in basic skills training as well as retraining.

A number of recent societal changes and phenomena have generated a fifth set of factors leading to more T&D, involving new areas or emphases. They include:

1. Cross-cultural training. The growth and increasing sophistication of international trade has created a need for training that provides North American employees with knowledge of facts and customs of the countries and cultures in which they will be working. (And, of course, organizations in Japan, Korea, France, and other foreign countries need to train their employees to cope with North American culture.)

2. Stress management training. As our society has become more complex and fast-moving and as the proportion of dual-career couples has grown, stress has become common. Employees must learn to "manage" it in order to minimize its damaging effects.

3. Wellness training. Just as employers are becoming increasingly concerned with controlling the rising costs of health care, more people want to be physically fit and to maintain a healthy lifestyle. One result has been a growing number of employer-sponsored programs on how to prevent heart disease, reduce cancer risk, lose weight, and avoid accidents. (Recall from previous chapters that safety was one of the major themes of the orientation training of the major personal products manufacturer in Case 8.1, and that Honda's first operating priority is safety.)

4. Combating sexual and racial harassment. Changing societal attitudes, as well as federal and provincial legislation, mean that employees and managers must be taught the meaning of harassment, what behaviour constitutes harassment, and how to deal with such incidents.

The sixth and final factor increasing T&D is the growing role of government in training. A study of Ontario in the mid-1980s found that government-sponsored training programs lasted nearly five times as long as employer-sponsored programs.[10] The pattern of funding and program emphasis has alternated between periods of growth and economic stabilization; recessions have led to programs of job creation and training the unemployed, while periods of rapid growth have produced programs to reduce labour shortages. Government programs can also easily direct specific portions of funds to designated groups, such as women, visible minorities, people with disabilities, and Native people. By providing increased training and work experience for members of such groups, these programs contribute to their employment equity.

THE ROLE OF T&D IN ORGANIZATIONAL STRATEGY AND EFFECTIVENESS

How does the training and development function contribute to organizational strategies and goal attainment? There are several answers because goals may be individual, organizational, or societal—or some combination of the three.

From the individual's perspective, human capital theory predicts that education, training, and development are valuable investments that yield returns such as higher expected income and greater employment security.[11] World economic and demographic trends are combining to put even greater pressure on those who lack basic and marketable skills. As one commentator says:

> Over the next 20 years the working age population in developing countries will rise by roughly 700 million—just about equal to the total current population of North America, Japan and Western Europe. Unskilled workers in the rich nations can expect that growth to exert a downward pressure on their wages.[12]

Jobs will flow to these nations, labour will migrate to the developed nations, or both. The recruiting problems of many Canadian organizations underline the value of all forms of learning, for both individuals and employers. So does the everyday experience of trying to find a good doctor, plumber, carpenter, or auto mechanic. Those with the knowledge and skill of their profession or trade are always in demand; the less competent are unlikely to draw many repeat customers.

At the organizational level, the role of training ranges from the basic goal of providing employees with the knowledge and skills necessary to perform to acceptable standards on their jobs to empowering workers so they can make decisions, solve problems, and tell management how to change the company.[13] It is appropriate to consider the role of training in achieving quality—a goal of such well-known employers as Xerox, Honda, and Motorola. W. Edwards Deming, a quality expert who taught top management in Japan in 1950, has suggested fourteen points for transforming American industry. Two of them are to "institute training" and to "institute a vigorous program of education and self-improvement."[14] He contends that workers should be taught the correct and best way to do their work the first time. (This suggests the use of well-qualified trainers, not just fellow workers who have not been trained how to train.) A related point is "drive out fear." Deming argues there is widespread resistance to knowledge, as new knowledge may reveal failings of the company.[15]

Another writer, who worked with Dr. Deming for many years, argues that many firms don't appreciate the benefits of training.[16] For example, some Canadian employers prefer to hire an experienced worker from the outside — often an immigrant — in order to avoid the time and expense of training. Some also fear that if they train an employee, he or she will leave, using the training elsewhere.[17] Yet immigration policy seems to vary with supply and demand for various types of skilled workers. And training can inspire great loyalty to an employer.

The strategic goal of high-quality products or service has led to many training programs. One of the best-known and most widely used programs in the world is the Crosby quality program. Essential parts of it are education and training for everyone from a company's top executives to its lowest-level employees.[18] Clearly, quality is but one example of an important organizational goal that cannot be successfully pursued without a substantial and continuing commitment to T&D. And quality has become a vital part of competitive strategy for organizations from "mom and pop" businesses to international giants. The link between the value of T&D to individuals and organizational goals is seen in the Honda motto: "Quality is our job security."

Another strategic goal for both employers and the Canadian economy is innovation. A 1987 study by the Economic Council of Canada (ECC) found that though retraining is an obvious and necessary organizational response to technological change, Canadian industry generally undertrains.[19] For example, retraining in response to the introduction of new technology was often very brief. The ECC researchers found, however, several examples of employers — including an aircraft engine manufacturer and a federal government publications bureau — that demonstrated how much a well-trained work force can fully exploit new technology. The authors concluded:

> Canada has no choice but to embrace technological change to survive. . . . However, to fully, rapidly and fairly exploit the potential benefits of technological change, Canada needs a cohesive program of labour market adjustment to develop a well-trained labour force in tandem with new technology.[20]

A recent survey of business and labour leaders by the Canadian Labour Market and Productivity Centre found that 60 percent of them saw education and training as either the most important or the second-most important factor in improving international competitiveness. On the other hand, some studies say only 30 percent of employers provide training.[21] Another source, which includes tuition assistance, time off, and formal courses from schools, trainers, and other sources as "training," claims 70 percent of employers provide some form of assistance.[22] (The apparent contradiction may be partly a matter of definition.) A Canadian Chamber of Commerce study found that one reason more companies don't train is the significant cost.[23] Perhaps the best reply to this finding is captured on a bumper sticker on a teacher's car: "If you think education is expensive, consider the costs of ignorance."

So far this section has discussed how T&D is an important part of individual, organizational, and even national goals and strategies. One can also view T&D in terms of how it can contribute to organizational effectiveness. For example, the availability of training and development opportunities can facilitate recruiting. Training and development can also be an important employee benefit for the retention of workers who value opportunities for growth and advancement. To the extent training is effective at raising performance levels, there should also be less need to dismiss employees for unacceptable performance.

Management may also seek to improve the effectiveness of an organization via a program of organization development, which makes use of various types of training methods. *Organization development (OD)* is a long-term process of changing employees' attitudes and behaviour so that members of the organization can interact better. By improving interpersonal relations within the organization, OD seeks to improve the effectiveness of an organization's operation and its ability to cope with change. Organization development programs are usually part of a larger program to create major changes in an organization. In such organization change programs, outside consultants and top management work with HRM managers to develop and implement training and OD programs. Some employers have instituted OD programs to improve employee relations, deter unionization, and reduce turnover.

One successful OD program used a variety of training methods and devices to reduce excessive turnover among blue-collar workers.[24] As part of an initial diagnosis of the company's ills, an investigation by outside consultants revealed that workers were troubled by poor pay and unsympathetic management. A first step, then, was for consultants to give managers feedback on worker attitudes in these areas. Based on this discussion, managers decided they should participate in a two-day team-building workshop to gain a more accurate picture of themselves and how they were seen by others. This workshop made use of a number of exercises, as well as the modelling of pertinent behaviour. After the team-building workshop, a supervisory-skills workshop was held for production managers who were very high in the unpopular "Theory X" (autocratic) management style. After these managers explored different supervisory styles via lecture-discussions and films, they role-played critical incidents at the plant. A number of blue-collar workers attended the workshop (but did not participate), and it was helpful for them to see their supervisors making honest attempts to improve. The authors who reported on this program noted a marked reduction in turnover among employees with a tenure of one month or more. They also noted much more positive job attitudes as a result of the intervention. However, some of the increased satisfaction may have resulted from pay raises that were approved during the time of intervention.

RELATION TO OTHER HRM FUNCTIONS

Figure 9.1 demonstrates the relationship of training and development to other HRM functions. For new employees, training follows orientation and precedes performance review. For current employees, performance appraisals often precede training, identifying those with performance deficiencies who could benefit from training and those whose potential makes them candidates for development.

Four HRM functions other than orientation provide direct inputs to training and development: job analysis, performance appraisal, selection, and career planning. Job analysis describes the activities and behaviours necessary to perform a job. The objective of the training program is to master these activities and behaviours. For example, according to the job description of a shipping clerk, Jane Simpson must pack parts for shipment. Thus, one objective of Simpson's training program is to master part-packing. The performance appraisal function, by specifying acceptable standards of performance, prescribes the level of performance necessary to master the required behaviour or activity. If a performance criterion were attached to Simpson's training objective, it might read: employee must be able to pack parts for shipment *at the rate of six per minute without causing any breakage*. The italicized portion of this objective indicates the level of performance necessary to master the required activity.

After training and some time on the job, an employee is usually evaluated in terms of performance. Such appraisals can serve as criteria for measuring the success of training programs. If, for example, after three months' employment Simpson is having difficulty performing her duties, this may indicate that her training program was not altogether successful. Of course, her poor performance may be caused by factors unrelated to the training program. For example, she may be poorly motivated, or perhaps her job is too difficult and should be simplified.

Selection information can be used to identify and place employees in appropriate training programs. For example, test scores or interviews often reveal strengths and weaknesses of newly hired employees. Recently, the distinction between selection and training has become blurred as numerous employers, such as Nissan, Toyota, Mazda, and Kimberly-Clark, have required applicants to take part in various types of training. Inclusion of training activities in the screening process reflects the importance many employers are placing on hiring people who are willing and able to learn. It is also an acknowledgement of the fact that jobs in competitive businesses

FIGURE 9.1
Training and Development: Relation to Other HRM Functions

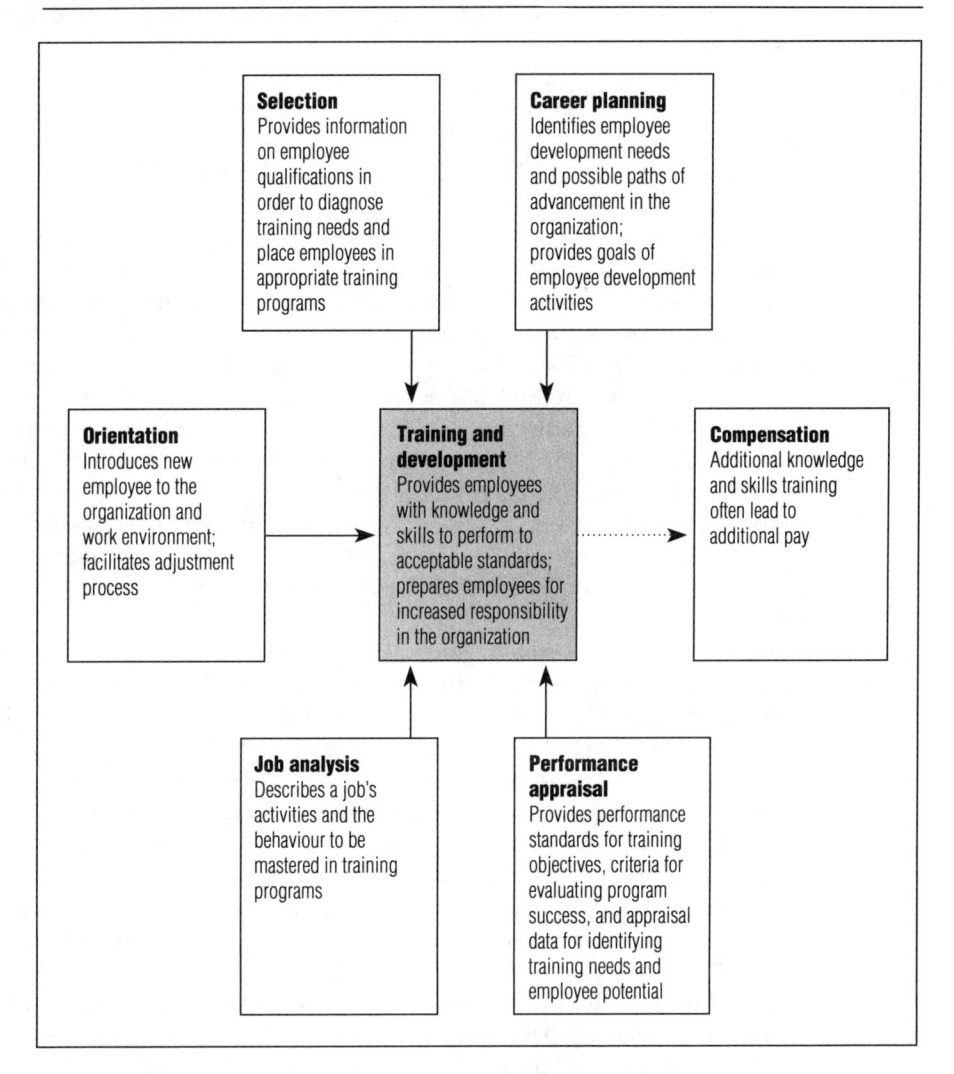

Selection
Provides information on employee qualifications in order to diagnose training needs and place employees in appropriate training programs

Career planning
Identifies employee development needs and possible paths of advancement in the organization; provides goals of employee development activities

Orientation
Introduces new employee to the organization and work environment; facilitates adjustment process

Training and development
Provides employees with knowledge and skills to perform to acceptable standards; prepares employees for increased responsibility in the organization

Compensation
Additional knowledge and skills training often lead to additional pay

Job analysis
Describes a job's activities and the behaviour to be mastered in training programs

Performance appraisal
Provides performance standards for training objectives, criteria for evaluating program success, and appraisal data for identifying training needs and employee potential

are not static and demand that employees learn and adapt to new requirements.

With regard to development, the career planning function identifies employee development needs and possible paths of advancement through the organization.

Finally, training and development are indirectly and sometimes directly related to compensation. Generally, higher levels of skill, knowledge, and education are associated with higher levels of pay. In Chapter 12, you will read about skill- or knowledge-based pay systems, which directly tie employees' job-relevant knowledge and skills to their pay level. This approach is very consistent with team-based management and facilitates employers' flexibility.

RESPONSIBILITIES FOR TRAINING AND DEVELOPMENT

Responsibilities for training and development are typically shared among HRM professionals and supervisory and management personnel. While supervisors and managers are responsible for making sure that employees in their departments are properly trained and developed, HRM professionals have major responsibility for training programs. A point to remember is that conflict can arise between the HRM department, which wants to assist employee development and promotion, and the operating department, which is concerned with production and the continuity of its employees. Some operating departments resent "intrusion" by the HRM department. To avoid such a conflict, HRM staff must demonstrate to operating departments the benefits of development programs. (This problem does not arise in many leading-edge firms, however, since their operations personnel work closely with T&D staff.)

Supervisors and managers generally participate in the training function by identifying training needs in their departments and by providing informal training and development for their subordinates. The supervisor's role is an important one. Long after formal training is over, the supervisor remains to communicate and reinforce appropriate work behaviours. Serving as a role model, the boss conveys verbal and nonverbal messages about organizational norms and values. He or she also assigns tasks and provides feedback on the adequacy of performance and what can be done to improve it. (The supervisor's important role in employee development is discussed further in Chapters 10 and 11, on career planning and performance appraisal.)

The Conference Board of Canada study of T&D found that 57 percent of responding firms had a separate T&D department. Larger employers were more likely to have separate departments, and the average firm allocated 0.4 percent of their staff to T&D. Thus, a typical firm with 1120 employees would have T&D staff of 4 full-time employees. Supporting the importance of T&D discussed earlier, most respondents indicated that their T&D staffs either remained constant or had grown over the previous two years. The report also found that T&D was organized as a centralized rather than a decentralized function in two-thirds of the firms. However, a number of employers, such as BC Hydro, were strong proponents of a decentralized staff, and decentralized divisional staffs were growing faster than corporate staffs. In firms with separate T&D departments, the function usually reports to a vice-president of HR or in some cases the CEO of the firm.

The study also found that the relationship between line management and the T&D staff has changed over time. The relationship has evolved from one in which line managers had little input or control over the content or delivery of training to one in which training staff work with line managers as their customers, doing what line managers need to meet business challenges and opportunities. This means that line managers have greater input into determining training needs, as well as the methods of delivery. Specifically, T&D staff handle almost half of design and delivery activities, outside consultants handle about a third, and line management is involved in the remainder. Finally, organizations are split on the practice of rotating line managers through the T&D function. While it is desirable to give T&D staff the perspectives and experience of line assignments and to give line managers T&D experiences, a rotation policy can lead to a training department "staffed by line 'experts' who are 'amateurs' in training." Some larger organizations are able to have the ideal combination of some training experts and also have some rotation.[25]

Five major responsibilities for training and development form the framework for this chapter. They are (1) determining training and development needs; (2) specifying training objectives; (3) choosing a training program; (4) implementing the program; and (5) evaluating the program.

DETERMINING TRAINING AND DEVELOPMENT NEEDS

Although the total number of Canadian organizations involved in T&D activities is not known, the Ontario Training Corporation has compiled a database called SkillsLink. This database has more than 71 000 listings from 1 200 training organizations in Ontario.[26] Despite the apparent wide availability of training resources, many training needs go unmet, especially at the supervisory level. It is not uncommon for an employee with no supervisory experience to be promoted to supervise a number of employees. Though many prepackaged training programs exist for supervisors and managers in areas such as decision making, problem solving, motivating employees, and setting goals, new supervisors often do not receive any supervisory skills training until after they have been in their jobs for some time.

On the other hand, a considerable amount of needless training takes place. It occurs for several reasons: (1) management identifies a performance deficiency and incorrectly labels it as a problem that can be remedied through a training program; (2) employees are taught material or skills they already know; and/or (3) an existing, popular training program is purchased by an organization and used, whether or not it satisfies an identified training or development need. The Conference Board study found an example of questionable training in the common practice of allowing employees to choose courses from a catalogue and a line manager approving it with little or no consideration of actual need. Additionally, some line managers still use training as a reward for desired behaviour, rather than as a means of changing behaviour.[27]

Unmet training and development needs can be identified, and needless, inappropriate training eliminated if a thorough training-needs assessment is conducted. The purpose of any such assessment is to discover and describe any individual, unit, or organizational performance problem for which training is an appropriate solution. Such a problem may be anticipated, as in the case of the introduction of new technology or of organizational restructuring. A training need exists whenever current or expected performance problems are caused by employees' deficiencies in knowledge or skills.

IDENTIFYING NEEDS

HRM professionals identify training and development needs by (1) monitoring organizational information, such as human resource flows and policy and procedural changes that affect the nature of jobs; (2) asking supervisors and managers about the training and development needs of their subordinates; and (3) accepting and analyzing training requests from managers and others.

Many training needs can be anticipated and identified by monitoring organizational information. For example, by monitoring the flow of employees into and through the organization, HRM professionals can identify the training needs of employees who are new, newly transferred, promoted, or bumped to lower-level jobs. Bumping to lower-level jobs sometimes occurs in unionized firms when layoffs are necessary. Because workers with less seniority are laid off first, vacancies sometimes occur in their typically lower-level positions. These vacancies must be filled by workers with greater seniority, many of whom formerly occupied higher-level positions. The need to train even "bumped-down" workers is illustrated by the story of an employee who was demoted to a job of machining burrs off connecting rods at a tractor manufacturing company. The employee did $25 000 worth of product damage his first day on the new job.[28]

Monitoring career planning information is helpful in determining the development needs of individual employees. Career planning identifies possible paths of advancement in the organization and also employee career goals. Performance appraisal information and selection data can also be used to identify likely candidates for promotion. When training needs are identified in advance of new assignments, development programs can be initiated to prepare employees for assuming new job responsibilities.

Training needs that come from changes in jobs can be identified and anticipated by monitoring policy and procedural changes which affect jobs. Changes such as the introduction of higher quality standards or new or additional work procedures and equipment require accommodation by employees, and often some training.

Finally, organizational operations can be monitored for signs of actual performance problems. When records indicate poor performance, a possible cause is employees' deficiencies in knowledge or skills. Sometimes evidence of a training need is ignored because a practice is accepted as normal. For example, the new manager of a five-year-old petroleum-based materials plant asked about the huge pile of pellets behind the facility. He was told it was off-specification material resulting from the periodic restarting of the equipment. Since the value of the material was several hundred thousand dollars and thus represented considerable waste to the company, he did a little investigating. He discovered that each shift supervisor had his or her own approach to restarting. After considerable discussion and experimentation, a more efficient start-up procedure was devised and a training program designed and implemented.

A second way to identify training needs is simply to ask supervisors, managers, or others about their present or anticipated requirements. Questionnaires, interviews, or both are ways of gathering this kind of information. Team-based organizations find that involving employees in both training-needs analysis and implementation of training contributes to successful training.

Performance problems are also often brought to the attention of T&D professionals by supervisors, managers, and others. Whether such problems actually represent training needs is the next question for T&D professionals to consider.

ANALYZING PERFORMANCE PROBLEMS

Jane Simpson has been identified by her supervisor as having a performance problem with one aspect of her job: packing parts. She is required to pack six parts per minute with no breakage. Unfortunately, after three months on the job, she is still able to pack only four parts per minute, and she breaks an average of two per day. Simpson has a performance problem, but does it require a training solution? R.F. Mager and P. Pipe, consultants and authors of several books on training, suggest a method for analyzing performance problems.[29] It consists of a series of questions representing key determinations. These are summarized in the flow diagram in Figure 9.2.

The first determination is whether the performance problem is important enough to merit attention. If it is, the next step is to determine whether the problem is caused by a deficiency in either skill or knowledge. A key question in this determination is "could the employee perform the required behaviour if his or her life depended on it?" If not, the problem is caused by a true knowledge or skill deficiency for which training may be an appropriate solution. If Simpson has been trying very hard but still is unable to master part-packing without breakage, her problem falls in this category.

The next determination is whether the employee has ever performed the task adequately. Simpson has not, so she falls in this category. If performance has never been adequate, a formal training program is an appropriate solution, assuming that the employee is trainable. If other shipping clerks are

FIGURE 9.2
Mager and Pipe's Flow Diagram for Determining Solutions to Performance Problems

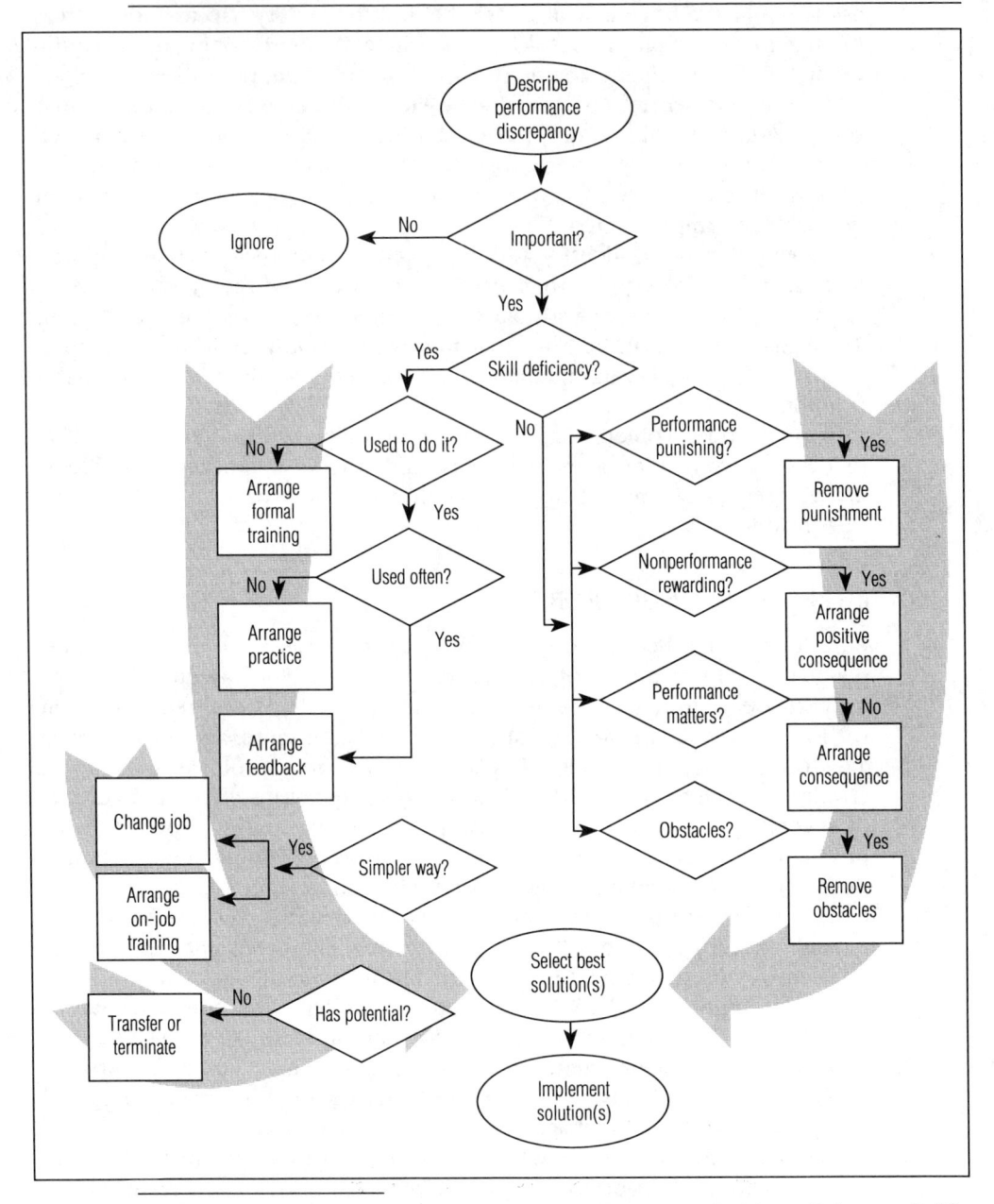

Source: R.F. Mager and P. Pipe, *Analyzing Performance Problems* (Belmont, Calif.: Lake Publishing Company, 1984). Reprinted with the permission of the publisher.

having the same problem as Simpson, another appropriate solution is to simplify the task so that employees' existing knowledge or skills are adequate. For example, using a different kind of packaging material might increase packing speed and also reduce breakage. Or the company might consider lowering performance standards to allow for some breakage and fewer parts packed per minute.

If, on the other hand, performance has been adequate in the past, the cause of a present deficiency may simply be lack of practice opportunities or inadequate performance feedback. Formal training programs are inappropriate in such cases. Appropriate solutions include providing opportunities for practice or more frequent feedback. Of course, if unpractised skills have been forgotten almost entirely, some amount of relearning has to take place before practice can be beneficial.

If the problem is not caused by a deficiency in skill or knowledge, what *is* the cause? Perhaps the employee lacks the necessary motivation to perform well. Or obstacles such as stress or personal problems may impede satisfactory performance. In cases like these, training is obviously not the solution. Performance problems that are not caused by deficiencies of knowledge or skills demand nontraining solutions, such as attaching positive consequences to desirable performance or removing obstacles to acceptable performance. Obstacles can often be removed by improving working conditions, sponsoring wellness programs, and/or referring troubled employees for counselling. Or, it may be necessary to impose discipline, even the threat of termination, in order to motivate correction of performance deficiencies.

SPECIFYING TRAINING OBJECTIVES

After determining training needs, T&D professionals specify training objectives, which describe what trainees will be able to do upon completion of training. Mager says that a useful instructional objective should (1) define the behaviour that will be accepted as evidence that the trainee has mastered the objective; (2) specify the important conditions under which the performance is expected to occur; and (3) specify a level of performance that will be considered acceptable.[30]

Since one kind of behaviour required for the job of shipping clerk is "assuring proper weight on all shipments handled," an objective for Jane Simpson's training program might be

> Given a standard mailing scale, the employee will be able to weigh packages accurately, i.e., within a gram of their actual weight 100 percent of the time.

In this instructional objective, the behaviour described is weighing packages. "Using a standard mailing scale" is the condition under which performance occurs. The level of performance considered necessary for mastery of the objective is "within a gram of their actual weight 100 percent of the time."

It is important to specify training objectives. Well-specified objectives define the content of training programs by providing clear statements of exactly what is to be learned. The success of training programs can be measured in terms of the extent to which training objectives are accomplished. And specifying training objectives provides trainees with a clear understanding of exactly what they will be expected to do after participation in the training effort.

Choosing a Training Program

Many choices confront the person charged with training responsibilities. One major decision is whether necessary training will be provided in-house (within the organization) or by outside organizations. Xerox Corporation decided that its redundant technicians should be schooled at a nearby technical institute, which customized classes to meet Xerox's needs. Participants were relieved of their work assignments for nine months in order to take a full class load (sixteen hours of courses each quarter). While attending classes, employees received full pay and were given computer terminals for use in their homes.[31] BC Hydro has been engaged in a substantial and continuing training program to reinforce its new corporate philosophy that focusses on "integrity, teamwork, commitment and innovation." A major part of the training effort is a five-day Generating Leadership program that is mandatory for all Hydro managers. The training involves analysis of one's leadership style and use of videotaped role plays demonstrating alternative leadership behaviours. Surveys of managerial behaviour six months after the training are compared to pretraining measures. BC Hydro also has a program for its supervisors. These programs were put together with the joint effort of Hydro T&D staff and external consultants.[32]

If in-house programs are used, T&D professionals can assemble the materials and plan the methods of presentation themselves, or they can order and implement prepackaged training programs. Prepackaged programs and outside training sessions must be selected carefully to ensure that their goals are consistent with the training objectives of the organization. Unfortunately, many companies choose programs without first conducting a needs analysis or formulating training objectives. With so many companies marketing books, cassettes, films, and programs on training, HRM professionals are constantly deluged with brochures and advertising for these products. The majority have much to offer, but managers who do not properly assess their T&D needs may be unwise consumers. Of course, nontraining benefits may accrue to offering some popular programs simply because employees appreciate and enjoy them. Given the expense of most training and development programs, however, a prudent organization exercises restraint in the number and types of programs selected.

The choice of a training program is determined by (1) the type of training content; (2) the extent to which the program incorporates key learning principles; (3) trainee characteristics; and (4) cost factors. These considerations are summarized in Exhibit 9.1.

TYPE OF TRAINING CONTENT

The content of the training program should be determined by the nature of the training need and specified training objectives. Content can be divided into four basic areas, each representing a type of behaviour or material to be learned: (1) information acquisition; (2) motor skills; (3) interpersonal skills and attitude change; and (4) decision-making and problem-solving skills. In practice, many programs incorporate more than one content area. For example, a program to help supervisors appraise performance may convey information about new appraisal techniques, develop interpersonal skills, and

EXHIBIT 9.1
Considerations in Choosing a Training Program

1. Area of training content (what type of behaviour or material is to be learned?)
    a. Information acquisition
    b. Motor skills
    c. Interpersonal skills and attitude change
    d. Decision-making and problem-solving skills

2. Extent to which the training program incorporates key learning principles
    a. Does program provide knowledge of results?
    b. Does program reinforce desired behaviour?
    c. Does method provide practice opportunities?
    d. Does method motivate the employee to learn and apply the new knowledge and skills to the job?
    e. Does the program facilitate transfer of new behaviour to on-the-job situations?

3. Trainee characteristics
    a. How many employees need training now? in the future?
    b. What level(s) of ability do trainees possess?
    c. What individual differences exist in employees who will be receiving training?

4. Cost of the program
    a. What is the size of the training and development budget?
    b. What does the program cost?

sharpen decision-making powers. A safety training program may combine information acquisition with motor skills by requiring that employees practise new safety behaviours.

Information Acquisition

One of the most common training needs is to provide employees with information relevant to their jobs. Such information frequently concerns new company policies, programs, or benefits; new laws and regulations affecting jobs; or new job performance standards. An underlying assumption of providing employees with information is that acquiring it will result in changes in behaviour. For example, a training program that provides HRM professionals with information about human rights legislation will, one hopes, result in compliance with the law. It may also result in changes in company policy and practices regarding the employment of members of visible minorities and other groups. Methods that seek to convey information must do so in such a way that it is retained for some time. Information must also be presented efficiently.

Motor Skills

Motor skills (or *psychomotor skills*, as they are sometimes called) are related to the performance of specific physical activities. Learning these skills involves learning to move various parts of the body in response to specific external and internal stimuli. Common motor skills are walking, riding a bicycle, tying a shoelace, throwing a ball, and driving a car.

To learn a motor skill, one must first acquire information so that one knows *what* one should do, then *how* to perform that action. Practice and performance feedback are necessary. For example, one cannot learn to drive a bus from simply reading a book or watching a film; one must actually perform the activity in order to master it. In the performance, one practises the necessary motor movements while receiving feedback and reinforcement from an instructor. Through practice and reinforcement, one learns to make certain motor responses at specific times in response to external stimuli, such as traffic flow and road signs, and to the internal stimuli from one's own muscles and nerves. Feedback provided by internal stimuli of this type is called *proprioceptive feedback*. It is very important for skilled motor movements, such as those required in equipment operation and use of tools.

Interpersonal Skills and Attitude Change

Interpersonal skills constitute the behaviour necessary for interaction with others in work and nonwork situations. Examples of interpersonal skills include listening, communicating, persuading, and showing understanding of others' feelings. Since interpersonal skills are frequently used to influence others, changing others' attitudes is included in this area of training content.

Acquiring interpersonal skills is also useful in developing leadership and bargaining skills.

Learning interpersonal skills is similar to learning motor skills in that both require opportunities to practise and to receive feedback on performance. Specifically, training in interpersonal skills involves learning to understand the behaviour of others and learning what to say and do in various situations. This is a common training content area for supervisors and managers.

Decision Making and Problem Solving

Decision making and *problem solving* focus on methods and techniques for making organizational decisions and solving work-related problems. This kind of learning improves trainees' abilities to define and structure problems, collect and analyze information, generate alternative solutions, and make an optimal decision from among alternatives. Training of this type is often provided to potential managers, supervisors, and professionals.

INCORPORATING KEY LEARNING PRINCIPLES

Since learning is the goal of any training effort, a second consideration in training-program choice is the extent to which a program incorporates the key learning principles of feedback, reinforcement, practice, motivation, and transfer. Some programs and methods, such as job instruction training, incorporate all five principles, while other methods, such as lectures and films, are limited in this regard. The extent to which a program or method incorporates a certain learning principle is important because, depending on the area of training content, certain learning principles may be more important than others.

Since one cannot actually observe learning taking place, its occurrence must be inferred. *Learning* is inferred to have taken place when a relatively permanent change in behaviour or behaviour potential occurs between two points in time as a result of reinforced practice or experience. The term *behaviour potential* recalls the fact that learning can take place even though a person has not had the opportunity to demonstrate that learning via performance. For example, individuals who have received training in cardiopulmonary resuscitation (CPR) may never need to use it to aid a heart attack victim. The potential to use it, however, exists as evidence of learning. The definition of learning as a "relatively" permanent change in behaviour calls attention to the fact that some forgetting of learned material is inevitable.

Feedback

The most basic learning principle is *feedback*, or knowledge about one's performance. It is difficult to imagine learning occurring without feedback. For example, imagine learning archery without being permitted to see if you hit the target. Feedback serves two major functions in the learning process:

it lets learners know whether they are performing correctly, and it reinforces desired behaviour.

Feedback informs trainees of the correctness or incorrectness of their responses to certain stimuli. If a student chooses alternative D in response to a multiple-choice question, feedback informs him or her if D is correct or incorrect. Ideally, feedback also informs the student of the correct response; one can learn from mistakes only if one knows what is wrong and how it can be corrected. Thus, this student should be provided with feedback that D is incorrect and that B is the correct alternative. Though learning is facilitated when such feedback is provided, relatively few training methods provide it. Feedback is also more informative and useful to the learner when it is given soon after responses are made and when it refers to specific responses to be learned rather than to factors of lesser importance in the learning situation. One training method that includes excellent informational feedback is programmed instruction. This method requires learners to answer questions based on small blocks of information. Each answer is followed immediately by feedback in the form of correct answers to the questions.

Reinforcement

Reinforcement has a greater impact on learning and performance than any other learning principle. The principle of reinforcement was stated nearly a century ago by E.L. Thorndike in his Law of Effect: responses that are closely followed by a "reinforcing state of affairs" tend to be strengthened and to occur more frequently in the future in response to the same stimuli.[33] In other words, the occurrence of desired behaviour can be increased by attaching *positive reinforcers* (desirable consequences) to it. A classic example of a reinforcer is the gold star a teacher affixes to a pupil's paper. Another example is a hockey coach's rewarding players for outstanding plays by placing visual symbols of accomplishment on their helmets. Gold stars and visual symbols provide recognition for desired behaviour. Such reinforcers gradually increase its occurrence.

Organizations use reinforcers such as recognition, praise, and bonuses to encourage desirable behaviour, but their primary use in training and development is to teach new behaviour. The process often used for this purpose is *shaping*, a systematic reinforcement of successively higher levels of performance. Suppose a teacher is teaching a child to read. The teacher shapes the behaviour (reading) first by reinforcing the student's recognition of the simplest words in the reader. As the child becomes more proficient, reinforcement is given for progressively more difficult words. Thus, the learner's new behaviour is shaped until an acceptable level of performance is reached.

The frequency of reinforcement is also important. Learning theory generally argues that a *continuous reinforcement schedule* (in which each correct response is reinforced) is most useful in learning new tasks. Such an approach is impossible to maintain in the work environment, however, because a supervisor is not always available to provide the necessary reinforcers. For this reason, many training programs begin partial, or intermittent, reinforcement schedules before an employee returns to the work environment to use newly learned behaviour on the job. An *intermittent reinforcement schedule* provides reinforcers for some correct responses but not for all. This approach is easier to maintain in the work environment and results in more consistent employee behaviour in the absence of reinforcers.

Perhaps one of the most useful forms of intermittent reinforcement is called variable ratio. A *variable ratio reinforcement schedule* is one in which employees are rewarded for desired behaviour on a random basis. For example, attendance may be improved by a program that gives employees a playing card for each day they arrive at work on time. At the end of each week, the employee with the best poker hand receives cash or some other form of reward. Employees perform the desired behaviour of coming to work on time, but they have only a random chance of being rewarded.

Although organizations find partial reinforcement useful in maintaining desirable behaviour, even this type of reinforcement is extrinsic. That is, trainees depend upon someone or something outside themselves for reinforcement. Ideally, learners provide themselves with reinforcement for correct behaviour. When people reinforce their own behaviour, reinforcers are intrinsic. Trainees can be taught to use intrinsic reinforcement by first learning the standards of correct behaviour from external reinforcement and feedback from the trainer. They also learn to obtain satisfaction from the correct behaviour itself. For example, after one has learned to read, reading becomes reinforcing in itself. Similarly, employees can find satisfaction in doing their jobs well.

Reinforcers are highly personalized; what one person finds reinforcing may not be reinforcing to another. For example, one person may find simple recognition to be a desirable consequence of good work, while another may need a more tangible reinforcer, such as an increase in pay. An employee who values autonomy may be reinforced by less supervision, while another finds close supervision more reinforcing. Thus, it is important to determine in advance what reinforcers will best suit one's purposes.

Feedback can be intrinsically rewarding. Most learners would prefer to get feedback on their performance (even when it is negative) than to have no knowledge of results. The reinforcement value of feedback is obvious from the importance most people place on keeping score when they play a game.

A recent newspaper article revealed what one city refuse collector found reinforcing about his work. The number and variety of reinforcers is rather surprising, given the nature of the job. The article is excerpted in Exhibit 9.2.

Practice

The learning of specific behaviour is the result of reinforced practice or experience. *Practice* is defined as repetition or rehearsal in order to remember or improve a response, a behaviour, or material. Feedback must reinforce practice so that the learner knows whether it is leading to the intended

EXHIBIT 9.2
What One Refuse Collector Finds Reinforcing about His Job

It is 7 A.M., and while most of the city is asleep, Babcock and his eight co-workers are getting ready to hit the streets to pick up what the rest of us have no use for—garbage.

"If anyone thinks my job is easy, I invite them to come on my truck," Babcock said during the dawn interview. "We're doing a hard job. I never thought I'd look down a street and feel satisfied by seeing empty garbage cans. We take a lot of pride in the department. We're like a family."

City officials are so pleased with the work of the sanitation department employees that three years ago they gave them a certificate of appreciation. Babcock and his co-workers proudly display the certificate if the occasion arises.

"I can see progress in my work and feel satisfied," said Babcock, adding that his line of work protects residents, particularly children, from disease and other troubles brought on by poor sanitation conditions.

Babcock, who previously worked in a factory, said he prefers collecting garbage. "You never knew where the product went," he said, adding that he enjoys contact with people and appreciates favourable comments from them.

"All it takes is one 'thank you' from the public to make your day," he said. "Sometimes one 'thank you' is better than a whole pay cheque. This doesn't mean we need a pat on the back every day."

Collecting refuse isn't easy, and this is one reason Babcock said he finds it rewarding. "It's good, hard, physical labour."

Source: G. Norman, "Collecting Trash Is a Dirty Job," *Daily Iowan* (Iowa City, Iowa), March 31, 1986. Reprinted with the permission of the *Daily Iowan*.

---

results. Without feedback, certain responses or behaviour may be practised and learned incorrectly. For example, beginning piano students who get no feedback may learn to play a piece of music incorrectly because they have no way of knowing that they are making errors.

Explaining practice is difficult because even psychologists who study human learning disagree about what constitutes it. For some people, practice requires physically performing an action, writing out material, or reading it aloud. For others, practice may be purely a mental activity. For example, a salesperson may mentally rehearse a sales presentation.

Though continuous reinforcement is important for learning new behaviour, practice is more instrumental in ensuring proper retention and performance. Generally, active practice is believed to be superior to the less active variety in facilitating the learning and retention of material. Retention of newly learned behaviour and material is also greater when practice is distributed rather than massed. *Distributed practice* means that practice sessions are interspersed with rest or other activities. Cognitive learning research suggests that the spacing between practice sessions should be gradually increased and that old material should be reviewed as new material is introduced.[34] *Massed practice* is practice with virtually no rest periods. Of course, massed practice is more time-efficient than distributed practice, a fact that probably explains why business training programs often violate the distributed-practice principle. (Massed practice is also popular with students who put off studying until the night before an exam.)

One question about practice concerns the "whole versus the part": material and behaviour can be rehearsed as a whole or divided into parts and practised separately. Generally, the "whole" method is superior, unless a task is complex and has a low degree of organization, in which case the "part" method may be more efficient. For example, a simple, repetitive piano piece can easily be learned as a whole, practising both right and left hands together from the start. A more difficult piece with greater variety may, however, be learned more effectively by practising first the right hand part, then the left hand part, and finally, playing both hands together. Depending upon the response to be learned, the "whole" method is sometimes not appropriate for learners of lesser ability.

A recent review of theory and research regarding recommendations for design of practice found a fairly high degree of commonality.[35] For example, recommendations from behavioural theory were similar to those from the most recent cognitive-based learning theory. The concept of automaticity is an example of a new concept from cognitive theory that is applicable to practice. *Automaticity* refers to practising a skill to the point at which it requires very little attention capacity of the brain. For example, typing is a skill that has been automatized by good typists but not by those who hunt and peck. Automaticity is important because recent research suggests that performance of complex tasks, such as computer programming and even reading, requires learning of some subtasks to this level.[36] The implication for practice is that it must proceed through three stages — speed, accuracy, and automaticity. For example, practice sessions in distinguishing letters from numbers would initially emphasize error-free performance, then speed, and finally, automaticity — that is, the ability to make these distinctions while performing a second task simultaneously.[37]

Any training method or program that does not permit trainees to control the pace at which material is presented is low on opportunities for practice. For example, the lecture method does not allow for practice opportunities. The learner in a lecture usually does not have time to repeat, even mentally, material he or she has just learned because new material is continually being presented. Of course, opportunity to practice is more important for learning motor skills than for learning the kind of material usually presented in a lecture.

Motivation

Training programs should help to motivate trainees to learn. Most learning processes have both intrinsic and extrinsic motivators. For example, learning to perform a new task may prove satisfying in itself because of pride in accomplishment, and this pride intrinsically motivates the trainee to continue learning and performing the newly learned task. On the other hand, the trainee may be extrinsically motivated to learn the new task because mastery will result in a desirable new job assignment.

An ideal training method would be very intrinsically motivating throughout the entire learning process. When trainees are intrinsically motivated, they are not dependent upon trainers or others to provide motivation for learning. Often, however, extrinsic motivators must be relied upon in the initial stages of learning. For example, praise and criticism used in the early stages of training are extrinsic motivators. Trainees are generally motivated to seek praise and avoid criticism. In time, they may come to internalize the standards necessary to receive praise; then good performance becomes intrinsically motivating and reinforcing. Such a process is most likely to occur in training methods and programs in which trainers provide close attention to and reinforce appropriate trainee behaviour. On-the-job training programs and well-run apprenticeship programs facilitate the transition from extrinsic to intrinsic motivation.

Several methods have been suggested for increasing trainees' intrinsic motivation to learn. These include stressing the future value of the material, providing feedback on progress toward the learning goals, and relating the material to "interesting, meaningful materials already studied outside the training program."[38]

A substantial body of research supports setting specific, hard goals to obtain the best effort and performance from people.[39] Training programs can and should make use of the goal-setting process to maximize performance gains.

Transfer of Learning

The bottom line in any training program or method is whether acquired learning is properly transferred to the job. When learning from one situation (such as a training program) is successfully applied to a different situation (such as the job), *positive transfer* is said to occur. Transfer can also be neutral or negative. *Neutral transfer* means that what has been learned is not applied to another situation. In *negative transfer*, learned behaviour or material has an adverse effect on performance. For example, a bicyclist may attempt to stop her new hand-braked bike with her foot because her old bike had coaster brakes. The driver of a new car may turn on his windshield wipers instead of his turn signal if the knobs' positions are the reverse of what they were in his old car. In each case, learned behaviour appropriate to an old situation results in poor performance in a new situation.

Assuring positive transfer is one of the most important aspects of a training program. A number of factors have been suggested as necessary for producing the transfer of learning to new situations, including the following:

1. Maximize the similarity between the learning and performance situation.
2. Practise the new task extensively (overlearning).
3. Provide a range of learning experiences so the trainee can generalize.
4. Identify key elements of the material or behaviour so that the learner is able to determine the appropriateness of transfer.
5. Emphasize knowledge of general principles.
6. Provide feedback on job performance and otherwise reinforce proper transfer of new materials and behaviour to the job.[40]

Overlearning, or practising a new task extensively, is particularly necessary when knowledge is critical but rarely used. For example, the individual who receives CPR training should probably overlearn the techniques; the chances of encountering a heart attack victim are remote, but if the need to perform CPR does arise, it is critical to remember the correct procedures.

Another situation in which overlearning is helpful is in learning a new response to an old or familiar stimulus. For example, imagine learning to drive in a country in which a red light means go and a green light means stop. In an emergency situation, a driver familiar with our red–stop, green–go associations would probably revert to the old responses (negative transfer), possibly causing an accident. Overlearning is one way to avoid such problems.

An organization should provide on-the-job performance feedback and other reinforcers for the proper transfer of newly learned materials and behaviour to the job. Newly learned behaviour and responses must be reinforced in the work environment or they will quickly be forgotten. A classic study illustrates this point. A training program for foremen designed to increase their consideration toward their subordinates was successful according to initial post-training measures. Within several months, however, the foremen had reverted to their pretraining behaviour. They did so simply because the newly learned behaviour had not been reinforced by the work environment and upper management. This study demonstrated that behaviour changed through training will not transfer or persist in the job situation unless the job and the organizational environment reinforce it.[41]

The importance of providing appropriate rewards to maintain new behaviour following organizational innovations, change, and restructuring is well documented. For example, when employers move to a team-based system that requires employees to learn multiple skills, a skill-based pay system is more appropriate than the traditional job-based pay. Ralph Kilmann argues that the appropriateness of the reward system is the most important factor in determining whether organizational change will last.[42]

Since transfer is an important factor, T&D professionals must consider how to achieve it in the training methods they choose, in the training program, and especially in the work environment itself. Planning for transfer can begin immediately after specification of the training objectives. Transfer should be regarded as the appropriate generalization of learned material to nontraining, on-the-job situations.

Trainee Characteristics

Also affecting choice of a training program are trainee characteristics — specifically, the number of employees who need training, their ability levels, and individual differences in training needs.

Number of Employees Who Need Training

Some training methods, such as teleconferences, lectures, films, videotapes, and programmed instruction, are easily adapted to large numbers of trainees. However, other methods, such as behaviour modelling, role play, job instruction training, and coaching, require low trainee/trainer ratios, in most cases fewer than ten trainees for every trainer. The coaching method, in which a supervisor coach provides guidance and feedback to subordinates, usually has only two to four trainees to every trainer. Most training methods can be used for small numbers of employees, but the more costly methods, such as interactive videodisk instruction and many types of simulations, require a large number of trainees over time in order to justify their initial expense.

If only a small number of employees need a certain kind of training or development, T&D professionals commonly use methods and programs that already exist within the organization or programs sponsored by other organizations. For example, trainees may enrol in workshops given by a university or community college or attend professional meetings. This approach avoids the costs associated with developing or purchasing a new program. If, on the other hand, large numbers of employees require training and the need is expected to recur, development costs can be justified more easily.

Trainee Ability Level

The ability level of trainees is another factor to consider in selecting a training method. For example, if reading ability is low, the level of written materials must be adjusted accordingly. A recent study by the Canadian Business Task Force on Literacy found that 24 percent of Canadians aged eighteen and over were functionally illiterate, with 100 000 illiterates added to the population each year through immigration and a flawed education system.[43] The study estimated that illiteracy costs Canadian companies between $4.5 billion and $10 billion every year as a result of accidents, low productivity, and lost earnings. The Task Force, composed of 32 major corporations, is working to make employers aware of this problem.

For employees with limited reading abilities, training materials may be modified and greater reliance placed on audio and video presentations, or basic skills training may be provided. For example, companies such as Chrysler Canada, Boeing Canada (de Havilland division), and Cummins ReCon (a Cornwall plant that reconditions diesel engines) have implemented night schools, remedial reading programs, and even home tutors to help illiterate workers and those with low-level reading and math skills.[44] De Havilland changed from a three-week training program that cost $675 per person but was not yielding employees with adequate skills, to a combination of night school and a more stringent selection process. This program cost de Havilland only $81 per person, and the graduation rate from night school increased to 70 percent. At Cummins ReCon, plant safety concerns led to the discovery that many workers' English skills were at a third-grade level and many lacked basic math skills. Cummins worked with the provincial government to pay for half of the training in English, math, and statistical process control. Even though the programs were voluntary and many were at night, employee participation was excellent. The training programs have been credited with decreasing accidents and increasing productivity.

In many organizations, a related problem is variation in ability level within a group of trainees. Imagine trying to design a training program for employees whose IQs range from 80 to 150. Some aspects of a company — such as company policies, performance standards, and income tax information — must be communicated to just such a diverse population. If the program is geared to a high intelligence level, employees of lesser intelligence will not understand much of the information presented. But if it is geared to a low level, employees of higher intelligence will likely be bored and perhaps insulted. Thus, training programs must take trainee ability levels into account and make an effort to gear program material appropriately.

Individual Differences in Training Needs

Trainees do not enter the training situation with identical needs, even if all are to learn the same behaviour or material. Differences in work experience and in levels of ability and motivation affect the amount and type of training an employee requires. For example, an employee with two years' experience as a telephone operator can master a new switchboard with less training than an employee who has never worked a switchboard.

To accommodate individual differences in needs, training can take a *criterion-referenced approach*, which assesses individual trainees before they enter the program. Trainees can start at slightly different points in the program, depending on how much they already know. Many North American organizations, including American Airlines, Xerox, and the U.S. Army, have successfully used this approach with substantial savings in training costs and time. American Telephone and Telegraph reported savings of $37.8 million from 1968 to 1973 as a result of switching to a criterion-referenced approach for telephone linesmen.[45]

Self-paced training programs recognize differences in levels of ability and motivation and enable trainees to work at their own speed. Programmed and computer-assisted instruction allow trainees to work at their own pace. These methods can also be easily adapted to a criterion-referenced approach.

COST FACTORS

Budgetary considerations play a major role in choice of a training program. Budget size is likely to increase as a function of the number of trainees, their organizational level (more dollars per trainee for higher-level trainees), and the extent of training needs. The Conference Board study referred to earlier found that larger employers, those whose ROI was higher, and those in certain industries such as transportation, communication, and public utilities tended to have larger per-capita training budgets than smaller firms, those with lower ROI, and those in other industries such as the retail trade. Larger firms tended to spend more of their training dollars on in-house facilities and staff trainers, while smaller firms spent a greater proportion of their budgets on consultants, outside courses, and off-the-shelf materials. The Board study also stated that Canadian firms spent an average of 48 percent of their budgets on T&D staff salaries and overhead, compared with 80 percent in the average U.S. organization. This tendency for Canadian firms to rely more on consultants and outside courses than U.S. firms held even when the size of the company was held constant.[46]

Larger budgets permit smaller class sizes, more and better training materials and equipment, and more and better trainers. A generous training budget should be used to maximize learning and the transfer of learning to the job situation. For example, a large budget could be used to divide a long two-day session into five four-hour sessions. A large budget could also permit hiring an excellent lecturer in place of showing a film or videotape. Of course, companies occasionally waste money on unnecessary items or purchase training programs that are more complicated than they need to be. If possible, increased expenditures for training programs should be evaluated to determine their effects on learning and performance. In some cases, the cheaper method may prove the better method.

Training costs can be a substantial problem since 98 percent of Canada's 1.1 million businesses have fewer than 100 employees. The Canadian Chamber of Commerce suggests co-operative programs between businesses and communities to reduce training costs. For example, one catalyst program in the Hamilton–Wentworth, Ontario, area linked 3500 girls from the eighth, ninth, and tenth grades with 400 women working in nontraditional occupations.[47]

TRAINING AND DEVELOPMENT METHODS AND AIDS

This section describes major methods and aids used in training and development programs. Although each is presented here under the heading of its primary use, many are appropriate for more than one content area. For a comparison of T&D methods according to several important criteria, see Table 9.1.

Information Acquisition

Methods and aids used primarily for the acquisition of information include lectures, seminars, films and videotapes, programmed instruction, computer-assisted instruction, and interactive videodisk instruction.

Lectures

In the lecture method, a trainer orally presents information to a group, which can range from very small to very large. Visual aids, such as a chalkboard or slides, are often used in conjunction with lectures. With the availability of cable and satellite television, companies can now broadcast live lectures to many remote locations simultaneously. Furthermore, technology has made it possible for lecturers to receive questions and comments from viewers in the hinterlands. Technological capabilities such as these make it possible to train many people more rapidly than ever before, while also substantially reducing travel costs for trainers, trainees, and their sponsoring organizations.

The lecture method has its shortcomings, even when the trainer is excellent. Except for questions from students, communication is one-way. For the most part, trainees sit passively listening or taking notes with little if any immediate feedback or reinforcement for learning or opportunities to practise the material being presented. Transfer of learning from lecture to the job depends on overlearning, verbal or pictorial identification of key features of the task, and emphasis on general principles. A lecture does not allow for varying ability levels of trainees, and the learning pace is structured by the instructor for the group as a whole. Despite its shortcomings, the lecture remains a common training method because of its low cost per trainee and the fact that trainees are familiar with and generally accept the method.

Seminars

Many agencies, firms, and universities offer seminars on topics of interest to employers. Seminars usually feature lectures, handouts, and some discussion among participants. Some seminars limit group size; others are open to large groups. Seminars are typically held in hotels, convention centres, or other locations outside the company. Increasingly, however, companies are bringing human resources consultants into the organization to conduct training sessions and seminars. Seminars are similar to lectures in terms of incorporating key learning principles. The value of a seminar depends on the expertise of the speaker and the relevance of the topic to the actual needs of the company.

TABLE 9.1
A Comparison of T&D Methods

TRAINING METHOD	CONTENT AREA OF PRIMARY USE	Feedback	Reinforcement	Practice	Motivation	Transfer	ACCOMMODATION OF INDIVIDUAL DIFFERENCES	INITIAL COSTS
Lectures	Information acquisition	Limited	Limited	Limited	Limited	Limited	Limited	Low
Seminars	Information acquisition	Limited	Limited	Limited	Limited	Limited	Moderate	Moderate-low
Films and videotapes	Information acquisition	Limited	Limited	Limited	Limited	Limited	Limited	Moderate
Programmed instruction	Information acquisition	Excellent	Moderate	Good	Good	Limited	Moderate-good	High
Computer-assisted instruction	Information acquisition	Excellent	Excellent	Excellent	Excellent	Limited	Good	High
Interactive videodisk instruction	Information acquisition, decision-making skills	Excellent	Excellent	Excellent	Excellent	Good	Excellent	High
Job instruction training	Motor skills	Good	Good	Good	Good	Excellent	Good	Low
Vestibule training	Motor skills	Good	Good	Good	Good	Good	Moderate-good	High
Apprenticeship training	Motor skills	Good	Good	Good	Good	Excellent	Good	Moderate

Method	Content areas							Cost
Coaching	Motor skills, interpersonal skills, decision-making skills	Moderate	Moderate	Limited	Good	Excellent	Excellent	Low
Video systems	Motor skills, interpersonal skills	Excellent	Good	Good	Excellent	Good	Good	Moderate
Conference/discussion	Interpersonal skills, information acquisition	Limited	Moderate	Limited	Good	Limited	Moderate	Moderate-low
Role play	Interpersonal skills	Good	Good	Good	Moderate	Good	Moderate	Moderate-low
Behaviour modelling	Interpersonal skills	Excellent	Good	Good	Moderate	Excellent	Moderate	High
T-groups	Interpersonal skills	Moderate	Moderate	Good	Moderate	Moderate	Moderate	Moderate-high
Case method	Decision-making skills	Moderate	Moderate	Good	Moderate	Moderate	Limited	Low
In-basket technique	Decision-making skills	Good	Moderate	Good	Good	Good	Limited	Low
Business games	Decision-making skills	Good	Moderate	Limited	Good	Moderate	Limited	Moderate-high
Internships	All content areas	Moderate	Moderate	Moderate	Good	Excellent	Limited	Low
Job rotation	All content areas	Moderate	Moderate	Limited	Good	Excellent	Moderate	Low

Films and Videotapes

Films and videotapes are prerecorded audiovisual presentations of material to be learned. They can be shown on either movie screens or television sets and are well-suited for use with any number of trainees. They can be purchased or rented ready made at affordable prices or prepared specifically for one firm. An advantage of films and videotapes over lectures is that they can show objects and processes in detail and in motion, facilitating transfer because visual images tend to be remembered longer than verbal ones and visual presentations can have greater similarity to the job situation.

Films and videotapes suffer some of the same disadvantages as the lecture method; namely, the audience is passive and has no opportunity for feedback, reinforcement, or practice. In addition, they are even more impersonal than lectures because there is no live instructor. Of course, videotapes or films are often used as only one part of a program that also includes live presentations; in such a case, the audiovisual and the lecture method are complementary.

Programmed Instruction

Programmed instruction presents information in small blocks on either printed pages or a computer screen. After reading each block of material, the learner must answer a question about it. Feedback in the form of correct answers is provided after each response. A major advantage of programmed instruction is that it is self-paced; each trainee can progress through the program at his or her own speed. It provides a high degree of reinforcement and knowledge of results and motivates most trainees in that they are actively engaged in the learning experience. Also, the material is structured, giving much opportunity for practice. Transfer of learning can be a problem, however, since the learning situation is so unlike the job situation. The development costs of programmed instruction are high but may be justified because the method is very flexible and can accommodate a number of employees at different times and in different locations. Research has shown that programmed instruction results in learning that is faster but not superior to that achieved with other methods.[48]

Computer-Assisted Instruction

Computer-assisted instruction (CAI) is similar to programmed instruction in that it uses a computer's storage and memory capabilities to individualize instruction. Thus, learners can begin at a level appropriate to their abilities (a criterion-referenced approach) and proceed at their own pace. The computer analyzes the learner's responses and determines what material is to be presented next. In terms of the learning principles, computer-assisted instruction is much like programmed instruction except CAI's feedback can be as rich and colourful as modern electronic games, complete with audio and visual displays. CAI development costs are high since programming costs are included,[49] but repeated use of a program may justify the costs. Research shows that computer-assisted instruction leads to faster but not necessarily superior learning. One recent study of CAI use for training in electronics found that it resulted in shorter learning times than conventional classroom training, with the same level of learning achievement. Learning times for CAI users were even shorter when two trainees teamed up to use the same computer.[50]

CAI is being used by a growing number of employers. For example, British Airways uses it to train employees to make reservations, using a new computer-based system; IBM uses it to teach new technicians basic data-processing principles; and the city of Dallas uses it to help people with disabilities learn computer programming.[51]

Interactive Videodisk Instruction

Interactive videodisk instruction (IVI) is similar to computer-assisted instruction, but it includes the graphic capabilities of television or films as well as the interactive capabilities of the computer. Interactive capabilities make criterion-referenced, self-paced learning possible since the content, level, pace, and sequencing of material all depend upon trainee responses. Through the use of branching, software can be designed to allow trainees to skip material they already know, review material not yet mastered, and cover material according to their own pace and style. Learners using this method are presented with video displays of work situations, such as an engine that needs adjustment or a fire in a chemical warehouse. After choosing from a set of responses to the situation, the trainee is shown the consequences, right or wrong, of the chosen alternative. These are vividly displayed in the form of audios and videos of actual situations.

Videodisk technology has been combined with computer graphics and simulators to approximate highly realistic work settings, such as airplane cockpits and ship bridges. The simulators duplicate controls and instruments and provide sensations a person would feel while actually operating the equipment. With the addition of video, trainees can also see and hear what they would actually experience as a result of their responses. Thus, pilot trainees can be taught how to land at major international airports, under all types of weather conditions, without ever leaving the ground.

Though one hour of material may be expensive, companies such as IBM, Ford, J.C. Penney, Hewlett-Packard, American Telephone and Telegraph (AT&T), and General Electric are making use of the method.[52]

Indeed, the use of both IVI and computer-based training has grown recently. One reason is that disks can be mailed to trainees anywhere. Though little research is available, many users claim a 30 to 50 percent reduction in training time and as much as an 80 percent increase in retention of material.[53]

HRM IN ACTION

BEYOND INTERACTIVE VIDEO: VIRTUAL REALITY

If you have used Mattel's Power Glove combined with a Nintendo game cartridge to play handball, you have experienced a form of "virtual reality." Virtual reality is a computer-generated world that creates an artificial environment that looks like and reacts like the real world. While interactive video technology allows learners to manipulate objects on a computer screen, "virtual reality turns you into a full participant in a three-dimensional setting that envelopes you completely." This electronic reality is created through use of a combination of a headset, which contains two very small liquid-crystal screens inside goggles, and a data glove, which contains sensors measuring hand position and finger movement. Signals from the headset and data glove go into a computer, which then generates appropriate displays and sensations, using stored equations.

Virtual reality is only in its infancy, but it has already been used in several ways. One example is the "virtual kitchen" developed by Matsushita Electric Works using U.S.-built headsets and gloves. This product is used to sell custom-built kitchens. A customer provides the dimensions of the kitchen along with a list of desired appliances, and the salesperson enters this information into a computer. The customer can then put on the headset and walk around, opening cabinets and even dropping and breaking dishes in the kitchen as it would be when built. This enables the customer to experience the new cabinets and appliances before they are built and to make desired changes. As you can imagine, the "virtual kitchen" is also a fascinating sales tool.

The applications of virtual reality for architecture, manufacturing, and entertainment are fairly obvious. This technology also holds tremendous possibilities for training. It can greatly enhance the realism of almost all types of skill and perceptual-skill training, including that required for pilots, equipment operators, and many medical workers. Virtual reality can give trainees experience and the opportunity to practise skills that would be either very dangerous or very costly to do in real life. For example, firefighters could practise safely in a wide range of conditions, such as dense smoke, different types of buildings and rooms, and the presence of various hazards.

In addition to offering opportunities to practise a wide range of skills under nearly realistic conditions, virtual reality is an extremely efficient medium for information presentation. "People comprehend images much faster than they can grasp columns of numbers or lines of text. Since about

> half the brain is dedicated to visual processing, virtual reality is the most natural way of all for people to understand and manipulate data and do so in three dimensions." Scientists using virtual reality report gaining new insights into chemical and physical phenomena that were not apparent from examining equations.
>
> Virtual reality is still a very new and very expensive technology, but as development proceeds and costs decline, it is certain to become a valuable training tool.
>
> ---
>
> Source: Based on G. Bylinsky, "The Marvels of 'Virtual Reality,'" *Fortune*, June 3, 1991. Used with the permission of *Fortune*.

MOTOR SKILLS

Learning motor skills requires practising demonstrated behaviours and receiving performance feedback. Methods and aids frequently used to teach motor skills include job instruction training, vestibule training, apprenticeship training, coaching, and video systems.

Job Instruction Training

Job instruction training is one of the oldest methods of on-the-job training, especially for manual jobs. This was the method used to train Jane Simpson for the job of shipping clerk. Job instruction training is sometimes referred to as Tell, Show, Do, and Review, because of its steps:

1. *Tell:* The trainee is told how to do the activity.
2. *Show:* The trainee is shown how to do it.
3. *Do:* The trainee has an opportunity to practise the activity.
4. *Review:* The trainee receives feedback and correction on practice attempts.

The person in charge of training is usually the immediate supervisor or an experienced co-worker. Job instruction training implements all the learning principles. It is an excellent method, though it may be somewhat costly in terms of a trainer's time since it requires close monitoring of trainees.

Vestibule Training

Vestibule training is very much like job instruction training except that it occurs off the job, away from the production area. It is usually employed to teach trainees how to use the machinery and tools that they will be using on the job. Although vestibule training uses the learning principles, it may present some problem for transfer of learning unless its machinery and tools are identical to those used on the job. Also, vestibule training cannot simulate work environment conditions such as noise, distractions from co-workers, and job pressures. Rather, it allows the employee to develop necessary skills in a pressure-free environment. And the absence of noise and other distractions may contribute to more rapid mastery of skills.

Apprenticeship Training

Apprenticeship training combines job instruction and vestibule training in that it provides instruction both on and off the job. This method is used in various skilled trades — industrial, construction, and others. The training includes work under the supervision of certified workers in the trade plus time spent in school, usually a community college. Training periods vary from three to five years and normally end with an examination that must be passed for certification. Provincial governments regulate the type and amount of instruction required for apprenticeship and pay rates in relation to those of certified workers. When training is provided in a unionized plant, the collective agreement sets out a schedule for it as well as the rates of pay for apprentices. It may also stipulate who is to be given preference when apprenticeship positions become available.

Though the apprenticeship method tends to develop well-qualified workers in the skilled trades, it has been criticized because the numbers trained have generally been smaller than the demand for these workers in Canada. Moreover, since apprentices have to be employed to receive instruction, their numbers fluctuate with the general level of employment. And because apprenticeship is time-consuming, it requires a very long lead time for human resource planning.

Coaching

Coaching is a method of on-the-job training commonly used for all kinds of trainees, from unskilled to managerial. In this method, a trainer or boss (the "coach") works with one or a few trainees, assigning tasks, monitoring performance, and providing reinforcement and feedback. Coaching is a continuous process of shaping a trainee's behaviour. The method is critically dependent upon quality of the coach—his or her ability to communicate; to motivate; and to provide supportive, noncritical, realistic performance feedback. It is important that coaches convey to trainees a clear statement of their job responsibilities. (Though that seems an obvious point, one expert estimated, based on a major 1982 survey, that salaries totalling $300 million had been paid to federal employees "confused about their job responsibilities."[54]) Coaches must also convey information about performance expectations and standards by which work will be judged.

As a training method, coaching incorporates all five learning principles, but practice opportunities may be limited since it is often difficult to learn and practise material in an organized way when one's employer is "running a business not a training centre." This method can also be costly if one person serves as a full-time coach for only a few trainees.

Video Systems

Companies with video systems that include cameras and recorders can videotape groups of trainees at practice or simulated sessions, then play back their actions for discussion. The playback segments of this method are often preceded, and perhaps followed, by prerecorded taped demonstrations by experts. These can be purchased or developed using the organization's own equipment. The demonstration segments of this method are like other film and videotape training materials, while playback of the practice sessions provides immediate performance feedback, which is very reinforcing. The opportunity to see one's performance on screen can also be a motivating factor. This method is frequently used to demonstrate and play back motor and interpersonal skills.

INTERPERSONAL SKILLS AND ATTITUDE CHANGE

The teaching of interpersonal skills, such as effective communication, listening, and techniques of persuasion, usually occurs in a small-group format. Feedback and practice opportunities are especially important. Methods for this training include conference/discussion, role play, behaviour modelling, and T-groups (sensitivity training).

Conference/Discussion

In the conference/discussion method, a directed discussion on a specific topic is conducted with a relatively small group of trainees. Trainees participate in a great deal of verbal interaction with the discussion leader and with one another. As a result, conference/discussion is useful for teaching and exploring difficult conceptual material and for changing attitudes and opinions. It provides much opportunity for feedback, reinforcement, practice, motivation, and transfer, largely through the active interchanges between participants.[55] Conference/discussion is a popular managerial training method, but it is more expensive than the lecture method since a group size of more than, say, twenty is impractical.

Role Play

Role play teaches interpersonal skills by having two or more trainees interact within the context of a realistic situation. The situation is defined in a case format so that each trainee receives the same information. Each trainee plays the role of a specific person in the situation, such as the boss or one of several subordinates.

Role play is a very useful method for learning interpersonal skills since trainees are actively engaged in a situation in which new behaviour can be practised. The trainer is very important to the success of this method since he or she provides feedback and reinforcement; videotaping the role plays can also facilitate feedback. The success of learning transfer depends on how well the role play approximates interpersonal situations on the job. The cost of the method is moderately high since a trainer cannot handle more than one or two small groups of role players.

Behaviour Modelling

Behaviour modelling, a relatively new method for teaching interpersonal skills and attitude change, is based on Albert Bandura's social learning theory.[56] The method is very specific in its training objectives. It teaches specific supervisory skills by (1) presenting a model or good example of the behaviour to be learned; (2) allowing trainees to practise the modelled behaviour; and (3) providing feedback and reinforcement on practice attempts. To the degree that the interpersonal skills learned prove useful on the job, some attitude change occurs. The use of this method requires the development of specific behavioural models, which are filmed or videotaped. Trainees view these films and receive opportunities to role-play the modelled behaviour. Feedback and reinforcement are provided by the trainer, other trainees, and videotaped playbacks of practice attempts. Because trainees are actively involved in the learning process and can easily see the value of the modelled behaviour in the simulated situations, they are easily motivated. Behaviour modelling has, in principle, the greatest number of transfer mechanisms of any method in Table 9.1. Behaviour modelling situations are designed to approximate on-the-job situations as closely as possible; ample opportunities for overlearning exist; and a variety of situations can be portrayed. Instructors and written materials provide the key elements of the skills to be learned, and general principles useful for transfer can also be acquired. To some degree this training method accommodates individual differences: it is sufficiently flexible to permit giving more time to slower learners, and trainees at different levels can be grouped. Behaviour modelling tends to be relatively expensive because group size must be limited to ten or twelve trainees.

Most studies on behaviour modelling have shown that trainees have positive reactions to this method and acquire new knowledge and skills as a result. Only a few studies, however, have demonstrated positive transfer of newly learned skills to the job. Of four behaviour modelling studies using objective measures of behaviour change on the job after training, only two found behavioural changes on the job, and these were attributed to supervisors' motivation to change.[57] In one of the studies, supervisors were directed and encouraged by their bosses to use their newly acquired skills; in the other, subordinates of the supervisors received identical training at the same time, although in separate groups.

T-Groups

The *T-group method* — also known as *sensitivity training* — uses a small number of trainees, usually fewer than twelve in a group, who meet with a passive trainer to gain insight into their own and others' behaviour. Meetings have no agenda, and questions deal with the "here and now" of the group process. Discussion focusses on "why participants behave as they do, how they perceive one another, and the feelings and emotions generated in the interaction process."[58]

T-groups are highly involving and give participants some opportunity to practise new behaviour, but the material to be learned is very unstructured; feedback and reinforcement are primarily in the hands of other group members, and transfer is difficult unless everyone on the job has also been in a T-group.

T-groups exemplify the faddishness of some training methods. They became very popular in the early 1960s but are now seldom used. Although research shows that they often produce desired changes in interpersonal behaviour and are useful for individual growth and development, they rarely have positive effects on organizational performance.[59]

DECISION-MAKING AND PROBLEM-SOLVING SKILLS

Training methods to improve decision-making and problem-solving skills generally attempt to structure situations in which trainees can put these skills to work. The methods include the case method, the in-basket technique, business games, internships, and job rotation.

Case Method

One of the oldest methods of teaching decision-making and problem-solving skills is the *case method*, which presents trainees with a long and detailed written description of a business or organizational problem and asks them to propose a solution. The object of the case method is to teach trainees how to analyze information, generate decision alternatives, and evaluate the alternatives. Cases can be analyzed by individuals or small groups. Feedback and reinforcement are provided through oral discussion in class or written comments from the instructor or class members. Through case analysis, trainees learn to transfer the appropriate principles to examples of "real" problems. Though there is little conclusive research evidence about effectiveness of the case method, it is widely used in business schools and industry. It is one of the least expensive methods of teaching decision-making and problem-solving skills.

A four-week business management course for managers at General Electric used an uncommon variation called the "living case" method. This method presents decision makers with data and materials about *unresolved present-day* challenges facing a company.[60]

In-Basket Technique

The *in-basket technique* is a simulation training method that puts the trainee in the role of a person who must suddenly replace a manager. The trainee receives background information about the organization and the person he or she is replacing, as well as letters, memos, and phone messages. He or she must organize the information, make decisions, and prepare memos and letters to handle the problems presented. In-baskets can be developed for almost any type of job involving managerial or professional decision making. The method is highly involved and covers major features of managerial jobs. Thus, it has good motivational properties and provides opportunities for transfer. Its value as a training technique depends on the amount of feedback and reinforcement provided, which varies among trainers. The in-basket technique is also a common component of assessment centres used to identify managerial talent.

Business Games

The most famous business game in existence is probably Parker Brothers' *Monopoly*. The business game technique requires trainees to make sequential decisions. It is a more dynamic method than case studies since the decisions made early in the game affect not only the outcome but the alternatives available later during play. Trainees work by themselves or in teams in which each member takes the role of manager of a functional area such as human resource management, finance, or marketing. Trainees usually regard business games as highly involving and motivating since, as in any game, they keep score and compete with each other. Modern business games commonly use a computer to analyze the trainees' decisions and provide their organizational consequences. A game can simulate an organization's entire operations over several years, or it may be restricted to one or two functions, such as marketing or manufacturing.

With the assistance of a grant from the Burroughs Corporation (now UNISYS), researchers at the University of Iowa developed an interactive business game in which trainees use computers to compete against each other or the computer. In the game, trainees play the part of a boot manufacturer who can advertise in various magazines displayed on the terminals. Trainees choose how they want to advertise the product, wait for consumer reaction, and respond to it. Problems with the product, such as short sole life, are introduced so that decisions must be made regarding remedial actions to take. This computer business game and others like it can be expanded to include multiple companies. In this case, each trainee takes the role of a different company, and the decisions of one trainee affect the market environment of all the other companies. Other games being developed at the University of Iowa simulate collective bargaining. In these games trainees sharpen their bargaining or negotiating skills.

Because of the nature of business games, trainees do not know the decision-making and problem-solving principles to be learned until after completing the game. They also do not get feedback or reinforcement from the instructor until afterwards, though many games do provide quarterly feedback on company performance. Business games are relatively expensive, if they are properly designed and well run, but they provide a unique method of teaching trainees how to analyze information, make decisions, and work within the context of those decisions.

Internships and Job Rotation

In addition to off-the-job methods for improving decision-making and problem-solving skills, two on-the-job methods are commonly used for acquiring these skills: internship and job rotation. They are usually used after trainees have completed all or part of their formal off-the-job training.

Internships are designed to teach professionals or managers the skills and knowledge to do their new jobs. In principle, they are similar to apprenticeships in the skilled trades, although they are not regulated by the provinces. Trainees learn by observing experienced professionals performing their jobs, by questioning these experienced workers, and by performing some tasks under supervision.

Job rotation programs move managers or managerial trainees from one job to another in the organization with the goal of familiarizing the trainees with each job or organizational unit. The length of time in each unit is usually three to twelve months.

Although transfer of learning is no problem for either of these methods, both may lack opportunities for the practice of critical but rare behaviour. Also, feedback and reinforcement depend on the supervisor. Learning on the job through internships and job rotation may place learners in pressure situations in which mistakes are very costly. However, since trainees help produce goods or services, these on-the-job methods are relatively inexpensive.

IMPLEMENTING THE TRAINING PROGRAM

Once needs analysis has helped determine the appropriate training content and the best, most efficient techniques and methods to use, training must be implemented. If it is to be delivered by company personnel, as opposed to outside consultants or school faculty, HRM professionals must plan that implementation. T&D professionals may deliver training themselves or, as described in the Repap case that opened the chapter, they may train the trainers. With the growth of team-based management, train-the-trainer approaches to delivery are becoming more common.

Federal–provincial cost-sharing programs are available, but there are some important new initiatives as a result of the new Training Board.[61] An employer who wants to explore the possibility of obtaining assistance for establishing or expanding a training program first contacts a Canada Employment Centre (CEC). The CEC assigns a T&D specialist to consider the request. CECS are also ready to supply advice and information on training content and methods. Provincial authorities have responsibility for the registration and certification of apprentices.

TRAINERS

Unless an organization employs enough trainers to meet all its training needs (and most do not), the implementation of training programs involves building a corps of competent trainers. Consulting organizations can provide trainers as needed. More often, however, managers, supervisors, and HRM staff within the organization serve as trainers. In some organizations, especially those with a team-based structure, knowledgeable employers who have received trainer training often train other employees.

A trainer is basically a teacher, and a teacher's primary goal is to influence students' attitudes and behaviour. Organizations too often assume that an experienced employee, supervisor, or manager is a good teacher, especially in the case of on-the-job training. Like any other interpersonal skill, training or teaching can and should be taught to those with training responsibilities. Generally, trainers should be taught how to organize and present their material, motivate and reinforce trainees, and prepare them to apply new material to the job. Training the trainers is an important responsibility of HRM professionals and T&D specialists.

TRAINING ROOMS

Training rooms should have certain characteristics. Specifically, they should be flexible, isolated, properly lit and ventilated, and able to accommodate computer equipment and a variety of training activities, such as videotape viewing, role plays, group discussions, and computer use. Furniture, including tables and chairs, should be easily moved to facilitate different training activities. Most management conferences, for example, use a U-shaped seating arrangement, while team tasks or small-group exercises cluster a few chairs around each of a number of tables. Isolation, both physical and psychological, is necessary to ensure that trainees are able to concentrate on learning, rather than worrying about work problems. Lighting control is necessary, particularly for film and video displays. And anyone who has fallen asleep in an overheated, stuffy classroom realizes the value of maintaining a comfortable temperature (between 22.5° and 24°C), humidity level (about 50 percent), and airflow (3.5 to 4.5 metres per minute).[62]

TRAINING PROGRAMS IN PRACTICE

One of the best and most comprehensive surveys of current training activities is *Training* magazine's annual investigation of U.S. employers. The 1990 report used a sample drawn from 12 000 businesses in the Dun and Bradstreet

Directory; responses were received from 2645 employers with at least 100 employees. Although the survey results cannot be said to be typical of Canada or even of the United States (the response rate was 22 percent), they provide a recent view of the training activities of a large number of employers. Specifically, this survey provides information on who receives training, the general types of training, sources of training, techniques and methods, and the areas viewed as critical challenges for T&D in the near future.[63] The Conference Board of Canada study of T&D differs from the *Training* survey in a number of ways. For example, the Board's survey includes 444 employers (a 19 percent response rate), excludes those with fewer than 200 employees (versus 100), includes 57 percent independently owned Canadian firms, and focusses on a few questions different from those in the *Training* survey.[64]

According to the *Training* survey, all categories of workers receive some form of training from most organizations. Middle managers were most likely to get some training (75.9 percent of respondents) and production workers least likely (33.3 percent of respondents). Other groups receiving training included first-line supervisors (73.3 percent), executives (67.3 percent), office and administrative personnel (66.7 percent), professionals (59.6 percent), customer service personnel (45.0 percent), and salespeople (40.4 percent). These percentages may not reflect the complete picture. For example, though only 33.3 percent of respondents provided training for production workers, that group averaged 195.4 employees trained per organization — the largest number reported — while middle managers averaged only 25.4 trained per organization. Moreover, the number of production workers trained was up substantially from 1989. Yet another picture of who receives training is apparent from the average number of hours of training per employee: It was about 33.0 hours per year for every category of employee except salespeople, who averaged 40.7 hours, and office and administrative personnel, who averaged 19.0 hours.

The Board survey reported that management and professional/technical employees received the highest number of median hours per capita, with 28; followed by executives, with 24; and all other employee categories (including sales, clerical, production, service, and trades), with 14 hours. Though there are differences in hours of training, much of the differences are likely attributable to the samples and survey methods used.

Table 9.2 shows the percentage of organizations in the *Training* survey providing various types of training. There was substantial training in areas where one might expect it, such as management and supervisory skills, technical and computer skills, communications, customer relations, and new methods, but there were also some surprises. More than half the employers provided wellness training. Despite all the recent publicity about illiteracy, only 35 percent offered remedial basic education; the most common area was writing, followed by reading and basic math.

Specific types of training reported included new-employee orientation (82.7 percent of organizations), interpersonal skills (68.2 percent), perform-

TABLE 9.2
General Types of Training

TYPE OF TRAINING	PERCENTAGE OF EMPLOYERS PROVIDING TYPE OF TRAINING
Management skills development	86.2
Technical skills knowledge	83.0
Supervisory skills	82.4
Communication skills	78.2
Basic computer skills	74.5
New methods/procedures	72.6
Customer relations/services	70.8
Executive development	69.1
Clerical/secretarial skills	68.2
Personal growth	65.6
Employee/labour relations	56.4
Wellness	52.8
Sales skills	47.5
Customer education	45.2
Remedial basic education	35.1

Note: $N = 2645$.

Source: Adapted from J. Gordon, "Where the Training Goes." Used with permission from the October 1990 issue of *Training* Magazine, p. 52. Copyright 1990, Lakewood Publications Inc., Minneapolis, MN. All Rights Reserved.

ance appraisals (71.8 percent), new equipment operation (64.4 percent), goal setting (63.7 percent), team building (58.3 percent), train the trainer (57.4 percent), safety (56.0 percent), managing change (45.9 percent), and outplacement/retirement planning (32.2 percent). The breadth and variety of training offered suggests that respondents to the survey were probably more progressive than typical employers. Both the general and the specific lists show current training content that goes far beyond the training that employees would need simply to perform their jobs. There was clearly both a development emphasis and an attempt to help employees maintain their physical and mental health. Surprisingly, differences related to organizational size were relatively small. Smaller employers (100 to 499 employees) and the largest (10 000 or more employees) differed *most* in offering remedial basic education (33.8 versus 49.5 percent), training in basic computer skills (73.5 versus 82.5 percent), and wellness training (51.3 versus 64.2 percent). The variations among organizations in different industries were, as one would expect, larger.

The types of training identified in the Board study were generally similar to those identified in the *Training* survey, but differed notably in the following areas. Assuming "computer training" is comparable to "basic computer skills," a larger percentage of Canadian employers offer such programs (90.0 percent versus 74.5), but a smaller percentage offer remedial basic education or literacy training (11 percent versus 35). Similarly, wellness training appears to be less popular in Canada than in the United States (24.0 percent versus 52.8), though stress management, a category in the Board survey but not in the *Training* one, is done by 50 percent of Board respondents.[65] Both surveys provide only general and relative information on the types of training employers are providing at a given time. Though there are many commonalities across employers, particularly at a given time, each employer has some training needs that are unique to its own particular goals and needs.

The *Training* survey also reported how much of the training was given by company staff, by external providers such as consultants, training firms, or schools, and by a combination of both. Generally, organization-specific material, such as new methods and procedures and technical skills, were provided exclusively by in-house staff, or, more often, by external sources in combination with in-house staff. In fact, except for areas such as new-employee orientation, performance appraisals, product knowledge, new methods, and customer education, the combination of in-house and external providers was more common than in-house alone for all types of training. This tendency was less common among Canadian employers in the Board survey, with the internal staff providing somewhat more of the training than the combination of in-house and external. The larger percentage of smaller firms in the U.S. sample may explain this discrepancy.

More than half the training received by all types of employees in the *Training* survey, except production workers, came from a combination of in-house and outside suppliers. Only executives and senior managers received as much as 20 percent of their training exclusively from outside suppliers. In general, the lower the level of employee, the greater the proportion of the training that came from within the organization.

Table 9.3 shows the percentage of organizations using various types of training methods and techniques. Note that videotapes were reported as being used by more organizations than were lectures. (Actually, videotapes passed lectures in the 1987 *Training* survey.) This, of course, does not necessarily mean that trainees spent more time watching tapes than listening to lectures. Overall, the table reflects a high use of visually oriented methods, from simple ones, such as slides, to expensive and complex ones, such as computer-based instruction. Indeed, the use of computers in training is growing sharply; between the 1985 and the 1990 survey, smaller organizations increased their use from 46 to 64 percent, whereas the largest employers went from 74 to 89 percent. Computers are also used to manage training activities — for example to keep track of trainees' courses and to schedule

TABLE 9.3
Use of Instructional Methods

METHOD	PERCENTAGE OF EMPLOYERS USING METHOD
Videotapes	88.7
Lecture	84.7
One-on-one instruction	72.2
Computers (in training)	66.0
Computer-based training (CAI and IVI)	41.0
Slides	55.6
Role play	54.4
Audiotapes	53.0
Films	47.8
Case studies	46.4
Self-assessment/self-testing instruments	39.8
Noncomputerized self-study programs	35.9
Video conferencing	11.6
Teleconferencing (audio only)	8.5
Computer conferencing	4.5

Note: $N = 2645$.

Source: Adapted from J. Gordon, "Where the Training Goes." Used with permission from the October 1990 issue of *Training* Magazine, pp. 51–69. Copyright 1990, Lakewood Publications Inc., Minneapolis, MN. All Rights Reserved.

classes. These and related uses grew from 33 to 55 percent, even among the smallest employers.

Finally, the *Training* survey asked, what "topic or trend would present the most critical challenge to your organization's training and development function over the next two to five years?" The top six responses were technological change, customer service, quality improvement, corporate culture, new market strategies and organizational missions, and productivity improvement.[66] Perhaps surprisingly, remedial or basic education was near the bottom; only 2.2 percent of the respondents named it (compared to the 16.2 percent who said technological change).

The Board survey asked a similar question regarding the major challenge facing T&D departments. The answers were a lack of resources in T&D (23 percent), getting increased commitment from senior management (13 percent), more individual and corporate needs analysis to facilitate linking T&D to corporate goals (10 percent), finding time for T&D (9 percent), and fostering a training culture (9 percent).[67]

Evaluating the Training Program

For years, psychologists and personnel researchers bemoaned the fact that many employers took on faith the effectiveness of their training and development programs.[68] If results from a U.S. Bureau of National Affairs survey are representative, researchers may finally have made their point that formal evaluation should be done. The study found that 70 percent of the surveyed companies conduct formal evaluations of their management and nonmanagement training programs. Of this 70 percent, more than 96 percent obtain trainee feedback; approximately 65 percent measure on-the-job performance changes; one-quarter examine changes in company performance, such as production volume, profits, sales, absenteeism, and turnover; and about 15 percent conduct before and after testing of trainees.[69] These findings are consistent with the Board survey, which found that some form of evaluation was done for about three-quarters of the training offered by responding firms. Most evaluation was at the basic reaction level, and only 35 percent of the training offered was evaluated in terms of its impact on results or work-related outcomes. The average employer allocates 4 percent of its T&D budget to evaluation activities.[70] Thus, it appears that many of today's organizations are evaluating their training programs.

Why Evaluate?

The major reason for evaluating training programs is to determine if they are accomplishing specific training objectives. For example, the success of a program to teach T&D specialists to write training objectives can be measured in terms of how well the specialists can write objectives after completing the program. A training program that does not change employees' knowledge, skills, or attitudes in the desired direction should be modified or replaced. Economists have attempted to measure the impact of training by comparing the before and after earnings of persons who undertook training with those who did not.

A second reason for evaluation is to ascertain whether changes in trainees' capabilities come from the training program. This point is particularly important when a training program is first begun, since good results may lead to its adoption for other employees. To determine whether a training program is responsible for changes in trainees, it is necessary to compare their performance, both before and after the program, with the performance of a control group. For example, a training program on managerial decision making can be given to one group of management trainees and not to another. If, after training, *both* groups demonstrate similar increases in decision-making skills, the improvement is not attributable to the training program. If, on the other hand, only those who participated in the training program demonstrate increases in their decision-making skills, then the program has probably had some degree of success.

Another reason to evaluate training programs is to explain failure if it occurs. A basically sound program may fail for many reasons. Perhaps the training objectives were too ambitious, or the program was not implemented properly because of circumstances beyond its planners' control (such as equipment breakdown or human failure). Depending on the reasons for a program's lack of success, the program may be either retained or discontinued.

Training programs should also be evaluated to determine their cost-effectiveness. Like any other human resource or business programs, training programs must demonstrate cost-effectiveness in order to justify their continuation. Basically, to be cost-effective, a training program must result in gains in employee performance or job-related behaviour that outweigh the costs of training. When training programs are evaluated for cost-effectiveness, programs can be compared to determine the least costly way of achieving desired results. For example, if both on-the-job training and a formal safety instruction program result in increased use of protective devices on the job, the organization will probably decide to retain the less costly program for meeting these training needs in the future.

CONDUCTING THE EVALUATION

The evaluation of training programs has four parts:

1. Setting training objectives.
2. Gathering pretraining data, sometimes called *baseline data* because they show the level, or base, of a trainee's performance before training.
3. Gathering data during and after training.
4. Comparing the pre- and post-training data. If possible, the results of this comparison should then be compared with those of a control group of similar employees who were not trained.

The process of evaluating training programs begins in the planning stages of training, with the specification of objectives. Training objectives, which are obtained from a needs analysis, provide standards for the evaluation of program effectiveness.

Baseline data are of three general types: (1) measures of knowledge or skill, obtained through tests or other standardized measures; (2) on-the-job behaviour and performance measures, such as individual production rates, error rates, customer complaints; and (3) organizational results measures, such as profitability, production costs, and scrap rate. The three types differ in their relationship to individuals; knowledge and skill measures accurately reflect an individual's pretraining performance, while organizational results data may be affected by many factors unrelated to the individual or how much was learned in training.

The third part of evaluation requires gathering data during and after training. By monitoring the progress of trainees during training, "bugs" can be worked out of the program. Post-training data, which can be gathered immediately after training and at various times thereafter, are usually of two types. The most commonly gathered are trainee reactions to the program, which are usually solicited by questionnaire. Unfortunately, information of this type is of little value in evaluating the effectiveness of training. It can, however, provide some guidelines for modifying the program in order to improve its organization, motivating effect, and use of materials. A generally negative reaction from trainees, especially regarding how much they feel they learned in the program, can indicate a need for major program changes.

The second type of post-training data demonstrates whether learning has taken place by comparing the pretraining and post-training test scores of trainees. Ideally, the same tests have also been given to a control group at the same times. When employees are randomly assigned to either a control or an experimental group and a true experiment is conducted, effectiveness of training can be scientifically examined. Even if premeasures cannot be obtained, comparison of post-training results from experimental and control groups provides excellent information on program effectiveness, as random assignment ensures that experimental and control groups are equivalent and that any differences result from the training program.

Since training objectives usually specify mastery of material or results to be used on the job, it is necessary to collect on-the-job performance data to determine whether learning has successfully been transferred to the job. In many cases, learning may be short-lived or may transfer unsuccessfully. Job performance and organizational results data must therefore be collected and analyzed for some time after training. Few organizations examine the effects of training programs beyond one year, but if performance returns to pretraining levels in a little more than that period, it may be difficult to justify the costs of training. (Such results may also indicate that training was not an appropriate solution to a performance problem.)

All this evaluation takes time and money, so many companies simply "take it on faith that training employees for new tasks pays off." Others, such as IBM Canada, employ all four of the evaluation steps just described.[71] For example, IBM uses "happy-face sheets" to measure student reactions at the end of a session, and tests are given at both the beginning and the end of courses, as well as six to nine months later. After some time, students are also asked to evaluate the contribution of training to revenue. Additionally, IBM has an annual skills assessment process to determine training needs. Thus, each employee has his or her own skills development plan.

It is possible to estimate the utility of a training program in much the same way as we estimated the utility of an additional predictor in the selection chapter (see Appendix 7A). A procedure has been developed by Jack Hunter and Frank Schmidt.[72]

Summary

Training and development is an important HRM function in both implementing organizational strategy and facilitating organizational effectiveness. The training and development area has experienced recent growth, and this trend can be expected to continue. The major contribution of training and development to organizational effectiveness is to help maintain a qualified work force. Training and development responsibilities are handled by HRM professionals, including T&D specialists, as well as supervisors, managers, and sometimes line employees.

Training programs should begin with a training-needs assessment in which organizational information is monitored and performance problems are analyzed. Although many organizations omit or cut short this assessment phase, it is necessary in order to develop specific behavioural training objectives, to select proper training methods and programs, and to formulate evaluation methods and measures. After training needs are determined and translated into objectives, programs or methods must be developed or selected. The choice of a training program is affected by four major considerations: (1) the nature of the material to be learned (information, motor skills, interpersonal skills and attitude change, decision-making and problem-solving skills); (2) the extent to which the program incorporates the key learning principles of feedback, reinforcement, practice, motivation, and transfer of learning; (3) characteristics of the trainees, including their number and abilities; and (4) budgetary constraints. Considerable care must be given to the actual operation of a training program. Sessions must be planned in advance for smooth execution, trainers may need to be trained, and programs should be co-ordinated with trainees' regular work activities to minimize disruption. Finally, evaluation of training programs should be planned well before training begins. A good evaluation procedure involves a control group and pre- and post-training measures of trainees' abilities, job behaviour, and/or organizational performance outcomes. The evaluation process should be regarded as an integral part of any training program. Information from evaluation is necessary to revise, improve, or completely change the content or methods of training programs used.

Review Questions

1. What major factors contribute to the increasing importance of T&D in attaining organizational strategic objectives and effectiveness?
2. Discuss the role of needs analysis in the training process. Why do many people regard it as the most important part of training?

3. In the past, training was often done by employees, though this approach had been criticized for a number of reasons. Today, line employees *are* conducting training in many leading-edge companies, such as Northern Telecom and Procter and Gamble. Discuss the advantages and disadvantages of using production or line employees as trainers.

Project Ideas

1. From your own experience, describe a learning situation in which you had to improve or master a certain skill or behaviour. Explain the learning process or the training situation involved. How did the process facilitate the key learning principles of feedback, reinforcement, practice, motivation, and transfer of learning? Which (if any) of the learning principles were more or less important to you or to the mastery of the task at hand? Why?

2. Read R.F. Mager's short, amusing paperback *Preparing Instructional Objectives*, 2nd ed. (Belmont, Calif.: Fearon-Pitman, 1975). Choose four jobs that you are familiar with and generate two useful training objectives for each (according to Mager's definition of "useful"). Write a brief paper relating how your training objectives demonstrate the key principles in Mager's book.

3. Consider each activity and behaviour required for the job of public-opinion collector as described in Manpower and Immigration Canada, *Canadian Classification and Dictionary of Occupations* (Ottawa: Information Canada, 1971).

    4199-214   PUBLIC-OPINION COLLECTOR (clerical) DPT:368
    public interviewer.
    GED: 3 SVP: 3 EC: B PA: L 4 5 6

    Interviews public and compiles statistical information on topics, such as public issues or consumer buying habits.
    Contacts people at their homes or places of business, approaches them at random on street, or contacts them by telephone following specified sampling procedures. Asks questions following outline on questionnaire, and records answers. Reviews, classifies and sorts questionnaires following specified procedures and criteria.
    May tally and prepare statistical reports on answers to questions.
    May participate in federal, provincial or local population surveys and be designated accordingly, Census Taker (gov. serv.)

    What methods could be used to train an inexperienced person in each kind of required behaviour? Select an optimal method for training in each and explain why you chose it over other possible methods. Assemble the optimal methods into a training package.

4. Examine training and/or business journals to find an article describing an organization's training program. Describe this program in a short report. What methods does it use? What are some of its advantages and disadvantages? Are there any situations in which it would not be appropriate? (If a number of oral reports are given on this topic, students can learn about a variety of real-world training efforts.)

▶▶▶ CASES

CASE 9.1 ▶ TRAINING AND DEVELOPMENT AT DELI-DELITE

Anne Dotsworth has recently joined the staff of Deli-Delite Industries, a Toronto-based food processing plant. As human resource specialist, she serves in an advisory capacity to the general manager, Harry Walsh. One of Dotsworth's first assignments is to recommend training and development programs for key personnel under Walsh. She has a budget of $3000 to work with.

Since Dotsworth is new to Deli-Delite, she begins by familiarizing herself with Walsh's five immediate subordinates. Reading through their personnel files she gives special attention to information regarding performance reviews, promotions, past training and development activities, and career aspirations. The most pertinent data are summarized into short composites for each employee, as follows:

- *Anton* (age 35) is the division's rising star. After he started in the sales force eight years ago, his exemplary performance quickly accelerated him through a position as regional sales manager to his current position of national sales manager. Anton has responsibility for all key accounts — that is, high volume accounts—and supervises a sales staff of fifteen. There has been a rumour that Deli-Delite's closest competitor has approached Anton with an attractive job offer.
- *Benson* (age 63) has been traffic manager for the division for ten years now, having joined the company at its inception at Walsh's request. Benson appears to enjoy the autonomy of his one-man operation and has no aspirations for advancement. Since no major breakthroughs have occurred in the transportation industry over the past five years and since his work has been satisfactory, Benson has been allowed to choose a personal development training course to attend each year. His in-laws live in Winnipeg, and Benson has always chosen to attend courses offered in that city, scheduling them to coincide with his wife's vacation.
- *Carmela* (age 38) is national brand manager and has six product managers reporting directly to her. Although hers is primarily a strategic planning

and supervisory function, she has been unable to fully relinquish day-to-day "firefighting" responsibilities to her subordinates. Hence, there are never enough hours in the day for Carmela and she is often short with her subordinates. A recent exit interview with a product manager indicated that Carmela didn't give him a chance to run his own product line.
- *Dixon* (age 55) is the division's production manager. His latest performance appraisal indicates that his analytical skills need sharpening. This became apparent when Dixon failed to grasp the significance of capital budgeting calculations that pointed out the infeasibility of a proposed equipment purchase. Dixon admitted never being particularly good with numbers and appeared reluctant to spend the time necessary to fully understand the financial ramifications of his proposal.
- *Ellwood* (age 53), a certified accountant, is the divisional controller. He is an extremely self-motivated, outgoing individual who has a thorough grasp of his job duties. His department runs smoothly and efficiently. Ellwood is working part-time on an MBA at a local university and Deli-Delite is paying his tuition. (This amount need not be included in the current T&D budget.) Even so, Ellwood is always eager to attend further courses so he can meet with other members of his profession or industry. Ellwood has specifically mentioned a forthcoming seminar for controllers offered by the York Executive Development program. According to Ellwood, all his buddies will be in attendance.

Dotsworth refers to the composites as she surveys a list of training and development opportunities prepared by her predecessor (Table 1). She is now ready to make some recommendations.

TABLE 1
Training and Development Opportunities for Deli-Delite Managers

TITLE	LOCATION	DURATION	COST	COURSE OUTLINE	SPECIAL FEATURES
Fundamentals of traffic	Toronto, Harbour Castle	2½ days	$810	How to manage traffic so it makes a real contribution to company profits How to best organize the traffic function What you should know about the rates and routing cycle How to translate transportation documents into valuable sources of information How to prevent claims, and how to proceed when you do get hit Motor carrier regulation—what you must know	

TABLE 1 *(continued)*

Title	Location	Duration	Cost	Course Outline	Special Features
Fundamentals of traffic *(continued)*				Modes of transportation and how each affects your costs and time records	
Management course for controllers	Toronto, Holiday Inn	3 days	$906	Managing yourself, your career, and your staff How to make time work for you How to recognize and avoid barriers to effective communications How to set realistic standards of performance for greater success Eliminating obstacles to problem solving and decision making Successful coaching and counselling techniques Dealing successfully with change	
Action tools for the middle manager	Winnipeg, Holiday Inn	4½ days	$1140	Managing your job and your career How to manage your time How to work with the people side of your job How to use delegation effectively to get things done How to make sure your message is understood How to develop and administer a departmental standards of performance program How to measure performance and review results The positive approach to problem solving and decision making How to use coaching and counselling to develop staff	
Making effective presentations	Toronto, Sutton Place	2 days	$468	Obstacles to effective communications Organizing speeches, proposals, and presentations Speaking and thinking on your feet Overcoming anxiety and developing stage confidence Using visual aids to enhance your message	Closed circuit television sessions Small group work
Effective speed reading	Toronto, Chelsea Inn	1 day	$186	Evaluation of your present reading speed Why a rapid reader has better comprehension and retention	Activity-oriented workshop

TABLE 1 *(continued)*

Title	Location	Duration	Cost	Course Outline	Special Features
Effective speed reading *(continued)*				Techniques for increasing reading speed and concentration Practical session to apply speed reading techniques	
Improving managerial skills	Toronto, Holiday Inn	3 days	$756	Your role as a manager How to motivatee employees (Theory X and Theory Y) Interpersonal relationships Communicating with employees Appraising performance Managing your time Delegating your work Decision making Planning and organizing	
Fundamentals of finance and accounting for nonfinancial managers	Toronto, Westbury Hotel	3 days	$960	The financial community—stock markets, banks, government, financial counsellors, internal financing Financial planning and control—profit planning and budgeting, evaluation of investment performance Nature and organization of business firms—promotion, organization, finance, management Financial statement analysis—understanding accounting language, reading annual reports	Presentations Case studies Informal discussions Role playing
Executive course in sales management	Toronto, Warwick Hotel	4½ days	$1044	Scope of the general sales manager's function and responsibilities Elements of effective sales planning Communicating within the sales organization The general sales manager and the management to the sales function Financial aspects of the general sales manager's function Pricing strategies and profit concepts Sales compensation as a tool to gain management objectives	

TABLE 1 *(continued)*

TITLE	LOCATION	DURATION	COST	COURSE OUTLINE	SPECIAL FEATURES
Wilderness seminar on stress management	Banff National Park	10 days	$1800	Learning to handle stress more effectively Entrants must pass a stiff physical examination	Mountaineering Canoeing River rafting

Source: Based on an exercise developed by E. Hill, H. Lichtman, and C. MacMillan.

TASKS AND QUESTIONS

1. Assume you are Dotsworth. Which of the listed training or development program(s), if any, do you feel might benefit Anton? Benson? Carmela? Dixon? Ellwood? Why?

2. Given your $3000 budget, which of the listed programs will you recommend and for which employees? Will some employees receive no training or development? Provide a brief rationale for your recommendations to Walsh.

CASE 9.2 ▶ ORGANIZATION OF TRAINING FOR NORTHERN TELECOM TEAMS

Northern Telecom (NT) is the world's leading manufacturer of digital communications systems and also produces office information-management systems. It has facilities in Canada, the United States, Malaysia, and Ireland. NT's current strategic goal is to strengthen its position as the leading manufacturer of fully digital telecommunications equipment. The company has established a strategic plan, called Vision 2000, to help it concentrate on five product areas it believes have the greatest growth potential for the year 2000. As part of this strategy, NT is changing its manufacturing operations through the introduction of new equipment and technologies. In addition, work teams are being created in selected product development and manufacturing areas.

NT's training is partly centralized and partly decentralized. Training for management and professional development, sales, and marketing is designed and delivered by the company's headquarters training unit. Other forms of training, particularly technical training, is decentralized to the division and plant levels. The headquarters unit designs and develops generic orientation and core technical materials, which can be used, modified, and added to by the divisions. Product complexity and unique operations make this decentralized approach the most effective one. NT advocates decentralization because each unit can best identify its training needs and can respond quickly to them.

This case focusses on one of NT's major divisions, the Integrated Network Systems Group (INSG). Its training is designed and developed at the group level and delivered centrally at the plant level by operations employees who have been trained and certified as trainers in a specific area. The training is organized on the basis of work operations for four areas: technical (technicians and engineers), operations (just-in-time inventory control and production), manufacturing (product assembly), and sales marketing. The INSG training staff works with division and plant operations managers, as well as with "subject experts" and operations staff trainers, to assess training needs, design and develop programs, provide train-the-trainer training and certification, and assess the effectiveness of training.

The location of technical training depends upon the product or equipment. Manufacturing and operations training is done at the plants; circuit and system training that requires equipment simulators is done at the division's central training facility in Raleigh, North Carolina.

A good example of the approach is the Rancho Bernardo, California, plant, a producer of semiconductors, where a 1984 audit found productivity and quality weaknesses. The plant was restructured by removing several layers of management and integrating functions such as finance, human resources, training, and manufacturing into "business councils." Under the new system, there is one council for each of the main activities, including fabricating, testing, and assembly. Each council has three to twelve work teams, and each team consists of engineers, technicians, operators, and a team manager.

Naturally, technical training was restructured to fit the new team structure. Top management regards excellent technical training as absolutely critical for the success of the teams. Team operators and technicians need to know not only how to operate, trouble-shoot, and maintain equipment in their units, but they must also keep up with the rapidly changing product and manufacturing technologies of semiconductors. Thus, teams are responsible for identifying and analyzing their own training needs and putting together and conducting their own training.

They are not left totally on their own, however. Each council has a technical training group that serves as consultants to its teams and stays up-to-date on new training methods and technologies. Another source of training material, both technical and nontechnical, is the HRM department library, which provides audio and video programs, interactive videos, self-paced printed material, and, of course, books and journals. Technical training also comes from outside sources. For example, a satellite of a local university gives engineering courses for technicians and engineers, and technical schools and community colleges provide courses useful for technicians and operators. Also, manufacturers of new equipment installed at the plant usually provide maintenance training for operators.

Of NT's nearly 49 000 employees worldwide, 900 are technical trainers and about 400 of these are in the INSG. These 400 trainers either have a background in adult education and instructional systems or are "subject experts" (technicians or engineers with an excellent knowledge of their specialty) with some adult education experience. These experts don't stay in training but use the work there as one step in their career; the advantages to INSG are that training stays very close to plant operations, and operations employees appreciate the importance and challenge of training.

INSG training staff work in three-person teams to respond to training needs. One member, the "subject expert," is responsible for training content and works most closely with operations. The second team member is an HR specialist, who organizes the training content for most effective learning. Finally, a media specialist assists in developing training materials.

Source: Based on A.P. Carnevale, L.J. Gainer, and E. Schulz, *Training the Technical Work Force* (San Francisco: Jossey-Bass, 1990), pp. 167–81. Used with the permission of Jossey-Bass Inc. and the American Society for Training and Development.

TASKS AND QUESTIONS

1. Describe how NT has organized training. Why did the company choose this approach? Do you believe it meets the firm's needs?

2. Would NT's approach to training be appropriate for other organizations? Why or why not?

3. NT's training programs are similar in many ways to those of Merck, Motorola, and Kimberly-Clark, Xerox, and other leading employers. How does NT's approach to training compare to that of an organization with which you are acquainted?

NOTES

1. "Old Hands, New Skills: Training the Trainers at Miramichi," in G. Betcherman, K. Newton, and J. Godin, eds., *Two Steps Forward: Human Resource Management in a High-Tech World* (Ottawa: Economic Council of Canada, 1990), p. 7. Reproduced with the permission of the chairman of the Economic Council of Canada, 1992.

2. "Old Hands, New Skills," pp. 7–13.

3. H.B. Bernard and C.A. Ingols, "Six Lessons for the Corporate Classroom," *Harvard Business Review*, vol. 66 (September–October 1988), pp. 40–47.

4. A.P. Carnevale, L.J. Gainer, and E. Schulz, *Training the Technical Work Force* (San Francisco: Jossey-Bass, 1990).

5. *Wall Street Journal*, February 9, 1990.

6. P.E. Larson and M.W. Blue, *Training and Development 1990: Expenditures and Policies*, Conference Board of Canada, Report 67-91, June 25, 1991, pp. 7–11.

7. N.M. Meltz, "The Evolution of Worker Training: The Canadian Experience," in L.A. Ferman, M. Hoyman, J. Cutcher-Gershenfeld, and E.J. Savoie, eds., *New Developments in Worker Training: A Legacy for the 1990s* (Madison, Wisc.: Industrial Relations Research Association, 1990).

8. A.P. Carnevale, L.J. Gainer, and J. Villet, *Training in America: The Organization and Strategic Role of Training* (San Francisco: Jossey-Bass, 1990), p. 165.

9. R.T. Pascale, *Managing on the Edge* (New York: Simon and Schuster, 1990), p. 249. Copyright © 1990 by Richard Pascale. Reprinted by permission of Simon & Schuster.

10. Meltz, "Evolution of Worker Training."

11. R.G. Ehrenberg and R.S. Smith, *Modern Labor Economics*, 3rd ed. (Glenview, Ill.: Scott, Foresman, 1988).

12. L.S. Richman, "The Coming World Labor Shortage," *Fortune*, April 9, 1990, p. 71. Reprinted with permission.

13. See L. Surtees, "Northern Telecom Embraces Work-Team System," *The Globe and Mail*, April 9, 1990.

14. W.E. Deming, *Out of the Crises* (Cambridge, Mass.: MIT Press, 1986), pp. 23–24. Consideration of all fourteen of Deming's points would be useful for students of HRM.

15. Deming, *Out of the Crises*, pp. 59–60.

16. R. Aguayo, *Dr. Deming: The American Who Taught the Japanese about Quality* (Don Mills, Ont.: Musson Book Company, 1990), p. 172.

17. Meltz, "Evolution of Worker Training."

18. P.B. Crosby, *Quality without Tears* (New York: McGraw-Hill, 1984); and P.B. Crosby, *Quality Is Free: The Art of Making Quality Certain* (New York: McGraw-Hill, 1974).

19. K. Newton and G. Betcherman, "Innovating on Two Fronts: People and Technology in the 1990s," *Canadian Business Review*, Autumn 1987, pp. 18–21. The Conference Board of Canada.

20. Newton and Betcherman, "Innovating on Two Fronts," p. 21.

21. M. Gibb-Clark, "Improved Training of Staff Becoming Essential Tool," *The Globe and Mail*, January 23, 1990.

22. Gibb-Clark, "Improved Training."

23. Gibb-Clark, "Improved Training."

24. J.E. Hautaluoma and J.F. Gavin, "Effects of Organizational Diagnosis and Intervention on Blue-Collar Blues," *Journal of Applied Behavioral Science*, vol. 11 (1975), pp. 475–98.

25. Larson and Blue, "Training and Development 1990," pp. 5–6 and 11–13.

26. Ontario Training Corporation, *SkillsLink*, 1991.

27. Larson and Blue, "Training and Development 1990," p. 12.

28. A. Kotlowitz, "Caterpillar Faces a Showdown with UAW," *The Wall Street Journal*, March 5, 1986.

29. R.F. Mager and P. Pipe, *Analyzing Performance Problems* (Belmont, Calif.: Lake Publishing Company, 1984).

30. R.F. Mager, *Preparing Instructional Objectives*, 2nd ed. (Belmont, Calif.: Fearon-Pitman Publishers, 1975).

31. R.A. Morano and N. Deets, "Professional Retraining: Meeting the Technological Challenge," *Training and Development Journal*, March 1985, pp. 99–101.

32. M. Cu-Uy-Gam, "Firms, Workers Making Most of Training Opportunities," *The Toronto Star*, June 9, 1989, p. 39.

33. B.M. Bass and J.A. Vaughan, *Training in Industry: The Management of Learning* (Monterey, Calif.: Brooks/Cole, 1966).

34. D.F. Salisbury, B.F. Richards, and J.D. Klein, "Designing Practice: A Review of Prescriptions and Recommendations from Instructional Design Theories," *Journal of Instructional Development*, vol. 8, no. 4 (1985), pp. 9–19.

35. Salisbury, Richards, and Klein, "Designing Practice."

36. J.R. Anderson, *Cognitive Psychology and Its Implications* (San Francisco: Freeman, 1980).

37. Salisbury, Richards, and Klein, "Designing Practice."

38. Bass and Vaughan, *Training in Industry*, p. 58.

39. E.A. Locke and G.P. Latham, *A Theory of Goal Setting and Task Performance* (Englewood Cliffs, NJ: Prentice-Hall, 1990).

40. I.I. Goldstein, *Training in Organizations: Needs Assessment, Development and Evaluation*, 2nd ed. (Monterey, Calif.: Brooks/Cole, 1986); and A.P. Goldstein and M. Sorcher, *Changing Supervisor Behavior* (New York: Pergamon Press, 1974).

41. E.A. Fleishman, E.F. Harris, and H.S. Burtt, *Leadership and Supervision in Industry*, Bureau of Educational Research report no. 33 (Columbus: Ohio State University, 1955).

42. R.H. Kilmann, *Beyond the Quick Fix* (San Francisco: Jossey-Bass, 1984).

43. L. Bambrick, "Book Warming," *Canadian HR Reporter*, June 21, 1989, p. 7.

44. L. Bambrick, "Companies Take Closer Look at Recruits," *Canadian HR Reporter*, August 16, 1989, p. 13; T. Crawford, "Firm's Production and Sales Soar after Training Scheme Introduced," *The Toronto Star*, January 28, 1990; and "Chrysler Workers to Get Paid for On-the-Job Literacy Training," *The Toronto Star*, December 13, 1991.

45. R.F. Mager, "The Winds of Change," *Training and Development Journal*, October 1977, pp. 12–20.

46. Larson and Blue, "Training and Development 1990," p. 9.

47. "Employee Training Can Be Started without Great Expense, Chamber Says," *The Globe and Mail*, January 25, 1990.
48. Goldstein, *Training in Organizations*.
49. J. Main, "New Ways to Teach Workers What's New," *Fortune*, October 1, 1984, pp. 85–94.
50. D.L. Dossett and P. Hulvershorn, "Increasing Technical Training Efficiency: Peer Training via Computer-Assisted Instruction," *Journal of Applied Psychology*, vol. 68, no. 4 (1983), pp. 552–58.
51. K.N. Wexley and G.P. Latham, *Developing and Training Human Resources in Organizations*, 2nd ed. (New York: HarperCollins, 1991), pp. 198–99.
52. Main, "New Ways to Teach Workers."
53. Wexley and Latham, *Developing and Training Human Resources*, p. 163.
54. G. Allen, "Politics in the Office," *Maclean's*, July 15, 1985, pp. 32–36.
55. Bass and Vaughan, *Training in Industry*.
56. A. Bandura, *Principles of Behavior Modification* (New York: Holt Rinehart and Winston, 1969).
57. G.P. Latham and L.M. Saari, "The Application of Social Learning Theory to Training Supervisors through Behaviour Modeling," *Journal of Applied Psychology*, vol. 64 (1979), pp. 239–46; and M. Sorcher and R. Spence, "The Interface Project: Behavior Modeling and Social Technology in South Africa," *Personnel Psychology*, vol. 35, no. 3 (Autumn 1982), pp. 557–82.
58. J.R. Hinrichs, "Personnel Training," in M.D. Dunnette, ed., *Handbook of Industrial/Organizational Psychology* (Chicago: Rand McNally, 1976), p. 856.
59. Hinrichs, "Personnel Training."
60. E.S. Andrews and J.L. Noel, "Adding Life to the Case-Study Method," *Training and Development Journal*, February 1986, pp. 28–29.
61. Meltz, "Evolution of Worker Training."
62. D. Laird, "What Should Training Rooms Be Like?" in D. Laird, *Approaches to Training and Development* (Reading, Mass.: Addison-Wesley, 1985), pp. 185–202.
63. C. Lee, "Industry Report, 1990," *Training*, October 1990, pp. 29–32.
64. Larson and Blue, "Training and Development 1990," p. 3.
65. Larson and Blue, "Training and Development 1990," p. 16.
66. J. Gordon, "Where the Training Goes," *Training*, October, 1990, pp. 51–69.
67. Larson and Blue, "Training and Development 1990," p. 21.
68. See, for example, J.P. Campbell, "Personnel Training and Development," *Annual Review of Psychology*, vol. 22 (1971), pp. 565–602; and Hinrichs, "Personnel Training."
69. [U.S.] Bureau of National Affairs, *Training and Development Programs Personnel Policies Forum Survey No. 140*, pp. 17, 20. Copyright 1985 by the Bureau of National Affairs, Inc.

70. Larson and Blue, "Training and Development 1990," p. 13.
71. M. Gibb Clark, "IBM Measures Up in Employee Training," *The Globe and Mail*, January 25, 1990.
72. J.E. Hunter and F.L. Schmidt, "Quantifying the Effects of Psychological Interventions on Employee Job Performance and Work-Force Productivity," *American Psychologist*, vol. 38 (1983), pp. 473–78.

SUGGESTIONS FOR FURTHER READING

- L.S. Baird, C.E. Schneier, and D. Laird. *The Training and Development Sourcebook*. Amherst, Mass.: Human Resource Development Press, 1983.
- A.P. Carnevale, L.J. Gainer, and E. Schulz. *Training the Technical Work Force*. San Francisco: Jossey-Bass, 1990.
- A.P. Carnevale, L.J. Gainer, and J. Villet. *Training in America: The Organization and Strategic Role of Training*. San Francisco: Jossey-Bass, 1990.
- I.L. Goldstein. *Training and Organizations: Needs Assessment, Development and Evaluation*, 2nd ed. Monterey, Calif.: Brooks/Cole, 1986.
- R.F. Mager and P. Pipe. *Analyzing Performance Problems*. Belmont, Calif.: Lake Publishing Company, 1984.
- N.M. Meltz. "The Evolution of Worker Training: The Canadian Experience." In L.A. Ferman, M. Hoyman, J. Cutcher-Gershenfeld, and E.H. Savoie, eds., *New Developments in Worker Training: A Legacy for the 1990s*. Madison, Wisc.: Industrial Relations Research Association, 1990.
- K.N. Wexley and G.P. Latham. *Developing and Training Human Resources in Organizations*, 2nd ed. New York: HarperCollins, 1991.

CHAPTER 10

CAREER PLANNING

- REASONS FOR CAREER PLANNING
- RELATION TO OTHER HRM FUNCTIONS
- WHAT PEOPLE WANT FROM THEIR CAREERS
- ELEMENTS OF CAREER PLANNING PROGRAMS
- CAREER PLANNING PROGRAMS
- CEIC AIDS FOR CAREER PLANNING
- FACILITATING CAREER PLANNING AND DEVELOPMENT
- CAREER PLANNING ISSUES
- HRM IN ACTION ▸ ACCOMMODATING A CHANGING WORK FORCE
- SUMMARY
- REVIEW QUESTIONS
- PROJECT IDEAS
- CASE 10.1 ▸ TUITION AID AND TURNOVER AT WESTFIELD CONSTRUCTION
- CASE 10.2 ▸ WORK AND FAMILY ISSUES
- NOTES
- SUGGESTIONS FOR FURTHER READING

TED MAXWELL HAS BEEN EMPLOYED AS a medical records clerk at a large hospital, City General, for twelve months. He has adjusted well to his job and to the work environment. Maxwell is happy with his decision to join the hospital staff, and the annual appraisal of his work indicated that he is doing a good job. Because Maxwell is happy with his job choice and with City General, he is beginning to wonder what kind of future he might have with the organization. Like many modern workers, Maxwell welcomes a challenge and the opportunity to grow and develop to his full potential. Too, Maxwell's superiors may be wondering how they can develop and utilize him to the best of his abilities in order to meet future staffing needs. The HRM function that seeks to reconcile individual career plans and needs with organizational needs is known as career planning, or career management.

Career planning includes (1) assessment of an employee's abilities and potential; (2) determination of logical paths of movement between jobs; and (3) efforts to channel individual career interests in directions compatible with the organization's future human resource needs.

Although the term "career development" is sometimes confused with "career planning," the two are not synonymous. *Career development*, as discussed in Chapter 9, refers to the process and activities involved in preparing an employee for future positions in the organization. Career planning is the topic of this chapter.

REASONS FOR CAREER PLANNING

Career planning is a relatively new HRM function, and established programs are rare except in very large or progressive organizations. Organizational involvement in career planning is increasing, however. Many job candidates — especially, but not only, those who are highly educated — want a career, not "just a job," and many employees have high expectations about gaining satisfaction from their work, now and in the future.

There are a number of reasons for career planning; the following are cited as influential by 225 companies that engage in career planning activities:

1. Desire to develop and promote employees from within.
2. Shortage of promotable talent.
3. Desire to aid individual career planning.
4. Strong expression of interest by employees.
5. Desire to improve productivity.
6. Affirmative action program commitments.
7. Concern about turnover.
8. Personal interest of unit managers.
9. Desire for a positive recruiting image.[1]

From this list, we see that the impetus behind career planning may come from either of two sources or both: (1) employers who strive to retain and effectively utilize their human resources; and (2) employees who desire satisfying work and personal growth.

The economic turbulence of the 1980s has led a number of writers such as Rosabeth Moss Kanter to argue that careers are "less likely to resemble the bureaucratic pattern of an orderly progression of ever-higher-level and more remunerative jobs."[2] Careers may instead consist of moves from one project to another or advances within a skill- or knowledge-based pay structure in which one remains in the same work team. Kanter believes that the future work environment — the post-entrepreneurial world — will be a blend of "creative entrepreneurs" and "disciplined, agile, innovative corporations." In such an unpredictable environment, where job security is uncertain, Kanter believes that employers must offer jobs and training and development opportunities that can increase employees' future employability — their "employability security." One example of this approach is at Motorola, which provides an education program to teach employees new skills at a cost of about $44 million per year, or about 2.4 percent of payroll.[3]

Even in the midst of downsizing and restructuring, career-related programs are not only possible but vitally important. Latack argues that restructuring leads to many redundant or inappropriately placed employees and that a "career management strategy" that ranges from in-placement to out-placement is necessary.[4] *In-placement* emphasizes employee retention and creative employee movement to other jobs. Closely associated with it are strategies such as retraining or cross-training, entrepreneurship focussing on creating new jobs, and job redesign. At the other extreme is *outplacement*, which focusses on helping employees exit. Proper handling of outplacement strategies is important for employers as they must rely on the commitment and best efforts of the survivors. Research by Brockner shows that when layoffs are done in a manner perceived by survivors as equitable, performance will not be adversely affected.[5] Additionally, employers who help employees increase their employability through a variety of training and development programs will find that in-placement is a more viable strategy and that outplacement, if it is necessary at all, is more accepted.

Effective Utilization of Human Resources

A primary reason for career planning is the organizations' need to make the best possible use of their most valuable resource—people—in a time of rapid technological growth and change. By developing employees for future positions, an organization is assured a supply of qualified, committed employees to replace higher-level employees who either terminate or advance. This facilitates internal staffing of the organization and reduces the costs of external recruiting and selection. In addition, a career planning strategy enables organizations to develop and place employees in positions compatible with their individual career interests, needs, and goals, thus promoting employee satisfaction and optimal use of employee abilities.

Though career planning programs can help employees channel their energies toward higher-level positions (giving them a sense of striving and upward mobility), they cannot be expected to guarantee such positions for all who choose to pursue them. For one thing, the number of higher-level positions, especially in management, is limited. For another, the number of experienced and deserving workers vying for limited positions has grown because of the aging of the work force. The realities of a sluggish economy, requiring staff cutbacks in many cases, have only made matters worse.

Problems of career blockage are especially acute among executives who find their paths blocked because of corporate reorganization, office politics, and sluggish company growth. Because of the lack of advancement opportunities, many such executives actively seek alternative employment.

Women as a group have recently begun to overcome career blockage problems. Formerly concentrated in domestic occupations such as nursing, women now represent 40 percent of employed managers and administrators, and 56 percent of professionals.[6] Women have been a major factor in labour force growth. Their increase in both traditionally female- and traditionally male-dominated professions is impressive. The number of women graduating with MBAs increased 344 percent from 1976 to 1986 in the United States.[7] Television coverage of the Persian Gulf conflict in early 1991 made us all aware of the large role women are playing as members of the armed services.

Women still contend with "glass ceilings" in many organizations, but changes are occurring, and challenges such as problems of child care and dual-career couples will have to be met.

The realities of employment equity, slowed economic growth, and downsizing mean that career planning must identify logical job sequences and activities that have less of the traditional emphasis on upward mobility. With upward mobility less of an option, career planning increases in importance as a vehicle for meeting employee demands for more satisfying work and employability security.

Employee Desires for Satisfying Work

In North America, the decades since World War II have seen a general increase in concern for the quality of life and work, in good times and in bad. Workers expect more than pay cheques from their jobs. Work is often viewed as a medium for satisfying personal needs, as an experience in which the employee grows to meet increasing challenges. This broad view of the role of work is evidenced by the federal and Ontario governments' establishment of quality of working life (QWL) programs. QWL centres, whose boards include representatives of management and organized labour, provide information and research data on ways in which unions and management can work together to redesign their organizations to offer more satisfying work experiences.

In part, the phenomenon of seeking satisfaction in work reflects the general prosperity of the postwar era. It is probably also a function of the rising general level of education. A 1978 survey, which received responses from 29 609 individuals who had graduated from Canadian universities and colleges in 1976, found that only 12 percent were not satisfied with their jobs.[8] Two-thirds of this group were underemployed and/or working in jobs that had nothing to do with their postsecondary programs. Respondents who were most satisfied were graduates of master's and PhD programs, presumably because they had been able to obtain interesting work.

The tendency to emphasize job satisfaction is not restricted to highly educated or professional workers. A more general survey of Canadians' feelings about their jobs in the 1970s found that the single most important consideration was interesting work.[9] This factor ranked ahead of such other job characteristics as enough authority, clearly defined responsibilities, competent co-workers, a lot of freedom, or good job security. Of the 34 characteristics listed, good pay ranked 17th and good fringe benefits 26th. The importance of interesting work did increase with the respondent's income level, but a very high percentage of low-income workers indicated that they put much value on job satisfaction. Interesting work was listed as important by 72 percent of the respondents whose incomes were at or near the poverty line and by more than 85 percent of those whose incomes were at middle-class levels.

If frustrated, employee needs for growth and advancement can lead to dissatisfaction and voluntary turnover. A study comparing employee satisfaction in 1981 versus 1977 found a decline in satisfaction over the four-year period for both men and women. The fall-off was attributed to two factors: lack of perceived opportunities for advancement and perceived inability to influence the decisions of superiors. Women experienced the greatest declines in satisfaction over the four-year period. Among men, the greatest declines were found among professional, managerial, and skilled workers.[10] Another study found that 42 percent of executive job-changers quit because they perceived better opportunities for career advancement elsewhere. An additional 23 percent left to assume greater responsibilities immediately.[11] Lack of advancement opportunities has also been linked to turnover among nurses, clerical workers, salesmen, and nonsupervisory plant workers, among others.

Recent surveys present a somewhat negative picture of employee satisfaction. For example, an analysis of a ten-year (1977–87) trend in employee attitudes by Hay Management Consultants found a significant decline in employees' ratings of their companies as places to work. One major reason for the decline was the perceived reduction in promotion opportunities, particularly among middle managers. Employees also felt less informed about what was going on in their organization — why various business decisions were made, where the company was going, and where their jobs fit in. And employees felt the information they did receive was not very credible.[12] A more recent survey by the Wyatt Company found that 75 percent of their 2300-person sample were satisfied with the content of their jobs.[13] Only 40 percent, however, felt that those in management positions had a genuine interest in their well-being and treated them with respect and dignity (though 70 of 98 senior managers felt they did). Only 54 percent of employees were satisfied with communication with management and just over 40 percent were satisfied with performance appraisals and career development and training. Men and union members were more satisfied than women and nonunion members. Clearly, the economic climate as well as various management practices have adversely affected employee attitudes.

The realities of the recession of the early 1980s tempered short-term aspirations but did not change basic societal attitudes. The career orientation of labour force entrants was evidenced in the 1981–82 *Career Planning Annual*;[14] most organizations advertising in this publication emphasized opportunities for career growth and development. A glance at recruitment ads in fall 1982 also suggested that not even that season's high unemployment rates had obviated the perceived importance of work as a challenge and a career. In just one edition of one daily paper, ads for many different jobs emphasized their potential for growth: "challenging, demanding, rewarding career opportunity" (caregiver for disturbed children); "ground floor opportunity to work yourself into the personnel department of a downtown hospital" (reception/clerk); "chance to grow with young company" (copy preparer for a typesetting and printing firm); "excellent dynamic opportunity" (telephone salesperson); and so on. To see how employers are describing positions today, examine the most recent issue of the *Career Planning Annual*.

The turbulence of the 1980s and early 1990s has undoubtedly left employees, from low-level blue-collar workers to executives, more concerned with having a job than with career advancement. A 1986 Harris–*Business Week* poll found that of the manager respondents from a sample of large companies, nearly half expected cuts in salaried employees. Another survey of top executives found that only slightly more than a third were confident about the future of big companies. Comparison of a 1975 and a 1985 Hay survey of middle managers found the percentage of those with a positive opinion of advancement opportunities had declined from 75 to 40 percent.[15] Clearly, the 1980s caused many employees to shift their career planning concerns from advancement to security.

Ironically, the very condition that led to layoffs, restructuring, and downsizing, namely, the need for organizations to be flexible and innovative in meeting global competition, is also demanding that companies invest more in developing their human resources. While career planning has traditionally helped employees move upward in well-defined career paths, turbulent business conditions require a more general and more flexible kind of planning that includes a wider array of potential jobs.

RELATION TO OTHER HRM FUNCTIONS

From an employee's perspective, career planning takes place after some amount of time on the job and after the organization has had a chance to appraise his or her performance. From an organizational perspective, career planning is an ongoing management function with close ties to performance appraisal, human resource planning (HRP), job analysis, and employee development (see Figure 10.1).

PERFORMANCE APPRAISAL

Performance appraisals inform employees of their strengths and weaknesses, their relative standing in the organization, and their chances for promotion or advancement. This information is essential to deciding on realistic individual career goals.

Such goals are often set within developmental performance appraisal interviews. Traditionally, organizations have used performance appraisal, formal or informal, to identify employees with the potential to advance to positions of greater responsibility. The underlying assumption is that employees with good performance records in one capacity will be good performers in another. Because of their past performance records, high-potential employ-

FIGURE 10.1
Career Planning: Relation to Other HRM Functions

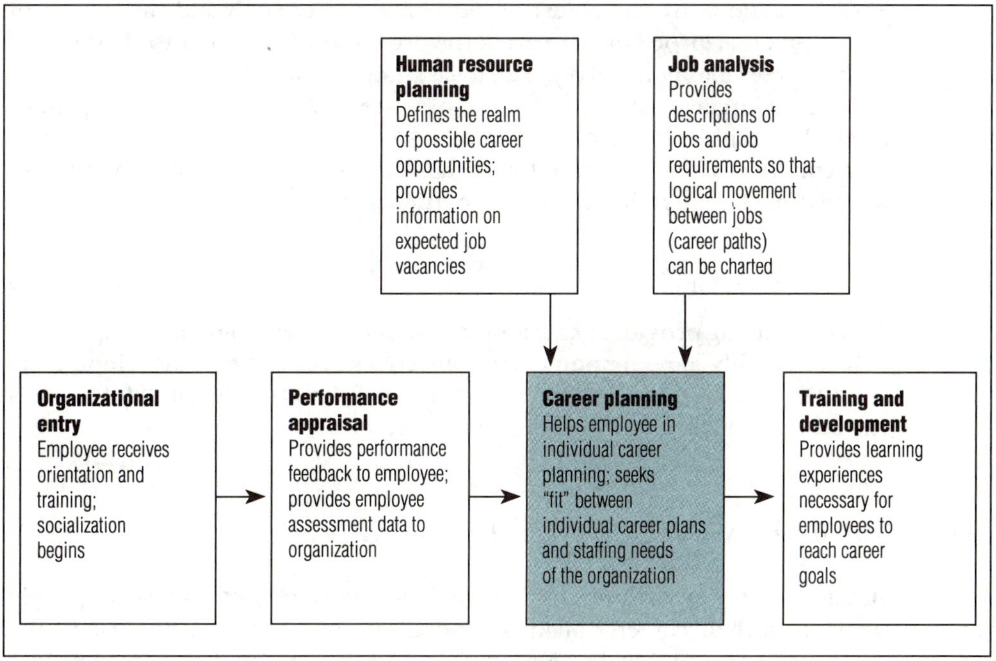

```
                    ┌─────────────────┐    ┌─────────────────┐
                    │ Human resource  │    │ Job analysis    │
                    │ planning        │    │ Provides        │
                    │ Defines the realm│    │ descriptions of │
                    │ of possible career│   │ jobs and job    │
                    │ opportunities;  │    │ requirements so that│
                    │ provides        │    │ logical movement│
                    │ information on  │    │ between jobs    │
                    │ expected job    │    │ (career paths)  │
                    │ vacancies       │    │ can be charted  │
                    └────────┬────────┘    └────────┬────────┘
                             │                      │
                             ▼                      ▼
┌──────────────┐  ┌──────────────┐  ┌──────────────┐  ┌──────────────┐
│Organizational│  │Performance   │  │Career planning│ │Training and  │
│entry         │  │appraisal     │  │Helps employee in│ development  │
│Employee receives│ Provides performance│ individual career│ Provides learning│
│orientation and│ │feedback to employee;│ planning; seeks│ experiences  │
│training;     │→ │provides employee│→ │"fit" between  │→│necessary for │
│socialization │  │assessment data to│ │individual career plans│ employees to│
│begins        │  │organization   │  │and staffing needs│ reach career │
│              │  │              │  │of the organization│ goals       │
└──────────────┘  └──────────────┘  └──────────────┘  └──────────────┘
```

ees gain access to career planning and development opportunities that will prepare them for future positions in the organization.

HUMAN RESOURCE PLANNING

From an organizational perspective, career planning reconciles individual career planning needs, interests, and goals with the organization's future staffing needs. In this way, the organization ensures that an adequate supply of well-trained and motivated employees will be available to fill job vacancies. Human resource planners provide predictions of expected job vacancies, data that career planners use to give employees reasonable expectations of their opportunities for advancement. Career planning also has valuable inputs for HRP. By providing information on the career plans of individuals, it contributes to management's knowledge of probable human resource flows throughout the organization.

JOB ANALYSIS

One of the responsibilities of career planners is to inform employees of career opportunities within the organization. This responsibility involves the charting of *career paths*, logical movements between jobs or from one job to a target position. A *target position* is one that an employee is striving to attain or one that the organization is preparing him or her to assume in the future. Target positions are the object of individual career goals and the subject of developmental efforts on the part of the organization. In order to chart career paths, career planners need job analysis information.

Specific target positions are a realistic career objective in some organizations. The rapid rate of change in many organizations, however, suggests that employees should strive for certain levels of responsibility within an occupational area, rather than for a particular position.

EMPLOYEE DEVELOPMENT

Career planning provides goals for the systematic development of employees. When mutually agreed-upon career objectives are specified, developmental activities can be selected and channelled in a direction meaningful to both the individual employee and the organization.

WHAT PEOPLE WANT FROM THEIR CAREERS

In addition to opportunities for growth and development, what do people want from their careers? Making generalizations is difficult because of the wide range of individual differences. Further, what people want from their careers tends to change over time: career advancements and advancing age spark new interests and change needs. Nonetheless, E.H. Schein has identified five dominant motives underlying people's career choices and long-range goals. He refers to them as "career anchors."[16]

SCHEIN'S CAREER ANCHORS

Schein's career anchors represent aspects of work that people especially value or need for personal fulfilment. They include the following:

1. Managerial competence: the individual desires opportunities to manage.
2. Technical/functional competence: the individual wants to use various technical abilities and special competencies.
3. Security: the individual is basically motivated by a need for job security or stability in the work situation.
4. Creativity: the individual is motivated by a need to create or build something.
5. Autonomy and independence: of primary interest to this person is the opportunity to work independently, without organizational constraints.

Career planning and development activities allow employees to grow in any of these desired directions.

CAREER STAGES

What people want from their careers also varies according to the stage of their careers. What may have been important in an early stage may not be in a later one. Researchers have identified four distinct career stages: trial, establishment/advancement, midcareer, and late career.[17] Each stage reflects different career needs and interests of the individual (see Table 10.1).

TABLE 10.1
Career Stages

STAGE	TASK NEEDS	EMOTIONAL NEEDS
Trial	Varied job activities Self-exploration	Make preliminary job choices Settle down
Establishment/ advancement	Job challenge Develop competence in a specialty area Develop creativity and innovation Rotate into new area after 3–5 years	Deal with rivalry and competition; face failures Deal with work–family conflicts Support Develop autonomy
Midcareer	Technical updating Develop skills in training and coaching others (younger employees) Rotation into new job requiring new skills Develop broader view of work and own role in organization	Express feelings about midlife Reorganize thinking about self in relation to work, family, community Reduce self-indulgence and competitiveness
Late career	Plan for retirement Shift from power role to one of consultation and guidance Identify and develop successors Begin activities outside the organization	Receive support and counselling to see work as a platform for others Develop sense of identity in extraorganizational activities

Source: Adapted from D.T. Hall and M.A. Morgan, "Career Development and Planning," in K. Pearlman, F.L. Schmidt, and W.C. Hamner, eds., *Contemporary Problems in Personnel*, 3rd ed. (New York: Wiley, 1983), p. 229. Copyright © 1983 John Wiley & Sons, Inc. Used with the permission of John Wiley & Sons, Inc.

Trial Stage

The trial stage begins with an individual's exploration of career-related matters and ends, usually at about age 25, with a commitment to a particular occupation. Until that decision is made, the individual may try a number of jobs and a number of employers. Unfortunately for many organizations, this trial and exploration stage results in high levels of turnover among new employees. Employees in this stage need opportunities for self-exploration and a variety of job activities or assignments.

Establishment/Advancement Stage

The establishment/advancement stage tends to occur between ages 25 and 44. The individual has made his or her career choice and is now concerned with achievement, performance, and advancement. This stage is marked by high productivity and career growth, as the individual is motivated to succeed in the organization and in his or her chosen occupation. Opportunities for job challenge and use of special competencies are desired. Employees in this stage strive for creativity and innovation through new job assignments. They also need a certain degree of autonomy so that they can experience feelings of individual achievement and personal success.

Midcareer Stage

The midcareer stage, which occurs roughly between ages 45 and 64, has also been referred to as the maintenance stage. It is typified by a continuation of established patterns of work behaviour. The person is no longer trying to establish a place within the organization but to maintain his or her position. This stage is sometimes viewed as a plateau,[18] but the individual in it may need some technical updating and should be encouraged to develop new job skills in order to avoid early stagnation and decline.

Late Career Stage

D.E. Super, whose work has defined career stages, refers to the late-career stage from 65 on as one of decline. He states: "You call it what you want — the Golden Years, the Sunshine Years, whatever. But I'm there; take my word for it, it's decline!"[19] In this stage, the career lessens in importance and the employee plans for retirement and seeks to develop a sense of identity outside the work environment.

Although the concept of career stages is a useful one, few of today's employees may be expected to progress through them step-by-step. Rather, the trend is toward multiple careers and midcareer changes.

ELEMENTS OF CAREER PLANNING PROGRAMS

In practice, career planning is a poorly defined function whose responsibilities often span a number of other HRM functions. For example, human resource planners may describe career opportunities in terms of estimates of projected job vacancies at time X. Supervisors may handle career counselling within the context of performance appraisal interviews. Developmental activities for reaching career goals may be prescribed by training and development specialists. Career planning is not necessarily new to organizations; what is new is an increased awareness of its potential value and the attempt by some organizations to integrate its diverse elements into a separate and definable HRM function.[20]

Though career planning programs differ, four distinct elements emerge: (1) individual assessments of abilities, interests, career needs, and goals; (2) organizational assessments of employees' abilities and potential; (3) communication of information about career options and opportunities with the organization; and (4) career counselling to set realistic goals and plan for their attainment. Effective career planning programs provide opportunities for employees to engage in all four elements.

INDIVIDUAL ASSESSMENTS

Many employees begin their working lives without any formal assessment of their abilities, interests, career needs, and goals. This phenomenon of entering jobs, occupations, and careers with little attention to planning is known as *career drift*. A *Psychology Today* survey of 2300 readers in the late 1970s found that career drift explained the job choice of many respondents: 40 percent had happened into their present occupation by chance; fewer than 25 percent were in an occupation of their choice, and the majority were thinking of making a major career change in the next five years. Further, nearly half the sample felt locked into their jobs with no avenues of escape other than termination. The authors of the survey concluded that the needs, desires, and dissatisfactions represented in this sample meant potential turnover and other problems for organizations unless they could provide more interesting and challenging jobs and careers.[21] A more recent but smaller sample study reported in *Personnel* adds support to the *Psychology Today* conclusion.[22] It found that the desire for more meaningful work and for a better fit between work and personal values was cited by managers as a reason for leaving current employment to start a new career. Those managers who stayed with their employers valued advancement opportunities, job security, and high income more than did those who chose to leave. The plant closings, layoffs, and relatively slow economic growth of the 1980s and early 1990s suggest that today's employees may have similar or even more pessimistic attitudes. Regardless of the economic climate, managers and HRM professionals must attempt to create opportunities for employees to do interesting and challenging work.

Since definitions of "interesting" and "challenging" vary from one employee to another, the career planning process must begin with the individual and an assessment of his or her abilities, interests, career needs, and goals.

Individual assessment of abilities, interests, career needs, and goals is basically a process of self-exploration and analysis. Individuals are frequently guided by self-assessment exercises (see Exhibit 10.1). The self-assessment process is primarily viewed as an individual responsibility; however, organizations can aid in it by providing the employee with materials and opportunities for self-exploration and analysis. A variety of self-assessment materials are available commercially, but a number of organizations, including Ontario Hydro, Corning, and General Electric, have developed tailor-made workbooks for employees' career planning.

Individual career planning exercises can be done independently by employees or in workshops sponsored by the organization. Workshops have the advantage of combining a number of career planning elements, including self-assessment, communication of organizational career and development opportunities, and one-on-one counselling to ensure that career goals are realistic. Planning for the accomplishment of career objectives, sometimes called "strategizing," may also be done at this time. Although workshops are a useful aid in individual career planning, they are still quite uncommon.

ORGANIZATIONAL ASSESSMENTS

A key issue in career counselling is whether an employee's goals are realistic in terms of organizational possibilities and the organization's assessments of his or her abilities and potential. Thus, accurate assessments of an employee's abilities and potential are important to both the organization and the individual.

Organizations have several sources of information for making assessments of their employees' abilities and potential. The first is selection information, including ability tests, interest inventories, and biographical information, such as education and work experience. The second is current job history information, including performance appraisal information, records of promotions and promotion recommendations, salary increases, and participation in various training and development programs.

Organizations have traditionally relied on performance appraisal data as the primary basis for assessing employee potential. This reliance assumes that past performance is a good predictor of future performance in a different capacity, an assumption that may be faulty for a number of reasons. First, performance appraisals do not always accurately reflect employees' abilities and actual performance. They are often coloured by evaluators' biases and by faulty instruments. Second, if the job requirements of the future position

EXHIBIT 10.1
Items from a Self-Assessment Exercise to Determine Personal Wants

Personal wants

Free time	Power	Fun work
Money	Independence	Security
Professional stature	Challenge	Freedom from worry
Friends	Prestige	Cultural opportunities
Geographic location	Recreation	Visibility
Climate	Educational facilities	Leadership
Expertness	Time with family	

1. Select the three personal wants above that are most important to you in your next job assignment and circle them.
2. Select the three personal wants above that are least important to you in your next career step and draw a line through them.
3. Add personal wants you don't find on the list.
4. Does your present job setting offer possibilities for satisfying what you want most in your next step? If yes, describe how. If no, what setting is indicated?
5. Do you want your next job assignment to satisfy your wants? If yes, how? If no, why not?
6. Decide what you want most in your next job assignment and describe it.
7. Describe the major activities you can do and will do to gain what you want, but don't use job titles or positions to describe what you will do. Describe the type of activities you'll perform to achieve what you want. List at least five activities you can perform now.
   Examples: I'll analyze data for financial records.
   　　　　　I'll collect more from creditors.
   　　　　　I'll marry the boss's daughter.
8. Do you need to develop some new skills or abilities to improve your potential for your next step? If so, what skills or abilities would you develop?
9. Can or must some of your wants be satisfied off the job? If so, what does this mean in terms of how you would consider any future positions?
10. Summarize what you personally want and what you can do and will do to satisfy your wants.

Source: Adapted from General Electric's *Career Action Planning Workbook* (Ossining, N.Y.: GE Management Development Institute, © 1973). Used with permission.

differ substantially from those of the present job, one cannot assume that the employee will be equally successful in the new role. Despite these potential problems, performance appraisal data will continue to be used in organizations. Effectiveness of performance appraisal for this purpose may be maximized by both training raters and using performance dimensions relevant to the job for which an employee is being considered.

A number of organizations have turned to methods such as psychological testing and assessment centres to assess more directly employees' potential for future positions.[23] Assessment centres evaluate employees on their abilities to perform tasks required in future positions. Assessors are trained; they tend to be managers familiar with the position for which centre participants are being evaluated. The methods used may include group discussions, role play, interviews, and an assortment of tests, but they always also use at least one simulation exercise.[24] For example, J.C. Penney Company's assessment centre in the United States has used phone calls from irate customers as a simulation exercise to assess participants' ability to handle complaints.[25] Each participant's behaviour is observed and evaluated. An overall evaluation is the result of the process.

Almost all employees who participate in assessment centres do so to determine whether they have any potential for management positions. Exhibit 10.2 lists and describes ten common performance dimensions on which centre participants are assessed.

A number of organizations created assessment centres during the 1970s, largely because of their usefulness in managerial selection. However, assessment centres are also a valuable tool in career planning. Assessment helps organizations determine possible avenues for employee development, and also aids employees in understanding their strengths and weaknesses so they can set more realistic career goals. As employment equity programs grow in Canada, more employers may use assessment centres to identify women and members of minority groups with the potential for development.

Assessment centres can, however, create some problems for an organization. Bell Canada, a pioneer in company-sponsored career planning, discontinued its use of appraisal centres in the 1960s because it found that results tended to categorize employees as having or not having potential, and individuals in the latter group became demoralized.[26]

CAREER INFORMATION WITHIN AN ORGANIZATION

Before an employee can set realistic career goals, he or she needs to know about options and opportunities, including information about possible career directions, possible paths of career advancement, and specific job vacancies. It is the responsibility of HRM professionals to develop career paths and to inform employees and those acting as counsellors about career opportunities in the organization.

EXHIBIT 10.2
Common Assessment Centre Dimensions

1. Oral communication skill — effective expression in individual or group situations (includes gestures and nonverbal communications)
2. Oral presentation skill — effective expression when presenting ideas or tasks to an individual or to a group when given time for presentation (includes gestures and nonverbal communication)
3. Written communication skill — clear expression of ideas in writing and in good grammatical form
4. Job motivation — the extent to which activities and responsibilities available in the job overlap with activities and responsibilities that result in personal satisfaction
5. Initiative — active attempts to influence events to achieve goals; self-starting rather than passive acceptance; taking action to achieve goals beyond those called for; originating action
6. Leadership — utilizing appropriate interpersonal styles and methods in guiding individuals (subordinates, peers, superiors) or groups toward task accomplishment
7. Planning and organization — establishing a course of action for self and/or others to accomplish a specific goal; planning proper assignments of personnel and appropriate allocation of resources
8. Analysis — relating and comparing data from different sources, identifying issues, securing relevant information, and identifying relationships
9. Judgement — developing alternative courses of action and making decisions that are based on logical assumptions and reflect factual information
10. Management control — establishing procedures to monitor and/or regulate processes, tasks, or the job activities and responsibilities of subordinates; taking action to monitor the results of delegated assignments or projects

Source: Adapted from W.C. Byham, "Starting an Assessment Center the Correct Way," *The Personnel Administrator*, February 1980, pp. 27–32. Used with the permission of *HRMagazine* (formerly *The Personnel Administrator*), published by the Society for Human Resource Management, Alexandria, Va.

Job vacancies are announced in company newspapers, by word of mouth, or through job posting. (As employment equity and affirmative action programs grow, job posting is likely to be required increasingly as a mechanism to promote fairness in internal recruiting.) In organizations where career planning is informal, employees learn about career options and opportunities from their supervisors within the context of developmental performance appraisal interviews.[27] Organizations with more established career planning programs make greater use of workbooks, workshops, and even recruiting materials to communicate career options and opportunities.

Career paths chart possible career directions and paths of advancement in an organization. They can be defined as logical movements between jobs or from one job to a target position. Career paths can be either traditional or behavioural. *Traditional career paths* are based on past patterns of actual movement by employees. They tend to be limited to advancement within a single function or organizational unit, such as purchasing, sales, or customer relations. Years of service to the organization largely determines the rate at which advancement can occur. For example, a salesperson might expect to advance to the position of account supervisor after five years, to sales supervisor after ten, to district manager after fifteen, and to regional manager after twenty-five.[28] A basic problem with traditional career paths is that they are based on an organization's past needs for human resources, which may not suit present and future purposes. With needs for human resources always changing because of technological advances, restructuring, and legal requirements, today's organizations must develop more flexible and more progressive patterns of career growth and development.

More flexible patterns of career movement are described by *behavioural career paths*, which are based on analyses of similarities in job activities and requirements. Where similarities exist, jobs can be grouped into job families, or clusters. Thus, all jobs involving similar work activities and comparable levels of required skills and abilities form one job cluster, regardless of job title. Consider Ted Maxwell's position of Medical Records Clerk I at City General Hospital (see Figure 10.2). Although Maxwell is in the Medical Records Department, his position is in the same job cluster as Personnel Records Assistant I, located in the Human Resources Department. The two positions require similar levels of skills and have similar work activities. Medical Records Clerk II and Personnel Records Assistant II constitute another job cluster; they require somewhat higher levels of skill and entail somewhat greater responsibility.

After job clusters have been identified, lines of logical progression between them can be charted. Career paths can be complex networks of lines of progression between jobs. Figure 10.2 presents two very simple career paths for Ted Maxwell. The traditional career path is straight on the diagram, from Medical Records Clerk I to Medical Records Clerk II to Senior Clerk, Medical Records, to Assistant Manager, Medical Records, and finally to Manager, Medical Records. However, since the Medical Records Clerk I position is in the same job cluster as Personnel Records Assistant I, another career option for Maxwell is to make a lateral move and assume a Personnel Records Assistant I position. This transition would be quite easy as the job requirements are similar. *Lateral moves* are moves across functions and organizational units at the same level; they need not be limited to the same job cluster. Strictly speaking, they are not career advancements, but they afford employees a chance for variety and growth in new career directions. By making the

FIGURE 10.2
Traditional and Behavioural Career Paths for a Medical Records Clerk I

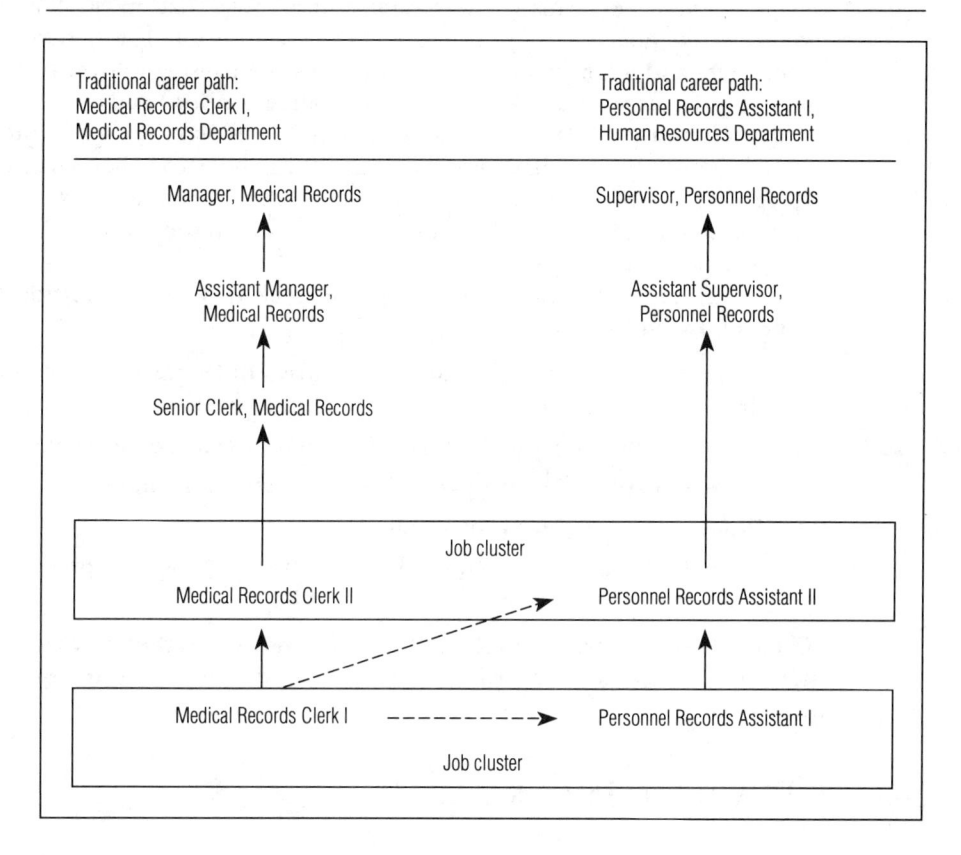

```
Traditional career path:                    Traditional career path:
Medical Records Clerk I,                    Personnel Records Assistant I,
Medical Records Department                  Human Resources Department
─────────────────────────────────────────────────────────────────────

         Manager, Medical Records              Supervisor, Personnel Records
                  ↑                                       ↑
         Assistant Manager,                     Assistant Supervisor,
         Medical Records                        Personnel Records
                  ↑                                       ↑
         Senior Clerk, Medical Records

                  ↑                 Job cluster           ↑
         Medical Records Clerk II              Personnel Records Assistant II
                  ↑                  ↗                    ↑
         Medical Records Clerk I  --------→   Personnel Records Assistant I
                                     Job cluster
```

lateral move, Maxwell would gain access to a new career path in a different department. The value of lateral moves as a means of providing employees with growth opportunities is increasing as layoffs and early retirements leave relatively young employees in many higher-level jobs. Thus, lateral moves are especially useful when opportunities for upward advancement in the organization are limited or blocked.

Focussing on job similarities across functions and organizational units brings to light new career options for employees and greater flexibility for the organization in using the human resources it has available. One organization, for example, was able to shift a number of its sales personnel to purchasing positions when sales declined in a major product line and opportunities became available in the purchasing department. This shift was undertaken when a job analysis showed behavioural similarities between the two previously distinct functions.[29]

CAREER COUNSELLING

It is in counselling sessions, most often with supervisors and managers in developmental performance appraisal interviews, that most employees explore career goals and opportunities in the organization. For these sessions, supervisors and managers need accurate assessments of employees' abilities and potential, as well as information about career options and opportunities in the organization. HRM professionals may be involved in some informal career counselling activities, but basically their role is to support the counselling activities of supervisors and managers. Thus, they must provide supervisors and managers with information as well as with the training they need to function effectively as counsellors.

In career counselling sessions, employees seek answers to questions such as the following:

1. What are my skills and what are the possibilities for developing them or learning new ones?
2. What do I really want for myself insofar as work is concerned?
3. What's possible for me, given my current abilities and skills?
4. What's really required for certain jobs?
5. What training will be required if I choose to pursue a certain career objective?[30]

When counsellors are equipped to help employees find the answers to such questions, realistic career goals can be set. Next, development strategies must be devised.

CAREER PLANNING PROGRAMS

Programs vary in the degree to which they emphasize the four elements of career planning. Some offer employees little assistance in self-assessment, while others aid this process by providing workbooks and workshops. Assessment centres are part of some programs, but most organizations rely on the judgement of supervisors and managers in assessing employee potential. Career path information is provided by some organizations, while others simply post job vacancies. Counselling in many organizations is informal, although some established programs provide staff positions for career counsellors. The ways in which organizations assemble career planning elements result in a variety of career planning programs.

WARNER-LAMBERT CANADA INC.

Warner-Lambert Canada Inc. attributes its impressive business results to its performance management system. The strength of this system is a commitment to employee involvement demonstrated through career planning and development. The personal career goals of the individual are related directly to the organization's business direction. Senior management gives feedback to employees on their plans based on attempts to balance what's best for the individual and the company's profit plans.[31]

GULF CANADA RESOURCES LTD.

Gulf Canada Resources Ltd. of Calgary has introduced a competency-based career development program based on the skills profile, an analysis of which skills are required to do which job.[32] The skills profile outlines the importance of each skill as it relates to the job, along with the competency level demanded for each skill. This approach challenges the assumption that senior employees require high competency in *all* skills. Thus, a junior-level executive might be the best person to fill a senior position because of high competency levels in certain required skills. From a motivational perspective, linking skills to job attainment allows employees to see a return on skill investment, even if it is reflected in a lateral move rather than a vertical promotion.

ONTARIO HYDRO

The same approach is being used at Ontario Hydro, which has committed itself to comprehensive career development even though it is downsizing its organization. Development is to be done by increasing the frequency of job rotations in order to establish a broad base of experience as a prerequisite for promotion. According to Don Tyler, director of Ontario Hydro's human resource division, the company is moving from the view that career development is a luxury to the view that career development is an essential tool for creating a committed and satisfied staff.[33]

CORNING, INC.

Corning's philosophy used to be that primary responsibility for career planning rested with each employee. As a result of a mid-1980s climate survey, however, it learned that nonexempt employees felt underutilized and overlooked. Corning also learned that the link between its performance development and review (PD&R) system and career planning was not functioning properly — employees were not very involved in the process, and administrative purposes of appraisal, such as pay decisions, had been emphasized at the expense of development.

Corning implemented a new career planning system that includes a computer software package, three videotapes, informative books, and a one-day supervisory training session. The software contains questions employees often ask about their own career development. By working through the four programs, employees address their values, skills, and interests, as well as how they are seen by their co-workers and supervisors, what goals are realistic for them and, finally, how to put together an achievable plan. The three videotapes support the software by presenting information regarding career planning at Corning, available planning tools, the career options open to nonexempt employees, and how to use this material to make a plan. The book describes jobs, career paths, pay information, and other information specific to jobs at Corning. Finally, the one-day supervisory training session provides knowledge and skills necessary for communicating effectively with subordinates.[34]

CEIC AIDS FOR CAREER PLANNING

Materials for the career planning programs just described were developed by large organizations for their own use. Companies, large and small, can also purchase aids for career planning. Canadian organizations have access to excellent career guidance materials prepared by the Occupational and Career Analysis and Development Branch of the Canada Employment and Immigration Commission (CEIC).[35] These materials include booklets profiling particular occupations; they describe the preparation, training, and personal qualities required for jobs in these occupations, along with their outlook for the future. The Careers Canada series of booklets focusses on particular provinces.

Employment and Immigration Canada (EIC) has also compiled detailed information on the fields of work of university and community college graduates, along with the projected labour market situation in a sizable number of occupations. The information was prepared by EIC's Canadian Occupational Projection System (COPS) and is presented in its volume *Job Futures: An Occupational Outlook to 1995*.[36]

Job Futures is divided into two parts. Part one lists the major occupations held by graduates two years after they received their degrees; the information is listed by field of study (23 university fields and 18 community college fields). Part two presents the labour market outlook for 174 occupations in 1995 as compared with the situation in 1989. For example, Personnel and Industrial Relations Management Occupations (*CCDO* Code 1136) are expected to grow at a rate of 3.4 percent, compared with 1.5 percent for all occupations. This rate means that between 1989 and 1995, 21 388 new job openings are expected in those fields.[37]

Individual employees interested in career planning can also be referred to an EIC computerized career information and exploration system called CHOICES. Since a person using it has to understand what he or she wants from a job, the first step is completing a questionnaire that pinpoints the individual's interests, aptitudes, and temperament; what environment, earnings, and other conditions of work he or she wants; and what education and training he or she has. This information is fed into the computer, setting some parameters. Next, the person answers a series of questions set by the computer. The responses set up a path and lead eventually to a suggested set of compatible occupations.

The CHOICES model is available in many Canada Employment Centres and university and community college guidance centres, where it can also be used to explore possible occupations, to obtain detailed information about specific occupations, or to compare two or three occupations that share characteristics with a particular one in which a person is interested. The program's background material comes from the job characteristics set out in the *Canadian Classification and Dictionary of Occupations* (see Chapter 5).

FACILITATING CAREER PLANNING AND DEVELOPMENT

Organizations can facilitate career planning in a number of ways. D.T. Hall categorizes the pertinent areas as (1) organizational entry; (2) the job; (3) the boss; (4) organizational structure and procedures; and (5) human resource policy. Exhibit 10.3 presents ways the organization can facilitate career planning within each of these areas.

ORGANIZATIONAL ENTRY

Efforts to facilitate career planning can begin before or at the time an individual takes a job. One of the earliest pre-entry points of influence is contacts between an employer and school placement staff or faculty, job counsellors, and others who may discuss career planning with potential job applicants. Increasingly, organizations are including career planning information in their recruiting messages and materials.

McCormack and Dodge, a company that makes computer software for finance, marketing, and various HRM functions, believes that employees can benefit from a variety of approaches to career development. Its programs consist of classroom work, internal job postings, formal mentoring, individualized development planning, and a trainee program. The technical trainee program was designed to help fill the company's need for well-qualified technical expertise. Recent graduates of software training programs or college graduates may enter the one-year program. During the year, trainees alternate classroom training with job rotation experience. Most of the classroom training is in-house and the job rotations last from four to twelve weeks. About half of the trainees come from outside the company and the other half are internal candidates interested in a more technical career track. Upon successful completion of the program, trainees are offered a job, and so far, the only problem with the program has been trainees' difficulty in choosing from their various job offers. McCormack and Dodge also uses job rotation for middle- and senior-level managers.[38]

EXHIBIT 10.3
Facilitating Career Planning

ORGANIZATIONAL ENTRY

1. Provide information on jobs and career opportunities to placement offices, career counsellors
2. Provide career planning information in recruiting materials

THE JOB

1. Make first job challenging
2. Sequence jobs so progression provides gradual acquisition of skills
3. Use job rotation to provide new challenge and growth opportunities

THE BOSS

1. Provide training to increase boss's ability to be an effective agent of career planning
2. Reward boss for career planning activities

ORGANIZATIONAL STRUCTURE AND PROCEDURES

1. Offer career planning services and programs
2. Work closely with human resource planning arm of the organization
3. Institute human resource accounting procedures

HUMAN RESOURCE POLICIES

1. Institute policies that promote career planning
2. Legitimize downward transfers and fallback positions
3. Provide incentives for employees to leave the organization
4. Involve families in career decisions

Source: Adapted from D.T. Hall and M.A. Morgan, "Career Development and Planning," in K. Pearlman, F.L. Schmidt, and W.C. Hamner, eds., *Contemporary Problems in Personnel*, 3rd ed. (New York: Wiley, 1983), p. 233. Copyright © 1983 John Wiley & Sons, Inc. Used with the permission of John Wiley & Sons, Inc.

THE JOB

Career planning and development can be facilitated in the job itself. Evidence from studies of a variety of organizations and occupations — including an automobile manufacturer, AT&T, the Roman Catholic church, managers in eight large organizations, and a sample of engineers — demonstrates the importance of a challenging and demanding first job.[39] Employees who have such a job tend to be more successful later in their careers. Despite this evidence, however, most organizations are unwilling to give challenging jobs to young, new employees. Some managers hold negative stereotypes of recent graduates as too theoretical, overambitious, immature, and inexperienced. One survey of 22 research and development organizations found that only one had a policy of giving new professional employees a difficult first job.[40]

Another use of the job as a development agent is logical sequencing of work experiences. Under such programs, employees acquire ever-increasing levels of skill and responsibility as they progress through a variety of job assignments.

Related to the job progression concept is *job rotation*, which allows employees to work in a variety of capacities and provides growth and development. A carefully planned and sequenced job rotation program can help meet employees' needs even when upward mobility is limited.

Job rotation is a fairly common method of management development at all levels. McCormack and Dodge uses job rotation for both technical trainees and experienced managers. Another organization that uses job rotation is Bell Canada, whose program includes rotating line managers into the personnel department and personnel officers into line management positions. Several other large organizations also rotate promising managers through the human resources department, and not merely as observers.[41] Job rotation is useful in providing managers with both knowledge and experience in different areas. Such moves both facilitate interdepartmental or divisional cooperation and have the potential of affording managers new challenges and opportunities to learn and grow in their careers. Programs of job redesign, such as job enrichment, also have the potential to satisfy employee development needs.[42]

THE BOSS

Another agent of career planning in organizations is the boss. The importance of the immediate supervisor, especially an employee's first boss, must not be underestimated. The boss assigns tasks, judges performance, provides feedback, rewards and punishes, and by such actions, defines the criteria for success. Exhibit 10.4 illustrates the important role of the boss and the anxiety and frustration that result when he or she fails to clarify success criteria.

The boss is also important because he or she serves as a model for the employee's own behaviour and future leadership style. Ironically, there is evidence that employees learn valuable lessons not only from good bosses but also from poor ones. A 1985 *Psychology Today* survey asked 73 successful executives to describe intolerable bosses they had worked for in the past. Fifty of the executives had had an "intolerable" boss, and four had worked under two. Interestingly, only eleven of the executives with intolerable

EXHIBIT 10.4
Criteria for Success at NASA

The rule in the astronaut corps is simple: Please the boss and you can fly. Annoy him and you stay on Earth. The trick is figuring out how best to play the game and that's one of the mysteries of NASA [the U.S. National Aeronautics and Space Administration].

Astronauts universally claim they have no idea why some are selected for flight after flight and others only rarely, but for the 95 active members of America's space corps there is a feeling of intense competition that touches every phase of their life.

It's a pressure that some credit with breaking up marriages and disrupting family life. Some astronauts drop out, deciding it's not worth it. Others hang on for decades, trying to find the formula that will put them into space.

"You never really know what the criteria are," said Alan A. Bean, a former astronaut who says he walked on the moon only after learning how to play the game. "You know that certain people get good assignments and others get bad ones and you learn to read the winds."

Bean said the pressure comes from the fact that if one wants to fly in space "NASA is the only game in town." Astronauts, he said, can't quit and go to another space agency.

"If you're going to play the game, you have to figure out the rules," he said. "Nobody will tell you the rules."

Some astronauts, he said, "catch on right away. Some never did catch on."

Source: Paul Recer, "Astronauts Unclear on Selection Process," The Associated Press, April 1, 1986. Reprinted with the permission of The Associated Press.

bosses quit their positions. Another seven tried to get their bosses removed, but only two succeeded. The remaining executives simply learned patience, coping behaviour, and how *not* to manage. Positive managerial guidelines that came out of the executives' negative experiences included: (1) give people recognition for what they accomplish; (2) give people responsibility, a chance to show what they can do; (3) look below the surface to understand people's actions; and (4) accept your responsibilities.[43]

Besides assigning tasks and rewards and serving as a role model, bosses often counsel individuals in career planning. Any one of these factors can have a strong impact on employee careers; taken together they make the boss, especially the first boss, a key to career progress. Research has shown that even the boss's expectations can have a substantial impact on a new employee's career expectations and performance. When the boss expects and demands more from employees, they come to expect and demand more from themselves.[44]

Unfortunately, many supervisors and managers fail to make the most of their potential to influence employees' careers in a positive direction. Some may feel unequal to the task, thinking they lack the ability to help develop their subordinates. This problem can be remedied through training. Hall suggests that managers receive training in job analysis and restructuring so that they can identify a challenging job or restructure one to make it more challenging. Additionally, they should receive training in interviewing and counselling skills, interpersonal skills, and performance appraisal, including providing constructive feedback.[45]

Supervisors and managers may be ineffective agents of career planning and development because they are not rewarded for such activities. Hall suggests that career planning be facilitated by rewarding managers for their career development activities. Or career development could be incorporated into a management by objectives (MBO) program, with successful goal attainment resulting in a pay increase or bonus. Also, organizations must ensure that managers are not unintentionally punished for career planning efforts. For example, time and money for employee assessment, career counselling, and training courses are sometimes charged against the manager's operating budget. Or, if career development results in subordinates' transferring, moving upwards, or perhaps even leaving the organization, these events may be perceived as a turnover problem for the organization.[46]

ORGANIZATIONAL STRUCTURE AND PROCEDURES

The most obvious way to facilitate career planning is, of course, to provide career planning services and programs. Although many organizations do this on an informal basis, established programs are still rare. Some organizations hesitate to involve themselves in career planning, believing that it would raise employees' expectations for advancement and thus lead to dissatisfaction and possible turnover. These risks may well exist, but they can be minimized. It depends to a large extent on the success of career counselling efforts and on the information provided by human resource planners. If expected job vacancies fail to materialize or if unforeseen changes force alterations in job structure, someone is likely to be disappointed. To avoid this, career planners and human resource planners need to keep lines of communication open. Finally, it is important for organizations to emphasize that the purpose of career planning is to provide employees with development and growth opportunities, not simply a means of upward mobility. When economic conditions restrict upward mobility, career planning activities may still increase the quality of working life for employees and the skill level and flexibility of an organization's work force.

In the post-entrepreneurial world described by Kanter, formal career planning programs may become less common or change form. Both employers and employees will benefit from programs designed to help employees acquire marketable knowledge and skills. Additionally, organizations that can provide challenging jobs, projects, and work assignments with growth opportunities and that give appropriate rewards should attract and retain quality employees. One way today's leaner organizations remain competitive is by using fewer people. A result is more opportunities for an individual to do a variety of assignments. Another result for many employees is longer hours. Perhaps surprisingly, job satisfaction tends to be highest among those who work the longest hours. But long hours can lead to employee burnout. To avoid burnout, many employers impose mandatory vacations, and others lock the building doors during holidays.[47]

HUMAN RESOURCE POLICY

Human resource policies can facilitate career planning. An internal recruiting policy, for example, enables employees to plan their careers with greater certainty than does a policy of external recruiting. Additionally, a policy of job posting promotes employees' awareness of openings and the qualifications for jobs. Making human resource forecasts available to employees also facilitates career planning. Compensation policy can affect career planning activities. For example, secrecy about compensation may reduce the financial incentives of higher-level jobs. Periodic, objective appraisals of performance are important to growth and should be encouraged by human resource policy.

A human resource policy legitimizing downward transfers and fallback positions can also promote career planning. A *downward transfer* is a move from an organizational level to a lower one. A *fallback position* is simply a job to which an employee can return if a new assignment does not work out. When organizations have a policy legitimizing downward transfers and fallback positions, employees can afford to accept more challenging assignments without risking the stigma of failure. Fallback positions are used in a number of progressive organizations, such as Continental Can and Procter and Gamble. Universities usually provide academic administrators a form of fallback by allowing them to return to tenured teaching positions. Despite this well-accepted practice in academe, business organizations often regard downward transfers as failures. Perhaps they would be more accepted if more organizations adopted Robert Townsend's recommendation that top executives step down after five years.[48]

Hall suggests two additional human resource policies to facilitate career planning: (1) providing incentives for an employee to leave the organization, and (2) involving families in career decisions.[49] Too often, retirement and benefit programs, as well as seniority systems, reward people for mere long-term organizational membership. The result is that employees who might benefit both themselves and the organization by leaving end up staying. As alternatives, organizations could offer such incentives as reimbursement for continuing education, career counselling, or midlife transition training sessions such as those held by the Menninger Foundation.[50]

The phenomenon of dual-career couples has created many other needs for policy innovations and modifications. For example, antinepotism policies should not constrain the recruitment of spouses; policies for reasonable parental and even elder care are needed; and alternative work arrangements, such as flexible hours, part-time jobs, and job sharing, should be developed.[51]

MENTORING

Another way career planning and development is facilitated in organizations is through the informal process of mentoring. *Mentoring* describes a relationship between a relatively inexperienced employee (a protégé) and an older, more experienced employee who provides advice, gives social support, and facilitates opportunities for the protégé to exhibit his or her competence.[52] Mentors also try to protect protégés from their mistakes and help them avoid career-threatening situations. Burke points out that mentors have several expectations of their protégés, including working hard on tasks, loyalty to their mentors, and sharing any organizational rewards as well as intrinsic satisfaction resulting from success.[53] Of course, not all mentoring relationships are successful.

Though mentoring is often a productive career planning and development process, organizations cannot simply run mentoring programs. They can, however, facilitate the mentoring process by providing opportunities for newer employees to interact with more senior staff, both in work-related activities and informally.

The potential value of mentoring is captured in a story told by Ruth Tibbs, an educator from Oklahoma. Three men were in a boat. A storm came up and the boat capsized. The first man walked across the water to shore almost effortlessly. The second man had a little more difficulty, but after going under a few times, he too made it to shore. The third man then started out, but he slipped under water many times. As the other two stood watching him, the first said, "Do you think we should tell him where the stones are?"[54]

One study of the career progress of a large sample of undergraduate business and MBA students found that mentored graduates, regardless of sex, had more promotions and higher salaries than those without mentors.[55] Though one cannot conclude that mentoring, by itself, caused this difference, there is ample evidence that it is a beneficial career development process.

CAREER PLANNING ISSUES

Employers face many career-related challenges in the years ahead. For example, women's increasing participation in the labour force is forcing many employers to examine the problems of dual-earner and dual-career families. The changing demographics of the labour force and employment equity legislation may compel many employers to develop women and minorities for jobs and career paths that have traditionally been occupied by white males. As mandatory retirement becomes a thing of the past, employers must find ways to make longer working lives both productive and satisfying. Finally, the higher education and aspiration levels of today's employees suggest that they will demand more career planning and development from employers.

HRM IN ACTION

ACCOMMODATING A CHANGING WORK FORCE

Changing demographics of the labour force have led many employers to develop innovative work arrangements and to help with child care in various ways. Such programs are necessary to accommodate the needs of working women and single parents with children, as well as those seeking part-time employment.

Two excellent examples are the day care programs associated with Alberta Children's Hospital (ACH) and Ontario Hydro. In both cases, employees were involved in the development of the day care centre and take part in running it.

The Alberta facility came about as the result of a year's joint effort by ACH employees, who were seeking on-site day care, and parents from nearby Knob Hill (KH) School, who were concerned about low enrolments. The ACH/KH program now consists of day care on a full-time, part-time, or drop-in basis for preschool-aged children of working parents. In addition, care is offered for elementary school children before and after school and during lunchtime and summer holidays. The day care currently operates at full capacity with 63 full-time placements in addition to 21 out-of-school placements. Fees are typical of similar programs in the area; hospital employees receive no special rates or subsidies. Though no formal evaluation has been done, ACH believes the facility has aided recruitment and reduced absenteeism and turnover.

Ontario Hydro established a nonprofit centre in its downtown Toronto headquarters in 1985. The centre, called Hydrokids, was planned by a group of Hydro parents and, though the firm contributed initial capital costs, the centre is now a separate, self-sustaining operation. Hydro employees' children are given priority, but children from the community are also eligible for placement. Hydro management was sympathetic to Hydrokids from the start, viewing it as a demonstration of the firm's commitment to affirmative action.

Another example of an innovative policy favouring the family is that of Lipton's International, a retailer of women's clothing. Lipton's changed its traditional sick-leave policy to a "family needs" policy, thereby allowing "associates" (as employees are called), to use their leave time to care for ill family members, as well as themselves. It is interesting to note that this policy was developed by the company's human resources team, which consists of a group of associates from different areas of the company who meet four or five times a year to propose new policies and practices based on ideas solicited from other associates.

> A final example of policies designed to accommodate a changing work force is London Life Insurance Company's job-sharing program. It began on an ad hoc basis in Vancouver in 1977 and became a company-wide policy in 1984. The informal program encourages supervisors to try job sharing for a few months when two "well-matched" individuals propose the arrangement. Though most shared jobs are clerical, two office managers run a small regional office and couples can share a job. A typical arrangement has one employee working Monday, Tuesday, and Wednesday of one week and only Monday and Tuesday of the next. In other cases, each of the paired employees works half-days or alternate weeks.
>
> The greatest challenge of instituting the London Life job-sharing program was to convince management that it would not create problems such as doubling training costs, adding administrative costs, or lowering the quality of customer service. This challenge was met, and additional costs proved minimal. The benefits to both employer and employees are positive. For example, employees have higher morale and energy, and it is now easier to solve staffing problems caused by illness, vacations, or heavy workload.
>
> Source: Based on Alberta Children's Hospital, "Canadian Organizations and Their Family-Related Programs," *Canadian Business Review*, Autumn 1989, pp. 22-26. Used with the permission of The Conference Board of Canada.

Of the many issues suggested above, dual careers have attracted considerable interest. To understand career issues, one must distinguish the dual-career family from both the traditional and the dual-earner family. In the *traditional family*, one spouse, usually the husband, engages in paid work while the other spouse works as homemaker and parent. Wives or husbands may help to facilitate their spouse's promotion and career progress through career support activities such as entertaining colleagues or clients and participating in community affairs. In *dual-earner families*, both spouses work outside the home for pay. One spouse may pursue a career while the other regards working as a temporary activity undertaken for economic reasons.[56] In January 1992, there were 3.5 million dual-earner Canadian families, up from approximately 1.3 million in the late 1960s.[57] This shift from the traditional family pattern is often caused by high levels of inflation, layoff, or desires for a higher standard of living. This pattern typically leaves the primary responsibilities for homemaking and/or parenting to the wife. From an employer's perspective, dual-earner families mean that wives may seek part-time jobs or jobs with convenient or flexible hours at organizations located near their residence. Wives of dual-earner families may have little interest in career planning and development activities because of their lower commitment to the labour force. Another consequence of this pattern is that the spouse is not available to support the career activities of the career-pursuing spouse.

A *dual-career family* is one in which each spouse has a commitment to a career as well as to a family life together.[58] The implication of this pattern is that neither spouse will subordinate his or her career to family demands but both maintain a commitment to family activities. Organizations encounter numerous career planning challenges with respect to dual-career employees. One of the most common challenges is dealing with a spouse's promotion opportunity that requires relocation. In the traditional career and the dual-earner families, the promotion opportunity is likely to be readily accepted. In the case of the dual-career family, acceptance of the promotion and relocation may depend upon obtaining a comparable job for the other spouse. In reality, this is often difficult or impossible, so the couple is forced to choose between the relative gains of accepting the new position and the consequences of not relocating. Large employers located in urban areas may have less difficulty than small employers in rural areas in locating alternative positions for spouses.

Other problems associated with dual-careers include conflicts in work and vacation schedules, career–family role conflicts regarding child care and sometimes the care of elderly relatives, and the stress of managing two careers.

Sekaran and Hall argue that family lifecycle stages, such as young parenthood and empty nest, may be either a good or a poor "fit" with the career stage of either spouse.[59] For example, the demands of young children may make it difficult to exert the required effort to be successful in the establishment career stage. The authors contend that employers must recognize this and allow for multiple career paths and more flexibility in the timing of promotions.

Relationships between work and family life have become more complex and difficult to manage in the past several decades. Burke and McKeen reviewed much of what is known and not known about these relationships.[60] For example, they say, work has a stronger effect on family life than vice versa; work schedules have a major impact on family life (a compressed work week and flexible working hours facilitate leisure and sharing family responsibilities); and there are numerous stress and role conflict issues associated with work and family life.

Despite all the attention given to families and dual-career couples, HR professionals are wise to remember that more than one-third of the North American work force is single. (Singles, of course, are a diverse group that includes the divorced, widowed, and separated, as well as those who have never married.) One study found singles were less satisfied with their lives and their jobs and more likely to be absent than married employees.[61]

SUMMARY

Career planning as a separate HRM function is a relatively new but growing phenomenon. Established programs are rare but increasing because of organizations' desire to ensure a supply of qualified replacements and to satisfy the desires of employees for career and growth opportunities. The turbulent 1980s and early 1990s raised issues of job security and created the need for employers to help employees plan and prepare for the possibility of eventual job loss or change.

Programs differ, but in general career planning has four elements: (1) individual assessment of abilities, interests, career needs, and goals; (2) organizational assessment of employees' abilities and potential; (3) communication of information concerning career options and opportunities with the organization; and (4) career counselling to help individuals set realistic goals and plan for their attainment. HRM professionals provide materials and opportunities for individual career planning, conduct assessments of employee potential, develop career paths, and inform employees and those acting as counsellors and mentors of career opportunities in the organization. HRM professionals also aid managers and supervisors in career planning and development efforts. Support functions include providing needed information, encouraging periodic and objective appraisals of employee performance, and training supervisors and managers to function effectively as career counsellors and agents of employee development. Career planners should develop a close working relationship with human resource planners so that employee expectations for advancement are reasonable and career goals realistic.

REVIEW QUESTIONS

1. The section of this chapter headed "Relation to Other HRM Functions" is, of course, theoretical and more prescriptive than descriptive of actual organization practice. How, if at all, has the turbulent business climate of the 1980s and early 1990s changed career planning and/or its relationship to other HRM functions?

2. In the leaner organizations of the 1990s, should career planners use traditional or behavioural career paths? Why? What are the advantages and disadvantages of one over the other?

3. Should organizations encourage mentoring? Describe any problems mentoring might present.

Project Ideas

1. Visit your university or college placement office, student counselling centre, or any other agency offering career planning and counselling services. Prepare a brief report describing the services it offers. For example, what are its standard operating procedures? Is a battery of tests given before the meeting with a counsellor? Is more than one trip required? What kinds of tests are given? What kind of feedback does the student receive? What qualifications do counsellors possess?

2. Work through the self-assessment exercise on personal wants in Exhibit 10.1. Record your responses. After you have finished, write a short paper evaluating the exercise. What do you think of it? Did it help you to clarify your wants and needs? Submit both your self-assessment report and your evaluation of the exercise to your instructor.

3. Obtain a workbook or other materials from a large organization that has some kind of career planning program. Prepare a written or oral report on the organization's career planning activities as described in the materials. If a workbook is available, describe its contents, including the nature of some of the career planning exercises.

▶▶▶ CASES

CASE 10.1 ▶ TUITION AID AND TURNOVER AT WESTFIELD CONSTRUCTION

From his office in mid-town Calgary, Howard Flanders, human resource manager for Westfield Construction Company, gazes at the setting sun as he contemplates a report from Alice Sims, manager of career planning and development. It describes the past six months of the company's career development and tuition reimbursement program. Currently, the program allows employees who take work-related postsecondary courses, undergraduate or postgraduate, to be reimbursed for their tuition if they receive at least a B grade. In the past, entry-level engineers have typically pursued undergraduate degrees, while higher-level engineers pursued MBA or graduate engineering degrees.

Flanders finds Sims' report disturbing. Basically, it documents an increased use of the tuition aid program and also a 15 percent increase over last year in quit rates among participants. Tuition recipients tend to be workers of high ability and motivation—people Westfield would choose to retain even in the worst of times. Quit rates seem to be higher among engineers than other types of workers, including project and cost analysts. (Career paths for these two types of employees are given in Figure 1.)

Not surprisingly, Sims' report also documents an increase in dissatisfaction with promotion and growth opportunities among engineers, the company's most vital human resource. Several engineers have complained, for example, that they had not even learned of some vacancies until others had been promoted to fill them. The following quotes are illustrative of the engineers' discontent:

"We're trained for construction, but now we 'build' pre-fabricated burger joints." (Engineer I)

"We used to do big projects, but now we do simple jobs an Engineer I could handle." (Engineer II)

"The tuition aid program is fine, but Westfield can't seem to utilize our added knowledge." (Engineer III, who quit six months after completing an MBA degree)

"When I first came here, the work was tough and challenging and good engineers could move up quickly; now even good engineers are stuck with routine projects and slow promotions." (Engineer IV, who left after ten years with the company)

FIGURE 1
Career Paths for Westfield's Engineers and Project and Cost Analysts

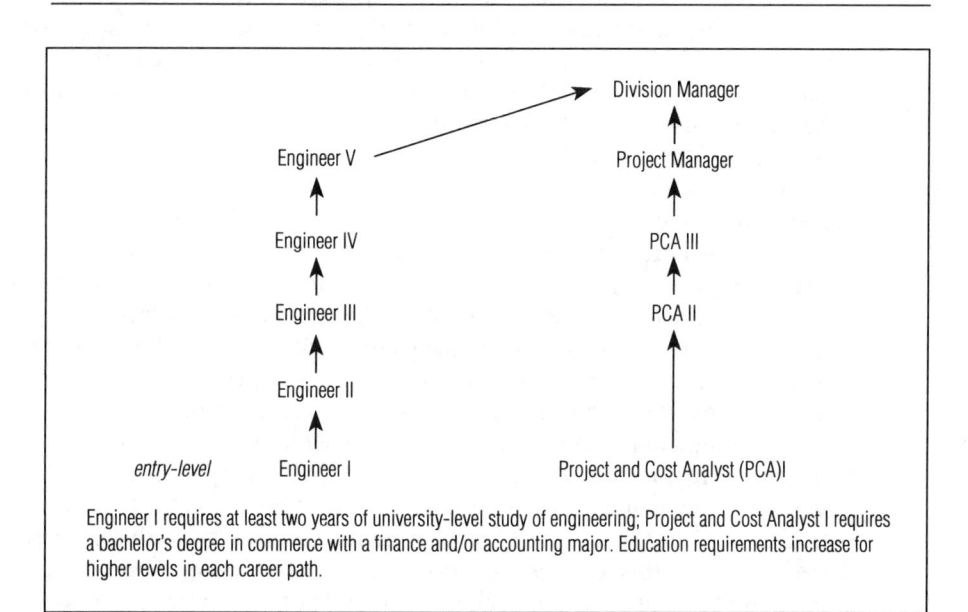

```
                                    Division Manager
                                          ↑
              Engineer V ─────────→  Project Manager
                   ↑                      ↑
              Engineer IV              PCA III
                   ↑                      ↑
              Engineer III             PCA II
                   ↑                      ↑
              Engineer II
                   ↑
entry-level    Engineer I        Project and Cost Analyst (PCA) I
```

Engineer I requires at least two years of university-level study of engineering; Project and Cost Analyst I requires a bachelor's degree in commerce with a finance and/or accounting major. Education requirements increase for higher levels in each career path.

Flanders understands why his engineers might miss the boom times. Still, he had hoped they would understand that business was slow in the entire construction industry. He had also hoped that employees would appreciate Westfield's policies of reducing hiring and offering early retirements in order to avoid layoffs.

In light of Sims' report, Flanders now wonders whether Westfield should modify its $250 000 per year tuition aid program or discontinue it entirely.

TASKS AND QUESTIONS

1. How has the slowdown at Westfield affected career planning and career-related issues? What actions other than modifying or discontinuing the tuition aid program might Flanders take to ease the situation?

2. What are some possible consequences of discontinuing the tuition aid program? What are some possible consequences of continuing or modifying it?

3. What do you feel Flanders should do about the tuition aid program? Why? What, if any, additional information would be useful in answering this question?

CASE 10.2 ▸ WORK AND FAMILY ISSUES

The pronouncement that workers' family-related needs are becoming increasingly intertwined with their workplace needs has become almost commonplace. Organizations are still struggling, however, with the specific challenges raised by that theoretical generalization. Three recent articles in business journals detail some examples.

One, in the *Canadian Business Review*, tells the story of a large public relations firm challenged by account executive Wendy Kimbrell, who announced she wanted to return to work only six weeks after giving birth to her first child. Because Wendy was a key person in the company, the president was delighted that she did not want the entire four-month maternity leave to which she was entitled. His delight became indecision, however, when he learned one of her requisites for early return: to bring her daughter to the office and nurse her when necessary. She proposed to keep the baby and a nanny in a small, unused room down the hall from her office.

The ramifications of the worker's proposal immediately rang caution bells in the president's mind. But being a "good" manager, he said he would think it over. Two issues motivated his caution. The first was whether Wendy could adequately balance her work with the demands of the baby. The second was whether this concession would establish a potentially complex and costly precedent. After all, more than half of the company's workers were women in their 20s and 30s.

Being aware that companies were increasingly establishing day-care centres, the president telephoned the ultimate fount of wisdom for executives, his attorney, to ask what such a venture might require.

The attorney warned of a number of potential problems. He raised the issue of whether the company could get insurance without making substantial renovations to meet what he imagined were rigid government standards for child-care facilities. He also asked about extra washroom and kitchen facilities and the firm's willingness to have staff members help with child care. In short, the attorney did not encourage adoption of the proposal.

Despite this uninspired advice, the company president decided to go along with his valued account executive's proposition on a trial basis. And he felt a considerable degree of relief when other employees approved. Indeed, some praised him for having given a positive response to what many considered a crucial problem.

The president's supportive instincts had some long-term positive results. Wendy's initial arrangement worked out, and within a year, four employees had an authentic child-care centre in operation across the street from company offices.

Related issues can be seen in a *Harvard Business Review* case study about a promotion decision in a metropolitan law firm known within the legal and corporate world as pre-eminent in corporate litigation. In September 1990, the firm's promotions committee met to consider three associates as partners. One was accepted without a ripple. A second was rejected. The third, Julie Ross, evoked such controversy that the decision was postponed until a meeting of the partnership could be called for an open discussion.

What was there about Julie Ross that generated indecision about her becoming a partner? She met the firm's seven-year employment requisite for partner consideration, and her file indicated exemplary performance. Her work had ranked among the best in the firm, displaying both keen insight into legal issues and top-notch courtroom litigation, and in the past two years, it was noted, she had shown a growing capability for attracting new business. The file also reported that Julie had a baby three years ago and she had "requested and was given a reduction in her client load."

During the promotions committee discussion about Julie, the chairman was reminded that many senior partners had voiced strong opposition to her part-time arrangement at the time it was negotiated. He responded that he had informed all the firm's attorneys in writing that they might negotiate similar arrangements on an individual basis but that no policy about part-time work would be formulated. He also reminded the committee that two other female junior associates had since negotiated part-time roles.

A female partner and member of the promotions committee voiced strong opposition to Julie's promotion on the grounds that she simply had not earned it. Using herself as an example, this woman asserted that working 70 or more hours a week in the interest of the firm was a crucial requisite for promotion.

A male committee member expressed concern about establishing a precedent if Julie were promoted. His argument was that to promote a part-time employee would broadcast a message that the firm no longer placed first priority on demonstrated motivation and dedication.

The committee chairman supported Julie for promotion, basing his decision on the fact that the new professional environment needs first-class female lawyers, even if some of them work only part-time. He also noted that part-time work was no longer only a female issue—many men have valid reasons for wanting to work part-time. And he concluded that promoting Julie would make the firm a more desirable place to work and thus make it easier to recruit and hold the best young talent.

A male committee member, who had spoken earlier in opposition to Julie's promotion, closed the discussion in almost passionate terms, claiming that it would be worth losing Julie and people like her to avoid upsetting the status quo in the firm.

Shortly after the promotions committee meeting, the chairman received a note from a male member:

> Nice handling of the discussion at the meeting. You've got a tough assignment ahead of you outlining for the partners the committee's divergent positions on Julie.
>
> I don't mean to complicate the matter, but to me the issue isn't simply about making Julie a partner. Her case will effectively establish the firm's policy on part-time work. The relevant issues here include flexible work schedules, motivation of both male and female associates, the reaction of the firm's clients, and the concerns of the existing partners.
>
> But even more important, our decision will reflect our beliefs as an organization about how the quality of one's personal life affects one's work at the firm.
>
> I think you know my position on this. I intend to spend more time with my family—I don't want to wait until retirement to begin enjoying my grandkids. Furthermore, I'm convinced that doing this will make the time I spend at the firm more productive.

In many respects, the above note to the chairman constitutes a manifesto about work and family issues in the corporate world. It is manifesto deserving consideration, analysis, and thought.

Finally, a *Management Review* article points out the growing importance of work and family issues. Such issues are evident at IBM, for example, which estimates that 63 percent of its work force are single parents or part of a dual-career couple. This trend is expected to continue in the next decade, as is growth in the number of workers with dependent parents. The authors contend that a large problem in an organization's coping with these inescapable demographics are managers who are older and/or lack understanding. In a Gallup/*Fortune* poll of working parents, for example, respondents ranked management training and sensitivity to work and family demands second in terms of workplace changes that would lessen work and family demands.

Source: Based on material from Paul McLaughlin, "Infants Terribles," *Canadian Business*, December 1988. Used with the permission of *Canadian Business*; G.W. Loveman, "The Case of the Part-Time Partner," *Harvard Business Review*, September–October 1990, pp. 12–29. Used with the permission of *Harvard Business Review*; and K. Cramer and J. Pearce, "Work and Family Policies Become Productivity Tools," *Management Review*, November 1990, pp. 42–44. © 1990. Used with the permission of the publisher, American Management Association, New York. All rights reserved.

TASKS AND QUESTIONS

1. Consider the issues raised here. Do you feel employers have the responsibility to accommodate to family-related needs? What are the advantages and disadvantages to both employer and employee of doing so?

2. To what extent do you see attitudes of some managers as a problem in coping with work and family conflicts? Cite instances in the case. How can training and organizational policies help remedy this problem?

3. Discuss the pros and cons of an employer-run child-care facility.

NOTES

1. J.W. Walker and T.G. Gutteridge, *Career Planning Practices* (New York: AMACOM, 1979).

2. R.M. Kanter, *When Giants Learn to Dance* (New York: Simon and Schuster, 1989).

3. J.C. Latack, "Organizational Restructuring and Career Management," in G.R. Ferris and D.M. Rowland, eds., *Research in Personnel and Human Resources*, vol. 8 (Greenwich, Conn.: JAI Press, 1990), pp. 109–39.

4. Latack, "Organizational Restructuring."

5. J. Brockner, "The Effects of Work Layoffs on Survivors: Research, Theory and Practice," in B.M. Staw and L.L. Cummings, ed., *Research in Organizational Behavior*, vol. 10, (Greenwich, Conn.: JAI Press, 1988), pp. 213–55.

6. Statistics Canada, *Labour Force Annual Averages 1990*, cat. no. 71-220, February 1991, p. B-39.

7. U. Sekaran, "Organizational Design for Facilitating Satisfying Work–Family Linkages through a Better Understanding of Couple Dynamics," *Canadian Journal of Administrative Sciences*, vol. 5 (1988), pp. 14–21.

8. W. Clark and Z. Zsigmond, *Job Market Reality for Post-Secondary Graduates*, Statistics Canada (Ottawa: Supply and Services Canada, 1981). Reproduced with the permission of the Minister of Supply and Services Canada, 1992.

9. M. Burstein, N. Tonhaara, P. Hewson, and B. Warrander, *Canadian Work Values*, Manpower and Immigration (Ottawa: Information Canada, 1975).

10. T. Atkinson, "Differences between Male and Female Attitudes toward Work," *Canadian Business Review*, Summer 1983, pp. 47–51.

11. P. Meyer, "Why Executives Change Jobs," *The Personnel Administrator*, vol. 24, no. 10 (October 1979), pp. 59–64, 72.

12. G.C. Johnson and R.J. Grey, "Signs of Diminishing Employee Commitment," *Canadian Business Review*, Spring 1988, pp. 20–23.

13. M. Gibb-Clark, "Canadian Workers Need Some Respect," *The Globe and Mail*, September 4, 1991, pp. B1, B6.

14. University and College Placement Association, *Career Planning Annual* (Toronto: UCPA, 1981).

15. Kanter, *When Giants Learn to Dance*, p. 301.

16. E.H. Schein, "How 'Career Anchors' Hold Executives to Their Career Paths," *Personnel*, vol. 52 (May–June 1975), pp. 11–24. © 1975. Used with the permission of the publisher, American Management Association, New York. All rights reserved.

17. D.T. Hall and M.A. Morgan, "Career Development and Planning," in M. Jelinek, ed., *Career Management for the Individual and the Organization* (Chicago: St. Clair Press, 1979).

18. D.E. Super, J. Crites, R. Hummel, H. Moser, P. Overstreet, and C. Warnath, *Vocational Development: A Framework for Research* (New York: Teachers College Press, 1957).

19. D.E. Super, personal communication to D.T. Hall.

20. M.A. Morgan, D.T. Hall, and A. Martier, "Career Development Strategies in Industry—Where Are We and Where Should We Be?" *Personnel*, March–April 1979, pp.13–30.

21. P.A. Renwick, E.E. Lawler III, and the *Psychology Today* staff, "What You Really Want from Your Job," *Psychology Today*, vol. 11 (May 1978), pp. 53–58, 60, 62, 65, and 118.

22. O.C. Brenner and M.G. Singer, "Career Repotters: To Know Them Could Be to Keep Them," *Personnel*, November 1988, pp. 54–60.

23. J. Koten, "Career Guidance: Psychologists Play Bigger Corporate Role in Placing of Personnel," *The Wall Street Journal*, July 11, 1978.

24. Task Force on Assessment Center Standards, "Standards and Ethical Considerations for Assessment Center Operations," *Personnel Administrator*, vol. 25, no. 2 (February 1980), pp. 35–38.

25. Koten, "Career Guidance."

26. Personal communication from Herbert Clappison and Margaret Briere, June 15, 1982.

27. J.W. Seybolt, "Career Development: The State of the Art among the Grass Roots," *Training and Development Journal*, vol. 33, no. 4 (April 1979), pp. 16–21.
28. J.W. Walker, *Human Resource Planning* (New York: McGraw-Hill, 1980), p. 311.
29. E.H. Burack and N.J. Mathys, *Career Management in Organizations: A Practical Human Resource Planning Approach* (Lake Forest, Ill.: Brace-Park Press, 1980), p. 127.
30. Burack and Mathys, *Career Management in Organizations*, p. 301.
31. Mary Ann Archer and Carolyn Brooks, "The Winning Partnership, Creating Effective Performance Management Programs," *Human Resources Professional*, September 1989, pp. 12–15.
32. Marjory Thompson, "Reshaping Work for the Six Million Dollar Man," *Canadian HR Reporter*, October 5, 1987, p. 8.
33. Thompson, "Reshaping Work."
34. Z.B. Leibowitz, B.H. Feldman, and S.H. Mosley, "Career Development Works Overtime at Corning, Inc.," *Personnel*, April 1990, pp. 38–46.
35. CEIC also has a short book discussing how to approach career choice: Catherine V. Davidson and L. Glen Tippett, *A Career Planning Guide* (Ottawa: Manpower and Immigration Canada, 1977).
36. Employment and Immigration Canada, *Job Futures: An Occupational Outlook to 1995, Volume 1: Occupational Outlooks* and *Volume 2: Experience of Recent Graduates*, 1990 ed., prepared by the Canadian Occupational Projection System (COPS) (Toronto: Nelson Canada, 1990).
37. Employment and Immigration Canada, *Job Futures*.
38. L.M. Carulli, C.L. Noroian, and C. Levine, "Employee-Driven Career Development," *Personnel Administrator*, vol. 34, no. 3 (1989), pp. 67–70.
39. M.D. Dunnette, R.D. Arvey, and P.A. Banas, "Why Do They Leave?" *Personnel*, May–June 1973, pp. 25–39; D.W. Bray, R.J. Campbell, and D.L. Grant, *Formative Years in Business* (New York: Wiley, 1974); D.T. Hall and B. Schneider, *Organizational Climate and Careers: The Work Lives of Priests* (New York: Seminar Press, 1973); B. Buchanan II, "Building Organizational Commitment: The Socialization of Managers in Work Organizations," *Administrative Science Quarterly*, vol. 19 (1974), pp. 533–46; H.G. Kaufman, "Relationship of Early Work Challenge to Job Performance, Professional Contributions, and Competence of Engineers," *Journal of Applied Psychology*, vol. 59 (1974), pp. 337–79; and D.E. Berlew and D.T. Hall, "Socialization of Managers: Effects of Expectations on Performance," *Administrative Science Quarterly*, vol. 11 (1966), pp. 207–23.
40. D.T. Hall and E.E. Lawler III, "Unused Potential in Research and Development Organizations," *Research Management*, vol. 12 (1969), pp. 339–54.
41. H.E. Meyer, "Personnel Directors Are the New Corporate Heroes," *Fortune*, vol. 93 (February 1976), pp. 84–88.
42. J.R. Hackman and G.R. Oldham, *Work Redesign* (Reading, Mass.: Addison-Wesley, 1980).

43. M.M. Lombardo and M.W. McCall, Jr., "The Intolerable Boss," *Psychology Today*, January 1984, pp. 44–48. Used with the permission of *Psychology Today*. Copyright © 1984 (Sussex Publishers, Inc.).
44. J.S. Livingston, "Pygmalion in Management," *Harvard Business Review*, vol. 47 (1969), pp. 81–89.
45. D.T. Hall, *Careers in Organizations* (Pacific Palisades, Calif.: Goodyear Publishing, 1976).
46. Hall, *Careers in Organizations*.
47. Kanter, *When Giants Learn to Dance*, p. 271.
48. R. Townsend, *Up the Organization* (New York: Knopf, 1970).
49. Hall, *Careers in Organizations*.
50. B. Rice, "Midlife Encounters: The Menninger Seminars for Businessmen," *Psychology Today*, vol. 12, no. 11 (1979), pp. 67–77.
51. Sekaran, "Organizational Design," pp. 19–20.
52. K.E. Kram, *Mentoring at Work: Developmental Relationships in Organizational Life* (Glenview, Ill.: Scott, Foresman, 1985).
53. R.J. Burke, "Mentors in Organizations," *Group and Organization Studies*, vol. 9 (1984), pp. 353–472.
54. R. Tibbs, Speech given at Tulsa Area Human Resource Management Association meeting, Tulsa, Oklahoma, April 17, 1991.
55. G.F. Dreher and R.A. Ash, "A Comparative Study of Mentoring among Men and Women in Managerial, Professional and Technical Positions," *Journal of Applied Psychology*, vol. 75 (1990), pp. 539–46.
56. L.A. Gilbert and V. Rachlin, "Mental Health and Psychological Functioning of Dual-Career Families," *The Counseling Psychologist*, vol. 15, no. 1 (1987), pp. 7–49.
57. Maureen Moore, *The Characteristics of Dual-Earner Families*, Statistics Canada, Labour and Household Surveys Analysis Division, cat. no. 13–588, no. 3 (Ottawa: Supply and Services Canada, July 1989), p. 9; and Statistics Canada, *The Labour Force*, January 1992, cat. no. 71–001, p. B-20.
58. R. Rapoport and R.N. Rapoport, *Dual-Career Families* (Harmondsworth: Penguin, 1971).
59. U. Sekaran and D.T. Hall, "Asynchronism in Dual Career and Family Linkages," in M.B. Arthur, D.T. Hall, and B.S. Lawrence, eds., *Handbook of Career Theory* (Cambridge: Cambridge University Press, 1989.)
60. R.J. Burke and C.A. McKeen, "Work and Family: What We Know and What We Need to Know," *Canadian Journal of Administrative Sciences*, vol. 5 (1988), pp. 30–40.
61. D.R. Austrom, T.T. Baldwin, and G.J. Macy, "The Single Worker: An Empirical Exploration of Attributes, Behavior, and Well-Being," *Canadian Journal of Administrative Sciences*, vol. 5 (1988), pp. 22–29.

Suggestions for Further Reading

- M.B. Arthur, D.T. Hall, and B.S. Lawrence, eds. *Handbook of Career Theory*. Cambridge: Cambridge University Press, 1989.
- G.R. Ferris and K.M. Rowland, eds. *Career and Human Resources Development*. Greenwich, Conn.: JAI Press, 1990.
- K.E. Kram. *Mentoring at Work: Developmental Relationships in Organizational Life*. Glenview, Ill.: Scott, Foresman, 1985.
- J.C. Latack. "Organizational Restructuring and Career Management." In G.R. Ferris and D.M. Rowland, eds., *Research in Personnel and Human Resources*, vol. 8. Greenwich, Conn.: JAI Press, 1990.
- R.M. Meltz and N.M. Meltz. *Taking Charge: Career Planning for Canadian Workers*. Toronto: Captus Press, 1992.

CHAPTER 11

PERFORMANCE APPRAISAL

- PERFORMANCE APPRAISAL: A DEFINITION
- THE PURPOSES OF PERFORMANCE APPRAISAL
- RELATION TO OTHER HRM FUNCTIONS
- RESPONSIBILITIES FOR PERFORMANCE APPRAISAL
- DESIGNING AN APPRAISAL SYSTEM
- GENERAL REQUIREMENTS OF PERFORMANCE APPRAISAL SYSTEMS
- PERFORMANCE APPRAISAL METHODS
- HRM IN ACTION ▸ PARTNERSHIP APPRAISAL
- A PERFORMANCE APPRAISAL SYSTEM: CORNING, INC.
- IMPLEMENTING AN APPRAISAL SYSTEM
- THE APPRAISAL INTERVIEW
- COLLECTING AND STORING APPRAISAL DATA
- SUMMARY
- REVIEW QUESTIONS
- PROJECT IDEAS
- CASE 11.1 ▸ PERFORMANCE REVIEW AT BERGHOFF'S
- CASE 11.2 ▸ PERFORMANCE MONITORING AT BELL CANADA
- NOTES
- SUGGESTIONS FOR FURTHER READING

ROSE ZUKROWSKI WAS A LITTLE NERVOUS AS she ate breakfast. She glanced at the clock; it said 6:30 A.M. As she gulped the last of her coffee, she thought, "I wonder how this appraisal session will go? Will Raj and Cynthia agree with how I've rated myself?" Rose was scheduled to receive her first annual peer review appraisal from two members of her work team. The appraisal session was scheduled for 8:00 A.M., just after the usual 30-minute team meeting.

As Rose pulled into the stream of traffic on the highway, she thought that this appraisal would certainly go better than the ones she had had with her old boss. He had varied from having almost nothing to say about her work to giving a long list of complaints, some about things over which she had no control. At least, she had been able to choose Cynthia as her reviewer, and Raj had been chosen by the other team members. Again, she assured herself: "There is no need to feel at all nervous. After all, I have trained and worked closely with all ten people in my team. Heck, we are almost like family." She attributed her nervousness to the many previous appraisals in which she did not know what to expect; the boss had done a poor job of listening to her, and she had walked out not knowing what to do to get a better evaluation next time.

As Rose turned into the plant parking lot, it occurred to her that Cynthia and Raj were a little nervous too. Raj had done only one other appraisal this year, and this would be Cynthia's first. Walking into the plant, she said to herself, "We have worked through a lot of problems as a team; this peer review should be no problem."

Rose was about to experience one of the newest forms of performance appraisal, peer review by members of the employee's own work team. Although various forms of peer review have long been used in some situations, such as the military and academia, today's approach is unusual in that it extends to brand new areas and replaces the traditional appraisal by the boss. Whether or not this form of appraisal will eliminate many of the problems common to the traditional appraisal is not yet clear.

In this chapter we discuss the many organizational purposes of appraisal, appraisal methods and instruments, and the appraisal interview itself. After reading this material, you can better judge how peer review appraisals compare with traditional ones.

PERFORMANCE APPRAISAL: A DEFINITION

Performance appraisal is the process of collecting, analyzing, evaluating, and communicating information relative to individuals' job behaviour and results. The performance of organizational units and organizations as a whole can also be assessed, but this chapter focusses on the appraisal of individuals.

Performance appraisal can be formal or informal. Users of formal systems schedule regular sessions in which to discuss an employee's performance. Informal appraisals are unplanned, often chance statements made in passing about an employee's performance. Most organizations use a formal appraisal system but also provide varying amounts of informal, day-to-day feedback on performance.

Some organizations use more than one appraisal system, applying a different method to different types of employees or for different purposes. Formal procedures are most prevalent for evaluating office workers and lower-level managers; top managers and production employees are evaluated less frequently.[1] In organizations without a formal appraisal system, employees must guess the employer's attitude toward them and their work from subtle or indirect indicators (for example, how the boss relates personally to them versus other employees or how large a raise is received in relation to others). In such a situation, employees are likely to be ineffective on the job and feel anxious and insecure simply because they are unsure of what is expected of them and how they are doing.

An example of a progressive performance appraisal system is that of the Canadian Imperial Bank of Commerce (CIBC).[2] The goal of CIBC's system, called The Employee Achievement Measure (TEAM), is to tie individual employee job success to the bank's success. A major strength of TEAM is the strong level of employee participation that begins in the planning phase. Within the framework of a unit's business plan, employees negotiate specific job performance targets related to their key responsibilities. Once agreement is reached, a "contract" is formed between employee and manager. Unlike many programs, where such contracts are recorded and then ignored by both manager and employee until next year's appraisal, at CIBC, both manager and employee monitor progress toward the goals and hold periodic progress sessions. When appraisal time is near, the employee completes a self-appraisal prior to the actual interview. At the interview, achievements are discussed and plans made for the next year. After the interview, employees can make comments about any part of the process and if agreement is not reached, the employee can make an appeal.

Since its launch in 1987, the program has generated good responses and strong commitment from both management and employees. Much of the success is undoubtedly due to the effort put into developing the system. Approximately 150 employees worked on the system in various project teams and committees. Finally, a training program and strong support from senior management proved invaluable. Organizations that put less time and effort into their performance appraisal systems are often disappointed with the results.

THE PURPOSES OF PERFORMANCE APPRAISAL

Although performance appraisal occurs on an individual level, it is a major component of the organizational control process. As such, it links the performance of lower-level units with that of higher-level units. Boards of directors or other planning groups begin the process by developing plans that include goals and objectives. These goals and objectives become the standards by which the performance of top management is evaluated. Similarly, top management develops goals for various strategic business units (SBUs) that affect the performance standards of their subordinate managers. Theoretically, this process continues down to the specific performance goals and standards of the lowest-level employee. Therefore, the lowest-level employees' meeting their performance standards enables higher levels in the organization to attain their goals.

The performance appraisal system is an important mechanism for communication and control of organizational goals, objectives, and values. This means that, to be effective, a performance appraisal system must have the full support of the highest level of management. For example, W. Edwards Deming, a founder of the quality control movement, argues that higher quality products can be produced at lower cost through commitment to quality from top management, rather than through more automation and mass inspections.[3]

The organizational purposes served by performance appraisal are many and varied. They can be classified into three major areas: administrative, employee development, and monitoring/assessment purposes.

ADMINISTRATIVE PURPOSES

Performance appraisals for administrative purposes provide employers with a rationale or basis for making many HRM decisions, such as those relating to pay, promotions, demotions, terminations, and transfers. For administrative purposes, a global, or overall, rating for each employee is usually desired in order to facilitate employee comparisons. Most appraisal methods, however, provide ratings of employees on a number of different factors of job performance. In order to be useful for administrative purposes, these multiple ratings must be combined into a composite rating for each employee. Composite ratings can be obtained in several ways. One is to add the ratings for each performance factor and use the total as a composite; another is to average the factors to obtain a mean. A more sophisticated composite weights each performance factor according to its contribution to job effectiveness. (Of course, job effectiveness itself is usually a composite measure.)

Salary increases and other decisions based on performance appraisal data are often conveyed to employees during regularly scheduled performance appraisal interviews.

EMPLOYEE DEVELOPMENT PURPOSES

When communicated to individual employees, appraisal data serve development purposes by providing employees with performance feedback. Such feedback reinforces desirable behaviour, while seeking to guide and motivate employees to improved performance where needed. Feedback also helps employees, especially new ones, clarify role expectations, performance expectations, and standards. For example, if employees find themselves rewarded for tasks that are not specified in their job descriptions, they will probably continue to do them since they have resulted in positive feedback. Similarly, tasks that are specified but go unnoticed or unrewarded may come to be ignored. Over time, employees' role perceptions change to include performance of unspecified but rewarded tasks and nonperformance of the tasks that have gone unnoticed.

Although appraisal interviews provide needed performance feedback, they do not occur often enough to meet employee needs for feedback. For this reason, it is good practice for managers and supervisors to provide their subordinates with frequent, informal feedback as well.

In contrast to administrative purposes, employee development purposes require evaluations of employee effectiveness on a number of job-related performance dimensions so that areas needing improvement can be readily identified. In this type of appraisal, performance is often measured against absolute standards, rather than that of other employees.

Because administrative and development appraisals differ so widely in their intent, it is suggested that they be conducted separately and use different methods. Unfortunately, many organizations attempt to use the same appraisal method for both administrative and development purposes. A large survey of 581 employers across Canada found that over 75 percent used the same appraisal for both development and administrative purposes.[4] Several researchers have noted the problem of conflicting objectives in appraisal interviews intended to serve the two purposes.[5] In such an interview, the evaluator must assume the role of both judge (administrative purpose) and helper (development purpose). Research at General Electric showed that when this conflict occurs, administrative issues, such as the amount of a pay increase, tend to dominate the interview.[6] This does little to further employee development. Some organizations have solved the problem by scheduling separate appraisals for each of the appraisal purposes.[7]

At a number of sophisticated employers, the employee development component of appraisal has evolved into a career planning and development process. At Corning, for example, the performance development and review (PD&R) system initially had some problems, such as lack of employee participation in the process, lack of time for the interviews, and lack of perceived ownership among employees in their development objectives. Instead of modifying the PD&R system to handle these issues, Corning developed a different system for development of its nonexempt employees.[8] (This system was described in Chapter 10.)

Monitoring/Assessment Purposes

Performance appraisal is one way organizations monitor quality of the work force. (More indirect ways include the costs of providing a service or product and customer satisfaction.) Organizations need to monitor work force quality to ensure that acceptable standards of performance are being maintained. If they are not, steps can be taken to simplify jobs, train workers, motivate workers, help them solve personal problems, or dismiss them, depending upon the reasons for poor performance.

Performance appraisal data are also collected, stored, and analyzed for program assessment purposes, such as validating selection procedures and determining the success of training and development programs. Records of employee performance can also show how effective recruiting, selection, and placement have been in supplying a qualified work force.

Appraisals for monitoring/assessment purposes should incorporate a number of reliable and representative measures of job behaviour and job results. This is to ensure that appraisal data are valid measures for use as criteria in studies of program effectiveness and in validation of the instruments and methods used in HRM decisions.

RELATION TO OTHER HRM FUNCTIONS

The relation of performance appraisal to other HRM functions is shown in Figure 11.1. An employee's first formal performance appraisal usually occurs after training and six months or a year on the job. Standards against which performance is evaluated are derived from job descriptions, which are developed through job analysis. As revealed in the previous section, performance appraisal data are used to determine training and development needs, validate predictors used in selection, assign pay, and evaluate program success. In human resource planning, they can be used to indicate likely human resource flows, pointing up future needs for human resources. For example, if an

FIGURE 11.1
Performance Appraisal: Relation to Other HRM Functions

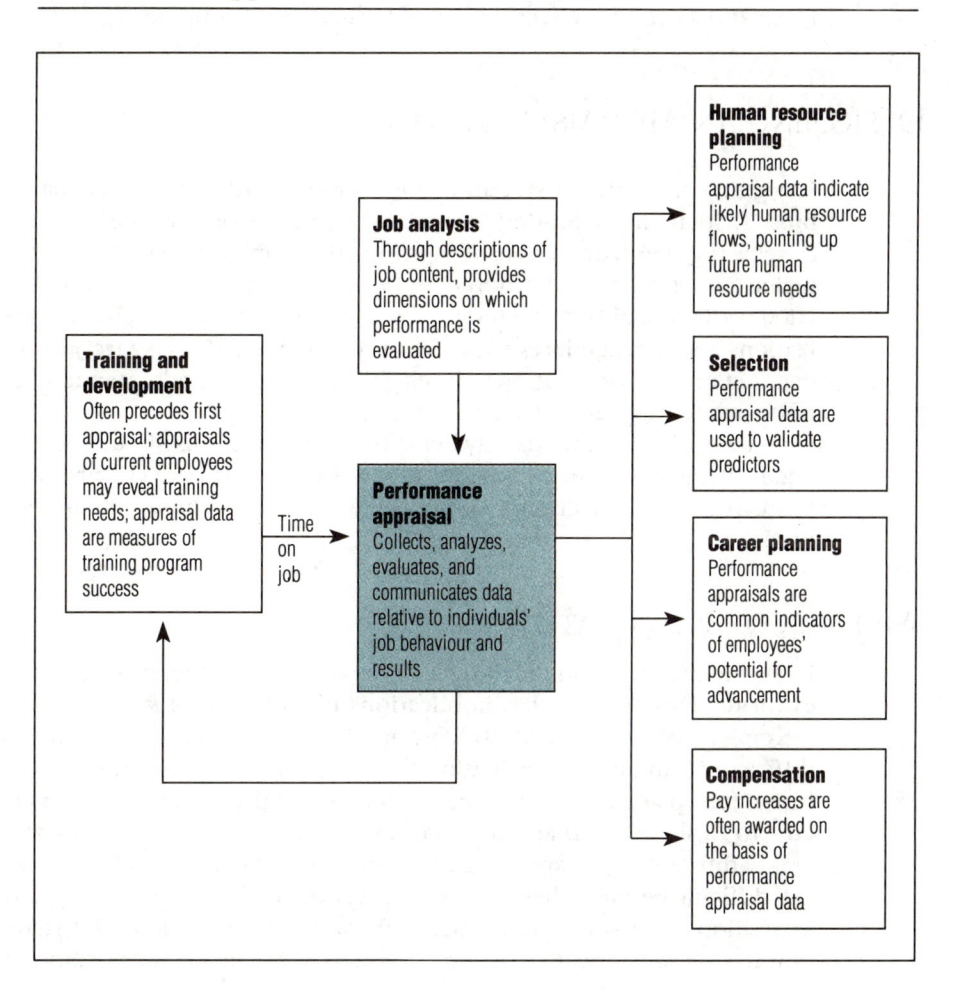

Job analysis
Through descriptions of job content, provides dimensions on which performance is evaluated

Training and development
Often precedes first appraisal; appraisals of current employees may reveal training needs; appraisal data are measures of training program success

Time on job →

Performance appraisal
Collects, analyzes, evaluates, and communicates data relative to individuals' job behaviour and results

Human resource planning
Performance appraisal data indicate likely human resource flows, pointing up future human resource needs

Selection
Performance appraisal data are used to validate predictors

Career planning
Performance appraisals are common indicators of employees' potential for advancement

Compensation
Pay increases are often awarded on the basis of performance appraisal data

organization has twenty middle managers capable of moving up, it will have little need to recruit externally to fill six executive positions.

Responsibilities for Performance Appraisal

With respect to performance appraisal, HRM professionals engage in activities related to three major areas of responsibility: (1) designing an appraisal system; (2) implementing the system; and (3) collecting, storing, and analyzing appraisal data for a variety of purposes. Designing an appraisal system requires determining organizational needs for appraisal and deciding which method(s) best suit those needs. Implementation activities include readying materials, training raters so that appraisal purposes and procedures are understood, and scheduling appraisal interviews. Finally, HRM professionals collect, store, and use appraisal data in order to monitor the quality of the work force and assess the effectiveness of various HRM programs.

Designing an Appraisal System

Designing an appraisal system is not a simple matter: there are many possibilities, including adopting an existing system from another organization, purchasing one from a consulting firm, developing one's own system, and hiring a consultant to develop one. Because of the number of options, some HRM professionals may be tempted to seek advice from neighbouring organizations about procedures they use or recommend. This is rarely wise, however, because organizations differ in their needs and intended uses for performance appraisal data.

In designing an appraisal system, HRM professionals should consider the needs of their own organization. Key considerations are (1) who should be evaluated; (2) what criteria should be used; and (3) how will appraisals be used.

Who Should Be Evaluated?

First, the organization must determine what types of employees it wants to evaluate. This decision has implications for the type of system chosen. For example, a system that effectively appraises managerial performance is quite different from one for evaluating the performance of clerical workers. Different jobs place different demands on appraisal systems. Jobs that are difficult to describe or that vary substantially in terms of activities and tasks create difficulties for appraising performance. Managerial jobs, for example, are difficult because they involve a great deal of variety, brevity, and fragmentation. One study found that half of a manager's activities lasted nine minutes or less, and that ad hoc contacts were much more common than planned encounters.[9] These facts suggest great difficulty in constructing adequate appraisal instruments. At the opposite extreme, some jobs have very little variation in performance. Many manufacturing, production-line, and continuous-process operations fall into this category. It simply does not make sense to install a formal appraisal system for employees whose performance is constrained by the equipment and processes used on the job. When interdependence among workers is high, as in the case of employees on a tractor assembly line or a refuse collection team, individuals do not have complete control over their own performance. Obviously, an appraisal system should not judge people on results that are beyond their control. In such cases, it makes more sense to consider other means of evaluation.

WHAT CRITERIA SHOULD BE USED?

Next, an organization must decide what criteria to use for evaluation. Does it want a system based on evaluating individual traits, behaviour, or job results? This decision depends in part on who is being evaluated and how the organization intends to use performance appraisals.

Early rating scales evaluated workers on individual traits or personal characteristics that were presumably related to job performance. Initiative, aggressiveness, reliability, and personality are examples of traits on which employees have been rated. One problem with such criteria is that traits themselves are difficult to define and may be subject to varying interpretations by evaluators. For example, what one evaluator perceives as desirable aggressiveness, another may see as undesirable hostility. Another problem is that organizations have often used trait rating forms for a wide variety of jobs, so some employees were rated on traits with little relevance to their jobs. The modern trend is away from trait rating toward evaluation of employees on their behaviour or in terms of results achieved.

Rating employees according to job behaviour is based on the assumption that effective and ineffective kinds of behaviour exist and have been identified for each job or type of job. A behaviour is judged effective or ineffective in terms of the results it produces (either desirable or undesirable). For example, a customer service representative could be judged on the way he or she calms irate customers. Evaluating employees on their behaviour is especially important for purposes of employee development.

Most managers would probably prefer to base appraisals on some form of results indices, such as the dollar volume of sales, amount of scrap, and quantity and quality of work produced, since these appear to be more objective measures of performance than standard rating scales. Thanks to the advent of computer surveillance and monitoring, many organizations are now able to collect highly detailed job results data for certain types of employees, including telephone operators, video display terminal and word-processing operators, reservations agents, truck and taxi drivers, and others. Bell Canada used one of the most sophisticated computer monitoring systems, which measured 76 characteristics of operator performance.[10]

Sometimes appraisals may, of necessity, focus on results rather than behaviour. For example, the content of managerial jobs is highly variable, making it difficult to specify appropriate behaviour for evaluation purposes. Thus many managers are measured according to results indices such as turnover, absenteeism, grievances, profitability, and production rates in their departments. These indices can also be used to evaluate the performance of organizational units. When results indices are used for appraisal purposes, appraisal instruments, such as rating scales, are rarely used.

How Will Appraisals Be Used?

A third question to consider in determining needs for a system is, how will appraisals be used? Will they be used to decide pay increases, to provide performance feedback to employees, to assess training needs, or to validate selection procedures? As we have seen, different purposes necessitate collection of different kinds of appraisal data and, therefore, affect choice of an appraisal instrument or system.

General Requirements of Performance Appraisal Systems

Regardless of an organization's specific needs for performance appraisal, if a system is to accomplish its objectives, it must meet five general requirements: reliability, validity, practicality, fairness, and impact. (Alert readers will notice that the criteria of reliability and validity, as well as some of the vocabulary of assessing their presence or absence, are the same as those used in selection methods, discussed in Chapter 7.)

Reliability

Reliability is the consistency of a measure over time and between raters. Consistency over time means that the passage of time should not affect the findings or results of an instrument. This form of reliability is not very crucial for performance appraisal since one expects to see changes in performance over time. Consistency between raters is a more important requirement of performance appraisal measures. It means that different raters using the method should have a reasonable amount of agreement on their evaluation of the same employee. Generally, research shows that well-trained raters become quite consistent in their ratings. The highest degrees of consistency should occur when raters observe a given employee from the same organizational position. Lower degrees of consistency are inevitable when evaluators differ in their perspectives and opportunities to observe. To handle differences in perspective, many appraisal forms record the nature of the relationship between evaluator and evaluatee and give greater weight to evaluators who have better knowledge. It is generally believed that an immediate superior is in the best position to evaluate the performance of a subordinate, though this is not always the case in practice. Reasonably high reliability is necessary for validity.

VALIDITY

An appraisal method or index is *valid* if it accurately measures job performance. The validity of appraisal measures must be established by demonstrating various relationships between appraisal scores or results and other job- and performance-related behaviour and/or results. Establishing the validity of an appraisal system is not a one-shot project. It is, or should be, a continuing attempt to understand how scores or ratings relate to other personnel and organizational performance indices. Depending on their purpose, performance ratings should correlate positively with promotion rate, with pay increases, and, to a lesser degree, with objective indices of performance, such as productivity and profitability.

The major aspect of validity in performance appraisal is content validity. An appraisal instrument has *content validity* to the extent that it includes most of the important job behaviours and/or results of the job. Many appraisal instruments attempt to cover too many different jobs. It is naive, for example, to expect an accounting department, a shipping and receiving department, and a production department to have common jobs, common job behaviours, and common performance goals. The only way the same instrument could be used in a variety of departments would be to include only the most general factors or those based on personal traits. And ratings of such factors are likely to be unrelated to actual job behaviour and/or performance.

Using appraisal instruments that attempt to cover too many jobs can result in some employees' being evaluated on criteria not related to their jobs, while other essential criteria are overlooked. Measures that evaluate employees on aspects of performance that are not job-related are said to be *contaminated*. Measures are called *deficient* if they fail to evaluate employees on certain criteria that are job-related. Content validity suffers when measures prove either contaminated or deficient.

Another threat to validity is rater errors, such as the halo effect, central tendency, severity, and leniency. The *halo effect* occurs when a rating on one dimension of an appraisal instrument substantially influences the ratings on other dimensions for the same employee; as a result, the evaluation is about the same across all performance dimensions. Errors of central tendency, severity, and leniency are said to be "constant" errors because a rater tends to make them in evaluating all subordinates. The *error of central tendency* is a lack of variation among ratings of different subordinates; most employees end up being rated as average. *Leniency* refers to an evaluator's tendency to rate most employees very highly across performance dimensions, whereas *severity*, also called *strictness*, is the tendency to rate most quite harshly. All these errors result in an inability to identify differences in performance among employees.

PRACTICALITY

To meet the requirements of practicality, an appraisal system must be acceptable to both evaluators and those being evaluated. If an appraisal system is unacceptable, its use will be resisted, and resulting appraisals and decisions will be suspect. Practicality dictates that an appraisal system must measure something significant to individuals and the organization. If it does not, it will have little utility for employees or the organization.

FAIRNESS

Employees must feel that appraisals are conducted fairly and that their consequences (raises, promotions, and so on) are fair. A system perceived as unfair will likely prove unacceptable to employees. For this reason, many unions given considerable attention to performance appraisal systems. Collective agreements may specify that any changes require consultation with the union and/or that the union has the right to review results. Grievances involving appraisals are not uncommon. To the extent that unions perceive performance appraisals as related to pay-for-performance or other variable pay systems, leaders such as the Canadian Auto Workers' Bob White are strongly opposed to them. Compensation experts doubt that such systems will come to organized labour in the near future.[11]

Results of a study by Meyer suggest that achieving perceived fairness in an appraisal system may be difficult because employees tend to rate their performances highly.[12] Meyer's study showed that 95 percent of employees in occupations ranging from accountants and engineers to blue-collar workers from several companies rated their own performances as "above average," and nearly 70 percent felt they were in the top 25 percent of their co-workers. Indeed, most attitude surveys show that 75 to 80 percent of employees believe they are above average.[13]

IMPACT

If, after spending valuable time conducting appraisals, supervisors and managers discover that employees with low ratings get the same rewards as those with high ratings, then the system loses its impact. Without impact, the system loses credibility, and practicality is likely to suffer.

PERFORMANCE APPRAISAL METHODS

Performance appraisal methods are numerous and varied. They are grouped, somewhat arbitrarily, in the following pages into those best suited to administrative purposes and those best suited to employee development purposes. Methods geared to administrative purposes include job results indices, the essay method, graphic rating scales, mixed standard scales, ranking, forced distribution, peer evaluation, and field review. Methods more suited to employee development include behavioural checklists, behaviourally anchored rating scales (BARS), management by objectives (MBO), and team-style peer review. Table 11.1 compares appraisal methods on a number of characteristics.

METHODS FOR ADMINISTRATIVE PURPOSES

The intent of methods for administrative purposes is to generate a global or composite rating for each employee in order to allocate pay and other organizational rewards. Methods for administrative purposes typically do not focus on individual strengths but rather seek to compare employees based on their performance levels.

Job Results Indices

Job results were already discussed briefly as one of three possible criteria on which to base appraisals. Though not an appraisal method per se, job results are a source of data that can be used, either singly or in conjunction with other methods, to appraise performance. Typically, an employee's job results are compared against some objective standard of performance. This standard can be absolute or relative to the performance of others.

Job results are especially useful for appraising the performance of higher-level workers, such as managers and professionals. Use in appraising lower-level employees, such as clerical workers, is growing, however, because of the increased use of computer surveillance and monitoring systems. One-fifth of the 834 delegates attending the 1983 Ontario Federation of Labour convention reported working under some form of electronic monitoring.[14] (Case 11.2 describes Bell Canada's computerized performance monitoring system, TOPS, and some of the controversy surrounding its use.)

One might think that because job results are quantifiable, using them would circumvent problems of validity and reliability. However, results indices are frequently subject to contamination and deficiency. For example, evaluating an insurance salesperson's performance on the basis of the face value of policies sold may be deficient since the measure does not reflect the many other useful and profitable activities the individual undertakes for the company. The index may also be contaminated if it does not take into account differences in sales territories that result in the salesperson's being evaluated on results that are outside his or her control.

In most organizations, it is very difficult to find objective indices that are not somewhat deficient or contaminated. Even those that are neither may have unacceptably low reliability over time because of unpredictable fluctuations in the characteristics being measured.[15] Other problems occur when numerous job results indices are combined to yield an overall rating for a

TABLE 11.1
Performance Appraisal Methods

		MAJOR PURPOSE: ADMINISTRATIVE (A), DEVELOPMENT (D)	TYPICAL CONTENT	FREQUENCY OF USE	DEVELOPMENT COSTS	USAGE COSTS	ACCEPTANCE BY RATER AND RATEES
	Job results indices	A	Results	Very common	Variable	Variable	Fair–low
	Essay	A	Variable	Common	Low	High	Fair
Rating scales	Graphic rating scales	A	Traits, behaviour	Very common	Average	Low	Fair
	Mixed standard scales	A	Traits, behaviour	Rare	High	Average	Low
	BARS	A, D	Behaviour	Uncommon but growing	High	Low	Good
Ranking methods	Straight ranking	A	Overall assessments	Fairly common	Low	Low	Low
	Alternative ranking	A	Overall assessments	Fairly common	Low	Low	Low
	Paired comparisons	A	Overall assessments	Uncommon	Low	Average	Low
	Forced distribution	A	Overall assessments	Uncommon	Low	Low	Low
	Field review	A	Behaviour results, traits	Uncommon	Average	High	Fair–good
	Peer evaluation	A	Overall assessments	Uncommon	Low	Low	Good
	Team-style peer review	A, D	Behaviour, results, overall assessments	Uncommon	High	Average	Good
	Behavioural checklist	A, D	Behaviour, traits	Common	Average	Low	Fair
	MBO	A, D	Results	Common in management	High	High	Good

person. For example, imagine having to weigh the importance of each of Bell's 76 performance measures in order to determine an overall assessment for each operator. This does not mean that job results indices are useless — only that their reliability and validity must be examined closely.

Essay Method

The essay method involves an evaluator's written report appraising an employee's performance, usually in terms of job behaviour and/or results. Essay appraisals are often justifications of pay, promotion, or termination decisions, but they can be used for development purposes as well. Since essay appraisals are to a large extent unstructured and open-ended, lack of standardization is a major problem; by nature, they are highly susceptible to evaluator bias, which may in some cases be discriminatory. Since the evaluator does not have to report on all job-related behaviour or results, he or she may simply comment on those that reflect favourably or unfavourably on an employee. Such a statement usually does not represent a true picture of the employee or the job, and content validity suffers. The essay method is unacceptable to most unions and does not form a sound database for justifying decisions about pay, promotion, and dismissal. Its development costs are very low, but its usage costs can be high because of the time supervisors and managers must spend writing and reviewing the essays. According to Thacker and Cattaneo's survey, no respondents reported using the essay method. It is likely, however, that it is used as a part of some other methods such as management by objectives (MBO), which was the most frequently cited appraisal method. Essays might also be used as part of developmental planning documents or as justification for any actions resulting from an appraisal.[16]

Graphic Rating Scales

One of the most common methods of performance appraisal, *graphic rating scales*, requires an evaluator to indicate the degree to which an employee demonstrates a particular trait, behaviour, or performance result. Thacker and Cattaneo found a type of graphic rating scale, the trait-oriented rating scale, to be the second most commonly used appraisal method in their sample (26.8 percent).[17] Rating forms are composed of a number of scales, each pertaining to a particular performance-related aspect, such as job knowledge, responsibility, or quality of work. Each scale is a continuum of scale points, or *anchors*, ranging from high to low, good to poor, most to least effective, and so forth. The scales usually have five to seven points, though they can have more or fewer. Graphic rating scales may or may not define their scale points. For example, scale points are not defined in the following five-point scale, which asks students to rate their professor on overall teaching effectiveness:

```
                                Very                    Very
                                poor                    good
                                 ←——————————————————→
      Teaching effectiveness:    1    2    3    4    5
```

This is an example of a poor graphic rating scale; not only are scale points undefined, but so is the concept of "teaching effectiveness." An evaluator must use his or her own definition of what is being measured and determine what constitutes very poor to very good performance. This results in a vague and subjective measure. Undefined measures and scale points leave room for broad interpretation by evaluators and more often than not result in low reliability.

There are better graphic rating scales; one example is given in Exhibit 11.1. This graphic rating scale, which is used to evaluate office employees, includes as performance dimensions traits or characteristics (appearance, personality, job knowledge), behaviour (responsibility, service awareness), and results (quality of work, quantity of work). Note that the form calls for an overall assessment of each ratee's promotion potential.

Rating scales should have the following characteristics:

1. Performance dimensions should be clearly defined.
2. Scales should be behaviourally based so that a rater is able to support all ratings with objective, observable evidence.
3. Abstract trait names such as "loyalty," "honesty," and "integrity" should be avoided unless they can be defined in terms of observable behaviour.
4. Points, or anchors, on each scaled dimension should be brief, unambiguous, and relevant to what is being rated. For example, in rating a person's flow of words, it is preferable to use anchors such as "fluent," "easy," "unimpeded," "hesitant," and "laboured," rather than "excellent," "very good," "average," "below average," and "poor."[18]

Carefully constructed graphic rating scales have a number of advantages.

1. Standardization of content, permitting comparison of employees.
2. Ease of development, and relatively low development and usage cost.
3. Reasonably good rater and ratee acceptance.

A disadvantage of most rating scales is that they are susceptible to several rating errors, including the halo effect, central tendency, severity, and leniency.

Mixed Standard Scales

In a *mixed standard scale*, each performance dimension has three statements relating to it: one illustrating good performance, one average performance, and one poor performance. Statements represent behavioural examples obtained from knowledgeable persons, usually supervisors. The evaluator's

EXHIBIT 11.1

Personnel Evaluation Report for Office Workers

Instructions to the evaluator:
This report should be an honest and objective evaluation of the employee's performance. The factors should be rated on the basis of current performance and not on future expectations. Avoid letting your appraisal of one quality influence your judgement on another. Do not give disproportionate weight to single, isolated deviations from the normal.

Name	Department	Date
Job title	Length of time on this job	

Quality of work (disregard quantity)

5	4	3	2	1
___Extremely neat and accurate.	___Good accurate worker. Makes few mistakes.	___Adequate, some improvement desirable.	___Barely up to minimum standards. Often inaccurate.	___Below minimum standards. Much room for improvement.

Quantity of work (disregard quality)

5	4	3	2	1
___Outstanding volume.	___Well above average volume.	___Adequate volume.	___Barely up to minimum standards.	___Below minimum standards. Much room for improvement.

Job knowledge (technical)

5	4	3	2	1
___Expert. Has superior knowledge.	___Well-rounded knowledge. Seldom needs assistance.	___Possesses acceptable knowledge.	___Knowledge is adequate to perform minimum job requirements.	___Very limited knowledge. Needs frequent assistance.

Responsibility (ability to plan and direct work)

5	4	3	2	1
___Plans and carries out own work in a superior manner. Self-sustaining.	___Plans and carries out work well. Requires little supervision.	___Requires occasional work direction.	___Carries out only the most obvious tasks without follow-up.	___Always waits to be directed.

Appearance (personal grooming habits)

5	4	3	2	1
___Outstanding. Makes excellent impression.	___Neat. Better than average impression.	___Presentable by average standards. Good impression.	___Fair appearance. Could use some improvement.	___Careless, unkempt.

Personality (ability to get along with others)

5	4	3	2	1
___Exceptionally pleasing. Very highly regarded.	___Favorable impression. Well-liked and accepted.	___Usually well-liked. Usually makes a favorable impression.	___Some difficulty gaining acceptance.	___Negative. Antagonistic. Arouses resentment.

Service awareness (ability to please public)

5	4	3	2	1
___Always pleases public. Goes out of way to serve them.	___Gets along with public. Seems to please them.	___Does an adequate job in public relations.	___Seldom goes out of way to please public.	___Does not try to satisfy. Appears disinterested.

Promotional potential (Check the appropriate statement below and explain reason for choice)

___Now ready for promotion or transfer (indicate job duties that you believe employee is capable of performing)
___Of maximum value to the company and of greatest personal effectiveness in present assignment
___Adequate in present job but not yet qualified for promotion
___Not adequate in present job—no potential for promotion

task is to indicate whether an employee fits the statement, is better than the statement, or is worse than the statement. Statements are randomly mixed, which tends to reduce rater errors by making it less obvious which statements reflect effective or ineffective performance.

Mixed standard scales have been applied in only a few settings. Research on mixed standard scales shows that while this method is not superior to other methods, it can result in less leniency in administrative decisions.[19] It can be unpopular with evaluators, however, because the rating process is time-consuming and the relative effectiveness of statements is hidden.

A mixed standard scale is shown in Exhibit 11.2. The nine statements in this scale relate to the three performance dimensions of efficiency, carefulness, and relations with other people.

Ranking

Ranking methods compare one individual with another, resulting in an ordering of employees in relation to one another. Rankings often result in overall assessments of employees, rather than in specific judgements about a number

EXHIBIT 11.2
A Mixed Standard Scale

Instructions: If the employee fits the statement, put a 0 in the space opposite the statement; if the employee is better than the statement, put a + in the space; if the employee is worse than the statement, put a – in the space.

_____Is on good terms with everyone. Can get along with people even in disagreement.

_____Employee's work is spotty, sometimes all right and sometimes not. Could be more accurate and careful.

_____Has a tendency to get into unnecessary conflicts with people.

_____Is quick and efficient, able to keep work on schedule. Really gets going on a new task.

_____The accuracy of employee's work is satisfactory. It is not often that you find clear evidence of carelessness.

_____Gets along with most people. Only very occasionally has conflicts with others on the job, and these are likely to be minor.

_____Is efficient enough, usually getting through assignments and work in reasonable time.

_____Work is striking in its accuracy. Never any evidence of carelessness in it.

_____Some lack of efficiency on employee's part. Employee may take too much time to complete assignments and sometimes does not really finish them.

Source: Adapted from F. Blanz and E.E. Ghiselli, "The Mixed Standard Scale: A New Rating System," *Personnel Psychology*, vol. 25 (1972), pp. 185–99. Used with the permission of *Personnel Psychology*.

of job components. *Straight ranking* requires an evaluator to order a group of employees from best to worst overall or from most effective to least effective in terms of a particular criterion. *Alternative ranking* makes the same demand, but the ranking process must be done in a specified manner (for example, by first selecting the best employee in a group, then the worst, then the second-best, then the second-worst, and so on). In *paired comparison*, a more sophisticated ranking method, each employee in a group is compared with every other member in the group through a series of comparing pairs.

An example can illustrate the three methods of ranking. Assume that an office manager is asked to rank the office's five secretaries in terms of overall performance. Using straight ranking, the manager judges Karen best, Lee second best, Holly third, Frank fourth, and Heather fifth. The same rank-ordering might or might not result using alternative ranking, but in either case evaluative judgements would have been made in a specified way. Assuming that the same rank-ordering results, the office manager first judges Karen best, then Heather worst, then Lee second best, then Frank next-to-worst, and finally Holly third best. Using paired comparison, any one of the secretaries, say, Karen, is first compared with any one of the others, say, Frank, and determined to be better or worse. Then Karen is compared with Lee or Holly or Heather, and the process continues until she has been compared with each of the others. The office manager then turns to one of the other secretaries and compares him or her with every other secretary in a similar manner. To determine rankings using the paired-comparison method, an evaluator simply adds the number of times each person was judged superior (for example, Karen was judged best four times and, therefore, is ranked first among the five secretaries).

The paired-comparison method can be quite time-consuming and laborious if there are a number of employees to be evaluated. The number of comparisons necessary can be found by the formula $N(N-1)/2$, where N is the number of employees. Paired comparison of ten employees, for example, requires that 45 comparative judgements be made.

Alternative-ranking and paired-comparison methods attempt to increase the reliability of rankings by structuring the way in which rank-orders are determined. Although reasonably successful, these methods are still subject to bias and error, which may be seen by comparing different raters' rankings of the same employee. Even when raters are equally familiar with the employees, they may vary in what they see as important components of job performance. Ranking methods usually do not specify the job components on which an evaluator should judge overall performance.

Comparative evaluation systems such as ranking are rarely popular. No matter how close a group of employees are in terms of level of performance, and no matter how well they perform on the job, some will rank high and some will end up at the bottom. Evaluators are often reluctant to make such comparisons. Also, rankings do not permit much comparison of employees across groups. For example, it is difficult to say whether the second-ranked employee in Unit A is as good as or better than the second-ranked employee in Unit B. One researcher has, however, suggested a method by which raters familiar with employees in different units can establish their relative rankings.[20] Despite the problems of ranking methods, they can be very useful in differentiating among employees if an organization has a very limited number of promotions or dollars to allocate.

Forced Distribution

Forced distribution is a form of comparative evaluation in which an evaluator rates subordinates according to a specified distribution. Unlike ranking methods, forced distribution is frequently applied to several components of job performance, rather than only one. Students who have been graded on a curve are already familiar with this method of appraisal. For example, a manager may be told that he or she must rate subordinates according to the following distribution: 10 percent low; 20 percent below average; 40 percent average; 20 percent above average; and 10 percent high. In a group of twenty employees, two would have to be placed in the low category, four in the below-average category, eight in average, four in above-average, and two in the highest category. The proportions can vary; for example, a supervisor could be required to place employees into the top, middle, and bottom thirds of a distribution. Forced distribution is primarily used to eliminate rating errors, such as leniency and central tendency, but the method itself can cause rating errors because it forces differentiation among employees even when performance is quite similar. Even if all employees in a unit are doing a good job, a certain number must be placed at the bottom of the continuum. For this reason, raters and ratees do not readily accept this method, especially in small groups or when group members are all of high ability. An example of this occurred at the medical research division of American Cyanamid. The company had used a forced-distribution system to appraise a highly educated staff of professionals, many of whom had graduate degrees. Managers dreaded the appraisal task and subordinates felt the results were unfair. Results of a two-year experiment in which the old system was replaced with a simple three-category system of "exceptional," "good," and "unacceptable" showed substantially improved attitudes and faith in appraisals.[21] It is perhaps not surprising that Thacker and Cattaneo's survey found fewer than 5 percent of respondents using the forced-distribution method.[22]

Peer Evaluation

In peer evaluation methods, employees judge the performance of their co-workers. Three methods of peer evaluation are peer rating, peer ranking, and peer nomination. *Peer ratings* are simply ratings of peers done by group members, rather than by a superior; any type of rating instrument can be used. Similarly, *peer ranking* is any ranking method in which group members assign rankings to one another. In *peer nomination*, each member of a well-defined group designates a number of group members as highest (and sometimes lowest) on a particular performance dimension. This frequently researched method has been shown to distinguish with a high degree of reliability and validity group members who are very high (or very low) on a performance dimension.[23] It has had a relatively long record of success in identifying successful officers in the armed services. Its use in nonmilitary situations has been limited, but evidence suggests its usefulness in making decisions about promotions. Of the other peer evaluation methods, peer ratings are most useful for performance feedback purposes, while peer rankings hold some promise for pay decisions since they compare co-workers with one another.

A peer-rating system was successfully implemented at Schreiber Foods, a food processing plant. The system was developed through extensive involvement of groups of hourly employees and managers and put into effect when a new performance-based pay system was implemented. When it was time to evaluate an employee, a supervisor would select five peers of the employee — co-workers who knew the ratee's job and not all of whom were friends (or enemies) of the ratee. The co-workers' evaluation forms were filled out and returned to the supervisor, who deleted the highest and lowest ratings and averaged the remaining three. The ratee was told only of the average rating, thereby preserving some degree of anonymity of the raters. As in other systems, supervisors received training both in rating and in conducting effective appraisal interviews, but peers received no training. Interestingly, the peer ratings were used for both administrative and developmental purposes. A survey of attitudes of both employees and managers showed that only 22 percent were dissatisfied with the system, and managers were slightly more in favour of the system than were employees. Also, attitudes were more favourable toward use of peer ratings for developmental than for pay purposes. Generally, the program demonstrated that peer ratings could be used successfully by hourly workers, but there were still a few concerns that needed to be addressed.[24]

Another form of peer evaluation, team-style peer review, is discussed later in this section.

Field Review

Field review is an appraisal by someone outside the employee's own department, usually someone from the corporate office or the HRM department. The process involves a review of the employee's records and interviews with the employee and sometimes with his or her superior. Field review is used primarily in making promotion decisions at the managerial level. It is also useful when comparable information is needed about employees in different units or locations. The method has two disadvantages:

1. An outsider is usually not very familiar with conditions in the particular work environment that may affect the employee's ability or motivation to perform.
2. An outside reviewer does not have the opportunity to observe the employee's behaviour or performance over time and in a variety of situations but only in a very short, artificially structured interview situation.

METHODS FOR EMPLOYEE DEVELOPMENT PURPOSES

Performance appraisals conducted for purposes of employee development should be very different from those conducted for administrative purposes. Because they are intended to guide and to motivate improved performance, appraisals for employee development should

1. Focus on a number of elements of job behaviour or results.
2. Have explicit or implicit standards of performance.
3. Be specific to a particular job or type of job.

Appraisal methods used for employee development include the behavioural checklist, behaviourally anchored rating scales (BARS), management by objectives (MBO), and team-style peer review. Though these methods meet the criteria of a development purpose, they can also be used for administrative purposes.

Behavioural Checklist

A behavioural checklist is a rating form containing statements that describe both effective and ineffective kinds of job behaviour relating to a number of dimensions determined to be relevant to the job. A rater is asked to check those statements that are descriptive of the employee's behaviour. To develop a behavioural checklist, a panel of experts rates a large number of behavioural statements relevant to a job or set of jobs. Statements that are reliably rated and represent the entire range of performance effectiveness are selected for inclusion in the checklist. Exhibit 11.3 presents a number of items that are part of a behavioural checklist for a salesperson.

If an appraisal is for administrative purposes, the rater is not told which types of behaviour are effective or ineffective; an HRM professional can tabulate any required overall assessment. If, however, the behavioural checklist is intended for development purposes, the rater must know which types of behaviour are effective and which are not, so he or she can make suggestions for the employee's improvement.

One of the first behavioural checklists was developed for salespeople at the Minnesota Mining and Manufacturing Company (3M).[25] More than 100

EXHIBIT 11.3
Items from a Behavioural Checklist for a Salesperson

Instructions: Please check those statements descriptive of the employee's behaviour.

____Calls on customers immediately after hearing of any complaints

____Discusses complaints with customer

____Gathers facts relevant to customers' complaints

____Transmits information about complaints back to customers and resolves problems to their satisfaction

____Plans each day's activities ahead of time

____Lays out broad sales plans for one month ahead

____Gathers sales information from customers, other salespeople, trade journals, and other relevant sources

____Transmits sales information to manager

____Is truthful in dealing with customers

____Is truthful in dealing with superiors

____Suggests new approaches to selling

____Systematically calls on all customer accounts

Source: Adapted from M.D. Dunnette, *Personnel Selection and Placement* (Belmont, Calif.: Wadsworth, 1966). Used with the permission of the author.

critical incidents of effective and ineffective behaviour were collected from sales managers and listed in thirteen categories.

Behavioural checklists are well suited to use in employee development because they focus on behaviour and results, are specific to the job for which performance is being rated, and use absolute rather than comparative standards. However, they can also be used for administrative purposes. An advantage of this method is that raters are asked to describe rather than evaluate a subordinate's behaviour; for this reason, behavioural checklists may meet with less resistance than some other methods. There may be some objection, however, to the lack of information about which types of behaviour are considered effective and ineffective. And if scale values are assigned to various kinds of behaviour in determining an overall evaluation for an employee, an evaluator may not like the fact that these values are kept hidden. To the extent that types of behaviour are not identified as either effective or ineffective, rater errors, such as leniency, severity, central tendency, and the halo effect, are minimized. An obvious disadvantage of behavioural checklists is that constructing the instrument demands an investment of much time and money.

HRM IN ACTION

PARTNERSHIP APPRAISAL

At Digital Computer, one of the largest computer manufacturers, many work groups have adopted the highly participative self-directed work team (SDWT) style of management. Digital recognized that the traditional boss-subordinate type of performance appraisal would be inconsistent with the highly participative culture of SDWTs. Therefore, a form of team appraisals was introduced. Called the "partnership appraisal," it involves both self-rating and peer ratings.

Partnership appraisal is done by a committee of five people: the evaluee, a committee chairperson chosen by the evaluee, two randomly selected members of the evaluee's team, and a management consultant. (Many SDWTs rely on internal managers for advice and expertise. Therefore, instead of a supervisor, teams utilize a management consultant, who may be an HRM manager.)

As is the case in any well-done traditional appraisal, the appraisal committee begins by making sure an up-to-date and complete job description with job specifications is available for the evaluee.

The appraisal begins in a high-tech manner with the secretary sending the evaluee an electronic mail message that appraisal time is in 30 days. The evaluee then selects the committee chair, usually someone he or she knows well. Again using electronic mail, the evaluee sends committee members information regarding his or her performance, accomplishments, and training over the past year. Members of the appraisal team use this information as well as their own knowledge of the evaluee to make inputs to the chairperson.

After the evaluee receives material from the committee, he or she prepares a self-appraisal and sends it to the chairperson. Within a week, the committee reviews all material, including the self-appraisal. At this point, the committee meets with the evaluee. (If necessary, a second meeting is held.)

At the meeting the committee arrives at a final rating, and the evaluee and committee members jointly set goals for next year. At this point, the chairperson prepares a report of the committee's actions; it is signed by all parties and sent to the human resource department.

Like most systems of appraisal, this one has a number of advantages and disadvantages. One of the major advantages is the multiple inputs to the process, including the worker, his or her peers, and the management

> consultant. Involvement of team members in the appraisal process is good training for leadership roles, and employees receive feedback and recognition from their peers. In addition, employees are involved in the goal-setting process. On the negative side, the appraisal requires considerable time and energy from team members; rating errors may be made; and feedback may be given in a negative, nonsupportive manner. To ensure such problems do not occur, team members must be trained in the appraisal process; the chairperson and management consultant must act as controls when necessary to prevent inaccurate, unfair, or overly harsh feedback; and the collaborative and participative nature of the process should be communicated frequently.
>
> Source: Based on C.A. Norman and A.Z. Zawacki, "Team Appraisal–Team Approach," *Personnel Journal*, September 1991, pp. 101–04. Used with the permission of *Personnel Journal*, Costa Mesa, California; all rights reserved.

Behaviourally Anchored Rating Scales

Behaviourally anchored rating scales (BARS), sometimes called *behavioural expectation scales*, are rating sales whose scale points are defined by statements of effective and ineffective behaviour.[26] They are said to be "behaviourally anchored" because statements describe a continuum of behaviour ranging from least to most effective. In the most common form of BARS, an evaluator must indicate which behaviour on each scale best describes an employee's performance. Exhibit 11.4 is a BARS scale for the knowledge and judgement dimension of a grocery checker's job.

In another form of BARS, evaluators record observations of each employee's behaviour throughout the year or the appraisal period. When it comes time to actually evaluate the employee, the evaluator refers to his or her written record and gives each observed behaviour its assigned BARS value. Thus, documentation in the form of a diary or written record is available both to justify administrative actions and to provide feedback to employees.

BARS differ from other rating scales in that scale points are specifically defined kinds of behaviour. Also, BARS are originally constructed by the evaluators who will use them. There are four steps in the BARS construction process:

1. Listing all the important dimensions of performance for a job or jobs.
2. Collecting critical incidents of effective and ineffective behaviour.
3. Classifying effective and ineffective behaviour to appropriate performance dimensions.

EXHIBIT 11.4

A BARS Scale for the Knowledge and Judgement Dimension of a Grocery Checker's Job

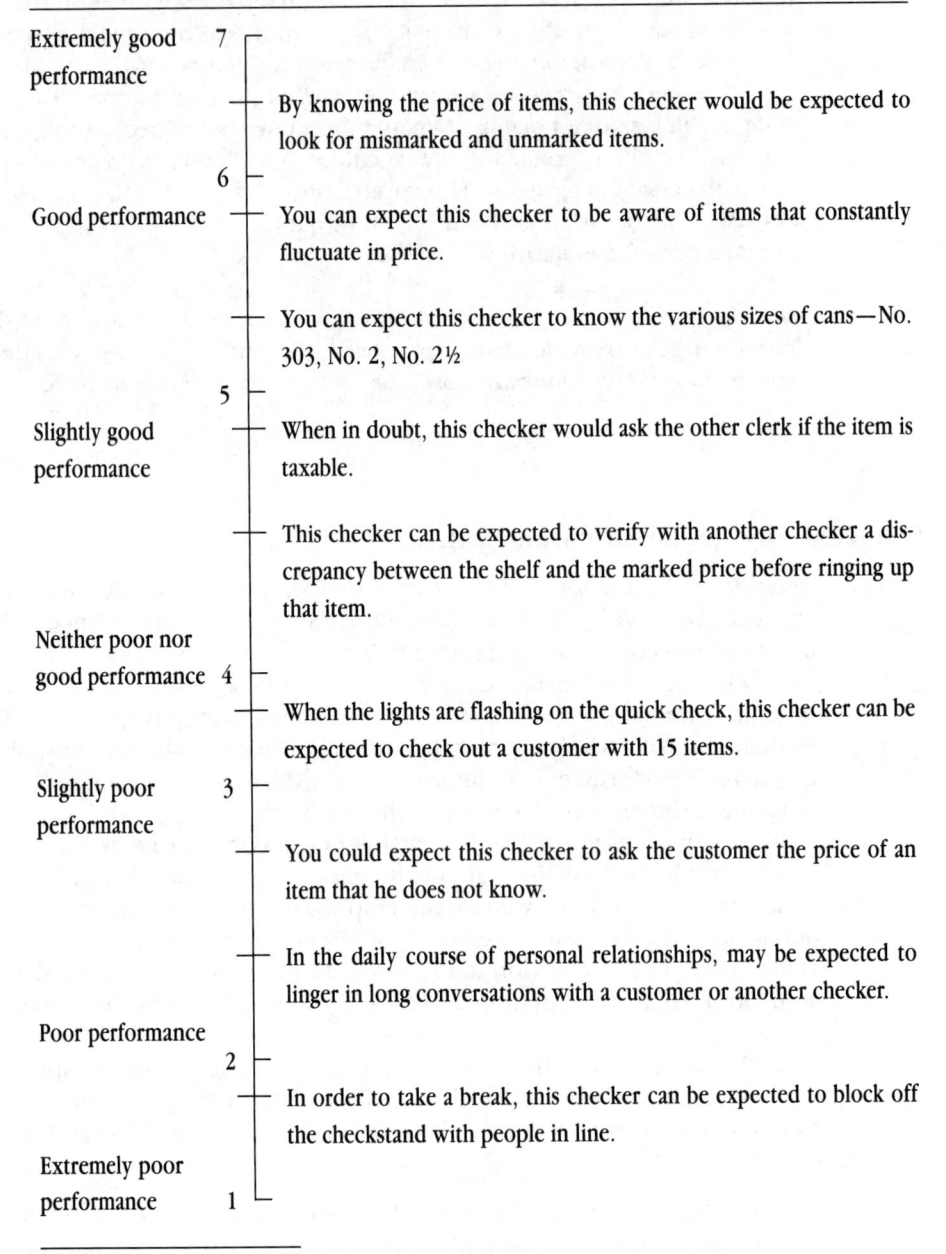

Scale	Rating	Behavioral Anchor
Extremely good performance	7	By knowing the price of items, this checker would be expected to look for mismarked and unmarked items.
Good performance	6	You can expect this checker to be aware of items that constantly fluctuate in price.
		You can expect this checker to know the various sizes of cans—No. 303, No. 2, No. 2½
Slightly good performance	5	When in doubt, this checker would ask the other clerk if the item is taxable.
		This checker can be expected to verify with another checker a discrepancy between the shelf and the marked price before ringing up that item.
Neither poor nor good performance	4	When the lights are flashing on the quick check, this checker can be expected to check out a customer with 15 items.
Slightly poor performance	3	You could expect this checker to ask the customer the price of an item that he does not know.
		In the daily course of personal relationships, may be expected to linger in long conversations with a customer or another checker.
Poor performance	2	In order to take a break, this checker can be expected to block off the checkstand with people in line.
Extremely poor performance	1	

Source: L. Fogli, C. Hulin, and M.R. Blood, "Development of First-Level Behavioral Job Criteria," *Journal of Applied Psychology*, vol. 55, no. 1 (1971), pp. 3–8. Copyright 1971 by the American Psychological Association. Reprinted with permission.

4. Assigning numerical value to each behaviour within each dimension (that is, scaling of behavioural anchors).

In the first step of the process, evaluators (and sometimes their subordinates) discuss and list all the important dimensions of performance for a job or jobs. For example, other performance dimensions for the grocery checker's job include conscientiousness, skill in human relations, skill in operation of the cash register, skill in bagging, organization of the checkout work, and skill in monetary transactions.[27] The construction process continues with a second group of evaluators, who observe, record, and collect examples of effective and ineffective job behaviour, which are called critical incidents. They make up the body of behavioural checklists and BARS forms. For some time, psychologists argued that these critical incidents must be very job-specific; however, recent studies have demonstrated that the BARS procedure can be applied to a reasonably broad group of jobs by making the descriptions of job behaviour less specific.[28]

When a large number of instances of effective and ineffective behaviour has been collected, a third group of evaluators is given the first group's list of job performance dimensions and the set of critical incidents. Their task is to match, or classify, specific behaviour to appropriate performance dimensions. Consider the following behaviour from Exhibit 11.4: "In the daily course of personal relationships, [the employee] may be expected to linger in long conversations with a customer or another checker." The third group of evaluators must decide to which performance dimension this behaviour belongs. Does it relate to the knowledge and judgement dimension or to skill in human relations? Behaviour must be classified into a given dimension by 60 to 80 percent of the evaluators in order to be included in the scale for that dimension. New dimensions may be added if there are a number of uncategorized critical incidents. Separate groups of evaluators are involved in this retranslation process to ensure that the words and terms used in the performance dimensions and the descriptions of behaviour have the same meaning for different people. Therefore, the third group of evaluators, those classifying the behaviour, are not biased by involvement in the earlier steps. The result is a set of behaviour/performance dimensions with each represented by a number of behavioural descriptions.

A final step in the BARS construction process is assigning scale values to each behaviour within each dimension. The critical incidents must represent the full range of performance in any one dimension: they cannot be clustered at one or both ends of the continuum but must be distributed evenly along it. High degrees of agreement among evaluators are required in this scaling procedure. Ideally, a fourth group of evaluators performs this step, but it could be done by either of the first two groups. (Actually, there is no evidence that one group of conscientious evaluators could not effectively handle all four steps.)

The Thacker and Cattaneo survey of the personnel practices of 581 Canadian employers found that only 2.4 percent use BARS, despite its superiority to the typical graphic rating scale.[29] In the United States, a Conference Board survey reported that about 9 percent of the 293 companies it surveyed used behaviourally anchored rating scales.[30] The authors suggested, however, that this may be an overestimate of BARS use. Of the sample appraisal forms they received, fully one-third did not correspond to the way in which they were classified on the respondents' surveys. Further, the most typical discrepancy involved appraisal forms that met the definition of a conventional rating sale but were mistakenly identified as BARS.

Like most new rating formats, BARS was designed to eliminate or reduce rating errors such as leniency and halo, while increasing the accuracy of ratings. A substantial amount of research has compared BARS to other appraisal methods. This research shows that BARS does not outperform other simpler, less costly methods, such as graphic rating scales, when it comes to reducing rating errors and increasing accuracy.[31] There is some evidence, however, that BARS improves evaluator attitudes toward performance appraisal.[32]

Management by Objectives

Management by objectives (MBO) is a method of appraising individuals on the basis of objective results indices, such as sales, letters word-processed, units constructed, customer complaints, errors in filing, amount of downtime, days sick, days tardy, and so on. MBO combines a goal-setting phase and a performance review phase. In the goal-setting phase, a superior and subordinate discuss the subordinate's job responsibilities and mutually agree on one or more results-oriented goals. Goals frequently focus on problem areas or special projects, rather than on routine aspects of the job. Ways of measuring progress toward goals are also specified at this time so the subordinate can assess how well he or she is doing.

An MBO form of an industrial firm is shown in Exhibit 11.5. This form is used in the goal-setting phase to record mutually agreed-upon target results and deadlines for each of six results measures. Actual results and deadlines are noted and assessed in subsequent performance review sessions.

Phase two is the performance review session, a regularly scheduled get-together between superior and subordinate for the purpose of assessing progress toward goals, revising goals, and/or setting new ones. For most managers, this interview is probably the most difficult part of the appraisal process because of the interpersonal skills required to make it a productive and motivating session. Skills appropriate for effective development interviews include active listening, acceptance of the subordinate's disagreement, openness to communication, and the ability to create a climate of trust. Basically, MBO casts the superior in the role of helper, rather than judge, and this may conflict with some superiors' day-to-day management style.[33]

There are, however, several aspects of MBO that make the performance review session somewhat easier and more acceptable to evaluators than

EXHIBIT 11.5
MBO Form for an Industrial Firm

KEY RESPONSIBILITY AREA	WEIGHT	MEASURES OF RESULTS	PERF. STD.	RESULTS Target	RESULTS Actual	DEADLINES Target	DEADLINES Actual
Product delivery	30%	Percent of deliveries on schedule	95%				
		Percent of customer complaints	3%				
Product quality	25%	Per cent of rejects	5%				
		Amount of rework	2%				
Operating efficiency	20%	Cost per unit per month	$37				
		Equipment utilization	90%				

Source: S.J. Carroll and C.E. Schneier, *Performance Appraisal and Review Systems* (Glenview, Ill.: Scott, Foresman, 1982). Reprinted with the permission of the authors.

appraisal interviews associated with other methods. First, since the subordinate clearly understands the goals or results on which the evaluation is based and since he or she also knows how progress is being measured, the review session often becomes something of a self-review or self-appraisal. Furthermore, many managers find it easier to evaluate a person on results or progress toward goals than to make judgements about personal attributes or the degree to which an employee exhibits particular job-related behaviour.

When a subordinate accomplishes MBO goals, he or she often expects some sort of tangible reward. Indeed, at the managerial and professional level, MBO is commonly tied to salary increases and bonuses, which are administrative concerns. Problems can result, however, if a raise or even a one-time bonus is attached to goal accomplishment. The goals achieved by various employees may vary greatly in their value to the organization. Should the lowest-performing employee in a department receive a large financial bonus for improving more than any other employee? Should the top-performing employee receive no award because of failure to accomplish a very difficult goal? Attaching financial rewards to MBO goals can create such problems, though proper planning and allocation of compensation funds can help to solve them.

MBO is a very popular method of performance appraisal, especially for evaluating managerial performance. The Thacker and Cattaneo survey found that nearly half of their sample, 45.6 percent, use MBO, primarily for management and white-collar professional employees.[34] The Conference Board survey of managerial appraisal systems in the United States found MBO to be the most frequently used method of performance appraisal for all 293 surveyed companies.[35] MBO is commonly used for both administrative and development purposes. Although some managers resent the excessive paperwork sometimes associated with MBO, they generally accept it as an appraisal method.[36]

A comprehensive review of 185 MBO studies, most of them case studies, found that MBO programs had generally positive effects on employee productivity and/or job satisfaction.[37] MBO appeared to be more effective in the short term (less than two years) and in private sector organizations. Other research on MBO has suggested that the key factor in performance improvement and employee satisfaction is the setting of moderately difficult goals, rather than the subordinate's participation in the goal-setting process.[38]

Latham and Wexley have identified three reasons why goal-setting affects performance.[39] First, goal-setting has a directive effect, channelling energy in one particular direction. Second, attaining goals requires putting forth effort, which is a major determinant of performance, according to Porter and Lawler's model of performance and satisfaction (see Chapter 2, Figure 2.2). Third, attaining difficult goals requires persistence, which may be viewed as "directed effort over time." In short, these authors conclude that "goal-setting is effective because it clarifies exactly what is expected of an individual."[40]

Based on their review of the literature on MBO, Carroll and Schneier have suggested nine factors contributing to MBO program failure.[41] These are given in Figure 11.2. They include lack of support from top management, lack of training for evaluators, and the setting of easy goals.

Some people go farther, saying that problems with MBO are not failures of its application but failures inherent in the system. At least one renowned management guru, W. Edwards Deming, argues against MBO. So does Honda, a company well known for its innovation and quality. In discussing one of his fourteen points for the transformation of American industry, "adopt and institute leadership," Deming says that managers must abolish the focus on outcomes such as MBO, zero defects, and other management by numbers.[42] Deming believes managers should really know the work they supervise and that a key part of their job is to remove barriers that make it impossible for the workers to do their work with pride. He further contends that many forms of performance appraisal focus on the end products and reward people who do well in the system but don't reward attempts to change the system.

In a very similar view, the manager at the Honda plant at Marysville, Ohio, says, "If the system is 80 percent of the problem, MBOs distract us from improving the system and subtly confine efforts to 'optimizing' that which is suboptimal."[43] This view is consistent with the Honda ethic: "To lead is

FIGURE 11.2
Factors Contributing to MBO Program Failure

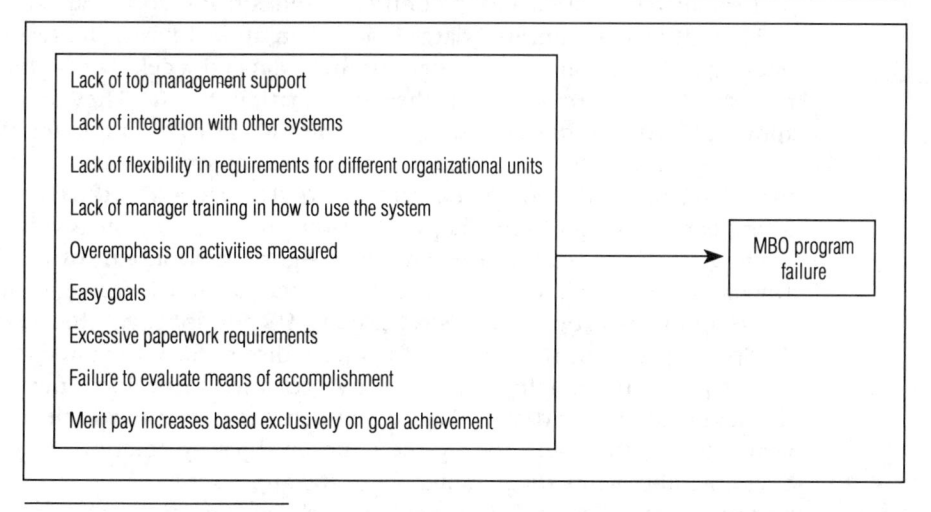

- Lack of top management support
- Lack of integration with other systems
- Lack of flexibility in requirements for different organizational units
- Lack of manager training in how to use the system
- Overemphasis on activities measured
- Easy goals
- Excessive paperwork requirements
- Failure to evaluate means of accomplishment
- Merit pay increases based exclusively on goal achievement

→ MBO program failure

Source: S.J. Carroll and C.E. Schneier, *Performance Appraisal and Review Systems* (Glenview, Ill.: Scott, Foresman, 1982). Reprinted with the permission of the authors.

to serve." Honda and many other team-based management systems teach employees empowerment. Empowerment means more than doing the job better; it means looking at and changing the system that affects how the job is done. Thus, as Deming argues, the "boss's job is to free up his subordinates," which is a near reversal of the traditional power relationship exemplified in MBO.[44]

Team-Style Peer Review

The rise of participative and team-style management has led to substantial employee involvement in both the development and use of performance appraisal systems. One of the leading consulting groups on self-directed work teams, or team-style management, Zenger-Miller and Orsburn, uses a peer review approach not unlike a group MBO. These peer reviews are done for administrative as well as developmental purposes.[45]

In this approach, the team develops an annual performance plan that includes objectives and standards team members have agreed to achieve during the year. Each team member negotiates an individual performance plan based on the team objectives and standard. The negotiation is done with two team members, one chosen by the team and the other by the person being reviewed. Each team member's performance plan is reviewed and approved by the HRM staff, both to ensure that legal requirements are met and to help coach and train the evaluators. Of course, before a work team has developed and matured to the point of responsible self-management, annual objectives are developed in collaboration with a manager and HR staff. Additionally, all team members receive training in setting and writing performance standards and in conflict resolution and appraisal skills.

Though formal appraisals are done on an annual basis, the team carries out ongoing coaching and review activities. Several weeks before the annual review, the two reviewers gather information for it. They prepare the appraisal form and have it reviewed by the HR staff. The employee also does a self-appraisal, which is brought to the actual appraisal session. Before the formal appraisal session, the two reviewers are coached by the HR staff. The intent is to make the actual appraisal rather like a problem-solving session. At the end of the session, the employee signs the appraisal form as well as any proposed action forms. (If an action, such as a pay increase, promotion, or discipline, is proposed, it is referred to HR for approval. In the event of disciplinary action, there is usually a peer disciplinary review committee.) At this point, the employee and the two reviewers develop a new plan for the next year; it includes any action that may have been recommended. Each year, the reviewer selected by the team changes by rotation. In this way, every member gains the perspective of the appraiser.[46]

At present, there is little if any research on how successful this form of appraisal is compared to more traditional methods. Judging from success stories of the world-class organizations using team-style management, however, peer review appraisal is likely to be as good as traditional methods.

A Performance Appraisal System: Corning, Inc.

Because of differences in intended use, most appraisals for administrative and for development purposes should use different methods and be conducted at different times. However, this section describes an appraisal system that took an alternative approach, one that was designed to include components specific to both administrative and development purposes.

Corning, Inc.'s Performance Management System (PMS) measured and developed the performance and potential of 3000 managers and professional employees.[47] The system included three major components:

1. Performance development and review (PD&R), to appraise performance and profile individual employees' strong and weak areas.
2. Management by objectives (MBO), to guide the efforts of employees and provide data on results to complement PD&R ratings.
3. Salary and placement review, to take administrative action based on PD&R and MBO data.

The system took several years to develop and represented a substantial step beyond the situation at Corning in 1968, when even appraisals for administrative purposes were based on casual exchanges between managers over the phone or in a bar. An initial step was development of the PD&R component, which involved construction of rating scales using a BARS-like procedure. Items in the rating scales were constructed to apply to a number of jobs, rather than to be job-specific. Some of the dimensions and behavioural items identified for supervisory performance are listed in Exhibit 11.6.

EXHIBIT 11.6
Selected Items from Corning's Performance Development and Review Behavioural Rating Scales

Subordinate participation: delegates authority and involves subordinates in decisions and in setting objectives

Involves subordinates in decision-making process

Permits subordinates to participate in decision-making process when appropriate

Consults with subordinates in setting their performance objectives

Delegates authority to subordinates

Control: maintains necessary discipline among subordinates and follows up on work assignments, taking corrective action if necessary

Fails to follow up on work assignments given others

Fails to take action when errors or faulty work are observed in subordinates

Permits subordinates to make poor presentations before other organizational units of higher level management

Maintains necessary discipline

Supportiveness: supports subordinates through appropriate utilization and development of their capacities

Builds confidence in subordinates by supporting their actions

Understands the capabilities and limitations of subordinates

Selects and places qualified personnel

Gives adequate instructions to subordinates when new methods are initiated or new work assigned

Unit's productivity: subordinates maintain a high level of quality in their work and accomplish large amounts of work

Subordinates accomplish a large amount of work

Maintains a high level of quality in the work of subordinates

Subordinates tend to be lax in their work, even to the point of poor quality results

EXHIBIT 11.6 *(continued)*

Conflict resolution: maintains co-operative and cohesive work group by effectively communicating company objectives and helping to resolve conflict

Takes action to settle conflicts among subordinates

Communicates objectives of company and organizational unit to subordinates

Helps subordinates settle their differences

Communicates with subordinatees by providing vital information affecting organizational unit and its members

---

Source: M. Beer, R. Ruh, J.A. Dawson, B.B. McCaa, and M.J. Kavanagh, "A Performance Management System: Research, Design, Introduction, and Evaluation," *Personnel Psychology*, vol. 31 (1978), pp. 505–35. Reprinted with the permission of *Personnel Psychology*.

Note that the dimensions of Corning's PD&R scales reflect the type of linking of organizational goals to employee performance discussed early in the chapter. Specifically, managers were responsible for productivity of their unit and for communicating company objectives in the course of conflict resolution. Other scales such as control and supportiveness captured important individual aspects of the manager's performance.

PD&R was used for both administrative and development purposes. For the former, the end of the rating form asked for a global evaluation of the person being rated. This was sent to the personnel department for use in salary and placement decisions. When used for development purposes, the behavioural rating scales were scored ipsatively. *Ipsative scoring* results in profiles of employees' strengths and weaknesses, as opposed to comparisons of one subordinate with another. These profiles proved useful as a basis for discussions between superiors and subordinates in developmental appraisal interviews. However, some managers had difficulty understanding the ipsative scale scores at first and misused them by attempting comparison of one employee with another. Eventually, many employees became familiar enough with PD&R to rate their own performances before the appraisal interview and to discuss discrepancies between their own ratings and those of their superior.

The second component of the Performance Management System was MBO, which Corning regarded as most useful for guiding the efforts of employees and for focussing on results. MBO, therefore, complemented PD&R by appraisal of results.

The third component was the salary and placement review. Though there was no prescribed method for this review, both PD&R and MBO data were fed into salary, promotion, and other HRM decisions. Corning policy required a PD&R before a salary increase could be processed.

Corning implemented this program with an extensive two-day training session. Much of this time was spent training managers to conduct appraisal feedback interviews effectively. In behaviour modelling training, the managers saw films of effective and ineffective interviews (role-played by Corning managers). The trainees then role-played a developmental interview, using PD&R scale scores as a guide. An unusual strategy for creating acceptance of the system was to include both managers and their subordinate managers in the same training sessions.

At this point one might conclude that Corning had developed the perfect method of performance appraisal. Yet, no matter how perfect a method seems to be from its description or from unsystematic information regarding its use, a vigorous evaluation of its effectiveness should be done. A study of four Corning divisions that used the system for one year was conducted, using a lengthy questionnaire survey. Although the survey results were generally very positive, they revealed some problems. One was confusion regarding how to use part of an interview guide concerning career development planning and training objectives; a committee was appointed to revise it. A somewhat more serious problem occurred in the use of PD&R for both developmental and administrative purposes. Using the same instrument for two such dissimilar purposes resulted in some resistance to appraisal by both evaluators and those being evaluated. Finally, the system was not being used universally throughout the organization; some managers neglected it because it had not received as much formal endorsement from higher management as they had expected.

The system was eventually put into use throughout Corning. The PD&R component was widely accepted and used as an aid to two-way communication between superiors and subordinates. Efforts were made to tie PD&R to career planning by developing lists of the types of behaviour important for various jobs. Such lists would permit employees to work on behaviour needing improvement in order to qualify for different jobs within the organization. Despite a few problems, Corning's Performance Management System was an uncommon example of the development, implementation, and evaluation of a performance appraisal system to serve both administrative and developmental purposes.

IMPLEMENTING AN APPRAISAL SYSTEM

HRM professionals have considerable responsibility for implementing appraisal systems. They must prepare necessary materials, schedule appraisals, see that they are conducted, and make sure that appraisal purposes are understood. One problem that often stands in the way of implementation and proper use of a system is resistance, especially on the part of evaluators.

THE PROBLEM OF EVALUATOR RESISTANCE

Many managers dread face-to-face appraisal interviews, especially when they must give negative feedback to a subordinate.[48] One executive recalls his first performance appraisal: "My boss had the appraisal on his desk and he said: 'I'm not supposed to show you this. But I have to go to the bathroom now and I'll be back in about fifteen minutes.' With that, he opened the file on his desk and left."[49]

As a result of their attitudes toward appraisal, many evaluators choose leniency over accuracy when faced with performance problems. This solves the short-run problem of having to confront subordinates with negative information but may in the long run damage trust in the system's fairness and its ability to allocate rewards based on performance criteria. Withholding negative information also denies employees feedback that may be instrumental to their improvement. And, if instances of poor job performance are overlooked during performance review, employees will surely come to believe that poor performance is acceptable. Imagine the chagrin of these same employees if they are subsequently dismissed. They may file a grievance or lawsuit against the company, believing that dismissal was "without cause." If it was, the organization is required to provide either reasonable notice of termination or compensatory pay.

One human resource manager tells of being asked by a supervisor to dismiss an employee for unacceptable job performance. In preparation for the chore, the manager examined the same supervisor's earlier performance evaluations of the subordinate. To his surprise, there was nothing in the record to indicate less than adequate performance! Neither the human resource manager nor the terminated employee was happy with the supervisor's earlier decisions to spare the unpleasantness of a negative evaluation.

Why do so many supervisors and managers dislike performance appraisal? There are a number of possible reasons. Many may simply dislike "playing God," passing judgement on others.[50] Some may doubt their skills in handling the appraisal interview, especially their ability to deal with subordinates' defensive and angry reactions to negative information. Others may not understand the system being used. For example, managers at Corning had difficulty at first interpreting ipsative scale scores. Evaluators may also distrust the appraisal process and fear that appraisal data will not be used fairly and objectively for pertinent HRM decisions.[51]

Occasionally, raters resist giving an accurate appraisal because it may have negative implications or consequences for them.[52] For example, armed service officers have been known to be reluctant to rate poorly performing subordinates accurately because an individual with a low evaluation may be very difficult to transfer to another unit. Raters may also have the fear of making future rater–ratee interactions unpleasant. Many managers and supervisors carefully consider the consequences of their appraisals, frequently taking the approach that is most rewarding, or less punishing, for themselves in the short run.

Because of evaluator resistance to performance appraisal, HRM professionals often find it necessary to build support for an appraisal system. There is some evidence that commitment of evaluators to an appraisal method or system is more important to the success of the system than is the sophistication of the system itself.[53] Commitment can be increased and resistance overcome by involving managers in the development of a system, providing training geared to an increased understanding and acceptance of the system, and making performance appraisal an important and rewarded part of every manager's job.

INVOLVING RATERS IN THE DEVELOPMENT OF A SYSTEM

There is no reason an appraisal system cannot be designed with the same careful, analytical approach used in the design of most products. For example, it is quite possible (and also beneficial) to solicit ideas from people who will use the product. The inclusion of users in the process generates a set of very practical design criteria and also lets product users know that their input is valued. By involving supervisors and managers who will be using an appraisal system in its design and construction, understanding of the system and commitment to it are greatly improved. Involvement at this stage also reduces the amount of training necessary for evaluators. Yet BARS and team-style peer review are the only appraisal methods that generally use this approach.

TRAINING RATERS

Substantial research supports the value of rater training as a means of improving the reliability and validity of appraisals.[54] Training can also be an important tool in gaining evaluator acceptance and understanding of the appraisal system. Evaluator training must accomplish two purposes. First, it must convince evaluators of the value of making accurate appraisals. This can be done by providing them with an understanding of the system and its importance to the organization. Training programs should explain how appraisals will be used and provide information on why accurate appraisals are essential for these purposes. Though beyond the scope of the training program, reinforcers and rewards should be provided and used as incentives for making fair, objective appraisals. The second training goal—one that is especially important to increase acceptance of the system—is to teach evaluators about the appraisal process and about handling the appraisal interview. Unless the first training goal is accomplished, time and effort will probably be wasted pursuing the second.

HRM professionals must train evaluators to handle the appraisal process, which has two components: (1) observing and collecting data on what is measured, and (2) making evaluative judgements. Evaluators should be instructed in the use of appraisal instruments and made aware of the types of rater error.

By definition, the evaluative process means comparing people with others or with some absolute standard. If a promotion decision is to be made, the evaluative process involves comparison of one candidate with another (assuming there are competing candidates). When appraisal data are used for development purposes, judgements are often more absolute than comparative.

The evaluative process is often more involved than making straightforward comparative or absolute judgements about people and their performance. Evaluators also make judgements about the reasons behind individual success and failure. These judgements affect organizational outcomes, such as rewards and punishments, for the employee. Stone and Slusher first suggested the applicability of attribution theory to the performance appraisal process.[55] *Attribution theory* describes how people explain their own and others' successes and failures. According to Weiner's classification scheme, people explain success or failure in terms of ability, effort, task difficulty, and luck.[56] Ability and effort are internal, "person" factors, while task difficulty and luck are external, "environment" factors. Attribution theory seeks to explain the circumstances under which behavioural consequences are attributed to one factor as opposed to another. For example, a ward supervisor sees a registered nurse fail in trying to give an elderly patient an intravenous injection. In order to form a judgement about the nurse, the supervisor explains the failure in terms of lack of ability, lack of effort, task difficulty, or bad luck. Whichever the supervisor decides is the reason for failure will affect outcomes for the employee (whether he or she will be punished, encouraged, or unaffected when it comes to performance review).

Evidence suggests that attributions of ability are made early in an employee's career.[57] These early attributions are important because a supervisor will assign tasks on the basis of perceived ability and because the employee may set his or her level of aspiration accordingly.[58]

Variations in performance corresponding to high and low incentives are likely to be explained as the results of effort rather than ability, task difficulty, or luck. For example, if the reward for achieving a certain objective is a large bonus, the reason for success is more likely to be perceived in terms of expenditure of effort. There is some evidence that effort is judged as greater following success than failure.[59] Other research suggests that if failure is attributed to lack of effort, rather than to lack of ability, more punitive action will be taken.[60] If almost everyone fails at a given task, a supervisor will probably explain this by regarding the task as very difficult, though some supervisors might say that all their subordinates are incompetent and lazy. Finally, unexplainable and unexpected failures and successes are usually attributed to luck. Although task difficulty and luck may have been causative factors in a person's performance, evaluators tend to attribute most behavioural consequences to ability and effort.[61]

Many inaccurate appraisals result from poor judgement or inappropriate use of available information about an employee's performance. A training program incorporating attribution theory could make evaluators aware of some of the factors influencing their judgements.

Most supervisors and managers could also benefit from training in effective handling of the appraisal interview. One survey of 227 Canadian manufacturers, however, found that very few organizations provide training for raters.[62] Yet in the 1990 *Training* magazine survey of more than 2600 U.S. organizations, performance appraisal was the second most frequent training topic reported; such training was done by almost 72 percent of respondents.[63]

THE APPRAISAL INTERVIEW

Appraisal interviews are scheduled with employees to communicate outcomes of the performance appraisal process, such as salary adjustments, promotions, and termination decisions (administrative purpose). They are also held to review performance, reinforce desirable behaviour, point out performance deficiencies, and develop plans for improvement (development purpose). Although many organizations use one interview for both administrative and development purposes, it is best to conduct separate interviews for these very distinct purposes.

PREPARING FOR THE INTERVIEW

Before the appraisal interview, a supervisor or manager should prepare by collecting, organizing, and reviewing data related to the subordinate's performance. There is also evidence that it is helpful for the subordinate to prepare for the meeting. Greater preparation by subordinates has been linked to higher levels of participation in the interview and to positive interview outcomes.[64] To allow adequate time for preparation, subordinates should be notified of appraisal interviews at least several days in advance. The interview should be held in a private place, free from interruptions, and adequate time should be reserved—at least half an hour for administrative interviews and more for development interviews.

The supervisor should also decide on the format of the meeting, which will vary according to an employee's performance level and job type. Cummings and Schwab suggest three different appraisal interview formats, or programs: DAP, MAP, and RAP.[65]

A *developmental action program* (DAP) approach is used in interviews with high performers who show potential for advancement. The focus here is on planning work, not evaluating performance. Subordinate and superior work together to set goals, determine performance standards, and decide on development needs. MBO is a form of DAP.

MAP, a *maintenance action program*, is appropriate for employees who perform acceptably but show little potential for advancement. The focus here is on maintaining acceptable performance. Under this approach, an employee is informed that his or her performance is acceptable but that there is little evidence of development potential.

A *remedial action program* (RAP) approach is taken with employees who have demonstrated consistently poor performance. This type of interview focusses on performance improvement, with the supervisor providing feedback on performance deficiencies and giving examples of acceptable and unacceptable performance. A RAP approach extends beyond the appraisal interview situation, since progressive discipline may be required if performance does not improve. General procedures to follow in a RAP approach are given in Exhibit 11.7.

APPROACHES TO THE APPRAISAL INTERVIEW

Maier describes three approaches to appraisal interviews: "tell and sell," "tell and listen," and "problem-solving."[66] They are outlined in Table 11.2.

Most managers take a "tell and sell" approach, which involves communicating appraisal results to employees and, through salesmanship, encour-

EXHIBIT 11.7
Procedure to Follow in a RAP Approach

1. Clear feedback to the individual about why the superior feels the performer has performance problems.
2. Frequent use of behavioural critical incidents to point out examples of poor and acceptable performance.
3. A highly specified, imposed program for corrective action, with performance measures and time perspectives clearly and formally established.
4. Monthly review sessions, more frequent if performance is continuing to deteriorate, with the focus of these sessions on the superior's communicating to the employee how the superior feels the employee is doing against the program established in the previous step.
5. If performance increases, then go to longer time intervals of performance specifications and measurement; if continual improvements over a sustained period occurs, then transfer the individual to a MAP.
6. If performance does not improve or decreases even further, then establish a highly specified sequence of events in terms of activities, measurements, and short-time perspectives, with the explicit conclusion being termination if no performance improvements are shown; this frequently results in voluntary self-termination. A key element here is the employee's understanding that he or she has moved into this phase; therefore, explicit communications to this effect are crucial.

Source: L.L. Cummings and D.P. Schwab, *Performance in Organizations: Determinants and Appraisal* (Glenview, Ill.: Scott, Foresman, 1973), p. 123. Reprinted with the permission of the authors.

aging them to begin a plan of improvement. A superior using this approach sits as a judge, assuming that subordinates need only be informed of their deficiencies in order to want to correct them.

In the "tell and listen" approach, a superior also serves as a judge but encourages feedback from the subordinate. The superior uses listening skills and reflects, or restates, feelings and reactions of the subordinate. This serves to reduce defensiveness because the subordinate feels he or she is understood and accepted.

TABLE 11.2
Three Approaches to Appraisal Interviews

	METHOD		
	Tell and Sell	Tell and Listen	Problem-solving
Role of interviewer	Judge	Judge	Helper
Objective	To communicate evaluation and get employee to change	To communicate evaluation and encourage discussion	To stimulate growth and development in employee
Assumptions	Employee desires to correct weaknesses if he/she knows them Any person can improve if he/she so chooses A superior is qualified to evaluate a subordinate	People will change if defensive feelings are removed	Growth can occur without correcting faults Discussion of job problems leads to improved performance
Reactions	Defensive behavior suppressed Attempts to cover hostility	Defensive behavior expressed Employee feels accepted	Problem-solving behavior
Skills	Salesmanship Patience	Listening and reflecting feelings Summarizing	Listening and reflecting feelings Reflecting ideas Using exploratory questions Summarizing

TABLE 11.2 *(continued)*

	METHOD		
	Tell and Sell	Tell and Listen	Problem-solving
Attitude	People profit from criticism and appreciate help	One can respect the feelings of others if one understands them	Discussion develops new ideas and mutual interests
Motivation	Use of positive or negative incentives or both (extrinsic in that motivation is not related to task content)	Resistance to change reduced	Increased freedom Increased responsibility (intrinsic motivation in that interest is inherent in the task)
Gains	Success most probable when employee respects interviewer	Develops favorable attitude to superior, which increases probability of success	Almost assured of improvement in some respect
Risks	Loss of loyalty Inhibition of independent judgement	Need for change may not be developed	Employee may lack ideas Change may be other than what superior had in mind
Values	Perpetuates existing practices and values	Permits interviewer to change views in the light of employee's responses Some upward communication	Both learn since experience and views pooled Change is facilitated

Source: N.R.F. Maier, "Three Types of Appraisal Interview," *Personnel*, vol. 34 (March–April 1958), p. 29. Reprinted with the permission of Mrs. A. Maier.

The objective of a "problem-solving" approach is to stimulate employee growth and development through discussion of job problems. Instead of eliciting defensiveness from subordinates, this approach prompts problem-solving behaviour. A superior using this approach listens, reflects feelings and ideas, and serves as a helper, rather than judge. Several studies show that subordinate reactions to performance review are most positive when a problem-solving approach is used.[67]

Characteristics of Effective Appraisal Interviews

Figure 11.3 (page 518) presents factors contributing to the effectiveness of performance appraisal interviews. We have already discussed some of these factors, such as skills acquired by training and adequate preparation. Other factors of importance are participation of the subordinate, supportiveness of the superior, and a goal-setting, problem-oriented approach.

Appraisal interviews are most effective when subordinates have high levels of participation and are allowed to voice their opinions.[68] Participation has been found to increase satisfaction with both the appraisal process and the supervisor conducting the appraisal. One expert suggests that a subordinate should talk eight or nine times more than the person conducting the interview. The supervisor should, of course, control and guide the interview through directive techniques, including proper use of questions.[69]

Appraisal interviews are also more effective when superiors are supportive and noncritical.[70] Supportiveness facilitates acceptance of appraisals, while criticism makes acceptance more difficult. Beyond a certain point, criticism may have a negative effect on performance. A classic study of 92 managers at General Electric found that an above-average number of criticisms from the boss resulted in both increased defensiveness and subsequent reductions in performance.[71]

Other key ingredients of effective appraisal interviews include setting specific goals and working toward solutions for problems that interfere with performance.[72]

The important role of the supervisor or manager is obvious at this point. Through their handling of the appraisal interview, supervisors and managers not only affect levels of employee motivation and job performance but also influence attitudes toward appraisals, management, and the organization. Exhibit 11.8 (pages 519–20) presents seven dimensions of behaviour that have been identified as important for the success of managerial appraisal interviews, including structuring and controlling the interview; establishing and maintaining rapport; reacting to stress; obtaining information; resolving conflict; developing the interviewee; and motivating the interviewee. These dimensions were identified by Borman, Hough, and Dunnette in their development of behaviourally anchored rating scales for interviewer behaviour.[73] Various kinds of effective and ineffective behaviour relating to each dimension are given in the exhibit.

FIGURE 11.3
Factors Contributing to the Effectiveness of Performance Appraisal Interviews

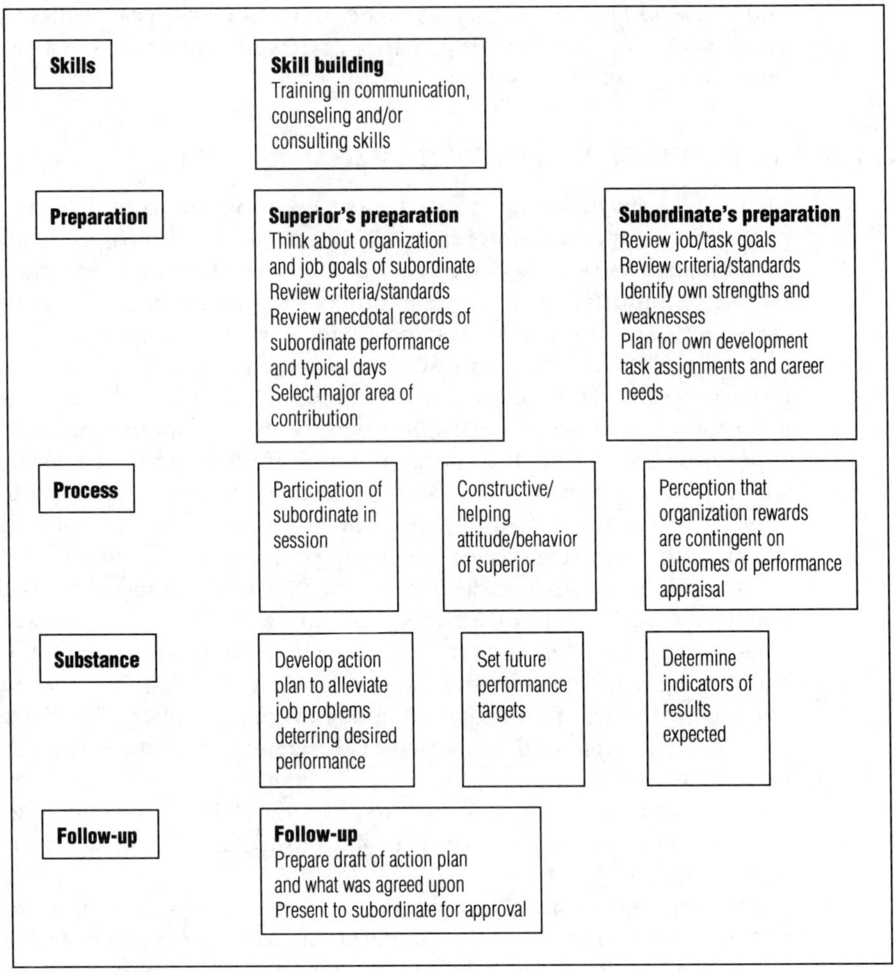

Skills	**Skill building** Training in communication, counseling and/or consulting skills		
Preparation	**Superior's preparation** Think about organization and job goals of subordinate Review criteria/standards Review anecdotal records of subordinate performance and typical days Select major area of contribution		**Subordinate's preparation** Review job/task goals Review criteria/standards Identify own strengths and weaknesses Plan for own development task assignments and career needs
Process	Participation of subordinate in session	Constructive/helping attitude/behavior of superior	Perception that organization rewards are contingent on outcomes of performance appraisal
Substance	Develop action plan to alleviate job problems deterring desired performance	Set future performance targets	Determine indicators of results expected
Follow-up	**Follow-up** Prepare draft of action plan and what was agreed upon Present to subordinate for approval		

Source: C.E. Schneier and R.W. Beatty, "Combining BARS and MBO: Using an Appraisal System to Diagnose Performance Problems," *The Personnel Administrator*, 1979. Reprinted with the permission of *HRMagazine* (formerly *The Personnel Administrator*), published by the Society for Human Resource Management, Alexandria, Va.

EXHIBIT 11.8
Seven Dimensions of Interviewer Behaviour

1. *Structuring and controlling the interview:* Clearly stating the purpose of the interview, maintaining control over the interview, and displaying an organized and prepared approach to the interview *versus* not discussing the purpose of the interview, displaying a confused approach, and allowing the interviewee to control the interview when inappropriate.

2. *Establishing and maintaining rapport:* Setting an appropriate climate for the interview, opening the interview in a warm and nonthreatening manner, and being sensitive to the interviewee *versus* setting a hostile or belligerent climate, being overly friendly or familiar during the interview, and displaying insensitivity toward the interviewee.

3. *Reacting to stress:* Remaining calm and cool even during an interviewee's outbursts, apologizing when appropriate but not backing down or retreating unnecessarily, and maintaining composure and perspective under fire *versus* reacting inappropriately to stress, becoming irate or defensive in reaction to complaints, and backing down inappropriately when confronted.

4. *Obtaining information:* Asking appropriate questions, probing effectively to ensure that meaningful topics and important issues are raised, and seeking solid information *versus* glossing over problems and issues, asking inappropriate questions, and failing to probe into the interviewee's perception of problems.

5. *Resolving conflict:* Moving effectively to reduce any conflict between the interviewee and other employees, making appropriate commitments and setting realistic goals to ensure conflict resolution, and providing good advice to the interviewee about his or her relationships with other employees *versus* discussing problems too bluntly or lecturing the interviewee ineffectively regarding the resolution of conflict, failing to set goals or to make commitments appropriate to effective conflict resolution, and providing poor advice to the interviewee about his or her relationships with other employees.

6. *Developing the interviewee:* Offering to help the interviewee develop professionally, displaying interest in the interviewee's professional growth, specifying developmental needs, and recommending sound developmental actions *versus* not offering to aid in the interviewee's professional development, displaying little or no interest in the interviewee's professional growth, failing to make developmental suggestions, and providing poor advice regarding the interviewee's professional development.

7. *Motivating the interviewee:* Providing incentives for the interviewee to stay with the organization and to perform effectively, making commitments to encourage the interviewee to perform his or her job well and to help the organization accomplish its objec-

EXHIBIT 11.8 *(continued)*

tives, and supporting the interviewee's excellent performance *versus* providing little or no incentive for the interviewee to stay with the organization and to perform effectively, failing to make commitments to encourage the interviewee's continued top performance, and neglecting to express support of the interviewee's excellent performance record.

Source: Adapted from Borman, Hough, and Dunnette, as appearing in H.J. Bernardin and R.W. Beatty, *Performance Appraisal: Assessing Human Behavior at Work* (Boston: Kent Publishing, 1984), pp. 279–80. Used with the permission of Marvin D. Dunnette.

COLLECTING AND STORING APPRAISAL DATA

Besides developing and implementing appraisal systems, HRM professionals collect and store appraisal data in order to monitor the quality of the work force and assess the effectiveness of various HRM programs. Records of appraisal data are also essential to protect the organization against charges of discrimination and unjust dismissal.

APPRAISAL DATA FOR PROGRAM ASSESSMENT

Program assessment purposes were discussed earlier; they include using performance appraisal data to assess the effectiveness of recruiting, selection, and placement procedures and to evaluate training and development programs. Studies of program effectiveness require "before" and "after" measurements. For recruiting, selection, and placement procedures, performance appraisal data may be used to help determine whether organizational predictors of success are, in fact, predictive of success. The effectiveness of training and development programs can be ascertained by controlled studies comparing employees' performance before and after participation in such programs.

The ideal appraisal system would yield numerous reliable and representative measures of job behaviour and job results. Numerous measures are necessary for several reasons. First, any single measure may be deficient in itself or contaminated by situational factors. Second, most jobs are too complex for one measure to cover their required behaviour or their results completely. Finally, different measures may be required for different organizational purposes, and these purposes may change over time. For example, the quantity of production may now be of major importance, but in the future the firm may wish to select employees who perform very high quality work.

The responsibility for data collection and storage is a vital one because data collected and retained in appraisal forms are often the only record of an employee's job performance.

Appraisal Data to Protect Against Charges of Discrimination and Unjust Dismissal

Appraisal data provide crucial documentation should personnel actions be contested on human rights grounds or on charges of unjust dismissal. For example, if an employee charges sex discrimination because she was denied a promotion, an employer can produce appraisal records that indicate the employee was less qualified than male candidates for the position.

Increasingly, Canadian courts and arbitrators are requiring employers to prove "just cause" for dismissing employees without notice. Without cause for dismissal, an employer must provide "reasonable" notice or compensatory pay.[74] "Reasonable" is a subjective term: its definition varies from one situation to another. For example, "reasonable" may mean a year in the case of a high-level executive or an older employee who has little chance of re-employment; it may be only a few months in the case of a more employable person. In order to prove "just cause" for dismissal, employers need sound performance data, usually evidence of fraud or gross misconduct.

In order for appraisal data to be useful for this purpose and for defending against charges of human rights violations, appraisal systems themselves must be "defensible." Based on their review of significant U.S. court cases involving performance appraisal, Lubben, Thompson, and Klasson offer a number of generalizations as to "what appears to constitute a defensible performance appraisal system." Among them are:

1. The overall appraisal process should be formalized, standardized, and, as much as possible, objective in nature.
2. The performance appraisal system should be as job-related as possible.
3. A thorough, formal job analysis for all employment positions being rated should be completed.
4. Evaluators should be adequately trained in the use of appraisal techniques that employ written qualification criteria for promotion or transfer decisions.
5. An evaluator should have substantial daily contact with the employee being evaluated.
6. The administration and scoring of the performance appraisals should be standardized and controlled.[75]

Summary

This chapter has examined the performance appraisal function and the use of appraisals in administrative decision making, employee development, work force monitoring, and program assessment. With respect to performance appraisal, HRM professionals have responsibility for designing appraisal systems, implementing them, and collecting and storing appraisal data for a variety of purposes. In designing an appraisal system, HRM professionals must determine the organization's particular needs for appraisal and whether the system or method meets the general requirements of reliability, validity, practicality, fairness, and impact. Implementing a system involves preparation of materials, scheduling, and taking steps to ensure that raters accept and understand the appraisal system. Evaluators often resist appraising performance, but much of this resistance can be overcome through rater training in appraisal methods and handling of the appraisal interview.

Review Questions

1. More and more employers are moving to participative and team-style management. What forms and methods of performance appraisal best fit this environment? What characteristics of a team environment versus a "traditional" environment are most important in choosing a method?

2. Assume you have the responsibility of evaluating the performance of others, a responsibility that includes making judgements that have considerable impact on their pay and career opportunities. What features of an appraisal method are most important to you? Which, if any, of the methods discussed in this chapter comes closest to meeting your set of desired or important features?

3. Do you believe the Corning appraisal system described in the chapter is appropriate for the team-based management system in use at several of that firm's plants? Why or why not? If not, what features of the system would you change and how?

Project Ideas

1. Describe an incident in which your performance was evaluated. Describe the appraisal itself (positive or negative? how determined? how conveyed to you?) and the resulting outcomes in terms of extrinsic rewards. Did you perceive the appraisal as fair? Why or why not? How did the actual outcomes compare with the desired or expected outcomes? Was your level of job satisfaction affected in any way as a result of the appraisal and its outcomes? How? Was there any effect on your subsequent performance? (The sharing of student experiences should demonstrate a variety of consequences associated with different types

of appraisals. The role of individual differences in reactions to performance appraisals and their outcomes should also be evident.)

2. Divide the class into three groups to develop behaviour/performance dimensions for use in BARS construction for a familiar occupation, such as cleaner, waiter, or drivers' training instructor. Group 1 should generate a list of performance dimensions, while Group 2 works to specify agreed-upon effective and ineffective behaviour relating to the job. When Groups 1 and 2 have completed their tasks, Group 3 should try to match the kinds of behaviour to the dimensions. When the process is complete, each group should discuss its experience in its assigned task. (Though any scales that might result from this class project will have no validity, students will gain an understanding of the BARS construction process.)

3. Role-play a performance appraisal interview between a superior and a subordinate. Maier's *The Role-Play Technique: A Handbook for Management and Leadership Practice* (LaJolla, Calif.: University Associates, 1975) is a good source for role-playing cases. After the role play, carefully examine the interview process and outcomes. Does the "boss" feel that his or her purposes were accomplished in the interview? Compare the subordinate's perception of the interview with the boss's. Were they the same? If not, explore why. In your discussion focus on behaviour that makes open communication and understanding between boss and subordinate easier. Development of good interview skills requires a knowledge of appropriate behaviour, opportunities for practice, and feedback and reinforcement. The role-playing setting is one method of developing interview skills.

4. Search relatively recent issues of *Journal of Applied Psychology, Personnel Psychology, Canadian Journal of Administrative Sciences, HR Magazine*, and other personnel or human resource management–related journals for articles on performance appraisal. Read, briefly summarize, and criticize several articles. This is an excellent way to get some ideas on recent theories, research, and practices in performance appraisal.

▶▶▶ CASES

CASE 11.1 ▶ PERFORMANCE REVIEW AT BERGHOFF'S

Raj Chandra, manager of men's clothing at Berghoff's Department Store, checks his watch as he paces nervously outside his boss's office. Marcus Berghoff, son of the owner, is late for the 11:00 A.M. appointment he made with Chandra yesterday. Chandra wasn't told the purpose of the meeting, only that the boss wanted to see him. He wonders if it has anything to do with the customer who came in last week demanding that he credit her account for a defective pair of jeans. He told the woman, Lucy Wilson, that it was against store policy to take back the jeans, since she had already washed them. He suggested instead that the store's seamstress could fix the jeans. But Wilson was insistent and Chandra finally gave in. Wilson was, after all, a very good customer. Only last month she had purchased six of Berghoff's finest silk ties.

The clock reads 11:15 when Chandra is finally called into Berghoff's office. He's never had the pleasure before, and he isn't sure he wants it now. Berghoff, an imposing man in his late 40s, sits at a large desk facing an uncomfortable-looking straight-backed chair, which is obviously meant for Chandra.

"Would you like a cup of coffee?" Berghoff asks amiably, motioning for Chandra to make himself comfortable.

"Why, yes, thank you." Chandra sits down.

Berghoff asks his secretary to bring Chandra a cup of coffee. "Nice weather we're having, isn't it?" he continues. "How are your wife and kids . . . you do have a wife and kids, don't you?"

"Yes, I do, Mr. Berghoff. They are very well, thank you."

"Well, Mr. Chandra, you've been with us for about a year now and I, uh, I guess it's about time we had our little talk."

"Fine, sir," says Chandra, "I guess it is about time." He wonders why he feels so nervous; sales are up in his department and he is confident of his ability to manage his eight subordinates.

"What I want to talk to you about . . ." Berghoff is interrupted by the ringing of his office phone.

Chandra sips his coffee while Berghoff makes a date to play tennis at the racquet club later that afternoon with someone named Frank.

"Now, as I was saying," he continues, "I want to talk to you about, uh . . . , about the fine job you've been doing. I see that you've exceeded your department's sales goals, profit is up, and theft is down. The two new clerks you hired and trained are working out well."

Chandra, feeling pleased, relaxes somewhat in his chair. "Thank you, I appreciate . . ."

"That doesn't excuse the fact, however," Berghoff interrupts. "that you flagrantly broke the rules. You know as well as I do we have a company policy against accepting returns that have been washed or worn. Rules . . ."

"I can explain . . ." Chandra begins.

"Rules," continues Berghoff, "aren't made to be broken. We didn't get where we are today by letting people return things they've already . . ."

"But I can explain!" Chandra interrupts in frustration.

"No explanations, no excuses!" says Berghoff, raising his voice and stamping his fist on the desk to punctuate his point. "We go by the book around here, in case you haven't noticed."

"I did notice, sir, but you see, she said . . ."

"I don't care what she said. You went against company policy. The next time you do something like this I'm going to have to dock your pay."

"Yes sssir," Chandra stammers. "Will there be anything else?"

Berghoff pushes his chair back from his desk, stands up, smiles, and walks around to Chandra. In a calmer mood, he places a hand on Chandra's shoulder and says, "I think you're going to work out just fine, son. Just don't break any more rules."

Chandra leaves the office, feeling both stunned and frustrated. Despite his accomplishments, the boss picked up on a little rule violation that could easily have been explained if only Berghoff had listened. As he returns to his department, Chandra wonders how long he can work for a boss who won't listen—one who values rules more than a manager's good judgement.

Back in his office, Berghoff heaves a sigh of relief, glad the encounter is over. "It's never easy to give a negative appraisal," he thinks, "but sometimes it has to be done."

TASKS AND QUESTIONS

1. Analyze Berghoff's handling of the review session. What were his mistakes and how might they be corrected?

2. Based on your analysis, restructure the review session and rewrite its dialogue to demonstrate how the interview could have been handled more effectively by Mr. Berghoff.

CASE 11.2 ▸ PERFORMANCE MONITORING AT BELL CANADA

The 20 operators on shift one morning in the fall of 1985 were all women, although Bell did employ some men, and they made anywhere from $293 to $431 weekly. On her VDT screen a young operator was checking out her own performance. The computer told her that she had taken 119 calls since starting work a little more than an hour ago, and that her average work time (AWT) per call of 25 seconds was two seconds better than the average so far that day.

Behind the operator stood her supervisor, Judy Wenman, who said the system was a big change from when she joined Bell as an operator thirteen years ago. Wenman, at the time manager of operator services, said that AWT wasn't recorded then because it could take as long as five minutes to place a call from Toronto to Montreal. Just prior to the introduction of Bell's Traffic Operator Position System (TOPS) in 1977, AWT was 85 seconds; it was now 25.

If an operator's TOPS statistics started to fluctuate, it was a signal to Wenman that something was wrong—usually in the operator's phone manner. That's where monitoring calls, a practice Bell had used for decades, came in handy. Upon being hired, Bell operators were warned that their calls would be listened to periodically. The company said it gave advance notice of the approximately 200 calls it monitored annually on each operator, and that it was done to improve service. "There are ways to speed up and still be polite. An operator doesn't have to hear about the customer's children or what's for dinner," said Mel James, director of information for Bell Canada, Ontario region. He defended eavesdropping because the company used it as a teaching tool, "not a club."

The Communications Workers of Canada (CWC) disagreed. George Larter, president of CWC's Local 50 in Toronto, said Bell targeted operators it thought were performing poorly. "Some aren't listened to at all; others are monitored without warning hundreds of times a year." Larter, an operator since 1976, refuted James's assertion that the dual monitoring system was not used to discipline employees: "At least three operators have been recently suspended without pay for as long as three days because of their AWT figures, or for what Bell calls 'improper operator practices.' "

James didn't deny that "in the wrong hands" the system was a weapon, but argued that TOPS and eavesdropping were just one part of Bell's employee evaluation and promotion process. "Anyone who lets the machine obsess them will naturally perform poorly, and maybe they are in the wrong job," he suggested. As for misuse, he said that any supervisor "cracking the whip needlessly" would quickly attract union attention. "We'd say to them, 'Hey cool it down there.' " Would the supervisor comply? Larter didn't think so. "Supervisors are nervous. They're surplus and they have to look good. Mr. James may say 'cool it,' but does he really expect them to?" At any rate, James said that because Bell was entirely computerized, no other way existed to measure employee performance. "There's no paper around anymore, so the machine keeps score. That's what makes them fearful."

Still, in the paper era, Bell couldn't gather the information it now did on its operators. With the touch of a key, managers could examine 76 measurements of an operator's performance, including the average number of seconds between the customer coming on the line and the operator depressing the first key; the average number of keystrokes required to get the requested listing; the average number of screenings pulled to find a listing; and the average time between the pushing of the last key and the customer dropping out of the system. With operators answering between 700 and 1000 calls per shift, it's remarkable that most operators' statistics hardly fluctuated. But for those riding out personal or financial troubles — or just a hangover — the computer was the first to know. Management was the second.

It was this type of record keeping that particularly concerned Larter and his fellow unionists. While the computer pinpointed an operator's down days, it of course had no way of recognizing the reasons why someone's performance was off. As Larter said: "By the time a performance review occurs, the circumstances that led to poor TOPS scores can be forgotten. The operator stands condemned."

In 1989, on a trial basis, Bell Canada ended electronic monitoring of most of its telephone operators in an attempt to reduce on-the-job stress. Employees' productivity is now measured across groups of operators, with performance goals set for each unit rather than on an individual basis. The group measure allows for differences in the speed at which individual employees work, while still ensuring they stay productive. The trial program is the result of a union–management study following a four-and-a-half-month strike by Bell employees in 1988 in which monitoring was a key issue.

Source: Adapted from L. Archer, "I Saw What You Did and I Know Who You Are," *Canadian Business*, November 1985, pp. 76–83; and Peter Menyasz, "Union Reports End to Bell Monitoring in Attempts to Cut On-the-Job Stress," *Canadian HR Reporter*, October 18, 1989, p. 3. Used with the permission of the publisher.

TASKS AND QUESTIONS

1. What were the major reasons behind Bell Canada's use of computer performance monitoring? Do you think Bell used the system mainly for administrative or development purposes? Which do you feel the system is better suited to and why?

2. Large numbers of employees and their unions oppose computer performance monitoring. What are some of the reasons for their opposition? What do you think of the idea?

3. Compare computer performance monitoring systems to performance appraisal processes that do not have computer monitoring. How are they alike and how are they different? How do computer monitoring systems measure up in terms of the requirements for all appraisal systems?

4. Identify the problems you see in using computer performance monitoring. How might these problems be alleviated?

NOTES

1. U.S. Bureau of National Affairs, "Employee Performance: Evaluation and Control," *Personnel Policies Forum*, no. 108 (February 1975); and R.I. Lazer and W.S. Wikstrom, *Appraising Managerial Performance: Current Practices and Future Directions* (New York: The Conference Board, 1977).

2. M.A. Archer and C. Brooks, "The Winning Partnership," *Human Resources Professional*, September 1989, pp. 12–15.

3. "An Interview with W. Edwards Deming", *Pacific Basic Quarterly*, Spring–Summer, 1985.
4. J.W. Thacker and R.J. Cattaneo, "The Canadian Personnel Function: Status and Practices," *Proceedings of the Administrative Sciences Association of Canada*, Supplement 2, *Personnel and Human Resources*, Toronto, June 1987, pp. 56–66.
5. D. McGregor, "An Uneasy Look at Performance Appraisal," *Harvard Business Review*, vol. 35, no. 3 (1957), pp. 89–94; and N.R.F. Maier, *The Appraisal Interview: Objectives, Methods, and Skills* (New York: John Wiley, 1958).
6. H.H. Meyer, E. Kay, and J.R.P. French, Jr., "Split Roles in Performance Appraisal," *Harvard Business Review*, January–February 1965.
7. Lazer and Wikstrom, *Appraising Managerial Performance*.
8. Z.B. Leibowitz, B.H. Feldman, S.H. Mosley, "Career Development Works Overtime at Corning, Inc.," *Personnel*, April 1990, pp. 38–40.
9. H. Mintzberg, *The Nature of Managerial Work* (New York: Harper & Row, 1973).
10. L. Archer, "I Saw What You Did and I Know Who You Are," *Canadian Business*, November 1985, pp. 76–83.
11. S. Boyes, "Unions Ward Off Incentive Pay," *Canadian HR Reporter*, May 3, 1989, p. 12.
12. H. Meyer, "The Pay for Performance Dilemma," *Organizational Dynamics*, Winter 1975, pp. 22–38.
13. M. Gibb-Clark, "Evaluating Work Performance of Employees," *The Globe and Mail*, February 28, 1989, p. B13.
14. D. Swift, "The Electronic Supervisor," *Maclean's*, June 17, 1985, pp. 32–33.
15. P.C. Wright, "Performance Appraisal, A Double-Edged Sword," *Industrial Management*, June 1982.
16. Thacker and Cattaneo, "The Canadian Personnel Function," p. 63.
17. Thacker and Cattaneo, "The Canadian Personnel Function," p. 63.
18. W.F. Cascio, *Applied Psychology in Personnel Management*, 4th ed. (Englewood Cliffs, NJ: Prentice-Hall, 1991).
19. H.J. Bernardin, L. Elliot, and J.J. Carlyle, "A Critical Assessment of Mixed Standard Scales," *Proceedings of the Academy of Management*, 1980, pp. 308–12; and T.L. Dickinson and P.M. Zellinger, "A Comparison of the Behaviorally Anchored Rating and Mixed Standards Scale Formats," *Journal of Applied Psychology*, vol. 65, no. 2 (1980), pp. 147–54.
20. P.F. Ross, "Reference Groups in Man-to-Man Job Performance Ratings," *Personnel Psychology*, vol. 19 (1966), pp. 115–42.
21. S.W. Gellerman and W.G. Hodgson, "Cyanamid's New Take on Performance Appraisal," *Harvard Business Review*, vol. 66, no. 3 (1988), pp. 36–40.
22. Thacker and Cattaneo, "The Canadian Personnel Function," p. 63.
23. J.S. Kane and E.E. Lawler III, "Methods of Peer Assessment," *Psychological Bulletin*, vol. 85 (1978), pp. 555–86.

24. G.M. McEvoy, P.F. Buller, and S.R. Roghaar, "A Jury of One's Peers," *Personnel Administrator*, vol. 33, no. 5 (1988), pp. 94–101.

25. W.L. Kirchner and M.D. Dunnette, "Identifying the Critical Factors in Successful Salesmanship," *Personnel*, vol. 34 (1957), pp. 54–59.

26. See P.C. Smith and L.M. Kendall, "Retranslation of Expectations: An Approach to the Construction of Unambiguous Anchors for Rating Scales," *Journal of Applied Psychology*, vol. 47 (1963), pp. 149–55.

27. L. Fogli, C. Hulin, and M.R. Blood, "Development of First-Level Behavioral Job Criteria," *Journal of Applied Psychology*, vol. 55, no. 1 (1971), pp. 3–8.

28. J.G. Goodale and R.J. Burke, "Behaviourally Based Rating Scales Need Not Be Job Specific," *Journal of Applied Psychology*, vol. 60 (1975), pp. 389–91; and M. Beer, R. Ruh, J.A. Dawson, B.B. McCaa, and M.J. Kavanagh, "A Performance Management System: Research, Design, Introduction, and Evaluation," *Personnel Psychology*, vol. 31 (1978), pp. 505–35.

29. Thacker and Cattaneo, "The Canadian Personnel Function," p. 63.

30. Lazer and Wikstrom, *Appraising Managerial Performance*.

31. H.J. Bernardin and R.W. Beatty, *Performance Appraisal: Assessing Human Behavior at Work* (Boston: Kent Publishing, 1984).

32. R.W. Beatty, C.E. Schneier, and J.R. Beatty, "An Empirical Investigation of Perceptions of Ratee Behavior Frequency and Ratee Behavior Change Using Behaviorally Anchored Rating Scales (BARS)," *Personally Psychology*, vol. 31 (1977), pp. 647–58; and J.M. Ivanevich, "A Longitudinal Study of Behavioral Expectation Scales: Attitudes and Performance," *Journal of Applied Psychology*, vol. 65 (1980), pp. 139–46.

33. R.J. Burke and D.S. Wilcox, "Characteristics of Effective Employee Performance Review and Development Interviews," *Personnel Psychology*, vol. 22 (1969), pp. 291–305.

34. Thacker and Cattaneo, "The Canadian Personnel Function," p. 63.

35. Lazer and Wikstrom, *Appraising Managerial Performance*.

36. Wright, "Performance Appraisal."

37. J.N. Kondrasuk, "Studies in MBO Effectiveness," *Academy of Management Review*," vol. 6, no. 3 (1981), pp. 419–30.

38. D.L. Dossett, G.P. Latham, and T.R. Mitchell, "The Effects of Assigned versus Participatively Set Goals, KR, and Individual Differences When Goal Difficulty Is Held Constant," *Journal of Applied Psychology*, vol. 64 (1979), pp. 291–98; and T.I. Chacko, "An Attributional Analysis of Participation and Knowledge of Result in a Goal-Setting Context," PhD dissertation, University of Iowa, 1977.

39. G.P. Latham and K.N. Wexley, *Increasing Productivity Through Performance Appraisal* (Reading, Mass.: Addison-Wesley Publishing Company, 1981).

40. Latham and Wexley, *Increasing Productivity*, p. 126.

41. S.J. Carroll and C.E. Schneier, *Performance Appraisal and Review Systems* (Glenview, Ill.: Scott, Foresman, 1982).

42. W. Edwards Deming, *Out of the Crises* (Cambridge, Mass.: MIT Press, 1986), pp. 54, 102.

43. R.T. Pascale, *Managing on the Edge* (New York: Simon and Schuster, 1990), p. 251. Copyright © 1990 by Richard Pascale. Reprinted with the permission of Simon & Schuster.
44. Deming, *Out of the Crises*.
45. J.D. Orsburn, L. Moran, E. Musselwhite, and J.H. Zenger, *Self-Directed Work Teams: The New American Challenge* (Homewood, Ill.: Business One Irwin, 1990), pp. 318–20.
46. Orsburn et al., *Self-Directed Work Teams*.
47. Beer et al., "A Performance Management System."
48. T.H. Stone, "An Examination of Six Prevalent Assumptions Concerning Performance Appraisal," *Public Personnel Management*, October 1973, pp. 166–70.
49. J. Terry, "In Praise of Appraisals," *Canadian Business*, December 1984, pp. 81–85.
50. McGregor, "An Uneasy Look."
51. H.J. Bernardin and R.W. Beatty, *Performance Appraisal: Assessing Human Behavior at Work* (Boston: Kent Publishing, 1984), p. 268.
52. A.L. Patz, "Performance Appraisal: Useful but Still Resisted," *Harvard Business Review*, May–June 1975, pp. 74–80.
53. E.E. Lawler III, *Pay and Organizational Effectiveness* (New York: McGraw-Hill, 1971).
54. H.J. Bernardin and C.S. Walter, "Effects of Rater Training and Diary Keeping on Psychometric Error in Ratings," *Journal of Applied Psychology*, vol. 62 (1977), pp. 64–69; pp. G.P. Latham, K.N. Wexley, and E.D. Pursell, "Training Managers to Minimize Rating Errors in the Observation of Behavior," *Journal of Applied Psychology*, vol. 60 (1975), pp. 550–55; Smith and Kendall, "Retranslation of Expectations"; and D.E. Smith, "Training Programs for Performance Appraisal: A Review," *Academy of Management Review*, vol. 11 (1986), pp. 22–40.
55. T.H. Stone and E.A. Slusher, "Attributional Insights into Performance Appraisal," *JSAS Catalog of Selected Documents in Psychology*, ms. no. 964, vol. 5, 1975.
56. B. Weiner, I. Frieze, A. Kukla, L. Reed, S. Rest, and R.M. Rosenbaum, "Perceiving the Causes of Success and Failure," in E.E. Jones, D.E. Kanouse, H.H. Kelley, R.E. Nisbett, S. Valins, and B. Weiner, eds., *Attribution: Perceiving the Causes of Behavior* (Morristown, NJ: General Learning Press, 1971).
57. H.H. Kelley, "The Process of Causal Attribution," *American Psychologist*, vol. 28 (1973), pp. 107–28; and E.E. Jones, L. Rock, K.G. Shaver, G.R. Goethals, and L.M. Ward, "Pattern Performance and Ability Attribution: An Unexpected Primacy Effect," *Journal of Personality and Social Psychology*, vo. 10 (1968), pp. 317–40.
58. A.K. Korman, "Expectancies as Determinants of Performance," *Journal of Applied Psychology*, vol. 55 (1971), pp. 218–22.

59. H.M. Jenkins and W.C. Ward, "Judgment of Contingency between Responses and Outcome," *Psychological Monographs*, vol. 70 (1, whole no. 594) (1965); and B. Weiner and A. Kukla, "An Attributional Analysis of Achievement Motivation," *Journal of Personality and Social Psychology*, vol. 15 (1970), pp. 1–20.

60. B. Weiner, H. Heckhausen, W.U. Meyer, and R.E. Cook, "Causal Attributions and Achievement Motivation: A Conceptual Analysis of Effort and Re-Analysis of Locus of Control," *Journal of Personality and Social Psychology*, vol. 21 (1972), pp. 239–48.

61. R.E. Nisbett, C. Caputa, P. Legant, and J. Maracek, "Behavior as Seen by the Actor and as Seen by the Observer," *Journal of Personality and Social Psychology*, vol. 27 (1973), pp. 154–64.

62. John F. Duffy and Andrew C. Peacock, "Contingency Factors in the Effects of Rater Training on Interrater Agreement: Some Lint in the Bellybutton," *Canadian Journal of Administrative Sciences*, vol. 3, no. 2 (December 1986), pp. 317–28.

63. J. Gordon, "Where the Training Goes," *Training*, October 1990, pp. 51–69.

64. R.J. Burke, W. Weitzel, and T. Weir, "Characteristics of Effective Employee Performance Review and Development Interviews: Replication and Extension," *Personnel Psychology*, vol. 3 (1978), pp. 903–19.

65. L.L. Cummings and D.P. Schwab, *Performance in Organizations: Determinants and Appraisal* (Glenview, Ill.: Scott, Foresman, 1973), pp. 118–26. Used with the permission of the authors.

66. N.R.F. Maier, "Three Types of Appraisal Interview," *Personnel*, vol. 34 (March–April 1958), pp. 27–39.

67. N.R.F. Maier, *The Appraisal Interview* (New York: Wiley, 1958); and H.H. Meyer and E.A. Kay, *Comparison of a Work Planning Program with the Annual Performance Appraisal Interview Approach*, Behavioral Research Report No. ESR17, General Electric Company, 1964.

68. Burke, Weitzel, and Weir, "Characteristics of Effective Employee Performance Review."

69. R.G. Johnson, *The Appraisal Interview Guide* (New York: AMACOM, 1979), pp. 72, 113.

70. Burke, Weitzel, and Weir, "Characteristics of Effective Employee Performance Review."

71. H. Meyer, E. Kay, and J.R.P. French, "Split Roles in Performance Appraisal," *Harvard Business Review*, vol. 43 (1965), pp. 123–29.

72. Burke, Weitzel, and Weir, "Characteristics of Effective Employee Performance Review.".

73. W.C. Borman, L.M. Hough, and M.D. Dunnette, *Performance Ratings: An Investigation of Reliability, Accuracy and Relationships between Individual Differences and Rater Error*, final report to the Army Research Institute for the Behavioral and Social Sciences, Alexandria, Va., 1978.

74. W. Trueman, "When Workers Take Root," *Canadian Business*, April 1984, pp. 82–85.
75. G.L. Lubben, D.E. Thompson, and C.R. Klasson, "Performance Appraisal: Legal Implications of Title VII," *Personnel*, May–June 1980. © 1980. Used with the permission of the publisher, American Management Association, New York. All rights reserved.

Suggestions for Further Reading

- H.J. Bernardin and R.W. Beatty. *Performance Appraisal: Assessing Human Behavior at Work*. Boston: Kent Publishing, 1984.
- S.J. Carroll and C.E. Schneier. *Performance Appraisal and Review Systems*. Glenview, Ill.: Scott, Foresman, 1982.
- G.R. Ferris and K.M. Rowland, eds. *Performance Evaluation, Goal Setting, and Feedback*. Greenwich, Conn.: JAI Press, 1990.
- R.G. Johnson. *The Appraisal Interview Guide*. New York: AMACOM, 1979.
- A.M. Mohrman, Jr., S.M. Resnick-West, and E.E. Lawler III. *Designing Performance Appraisal Systems*. San Francisco: Jossey-Bass, 1989.

video CASE

ALL IN A DAY'S WORK

The vision of the traditional Canadian family has changed with each generation. The image of the father going off to work, as the sole income-earner, while the wife stays at home to care for the house and the family is no longer realistic. In the 1990s, double-income families are common, with both parents having to reconcile their commitments to their jobs with the needs of their families. While demographics reflect this new domestic fact, statistics also show a rapid increase in the number of single-parent families as a result of divorce and of single women opting to raise children on their own.

Children are not the only family members who require care and support. Many families have to care for elderly or disabled parents and relatives. It is projected that by the year 2036, one in four Canadians will be 65 years of age or older, and the needs of these individuals will have to be met by their children or younger relatives.

Employees often become frustrated when trying to balance work and family responsibilities. People who want to develop their careers while raising young families or caring for elderly relatives face difficult decisions. These people often feel guilty for not spending more time with their families, especially in times of need. Such conflict often results in increased absenteeism, low morale, and decreased productivity at the workplace.

Employers wishing to recruit and retain valuable employees must be prepared to formulate flexible, creative, and innovative policies and programs that will better enable employees to balance their family obligations and their work-related commitments. Xerox Canada Ltd. has implemented various family-supportive programs in an effort to assist their employees. One such program is the child-care information and referral service. This service enables employees to receive personal child-care advice, information, and referrals at their workplace.

An open and communicative environment can be the first line of defence for both employer and employee against conflicts between work and family obligations. Line managers and supervisors should be encouraged to become more aware of work and family issues. Part-time work, flexible hours, and company-run day-care centres are examples of further steps that a company might take. Once implemented, these programs have obvious mutual benefits for the employee and the employer in terms of less stress, reduced absenteeism, higher motivation, and increased productivity.

Source: Based on "All in a Day's Work," video package and *Work and the Family: The Crucial Balance*, March 1991, used with the permission of the Ontario Women's Directorate and Xerox Canada Ltd.

Discussion Questions

1. Why is it necessary for corporations and other organizations to develop policies to help employees balance work and family responsibilities?

2. Outline some of the consequences of organizations' not responding to changes in our society and, ultimately, in the workplace.

3. You are a management consultant. Outline some recommendations that would alleviate the conflict between work and family obligations.

ORGANIZATIONAL GOALS AND OBJECTIVES AND STRATEGIC PLANNING
SURVIVAL AND GROWTH
PRODUCTIVITY
PROFITS
SERVICE

JOB ANALYSIS
PROVIDES PLANNERS WITH JOBS' REQUIREMENTS FOR HUMAN RESOURCES

STRATEGIC HUMAN RESOURCE ANALYSIS
USES HRM EXPERTISE AND EXPERIENCE TO ASSIST IN DEVELOPING ORGANIZATIONAL OBJECTIVES AND TO PROPOSE ALTERNATIVES TO OBTAIN THESE OBJECTIVES

HUMAN RESOURCE PLANNING
SPECIFIES NUMBER AND KIND OF EMPLOYEES NEEDED

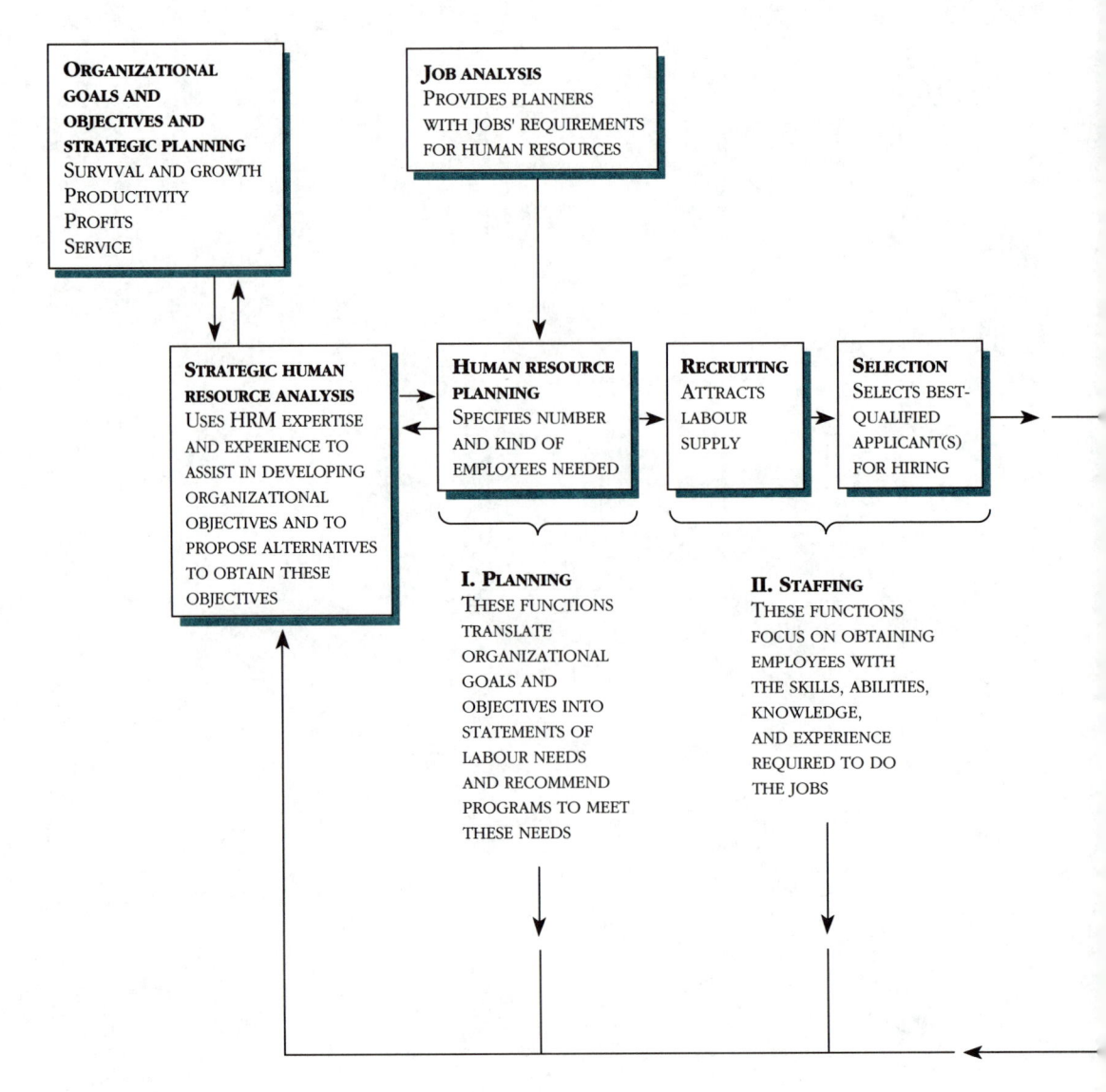

RECRUITING
ATTRACTS LABOUR SUPPLY

SELECTION
SELECTS BEST-QUALIFIED APPLICANT(S) FOR HIRING

I. PLANNING
THESE FUNCTIONS TRANSLATE ORGANIZATIONAL GOALS AND OBJECTIVES INTO STATEMENTS OF LABOUR NEEDS AND RECOMMEND PROGRAMS TO MEET THESE NEEDS

II. STAFFING
THESE FUNCTIONS FOCUS ON OBTAINING EMPLOYEES WITH THE SKILLS, ABILITIES, KNOWLEDGE, AND EXPERIENCE REQUIRED TO DO THE JOBS

INPUT FROM MAJOR AREAS OF HRM RESPONSIBILITY

PART FOUR

Employee Maintenance

Orientation
Provides new employees with information about the job, what to expect, and what is expected

Training and development
Maintains acceptable levels of performance, involves employees in work practice decisions, and prepares employees to advance

Career planning
Seeks to reconcile individual career goals with organizational needs for human resources

Performance appraisal
Measures employees' performance on the job

III. Employee development
These functions seek to ensure that employees possess the knowledge and skills to perform satisfactorily in their jobs or to advance in the organization

Compensation
Develops and administers pay policies to facilitate attraction and retention of employees

Benefits
Administers compensation other than direct pay

Health and safety
Provides employees with a workplace free from health and safety hazards

Labour relations (unions)
Gives employees a collective voice in decisions affecting employment

Adequate number of competent employees with needed skills, abilities, knowledge, and experience to further organizational goals

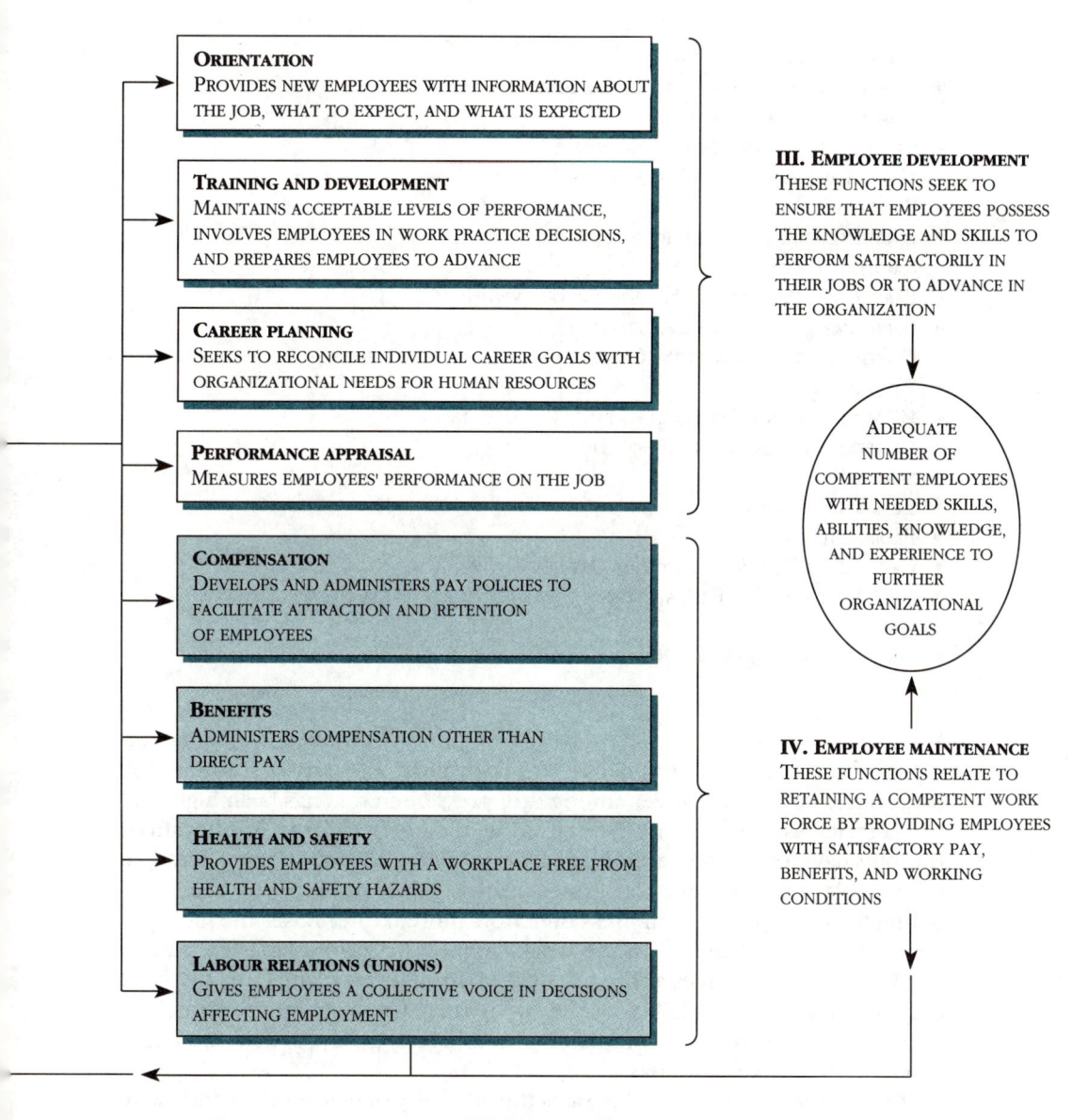

IV. Employee maintenance
These functions relate to retaining a competent work force by providing employees with satisfactory pay, benefits, and working conditions

Input from major areas of HRM responsibility

CHAPTER 12

COMPENSATION

- COMPENSATION: A DEFINITION
- COMPENSATION AND ORGANIZATIONAL EFFECTIVENESS
- COMPENSATION RESPONSIBILITIES
- RELATION TO OTHER HRM FUNCTIONS
- MAJOR LAWS AFFECTING COMPENSATION
- PAY SURVEYS
- HRM IN ACTION ▶ PAYING BY SKILL
- JOB EVALUATION SYSTEMS
- PRICING THE PAY STRUCTURE: ASSIGNING PAY TO JOBS
- USING PAY TO MOTIVATE EMPLOYEES
- CONTROLLING COMPENSATION COSTS
- PAY EQUITY
- HRM IN ACTION ▶ PAY EQUITY AT THE ROYAL BANK
- COMPENSATION ISSUES AND INNOVATIONS
- SUMMARY
- REVIEW QUESTIONS
- PROJECT IDEAS
- CASE 12.1 ▶ PAY EQUITY AT *THE OTTAWA CITIZEN*
- CASE 12.2 ▶ SALARY PROGRESSION AT SHELL CANADA'S SARNIA CHEMICAL PLANT
- NOTES
- SUGGESTIONS FOR FURTHER READING

WALT LESTER, HUMAN RESOURCES MANAGER AT Supply Unlimited, a manufacturing firm in Nova Scotia, has decided to re-evaluate the pay level of the drill press operator job. Turnover among drill press operators has been high, and exit interviews point to insufficient pay as the likely culprit. To re-evaluate the job's pay, Lester compares the drill press operator job at Supply Unlimited with similar jobs in other companies nearby. When he discovers that competing firms are paying drill press operators more, Lester raises the job's pay from Level 3 and Level 4. In the weeks immediately following the raise in pay level, Lester receives approximately 60 formal complaints, mainly from employees one pay grade below the twenty drill press operators whose pay rate was increased. The complaining employees believed that their jobs should also receive more pay.

Walt Lester's experience illustrates the difficulty of determining and maintaining pay structures that meet the demands of both external and internal equity. *External equity* is the fairness of pay and other rewards as perceived in relation to similar jobs outside the organization; it emphasizes competitiveness in the labour market. *Internal equity* is the fairness of pay and other rewards as perceived in relation to other jobs within the organization. In raising the pay grade of the drill press operator job, Lester had increased its external equity, but disrupted the internal equity of the pay structure. An organization's *pay structure* is the set of pay levels associated with jobs in the organization. As such, it defines *pay differentials*, which are the relationships between jobs in terms of pay. For example, a Labour Grade 4 job might pay $1 per hour more than a Labour Grade 3 job.

If the Supply Unlimited plant were located in Ontario, Walt Lester would have to consider not only the internal equity issues when responding to external labour market pressures but also that province's Pay Equity Act. Since the drill press operators are primarily male, if a skill shortage existed the act would permit Lester to pay more for these jobs than their value based on job content if he had prepared an amended pay equity plan declaring the use of the exemption. He would, however, have to be able to substantiate the skills shortage if challenged. Moreover, the additional pay resulting from the skill shortage should be paid as extra compensation because pay equity assumes that all skill shortages are temporary.[1]

For human resource professionals, balancing internal equity, external equity, and pay equity requires a thorough understanding of the principles of compensation together with an up-to-date knowledge of pay legislation.[2]

COMPENSATION: A DEFINITION

Compensation is any form of payment given to employees in exchange for work they provide their employer. Financial payment made at or near the time work is performed is called *direct compensation*. Examples of direct compensation are wages, salaries, overtime pay, commissions, pay for performance, and bonuses. *Wages*, which are usually distinguished from salaries, are direct compensation received by employees who are paid according to hourly rates. Employees paid on a monthly, semimonthly, or weekly basis receive *salaries*; their pay does not vary with number of hours worked.

Besides earning a wage or a salary, most employees are also compensated for their efforts by certain benefits, such as paid vacation days and holidays, various forms of insurance, and pensions. These are forms of *deferred*, or *indirect*, *compensation*.

This chapter discusses direct compensation. The following chapter deals with forms of indirect compensation.

COMPENSATION AND ORGANIZATIONAL EFFECTIVENESS

Organizational effectiveness has been defined as "an organization's capacity to acquire and utilize its scarce and valued resources as expeditiously as possible in the pursuit of its operational goals."[3] Compensation contributes to organizational effectiveness in five basic ways. First, it can attract qualified applicants to the organization. Other things being equal, an organization that offers a higher level of pay can attract a larger number of qualified applicants than its competition. Thus, it benefits from a lower selection ratio, which enables it to hire the most highly qualified of a relatively large number of applicants. (Of course, this assumes that the organization uses valid selection procedures.) More highly qualified applicants are more likely to be highly productive employees. When worker productivity is high, a smaller number of workers can achieve the same output, thus reducing the employer's total labour costs and increasing organizational profitability.

Second, compensation helps to retain competent workers in the organization. Although retaining workers is contingent on many factors, compensation policies help by maintaining a fair internal pay structure, as well as by keeping pay and benefits competitive (ensuring external equity). Turnover is thus reduced, along with costs associated with recruiting, selecting, and training replacements. ISECO Safety Shoes of Mississauga, Ontario, is one company that credits its record of low turnover to a compensation plan featuring profit sharing, bonuses, and generous benefits. ISECO's compensation plan is described in Exhibit 12.1.

Third, compensation can motivate employees to put forth their best efforts. For example, many manufacturers and sales organizations use monetary incentives to attain higher levels of production or sales without hiring additional employees. Monetary incentives provide employees with additional pay as a reward for higher levels of performance. When employees put forth their best efforts, the average productivity of labour increases. With increased productivity, fewer employees are needed to achieve the same level of output. Thus, labour costs are reduced and organizational profitability increased. Note the way ISECO's plan serves to motivate workers. Several recent studies have shown positive links between pay and performance. Work by Leonard, by Gibbons and Murphy, and by Abowd has shown that tying executive compensation to measures of corporate performance leads to improved corporate performance. Ehrenberg and Bognanno, Asch,

EXHIBIT 12.1
ISECO Reaps Benefits from Compensation Plans

If low turnover is a key measure of employee satisfaction, ISECO Safety Shoes of Mississauga, Ont., is a very satisfying place to work. It's a rare year when even one of the national staff of 100 leaves ISECO, says Randy Munnings, the company's secretary treasurer. He attributes a good deal of the record for low turnover to a compensation schedule featuring cash and benefits. Then there are the special perks for sales staff, such as merchandise and vacation trips.

Munnings's uncle George founded the company 45 years ago (his father, Bob, joined the company two years later) to sell steel-toed safety shoes directly to customers from specially

EXHIBIT 12.1 *(continued)*

equipped trucks. ISECO currently has about 40 trucks and 11 stores across the country and distributes products from about 10 safety-shoe manufacturers. With annual sales of about $14 million, the company has earned its own rewards by paying close attention to how it compensates employees. "Our attitude is that we're a privately owned company and we don't have to satisfy shareholders," says Munnings. "So we share as much of the profit as possible with the employees." The standard profit-sharing plan is based on a percentage of the previous year's after-tax profits. It generally amounts to about 8% of an employee's salary.

The noteworthy difference in ISECO's approach is its deliberate emphasis on relating individual performance directly to company performance. Instead of sharing profits in one lump sum after the year-end, Munnings says the company gets maximum psychological benefit from the payment by distributing it quarterly; that way employees get four reminders annually. Although each employee is entitled to a different amount in the profit-sharing scheme based on individual salary, Munnings figures profit sharing linked to salary works in a company the size of ISECO, since it removes the need for complex calculations, and since salaries already reflect employee value and years of service.

In most heavily sales-oriented companies, commissions earned are in themselves an incentive. ISECO gives its sales staff a guarantee of about $200 a week and a percentage of sales and looks after maintenance of the trucks. In addition, Munnings started a special bonus plan two years ago, enabling the sales force to earn points based on performance. "The main feature is that we don't pay cash," he says. "After a certain number of points are accumulated, employees can exchange them for merchandise or a trip or something like that." Again, he figures ISECO gets maximum results for its outlay through the plan. "Our thinking was that, if we paid them in cash, it would go to pay grocery bills or something," he says. "But if we pay in merchandise or other goods, the incentive is there as a reminder for a longer time."

Because top management at ISECO is family—Munnings's father is president, and his cousin Garry is vice-president—the company doesn't have a special executive-compensation plan. However, ISECO looks after salaried people well. The company pays ... all of their major medical coverage for prescription drugs and semiprivate hospitalization and all of a long-term disability insurance plan. ISECO also matches employee contributions to the company's pension plan and covers the administrative costs for a group registered retirement savings plan.

With a far-flung work force, Munnings says communications can sometimes be a problem, especially since most of the salespeople are on the road every day. But he points out that the low turnover resulting from a good compensation package itself leads to good communications. "It's sort of a joke that we try to make things so good for employees that they can't afford to leave," he says. "But because few of them do, we know most employees personally."

Source: Wayne Lilley, "More Money," *Canadian Business*, April 1985, p. 52. Reprinted with the permission of the author.

Kahn and Sherer, and Hamermesh found that systems that provide explicit or implicit incentives for high levels of performance can motivate individuals to increase their effort levels.[4] (However, Asch also found that under certain circumstances quality can suffer and that those who have little chance of benefiting from the incentives appear to reduce their work effort.)

Fourth, compensation systems are important to the effectiveness of organizations since they help to define organization structure and culture.[5] For example, when an organization adds a new line of business, it may need to change its compensation system. New lines of business often require a different set of behaviour and culture than current business lines, and the compensation system can redirect behaviour to meet changed conditions. Similarly, an organization seeking to downsize and have a more flexible work force may seek to change from a traditional job-based pay system to a skill-based pay system. *Job-based systems* pay people for the job they occupy, while *skill-based systems* reward the range of skills and job-related knowledge. Thus, the change in reward systems is consistent with and supports the new strategy and related structure and culture changes.

Finally, minimizing the costs of compensation can also contribute to organizational effectiveness since compensation is a significant cost for most employers.

COMPENSATION RESPONSIBILITIES

HRM professionals engage in a number of compensation activities to facilitate the goals of attracting, retaining, and motivating employees while trying to control compensation costs.

First, in order to ensure that compensation packages are competitive, HRM professionals conduct pay or wage surveys. Pay or wage surveys are a way of collecting and analyzing information about jobs and their pay for the purpose of making pay comparisons between similar jobs in different organizations. Second, to facilitate retention, compensation specialists conduct job evaluations. Job evaluations use selected criteria to compare jobs within an organization, providing a rationale for paying one job more than another. Third, in order to motivate employees, compensation specialists design incentive systems, which attach rewards to desired levels of performance. (Chapter 2 discussed incentive systems.) Finally, HRM professionals implement systems of compensation cost control, including budgets, audits, and compensation guidelines.

RELATION TO OTHER HRM FUNCTIONS

Compensation is related in some way to almost every other HRM function. The most direct relationships are depicted in Figure 12.1.

FIGURE 12.1
Compensation: Relation to Other HRM Functions

```
                    ┌─────────────────────┐
                    │ Job analysis        │
                    │ Provides necessary  │
                    │ data for conducting │
                    │ job evaluations and │
                    │ wage surveys        │
                    └──────────┬──────────┘
                               │
                               ▼
┌─────────────────────┐ ┌─────────────────────┐ ┌─────────────────────┐
│ Human resource      │ │ Compensation        │ │ Recruiting/selection│
│ planning            │ │ Provides direct     │ │ Compensation can be │
│ Specifies human     │→│ financial payment to│→│ used to attract     │
│ resource goals,     │ │ employees in exchange│ │ applicants to the   │
│ which can be        │ │ for the work they   │ │ organization; high  │
│ furthered by        │ │ provide their       │ │ pay may facilitate  │
│ compensation        │ │ employer            │ │ low selection ratios│
│ policies and        │ └─────────────────────┘ └─────────────────────┘
│ programs            │           │
└─────────────────────┘           ▼
                        ┌─────────────────────┐
                        │ Benefits            │
                        │ Level of direct     │
                        │ compensation        │
                        │ received often      │
                        │ affects amount and  │
                        │ type of benefits    │
                        │ received            │
                        └─────────────────────┘

┌─────────────────┐  ┌─────────────────┐  ┌─────────────────┐
│ Performance     │  │ Labour relations│  │ Career planning │
│ appraisal       │  │ Agreements      │  │ Compensation    │
│ Is often a      │  │ negotiated      │  │ associated with │
│ factor in pay   │  │ between labour  │  │ higher-paying   │
│ increases and   │  │ and management  │  │ jobs may        │
│ promotion       │  │ specify the     │  │ influence career│
│ decisions;      │  │ amount and form │  │ plans and       │
│ performance     │  │ of compensation │  │ development     │
│ appraisal data  │  │ paid to         │  │ activities of   │
│ are needed to   │  │ employees       │  │ employees       │
│ use pay as a    │  │                 │  │                 │
│ motivator       │  │                 │  │                 │
└─────────────────┘  └─────────────────┘  └─────────────────┘
```

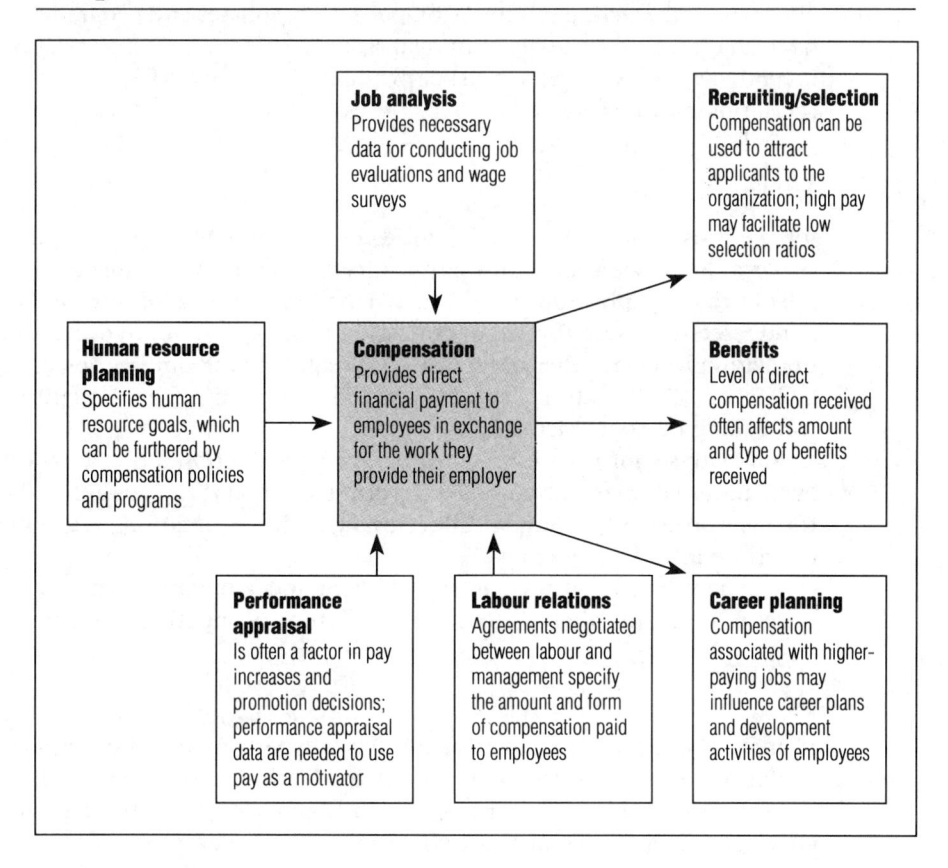

An employee receives his or her pay after a period of time on the job, usually a week to a month. However, the typical employee's first contact with compensation is during recruiting. Pay can be an important factor in whether an applicant accepts a job offer.

HRM functions that directly influence compensation policies and practices include (1) human resource planning, (2) job analysis, (3) performance appraisal, and (4) labour relations. Also, compensation directly influences other functions: (1) recruiting and selection, (2) benefits, and (3) career planning and development.

HUMAN RESOURCE PLANNING

Human resource planning specifies human resource goals, which can be furthered by compensation policies and programs. The number and type of employees needed have a substantial effect on an employer's compensation costs. If, for example, human resource planners project a need for a scarce type of labour, such as tool and die makers, compensation budgets have to allow for high starting salaries. Compensation policies and programs can also have an effect on the goals of human resource planners. If, for example, pay incentive systems increase worker productivity, then HRP goals for external recruiting may be reduced.

JOB ANALYSIS

Job analysis is basic to three activities of the compensation function: wage surveys, job evaluations, and pay equity programs. Wage surveys compare jobs in the organization with similar jobs in other organizations. They are conducted to ensure that an organization's pay is competitive and equitable in relation to what other organizations are paying for similar jobs. Complete and accurate job analysis data are essential to determine the similarity of jobs for making pay comparisons.

Job analysis information is also basic to conducting job evaluations. Job evaluations compare jobs on selected criteria so that they can then be ordered for the purpose of assigning differential pay. Job evaluations are conducted to ensure internal pay equity.

The comparison of the earnings of men and women for pay equity purposes relies on job analysis to determine which occupations are comparable.

PERFORMANCE APPRAISAL

If an organization chooses to use a pay-for-performance or merit system, performance appraisals may be used to determine the magnitude of pay increases or who receives promotion to a higher-paying job. Valid performance appraisals are essential for effective utilization of merit increase dollars.

LABOUR RELATIONS

Agreements negotiated between labour unions and management affect the amount and form of compensation. Under provisions of labour relations acts, unionized employers must negotiate with union representatives who speak for the organized workers. Specifically, management must negotiate wages, benefits, and the conditions of employment, such as working hours, production standards, and so on. The unionized employer thus has less flexibility in compensation than does the nonunion employer.

RECRUITING/SELECTION

Compensation can be used to attract applicants to the organization; attractive pay packages may facilitate low selection ratios and the hiring of high-quality personnel.

BENEFITS

A form of indirect compensation, benefits are closely tied to the compensation function. In some instances, the amount of direct compensation an employee receives affects the amount and type of benefits received. The Unemployment Insurance system, for example, uses the employee's pay to determine the amount of benefits.

CAREER PLANNING AND DEVELOPMENT

Compensation influences an employee's career plans. The higher pay associated with higher-level jobs can motivate an employee to prepare for a position of greater responsibility in the organization.

MAJOR LAWS AFFECTING COMPENSATION

In using compensation to serve its various organizational purposes, employers must work within the framework of many laws and regulations. Among the most important are labour standards legislation, human rights legislation, and income tax laws.

EMPLOYMENT STANDARDS AND HUMAN RIGHTS LEGISLATION

Chapter 3 included a survey of legislation related to labour standards and human rights. Labour or employment standards acts mandate and regulate minimum wages, maximum hours of work and overtime pay, paid vacations and holidays, and so on. Their provisions are normally enforced by the appropriate department of labour.

Equal pay provisions apply to male and female employees performing the same or similar work under the same or similar conditions. In some provinces these provisions are in the human rights acts; others include them in employment standards legislation. Nine Canadian jurisdictions have legislation providing for pay equity or equal pay for work of equal value in the public sector. Ontario also applies its act to private employers with ten or more employees. The criterion is an assessment of the value of work performed by employees in the same establishment.

Human rights legislation prohibits various types of discrimination in employment practices. Except as provided in minimum wage legislation, forbidden practices include paying different wages to persons on the basis of race, religion, ethnic or national origin, marital status, or age. Human rights provisions are normally enforced by human rights commissions.

Employment standards and human rights legislation exist in each of Canada's thirteen jurisdictions (the ten provinces, the two territories, and the federal jurisdiction, which covers industries such as transportation and communications). Since the laws and their interpretations by regulatory bodies are different in each jurisdiction, and since the legislation and regulations undergo frequent revision, HRM professionals must continually monitor the changing legal environment as it relates to compensation.

INCOME TAX LAWS

Federal and provincial laws have an important impact on employee take-home pay and often affect an employer's compensation policies and practices. The effect of income tax laws has been a major factor in developing compensation programs for highly paid executives. Because such employees are in high income tax brackets, salary increases often result in very little additional take-home pay. For this reason, executive pay specialists have developed forms of compensation that reduce the impact of taxes on executive income. Examples include stock options and methods of deferred pay, such as profit-sharing plans and generous pensions.

Although inflation has declined markedly since the beginning of the 1980s, even with little inflation there are still implications for tax laws on the pay of all employees. Until 1982, the federal government fully indexed tax brackets to prevent the erosion of income through inflation's pushing people into higher brackets. In that year, however, the adjustment was held to 6 percent, less than the rate of inflation. In the middle-income brackets especially, a pay increase can move an employee into a higher tax bracket. These circumstances reduce the effectiveness of the pay raise as a means of motivating employees.

PAY SURVEYS

Traditionally, employers have used money to attract an adequate supply of qualified applicants. Whether an organization chooses to be a wage leader or to offer only the market rate for new employees, it must have accurate information about the pay rates for relevant jobs in other organizations. This information is obtained through pay surveys, which enable an employer to learn the going rates for jobs included in the survey. Most organizations obtain pay survey data for only their "key jobs." Key jobs have the following characteristics: (1) they are representative of the organization's pay structure; (2) their job content is relatively stable and well known; (3) they include substantial numbers of employees; and (4) they have not recently undergone large changes in pay level. Data from pay surveys are used both to attract employees and to retain them by ensuring external equity.

Pay surveys are particularly important to employers since they are a major means of determining not only the worth of jobs but also the validity of job evaluation methods. Though pay surveys and job evaluation are separate components of compensation, it is common practice for employers to compare the rankings of jobs produced by job evaluation to that found in pay surveys. Several researchers argue the importance of pay surveys and how they are done in determining the comparable worth of jobs.[6]

Many pay surveys are published by private and government agencies. An employer can also gain such information by participating in local pay surveys conducted by other organizations. If existing pay surveys prove ill-suited to an organization's purposes, it can conduct its own.

CONDUCTING A PAY SURVEY

In order to provide maximum benefit, the makers of a pay survey must follow six steps:

1. Specify purpose of the survey.
2. Specify the jobs to be surveyed, their descriptions or specifications, and the information needed from survey participants.
3. Select comparison employers for inclusion in the survey.
4. Select a survey method and design a survey instrument.
5. Administer the survey.
6. Analyze and display survey data.

An employer can have a number of reasons for wanting to conduct a pay survey. One common one is to examine the competitiveness of hiring wage rates for entry-level jobs. Another common purpose is to compare pay levels for higher-level jobs with those in other organizations. The intended purpose of a pay survey has implications for its design and administration. For example, one must pose different questions in a survey to examine the competitiveness of hiring wages for entry-level jobs and in a survey to investigate the appropriateness of pay differentials among jobs.

Depending on the intent of the survey, different jobs are selected for comparative purposes. If the purpose of the survey is to evaluate a firm's competitive position in the labour market, only entry-level jobs need be included. However, if the survey's purpose is to compare the pay structure to competitors', it is important to include a representative sample of jobs throughout the firm. Information commonly requested in pay surveys includes the number of employees in each surveyed job; pay ranges and midpoints for each job; the basis for advancement to higher pay levels; and the actual pay for each job occupant. Surveys sometimes also seek additional information, such as the nature of fringe benefits provided for various jobs.

HRM managers may also telephone other managers to check whether they have adjusted the pay level for one or more jobs since the last pay survey.

Employers selected for a pay survey are generally in the same industry and local labour market as the employer conducting the survey. When private or public surveys are used, employers may utilize pay data from other companies within either their industry or their local or regional labour market. Labour unions generally prefer that employers compare wage rates with

HRM IN ACTION

PAYING BY SKILL

Increasingly, firms are introducing skill-based pay, as opposed to the conventional system of job-based pay in which employees are paid for the particular jobs they perform, not for their ability to perform other tasks. Initially the firms that introduced skill-based pay did so to get out of the strait-jacket of rigid job classifications. They hated the way each worker was hired, trained, and paid to perform a particular narrow task. If a light bulb needed changing in a car-assembly plant, an engineer had to be summoned to put up the scaffolding before an electrician could screw in the bulb. Then the engineer had to return to dismantle the scaffolding.

Such restrictions were written into legally enforceable contracts. Unions were determined to prevent firms from undermining them by "enlarging" the job of a machine-minder earning $10 an hour to include the routine maintenance and repairs tasks reserved for an engineer earning $15. The only way out was to agree to pay the machine-tender more to acquire and use these semi-skills: in effect to buy out the restrictive practices. The increase in compensation costs was more than offset by higher productivity.

Skill-based pay techniques are also being introduced in nonunionized firms with long histories of good employee relations in order to attract young workers, whose numbers are dwindling because of demographic trends. In addition, skill-based pay is a way of rewarding employees in an organization with a high proportion of older workers who are at the top of their pay scales. Polaroid Corporation is an example of a firm with a lot of good but not very happy employees. They are now being rewarded not only for the skills and knowledge they apply at work, but for their individual performance and contribution to team goals. The goal at Polaroid is a better-motivated, more flexible, and more highly skilled work force.

Even small firms have benefited from skill-based pay. CPS, a 130-employee printing-inks manufacturer in Dunkirk, New York, found that cross-training broke down barriers in job categories and slowed turnover dramatically. Though the approach has been successfully applied on the shop floor, it is not easy to develop an equivalent scheme for office workers. However, the trend toward such a development seems clear. A 1991 survey of U.S. firms by Noble Lowndes found that nearly half were altering their pay practices. Some of the changes, such as sign-on bonuses, were

> viewed as fads, whereas skill-based pay looked like it would thrive. Later in this chapter we will examine two Canadian skill-based pay systems: those of Northern Telecom and Shell Canada.
>
> Source: Adapted from "Pay Practices Altered," *The Economist*, as reported in *The Globe and Mail*, July 22, 1991. Used with the permission of *The Economist*.

those of other unionized firms in the same industry. This is because the pay levels of such jobs are often higher than for the same or similar jobs in local nonunion firms. Generally, it is necessary to utilize competitors in other geographic areas in order to make pay comparisons for highly skilled and specialized jobs.

In theory, organizations could use industry surveys for jobs that are unique to their industry, while also using local wage surveys for jobs that are common to many employers, such as secretary, truck driver, and custodian. In practice, however, many industries, such as banking, hospitals, and breweries, use industry wage survey data for all jobs, not just those specific to the industry. This may result in problems of external equity, since some common jobs tend to be paid more in some industries than in others. For example, a secretary may be paid more at a bank or a brewery than at the hospital or hotel down the street.

In deciding how many organizations to include in a pay survey, the designer must consider the number of organizations with which the employer actually competes for various types of labour. Cost and time considerations also affect the decision of how many organizations to survey. One compensation manager suggests that a pay survey include at least ten but no more than thirty organizations.[7]

Since employers often use the results of pay surveys to demonstrate to employees the fairness of their pay in relation to that given by other organizations, it may be beneficial to give employees a voice in selecting the organizations to be included in such surveys. Participation of this sort can tend to persuade employees of the external equity of their pay. Of course, employers who cannot afford to pay at or above the market wage level may choose not to allow employee involvement in the survey process.

The choice of a survey method depends on the number of jobs to be surveyed, the geographic area of the potential respondents, and time and cost constraints. In some cases, employers may find that surveys available from government or private compensation firms are adequate for their needs.

However, government surveys may not be available when needed. Surveys by private firms tend to be more timely but may cost several hundred dollars or more. Both types of surveys have the disadvantage that an employer is not able to choose or even know which organizations are included in the survey. For these reasons, many employers choose to conduct their own survey, using one or more survey methods.

Questionnaires are most appropriate for surveying large numbers of jobs. Mailed questionnaires are the most common survey method, but when a relatively small amount of information is needed quickly, a telephone survey may be practical. One seldom-used but potentially valuable method of gathering pay information is a conference at which managers from different companies exchange wage and salary information. This method is superior to the questionnaire since ambiguities can be clarified on the spot and data collected rapidly. Further, pay data are easily exchanged in the conference situation.

The survey instrument must be simple, understandable, and easy to complete to encourage co-operation from respondents. It must include adequate descriptions of the jobs being surveyed so that respondents can provide information for comparable jobs in their organizations. Comparability of jobs is crucial to the usefulness of the pay survey, since differences in pay are meaningful only when jobs are similar in content.

The first step in the administration of a pay survey is to notify potential participants that the survey is being conducted and that they are being included. An explanation of the purposes of the survey should be provided. To encourage participation, employers who participate should be promised survey results. In the case of mailed questionnaires, follow-up phone calls are often required to ensure an adequate response rate.

The final step in a pay survey is to analyze and display the data. Data from the survey must be summarized and presented to management and/or employees in an understandable and useful way. Exhibit 12.2 is an example of the results of a pay survey for 32 clerical positions. The survey is conducted annually by the Board of Trade of Metropolitan Toronto. The survey results show the number of firms reporting persons employed in the particular positions, the number of employees, and the various measures of salaries according to their distribution within the salary ranges. The final column presents the weighted average salary for each clerical position. The highest salaries are for senior credit and collection clerk, executive secretary/administrative assistant, senior secretary, senior payroll clerk, and senior accounting clerk. The lowest salaries are for file clerk, junior accounting clerk, messenger–mail clerk, and junior typist. The range (or spread) between the lowest and highest salaries is smallest for occupations at the bottom end of the scale and largest for those at the upper end.

Conducting a pay survey is a complex, costly, and time-consuming process. For this reason, employers should thoroughly examine existing pay surveys before deciding to conduct one of their own.

CHAPTER 12 COMPENSATION 551

EXHIBIT 12.2
Results of a Pay Survey for Clerical Jobs

Adjustments to salary ranges during twelve-month period ending April 1, 1991
% of reporting firms that use salary ranges 66.7
% of reported employees covered by ranges 78.2
% of firms with ranges that made adjustments to these ranges during last 12 months . 75.0
% of employees covered by ranges, whose ranges were affected by adjustments 82.0
Average percentage increase in ranges during last twelve months 3.7

PRINTING/PUBLISHING

	1991	1990
Firms Reporting	18	25
Employees Reported	862	908

	Total No. of Firms	Total No. of Employees	Salary Ranges		Actual Salaries (Annual Rate)					Weighted Average
			Average Min.	Average Max.	1st Decile	1st Quartile	Median	3rd Quartile	9th Decile	
Messenger—Mail Clerk	9	35	17.5	22.7	17.0	18.0	20.0	22.5	24.5	20.5
File Clerk	7	11	16.0	21.6	16.5	16.5	18.5	19.5	20.5	18.5
Shipping & Receiving Clerk	12	22	18.8	25.9	18.5	19.5	22.5	26.5	28.5	22.6
Traffic Clerk	5	12	23.2	31.1	19.0	21.0	26.0	29.5	30.5	24.8
Personnel Clerk	7	8	21.9	31.2			25.5			25.9
Payroll Clerk	7	14	20.7	27.3	20.0	22.0	26.0	27.0	27.0	25.1
Payroll Clerk—Senior	11	16	24.9	34.8	25.0	25.5	29.0	33.0	37.0	29.4
Credit & Collection Clerk	9	30	22.4	29.4	20.0	22.0	23.0	26.0	35.0	24.5
Credit & Collection Clerk—Sr.	6	18	24.7	33.5	21.0	24.5	39.0	39.0	39.0	32.3
Clerk—Junior	12	61	18.5	25.3	18.0	19.5	21.5	23.5	25.0	21.5
Clerk—Intermediate	14	54	21.2	30.0	20.5	21.5	23.0	26.0	28.5	23.7
Clerk—Senior	12	31	24.1	34.5	22.5	25.0	27.5	31.5	33.0	27.8
Accounting Clerk—Junior	11	28	18.8	25.4	18.0	19.0	20.5	21.0	22.5	20.4
Accounting Clerk—Intermediate	14	50	21.3	29.5	21.5	22.5	23.0	24.0	28.0	24.0
Accounting Clerk—Senior	10	21	24.9	34.4	25.0	26.0	28.5	31.5	34.0	29.1
Data Entry Operator	13	55	19.4	26.7	19.0	20.0	21.5	23.5	24.0	22.2
Typist—Junior	3	9	20.6	25.1			20.5			20.6
Typist—Senior	5	16	21.2	26.7	21.0	22.5	24.5	27.0	28.0	24.2
Word Processing Operator	3	6	17.5	24.0			22.5			22.7
Word Processing Operator—Sr.	1	1								
W.P./Desktop Pub. Specialist	2	3	21.7	30.5			26.0			25.3
Secretary	14	79	21.1	29.8	21.0	22.0	24.0	27.0	30.5	25.0
Secretary—Senior	12	56	23.6	34.0	25.5	27.0	28.5	36.0	36.0	30.2
Executive Sec./Admin. Assistant	14	48	26.4	37.8	25.5	27.5	31.0	35.0	39.0	31.6
Customer Service/Order Entry Clerk	10	43	21.4	29.6	20.5	21.0	23.0	25.5	29.5	24.1
Customer Service Representative	14	80	24.0	34.0	20.5	23.0	27.5	35.0	35.0	28.3
Teletype Operator	1	1								
Switchboard Operator/Receptionist	18	54	20.0	27.1	20.0	21.0	22.0	25.5	36.0	24.0

Source: The Board of Trade of Metropolitan Toronto, *1991 Clerical Salary Survey*, Thirty-ninth Annual Salary Review (Toronto, 1991), p. 20.

MAJOR PAY SURVEYS

Employers can use a number of existing pay surveys to learn the market rates of pay for certain jobs. Labour Canada and the federal government's Pay Research Bureau (PRB) are important sources of pay surveys for many types of jobs (see Table 12.1). Most provincial government departments of labour publish the pay rates contained in collective agreements within their jurisdictions. In addition, various private groups and associations conduct their own surveys, which usually focus on selected occupations or industries. These include the Administrative Management Society, Bell Canada, and the Conference Board of Canada. The cost of obtaining a pay survey's results ranges from mere participation in the survey to more than $600. A complete listing of sources of pay information, along with a summary of the contents and the cost of each, is in Labour Canada's *Collective Bargaining Informa-*

TABLE 12.1
Federal Government's Wage and Salary Surveys

SPONSORING ORGANIZATION	TYPE OF EMPLOYEES &/OR INDUSTRIES SURVEYED	GEOGRAPHICAL AREAS SURVEYED	FREQUENCY OF SURVEY
Labour Canada Collective Bargaining Review	All (except construction) for lowest labour classification and top rated nonsupervisory tradesmen	Federal labour jurisdiction and provinces	Monthly
Pay Research Bureau (PRB) Rates of pay in industrial and other organizations	Mining, manufacturing, transportation and communication, public utilities, trade, finance and insurance, service; 14 occupational groups in five classes	Atlantic, Quebec, Ontario, Prairies, British Columbia, plus major metropolitan areas	Annual
Pay Research Bureau (PRB) Anticipated and actual recruiting rates for university and community college graduates	No industry breakdown; various engineering, science, arts and commerce, and business administration graduates	Canada-wide	Annual
Statistics Canada Survey of employment payrolls and hours	All industries at the most detailed level, except agriculture, fishing and trapping, private household services, religious organizations, and military services	Provinces, census divisions, economic regions (of Ontario and Quebec), and metropolitan and urban areas that had a population of 25 000 or more in 1981	Monthly
Labour Canada Bureau of Labour Information	Provides information on wages and salaries in collective agreements in Canada	Federal labour jurisdiction and provinces	No separate surveys, but provides information from existing collective agreements

tion Sources.[8] In addition, Labour Canada's Bureau of Labour Information provides free, comprehensive information on wages and working conditions contained in collective agreements covering 500 or more employees (call 819-997-3117 or 800-567-6866).

An employer can sometimes obtain information regarding local pay surveys from a local board of trade or chamber of commerce. Many unions conduct periodic pay surveys; it is useful for employers who operate under collective agreements to have detailed information about such surveys, especially during contract negotiations.

Before deciding to use an existing survey, an employer should consider a number of factors. First, does it provide the information the organization needs? If one survey does not meet an employer's needs, perhaps several surveys can provide the needed information. Second, to what degree are the surveyed organizations representative of those with which the employer wishes to make pay comparisons? If the fit is not close, using the survey data can lead to false conclusions regarding the competitiveness of pay levels. Third, does the existing survey provide job descriptions that are detailed enough to permit comparison with jobs in the organization? Most standard pay surveys include only "key jobs." For example, machinist is a key job for metal fabricating firms, while secretary is a key job for many different types of employers. Although the content of key jobs is usually similar to related jobs in many organizations, reliance upon a general pay survey means that an employer may have to interpolate pay ranges for jobs that are not included in the standard list. Many employers have at least a few jobs that are unique to their organizations and are, therefore, impossible to compare with identical jobs elsewhere. Finally, in using an existing survey, attention must be given to the form of pay specified in the survey. For example, most surveys use an *average wage rate*, which is defined as the weighted average or mean of straight-time rates paid on a time basis in an occupation. The wage rates in an occupation are multiplied (weighted) by the number of employees receiving each rate, and the sum of these products is divided by the total number of employees reported in the occupation. To make a valid pay comparison with surveys reporting this form of pay, the employer must use the same definition for each job being compared.

USING PAY SURVEY INFORMATION

Though procedures for conducting pay surveys and for analyzing and displaying survey data are fairly standard, little is known about how managers actually use pay survey information to determine levels of pay. It is likely that different compensation policies affect the use that is made of pay survey information. For example, one HRM manager of a unionized auto parts plant adheres to a corporate policy of keeping pay levels at or only slightly below that of his average-paying local competitors. This manager surveys only a few competitors several months before negotiations and disregards pay levels of the highest and lowest paying among them. On the other hand, a highly profitable, nonunion manufacturer surveys only the better-paying employers in its local labour market. It does this at least twice a year because it has a policy of being a wage leader. This employer grants a pay increase anytime a competitor gets close to its pay levels. Thus, the different compensation policies of these two organizations lead one employer to take a vital interest in its highest-paying competitor, while the other chooses to ignore it.

JOB EVALUATION SYSTEMS

The major factor contributing to retention of employees is job satisfaction. As we saw in Chapter 2, job satisfaction has several components, one of which is pay. Dissatisfaction with pay is one factor leading to employee turnover.

One theory used to explain satisfaction with pay is equity theory, also discussed in Chapter 2. *Equity theory* postulates that people compare their inputs (abilities, effort, experience, education) and outcomes (pay, benefits, and other rewards) to the inputs and outcomes of other, comparable persons.[9] The amount of a person's inputs in relation to his or her outcomes is the *ratio of exchange*. An employee who believes that his or her ratio of exchange is not equal to that of a comparable person is likely to perceive the situation as inequitable.

Inequities can be perceived among the pay of co-workers in the same job and among employees in different jobs in the same organization. For example, many employees feel it is inequitable that co-workers receive more pay for the same work simply because they have been on the job longer. In the second kind of perceived inequity, a university-educated reporter might complain about making less money than a printer who works for the same newspaper.

Job evaluation systems are useful in achieving internal equity of pay between different jobs in the organization. Internal equity may be distinguished from employee equity, which is the perceived fairness of pay among workers in the same job or pay grade. Employee equity, which is discussed in a later section, is maintained through seniority, merit, and pay-for-performance systems. Job evaluation systems are also central to the pay equity process.

THE JOB EVALUATION PROCESS

The process of *job evaluation* uses selected criteria to compare jobs within an organization so that they can be ordered for the purpose of assigning differential pay. Job evaluation systems provide a rationale for paying one job in an organization more or less than another. The job evaluation process involves five steps:

1. Collect job analysis data.
2. Prepare job descriptions and job specifications.
3. Choose compensable factors.
4. Develop or choose a job evaluation method.
5. Evaluate jobs.

The first step is to collect job analysis data. This information must be collected through a method of job analysis that completely and accurately captures the content and employee requirements of the jobs. Since job evaluation compares the content of jobs, it is also important to use a job analysis method that captures the similarities and differences between jobs. Some methods of job analysis are better suited than others for conducting job evaluations; methods that are well suited are functional job analysis (FJA), the Position Analysis Questionnaire (PAQ), and work analysis methods for manual, repetitive jobs.

The job descriptions and job specifications that result from job analysis should state clearly and completely the content and employee requirements of jobs. Ambiguous, incomplete job descriptions can result in some jobs being incorrectly evaluated.

The third step in job evaluation is choosing the compensable factors on which jobs will be compared. *Compensable factors* are those factors an organization values and chooses to reward through differential pay. Examples of common compensable factors are skill, knowledge, responsibility, effort, and working conditions. Pay equity legislation uses as the criterion for determining the value of particular work the composite of the skill, effort, and responsibility normally required in the performance of the work and the conditions under which the work is normally performed.[10] All four factors must be considered for pay equity, and the system must be "gender neutral," that is, not weighted to the kinds of factors that are associated with traditionally male or female jobs.

If a factor is to be useful in job evaluation, it must meet four conditions.[11] First, it must be present in different amounts among jobs. For example, working conditions may be a useful compensable factor for comparing jobs that do actually have different working conditions—say, those of a mining company with employees working underground, above ground, and in offices. On the other hand, working conditions would not be a useful compensable factor for evaluating clerical jobs in an air-conditioned insurance office in which all workers are exposed to the same temperature, humidity, lighting, and noise levels.

The second condition is that there be no overlap in meaning between factors. If all jobs are consistently evaluated at the same level on two different factors, a high degree of overlap between the two is likely. Thus, the two factors measure essentially the same aspect of a job and receive an inappropriate weight in relation to other aspects. An example of overlap occurred in an evaluation done by a large retail clothing company. It used financial responsibility and decision making as two of its compensable factors. When the evaluators discovered that most jobs had nearly identical levels of these two factors, the decision-making factor was retained and slightly modified to include financial decisions. Thus, the two factors were combined into one and the overlap problem was solved.

The third condition is that some degree of the factor must be present in all jobs. Quite simply, it is unfair to compare jobs for pay purposes on a factor appropriate to some jobs but not to others.

A fourth condition for the usefulness of compensable factors is that management, employees, and the union should be involved in choosing the ones that will affect pay. Recent research shows that employees have considerable interest in participating in decisions affecting their pay.[12] Compensation specialists agree that when management begins a job evaluation program, employees and their union representatives should be included on an evaluation committee. Since job evaluation involves many value-laden decisions and has a significant impact on pay, it is generally better to include employees in the inevitable discussions and arguments before a job evaluation system is implemented rather than afterwards. Some unions, however, resist becoming involved in the job evaluation process, fearing that their involvement may be interpreted as support and acceptance of the results. Such unions often prefer to let management conduct the job evaluation; then, if aspects of the outcome prove objectionable, the union can file a grievance.

If an organization develops its own job evaluation system, it must select compensable factors. If, on the other hand, it chooses to use one of the many ready-made systems available from compensation consulting firms, government agencies, or industry associations, the compensable factors will already have been selected. For example, the Hay Guide Chart-Profile method employs three factors: knowhow, problem solving, and accountability. Though ready-made plans have established compensable factors, modification of factor weights or other details may be made to fit a particular employer's situation. Ready-made systems have benefits such as savings in time and effort, but these advantages should not prevail over developing a more appropriate, custom-made system if necessary. Whether an employer chooses a custom-made or a ready-made system depends upon (1) the uniqueness of the organization's jobs, (2) the number and variety of jobs to be evaluated, and (3) the financial resources available.

After an evaluation method is developed or chosen, it is implemented and jobs are evaluated. Employers purchasing ready-made plans typically receive professional assistance in all aspects of the evaluation process, including job analysis, training in use of the system, and advice on administrative problems following plan implementation. Though methods of evaluating differ, they all basically involve determining how much of each compensable factor is present in each job. Thus, jobs can be ordered in terms of their relative worth to the organization.

Even with an excellent job evaluation system, the evaluation process contains subjective value judgements. Since a major criterion of the effectiveness of a job evaluation system is how well it is accepted by employees, compensation experts advocate using a compensation committee with employee representation. Compensation committees are used in the implementation stage to determine how many points or what relative value should be assigned to each job. Disagreements or grievances regarding evaluation of particular jobs are also sometimes resolved by compensation committees consisting of management, HRM professionals, and employee representatives. Under Ontario's Pay Equity Act, pay equity officers are available to settle disputes.

JOB EVALUATION METHODS

There are five basic methods of job evaluation: ranking, level description, factor comparison, point methods, and market pricing. Many variations of these methods exist in practice, but the five basic approaches are described here.

Ranking

The simplest and most basic form of job evaluation is ranking. *Ranking* is a method of ordering jobs from least valued to most valued in an organization. It involves subjective judgements of relative value. The judgements are made by the chief executive officer, perhaps with the assistance of other managerial personnel. Ranking does not require a set of complete job descriptions because those doing it should be thoroughly familiar with the content of the jobs. The compensable factors are not explicit but underlie the subjective judgements about the relative worth of jobs.

The ranking method is most appropriate for small organizations and for those with a limited number of different jobs. It has advantages in that it can be done quickly and inexpensively. An obvious disadvantage is that it is entirely subjective and has no explicit rationale or documentation for the results. This makes the method less useful for establishing internal equity in an organization's pay structure, for defending against pay discrimination suits, and for pay equity purposes. The problem with using the ranking method for pay equity purposes is that many jobs are associated with one gender or the other. The ranking method can be adopted for pay equity purposes if a separate ranking is done for each of the four criteria: skills, effort, responsibility, and working conditions.

Level Description

The *level description* or *classification method* places jobs in a hierarchy, which is a series of descriptions of job grades. *Job grades* are general descriptions of types of jobs. Grades are differentiated according to the degree to which the jobs possess a set of compensable factors. For example, the federal government identifies 74 occupational groups and 153 subgroups, each with different factors that are important for determining levels of pay for different jobs. Thus, evaluation of a job analyst (classification officer), which belongs to the personnel administration group, considers three: knowledge, decision making, and managerial responsibility.[13] Each factor is assigned points, and their sum determines the job's level within the government's seven-level system. Jobs in other occupations receive points for different factors; for example, hazard and environment are weighted for general labour and trades.

In using a level system, a job evaluator compares the job's description to descriptions of job grades in the job classification system. When a close match is found between the job's description and one of the job grade descriptions, the job can be placed in the hierarchy and assigned a pay scale. To illustrate how the level system is used, suppose you are considering the purchase of a new General Motors car. You have a brochure that has a description of all GM models, ranging from the bottom of the line to the top. Now assume that GM introduces a new model that is not included in the brochure. In order to determine where it fits into the existing hierarchy of models, you could obtain a description of the new model and compare it with the descriptions of other GM models in the brochure.

The *classification* method also requires adaptation to meet pay equity needs. As the Ontario Pay Equity Commission points out,

> just as specific jobs tend to be associated with one gender or the other, so do job families. The clerical job family is dominated by females, while the managerial job family is dominated by males. The practice of avoiding comparisons of jobs in different job families has been one of the reasons for job inequities. . . . To avoid this problem, [grade descriptions are prepared] rather than classification descriptions. Grade descriptions are more general. For example, a class description for clerical jobs would include the skill of typing.[14]

The level description method of job evaluation is available to employers at minimal cost from the *Canadian Classification and Dictionary of Occupations* and the new *National Occupational Classification* published by Employment and Immigration Canada. Nevertheless, very few private employers use the method, perhaps because they find the *CCDO*'s two volumes of job descriptions cumbersome.

Factor Comparison

Factor comparison is a quantitative method of job evaluation that evaluates jobs according to several compensable factors. It is a sophisticated method of ranking in which jobs are compared with each other across several factors.

The method has five steps. In the first, a job evaluation committee selects and rank-orders the key jobs in the organization. When the key jobs have been ranked, each is assigned a monetary value, which is its current going wage. Table 12.2 shows the monetary values assigned to six key jobs in a machinery manufacturing plant and their compensable factors. In this first step, monetary values ranging from $7.54 to $16.06 have been assigned to the six key jobs.

In the second step, the evaluation committee rank-orders compensable factors according to their relative importance in each job. Though the committee may select its own compensable factors, the most commonly used are mental requirements, skill requirements, physical effort, responsibility, and working conditions. In the example, skill is ranked most important in the machinist's job, and working conditions are least important. In the labourer's job, physical effort is most important and mental requirements are least important.

TABLE 12.2

Monetary Values Assigned to Key Jobs and Compensable Factors

		MONETARY VALUE ASSIGNED TO COMPENSABLE FACTORS				
JOB	MONETARY VALUE OF KEY JOB	Mental Requirements	Physical Effort	Skill	Responsibility	Working Conditions
Machinist	$16.06	$2.25	$1.88	$8.54	$1.85	$1.54
Electrician	15.61	2.29	2.15	7.16	1.90	2.11
Drill press operator	11.33	1.93	1.49	5.31	1.50	1.10
Inspector	10.20	1.74	1.34	4.78	1.35	0.99
Tool crib attendant	9.09	1.29	2.19	2.89	1.29	1.43
Labourer	7.54	0.97	2.18	1.57	0.99	1.83

The third step involves the assignment of a monetary value to each factor for each key job so that the total equals the overall value assigned to the job in the first step. For example, of the $16.06 monetary value assigned to the machinist's job, $2.25 is allocated to mental requirements, $1.88 to physical effort, $8.54 to skill, $1.85 to responsibility, and $1.54 to working conditions.

The fourth step is development of job factor comparison scales based on information from step three. Table 12.3 shows job factor comparison scales for physical effort, mental requirements, and skill for the key job in the machinery manufacturing plant. Note that each scale is weighted by the highest monetary value assigned to it. Skill is the most heavily weighted, and physical effort and mental requirements are weighted approximately equally. Thus, skill is the most important of the compensable factors.

The final step in the factor comparison method is to use the factor comparison scales to evaluate other, non-key jobs in the organization.

There are advantages to this method. First, it "fits" the organization very well because it must be custom-built by each employer. Second, it is easy to use because evaluators rate jobs in terms of well-known jobs in their own organization.

The factor comparison method also has several disadvantages. The most important is that as the content of key jobs changes, the system becomes less accurate. And this method may formalize any existing pay inequities since it assumes that the existing pay rates for key jobs are correct. Finally, the complexity of the factor comparison method makes it difficult for employees to understand and accept.

This method is limited primarily to manufacturing and manual, blue-collar jobs. The disadvantages just mentioned, as well as the applicability of the

TABLE 12.3
Three Job Factor Comparison Scales

MONETARY VALUE	PHYSICAL EFFORT	SKILL	MENTAL REQUIREMENTS
$8.50		Machinist	
7.20		Electrician	
5.30		Drill press operator	
4.80		Inspector	
2.90		Tool crib attendant	
2.20	Tool crib attendant		
	Labourer		Electrician
2.15	Electrician		Machinist
	Machinist		Drill press operator
1.50	Drill press operator	Labourer	Inspector
1.40	Inspector		Tool crib attendant
1.00			Labourer

method to a declining occupational group, mean that factor comparison is not commonly used. In fact, the authors of one compensation text estimated that this method was the least popular of the conventional methods listed in a 1987 survey of salary management practices.[15] "The traditional method of doing factor comparisons is unacceptable for pay equity purposes, because it traditionally incorporates current salaries. It is possible to adapt the factor comparison method, however. But since this method is the most complex and least common, it is best to avoid using it unless it is already in place."[16]

Point Method

The most complex and yet most frequently used of the major job evaluation methods is the *point method*, sometimes called the *point factor method* or *point rating*, which is similar to the factor comparison method in that separate scales are developed for each compensable factor. The two methods differ primarily in that the factor comparison method is based upon a set of key jobs existing in one organization at one point in time, while the point method is independent of jobs in a particular organization. Since point systems are usually not unique to a specific organization, they are used in many ready-made job evaluation systems.

Scales based on the point method are more precise and accurate than factor comparison scales because point systems are universal compensable factors which are further divided into subfactors and degrees. *Universal factors* are compensable factors common to many different jobs in an occupational group, such as management or manual labour jobs. Typically, the factors receive different weights to reflect greater or lesser degrees of importance, as compared to other factors. A common method of assigning different weights to factors is by allocating a larger number of maximum possible points to one factor as opposed to another. For example, if a job evaluation system has 1000 possible points, a professional services employer, such as a CPA firm, might emphasize responsibility by assigning 400 points to the highest level of responsibility, 300 to skill, 200 to effort, and 100 to working conditions.

One example of a ready-made point system from the United States is the American Association of Industrial Management's National Position Evaluation Plan. As shown in Exhibit 12.3, it has four universal factors: (1) skill, (2) effort, (3) responsibility, and (4) job conditions. Each of these factors is further divided into subfactors. For example, "skill" is divided into "knowledge," "experience," and "initiative and ingenuity." Subfactors are further divided into degrees, which are defined so that the job evaluator can determine how much of each is present in the job or jobs being evaluated. Under this plan, each degree of a subfactor has a fixed point value. For example, a job with fifth-degree knowledge requirements receives a point value of 70; a job with first-degree knowledge requirements receives a point value of 14. The point values assigned to each subfactor of a job are then totalled across factors, allowing jobs to be placed in a hierarchy according to their total point value. For pay administration purposes, jobs within certain point ranges are grouped together and assigned labour grades. The checking of point ranges is very important because if clear, precise distinctions are not made between levels of subfactors, gender bias could be introduced since this method uses more subfactors. "The more room for ambiguity, the more likely it is for bias to occur. Further, the description of each level must apply equally to the content found in the female and male jobs under evaluation. When examples of equipment appear, for instance, make sure that equipment used in both men's and women's jobs is listed."[17]

The federal government uses the point method to evaluate some of its jobs. One reviewer explains, "In general, point-rating is used where the duties and responsibilities of positions in an occupational group or subgroup are heterogeneous. Level description is used if they tend to be homogeneous."[18]

The point method is the most accurate of the job evaluation systems. It remains relatively stable over time, unlike the factor comparison method, whose key jobs are subject to change. The accuracy and comprehensiveness of the point method mean that employee acceptance is relatively high, increasing the chances that workers will perceive their pay as internally equitable. It also has advantages for pay equity purposes in that it can demonstrate any existing gender bias. "Point ranges should be consistent, and they should be checked to ensure that they do not routinely work against jobs of one gender versus the other. For example, is the point cut-off always placing female (or male) jobs at the top of lower groupings? This could

EXHIBIT 12.3
Point System of the American Association of Industrial Management

POINTS ASSIGNED TO FACTOR DEGREES AND RANGE FOR GRADES

Factor	1st Degree	2nd Degree	3rd Degree	4th Degree	5th Degree
Skill					
1. Education	14	28	42	56	70
2. Experience	22	44	66	88	110
3. Initiative and ingenuity	14	28	42	56	70
Effort					
4. Physical demand	10	20	30	40	50
5. Mental or visual demand	5	10	15	20	25
Responsibility					
6. Equipment or process	5	10	15	20	25
7. Material or product	5	10	15	20	25
8. Safety of others	5	10	15	20	25
9. Work of others	5	10	15	20	25
Job conditions					
10. Working conditions	10	20	30	40	50
11. Hazards	5	10	15	20	25

Score Range	Grades	Score Range	Grades
139	12	250–271	6
140–161	11	272–293	5
162–183	10	294–315	4
184–205	9	316–337	3
206–227	8	338–359	2
228–249	7	360–381	1

1. EDUCATION

This factor measures the basic trades training, knowledge or "scholastic contact" essential as background or training preliminary to learning the job duties. This job knowledge or background may have been acquired either by formal education or by training on jobs of lesser degree or by any combination of these approaches.

1st Degree

Requires the use of simply writing, adding, subtracting, whole numbers and the carrying out of instructions; and the use of fixed gauges and direct reading instruments and devices in which interpretation is not required.

2nd Degree

Requires the use of commercial English, grammar and arithmetic such as addition, subtraction, multiplication and division, including decimals and fractions; simple use of formulas, charts, tables, drawings, specifications, schedules, wiring diagrams, together with the use of adjustable

EXHIBIT 12.3 *(continued)*

measuring instruments, graduates and the like requiring interpretation in their various applications; or the posting, preparation, interpretation, use and checking of reports, forms, records and comparable data.

3rd Degree

Requires the use of shop mathematics together with the use of complicated drawings, specifications, charts, tables, various types of adjustable measuring instruments and the training generally applicable in a particular or specialized occupation. Equivalent to 1 to 3 years applied trades training.

4th Degree

Requires the use of advanced shop mathematics, together with the use of complicated drawings, specifications, charts, tables, handbook formulas, all varieties of adjustable measuring instruments and the use of broad training in a recognized trade or craft. Equivalent to complete, accredited, indentured apprenticeship or equivalent to high school plus a 2-year technical college education.

5th Degree

Requires the use of higher mathematics involved in the application of engineering principles and the performance of related, practical operations, together with a comprehensive knowledge of the theories and practices of mechanical, electrical, chemical, civil or like engineering field. Equivalent to complete 4 years of technical college or university education.

Source: American Association of Industrial Management, National Headquarters, Springfield, Massachusetts. Reprinted with permission.

indicate gender bias in the evaluation of jobs and not necessarily how the point range have been established."[19] One disadvantage of the method is that administrative costs may be too high to justify its use in small and medium-size organizations.

Market Pricing

The *market pricing method* is entirely different from the other four methods of job evaluation; it relies entirely on the labour market to determine how much jobs should be paid. It is not concerned with internal equity of pay, compensable factors, or assigning relative worth to jobs except in relation to the going rate in the labour market. In order to evaluate jobs using the market pricing method, an employer must conduct a pay survey to determine the market price for each job.

The market pricing method may be impractical for a number of reasons. First, going rates may vary depending upon what comparison firms are included in the survey. The inclusion or exclusion of one high- or low-paying firm in the pay survey, for example, could make hundreds or even thousands of dollars difference in pay for a job. Second, it may prove difficult to obtain pay information about some of the less common jobs in an organization. Third, market prices of jobs vary from time to time, making it difficult to maintain a stable pay structure or predict labour costs with this method. Fourth, the market prices of jobs may cause pay equity problems if the relationships between female job classes and male job classes differ externally from what they have been found to be internally. Also, if there is an undervaluing of female job classes either externally, or internally, it is reflected in current salaries. However, salary surveys can assist the pay equity process if there is a gender-neutral job comparison system in place. Finally, the market pricing method may cause problems with internal equity, especially for persons in jobs for which demand has declined. When demand declines, the going rate for the job declines. This situation could actually result in pay *reductions* for some employees. Furthermore, many employees might be disturbed to know that their pay is determined by the going rate in the labour market and not by factors more under their control.

The theoretical advantage of the market pricing method is that employees are paid their market value and employers can obtain needed labour at current market prices. In reality, use of market pricing is probably limited to unskilled, nonunion labour and to independent professionals, such as lawyers and architects. Market forces are, however, used to some employers' advantage in recessions when they negotiate wage concessions with unions.

Policy-Capturing Method

"In this method, jobs are not described and then evaluated. Instead, a detailed, closed-ended questionnaire is administered to obtain information about the jobs. The compensable factors are reflected in the questionnaire." The statistical procedure relates quantifiable job information from the questionnaire to the job salaries and includes in the regression equation a factor for the percent female. This permits the identification of gender bias, which can subsequently be removed. This approach was developed by the State University of New York (SUNY) for the state of New York to assess salaries of women's jobs.[20]

Job evaluation methods are summarized in Table 12.4. Job evaluation factors that may favour male or female job classes are shown in Table 12.5.

PRICING THE PAY STRUCTURE: ASSIGNING PAY TO JOBS

The result of any job evaluation process is a hierarchy of jobs in terms of their relative value to the organization. The practice of assigning pay to this hierarchy of jobs is called pricing the pay structure. This practice involves a number of policy issues, including (1) how the organization's pay levels relate

TABLE 12.4
Major Job Evaluation Methods

METHOD	WHAT FACET OF JOB IS EVALUATED?	HOW IS JOB EVALUATED?	TYPE OF METHOD	MAJOR ADVANTAGE(S)	MAJOR DISADVANTAGE(S)
Ranking	Whole job (compensable factors are implicit)	Ordered subjectively according to relative worth	Nonquantitative	Relatively quick and inexpensive	Entirely subjective
Level description	Whole job	Compared to descriptions of job grades	Nonquantitative	Readily available and inexpensive	Cumbersome system
Factor comparison	Compensable factors of job	Compared to key jobs on scales of compensable factors	Quantitative	Easy to use	Hard to construct; inaccurate over time
Point method	Compensable factors of job	Compared to standardized descriptions of degrees of universal compensable factors and subfactors	Quantitative	Accurate and stable over time	May be costly
Market pricing method	Whole job	Compared to similar jobs in terms of going rate of pay	Quantitative	Avoids management bias; simple to use	Promotes instability of pay structure; may lead to perceived inequities

to the market; (2) what the organization pays for; (3) how it pays, and (4) what steps the organization takes to ensure that pay is administered in a bias-free manner.[21]

How should an organization's pay levels relate to the market? An organization can choose to be a wage leader, to match the going rates in the market, or to pay less than the market. We have already discussed implications of this policy decision for the recruiting and selection functions. An implication of the earlier discussion is that the wage policy decision is substantially affected by an employer's ability to pay high wages. Ability to pay is related to many factors, including profitability, industry, and organization size. Some employers recognize the need to be wage leaders for some occupations or jobs that are vital to their business, while they cannot afford to be wage leaders for all jobs. In such a situation, an organization may adopt a *mixed wage policy* in which it is a wage leader for some jobs while only matching

TABLE 12.5
Job Evaluation Factors That May Favour Male or Female Jobs[a]

FAVOURS MALE JOBS			FAVOURS FEMALE JOBS	
Highly	Moderately	NEUTRAL	Moderately	Highly

Skill

Experience	Breadth of know-how	Communication	Accuracy	Dexterity
	Depth of know-how	Co-ordination	Information ordering	Typing and keyboarding skills
	Differentiating sounds	Complexity of job	Scanning and attention to detail	
	Education	Differentiating smells		
	Knowledge	Differentiating tastes		
	Knowledge of machinery, tools and materials	Ingenuity		
		Initiative		
		Judgement		
		Level of skill		
		Originality		
		Training period		
		Verbal comprehension		
		Verbal expression		

Effort

	Numerical calculations	Co-operation	Concentration	
	Physical effort	Decision making		
	Physical skills	Fatigue		
	Problem solving	Mental effort		
		Planning		
		Stamina		
		Versatility		

Responsibility

	Responsibility for cash or assets	Accountability	Contacts: Internal, external	Caring
	Responsibility for equipment	Confidential data/information	Human relations responsibility	
	Responsibility for products	Effect of decisions	Public relations responsibility	
	Responsibility for standards	Responsibility		
		Responsibility for materials		
		Safety of others		
		Supervision of subordinates		

TABLE 12.5 *(continued)*

	FAVOURS MALE JOBS		NEUTRAL	FAVOURS FEMALE JOBS	
	Highly	Moderately		Moderately	Highly
		Working conditions			
Heavy lifting			Monotony		
Physical hazards					
Spatial ability					
Unpleasant working conditions					

^a Adapted from research conducted in the United Kingdom.

Source: Pay Equity Commission, *How to Do Pay Equity Job Comparisons* (Toronto: March 1989), p. 36. Reprinted with permission.

the going rate for others. Though a mixed wage policy has the advantage of controlling labour costs, it runs the risk of creating internal inequity.

What does an organization want to pay for? Most organizations use a combination of factors, with job content being a major one. Basing pay on job content means that rates are determined on the basis of the presence of certain compensable factors in jobs. Once pay rates for jobs have been established, individuals may receive increases based on other factors, such as seniority, performance, and cost of living.

How does an organization pay? Basically, an organization has to decide whether to have a single rate or a range of pay for each job. A single rate of pay means that all employees in a job receive the same rate of pay regardless of other factors. In practice, single pay rates are rare. Most employers prefer to use pay ranges, which allow for variations in pay to individuals in the same job. Such variations can be based on differences in performance, on employee qualifications, and/or on seniority. Whatever the basis for differences in pay between employees in the same pay grade, they must be perceived as fair in order to maintain employee equity. When pay ranges are used, an employer must decide the basis both for starting pay and for how employees progress through pay ranges. Once such policy decisions have been made, pay can be assigned to the hierarchy of jobs.

Pricing jobs is difficult because there are many factors to be considered. For example, the American Society of Personnel Administration (ASPA) says,

> The resulting pay structure should reflect the organization's objectives; the market place; internal job values; the mix of pay and benefits; its philosophy on how it wishes to pay versus the market; compensation policies, practices, and procedures; the entity's approach to organizational structure; and the economic ability of the organization to pay at a given level.[22]

In developing a pay structure, similar jobs are grouped together in pay grades. Pay grades determine the magnitude of difference between levels of work and make compensation administration easier for employers. But employees must perceive the pay grades as equitable, and this can be a problem because jobs in the same pay grade can be fairly different from one another. For example, a secretary, a security guard, and an assembler may be in the same pay grade.

A major decision is determining the number of pay grades in the structure. Two factors affecting this decision are the number of different work levels the organization chooses to recognize and the difference in compensation for the highest-paid and the lowest-paid jobs in the pay structure. The larger the difference, the more grades the organization needs. The number of pay grades in an organization also has implications for employees' career advancement. A pay structure with relatively few grades provides limited financial incentives for advancement.

Each grade has a midpoint and a range of pay. The *midpoint* is usually paid to an employee who is performing at an acceptable and fully competent level; it is usually determined by wage survey data from similar jobs. The *pay range* defines the upper and lower limits of pay for jobs in a grade. Individual levels of pay within the range reflect differences in seniority and/or performance. The size of a pay range may vary, but it is often about 20 percent from the midpoint in both directions. For example, if the midpoint for a secretary is $25 500 per year, the pay range might be $20 400 to $30 600. In many organizations, the size of the pay range increases for higher-level jobs. For example, a pay range of 30 percent from the midpoint may be used for supervisors. The rationale is that higher-level jobs have a greater performance potential and that employees tend to remain in higher-level positions longer.

The pay range has to be large enough to give individuals incentive to work their way through it over time. For example, the 1991 collective agreement between the Ontario Hospital Association and the Ontario Nurses Association provided for major changes in the pay range for registered nurses. An earlier study had shown that the narrow range between the lowest and the highest pay rates was a factor in the extreme shortage of nurses in the 1980s.[23] The 1991 contract enlarged the range by giving no increase to nurses with less than two years' experience, and 29.3 percent over a two-year period for nurses with nine or more years' experience. By April 1, 1992, the range in the annual salary would widen from $7400 ($32 800 starting to $40 200 at the top) to $19 200 ($32 800 starting to $52 000 at the top).[24]

Most employers have some degree of overlap among their pay grades. The highest-paid employees in one pay grade may receive more than the lowest-paid of the next-higher grade. Such an overlap allows an organization to reward employees for performance or seniority without promoting them. However, too much of an overlap could reduce the incentive for employees to attempt to upgrade themselves.

Developing a basic pay structure usually has to be done only once, but periodic assessments must be made to determine the competitive position of the pay structure over time. One way to compare two or more organizations' wage or pay levels is to portray each one's pay grades graphically and draw a line between the midpoints. This line, called a *pay policy line*, represents an organization's pay level. The pay policy lines can then be compared to ascertain each organization's competitive position in the labour market. A common way organizations respond to increases in cost of living or competitors' pay increases is simply to raise their pay policy line. This results in an increase in the midpoints of pay ranges.

Figure 12.2 depicts one firm's pay grades and pay policy line. In this case, although there is some overlap between pay grades, the size of the pay range does not increase for higher-level jobs.

FIGURE 12.2
One Organization's Pay Grades and Pay Policy Line

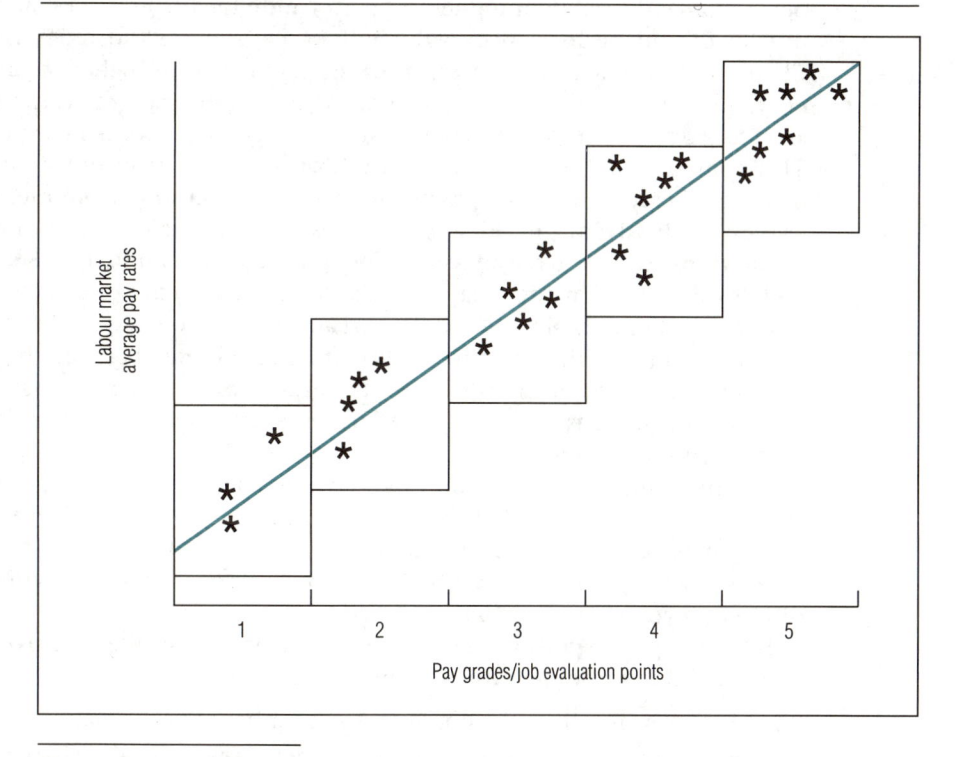

Source: American Compensation Association/Society for Human Resource Management, *Elements of Sound Base Pay Administration* (1981). Published by the American Compensation Association, Scottsdale, Ariz., and the Society for Human Resource Management, Alexandria, Va. Reprinted with permission.

Using Pay to Motivate Employees

Most employees are paid for their time or the number of hours they work. In this case, pay is not contingent upon levels of individual performance. What, then, motivates employees to perform even to acceptable levels?

Employees can be motivated by their boss, by co-workers, or by the non-financial rewards of work, such as intrinsic satisfaction derived from the job. This section deals with an alternative approach to motivating employees: pay for performance.

Pay for performance means that an employee's pay is contingent upon some level of performance specified by the organization. In its *Compensation Planning Outlook 1990* survey, the Conference Board of Canada found that performance-pay management, combined with variable compensation, was a significant priority for many organizations.[25]

There are three basic approaches to pay for performance. The first is *merit pay*, in which pay increases are based on subjective evaluations of employees' performance. In determining merit pay for individual employees, superiors usually fill out performance evaluation forms, such as those described in Chapter 11. The second approach makes promotion to higher-paying jobs contingent upon superior performance. Again, superior performance is usually judged by the employee's boss, using a system of performance appraisal. This approach is most commonly used for white-collar, professional, and managerial employees. As a pay-for-performance method, promotions have two major disadvantages. First, employees compete against one another for promotions, which may reduce co-operation among employees. Second, a high level of performance may not lead to promotion because such opportunities are limited. Many Canadian organizations are likely to have fewer promotion opportunities in the 1990s than in the past because they have become leaner organizations with flatter structures, because successful early retirement programs mean fewer retirements, and because high unemployment means lower turnover.

The third approach to linking pay to performance is to make pay directly proportionate to criteria such as the number of units produced, sales volume, or the profitability of the organization. This type of system is called an *incentive pay system* because the level of monetary reward associated with different levels of performance is specified in advance.

If linking pay to performance is to be useful in motivating employees, the work situation must meet five conditions:

1. The jobs must have the potential for meaningful performance variation.
2. Employees must have — and *believe* they have — the ability to perform at higher levels.
3. Employees must be motivated by money.
4. Employees must perceive an equitable pay–effort bargain.
5. Employees must perceive that the system is fairly administered.

Jobs must have the potential for meaningful variations in performance if pay is to be used as a motivator. Some jobs have very little of this potential because of their narrow scope and/or because employees have limited control over work activities. For example, jobs with a low standard deviation of performance (SD_y) have little potential for variation. In such jobs, performance variations have relatively little impact on the firm's profitability. Examples include library assistants, janitors, and garbage collectors. A job with a low SD_y is not a good candidate for an incentive pay system because performance cannot be greatly influenced by linking it to pay. On the other hand, a job with a high SD_y may be an effective place to link pay to performance. For example, significant differences in performance can result if pay is used to motivate sales representatives, human resource and production managers, and individually paced production workers.

Pay-for-performance systems are useful only if employees have the ability to perform at higher levels and believe that they can achieve higher levels of performance. Since performance is a combination of abilities and effort, pay-for-performance systems have only limited effectiveness with low-ability employees. This points up the importance of the recruiting and selection functions in hiring high-ability employees and of the training function in developing skills. Employees themselves must believe that they have the abilities necessary to perform at higher levels. If employees do not believe this, they will not be motivated to achieve higher levels of pay.

Pay-for-performance systems offer employees the opportunity to obtain money beyond their standard level of pay. To be useful as a motivator of performance, money must be a valued reward. Individuals differ in the value they assign to money. Even employees who view money as a valued reward may choose not to pursue it because they value other rewards or outcomes more highly.

People are motivated by money for many different reasons. The need to provide the basic necessities of life motivates most people. Some also view money as instrumental in satisfying noneconomic needs, such as status, power, and affiliation with desired groups. It is often seen as a symbol of personal success and achievement.

The power of money to motivate individuals varies from time to time. A survey of more than 5000 *MBA* magazine readers found that money was the most important thing wanted from a career by the 35-to-39 age group but not by those under 30 or over 45.[26] For some employees, money is a more powerful motivator in times of greater financial need. One Canadian manufacturer found that employees transferred into and out of pay-for-performance jobs as a function of their need to pay for large items they had purchased. Although employees must value money if pay-for-performance systems are to be effective, employers have very little control over this factor.

Employees must also feel that the additional pay offered is worth any extra effort they have to expend to get it. The ratio of pay to effort is known as the *pay–effort bargain*. Each employee has a certain ratio of exchange between pay and effort which he or she considers equitable. For example, one employee may believe it is fair to be paid $1 for each unit produced above standard, while another employee may perceive that amount to be too low and hence unfair. The employee who perceives the ratio of pay to effort as unfair may have a lower level of ability, which would require him or her to exert more effort to produce each additional unit. How an employee perceives the pay–effort bargain is also influenced by how much he or she needs and desires money.

Management determines the amounts of additional pay offered to different levels of performance on the basis of product costs, considering the value of additional production in relation to the costs of the pay-for-performance system. Such considerations set upper limits on what an employer can pay for higher levels of performance and additional levels of production.

A final condition to be met in using pay to motivate performance is that employees must perceive that the system is administered fairly. They must believe that if they achieve the specified levels of performance, they will receive the promised rewards. The method of measuring performance must be reliable and valid. If performance measures are inconsistent or inaccurate, employees will regard the system with distrust and suspicion.

Employees working under pay-for-performance systems often fear that standards will be raised if they consistently produce at high levels or earn too much. These fears are heightened by the changes that the introduction of new equipment and methods frequently requires in these systems. When such changes become necessary, employees must fully understand them and why they are necessary. One way of facilitating understanding is to involve employees via compensation committees in decisions affecting their pay.

Pay-for-performance systems are summarized in Table 12.6.

MERIT PAY SYSTEMS

The most commonly used pay-for-performance system is merit pay. Under merit pay systems, superiors make subjective appraisals of their subordinates' performance. These appraisals are then used to determine the magnitude of an employee's pay increase. Merit pay systems have been criticized by many authors as unreliable, invalid, and unfair.[27] Additionally, the size of merit budgets fluctuates, increasing in good times and decreasing in lean ones. This means that the amount of merit pay an employee receives may depend more on the financial status of the employer than on the employee's performance.

Assuming that an employer has an adequate performance appraisal system, some mechanism must be developed to translate appraisals into merit increases. One frequently used mechanism is the merit increase guidechart. Guidecharts, which are developed by individual employers, vary in complexity, but most include two dimensions: performance level and position in the pay range relative to the midpoint. Position in the pay range (whether above or below the midpoint) is important because employers use this infor-

TABLE 12.6
Summary of Pay-for-Performance Systems

LEVEL OF PERFORMANCE MEASUREMENT	TYPES OF PLANS	METHOD OF PAY DETERMINATION
Individual	Merit	Performance appraisal data Merit guidechart
	Promotion	Performance appraisal data
	Straight piece rate	Number of units produced × $ per unit
	Standard hour plan	Standard time for task × hourly rate of pay
Group	Group piece rate or group standard hour plans	Same as individual plans, but members receive equal pay
Company	Productivity sharing plans Scanlon Rucker Improshare	Employees as a group receive bonuses for improvements in productivity over a base period
	Profit-sharing plans Current distribution Deferred payment Combination	Employees receive some portion of profit based on set formula
	Cost savings plan	Reductions in costs (excluding those due to technological change) are shared by the company and its employees

mation to assign pay and control compensation costs. For example, most employers try to move excellent performers to the midpoint of the pay range rapidly, whereas employees above the midpoint generally receive smaller percentage pay increases in order not to exceed the pay range maximum. Therefore, as shown in the example of a simplified guidechart in Table 12.7, employees below the pay range midpoint receive larger merit raises than those above the midpoint. Excellent performers at the top of the pay range are prime candidates for promotion.

Note that, in the guidechart, performance level is specified in terms of distribution of performance, from below average (bottom 10 percent) to average (70 percent) to excellent (top 20 percent). A 1990 Conference Board of Canada survey found that more than 60 percent of the surveyed firms claim to use "merit only" as a salary increase criterion.[28] There are, however,

TABLE 12.7
A Simple Merit Increase Guidechart

CURRENT SALARY	BELOW AVERAGE PERFORMANCE (LOWER 10%)	AVERAGE PERFORMANCE (MIDDLE 70%)	EXCELLENT PERFORMANCE (UPPER 20%)
Above midpoint	0	4%	8%
Below midpoint	0	5%	10%

two major limitations to a merit pay approach as a performance-linked strategy. First, merit pay rewards only individual performance, whereas the nature of work is changing to become increasingly interdependent, with shared responsibilities. Second, there is criticism as to whether merit pay increases based on subjective appraisal of employee performance have real motivational value.[29] While performance level and position in the range are important to merit pay decisions, other factors, such as financial resources and state of the labour market, may also affect decisions.

INCENTIVE PAY SYSTEMS

All incentive pay systems link pay directly to measured job outcomes. Such systems can be categorized in terms of the level at which performance is measured, including (1) individual level, (2) group level, and (3) plant-wide or company level. In each case, additional pay is awarded when the performance or production levels exceed some minimum specified by the organization.

Individual-Level Incentive Pay Systems

Under an individual-level system, employees who perform at minimal levels receive their standard pay for the job, but those who perform above these levels receive incentive pay. Two common examples of individual incentive pay plans are the straight piece rate and the standard hour plan. Standard hour plans are used when the time to complete one unit is relatively long, while piece rates are used for parts that can be made rapidly.

For straight piece rates, pay is determined by multiplying the number of units produced by a number of dollars or cents. If, for example, a job pays $0.50 per unit and an employee produces 100 units, he or she earns $50. Piecework is the most frequently used incentive system because it is the most easily understood and accepted by employees. One disadvantage of this method is that setting the rate of pay requires careful study and must often be negotiated with the union. And, since the rate is expressed in monetary terms, it must be changed whenever wage rates are increased. The rate must also be no less than the minimum wage rate specified in the relevant jurisdiction.

The standard hour method is essentially the same, but standards are set in terms of hours. Industrial engineers determine standard times to complete various jobs or tasks. Also specified is the amount an employee is to be paid for the standard level or 100 percent of production. For example, if the standard for assembling a compact disk player is thirty minutes and assemblers work eight hours, sixteen players should be assembled in an eight-hour day. Assuming employees are paid $10 per hour, an employee assembling the standard sixteen would earn $80. The standard hour plan rewards faster employees by paying them at their hourly rate for additional units produced. Thus, an employee assembling four units above standard in an eight-hour day would be paid for two extra hours of production, or a total of $100.

The John Deere Company, a major U.S. manufacturer of construction and farm equipment, has had great success with the standard hour system. It is not uncommon to find some Deere employees producing consistently at 150 to 180 percent of standard. The company's success with the system has come about through use of a large staff of well-trained industrial engineers who have developed and monitored the system.

Incentive pay systems have proven effective in increasing productivity. Because the link between individual performance and incentive pay is most direct in individual incentive systems, they result in larger increases in productivity than do group or company-wide systems. However, individual incentive pay systems are costly to set up and to monitor. Further, they are limited to jobs in which individual performance can be measured objectively and to jobs that require little interdependency of workers to accomplish a common task.

Individual wage incentive systems for unionized blue-collar workers are becoming less common in Canada. Data on collective agreements covering 500 or more employees in industries other than construction show that the percentage with wage incentive provisions declined from 19.8 to 13.7 percent between 1973 and 1980, and to 10.3 percent in 1989. Similarly, the number of employees covered by such provisions declined from 14.5 to 11.9 percent to 6.6 percent in 1989.[30] For executives and managerial employees, on the other hand, the use of variable compensation, usually involving an incentive/bonus mix, is increasing.[31] A study of 16 000 managers at 250 large corporations in the United States found that economic and market measures of the performance of firms are improved when there is an increase in the pay-for-performance component of managerial compensation.[32] What seems to be happening is a shift in compensation emphasis that reflects more closely the desired short-term and long-term focus of employees at different organizational levels.

Group-Level Incentive Pay Systems

If it proves difficult or impossible to measure individual output or if the need for co-operation within work groups is high, employers can use group-level incentive pay systems. Such a system links incentive pay to group performance. All members of a work group receive the same amount of incentive pay, which is determined by the level of group output. The measurement of output is similar to that used for individual incentive systems, but what is measured represents the collective efforts of a number of workers.

In a survey of group incentive programs in 144 companies located primarily in the United States and Canada, Towers Perrin reported that group incentives work. Such programs must, however, contain operational measures so that employees can understand the relationship between their actions and the plan objectives, that is, that changes in their on-the-job behaviour can affect the results of their team, their unit, even their division. There must also be a recognition that the most effective plans look at performance from a broad, strategic perspective. The support of both senior management and employees is critical in ensuring the success of group incentive plans. Neither size of firms nor union status affects how well group incentive plans work. Seventy-three percent of those surveyed reported that a primary reason for adopting their plan was the role it played in supporting their human resource strategy. The keys to success are in the ability of a plan to encourage improvements in quality and productivity, to promote teamwork among employees, and to encourage greater employee participation. While the use of group incentives is rising, almost two-thirds are "blended" plans, meaning payouts are either based on a combination of financial and operating improvements and results, or drawn from a bonus pool funded on the basis of financial results alone, with the distribution of rewards linked to the achievement of operational targets.[33]

A variation of blended plans is the variable compensation approach. Variable compensation includes the use of stock-based programs and cash-based vehicles, such as profit sharing, productivity gain-sharing, and cash incentives or bonuses. Like merit pay, a variable compensation approach is performance-linked, but unlike merit pay this approach can incorporate the performance of individuals, groups, business units, and both corporate financial and stock price performance. The Conference Board of Canada reported in 1990 that nine out of ten of the respondents to their strategic rewards management research felt that variable compensation would have a role of considerable importance in the next two years. The reason given for the increased importance was the objective of improving business performance through changed employee behaviour. Seventy-nine percent of the organizations surveyed claimed that compensation planning is a part of their strategic planning process.[34]

Plant-Wide or Company Systems

Plant-wide or company systems base incentive pay on the performance and organizational results of all employees. The goal of plant-wide systems is not only to motivate employees, but also to improve co-operation and participation in organizational decision making. Plant-wide incentive systems are appropriate where individual-level incentive systems have failed or are not possible, where close supervision and close monitoring of quality is difficult, and particularly where co-operation and teamwork are important to organizational success.

There are two basic types of plant-wide systems: gain-sharing plans and profit-sharing plans. *Gain-sharing plans* share productivity gains and/or cost savings with employees; *profit-sharing plans* provide employees with some share of a company's profits.

All gain-sharing plans are similar but use different formulas to calculate productivity or labour savings. The amount an individual receives is based on his or her job grade or classification, rather than on individual contributions. Thus, all employees in the same job receive the same amount of incentive pay, and employees in lower-paying jobs receive a smaller share of the incentive pay fund than do those in higher-paying jobs. A recent compensation survey found that 8 percent of large and medium-size Canadian organizations had productivity- or gain-sharing plans, and another 4 percent would be introducing them soon.[35]

Three well-known productivity-sharing plans are the Scanlon, Rucker, and Improshare plans. They have similar formulas for calculating labour savings, though the Rucker formula is somewhat more complex. We will discuss only the Scanlon Plan here.

In the Scanlon Plan, a ratio of the total labour costs to the sales value of production is obtained from past company data. If, through suggestions, changes, and effort, employees either reduce payroll costs or increase production, they receive a share of the resulting savings.[36] The amount an individual employee receives is based on his or her job classification and pay. Implementing the Scanlon Plan requires two committees: a production committee and a screening committee. A production committee, which includes several employees and a management representative, is usually installed in each major department. Its function is to produce suggestions for improvements and cost reductions. The screening committee consists of members of top management and worker representatives; they discuss problems and changes in the plan and the company's competitive position. Labour's share of the savings, usually 50 to 75 percent, is often a matter for bargaining with management.

Gain-sharing plans work best when high levels of interdependence are necessary between employees and departments and when individual or small-group incentive systems are too difficult or costly to install. Case studies suggest that such systems are successful in small organizations that have stable product lines, good supervisors, good union–management relations, and committed top managers who are willing to work with employees on problems.[37]

A variant to productivity sharing is a cost-savings plan. Cost-savings plans can take a variety of forms. Generally, allowable costs such as those for labour, scrap, and downtime are determined during a base period. Reductions in those costs, usually excluding savings resulting from technological change, are then shared by the company and its employees.[38]

Profit-sharing plans have been in existence for nearly a century but have recently received renewed interest, especially since the publication of Martin Weitzman's *The Share Economy* in 1984.[39] One-fifth of a sample of large and medium-size Canadian firms have profit-sharing plans.[40] There are three basic types of profit-sharing plans: the current distribution or cash plan, the deferred payout plan, and the plan combining both cash and deferred payout. Discussion of current distribution plans is appropriate to this chapter. (Deferred payouts are generally a substitute for or augmentation of pension plans, which are a kind of benefit, the subject of Chapter 13.)

Current distribution plans distribute some portion of company profits, in cash or stock, to eligible employees on a regular basis, such as quarterly or annually. Exhibit 12.4 describes the profit-sharing plan of IPSCO Inc. of Regina. It illustrates some typical features of profit-sharing plans, as well as some novel ones.

One of the foremost advocates of all forms of profit sharing, Don Nightingale, professor of management at Queen's University, argues that there is a need for such plans in today's economy. Specifically, he views profit sharing as an important means to greater participation, co-operation, and commitment in organizations.[41] Higher levels of commitment and co-operation are likely to make Canadian businesses more competitive with foreign companies. A survey of 83 member firms of the Profit Sharing Council of Canada found profit sharing an excellent means of improving employee morale as well as profitability. And 84 percent of the surveyed firms said that the plan was a good means of attracting and and retaining desirable employees.[42]

Profit-sharing plans are appropriate in many situations and have been used successfully by a number of large organizations. But they are likely to be unsuccessful when profit levels fluctuate substantially from year to year because of factors beyond the control of employees and managers. Profit sharing may also not work well in capital-intensive industries or in large organizations.[43] A case in point is the automobile industry. Following the 1981–82 recession, the Big Three firms (General Motors, Ford, and Chrysler) argued with the United Auto Workers (UAW), trying to convince the union to replace their decades-old wage rate increase, known as the annual improvement factor, with profit-sharing plans. The U.S. union accepted the scheme. But the Canadian branch of the UAW refused to agree to profit

EXHIBIT 12.4
Profit Sharing at Ipsco Inc.

Until this past winter, Roger Phillips, the gruff CEO of Ipsco Inc. of Regina, was not a fan of profit-sharing plans. Since developing his own profit-sharing scheme, however, Phillips has become a believer. And if the steel manufacturer's novel program works as well as he envisions, its components may soon turn up in other companies' compensation programs as well.

One of the approaches that Phillips found attractive was the idea that profits could be shared in the form of Ipsco stock instead of cash. Equally appealing was the idea of getting participants to contribute money to the profit pool used to buy Ipsco shares. "We think people will appreciate the plan more if their own money is invested," says Phillips. Ipsco asks profit-sharing participants to put from $200 to $500 of their own money into the plan through payroll deductions. The employees' money is then put together with the profit-sharing pool to buy Ipsco shares on the open market. The $200 contributor gets two-fifths of the shares allotted to a $500 contributor. "Most employees can handle that much," says Phillips, "and those who are eligible can shield their share purchase in a group registered retirement savings plan, so there's a tax deduction involved."

The Ipsco plan differs from conventional approaches in other ways as well. For one thing, all participants share equally in the profits. "Most plans divide up what's going to be shared according to salary," says Phillips. "But that means the more you make, the more you earn from profit sharing, and we didn't think that was necessarily equitable." Another uncommon variation is that the shares bought by the plan are vested right away. "Naturally, we hope they hang on," Phillips says. "But employees are able to sell their shares at any time."

One of Phillips' initial objections to profit-sharing plans was the suggestion by some consultants that there should be a guaranteed payout whether there were profits or not. He has skirted that condition and, at the same time, attempted to impress profit-sharing participants with the role of Ipsco's nonemployee shareholders who risked investment money in the company. "Most of the plans we looked at designate a certain percent of profit for sharing, but they start at zero," says Phillips. "We recognize that our shareholders have first call on dividends, so we based our pool formula on after-tax dollars less dividends; 10% of that net figure is allocated to the profit-sharing plan." Of course, once the Ipsco plan is up and running, employees will benefit from those dividends.

Source: Wayne Lilley, "More Money," *Canadian Business*, April 1985, p. 55. Reprinted with the permission of the author.

---

sharing, and after a strike against General Motors in 1984, the Big Three retained annual increases for unionized workers in Canada. A recent study has shown that Canadian auto workers received greater earnings increases without profit sharing than did their American counterparts with profit sharing, and at the same time productivity was higher in Canada than in the United States.[44]

Economists have hypothesized that firms with profit-sharing plans should exhibit fewer layoffs and greater employment stability than firms without such plans because profit sharing would provide for more flexible compensation levels. Thus, firms with profit sharing would tend to reduce compensation more than they would reduce employment. Some support, albeit weak, has been found between the existence of profit-sharing plans and an increase in employment stability.[45]

The many different plant and company-wide incentive pay systems all have the disadvantage of a weak link between each employee's efforts and his or her share of the incentive pay fund. Also, some methods are complex and difficult to explain to employees. Incentive pay may be relatively infrequent; when it comes, it is often included in a regular paycheque, and the employee is unable to differentiate it, a fact that can reduce the ability of incentive pay to motivate employees. One way to overcome this disadvantage is to keep incentive pay separate from regular pay. For example, ISECO Safety Shoes provides profit-sharing cheques quarterly to get "maximum psychological benefit from the payment" (see Exhibit 12.1). It also communicates to employees the formula on which incentive pay is based. Clearly identifying incentive pay and making sure that employees know how they earned it is important to success of plant and company-wide incentive systems. Also, management's philosophy must encourage employee participation and sharing in organizational decisions.

Information on organizations with profit-sharing plans can be obtained from the Profit Sharing Council of Canada, Etobicoke, Ontario.

CONTROLLING COMPENSATION COSTS

Since compensation costs represent a major part of an employer's labour costs, minimizing them is one way to facilitate organizational effectiveness. Recessionary pressures and strong competitive pressures have made control of labour costs a major goal at many organizations. Efforts to control labour costs can create difficulties in realizing the compensation objectives of attracting and retaining quality employees and effectively using pay to motivate employees to attain higher levels of performance. Even when there is less pressure to enforce cost control, employers differ greatly in terms of their ability to pay high wages.

FACTORS AFFECTING BUDGET ALLOCATIONS

Whatever the size of an employer's compensation budget, certain portions of it must be allocated to wages and salaries, benefits, overtime, and special programs, such as pay-for-performance systems and attractive recruiting packages. The allocation of compensation funds to these areas is influenced by several factors: (1) laws and regulations affecting compensation; (2) job evaluation systems; (3) unions; and (4) human resource policies. We have already seen how laws and regulations and job evaluation systems pose constraints on compensation. In Chapter 15, we will discuss how unions affect the determination of compensation. Here we will consider the impact of human resource policies.

An organization's human resource policies have a major effect on how compensation is allocated since they determine the relative importance of alternative goals. For example, does an employer choose to be a wage leader and attract the best-qualified applicants, or to pay less and allocate the difference to an incentive pay system for the purpose of increasing productivity? In times of increased product demand, are compensation funds allocated to the hiring of new employees or are present employees paid overtime for extra hours worked? Such policy questions affect how compensation funds are allocated.

Although human resource policies influence the allocation of compensation dollars, these policies themselves are often influenced by budgetary constraints. Situations often arise that force employers to choose which human resource goals are most important to the organization.

A common conflict in human resource policies is that between offering competitive wages for hiring positions and maintaining internal equity. Organizations must offer competitive pay in order to attract adequate numbers of competent employees. However, a competitive hiring wage often conflicts with the goal of maintaining internal equity in the pay structure. The problem is caused by market forces pushing up the pay rates of certain jobs more rapidly than many employers can afford to increase the pay of experienced employees in the same or similar jobs. Thus, experienced employees often find themselves earning an amount very close to the starting pay of a new employee. This narrowing of the pay differentials between jobs is called *compression*. It often results in experienced employees' feeling that the pay structure is inequitable, that their years of experiences and service count for very little. Compression was found to be a problem in 90 percent of the organizations in one survey.[46] Ideally, employers would simply raise the pay of experienced employees to meet the higher rates of the labour market, but such a policy would greatly increase costs and would also disrupt internal pay relationships, which have been carefully constructed through job evaluation.

MONITORING COMPENSATION ADMINISTRATION

After compensation budgets have been allocated, steps must be taken to ensure that the compensation system is achieving its goals and that compensation costs remain within allocated amounts. The mechanisms commonly used for this purpose include (1) the compa-ratio and other indices, (2) budget, and (3) periodic audits of wages.

Compa-Ratio and Other Indices

The *compa-ratio* is an index of the relationship of an employee's actual pay to the midpoint of the pay grade. In order to calculate a compa-ratio, divide current pay by the midpoint of the pay grade. This index may be used to indicate the relative position of an individual employee's pay or the relationship of the average employee pay to the pay grade midpoint. A compa-ratio for a company could also indicate the relationship between the average of all employees' pay to the average midpoint of all pay grades in the company. Though compa-ratios of 1.0 are often desirable, there are many valid reasons why the compa-ratio for a pay grade or company may be more or less than 1.0. A compa-ratio of less than 1.0 may result from having many newly hired employees in a pay grade, many poorly performing employees, or rapid promotion of employees to higher pay grades. Compa-ratios of more than 1.0 may result from the opposite conditions: namely, many high-seniority employees, high-performing employees, low turnover, and slow promotions. A rapidly growing organization is more likely to have low compa-ratios than is a stable or declining organization.

Other potential indices of the effectiveness of a company's compensation policies and practices include the ratio of labour costs to total product or service costs, the voluntary turnover rate, the average number of applicants per vacancy, and the average length of time to fill a vacancy.

Budgets for Managers

Managers can be required to hold compensation costs in their departments to specified limits. Within these limits, the managers must decide how to allocate funds among their subordinates. For example, if product demand increases, a manager can choose either to allocate funds to additional personnel or to pay present employees overtime for extra hours. Some employers have separate budgets for pay increases. Budgets often force managers to choose between rewarding high-performance employees with large pay increases and providing smaller increases to a large number of employees. As a part of their cost control and performance appraisal systems, some organizations periodically review managerial decisions relating to pay increases. Such reviews also help maintain some degree of consistency in the compensation administration of managers in a single organization.

Periodic Audits of Wages and Hours

Detailed records document proper and fair compensation practices and provide useful data for monitoring the way in which pay is used. For example, periodic audits may reveal incomplete or inaccurate compensation records or excessive use of overtime. The latter sometimes indicates that a particular department is not functioning as efficiently as it should. When compensation problems are discovered, steps can be taken to alleviate them.

PAY EQUITY

As explained in Chapter 3, the concepts of *pay equity*, and of *equal pay for work of equal value* or *comparable worth* are similar in that they involve the payment of equal wages to men and women for jobs of equal or comparable value to an employer. They differ primarily in that pay equity puts more legal pressure on the employer to achieve an equitable situation. In this chapter, where the focus is on how equality is calculated, they can be considered synonymous. The idea of pay equity is a logical extension of the concept of *equal pay for equal work* that underlies legislation requiring that men and women who are performing substantially the same job receive equal pay. Advocates of the concept of equal value go farther, saying that employers should pay equal wages to female employees who hold jobs that are different from male jobs but that are of equal or comparable worth in a composite of skill, effort, responsibility, and working conditions. The application of pay equity will work, they argue, to remove differences in pay based on gender bias inherent in traditional methods of compensation calculation. These adjustments will partially redress the difference in the average earnings of men and women in the workplace. Other initiatives, such as enforcement of employment equity and wide availability of day care, will further reduce this discrepancy, it is hoped.

Table 12.8 summarizes the major elements of the pertinent legislation in each of the nine Canadian jurisdictions that imposes pay equity or equal pay for work of equal value on at least some public sector employers. The most comprehensive approach is that of Ontario's Pay Equity Act of 1987, which covers not only all of the province's public sector but also its private sector employers that have ten or more employees.[47] This section begins with a brief overview of that act, considers how job classes are compared and pay equity implemented, examines the proportional value comparison method, and considers the implications of pay equity for human resource professionals.[48]

TABLE 12.8
Major Provisions of Pay Equity Legislation in Canada

	LEGISLATION	ENACTED	EFFECTIVE DATE	LEGISLATION APPLIES TO
CANADA	Canada Human Rights Act	14/7/77	1/3/78	Federally regulated employers
ONTARIO	Pay Equity Act	16/6/87	1/1/88	All public sector employers, and private sector employers with 10 or more employees
QUEBEC	Charter of Human Rights and Freedoms	6/75	6/75	Provincially regulated employers
NOVA SCOTIA	An Act to Provide for Pay Equity	25/5/88	1/9/88	Civil service, corrections employees, highway workers, hospital employees, Crown corporations, school boards
MANITOBA	Pay Equity Act	11/7/85	1/10/85	Civil service, every Crown entity and external agency
NEW BRUNSWICK	Pay Equity Act	22/6/89	22/6/89	Employees in Part 1 of the First Schedule of the Public Service Labour Relations Act
PRINCE EDWARD ISLAND	Pay Equity Act	17/5/88	1/10/88	Civil service, Crown corporations, university and colleges, and health and care facilities
YUKON	Human Rights Act	12/2/87	1/7/87	Government of the Yukon and municipalities and their corporations, boards and commissions
NEWFOUNDLAND	None — Pay Equity Agreement with public sector unions	Announced 8/4/88	Agreement reached 24/6/88	Public sector employers and members of Association of Allied Health Professionals, International Brotherhood of Electrical Workers, Canadian Union of Public Employees, Nfld. Association of Public Employees and Nfld. and Labrador Nurses' Union

TABLE 12.8 *(continued)*

	FEMALE-DOMINATED JOB CLASSES	**MALE-DOMINATED JOB CLASSES**	**ADMINISTRATIVE BODIES**	**IMPLEMENTATION MODE**
CANADA	70% of the occupation group if fewer than 100 members	70% of the occupation group if fewer than 100 members	Canadian Human Rights Commission	Complaint based
	60% of the occupation group if 100–500 members	60% of the occupation group if 100–500 members		
	55% of the occupation group if more than 500 members	55% of the occupation group if more than 500 members		
ONTARIO	Job class in which 60% or more are female	Job class in which 70% of more are male	Pay Equity Commission	Proactive, and complaint based
	Class determined by a review officer, tribunal, or upon agreement of the parties; allowances for historical incumbency and gender stereotyping considerations	A class that a review officer or tribunal deems as a male job class or that the employer and bargaining agent agree on as a male job class		
QUEBEC	Not defined	Not defined	Commission des droits de la personne	Complaint based
NOVA SCOTIA	10 or more employees where 60% or more are female	10 or more employees where 60% or more are male	Pay Equity Commission	Proactive
MANITOBA	10 or more incumbents of whom 70% or more are women	10 or more incumbents of whom 70% or more are men	Pay Equity Bureau	Proactive
	Public sector employers with more than 500 employees and bargaining agents may agree on a female-dominated class	Public sector employers with more than 500 employees and bargaining agents may agree on a female-dominated class		
	In public sector with fewer than 500 employees if stated in regulations	In public sector with fewer than 500 employees if stated in regulations		

TABLE 12.8 (continued)

	FEMALE-DOMINATED JOB CLASSES	MALE-DOMINATED JOB CLASSES	ADMINISTRATIVE BODIES	IMPLEMENTATION MODE
NEW BRUNSWICK	10 or more incumbents of whom 60% or more are women. The bargaining agent can make application to have classes with fewer than 10 incumbents included. Allowances for historical incumbency considerations	10 or more incumbents of whom 70% or more are men. Allowance for historical incumbency considerations	Pay Equity Bureau (representing employer only); committee representing employers and labour to be established	Proactive, and complaint based (limited)
PRINCE EDWARD ISLAND	60% or more of the incumbents are women. Allowances for historical incumbency and gender stereotyping considerations	60% or more of the incumbents are men. Allowances for historical incumbency and gender stereotyping considerations	Pay Equity Bureau	Proactive, and complaint based
YUKON	Not defined	Not defined	Human Rights Commission	Complaint based
NEWFOUNDLAND	5 or more employees where 60% or more are female. Allowances for historical incumbency considerations	5 or more employees where 60% or more are male. Allowances for historical incumbency considerations	Pay Equity Steering Committee	Collective agreement

	MANDATORY FILING OF PAY EQUITY PLANS/ REPORTS	VALUE DETERMINATION	EXCEPTIONS	INFORMATION-SHARING PROVISION
CANADA	No	Skill, effort, responsibility, and working conditions	Individual performance rating, seniority, red-circling rehabilitation assignment, demotion, reassignment due to changes, internal labour surplus or shortage, geographical/regional differences	No

TABLE 12.8 *(continued)*

	MANDATORY FILING OF PAY EQUITY PLANS/ REPORTS	VALUE DETERMINATION	EXCEPTIONS	INFORMATION-SHARING PROVISION
ONTARIO	No mandatory filing. Plans of public sector employers and private sector employers with 100 employees or more must be posted	Skill, effort, responsibility, and working conditions	Formal seniority system, temporary training development or assignment, merit compensation plan, gender-neutral red-circling, skill shortages, bargaining strength	Not in act; established by case law
QUEBEC	No	Skill, effort, responsibility, and working conditions	Experience, seniority, years of service, merit, productivity, overtime	No
NOVA SCOTIA	Yes	Skill, effort, responsibility, and working conditions	Formal seniority system, temporary training or development or assignment, merit pay plan, skills shortage causing temporary inflation	Yes
MANITOBA	Yes	Skill, effort, responsibility, and working conditions	May be negotiated between parties	Yes
NEW BRUNSWICK	No	Skill, effort, responsibility, and working conditions	Formal seniority system, temporary employee training or assignment, merit pay plans, red-circling and skill shortages	Yes
PRINCE EDWARD ISLAND	Yes	Skill, effort, responsibility, and working conditions	Formal performance appraisal system, seniority system, skills shortage	Yes
YUKON	No	Skill, effort, responsibility, and working conditions	None	No
NEWFOUNDLAND	None	Skill, effort, responsibility, and working conditions	Service, temporary training or development, red-circling, skills shortages	Yes

TABLE 12.8 *(continued)*

	IMPLEMENTATION DATE	DEFINITION OF PAY	WAGE ADJUSTMENT TIME FRAME
CANADA	Effective 1/3/78	Any form of payment for work performed includes salaries, commissions, vacation pay, dismissal wages, bonuses, value for board, rent, housing, lodging, payments in kind, employer contributions to pension funds or plans, long-term disability, health insurance, or other	None
ONTARIO	Pay equity plan Public sector: 1/1/90 Private sector: 500+ employees: 1/1/90 100–499 emp.: 1/1/91 50–99 emp.: 1/1/92 10–49 emp.: 1/1/93 Pay equity adjustments Public sector: 1/1/90 Private sector: 500+ employees: 1/1/91 100–499 emp.: 1/1/92 50–99 emp.: 1/1/93 10–49 emp.: 1/1/94	All payments and benefits paid or provided to or for the benefit of an employee	For the public sector, adjustments are to be 1% per year for 4 years; in the 5th year remainder is paid. In the private sector, 1% per year until pay equity is achieved
QUEBEC	Effective 6/75	Salary and wages do not include compensation or benefits of pecuniary value with the employment	None
NOVA SCOTIA	5 months after pay equity process begins (6/88 or 6/89 depending on employer) to determine job evaluation system; 21 months to apply the evaluation system and to compare classes; 24 months to make adjustments	Salary or compensation does not include benefits such as value of living, residential, auto or clothing allowances, gratuities, overtime, or payments in lieu of overtime	Adjustments divided equally over 4 successive years
MANITOBA	Job evaluation development report, 30/7/86; pay equity adjustments, 30/10/87	Any form of remuneration payable or benefit provided by an employer	Up to 1% over 4 consecutive years

TABLE 12.8 *(continued)*

	IMPLEMENTATION DATE	DEFINITION OF PAY	WAGE ADJUSTMENT TIME FRAME
NEW BRUNSWICK	Phase 1: 12 months following commencement of the act, to negotiate comparison systems and classes; Phase 2: 24 months to apply system and identify inequities; Phase 3: 28 months to make adjustments	Straight-time wages and salary	1% per year for 4 years
PRINCE EDWARD ISLAND	Stage 1: 9 months to negotiate job evaluation system and fix classes; Stage 2: 21 months to apply system and compare classes and agree on quantum of adjustments; Stage 3: 24 months to allocate wage adjustment; Stage 4: 24 months to make adjustments	All forms of pay and benefits paid or provided, directly or indirectly	1% per year until pay equity is achieved
YUKON	Effective 1/7/87	Any form of payment for work performed includes salaries, commissions, vacation pay, dismissal wages, bonuses, value for board, rent, housing, lodging, payments in kind, employer contributions to pension funds or plans, long-term disability, health insurance, or other	1% per year until pay equity is achieved
NEWFOUNDLAND	6 months to select job evaluation system and identify classes, a further 12 months to apply system and compare classes, a further 3 months to determine allocation of adjustments. Adjustments retroactive to 1/4/88	Hourly rate excludes shift differential, contract or uniform allowances, overtime	1% of payroll per year for 4 years with remainder paid in 5th year

Source: Adapted from *Labour Research Exchange*, no. 5, December 1989 (Ottawa: Canadian Labour Market and Productivity Centre, 1989). Used with the permission of the publisher.

The Ontario Pay Equity Act

The purpose of the Ontario Pay Equity Act is to redress systemic gender discrimination in compensation for work performed by employees in female job classes. A job class in which most of the workers are women is compared to one in the same establishment in which most of the workers are men. The two classes must be of equal or comparable worth to the employer. The criterion for comparison is a composite of skill, effort, and responsibility normally required in the performance of the work and the conditions under which it is normally performed. Pay equity is attained when the job rate for the female job class is at least equal to the job rate of the male class. The *job rate* is defined as the highest rate of pay for a job class; it includes wages or salary and benefits. When the comparison identifies a difference in job rates, the employer must make adjustments over a period of time to bring the rate of the female job class up to at least the level of the male job class.

If the establishment has no equal or comparable male job class, the comparison is to a male class that has a higher job rate but performs work of lower value. For unionized employees, female job classes are first compared with male job classes in the same bargaining unit. If no male class in the bargaining unit is of equal or comparable value, then the female job class is compared to male job classes that are part of other bargaining units or that are not unionized.

PREPARING A PAY EQUITY PLAN

A pay equity plan is required for each bargaining unit and for that part of the establishment that is not in any bargaining unit. The employer and the bargaining agent must negotiate a gender-neutral comparison system and a pay equity plan for the bargaining unit.

Detailed guidelines for employees for implementing pay equity have been prepared by the Pay Equity Commission of Ontario, as well as by private organizations (such as Pay Trends, Inc. in its monthly publication *Pay Equity Guide*). The Pay Equity Commission's publication *How to Do Pay Equity Job Comparisons* sets out the process in three stages:

1. Identify female and male jobs or job classes.
2. Compare jobs in terms of skill, effort, responsibility, and working conditions.
3. Provide the same compensation to female job classes that are equal or comparable.

For the purposes of Stage 1, the jobs within a pay equity plan are grouped into classes based essentially on similar duties and responsibilities. Each job class in the establishment is determined to be male, female, or gender-neutral. Generally, a class is considered female if 60 percent or more of the incumbents are women, and male if 70 percent or more of the incumbents are men.

HRM IN ACTION

PAY EQUITY AT THE ROYAL BANK

The Royal Bank of Canada has become the first bank to sign an employment equity agreement with the Canadian Human Rights Commission, but a bank spokesman says the new deal is not far off the bank's existing programs.

The agreement follows a two-year commission review of the bank's policies and practices and sets targets and timetables for the hiring and promotion of Native people, women and visible minorities. The commission will monitor the bank's progress over the next three years.

The goals set out in the agreement "in some cases are very close to what we already have [in the bank's employment equity plan]," said Lynda White, manager of employment equity for the Royal Bank.

"In the agreement that we have, I look at the goals for women executives and visible minorities and they reflect our own goals."

The bank has 37 943 full-time employees. The hiring targets in the agreement apply to full-time employees only.

The agreement sets a goal of hiring 2.25 per cent Native people a year in the clerical area, she said. "Last year we hired at 2.2 per cent. Given that, I would think that we can do better" than the goal set in the agreement.

"I think there are things [in the agreement] that are additional," said human rights commissioner Max Yalden. "I think there are numbers that might increase more than they otherwise would have."

A statement from the commission indicated that promoting more women to senior ranks and an expanded support system for Native employees were improvements made in the new agreement.

Canadian banks have been the target of criticism by women's groups, disabled groups and others for their failure to hire Native people and promote women and visible minorities. One study showed that in 1988, women in banking made only 57 cents for every dollar earned by men, an increase of less than 1 per cent from 1987.

The Royal Bank's review did not arise from a specific complaint but was part of a commission effort to improve employment equity generally in the private sector, a commission official said.

Ms. White said that in 1990, women made up 75 per cent of the Royal Bank's employees, about the same as in 1987. About 5 per cent were in upper management, she said, up from 1 per cent in 1987. In middle management, they were 49 per cent of the employee force.

> Visible minorities constituted 11.6 per cent of the bank's employees in 1990, she said, up from 7.8 per cent in 1987. They also made up 49 per cent of middle management employees, she said. She gave no figure for visible minorities in upper management.
>
> Native people made up 0.6 per cent of employees in 1990, up from 0.1 per cent in 1987, she said.
>
> Statistics were not available for 1991.
>
> Asked how fast those numbers would change and what goals the bank would strive to meet, Ms. White said that information is confidential. "Most of it is expanding on things that are already in place."
>
> The commission is currently doing reviews with the Bank of Nova Scotia, the Toronto-Dominion Bank, the Bank of Montreal and the Canadian Imperial Bank of Commerce, a commission spokesman said.
>
> ---
>
> Source: "Pay Equity at the Royal Bank," *The Globe and Mail*, June 17, 1991. Reprinted with the permission of *The Globe and Mail*.

A job class may also be identified as male or female because of historical gender incumbency or because the field of work is gender-stereotyped.

Stage 2 requires assigning values to the job classes using one of the evaluation systems described earlier in this chapter. The important difference is that each part of the process must be gender-neutral. This means that the evaluation system itself must not give greater emphasis to factors more frequently found in male jobs or ignore or undervalue factors associated with female work. That sounds obvious, but history has shown that gender bias can enter the process at a number of points:

1. The collection of data (what's collected and how).
2. The selection of a comparison system (its factors, level descriptions, and weights).
3. The application of the system (the subjective decisions made).

Some of these errors are very easy to fall into. For example, the Pay Equity Commission points out some job requirements of predominantly female jobs that are frequently overlooked or ignored:

> Skills: Writing correspondence for others; proofreading and editing others' work; and training and orienting new staff.
>
> Efforts: Deciding the content and format of reports and presentations to client; and developing work schedules for subordinates.
>
> Responsibilities: Caring for patients, children, and institutionalized people; and acting on behalf of absent supervisors.

Working Conditions: Stress from open office noise; crowded conditions; exposure to disease; and stress from caring for ill people.

Stage 3 in the pay equity process is to ensure that the same compensation is provided for jobs that are equal or comparable. Public sector employers must complete all necessary adjustments within five years. There is no time limit for private sector employers, but they must prepare a schedule of payments demonstrating that 1 percent of the previous year's total payroll is being devoted to pay equity adjustments.

The Pay Equity Commission concludes: "Now, pay equity provides organizations with an opportunity to examine their compensation systems and ensure that they are fulfilling the intended objective to give women equal pay for work of equal value. Because ultimately, pay equity is a question of fairness."[49]

Other Comparisons

The Ontario Pay Equity Act provides only for job-to-job comparisons between female and male job classes in the same establishment. This approach is not always sufficient. An establishment may not have appropriate male comparison classes for most, even all, of its female job classes. One alternative is the *proportional value* or *indirect comparison method*, which allows relative comparisons to be made between all female jobs and all male jobs in the same establishment. Manitoba's Pay Equity Act requires the use of this approach. Another alternative is the proxy comparison method; it allows public sector organizations to use information for pay equity comparisons from other public sector organizations that are not predominantly female. The state of Minnesota includes a proxy comparison method in its pay equity legislation.[50]

The Ontario government is considering a bill that would include use of the proportional value comparison method in both the private and the public sector and the proxy comparison value method in the public sector. The addition of these two comparison methods would expand Ontario pay equity coverage to approximately 240 000 more working women.

Further Considerations

Pay equity has implications for HR professionals beyond establishing a pay equity plan. First, most jurisdictions provide a complaint mechanism and an administrative body to investigate the complaints. In Ontario, at least, it is strongly recommended that employers also establish an internal appeals committee composed of managerial and employee representatives.[51] Individuals would have recourse to the internal appeals committee before proceeding to the investigative body (in the case of Ontario, a pay equity officer) if the internal committee did not deal satisfactorily with their complaint.

Second, there is every likelihood that pay equity will expand to other jurisdictions in Canada within the public sector and possibly the private sector.[52] It is also likely that changes will take place in existing pay equity legislation and its application. Third, it should be noted that pay equity addresses only female-to-male compensation inequities. Once it has been addressed, HR practitioners should be alert for other internal equity considerations: female to female, male to male, and male to female.

Thus, HR professionals must keep themselves up-to-date on pay equity. In addition to reading current professional literature on the subject, they should obtain material specific to the jurisdiction in which they work by contacting the pay equity administrative agency (see Table 12.8) or their provincial human rights commission.[53] Even in those jurisdictions in which pay equity legislation does not apply to the private sector, employers might consider changes in compensation practices relating to pay equity issues for both negative and positive reasons. The negative reason would be to avoid a sizable compensation adjustment in the face of new legislation, and the positive reason would be to capture some possible job satisfaction gains from female employees by being proactive.

COMPENSATION ISSUES AND INNOVATIONS

By its very nature, compensation is an HRM function subject to conflicting pressures from many sources, including management seeking to control labour costs; employees and unions seeking higher pay; the government seeking to control inflation and ensure minimum, nondiscriminating pay; and the forces of product and labour markets. From these conflicting pressures emerge problems such as cost-of-living adjustments and pressures to move away from a single wage system.

Like most industrialized countries, Canada entered the 1980s with double-digit price increases and double-digit wage increases. This upward spiral was primarily the result of oil price increases by the Organization of Petroleum Exporting Countries (OPEC) in 1973 and 1979. The economic slump of 1981–82 led to a sharp reduction in both the rate of inflation and wage settlements as unemployment rates soared to 13 percent. In order to prevent upward wage pressure on prices, the federal government announced that it would hold its own employees' increases to 6 and 5 percent, respectively, in 1982/83 and 1983/84; it pleaded with the private sector to do the same, and several provincial governments followed suit. Unionized workers met increased resistance at the bargaining table, resulting in smaller wage increases. The remainder of the 1980s witnessed comparatively low inflation rates of 4 to 5 percent per year; wage increases were approximately the same. At the beginning of the 1990s, recession came again, and the federal government again limited wage increases for its employees: to 3 percent in 1991/92 and 0 percent in 1992/93. These low rates were consistent with the high priority both the government and the Bank of Canada gave to reducing inflation.

For HRM professionals, the pressure to contain wage increases have meant a continuing need to monitor compensation costs closely. A number of innovative compensation practices have developed as organizations have changed to meet competitive and recessionary pressures. Examples of innovations include two-tier wage systems, lump-sum pay increases, and skill-based pay.

TWO-TIER WAGE SYSTEMS

In the early 1980s, as a way of reducing labour costs, a number of unionized U.S. employers negotiated contracts with two-tier wage systems. Some Canadian employers followed the American lead. A *two-tier wage system* reduces starting pay for new employees hired after some date, while maintaining or raising pay for current employees. In some two-tier systems, the pay levels of newly hired employees never reach those of current employees; in others, the two pay scales meet after a number of years.

The 1985 agreement between Sunbeam Corporation (Canada) and the United Electrical Workers is an example of a two-tier wage system in which the two scales do not meet. The agreement reduced the hiring rate for new employees by $2.00 an hour to $5.42. The 60 laid-off employees were to be recalled before there were any new hires.[54] Those persons who were recalled were to return at their old rates. An example of a two-tier agreement in which the new hire rates rise toward the rates of previously hired employees was the 1986 agreement between Air Canada and the International Association of Machinists. New employees in eight unskilled jobs had their starting pay reduced to $7.00 an hour for their first year. In the second year they earned a rate halfway between $7.00 and the previous rate. After two years they moved to the previous entry rate and progressed at six-month intervals from there.[55] The eight jobs and the rates were

	New entry rate	*Old entry rate*
Cleaner blaster	$7.00	$10.42
Toolroom issuer	$7.00	$10.27
Cleaner	$7.00	$10.19
Commissary attendant	$7.00	$ 9.96
Building attendant	$7.00	$ 9.77
Station attendant	$7.00	$ 9.58
Stockkeeper	$7.00	$ 9.58
Cargo communications operator	$7.00	$ 8.09

Hughes Aircraft, which used a two-tier system, found that morale, productivity, and quality declined to such an extent that it had to raise starting pay and modify the plan.[56] In general, two-tier wage plans have declined in popularity because both high- and low-wage groups fear that the plans will hold down their wages and the plans have resulted in divisiveness among employee groups where people doing the same work side-by-side are receiving markedly different wage rates.[57]

Two-tier wage systems are more likely to work when wages for new hires are generally competitive, when workers realize they would not have jobs if it weren't for the system, and when a new location is used for introduction of the plan, at least initially.

LUMP-SUM PAY

Lump-sum pay means giving an employee the total amount dollars of his or her pay increase at one point in time. Compensation expert Edward E. Lawler III has argued for such increases as a way of making rewards for increased performance more visible to employees.[58] Since the 1981-82 recession, employers have increasingly used lump-sum payments as a cost control mechanism.[59] By using this approach rather than raising base pay by some fixed percentage, the employer is not committed to a higher base pay in the future. A compromise may be the best approach; for example, a small increase in base pay can be accompanied by a lump-sum payment that is contingent upon accomplishment of a certain performance goal.

In Canada, unions have tended to oppose lump-sum payments. A major example of this opposition occurred in the automobile industry in 1984, when the Canadian branch of the United Auto Workers (UAW) opposed giving up the traditional annual improvement (AIF). Canadian auto workers in assembly plants retained the AIF, whereas their American counterparts agreed to profit sharing and lump-sum payments. The differences in views over this issue caused the Canadian branch of the UAW to form its own independent union in 1985, the Canadian Auto Workers (CAW).[60]

SKILL-BASED PAY

A final innovation, skill-based pay, is a substantial departure from the traditional job evaluation method of establishing pay differentials. In a *skill-based pay system*, employees are paid on the basis of the number and level of jobs they can perform. All new employees earn a starting rate until they have mastered one job. At this point, they are paid a "one-job" rate. The process continues until the employee has learned to perform all jobs in the organization, which entitles him or her to receive the highest rate of pay. Thus, employees are paid on the basis of what they know and the skills they possess, rather than on the particular job to which they are assigned. The advantage of this type of system is that it encourages employee growth and development and provides the organization with a skilled, flexible work force.

In the early 1980s, Shell Canada worked with the Energy and Chemical Workers' Union to develop a skill-based pay system for a new plant it was opening in Sarnia, Ontario. That system is described in a case study at the end of this chapter.

One obvious disadvantage of skill-based pay is that labour costs may be relatively high if a large proportion of the work force reaches the top skill-pay level. To avoid this problem, the skill-based pay system used for Northern

Telecom's 2500 field technicians and engineers provides for merit pay as well as skill pay. Fast Forward, as the system is called, is intended to improve customer satisfaction, to increase commitment to Northern Telecom and avoid unwanted turnover, and to place employees performing essentially the same work on a single pay system. The system, designed by a development team, established four separate blocks based on seven key dimensions of work. Skills in each of the dimensions are ranked from most to least complex, and an employee must complete all skills in one block before moving to the next. Minimum salaries are matched to the market. For the technician family of jobs, there is a 270 percent spread, with segments that correspond to the skill blocks. In addition, employees are reviewed annually (on the individual's anniversary employment date) for pay treatment based on performance. In 1991, a one-time "merit cash" payment was awarded to Fast Forward participants who were performing at or near their targets. Special titles were also added to denote skill levels. Two years after Northern Telecom's introduction of skill-based pay for field service technical personnel, the plan was generally deemed to be meeting its objectives. The overall customer satisfaction rating had risen from 72 to 75 (out of a possible 100). Installation ratings, a target of the program, were up from 70 to 74. Termination, voluntary and involuntary, had fallen from 16 to 7 percent, and voluntary technician resignations had been cut in half. Complaints about salary differences had all but disappeared with all employees being paid on a common system.[61]

SUMMARY

This chapter has discussed the role of compensation in facilitating the human resource goals of attracting, retaining, and motivating employees. The related activities of HRM professionals and compensation specialists include pay surveys, job evaluations, pricing jobs, and pay-for-performance systems. As employees' needs and desires change and as organizations experience continuing competitive, technological, economic, and legal pressures, especially with the expansion of pay equity legislation, attaining the goals of attracting, retraining, and motivating employees will become increasingly difficult. HRM professionals must work with management to develop new and innovative pay methods to meet the goals while controlling compensation costs.

REVIEW QUESTIONS

1. Why are pay surveys an important input in developing an organization's compensation policy?

2. Why is a job evaluation process the most important component of an organization's compensation policy?

3. Explain what is meant by the ratio of exchange between an employee's input and his or her compensation outcomes. Discuss the implications of this concept for an organization's compensation policy.

4. Discuss how pay can be used to motivate employees. Include discussion of the difficulties that can arise from doing so.

5. Explore the implications of pay equity legislation for an organization's compensation policy. (The law in a particular jurisdiction could be considered.)

Project Ideas

1. Have you ever experienced dissatisfaction with pay or other rewards received from an employer? Discuss your experience. Why were you dissatisfied? Describe your dissatisfaction in terms of the ratio of exchange between inputs and outcomes. With whom did you compare yourself? What could your employer have done to alleviate the inequitable situation? What did he or she do? What could you have done to resolve the inequity? What did you do?

2. Search through recent newspapers or news magazines for incidents revealing workers' dissatisfaction with pay or other rewards. Find at least three incidents related to dissatisfaction with different aspects of pay — for example, the amount of pay, the form of pay (direct versus benefits), the administration of pay (not receiving pay or other rewards due). For each incident, describe the nature of the complaint, the employees' demands, and the resolution of the situation, if any. Note the type of employee making the complaint (labour type, sex, individual or group, union or nonunion). What would be the implications for the organization of meeting the employees' demands as stated?

3. Interview a compensation manager or HRM professional who has major compensation responsibilities. Ask about pay problems he or she has encountered. How have they been handled? If a number of students do this project, half should visit unionized employers and half nonunionized. If different types of organizations are visited, a range of compensation problems should be revealed. This variety can be demonstrated to the class as a whole by each student's giving a brief oral report.

4. One major issue in compensation is whether pay rates or levels for jobs should be open or secret. Some employers feel so strongly about keep-

ing pay secret that they have policies prohibiting employees from discussing pay; in some cases, workers have been fired for talking about their pay with others. Research regarding the effects of open and secret pay has not provided definitive answers on which is the better approach. Discuss in a short report the possible pros and cons of each approach. Do not limit your discussion to the compensation area; include the implications of open and secret pay for other HRM functions, such as career planning, training and development, worker satisfaction, and so on. If several students choose this project, a debate could be arranged.

5. Analyze the impact of profit sharing on human resource practices in an organization in your local area. (If you cannot identify such an organization, contact the Profit Sharing Council of Canada for assistance. The address is 5146-A Dundas Street West, Suite 3, Etobicoke, Ontario, M9A 1C2, and the telephone number is 416-231-9438.) Describe the nature of the profit-sharing plan in which employees are included, its history, and its impact. Attempt to determine the measure the organization uses to assess the effects of profit sharing. Describe the overall HR impact of the plan.

6. If your province has legislation requiring pay equity, contact the HR manager of a local organization subject to the law and ask him or her to suggest someone who could be interviewed on that organization's experience with pay equity. Prepare a report describing the steps and people involved in the implementation of pay equity in the organization and the specific aspects of the implementation plan, including the timetable and the resulting pay levels. Also describe the reaction of the employees whose salaries were changed or not changed and the general implications of the pay equity program for human resource management. If several students pursue this project with different organizations, the class can hear reports on a variety of situations.

▶▶▶ CASES

CASE 12.1 ▶ PAY EQUITY AT *THE OTTAWA CITIZEN*

For *The Ottawa Citizen*, a large newspaper with over 900 employees and eight union contracts, the task of meeting the requirements of the Pay Equity Act of Ontario seemed monumental. We were faced with the posting of nine pay equity plans — eight for our bargaining units and one for non-union employees. These all had to be done by December 31, 1989. In hindsight the task was indeed substantial. Fortunately, with careful planning the snags were kept to a minimum and the objective was achieved on time. This article will highlight the process followed and some of the lessons learned.

Because seven of our bargaining units had no female job classes as defined by the act our primary goal was to complete a pay equity plan for the remaining bargaining unit (the Ottawa Newspaper Guild) and another for the non-union group. The Guild unit included over 400 employees in 65 separate job classes within several departments. Fifteen of these job classes were female. On the non-union side 95 job classes existed, including supervisory and mid-level management positions. Thirteen of these were female.

To start the process a new coding system was developed to identify job classes. Plans were made for ongoing communication about pay equity with management, union leaders and staff. We suggested to the Guild that there be a single steering committee to oversee the pay equity process for both union and non-union employees. This was agreed to on the condition that the evaluation of Guild jobs and non-Guild jobs be done separately and that there be no sharing of Guild data with non-Guild committee members. The eleven-member steering committee consisted of five managers, three Guild employees, the Guild's local executive officer, one non-union employee and an external consultant.

What was the role of the steering committee? Basically, this committee was responsible for meeting the requirements of the pay equity legislation. Its prime duties included:

- Communication.
- Choosing a consultant.
- The job evaluation system.
- The job questionnaire.
- The weighting of job factors.
- The final plans.

The committee agreed on the importance of communicating with management and staff to explain what pay equity was — and wasn't! Communication activities in the early stages included:

1. Information meetings for all managers and supervisors.
2. Information meetings for staff (well advertised through pay envelope inserts; voluntary but on company time).
3. Articles in the company newsletter.
4. Distribution of Pay Equity Commission literature.
5. Bulletin board postings of names and phone numbers of steering committee members.

The starting point for all information meetings was to clarify the following terms:

- Equal pay for equal work.
- Equal pay for work of equal value (pay equity).
- Employment equity.

Many people appeared to be confused about these different concepts. The meetings then covered the process to be followed during the coming months to develop our pay equity plans. Questions were encouraged throughout the presentations. In spite of substantial publicity regarding these staff information meetings on company time, only 5% of employees chose to attend. This was somewhat surprising to us. Other companies, however, have found similar limited interest in such meetings.

Because the *Citizen* did not have formal job descriptions in place, it was necessary to develop a comprehensive questionnaire to gather the essential information about each job. This questionnaire was prepared by our external consultants and refined by the steering committee. The committee had to make sure the language of the questions was appropriate for our situation and that the questions themselves were adequate to capture the necessary data for 160 different jobs.

A pilot test of the draft questionnaire was carried out on 25 jobs. Revisions were then made to reduce confusion in some questions. The final questionnaire, used for both union and non-union jobs, was a somewhat overwhelming 40-page document requiring approximately three hours to complete.

Rather than having every incumbent in a job class complete a separate questionnaire, we offered employees the chance to work together in groups of two to five to complete questionnaires. Also, in jobs which had many incumbents (for example, reporters), a few of these incumbents were invited to complete individual questionnaires in order to represent their job class. In such situations, however, letters were sent out to all members of the job class explaining what was happening and offering all those who had not been chosen the chance to fill out questionnaires if they wished to. A few employees did accept this offer.

Questionnaires were completed during working hours. A review of the completed questionnaires was carried out by the supervisors involved and, in the case of Guild jobs, by members of the Guild executive also. Any comments either group wished to make were put in writing and held for later consideration by the job evaluation committees.

A point of interest in setting up the procedures for reviewing the questionnaires was whether or not supervisors should know who had filled them out. The Guild had a concern that some employees might be somewhat inhibited in completing their questionnaires if they knew their supervisor would be seeing their answers. To alleviate this concern a simple numerical code was used so that no employee names appeared on the questionnaires themselves. This arrangement worked smoothly and helped, in the evaluation stage, to keep the focus on the jobs under consideration rather than on specific incumbents.

Three committees were set up to evaluate jobs. Two separate six-member committees, each with equal representation from management and staff, reviewed non-union and Guild jobs during the summer of 1989. The three staff members on the non-union evaluating committee were chosen by management. An attempt was made to choose people who were respected by their peers and who had a wide knowledge of jobs throughout the paper. The staff members on the evaluating committee for Guild jobs were chosen by the Guild. They, too, were knowledgeable and respected by their peers. A third committee consisting of three managers and one senior staff person was formed to evaluate management jobs.

Leadership for the three committees was provided by our outside consultant who gave training in evaluating jobs, got the process under way, and then monitored the committees' output daily by fax reports and telephone. The human resources manager served as one of the management members on all three evaluation committees to help ensure that the evaluations were consistent from committee to committee.

For most jobs the questionnaires themselves, together with the knowledge the committee members had of the jobs, provided sufficient information. For some jobs, however, the committees set up interviews with incumbents and/or their supervisors to gain additional information or to clarify what had been said in the questionnaires. A point factor system was used to evaluate each job on eleven separate elements covering the four job factors specified in the Pay Equity Act, i.e., knowledge and skills, effort, responsibility and working conditions.

The evaluation committees operated with a high level of efficiency and seriousness of purpose. There seemed to be a real desire to understand each job thoroughly and to be fair in the evaluations reached. During a typical day, between six and nine jobs were evaluated. The committees operated on a consensus basis. There was no majority rule. When disagreements arose over the points to give a particular factor in a certain job it sometimes was necessary to defer a decision pending more information and/or comparisons with other jobs yet to be evaluated. In the end, though, consensus was always reached. On a number of occasions a committee member in disagreement with the other five members would eventually sway the committee over to his or her viewpoint.

After the committees had completed their preliminary evaluations and gone through a "sore thumbing" process to identify and correct anomalies, the results were passed on to the steering committee for their review. At this point the steering committee broke into two groups — one to consider the Guild data, the other to review the non-union data. Senior management also reviewed the data thoroughly.

As a result of these reviews the evaluation committees were asked to reconsider a number of jobs. Some changes were made by the committees after further reflection. Many evaluations, however, remained unchanged.

While senior management had the right to overrule the evaluation committees' decisions for non-union jobs, in the end all evaluations as presented by the evaluation committees were accepted unchanged.

Some members of the non-union evaluation committee had expressed concerns that management might overrule some of their evaluations. They were pleased to see that this did not happen. For Guild jobs, of course, management did not have the right to change any evaluations unilaterally because the evaluations themselves were part of the negotiating process with the Guild.

Once the evaluations were in place it was time to apply a weighting scheme to the eleven elements evaluated for each job. We had anticipated choosing a weighting scheme early in the pay equity process. It turned out to be almost the last step, however, as neither management nor the Guild seemed anxious to make a decision before having the raw job evaluation data in hand.

With a computer software program we were able to look at the impact of many different weighting schemes. We ended up with almost too much data and too many choices! The Guild was given printouts of any weighting scheme they wished, together with any banding of points, i.e., the range of points within which male and female jobs classes would be considered comparable for pay equity purposes. Surprisingly, the fifteen or so weighting schemes and numerous banding arrangements experimented with did not provide significant differences in the resulting pay equity comparisons.

Two weeks before the posting deadline we were able to negotiate a final pay equity plan with the Guild and to proceed with arrangements to post all nine union and non-union plans. An issue we had been concerned about was the possibility of having to look outside the Guild for male comparators for some of the female Guild job classes. This would have meant facing the question of the acceptance of the non-union committee's evaluations by the Guild. Fortunately, this did not arise as an issue because satisfactory male comparators were found within the Guild for all female Guild job classes.

The Guild pay equity plan, incidentally, included some modest increases which went beyond the requirements of the act, which helped to maintain internal equity.

We were now at a critical point in the communication process. There were several things to be done before posting:

1. A meeting was held with all managers and staff to brief them on what was happening and to answer their questions. It was suggested that employee questions about the plans after posting should be passed on to the human resources manager. Ideally, the managers and supervisors should have been trained to answer all questions about the pay equity

plans. However, this was not practical considering the time pressures we faced.

2. A letter to all employees from our publisher was inserted in the pay envelopes. It summarized the work done on pay equity and notified non-union and Guild employees they would be receiving personal letters in a few days with further pay equity details.

3. Almost 600 personal letters were sent to non-union and Guild employees explaining how pay equity would or would not affect their pay rates. There were three different letters, each with a separate version for non-union and union employees:
   a. One to those employees in female job classes that would be getting a pay equity increase. Each letter was personally addressed and indicated the male comparator used and the amount of the pay equity increase to be given.
   b. One to those who were in female job classes that would not be getting a pay equity increase because the current rate was higher than that of the male comparator.
   c. One to those in male or gender-neutral job classes that would not be eligible, therefore, for a pay equity increase.

In the non-union area 14% of the female job classes received pay equity adjustments ranging from $0.16 to $8.06 per hour. In the Guild plan 23% of the female job classes received adjustments from $0.55 to $3.57 per hour. Overall, almost 20% of employees under these two plans received a pay equity increase. Most of the increases tended to be at the lower end of the ranges mentioned above. The largest increase, $8.06 per hour, was for a specialized job class with a single female incumbent.

Rather than wait a year to give these pay equity increases our publisher decided to give half the increase a year early, i.e., on January 1, 1990. The remainder will be given January 1, 1991.

Employee interest in the posted plans was considerable at first. There were very few questions asked, however, over the weeks that followed. In two or three cases people wanted clarification as to which pay equity job class they were in. In another case a male, the single incumbent in his Guild job class, expressed disappointment that he had not received an increase when a somewhat similar female job class had got an increase. This was a matter of internal equity rather than pay equity under the act. (Internal equity is a matter we are currently looking at both in the non-union area and in negotiations for a new Guild contract.)

Another question came from a female employee whose job class had received a pay equity increase somewhat smaller than that of another female job class. Historically, the two job classes had been perceived as being on a par. Why, she asked, was the increase less for her job class? The explanation given to her centred around a discussion about each of the eleven job elements considered by the evaluation committee to help her understand that the two jobs were not, in fact, on a par in all eleven areas.

On reflection, there is little we would have changed in the process we followed. No doubt a simpler, shorter questionnaire would have been appreciated by many employees! The success of our implementation, I would say, hinged on our open and frequent communication (even in the face of seeming indifference by many staff members), detailed planning of every step (with the help of a super-organized staff assistant), and the careful selection of committee members, i.e., people who could be counted on to get the job done and who would have the confidence and respect of their peers.

The Pay Equity Act, while not perfect, did force us to focus on an issue that needed addressing. We uncovered some female jobs that had been clearly underpaid relative to other jobs of comparable worth. These inequities are being corrected. Our goal is to be fair and equitable in our pay practices. The process to achieve this is ever ongoing!

Source: Ross Dixon, human resources manager, *The Ottawa Citizen*, "Pay Equity at *The Ottawa Citizen*," *Pay Equity Guide*, vol. 3, no. 10 (October 1990), pp. 83, 87–90. Reprinted with the permission of the author and the publisher.

TASKS AND QUESTIONS

1. Discuss the lessons for human resource professionals from the implementation of pay equity at *The Ottawa Citizen*.

2. How could the HR department have prevented questions such as that from a female employee whose job class had received a pay equity increase somewhat smaller than that of another female job class?

CASE 12.2 ▸ SALARY PROGRESSION AT SHELL CANADA'S SARNIA CHEMICAL PLANT

In the Sarnia chemical plant of Shell Canada, the salary progression is based on demonstrated knowledge and skill rather than on specific tasks being performed. This includes process operating areas, craft skills, laboratory and warehousing.

As set out in the employee *Good Work Practices Guidebook*, dated January 1992, the plant has been divided into ten process areas, each with a particular job knowledge cluster (JKC). An individual progresses through the compensation system in twelve phases. The skill and experience required in a phase depend on the nature of the particular process. Table 1 provides an example of a regular progression for a new team member. Not shown in the table is a separate system of progression for lab team members. Also included in the table is the schedule of basic monthly salaries for each phase as set out in the collective agreement between Shell Products Canada Limited (Sarnia Chem-

TABLE 1

PROGRESSION SYSTEM BY PHASE	MONTHLY SALARIES FROM FEBRUARY 1, 1993	EQUIVALENT HOURLY SALARY RATE
1. Entry	$2762	$17.03
2. Basic A and 18 weeks' service	2856	17.61
3. 1 Process JKC and Basic B 1–2	2986	18.41
4. 2 Process JKCs and Basic B3–5	3118	19.22
5. 1 Other skill JKC + 24 months in that other skill + all Basic B	3250	20.04
6. 3 Process JKCs	3383	20.86
7. 4 Process JKCs	3509	21.63
8. 2 Other Skill JKCs + additional 24 months after completion of JKC-1	3677	22.67
9. 5 Process JKCs	3841	23.68
10. 5 Process JKCs + 1 year minimum on 5th Process JKC	3967	24.46
11. 6 Process JKCs	4102	25.29
12. 6 Process JKCs + year minimum on 6th Process JKC and 6 years' minimum employment	4236	26.12

Note 1: All persons being paid at a rate higher than that to which they are entitled according to the progression qualifications will be expected to complete those qualifications before further increases are forthcoming.

Note 2: The top rate in our plant is through the acquisition of Basics, 6 Process JKCs and 2 Other Skill JKCs. It is expected, however, that the opportunity will exist for team members at the top rate to train on and learn all the process areas in the plant in time.

Source: Shell Canada Products Limited, Sarnia Chemical Plant, *Good Work Practices Guidebook*, January 1992, section 1, p. 7; Agreement between Shell Canada Products Limited (Sarnia Chemical Plant) and the Energy and Chemical Workers' Union, Local 800, effective February 1, 1992, to January 31, 1994, Schedule "A."

ical Plant) and the Energy and Chemical Workers' Union, Local 800, February 1, 1992, to January 31, 1994.

A phase level increase can be obtained by demonstration of knowledge and skill in the JKC area. The team member must, however, spend twelve consecutive months in the area even if qualified sooner. Six years is the minimum time to the top rate.

The JKCs have been grouped into sections, the intent being that a team member who begins his process training in a particular section will complete all the clusters in that section before moving to another. Exceptions may have to be made, depending on team requirements. If because of circumstances beyond a team member's control (for example, team member attrition), a change of this nature must be made, and the team member is not meeting his progression timetable, accommodation is made on an individual basis. Guidelines have been developed to handle these special situations.

Shell introduced this compensation system when the chemical plant was opened in 1979, but the planning for the system began 1975. The principle for payment was developed with the union and is set out in the foreword to the collective agreement. The compensation system is part of the participative management approach at the chemical plant. A statement of that approach, Revision 1, dated August 1991, contains the following under the heading 'Philosophy':

1. Participative management is a style of leadership that encourages maximum participation and involvement by employees in decisions that affect their working lives.

2. Management has the ultimate accountability and responsibility for plant operations and activities, but shares power with the organization through participative management. Participative management is most effective when power is shared.

3. Participative management is not an abdication of managerial responsibility for the business.

4. Participative management implies taking risks and learning from failures.

5. Participative management should evolve toward higher levels of employee involvement, while still recognizing that the appropriate degree of involvement is dependent on the circumstances of the situation.

Guidance for the application of the principle is provided in the *Good Work Practices Guidebook*.

In addition to the pay for skill, the successful implementation and sustenance of the Shell plant's organizational design over a period of almost a decade and a half is based on several support systems. These include effective employee recruitment, role clarification, relevant social skills training, and development of mechanisms for self-management. There is a co-ordinator within each of the work teams who is a carefully chosen facilitator and who acts as a link between organized labour and management. In addition, there is a Team Norm Review Board (TNRB) consisting of one representative from each team, one team co-ordinator, one operations manager, the union vice-president, and a representative from human resources.

The TNRB edits, interprets, and disseminates norms throughout the plant, suggests modifications, and receives recommendations from teams. This board operates by "consensus to support," with each member having veto power. All teams meet regularly to review and assess progress. Minutes of all sessions are distributed to everyone in the plant. Any issues not resolved at the team level are referred to the TNRB, management, or the union/management committee. The design is never complete, and since the opening of the plant in 1979, numerous modifications of the original design have been implemented.

Source: Based on Peter P. Kingyens, "Shell Canada Products Limited, Sarnia Manufacturing Centre Chemical Plant," presented at the Work in America Institute, Productivity Forum Symposium, *New Roles for Unions*, New York City, January 15, 1992 (Scarsdale, NY: Work in America Institute, 1992); *Good Work Practices Guidebook*, Shell Canada Products Limited, Sarnia Chemical Plant, January 1992; Norm Halpern, "Novel Organization Working at Shell Canada Facility," *Oil and Gas Journal Report*, March 25, 1985, pp. 89–90, 93; and Agreement between Shell Canada Products Limited (Sarnia Chemical Plant) and the Energy and Chemical Workers' Union, Local 800, effective February 1, 1992, to January 31, 1994. The authors would like to thank Peter P. Kingyens, President, Energy and Chemical Workers' Union, Local 800, for providing the most recent material on Shell Canada's Sarnia Chemical Plant.

TASKS AND QUESTIONS

1. Shell Canada's Sarnia Chemical Plant has had a system of compensation based on acquired skill since 1979. Discuss possible reasons why most organizations have not followed this approach to compensation, even though both Shell and the Energy and Chemical Workers' Union are pleased with the results.

2. Discuss how the Team Norm Review Board complements the pay-for-skill approach to compensation in enhancing productivity.

NOTES

1. Nan Weiner, "How to Build Pay Equity into Your Overall Compensation System," *Pay Equity Guide*, vol. 3, no. 10 (October 1990), p. 83.

2. For a detailed examination of the principles of compensation, see George T. Milkovich and Jerry M. Newman, *Compensation* (Homewood, Ill.: Richard D. Irwin, 1990).

3. R.M. Steers, *Organizational Effectiveness: A Behavioral View* (Santa Monica, Calif.: Goodyear Publishing Co., Inc., 1977), p. 5.

4. The following articles are all from *Industrial and Labor Relations Review*, vol. 43, no. 3 (February 1990, special issue): Jonathan S. Leonard, "Executive Pay and Firm Performance," pp. 13-S–29-S; Robert Gibbons and Kevin J. Murphy,

"Relative Performance Evaluation for Chief Executive Officers," pp. 30-S–51-S; John M. Abowd, "Does Performance-Based Managerial Compensation Affect Corporate Performance?" pp. 52-S–73-S; Ronald G. Ehrenberg and Michael L. Bognanno, "The Incentive Effects of Tournaments Revisited: Evidence from the European PGA Tour," pp. 74-S–88-S; Beth J. Asch, "Do Incentives Matter? The Case of Navy Recruiters," pp. 89-S–106-S; Lawrence M. Kahn and Peter D. Sherer, "Contingent Pay and Managerial Performance," pp. 107-S–102-S; and Daniel S. Hamermesh, "Shirking or Productive Schmoozing: Wages and the Allocation of Times at Work," pp. 121-S–133-S.

5. E.E. Lawler III, "The Strategic Design of Reward Systems," in R.S. Schuler and S.A. Youngblood, *Readings in Personnel and Human Resource Management*, 2nd ed. (St. Paul, Minn.: West Publishing, 1984), pp. 253–69.

6. S.L. Rynes and G.T. Milkovich, "Wage Surveys: Dispelling Some Myths About the 'Market Wage'," *Personnel Psychology*, vol. 39 (1986), pp. 71–90.

7. B.R. Ellig, "Salary Surveys: Design to Application," *The Personnel Administrator*, vol. 22, no. 8 (1977), pp. 41–48.

8. Labour Canada, *Collective Bargaining Information Sources* (Ottawa: Supply and Services Canada, 1988 and periodic updatings), section 1.

9. J.S. Adams, "Inequity in Social Exchange," in L. Berkowitz, ed., *Advances in Experimental Social Psychology*, vol. 2 (New York: Academic Press, 1965).

10. Labour Canada, *Employment Standards Legislation in Canada*, 1991 ed. (Ottawa: Supply and Services Canada, 1991), p. 48.

11. D.W. Belcher, *Compensation Administration* (Englewood Cliffs, NJ.: Prentice-Hall, 1974), p. 136.

12. E.E. Lawler III, "The New Pay," in R.M. Fulmer, *New Management* (New York: Macmillan, 1987).

13. *Classification and Selection Standard for the Personnel Administration Group* (Ottawa: Information Canada, 1975).

14. Pay Equity Commission, *How to Do Pay Equity Job Comparisons* (Toronto, March 1989), p. 33.

15. Milkovich and Newman, *Compensation*, p. 106.

16. Pay Equity Commission, *How to Do Pay Equity Job Comparisons*, p. 35.

17. Pay Equity Commission, *How to Do Pay Equity Job Comparisons*, p. 34.

18. L.J. Nozzolillo, "The Classification and Pay System in the Public Service of Canada," *The Labour Gazette*, May 1976, p. 262.

19. Pay Equity Commission, *How to Do Pay Equity Job Comparisons*, p. 35.

20. Pay Equity Commission, *How to Do Pay Equity Job Comparisons*, p. 35.

21. American Society of Personnel Administration/American Compensation Association, *Elements of Sound Base Pay Administration* (Scottsdale, Ariz.: American Compensation Association, and Alexandria, Va.: ASPA, 1981).

22. ASPA/ACA, *Elements of Sound Base Pay Administration*, p. 13.

23. Noah M. Meltz with Jill Marzetti, *The Shortage of Registered Nurses: An Analysis in a Labour Market Context* (Toronto: Registered Nurses Association of Ontario, 1988).
24. Ontario Nurses Association, *The ONA News*, vol. 18, no. 3 (March 1991).
25. Judith Lendvay-Zwickl, *Compensation Planning Outlook 1990* (Ottawa: Conference Board of Canada, 1989), p. 3.
26. "MBAs Look at Their World," *MBA* July-August 1977.
27. N.B. Winstanley, "Are Merit Increases Really Effective?" *The Personnel Administrator*, April 1982, pp. 37–41.
28. Patricia L. Booth, *Strategic Rewards Management: The Variable Approach to Pay* (Ottawa: Conference Board of Canada, 1990), p. 2.
29. Booth, *Strategic Rewards Management*, p. 2.
30. W.D. Wood and Pradeep Kumar, eds., *The Current Industrial Relations Scene in Canada, 1981* (Kingston, Ont.: Industrial Relations Centre, Queen's University, 1981), p. 352; and David Arrowsmith and Melanie Courchene, *The Current Industrial Relations Scene in Canada: Collective Bargaining Reference Tables* (Kingston, Ont.: Industrial Relations Centre, Queen's University, 1989), p. 38.
31. Booth, *Strategic Rewards Management*, p. vi.
32. Abowd, "Does Performance-Based Managerial Compensation Affect Corporate Performance?"
33. Towers Perrin, *Achieving Results Through Sharing: Group Incentive Program Survey Report* (Toronto, 1990), pp. 1–4.
34. Booth, *Strategic Rewards Management*, pp. 2–3.
35. *Compensation Planning Outlook 1990*, p. 5.
36. B.E. Moore, *A Plant-Wide Productivity Plan in Action: Three Years of Experience with the Scanlon Plan* (Washington, DC: National Center for Productivity and Quality of Working Life, 1975).
37. T.H. Patten, Jr., *Pay: Employee Compensation and Incentive Plans* (New York: The Free Press, 1977).
38. Gordon Betchaman, Keith Newton, and Joanne Godin, eds., *Two Steps Forward: Human Resource Management in a High-Tech World*, Economic Council of Canada (Ottawa: Supply and Services Canada, 1990).
39. Martin Weitzman, *The Share Economy* (Cambridge, Mass.: Harvard University Press, 1984).
40. *Compensation Planning Outlook 1990*, p. 5.
41. D. Nightingale, "Profit Sharing: New Nectar for the Worker Bees," *The Canadian Business Review*, Spring 1984, pp. 11–14.
42. D. Nightingale, *Workplace Democracy* (Toronto: University of Toronto Press, 1982), pp. 159–60.

43. Nightingale, *Workplace Democracy*, pp. 159–60.
44. Harry C. Katz and Noah M. Meltz, "Profit Sharing and Auto Workers' Earnings: U.S. versus Canada," *Relations Industrielles/Industrial Relations*, vol. 46, no. 3 (1991), pp. 515–30.
45. James Chelius and Robert S. Smith, "Profit Sharing and Employment Stability," *Industrial and Labor Relations Review*, vol. 43, no. 3 (February 1990, special issue), pp. 256-S–73-S.
46. R.W. Merry, "Labor Letter," *The Wall Street Journal*, March 21, 1978.
47. Kenneth A. Kovach and Peter E. Millspaugh, "Comparable Worth: Canada Legislates Pay Equity," *Academy of Management Executive*, vol. 4, no. 2 (1990), pp. 92–101.
48. We are indebted to Murray C. Lapp, director, Review Services, Ontario Pay Equity Commission, for his very helpful comments on this section.
49. Pay Equity Commission, *How to Do Pay Equity Job Comparisons*, p. 45.
50. Nan Weiner, "Proxy Comparison to Be Applied to Ontario Public Sector," *Pay Equity Guide*, vol. 4, no. 2 (February 1991), pp. 9, 12–13.
51. "What Should Employers Know about the Pay Equity Complaints Procedure?" *Pay Equity Guide*, vol. 3, no. 5 (May 1990), p. 39.
52. "Public Sector Pay Equity Spreads across Canada," *Pay Equity Guide*, vol. 4, no. 2 (February 1991), p. 9.
53. For example, the Pay Equity Commission of Ontario issues a newsletter, *Pay Equity Implementation Series*, in addition to guidebooks. *The Pay Equity Guide*, published monthly by Pay Trends Inc., of Toronto, features the latest developments in legislation and practice.
    Two recent studies are: Nan Weiner and Morley Gunderson, *Pay Equity: Issues, Options and Experiences* (Ottawa: Supply and Services Canada, 1990); and David W. Conklin and Paul Bergman, *Pay Equity in Ontario: A Manager's Guide* (Halifax: The Institute for Research on Public Policy and the National Centre for Management Research and Development, The University of Western Ontario, 1990).
54. CLV Reports, *Facts and Trends in Labour Relations*, 1985.
55. CLV Reports, *Facts and Trends in Labour Relations*, February 3, 1986.
56. D. Wessel, "Split Personality," *Wall Street Journal*, October 14, 1985.
57. *Compflash: New Developments in Compensation and Benefits* (American Management Association, July 1990), p. 2.
58. E.E. Lawler III, "Workers Can Set Their Own Wages—Responsibly," *Psychology Today*, February 1977, pp. 109–12.
59. Margot Gibb-Clark, "Firms Tend to Favour Bonus over a Raise," *The Globe and Mail*, August 24, 1987.
60. Katz and Meltz, "Profit Sharing and Auto Workers' Earnings."
61. Peter V. Leblanc, "Fast Forward," © American Compensation Association (ACA), 1990.

Suggestions for Further Reading

- John M. Abowd. "Does Performance-Based Managerial Compensation Affect Corporate Performance?" *Industrial and Labor Relations Review*, vol. 43, no. 3 (February 1990) special issue, pp. 52-S–73-S.
- David Arrowsmith and Melanie Courchene. *The Current Industrial Relations Scene in Canada: Collective Bargaining Reference Tables*. Kingston, Ont.: Industrial Relations Centre, Queen's University, 1989.
- Patricia L. Booth. *Strategic Rewards Management: The Variable Approach to Pay*. Ottawa: Conference Board of Canada, 1990.
- James Chelius and Robert S. Smith. "Profit Sharing and Employment Stability." *Industrial and Labor Relations Review*, vol. 43, no. 3, (February 1990, special issue), pp. 256-S–73-S.
- David W. Conklin and Paul Bergman. *Pay Equity in Ontario: A Manager's Guide*. Halifax: The Institute for Research on Public Policy and the National Centre for Management Research and Development, The University of Western Ontario, 1990.
- C.H. Fay and R.W. Beatter, eds. *The Compensation Sourcebook*. Amherst, Mass.: Human Resource Development Press, 1988.
- *Industrial and Labor Relations Review*, vol. 43, no. 3 (February 1990), Special issue, "Do compensation policies matter?" See, for example, articles by Abowd and by Chelius and Smith, noted here.
- Pradeep Kumar, David Arrowsmith, and Mary Lou Coates. *The Current Industrial Relations Scene in Canada, Canadian Labour Relations: An Information Manual*. Kingston, Ont.: Industrial Relations Centre, Queen's University, 1991.
- Judith Lendvay-Zwickl. *Compensation Planning Outlook 1990*. Ottawa: Conference Board of Canada, 1989. See also subsequent annual editions.
- George T. Milkovich and Jerry M. Newman. *Compensation*. Homewood, Ill.: Richard D. Irwin, 1990.
- Pay Equity Commission. *How to Do Pay Equity Job Comparisons*. Toronto: March 1989.
- *Pay Equity Guide*. A monthly published by Pay Trends Inc., Toronto. The August 1991 issue includes a lead article titled "Three Emerging Challenges in Bargaining with Unions."
- Nan Weiner and Morley Gunderson. *Pay Equity Issues, Options and Experiences*. Ottawa: Supply and Services Canada, 1990.

CHAPTER 13

BENEFITS

- GROWTH OF EMPLOYEE BENEFITS
- HOW BENEFITS CONTRIBUTE TO ORGANIZATIONAL EFFECTIVENESS
- RELATION TO OTHER HRM FUNCTIONS
- BENEFITS AND THE HRM PROFESSIONAL
- CATEGORIES OF BENEFITS AND TYPES OF PROTECTION
- UNIVERSAL BENEFITS
- MANDATORY BENEFITS
- DISCRETIONARY BENEFITS FOR EMPLOYEE PROTECTION
- HOLIDAY AND VACATION PAY
- EMPLOYEE SERVICE BENEFITS
- CAFETERIA BENEFITS: AN INDIVIDUALIZED APPROACH
- HRM IN ACTION ▶ THE EVOLUTIONARY WAY TO FLEXIBLE BENEFITS
- CONTROLLING BENEFIT COSTS
- ISSUES IN THE BENEFITS AREA
- SUMMARY
- REVIEW QUESTIONS
- PROJECT IDEAS
- CASE 13.1 ▶ INDEXED PENSIONS AT INCO
- CASE 13.2 ▶ ENHANCING PRODUCTIVITY THROUGH ON-SITE CHILD CARE
- NOTES
- SUGGESTIONS FOR FURTHER READING

LEAH HOLSTEIN HAS BEEN A RESEARCH CHEMIST AT Monsanto Canada for the past six years. She has never considered leaving Monsanto because she enjoys her work, has opportunities for growth and advancement, and feels she is compensated fairly. Besides an ample pay cheque, Holstein receives a generous benefit package, including paid vacations and holidays, supplemental medical benefits, dental assistance, life insurance, a pension plan, and a tuition payment program. Career development is also included as a benefit in Monsanto's package.

Holstein is unusual in one sense: she understands and appreciates the value of the wide range of benefits provided by her employer. Most employees don't, as evidenced by a survey of 850 employees that revealed that only 5 percent had any idea how large a proportion of company payroll went to pay for their benefits.[1] An important function of HRM professionals and benefits specialists is to help employees understand and appreciate the value of their benefit packages. Such understanding is necessary if organizations are to achieve maximum benefit from the benefits they offer.

In addressing benefits as an HRM area, this chapter deals with five categories: (1) those provided directly by government; (2) those mandated by federal and provincial law for total or partial provision by employers; (3) those provided at an employer's discretion; (4) those providing pay for time not worked; and (5) those providing employees with a variety of services. Within certain constraints, each organization chooses from among the wide range of benefits available to assemble a benefit package uniquely its own.

GROWTH OF EMPLOYEE BENEFITS

Benefits first gained popularity during World War II when the imposition of wage ceilings made it necessary for employers to find alternative means of attracting, rewarding, and retaining employees. Since that time, the scope and importance of benefits have grown tremendously. According to data from private surveys (see Table 13.1), in 1989 the average Canadian employer's outlay on fringe benefits was 33.5 percent of direct labour costs; it had been 15.1 percent in 1953.[2] This increase reflected particular growth in paid time off (vacations, holidays, coffee breaks, and rest periods), to 13.9 percent of the total, and in pension and welfare plans, to 8.6 percent. There was also growth in the proportion attributed to payments required by law (5.3 percent) and to such things as bonuses and profit sharing (2.9 percent). The findings of an earlier Statistics Canada survey were similar: it set the costs of benefits in 1978 at 34 percent of the basic pay for regular work.[3] Table 13.1 also shows that total employee benefit costs by industry vary from a low of 25.6 percent in the chemicals industry to a high of 41.6 percent in the petroleum pipeline industry.

The growth of benefits has two major causes. First, the growth of unions and collective agreements has spurred benefit expansion. Second, as we shall

TABLE 13.1

Employee Benefit Costs by Type of Benefit and Major Industry Group in Canada, 1953–1989

	\multicolumn{6}{c}{PERCENTAGE OF GROSS PAYROLL}
	1953	1961	1971	1984	1986	1989
Total[a]	15.1	22.8	29.0	32.5	36.3	33.5
Paid Absence	5.9	11.6	14.6	14.9	15.2	13.9
Vacation	3.4	4.5	5.5	6.4	6.5	6.0
Holidays	2.4	2.8	3.5	3.8	3.7	3.6
Rest periods	na	3.4	4.2	3.9	3.9	3.6
Bereavement, jury duty	na	0.1	0.1	0.1	0.2	0.2
Other	0.1	0.8	1.2	0.8	0.8	0.5

TABLE 13.1 *(continued)*

	\multicolumn{6}{c}{PERCENTAGE OF GROSS PAYROLL}
	1953	1961	1971	1984	1986	1989
Payments Required by Law	1.5	3.0	2.3	4.4	5.5	5.3
Unemployment Insurance	0.8	0.8	0.6	2.1	2.3	2.3
Workers' Compensation	0.7	0.7	0.6	1.2	2.0	1.6
C/QPP			1.1	1.2	1.3	1.4
Payments for Pension/Welfare and Related	5.5	7.2	9.8	10.5	11.0	9.9
Pension plans	4.0	4.3	3.8	4.1	4.1	3.6
Welfare plans	1.4	2.2	5.4	5.2	5.4	5.0
Other (e.g., severance)	0.1	0.7	0.6	1.1	1.5	1.3
Bonuses and Profit Sharing	1.7	1.3	1.3	1.7	3.1	2.9
Other Non-Cash Benefits	0.5	1.2	1.1	1.0	1.4	1.5
Manufacturing	14.3	23.4	29.6	33.8	35.5	32.2
Food, beverage, tobacco	18.0	27.2	33.0	35.2	39.3	35.6
Textile, footwear	13.7	18.5	24.6	31.7	26.0	29.4
Pulp, paper	12.4	20.8	27.5	37.9	36.0	35.4
Primary metals, fabrication	12.1	18.2	31.5	35.7	45.3	30.2
Petroleum, pipeline	19.0	25.9	26.7	37.1	38.6	41.6
Chemicals, allied	13.0	26.0	36.6	33.3	43.6	25.6
Others	13.6	23.5	27.6	34.0	29.9	30.3
Non-Manufacturing	17.5	26.5	28.4	31.3	37.0	34.6
Mining	na	na	na	33.5	39.6	37.8
Construction	na	na	na	26.8	39.1	28.6
Utilities	18.8	28.2	32.7	38.0	36.0	34.0
Transportation	11.4	23.8	25.8	32.5	39.7	36.5
Trade	16.5	20.6	na	27.1	33.7	31.4
Finance, insurance	24.0	28.9	30.2	31.6	31.5	34.7
Hospitals	na	na	24.3	28.5	32.2	34.0
Education	na	na	na	29.8	38.0	37.8
Government	na	na	na	31.0	33.0	34.8
Municipalities	na	na	29.1	33.1	37.6	35.1
Other	9.9	na	30.6	32.0	46.7	36.1

[a] Excludes Old Age Security expenditures except in 1953 survey.
Note: This is a biennial survey.

Source: Peat, Marwick, Stevenson and Kellogg, *Employee Benefit Costs in Canada*, Toronto, selected annual reports. Reprinted with permission.

see in the next section, certain benefits have inherent cost advantages to the organization. Moreover, some benefits provide forms of compensation that are not taxable to employees; recent changes in the tax laws have reduced some of these possibilities, but a number remain.

How Benefits Contribute to Organizational Effectiveness

Benefits contribute to organizational effectiveness by

1. Helping to attract and retain employees.
2. Controlling costs by making an organization's compensation dollars go farther.
3. Enhancing an organization's image as a caring employer.

Attracting and Retaining Employees

Most organizations use benefits as they do direct compensation to attract and retain a qualified work force. Scant research evidence exists, however, to support the view that benefits are useful in achieving this purpose. In fact, several investigations of pensions and turnover in the United States found very little relationship between them.[4] On the other hand, some organizations have been able to motivate their employees by providing unusual benefits, such as wilderness excursions and one-day courses on personal financial planning (see Exhibit 13.1).

The need to provide an attractive benefit package stems largely from an organization's need to remain competitive. Many employers find that they must frequently add to their benefit packages in order to remain competitive. Also, "pattern bargaining," in which a single large union negotiates a contract with a major employer and then uses it as a model for other employers, tends to make benefits proliferate. For example, indexed pension plans are an increasingly common demand of employees and their unions.

Unlike direct pay, benefits are rarely used to motivate employees to desirable work behaviour and performance. In order for benefits to be used as motivators, they must be contingent upon certain levels of job performance or work behaviour. But benefits are generally provided to all employees as a condition of employment, without regard to level of performance or contribution to the organization. (Exceptions are some kinds of benefits provided executives in lieu of increases in direct compensation and some of the types of nonpay incentives described in Exhibit 13.1.)

Benefits that are perceived as inadequate can be a source of dissatisfaction, contributing to poor job performance and possible turnover. One waitress, for example, was upset when she learned that her five-day absence from work because of illness had cost her two paid vacation days. The employee was eligible for ten "sick days," but the employer's policy was that the first two days of any absence had to be covered by accrued vacation days unless hospitalization occurred on the first day of absence. This policy, which was designed to reduce abuse of sick pay benefits, provoked such negative feelings in the employee that she left to take a position in a restaurant with a more lenient sick pay policy.

EXHIBIT 13.1
Benefits as Employee Motivators

It didn't surprise the employees of Drexis Inc. to find themselves gathered around a 2½-metre topiary of Mickey Mouse near the entrance to Disney's Tomorrowland one morning last year. After all, working for Drexis often resembles living in never-never land. Founder Drew McDougall, 33, wants Drexis to be the largest computer rental firm in North America, and he needs employees to perform with almost superhuman loyalty and gusto right through frequent 14-hour days and weekends. In return, he rewards them, not only in salary and benefits but in imaginative perks.

Like many other small, fast-growing companies, Drexis has, in addition to the usual array of employee benefits, a share-ownership plan, a profit-sharing plan and frequent barbecues on the patio of the company's downtown Toronto head office. But in 1987, McDougall issued a challenge to his 12 employees: If they could increase Drexis's sales over the previous year by 100%, McDougall would take them, along with their spouses and children, to Disney World in Florida. The four-year-old company's sales proceeded to jump to $1.1 million from $437 000 the previous year. Not a bad return on the $10 000 that McDougall spent on the junket.

If you have yet to see such show-biz tactics, they may be on the way. The nature of compensation is changing and companies of all sizes want more bang for their buck. Instead of stuffing an extra $50 into an employee's pay envelope, executives are racking their brains to come up with splashy new hoopla to reward staff, boost morale and increase sales.

Geoff Genovese, president of Incentive Design Co. in Toronto, employs a staff of 50 people who do nothing but organize such programs for medium-sized and large companies. With the economy slowing down, Genovese says his business has never been better.

Companies that might spend $1 million on advertising in a strong economy are taking a portion of their advertising budgets and plowing the money into incentive programs. "An advertising program is a fixed expense," says Genovese, whose company's sales reached $15 million last year. "If you don't reach your sales target, you still have to pay. Smart companies take that fixed expense and turn it into a variable expense. If your sales staff reaches its goals, you spend half a million dollars to reward them. If they don't, you still might spend $100 000 on promotion. But the rest goes to the bottom line."

For tax reasons, many companies try to combine business with pleasure. In Hong Kong, for example, Pitney Bowes held several motivational sessions and product launches.

The best perks reward the companies that offer them as well as their employees. Ron Estey, president of Avatar Communications Inc. in Mississauga, Ont., recently spent about $12 000 to take his 12 employees on a weeklong Outward Bound excursion into the wilderness. "It was a way to reward and recognize our employees," says Estey. "It gave them a sense of their importance to the company. But there was also a clear motivational component to the trip, involving team building and developing an understanding of group processes."

EXHIBIT 13.1 *(continued)*

Some companies choose more pragmatic ways to pat employees on the back. Luscar Ltd., a 75-year-old mining company based in Edmonton, provides its 1200 employees with personal financial planning services. Developed by Luscar and Royal Trust, the program includes a one-day course on reducing taxes, increasing savings and planning for retirement. More than half the company's employees and over 300 spouses have participated. "It's been really well received," says Ken Meen, manager of organization and development.

Larger companies still offer more conventional perks as well, such as special benefit plans and club memberships. But even at this level, perks are getting jazzier. Some firms offer sabbaticals of several months, encouraging executives to visit companies in other countries and allowing them to choose the way they spend their time rather than dictating an itinerary. It's not a vacation, but it rejuvenates the executives and expands their intellectual horizons as well. As more corporations sponsor arts programs, there's also a growing trend toward company-paid outings to the ballet or symphony for employees and their spouses.

Smaller companies with less cash to toss around have to use more imagination.

McDougall is now one of the many employers who pays a masseuse about $25 a half-hour to visit Drexis's offices and give each employee a shoulder massage. Afterwards, he holds an informal meeting, with hamburgers and hot dogs, to discuss the company's progress. "It's money well spent," he says. "You couldn't get the same response by giving someone $30." But while a perk may cast the company that awards it in an altruistic light, the company usually stands to gain more than its employees. "If you ask most employees what they'd rather have, 99% would say the cash," observes Genovese. But cash flows like water, and few people remember where it comes from. A company gets far more mileage from a trip to Switzerland or a night at the ballet. "Give them the cash," says Genovese, "and they'll just pay off their Visa like everybody else."

Source: Bruce McDougall, "Perks with Pizzazz," *Report on Business Magazine, The Globe and Mail*, June 1990, pp. 77–79. Reprinted with the permission of the author.

This example is extreme: most employees do not terminate simply because they are dissatisfied with their benefit package. However, it does illustrate the importance of maintaining benefit programs and policies that employees perceive as adequate and desirable. Employees' out-of-pocket costs for benefit programs is also important. A recent study found that increasing the cost of benefits borne by employees lowered the level of benefits satisfaction.[5]

COST SAVINGS

A second purpose served by benefits relates to cost control. Both employer and employee gain when a proportion of the organization's compensation dollars is allocated to benefits. The major advantage is that payments for benefits are sometimes tax-deductible for the employer but the benefits are not taxable income to the employee.

A further cost advantage is an economy of scale. An organization can provide its employees with certain benefits that might otherwise have to be purchased out of their take-home pay at a higher cost to them than to the organization. For example, an organization can purchase life, disability, and supplementary health insurance at reduced group rates, whereas an individual would pay more for this protection. Thus, an organization's compensation dollars can go farther in terms of what an employee receives when a certain percentage is set aside for benefits. Of course, insurance protection provided by an employer out of available compensation funds is a bargain for the employee only if he or she values and desires the protection.

This points up one disadvantage of employee benefits: inasmuch as employees do not have a say in selecting their individual benefits, benefits can be regarded as a forced allocation of their income. Given the option, the employee might not have chosen to spend that amount in the prescribed manner, preferring to allocate the cash in a different way. Life insurance is a good example. In many instances, an unmarried employee has no need for life insurance yet must accept it as part of the total compensation. Pension funds are another example. Though it is generally agreed that individuals should provide for their own retirement, they vary widely in the relative weights they assign to current income and future security. Because of the wide variation in the benefits employees want, some companies are giving them choices (flexible benefits), as discussed later in the chapter.

THE ORGANIZATION'S IMAGE

Benefits also serve to enhance an organization's image as a caring employer, concerned with the welfare of its employees, an image that can be very useful in recruiting. Benefits are essentially a means of providing for certain needs of employees and protecting them against certain risks. Though an employer's motives for providing benefits may not be entirely altruistic or humanitarian, they can at least be regarded as an exercise in enlightened self-interest: that is, in pursuing the organization's own best economic interests, the employer also accomplishes something which is of benefit to others and to society in general.

RELATION TO OTHER HRM FUNCTIONS

The relationship of benefits to other HRM functions is portrayed in Figure 13.1. The benefits area is related in varying ways to compensation, recruiting, orientation, and labour relations.

FIGURE 13.1
Benefits: Relation to Other HRM Functions

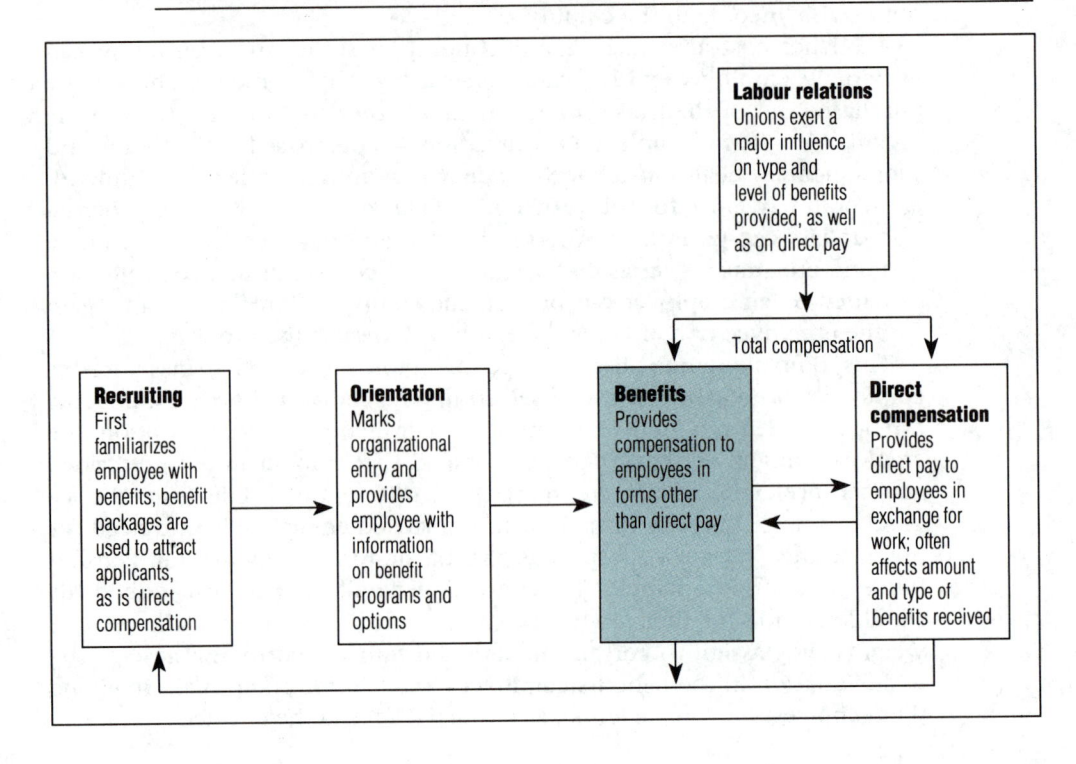

Labour relations
Unions exert a major influence on type and level of benefits provided, as well as on direct pay

Total compensation

Recruiting
First familiarizes employee with benefits; benefit packages are used to attract applicants, as is direct compensation

Orientation
Marks organizational entry and provides employee with information on benefit programs and options

Benefits
Provides compensation to employees in forms other than direct pay

Direct compensation
Provides direct pay to employees in exchange for work; often affects amount and type of benefits received

DIRECT COMPENSATION

Since benefits are a form of compensation, benefits as an HRM function is closely related to the direct compensation function. The proportion of total compensation spent on benefits as opposed to wages and salaries is determined by the employer. The typical range among industries is 26 to 42 percent.[6] Like direct pay, benefits are usually received only after organizational entry and some amount of time on the job. However, some benefits, such as relocation expenses, are commonly provided before organizational entry.

RECRUITING

An employee generally first gains familiarity with an employer's benefit package during the recruiting process. There is very little research examining the influence of benefits on an employee's decision to join an organization, but it is generally believed that employers must offer packages competitive with those of their competitors in the labour market if they are to be successful in recruiting qualified applicants.

ORIENTATION

Company benefits, including those options that require employees' decisions and signatures, are explained in greater detail during orientation sessions, which are usually held on the first day at work or shortly thereafter. Presentations by benefits specialists are quite common at this time. Although an orientation session may be a convenient time to acquaint employees with their benefit programs and options, it may not be the best time to do so. Research has shown that employees' concerns at this time focus mainly on what is expected of them and whether they will be able to perform successfully.[7] For this reason, some organizations schedule separate orientation sessions, dealing specifically with benefits, at a somewhat later date.

LABOUR RELATIONS

Unions exert a major influence on the type and level of benefits an employer provides. Benefits are as important an area of labour–management negotiations as are wages. The addition of particular benefits, such as a dental care plan or an extra holiday, can be the key to settling a collective agreement. After a one-week strike in the fall of 1990, Ford of Canada signed a three-year agreement with the Canadian Auto Workers (CAW) that included $100 million for worker security, more paid time off (including the development of three four-day weekends, eight hours added to the vacation schedule, and a vacation with families), health care improvements (increased insurance coverage for vision care, chronic care, and dental care), and the establishment of a social justice fund to assist such efforts as food banks and relief in time of national disasters.[8] This agreement became the basis for CAW contracts with General Motors and Chrysler.

BENEFITS AND THE HRM PROFESSIONAL

Many medium-sized and large organizations employ benefits specialists to handle the unique problems of the benefits area. Exhibit 13.2 is an example of a recruitment ad for a compensation and benefits manager, a particular kind of benefits specialist. It is instructive to note that this ad seeks to attract applicants by offering "an attractive remuneration package together with real scope for career and professional advancement."

According to the ad, the job responsibilities "include managing/supervising the Payroll department, designing policies relating to employee compensation and preparing and submitting the compensation budget." This is consistent with the organization's need to administer its benefit package and to comply with government regulations.

Many small and medium-sized organizations do not employ benefit specialists but assign these responsibilities to HRM generalists. These generalists are sometimes aided by plan fiduciaries (representatives of organizations that hold plan assets) and outside benefits consultants.

EXHIBIT 13.2
Ad for a Compensation and Benefits Manager

REAP THE
BENEFITS

At Sharp, our products are engineered to meet the sophisticated needs of business and home environments ... both today and in the future. Our success is rooted in the talent and commitment of our employees, where exceptional efforts lead to exceptional opportunities.

Manager, Compensation & Benefits

This challenging role calls for an experienced management professional to develop and manage our compensation, benefits and commission program. Your diverse responsibilities will include managing/supervising the Payroll department, designing policies relating to employee compensation and preparing and submitting the compensation budget.

Your B.B.A. or degree in Social Science, with a minor in Business Administration, is enhanced by a thorough knowledge of current compensation theory and practices. Familiarity with spreadsheets and database is essential. Experience managing a national payroll is a definite asset.

We offer an attractive remuneration package together with real scope for career and professional advancement. Please send your resume, in confidence, quoting **Reference # KD11**, by **April 27, 1992**, to: Human Resources, Sharp Electronics of Canada Ltd., 335 Britannia Road East, Mississauga, Ontario L4Z 1W9. Fax: (416) 568-7141

No telephone calls or agency solicitation please.

SHARP®
FROM SHARP MINDS COME SHARP PRODUCTS™

Source: Advertisement appearing in *The Toronto Star*, April 18, 1992. Reprinted with the permission of Sharp Electronics of Canada Ltd.

Categories of Benefits and Types of Protection

The wide variety of employee benefits can be divided into five major categories: (1) universal benefits; (2) mandatory benefits; (3) discretionary benefits for employee protection; (4) pay for time not worked; and (5) employee services. Benefits in the first category cannot truly be called employee benefits because employment (or lack of employment) is not what entitles an individual to receive any of them. They are discussed here, however, because, with mandatory and discretionary benefits, they offer employees protection against certain risks, including risks of superannuation, untimely death, disability, medical expenses, and unemployment.

Superannuation

Superannuation refers to the risk of outliving one's ability to earn an income. Protection against the risk reduces the economic loss associated with retirement by providing a regular source of income to former employees in their retirement years. Superannuation is a risk faced by virtually everyone who depends upon his or her personal efforts to provide the resources for life, and the employment situation provides an opportunity to protect against it. Protection against this risk is provided under the Canada Pension Plan and the Quebec Pension Plan (CPP and QPP), the federal government's Old Age Security benefits, and employer-sponsored pension and retirement plans, as well as by personal savings and investments.

Untimely Death

Death is said to be untimely when it occurs before an individual's productive years are over, thus causing an economic loss to surviving dependants. (The untimely death of a single employee with no dependants is associated with no risks except funeral expenses.)

Certain programs protect against untimely death, in the form of payments to eligible survivors. Protection is provided by the mandatory CPP or QPP and by voluntary programs, such as group life insurance and the death benefit in private pension plans.

Disability

Disability can take two forms: total or partial. A totally disabled worker is one who cannot undertake any employment; a partially disabled worker cannot perform the job held before the accident or illness but can perform some work for the same or another company.

The risk of disability poses a far greater threat than does untimely death. First, all employees face this risk. Only those who have dependants need protection from death, but everyone is his or her own dependant in cases of disability. Moreover, from an economic standpoint, the loss associated with disability is greater than that resulting from death since a disabled employee still incurs living expenses, often greatly increased expenses. Further, disability may be partial, permitting some work—but often only with aids and after retraining, which can be very expensive. Finally, the likelihood of becoming disabled exceeds that of dying. Statistics indicate that young workers are approximately three times more likely to become disabled before retirement age than they are to die.[9] Protection against disability is provided by the mandatory CPP or QPP and workers' compensation and by group disability plans, which are provided at an employer's discretion. Unemployment Insurance also provides short-term protection against the loss of earnings because of accident or illness.

Medical Expenses

Modern health care is expensive, and costs are increasing rapidly. Services are available today that could not be purchased at any price a decade ago. Basic protection against the risks of health care costs is provided by provincial government insurance plans under a federal–provincial cost-sharing agreement. Additional protection may be afforded by supplementary health insurance, offered at an employer's discretion.

Unemployment

People are unemployed for numerous reasons. Some, such as quitting or dismissal for misconduct, are generally within an employee's control. Others, such as market shifts or automation, are not. Unemployment Insurance (UI) offers compensation for unemployment that is outside a person's control. It also provides benefits when a worker's ability to earn is interrupted by sickness, nonoccupational accident, pregnancy, or quarantine.

Universal Benefits

Universal benefits are those that governments provide without requiring direct contributions from either employees or employers. The universal benefits in Canada that protect against the risks discussed are Old Age Security (OAS), the Guaranteed Income Supplement (GIS) to OAS, and provincial supplements to these programs. In addition, basic health insurance is a universal benefit in five provinces; in the others, the premiums are paid by individuals and/or employers. (See Table 13.2.)

Old Age Security

On January 1, 1952, the federal government's Old Age Security Act first gave Canadians universal pensions as a matter of right, with no means test. Initially, the program provided a pension of $40 a month to everyone from age 70.

TABLE 13.2
Universal Benefit Programs

PROGRAM	REGULATORY BODY	RISK COVERED	NATURE OF BENEFITS	FUNDING
Old Age Security (OAS)	Federal government	Superannuation	Universal pension; monthly payments from age 65 (indexed to Consumer Price Index); subject to residence requirements	Federal government
Guaranteed Income Supplement (GIS) to OAS	Federal government	Superannuation	Monthly payments from age 65 to ensure that all recipients of OAS receive a minimum income; subject to income test	Federal government
Provincial supplements	Ont., NS, Man., Sask., Alta., BC	Superannuation	Monthly payments to guarantee minimum income to old people; subject to residence and means tests	Provincial governments
Provincial health insurance plans in Nfld., PEI, NS, NB, Man., and Sask.	Provinces	Hospital and medical expenses	Most basic hospital and medical-care costs	Federal block and per capita grants, plus general tax revenues in these provinces. (Health insurance is supported by federal money supplemented by payroll tax in Quebec, Manitoba, and Ontario and by individually paid premiums in other provinces)

The benefit has since been raised in amount (it is partially indexed to the Consumer Price Index), and the commencement age has been reduced to 65. A full pension requires residence of forty years after age 18, and, in most circumstances, ten years of continuous residence in Canada prior to the date of application. People whose adult residence in the country has been shorter receive a proportionate pension. This benefit is taxable to the individuals who receive it.

GUARANTEED INCOME SUPPLEMENT

A guaranteed monthly income supplement (GIS) was added to the Old Age Security plan effective January 1, 1967. It was intended as a transitional support to ensure that all recipients of the OAS pension would receive a minimum monthly income until the Canada and Quebec Pension Plans matured. Instead, the GIS became a permanent part of the social security system because full indexing in a time of inflation increased the number of pensioners who could qualify under the required income test.

The GIS is reduced by $1.00 for each $2.00 of income an elderly person receives in addition to the OAS benefit. A pensioner's husband or wife age 60 to 65 may qualify for a spouse's allowance, subject to an income test that reduces it $4.00 for every $400 of the couple's income.

As of May 1, 1991, the basic OAS pension was $326.37 monthly while the single-person GIS was $430.65 for a maximum federal pension of $793.02. For a married couple, the maximum, including the GIS, was $1285.99 per month. Cost-of-living adjustments are made quarterly.

Several provinces provide older people minimum income supplements in addition to federal benefits, subject to a means and a residence test.

PROVINCIAL HOSPITAL AND MEDICAL INSURANCE PLANS

Basic health care in Canada is covered by provincial insurance plans, which receive considerable federal funding. The system began July 1, 1958, when the federal government began sharing the cost of provincial hospital insurance plans that were available to all residents and operated by a public nonprofit agency. It was extended to providing insured medical care services in 1966.

The method of financing under the Canada Health Act, which became effective on April 1, 1984, sets out five conditions that a provincial health program must meet to be eligible for the full cash portion of the federal contribution for insured health services. The conditions are (1) administration on a nonprofit basis by a provincial public authority; (2) comprehensiveness (coverage of all necessary hospital and medical services, including surgical-dental services provided in hospitals); (3) universality; (4) portability within Canada and for services outside Canada at the home province rates; and (5) accessibility. The federal government can impose financial penalties on provinces that do not abide by these rules. Most user fees are not acceptable, although the act allows provinces to charge a user fee for hospitalization for chronic care if the individual is more or less permanently resident in the hospital.[10]

The hospital plans provide unlimited time in hospital that is medically necessary but do not cover private duty nurses or semiprivate accommodation. The medical plans cover services by physicians, surgeons, and anaesthetists, as well as diagnostic X-rays and laboratory tests. Limited coverage is provided for optometrists and practitioners such as chiropractors, osteopaths, and podiatrists. Many provinces have added dental care for children and/or prescription drugs for elderly people.

The provincial funding mechanism varies. The Northwest Territories, Saskatchewan, New Brunswick, Nova Scotia, Prince Edward Island, and Newfoundland finance their plans from general revenues, plus the federal grants. Quebec, Manitoba, and Ontario levy on employers a special tax equal to 3.0, 1.5, and 0.98 to 1.95 percent respectively (the Ontario tax rate varies with payroll size). British Columbia, Alberta, and the Yukon require monthly premiums from individuals or families. If an employer pays the premium in those jurisdictions, the amount is considered taxable income for the employee.

Because of this variation in funding mechanisms, provincial health insurance must be regarded as a true universal benefit only in those provinces that finance their share of costs from general revenues. In Quebec, Manitoba, and Ontario, the payroll tax makes it a mandatory benefit, and in the other jurisdictions it is a government-offered service with economies of scale and other benefits.

MANDATORY BENEFITS

Mandatory benefits are those that an employer must provide under federal and/or provincial laws. Mandatory benefits include retirement, disability, survivors' and death benefits under the Canada (or Quebec) Pension Plan; disability benefits and spouses' and dependants' pensions under workers' compensation; unemployment compensation; and health insurance in Quebec, Manitoba, and Ontario. (See Table 13.3.) The payment of mandatory benefits amounted to 5.3 percent of the average employer's gross annual payroll in 1989.[11]

CANADA AND QUEBEC PENSION PLANS

The Canada Pension Plan and Quebec Pension plan (CPP and QPP) were introduced on January 1, 1966. (Quebec opted out of the federal plan but introduced its own with identical main features.) The plans are not subsidized by the government; they are based on contributions by the employer and the employee, each of whom contributes 2.3 percent of pensionable earnings up to a maximum, which was $30 500 in 1991.[12] Contributions are deducted from employees' pay and remitted once a month by the employer, together with his or her contributions. All employees and the self-employed (who remit 4.4 percent of earnings themselves) pay into the fund between the ages of 18 and 65; a person may continue to contribute to age 70.

The retirement pension, equal to 25 percent of the contributor's earnings in the previous three years, is paid at or after the age of 65; in 1991, the maximum pension was $604.86 per month. A disability pension, with a maximum of $743.64 per month in 1991, is payable to a person who has contributed for at least five years and is suffering from a disability that prevents gainful occupation. It is paid for the duration of the disability or until age 65, when the person receives the retirement pension. Survivors' benefits

TABLE 13.3
Mandatory Benefit Programs

PROGRAM	REGULATORY BODY	RISK COVERED	NATURE OF BENEFITS	FUNDING
Canada (and Quebec) pension plans	Federal (Quebec) government	Superannuation Disability Untimely death Costs of raising orphans Death	Monthly payment Monthly payment Percentage of deceased spouse's monthly retirement benefit Monthly payment Lump sum six times the monthly retirement benefit	Payroll tax paid by employer and employee
Workers' compensation	Provinces	Injury Untimely death resulting from employment Disability resulting from employment Medical, hospital, all related expenses (work-related injuries or illnesses)	Weekly benefit Dependents receive a pension plus lump sum Weekly benefit Expenses covered	Employer premiums levied on the statement of wages for the previous year and estimate of payroll for current year
Quebec health insurance Manitoba health insurance Ontario health insurance	Province of Quebec Province of Manitoba Province of Ontario	Hospital and medical expenses	Most basic hospital and medical-care costs	Federal block and per capita grants, plus 3% payroll tax in Quebec, 1.5% in Manitoba, and 0.98–1.95% in Ontario (Federal money is supplemented by general tax revenues in Nfld., PEI, NS, NB, and Sask. and by individually paid premiums in other provinces)
Unemployment insurance	Canada Employment and Immigration Commission	Interruption in employment due to: work shortage, sickness, nonoccupational accidents, pregnancy, quarantine	Payments for a limited period of time	Premium levied on employees and employers

vary with the age of the surviving spouse and whether there are any dependent children. There is also a death benefit.

Canada (or Quebec) Pension Plan payments by employers are deductible as costs, and employee payments are non-refundable tax credits. C/QPP benefits are taxable.

WORKERS' COMPENSATION

Every province and territory in Canada has a workers' compensation act, which mandates compensation to a worker (or the family) for injury or death arising from employment. Hospital, medical, and related expenses are also paid, and disabled workers receive full rehabilitation services from workers' compensation boards. The funding mechanism is a premium levied on employers. It is calculated on the statement of wages for the previous year and an estimate of payroll for the present year. The rate varies with the type of industry and hence the hazards involved. In 1988 it ranged from 20¢ per $100 of annual payroll in nonhazardous work to $10 or more per $100 for various types of mining and nearly $21 for stevedoring.

Disability compensation for an accident or illness is 75 percent of average gross earnings, subject to minimums and maximums that vary among provinces. In 1988, the lowest maximum annual earnings base was $22 000 in Prince Edward Island and the highest was $48 000 in Saskatchewan. If the disabling accident leaves the employee with a permanent disability affecting his or her future earnings, a lifetime pension may be payable. It can range from 15 or 20 percent of gross earnings if the permanent disability is partial to as much as 75 percent of gross earnings or 90 percent of net earnings if the disability is total.[13]

The employer's contribution is a deductible operating expense, but it is not taxable income for workers. Workers' compensation payments are not taxable to the recipients.

UNEMPLOYMENT INSURANCE

Unemployment insurance (UI) was introduced to Canada in 1942. Although most social welfare measures are a provincial responsibility, the British North America Act was amended in 1940 to give the federal government exclusive jurisdiction in matters relating to unemployment insurance.

The program now covers all employees under age 65 except employees of a provincial or foreign government and casual workers. Funding is through premiums levied on both employers and employees. On July 1, 1991, an employee paid 2.8 percent of gross pay of up to $680 per week, and the employer paid 1.4 times that amount. The premiums are tax-deductible for employers and are eligible for a tax credit for employees. On the other hand, UI benefits are taxable.

UI benefits cover interruptions in employment income caused by loss of job or by a layoff but not by a strike or lockout. A claimant must be genuinely unemployed and cannot, without good cause, refuse to apply for a suitable situation or a designated training program.

To qualify for benefits, the worker must usually have made regular contributions to the fund for at least 20 weeks during the "qualifying period," which is the lesser of the 52 weeks preceding the claim or the number of weeks since the start of the last claim. After a two-week waiting period, the claimant receives 60 percent of his or her average weekly insurable earnings. (In 1991, given maximum weekly insurable earnings of $680, the maximum UI benefit was $408.) An "initial benefit" is payable for the lesser of the number of weeks of contributions in the qualifying period or 25 weeks. This may be extended to as much as 50 weeks, depending on the contribution record, the regional unemployment rate, and whether layoff was the cause of unemployment.[14]

Major revisions to the Unemployment Insurance Act in 1971 increased benefits, reduced the qualifying period for layoff benefits, shortened the waiting period, and introduced coverage for interruptions in employment caused by sickness, nonoccupational accident, quarantine, or pregnancy. A controversy soon arose over whether the more generous provisions had resulted in a higher measured rate of unemployment. Economists estimated that they had raised it 0.8 to 1.9 percentage points, a finding based on the fact that between 1971 and 1972 the job vacancy rate doubled, indicating a strong demand for workers, yet the unemployment rate remained unchanged.[15] The suggestion that the UI revisions might have affected unemployment so incensed trade unionists that their representatives on the Economic Council of Canada refused to sign a study that reached this conclusion.[16] (The Council had noted that the increase in unemployment could have positive aspects from society's perspective if workers used their unemployment time to search for better jobs, ones that they would presumably hold for a longer duration.) In 1975, the regulations for drawing UI benefits were tightened by extending the qualifying period.

In 1981, another controversy arose when the government introduced a program of work-sharing through UI. Employers who would otherwise have to lay off some employees could put all of them on a part-week basis; all of them could receive UI benefits without using up any of their UI eligibility. Both central union and central employer associations were critical of the program. The former felt that by reducing measured unemployment, it took pressure off the government to fight the recession, and the latter worried about its effects on productivity. But the evident popularity of work-sharing with the workers and employers who participated in it eventually reduced the opposition, and the program was expanded to 8780 firms and more than 200 000 employees.[17] As expected, the number of firms and employees involved in work sharing declined following the general decrease in unemployment in the period following the 1982–83 recession but expanded again during the recession of the early 1990s.[18]

In 1990, the Conservative federal government implemented major revisions to the Unemployment Insurance Act after vigorous opposition in both the House of Commons and the then Liberal-dominated Senate. The revisions were partly based on the report of the Forget Commission, which examined the unemployment insurance system in Canada.[19] The revisions included lengthening the qualifying period (though it still varies according to the unemployment rate of the area); increasing premiums for both employees and employers in order to eliminate federal contributions to the UI fund; for those who quit work without "just cause" or are fired, doubling the disqualification period from one to six weeks to seven to twelve and reducing benefits from 60 percent to 50 percent of insurable earnings; extending UI eligibility to workers age 65 and over; improving benefits for maternity, parental, sickness, and adoption leaves, including having a labour dispute no longer disqualify a worker for these special benefits if the leave began before the strike; and providing $800 million for increased training and other initiatives to help the unemployed.[20]

The UI changes have general implications for all employees and specific implications for maternity leave policies, depending on the jurisdiction's employment standards legislation. In Ontario, for example, a woman who has been employed at the same company for at least thirteen weeks before the expected birth date is entitled to a maternity leave of seventeen weeks. In some other provinces and the territories, an employee must have worked continuously for at least one year to qualify for an eighteen-week maternity leave. British Columbia also mandates an eighteen-week maternity leave but does not specify a qualifying period. These differences also affect when the employer expects to receive advance notice of leave and, if no notice is given, when the leave can be deemed to start and end. These issues are important because the Supreme Court of Canada stated in *Brooks* v. *Canada Safeway* that it was against human rights legislation to refuse to provide benefits during the seventeen-week period surrounding childbirth. For HRM professionals, knowledge of the implications of changes in legislation is important for handling benefits during leave and other eventualities.[21]

SUPPLEMENTARY COVERAGE

Some employers, at their own discretion, supplement government unemployment insurance by offering plans that provide additional weeks' coverage. The best-known examples have been in the auto industry. The ultimate expansion of such plans is the guaranteed annual wage provided by some large U.S. employers such as Hormel and Procter and Gamble. Under such plans, an employee is entitled to a full year's pay, whether continuously employed or not.

HEALTH INSURANCE

As we have already noted, basic health insurance is, strictly speaking, a mandated benefit only in Quebec, Manitoba, and Ontario, where the provincial financing for the plan is raised by a payroll tax. Other provinces augment federal funding from general tax revenues (making the insurance a universal benefit) or through premiums paid by individuals and families. The latter jurisdictions, however, usually use payroll deductions to collect the premiums. The cost to employers of administering these deductions may be considered a mandated benefit to employees.

DISCRETIONARY BENEFITS FOR EMPLOYEE PROTECTION

In addition to mandatory benefits, many employers provide a variety of discretionary benefits for employee protection, including private pension plans and group life, disability, and supplementary health insurance. Such benefits accounted for 9.9 percent of the average employer's total compensation costs in 1989.[22]

PRIVATE PENSION PLANS

Some employers sponsor private pension plans that supplement CPP (or QPP) benefits. Although the primary purpose of a pension plan is to protect against the risks associated with retirement, many plans also pay a death benefit if the employee dies before retirement.

Basically, private pension plans operate as follows. During the course of employment, contributions are made to the pension fund, either by the employer alone or jointly by employer and employee. The accumulated money, representing contributions on behalf of many employees, is invested and allowed to accumulate interest, dividends, and/or capital gains. Upon retirement, an employee receives income from the fund. Most pension plans are *defined-benefit plans*, in which the amount received is calculated on some combination of the employee's years of service to the company and his or her average earnings, usually in the few years just prior to retirement. An alternative approach is the *defined-contribution plan*, in which a specified amount is paid into the plan and retirees receive pension income based on what the fund has earned.

Pension plans may have been prompted by humanitarian reasons, but their growth can be attributed to the inherent tax advantages for both employer and employee. Employers may usually deduct contributions to the plan from income before taxes. As of January 1, 1991, the annual limits on the amount that can be contributed to an individual's tax-deferred savings for retirement were increased for some Canadians. The new limits of 18 percent of earnings but not more than $15 500 apply to company-sponsored plans and to contributions to individual registered retirement savings plans (RRSPs). Unused RRSP deductions may be carried forward.

Private pension plans are regulated by the Canadian Association of Pension Supervisory Authorities (CAPSA), which was established to promote uniformity and ease in the administration of provincial pension benefits acts. The acts are uniform in their essentials, although Manitoba's, Ontario's, and Saskatchewan's have some variations to give employees further protection. An organization that operates a pension plan covering its employees must register the plan with provincial authorities. For contributors to obtain full income tax relief, the plan must also be registered with the federal minister of national revenue.

Pension plans are either vested or nonvested. A plan is said to *vest* for an employee when the individual has the right to retain the pension (or the value thereof) even if he or she leaves the employment of the plan sponsor. The Pension Benefits acts, which apply to all pension plan members in Canada, have established standards of vesting. A private pension plan must vest for an employee who has at least ten years of service with an employer and has attained age 45.

Under the federal Pension Benefits Standards Act of 1985 (PBSA), the "45 and 10 rule" continues to apply to pensions accrued up to December 31, 1986; pensions accrued from January 1, 1987, onwards are vested in any employee, regardless of age, who has been a member of the plan for two continuous years. Ontario's vesting rule is the same as that in PBSA. In Manitoba, vesting for benefits accrued in the years 1985 to 1989 inclusive is required if the member has five years of service; for benefits accrued from January 1, 1990, vesting is required after two years of plan membership. In Saskatchewan vesting applies when the years of service plus age add to 45 or more so long as there is a minimum of one year's service. The employee who terminates before retirement age and meets the vesting conditions is entitled to a deferred annuity commencing when he or she reaches normal retirement age (usually age 65).[23]

Private pension plans may, of course, vest more quickly than required by law. A plan in which the employee obtains a nonforfeitable right as soon as participation begins is said to vest immediately.

Industry-wide or multi-employer pension plans have been established by union negotiation in many industries, such as construction, transportation, forestry, and retail trades, where there are a large number of small employers or where employees move frequently among different employers. In these plans the employee continues to be a member of an industry-wide plan and pension credits earned with various employers accumulate as if he or she had worked for only one employer.[24]

Once a pension plan becomes vested, the contributions are "locked in"; that is, they cannot be withdrawn as a cash sum before a terminated employee is eligible to receive the deferred annuity, except in cases of mental or physical disability or if the deferred benefit is less than some minimum ($25 per month in most provinces). Before vesting takes place, contributions can be withdrawn.

The regulations provide that private plans must be funded so as to meet various solvency tests and that their benefits, conditions, and financial arrangements be well disclosed to the participants. The employer must send every employee, when he or she becomes eligible or joins the plan, a written explanation of it, including the plan members' rights and duties under the plan. The employer must also give each member regular statements of his or her entitlement; this information must be provided annually or when a plan is amended in Manitoba, Ontario, Alberta, and the federal jurisdiction, and at least once every three years in the other jurisdictions. A member who terminates employment or retires must be given a statement of the available benefits and options. A member is also entitled to ask to examine or to receive a copy of the plan text and amendments.

In 1980, Ontario added provisions to its act to protect pension rights of employees in the event of plant closure. If the employer is insolvent, payments are to be made from a Pension Benefit Guarantee Fund financed by contributions from all employers in the province. When a shortfall occurs in the pension plan of a bankrupt company, the fund guarantees employees' pensions of as much as $1000 a month.[25]

As is discussed in more detail later, the indexing of pensions was a major issue in Canada in the 1980s. Exhibit 13.3 and Case 13.1 describe major gains unions attained in indexed pensions in such industries and firms as pulp and paper, autos, Air Canada, and Inco. For organizations, indexed pensions mean increased charges on pension plan funds, which in turn requires a more careful monitoring of the available resources.

EXHIBIT 13.3
Private Sector Indexed Pensions

In the late 1980s, one of the major issues in the field of benefits was indexed pensions. Several unions negotiated inflation protection for pensions and the government of Ontario established a one-person task force under Professor Martin Friedland of the University of Toronto to examine the issue. Although the task force reported in 1988, by 1992 none of the recommendations had been implemented. A change in government in 1990, the severe recession in the early 1990s, and the decline in inflation to very low levels have delayed a provincial government program of inflation-protected private pensions.

The recommendations by the task force would not provide any inflation protection for pension credits accrued when pension indexing legislation becomes effective or for existing pensioners.

The proposal would increase credits earned after the law takes effect by 75 per cent of the rise in the Consumer Price Index, less 1 per cent. For example, a 10 per cent inflation rate would bring a 6.5 per cent increase in the level of earned benefits.

Contrast this with the pension terms negotiated by the unions with the pulp and paper industry, the auto industry, Air Canada and Inco Ltd. of Toronto.

The first union-negotiated agreement was between the Canadian Paperworkers Union and Abitibi Price in June, 1987. It provided for inflation adjustments over six years to cover 50 per cent of the annual rate of inflation, with a cap of 5 per cent a year.

EXHIBIT 13.3 *(continued)*

The auto agreements negotiated last fall by the Canadian Auto Workers and the Big Three auto manufacturers provided for pension increases that are 90 per cent of the rise in the Consumer Price Index, with a cap of about 6 per cent a year.

The indexing is retroactive to cover past as well as future credits. The auto pension agreements are for a term of six years.

Although the indexing did not apply to workers on pension at the time the agreement was signed, the CAW won substantial increases in their pensions over the life of the agreement.

The next agreement was between the International Association of Machinists and Air Canada. It calls for pensions to increase by 50 per cent of the rise in the CPI, with a maximum increase of 4 per cent.

The indexing covers workers already retired as well as future retirees. That agreement was for four years.

The most recent agreement for indexing pensions was negotiated by Inco Ltd. and the United Steelworkers of America. It broke new ground by indexing pensions for life, rather than guaranteeing inflation protection for the life of the agreement.

The indexing at Inco covers workers on pension when the agreement was negotiated and future retirees. It also covers survivor benefits.

The first adjustments are effective on July 1, 1989. They provide about 80 per cent inflation protection if inflation is in the range of 3.5 to 6.5 per cent a year. If inflation exceeds 7 per cent, the adjustment will be capped at 5 per cent.

For workers who take early retirement, the indexing begins at age 65 or three years after retirement, whichever comes first.

Source: Adapted from Wilfred List, "Labor Settlements Overtake Government Proposals," *The Globe and Mail*, August 1, 1988. Used with the permission of the author.

GROUP INSURANCE PROGRAMS

Group insurance programs are another way in which employers can voluntarily provide protection to employees. Under them, an employer contracts with an insurance company to provide employees certain protection, including life, disability, or supplementary health insurance. A wide variety of group policies are available. Many are paid in full by employers (noncontributory plans), but others require employee contributions (contributory plans). Group plans do not allow for individual selection of benefit levels. Rather, a prearranged formula, such as a percentage of annual income, determines how much of a particular benefit each employee can receive under the plan.

The major advantage of group insurance is its cost. Administrative costs are reduced when the agent deals with a group rather than with individuals. And since the agent is handling a large amount of insurance at one time, acquisition costs are much lower. The agent's commission, which is figured as a percentage of the annual premium, is often 40 to 60 percent in individually written business but generally only about 5 percent of group business. A final cost savings to the organization is realized through operation of income tax laws. An employer can deduct the cost of group term life insurance (up to $25 000 per employee) as a necessary business expense, but the employee need not report it as income.

Automatic availability may be the primary advantage of group insurance for those employees who would be unable to acquire coverage otherwise. From an insurance company's perspective, it is reasonable to provide coverage to "uninsurable" individuals because the larger number of good risks being insured at the same time offsets them. This "risk pooling" is a major advantage of the group technique.

Group Life Insurance

Several types of group life insurance are available, but the primary choice is between a term and a cash-value policy. *Term insurance* provides the beneficiary with the face value of the policy upon the death of the insured. *Cash-value* (or *whole life*) *insurance* pays the face value and also accumulates cash values, which are also payable to the beneficiary. The premiums for term insurance are considerably lower than those for cash-value, and term is the type often offered by employers. In fact, insurance companies often insist on term insurance's being part of a benefits package that includes other kinds of group insurance.

A relatively recent and increasingly popular development in group life insurance has been the addition of survivors' benefits, which are payable periodically to a surviving spouse. They may be payable for life or until remarriage, perhaps being limited by length of service of the deceased worker. A policy may also include contingent benefits, which are payable to children in the event of the death of the surviving spouse.

The Pay Research Bureau's 1990 survey reported that all the employers it covered had a group life insurance plan, provided such a plan under a flexible benefits package, or contributed to union-sponsored plans.[26]

Group Disability Insurance

Group disability coverage is needed to fill gaps left by CPP (or QPP) and workers' compensation. The government pension plans cover only total disability and provide only a "floor" of protection. Workers' compensation pays only for work-related disabilities. UI benefits for sickness or accident are available only for a short time. Group disability benefits are desirable to increase available benefits, to provide for temporary and partial disability, and to provide some medium-term benefits, particularly for nonoccupational disabilities.

A survey of industrial employers in Canada found that 94 percent had long-term disability plans for management and professionals, 87 percent for office employees, and 79 percent for nonoffice employees. The usual long-term plan has a waiting period of 17 to 26 weeks, during which the disabled employee is either fully or partially covered by a short-term disability plan. Long-term disability benefits typically range from 60 to 70 percent of earnings with a maximum monthly benefit payable until retirement age if the employee is totally or permanently disabled. The amount of payment is reduced by any disability income received from other plans.[27]

Group Health Insurance

Since basic hospital and medical services are provided under provincial plans, the private health insurance offered in Canada is what is frequently referred to as supplementary or extended health care plans. Typical plans cover private hospital rooms, nursing home accommodations, the cost of private duty nursing and other paramedical services, ambulances, emergency health expenses in foreign countries, prescription drugs, and medical supplies and appliances, including hearing aids and eyeglasses. Such plans usually specify a certain deductible and may pay less than 100 percent of the remaining expenses.

Recently, dental plans have become a popular new offering; their benefits range from basic dental care to major restorative care (crowns, inlays, fixed bridges, and dentures) and orthodontics. Vision care is a less common feature of benefit packages, but coverage is increasing. In 1990, 45 percent of establishments surveyed had no coverage for prescription eyeglasses or contact lenses.[28]

Employers' contributions to health insurance plans may be charged as operating expenses for tax purposes. However, employees' contributions to nongovernmental plans are not deductible from taxable income, and several types of employer contributions are added to it for tax purposes.

Deferred Profit Sharing

Deferred profit-sharing plans are another benefit that has traditionally been given to executives and senior managers in the form of stock purchase options.

HOLIDAY AND VACATION PAY

Employees receive benefits in the form of pay for time not worked, such as paid vacation days, paid holidays, paid "sick days," lunch or rest periods, coffee breaks, and paid leaves of absence for jury duty. Some of these benefits are mandated by the relevant jurisdiction's employment standards legislation. Others are given at the employer's discretion. Some discretionary benefits may, however, be virtually required by common practice in the industry or locality. In unionized organizations, collective agreements normally specify benefits in detail. Pay for time not worked cost the average Canadian employer 13.9 percent of gross annual payroll in 1989.[29]

HOLIDAYS

As we saw in Chapter 3, employment standards in all jurisdictions require specified paid holidays — from five in Newfoundland and Prince Edward Island to nine in four provinces, the two territories, and the federal jurisdiction. Many employers go beyond the legal minimum, particularly employers covered by collective agreements. Industry or local practice is also important —even clerical workers in the oil industry claim their "golden Fridays," and many offices in large metropolitan centres close on Friday afternoons in the summer, despite ubiquitous air conditioning, because of employees' demands for time off during the short Canadian season. Not unrelated is the particularly Canadian trend of setting holidays on Mondays so that employees may have long weekends.

Also growing in popularity is the "floating" holiday, which varies from year to year or from employee to employee. One type, a "personal" holiday, allows an employee to take off any day with supervisory approval. Another type is chosen by an employer, usually to give employees a long weekend or extra days off during the holiday season.

VACATIONS

Even the newest employee is generally entitled to holiday benefits, but paid vacations must be earned through length of service to an employer. In most jurisdictions, vacation days accrue at a rate of about one day per month of service, entitling an employee to two weeks of paid vacation after one year's employment. It is common to require an employee to work six months to a year before vacation can be taken. Generally, office and managerial employees become eligible for paid vacation days sooner than do production and maintenance employees. Regardless of job level, the length of paid vacations increases with length of service, and many firms go beyond the legal minimums. Many offer three weeks after three, four, or five years of service (depending upon job type); four weeks after five to nine years; and five after fifteen to twenty years. Forty-one percent of nonoffice employees who were included in a recent survey were entitled to six weeks after twenty or more years of service, and 17 percent received seven weeks after twenty-five years of service.[30]

Many firms provide additional vacation entitlement in various circumstances. Some reward long-service employees with additional days of leave after specified years of service. Others offer additional paid days for special reasons, such as an employee's taking the vacation in the winter, working in an isolated region, or reaching a given age. These additional vacation days are usually available only for the particular period or occasion and are not an annual entitlement.

The 1990 agreement between the Ford Motor Company of Canada and the Canadian Auto Workers provides for a $100 million compensation fund to cover the cost of such options as special early retirement programs, special income supplements of up to three years for workers who lose their jobs, and severance payments ranging from $25 000 to $65 000, depending on the seniority of workers. Ford of Canada also agreed to provide all employees with more time off the job and annual vacation bonuses of $500.[31]

EMPLOYEE SERVICE BENEFITS

In addition to compensation for time not worked and mandatory and discretionary benefits, employees frequently receive various kinds of service benefits, ranging from savings plans, stock purchase plans, credit unions, and tuition loans to recreational facilities and programs, use of company cars and parking privileges, and company discounts. This type of benefit accounted for 4.4 percent of the average Canadian employer's total compensation costs in 1989.[32]

Employee service benefits generally differ according to job level. For example, stock options and deferred pay plans are especially attractive to employees in higher-paying jobs. Executives commonly have their own special benefits, called *perquisites* or *"perks,"* which include such items as physical examinations, special parking and company cars, transportation for spouses who travel on company business, and memberships in luncheon clubs and country clubs.[33]

Increasingly, organizations are providing career counselling services and educational assistance as employee service benefits. Many offer employees time off the job with pay for participation in developmental activities, such as workshops and professional meetings, and some make low-interest loans available to employees who wish to continue their education. For example, IBM has a 100 percent tuition-assistance plan for its employees that covers any subject that is job-oriented or taken toward the completion of a degree.[34]

As Case 13.2 indicates, organizations are also finding that productivity can increase when child care is provided on-site.

Another form of service that has been growing rapidly in Canada is Employee Assistance Programs (EAPs). Initially EAPs tended to focus on alcoholism but have since been broadened to include drugs and psychosocial problems. Unions and management have increasingly been co-operating in dealing with these problems. (Types of approaches used by EAPs are discussed in Chapter 14.)

Cafeteria Benefits: An Individualized Approach

Although most employers offer a variety of benefits, their employees rarely have any choice in what they receive as a part of their total compensation. Benefits are generally selected for employees by management or, in the case of unionized employers, by union representatives. One study found that many union representatives do not have a good idea of the benefits desired by their constituents.[35] Another study reported that, when given the opportunity, 80 percent of the respondents had made changes in their benefit packages.[36]

The benefits in the benefit packages and the options in group insurance plans are geared to the needs and interests of the "average" employee. Even if such an employee really existed, there would be many others whose individual needs and interests were poorly met by benefits selected for them.

A moderate amount of research in the United States has examined employees' preferences for various forms of benefits. Several studies of blue- and white-collar workers found as much or more interest in some types of benefits, especially more vacations and increased medical insurance, as in additional increases in wages and salaries.[37] Canada's universal health insurance plans undoubtedly remove much pressure for that benefit.

At the executive levels, Canadians receive a smaller percentage of their total compensation in the form of benefits than do their U.S. counterparts. However, Canadian companies are far more generous with executive disability benefits and with medical and dental plans. And they are more likely to offer such perks as company cars right down to the middle-management level because perks have had preferred status in this country.[38] About two-thirds of the larger companies in Canada have a supplementary, unregistered (that is, nonqualified) retirement plan.[39]

Several studies have found that age, sex, number of children, and job type affect employees' preferences for benefits. For example, preference for pensions increase with age, and employees with children rate medical insurance higher than do employees without children.[40] Also, younger workers favour dental plans more than do older employees.[41]

One means of allowing employees to have some say in the type of benefits they receive is a system known as *cafeteria benefits*, *flexible benefits*, or *flex plans*, in which employees can choose the combination of cash and benefits they want included in their total pay packages. It is highly unusual for an organization to allow an employee to decide the proportion of total compensation that will be spent on benefits. It is somewhat more common, however, to allow employees to choose from various benefit alternatives. This system generally places a limit on the total dollar value of benefits which can be selected; sometimes the employee is entitled to cash payments to the extent that the value of selected benefits does not reach the limit.

Cafeteria or flexible benefits are not common, but, as Exhibit 13.4 indicates, many Canadian companies are considering them. Several U.S. organizations have used the approach successfully, among them American Can and

HRM IN ACTION

THE EVOLUTIONARY WAY TO FLEXIBLE BENEFITS

At Noranda Inc. and Canadian General-Tower Ltd., some employees can trade vacation time for extra cash or for other benefits such as more dental coverage.

About 30 percent of Canadian General Tower employees do so, reports Don Mattason, vice-president of corporate human resources for the vinyl films and coated fabrics maker.

Nobody is allowed to trade all their vacation time: employees must keep at least two weeks because the company believes they otherwise might suffer from burnout. That policy also matches a requirement in employment standards legislation in many provinces.

Noranda's program is still at the pilot stage. So far, it applies to about 490 of the company's 55 000 employees, says Pat Wiggins, manager of benefits. And there is a slight difference from Canadian General Tower's approach.

Employees with four weeks a year of holiday can only trade one week, retaining three, although those who have only three weeks' vacation can trade down to two.

Long-term staff with five weeks' vacation can trade two weeks and those with six weeks can use three toward extra credits for other benefits. So far, about 20 per cent of employees in the pilot group have traded their vacation time for other benefits.

The vacation trades are part of flexible benefits plans that give employees options so they can tailor the types and levels of coverage to their needs.

In both companies mentioned here, one week of vacation is worth 2 per cent of annual salary. At Toronto-based Noranda, it can buy additional life insurance, better long-term disability coverage or life insurance for dependents.

The Canadian General Tower version also allows employees to trade up to several levels of better pension coverage. Noranda has so far not included pensions, but a task force is looking at whether it is realistic to include them in the flexible benefits plan.

Both companies went to flexible benefits for similar reasons.

"We often wondered how people react to benefit plans," Mr. Mattason says. "Did they meet their needs? We didn't know. We had never asked." As part of the changeover, his company met with all employees in small groups to ask what they thought of their benefits and what they would like.

> Noranda wanted to create more awareness among employees of what the company is offering, Ms. Wiggins says.
>
> Flexible plans often initially cost companies about 5 per cent more than traditional benefits, says Dean Connor, a principal with William M. Mercer Ltd. consultants.
>
> This is the price companies must pay if they want to ensure employees don't lose any benefits they are entitled to before.
>
> But many companies are willing to live with the expense because the flip side is more employee appreciation once they are aware what the company provides in benefits, Mr. Connor says.
>
> Noranda has found its plan hikes payroll costs 0.38 per cent, while Canadian General Tower has been able to keep costs the same.
>
> Converting to flexible benefits is a bit like opening the hood of a car, Mr. Connor says. Employees will see inside and learn a lot more about things like whether their plan incorporates bigger subsidies to married employees than to those who are single for dental or medical benefits. (The minority do, he says.)
>
> Although flex plans are growing in popularity, Mr. Connor says they are not suitable for all companies. If employees are content with the existing benefits plan, it is not worth going through all the planning for the changes.
>
> The process can be lengthy, companies who have gone through it report.
>
> In Noranda's case, planning took 18 months, says Ms. Wiggins, though she considered the work enjoyable.
>
> At Canadian General Tower, part of the preparation time involved employees, a process Mr. Connor strongly recommends.
>
> As well, he suggests, "Don't try to change everything at once. You don't have to flex every single benefit this way to Sunday in order to have a flex plan. View it as an evolutionary, not a revolutionary process, one of continuous improvement."
>
> ---
>
> Source: Margot Gibb-Clark, "Flex Benefits Let Employees Tailor Coverage," *The Globe and Mail*, June 24, 1991. Reprinted with the permission of *The Globe and Mail*.

TRW.[42] These companies allow employees to choose whether they want more or less of certain types of benefits after a predetermined core of coverage has been provided. This type of system is also used for nonunionized staff at Cominco Ltd., a large Vancouver-based mining operation. Canadian Tire and Nova Corporation also have flexible benefit plans.

EXHIBIT 13.4
Cafeteria Benefits in Canada

Tim Liang was faced with some tough choices when Canadian Tire Corp. enrolled him in its new benefits plan.

Should he get more medical coverage or opt instead for additional vacation time?

How much life insurance do he and his wife, Marisa, need?

Would they be better off with a top-notch dental care plan or extra insurance against losing limbs or eyes in an accident?

Should the company pay for his disability insurance or, for income tax reasons, should the premiums come out of his own pocket?

Liang, a 34-year-old computer analyst, says he didn't mind being forced to make so many decisions instead of, as in the past, simply being handed a list of benefits the company would provide.

"It's great," he said in a recent interview at Canadian Tire's midtown home office. Selecting benefits "gives employees more choice and say about what they'd like to have."

Liang is among about 1400 employees of the auto-parts retailer who, on April 1, will officially join the growing ranks of workers with flexible benefit plans. The firm will enrol another 1400 employees next fall.

The company is one of only about 40 in Canada with full-fledged flex systems—nicknamed cafeteria-style plans.

None of the firms is unionized and union spokesmen have strong reservations about the plans, arguing they'll make it harder to win further improvements in company-paid benefits, and gradually lead to more benefit costs being dumped on workers.

Some doubt flex plans will make big inroads in Canada: "My general impression is that it's a big yawn. . . . I don't think they've been able to sell that snake oil to very many folks," said John O'Grady, a researcher with the Ontario Federation of Labor.

But more than 900 U.S. firms have already adopted flex plans, a recent survey suggests 58 per cent will have them within 10 years and supporters insist Canada is already well along the same trail.

"There's a whole slew of companies in the process of looking at them," said Madeleine Gaul, a principal with the consulting firm William M. Mercer Ltd.

For every firm that has one up and running, two or three are considering them, "so the momentum is building more and more," agreed Frank Livsey, a founding partner of Hewitt Associates and pioneer of flex plans in Canada.

In a recent survey by Hewitt and Benefits Canada, 85 per cent of 300 Canadian employers predicted use of flexible benefits will increase during the next 10 years and only 2 per cent disagreed.

EXHIBIT 13.4 (continued)

The trend is being fuelled by changes in the workforce, along with a desire to control the soaring cost of benefits — which now add an average 37 per cent to the average payroll in Canada.

Firms with global operations also believe flex plans may enable them to design pay plans that eliminate national borders, said Ken Feltman, executive director of the Employers Council on Flexible Compensation in Washington, D.C.

Cutting costs is the major motive behind flex plans in the United States where, without medicare, health insurance premiums are rising astronomically. Canadian firms say they're mainly concerned with making their benefits more efficient and useful to workers. But here, too, they could eventually be used to cut the employer's share of costs.

Proponents of flexible benefits say traditional plans, with everyone at a company getting the same benefits, were designed for the 50s-style of work force, dominated by men with wives at home raising children.

Now, less than 20 per cent of the current workforce fits the Leave-it-to-Beaver mold. Most employees are single, with or without children, or have a spouse also working outside the home.

The benefits they need depend on their individual circumstances.

Young singles want more cash and vacation time, employees with families need medical and life insurance, while older workers are most concerned with pensions, consultants say. Working couples, with benefits provided by both employers, want to avoid duplication.

Cafeteria-style plans are seen as a way to satisfy them all.

Source: "Benefits on the Menu," *The Toronto Star*, March 25, 1990. Reprinted with permission — The Toronto Star Syndicate.

Cafeteria benefits are not more widely used partly because of the costs of developing and administering such a system and partly because certain cost advantages of group insurance may be lost. Also, allowing individuals to choose their own packages may make it more difficult to predict and budget for benefit costs.

Another reason for the limited use of such programs is the opposition of unions. Union leaders believe that flexible benefit plans make it harder to bargain for improvements in benefits and gradually lead to shifting more of the benefit costs to employees by adding new benefits as options without increasing credits for them. At Cominco, however, the value of credits has kept pace with benefit costs.[43]

A cafeteria-style approach has two important advantages. First, it allows employees to have the benefits they need and desire most. Second, by their active involvement in benefits selection, employees become more aware of the benefits they have and of their costs. Such awareness can increase employees' appreciation of an employer's financial contribution on their behalf. Use of such a system does, however, impose a substantial responsibility upon the employer — and specifically on HRM professionals — to see that the nature of the program and of each optional benefit is adequately costed and communicated to employees. It may be necessary to conduct a survey of employee preferences for benefits,[44] to hold a number of meetings, to prepare brochures and/or videotapes, and perhaps to hold individual conferences to answer questions and record choices and changes in them. Changes in tax legislation can have a significant effect on the choice of benefits in a cafeteria program.

Controlling Benefit Costs

Benefit costs, like any other costs, must be controlled if an organization is to remain profitable. The costs of employee benefits and services have risen to nearly 33.5 percent of total compensation costs, though they appear to have eased slightly from the high point of 36.3 percent in 1986. Some costs are for government-mandated programs, but many benefits and services are provided at the discretion of an employer or are negotiated through collective bargaining. Most employers find it difficult to eliminate existing benefits and to control the amounts that must be spent if certain benefits are to be made available. Some steps can be taken, however, to reduce benefit costs and get the most from benefit dollars. An obvious one is to provide benefits that the majority of employees value and eliminate those in which they have little interest. A questionnaire survey can be used to elicit employees' preferences for various benefit offerings. If a new benefit appears attractive to them, instead of simply adding it to the list, an employer might use it to replace a less-attractive one in the package.

A second approach, used increasingly, is to have employees contribute a certain amount towards the purchase of discretionary benefits. This system accomplishes two purposes. First, the desired coverage can be provided at a lower cost to the organization but still as a bargain to the employee, who would pay more for it as an individual purchaser. Second, using a contributory approach promotes communication and creates an awareness and appreciation of the employer's contributions to benefits coverage on the employees' behalf. A third approach to cost containment is through savings by means of group insurance.[45]

Issues in the Benefits Area

HRM professionals face a number of issues and problems in the benefits area. Foremost among these are avoiding sex and age discrimination in benefits administration, controlling rising benefit costs, and keeping up with changes in the tax laws.

As a form of compensation, benefits must be provided equally to all employees regardless of sex, age, race, religion, or ethnic origin. For many benefits, maintenance of equality is relatively straightforward. However, in areas such as pensions and disability and health insurance, the road to equality between men and women is less clear. One problem with relation to pension plans is that women have a longer lifespan than men. Thus, they reap the benefits of pension plans for a longer time after retirement than do men, increasing benefit costs to employers.

Another problem is remaining aware of the current costs of benefits. Benefit packages can offer incentives for employees to remain with a company, but the costs of these incentives can change, sometimes quite suddenly. The June 1982 federal budget (as well as subsequent budgets), by making many benefits taxable, reduced many of the advantages of using them to reward certain groups of employees. Thus, a government effort to close what were viewed as tax loopholes forced employers to realize that nonsalary forms of compensation have to be examined continually for their cost implications to both companies and employees. Such an examination is related, for example, to the government policy, instituted in the 1991 taxation year, that changed the rules for contributions to RRSPs. For many employees, the changes linked more closely the individual's annual limit on contribution to this means of tax-sheltered retirement savings and his or her contribution to a company pension plan. The 1992 federal budget provided an additional benefit to some Canadians by permitting the use of RRSPs as a downpayment on the purchase of a first home.

Canada's pension system has a number of deficiencies that are likely to grow unless the implications of changes occurring on the structure of the work force are addressed. The continuing increase in employment in the service industries and the gradual aging of the population are the two primary underlying factors affecting the pension system. Growth in the service sector has carried with it the bulk of the increases in female employment and in part-time work (which is largely by women). Private pensions have not generally been available to most part-time workers, and even those women who work full-time end up with lower private pension benefits than men because, on average, their salaries are lower.[46] Hence, issues for the future include the extent to which pensions are insufficient and to which coverage of the system is uneven.

The aging of the population will increasingly put upward pressure on pension benefits that will not be fully offset by a decline in the costs of schooling and other child-related expenditures. The lack of protection of private pensions from inflation is also an issue that has to be considered.

A final pension issue concerns the ability of firms to withdraw money from pension funds over and above what is deemed necessary to meet anticipated employee pension needs. HRM professionals should follow developments here closely. In 1986, the courts held in *Dominion Stores* and *Dominion Securities Pitfield*[47] that money withdrawn from employee pension plans must be returned. For Dominion Stores, the amount was $38 million and for

Dominion Securities, $1.7 million. On the other hand, in a 1987 court decision, Ontario Hydro was permitted to use $72 million in accrued surpluses as the bulk of its 1986 contribution to an employee pension plan.[48]

The issues of large surpluses in many employment pension plans and of inflation protection led the Ontario government to appoint, in late 1986, the Task Force on Inflation Protection for Employment Pension Plans (the Friedland Task Force). The Friedland report recommended that pensions be indexed at 1 percent less than 75 percent of the Consumer Price Index. The Ontario Pension Benefits Act of 1987 responded by saying that pension benefits should be inflation-related, though no specific formula was provided.[49] The act also froze pension surpluses, permitting an employer to withdraw them only for use in contributing to employee pension plans.

In December 1989, the Supreme Court of Canada ruled against Ontario Hydro's using its pension fund surplus to take a contribution holiday. The decision said the court could

> see no realistic distinction between the corporation giving itself an accounting credit in place of actual payment of its required contribution, and the corporation directly withdrawing surplus from the fund. The result is the same in both cases — the fund's surplus is reduced or eliminated.[50]

Since the Ontario Hydro plan is in the form of a legislative statute, it may be viewed as an exception, but there remains considerable doubt about the ability of any employer to take a holiday from contributions to its pension fund.

There is also debate in Quebec over what to do with a pension plan surplus. Both employers and unions oppose the provincial government's proposal to end the current moratorium and impose an equal splitting of pension surpluses. The unions see pensions as deferred wages and believe that all the funds belong to employees. Employers do not consider pensions as salaries and want the moratorium removed.[51] Unions also see the control of the surplus linked with questions of indexation and management of pension funds.

How the issue of surpluses is settled will clearly affect benefits planning.[52] A 1988 Pension Commission survey showed that 62 percent of plans with more than 1000 members had a surplus.[53] Further changes in Ontario's pension legislation are planned. This area is a very complex one in which companies need specialized advice.

The provision of pensions for part-time employees will certainly be an issue for future consideration. So will employee participation in deciding on pension fund investments. Unions are asking for co-management of pension funds.[54] There has also been a growing interest in "socially responsible" pension investment funds — funds that build their investment portfolios taking into consideration such factors as the share issuer's environmental consciousness and the state of its labour–management relations. Just as environmental concerns have become an increasing part of society today, so it is likely that social investing will become a greater consideration in the investment decisions of pension funds.[55]

Since benefits represent approximately one-third of total compensation costs, HRM professionals must monitor the impact of various benefit programs on costs, on human resource effectiveness, and on employee satisfaction. In addition, HRM professionals will likely be active in developing new proposals in this area. Thus, they will want to stay informed of the latest developments in this complex field.[56]

Summary

This chapter has focussed on five categories of benefits provided employees: universal benefits; mandatory benefits; discretionary benefits; pay for time not worked; and employee service benefits. Although many organizations provide generous benefit packages, most employees have little control over the types of benefits they receive. The cafeteria approach, which seeks to remedy this problem by giving employees a choice in benefit selection, has limited though increasing use by organizations. Although benefits are used by organizations to attract and retain employees, there is little research evidence that they are successful in achieving this purpose. It is generally accepted, however, that attractive pay and benefit packages are necessary if an organization is to maintain a competitive position. In the past, because of the favourable tax treatment afforded a number of benefit programs, both employers and employees could benefit by having a certain proportion of an organization's compensation dollars set aside for benefits. Cost advantages still exist, even though changes in the tax laws have reduced the value of many benefit programs.

Review Questions

1. On average, benefits equal about one-third of direct labour costs. How can organizations control these costs yet have them contribute to organizational effectiveness?

2. Since legislated benefits differ from one Canadian jurisdiction to another, to what extent are benefit calculations likely to enter into decisions to transfer employees from one province to another.

3. What are the advantages and disadvantages to an organization of changing from a fixed to a flexible benefits program? Describe what is meant by each type of program.

4. Mandatory retirement has become a major issue in benefits administration in Canada. Some provinces, such as British Columbia, preclude a mandatory retirement age; others, such as Ontario, permit it. Discuss the arguments for and against mandatory retirement.

Project Ideas

1. Design an optimal benefit and service program to fit your own needs. Explain why you selected particular benefits and services and why you rejected other options. Compare your benefit preferences with those of other students.

2. Acquire a booklet describing employee benefits from a local employer (perhaps from your university or college). Relate the plans discussed therein to the material presented in the chapter, noting, where applicable, the choices that had been made by the employer. Comment on the extent to which the programs are clearly described. Are benefits being used to enhance the organization's image as a caring employer?

3. Find a firm with a pension plan. Discuss with the employee benefits manager the reasons for the plan's provisions (for example, the amount of contributions by employer and employee, the basis for calculating benefits, and who administers the plan).

4. Interview an HRM professional of a local organization. Ask about its benefit program, its changes in the past several years, the implications of any recent tax changes, and what methods are used to communicate the program to employees. Be sure to find out if the organization is unionized.

5. Develop a hypothetical company and ask one or more insurance companies or agents to recommend benefit coverages and perhaps provide cost estimates. (If this activity is done as a class project, many insurance companies may be willing to go to this trouble, particularly since they will be assisting individuals who may well be their corporate clients in the near future.)

▶▶▶ CASES

CASE 13.1 ▶ INDEXED PENSIONS AT INCO

More than 6300 hourly paid employees at Inco Ltd. will vote tomorrow on a tentative agreement containing unprecedented provisions for indexed pensions and the first across-the-board raise in a decade.

Leo Gerard, Ontario director of the United Steelworkers of America, said only two of 150 union stewards voted against the proposed three-year contract at a meeting yesterday. The union stewards are usually much more militant than the general membership.

The highlight of the proposed contract is inflation protection for pensions up to an inflation rate of 7 percent.

With an inflation rate between 1 and 2 percent, pension benefits would increase by 1 percent. Eight other increases are provided for until the inflation rate exceeded 7 percent, when benefits would jump by 5 percent.

"This covers approximately 80 percent of the inflation rate," Mr. Gerard said.

All Inco retirees and all survivors of Inco workers killed on or off the job would receive the inflation protection. Before 1972, the widows of such workers were not entitled to any pension benefits from the nickel giant. Inco has agreed to establish a special $1-million fund for these widows.

"To my knowledge, this is the first time [such an inflation protection package] has ever been negotiated in Canada," Mr. Gerard said. "It was not negotiated under a special pension contract, but on a lifetime plan; it is in place for life and we don't have to renegotiate it."

He said the pension plan surplus of about $48-million will be used to index benefits.

The proposed contract would allow workers to retire after 30 years with no reduction in benefits. Pension benefits for all employees would increase by 50 percent by the end of the contract.

In the first year of the deal, a 55-year-old Inco worker with 30 years' service would retire on a basic pension of $1,320 a month.

Over the life of the contract, the average wage would increase to $18.99 an hour from $15.58 an hour. The base rate would jump by $1 an hour on the first day of the contract and $1.42 an hour from the cost-of-living-allowance would be folded into the base wage from June 1. COLA increases of 25 cents an hour would kick in for the second and third years.

Under a new nickel-price-bonus plan, every Inco worker would receive about $2080 on the second payday after ratification. Further proposed bonus payments, to be paid quarterly, range from $46 to $2678, depending on the price of nickel. It is now selling for about $7 (U.S.) a pound.

After a membership meeting yesterday, Dave Campbell, president of Steelworkers Local 6500, which represents Inco's hourly rated workforce, said:

"I have been in this union a long time, and for the first time there was a standing ovation for the bargaining committee."

Mr. Gerard and Mr. Campbell expect the tentative agreement to be ratified.

Source: Terry Pender, "Tentative Inco Contract Contains a Unique Clause for Pension Protection," *The Globe and Mail*, May 30, 1988. Reprinted with the permission of the author.

TASKS AND QUESTIONS

1. Describe the unique features of the 1988 Inco pension plan.
2. Discuss the reasons for the favourable employee reaction to this plan.
3. From a company perspective, did the plan have any negative features?

CASE 13.2 ▶ ENHANCING PRODUCTIVITY THROUGH ON-SITE CHILD CARE

The slide shows Ontario Hydro president Robert Franklin sitting around a table with several small children, a huge grin on his face.

"That's the happiest anybody remembers seeing him," joked Etta Wharton, manager of employment equity for the utility.

The picture was taken, she explained, when Hydro opened an on-site day care centre for its employees. Mr. Franklin said at the time he felt such a centre made employees more productive, she reported at a conference last week on balancing work and family needs.

"To us, family responsive programming is not corporate philanthropy," said Fern Stimpson, director of corporate human resources for Manulife Financial Holdings Ltd. "We see it as a win-win situation, with a real opportunity for both corporations and employees to come out ahead."

Companies feel they are facing a conundrum, said Mark Daniel of the Conference Board of Canada as he opened the session: On the one hand they need higher productivity from their employees as they face increased competitive pressures. On the other hand, their employees are feeling stress and a sense of "I'm dancing as fast as I can."

The result is more companies are looking at their staff as "whole people," realizing productivity on the job depends on what happens outside.

And what happens outside today is that the majority of workers have responsibilities to care for family members, be they children or elderly parents.

Companies present at the meeting, co-sponsored by the conference board, Labour Canada and Status of Women Canada, offer a wide range of initiatives — from the opportunity to work at home, to sessions telling parents their legal responsibilities toward nannies.

Ontario Hydro recently retroactively restored service credits lost by women who took maternity leaves before 1981.

Several speakers said they felt offering a flexible work environment or family benefits also helps in recruiting and retaining staff, an increasing concern with the labor shortages expected to materialize in this decade.

Yet workplaces with the latest in technology are sometimes still in the horse and buggy age when it comes to attitudes toward workers, said Mary Collins, federal Minister for the Status of Women.

"I reject unequivocally that offering family benefit programs is anathema to sound business practices," she said. "As employers, making full use of your worker potential is integral to the bottom line. And to do so requires programs which acknowledge the demographics."

This includes a labor force in which women with children under three are the single biggest group of entrants, said Judy MacBride-King, a consultant to the conference board.

Another important issue is changing corporate culture so people don't feel they will be thought less of if they take advantage of work-sharing or other options, said Fran Sussner Rodgers, president of Work/Family Directions Inc. in Massachusetts.

Source: Margot Gibb-Clark, "How Children Can Make a Company More Productive," *The Globe and Mail*, April 4, 1990. Reprinted with the permission of *The Globe and Mail*.

TASKS AND QUESTIONS

1. Outline the pros and cons of offering child care on-site at the workplace.
2. Discuss whether employees should pay all, a part, or none of the costs of providing child care at a place of employment.
3. If you were an HR manager, how would you assess the demand for child care in your organization? How would you determine how much the company should contribute to the cost of a child-care program?

NOTES

1. Brent King, "Many Employees Don't Know What Their Firm's Benefits Are Worth," *Financial Post*, December 3, 1983.
2. *Employee Benefit Costs in Canada 1989* (Toronto: Peat, Marwick, Stevenson and Kellogg, 1989); and *Employee Benefit Costs in Canada 1953* (Toronto: The Thorne Group Ltd., 1953). For data from 1957 to 1975/76, see Sylvia Ostry and Mahmood A. Zaidi, *Labour Economics in Canada*, 3rd ed. (Toronto: Macmillan of Canada, 1979), pp. 202–3.

3. Statistics Canada, *Employee Compensation in Canada: All Industries, 1978* (Ottawa: Supply and Services Canada, 1980), p. 46.

4. D.J. Wynn, "Employee Mobility: Relationship to Pensions," *Public Personnel Review*, vol. 32 (1971), pp. 219–22.

5. George F. Dreker, Ronald A. Ash, and Robert D. Bretz, "Benefit Coverage and Employee Cost: Critical Factors in Explaining Compensation Satisfaction," *Personnel Psychology*, vol. 41 no. 2 (Summer 1988), pp. 237–54.

6. Pradeep Kumar, David Arrowsmith, and Mary Lou Coates, *Current Industrial Relations Scene, Canadian Labour Relations: An Information Manual* (Kingston: Industrial Relations Centre, Queen's University, 1991), p. 373.

7. E.R. Gommersall and M.S. Myers, "Breakthrough in On-the-Job Training," *Harvard Business Review*, vol. 44 (July-August 1966), pp. 62–71.

8. Canadian Auto Workers, *CAW/Ford Report*, September 1990.

9. O.D. Dickerson, *Health Insurance* (Homewood, Ill.: Richard D. Irwin, 1968), p. 16; and material compiled by the Life Underwriters Training Council, Washington, DC.

10. Lawrence E. Coward, *Mercer Handbook of Canadian Pension and Welfare Plans*, 9th ed. (Don Mills, Ont.: CCH Canadian, 1988), pp. 193–96.

11. *Employee Benefit Costs in Canada 1989*.

12. $3000 is deducted from earnings to calculate the contribution.

13. Coward, *Mercer Handbook*, pp. 187–91.

14. *The Canadian Master Labour Guide* (Don Mills, Ont.: CCH Canadian, 1991), p. 777.

15. Frank Reid and Noah M. Meltz, "Causes of Shifts in the Unemployment-Vacancy Relationship: An Empirical Analysis for Canada," *Review of Economics and Statistics*, vol. 61 (1972), pp. 470–75.

16. Economic Council of Canada, *People and Jobs* (Ottawa: Information Canada, 1976).

17. Frank Reid and Noah M. Meltz, "Canada's STC: A Comparison with the California Version," in Ramelle MaCoy and Martin V. Morand, eds., *Short-Time Compensation: A Formula for Work Sharing* (New York: Pergamon Press, 1984), pp. 106–19.

18. Alan Freeman, "Ottawa Doubles UI Work-Sharing Money," *The Globe and Mail*, September 19, 1990; and Leslie Papp, "Bridging the Gap, Labor, Management Find Innovative Ways to Keep Peace in Tough Times," *The Toronto Star*, March 7, 1992.

19. Commission of Inquiry on Unemployment Insurance, *Report* (The Forget Commission Report) (Ottawa: Supply and Services Canada, 1986).

20. Minister of Employment and Immigration, Ottawa, October 22, 1990; "Bill C-21 Becomes Law," *CAW Contact* (Toronto), special edition, 1990.

21. *Brooks* v. *Canada Safeway Limited*, 89 Canadian Labour Law Cases (S.C.), 17012. See also Susan E. Fremes, "A Parental Postscript," *Benefits Canada*,

vol. 15, no. 4 (April 1991), pp. 27–30; and Mary A. Porjes, "What Leave Am I Required by Law to Give Employees Going on Maternity Leave?" *Benefits Canada*, vol. 15, no. 4 (April 1991), p. 13.

22. *Employee Benefit Costs in Canada 1989.*
23. Coward, *Mercer Handbook*, pp. 43–46 and 102–3. British Columbia's proposed legislation is to take effect on January 1, 1993. See Frederick L. Abbott, "Last but Not Least," *Benefits Canada*, vol. 14, no. 7 (September 1990), pp. 31–33.
24. Coward, *Mercer Handbook*, pp. 43–46 and 102–3.
25. Margot Gibb-Clark, "Experts Advise Cautious Eye on Worker Pension Funds," *The Globe and Mail*, April 2, 1988.
26. Pay Research Bureau, Public Service Staff Relations Board Canada, *Benefits Survey: Program Incidence and Characteristics, January 1, 1990* (Ottawa: Pay Research Bureau, 1990), pp. 13–20.
27. Pay Research Bureau, *Benefits Survey*, pp. 51–55.
28. Pay Research Bureau, *Benefits Survey*, pp. 32–33.
29. *Employee Benefit Costs in Canada 1989.*
30. Pay Research Bureau, *Benefits Survey*, pp. 78–79.
31. Virginia Galt, "Ford, CAW Reach Deal," *The Globe and Mail*, September 22, 1990.
32. *Employee Benefit Costs in Canada 1989.*
33. L. Maloney, "Business Perks That Rile the White House," *U.S. News & World Report*, March 27, 1978, pp. 33–34.
34. Glenn J. Gooding, "Career Moves—For the Employee, for the Organization," *Personnel*, April 1988, p. 114.
35. E.E. Lawler III and E. Levin, "Union Officers' Perceptions of Members' Pay Preferences," *Industrial and Labour Relations Review*, vol. 21 (1968), pp. 509–17.
36. Berwyn N. Fragner, "Employees' Cafeteria Offers Insurance Options," *Harvard Business Review*, November-December 1975, pp. 7–10.
37. S.M. Nealey, "Pay and Benefit Preference," *Industrial Relations*, vol. 3 (1964), pp. 17–28; S.M. Nealey and J.G. Goodale, "Worker Preferences among Time of Benefits and Pay," *Journal of Applied Psychology*, vol. 52 (1967), pp. 357–61; J.R. Schuster, "Another Look at Compensation Preferences," *Industrial Management Review*, 1969, pp. 1–18; and J.B. Chapman and R. Ottemann, "Employee Preferences for Various Compensation and Fringe Benefit Options," *The Personnel Administrator*, vol. 20 (1975), pp. 31–36.
38. Helen Kohl, "Surprise Packages," *Canadian Business*, August 1982, p. 84.
39. *Across the Border: Comparing Compensation and Benefits in the U.S. and Canada 1989/1990* (Toronto: Hewitt Associates, 1990), p. 26.
40. Nealey, "Pay and Benefit Preference"; Nealey and Goodale, "Worker Preferences"; and Schuster, "Compensation Preferences."
41. Chapman and Ottemann, "Employee Preferences."

42. A. Schlachtmeyer and R. Bogart, "Employee-Choice Benefits—Can Employees Handle It?" *Compensation Review*, third quarter, 1979, pp. 12–19; and Fragner, "Employees' Cafeteria."

43. "Benefits on the Menu," *The Toronto Star*, March 25, 1990.

44. V.J. Pruegger and T.B. Rogers, "How to Predict Flex Benefits Costs," *Benefits Canada*, vol. 14, no. 1 (January-February 1990), pp. 15–20.

45. Angus Kyle, "Financial Management Key to Group Benefits," *Benefits Canada*, vol. 15, no. 2 (February 1991), pp. 15–19; and Liam Dixon, "Containing Health Care Costs," *Benefits Canada*, vol. 15, no. 2 (February 1991), pp. 24–26.

46. Virginia Galt, "Action Urged to Remedy 'Holes' in the Pension System," *The Globe and Mail*, June 5, 1985.

47. *Pension Commission of Ontario and Dominion Stores Limited* v. *Donald Collins et al.*, August 18, 1986 (S.C.O.); also summarized in CCH *Canadian Employment Benefits and Pension Guide Reports*, para. 8019 (Ont.HC); and *R.C. Heiliq et al.* v. *Dominion Securities Pitfield Ltd. et al.* (1986) 55 O.R. (2nd) 783; 29 D.L.R. (4th) 762 (H.C.J.); also summarized in CCH *Canadian Employment Benefits . . .*, para. 8020. See also Mark Kingwell and Lorne Slotnick, "Return Pension Funds, Dominion Stores Told by Court," *The Globe and Mail*, August 19, 1986; and Rich Haliechuk, "Firm Accused of 'Pirating' Pension Fund,' *The Toronto Star*, August 30, 1986.

48. *Canadian Union of Public Employees—C.L.C. Local 1000* v. *Ontario Hydro* (1987) 59 O.R. (2nd) 31 (Div. Ct.).

49. Task Force on Inflation Protection for Employment Pension Plans, *Report* (The Friedland Report) (Toronto: Queen's Printer for Ontario, 1988).

50. The Supreme Court of Canada denied Ontario Hydro leave to appeal a decision by the Ontario Court of Appeal which ruled that the existence of a surplus in and of itself did not permit Hydro to take a contribution holiday. See *Re: Canadian Union of Public Employees—C.L.C. Local 1000 v. Ontario Hydro* (1989), 68 O.R. (2nd) 620; also summarized in CCH *Canadian Employment Benefits and Pension Guide Reports*, para. 8107, September 1991. Peter Hirst, "On Death Row," *Benefits Canada*, vol. 14, no. 3 (April 1990), pp. 39–42.

51. Antoine Di-Lillo, "Surplus Standoff," *Benefits Canada*, vol. 15, no. 4 (April 1991), pp. 15–16.

52. John O'Grady, "Labor's New Deal," *Benefits Canada*, vol. 15, no. 4 (April 1991), pp. 49–55.

53. Margot Gibb-Clark, "Little Progress on Issue of Pension Surpluses," *The Globe and Mail*, July 17, 1990.

54. Ed Finn, "The Case for Co-Management," *The Facts* (Canadian Union of Public Employees), vol. 11, no. 2 (Fall 1989), pp. 30–32.

55. Tony Michael, "For Love or Money—Social Investing," in Mary E. Brennan, *Canadian Employee Benefit Plans, 1989*, report of 22nd Annual Canadian Employee Benefits Conference, November 25–29, 1989, New Orleans, La. (Brookfield, Wisc.: International Foundation of Employees Benefit Plans, 1990), pp. 22–27.

56. Sources of information on new developments in the benefits field in Canada include *Benefits Canada, Pension Investment/Employee Benefits*, published monthly by Maclean Hunter; *Canadian Employment Benefits and Pension Guide Reports*, published by CCH Canadian, Don Mills, Ont., and updated regularly; and *The Employment Law Report*, Concord Publishing, Toronto.

SUGGESTIONS FOR FURTHER READING

- *Benefits Canada*. A monthly publication with short articles on current issues in the benefits field in Canada. See, for example, the Kyle, O'Grady, and Pruegger and Rogers articles noted below.
- Mary E. Brennan, ed. *Canadian Employee Benefit Plans, 1989*. Report of 22nd Annual Canadian Employee Benefits Conference, November 25–29, 1989, New Orleans, Louisiana. Brookfield, Wisc.: International Foundation of Employee Benefit Plans, 1990.
- CCH Canada. *Canadian Employment Benefits and Pension Guide Reports*. Don Mills, Ont. Updated regularly.
- Lawrence E. Coward. *Mercer Handbook of Canadian Pension and Welfare Plans*. 9th ed. Don Mills, Ont.: CCH Canadian, 1988.
- George F. Dreker, Ronald A. Ash, and Robert D. Bretz. "Benefit Coverage and Employee Cost: Critical Factors in Explaining Compensation Satisfaction." *Personnel Psychology*, vol. 41, no. 2 (Summer 1988), pp. 237–54.
- Angus Kyle. "Financial Management Key to Group Benefits." *Benefits Canada*, vol. 15, no. 2 (February 1991), pp. 15–19.
- John O'Grady. "Labor's New Deal." *Benefits Canada*, vol. 15, no. 4 (April 1991), pp. 49–55.
- Pay Research Bureau, Public Service Staff Relations Board of Canada. *Benefits Survey: Program Incidence and Characteristics, January 1, 1990*. Ottawa: Pay Research Bureau, 1990.
- V.J. Pruegger and T.B. Rogers. "How to Predict Flex Benefits Costs." *Benefits Canada*, vol. 14, no. 1 (January-February 1990), pp. 15–20.
- Task Force on Inflation Protection for Employment Pension Plans. *Report* (The Friedland Report). Toronto: Queen's Printer for Ontario, 1988.

Chapter 14

Employee Health and Safety

- Organizational Benefits of a Safe and Healthy Workplace
- Relation to Other HRM Functions
- Health and Safety Responsibilities
- The Ontario Occupational Health and Safety Act
- Workers' Compensation
- Ensuring a Safe and Healthy Workplace
- Special Health Problems
- HRM in Action ▸ Should Compensation Benefits Be Paid for Work Stress?
- HRM in Action ▸ Drug Testing at Imperial Oil
- Summary
- Review Questions
- Project Ideas
- Case 14.1 ▸ Employee Fitness at Canada Life
- Case 14.2 ▸ A Workplace Policy for AIDS
- Notes
- Suggestions for Further Reading

THE ROLE OF HEALTH AND SAFETY as an HRM function is to maintain a safe and healthy work environment for employees. Speakers at a 1991 conference on health and safety organized by Labour Canada were told, according to one news report:

> Workplace accidents and occupation-related illness cost $4-billion a year in compensation payments alone.... The total cost is more than $8-billion a year when indirect expenses are taken into account.... There also is an incalculable social toll resulting from the estimated 1000 deaths and thousands of injuries caused by workplace accidents each year.
>
> Speakers at the conference... lamented the apparent lack of public concern about occupational health and safety. But health and safety advocates will have to "struggle to make progress" until the public regards unsafe working conditions to be as socially unacceptable as smoking, impaired driving or pollution, said Hugh Walker, managing director of Alberta Occupational Health and Safety.
>
> Mr. Walker said there is no general recognition in most businesses that poor occupational health and safety "is a high-cost item." Furthermore, many businesses "do not yet see workers as valuable assets, they still see their workers as costs to be minimized."[1]

Nowhere is the challenge of maintaining a safe and healthy work environment greater than on Canada's hazardous oil-drilling rigs. In February 1982, one of Canada's most publicized disasters occurred with the sinking off Newfoundland of the *Ocean Ranger*, an oil-drilling rig, and its entire 84-man crew. According to the commission investigating the tragedy:

> The problems began when a wave broke a porthole in the rig's nerve centre, the ballast control room, soaking the electrical controls that kept the vessel upright in the water.
>
> As a result, four hours later the control panel malfunctioned and allowed water to surge into one of the two gigantic underwater pontoons that supported the rig. When the Ocean Ranger then began to tip forward, untrained crewmen tried to correct the alarming list, but instead made it worse. As the rig leaned into the sea, water rushed inside through openings in two anchor chain compartments. By 1:30 a.m. on Feb. 15, roughly 5½ hours after the control centre porthole had broken, the crew began to abandon ship. But one of the four lifeboats was already underwater, and, lacking the protection of cold-weather survival suits, all hands perished.[2]

The commission blamed the rig's owner "for a variety of lapses, including ignoring regulations, training crewmen inadequately, and not providing survival suits."[3] Two years after the accident, the owner agreed to an out-of-court settlement of $440 000, tax free, to each crewman's family.[4] This incident illustrates not only the high human costs but also some of the financial repercussions of inattention to safety.

ORGANIZATIONAL BENEFITS OF A SAFE AND HEALTHY WORKPLACE

A safe and healthy workplace helps to maintain a productive and satisfied work force. A safe work environment facilitates productivity by reducing time lost due to work-related accidents and illnesses, as well as time lost due to labour disputes and work stoppages focussed on safety concerns. In just one year in British Columbia, for instance, 46 labour disputes with some of the province's largest public and private employers involved health issues such as first aid facilities, staffing levels, inspections, personal safety equipment, and pollutant levels. Disputes on these issues resulted in 75 000 lost days of worker production.[5] A thousand employees of McDonnell Douglas Canada in Brampton, Ontario, refused to work in 1987 when a report from the Ontario Ministry of Labour condemned the company for 200 infractions of the province's health and safety act.[6]

A safe and healthy workplace can eliminate worker dissatisfaction with unsafe and unhealthy working conditions. That workers care about health and safety is evidenced by the large number of labour disputes arising from safety concerns. Indeed, one occupational health and safety agency administrator has said that "health and safety is now the 'No. 1 priority' of unions."[7]

Besides facilitating productivity and worker satisfaction, maintaining a safe and healthy workplace helps reduce costs associated with work-related accidents and illnesses. An *accident* is defined as an unexpected or unplanned event that results in an injury, property damage, or material loss at a workplace. Statistics Canada reported that in 1987 there were an estimated 1.1 million accidents in the workplace.[8] According to the Occupational Health and Safety Branch of Labour Canada, in 1986 Canada had 762 work-related accidents that resulted in death and 598 424 disabling injuries. The total direct cost of these accidents, including medical and related costs, compensation for lost earnings, and pensions, was $3.13 billion, or an estimated $318 per Canadian worker. Although fatalities per 100 000 employees were halved, from 16.3 to 8.3, between 1965 and 1989, disabling injuries per 100 employees almost doubled, from 3.7 to 6.3.[9] (This increase in injuries occurred despite the general shift in employment from manufacturing to services.) Actual costs to organizations are even higher, since accidents and illnesses invariably result in production losses. A study by the Economic Council of Canada suggested that indirect costs could range from two to ten times the direct costs.[10]

Maintaining a safe and healthy workplace also helps control health care costs, since employers experience a rise in disability and other health- and accident-related insurance expenditures as the number of work-related injuries increases. And since premiums for workers' compensation are rated by industry, inattention to matters of health and safety can result in all employers in an industry having to pay more.

Disabling injuries and illnesses also deprive an employer of the full working life of an employee. A copper refinery lost the services of one loyal and enthusiastic worker when a platform collapsed under her. According to one of her co-workers, "Out of ten guys, Sally did more work than nine of them."[11] Furthermore, unsafe working conditions often lead to voluntary turnover when employees become anxious about work-related hazards. Having to replace workers who die, become disabled, or quit because of unsafe working conditions increases an organization's recruiting, selection, and training costs.

Finally, accidents often result in physical damage to material, equipment, and property, as well as in loss of life to employees, customers, and others. The actual costs of such damages can be quite high, but even costlier is the damage done to an organization's image. For example, in 1987, as part of a "total wellness and zero accident" program, Mazda opened a fitness centre in Flint Rock, Michigan, the first indoor health and recreation facility built by a Detroit automaker for the use of hourly workers. The idea was that health was going to be enhanced at Mazda. The whole program was swept into oblivion, however, by a drive to reach full production during the summer of 1988. The introduction of a second shift brought with it an increase in worker injuries to 42.6 days lost per 100 workers, almost a third higher than the industry average. The Flat Rock plant became the focus of negative publicity as a result of its high injury rate.[12]

An organization found guilty of practising or perpetuating unsafe or unhealthy working conditions often pays a price in business losses and in the ability to attract qualified applicants for job vacancies.

RELATION TO OTHER HRM FUNCTIONS

The health and safety function is directly related to seven other HRM functions: selection, training, performance appraisal, job analysis, recruiting, benefits, and labour relations. These relationships are shown in Figure 14.1.

SELECTION

The selection function facilitates health and safety by selecting applicants who are physically and mentally able to perform the job. Research shows very little support for an identifiable personality trait predictive of unsafe work behaviour ("accident proneness"). Selection procedures can, however, screen applicants for physical and mental impairments that could conceivably increase the likelihood of accident or illness.[13] For example, a relationship has been established between vision and accident occurrence: employees who pass vision standards for their jobs have significantly fewer accidents than employees who fail vision requirements.[14] It is safe to assume that an employee who fails to meet any selection standard important to performance in his or her job (such as co-ordination, hearing, or physical strength) has a greater risk of accident or injury in the performance of job duties. Research also indicates that older workers are much less likely than younger workers to have an accident.[15] Though younger applicants may not be rejected simply because of their age, in the interest of safety they could be assigned to less hazardous jobs.

TRAINING

Training facilitates health and safety by educating workers in safe work procedures and behaviour. Training is one of the major components in organizational programs to promote safety awareness among employees. The value of safety training for new employees or employees on a new job is supported by data indicating that accident rates are highest during the first months on a new job. This relationship holds regardless of age or sex of the worker.[16]

Training programs should be conducted for both supervisors and their subordinates. Program content for supervisors should emphasize knowledge and enforcement of safety rules and regulations, as well as recognition and control of hazards in the workplace. Programs for subordinates should be more specific, emphasizing rules and safe work behaviours.

CHAPTER 14 EMPLOYEE HEALTH AND SAFETY 661

FIGURE 14.1
Health and Safety: Relation to Other HRM Functions

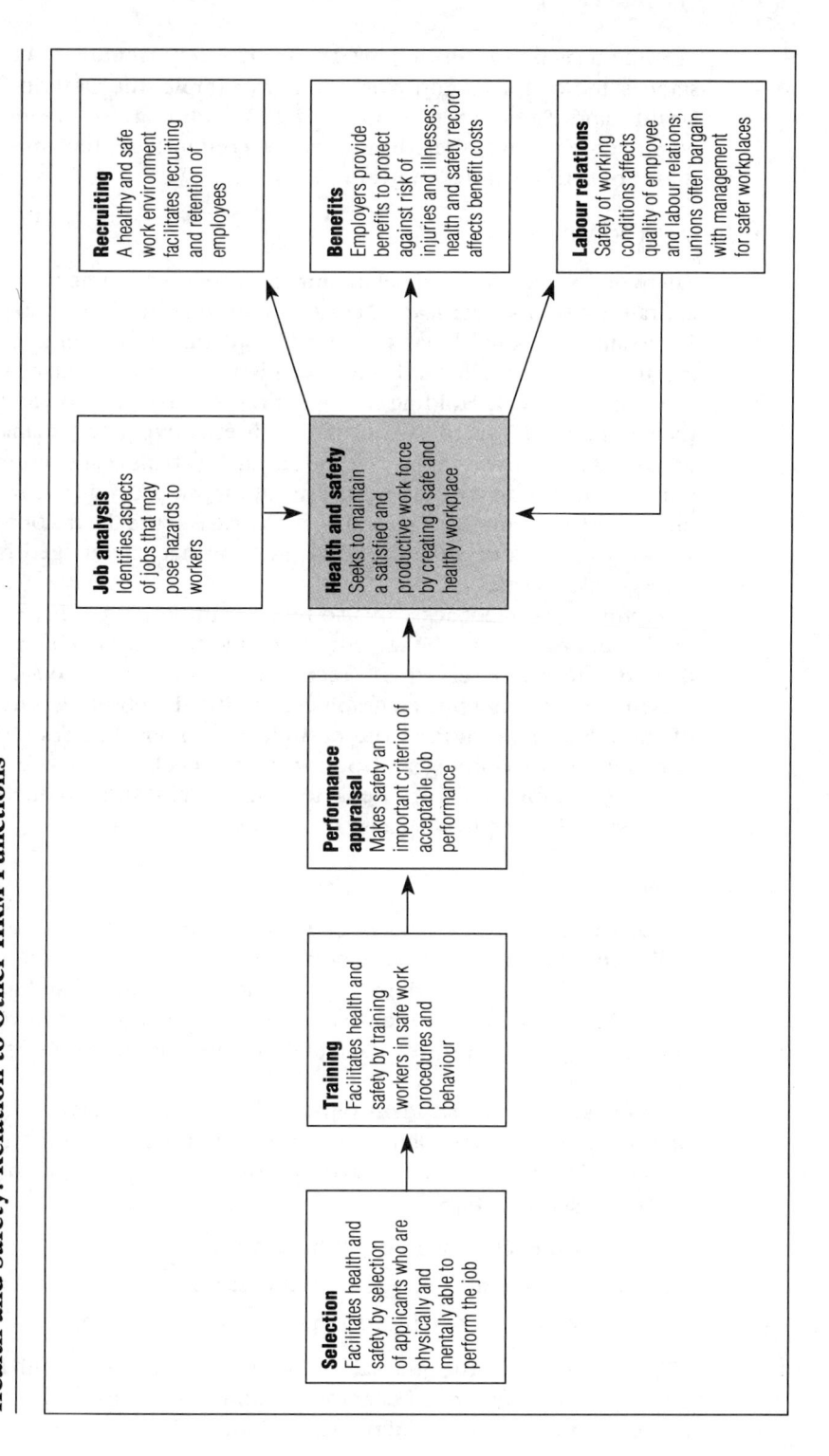

Selection
Facilitates health and safety by selection of applicants who are physically and mentally able to perform the job

Training
Facilitates health and safety by training workers in safe work procedures and behaviour

Performance appraisal
Makes safety an important criterion of acceptable job performance

Job analysis
Identifies aspects of jobs that may pose hazards to workers

Health and safety
Seeks to maintain a satisfied and productive work force by creating a safe and healthy workplace

Recruiting
A healthy and safe work environment facilitates recruiting and retention of employees

Benefits
Employers provide benefits to protect against risk of injuries and illnesses; health and safety record affects benefit costs

Labour relations
Safety of working conditions affects quality of employee and labour relations; unions often bargain with management for safer workplaces

PERFORMANCE APPRAISAL

Some jurisdictions have laws requiring safety training in certain circumstances and/or for certain workers. For example, the Ontario Occupational Health and Safety Act requires special training for members of joint employer–employee health and safety committees; the training program must be certified and is subject to inspection.[17]

Safe work procedures and behaviour can also be encouraged by performance appraisal systems that make safety an important criterion of job performance. For example, if a unit's safety record is one dimension for appraising managerial performance, that unit's manager is motivated to demand subordinates' attention to safety. Holding managers responsible for the safety records of their units is one factor associated with effective safety management programs.[18] Alternatively, appraisal and reward systems that overemphasize productivity may lead to a disregard for safe work procedures. Employees and union leaders claim that this had been the case in the deaths of several miners working under a production bonus system that encouraged production at the expense of safety.[19]

Performance feedback can also be used in programs that encourage safe work behaviour. The behaviour of employees in a vehicle maintenance department was observed and recorded with attention to safety. Feedback was in the form of a posted graph comparing the observed safety behaviour of the department against the desired behaviour. The study found that a combination of training and performance feedback on safety dimensions resulted in improved work behaviour and a substantial reduction over previous years in time lost because of accidents.[20]

JOB ANALYSIS

Job analysis identifies aspects of jobs that may pose hazards to workers. Following the identification of such hazards, jobs may be modified to eliminate hazards, or safe work procedures can be developed and specified in job descriptions. The use of required safety equipment and protective devices, such as goggles, ear protectors, and hard hats, should also be specified in job descriptions.

Job descriptions that identify hazards and specify safe work procedures provide guidelines and objectives for safety training programs. Instructions for completing a job safety analysis form are given in Exhibit 14.1. The analysis has three steps:

1. Break the job down into its basic steps.
2. Identify potential accidents and hazards associated with each step.
3. Recommend safe job procedures for each job step.

When completed, the job safety analysis serves as an aid in instructing employees in safe work behaviour. Exhibit 14.2 shows the safety analysis guide completed for a banding pallets job.

EXHIBIT 14.1
Instructions for Completing a Job Safety Analysis Form

Job Safety Analysis (JSA) is an important accident prevention tool that works by finding hazards and eliminating or minimizing them *before* the job is performed, and *before* they have a chance to become accidents. Use your JSA for job clarification and hazard awareness, as a guide in new employee training, for periodic contacts and for retraining of senior employees, as a refresher on jobs which run infrequently, as an accident investigation tool, and for informing employees of specific job hazards and protective measures.

Set priorities for doing JSAs: Jobs that have a history of many accidents, jobs that have produced disabling injuries, jobs with high potential for disabling injury or death, and new jobs with no accident history.

Here's how to do each of the three parts of a Job Safety Analysis.

SEQUENCE OF BASIC JOB STEPS

Break the job down into steps. Each of the steps of a job should accomplish some major task. The task will consist of a *set* of movements. Look at the first *set* of movements used to perform a task, and then determine the next logical *set* of movements. For example, the job might be to move a box from a conveyor in the receiving area to a shelf in the storage area. How does that break down into job steps? Picking up the box from the conveyor and putting it on a handtruck is one logical set of movements, so it is one job step. Everything related to that one logical set of movements is part of that job step.

The next logical *set* of movements might be pushing the loaded handtruck to the storeroom. Removing the boxes from the truck and placing them on the shelf is another logical set of movements. And finally, returning the handtruck to the receiving area might be the final step in this type of job.

Be sure to list *all* the steps in a job. Some steps might not be done each time—checking the casters on a handtruck, for example. However, that task is a part of the job as a whole, and should be listed and analyzed.

POTENTIAL HAZARDS

Identify the hazards associated with each step. Examine each step to find and identify hazards—actions, conditions and possibilities that could lead to an accident.

It's not enough to look at the obvious hazards. It's also important to look at the entire environment and discover every conceivable hazard that might exist.

Be sure to list health hazards as well, even though the harmful effect may not be immediate. A good example is the harmful effect of inhaling a solvent or chemical dust over a long period of time.

It's important to list *all* hazards. Hazards contribute to accidents, injuries and occupational illnesses.

In order to do part three of a JSA effectively, you must identify potential and existing *hazards*. That's why it's important to distinguish between a *hazard*, an *accident* and an *injury*. Each of these terms has a specific meaning:

HAZARD—A potential danger. Oil on the floor is a hazard.
ACCIDENT—An unintended happening that may result in injury, loss or damage. Slipping on the oil is an *accident*.
INJURY—The *result* of an accident. A sprained wrist from the fall would be an injury.

Some people find it easier to identify possible accidents and illnesses and work back from them to the hazards. If you do that, you can list the accident and illness types in parentheses following the hazard. But be sure you focus on the *hazard* for developing recommended actions and safe work procedures.

RECOMMENDED ACTION OR PROCEDURE

Using the first two columns as a guide, decide what actions are necessary to eliminate or minimize the hazards that could lead to an accident, injury, or occupational illness.

Among the actions that can be taken are: 1) engineering the hazard out; 2) providing personal protective equipment; 3) job instruction training; 4) good housekeeping; and 5) good ergonomics (positioning the person in relation to the machine or other elements in the environment in such a way as to eliminate stresses and strains).

List recommended safe operating procedures on the form, and also list required or recommended personal protective equipment for each step of the job.

Be specific. Say *exactly* what needs to be done to correct the hazard, such as, "lift, using your leg muscles." Avoid general statements like, "be careful."

Give a recommended action or procedure for *every* hazard.

If the hazard is a serious one, it should be corrected immediately. The JSA should then be changed to reflect the new conditions.

Source: *Accident Prevention Manual for Business & Industry*, 10th ed. (Chicago: National Safety Council, 1992). Reprinted with the permission of the National Safety Council.

EXHIBIT 14.2
A Form for a Job Safety Analysis Training Guide

JOB SAFETY ANALYSIS	JOB TITLE (and number if applicable): Banding Pallets	PAGE 1 OF 2 JSA NO 105	DATE: 00/00/00	☒ NEW ☐ REVISED
INSTRUCTIONS ON REVERSE SIDE	TITLE OF PERSON WHO DOES JOB: Bander	SUPERVISOR: James Smith	ANALYSIS BY: James Smith	
COMPANY/ORGANIZATION: XYZ Company	PLANT/LOCATION: Chicago		DEPARTMENT: Packaging	REVIEWED BY: Sharon Martin
REQUIRED AND/OR RECOMMENDED PERSONAL PROTECTIVE EQUIPMENT:	Gloves - Eye Protection - Long Sleeves - Safety Shoes			APPROVED BY: Joe Bottom

SEQUENCE OF BASIC JOB STEPS	POTENTIAL HAZARDS	RECOMMENDED ACTION OR PROCEDURE
1. Position portable banding cart and place strapping guard on top of boxes.	1. Cart positioned too close to pallet (strike body & legs against cart or pallet, drop strapping gun on foot).	1. Leave ample space between cart and pallet to feed strapping - have firm grip on strapping gun.
2. Withdraw strapping and bend end back about 3".	2. Sharp edges of strapping (cut hands, fingers & arms). Sharp corners on pallet (strike feet against corners).	2. Wear gloves, eye protection & long sleeves - keep firm grip on strapping - hold end between thumb & forefinger - watch where stepping.
3. Walk around load while holding strapping with one hand.	3. Projecting sharp corners on pallet (strike feet on corners).	3. Assure a clear path between pallet and cart - pull smoothly - avoid jerking strapping.
4. Pull and feed strap under pallet.	4. Splinters on pallet (punctures to hands and fingers). Sharp strap edges (cuts to hands, fingers, and arms).	4. Wear gloves - eye protection - long sleeves. Point strap in direction of bend - pull strap smoothly to avoid jerks.
5. Walk around load. Stoop down. Bend over, grab strap, pull up to machine, straighten out strap end.	5. Protruding corners of pallet, splinters (punctures to feet and ankles).	5. Assure a clear path - watch where walking - face direction in which walking.
6. Insert, position and tighten strap in gun.	6. Springy and sharp strapping (strike against with hands and fingers).	6. Keep firm grasp on strap and on gun - make sure clip is positioned properly.

Source: *Accident Prevention Manual for Business & Industry*, 10th ed. (Chicago: National Safety Council, 1992). Reprinted with the permission of the National Safety Council.

RECRUITING

The recruiting and retention of employees is facilitated when organizations demonstrate a protective concern for the safety and well-being of their employees. Whereas a good health and safety record may help in recruiting, a reputation for dangerous or unhealthy working conditions will surely discourage many potential applicants.

BENEFITS

Concern for health and safety has prompted employers and governments to provide a variety of benefits to protect workers against the risks of untimely death, disability, medical expenses, and unemployment from causes outside an employee's control (for example, shutdowns because of accidents and termination for health reasons). The cost of many discretionary benefits is affected by an employer's health and safety record since employers with poorer records must pay higher rates. Mandatory workers' compensation is industry-rated; a poor record by a few employers can force up the rate for every employer in the industry.

Some organizations also provide employee service benefits geared to maintaining a healthy work force. Examples include periodic physical examinations, fitness programs, antismoking campaigns, workshops on stress, alcohol and drug abuse programs, marital counselling, and behavioural therapy.[21]

LABOUR RELATIONS

Relations between labour and management can be strained by employees' concerns about health and safety. Worries about safety may give rise to strikes, as noted earlier. During labour negotiations, unions often voice employees' safety concerns to management and bargain for safer working conditions and other safety measures. For example, the Canadian Automobile Workers' collective agreements with Canadian automobile manufacturers now provide for a full-time worker-inspector in all plants with more than 600 employees, and plants with more than 10 000 workers must have two. This representative, who is appointed for an indefinite term by the president of the union, must be given an office by the company; he or she maintains a close but independent relationship with the company's safety committee.

HEALTH AND SAFETY RESPONSIBILITIES

Large organizations in industries with potentially hazardous equipment or materials (such as manufacturers and chemical producers) often have separate safety departments headed by a safety engineer. In the majority of companies, however, health and safety responsibilities are assigned to HRM professional staff, which may include safety specialists and medical professionals, such as industrial nurses or hygienists. Full-time safety specialists are most common in large manufacturing companies, public utilities, transportation and distribution industries, and in sectors of the resource industry such as oil drilling. They are least common in banks, nonprofit organizations, and insurance companies. In general, HRM professionals help organizations comply with health and safety standards set by legislation, as well as by employers.

All Canadian jurisdictions have health and safety legislation that requires employers to accept certain responsibilities for workers' safety and take various actions toward maintaining it. Most of the laws mandate an employer with a specified number of employees in a workplace — Ontario's act sets the number at 20 in most cases — to establish a joint management–worker health and safety committee. At other workplaces—Ontario specifies smaller establishments (five to nineteen workers) and places such as construction sites—the workers are to choose their own health and safety representative. In Alberta and Newfoundland, committees are not required in a workplace unless so named by the Minister of Labour.[22]

Health and safety legislation affects HRM professionals in a number of ways. When an employer is required to provide information, instruction, and supervision to a worker to protect his or her health and safety, this task often falls to HRM staff. So does meeting the requirements of giving assistance, co-operation, and certain information to the joint health and safety committee or to the safety representatives in smaller workplaces. Other major responsibilities of HRM staff, often HRM generalists, include record keeping, posting of notices, communicating and enforcing health and safety rules, monitoring the work environment, and safety training.

Safety management also includes identifying and changing hazardous working conditions, as well as evaluating the effectiveness of health and safety efforts. Some related activities extend beyond HRM department boundaries. For example, the purchasing department must consider safety issues when purchasing new equipment. The comptroller and top management must be willing to support health and safety training and the costs of purchasing and installing safety equipment.

THE ONTARIO OCCUPATIONAL HEALTH AND SAFETY ACT

All Canadian jurisdictions have legislation dealing with occupational health and safety. Their regulations are similar except that Prince Edward Island's and Nova Scotia's have no provision for joint health and safety committees. For the most part, we will discuss the Ontario Occupational Health and Safety Act because it is generally regarded as the country's most comprehensive health and safety act and because its 1990 revisions may influence legislation in other jurisdictions in Canada.[23]

HISTORY OF THE ONTARIO LEGISLATION

In 1974, following union allegations of serious health and safety problems in the mining industry, Ontario established the Royal Commission on the Health and Safety of Workers in Mines, chaired by Professor (later President) James Ham of the University of Toronto. The commission's report in 1976 made sweeping recommendations, including

1. The consolidation with the Ministry of Labour of various inspection, health, and safety units from various other ministries.
2. Mandatory establishment of joint worker–management health and safety committees.
3. Safety-related qualifications for supervisors and workers.
4. Safety-related duties of employees.
5. The provision of defined medical surveillance and services and the keeping of occupational health and safety records.[24]

In addition, the Ham Report found "a serious lack of openness on matters of the health and safety of workers in mines. . . . Workers have a right in natural justice to know about the risks and consequences of the risks that they undertake at work."[25]

Because the commission felt workers had too few opportunities to contribute their insights to the assessment of work conditions and decision making on issues of health and safety, it recommended removing these issues from the "adamantly confrontational character of Canadian labour–management relations" and establishing joint committees in the hope that "a new measure of labour–management co-operation can emerge."[26]

The Ham Report provided the major impetus for the Ontario Occupational Health and Safety Act of 1978, which consolidated previous legislation and introduced new principles concerning the control of toxic substances and the participation of workers in health and safety programs. During the decade after the act was passed, it was the subject of increasing complaints from organized labour. In particular, the unions said, the joint committees were not effective, and although workers had been given the right to refuse to work if they believed that any equipment might endanger themselves or another worker, the law did not go far enough. The unions wanted specifically trained workers to be given the right to shut down any workplace they considered unsafe. After more than two years of vigorous debate and redrafting of legislation, fundamental changes to the act were passed in June 1990.

PROVISIONS OF THE ONTARIO LEGISLATION

The Ontario Occupational Health and Safety Act (OHSA) of 1990 covers all workplaces and workers under the province's jurisdiction except farming operations and farm and domestic workers. (Ontario workplaces under the federal jurisdiction, such as post offices, banks, Bell Telephone, and airlines, are, of course, covered by the Canada Labour Code.) As described in explanatory material published by the Ontario Ministry of Labour and the Industrial Accident Prevention Association,[27] the act sets out the respective rights and responsibilities of employers, supervisors, and workers for maintaining occupational health and safety. It also mandates the formation of joint committees, specifies the training and certification of committee members and the designation of health and safety representatives, and sets procedures for inspection and record keeping.

Employers' Responsibilities

For a workplace employing six or more workers, the employer must prepare a written occupational health and safety policy, review it at least annually, and post it in a conspicuous location in the workplace. (The Ministry of Labour's guide to the act shows how to prepare an occupational health and safety policy.) The employer is also required to develop and maintain a program to implement the policy.

An employer is required to inform workers and supervisors of any health or safety hazards in a job. The employer must also provide workers with information concerning measures to be taken for their protection. It is also the employer's duty to ensure that equipment, materials, and protective devices are provided, maintained, and used as prescribed. Employers must also be sure that all supervisors are "competent persons"—qualified because of knowledge, training, and experience to organize work and its performance; familiar with regulations that apply to the work; and knowledgeable about actual or potential dangers in the workplace.

Copies of the act must be posted both in English and in the majority language of the workplace; explanatory material produced by the Ministry of Labour must also be posted. Assistance and co-operation must be given to the joint committee or to workers' health and safety representatives. They must also be given certain information, such as the results of reports and copies of written occupational health and safety reports that are in the employer's possession.

An occupational health service must be maintained and records kept of exposure to toxic substances. Where so prescribed, an employer may permit in the workplace only those employees who have undergone specified medical examinations, tests, or X-rays and are physically fit to do the work. A worker is not, however, required to participate in a prescribed medical surveillance program without his or her consent.

Supervisors' Responsibilities

A supervisor, defined as a person who has charge of a workplace or authority over a worker, is required to ensure that employees work in the manner prescribed and use prescribed protective devices and equipment. He or she also has the duty of advising workers of potential or actual hazards "of which the supervisor is aware."

Employees' Responsibilities and Rights

Employees must use or wear the safety equipment, protective devices, or clothing that their employers require. They must work in compliance with the provisions of the act and regulations, which include reporting to the employer or supervisor any absence of or defect in equipment or protective devices that might endanger themselves or other workers. Employees may not operate any equipment in a manner that might endanger themselves or other workers. (This prohibition includes pranks or other unnecessary conduct that could pose a danger.)

On the other side of the coin, an employee has the right to refuse work that he or she believes would endanger himself or herself or another worker. This right applies to danger perceived from the physical conditions of the workplace or any machine.

When a worker invokes the right of refusal, an established procedure, diagrammed in Figure 14.2, is set in motion. The worker reports the circumstances to the supervisor and then remains in a safe place near the work station. The supervisor must investigate in the presence of the complainant and a workers' representative. If the problem is not resolved, it is reported to a Ministry of Labour inspector, who investigates as soon as possible. Meanwhile, the worker may be assigned other duties, subject to the terms of any collective agreement, and another worker may be assigned to the work, provided he or she has been informed of the first worker's refusal and the reasons for it.

Saskatchewan's legislation, in contrast to Ontario's, has the joint health and safety committee itself investigate when an individual refuses unsafe work. If the members decide unanimously that the refusal is justified, the matter is settled. Otherwise, an inspector can be called in.

Joint Health and Safety Committees

With some exceptions, all workplaces where 20 or more persons are regularly employed or where workers are involved with toxic substances must establish a joint health and safety committee. It must have at least two members (at least four in a workplace where 50 or more workers are employed) and at least half the members must be nonmanagerial workers selected by the workers or, where applicable, by the union. The committees must have two co-chairs, one selected by the worker members and one by the management members. At least one management member and one worker member must be certified by the new workplace health and safety agency, in accordance with training criteria established by the agency.

The members of the joint committee are to identify hazardous situations and make recommendations to the employer on issues of health and safety.

FIGURE 14.2
Ontario's Procedure When a Worker Has Reason to Believe Work Is Likely to Endanger Self or Another Person

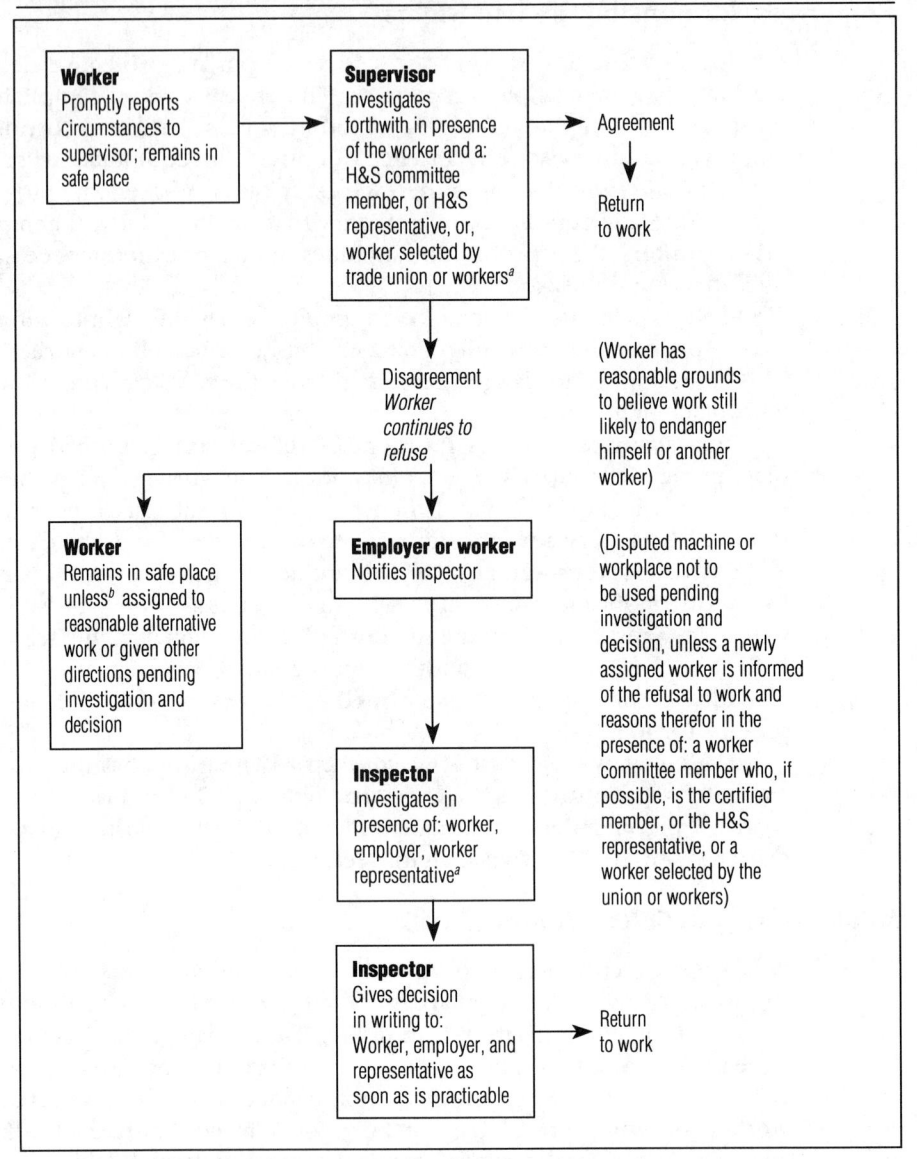

```
┌──────────────┐     ┌──────────────────┐
│ Worker       │     │ Supervisor       │
│ Promptly     │ ──▶ │ Investigates     │ ──▶ Agreement
│ reports      │     │ forthwith in     │         │
│ circumstances│     │ presence of the  │         ▼
│ to supervisor│     │ worker and a:    │      Return
│ remains in   │     │ H&S committee    │      to work
│ safe place   │     │ member, or H&S   │
└──────────────┘     │ representative,  │
                     │ or, worker       │
                     │ selected by      │
                     │ trade union or   │
                     │ workersᵃ         │
                     └──────────────────┘
                              │
                              ▼
                        Disagreement
                        Worker
                        continues to
                        refuse
```

┌──────────────────┐   ┌──────────────────┐
│ Worker   │   │ Employer or   │
│ Remains in safe │   │ worker   │
│ place unlessᵇ   │   │ Notifies   │
│ assigned to   │   │ inspector   │
│ reasonable   │   └──────────────────┘
│ alternative work │   │
│ or given other   │   ▼
│ directions   │   ┌──────────────────┐
│ pending   │   │ Inspector   │
│ investigation   │   │ Investigates in │
│ and decision   │   │ presence of: │
└──────────────────┘   │ worker, employer,│
                         │ worker   │
                         │ representativeᵃ │
                         └──────────────────┘
                                  │
                                  ▼
                         ┌──────────────────┐
                         │ Inspector   │
                         │ Gives decision   │ ──▶ Return
                         │ in writing to: │   to work
                         │ Worker, employer,│
                         │ and   │
                         │ representative   │
                         │ as soon as is   │
                         │ practicable   │
                         └──────────────────┘

(Worker has reasonable grounds to believe work still likely to endanger himself or another worker)

(Disputed machine or workplace not to be used pending investigation and decision, unless a newly assigned worker is informed of the refusal to work and reasons therefor in the presence of: a worker committee member who, if possible, is the certified member, or the H&S representative, or a worker selected by the union or workers)

ᵃ One of whom must be made available; the representative is entitled to pay for time spent here.
ᵇ Subject to terms of any collective agreement.

Source: Industrial Accident Prevention Association, *A Guide to the Provisions of Ontario's Occupational Health and Safety Act*, 9th ed. (Toronto: IAPA, 1990), p. 21. Reprinted with permission.

In addition, they are to obtain information from the employer concerning the identification of health and safety hazards and the experience of similar industries of which the employer has knowledge. One of the worker-members of the committee, if possible the certified member, is to inspect the physical condition of the workplace not more than once a month. A worker-member is also to investigate cases of critical injury or fatality and report the findings to the Ministry of Labour, as well as to the joint committee. A worker-member may be required to be present during a refusal-to-work situation or at the beginning of any safety tests or industrial hygiene testing. Certified members have additional powers and duties: to stop work in certain circumstances (described below), to investigate complaints that "dangerous circumstances" exist, and to carry out inspections.

The joint committee meets at least once every three months. Its members must be paid for the time they spend preparing for and attending meetings and carrying out other OHSA duties. Certified members must be paid for the time they spend on their special duties.

Health and Safety Representatives

A workplace or construction project where six to nineteen workers are regularly employed need not have a joint committee but must have a health and safety (H&S) representative chosen by the workers, or by the union if there is one. H&S representatives have essentially the same powers as joint committee members: that is, the power to identify workplace hazards, obtain information from the employer, be consulted about workplace testing, make recommendations to the employer, investigate work refusals, investigate accidents, and request information from the Workers' Compensation Board.

The Right to Stop Work

One of the most controversial changes of the 1990 amendments to the OHSA gives the certified worker and employer members of the joint committee the right in certain circumstances to insist that the employer stop work in the workplace. If, following consultation, the two certified members agree that a provision of the act has been contravened, that the contravention poses a danger, and that any delay in controlling it may seriously endanger a worker, they may issue a stop-work direction jointly. If they disagree, either one can request an inspector to investigate and provide the certified members with a written decision, which may include a stop-work direction. Following safe compliance and resolution, the employer may request a stop-work cancellation from either the two certified members or the inspector.

Under circumstances perceived as seriously unsafe, either certified member or an inspector can apply to an official known as the health and safety adjudicator, who can declare that the employer is subject to the work-stoppage procedure or recommend to the Ministry of Labour that an inspector be assigned to the workplace as a health and safety overseer for a specified period. After remedying the situation, the employer may ask either the certified member or the inspector to cancel the stop-work direction.

Inspection and Enforcement

The Ministry of Labour appoints inspectors to enforce OHSA regulations. They have the power to enter any workplace at any time without notice; to inspect and copy records and other material; to conduct tests; and to require an organization to provide, at its expense, reports from a professional engineer on the load limits of a floor, roof, or temporary structure. If an inspector finds that a provision of the act has been contravened, he or she can direct compliance, limit or stop work, or clear a workplace and isolate it by barricades, depending on the degree of hazard.

Any person within an organization, regardless of position, who fails to comply with any part of the legislation is liable to a fine and/or a jail sentence. However, strict liability has been modified by allowing accused employers, supervisors, and constructors to defend themselves by proving that they have "taken every precaution reasonable in the circumstances" for the protection of workers.[28] Moreover, a recent Ontario Court of Appeal decision shifted the burden to the prosecution to prove beyond a reasonable doubt that the accused was negligent.[29]

Information and Record Keeping

To encourage the active participation of workers and their representatives in workplace health and safety programs, OHSA requires employers to provide health and safety information to workers and their representatives. Table 14.1 provides a list of types of information, when and how it is to be provided, and to whom. The act also requires that reports be sent to the Ministry of Labour and to the joint labour–management committee concerning fatal or critical injuries, disabling injuries, other injuries that require medical attention, occupational illnesses, and toxic substances.

IMPACT OF HEALTH AND SAFETY LEGISLATION ON ORGANIZATIONS

Since the mid-1970s, health and safety legislation in Canadian jurisdictions has tended to increase the awareness of health and safety among employees, employers, and the public. However, a 1981 report of a federal–provincial commission enquiring into safety in the mines found that several companies had failed to establish clear goals or accountability for accident prevention and did not recognize the value of consulting with employees either for input into decision making or as a mechanism to improve workers' attitudes.[30] Such findings apparently led to the requirement of the 1990 OHSA that employers prepare a written occupational health and safety policy, put it in a conspicuous place, and have a program to implement the policy.

Disagreements continue to exist over how much certainty of hazard an employee must have to exercise the right to refuse to work. The labour relations board in the federal jurisdiction, which has a refusal provision

TABLE 14.1
Ontario Regulations on Access to Health and Safety Information

Type of Information	When and How Provided	To Whom
Names and work locations of JHSC members	Permanently posted in the workplace	Workers
Copy of the act and any explanatory material published by the ministry	Permanently posted in the workplace, in English and majority language	Workers
Copy of written health and safety policy	Prominently posted in the workplace	Workers
Results of health and safety reports and copies of written reports	To be made available to:	JHSC or H&S rep
If prescribed, to keep exposure records of workers, who have access to those records	To be made available	To each worker, his or her exposure record
Where required to do air sampling under regulation, air sampling results	Post in workplace	Workers
Measures and procedures, when required to have these by regulation	When applicable, in writing	Affected workers
Director's order made under S.33	Post in workplace, and on receipt from director, copies to:	Workers, JHSC or H&S rep
A ministry inspector's order or report	Post in workplace, with copies to:	Workers, JHSC or H&S rep
Employer's notice of compliance with inspector's order	Post in workplace	Workers
Notices required to be sent to ministry in cases of injury, death or accident	At the same time as provided to the ministry, copies to:	JHSC members or H&S rep, and trade union
Necessary information required by JHSC member or H&S representative for carrying out workplace inspections	As required for inspection	Designated worker JHSC member or H&S rep

TABLE 14.1 (continued)

TYPE OF INFORMATION	WHEN AND HOW PROVIDED	TO WHOM
Health and safety experience and work practices of similar industries, of which the employer is aware	As requested	JHSC members or H&S rep
Annual summary of workplace injury experience received by employer from WCB in response to request from any person in the workplace	Post in workplace	Workers
Where a designated substance regulation applies, assessment results	Copies to:	Each JHSC member
Control program for designated substance, where applicable	Copies to: Acquaint with its provisions: and make available in English and majority language:	Each JHSC member, Affected workers Workers
Inventory of hazardous materials and hazardous physical agents	Copies to be made available to:	Workers, JHSC or H&S rep
Floor plan showing names and locations of all hazardous materials	To be accessible to:	Workers
Notice of location of floor plan	Post in workplace	Workers
Unexpired material safety data sheets (MSDSs)	To be made available to:	Workers, JHSC or H&S rep
Hazardous materials assessment	To be made available to:	As above
Information on things that emit hazardous physical agents	To be made available to:	As above
Warning signs in locations of above	Post in locations	Workers

Source: Industrial Accident Prevention Association, *A Guide to the Provisions of Ontario's Occupational Health and Safety Act*, 9th ed. (Toronto: IAPA, 1990), pp. 28–29. Reprinted with permission.

similar to Ontario's, ruled in one case that a possible hazard in the normal operation of a job is not sufficient justification for refusal to work. A Bell Canada employee had refused to work with a sealant used in cable systems; initial tests at the University of Western Ontario had been inconclusive as to whether the compound was carcinogenic. A federal safety office found there was no imminent danger, and the worker's refusal was ruled unjustified. The union staff representative said the board's decision contained the dangerous implication that "if scientific research discloses hazards in the chemicals or compounds that have been used normally for years, workers would be precluded from invoking the imminent danger clause."[31]

Another problem is that workers and their representatives do not always understand or follow health and safety legislation. The 1981 commission reported that many workers were bypassing first-line supervision in firms' responsibility systems (with apparent approval of union locals) and that several local unions were failing in their responsibilities by not recognizing the extent of their influence over individual workers. Unions were also faulted for concentrating on identifying workplace hazards instead of trying to eliminate unsafe work practices. The report affirmed the importance of joint health and safety committees but found that they were not functioning as they should be. Noting that the role of a safety department is essential, but rarely understood, the report recommended that the safety department play an advisory and an auditing role, facilitating the integration of what it termed the direct and indirect responsibility systems within an organization.[32] A need for training in safety practices is also relevant to the functioning of joint committees and was incorporated into the 1990 revisions of OHSA.

WORKERS' COMPENSATION

An accident in the workplace will likely be followed by a claim to the workers' compensation board in the relevant jurisdiction. Exhibit 14.3 sets out suggested steps for employers to take in response to such a claim.

Since each province and territory has its own workers' compensation legislation (see Chapter 13), HRM professionals must be familiar with the relevant acts and procedures relating to claims. In addition, it is advisable to keep informed of new developments affecting workers' compensation.[33] For example, Ontario's BIll 162, which became law in 1990, imposed on every covered employer that regularly employs 20 or more workers the obligation to re-employ a worker injured in a work-related accident. If the worker can perform the essential duties of the old job, then that job (or comparable work) must be offered. If the worker suffers from a continuing disability, the first suitable job that becomes available must be offered.[34]

Elaine Newman, a workers' compensation consultant, offers HRM professionals some general advice about their attitude toward workers' compensation:

Think about workers' compensation problems in the context of the agenda you have set for your human resources department. Remember that when serious injury occurs, you are dealing with a crisis period. What is the corporate message you choose to send to that worker in those circumstances?

There is no doubt that the workers' compensation system is an expensive cost of doing business. There is little doubt that it will become more expensive. Employers in Ontario are now required to re-employ the injured worker, and this new requirement provides a choice. Are you going to bring your adversarial best to fighting this obligation? Or are you going to devote your resources to the kind of management plan that will turn this obligation into a cost-efficient aspect of conducting business?[35]

EXHIBIT 14.3
12 Steps That Employers Can Take in Response to a Worker's Compensation Claim

1. Keep detailed written records of the accident and the injury.
2. Interview the worker in person if possible.
3. Interview any witnesses to the accident.
4. Go to the scene of the accident and review the event.
5. Check information in the worker's personal file before completing the accident report form.
6. Investigate any previous similar disabilities that occurred before the worker was employed by your organization.
7. Check if the accident was caused by the negligence of someone other than one of your workers.
8. Find out if the worker had been involved in a pedestrian or car accident within the last five years.
9. Investigate any work-related difficulties, such as labour disputes, grievances, layoffs, or disciplinary proceedings, involving the worker.
10. Check whether the worker has been continuously employed by your organization for a period of one year or more.
11. Investigate any important inconsistencies between the worker's version of the accident and the version provided by any witnesses, supervisors, or managers.
12. Rely on your own common sense.

Source: Adapted from *Workers' Compensation, Managing Claims*, vol. 1, no. 2 (Toronto: Concord Publishing, February 1990). Reprinted with the permission of the publisher.

Ensuring a Safe and Healthy Workplace

This section focusses on strategies used by organizations and HRM professionals to ensure a safe, healthy workplace, including (1) controlling physical hazards, (2) promoting safety awareness, and (3) promoting good health.

The Workplace Hazardous Materials Information System (WHMIS) was established by federal legislation, effective October 31, 1988, for the protection of workers regularly exposed to hazardous materials or products in the workplace. WHMIS is a nationwide right-to-know system that requires the disclosure of full information as to the identification and chemical composition of hazardous materials or products that are used, handled, or stored in the workplace, as well as any health hazards associated with exposure to such materials or products. It also requires proper training programs for workers in the safe handling of such materials or products, preventative and emergency measures, and emergency treatment. Complementary implementing legislation and regulations have been enacted by each provincial and territorial government.[36]

Controlling Physical Hazards

The most direct approach to controlling physical hazards is to eliminate them, but this is not always possible. Some hazards, such as those inherent in oil-drilling equipment and locales, cannot be eliminated. However, steps can be taken to reduce their potential for causing accidents. For example, drilling operations can be suspended in periods of high wind; equipment can be maintained so that it functions properly; crew members can be alerted to the potential hazards of operating equipment; and shifts can be shortened so as to reduce fatigue and tedium, which contribute to accidents. In oil drilling and other industries, safety inspections can ensure that employees follow safety rules and use protective devices, and that machinery and the workplace are free from hazards.

Accident-causing hazards have been recognized for some time, but only in recent years have occupational threats to employees' health, both physical and mental, been recognized. Occupational illnesses are difficult to analyze and control because they develop relatively slowly. It is generally known that exposure to radioactive materials, coal dust, asbestos, and other substances can lead to illness and often death; literally thousands of other materials and substances are also now identified as hazardous. Indeed, medical research has uncovered health hazards in most occupations in modern society. The problem can be so complicated that Ontario's Royal Commission on Matters of Health and Safety Arising from the Use of Asbestos identified the need for a panel on industrial diseases. The group established in response to this recommendation, the Industrial Diseases Standards Panel, has dealt with such issues as criteria for evaluating evidence of the carcinogenicity in humans of occupational exposures; the scheduling for Workers' Compensation Board disability awards of workers with asbestosis; benefits to the survivors of deceased workers who had received partial disability awards for asbestosis; and recognition of psychological as well as physical disability as a compensable condition among claimants suffering from asbestosis.[37]

Employers' efforts to control physical health hazards should include regular monitoring of the work environment and regular physical examination of employees. For example, underground mining requires constant checking of the air quality and levels of coal dust. Grain milling and processing also require testing of dust levels, not only for health reasons but also to avoid explosions and fires. Company physicians and medical personnel should monitor a wide range of matters relating to employees' health, from routine hearing tests and chest X-rays to incidents of infertility and abnormal childbirth. The last is a particularly sensitive issue since employers are prohibited from discriminating against women. Although an employer must not deny a pregnant woman access to any job, certain jobs, such as video display terminal operator, may involve exposure to materials or conditions thought to be hazardous to unborn children.[38]

As employers discover that certain processes and materials are hazardous to the health and well-being of employees, they must develop ways to eliminate or reduce the danger. Some organizations have eliminated hazards by a very obvious and direct approach: they have substituted robots for people in high-risk jobs ranging from feeding metal blanks into a furnace and removing hot castings to shearing sheep and welding and painting automobiles. General Motors provides special instruction of up to 100 hours for the 1000 employees working with robots. The instruction includes how to operate and maintain these and other highly automated machines safely.[39]

The primary means used by organizations to reduce physical hazards is requiring the use of safety devices and protective equipment. Safety devices should meet three criteria. They should be foolproof, should not become disengaged, and should not interfere with production. In many cases, new equipment meets these criteria better than do "add-on" safety devices for existing equipment.

Unfortunately, personal safety equipment is sometimes unpopular with employees, and they object to using it. Despite the unpopularity of safety devices and equipment, nearly all employers require their use to protect employees against work-related injuries and illnesses. Failure to use safety equipment is illegal under occupational health and safety acts. In most organizations, employees can be disciplined and even fired for failure to use required safety equipment. Also not uncommon are disagreements between employers and employees about whether safety equipment reduces hazards more than it imposes additional dangers. For example, in 1982, garbage collectors in Toronto went on an illegal strike against the imposition of wearing fluorescent red and yellow vests. The workers claimed the jackets were a safety hazard, while management said they would reduce injuries from passing automobiles, as they had in a neighbouring jurisdiction. The strike was resolved by an agreement to have the Ontario Labour Relations

Board decide the issue and, in the interim, to have the garbage collectors wear strips of reflective tape on their uniforms in lieu of the vests.[40]

Clearly, rules and regulations about the use of safety equipment, unless accepted by most employees, can strain supervisor–subordinate relations. Increased acceptance of safety rules and regulations, including the use of safety equipment, is a common goal of organizational safety programs.

PROMOTING SAFETY AWARENESS

Organizations can focus attention on matters of safety in a number of ways, including using health and safety committees; recording and posting safety performance records; providing recognition and awards to individuals and units with good safety records; creating rules and regulations regarding work behaviour and the use of safety equipment; and giving safety training programs. In addition to these company-sponsored efforts, a number of organizations, such as the Industrial Accident Prevention Association and the Construction Safety Association, actively promote safety consciousness through seminars, television advertising, joint meetings with various organizations, and safety programs in schools. Promotion of public awareness of occupational health and safety is also a function of the workplace health and safety agency established by the 1990 OHSA.

Most organizations with safety programs combine a variety of approaches. Whatever methods are used, the commitment and participation of top management are key ingredients in the success of occupational safety programs.[41] Managerial commitment to safety is in evidence at B.C. Tel, whose highly successful program is described in Exhibit 14.4.

The most effective approach to promoting health and safety in the workplace is through team-based approaches (see Case 8.1).

Health and Safety Committees

As already noted, most jurisdictions require joint worker–management health and safety committees in most workplaces. Where these committees are not required, organizations often have their own safety committees, which have worker members but are usually headed by a safety specialist, the HRM department head, or an operations manager.

Depending on the relevant legislation, the union situation, and company policy, health and safety committees usually focus on one or more of the following functions:

1. Health and safety policy — reviewing health and safety records, investigating accidents, and making recommendations for safety procedures and expenditures.
2. Inspection — conducting periodic safety inspections of the establishment.
3. Education — promoting interest in and compliance with safety rules and methods.

EXHIBIT 14.4
B.C. Tel's Effective Driver Safety Program

B.C. Tel drivers are on the road throughout the province all year long—on snow-covered gravel roads in the remote north, in a major city with the country's worst traffic-accident record and in isolated, hard-to-reach rural communities. The nature of the telecommunications industry also requires employees to drive a wide variety of vehicles, from passenger cars to specialized manlift vehicles to tractor/trailers.

With 7000 employees driving 4000 company vehicles, the need for a good fleet safety program is paramount at B.C. Tel, the telephone company that serves 99 per cent of British Columbia's population. Company drivers cover more than 52 million kilometres—almost 1300 times around the world—every year. Yet at 3.3 preventable motor vehicle accidents for every million kilometres driven, B.C. Tel logs one of the lowest preventable motor vehicle accident rates in the province. Not one company driver has been killed in a B.C. Tel motor vehicle accident. The reason? A strong fleet safety program promotes safety awareness 24 hours a day.

Establishing Company Policy
The first step in developing a fleet safety program is to establish a management policy that outlines two things: the company's philosophy about fleet safety and the objectives behind a fleet safety program. For the best results—and to help establish integrity and credibility—the policy should have the support of senior management and be communicated to all fleet drivers.

A policy reflects the company's attitude about fleet safety. In so doing, it provides guidelines for programs and actions. For example, B.C. Tel's fleet safety policy stresses to all driving employees that, just as they are expected to act as professionals in their job functions, they are also expected to be professional when driving. In fact, driving is considered part of many employees' job responsibilities.

Employees who drive a company vehicle are considered, in a sense, "marked" persons; they represent the company to the people who see them. Employee driving habits thus have a direct impact on the public's perception of the company.

Beyond the interests of the company, B.C. Tel's policy also emphasizes every driver's obligation to himself or herself, to family members, to passengers, other drivers and pedestrians—off as well as on the job.

Determining Driver Eligibility
Before any driver is allowed behind the wheel of a company vehicle, a driver's licence audit is strongly recommended. The audit reviews an employee's or prospective employee's driving record to screen out potential problem drivers. Driving a company vehicle is considered a privilege—not a right—at B.C. Tel. A good driving record, in our experience, is one indicator of a positive employee attitude.

EXHIBIT 14.4 *(continued)*

B.C. Tel instituted licence audits in 1969. Checks are completed through the Motor Vehicle Branch of the provincial government. The branch will confirm whether or not the individual has a valid provincial driver's licence and how many outstanding demerit points are registered against the driver. To be accepted as a fleet vehicle driver at B.C. Tel, applicants must have no more than six demerit points currently outstanding or no outstanding demerit points accumulated in the past two years.

Building Awareness and Confidence

Although the other program components are valuable, safety training is the foundation upon which an effective fleet safety program is built. Driver education provides employees with the skills they need to be more aware and confident on the road. It's more cost-effective to train drivers first than it is to pay later for their mistakes. To ensure high standards and consistency of information, all fleet safety courses should be conducted by certified instructors.

Maintaining the Fleet

While driving behaviour is a critical component of fleet safety, so too is vehicle engineering and maintenance. Drivers can only be as safe as their vehicles allow them to be.

A computerized tracking service called Mainstream, provided to B.C. Tel by a contract company, keeps a running record of maintenance and repair work done on each of the company's 4000 vehicles. This kind of system can generate numerous useful reports, such as how much the company spends on repairs for every kilometre driven.

Vehicle cleanliness also reflects the company's image and attitude towards safety. The majority of B.C. Tel vehicles are washed bi-weekly at night while they sit unused in company compounds. Another option is to provide employees with a car-wash budget.

Keeping Records

One of the main objectives behind implementing a fleet safety program is to maintain—and in most cases, improve—your company's motor vehicle accident record. Identifying areas for improvement requires an accurate, detailed record-keeping system that tracks driving performance from several perspectives. At B.C. Tel, for instance, permanent motor vehicle accident (MVA) statistics are recorded by month, by geographic area, by type of accident and by individual driver.

The primary advantage of good record-keeping is that it provides analytical tools and concrete support for management presentations and program development. For example, if one particular region has a higher accident rate than another, the safety department can present these facts to management as incentive to introduce special area safety campaigns. Likewise, if accidents are shown to occur more often in winter, promotions can be developed to increase

EXHIBIT 14.4 *(continued)*

driver awareness at these times. B.C. Tel distributes dashboard tags with winter driving tips as a result of past winter driving records.

The benefits of a good driver safety program are many. At B.C. Tel we receive the maximum fleet discount from our insurers and also qualify for an additional safe driving rebate, resulting in a significant reduction in insurance costs. We also feel confident that we are protecting our employees, their families, the public and the company from unnecessary pain, injury, death or financial loss due to traffic accidents.

Source: Ed DeRocher, "The Driving Force at B.C. Tel," *Occupational Health and Safety Canada*, vol. 7, no. 1 (January/February 1991), pp. 52–57. Reprinted with permission.

Recording and Posting Safety Performance Records

Most health and safety laws require that an employer post notices of pertinent regulations and related information. Employers can also use posting as a form of feedback to employees on their safety performance. One study credited the public posting of departmental safety performance levels with improving the safety record in a wholesale bakery.[42]

Safety Recognition and Awards Programs

Recognition programs reward individual or group safety performance, or both. Typical rewards are plaques, certificates, and recognition in in-house publications. In the bakery just mentioned, subordinates demonstrating safe work behaviour received praise from their supervisors, who, as a part of the safety program, had received training in positive reinforcement techniques.

Safety Rules and Regulations

Almost all organizations have some rules and regulations regarding safe work behaviour. They are communicated to employees via supervisors, bulletin boards, and employee handbooks.

Rules and regulations should be developed from the results of detailed job analyses. The job safety training guide shown in Exhibits 14.1 and 14.2 provides an excellent source of specific safe job procedures and may be used to prepare rules and regulations. For example, Exhibit 14.2 suggests that banders and others using this equipment should be required to wear long-sleeved shirts, gloves, and eye protection. Also, employees should ensure a clear space in which to work. Safety rules and regulations developed in this way are specific to jobs, rather than overly general, and they are also consistent with training. It is also easier to develop incentive programs when proper and safe work behaviour has been specified in this way.

Employers are responsible for compliance with the relevant health and safety act, and they must make certain that employees know and follow its regulations and other safety rules. Many organizations impose penalties on employees for violation of safety rules and terminate for serious or repeated infringement. Of course, as with any rules and regulations, those responsible for ensuring compliance must consider specific cases. For example, violations of some rules represent considerable danger to many people, while others may involve only a very low risk of minor injury. Some rule violators may be new employees who are unfamiliar with the rules or good employees who usually obey the rules, while others are frequent violators. Most supervisors would treat these different cases differently. One of the most effective means of obtaining compliance with health and safety regulations is through employees' knowledge and commitment, which can often be obtained through safety training programs.

Safety Training Programs

Safety training programs identify hazards and teach workers how to avoid or handle them. The role of safety training is generally the same as that of any other training program: to ensure employee performance at a specified level. In this case, specified levels include attention to safety.

A safety training program is developed and conducted like any other training program. First, problems are identified via job analysis as already discussed, or by inspection, monitoring of the work environment, and/or by accident and injury reports. Next, problems are examined to determine appropriate solutions, either training or elimination of the hazard. If training is indicated, a program may be designed, aimed at mastery of safe behaviour on the job. The Ontario Workers' Health and Safety Centre has created a four-part, 120-hour core training module for the certification of members of joint health and safety committees. The four packages cover awareness training about hazards that exist and available control measures; functional skills to participate effectively in the committee and carry out its duties; understanding the legislation and the duties of all workplace parties; and instructional skills to equip members with the ability to communicate information to fellow workers.[43]

Workers learn safe work procedures through any number of training methods. To facilitate transfer and maintain desired levels of safety performance after training, arrangements should be made to reinforce or otherwise reward employees for safe behaviour on the job. The importance of trained supervisors and committed top management has already been mentioned. In addition, research suggests that incentive systems encourage the continued use of safe work behaviour.[44]

Training for job safety can begin as early as orientation. Research shows that new employees are most susceptible to accidents and should be informed at the earliest opportunity of hazardous areas and practices.[45] During orientation, they can be informed of health and safety regulations and told of their importance to personal health and safety. A new employee can also be encouraged to ask for assistance from the supervisor or an experienced employee should a potentially hazardous situation arise. Orientation is also a good time to convey proper attitudes toward health and safety matters. Attention to health and safety at this stage lets employees know about management's concern for their safety and well-being. However, since orientation is a time when employees must absorb a great deal of information, it is advisable to also include safety in job training programs.

Ideally, health and safety training should be an integral part of job training, whether on or off the job. It is easier to teach employees how to do the job safely in the first place than to get them to "unlearn" old habits and replace them with new ones. Special safety training programs may, of course, be helpful at any time during the course of employment. Periodic safety training programs help to renew employees' attention to health and safety concerns and are especially useful when new equipment or procedures are introduced or safety regulations change.

Another common goal of safety training programs is to encourage managers and supervisors to concern themselves with matters of health and safety by developing safe working conditions, spending time and money on safety training for employees, and creating and enforcing safety rules and procedures. Managers and supervisors often need to be "sold" on health and safety interests, since they sometimes interfere with short-run production and profitability goals. For example, the deaths of seven young Ontario forestry workers in a prescribed burn in 1979 were blamed on the failure of supervisors to follow basic safety rules. An official enquiry into the accident concluded that "fire bosses may have been more concerned with filling their quota of prescribed burns for the season than for safety.[46] A real problem in encouraging managerial commitment to safety is that managers and supervisors are often rewarded not for attention to safety but for controlling costs and promoting production and profitability. Therefore, many prefer to avoid the certain costs of a safety program, gambling that few or no accidents will occur. When this attitude prevails at managerial levels, it is likely to filter down to employees at all levels.

Training or education directed toward "selling" management on the value of safety programs and training is a key first step in creating an awareness of health and safety among employees. They can be taught to take a positive attitude toward safety through positive reinforcement from their superiors for safe work behaviour. Through performance appraisal and reward systems, management can ensure that employees are not forced to choose between safe and highly productive work behaviour.

PROMOTING GOOD HEALTH

Besides efforts to control physical hazards in the workplace and to promote safety awareness, some organizations sponsor programs that promote good health among workers. An Ontario study by Danielson and Danielson explored health promotion activities in a random sample of 680 organizations of 50 or more employees.[47] Table 14.2 shows the prevalence of certain types of programs across all surveyed organizations and among a subset of organizations with 500 employees or more. Note that most common were drug and alcohol counselling, exercise and fitness programs, and mental health counselling; these and other health promotion programs were more prevalent in the large organizations.

Health promotion programs are becoming more common. In Ontario in 1984, there were 850 companies with such programs; by 1987, the number was estimated to be at least 1000, with 40 percent provided to firms by private consultants. The programs included not only basic fitness but also seminars on back problems, eating disorders, burnout, cancer detection, hypothermia, and retirement planning. Imperial Oil had a session on problems relating to marriage, divorce, and reconstituted families. Northern Telecom offered a seminar on ski safety. Canada Life Assurance had a noon fitness class. Companies have found that improving the health of their employees can reduce absenteeism and turnover and can increase productivity.[48]

The Mental Health and the Workplace Project, initiated by the Canadian Mental Health Association (CMHA) in 1982, goes farther. After interviewing

TABLE 14.2
Types and Prevalence of Health Promotion Programs

TYPE OF PROGRAM	ORGANIZATIONS WITH >50 EMPLOYEES %	ORGANIZATIONS WITH >500 EMPLOYEES[a] %
Smoking cessation	4.1	11.9
Weight control/nutrition	6.4	18.5
Mental health counselling	10.4	29.7
Exercise and fitness	13.0	36.0
Drug and alcohol counselling	13.6	39.0
Stress management	5.3	15.2
	(n = 680)	(n = 48)

[a] This column of figures is a subset of the column directly to the left of it, that is, the 48 organizations with more than 500 employees are a subset of the 680 organizations with more than 50 employees.

Source: Reprinted with the permission of Lexington Books, an imprint of Macmillan, Inc., from *Healthier Workers: Health Promotion and Employee Assistance Programs*, by Martin Shain, Helne Suurvali, and Marie Boutilier. Copyright © 1986 by Lexington Books.

more than 1400 working Canadians in five pilot projects across the country, the CMHA Project proposed an agenda for health awareness and personal responsibility, as well as employer initiatives, to create healthier working conditions and environments. The objective is for human resource managers to add to the traditional approach of crisis intervention (for example, alcohol detoxification, personal counselling) an approach of preventive orientation to help people avoid crisis. The new workplace-based health programs include health risk appraisals, fitness, nutrition, smoking cessation programs, as well as promotion of health awareness.[49]

Programs that provide counselling and other forms of assistance to employees on a variety of topics, primarily alcoholism and drug abuse, are known as *employee assistance programs (EAPs)*. One drug expert with Health and Welfare Canada has estimated that EAPs are available to 12 percent of employees in the private sector and as many as 40 percent of all employees.[50] An important component of EAPs is often the identification of workers in need of assistance. In a survey of 45 Ontario organizations known to have EAPs, researchers talked with respondents "who held the greatest day-to-day responsibility for EAP." This person was likely to be a nurse, an EAP coordinator, a medical director, or the human resource manager. EAPs were under the auspices of HRM departments in nearly half the organizations and in medical departments in nearly a third.[51] Table 14.3 presents the type of problems EAPs in these organizations are equipped to handle. Note that most programs address a variety of concerns, but all assist employees with alcohol and drug-related problems. Programs have also been established for some professions. Exhibit 14.5 (pages 688-89) describes British Columbia's Interlock program for lawyers and chartered accountants.

SPECIAL HEALTH PROBLEMS

Several health problems are of special concern to today's employers. They include job stress, smoking, alcoholism, the use of drugs, and AIDS.

JOB STRESS

The Canadian Institute of Stress in Toronto has found that highly stressed workers have an absence rate that is almost three times greater than normal expectations. A 1991 survey by this institute and the Ontario Ministry of Labour, involving more than 60 000 firms, found that the typical employer believes that more than 25 percent of all sick time is the result of worker stress. Work site stress both erodes productivity among existing employees and creates additional costs through accelerated turnover.[52]

Job stress occurs when some element of the work environment has a negative impact on an employee's mental health and well-being. For example, stress may occur when role and job expectations are unclear or when a job

TABLE 14.3
Problems EAPS Are Meant to Handle

TYPE OF PROBLEM	NUMBER AND PERCENT OF EAPS HANDLING PROBLEM	
	n	%
Alcohol	45	100.0
Drugs	45	100.0
Cross addiction	45	100.0
Domestic	32	71.1
Mental health	32	71.1
Legal	30	68.2
Financial	33	73.3
Housing	30	68.2
Daycare	31	70.5
Work problems	31	68.9
Other[a]	25	64.1

[a] Other problems include physical health, retirement and career planning, leisure, education, anxiety, "life-style-related" problems, bereavement, and wife abuse.

Source: Reprinted with the permission of Lexington Books, from *Healthier Workers: Health Promotion and Employee Assistance Programs*, by Martin Shain, Helne Suurvali, and Marie Boutilier. Copyright © 1986 by Lexington Books.

makes demands that an employee cannot meet. The boss can be a source of stress, as can a demanding work schedule. Interruptions, lack of advancement opportunities, lack of input into decisions, and lack of communication from the supervisor are common stressors among secretaries.[53]

Exhibit 14.6 (page 690) describes how electronic monitoring of Bell Canada telephone operators was one of the biggest causes of stress for workers (see also Case 11.2). The factors related to stress and employee health are numerous and their relationships complex. Although certain occupations are recognized as being more stressful than others, stress is largely an individual matter: what is stressful to one person may not bother another.

Job stress often results in physical complaints, such as ulcers, headaches and backaches, and increased use of alcohol and drugs. The end result for organizations is increased absenteeism and reduced worker productivity. In high-stress occupations, such as air traffic control and health care, prolonged job stress often leads to burnout, a three-phase process characterized by emotional exhaustion, negativism, and lowered self-esteem. A labour arbitrator in Nova Scotia has ruled that burnout is a form of work-related injury, compensable under workers' compensation.[54]

To counter the effects of job stress and burnout, a growing number of organizations are sponsoring stress-management workshops and exercise programs for workers. EAPs also help employees deal with stress related to

EXHIBIT 14.5
British Columbia's Interlock Programs for Lawyers and Accountants

The argument got heated and Charles lost control. It didn't help at all that Charles, a lawyer, was suffering emotional problems during the dispute with his client. The upshot was that Charles struck the client, and in short order the Law Society of British Columbia was involved.

For Charles, the consequences could have been serious. If the law society ruled against him, it had the power to impose a fine and suspend his licence to practise. But Charles was spared such an ordeal because of an arrangement between the legal body and Interlock, a pioneer in the employee assistance movement in B.C.

Interlock is a non-profit diagnostic, counselling and referral service to which the law society's 7200 members can turn for help in dealing with their personal problems. Although Charles was given the option of seeking help as an alternative to disciplinary action, most lawyers who use Interlock's services do so voluntarily and anonymously, with complete assurance of confidentiality.

Similarly, British Columbia's 5000 chartered accountants have access to Interlock through a contract between the B.C. Institute of Chartered Accountants and the privately operated employee and family assistance service. The institute has not followed the law society model of linking its disciplinary process to a counselling program, although it is being considered.

Interlock, which grew out of a government-financed alcoholism and drug abuse treatment organization, now serves 35 000 employees and members of about 80 companies, institutions and professional groups in British Columbia. Its board of directors is drawn from the ranks of labor, management and community representatives. Interlock's focus is on diagnosis, referral to appropriate community agencies for treatment, and followup by Interlock's staff. All of the counsellors have a Master's or Ph.D. in psychology or social work, and most of the counselling is done in-house (rather than being referred to outside agencies). The clinic's counsellors also provide therapy for about 30% of the people they see in Interlock's facilities in Vancouver, Kelowna, Victoria and Prince George.

Fees are usually based on the number of employees within a firm. However, the agreements with the law society and the institute provide for fee for service, with the costs paid by the two organizations, which are billed without any disclosure of the names of the clients.

The arrangement between the Institute of Chartered Accountants and Interlock had its genesis in a fund established by an institute member for the prevention of alcoholism and treatment of alcoholics. Before selecting Interlock, the fund's trustees interviewed health care agencies and firms specializing in psychological counselling. After discussions with Interlock,

EXHIBIT 14.5 *(continued)*

the plan was enlarged to deal with a whole range of emotional problems—from marital difficulties to general depression and even financial woes.

Barrie Jones, secretary to the trustees who administer the fund, says a professional who is addicted to alcohol either denies he has a problem or feels he is intelligent enough to handle it on his own. The institute's monthly publication has carried articles designed to shatter that belief and to draw attention to the availability of help through Interlock. A recent article offered a personal account of an accountant's drift to alcoholism. It began: "My name is X and I am an alcoholic. I am also a chartered accountant." The article prompted a surge of interest in Interlock.

Linda Korbin, regional director of Interlock, observed in 1992 that alcohol and drug concerns are only a part of Interlock's activities. "A great deal of our work is also around stress-related problems and marital/relationship and family problems. We are also focussing on wellness programs in the workplace, and responding to critical incidents (trauma) with training programs for supervisors who have to intervene with a troubled employee."

The accountants have had ten years' experience with Interlock and the lawyers nearly eleven years. For both groups the success of the program can be measured by the rehabilitation of alcoholics, and assistance provided in dealing with personal problems of lawyers and accountants that often interfered with the quality of service to clients. Says Frank Maczko, secretary of the law society: "A disrupted personal life makes for an impaired practitioner." Among cases where lawyers were referred to Interlock by the law society was one involving a lawyer who turned up drunk in court, and another of a lawyer who had been convicted on a drug charge. "If we hadn't intervened they might have found themselves in even worse trouble," Maczko says.

But there is still the nagging question of how far an organization should inject itself into a member's or employee's personal life. "Rehabilitation is certainly better than punishment," notes Maczko. "The issue is one of balancing individual rights and our duty to protect the client's interests. No one is forced to take treatment. But we have a right to prevent someone from practising if the use of drugs or alcohol addiction is a threat to clients."

Still, of 250 law society members who used Interlock's services in 1991, only five were directed to the clinic by the society. The level of voluntary referrals for all 650 persons among Interlock's client firms and organizations is even higher at 95%.

A survey by Interlock of its clients suggests that the vast majority were pleased with the help they had received. Says Interlock executive director David Ayers: "Employees are being helped in resolving their personal problems, and in the process their life at home and at work is being made more productive and pleasant. What more could you ask for?"

Source: Wilfred List, "Helping Out the Problem Employee," *Report on Business Magazine, The Globe and Mail*, September 1986, p. 72. Reprinted with the permission of the author; and updated information provided by Linda Korbin, regional director of Interlock, April 1992.

EXHIBIT 14.6
Monitoring as a Cause of Stress at Bell Canada

Bell Canada has ended electronic monitoring of telephone operators in some areas after a joint union–management study showed surveillance to be one of the biggest causes of stress for workers.

The study, done jointly with the Health and Safety Institute of Quebec, was agreed to in the last round of bargaining between Bell — which operates phone services in Quebec and Ontario — and the Communications Workers of Canada, which represents Bell employees.

Bell has stopped monitoring in some offices on a test basis after the study recommended assessing group production instead of individual workers.

"I am hearing from operators that they feel better working this way," said Gary Cwitco, a staff worker with the union.

Donald DiTecco, who is an internal consultant for Bell, said the study has put the introduction of new technology in perspective.

"The important thing for this study is to get people to see how we are allowing jobs to evolve with new technology without planning the design of the jobs," he said.

The two were interviewed after presenting their findings from the study to a conference on work with video display terminals, which has attracted 1500 delegates from 30 countries.

Mr. DiTecco said new technology is being allowed to dictate management techniques. In the case of operators, the ability to measure and compare each operator's speed in handling calls has led to enormous emphasis being placed on "average work time."

That has led supervisors to focus on slower employees, creating more stress, which can be related to more health problems and absenteeism and, ultimately, lower production over all.

The study found that two-thirds of operators consider their job to be stressful and 35 per cent say job stress is a severe problem.

Seventy per cent of operators said the conflict between pressure to work quickly and pressure to give good service was the most stressful aspect of the job.

Electronic monitoring of performance, the pressure to work faster, and the placing of calls by machines — which automatically feed operators a new call when they have finished the previous one — were the other top sources of job stress.

Source: Jane Coutts, "Bell Stops Snooping on Its Operators," *The Globe and Mail*, September 14, 1989. Reprinted with the permission of *The Globe and Mail*.

---

a variety of concerns. Another, more basic approach is to reduce, as much as possible, the number of stressors in the workplace. For example, noise levels might be reduced and job expectations clarified, supervisors might be provided with interpersonal skills training, and work loads might be reduced.

HRM IN ACTION

SHOULD COMPENSATION BENEFITS BE PAID FOR WORK STRESS?

Work-induced stress has been dubbed "the end-of-century affliction." It is known to affect workers' health—but the issue of whether a resulting condition should be compensable is a legal and ethical minefield.

Today [October 22, 1991], the Ontario Workers' Compensation Board ventures into that minefield by launching public hearings into whether it should pay compensation benefits for "disablements arising from workplace stressors."

Labour and management are polarized on the issue: workers' representatives say Ontario should follow the lead of several U.S. states and pay for emotional disabilities caused by work; employers argue against such compensation, fearing a flood of questionable claims and a corresponding increase in their WCB assessments.

Compensation for emotional disorders, while not unheard of in Canada, is rare. Workers' compensation boards in Saskatchewan and Quebec have allowed some claims for chronic stress. In many jurisdictions, including Ontario, "the workplace stressor must be a sudden, shocking and life-threatening event to be considered for compensation."

The Ontario board says it is "pioneering" in Canada with its hearings to determine whether the eligibility for compensation should be substantially broadened and whether emotional disorders brought on by work should be formally recognized.

There have been a few decisions granting stress compensation to Ontario claimants, including a recent one awarding benefits to a factory worker who became incapacitated as a result of long-term racial and sexual harassment on the job.

Pre-submissions to the board indicate that it is in for a lively debate at its public hearings across Ontario over the next three months. To assist in the debate the WCB has suggested that, in determining whether there is a disability, "a diagnosis of a psychiatric disorder in accordance with generally accepted psychiatric terminology is preferred and would be the most persuasive evidence."

Some of the disorders likely to arise in "workplace stressor" claims are mood disorders, anxiety disorders, sleep problems, sexual disorders and psychological factors affecting physical condition, the WCB said in a policy proposal distributed in advance of the hearings.

"Since generic terms such as 'emotional exhaustion' or 'stress' in themselves do not necessarily denote a disability, these will not be sufficient to establish a compensable condition."

Once a disability is established, there is the delicate exercise of determining whether it is more related to work life than home life.

The board concedes "there are significant gaps in the current knowledge base about workplace and non-workplace stressors and the interaction between them."

Several employers, in pre-submissions, said it is nearly impossible to pinpoint the factors that might push an employee over the brink. One employers' group said that while there has been some scientific study of workplace stressors, there has not been much research into the relationship between them and such non-work stressors as divorce, bereavement and alcoholism.

Bell Canada said flatly: "The WCB attempting to enter this area of claims in the admitted absence of solid scientific evidence or a well-known body of medical literature is not only questionable, but quite possibly irresponsible."

Employers argue that there would have to be an intrusive investigation into a employee's personal life to rule out other factors before a claim for a work-induced disability was allowed. That could create legal and ethical problems.

Some factors generally accepted as workplace stressors are the machine-pacing of work, monotonous work and lack of control over work, "particularly under conditions of high responsibility," the WCB said in its policy proposal.

One of the most contentious issues to be determined is whether personnel matters, such as discipline and layoffs, should be acknowledged as workplace stressors for the purpose of compensation.

The Ontario Public Service Employees Union submits that demotions, suspensions and dismissals should be considered "significant stressors."

"The law says that if a disability arises out of, and in the course of, employment, that disability is compensable. . . . A disability which arises from closures, layoffs, dismissals or other government programs comes out of, or in the course of, employment. It must therefore be compensable," OPSEU wrote in a submission to the WCB.

That position set off alarm bells with employers, prompting the Skyline Ottawa Hotel, for one, to warn that "if this floodgate is opened, you will be swamped with claims and employers will be bankrupted.

"In our opinion, while disciplinary actions are upsetting, they are a normal part of day-to-day work life and can in no way be described as "unusual,' " the hotel said in its submission.

Whatever the outcome of the hearings, the impact of stress on the workforce is an issue of growing concern to such bodies as the Geneva-based International Labour Organization, which recently reported:

"The end-of-the-century affliction, stress, continues to ravage all levels of society. It first spreads within the world of work, where the pressure

> of competition is one of its chief causes. But monotony can be just as harmful as excessive diversity or work overload, and stress-related illness can affect manual workers as well as executives."
>
> Source: Virginia Galt, "Ontario to Probe Issue of Work Stress," *The Globe and Mail*, October 22, 1991. Reprinted with the permission of *The Globe and Mail*.

SMOKING

It has been estimated that smokers cost their employers between $1000 and $4500 more per year than do nonsmokers. These costs include higher absenteeism, higher insurance rates, higher cleaning costs, and higher ventilation costs. Several large U.S. firms estimate that smokers are absent five to six more days a year than nonsmokers, and insurance discounts of up to 35 percent may be available for companies that do not have smokers, a major cause of industrial fires.[55]

To reduce the costs and risks associated with smoking, and also to appease growing numbers of nonsmokers who object to second-hand smoke, many organizations have established policies that restrict or prohibit smoking in offices. The cities of Vancouver and Toronto have passed bylaws curbing smoking, and many organizations, such as Bowater Mersey Paper Co. Ltd. of Liverpool, Nova Scotia, and Maritime Telegraph and Telephone Co. Ltd. of Halifax, are voluntarily choosing to limit smoking to designated areas. Such actions have led to predictions that "smoke [will be] out of the workplace within five years."[56]

Companies that have implemented smoking policies report little employee resistance, but experts agree that successful programs require commitment from top management and consultation with employees prior to policy implementation. In order to obtain employee input, organizations often conduct surveys or establish employee committees.

ALCOHOLISM

Alcoholism is both a health problem and a performance problem in organizations. A survey by Statistics Canada of exposure to accidents from January 1985 to January 1988 reported that persons who consumed seven drinks or more per week had a work-related accident rate three-and-a-half times that of nondrinkers. Persons who regularly consumed between one and six drinks per week had somewhat less than twice the accident rate of nondrinkers.[57] Alcoholism costs the economy in reduced productivity and increased time off work. According to an estimate by the Harvard School of Public Health, problem drinkers miss an average of 22 work days per year and are at least twice as likely as nondrinkers to have accidents.[58] The direct and indirect costs of alcoholism to employers include the costs of absenteeism, accidents, bad decisions, fighting, discharges, garnishment of pay, increased benefit costs, lower productivity, and supervisors' lost time in dealing with alcoholic workers.

Managers are slightly more likely than other employees to become alcoholics since it is often easier for a manager to conceal a drinking problem. Managers also come into more frequent contact with alcohol in the context of business luncheons, dinners, and meetings. Several years ago, a Ford Motor Company executive sued his employer, arguing that his job, which involved many luncheons and parties at which virtually everyone drank, had caused his drinking problem.

Employers should have a policy regarding alcoholism, and it should be applicable to both managerial and nonmanagerial employees. The policy should be a realistic and supportive one, since strict, punitive policies often cause an alcoholic to hide the problem as long as possible rather than ask for help. Employers, of course, cannot tolerate alcoholic employees, especially those in responsible or potentially hazardous jobs, and should terminate any who fail to respond to rehabilitation.

In addition to offering supportive policies, employers can make available employee assistance programs (EAPs) on alcohol abuse. Evidence shows economic as well as ethical benefits are inherent in establishing such programs. In the United States, a study of McDonnell Douglas concluded that treating employees for alcoholism through the company EAP saved four dollars for every dollar spent. Kimberly-Clark said it had a recovery rate of about 65 percent, Dupont reported a 70 percent recovery rate, and the success rate for airline pilots was above 90 percent, according to the Employee Assistance Professionals Association. Motivation is the key and airline pilots are the most highly motivated. A spokesperson for the association observed that "when alcoholics get sober, they experience a dramatically improved quality of life. If their employers helped them achieve that . . . they develop a loyalty to their employer that can't be measured."[59]

Finally, employers should examine their policies and practices in other areas to be sure that they are not contributing to an alcohol problem. For example, the human resource manager of a large personal-products manufacturing plant became concerned at the number of hung-over employees at work on Fridays; he discovered that the major cause was the company-sponsored bowling league, which met on Thursday nights. The manager handled the problem by announcing that if employees did not come to work in better condition on Fridays, the bowling league would have to be discontinued.

DRUG USE

Drug use, including abuse of prescription drugs, is a growing problem for employers in Canada. The Task Force on Employment-Related Drug Screening, established by the Addiction Research Foundation of Ontario, estimated that in 1987 Ontario had 200 000 workers with a drug or alcohol problem, causing a $1 billion a year loss to the economy. Eleven percent of all Ontario adults used marijuana, according to a 1984 survey, and 3 percent used cocaine; for younger adults, the figures were 28 percent using marijuana and 7 percent cocaine.[60]

Employees who are drug users do not perform as well as they otherwise might; they also have higher rates of accidents and absenteeism and receive three times the average level of sick benefits.[61] Drug use may also lead to theft and drug dealing in the workplace, as users are driven to support their expensive habit.

No industry or occupation is immune to drug use; it is especially prevalent among young adults, with cocaine being the preferred drug of professionals and executives. As stated in *Time*:

> Cocaine is an increasingly popular drug to use at work, partly because the intense high it generates often gives users the false feeling that they can do their jobs better and faster. Moreover, cocaine is easy to hide. It is generally snorted rather than smoked, and does not give off an odor as marijuana does.[62]

Many Canadian and U.S. companies are having to come to terms with drug use in their organizations. Most companies have rules against drug use and many have begun employee assistance programs or equipped existing programs to deal with problems of drug abuse and cross addiction, addiction to both drugs and alcohol. Programs generally involve both counselling and referral to hospital for treatment.

A much-debated strategy is testing for drug use, during the selection process and/or during employment. The issue is a contentious one for employers trying to deal with the growing problem of drugs in the workplace.[63] There are questions both about the accuracy of tests and about the legality of making them mandatory. The Task Force on Employment-Related Drug Screening found that drug testing could be done legally and that the tests could be accurate. It also found, however, that there was no evidence that moderate use of alcohol or drugs increases the risk of accidents at work. More recent evidence, published in 1991 and noted above, found that moderate use of alcohol did increase the risk of accidents. Accordingly it recommended that testing be limited to employees in jobs that pose a risk to other workers or the public. Although employers have the right to screen potential employees, employees covered under a union contract or nonunionized employees who worked for a company before testing was introduced may have the right to refuse to undergo tests. If a unionized employee refused, he or she would probably win any grievance that resulted from discipline by the employer. For a nonunion employee, a drug test could be considered a change in the terms and conditions of employment and would have to be implemented with adequate notice, according to Robert MacDermid, a lawyer who advised the task force on the legal aspects of testing.[64] Drug testing is also relevant to the selection of employees, which is discussed in Chapter 7.

HRM IN ACTION

DRUG TESTING AT IMPERIAL OIL

Imperial Oil Ltd. will begin mandatory testing of employees, including some executives, for drug and alcohol use . . .

The company, which employs more than 11 000 people, says it is updating its drug and alcohol policy because of increased employer responsibility for workplace health and safety and environmental protection.

New employees will be tested before job offers are confirmed. Workers in safety-sensitive positions, such as drilling-rig supervisors, will be subject to random tests. Seven per cent of Imperial employees hold such safety-sensitive jobs.

Executives, including chairman Arden Haynes and down to the level of general manager or refinery plant manager, also will be tested.

The reasoning for testing executives is that they make financial decisions, explained Barbara Hejduk, manager of public affairs. "It's also a leadership issue," she said.

About 10 per cent of Canada's adult population is believed to suffer from alcohol or drug problems, said Jacques Perras of the Ottawa-based Alliance for a Drug Free Canada. "Of course that doesn't mean they are all impaired at work."

Imperial is not the first Canadian company to introduce on-the-job drug testing, but it is considered a corporate leader in the field of human resources. The Toronto-Dominion Bank and the Winnipeg police force also do some employee drug testing. As well, there have been proposals to test federally regulated transportation workers.

[Recently,] Exxon Corp. of New York, the parent of Imperial, agreed to a settlement of more than $1-billion (U.S.) to the Alaska and U.S. governments for damages caused when the Exxon Valdez went aground in 1989. The captain was accused of drinking on shore before the ship sailed. He was acquitted of state charges of operating his ship while drunk.

Imperial's program, described as one of the most comprehensive in the country, has already been criticized by opponents who question the reliability of drug tests and whether they are an invasion of privacy and a violation of Canada's Charter of Rights and Freedoms.

"These people have no business trying to implement this sort of intrusive regime," said Brian Edy, president of the Alberta Civil Liberties Association. "Imperial should be ashamed of themselves."

Mr. Edy, a Calgary lawyer, said drug testing is "grossly inaccurate," and can't determine whether a worker is doing a job properly.

However, Mr. Perras of the anti-drug organization said the program appears very thorough. "Our policy is one of neutrality with respect to testing but we applaud the fact that Imperial talked to employees at all levels in the company, including labour unions." The anti-drug alliance is supported by member businesses, including Imperial.

Imperial's policy sets out basic standards for all employees, including a ban on alcohol and illegal drugs on company premises, and prohibits a blood-alcohol concentration of more than .04 per cent for anyone on company business. A person weighing less than 73 kilograms reaches that level after consuming one drink an hour.

A zero blood-alcohol reading is mandatory for workers in safety-sensitive positions. However, drinking will be allowed at company social functions under certain guidelines.

Penalties range from dismissal for drug trafficking and use on company property to a warning and referral for treatment if evidence of substance abuse turns up.

Imperial plans to use backup drug tests where a positive reading is obtained, a procedure that Mr. Perras said increases reliability to "99.9 per cent." Test results would be reviewed by a qualified doctor and discussed with the applicant or employee before being communicated to management.

Source: Margot Gibb-Clark, "Imperial Oil to Test Staff for Drugs," *The Globe and Mail*, October 5, 1991. Reprinted with the permission of *The Globe and Mail*.

The arguments continue. Unions and civil libertarians vigorously opposed drug testing in the workplace,[65] and in fact, mandatory drug testing may be a violation of human rights legislation.[66] In addition there are doubts that random drug testing of employees would survive a court challenge based on the Charter of Rights and Freedoms. Accordingly the federal government has ruled out random drug and alcohol testing of employees in the federal jurisdiction in safety-sensitive positions.[67]

HRM professionals will have to review the latest research findings as well as recent court decisions before deciding how to proceed on this sensitive issue. A recent examination of the legal implications of employment-related drug testing in Canada concluded that employers considering a drug-testing program should avoid pre-employment drug testing for most jobs. Employers should test existing employees in most jobs only upon a reasonable suspicion of drug use. Employers should also limit the extent of invasion into employees' privacy if employees test positive, and should try to assist them before taking any disciplinary action.[68]

AIDS

A growing health-related problem for employers is AIDS. Public fear of the disease and the legal problems of coping with its victims (or possible victims) may be greater hazards than the illness itself.

Employers are aware of the problems. In a recent survey of corporate decision makers, two-thirds expressed concern about AIDS. Forty percent indicated that AIDS will have an impact on their business in the future, and 21 percent said they probably have AIDS cases in the workplace. Nevertheless, only a few employers have developed policies on AIDS-related issues.[69] Such policies should relate both to current employees and to the selection of employees. Professor Hem Jain attributes employers' reluctance to prepare policy statements to a belief that AIDS is treated like any other disease or condition, a concern that issuing a statement might obligate them to an unwise course of action, and to the view that legal and medical facts are still changing. Jain argues, however, that it is important for firms to prepare such a statement both because fear of contracting AIDS has reached crisis proportions, creating misunderstanding, and because

> co-workers' anxieties concerning working with AIDS victims are understandable, considering the myths and misconceptions about AIDS so widespread among the general public. Management must be sensitive to such concerns. Management should have written policies, which should give adequate consideration to the rights of the AIDS victims as well as to the rights and concerns of fellow employees and provide a safe working environment.[70]

An Ontario Bar Association Committee concluded that under the province's human rights code a person with AIDS would be considered to have a physical disability, as would an HIV-infected person with no symptoms. Accordingly, employers should conclude that HIV-infected persons, with or without the symptoms of AIDS, have explicit rights under the Human Rights Act, as well as their common law civil rights.[71] A federal arbitration board held in 1987 that a suspension of an airline flight attendant who was suspected of having contracted AIDS was a breach of the collective agreement; the employee, it ruled, "had the right to continue to work as long as he was physically able to do the job and did not pose a risk to others."[72]

Mandatory testing for AIDS is regarded as a serious intrusion on individual rights in Canada. Thus, the Canadian Human Rights Commission forbids mandatory AIDS tests for employees or prospective employees unless workers have been exposed to infected blood or body fluids. People with AIDS cannot be dismissed from employment unless they are unable to perform their work.

AIDS is a sensitive issue in the employment relationship. Jain points out that "it is in the enlightened self-interest of employers to have policies aimed at finding solutions which could accommodate the rights of AIDS victims and the fears of fellow employees in order to prevent workplace disruptions and loss of productivity." He suggests that any policy emphasize the importance of workplace education programs to prevent the spread of the disease and to increase employee understanding and acceptance of people with AIDS.[73] (Case 14.2 contains a sample policy statement on AIDS.)

SUMMARY

This chapter has examined the role of health and safety in organizations, the requirements and impact of legislation on employers and on human resource management, various approaches to health and safety, and the special health problems of job stress, smoking, alcoholism, drug use, and AIDS. Organized labour has been promoting more stringent health and safety legislation. This activity has led to several government commissions, which, in turn, have led to more legislation in this field. With increasing awareness of the dangers to health and safety in both the workplace and the environment, it is likely that HRM professionals will face greater responsibilities in this area during the coming years.

REVIEW QUESTIONS

1. What role can human resource professionals play in increasing senior management's awareness of the costs to an organization of unsafe conditions?

2. Joint labour–management committees are an important feature of health and safety legislation in Canada. Explain the importance of these committees for improving conditions in the workplace.

3. Discuss how employers should respond to a workers' compensation claim. Use an example.

4. Explain why employers are concerned about having workplace stress eligible for workers' compensation.

5. Drug testing in the workplace is an issue that has divided civil libertarians and employers. Discuss the pros and cons of mandatory drug testing.

PROJECT IDEAS

1. Peruse some trade journals or journals related to health and safety, and locate an article on one organization's safety program. Make sure that the article you choose provides a good description, rather than a sketchy one. Describe the program in a short written or oral report.

2. Contact a company, by either phone or mail, and request copies of its rules and regulations relating to employees' health and safety. Find out what other measures the employer takes to ensure a healthy and safe workplace for employees. Share the information you obtain in a report to your classmates.

3. Obtain a copy of the health and safety regulations of some Canadian jurisdiction other than Ontario. Summarize the major provisions and compare them with those of Ontario's Occupational Health and Safety Act, which is discussed in this chapter. Write a short essay discussing the relative merits of each jurisdiction's approach to health and safety from the perspective of the employer and of the employee.

4. As a class project, arrange for a visit to a local employer, preferably a manufacturer or other organization where health and safety may be major problems. If possible, tour the organization with a person responsible for safety (arrangements will need to be made in advance). Pinpoint as many potential hazards as you can and find out how the organization protects its workers from them.

▶▶▶ CASES

CASE 14.1 ▶ EMPLOYEE FITNESS AT CANADA LIFE

A ground-breaking study of an employee fitness and lifestyle program at Canada Life Assurance Co. in Toronto, which tracked fitness levels over 10 years, has found significant improvement in fitness and lower risk of heart attack among active participants.

The study is unique because there [are] no other research data dealing with employee fitness programs that provide a comparison of fitness levels and cardiovascular risk factors among the same group of individuals over such a long period of time.

Employees who were most active also had the lowest levels of absenteeism, the study found.

A striking sidelight of the data was the finding that smoking is a factor influencing absenteeism. It was estimated that, on average, smokers were absent 16 days more than non-smokers over the 10-year period.

But the job level of individuals appeared to influence absenteeism most, with lower absenteeism among those on the higher rungs of the hierarchical ladder.

Still, the study states that reducing absenteeism can be a prime reason for companies to initiate an employee fitness and lifestyle program.

Ontario's Ministry of Tourism and Recreation, which financed the study jointly with Canada Life, plans to use the results to promote such programs.

More than 800 Ontario companies, with a total of 40 000 employees, have some form of fitness or wellness program, ranging from provision of elaborate fitness centres to subsidized memberships in private health clubs.

Canada Life was one of the first employers in Canada to introduce an on-site employee fitness program in 1978 as part of a research project then sponsored by the federal government.

The company employs about 1500 workers in its head office in Toronto; about one-third of them participate in programs during non-working hours, with the majority enrolled in fitness classes. Employees are charged $12 for each 10- to 12-week program, or about $60 a year.

The study at Canada Life measured fitness levels of 126 employees who have been with the company since the project began. It also included 27 employees from another company as a control group.

The study, under the direction of Michael Cox and Jan Walker, compared cholesterol levels and found that the most active individuals had a reduced risk of heart attack, compared with those who were inactive.

Dr. Cox is director of the human performance division of the Graduate Sports Medicine Centre in Wayne, Pa.

The current findings contradict those of an earlier study seven years after the fitness program at Canada Life was launched. That study, published in early 1988, concluded that the results of the program were disappointing.

It said a longer period of more intensive exercise than the participants were getting in the 30-minute luncheon workout was required for significant improvement in fitness.

Dr. Cox said the earlier study was flawed and did not take into account a broad range of factors relating to fitness and categories of participants.

The results of the current study are said to be more conclusive, particularly regarding cardiovascular fitness.

"Reduced risk [of heart attacks] was evident even among those with moderate levels of activity," the study states.

"There is no question about the cost of coronary disease for companies in terms of lost working hours due to premature death, retraining, sickness and bereavement."

The study also notes that the most active groups showed better attitudes to health, lower stress levels and less smoking.

In making a case for the relationship between employee fitness programs and absenteeism, the study says the 41 people in the most active groups had a decrease in absenteeism of 0.78 days a year. This saved the company $51 487 over the 10 years.

"These results are evidence that much of what has been thought of as historically unavoidable absence is, in fact, avoidable," the study states.

Source: Wilfred List, "Study Shows Employee Fitness Programs Work," *The Globe and Mail*, November 27, 1989. Reprinted with the permission of the author.

TASKS AND QUESTIONS

1. Prepare a case justifying company fitness programs.
2. Discuss why only approximately 1 percent of Ontario's workers have some form of fitness or wellness program available through their employer.

CASE 14.2 ▶ A WORKPLACE POLICY FOR AIDS

The following is an example of a specific policy with respect to AIDS. It is based on the policy developed by the Municipality of Metropolitan Toronto.

_____recognizes and respects the rights of all its employees as these rights have been developed and defined under federal and provincial laws, collective agreements and management policies. The _____has an obligation to provide a safe work environment for its employees and the safe delivery of services to its clients. At the same time, it is recognized that employees handicapped by illness have a right to pursue those activities which their conditions allow, including continuing to work. As long as these employees are able to perform the essential duties of their jobs in a satisfactory manner, and medical evidence indicates that their continuing to work does not pose a safety or health hazard to themselves or others, the _____will deal with them, if and when the need arises, according to the usual procedures governing personnel decisions.

It is recognized that AIDS is an extremely serious medical condition, and that no medical cure, nor a vaccine to prevent its spread, has yet been found. For these reasons, many people have deep concerns about contracting AIDS, and need assurance that their safety will be protected.

The _____is committed to addressing these concerns with sensitivity, and through an ongoing programme of information and education for its employees.

While the best available medical opinion indicates that AIDS cannot be contracted through casual contact or most workplace activities, _____will review all situations where employees may, in the course of their duties, be exposed to the bodily fluids of others, and co-ordinate the implementation and regular review and amendment of safety procedures, and the provision of clothing and devices to give effect to such procedures.

Where procedures have been duly established, _____ will give its full support to the taking of precautions and the use of protective clothing and equipment called for by the procedures.

As with other diseases, the worst enemies in battling AIDS are fear and ignorance. _____ undertakes to obtain and utilize the most up-to-date and authoritative medical information available for the purpose of educating and protecting its employees and members of the public with whom they deal.

Source: Policy with Respect to AIDS—For the Municipality of Metropolitan Toronto, as reported in Hem C. Jain, "AIDS: Need for Policy in the Workplace," *Relations Industrielles/Industrial Relations*, vol. 44 no. 4 (Autumn 1989), p. 864. Reprinted with the permission of the publisher.

TASKS AND QUESTIONS

1. Do you believe this statement represents an appropriate balance among the concerns of people with AIDS, co-workers, and employers? If not, how would you amend the wording of the statement?

2. What additional steps should employers take to prepare for the possibility that some employees may contract AIDS?

NOTES

1. Virginia Galt, "Workplace Accident Tab $4-Billion," *The Globe and Mail*, March 14, 1991.
2. M. Clugston, "A Preventable Tragedy," *Maclean's*, August 27, 1984, p. 45.
3. Clugston, "A Preventable Tragedy," p. 45.
4. B. Woodworth, "Settling the Rig Disaster," *Maclean's*, January 9, 1984, p. 25.
5. C.E. Reasons, L.L. Ross, and C. Paterson, *Assault on the Worker: Occupational Health and Safety in Canada* (Toronto: Butterworths, 1981), p. 243.
6. Rosemary Todd, "Aircraft Plant Workers Stop Work Over Safety," *The Globe and Mail*, November 18, 1987.
7. K. Govier, "Eminence Gray," *Canadian Business*, March 1986, pp. 31–34, 107–12.
8. Statistics Canada, *Accidents in Canada*, cat. no. 11–612E, no. 3, General Social Survey Series (Ottawa, 1991), p. 65.
9. Labour Canada, *Canadian Employment Injuries and Occupational Illness*, 1972–1981 ed. (Hull, Que.: Supply and Services Canada, 1984), p. xiii; and Labour Canada, Occupational Safety and Health Branch, *Occupational Injuries and Their Cost in Canada 1987–1989* (Ottawa, May 1991), tables 1A and 2A.

10. P. Manga et al., *Occupational Health and Safety: Issues and Alternatives*, Technical Report Series no. 6 (Ottawa: Economic Council of Canada, 1981).

11. A. Moses, "Mine Worker Remembered as Extraordinary Woman," *The Globe and Mail*, December 19, 1980.

12. Joseph J. Fuchini and Suzy Fuchini, *Working for the Japanese: Inside Mazda's American Auto Plant* (New York: The Free Press, 1990), pp. 172–75.

13. F. Lindsay, "Accident Proneness — Does It Exist?" *Occupational Safety and Health*, vol. 10, no. 2 (February 1980), pp. 8–9.

14. N.C. Kaphart and J. Tiffin, "Vision and Accident Experience," *National Society News*, vol. 62 (1950), pp. 90–91.

15. N. Root, "Injuries at Work Are Fewer Among Older Employees," *Monthly Labor Review*, vol. 104, no. 3 (1981), pp. 30–34.

16. F. Siskind, "Another Look at the Link between Work Injuries and Job Experience," *Monthly Labor Review*, vol. 105, no. 2 (1982), pp. 38–40.

17. Ontario, Ministry of Labour, Occupational Health and Safety Division, *The New Occupational Health and Safety Law for Ontario: How Bill 208 Affects You* (Toronto, 1990). For example, under the uniform Workplace Hazardous Materials Informations System (WHMIS) that came into force countrywide in October 1988, employers that use hazardous materials in the workplace must provide training for any workers likely to be exposed to them. Charles E. Humphrey and Cheryl A. Edwards, *The Employer's Health and Safety Manual* (Don Mills, Ont.: De Boo, 1990), pp. 8-29–8-30.

18. M.J. Smith, H.H. Cohen, A. Cohen, and R.J. Cleveland, "Characteristics of Successful Safety Programs," *Journal of Safety Research*, vol. 10 (1978), pp. 5–15.

19. M. Lowe, "Union Leaders Suspect Bonus Hinders Safety," *The Globe and Mail*, September 18, 1980.

20. J. Komaki, A.T. Heinzmann, and L. Lawson, "Effect of Training and Feedback: Component Analysis of a Behavioral Safety Program," *Journal of Applied Psychology*. vol. 65, no. 3 (1980), pp. 261–70.

21. "Lending a Helping Hand Can Also Aid Bottom Line," *The Globe and Mail*, August 1, 1988.

22. *The Canadian Master Labour Guide*, 6th ed. (Don Mills, Ont.: CCH Canadian, 1991), p. 755.

23. For discussion of earlier health and safety issues in Canada, see G.B. Reschenthaler, *Occupational Health and Safety in Canada: The Economics and Three Case Studies* (Montreal: Institute for Research on Public Policy, 1979), p. xiv; and Albert Broyles and Gil Reschenthaler, *Occupational Health and Safety: Issues and Alternatives*, Technical Report no. 6 (Ottawa: Economic Council of Canada, 1981).

24. Ontario, Royal Commission on the Health and Safety of Workers in Mines, *Report*, James Ham, chair (Toronto: Ministry of the Attorney General, 1976), pp. 254–55.

25. Ham Commission, *Report*, pp. 249–50.

26. Ham Commission, *Report*, p. 250.
27. Ontario, Ministry of Labour, Occupational Health and Safety Division, *A Guide to the Occupational Health and Safety Act* (Toronto: Queen's Printer for Ontario, 1990); and Industrial Accident Prevention Association, *A Guide to the Provisions of Ontario's Occupational Health and Safety Act*, 9th ed. (Toronto: IAPA, 1990).
28. See Ontario, Ministry of Labour, Occupational Health and Safety Division, *A Guide for Joint Health and Safety Committees and Representatives in the Workplace* (Toronto: Queen's Printer for Ontario, 1983; reprinted 1988).
29. Scott Thompson, "The Benefit of Doubt," *Occupational Health and Safety Canada*, vol. 7, no. 1 (January-February 1991), pp. 70–75.
30. Joint Federal–Provincial Inquiry Commission into Safety in Mines and Mining Plants in Ontario, *Towards Safe Production*, vol. 1 (Toronto: Ontario Ministry of Labour, 1981), pp. 14–15.
31. Wilfred List, "Worker Can't Refuse Normal Job If Safety in Dispute, Board Rules," *The Globe and Mail*, December 17, 1981.
32. Commission into Safety in Mines and Mining Plants in Ontario, *Towards Safe Production*, pp. 14–15, 19.
33. Two examples of monthly publications on developments in workers' compensation are *Workers' Compensation, Managing Claims* (Toronto: Concord Publishing); and *Occupational Health and Safety Canada*.
34. Elaine Newman, "Ontario's Bill 162, Are You Ready?" *Occupational Health and Safety Canada*, vol. 6, no. 1 (January-February 1990), pp. 100–104.
35. Newman, "Ontario's Bill 162," p. 104.
36. *The Canadian Master Labour Guide*, p. 750.
37. Ontario, Ministry of Labour, Industrial Disease Standards Panel, *First Report to the Workers' Compensation Board on Certain Issues Arising from the Report of the Royal Commission on Asbestos* (Toronto, September 1988) and *Annual Report 1987–1988* (Toronto, 1989).
38. At present, opinions are divided as to whether or not there is danger from VDTs. A recent University of Toronto study of 800 laboratory mice, subjected to varying levels of low-level electromagnetic radiation similar to the kind emitted by VDTs, concluded that there is no effect on the number of miscarriages, stillbirths, or fetal deformities. Lee-Ann Jack, "VDTs, What Does the Latest Research Reveal?" *Occupational Health and Safety (OH&S) Canada*, March/April 1990, pp. 53–54.
39. Suzanne McGee, " 'Unthinking' Robots Pose Safety Threat to Workers," *The Financial Post*, June 21, 1986.
40. Ross Laver, "Compromise Reached, Garbagemen Returning," *The Globe and Mail*, May 26, 1982.
41. F.C. Rinefort, "A New Look at Occupational Safety," *The Personnel Administrator*, vol. 22 (November 1977), pp. 29–36; Smith et al., "Characteristics of Successful Safety Programs," and D. Zohar, "Safety Climate in Industrial Organizations: Theoretical and Applied Implications," *Journal of Applied Psychology*, vol. 65, no. 1 (1980), pp. 96–102.

42. J. Komaki, K.D. Barwick, and L.R. Scott, "A Behavioral Approach to Occupational Safety: Pinpointing and Reinforcing Safe Performance in a Food Manufacturing Plant," *Journal of Applied Psychology*, vol. 63 (1978), pp. 434–45.

43. Lee-Ann Jack, "Coming to Grips with Bill 208," *Occupational Health and Safety Canada*, vol. 6, no. 4 (July-August 1990), pp. 51–59.

44. R.S. Haynes, R.C. Pine, and H.G. Fitch, "Reducing Accident Rates with Organizational Behavior Modification," *Academy of Management Journal*, vol. 25 (1982), pp. 407–16; and R.A. Weber, J.A. Wallin, and J.S. Chhokar, "Reducing Industrial Accidents: A Behavioral Experiment," *Industrial Relations*, vol. 23 (1984), pp. 119–25.

45. N. Root and M. Hoefer, "The First Work-Injury Data Available from New BLS Study," *Monthly Labor Review*, vol. 102, no. 1 (1979), pp. 76–80.

46. M.K. Rowan, "Ignoring Rules Led to Seven Deaths, Ministry Tells Inquest into Test Burn," *The Globe and Mail*, December 18, 1980.

47. D. Danielson and K. Danielson, *Ontario Employee Programme Survey* (Toronto: Ontario Ministry of Culture and Recreation, 1980).

48. Patricia Sarjeant, "Firms Find Wealth in Aiding Worker Health," *The Globe and Mail*, March 19, 1987.

49. Peter Clutterbuck, "Health and Safety in the Workplace," *The Human Resource*, February/March 1988, pp. 9–11.

50. D. Lees, "Executive Addicts," *Canadian Business*, February 1986, pp. 52–56, 105–6.

51. M. Shain, H. Suurvali, and M. Boutilier, *Healthier Workers: Health Promotion and Employee Assistance Programs* (Lexington, Ky.: Lexington Books, 1986), pp. 76–79.

52. Richard Earle, "Stress Taking Toll on the Bottom Line," *Canadian HR Reporter*, vol. 4, no. 1 (February 13, 1991, special report on employee wellness), p. 1.

53. "Secretaries and Stress," *The Wall Street Journal*, March 18, 1986.

54. M. Strauss, "Burnout Compensable as Work-Related Injury, NS Arbitrator Rules," *The Globe and Mail*, June 4, 1985.

55. Craig McInnes, "Business Smells Profit in Bid for Clean Workplace," *The Globe and Mail*, November 2, 1987.

56. McInnes, "Business Smells Profit."

57. Statistics Canada, *Accidents in Canada*, p. 36.

58. C.A. Filipowicz, "The Troubled Employee: Whose Responsibility?" *The Personnel Administrator*, June 1979, p. 18.

59. Jim Castelli, "Addiction," *HR Magazine*, April 1990, p. 58.

60. Craig McInnes, "Drug Testing Found Effective in Improving Workplace Safety," *The Globe and Mail*, March 31, 1987.

61. Estimate of the Research Triangle Institute, North Carolina, as reported in J. Castro, "Battling the Enemy Within," *Time*, March 17, 1986, pp. 52–61; and Estimate of the U.S. Alcohol, Drug Abuse and Mental Health Administration, 1984, as reported in Lees.

62. Castro, "Battling the Enemy Within," p. 54.
63. Nancy Bramm, "Message in a Bottle," *Benefits Canada,* vol. 15, no. 2 (February 1991), p. 11.
64. McInnes, "Drug Testing."
65. Elaine Carey, "An Invasion of Privacy? Drug Testing," *The Toronto Star*, April 19, 1987.
66. Raj Anand, "Workers Can Use Rights Laws to Challenge Drug Testing," *Canadian Human Rights Advocate*, August 1988, pp. 6–7; and The Privacy Commissioner of Canada, *Drug Testing and Privacy* (Ottawa 1990).
67. *CLV Health and Safety Forum*, November 19, 1990, p. 3.
68. Anthony N. Bota, *Employment Related Drug Testing* (Kingston, Ont.: Industrial Relations Centre, Queen's University, 1989).
69. Andrew Nikiforuk, "How Sex, Death and Fear Spell Profits and Losses," *Canadian Business*, vol. 61, no. 5 (May 1988), pp. 58–63, 107–15.
70. Hem C. Jain, "AIDS: Need for Policy in the Workplace," *Relations Industrielles/Industrial Relations*, vol. 44, no. 4 (Autumn 1989), pp. 862–63.
71. Jain, "AIDS: Need for Policy in the Workplace," p. 855.
72. Jain, "AIDS: Need for Policy in the Workplace," p. 855.
73. Jain, "AIDS: Need for Policy in the Workplace," p. 863.

SUGGESTIONS FOR FURTHER READING

- Anthony N. Bota. *Employment Related Drug Testing*. Kingston, Ont., Industrial Relations Centre, Queen's University, 1989.
- Hem C. Jain. "AIDS: Need for Policy in the Workplace." *Relations Industrielles/Industrial Relations*, vol. 44, no. 4 (Autumn 1989), pp. 850–65.
- Labour Canada, Occupational Safety and Health Branch. *Occupational Injuries and Their Cost in Canada 1987–1989*. Ottawa, May 1991.
- P. Menga, Albert Broyles, and Gil Reschenthaler. *Occupational Health and Safety Issues and Alternatives*. Technical Report Series no. 6. Ottawa: Economic Council of Canada, 1981.
- *Occupational Health and Safety Canada*. Usually monthly.
- Ontario. Ministry of Labour. Occupational Health and Safety Division. *A Guide to the Occupational Health and Safety Act*. Toronto: Queen's Printer for Ontario, 1990.
- The Privacy Commissioner of Canada. *Drug Testing and Privacy*. Ottawa, 1990.
- C.E. Reasons, L.L. Ross, and C. Paterson. *Assault on the Worker: Occupational Health and Safety in Canada*. Toronto: Butterworths, 1981.

- M.J. Smith, H.H. Cohen, A. Cohen, and R.J. Cleveland. "Characteristics of Successful Safety Programs." *Journal of Safety Research*, vol. 10 (1978), pp. 5–15.
- *Workers' Compensation Managing Claims*. Concord Publishing, Toronto. Monthly.

CHAPTER 15

LABOUR RELATIONS

- UNIONS: A DEFINITION
- LABOUR RELATIONS AND PUBLIC POLICY
- LABOUR RELATIONS AND ORGANIZATIONAL EFFECTIVENESS
- RELATION TO OTHER HRM FUNCTIONS
- RESPONSIBILITIES FOR LABOUR RELATIONS
- LABOUR UNION GOALS
- LABOUR UNIONS: STRUCTURE
- THE TRANSITION FROM EMPLOYEE RELATIONS TO LABOUR RELATIONS
- HRM IN ACTION ▸ CAW GAINS VOLUNTARY RECOGNITION FROM TEAM-BASED CAMI PLANT
- COLLECTIVE BARGAINING
- THE GRIEVANCE PROCEDURE
- DISSATISFACTION AMONG UNION MEMBERS
- IMPROVING LABOUR RELATIONS
- HRM IN ACTION ▸ EMPLOYEE INVOLVEMENT AT INMONT
- SUMMARY
- REVIEW QUESTIONS
- PROJECT IDEAS
- CASE 15.1 ▸ UNIONS UNITE FORCES AGAINST NORTHERN TELECOM
- CASE 15.2 ▸ MEETING EMPLOYEE NEEDS FOR FLEXIBILITY
- NOTES
- SUGGESTIONS FOR FURTHER READING

IT HAD BEEN TWO DAYS SINCE Rob Williams, human resource manager of a medium-sized manufacturing plant, received notice that the United Steelworkers had applied to the provincial labour relations board for certification to represent the plant's 80 hourly employees. Williams felt that unionization of the factory workers would limit his policy-making flexibility and authority by requiring agreement between management and the trade union on many HRM issues. He would have liked to try to persuade the employees not to support unionization, but he knew he had to be very careful.

First, labour relations laws in Canada prohibit employers from coercing, intimidating, or promising something to employees to prevent them from joining a union. Employers are allowed to voice their opinions on the advisability of unionization, but they must avoid any action or statement which could be deemed an unfair practice. Hence, Rob Williams realized he must not say too much. Second, a union usually applies for certification only when it has signed up at least enough employees to require a representation vote. And quite likely, the Steelworkers had a percentage so high that the board would certify without a vote. Rob Williams knew that if the union had the support of a majority of the employees and so won certification, he would simply have to make the best of it. An aggressive campaign on his part now might alienate the workers and poison the atmosphere when collective bargaining began.

Williams's estimate of the probabilities was correct. When the union submitted its list of members to the labour relations board, it did have a percentage of the bargaining unit sufficiently large to be certified without a representation vote. The employer filed no formal objection, and the board certified the new local of the United Steelworkers as the exclusive bargaining agent for the plant's hourly employees. The union then gave notice that it wanted to begin collective bargaining.

Incidents like this occur hundreds of times each year in Canadian places of employment that range from manufacturing plants to nursing homes. The union wins the right to represent employees in the majority of certification applications. For example, in Ontario during the fiscal year 1988/89, unions were certified in 649 out of 944 applications: 69 percent of the total. Of the 295 not certified, 162 were withdrawn. Only 145 applications (15 percent of the total) were for cases in which the union had signed up 45 to 55 percent of the employees in the prospective bargaining unit, and so a representation vote was conducted; the union won 79 of these votes and lost 66.[1] In most of the other cases, more than 55 percent of the employees involved had signed with the union before the application for certification was filed.

Across the country, similar situations prevail, although there are variations in the percentages at which a representation vote must or is likely to be called. With the exception of Nova Scotia, Alberta, and British Columbia, a provincial labour relations board certifies a union whenever it has reason to believe a majority of the bargaining unit's employees favour it. And whether an application for certification is successful or not, the fact of the bid usually affects management's personnel policies.

UNIONS: A DEFINITION

Trade unions are organizations of employees who have joined together to obtain a stronger voice in decisions affecting their wages, benefits, working conditions, and other aspects of employment than they would have as individuals. (In Canada, the terms "trade union" and "union" are used synonymously. For the sake of brevity, we often use "union.") Union members elect officers and officials, who represent the group's collective views to management. Through collective bargaining, union representatives negotiate *collective agreements* that spell out the terms and conditions of employment with management. Collective agreements also structure and define the nature of the relationship between labour and management.

Collective bargaining is a rule-making process that seeks to maintain a balance of power between labour and management so that they can come to terms and resolve their differences. Unions provide a system of justice through the grievance procedure to ensure that employees are treated according to terms specified in the collective agreement. If an employee feels that rights or privileges under the agreement have been violated, he or she may file a formal complaint, or *grievance*, against management. Union officials support and assist employees during the grievance process.

Like other organizations, a union depends upon its members for its continued existence and for financial support through the payment of dues. Therefore, a union attempts to persuade employees of its value by engaging in activities such as speeches, informal discussions, and dissemination of literature informing them of what it can do to improve pay and other conditions of employment. Some unions also offer apprenticeship and a variety of educational and social programs.

LABOUR RELATIONS AND PUBLIC POLICY

The term *labour relations* describes all interactions between labour and management in situations in which employees are represented by a trade union.[2] Unionized employees are often referred to collectively as *organized labour*. In the absence of a union, the structure and nature of interaction between labour and management is called *employee relations*. Employee relations are characterized by managerial control over the making and interpretation of human resource policies. In employee relations, management deals with employees individually rather than collectively.

Labour relations in the 1990s can best be understood by examining the history of trade unions and labour laws. In the Canadian context, labour laws are primarily provincial laws since the provinces have jurisdiction over labour relations for approximately 90 percent of the Canadian work force. Federal government jurisdiction applies to federal government employees and employees of banks, air, rail and sea transportation, grain elevators, and federal Crown corporations. The jurisdictional split is the same as for human rights and labour standards, as discussed in Chapter 3. Laws reflect the dominant values of society at a given point in time. Thus, the role of unions in society has changed as values and laws have changed. The history of unions can be traced from the free-market period, during which they were regarded as criminal conspiracies, to the era of World War II, when collective bargaining became the approved mechanism for labour–management negotiations and resolutions of conflict. In recent years the trend has been toward granting of the right to collective bargaining and the right to strike to more groups of employees, particularly employees in the public sector.

THE FREE-MARKET PERIOD

The free-market approach regards the employee–management relationship primarily as an exchange in which each person bargains individually with management. During this early period in union history, public policy did not support organized labour. In fact, unions were regarded as criminal conspiracies. The Trade Unions Act of 1872 did exempt "registered" unions from the charge of criminal conspiracy, but since no labour organization apparently ever did register, the first "charter of Canadian labour rights" came to nothing.[3] Moreover, the Criminal Law Amendment Act passed at the same time provided severe penalties for most forms of picketing and union pressure.

THE IDI ACT OF 1907

Despite their barely legal status, unions continued to grow in turn-of-the-century Canada. A landmark came in 1907, when the Industrial Disputes Investigation (IDI) Act introduced the principle of compulsory delay of work stoppages, a principle still present in most Canadian labour legislation. The act, which was passed after a coal-mining strike in the West resulted in a major emergency, provided for investigation and conciliation by a tripartite board — that is, a board with a representative of labour, a representative of management, and a neutral chairman. The board was given legal power to investigate disputes, to compel testimony, to determine the cause of dispute, and to recommend a settlement. This approach was developed by William Lyon Mackenzie King, who, as deputy minister of labour, found that publicity could be a useful weapon in settling a labour dispute. As historian Desmond Morton points out, on the strength of the IDI Act, King won a seat in Parliament in 1908 and soon became Canada's first full-fledged minister of labour. He later became prime minister.[4]

Although the IDI Act did give unions in the federal jurisdiction a form of recognition while the boards were conducting their investigations, it also undercut the power of the measures by which trade unionists attempted to achieve their goals. "An arrangement that gave employers time to continue operations, stockpile, train strikebreakers, and victimize union activists left workers at a serious disadvantage."[5]

WORLD WAR I AND THE EXTENDED IDI ACT

During World War I, the IDI Act was extended to cover disputes between workers and employers in industries producing military supplies. However, with full employment and rampant inflation, labour unrest increased, and in October 1918, strikes and lockouts were simply prohibited in major war industries. Although this prohibition was rescinded shortly after the end of the war, the scope of the IDI Act was extended to empower the federal minister of labour "to establish on the request of a municipality or on his own initiative, boards of conciliation and investigation to settle disputes in which strikes threatened, as well as to settle strikes already in progress."[6]

In 1925, in *Toronto Electric Power Commissioners* v. *Snider et al.*, the courts and the Privy Council declared that the federal government had acted beyond its proper constitutional jurisdiction. The Parliament of Canada then amended the IDA Act to make it apply only to disputes within its jurisdiction, but it also provided that the act could be extended to any province that passed enabling legislation. All the provinces except Prince Edward Island passed such legislation between 1925 and 1932.

THE WAGNER ACT IN THE UNITED STATES

Meanwhile, the union movement had had no better legislative support in the United States than in Canada from the nineteenth century through the 1920s. During the Depression, however, the Americans swung to a more pro-labour stance. Of the several labour laws they passed during this period, the most important was the National Labor Relations Act of 1935, usually called the Wagner Act, after its sponsor, Senator Robert Wagner. As historian Stuart Jamieson explains, its principles were eventually influential north of the border:

> The almost revolutionary change in government attitude and policy toward organized labour in the United States during the 1930s had a delayed impact in Canada. The Wagner Act of 1935 firmly established the by now well-known principles of guaranteeing workers the freedom to organize into unions of their own choosing, free from employer interference or attack; of establishing labour relations boards to investigate complaints of unfair labour practices, to prosecute offenders, and to conduct supervised elections to decide certification of unions representing the majority of workers in appropriate bargaining units; and of requiring recognition and bargaining by employers with properly certified unions. Notably absent from the act were measures to aid unions and employers to negotiate agreements, to regulate the contents of agreements, or to restrict the use of strikes or lockouts. Through the device of certification, however, it did have the effect of sharply reducing the issues of recognition and jurisdiction as major causes of strikes.[7]

The latter 1930s in Canada saw a considerable amount of new labour legislation, encouraged by changing attitudes and the support organized labour received from the States. Most provincial legislatures passed new labour laws; many of these adopted some of the Wagner Act principles, such as freedom of association, and required collective bargaining where desired by a majority of a unit's workers. Most, however, retained the basic IDI Act restrictions, and most lacked effective mechanisms for enforcement. The federal government let the IDI Act stand but did make it an offence under the Criminal Code for an employer to discharge workers for union activity.

WORLD WAR II AND PC 1003

World War II brought another tight labour market, but the federal government again extended the IDI Act, with its compulsory conciliation and "cooling off" period, to industries deemed essential to the war effort. Wartime orders-in-council did add recognition of the right to join unions and encouragement of collective bargaining, but full employment plus vigorous organizing campaigns by industrial unions produced what Jamieson terms "a new peak of intensity and bitterness in 1943."[8] Time lost through strikes approached the heights reached in 1919.

The passage of the Ontario Collective Bargaining Act of 1943 led the way for subsequent federal legislation. It began in 1944 with a new, blanket order-in-council, PC 1003, which included the main principles of the Wagner Act: guarantees of labour's right to organize; selection of units appropriate for collective bargaining; certification of bargaining agents; compulsory collective bargaining; and labour relations boards to investigate and correct unfair labour practices. Nevertheless, the order retained the IDI Act's compulsory conciliation and "cooling off" procedures.

After the war, in 1948, Parliament passed the Industrial Relations and Disputes Investigation (IRDI) Act; it was almost identical to PC 1003 but applied only to the much smaller peacetime jurisdiction of the federal government. However, the provinces (except for Prince Edward Island) soon passed new labour relations acts modelled on PC 1003. Since then federal and provincial legislation has evolved to take into consideration the responsibilities of unions as well as their rights, following aspects of the Taft-Hartley and Landrum-Griffin acts in the United States.

THE PUBLIC SERVICE STAFF RELATIONS ACT OF 1967

Although some provincial governments' employees had earlier won the right to collective bargaining and the right to strike (Saskatchewan's in 1944 and Quebec's in 1964), the granting of the rights by the federal government had a major impact on organized labour across Canada. In 1967, Parliament passed the Public Service Staff Relations Act (PSSRA), which enabled workers in bargaining units to opt for compulsory conciliation or the right to strike. With the exception of Ontario and Alberta, the provinces followed in granting their employees the right to strike.

THE GROWTH OF ORGANIZED LABOUR

The growth of unions in Canada and the United States is portrayed graphically in Figure 15.1. As the graph shows, union membership in Canada has had two periods of rapid growth: the 1940s through the early 1950s, and the late 1960s through the 1970s. The first reflected the late-1930s establishment in Canada of industrial union-organizing committees, most as branches of the

FIGURE 15.1
Union Shares of the Nonfarm Labour Force in Canada and the United States

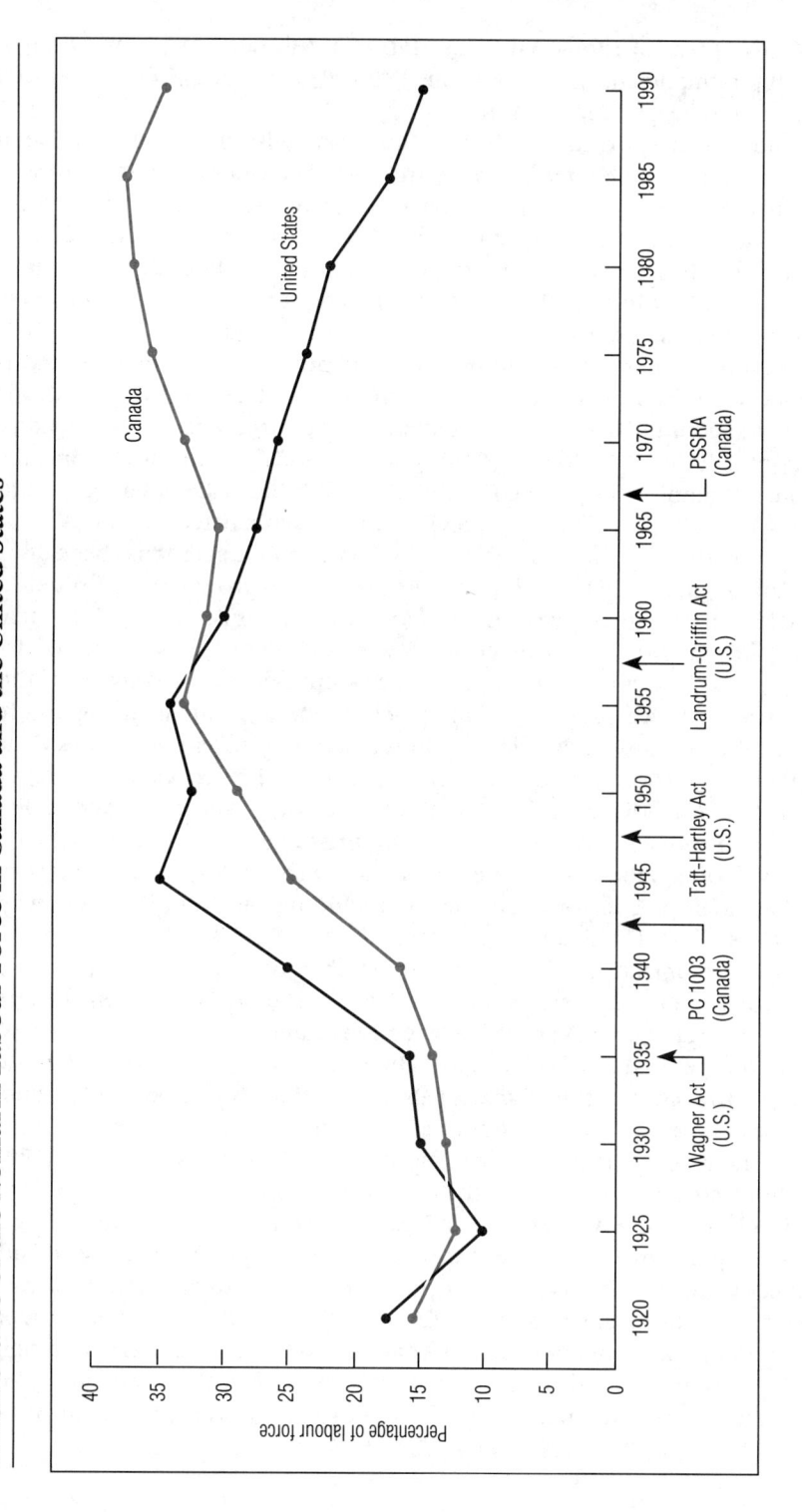

Source: Noah M. Meltz, "Labor Movements in Canada and the United States," in Thomas A. Kochan, ed., *Challenges and Choices Facing American Labor* (Cambridge, Mass.: MIT Press, 1985), p. 318; and "Unionism in Canada, U.S.: On Parallel Treadmills?" *Forum for Applied Research on Public Policy*, vol. 5, no. 4 (Winter 1990), pp. 46–52. Reprinted with permission.

CIO (Congress of Industrial Organizations), followed by the wartime boom in employment and by legislation (PC 1003) that required recognition of unions and bargaining with them.

The second spurt in membership contrasts with the steady decline in the percentage of the labour force organized in the United States. Before 1955, the percentage of workers unionized south of the border exceeded that in Canada. By 1990, the Canadian rate (36 percent) was more than double the American (16 percent). The second growth period began in 1967 and was dominated by the organization of public employees, including professional and white-collar workers. The spur was the federal PSSRA and provincial legislation permitting the unionization of provincial, municipal, and other public-sector workers, such as teachers and hospital staff. By 1990, the public sector accounted for three of Canada's five largest unions: the Canadian Union of Public Employees (CUPE); the National Union of Provincial Government Employees (NUPGE); and the Public Service Alliance of Canada (PSAC). In 1965, NUPGE and PSAC had not even existed as unions.

Although the growth of unionization in the public sector has been dramatic in Canada, union membership in this area has also grown in the United States. The big difference between the two countries has been falling U.S. membership rates in other sectors in contrast with stability or slower rates of decline in Canada. The most important factors identified as the sources of the difference are more supportive labour legislation and much stronger enforcement of it in Canada than in the United States. Also important are Canada's higher proportion of public-sector employees; differences in cultural values such that Canadians accept a greater role for government and collective action; the presence of 13 strong labour jurisdictions in Canada (in the United States, federal labour laws override those of the states); and the importance in Canadian politics of third parties, including the New Democratic Party, which is aligned with and supportive of unions.[9]

With unionization of the public sector having reached a high level of 71 percent,[10] many experts expect the Canadian union movement to attempt again to organize workers in banks and insurance companies, sectors where it has not yet had notable success. The one major gain in the banking sector was the first contract the Canada Labour Relations Board ordered be imposed in 1986 on the Canadian Imperial Bank of Commerce after its Visa unit workers were on strike for seven months. The contract was renewed in 1987 without strike. One expert studying banks concluded earlier: "Collective action is more likely to emerge in heavily unionized centres than elsewhere, providing that bank employees are sufficiently dissatisfied to have considered collective means of solving work problems."[11] Organizing also took place in the mid-1980s in department stores with the certification of retail workers in a number of branches of Eaton's and Simpsons. (Since bargaining rights in all but one of the Eaton's locations were subsequently terminated, there is likely to be little momentum for further organization of this sector.)

Whatever sector one considers, it is clear that Canadian organized labour faces many challenges, including uncertain job opportunities, the problems of organizing small groups of employees in widely scattered areas, and the example of the United States where the union movement has been slowed by some of the 1960s' and 1970s' social legislation (which gave government guarantees in areas affecting wages, benefits, and working conditions, where workers had depended on unions for protection) and by the increasing hostility of management and legislators. Nevertheless, with almost 40 percent of Canadian employees covered by collective agreements, HRM professionals are likely to have to deal with unions.

LABOUR RELATIONS AND ORGANIZATIONAL EFFECTIVENESS

Many managers feel, as Rob Williams did, that when a union represents some or all of their employees, the organization is less flexible and less effective and managers have less power. These feelings may not be entirely justified.

Opponents of unions argue that they have a negative impact on organizational effectiveness because they raise wages above competitive levels, impose inefficient work rules, and lower output through strikes. The opposite view is that unions increase effectiveness by reducing turnover and inducing management to adopt more efficient policies and practices.[12] One far-ranging examination of research on the impact of unions provides support for the second view. It cites a detailed study that found that the unionized workers had significantly lower turnover than comparable nonunion workers, and that productivity was 20 to 25 percent higher in unionized manufacturing industries, although unionized bituminous coal industries had lower productivity than did their nonunionized counterparts. (During the period studied, the United Mine Workers Union suffered a number of internal problems, which may have resulted in the relatively low productivity.) Another study, of the cement industry, found productivity gains in unionized firms; it attributed one-fifth of the increase to reduced turnover and the remainder to changes in management personnel and in HRM policies.[13] Although in general the evidence suggests that unions raise productivity, it may not be surprising that a study of Canadian manufacturing industries found that unions reduce profitability. This seems to have occurred because the effects of unions in raising wages exceeded the effects in raising productivity.[14]

Of course, in the final analysis, the effects of unionization on organizational effectiveness depend both on the development of an effective working relationship between labour and management and on management's ability to make efficient use of labour, capital, and technology. According to an old saying, "Management usually gets the union it deserves."

RELATION TO OTHER HRM FUNCTIONS

As shown in Figure 15.2, unions exert an influence on many HRM functions. Unions give employees a collective voice in bargaining for wages, benefits, and other conditions of employment. They also provide employees with a formal grievance procedure for disputes regarding the interpretation of the collective agreement and complaints about conditions of employment.

FIGURE 15.2
Labour Relations: Relation to Other HRM Functions

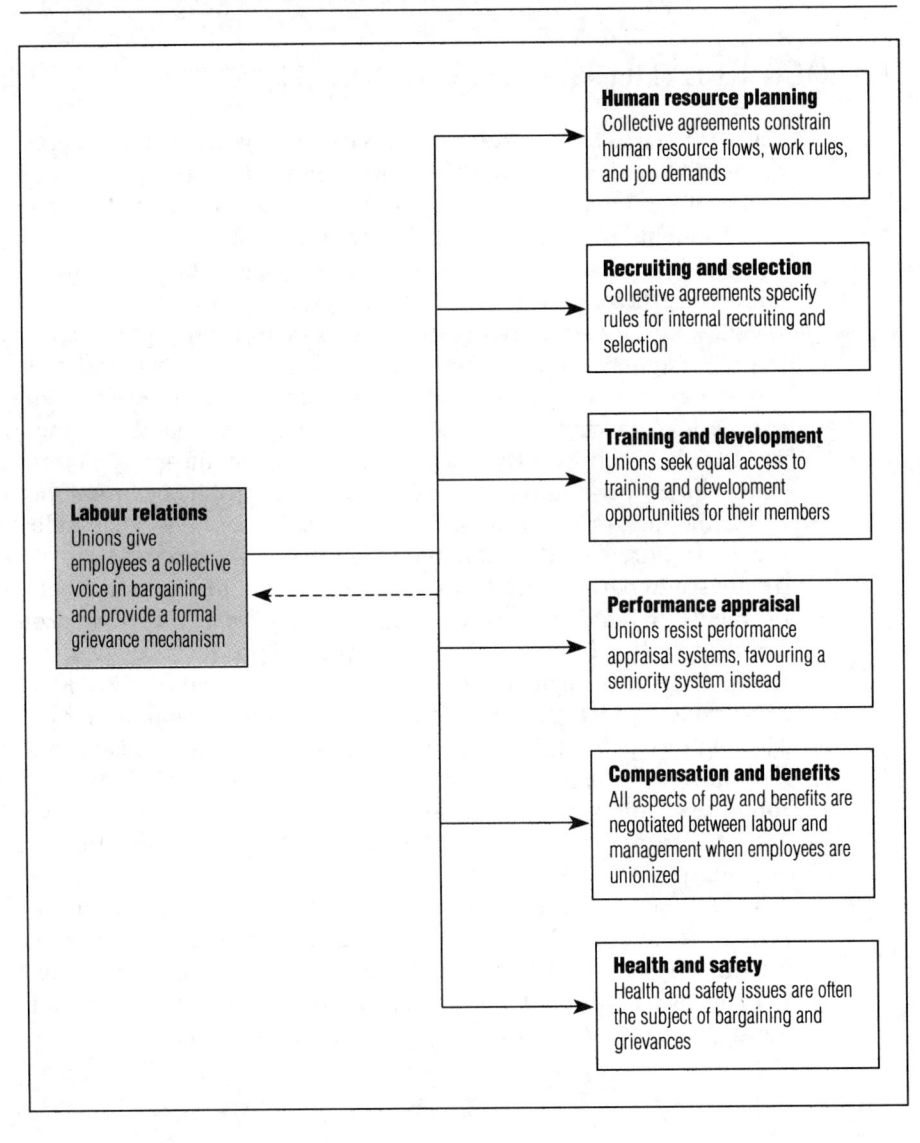

Labour relations
Unions give employees a collective voice in bargaining and provide a formal grievance mechanism

Human resource planning
Collective agreements constrain human resource flows, work rules, and job demands

Recruiting and selection
Collective agreements specify rules for internal recruiting and selection

Training and development
Unions seek equal access to training and development opportunities for their members

Performance appraisal
Unions resist performance appraisal systems, favouring a seniority system instead

Compensation and benefits
All aspects of pay and benefits are negotiated between labour and management when employees are unionized

Health and safety
Health and safety issues are often the subject of bargaining and grievances

The major influence of unions on HRM policies relates to how human resources are used and maintained in the organization. In a unionized firm, policies on virtually all aspects of employment must be agreed upon by labour and management through the collective bargaining process. Since collective agreements specify rules and standard operating procedures, one result of unionization is increased consistency in HRM policies and practices. For example, when employees are unionized, pay is administered either across-the-board (everyone in a particular job category receives the same amount) or according to very objective criteria (everyone is paid according to, for example, the number of units assembled). Under some collective agreements, seniority is another dimension to be considered.

HUMAN RESOURCE PLANNING

Collective agreements affect human resources flows through the organization by specifying criteria for promotions, transfers, and layoffs — for example, who will be laid off first in the event of reductions in the work force, and who will qualify to fill job vacancies. (Ability usually remains an important criterion in such decisions, but management must be in a position to substantiate its judgement.) Some agreements allow unions to object to work rules such as production standards and the introduction of new equipment and work methods. Others specify and limit the tasks to be performed in some jobs. All of these factors and others impose constraints upon human resource planners.

RECRUITING AND SELECTION

The major impact of unions on recruiting and selection is on policies relating to internal movement. Generally, unions try to make seniority the major criterion of internal recruiting and selection, while management usually prefers promotions based on individual merit or past job performance. Collective agreements usually settle on a compromise: when two workers being considered for promotion have approximately equal ability and experience, preference must go to the one with more seniority. In some industries, most notably shipping and construction, unions also maintain substantial control over external recruiting since employers may hire only union members. Such agreements are called closed shop agreements or contracts. This control increases when unions, like the longshoremen's, run their own hiring halls.

Unions sometimes sponsor apprenticeship programs to train people in skilled occupations, and employers often recruit new employees from such programs.

TRAINING AND DEVELOPMENT

Unions take an interest in training and development. They try to ensure that their members receive equal opportunities for programs because participation can lead to higher-level jobs and higher-level pay. Unions may also participate with management in developing training programs, and in some construction trades, the unions run the apprenticeship programs themselves.

Performance Appraisal

Because unions favour seniority-based systems, they strongly resist all forms of performance appraisal based on individual merit or other performance measures. In regard to employee discipline, unionized employees have a formal mechanism for complaints or grievances. Although nonunion employers may also have a grievance procedure, only the presence of a union ensures that employee complaints are considered seriously and that no reprisals are taken by management.[15]

Compensation and Benefits

In a unionized firm, the employer must negotiate all aspects of wages and benefits, including increases, with union representatives. Most collective agreements also specify which workers should be offered overtime first (usually those with the most seniority). All aspects of wages and benefits are subject to the grievance procedure during the term of the agreement.

Health and Safety

Since matters of health and safety are conditions of employment, they are subject to negotiation with management, subject to the jurisdiction's health and safety legislation. Union representatives can also file grievances regarding health and safety during the term of a collective agreement. In jurisdictions that mandate joint worker–management health and safety committees, the regulations usually provide for worker representation through the union, if one exists.

Influences on Unions

The dotted arrow in Figure 15.2 indicates that human resource policies also have an influence on union activities. For example, employees' dissatisfaction with certain aspects of employment may result in grievances and in contract demands at the bargaining table. Human resource policies exert another type of influence on unions: if policies are acceptable to employees who are not yet unionized, employees are less susceptible to union organizing attempts. On the other hand, policies that are poorly received may give rise to organizing attempts.

Responsibilities for Labour Relations

The major role of HRM professionals in labour relations is to preserve management rights and to ensure that an adequate supply of qualified labour is available at the least possible cost. The term *management rights* refers to management's freedom and autonomy to run the organization efficiently, including the right to hire, promote, discharge, and discipline employees for justifiable reasons; the right to determine production schedules and plant locations; and the right to make all other business decisions as long as they do not conflict with the other terms of the collective agreement. In unionized organizations, HRM labour relations specialists perform two major functions: they represent management in collective bargaining and they handle all grievances and contract-related disputes.

The major part of collective bargaining is contract negotiations, and labour relations specialists often begin preparing for them many months before an existing agreement expires. This preparation requires a great deal of planning and research in order to predict the employer's business future, anticipate union demands, and develop offers to the union. Research may include examining other collective agreements in the same industry and/or geographical area; conducting wage and benefit surveys; analyzing organizational productivity, labour costs, and profitability; and forecasting future demand for the organization's products or services. Labour relations specialists often head the management bargaining team and always act as expert advisers in contract negotiations. When a tentative agreement has been reached, labour lawyers, who are often employed by large organizations, finalize the language of the collective agreement so that its conditions are properly stated. The agreement is very important to both management and labour since it specifies the terms and nature of labour–management relations for periods of as much as three years.

Also an important part of labour relations is the handling of grievances and the day-to-day administration of the collective agreement. Administration requires careful monitoring of all human resource policies and grievances to ensure that no precedents are set that would adversely affect management rights. Thus, supervisors must know the collective agreement, how to interpret it, and how to be consistent in its administration. Labour relations specialists also represent management in all grievances.

In order to illustrate some of the activities of HRM professionals in unionized organizations, the following typical day is described by John Duke, the industrial relations manager of a manufacturing plant of about 500 employees. Duke reports to the plant manager and manages a human resources department of five employees. A major part of his day is devoted to union-related activities.

      7:30–7:45 A.M. Held meeting with employees of my department.
      7:45–8:00 Read the day's mail.
      8:00–9:00 Discussed problem with employee regarding workers' compensation claim. Met with maintenance supervisor regarding grievance field in his department. Discussed problem with employee regarding scheduling and overtime.
      9:00–10:00 Met with staff.
      10:15–10:30 Discharged employee for insubordination.

10:30–11:00 Held telephone conversation with lawyer regarding grievance arbitration case. Met with five employees regarding scheduled overtime.
11:00–12:00 Held telephone conversation with lawyer regarding a hearing before the provincial labour relations board. Discussed human resource problem with a department head. Prepared for grievance meeting later in the day with union.
12:00–12:30 Lunch.
12:30–1:15 P.M. Met with chief union steward regarding procedure for scheduling overtime. Met with a supervisor regarding new safety procedures.
1:15–2:00 Met with four supervisors regarding interpretation of collective agreement. Met with union business agent to discuss meeting today plus other problems.
2:00–3:15 Union meeting (handled three grievances).
3:15–3:45 Dictated to secretary.
3:45–4:30 Met with three supervisors regarding interpretation of the collective agreement. Met with general manager of the plant.
4:30–5:15 Investigated and took disciplinary action against three employees on second shift.
5:15–6:00 Handled miscellaneous paperwork.
Comment: As on any typical day, I received 15 to 20 telephone calls from people inside or outside the plant. I also spent two hours in the evening preparing for a grievance arbitration.

LABOUR UNION GOALS

The goal of any trade union is to improve the welfare of its members, who are workers. It is possible to take several approaches to this goal. Broadly speaking, a union can concentrate on representing its members' interests to employers through collective bargaining, or it can attempt to better their lot through political action. Historically, unions in the United States have emphasized the employment relationship, and the AFL-CIO is not affiliated with any political party. The European labour movement, on the other hand, emphasizes social reform through the political process, often allying itself with or forming political parties. The split is by no means total: European unions do concern themselves with wages and other terms of employment, while U.S. labour organizations lobby for or against specific legislation and attempt to influence the outcome of elections by supporting one party or another (an approach that Samuel Gompers, founder of the AFL, referred to as "rewarding your friends and punishing your enemies"). Nevertheless, the difference in approach is clear, with U.S. labour often being called "job conscious" and European "class conscious."

As in other fields of endeavour, Canadians have combined aspects of the American and the European approaches, although their pattern comes closer to mirroring that of the United States, with the Canadian trade union movement being a somewhat tempered form of business unionism. Certainly, the goals of Canadian unions at the bargaining table can be described as "job conscious," rather than "class conscious," in that they emphasize wages, benefits, working conditions, and job security. On the other hand, central labour organizations, such as provincial federations of labour and the 2.36-million-member Canadian Labour Congress (CLC), have pressed for legislated improvements in minimum wages, social benefits such as pensions and health care, and health and safety standards in workplaces, and this pressure has been applied partly through affiliation with the New Democratic Party, of which it was a co-founder, and support for the NDP's predecessor, the Co-operative Commonwealth Federation.

In the early 1990s, the NDP held power in three provinces, Ontario, British Columbia, and Saskatchewan, representing over half the population of Canada. The NDP also led the opposition in Alberta and Manitoba. In Quebec, the opposition Parti Québécois had close ties with some unions.

Support for the NDP has not, however, found favour with all Canadian unions, particularly the craft unions in the skilled construction trades. In 1982, ten of them left the CLC and formed a new congress, the Canadian Federation of Labour (CFL). Although the specific issue on which they broke away was a question of jurisdiction, the CFL has followed the American approach of not being formally linked with a political party.

Of course, in another sense, all Canadian unions, like unions everywhere, are political in that union leaders are elected by union members. To retain their positions, union leaders must not only bargain effectively with management; they must also satisfy the needs of those they represent. In an effort to satisfy these needs, the NDP government in Ontario proposed major changes in labour legislation with the objective of encouraging the growth of union membership and thereby furthering labour–management co-operation.[16]

LABOUR UNIONS: STRUCTURE

Labour organizations in Canada exist at three levels: (1) local unions; (2) national and international unions; and (3) central labour congresses. Although the organizational chart in Figure 15.3 shows the Canadian Labour Congress at the top of a pyramid, primary authority rests at the local level because individual unions have the responsibility for organizations and collective bargaining.

LOCAL UNIONS

A *local union*, the basic unit of labour organization, is formed in a particular plant or locality. Locals in Canada are of three kinds. By far the most prevalent is the *local of an international or national union*, which is affiliated with a national or international union. The local receives dues from its members, pays per-capita dues to the parent union, and receives services in return. A

FIGURE 15.3
The Structure of the CLC-Affiliated Segment of the Canadian Labour Movement

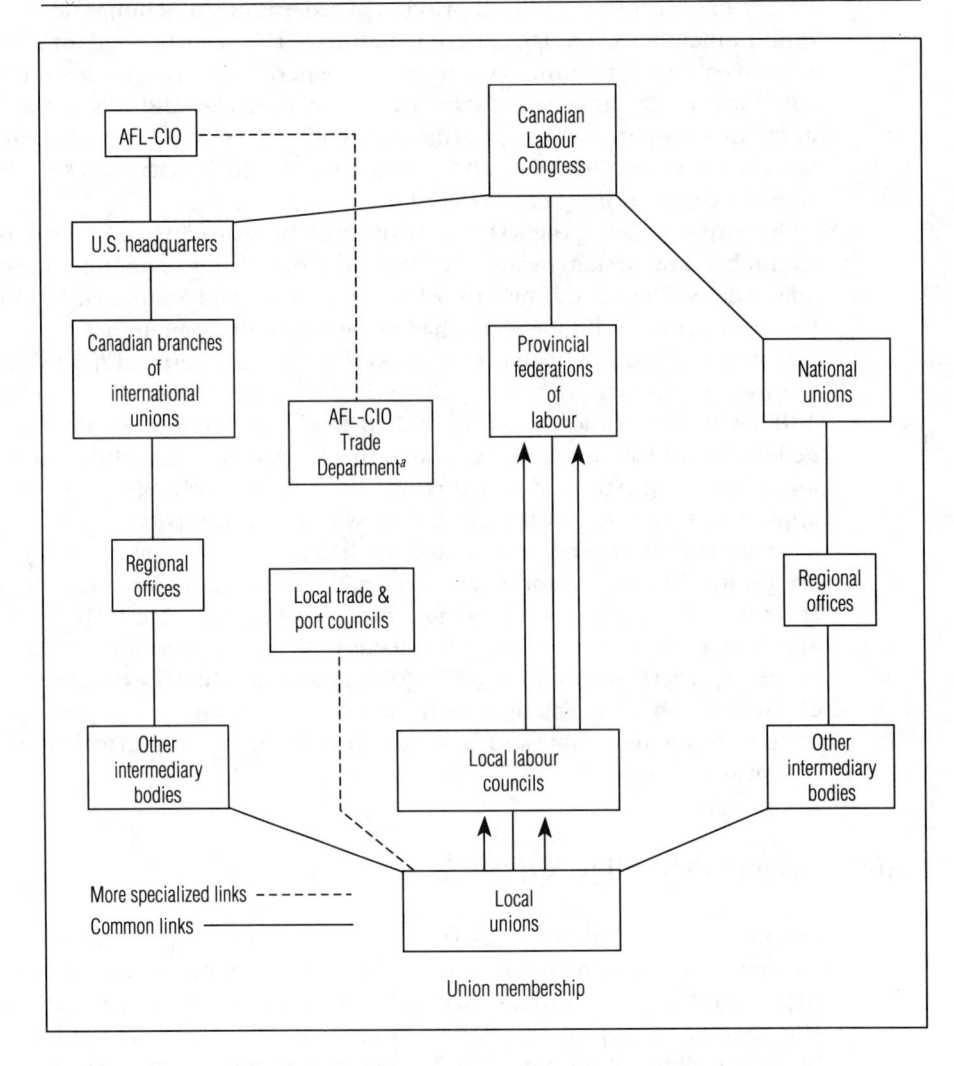

[a] Since the separation of the Building Trades from the Canadian Labour Congress, and the formation of the Canadian Federation of Labour in 1982, none of the unions in the AFL-CIO Trade Department is affiliated with the Canadian Labour Congress.

Source: John Crispo, *International Unionism, A Study in Canadian–American Relations* (Toronto: McGraw-Hill, 1967), p. 167. Reprinted with the permission of the author.

second kind of local is one *directly chartered* by a central labour congress. Dues are paid directly to the congress and services are received from it. Directly chartered locals covered 1.2 percent of all union members in 1990. *Independent locals* are units not formally affiliated with any other labour organization. Their membership totalled 3.4 percent of organized workers in 1990.[17]

It is with local unions, no matter what their type, that individual employers and employees usually interact on a day-to-day basis. Though locals vary considerably in membership size, they are usually confined to a specific municipality or other geographic area, representing workers in a single industry or kind of job and frequently bargaining with a single employer. Each has officials, including stewards, and elected officers. *Stewards* are the lowest-level officials; they act as the union's representatives on a daily basis to be sure that management complies with the collective agreement. They also represent employees in grievances against management. Like most union officials, stewards are employees who are not paid for their union activities. Besides elected officials, unions have committees to handle functions such as organizing and membership, recreation, and community relations. An important committee is the executive committee, which often handles contract negotiations with management as well as major grievances.

Workers in unionized organizations have various degrees of freedom to join or not join the union. Under *closed shop agreements*, only union members can be hired for employment. In *union shop agreements*, employees must become union members within 30 days of their date of hire. Under *Rand formula*, or *agency shop agreements*, employees may refuse to join a union but must still pay it dues (on the grounds that it represents and benefits all the bargaining unit's employees, not just union members). No Canadian jurisdiction has an equivalent of American "right-to-work" laws, which make union membership completely voluntary. To the contrary, some jurisdictions, such as Ontario, give unions the right to require employers to deduct the amount of regular union dues from the wages of each employee in the bargaining unit, whether he or she is a member of the union or not.

Members' level of interest in local unions is often low. One U.S. study found that attendance at meetings was generally very poor but increased substantially for discussions of collective-agreement demands, ratification votes, and election of officers.[18] One author has suggested that most union members have little interest in participating in its activities, but just want the organization to function effectively as their representative in matters of pay, benefits, and working conditions.[19] On the other hand, the mechanism of the local union always exists to permit a great deal of grass-roots participation if members believe the situation demands it. This normally occurs at contract negotiation time since 80 percent of collective bargaining in Canada is between single unions and single employers.[20] Whether union members take advantage of their opportunities to participate seems to depend on their perceptions of both the elected representatives and the organization that employs them. In one insightful paper, North American unions are depicted as combining features of an army and of an old-fashioned town meeting.[21]

NATIONAL AND INTERNATIONAL UNIONS

In most parts of the world, one can find unions that are restricted to one country as well as unions or alliances of unions that cross international boundaries. In Canada, however, the terms "national union" and "international union" have a specialized meaning. A *national union* is an organization that charters locals only in Canada. Well-known examples are the Canadian Union of Public Employees (CUPE), the National Union of Provincial Government Employees (NUPGE), the Public Service Alliance of Canada (PSAC), Centrale de l'enseignement du Québec (CEQ), the Canadian Paperworkers Union (CPU), the Ontario Nurses Association (ONA), and the Canadian Union of Postal Workers (CUPW).

An *international union*, on the other hand, charters locals in both the United States and Canada. Well-known international unions include the United Steelworkers of America, the United Food and Commercial Workers International Union (UFCW), and the International Brotherhood of Teamsters, Chauffeurs, Warehousemen, and Helpers of America.

The United Automobile Workers (UAW) used to charter locals in both countries, but in 1986 all but one of the Canadian locals formed a new national union, the Canadian Automobile Workers (CAW), with 140 000 members. The Canadian union received $43 million from the UAW as the Canadian share of strike funds and other resources that were held by the international.

Both international and national unions may be organized as craft unions, such as the United Brotherhood of Carpenters and Joiners or the CEQ; as industrial unions, such as the CAW or CUPE; or as a mixture of craft and industrial, such as the Teamsters. *Craft unions* are organized around a particular skill, craft, or profession; they attempt to organize all employees in a specific occupation, such as carpenters, machinists, musicians, printers, and nurses. *Industrial unions* are organized on the basis of a product, service, or industry: they organize employees primarily in a specific industry, such as steel, automobiles, or government.

In many ways, national and international unions, craft or industrial, function alike. They are large groups—varying from 1000 to 380 000 Canadian members—that provide structure and support for their local affiliates. Often they help locals in bargaining by providing experienced negotiators, and they fund and support many organizing campaigns. The structure and government of nationals and internationals are similar to those of locals, but their officers and professional staffs are paid, full-time employees of the union. Money to run the nationals and internationals comes from dues collected by the local affiliates.

The difference between national and international unions is basically one of the locus of power. All international unions have their headquarters in the

United States, although most elect a Canadian vice-president or some other senior official to ensure Canadian representation at the executive-committee level. The relative merits of international versus national unions have been debated for almost a century in Canada. After a detailed examination of the subject in 1966, John Crispo concluded:

> Where effective alternative forms of unionism are available, Canadian workers sometimes look more critically upon the role played by international unions. To date, however, relatively few of them have chosen to abandon them. This attitude indicates that the Canadian workers who have become members of international unions remain convinced that they represent a good investment.[22]

This statement is still valid more than 25 years later, although the creation of the CAW may suggest a greater possibility that other international unions will separate. The major development since the late 1960s is that national unions have grown rapidly, particularly in the public sector, sharply increasing their share of the organized labour force. In 1965, 70.8 percent of Canadian union members belonged to international unions and 24.5 percent to national unions. By 1990, it was 31.8 percent and 63.6 percent respectively.[23]

THE CLC AND OTHER CENTRAL LABOUR CONGRESSES

Several large labour congresses serve as unifying bodies for Canadian labour unions. Most national and international unions belong to them; notable exceptions are the Teamsters and the Centrale de l'enseignement du Québec. The largest congress is the Canadian Labour Congress (CLC); in 1990, 59 percent (2.36 million) of Canada's 4 million union members were affiliated with it. The country's next-largest labour congress is the Confederation of National Trade Unions (CNTU), with 211 800 members. There are also two small groups, the Centrale des Syndicats Démocratiques (CSD), a CNTU breakaway with 60 596 members, and the Confederation of Canadian Unions (CCU) with 32 394 members. A recent addition is the Canadian Federation of Labour (CFL) formed in 1982 by ten international construction trade unions, totalling 211 314 members, which left the CLC after various contentious issues culminated in a jurisdictional dispute.

Resolution of jurisdictional disputes is one of a number of functions of the central labour congresses. Others include assisting affiliates in collective bargaining through technical expertise and support, furthering the political interests of organized labour, and representing Canadian labour in international organizations. The congresses also directly charter a few locals.

THE TRANSITION FROM EMPLOYEE RELATIONS TO LABOUR RELATIONS

This section examines the transition from nonunion status (employee relations) to union status (labour relations). It discusses employee relations briefly, and then considers factors related to unionization. Finally, the union organizing process is described. Figure 15.4 illustrates the movement.

Employee Relations

The majority of employers are not unionized and fewer than 40 percent of the country's paid, nonagricultural workers are unionized or covered by collective agreements. Therefore, most employers and employees function in an employee relations environment, as opposed to a labour relations environment. An employee relations environment is characterized by an employer, who is in a dominant power position, interacting with employees on an individual basis. It is the employer who dictates all the conditions of employment except those set by employee standards acts and other pertinent legislation. Some senior executives do have written, legal contracts, but in most nonunion situations, employer and employee develop an unwritten psychological contract.[24]

The psychological contract is a set of expectations held by both employer and employee. Employers expect employees to provide a "fair" day's work, to accept the authority of the organization, and to come to work regularly. Employees expect, in return for their services, a "fair" day's pay and good working conditions and benefits. These expectations have been rising since the postwar era. Today's employees also expect many intangibles, including a mechanism through which unfair or biased actions by supervisors or other employees may be appealed; an equitable system of judging and rewarding job performance; an explanation of the employer's goals, policies, actions, and any changes affecting employees; at least some participation in decisions affecting their jobs; and more challenging jobs.

Maintaining the psychological contract is an essential part of good employee relations. The terms of a psychological contract require a period of interaction and communication between employer and employee. Over time, a climate of trust is developed if both parties are consistent and fair in their actions; keep their explicit and implicit promises; and maintain honest, two-way communication. It is especially important for management to be consistent and fair. A climate of trust is usually easier to develop and maintain in small organizations, where managers can know their employees personally. Of course, a climate of trust is not unique to nonunionized settings, but it is especially important in them. Repeated and serious violations of the psychological contract by management cause dissatisfaction, distrust, and a feeling of powerlessness among employees, which often lead them to seek a union to restore equity and fairness in the workplace.

Factors Related to Unionization

The previous section suggests that good employee relations reduce the tendency for employees to join a union. A number of other factors are related

FIGURE 15.4
From Employee Relations to Labour Relations

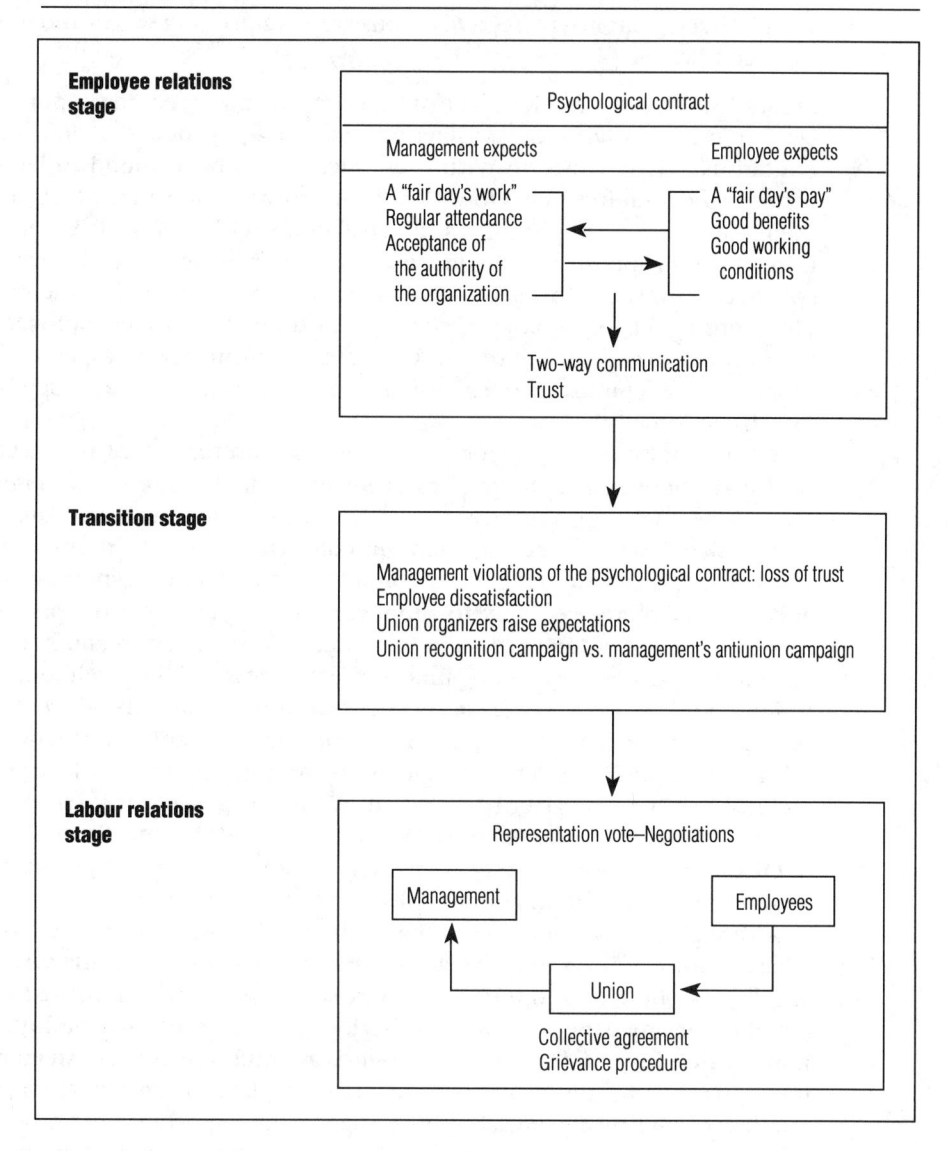

Employee relations stage

Psychological contract

Management expects	Employee expects
A "fair day's work" Regular attendance Acceptance of the authority of the organization	A "fair day's pay" Good benefits Good working conditions

Two-way communication
Trust

Transition stage

Management violations of the psychological contract: loss of trust
Employee dissatisfaction
Union organizers raise expectations
Union recognition campaign vs. management's antiunion campaign

Labour relations stage

Representation vote—Negotiations

Management ← Union ← Employees

Collective agreement
Grievance procedure

---

to unionization. Survey results indicate that the propensity to unionize is related to the following situations and attitudes:

1. Job dissatisfaction, especially with wages, benefits, and working conditions.
2. Perceived inequities in pay.

3. Lack of desired amount of influence or participation on the job, and perceptions of inability to influence working conditions.
4. Beliefs about how effective unions are in improving wages and working conditions.

Figure 15.5 shows a model of the propensity for employees to support unionization. It begins with job satisfaction regarding pay, benefits, and working conditions. Dissatisfaction with these factors has been found to be highly related to pro-union behaviour.[25] Another study found that perceived pay inequities were as important as dissatisfaction with levels of pay in determining the propensity to favour unionization.[26] From the employee's perspective, both these forms of dissatisfaction may be viewed as the result of violations of the psychological contract. Additionally, some employees may have a high degree of interest in having some influence in aspects of their work. If the employer does not accommodate them, the result is job dissatisfaction.

When employees experience job dissatisfaction for any of these reasons, they may choose either to quit or to remain on the job and work to improve conditions. In the terms used by Albert Hirschman, the alternatives are "exit" and "voice," with voice representing collective action to improve conditions.[27] Workers who have more commitment to the job generally remain, and some of them are likely to support union organizing attempts. Within this group, the tendency to support a union depends upon another factor: the individual's perception of union effectiveness, of the likelihood that a union could improve wages and other working conditions. Moreover, the propensity to unionize is higher in medium-sized organizations (companies with more than 200 and fewer than 1000 employees). As already suggested, a climate of trust is easier to maintain in small organizations. On the other hand, large employers, such as Dominion Foundries and Steel Company (DOFASCO), are more likely to be able to afford to pay high wages and benefits and to maintain good employee relations programs.

Although the model suggests that only job dissatisfaction or a frustrated desire or influence on the job leads to unionization, this is not the case. Some employees choose to join unions for reasons completely unrelated to pay, benefits, or any aspect of job satisfaction. For example, an employee may join because his or her relatives or friends are union members. An employee may have been a union member at another place of employment. Or an employee's political persuasions may suggest the importance of unions. And, of course, if a company is already unionized, employees must join the union under a union shop agreement; in other situations, they may joint because of peer pressure.

Certainly a factor affecting the propensity to unionize is union strength in certain industries and certain parts of the country. Unions have traditionally represented employees in approximately half of all manufacturing firms and have been strong in resource industries and construction. During the 1970s, union penetration remained stable in these areas, though it began to decline

FIGURE 15.5
Factors Affecting Propensity to Unionize

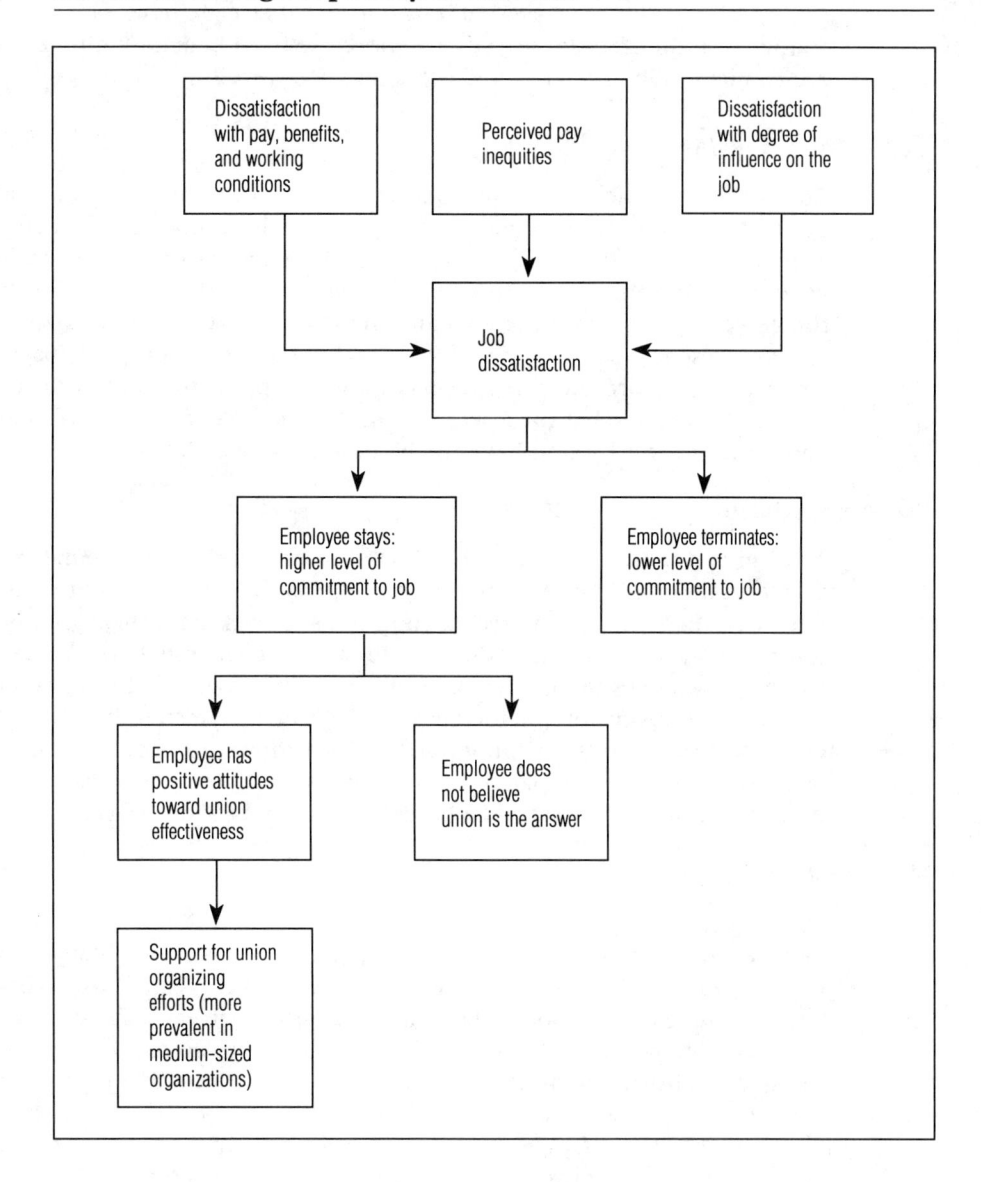

```
┌─────────────────┐    ┌─────────────┐    ┌─────────────────┐
│ Dissatisfaction │    │ Perceived pay│    │ Dissatisfaction │
│ with pay,       │    │ inequities  │    │ with degree of  │
│ benefits, and   │    │             │    │ influence on the│
│ working         │    │             │    │ job             │
│ conditions      │    │             │    │                 │
└────────┬────────┘    └──────┬──────┘    └────────┬────────┘
         │                    │                    │
         │                    ▼                    │
         │           ┌─────────────────┐           │
         └──────────▶│      Job        │◀──────────┘
                     │ dissatisfaction │
                     └────────┬────────┘
                              │
              ┌───────────────┴───────────────┐
              ▼                               ▼
    ┌──────────────────┐            ┌──────────────────┐
    │ Employee stays:  │            │Employee terminates:│
    │ higher level of  │            │ lower level of   │
    │ commitment to job│            │ commitment to job│
    └────────┬─────────┘            └──────────────────┘
             │
     ┌───────┴────────┐
     ▼                ▼
┌─────────────┐  ┌─────────────┐
│ Employee has│  │Employee does│
│ positive    │  │ not believe │
│ attitudes   │  │union is the │
│ toward union│  │ answer      │
│effectiveness│  │             │
└──────┬──────┘  └─────────────┘
       │
       ▼
┌─────────────┐
│Support for  │
│union        │
│organizing   │
│efforts (more│
│prevalent in │
│medium-sized │
│organizations)│
└─────────────┘
```

in the 1980s. In the 1970s, it was in the service industries and the public sector that it shot upwards, led by the growth of CUPE, NUPGE, PSAC, teachers' federations, nurses' associations, and the Service Employees International Union (SEIU). By 1979, the public sector was the most organized in Canada, with 67.7 percent of its workers unionized.

Today Newfoundland and Quebec are the most highly unionized provinces in Canada, whereas Nova Scotia and Alberta are the least.[28] These data suggest that employees in industries and provinces that already have a high concentration of unionized employees are more likely to become unionized than are employees in industries and areas with low levels of unionization.

THE UNION ORGANIZING PROCESS

The previous section examined factors leading to employees' propensity to unionize. This section examines activities and legal constraints associated with union organizing campaigns. Figure 15.6 portrays the union organizing process in Ontario. Other jurisdictions vary only in detail, most notably in the percentage of union membership the labour relations board requires to call a representation vote or to certify without a vote. Table 15.1 (page 734) summarizes, by province, the levels of union support required for certification. Saskatchewan has the lowest required rank, 25 percent; Newfoundland and Prince Edward Island have the highest, at 50 percent.

Process Initiation

The union organizing process is initiated in one of two ways. First, as suggested in the previous section, employees may become sufficiently dissatisfied with their pay and working conditions to seek help through a union. Alternatively, representatives of a national or international union may contact employees at the local level. Established unions often allocate money to organize employees in specific geographical regions or in industries considered good candidates for unionization. Though unions need new members to grow, organizing campaigns can be expensive. Therefore, most unions try to organize only where they feel they have a good chance of success.

Membership Campaign

In the second step of the organizing process, the union tries to convince members of a potential bargaining unit to join the group and obtains a signed membership card from each willing worker. These cards are important because the relevant labour relations board will check each signature against a sample obtained from the employer. Some boards also require the filing of receipts to ensure the new members have made at least token payments as evidence of their wish to have the union represent them.

An organization can agree to recognize voluntarily the union as the exclusive bargaining agent for certain of its employees. If this recognition is given, collective bargaining may begin. However, employers rarely give voluntary recognition to a union; most wait for the appropriate labour relations board to make the decision for them.

Union organizers often face a difficult task in gaining access to employees in order to convince them to become union members. By law, employers need not permit any organizations to solicit on company property or time.

FIGURE 15.6
Union Organizing Process under the Ontario Labour Relations Act

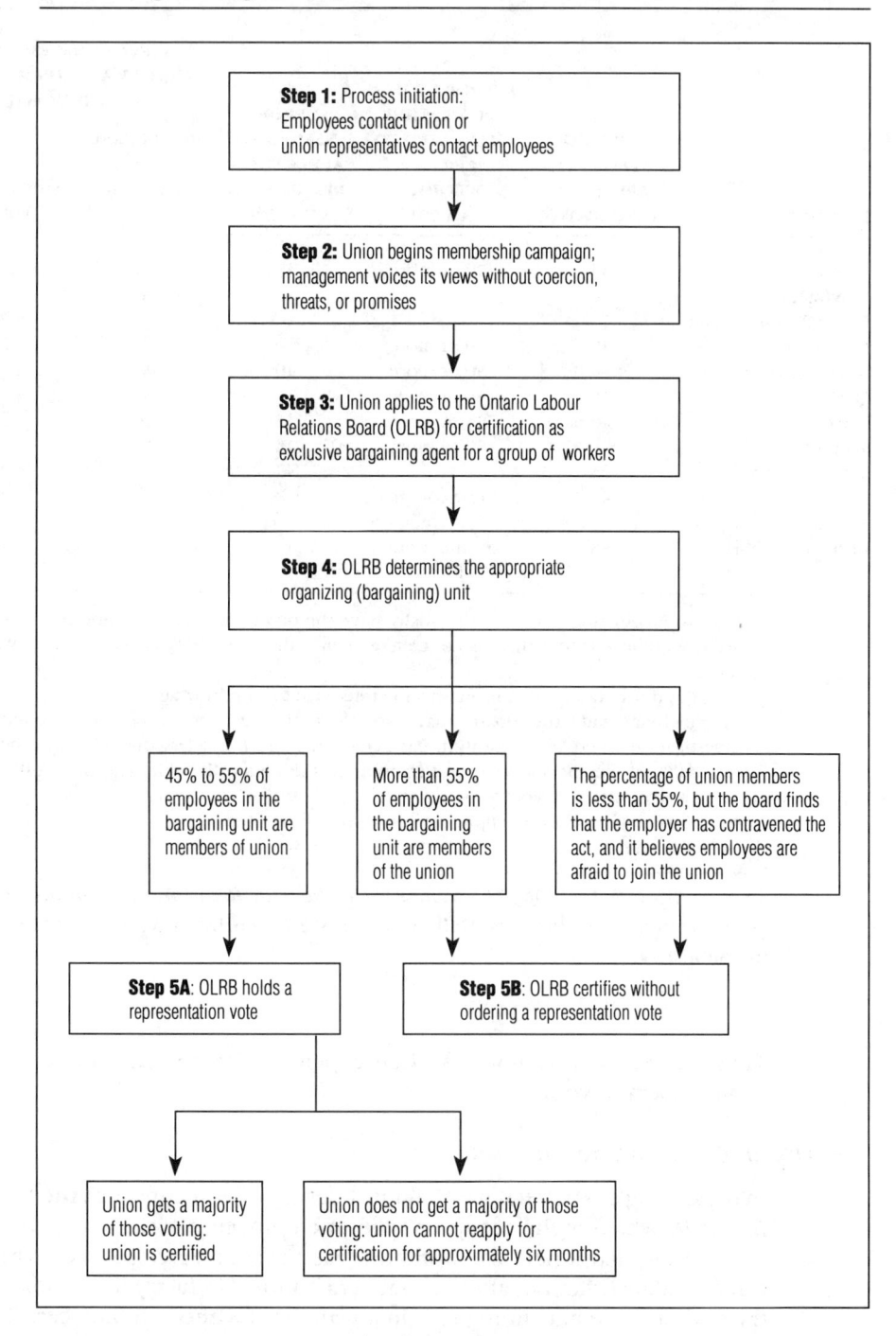

Step 1: Process initiation: Employees contact union or union representatives contact employees

Step 2: Union begins membership campaign; management voices its views without coercion, threats, or promises

Step 3: Union applies to the Ontario Labour Relations Board (OLRB) for certification as exclusive bargaining agent for a group of workers

Step 4: OLRB determines the appropriate organizing (bargaining) unit

- 45% to 55% of employees in the bargaining unit are members of union
- More than 55% of employees in the bargaining unit are members of the union
- The percentage of union members is less than 55%, but the board finds that the employer has contravened the act, and it believes employees are afraid to join the union

Step 5A: OLRB holds a representation vote

Step 5B: OLRB certifies without ordering a representation vote

- Union gets a majority of those voting: union is certified
- Union does not get a majority of those voting: union cannot reapply for certification for approximately six months

TABLE 15.1

A Comparison of Provisions Dealing with Certification

Jurisdiction	% Support Needed to Apply for Certification	% Support Where Boards are Mandated to Certify Without a Vote	% Support Needed to Apply for a Prehearing Vote[a,b]	% Support Necessary to Certify a Union When a Vote is Taken 50% of those in the bargaining unit	50% of those voting
Federal	35	50 or more	35		X
Newfoundland[c]	50		40	X	
Prince Edward Island	50		N/S		X
Nova Scotia	40	50 or more	N/S[d]		X
New Brunswick	40–60	50 or more	40	X	
Quebec	35	50 or more	35	X	
Ontario	45–55	55 or more	35		X
Manitoba	45–55	55 or more	45	X	
Saskatchewan	25		N/S		X
Alberta	40	must conduct a vote	N/S		X
British Columbia	45	must conduct a vote	45		X

[a] In most jurisdictions, the boards usually have the power to certify the union or bargaining agent without a vote if there is concrete evidence that over 50% of the members want the union.
[b] Includes those statutes that make specific reference to a prehearing vote.
[c] In Newfoundland, the Board may direct its chief executive officer to conduct an investigation where an application has been made and if not less than 40% and not more than 50% of members are in good standing in the union, the chief executive officer shall cause a representation vote to be taken.
[d] Nova Scotia subjects every application to a prehearing vote.
N/S—Not specified.

Source: Alton W.J. Craig, *The System of Industrial Relations in Canada*, 3rd ed. (Scarborough, Ont.: Prentice-Hall, 1990), p. 125. Reprinted with the permission of the publisher.

Thus, membership campaigns often depend on organizers who are already company employees.

Determining the Bargaining Unit

In organizing employees, a union must define what it considers the *bargaining unit*, which is the group or type of employee it seeks to represent. As we already mentioned, each union seeks to organize employees within its traditional jurisdiction, along certain craft and/or industry lines. Unions also try to define the bargaining unit in a way that favours winning certification (by including job categories in which a high proportion of workers favour unionization and excluding those in which unionization is unpopular) and that will give it the most bargaining power if the union is certified. Thus, the union prefers a bargaining unit in which employees have common skills, needs, and work experiences and are important enough to the employer to disrupt the organization through a strike. Management, on the other hand, prefers a bargaining unit defined so as to make it less powerful and less likely to win certification for the union.

Because union organizers and management each have vested interests in defining the bargaining unit, the final determination is left to the appropriate labour relations board. The complex decision involves many factors. For example, the Ontario Labour Relations Board only occasionally carves out craft units; in general, it decides on an appropriate industrial unit by considering: (1) the desires of the employer and the union; (2) the community of interest among employees (that is, the nature of work performed, the conditions of employment, and the skills required); (3) the organizational structure of the employer; (4) the desire not to split one employer's work force into too many bargaining units; (5) the general policy of not putting office staff and production workers in the same bargaining unit.[29]

The Representation Vote

Before certifying a union as a bargaining agent, the relevant labour relations board needs to ascertain that a majority of the workers in the unit favour the union. If the membership count alone gives it this certainty, it will certify the union automatically. If there is some question, it calls for a representation vote. The percentages of workers needed for automatic certification and for calling a representation vote vary from jurisdiction to jurisdiction. As Table 15.1 indicates, the Canada Labour Relations Board (federal jurisdiction), for example, certifies automatically if more than 50 percent of the workers have taken membership in the union, and it orders a representation vote if 35 to 50 percent are members. Ontario's board usually requires more than 55 percent membership for automatic certification and 45 to 55 percent for a representation vote. Ontario's NDP government, as part of a proposed package of reforms to the Labour Relations Act in 1992, suggested lowering the rate for automatic certification to more than 50 percent, and to between 40 and 50 percent for a representation vote.

If the board does require a representation vote, it is taken by secret ballot under the supervision of a returning officer sent by the board. In many provinces, the union and the employer may each send a scrutineer to each polling place. The union wins the representation vote if more than half of those voting favour it.

Management Responses to Unionization

No employer may interfere with the formation or selection of a union by employees. The employer is free to express his or her views, but that expres-

HRM IN ACTION

CAW GAINS VOLUNTARY RECOGNITION FROM TEAM-BASED CAMI PLANT

Only about 300 out of an eventual work force of 2000 have been hired, but the Canadian Auto Workers union has quietly become the bargaining agent for employees of CAMI Automotive Inc. in Ingersoll, Ont.

The legal certification of the union had the complete, if tacit, approval of Suzuki Motor Co. Ltd. of Japan and General Motors of Canada Ltd. of Oshawa, Ont., the 50-50 joint-venture owners of the kilometre-long plant on the edge of a pleasant Southern Ontario town hitherto best known for the cheese that bears its name.

Day 1 of production is set for April at the first completely new auto assembly factory in Canada to start operation with a working sheet-metal stamping plant on site — in effect a complete, integrated auto plant.

(When full production is reached — by 1990, CAMI hopes — the plant will be able to produce 200 000 Tracker and Sidekick light utility vehicles and Swift, Sprint and Firefly sub-compact cars a year.)

The CAW celebrated the certification with a brief and restrained news release; CAMI management made no official statement. Nevertheless, CAMI personnel vice-president and legal counsel James Cameron said in an interview that the uncontested certification gave CAMI management one luxury during the immensely complicated build-up to running an auto plant that other Japanese car makers have not had in North America.

"Because we've recognized the CAW, we don't have to worry about anti-union or pro-union bias [among potential employees]."

In fact, in the fall of 1986, Suzuki and the CAW signed an unusual agreement to ensure that vehicles made at Ingersoll would bear the union label in return for union flexibility on Japanese-style "team concept" work rules. That deal, the terms of which are being kept confidential by both parties, will form the basis of the first contract at CAMI once more workers are hired and a bargaining committee is formed.

Based on the preliminary agreement, union officials say, the eventual contract will be not unlike the traditional deals negotiated with the Big Three North American car makers, with wages "very close" to those in the Big Three's contracts — usually about $12 to $13 an hour.

But in the meantime, according to Mr. Cameron, CAMI's managerial office staff — made up of about 40 people from Suzuki, including the president and operating and executive vice-presidents, and 30 from GM — can concentrate on weeding through the "many thousands" of applicants for assembly jobs.

"We're looking for people that share our values, that are trainable, creative," he said. "What we want is to develop our own culture, our own way of doing things. This is not Suzuki, this is not GM; it is our own unique organization."

The search for "team players" is not a simple one, Mr. Cameron said. CAMI uses a complicated, seven-step selection process that starts with one of the most detailed application forms outside the secret service and takes 20 hours over several days of an applicant's time devoted to hands-on skills testing, group skills analysis, a medical examination and more.

In addition, he said, CAMI is aggressively seeking likely candidates, combining campus job fairs and setting up recruiting booths at shopping malls and county agricultural exhibitions.

So how does the union react to a rigorous selection process, complete with questions designed by a U.S. consulting firm to weed out lone wolves and others?

Without much concern, said CAW national representative Ron Pellerin. For one thing, "CAMI has hired people that have been very active union people.

"They've hired people, of course, that have had no experience in the work force at all, they've hired people that came from different industries and different types of jobs. But there's also a good blend of previous union activists and union members in there."

For another, past industry experience shows that "the reality of production" soon overcomes complicated hiring procedures.

RECENT DEVELOPMENTS

In the fall of 1992, CAMI was the scene of the first strike in North America involving a Japanese auto manufacturer. There were two issues in the strike: elimination of the gap in the wage rate between CAMI and the Big Three auto makers; and changes in work practices, which the CAW believed had deteriorated since the plant began its operations. The somewhat acrimonious strike lasted five weeks and followed changes in management personnel. The new three-year contract will give CAMI employees the same wages and benefits negotiated in 1990 for Canadian employees of GM, Ford, and Chrysler. Work-team leaders will be elected by workers instead of being appointed by management. Spokespersons for management and the union were encouraged by the settlement, which was ratified by a vote of 94 percent of the members. The company's representative, Susan Nicholson, observed, "We feel we've made some positive improvements that reinforce the CAMI values." CAW president

> Buzz Hargrove was extremely pleased with the agreement, "We've come a long way and now we just want to get back on the shop floor and start a relationship that's based on respect, not paternalism."
>
> Source: Excerpt from David Climenhaga, "CAW to Represent CAMI Plant's 'Team Players,'" *The Globe and Mail*, November 8, 1988, p. B5. "Recent Developments" section adapted from Danielle Bochove, "CAMI Workers Ratify Deal, Ending Month-Long Strike," *The Globe and Mail*, October 19, 1992. Used with the permission of *The Globe and Mail*.

sion must not involve coercion, intimidation, threats, or undue influence. Undue influence includes promising benefits to employees if they do not join a union. It also includes making threats against employees, such as threats of closing down, of moving the firm's facilities elsewhere, or of ending certain employee benefits. "If the board feels that a vote is not likely to disclose the true wishes of the employees because of undue coercion, it will grant certification;"[30] illegal anti-union statements by an employer may be sufficient evidence of undue coercion. Once a union has applied for certification, the terms and conditions of employment cannot be changed without its approval.

Additionally, an employer may not fire or penalize an employee for organizing or other union activity; if a complaint of this sort of harassment is upheld, the employee can be ordered reinstated with back pay or reimbursed for lost wages. Moreover, a labour board may order remedies, including access to the employees for the union, to moderate the impact of this or other illegalities by the employer. Management may, however, use labour lawyers to disallow, delay, or block the signing of members or certification votes. Generally, the longer the time between the membership campaign and the vote, the less likely the union is to win certification.

Alternatively, an employer is forbidden to support a union in any way. If there has been such support, the union will not be certified. (This regulation prevents company, or employer-controlled, unions.)

Organizing campaigns are a very difficult and stressful time for most HRM professionals and management. Many employers view the organizing process as an invasion of their territory and rights. In fact, management resistance to unionization has produced a lucrative consulting business for many labour lawyers and consulting firms.[31]

One popular seminar for managers, entitled "Making Unions Unnecessary," focusses on the following areas:

1. Management commitment to and communication of a nonunion objective.

2. Basic assumptions of nonunion companies, including shaping employee thinking and avoiding human resource policies that teach people to "think union."
3. Pay policy, including avoiding problems in performance reviews and the danger of poorly handled merit reviews.
4. Benefit programs, including overcoming communication and administrative problems.
5. Problem solving, including consistency and due-process approaches to discipline.
6. Communication programs, including discussion methods such as meetings, employee handbooks, newsletters, attitude surveys, and the use of survey results.
7. Value system analysis, including management and employee values and a workshop on management flexibility.[32]

In brief, this seminar covers many of the aspects of good employee relations that we discussed earlier. Alternative approaches are also presented, especially by associations of human resource professionals, which accentuate the positive by focussing on the benefits to organizations of good employee relations. Such positive approaches are also central to programs dealing with total quality.

Perhaps it is not surprising that some employers make no effort to improve their employee relations until threatened with unionization. After all, many employers did not attempt to avoid discrimination in their hiring practices until the introduction of human rights codes, and many gave inadequate attention to employees' health and safety before the passage of relevant legislation. Although such techniques may be useful for improving employee job satisfaction and reducing the propensity to unionize, they are rarely effective once an organizing campaign has been set in motion.

Should management be so concerned about unionization? As we have seen, some experts feel that it may actually contribute to organizational effectiveness by reducing turnover and encouraging managerial efficiency. On the other hand, it was also observed that unionization seems to lower profitability, although the authors of the study that stated this conclusion observed that there were other possible explanations, in addition to unions raising wages more than they raise productivity. For example, the authors mentioned the possibility that unionized firms may have a greater incentive than non-unionized firms to keep recorded profits low.[33]

A review of the industrial relations literature concluded that firms in North America appear to use three general strategic approaches toward unions: acceptance, replacement/suppression, and avoidance/substitution. In the first approach, companies accept the legitimacy and/or the inevitability of collective bargaining and attempt to negotiate the most favourable settlement to support company objectives. In the second approach, firms attempt to reduce the role of unions by relocating, contracting out, promoting technological change, or encouraging the decertification of the existing union. The third approach involves preparing to counter union organizing, progressive human resource management policies, employee participation, and work restructuring programs.[34]

COLLECTIVE BARGAINING

After a trade union wins the right to represent a group of employees, union and management representatives must negotiate a collective agreement.[35] Both employer and union representatives have a legal obligation to begin collective bargaining in good faith.

Both parties value negotiating a favourable collective agreement since it defines conditions of employment and provides the structure of the labour–management relationship for one or several years. Union leaders are motivated to negotiate a favourable agreement for their members since doing so will help them win re-election. Management is motivated to negotiate an agreement that keeps labour costs to reasonable levels and preserves its right to operate the organization efficiently. Since contract negotiations are vitally important, both parties usually spend much time and effort preparing for and executing negotiations.

Before negotiations begin, both labour and management (including HRM professionals) engage in a number of preparatory activities. Representatives from the national or international union sometimes aid locals in preparing for negotiations. The union gathers information on:

1. Recent contract settlements, in the local area and industrywide.
2. Grievances under the previous contract, if one was in effect.
3. Interests and demands of union members.

HRM professionals and management also collect information on other relevant settlements. They examine grievances to determine if changes in the collective agreement could reduce grievances, and they try to forecast future economic conditions to determine how much can be offered the union.

HRM professionals involved in negotiations may find useful a 1987 code of conduct for both parties during certification and collective bargaining.[36] It was prepared by a group of union and management representatives under the auspices of the Niagara Institute.

THE BARGAINING PROCESS

The actual bargaining process begins when union and management teams meet at the bargaining table.[37] The union negotiating team generally consists of the local union's officers, its negotiating committee, and one or more specialists from the national or international union's staff. Members of the management negotiating team vary but usually include one or more production or operations managers, a labour lawyer, and a compensation specialist and/or a benefits specialist. The chief labour relations specialist usually heads the management team.

If a previous collective agreement has been in effect, the union team usually begins by presenting its proposed changes, additions, and deletions. If no contract exists, the union simply states its demands. Initially, unions frequently demand fairly large increases in wages, benefits, and other items. Both labour and management know that haggling and compromise are a traditional part of collective bargaining. After hearing the union's initial proposals, management offers a counterproposal that is usually less than it realistically expects to end up with. If many issues are to be negotiated, groups of related issues are often handled separately. For example, issues related to health and safety may be separated from hourly wages and benefits, while changes in the grievance procedure constitute yet a third area. Negotiations often begin with the least controversial issues and proceed to the more difficult ones. Separate issues may be combined or tradeoffs made between various issues in order to reach an acceptable agreement. Management may, for example, agree to a higher wage and benefit package if the union agrees to a longer contract. Although this strategy would mean higher labour costs for management, its ability to maintain uninterrupted operations over a longer time would also increase.

Contract negotiations are sometimes difficult, unpleasant, and lengthy, but negotiators are legally required to bargain in good faith. This does not mean, however, that an agreement must be reached; it simply means that the negotiating parties must try their best to reach some agreement. Merely going through the motions of negotiating without taking any real steps toward reaching accord is an example of failure to bargain in good faith, which is considered an unfair labour practice.

IMPASSES AND RESOLUTIONS

Even when both parties bargain in good faith, negotiations can become deadlocked. The result is often that labour calls a *strike*, a partial or complete withdrawal of services. Most employees have the legal right to strike, except those in certain public-sector jobs, such as fire fighting and law enforcement, deemed "essential" by particular jurisdictions. This right is limited, however, by time; in most jurisdictions, labour laws prohibit strikes: (1) before a union is certified; (2) during the term of a collective agreement; and (3) before the jurisdiction's mandatory conciliation procedures and cooling-off period have been accomplished. A strike during one of these prohibited periods or by workers who do not have the right to strike is termed an *illegal strike* and may leave the union and/or its individual members open to fines and its leaders to prison sentences.

Management may react to an impasse with a *lockout*, a refusal to allow employees to work. This right, too, may be exercised only after the exhaustion of the conciliation process and the following cooling-off period.

Although the strike and the lockout may be legitimate forms of bargaining, it is clear that both are disruptive.[38] In the private sector, both sides suffer an economic loss when either response is taken. In the public sector, management may or may not suffer financial loss, but authorities there are subject to public criticism when there is a loss of services, such as municipal transport or postal service. Canadian labour law, therefore, puts considerable emphasis on *mediation*, which is basically efforts by a neutral third party to establish communication between a union and management and assist them in coming to an agreement.

Mediation can be of two types: compulsory conciliation and voluntary mediation. *Compulsory conciliation* is a remnant of the cooling-off and public-information approach developed by W.L. Mackenzie King in the Industrial Disputes Investigation Act of 1907; most provinces require the intervention of a conciliation officer as a last-ditch effort to avoid a strike. The conciliation officer is appointed by a labour relations board, and he or she reports back to it on the success or failure of the effort to reconcile the parties. When the report has been made to the board, the union is free to strike and management to lock out after a stipulated cooling-off period (generally a week).

Voluntary mediation is an option whereby both sides request the services of a third party to assist them in negotiations. Often the conciliation officer or mediator acts as a messenger, trying to get both parties back to the bargaining table. Situations of this type are most common with parties who have little negotiation experience.

Another form of third-party intervention for impasse resolution is *interest arbitration*. In situations in which no collective agreement exists or in which a change is sought in an agreement, an arbitrator acts as a judge to decide on new terms. Interest arbitration occurs most often in the public sector where several provinces do not permit government employees to strike (Alberta, Prince Edward Island, Nova Scotia, and Ontario). Fire and police employees are denied the right to strike in most of these and other jurisdictions.[39] The traditional approach to interest arbitration is through a single arbitrator or a tripartite board, which receives submissions from management and the union, then decides on the wages, benefits, and other conditions of employment. A variation that has been experimented with is final-offer selection, where an arbitrator chooses either the management's proposal or that from the union. This process is intended to bring the parties closer together by discouraging unreasonable behaviour.[40]

Though some impasses do occur in contract negotiations and sometimes result in well-publicized strikes and lockouts, these drastic actions are relatively rare. Collective agreements are achieved without strikes or lockouts in more than 90 percent of negotiations.[41] In most cases, labour and management negotiate a tentative agreement, which is then approved or ratified by a vote of union members. Of course, the members have the right to reject an agreement negotiated by their representatives, but this situation does not occur often. If employees vote not to accept an agreement, labour and management usually return to the bargaining table. Rejection of a tentative agreement could also lead to a strike. This occurred in 1991 in the Toronto Transit Commission negotiations with the Amalgamated Transit Union.

HRM professionals often view the actual negotiation process as exciting and challenging. One reason may be that it has an atmosphere of a long poker game played for very high stakes. Bargaining may proceed at a very leisurely pace until the expiration date of the existing agreement, at which time the process begins to move rapidly, continuing for several consecutive days and nights. In good bargaining relationships, labour and management may not like each other, but they respect each other.

THE GRIEVANCE PROCEDURE

Though collective agreements are written precisely and are very specific on many aspects of wages, benefits, hours, and working conditions, disputes sometimes arise regarding the interpretation of provisions. For this reason, virtually every agreement provides a grievance procedure specifying how problems of interpretation and application will be resolved. The grievance procedure is an important part of a labour agreement everywhere in the world, but it is especially important in Canada, where most jurisdictions do not permit a union to strike or management to lock out during the term of a contract. In these jurisdictions, the grievance procedure is supposed to offset the loss of these stop-work mechanisms, so if such a procedure is omitted, model wording from the relevant labour relations act is deemed to be included in the collective agreement.

Given such a procedure, a *grievance* is a formal complaint by an employee (the "griever") regarding any event, action, or practice that he or she believes violates the collective agreement. Grievances may, for example, arise from the dismissal or promotion of an employee, from the reassignment of an employee from one job to another, from the addition of duties, from the assignment of overtime to or the laying-off of particular employees, from practices relating to health and safety, and so on.

Figure 15.7 shows the four steps in a typical grievance procedure.[42] In the first, the griever seeks the assistance of the union steward in filing a grievance against management. If the steward agrees that the contract has been violated, a written grievance is filed and presented to the supervisor for a decision. He or she may "accept" the grievance, settling it on the spot. Or the grievances may be "denied." In that case, the griever has two choices. He or she can accept the supervisor's denial and let the matter drop. Alternatively, the supervisor's decision may be rejected, in which case the grievance moves to the second step.

In practice, the first step of the grievance procedure can vary considerably. Some procedures do not require a written grievance, and some begin with a

FIGURE 15.7
Typical Grievance Procedure

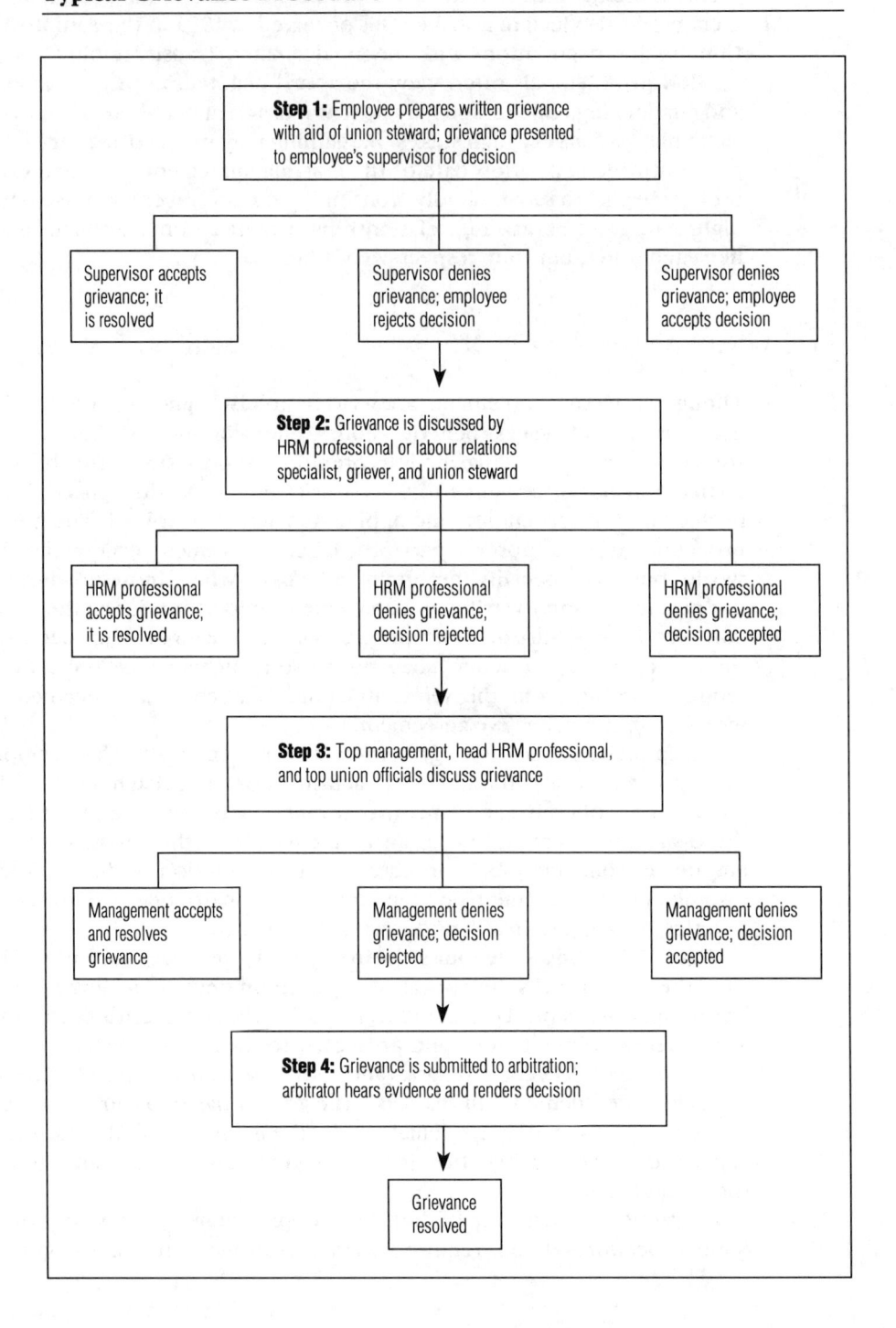

Step 1: Employee prepares written grievance with aid of union steward; grievance presented to employee's supervisor for decision

- Supervisor accepts grievance; it is resolved
- Supervisor denies grievance; employee rejects decision
- Supervisor denies grievance; employee accepts decision

Step 2: Grievance is discussed by HRM professional or labour relations specialist, griever, and union steward

- HRM professional accepts grievance; it is resolved
- HRM professional denies grievance; decision rejected
- HRM professional denies grievance; decision accepted

Step 3: Top management, head HRM professional, and top union officials discuss grievance

- Management accepts and resolves grievance
- Management denies grievance; decision rejected
- Management denies grievance; decision accepted

Step 4: Grievance is submitted to arbitration; arbitrator hears evidence and renders decision

Grievance resolved

discussion between the griever and the supervisor with the union steward present. Grievances may be very minor (such as a supervisor's performing the work of a subordinate) or very significant (such as a denial of a promotion, a disciplinary layoff, or a dismissal). The number of grievances filed in an organization is related to many factors, such as leadership style and consistency in the application of company policies.[43] Many employers do not encourage supervisors to settle potentially costly and significant grievances at the first step because a precedent could be set that would lead to demands by the union for similar practices in other parts of the organization.

At the second step, the union steward usually takes the written grievance to the labour relations specialist or HRM professional. In deciding on the grievance, the HRM professional considers many factors: management's interpretation of the contract; the details of the grievance; previous related grievances; the potential costs and benefits of accepting or denying the grievance; and the relevance of the jurisdiction's human rights, occupational health and safety, and other legislation. Most routine grievances are settled at this point, with management either accepting the grievance and admitting a mistake or denying it and convincing the union not to pursue it to the next step. Potentially significant and costly grievances may go to the third step. So may those in which the union refuses to accept a denial.

In the third step of the grievance procedure, top management and top union officials discuss the grievance. It is common practice for an HRM professional at a plant of a multiplant location to bring in the firm's head HRM officer and often other top-level managers. The local union may be assisted by representatives from the national or international office. At this stage, grievances are often of major significance because the decision may affect the interpretation of a major contract provision.

The fourth step of the grievance procedure involves the use of a neutral third party—an arbitrator or a tripartite arbitration board—to render a decision on the grievance. This type of arbitration is properly called *rights arbitration*. Since the arbitrator or the arbitration board plays a determining role in grievances that reach this level and since these grievances are usually important to one or both parties, both labour and management want a fair and unbiased person as arbitrator. Single arbitrators are usually selected from a list of persons agreed to by both sides. If an arbitration board is to be used, each party appoints one person and these two appoint a third, who serves as chairperson. If the two parties cannot agree on a chairperson within a given time limit, the labour relations board is empowered to appoint one. A majority of the arbitration board decides the issue, but if there is no majority the decision of the chair governs. Labour and management generally share arbitrators' fees.

Most collective agreements are very specific about the grievance procedure and include time deadlines for each step, exactly who is to be involved at each, and the way in which arbitrators are to be selected.

Processing grievances can be quite costly for an employer, as well as the union, even if most grievances are denied. Since an employee and the union have the right to pursue a grievance through the final step, no matter how trivial or unjust it may be, the HRM professional is under an obligation to respond. A large number of grievances often indicates dissatisfaction and problems in an organization. However, the fact that very few grievances are filed against a company does not necessarily indicate that its employees are satisfied. Some HRM professionals feel that the existence of a small number of nontrivial grievances is an indicator of a healthy labour–management relationship since some differences of interpretation of an agreement's terms are certain to arise in any normal situation.

It is also worth remembering that the grievance procedure is very important to the job satisfaction of individual employees since it provides them with a mechanism for seeking justice in the workplace. A survey of union members across the United States found that they viewed handling grievances as the most important activity of the union.[44] Employers seeking to avoid unionization are often aware of employees' desire for a grievance procedure, and sometimes attempt to provide one. Such has been the case in the United States, where two out of three nonunion firms provide some kind of an internal complaint or "voice" system.[45] To be effective, a grievance procedure must have the support of a power independent of management. The Canada Labour Code provides such a procedure in the federal jurisdiction.

Dissatisfaction among Union Members

So far, we have discussed unions as a means by which employees can influence management policies and practices. But unions are fallible, human organizations, and members sometimes become dissatisfied with their performance at the bargaining table, in the grievance process, or in other situations. There are several ways for union members to act on their dissatisfactions. One is through the democratic process and the election of new officers. Another is through an appeal procedure, if one is provided in the union's constitution. A member who believes a union is not abiding by its own constitution can take it to court. Labour relations boards also offer avenues of redress. For example, in some jurisdictions, a member who requests a copy of the union's last audited financial statement and does not receive it can complain to the labour relations board, which can order that a copy be provided to both the employee and the board itself.

Another route to resolving dissatisfaction is for the employees of a bargaining group to change unions or to decide not to be represented by a union at all. Changing unions involves having a second union apply for certification. If a collective agreement is in effect, the application must be made during the "open period" provided for such applications (usually the last two months of an agreement). Other timing restrictions, which vary among jurisdictions, exist for other situations; for example, a new union may have to wait for several months if a legal strike has begun.

Employees can also apply to have their union decertified by applying to terminate its bargaining rights. This application can be filed during the open period; it can also be brought if the union fails to notify the employer of its desire to bargain within a stated time after certification or fails to start bargaining after giving notice (60 days is a common allotment for both periods). An application for termination must be accompanied by a petition signed by a number of the employees in the bargaining unit (45 percent in Ontario). After conducting an enquiry to make certain the petition is a voluntary expression of employees' sentiments and that no member of management was involved in it, the labour relations board conducts a representation vote. A majority vote against the union is not uncommon in such cases.

A union's failure, within stipulated times, to give notice of its desire to bargain after certification or to begin bargaining after giving notice can also open the way for an employer's applying to terminate its bargaining rights. On receipt of such an application, the labour relations board holds a hearing to determine whether the union has a reasonable explanation for the delay. An employer's application for termination is granted only when the union is "clearly 'sleeping' on its rights," and even then the board may hold a vote among the employees to ascertain their feelings.[46]

The details of termination and decertification vary among jurisdictions, but the various acts acknowledge two premises: (1) a union that fails to exercise its rights may lose them; and (2) a union that no longer represents the majority of employees in a bargaining unit may lose its rights — subject to the concern that a challenge must be made in a timely fashion and should not unduly impair the bargaining process.[47]

IMPROVING LABOUR RELATIONS

The late 1970s marked the starting point for two major efforts to improve labour relations in Canada: preventive mediation and quality of working life (QWL) programs. Some useful sectoral programs have also emerged.

The fact that preventive mediation and QWL programs both began in Ontario in 1978 is significant for that year marked the end of three years of the Anti-Inflation Board (AIB), which had administered a program of wage and indirect price restraint. The AIB was introduced to slow the rampant inflation of 1974 and 1975, which had been accompanied by a world-leading record of time lost through strikes. Although one million people observed the National Day of Protest against the AIB on October 14, 1976, the number of strikes decreased sharply thereafter as the AIB did not budge in its wage decisions.[48] With the imminent phasing out of the AIB, there were fears that a wage–price explosion would follow as it had the price freeze in the United States in 1971. No wage–price explosion occurred in Canada but there was concern with the connection between wage negotiations and price increases. "There has to be a better way to manage labour–management relations" was a view often voiced in the late 1970s. It is only speculation, but perhaps the tumultuous events of the mid-1970s led to the search for "better ways."

Preventive mediation, QWL, and sectoral labour–management co-operation are intended to be better ways.

PREVENTIVE MEDIATION

Preventive mediation (PM), which was developed by the Federal Mediation Service in the United States, was introduced by the Ontario Ministry of Labour in 1978 as a way of preventing needless and futile work stoppages caused more by poor attitudes and a breakdown of communications than by a dispute over contract issues.[49]

PM has three components. The first is the establishment of joint action committees, made up of small groups of management and union representatives who meet together on a regular basis, initially monthly, to discuss problems of mutual concern. The second component is the Relationships by Objectives program (RBO), in which representatives of management and the union spend three days away from the workplace examining the problems that have been identified as affecting their relationships and developing specific plans for resolving them. A follow-up meeting is arranged 60 to 90 days later to ensure progress on the plans. The final component is a one-day joint training program designed to review techniques to improve attitudes and understanding of the roles of the parties.

The key to preventive mediation is a mutual desire on the part of the parties to solve their problems. A notable success story is that of Budd Canada and the United (now the Canadian) Auto Workers. They succeeded in changing a confrontational relationship of wildcat (illegal) strikes and an enormous number of grievances to an attitude of joint problem solving.[50]

The government of Ontario has reaffirmed its confidence in the value of preventive mediation by including an expansion in the program as part of its 1992 proposals for reform to the Labour Relations Act.[51]

QUALITY OF WORKING LIFE

Quality of working life (QWL) programs have been designed to increase the humanization of work through the redesign of the way tasks and jobs are organized and through employee involvement in decision making. The various terms for QWL include quality circles, employee involvement, work redesign, and labour–management participation teams. The key to QWL is a change in managerial attitudes and practices, away from an authoritarian style toward a consultative and advisory role.[52] The rationale is that both parties benefit from QWL. By involving employees in decision making and greater identification with the product, it is expected there will be greater motivation and increases in productivity, as well as greater job satisfaction. Although there has been considerable employee interest in the QWL process,[53] there are many sceptics among both management and unions. The net result is that even after a decade in which public policy encouraged QWL initiatives, only 12.9 percent of collective agreements in Canada, covering 12.3 percent of unionized employees, had QWL provisions.[54]

For management, there are the positive prospects of improved productivity and product quality and more satisfied employees. However, a potential cost is that the role of first-line supervisors may be modified significantly through shared decision making, compromising their flexibility to act in the pure interests of management. For unions, the opportunity for increased union and employee influence at the plant level also has a potential cost; employee involvement and identification with management may undermine the role of the union in the eyes of union members.[55]

Several government agencies in Canada existed for about a decade to encourage QWL. Labour Canada had a QWL division that supported initiatives, disseminated information through a newsletter, and sponsored conferences and studies. It was discontinued in 1986, as a result of federal government cutbacks, but in its collective agreements information retrieval system, Labour Canada continues to analyze QWL provisions within collective agreements. The Ontario Ministry of Labour had a Quality of Working Life Centre that undertook a variety of studies and published a news journal. It was disbanded in 1988, four years after the Ontario Federation of Labour withdrew its support on the grounds that QWL could be used to prevent unions from organizing.

There are opposing views within the labour movement.[56] The most successful QWL program in Canada has been at the Shell chemical plant in Sarnia (see Case 12.2). The company involved the union from the beginning in planning the new plant, and the result has been a nontraditional organizational structure in which employees help design their jobs and are paid on the basis of the skills they have acquired. Management and the union prepared and continually update a statement of philosophy that includes a commitment to the joint optimization of the plant's social and technical systems and to the belief that "employees are responsible and trustworthy, capable of working together effectively and making proper decisions related to their spheres of responsibilities and work arrangement — if given the necessary authorities, information and training."[57]

As in the case of preventive mediation, the most important element in the success of QWL has been commitment by both management and labour. The number of QWL programs has never been large (in mid-1984, the Ontario QWL Centre identified a few more than 30 organizations in which union and management were involved in the process), and not all of them were successful. Even in the Shell organization, the QWL program has not spread. Just down the road from the chemical plant, Shell operates a refinery that has the same union as the chemical plant, but this older plant does not have a QWL program. Instead, there is a traditional labour–management relationship epitomized by a lengthy collective agreement, in contrast to the eleven-

EXHIBIT 15.1
CAW Guidelines on the Reorganization of Work

The workplace is changing, but the outcome of the change is not predetermined. Much is new in the workplace, but what is not is that management has its agenda and we have ours. Management has articulated its program—packaged as the team concept—as empowering workers and reforming the workplace. This theme of industrial democracy is not new to us. Our union was born out of and continues to be built on demands for a more democratic workplace. And the barrier to workplace democracy continues to be management. Their obsession with getting more with less subordinates workers' rights and working conditions to a narrow preoccupation with reducing costs, reducing staff, and eliminating any free time.

We reject managerial efforts, under whatever name, that jeopardize workers' rights, undermine workplace conditions, and erode the independence of the union.

1. We reject the use of Japanese Production Methods, which rigidly establish work standards and standard operations thereby limiting worker autonomy and discretion on the job.
2. We reject the use of techniques such as *kaizening* (pressure for continuous "improvement") where the result is speed-up, working intensification, and more stressful jobs.
3. We oppose workplace changes that limit mobility, weaken transfer rights, and erode seniority provisions.
4. We reject the introduction of alternative workplace structures and employee-based programs that purport to represent workers' interests while circumventing the union.
5. We reject efforts to shift compensation from wages to incentives and to individualize the rewards of productivity improvements.
6. We oppose the process of union nomination or joint appointees to new jobs created to perform company functions.
7. We oppose initiatives that undermine worker solidarity — structures that require conformity to company-determined objectives and that divide workers into competing groups internally, nationally, and internationally.
8. We oppose the use of peer pressure in company campaigns to discipline and regulate the behaviour of workers.
9. We reject workplace reorganizations that threaten job security by subcontracting or transferring work outside the bargaining unit.
10. We oppose efforts to render workplaces so lean that there is no place for workers with work-related, age-related, or other disabilities.
11. We oppose efforts to involve and reward workers in the systematic elimination of jobs or the disciplining of other workers.

We support efforts to involve and empower workers, to increase worker dignity, to produce quality products with pride, to make jobs more rewarding and workplaces more democratic.

EXHIBIT 15.1 *(continued)*

These objectives will be achieved through our own agenda for change, our own demands around:

- training
- technology
- improving jobs
- improving the work environment
- guaranteeing health and safety
- strengthening mobility rights
- strengthening affirmative action
- strengthening the union.

Source: *CAW Statement on the Reorganization of Work* (Toronto: Canadian Auto Workers, 1990), pp. 9–10. Reprinted with permission.

page agreement for the chemical unit. Nevertheless, given increased international competition on the one hand and a more highly educated work force on the other, there is no question that the interest and need for worker participation will find an outlet in various programs, regardless of what such programs are termed.[58]

As shown in Exhibit 15.1, the Canadian Auto Workers (CAW) has set out guidelines on the types of employee involvement in the workplace that it rejects and the types that it supports. Not all unions believe QWL to be as threatening as does the CAW. In 1992, the United Steelworkers of America reached agreement with Algoma Steel on an innovative employee buyout of the debt-ridden company. The buyout gives the union control of the company, which is to be restructured and downsized. Included in the program are wage and benefit cuts and employee involvement. Leo Gerard, Canadian director of the United Steelworkers of America, observed that

> Algoma Steel represents more than the largest experiment in worker ownership in North American history—it is destined to be Canada's most significant experiment for decades to come in workplace redesign, in new non-hierarchical management style in a heavy-industrial setting, and in shop floor empowerment.[59]

Employee empowerment is a term introduced in the 1990s that seems to be replacing 'quality of working life' as a buzzword for employee involvement. The term is interesting in that it appears to be an acceptance by management of a long-held union concept. As the CAW statement indicates, the term can mean different things to management and unions, although both would agree that it focusses attention on the role of employees in an organization.

HRM IN ACTION

EMPLOYEE INVOLVEMENT AT INMONT

Successful employee involvement requires more than the establishment of quality circles. This has been demonstrated by the experience of the graphics division at Inmont Canada. In 1982, the corporate office decided to initiate a quality circle program and hired a consulting firm to help introduce it. Presentations were made to management and supervisors to outline the process and discuss any concerns. A steering committee was established, two part-time facilitators were hired, and with the support of the union, a meeting was held to orient employees to the quality circle process. Within two years, four of the five quality circles had disbanded and the steering committee had stopped meeting.

The general manager decided to hire a program facilitator and reviewed the program. The facilitator conducted interviews with employees and management to see why the program failed and what could be done to revive it. He found that management gave no support to the program after it was launched and that the employees received no training or information beyond what was initially provided. In addition, part-time facilitators were not able to devote sufficient time to the program.

The general manager supported the revival of the concept, and mandatory orientation meetings were held among managers. A new steering committee was formed with plant managers and union representatives, and it later involved team members. The committee established general policies for the operation of the quality circle, including the requirement that management respond to circle suggestions and questions within five working days. Training was provided for every supervisor or manager who might become a circle leader. Training involved leadership, participative management, and consensus development. By the summer of 1985, there were 10 teams in which 65 employees participated.

Many work-related problems were resolved by the quality circles, and trust was developed between management and employees. A survey conducted in the summer of 1985 indicated that the program was viewed as being very positive. In addition, employee attitudes and communication within departments appeared to be improved.

Source: Adapted from Laurie P. Richer, *An Evaluation of Employee Involvement Initiatives in Canada*, Research Essay Series No. 36 (Kingston, Ont.: Industrial Relations Centre, Queen's University, 1991). Used with the permission of the publisher.

SELF-DIRECTED WORK TEAMS

Self-directed work teams, a development related to QWL programs, are identified with new ways of organizing work forces that were pioneered in Sweden and Japan. Self-directed work teams are not an end in themselves, but rather a means to an end. Their objective may be to improve the competitive quality of products and services or to help implement a just-in-time inventory system. Work teams may be introduced throughout an entire organization, or only in part of it.[60] Whatever their objective and extent, the most fundamental change they bring about is in the relationship between workers and managers. There is often great difficulty in transforming the manager–worker relationship from a "control orientation" to what has been described as a "learner role."[61] One recent study[62] identified nineteen tools and techniques for implementing teams:

1. Employee Involvement: Alternatives to Self-Direction
2. The Steering Committee
3. The Feasibility Study
4. Developing a Mission Statement
5. Design-Team Training
6. Designing and Implementing Awareness Training
7. Workplace Analysis
8. Team Member Training
9. Manager and Supervisor Transition Training
10. Hand-off Plans for Supervisory and Support Group Tasks
11. Team Member Role Expansion Plan
12. Peer Disciplinary Review Committee
13. Recognition and Reward Techniques
14. Mature Team–New Team Coaching Session
15. A Group Problem-Solving Process
16. Cluster Meeting
17. Peer Performance Appraisal
18. Repotting Workshop
19. Diffusion Strategies

Not all teams work, however, so organizations considering introducing teams should consult the growing literature in the field on what approaches, and in which situations, teams have proven successful.[63]

SECTORAL LABOUR–MANAGEMENT CO-OPERATION

Although organized labour in Canada has generally been wary of co-operative projects, such as QWL, in individual workplaces, there are some examples of labour–management co-operation at the industrial-sector level. The most far-reaching is the Canadian Steel Trade and Employment Congress, a program funded by the federal government and operated by the United Steelworkers of America and steel industry officials to assist laid-off steelworkers through job counselling and retraining. Another example is the Sectoral Skills Council of the Canadian Electrical and Electronics Manufacturing Industry, funded by Employment and Immigration Canada and run by management and labour representatives of the industry; it has focussed on human resource requirements and training.[64] In addition the Canadian Labour Market and Productivity Centre, which is jointly run by labour and management representatives, conducted an in-depth examination of labour force development strategy, including such issues as apprenticeship, co-operative education, and human resource planning, in 1989/90.[65]

Joint industrial-sector and national initiatives may be a way of building some union–management co-operation into the adversarial system that characterizes industrial relations in Canada.[66] But collective bargaining will continue to be the focus of union–management relations at the individual workplace.

SUMMARY

Although fewer than 40 percent of the nation's paid workers belong to a union and are covered by a collective agreement, labour relations is a major HRM function. Since the establishment of collective bargaining as the accepted mode of conflict resolution between labour and management, unionized employers have had to direct some of their resources to maintaining good labour relations, which include negotiations, administering the collective agreement, and processing and resolving grievances. Unionized employers usually have one or more labour relations specialists to deal with the many details associated with unionized employees.

Membership in labour organizations has been increasing in most geographic and industrial areas of Canada, especially in the public sector, for several decades, although the overall unionized proportion declined slightly in the 1980s. How organized labour will meet the challenges of the future and use its strong voice is yet to be seen. Labour relations and collective bargaining are a complex and specialized part of the HRM function.

Review Questions

1. Discuss the ways labour relations legislation has affected labour–management relations in Canada since World War II.

2. Describe the process by which unions are certified as representatives of employees. Does it make any difference to management whether a union is certified on the basis of membership cards or through a vote supervised by government officials? Discuss.

3. Some people say that "if employees are treated fairly, they are less likely to unionize." Discuss. Include in your answer reasons why employees join unions and the role unions play in representing them in their dealings with employers.

4. As noted in the chapter, academic economists debate whether or not unions raise productivity in the workplace. Present arguments for and against the view that unions are responsible for increases in productivity.

5. How does the presence of a union in the workplace alter the relationship between management and its employees?

6. What must be done by unions and by management to develop a constructive relationship through which both will benefit?

Project Ideas

1. For several weeks, read local and/or national newspapers for reports of labour–management negotiations, strikes, or the terms of collective agreements. At least three or four examples of disputes and settlements should be found. Report for each case the employer and the union involved, the issues of the dispute or settlement, whether the strike was legal, and whether a conciliation officer, an arbitrator, or an arbitration board was involved. Also note how many cases were in the public sector and how many in the private.

2. Obtain a copy of a collective agreement between a local employer and a union. (Your instructor could assist you in this.) When you read the agreement, note each provision that may restrict management's flexibility and speed in running the organization. Also note the provisions describing employees' pay, benefits, and job security, and those that provide for safe working conditions. Consider how many of these provisions would have been included in a "psychological contract." Summarize your observations in a brief written or oral report to the class.

3. Organize a debate between two groups of students on the proposition that employees should be members of a union. The debate should be as factual as possible, rather than based upon opinions and attitudes.

4. Invite a local union officer or official to class to discuss the activities of his or her group and some collective bargaining experiences. An officer or official with several years of experience should be able to provide the class with excellent insights into labour relations.

5. Examine the labour relations act in your province and summarize the main requirements for a union's becoming certified as the exclusive bargaining agent of a group of employees. If the provincial labour relations board holds regular hearings in your city, attend a hearing on an application for certification. Note the major points at issue between union and management, such as the definition of the bargaining unit, and whether there was management interference with the attempt to organize the employees. Share your findings with the class in a brief written or oral report.

▶▶▶ CASES

CASE 15.1 ▶ UNIONS UNITE FORCES AGAINST NORTHERN TELECOM

Claiming that Northern Telecom Ltd. has engaged in extensive anti-union practices worldwide, a group of international labour organizations will hold a special convention in Toronto next week to develop a global strategy to fight back.

"We will look at Northern Telecom's union practices internationally," said a spokeswoman for the Canadian Auto Workers. "They've been quite anti-union and have frequently opposed efforts to organize non-union workers and plants."

The three-day gathering starting Wednesday marks a rare bid by national labour movements to address changes wrought by the rise of global corporations.

"We see their chief objectives as seeking to respond to the migration of labour-intensive work in high-cost countries to lower-cost countries and wanting to translate the tremendous growth in telecommunications to increased membership," said James Marchant, vice-president of industrial relations at Northern Telecom Canada.

The meeting will bring together the top leadership and representatives of the CAW, the Communications and Electrical Workers of Canada (CWC) and the Communications Workers of America (CWA), in addition to labour organizers from Europe and Malaysia. It is being conducted under the auspices of two Geneva-based international unions, the Post Telegraph and Telephone International (PTTI) and the International Metalworkers Federation.

The telecommunications equipment manufacturer is one of five global companies that have been targeted by the PTTI for a co-ordinated organization drive of non-union plants.

Mississauga-based Northern Telecom faces a volley of accusations from the unions, including charges that it has relocated low-skilled jobs from Canada to plants offshore; engaged in union-busting activities in the United States; fired strike leaders at its joint venture plant in Turkey; and attempted to decertify unions at its British plants acquired during the acquisition of STC PLC last February, the CAW spokeswoman said.

"This is a global problem, so it requires a global approach," Joe Hanafin, national representative of the CWC, said in a telephone interview.

"The message we want to give Northern Telecom is that cultivating an image of good corporate citizenship is not enough," he said. "The company must improve its labour relations wherever it goes."

Union membership at Northern Telecom has been affected in recent years by major changes in employment patterns at many of its largest plants.

Although the employment level at the company's sprawling factory in Bramalea near Brampton, Ont., has remained constant at about 4000 over the past five years, membership in union locals has declined as the number of hourly shift workers has fallen to 2300.

Company statistics show a growing shift toward more higher-skilled, non-union workers, such as software experts and manufacturing engineers — or "white-collar-type factory jobs," Ken Law, manager of the Bramalea plant, said in a recent interview.

The proliferation of work teams at plants throughout Northern Telecom's empire, including Calgary, Bramalea and Research Triangle Park, N.C., has eroded traditional job classifications. The number of job descriptions on the Bramalea factory floor has been reduced to 110 from the 180 positions in 1988 and is expected to be winnowed to 50 by 1993, Mr. Law said.

Northern Telecom has 49 000 employees (excluding the 11 000 employees at STC PLC) who work at 42 plants throughout the world.

The bulk of the company's union membership is in Canada where 40 per cent of its employees are represented under collective agreements with the CAW and CWC.

The CAW represents 4300 workers at plants in Bramalea, London, Belleville and Kingston, Ont., and in Saint John. The CWC represents 3500 employees.

But only 400 of the company's 22 000 U.S. employees — a group of installers — are covered by a contract with the CWA.

The rest of Northern Telecom's employees at its plants in the United States, Malaysia, Australia, Ireland, France, China and Thailand are not unionized.

A company spokesman denies Northern Telecom has actively resisted the unions.

"In the end, it's the employees who decide whether they want a union," said John Lawlor, spokesman for Northern Telecom Canada. "The numbers speak for themselves."

He said the union's charge about union-busting tactics in the United States stems from a 10-year-old court case in Tennessee relating to an "overzealous" Northern Telecom plant manager who bugged the phones of union organizers and who was dismissed for his actions.

Mr. Lawlor also said it is "unfair to blame Northern Telecom" for actions that the Netas plant management in Turkey may have taken because the company does not control the plant. Northern Telecom owns 31 per cent of the venture.

Mr. Marchant added that the Turkish ministry of justice ordered Netas to fire 20 workers, including 11 union stewards, after they illegally took over a company cafeteria in 1988. He said the protest occurred after membership levels fell below the number required for the union to negotiate for employees.

Mr. Marchant said STC's previous difficulties with a union at a plant in South Wales have been resolved and, following an agreement reached three weeks ago, the union will not be decertified (as allowed under British law).

"We are neither anti-union nor union-free," he said.

But the chief concern of the unions in Canada relates to Northern Telecom's domestic employment levels in the wake of globalization and as a result of major workplace changes, Mr. Hanafin said.

Although the 40 000-strong CWC broke from the 800 000-member CWA in 1972, the two unions forged an alliance last year to fight moves by transnational corporations, including Northern Telecom and rival American Telephone and Telegraph Co., to move jobs to countries that pay lower wages.

Source: Lawrence Surtees, "Unions Unite Forces Against Northern Telecom," *The Globe and Mail*, October 18, 1991. Reprinted with the permission of *The Globe and Mail*.

TASKS AND QUESTIONS

1. What is causing the decline in the proportion of Northern Telecom's employees who are unionized? Include in your answer the changes in total company employment and the number unionized.

2. Describe the approach the unions are taking in their efforts to offset the decline in the share of organized workers at Northern Telecom.

3. Present arguments for and against the view that Northern Telecom has made a strategic decision to decrease the proportion of its employees who belong to unions.

4. Why would an organization have as a primary strategic goal reduction of the proportion of its employees who are unionized? Discuss this question, taking into consideration the costs and benefits that may be involved.

CASE 15.2 ▸ MEETING EMPLOYEE NEEDS FOR FLEXIBILITY

Julie White, national manager of public affairs for Levi Strauss & Co. (Canada) Inc., was on the way from her Toronto home to the airport for a big meeting in Edmonton when suddenly business didn't seem her most important priority.

Mrs. White had become guardian to her niece when her sister died two years earlier. The day of the meeting was the anniversary of her sister's death and she had left the child sitting sadly on the end of her bed as the cab honked outside.

Although she had promised to return that night, she was haunted by the forlorn image she had left behind, and asked the cab driver to turn around. Because Levi Strauss has set up a number of work–family balance policies, she was able to put her personal priorities ahead of business and take the day off. She says the colleagues waiting for her in Edmonton were disappointed — her contribution was a big part of the agenda — but understanding.

Mrs. White was doing a balancing act that Anne Swarbrick, Ontario's minister responsible for women's issues, described at a recent conference on work and family as "kind of like being a juggler on a teeter-totter."

It is a worthwhile balancing act, David McCamus, the chairman of Xerox Canada Ltd. of Toronto, told the same conference. He said his company has found that allowing staff to make decisions about their lives is highly motivating.

And the key to offering good customer service and thus creating a competitive advantage for your company is to have highly motivated people, he added.

There is no one solution to help workers balance their home and work responsibilities, said Armine Yalnizian of the Social Planning Council of Metropolitan Toronto. Canada will need "an enormous cafeteria of approaches for people to pick from."

For example, workplace day care is not the solution for everyone. It may take children out of their own communities or reduce their parents' mobility if they change jobs, said Nancy Riche, executive vice-president of the Canadian Labour Congress.

Annie Labaj of the Canadian Auto Workers said that in some of her union's plants, parents work night shifts or commute two hours each way to their jobs. They do not want to have to rouse children at 3 a.m. to take them home, or subject them to the long commute, she said.

Workplace day care centres don't solve the problem of after-school care or what to do with very young infants or sick children either, said Fern Stimpson, assistant vice-president, employee support services at Manulife Financial.

Manulife used to provide grants to a day-care centre near its Toronto offices. Now it spends its resources offering a variety of information and referral services. These run from noon-hour seminars on streetproofing a child to a computerized on-line referral service for advice about care for both children and elderly relatives. The on-line information is accessible 24 hours a day at Manulife offices.

Both Union Gas Ltd. Chatham, Ont. and Levi Strauss of Markham, Ont., set up focus groups to ask employees about their needs. Sometimes these needs are small, Mrs. White of Levi Strauss said. In her company, staff wanted more telephones in the cafeteria so they could phone home to check on their children.

However, Levi Strauss is also taking on bigger projects, for example trying to get away from assembly line production of jeans and into work teams because assembly lines do not lend themselves to flexible work schedules.

Some other solutions are mentioned in the Ontario government booklet, *Work and Family, The Crucial Balance*:

- Warner-Lambert Canada Inc. has a flexible hours plan called "bes-time." Twice a year, its employees negotiate with their department head for the hours they want to work. They must keep that schedule for six months but can then renegotiate if they wish.
- 3M Canada Inc. in London, Ont., negotiated permanent weekend shifts with the CAW. CAW members can work 12 hours each on Saturday and Sunday and be paid for a full work week with all benefits.
- In Toronto, Manpower Temporary Services uses a computerized information system to help its temporary employees find suitable child-care arrangements.

According to Debbi Gordon, a counsellor with Family Services of Metropolitan Toronto, there is a common refrain in what employees want with respect to trying to balance work and family responsibilities. It could be compressed into three phrases: They want to be treated as adults, as partners and with dignity.

Source: Margot Gibb-Clark, "Juggling Priorities Can Be Worthwhile," *The Globe and Mail*, May 13, 1991. Reprinted with the permission of *The Globe and Mail*.

TASKS AND QUESTIONS

1. From an HRM perspective, discuss the advantages and disadvantages of the increased employee flexibility presented in the article.

2. Discuss the connection between employee programs that offer greater flexibility and employees' concerns with being treated as adults, as partners, and with dignity.

NOTES

1. Ontario Labour Relations Board, *Annual Report 1988–89* (Toronto, 1989), pp. 78, 83.

2. For a detailed examination of labour relations in Canada, see John Anderson, Morley Gunderson, and Allen Ponak, *Union–Management Relations in Canada*, 2nd ed. (Don Mills, Ont.: Addison-Wesley, 1989); and Alton W.J. Craig, *The System of Industrial Relations in Canada*, 3rd ed. (Scarborough, Ont.: Prentice-Hall Canada, 1990). For labour relations in the United States, see Thomas A. Kochan and Harry C. Katz, *Collective Bargaining and Industrial Relations*, 2nd ed. (Homewood, Ill.: Irwin, 1988).

3. See Desmond Morton, *Working People: An Illustrated History of the Canadian Labour Movement*, 3rd ed. (Toronto: Summerhill Press, 1990), p. 27.

4. Desmond Morton, "The History of Canadian Labour," in Anderson, Gunderson, and Ponak, *Union–Management Relations in Canada*, p. 162.

5. Morton, "History of Canadian Labour," p. 162.

6. Stuart Jamieson, *Industrial Relations in Canada*, 2nd ed. (Toronto: Macmillan, 1973), p. 120. Reprinted with the permission of the author.

7. Jamieson, *Industrial Relations in Canada*, pp. 120–21. Reprinted with the permission of the author.

8. Jamieson, *Industrial Relations in Canada*, p. 122.

9. Noah M. Meltz, "Labor Movements in Canada and the United States," in Thomas A. Kochan, ed., *Challenges and Choices Facing American Labor* (Cambridge, Mass.: MIT Press, 1985), pp. 315–37; J.B. Rose and G.N. Chaison, "The State of the Unions: United States and Canada," *Journal of Labour Research*, Winter 1985, pp. 97–112. Seymour Martin Lipsett, "North American Labor Movements: A Comparative Perspective," in Seymour Martin Lipsett, ed., *Unions in Transition: Entering the Second Century* (San Francisco: ICS Press, 1986), pp. 421–52. See also Pradeep Kumar, "Union Growth in Canada: Retrospect and Prospect," in W. Craig Riddell, research co-ordinator, *Canadian Labour Relations* (Toronto: University of Toronto Press, 1986), pp. 95–160; Peter Bruce, "Political Parties and Labor Legislation," *Relations Industrielles/Industrial Relations*, vol. 28, no. 2 (Spring 1989), pp. 115–41; Gary N. Chaison and Joseph B. Rose, "Continental Divide: The Direction and Fate of North American Unions," in David Lewin, David Lipsky, and Donna Sockell, eds., *Advances in Industrial and Labor Relations* (Westport, Conn.: JAI Press, 1990); Leo Troy, "Is the US Unique in the Decline of Private Sector Unionism?" *Journal of Labor Research*, vol. 11 (Spring 1990), pp. 111–43; Seymour Martin Lipsett, *Continental Divide: The Values and Institutions of the United States and Canada*

(New York: Routledge, 1990); and Noah M. Meltz, "Interstate vs Interprovincial Differences in Union Density," *Relations Industrielles/Industrial Relations*, vol. 28, no. 2 (Spring 1989), pp. 142–58.

10. Meltz, "Interstate vs Interprovincial Differences," p. 149.

11. Graham S. Lowe, *Bank Unionization in Canada: A Preliminary Analysis* (Toronto: Centre for Industrial Relations, University of Toronto, 1980), p. 104.

12. Anderson, Gunderson, and Ponak, *Union–Management Relations in Canada*, pp. 359–63.

13. P.B. Freeman and J.L. Medoff, *What Do Unions Do?* (New York: Basic Books, 1984), p. 166.

14. Dennis R. Maki and Lindsay N. Meredith, "The Effects of Unions on Profitability: Canadian Evidence," *Relations Industrielles/Industrial Relations*, vol. 41, no. 1 (1986), pp. 54–68.

15. The Canada Labour Code contains a provision for grievance by workers of nonunion employers in cases of unjust dismissal.

16. Ontario, Ministry of Labour, *Proposed Reform of the Ontario Labour Relations Act*, a discussion paper from the Ministry of Labour (Toronto, November 1991).

17. Labour Canada, *Directory of Labour Organizations in Canada, 1990/91* (Hull, Que.: Supply and Services Canada, 1990), p. xiii.

18. L.R. Sayles and G. Strauss, *The Local Union*, rev. ed. (New York: Harcourt, Brace and World, 1967).

19. J.A. Fossum, *Labor Relations: Development, Structure, and Process* (Dallas: Business Publications, 1979), p. 81.

20. Craig, *System of Industrial Relations in Canada*, p. 155.

21. A.J. Muste, "Army and Town Meeting," in E. Wight Bakke, Clark Kerr, and Charles W. Anrod, eds., *Union, Management and the Public* (New York: Harcourt, Brace and World, 1967).

22. John Crispo, *International Unionism: A Study in Canadian–American Relations* (Toronto: McGraw-Hill, 1967), p. 322. Reprinted with the permission of the author.

23. Canada, Department of Labour, *Labour Organizations in Canada* (Ottawa: Queen's Printer 1966), p. xii; and Labour Canada, *Directory of Labour Organizations in Canada*, p. xiv. The remainder were directly chartered unions and independent local organizations, which totalled 4.6 percent in 1990.

24. E.H. Schein, *Organizational Psychology*, 2nd ed. (Englewood Cliffs, NJ: Prentice-Hall, 1970).

25. J.G. Getman, S.B. Goldberg, and J.B. Herman, *Union Representation Elections: Law and Reality* (New York: Russell Sage, 1976); W.C. Hamner and F.J. Smith, "Work Attitudes as Predictors of Unionization Activity," *Journal of Applied Psychology*, vol. 63 (1978), pp. 415–21; and C.A. Schriesheim, "Job Satisfaction, Attitudes toward Unions and Voting in Union Representation Elections," *Journal of Applied Psychology*, vol. 65 (1978) pp. 548–52.

26. T.A. Kochan, "How American Workers View Labour Unions," *Monthly Labor Review*, vol. 10 (April 1979), pp. 15–22.

27. Albert Hirschman, *Exit, Voice and Loyalty* (Cambridge, Mass.: Harvard University Press, 1970).

28. Statistics Canada, *Annual Report of the Ministry of Industry, Science and Technology under the Corporations and Labour Unions Returns Act Part II—Labour Unions 1989* (Ottawa: Ministry of Industry, Science and Technology, 1992), p. 49.

29. Ontario, Ministry of Labour, *A Guide to the Ontario Labour Relations Act* (Toronto, 1986), p. 21. © Reproduced with permission from the Queen's Printer for Ontario.

30. Ontario, Ministry of Labour, *Guide to the Ontario Labour Relations Act*, pp. 35, 48–49.

31. D. Martin, "Labor Nemesis," *The Wall Street Journal*, November 19, 1979.

32. C.L. Hughes, "Making Unions Unnecessary," Executive Enterprises Seminar, New York, 1979.

33. Maki and Meredith, "The Effects of Unions on Profitability," p. 57.

34. John C. Anderson, "The Strategic Management of Industrial Relations," in Anderson, Gunderson, and Ponak, *Union–Management Relations in Canada*, pp. 102–103, 110–19.

35. For a discussion and examples of different clauses of collective agreements in Canada, see Jeffrey Sack and Ethan Poskanzer, *Contract Clauses: Collective Agreement Language in Canada*, 2nd ed. (Toronto: Lancaster House, 1985).

36. Special Labour–Management Study Group, *Code of Conduct for Labour–Management Relations, "The Search for a Better Way,"* a summary of discussions and proceedings over the period February 1986 to October 1987 (Niagara-on-the-Lake, Ont.: The Niagara Institute, 1987).

37. For a dramatization of the process, see *The Collective Bargaining Process*, a four-part videotape prepared by the Centre for Industrial Relations and the Media Centre, University of Toronto, 1979.

38. For a dramatization of events associated with a strike, see *Anatomy of a Strike*, a videotape prepared by the Centre for Industrial Relations and the Media Centre, University of Toronto, 1983.

39. Meltz, "Interstate vs. Interprovincial," p. 154.

40. Allen Ponak and Mark Thompson, "Public Sector Collective Bargaining," in Anderson, Gunderson, and Ponak, *Union–Management Relations in Canada*, pp. 394–98.

41. Craig, *System of Industrial Relations in Canada*, p. 182.

42. For a dramatization of the process (using a grievance over dismissal), see *The Grievance Arbitration Process*, a videotape prepared by the Centre for Industrial Relations and the Media Centre, University of Toronto, 1975.

43. D. Peach and E.R. Livernash, *Grievance Initiation and Resolution: A Study in Basic Steel* (Boston: Graduate School of Business, Harvard University, 1974); and E.A. Fleishman and E.F. Harris, "Patterns of Leadership Behavior Related to Employee Grievances and Turnover," *Personnel Psychology*, vol. 15 (1962), pp. 43–56.

44. T.A. Kochan, *Collective Bargaining and Industrial Relations* (Homewood, Ill.: Irwin-Dorsey Ltd., 1980), p. 168.

45. R. Berenbeim, *Nonunion Complaint Systems: A Corporate Appraisal*, Conference Board Report no. 770 (New York: Conference Board, 1980). For more information on grievance procedures, see the following articles in *Labor Law Journal*, vol. 41, no. 8 (August 1990): Douglas M. McCabe, "Corporate Nonunion Grievance Procedures: Open Door Policies — A Procedural Analysis," pp. 551–57; Mark J. Keppler, "Nonunion Grievance Procedures: Union Avoidance Technique or Union Organizing Opportunity?" pp. 557–63; George W. Bohlander and Ken Behringer, "Public Sector Nonunion Complaint Procedures: Current Research," pp. 563–68.

46. Ontario, Ministry of Labour, *A Guide to the Ontario Labour Relations Act*, p. 59.

47. This comment was provided by Rick MacDowell, a vice-chairman of the Ontario Labour Relations Board and the author of *A Guide to the Ontario Labour Relations Act*, Mr. MacDowell also provided much-appreciated help on other parts of the chapter.

48. Frank Reid, "Wage-and-Price Controls in Canada," in John Anderson and Morley Gunderson, *Union–Management Relations in Canada* (Don Mills, Ont.: Addison-Wesley, 1982), pp. 482–502.

49. Ontario, Ministry of Labour, "Ontario Initiatives with Respect to Preventive Mediation and, Quality of Working Life," in W. Craig Riddell, research coordinator, *Labour–Management Co-operation in Canada* (Toronto: University of Toronto Press, 1986), pp. 57–71.

50. Ontario, Ministry of Labour, "Ontario Initiatives," p. 62.

51. Ontario, Ministry of Labour, *Proposed Reform of the Ontario Labour Relations Act*.

52. Ontario, Ministry of Labour, "Ontario Initiatives," pp. 62–71; Keith Newton, "Quality of Working Life in Canada," in Riddell, *Labour–Management Co-operation in Canada*, pp. 73–86; and Riddell, "Labour–Management Co-operation in Canada: An Overview," in Riddell, *Labour–Management Co-operation in Canada*, pp. 16–20. See also Don Nightingale, *Workplace Democracy: An Enquiry into Employee Participation in the Modern Organization* (Toronto: University of Toronto Press, 1981); and J.B. Cunningham and T.H. White, eds., *Quality of Working Life: Contemporary Cases* (Ottawa: Department of Labour, 1984).

53. T.A. Kochan, H.C. Katz and N. Mowes, *Worker Participation and American Unions: Threat or Opportunity?* (Kalamazoo, Mich.: W.E. Lepjohn Institute for Employment Research, 1984).

54. Pradeep Kumar, David Arrowsmith, and Mary Lou Coates, *The Current Industrial Relations Scene in Canada, Canadian Labour Relations: An Information Manual* (Kingston, Ont.: Industrial Relations Centre, Queen's University, 1991), p. 248.

55. Riddell, *Labour–Management Co-operation in Canada*, p. 19.

56. Don Wells, *Soft Sell: Quality of Working Life Programs and the Productivity Race* (Ottawa: Canadian Centre for Policy Alternatives, 1986).

57. Agreement between Shell Canada Product Limited (Sarnia Chemical Plant) and The Energy and Chemical Workers Union, Local 800, effective February 1, 1992, to January 31, 1994, p. 3.

58. Roy J. Adams, "Two Policy Approaches to Labour–Management Decision Making at the Level of the Enterprise," in Riddell, *Labour–Management Co-operation in Canada*, pp. 87–109; and Thomas A. Kochan, Harry C. Katz, and Robert B. McKersie, *The Transformation of American Industrial Relations* (New York: Basic Books, 1986), pp. 239–40.

59. Marian Stinson, "Algoma Redesigns the Workplace," *The Globe and Mail*, June 1, 1992.

60. Jack D. Orsburn, Linda Moran, Ed Musselwhite, John H. Zenger, with Craig Perrin, *Self-Directed Work Teams: The New American Challenge* (Homewood Ill.: Business One, Irwin, 1990), p. x.

61. Larry Hirschhorn, *Managing in the New Team Environment: Skills, Tools, and Methods* (Don Mills, Ont.: Addison-Wesley, 1991), p. 3.

62. J. Richard Hackman, ed., *Groups that Work (and Those that Don't)* (San Francisco, 1990).

63. Orsburn et al., *Self-Directed Work Teams*, pp. xv–xvi.

64. Sectoral Skills Council, Canadian Electrical and Electronics Manufacturing Industry, *Proceedings of the Fourth Human Resources Seminar*, December 4–5, 1990, Ottawa.

65. Canadian Labour Market and Productivity Centre Task Force on Labour Force Development Strategy, *Report* (Ottawa: CLMPC 1990).

66. Noah M. Meltz, "A Canadian Perspective on a New Era in Industrial Relations," in *New Departures in Industrial Relations: Developments in the U.S., U.K., and Canada*, Occasional Paper (Washington, DC: British North America Committee, 1988), pp. 31–38.

SUGGESTIONS FOR FURTHER READING

☐ Roy J. Adams. "Industrial Relations: Canada in Comparative Perspective." In John C. Anderson, Morley Gunderson, and Allen Ponak, eds., *Union–Management Relations in Canada*, 2nd ed. Don Mills, Ont.: Addison-Wesley, 1989.

☐ John C. Anderson, Morley Gunderson, Allen Ponak, eds. *Union–Management Relations in Canada*, 2nd ed. Don Mills, Ont.: Addison-Wesley, 1989.

☐ Peter Bruce. "Political Parties and Labor Legislation." *Industrial Relations*, vol. 28, no. 2 (Spring 1989), pp. 115–41.

☐ Canadian Labour Market and Productivity Centre. Task Force on Labour Force Development Strategy. *Report*. Ottawa: CLMPC, 1990.

- Gary N. Chaison and Joseph B. Rose. "Continental Divide the Direction and Fate of North American Unions." In Donna Sockell, David Lewin, and David Lipsky, eds., *Advances in Industrial and Labor Relations*, vol. 5. Greenwich, Conn.: JAI Press, 1991, pp. 169–205.
- Richard P. Chaykowski and Anil Verma, eds. *Industrial Relations in Canadian Industry*. Toronto: Dryden, 1992.
- Alton Craig. *The System of Industrial Relations in Canada*, 3rd ed. Scarborough, Ont.: Prentice-Hall, 1990.
- Thomas A. Kochan, Harry C. Katz, and Robert B. McKersie. *The Transformation of American Industrial Relations*. New York: Basic Books, 1986.
- Pradeep Kumar. "Union Growth in Canada, Retrospect and Prospect." In W. Craig Riddell, research co-ordinator, *Canadian Labour Relations*. Toronto: University of Toronto Press, 1986.
- Pradeep Kumar, David Arrowsmith, and Mary Lou Coates. *The Current Industrial Relations Scene in Canada, Canadian Labour Relations: An Information Manual*. Kingston, Ont.: Industrial Relations Centre, Queen's University, 1991.
- Noah M. Meltz. "Interstate vs Interprovincial Differences in Union Density." *Relations Industrielles/Industrial Relations*, vol. 28, no. 2 (Spring 1989), pp. 142–58.
- Noah M. Meltz. "Unionism in Canada, U.S.: On Parallel Trendmills?" *Forum for Applied Research and Public Policy*, vol. 5, no. 4 (Winter 1990), pp. 46–52.
- Desmond Morton. *Working People: An Illustrated History of the Canadian Labour Movement*, 3rd ed. Toronto: Summerhill Press, 1990.
- *Relations Industrielles/Industrial Relations*. A quarterly journal published by the Department of Industrial Relations, Laval University.
- W. Craig Riddell, research co-ordinator. *Canadian Labour Relations*. Toronto: University of Toronto Press, 1986.
- Lee Troy. "Is the U.S. Unique in the Decline of Private Sector Unionism?" *Journal of Labor Research*, vol. 11 (Spring 1990), pp. 111–43.

video CASE

AN EVEN BREAK

As the make-up of Canadian society has changed, the work force has become more diversified than it was only a generation or two ago. Two main factors have contributed to this change. First, since World War II, immigrants from all over the world have been attracted to Canada with hopes of a better life and better opportunities. Second, many women have chosen to work outside the home and now constitute almost half of the Canadian work force. Employers must now accept more responsibility than was previously expected or legislated to prevent discrimination on the basis of race, religion, sex, marital status, and so on, when it comes to decisions affecting hiring, pay, or promotions. Equal rights are now entrenched in the human rights legislation of every Canadian jurisdiction and are part of the Constitution of Canada, in the Charter of Rights and Freedoms.

Today, women are not limited to jobs that pay poorly and present little opportunity for advancement. They are now working in many fields and occupations traditionally considered male domains. Pay equity legislation was enacted to prohibit sexual discrimination in wages. Under pay equity, a woman doing the same or a comparable job as a male colleague, one requiring equal skill, effort, and responsibility and performed under similar working conditions, should expect to be paid the same wage.

Visible minorities and people with disabilities also face challenges in trying to overcome discrimination in the workplace. Affirmative action programs have attempted to remedy past hiring and promotion behaviour by taking positive action to recruit, hire, and advance members of target groups in jobs where they have been under-represented in the past. But such programs can be controversial, as there is a fine line between affirmative action and reverse discrimination and hiring quotas.

Affirmative action, equal employment opportunity, and employment equity are three closely related concepts dealing with human rights in employment that are intended to protect the rights of women, minorities, and people with disabilities. All potential employees and hired employees should be treated fairly. Fair treatment will ensure that all people are given the chance they deserve to prove they can do the job, without the obstacle of discrimination.

Employers and managers must be willing to re-examine and re-evaluate their employment practices on an on-going basis to ensure that they are fair. The departure from traditional practices, which largely excluded women, minorities, and people with disabilities, will allow all groups fair access to jobs.

Source: Based on "An Even Break," video segment used with the permission of the Ontario Women's Directorate and The Oshawa Group.

Discussion Questions

1. What is systemic discrimination? Give an example of systemic discrimination presented in the video.

2. Would the company profiled in the video benefit from an equal opportunity policy?

3. What advantages, if any, does the implementation of an affirmative action policy offer a company and its employees?

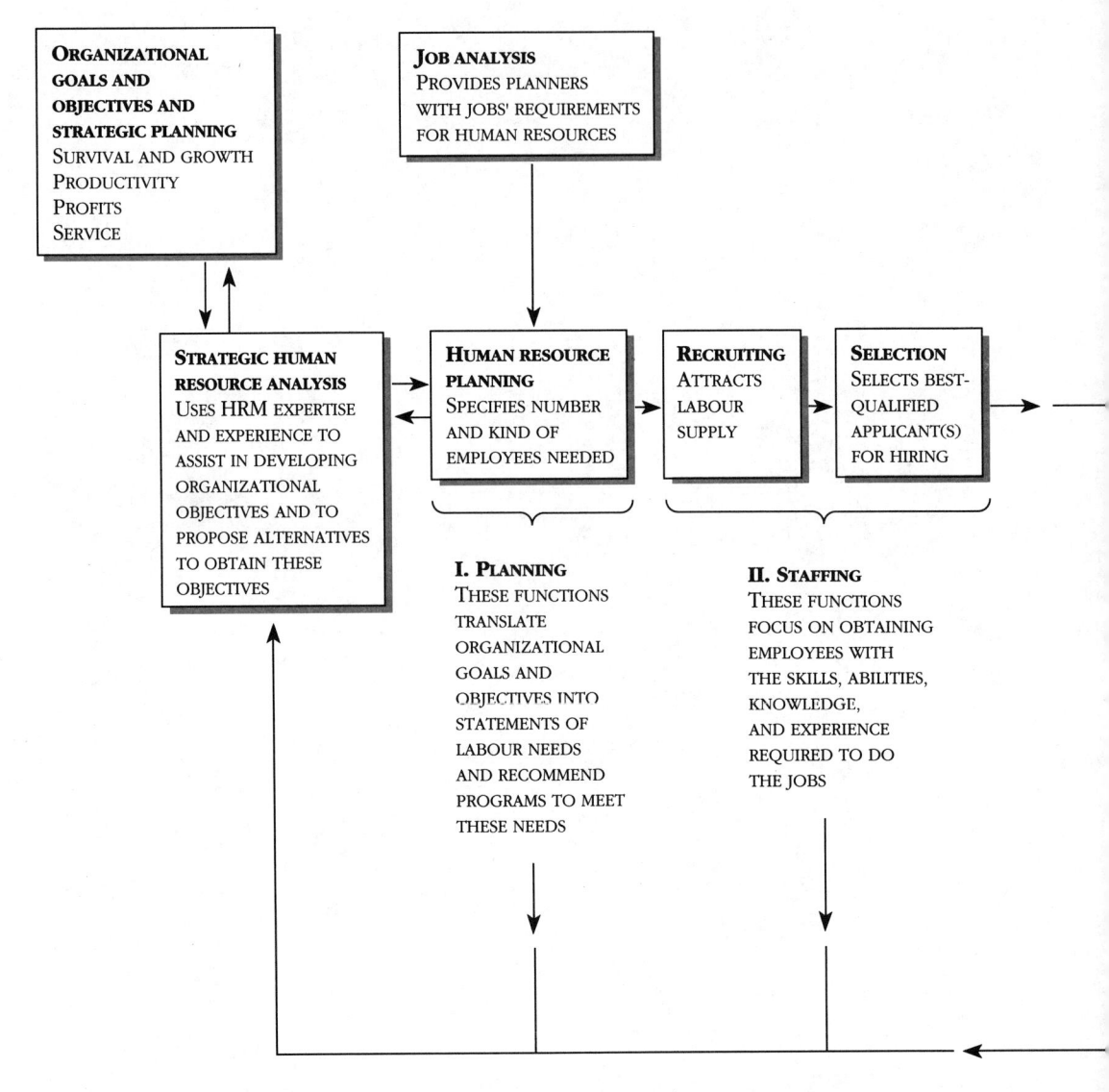

ORGANIZATIONAL GOALS AND OBJECTIVES AND STRATEGIC PLANNING
Survival and growth
Productivity
Profits
Service

JOB ANALYSIS
Provides planners with jobs' requirements for human resources

STRATEGIC HUMAN RESOURCE ANALYSIS
Uses HRM expertise and experience to assist in developing organizational objectives and to propose alternatives to obtain these objectives

HUMAN RESOURCE PLANNING
Specifies number and kind of employees needed

RECRUITING
Attracts labour supply

SELECTION
Selects best-qualified applicant(s) for hiring

I. Planning
These functions translate organizational goals and objectives into statements of labour needs and recommend programs to meet these needs

II. Staffing
These functions focus on obtaining employees with the skills, abilities, knowledge, and experience required to do the jobs

Input from major areas of HRM responsibility

PART FIVE

Issues and Challenges in Human Resource Management

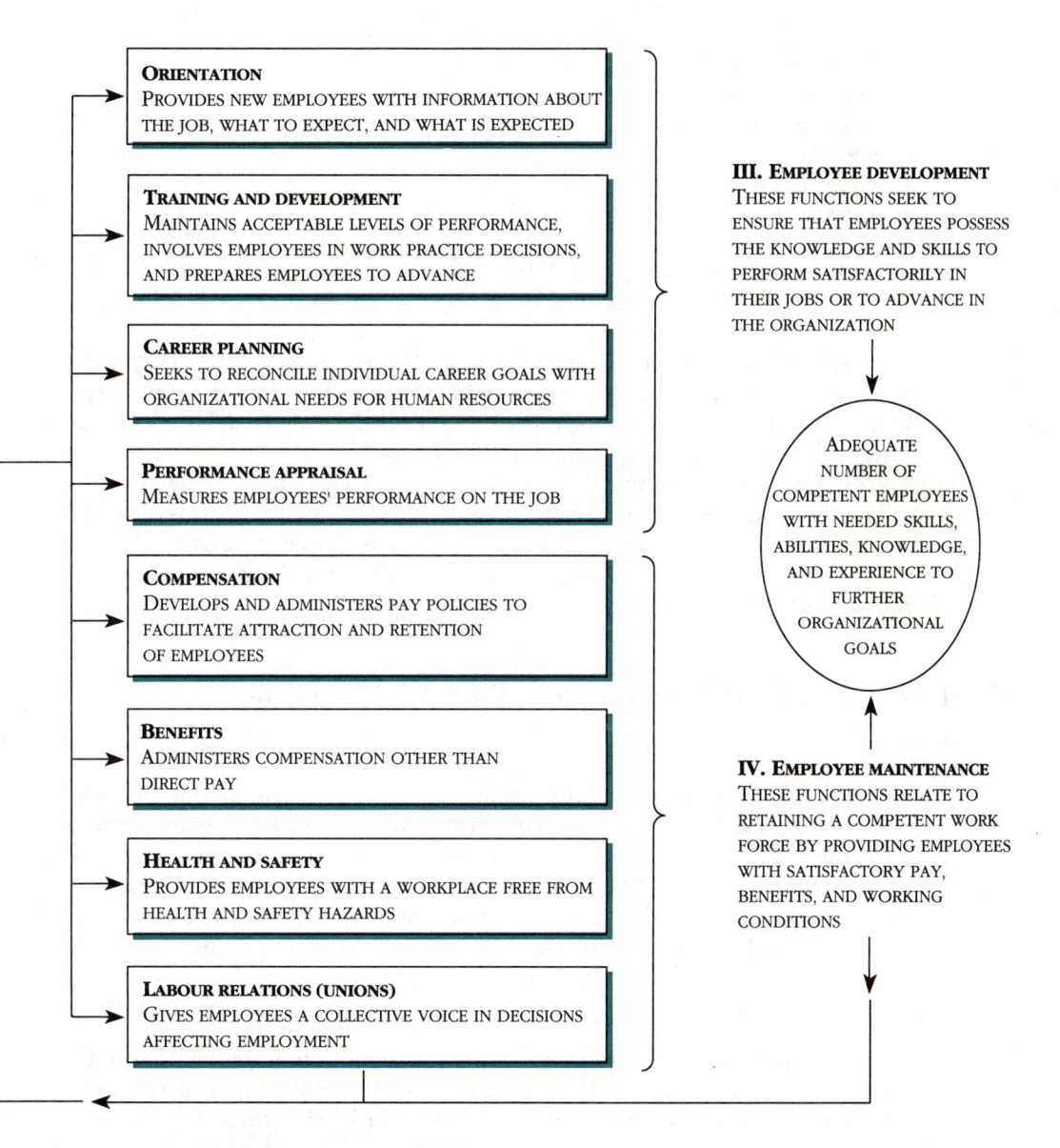

ORIENTATION
Provides new employees with information about the job, what to expect, and what is expected

TRAINING AND DEVELOPMENT
Maintains acceptable levels of performance, involves employees in work practice decisions, and prepares employees to advance

CAREER PLANNING
Seeks to reconcile individual career goals with organizational needs for human resources

PERFORMANCE APPRAISAL
Measures employees' performance on the job

III. EMPLOYEE DEVELOPMENT
These functions seek to ensure that employees possess the knowledge and skills to perform satisfactorily in their jobs or to advance in the organization

COMPENSATION
Develops and administers pay policies to facilitate attraction and retention of employees

BENEFITS
Administers compensation other than direct pay

HEALTH AND SAFETY
Provides employees with a workplace free from health and safety hazards

LABOUR RELATIONS (UNIONS)
Gives employees a collective voice in decisions affecting employment

Adequate number of competent employees with needed skills, abilities, knowledge, and experience to further organizational goals

IV. EMPLOYEE MAINTENANCE
These functions relate to retaining a competent work force by providing employees with satisfactory pay, benefits, and working conditions

INPUT FROM MAJOR AREAS OF HRM RESPONSIBILITY

CHAPTER 16

THE FUTURE OF HUMAN RESOURCE MANAGEMENT

- HUMAN RESOURCE MANAGEMENT AS A STRATEGIC FUNCTION
- HRM IN ACTION ▸ KEEPRITE GAINS FROM CO-OPERATION
- WHAT LIES AHEAD?
- SUMMARY
- REVIEW QUESTIONS
- PROJECT IDEAS
- NOTES
- SUGGESTIONS FOR FURTHER READING

SPEAKING OF ORGANIZATIONAL EFFECTIVENESS, Peter Drucker says: "Organizations are not more effective because they have better people. They have better people because they motivate to self-development through their standards, through their habits, through their climate."[1]

This textbook has focussed on the role of human resource management in maintaining and increasing organizational effectiveness. In this final chapter we examine ten challenges that face human resource management as a strategic function and what lies ahead for each of the functions that comprise HRM.

HUMAN RESOURCE MANAGEMENT AS A STRATEGIC FUNCTION

During the past two decades, the human resource management function has been transformed from a primary concern for wage and salary administration and collective bargaining to a strategic function within the upper echelons of management. The 1990s are likely to see an intensification of the strategic nature of the HRM function, with some changes in the primary thrusts and approaches. These changes are set out in the following ten points.

1. HRM AS A PROFESSION

The upgrading of the human resource management function is being accompanied by an upgrading in the education and training of human resource professionals. There has been a proliferation of university and college courses on various aspects of HRM, and the professional associations themselves have moved toward formal accreditation processes. As discussed in Chapter 1, the Ontario legislature passed legislation in 1990 giving the Human Resources Professionals Association of Ontario the authority to grant the designation Certified Human Resources Professional (CHRP) to people who complete a specified program of education and training. Although programs of HR preparation existed before, the new designation represents recognition of the profession and, by implication, its importance for organizations. Other provinces are likely to provide accreditation mechanisms within the decade.

2. HRM AND THE RELATION BETWEEN EFFICIENCY AND FAIRNESS

The literature on industrial relations has recently included discussion of the need for balancing of efficiency (increasing productivity and cost consciousness) and equity (fair treatment of employees) in the workplace. Jack Barbash maintains that this balancing has to be done by some agency, whether by unions, by the government, or by employers themselves.[2] Noah Meltz suggests efficiency can in fact be enhanced by attention to equity.[3] One of the mechanisms by which both fairness and efficiency can be enhanced is through employee involvement in such programs as Quality of Working Life and union–management co-operation, as discussed in Chapter 15.

For the nearly 40 percent of Canadian employees covered by collective agreements, the union is the agent to stress fair treatment. For the remaining 60 percent, the government sets what it believes to be minimum standards of fairness in the terms and conditions of employment (through legislation covering employment standards, human rights, pay equity, and employment equity — see Chapter 3). The majority of organizations go beyond the government-set minimums. One reason is the operation of competition within labour markets; to hire and retain qualified employees, most organizations have to provide compensation and terms of employment better than the government minimums. In addition, there is some recognition that the way employees are treated can affect productivity and thereby the efficiency of the organization.

One result of this recognition is the employer-led introduction of such workplace practices as QWL programs, employee involvement programs, the consultation of employees, and team-based organization.[4] The latest terminology for these initiatives is employee empowerment. As discussed in Chapter 15, many unions in Canada see these developments as intended to undermine unions.[5] (Unions in the United States have tended to be more cooperative, but recall that they represent fewer than 17 percent of employees there, putting them in a much weaker position than they enjoy in Canada.) Yet, in spite of the rhetoric, most Canadian unions tend to be pragmatic.

For HRM professionals, the challenge is whether there is to be recognition of the importance of balancing efficiency and fairness concerns in nonunion workplaces and of sharing such balancing with the union in unionized workplaces. Employers can adopt one of the three approaches to unions (or a combination) mentioned in Chapter 15: acceptance, substitution, or avoidance.[6]

Union accommodation is typified by the relationship between the Big Three auto companies and the Canadian Auto Workers. Union substitution was exemplified by a Toronto auto parts firm that shifted work from its unionized plant to its nonunionized plant and then closed the unionized plant. (The Ontario Labour Relations Board ordered the unionized plant to be reopened and as many former employees rehired as were needed to fill the available orders.[7]) Union avoidance is represented by employers who establish plants in traditionally nonunion regions to reduce the probability of being unionized.

For HRM professionals, an awareness of these issues and of their long-run implications for any organization is important.

3. Increasing Employee Consultation

Political analysts tell us that a factor underlying many recent political defeats has been the belief that the people have not been adequately consulted. This desire for consultation and contribution affects all parts of society, including the workplace. Consultation can take several forms. It takes place in unionized workplaces through collective bargaining and sometimes through continuing labour–management committees. Some consultation occurs in nonunion workplaces through health and safety committees or through employer-operated grievance systems. There may also be employee involvement programs, QWL programs, quality circles, team-based organization, or other mechanisms for some employee feedback to management. Management in nonunion establishments may also survey employees.

Whatever the vehicle used, employees of the 1990s want to be consulted on major changes affecting the workplace. This is not to say that there is increased interest in a joint sharing of management functions. Rather, the interest seems to be in consultation and, in the case of unions, bargaining over those aspects of company policies that directly affect the terms and conditions of employment, including long-term investment policy and pension fund investments.

The increased interest in consultation has enormous implications for HRM professionals. They are expected not only to deal with employees but also to be able to anticipate their concerns and develop policies for dealing with them without sacrificing the interests of the organization. Two areas that have a very high profile today and require some consultation are pay equity and employment equity.

4. The Difficulty of Dealing with People

We observed earlier in this book that organizations that look on their employees as resources, rather than as costs, are most likely to be productive. At the

HRM IN ACTION

KEEPRITE GAINS FROM CO-OPERATION

Marty Allgood is a tall, stalky man with long fuzzy hair and a dark smudge on his shirt.

You could mistake him for a tough biker until he smiles and begins to talk about teamwork and how it saved the KeepRite air conditioner factory from extinction.

"The teams were formed to solve the problems in the factory that have been bugging us for years and years and we haven't been able to put our fingers on," Allgood says.

Thanks to some of the teams' ideas, hourly employees at KeepRite can now believe Ottawa when it starts to advertise its prosperity campaign with the slogan "yes, we can."

Executives of Toronto-based Inter-City Products Corp. put KeepRite and a newly acquired sister factory in Red Bud, Ill., under a microscope this past summer.

Inter-City owned three main factories, including one in Lewisburg, Tenn. But it needed only two to hold the title of North America's second-largest maker of home and commercial air conditioners and furnaces.

KeepRite had a few problems. Its base wages, at nearly $16 an hour, and benefits were 30 per cent higher than the factory in Illinois, which Inter-City bought in June from SnyderGeneral Corp.

Freight costs to the hot southern U.S. states—the prime markets for air conditioners—were also 20 per cent higher from Canada. Local taxes were four times higher.

Yet KeepRite had a competitive edge.

That edge did not come from the five-year wage pact with a two-year wage freeze or the elimination of piecework incentives worth $4 an hour to some workers, although that helped.

It was mainly that KeepRite had greater productivity, flexibility, quality and a shorter cycle time, the time between receiving an order and delivering a finished product.

Plant manager Don Kivell says that wouldn't have been the case four years ago. "We had problems like you wouldn't believe: grievances, confrontation all day, every day. Our inventories were out of control."

He credits Brian Bennett, Inter-City's senior vice-president of operations and logistics, for the vision that put KeepRite on the path of becoming world-class.

An Etobicoke consulting company, Cycle Time Management Inc., provided the road map and acted as navigator. Workers like 15-year veteran Allgood did the driving.

"If we're not the best in the world, we're going to be," says a determined Allgood, one of many who volunteered to attend weekly meetings, often during lunch breaks.

A goal was set to cut the time between the receipt of an order and delivery of a finished air conditioner from 22 days to five within five years. Teams of hourly and salaried employees set about to find out how.

"We've basically achieved [that goal] in three years," says Kivell, who came to KeepRite four years ago after working for farm equipment, appliance and auto parts companies.

The time to change dies on stamping machines, which ranged up to four hours, was cut to as little as 10 minutes. Funds tied up in work-in-process inventory were cut from $21 million to $3 million.

". . . They have virtually doubled the plant's capacity without increasing the size of the plant or the work force," boasts Inter-City president H.J. Forrest.

Today at KeepRite, local dignitaries have been invited to celebrate the start of production of a new roof-top air conditioner/furnace for commercial buildings.

Over the next several months, production of all commercial products is to be moved to KeepRite, while Inter-City's Tennessee plant will build all residential models.

Some stock analysts like Glynn Williams at Gordon Capital Corp. expect the plant changes and an upturn in the economy to benefit Inter-City's bottom line.

In a recent report, he predicted Inter-City's stock price could double within a year. The company lost $2.9 million on sales of $286 million in the first six months of 1991.

At KeepRite, Allgood, Ron Sarkadi and George Madgwick were three of five hourly workers who participated in finding one of that plant's biggest time savers.

Three days were once required for the oil used during stamping to evaporate from the compact aluminum fins of air conditioner cores or radiators. So they were stacked up all over the factory to dry.

The team came up with the idea of riding the cores on a little merry-go-round above some high-volume fans. The whole setup, using materials on hand, cost about $3000, cut drying time to 10 minutes and saved nearly $500 000 a year.

The workers prepared their own video, script and manual and the company sent them to a productivity conference in Florida to show others what they had accomplished.

> Other teams of hourly workers have been assigned to buy new equipment and rearrange the layout of the factory.
> "Participation was the key," says Bennett. "The guy who does the job probably knows how to do it best and the trick then is to create the right environment and atmosphere for him to share his ideas."
>
> Source: James Daw, "KeepRite Keeps Its Edge with Employee Teamwork," *The Toronto Star*, November 1, 1991. Reprinted with permission—The Toronto Star Syndicate.

same time, it is important to note that every employee, including those who staff the HRM functions, has his or her own aspirations, skills, and experience. The larger the organization, the more difficult the HRM challenge because of the need for consistency and fairness in the treatment of employees. Employee relations problems, like labour relations problems, can never be totally "solved." There will always be myriad issues confronting HR professionals. The challenge is to recognize aspirations, skills, and experience and channel them to the mutual benefit of the organization and the individual employee.

5. THE INCREASING COMPLEXITY OF HR FUNCTIONS

This book has provided an overview of the human resource management field in Canada. It has not, however, been possible to present all of the complexities of every subject. In fact, separate books have been written on the subject of each chapter. And each such subject has expanded enormously during the past decade, partly because of fluctuations and trends in the economy and partly because of changes in social values, legislation, and technology.

The increased complexity of HR functions means that HRM professionals must make greater efforts not only to understand the details of new developments but also to continue to view each of the increasingly complex functions as part of a larger HRM system.

6. COST CONSCIOUSNESS

The increase in competitive pressures has meant demands for greater efficiency and productivity. One manifestation of this demand is increased cost consciousness — organizations' desire for greater control over costs. Since labour costs are a major portion of total costs, particularly in service organizations, this desire has meant a larger role for HRM professionals in maximizing the effectiveness of wage and benefit expenditures. At the same time, as already noted, HRM professionals are challenged to have workers who believe they are being fairly treated.

7. QUANTIFICATION OF THE IMPLICATIONS OF HRM POLICY

Increasing cost consciousness requires that HRM professionals enhance their ability to quantify the implications of HR policies. It is straightforward to estimate the cost of granting a specific wage increase or raising company contributions to a pension plan. It is harder to calculate the benefits from expenditures on training and still harder to quantify the returns from establishing a career planning program or an employee-assistance program. Yet these are the kinds of calculations that top executives deem important. To do them requires HRM professionals to have a knowledge of strategic corporate decision making as well as the results of research on the effects of particular HR policies.

8. HRM AS A PROACTIVE FUNCTION

In the past, management's roles in wage and salary administration and collective bargaining were regarded as primarily responsive to union demands or employee pressure. As a result of increased competition and the elevation of the HRM function within organizations, HRM is now increasingly proactive in its approach to long-range policy. Instead of taking a passive, "give as little as possible" approach to collective bargaining and wage and salary determination, HRM professionals must look to the long run and develop a strategy consistent with the overall corporate approach.

Such an approach is a two-way street. HR managers must not only determine the HR implications of various corporate strategies but also be proactive within the strategy-formation process, developing proposals for initiatives that arise from the potential of the organization's human resources.

9. THE DEVOLUTION OF HR FUNCTIONS

Associated with HRM's taking a greater strategic role has been a devolution of HR functions to line managers, as was found in the Conference Board of Canada's survey on HR practices.[8] The pattern for the 1990s seems to be HRM that increasingly trains line departments to handle many of the staffing functions and more of the grievance process. The advantage of this devolution is that it involves a broader segment of the organization and can increase the effectiveness of HR practices. At the same time, HRM professionals must be ready to provide appropriate training and backup if the devolution is to succeed.

10. HRM AND TRAINING THE WORK FORCE

It is axiomatic among Canadian policy makers that if Canadian society is to maintain and enhance its high standard of living, it will have to increase its rate of productivity growth. It is also accepted that one key is a more highly educated work force. The new Unemployment Insurance Act earmarks $800 million for training, but studies have shown that the greatest need is for increased training expenditures by private employers.[9] Various proposals have been made to encourage private investment in training, including a levy-grant system,[10] and joint labour–management control of training funds.[11] The new federal training act, which established the labour–management-run Canadian Labour Force Development Board, will encourage training.

For HRM professionals, the challenge of the 1990s will be to develop or purchase effective training programs. "Effective" must mean both technically efficient and relevant to both the needs of the organization and the desires of the individuals taking the training. The employer wants workers to acquire the skills necessary for the organization but not those that might encourage individuals to seek post-training employment elsewhere. Employees also want to acquire skills specifically relevant to the organization, but they also want more general skills, some of which may be portable. The HRM professional must balance the training needs of the organization and the desires of the individual. As we discussed in Chapter 14, employers are becoming increasingly responsive to a wider range of employee needs, and this responsiveness pays off for the organization in workers' greater commitment and greater overall productivity.

Notice how interrelated these ten themes are. The enhanced role and credibility of the HRM function carries with it a number of major implications for the practice of human resource management in the 1990s.

WHAT LIES AHEAD?

Chapters 1–3 discussed economic and labour force trends in Canada, as well as recent changes in legislation. These developments will affect the extent to which the profession of human resource management in Canada meets the ten challenges that have been identified for the 1990s. Meeting these challenges requires changes in each of the functions that were set out in Figure 1.1 as comprising human resource management. Let us look briefly at each function.

HUMAN RESOURCE PLANNING AND JOB ANALYSIS

Human resource planning (HRP) will become a more challenging and complex function for HRM managers than ever before. Labour force demographics, pay and employment equity legislation, rapid technological changes, and intense competition combine to produce a most challenging set of human resource constraints and goals. During past decades, the techniques of human resource planning have worked best in medium to large organizations with fairly stable, predictable product or service markets, such as Ontario Hydro. Today, product demand is less stable for many employers than in the past; moreover, shortened product life cycles, technological innovations, and new, more flexible organizational structures are modifying the nature of many tasks and jobs.

These environmental and organizational changes have at least several implications for HRP and job analysis. First, as just suggested, the nature of jobs has changed in the direction of a greater variety and range of activities and responsibilities. This shift affects selection, training, career planning, and compensation. Second, the time horizon for planning must be shorter than in the past to meet demands of rapidly changing markets and agile competitors. Third, the options for meeting human resource goals have increased for many employers. For example, use of temporary employees, part-time employees, retired workers, telecommuting, subcontracting, and other options are more common. Fourth, although labour shortages have become labour surpluses, the pressures of employment equity have increased the importance of innovative recruiting programs as well as training and development. These programs are necessary to meet staffing goals for workers with specific skills as well as targets for visible minorities, women, Native people, and people with handicaps.

Several of the ten factors affecting HRM discussed at the beginning of this chapter are having clear impacts on HRP. For example, the pressures for cost effectiveness, efficiency, and fairness are evident. Additionally, the need to be proactive and to make more extensive use of training reflects the greater complexity and challenge of this function. The responsibility for human resource planning, unlike several other functions, will not become shared with supervisors and employees. In fact, HRP will assume a more strategically important role in organization management than in the past.

RECRUITING

Recruiting will experience significant changes in this decade as the number of entrants to the labour force declines sharply and many applicants lack the knowledge and skills required by employers facing a highly competitive environment. We argued in Chapter 6 that although recruiting has traditionally been a matter of employers' going into the labour market and reaping the necessary workers, it is increasingly clear that employers must first sow human resources. Therefore, many far-sighted employers are establishing closer relations with schools and with special groups such as those involving members of ethnic minorities. Although traditional methods of recruiting, such as help-wanted signs and newspaper ads, may yield some applicants, recent evidence suggests that many of these applicants will lack the basic skills of reading, math, and writing. The result is that recruiting has become a more complex HRM function requiring planning and a close, long-term relationship with schools, colleges, and universities. The possible shortage of specially qualified labour must also be met by making greater use of apprenticeships, co-op programs, internships, and career information programs. An additional challenge facing recruiting is employment equity. Both public and legislative pressure will compel many employers to develop and seek applicants from nontraditional groups.

SELECTION

The selection function is undergoing numerous and conflicting pressures. On the one hand, competitive pressures to increase productivity and cut costs demand that employers select the most talented applicants. On the other hand, shortages of specific types of labour, together with employment equity legislation, mean that employers may have to rely on training more than selection to achieve these goals. Although these pressures conflict, they are not incompatible. The selection function can serve to identify the talented, highly motivated people necessary for the growing number of team-oriented organizations; it can also be used as a diagnostic tool to identify applicants with ability who would benefit from training.

During the 1970s and much of the 1980s, the huge cohorts of baby boomers in the labour market enabled employers to use selection procedures to hire the most talented from a large labour pool. The recession of the early 1990s again created large labour pools, allowing team-style management employers to use extensive, multistep selection procedures to hire people with strong basic skills, problem-solving capacity, interpersonal skills, and the willingness to learn continually. Such favourable selection ratios as those enjoyed by Honda, Mazda, and other team-style employers may not be possible for all organizations in the future if unemployment declines in the mid-1990s and more employers pursue team-style management.

The extensive selection procedures, especially for team-based organizations, have increased reliance on both interviews and simulated work exercises. These methods have added complexity to the HRM function in two ways. First, these procedures are more complex and time-consuming than mere application forms and ability tests. Second, much of the selection process is conducted by supervisors and even operative employees. This devolution of the selection function means that HRM staff must train employees to do what the former have traditionally done. Additionally, they must ensure that the selection process is done in a consistent and equitable manner.

ORIENTATION

As labour markets tighten in the mid-1990s and the costs of turnover continue to increase, the role of orientation in the socialization process will continue to grow. By helping new employees to adapt rapidly to their new jobs and the organization, orientation contributes to the cost-control and efficiency goals of employers facing a highly competitive environment. Some progressive employers, such as the one described in Case 8.1, use lengthy orientation periods to be sure new hires fully understand and accept the organization's culture.

More and more organizations are moving toward participative cultures, emphasizing empowerment; they require a greater commitment from employees than many traditionally managed organizations. Strong orientation programs help to strengthen and clarify what is expected and may weed out those who can't fit the culture.

TRAINING AND DEVELOPMENT

Training and development are becoming essential to employers' human resource programs. With the impact of the new information technology, government, business, and educators must help workers acquire the flexibility necessary to adapt to rapid change. In the future, employees may have three, four, or more different careers during their working lives. Moreover, the length of the average working life may increase because of shortages of younger employees, higher desired incomes, improved health care, and an increase in part-time employment. Training methods will make increased use of computers, video recordings, and other electronic equipment, which allow people to learn at their own pace and without being at work. Employers may develop closer relations with colleges and universities for the provision of training programs, as the costs of training increase and as educational institutions face declining enrolments caused by the low birth rates of the past quarter-century.

Training and development will play a highly significant role in helping HRM professionals meet many of the ten challenges and issues discussed earlier. For example, well-designed training programs can help employees gain the knowledge and skills to be more efficient and enable both employees and managers to conduct fair appraisals of their peers and subordinates. As a part of the devolution of HRM, staff in progressive organizations must advise and train employees in the skills of training, appraising, and rewarding or disciplining their peers. Such training used to be reserved for supervisors and managers, but the growth of team-style management requires that it be more extensive. Such efforts reflect both the increasing complexity and the growing proactiveness of the HRM function. In short, training and development can and should contribute to strategic organizational goals, such as becoming a world-class competitor.

CAREER PLANNING

The economically turbulent 1980s and early 1990s were particularly damaging to traditional careers and, consequently, to some career planning activities. As even giant employers such as IBM downsized to remain competitive, many traditional career paths vanished along with job security. This situation has created enormous HRM challenges. How can employees be motivated when promotion opportunities are severely limited? What type of training and development activities will maximize job security for employees and still provide employers with flexible, highly trained workers? As discussed in Chapter 10, many social phenomena — dual-career couples, working single parents, and the effects of family–work conflicts — are also affecting work life and career decisions. Career planning is a good example of the growing complexity of the HR function and presents many examples of the efficiency and equity issues described at the beginning of this chapter.

Performance Appraisal

HRM staff have traditionally been responsible for developing and administering performance appraisal systems, which have long had to serve administrative, development, and assessment functions. Several factors lead us to believe that performance appraisals will become more vital than ever as the 1990s progress. First, as Quinn Mills of Harvard University argues, the measurement of performance is a crucial component of a competitive management strategy.[12] HRM staff must provide reliable, relevant, and innovative methods of measuring job performance. In the past, appraisal data were used primarily by management, but the growth of participative and empowerment programs have led to more self-appraisal and peer-appraisal systems.

Second, cutting-edge performance appraisal systems are required to meet several of the ten challenges discussed at the beginning of this chapter. For example, a well-designed appraisal system is necessary to attain both efficiency and fairness, and it facilitates meeting competitive pressures by helping in the measurement of costs and benefits of both organizational and HRM policies and practices. Additionally, the peer-review rating procedures found in many team-style organizations require the devolution of HRM and thus increase the need to train the work force.

Performance appraisal is an excellent example of how HRM can operate in a proactive manner. Rather than waiting for line management to request a new or modified appraisal system, HRM staff can suggest and advocate innovative approaches to appraisal that are consistent with organizational strategies.

Compensation

Since the mid-1970s, the compensation function has given HRM professionals one of their greatest challenges. At first, it came from sharp increases in inflation, which combined with low productivity growth to stretch the ability of many employers to provide cost-of-living adjustments. While average employees demanded pay increases that kept up with inflation, management sought to use pay to motivate and reward above-average performers. The conflict between these two goals has eased somewhat as the rate of inflation has declined. However, the introduction of pay equity legislation again brings the compensation function to the fore. Some of the organizations most affected are those with 500 or more employees. These organizations are the ones most likely to employ HRM professionals, who will be leading players in the implementation of pay equity.

Compensation issues are also central to many of the ten challenges set out at the beginning of the chapter. Efficiency versus fairness, cost consciousness, a proactive approach, training—all have implications for compensation. Fairness in compensation can affect overall compensation costs unless offset by productivity gains. Training can be encouraged if there are appropriate compensation rewards for successful attainment of higher levels of skill, as in the case of Shell Canada's chemical plant in Sarnia.

The issue of profit sharing is also one that has implications for HRM professionals. Martin Weitzman's book *The Share Economy*[13] has prompted debate over the extent to which firms should move away from fixed wages toward profit sharing. One of the major factors behind the split of the Canadian Auto Workers from the UAW was the refusal to accept in Canada the profit sharing that had been negotiated in the United States. A recent article by Katz and Meltz found that Canadian auto workers were better off without profit sharing.[14] However, this finding seems to go against the view that there should be more pay for performance. The debate will undoubtedly continue, and HRM professionals will be called on for advice.

BENEFITS

The major challenge in the benefits area will be a continuation of the rapid rise in costs. Employers will undoubtedly continue to seek ways of reducing costs, such as requiring employees to make contributions to programs such as supplementary health care and life insurance. It is also likely that employers will make greater use of benefits as a method of retaining valuable employees. This trend may result in increased efforts to use some types of benefits as job performance incentives. Employees are likely to place increased importance on leisure time, opportunities for education and development, and supplementary health care benefits.

HEALTH AND SAFETY

Illnesses and accidents are costly to individuals, employers, and the economy since they often cause a productive employee to become nonproductive and dependent. This fact, plus increasing government regulation in and union attention to the area, is encouraging employers to develop more and more extensive health and safety programs. Moreover, since the rate for accidents that are not work-related is higher than the work-related rate, wise employers may increasingly invest in programs to maintain the health and safety of workers off the job as well as on it.

LABOUR RELATIONS

Labour relations in Canada is facing several challenges in the 1990s. Economic forces are putting downward pressure on the extent of unionization as structural changes reduce the number and proportion of jobs in the highly unionized manufacturing sector. Not only is there pressure on union density, but increased international competition is forcing changes in the relationship between unions and management. To meet the competition, productivity has to be increased; one of the ways this can be done is through greater union–management co-operation.

Governments are fostering enhanced co-operation, both through changes in labour legislation and through the provision of funds to sectoral initiatives such as the adjustment and retraining program jointly run by the United Steelworkers of America and the steel industry.

Other issues in labour relations that will have HRM considerations include continuing interest in employment security and income security. If the rate of inflation remains low, and the rate of unemployment remains high, there will be less pressure for cost-of-living allowances and probably fewer strikes. The key will be the extent to which a positive labour–management environment can be created.

❑ ❑ ❑ ❑

SUMMARY

Human resource management has come of age. The strategic nature of HRM functions has been recognized in Canada as having a central role to play within organizations. There are, however, challenges ahead. Ten challenges facing human resource management were discussed in this chapter, along with implications for the specific human resource management functions that have been examined in this textbook.

By combining an understanding of the detailed aspects of HRM with an overview of how the functions fit together from a strategic management perspective, students of human resource management will ultimately be better able to enhance organizational effectiveness, while treating employees with fairness.

REVIEW QUESTIONS

1. Identify the three most important changes in the HRM function in the 1990s. Explain why you have singled these out of the ten discussed.

2. The text provides a brief explanation of why the human resource planning (HRP) function will likely be more concentrated at the executive level, rather than devolving to the staff, as is expected to be the case for most of the HR functions. Explain why HRP will move in a different direction.

3. Discuss why firms have underinvested in training in Canada even though it is acknowledged that training is important for the economy. What role can HR officials play in encouraging training, both within organizations and in society as a whole?

4. Discuss ways in which human resource managers can use the results of experiences in the specific HR functions to influence the overall strategic policies of organizations. Your answer should make use of the diagram that shows the interrelationships of the various human resource functions.

Project Ideas

1. There has been considerable discussion concerning the desirability and costs of pay equity. Organize a debate on this issue.

2. What are the particular problems of an HRM professional in an organization that sees cost advantages in increasing the proportion of its staff who work part-time, yet has little turnover and an aging work force? How might the HRM professional determine whether the perceived cost advantages of increasing the number of part-time staff would be offset by the negative impact on long-service workers? Share your thoughts with the class in a brief oral report.

3. Given the frequent regulatory and legislative changes in employment standards and human rights legislation, these areas seem to lend themselves to computerized record keeping. Discuss the subject with a human resource manager of a company (try to find one that operates in more than one province) or with the head of an HRM professional association in your area.

Notes

1. Peter F. Drucker, *The Effective Executive* (New York: Harper Colophon Books, 1985), p. 170.

2. Jack Barbash, "Equity as Function: Its Rise and Attribution," in Jack Barbash and Kate Barbash, eds., *Theories and Concepts in Comparative Industrial Relations* (Columbia, SC: University of South Carolina Press, 1989), pp. 114–22.

3. Noah M. Meltz, "Industrial Relations: Balancing Efficiency and Equity," in Barbash and Barbash, *Theories and Concepts in Comparative Industrial Relations*, pp. 109–13.

4. Anil Verma, "Restructuring in Industrial Relations and the Role for Labor," paper presented to the conference on Labor in a Global Economy, September 20–22, 1990, Portland, Or. (Toronto: Centre for Industrial Relations, University of Toronto, 1990).

5. Don Wells, *Soft Sell: Quality of Working Life Programs and the Productivity Race* (Ottawa: Canadian Centre for Policy Alternatives, 1986).

6. John C. Anderson, "The Strategic Management of Industrial Relations," in John C. Anderson, Morley Gunderson, and Allen Ponak, eds., *Union–Management Relations in Canada*, 2nd ed. (Don Mills: Ont.: Addison-Wesley, 1989), pp. 99–124.

7. Jane Coutts, "Plant Must Reopen, Board Tells Employer," *The Globe and Mail*, March 2, 1990.

8. P.P. Bendimadhu, *Human Resources Management: Charting a New Course* (Ottawa: The Conference Board of Canada, May 1989).

9. Noah M. Meltz, "The Evolution of Worker Training: The Canadian Experience," in Louis A. Ferman, Michel Hoyman, Joel Cutcher-Gershenfeld, and Ernest J. Savoie, eds., *New Developments in Worker Training: A Legacy for the 1990s* (Madison, Wisc.: Industrial Relations Research Association, 1990), p. 304.

10. Roy J. Adams, "Towards a More Competent Labour Force: A Training Levy Scheme for Canadians," *Relations Industrielles/Industrial Relations*, vol. 35, no. 3 (1980).

11. Canadian Labour Market and Productivity Centre, Task Force on Labour Force Development Strategy, *Report* (Ottawa: CLMPC, 1990).

12. D. Quinn Mills, "Planning with People in Mind," *Harvard Business Review*, vol. 63, no. 4 (1985), pp. 97–105.

13. Martin L. Weitzman, *The Share Economy* (Cambridge, Mass.: Harvard University Press, 1984). See also Christopher Beckman, "Will Profit Sharing Reduce Unemployment?" *Canadian Business Review*, Summer 1986, pp. 50–55.

14. Harry C. Katz and Noah M. Meltz, "Profit Sharing and Auto Workers' Earnings, The United States vs. Canada," *Relations Industrielles/Industrial Relations*, vol. 46, no. 3 (1991), pp. 515–30.

SUGGESTIONS FOR FURTHER READING

- W.F. Cascio. *Costing Human Resources: The Financial Impact of Behavior in Organizations*, 3rd ed. Boston: PWS-Kent, 1991.
- "Managing an Increasingly Diverse Workforce." A series of seven articles in the *Canadian Journal of Administrative Sciences*, vol. 8 (June 1991).
- J.W. Walker. *Human Resource Strategy*, 2nd ed. New York: McGraw-Hill, 1992.

video CASE

QUAD GRAPHICS, INC.

Harry Quadracci's day dreams about his career after law school probably didn't include a vision of himself on stage leading amateur performers in songs from *Pirates of Penzance*. He found himself performing as part of his role as the C.E.O. of Quad Graphics, the full-color printing company he started in 1970 when he quit his position as a labor negotiator for a large Wisconsin printing company owned by his father. The annual stage performance is an integral part of the company's spirited, team-oriented culture. Quad Graphics had grown to employ approximately 3 300 people and generated annual sales of one-half billion dollars. Its clients included *Newsweek*, *Time*, *U.S. News & World Report*, *Playboy*, *Lillian Vernon*, and *James River Traders*.

Quadracci had always resisted hard-nosed, antilabor management tactics. In starting his own firm, he was anxious to employ an entirely new strategy for human resource management.

He built his organization based firmly on trust. The book *The 100 Best Companies to Work for in America* (Signet 1987) honors Quad Graphics, highlighting the ways it implements trust to form the backbone of its culture:

- Trust in teamwork. Employees trust that together they will accomplish more than they would individually.

- Trust in responsibility. Employers trust that each worker will carry his/her fair share of the load.

- Trust in productivity. Customers trust that Quad Graphics' work will represent the most competitive levels of pricing, quality, and innovation available.

- Trust in management. Shareholders, customers, and employees trust that the company will make decisive judgments for long-term success rather than focusing only on short-term goals like today's profit.

- Trust in Thinking Small. Quad Graphics people all trust in each other: they regard each other as persons of equal value; they respect the dignity of individuals by recognizing individual accomplishments, as well as the feelings and needs of individuals and their families; they all share the same goals and purposes in life.

These principles illustrate that, at Quad Graphics, trust is more than an empty promise.

Quad Graphics has far fewer rules and regulations than most companies of its size, and that's no accident. It's the way the founder likes to run the show. Quadracci calls his personal and direct style of management, expressly avoiding formalized rules and regulations, "Theory Q." As opposed to the traditional American top-down "Theory X" style or the Japanese participatory "Theory Z," Quadracci maintains the attitude that communications should be personal, vocal, and spontaneous, and that one should avoid the shelter of more formal, traditional limits such as job descriptions, time clocks, policies, and procedures.

Quadracci works to ensure that employees are happy and satisfied in their work, and also that they are challenged. Most of Quad's employees have completed high school educations at most. Quadracci believes that the key to corporate growth is these individuals' growth via ongoing training and development. The burden of this training and development falls mostly on peers. Employees train one another.

Each week nearly 1 000 people complete the various training courses Quad Graphics sponsors in a remodeled former elementary school building. With the exception of new recruits, who are paid to attend what amounts to basic training, the vast majority attend classes on their own time. Graduates of previous Quad classes teach their peers.

After completing basic training, part of an employee's job is to begin learning other jobs. This way all employees can contribute to improving the firm's management and productivity. This sense of shared purpose driven by individual responsibility nurtures a vital, creative work environment. Passing knowledge among fellow workers makes everyone's job easier and stimulates employees' growth in new directions. As many decisions are made on the plant floor as possible in the belief that the best ideas come from the people doing the work.

Each division operates as a separate company. Most divisions hire their own workers to suit their own needs, and most newly hired employees are referred by current employees. In 1984, the in-house newspaper reported that 39.5 percent of all employees were somehow related to other employees. This was called the "ouchi rating," taken from a Japanese term that translates roughly as "part of the family." At the time of the in-house article, the median age of Quad Graphics employees was 27 years old.

The sharing of authority that brings decision making to the ground floor of the organization attracts and holds these employees, as do the foundation of trust and the focus on education. A number of other conditions keep employment at Quad Graphics attractive. For one, employees own approximately 40 percent of the company. They share in its profits via a plan that links take-home pay to efficiency.

Quad Graphics' unusual shift schedule is attractive, as well. Each employee works three 12-hour shifts a week and every other Sunday (at double salary). This amounts to pay for 48 hours per week while working 42 hours.

The culture of equality among peers also helps individuals flourish. Plant managers wear the same uniforms everyone else does. Every employee gets a clean, dark blue uniform daily.

The company welcomes individual advice and input, encouraging employees to "get big by thinking small." Quad employees have developed improvements in production equipment and generated new business ideas, as well. Employees have even initiated entire new operating units like ink manufacturing, equipment repair, and Quad Tech, a high-tech division that develops new printing technologies for sale to other printers.

The company allows all managers to use its 57th Street apartment in Manhattan for visits to New York City. The company even picks up the air fare for two. This exposes young managers from Wisconsin to the home turf and daily operations of most of their clients.

Harry Quadracci pays close attention to the physical environment of the company, believing that it can be an important tool to promote employee creativity and voluntarism. These attitudes can deteriorate when employees run machines that run machines. Most Quad Graphics employees monitor computers that take over many of the mechanical tasks once performed by people. To combat [the] boredom this separation from the work might cause and to promote a joyful work place, a popcorn machine on the shop floor is available to anyone at any time. Overhead pipes and machines throughout the factory are painted in a rainbow of colors.

The company supports workers' interests outside the narrow limits of their jobs, as well. Employees have set up child-care facilities and food service facilities at Quad. They built up physical fitness programs that encourage teamwork and comradeship along with better health. Also, Quad pays employees $30 to attend a seminar to help them quit smoking. Those who quit for a year receive a bonus of $200.

A symbol of the firm's convivial team atmosphere, the stage show led by Quadracci has become a traditional part of the annual Christmas party. All managers participate, and the performers rehearse on their own time. The affairs have centered on a number of themes. In 1984, the party took the form of a sit-down dinner for 2200 employees and their guests at the firm's new Sussex, Wisconsin, plant. The show that year followed a circus parade theme, with all managers dressed as clowns and Quadracci, dressed as a ringmaster, riding in on an elephant.

Quad Graphics' state-of-the-art printing plants, phenomenal growth, and unique philosophy of management promote employees' sense of shared purpose. Besides churning out the product, technology helps the firm create a better, happier, more satisfying work environment for its workers. This combination of personal vision and technical development has made Quad Graphics a very successful company, and one employees like to work for.

Source: Excerpt from *Organizational Behavior*, Second Edition, by Robert P. Vecchio, copyright © 1991 by The Dryden Press. Reprinted with the permission of the publisher.

Discussion Questions

1. What is Quadracci's opinion regarding the selection of appropriate communication factors? Does he favour any particular communication factor over others? Why?

2. Quad Graphics scores high on employee job satisfaction. What are the benefits of this condition?

3. To what factors do you attribute the high degree of job satisfaction at the company?

INDEX

Abella Commission, 26
Ability, 56–57
Absenteeism, 16–17, 67–70
 controlling (example), 71–72
 job satisfaction and, 65
 QWL programs and, 70
 rewards and, 70
 turnover and, 73–74
Accidents (workplace), 659, *see also* Employee health and safety
Act Respecting Employment Equity, *see* Bill C-62
Advertising, recruitment method, 253–56
Affirmative action, 767
 defined, 108
 as reverse discrimination, 102, 109
 women and, 109
AFL, *see* American Federation of Labour
Age
 discrimination, 91, 99
 labour force participation and, 48
Agency shop agreements, 725
AIB, *see* Anti-inflation Board
AIDS testing, 320, 698–99
 workplace policy (example), 702–703
Alberta Children's Hospital, 462
Alcoholism, 693–94
Allen, John, 279
Alternative ranking, 493
American Business Conference, 60
American Federation of Labour (AFL), 722
Anchors, 489
Annual vacation with pay, 117
Anticipatory socialization, 351
Anti-inflation Board (AIB), 747
Appraisal interviews, *see* Performance appraisal interviews
Apprenticeship training, 408
Assessment centre, 322
AT&T, 140
Attitude change, 409–411

Attitude surveys, job satisfaction, 66
Attraction process, *see* Recruiting
Attribution theory, performance appraisal, 512
Auberge, Jacques, 83
Audits, of wages and hours, 582–83
Automaticity, 395
Average wage rate, 553

Baby boom, 74
Baby boomers
 baby bust and, 53
 labour force participation and, 48, 74
Background/reference checks, 318
Bargaining, *see* Collective bargaining
Bargaining unit, 734–35
BARS, *see* Behaviourally anchored rating scales (BARS)
Base rate, 286–87
 managerial jobs, 321
Basic rate of success (selection), 286
BC Hydro, 388
B.C. Tel, effective driver safety program, 680–81
Behavioural career paths, 450, 451
Behavioural checklist, 496–97
Behaviourally anchored rating scales (BARS), 499–502
Behaviour description interview, 308
Behaviour modelling, 410
Behaviour potential, 391
Bell Canada, 525–27, 690
Benefits, 14, 784
 cafeteria, 640–45
 in Canada vs. U.S., 640
 company image and, 619
 costs, 614–15, 618–619, 645
 disability, 623–24
 discretionary services, 623
 economy of scale and, 619

employee assistance programs, 639
employee services, 623, 639
flex plans, 640
growth of, 614–615
guaranteed income supplement (GIS), 625–26
holiday and vacation pay, 637–39
labour relations and, 621
mandatory, 623, 627–32
medical expenses, 624
as motivator, 616, 617–18
old age security, 624–25
organizational effectiveness, 616–19
orientation and, 621
part-time work and, 51
pay for time not worked, 623
perquisites, 639
provincial hospital/medical insurance plans, 626–27
relation to other HRM functions, 619–21
specialists and, 621
stock options, 639
superannuation, 623
unemployment, 624
unemployment insurance, 629–31
universal benefits, 623, 625
untimely death, 623
women and, 645–46
workers' compensation, 629
Berghoff's Department Store, 523–25
BIB, *see* Biographical inventory blank (BIB)
Bidding, 251–52
Bill C-62, 52
Biographical inventory blank (BIB), 300, 301
Bona fide qualifications, 99
Brandt, Gord, 121
Brief job analysis method, 210
Brooks v. Canada Safeway, 631
Burlingham, Garth, 234
Business climate, effect of on HRM, 22
Business games, 412

CAD/CAM systems, 34–35
Cafeteria benefits, 640–45, *see also* Benefits
CAI, *see* Computer-assisted instruction (CAI)
Cameron, Roger, 368
CAMI Automotive Inc., 735–37
Canada at the Crossroads, 28–29
Canada Employment Centres (CECs), 260–61, 413
Canada Health Act, 626
Canada Life, 700–702
Canada Pension Plan, 623, 627–29
Canada–U.S. Free Trade Agreement, 3, 22
  effect on branch plants, 5
Canadian Association of Pension Supervisory Authorities (CAPSA), 632
Canadian Auto Workers (CAW), 596, 621, 736–37, 748
  guidelines on reorganization of work, 750–51
Canadian Classification and Dictionary of Occupations (CCDO), 146, 162, 186, 196
  example description, 197
  FJA method used by, 201
Canadian Employment and Immigration Commission (CEIC)
  aids for career planning, 454–55
Canadian Federation of Labour (CFL), 723
Canadian General-Tower Ltd., 641
Canadian Imperial Bank of Commerce (CIBC), 477–78
Canadian Institute of Stress, 686
Canadian Labour Congress (CLC), 723, 727
Canadian National Rail (CN), 110
Canadian Occupational Projection System (COPS), 18, 162
Canadian Steel Trade and Employment Congress (CSTEC), 23
Canadian Tire Corp., 643–44
Canadian Union of Public Employees (CUPE), 716, 726

CanTech Electronics, 344–46
Career anchors, 442–43
Career blockage, 437
Career counselling, 452
Career drift, 445
Career Options, 259
Career paths, 442
  behavioural, 450, 451
  traditional, 450, 451
Career planning, 13, 782–83
  CEIC aids for, 454
  CHOICES, 454
  dual careers, 463
  employment development, 442
  in human resource planning, 138, 441
  human resource policy and, 460
  in-placement, 436
  job analysis and, 192–93, 441–42
  Job Futures, 454–55
  management by objectives (MBO) programs, 459
  mentoring, 461
  monitoring information, 384
  organizational entry, 455
  organizational structure and procedures, 459–60
  outplacement, 437
  performance appraisal and, 440–41
  programs, 452
  QWL programs, 438
  reasons for, 436–37
  relation to HRM functions, 440–42
  satisfaction in work, 438–40
  Schein's career anchors, 442–43
  stages, 443–44
  supervisor as agent in, 457–58
  target position, 442
  women and, 437, 439
Career Planning Annual, 439–40
Career planning programs, *see also* Career planning
  career information, 448–51
  individual assessments, 445–46
  organizational assessments, 446–48

Case method, 411
Cash-value insurance, 636
CAW, *see* Canadian Auto Workers (CAW)
CCDO, *see Canadian Classification and Dictionary of Occupations (CCDO)*
CECs, *see* Canada Employment Centres
Certification (unions), 734
Certified Human Resources Professional (CHRP), 6, 21, 773
CFL, *see* Canadian Federation of Labour (CFL)
Charter of Rights and Freedoms, 94
CHOICES, 454–55
Chouinard, Yvon, 338–39
CHRP, *see* Certified Human Resources Professional (CHRP)
CIO, *see* Congress of Industrial Organizations (CIO)
C-JAM, *see* Combination job analysis method (C–JAM)
Classification method, 557
CLC, *see* Canadian Labour Congress (CLC)
Closed shop agreements, 725
CNTU, *see* Confederation of National Trade Unions
Coaching, 408–409
Cognitive ability tests, 311–12
Collective agreements, 710
Collective bargaining, 711, *see also* Grievances; Labour relations; Unions
  compulsory conciliation, 742
  impasses and resolutions, 741–43
  interest arbitration, 742
  mediation, 742
  open period, 746
  process, 740–41
Collective Bargaining Information Sources, 551
Combination job analysis method (C-JAM)
Communications Workers of America (CWA), 757
Company pay systems, 577–80
Comparable worth, 114

Index

Compa-ratio index, 582
Comparison employee, 59
Compensation, 7, 13–14, 783–84, *see also* Job evaluation; Pay surveys
  cost-savings plans, 578
  defined, 539
  direct and indirect, 539
  employment standards, 545–46
  equal pay and, 545
  gain-sharing plans, 577
  in human resource planning, 138
  human rights legislation, 545–46
  incentive pay system, 570, 574–80
  income tax laws and, 546
  job analysis and, 193
  job- vs. skill-based systems, 542, 547
  laws affecting, 545–46
  merit pay, 570, 572–74
  organizational effectiveness and, 539–42
  pay for performance, 570–72
  plant-wide or company pay systems, 577–80
  pricing the pay structure, 564–69
  profit-sharing plans, 577
  promotions, 570
  relation to other HRM functions, 542–45
  responsibilities, 542
  skill-based pay, 596–97
  wages and salaries, 539
Compensation costs
  audits of wages and hours, 582–83
  budget allocations, 580–81
  budgets for managers, 582
  compa-ratio index, 582
  compression, 581
Competition, 28–29
Compression, 581
Compulsory conciliation, 742
Computer-assisted instruction (CAI), 404–405
Computers
  recruiting and, 263–64
  use of in human resource management, 18

Computer simulation, 155, 169
Conference Board of Canada, 2
Conference/discussion method, 409
Confirmatory processes, 306
Congress of Industrial Organizations (CIO), 716
Constitution Act, 94
Continuous reinforcement schedule, 392–93
Contracts, 297
Construct validity, 297–98
Contamination, 485, 487
Content validity, 298, 485
Contingency-based rewards, 64
Co-op programs, 259
COPS, *see* Canadian Occupational Projection System (COPS)
Corning, Inc., 361–62
  career planning program, 453–54
  performance appraisal system, 506–509
Correlation coefficients, 291–92
Cost-savings plans, 577
Craft unions, 726
Criterion measures, 290
Criterion-referenced approach (training), 399
Criterion-related validity, 295–97
Critical incidence technique (job analysis), 199–200
Crosby quality program, 378
Cross-cultural training, 476
Crutchfield, Sally, 83
CSTEC, *see* Canadian Steel Trade and Employment Congress (CSTEC)
Cummins ReCon, 399
CUPE, *see* Canadian Union of Public Employees (CUPE)
CWA, *see* Communications Workers of America (CWA)

DAP, *see* Developmental action program (DAP)
Decision making (teaching), 391, 411–13
  business games, 412–13
  case method, 411
  in-basket technique, 412
  internship/job rotation, 413

Deferred profit sharing, 637
Deficient measures (validity), 485
Defined-benefit plans, 632
Defined-contribution plans, 632
Delayering, 133
Deli-Delite Industries, 424–28
Delphi method, 153–54
Deming, W. Edwards, 377–78
Demographics, 40
Demotion, 146
Developmental action program (DAP), 513
Development strategy, 10
Differential validity, 316
Digital Computer, 498–99
Dipboye, Robert, 306–307
Direct compensation, 539
Direct observation (job analysis), 196–99
Disability
  costs, 659
  group insurance, 636–37
  total vs. partial, 623–24
Disciplinary sanctions (worker behaviour), 67, 68, 69
Disconfirmatory processes, 306
Discouraged workers, 44
Discretionary benefits, 623
  group insurance programs, 634–37
  private pension plans, 632–34
Discrimination, 91–92, 767, *see also* Human rights legislation
  Abella Commission (1984), 52
  affirmative action, 102
  age, 91, 99
  indirect, 96
  by job recruitment agencies, 98
  O'Malley decision, 96–97
  performance appraisal data and, 521
  private employment agencies, 262
  prohibited grounds of, 100
  in recruitment, 254
  reverse, 102, 109
  sexual harassment, 97–98
  systematic, 96
  in workplace, 96
Distributed practice, 395
Dominion Stores, 646–47

Downsizing, 5
Downward transfer, 460
DPT, 201
Drexis Inc., 617
Drucker, Peter, 133
Drug use/drug testing, 694–97
Dual-career couples, 460
Dual-career family, 464
Dual careers, 463
Dual-earner families, 463
Duke, John, 721–22
Dunnette, M.D., 211–12
Duties, 188

EAPs, see Employee assistance programs (EAPs)
Education, quality of in Canada, 25
EEO, see Equal Employment Opportunity (EEO)
Effort, 58–61
　expectancy theory and, 60–61
　motivation and, 58–59
　value of rewards and, 60
Effort → performance relationship, 61
Element, 189
Employee
　Canadian vs. American, 80–83
　consultation, 774
　decision-making, 133
　gold collar, 240
　older age, 74–78
　participation in work design, 133
Employee Achievement Measure, The, (CIBC), 478
Employee assistance programs (EAPs), 639, 686, 694, see also Employee health and safety
Employee behaviour, see Work behaviour
Employee benefits, see Benefits
Employee-determined changes (validity), 212
Employee development, 479
　performance appraisal and, 496–506
Employee empowerment, 751
Employee health and safety, 784, see also Ontario Occupational Health and Safety Act (OHSA)

access to health and safety information, 673–74
accident, 659
AIDS, 698–99, 702–703
alcoholism, 693–94
controlling physical hazards, 677–79
drug testing, 694–97
drug use, 694–97
employee assistance programs (EAPs), 686, 687
health and safety committees, 679
Interlock program (BC), 688–89
job analysis and, 193
job stress, 686–90, 691
Ontario Occupational Health and Safety Act, 666–72
organizational benefits of, 658–60
performance records, 682
promoting health awareness, 684–86
promoting safety awareness, 679
recognition and awards programs, 682
relation to other HRM functions, 660–65
responsibilities for, 665–66
rules and regulations, 682–83
safety training programs, 683–84
smoking, 693
Employee records, 15
Employee referral, 252–53
Employee relations, 711
　transition to labour relations, 729
Employee service benefits, 623, 639
Employment Earnings and Hours, 41
Employment equity, 23
　Bill C-62, 52
　at Canadian National Rail (CN), 110
　defined, 108
　effect of on recruiting, 244
　Federal Contractors Program, 52
　Legislated Employment Equity Program, 52

Employment Equity Act, 96
　human resource information systems and, 143
　purpose of, 109
Employment growth, projected in Canada, 53–54
Employment interviews, 304–311
　behaviour description interview, 308
　confirmatory/disconfirmatory processes, 306
　factors affecting, 306
　human rights concerns, 310
　improving, 307–308
　interviewer in, 307–308
　plan for, 309
　reliability of, 305
　role of, 311
　validity, 305
Employment legislation, 91–92
　provincial, 93
Employment/population ratio, 43
Employment standards legislation, 5, 23, 95
　annual vacation with pay, 117
　compensation and, 545–46
　equal pay for men and women, 114–15
　holidays, 117
　hours of work, 115–16
　minimum age for employment, 113
　minimum wage rates, 113–14
　parental leave, 118
　recovery of unpaid wages, 119
　statutory school-leaving age, 112–13
　termination of employment, 117–18
　weekly rest days, 116
Employment termination, 92, 117–18
Engler, Jim, 215–16
Entry-level jobs, 146
E → P relationship, see Effort → performance relationship
Equal employment opportunity (EEO), 108–109
Equal pay for equal work, 114
Equal pay for work of equal value, 114

vs. pay equity, 583
Equity, internal vs. external, 538–39
Equity theory, 59
  job evaluation and, 554
Error of central tendency, 485
Essay method, 489
Essex Engine, 39–40
Executive jobs, 20
Executive search firms, 262–63
Expectancy tables, 294
Expectancy theory, 60–61
  in businesses and schools, 60
Expert systems, and job analysis, 195
External equity, 554
  defined, 538–39
Extrinsic rewards, 63–64, *see also* Rewards

Face validity, 313
Factor comparison method, 558–60
Fallback position, 460
False negative error, 288, 289
False positive error, 288, 289
Federal Contractors Program, 52
Feedback, 64
  defined, 391–92
Fertility rates, 74, 75
Field review, 495–96
Films and videotapes (training aids), 404
FJA, *see* Functional job analysis (FJA)
Flex plans, 640, 641
Floating holidays, 638
Flyer Industries, 329–30
Forced distribution, 494
Ford Motor Company, 39–40
  Employee Involvement program of, 70
Forecasts (human resource needs), 149, *see also* Human resource needs (forecasting)
  approaches to, 149–56
  Stone and Fiorito models, 156
  use of in organizations, 156
Franklin, Robert, 651
Free trade, 3
Friedland, Martin, 634
Functional job analysis (FJA), 201–204, 556

Gain sharing rewards, 64, 577
Gamma Heavy Machinery Company, 34–35
GATB, *see* General aptitude test battery (GATB)
GED, *see* General educational development (GED) scale
General aptitude test battery (GATB), 311, 312
General educational development (GED) scale, 201
Goal programming, 168
Goal setting, 61, 62
Gold collar employees, 240
Gompers, Samuel, 722
Government legislation, *see also* Employment standards legislation; Human rights legislation
  and HRM, 23–25, 92
Graduate Workforce Professionals, 259
Graphic rating scales, 489–90
Gray, Cynthia, 83
Grievance, 711
Grievance procedure, 743–46, *see also* Collective bargaining; Labour relations; Unions
  rights arbitration and, 745
  voice system, 746
Group insurance programs
  deferred profit sharing, 637
  disability insurance, 636–37
  health insurance, 637
  life insurance, 636
Guaranteed monthly income supplement (GIS), 625–26
Gulf Canada Resources Ltd., 453

Halo effect, 485
Headhunters, 262
Health and safety, 14, *see also* Employee health and safety
  promoting awareness of, 679, 684–86
  types of programs for promoting, 685
Health insurance, 631–32, *see also* Benefits
  costs, 614–15, 618–19, 645, 659
  group, 637

Holiday pay, 638
Holidays, 117
Holstein, Leah, 613
Horizontal percent method, 299
How to Do Pay Equity Job Comparisons, 590
HRIS, *see* Human resource information system (HRIS)
HRM audit, 170–72
  benefits, 172
  levels, 170
  reasons for performing, 170
HRP, *see* Human resource planning (HRP)
HRPAO, *see* Human Resources Professionals Association of Ontario (HRPAO)
Human resource flows
  analysis of, 146
  stochastic models, 147–48
  transition matrix, 147
Human resource information system (HRIS), 143
  employment equity and, 143
  recruiting and, 252
  skills inventories and, 146
  typical data for, 145
Human resource management (HRM)
  areas of responsibility in, 6
  avoiding liability for workplace harassment, 101–102
  business climate and, 22
  complexity of functions, 777
  computers and, 18
  consultative role of, 17
  context of change affecting, 22–27
  cost consciousness and, 777–78
  departments, 16–17
  devolution of functions of, 778
  education and experience requirements in, 20–21
  efficiency and fairness, 773–74
  growth of profession, 17–18, 19
  historical development of, 4–6
  impact of technology on, 23
  issues confronting in next five years, 30

labour force changes and, 25–27
legislation and, 23–24, 91–92
nature of jobs in, 18–20
in private organizations, 3
proactive function of, 4, 778
as profession, 772–73
professionalization of, 6
professional organizations, 21–22
in public organizations, 3
responsibilities, 16–17
role of, 8
specialization in, 18–19
strategic function of, 3, 772
women and, 47
workforce training and, 779
unions and, 4
Human resource managers, 3–4
Human resource needs (forecasting)
bottom-up approach, 152
computer simulation, 155
delphi method, 153–54
management succession planning, 151
multiple regression equation, 152
planning for status quo, 149–51
predictor variables, 152
rules of thumb, 151–52
scenarios, 154–55
unit forecasting, 152–53
Human resource planning (HRP), 10, *see also* Human resource needs (forecasting)
defined, 134
delayering, 133
development strategy, 10
evaluating effectiveness of, 169–70
examining alternatives, 136–37
forecasting future needs, 149–56
hiring outside organization, 161–63
job analysis and, 189–90
national labour projections and, 162
organizational effectiveness, 136
process of, 141–43

projections of supply and demand, 141, 143–48, 156–58
purposes of, 135–37
recruiting, 138, 139
relation to other HRM functions, 137–39
reshaping the workplace, 133
revitalization, 133
setting goals and objectives, 136
shortages, 160
staffing strategy, 10
strategic human resource analysis, 137, 138
succession planning, 134
unemployment rate and, 40, 41
utilizing present employees, 160
Human Resource Revolution: Communicate or Litigate, 26
Human resources
business plans and, 150
forecasting future needs, 149
maintenance of, 7
Human Resources Professionals Association of Ontario (HRPAO), 6, 21–22, 773
act respecting, 21
objectives of, 21
Human resource supply
assessing, 143
forms for projecting, 144
Markov analysis, 148
projecting using human resource flows, 147–48
Human rights, 95
Human Rights Act, 96
Human rights commissions, 107–108
Human rights legislation, 766–67
bona fide qualifications, 99
codes, 98–102
compensation and, 545–46
discrimination, 96
employment interviews and, 310
enforcement, 107–108
jurisdictions, 98–102
purpose of, 96
reasonable cause clauses, 99

sexual harassment, 97–98
Human rights policies, 5
Hylck, Jean, 83

IBM, human resource planning at, 134
IDI Act, *see* Industrial Disputes Investigation (IDI) Act
Imperial Oil, drug testing at, 696–97
In-basket technique, 412
Incentive pay system, 570
group-level, 576
individual-level, 574–75
plant-wide or company, 577–80
Inco Ltd., 650–51
Income tax laws, 546
Indirect comparison method, pay equity, 593
Indirect compensation, 539
Indirect discrimination, 96
Individual assessments, 445–46
Industrial Disputes Investigation (IDI) Act, 712–13, 714
Industrial Relations and Disputes Investigation (IRDI) Act, 714
Industrial unions, 726
Information acquisition, 390
Information Systems for Employment Equity: An Employer Guide, 112
In-house training programs, 388
Inkester, Norman, 249
Inmont Canada, 751
In-placement, 436
Insurance, *see also* Benefits
cash value, 636
disability, 636–37
group programs, 634–37
health, 637
life, 636
term, 636
Interactive videodisk instruction (IVI), 405
Interest arbitration, 742
Interest inventories, 315–16
Inter-individual differences, 57
Intermittent reinforcement schedule, 393
Internal equity, 554
defined, 539
Internalization, 64

International unions, 726
Internship, 413
Interpersonal skills, 390
  behaviour modelling, 410
  conference/discussion method, 409
  role play, 409–410
  T-group (sensitivity) method, 411
Interviews, *see* Employment interviews
Interview techniques (job analysis), 200
Intra-individual differences, 57
Intrinsic rewards, 63–64, *see also* Rewards
Involuntary part–time work, 51
Involuntary turnover, 70
Ipsco Inc., 579
IRDI, *see* Industrial Relations and Disputes Investigation (IRDI) Act
ISECO Safety Shoes, 540–41
IVI, *see* Interactive videodisk instruction (IVI)

JCI, *see* Job component inventory (JCI)
JDI, *see* Job Description Index (JDI)
Job
  career planning and, 456–57
  defined, 186
  duties, 188–89
  element, 189
  entry-level, 146
  vs. position, 186–87
  tasks, 189
Job analysis, 12, 62–63
  career planning and, 192–93
  compensation and, 193
  as constraint, 213
  defined, 185
  employee health and safety, 193
  expert systems and, 195
  in human resource planning, 138, 189–90
  methods of, *see* Job analysis methods
  orientation and, 191–92
  performance appraisal and, 192
  recruiting and, 191
  relation to other HRM functions, 189–94
  responsibility for, 194–96
  selection and, 191
  team organization and, 213
  training and development and, 192
  unions and, 193–94
Job analysis methods
  brief job analysis method, 210
  combined observation/interview approaches, 201–210
  comparison of, 198
  critical incident technique, 199–200
  DPT rating, 201
  employee-determined changes (validity), 212
  environmental conditions, 202
  functional job analysis (FJA), 201–204
  GED scales, 201
  human judgement and, 212
  interview techniques, 200
  JCI, 209–210
  job inventories or checklists, 206, 207
  multi-method job design questionnaire, 210
  observation, 196–200
  physical activities, 202
  position analysis questionnaire (PAQ), 206–209
  questionnaires, 205–210
  reliability, 210, 211
  situation-determined changes (validity), 212
  SVP rating, 201
  technical conferences, 200
  time-determined changes (validity), 211–12
  validity, 210, 211–13
  VERJAS method, 204, 209
  work methods analysis, 199
Job analyst, 196
Job-based systems (compensation), 542
Job component inventory (JCI), 209–210
Job description, 185, 186, 194
  example of, 188, 197
Job Description Index (JDI), 66
Job evaluation
  factor comparison, 558–60
  functional job analysis (FJA), 555
  level description method, 557–58
  market pricing method, 563–64
  methods, 555, 557–64
  point method, 560–63
  policy-capturing method, 564
  position analysis questionnaire (PAQ), 555
  ranking, 557
Job Futures: An Occupational Outlook to 1995, 454
Job grades, 557
Job information, 226
Job information statement, 226
Job instruction training, 407
Job performance and satisfaction, 55–66
  Porter and Lawler's model, 56
Job result indices, 487–89
Job rotation, 413
  career planning and, 457
  job progression and, 457
Job safety analysis training guide, form, 663, 664
Job-sample tests, 298, 312–13
Job satisfaction, 55–56, 65–66
  absenteeism and, 65
  career planning and, 438–40
  compensation and, 554
  equity theory and, 554
  Job Description Index and, 66
  measuring, 66
  unionization and, 729, 730
  voluntary turnover and, 65
  women and, 439
Job-simulation exercises, 313
Job skills inventory, 146
Job specification, *see* Job analysis
Job stress, 686–90, 691
Job tryouts, 281, 320–21
Jobs
  key, 546
  types of in HRM, 18–19
Job task inventory (JTI), 216
Joint action committees, 748

Kanter, Rosabeth Moss, 436
Key jobs, compensation, 546
King, Lyon Mackenzie, 712
Kuder preference record, 315

Labatt Breweries of Canada, 31–33
Labour
 national projections and HRP, 162
 shortage and surplus, 134–35, 156–64
Labour force, 42
 age of employees, 25–26, 74–76
 baby boomers and, 48
 changes in, 25–27, 376
 data, 45–55
 democratization of, 26
 education of, 25
 participation rates, 45–48, 50
 part-time workers, 50–52
 provincial differences, 49–50
 secondary, 246–47
 terminology, 43–45
 trends and characteristics of, 45–48
 union shares of nonfarm, 715
 women in, 26
Labour force statistics, 40
 Native people and, 52
Labour Force, The, 41, 42
Labour law jurisdictions, 93–94
Labour market
 effect of on recruiting, 244–47
 tight vs. loose, 245
Labour relations, 14–15, 785, *see also* Unions
 contract negotiations, 721
 defined, 711
 employee empowerment, 751
 employee relations and, 728
 free-market period, 712
 growth of organized labour, 714–17
 Industrial Disputes Investigation (IDI) Act, 712–13, 714
 joint action committees, 748
 lockouts, 741
 management rights, 720–21
 organizational effectiveness and, 717
 PC 1003, 714
 preventive mediation, 748
 Public Service Staff Relations Act (1967), 714
 quality of working life (QWL) programs, 747, 748–50

relationships by objectives (RBO) programs, 748
 relation to other HRM functions, 718–20
 responsibilities for, 720–22
 sectoral labour-management co-operation, 753–54
 self-directed work teams, 753
 strikes, 741
 Wagner Act, 713
Labour Research Resource Manual, 41
Labour shortage, 134–35, 156–64, 166, 167
Labour standards legislation, *see* Employment standards legislation
Labour surplus
 cost-saving measures, 165–66
 permanent reductions, 164–65
 planning for, 164–66
 redistribution of workers, 165
Labour unions, *see* Unions
Language tests, 314
Law of Effect, 392
Learning
 defined, 391
 positive vs. negative, 396
 transfer of, 396–98
Lectures, 401
Legislated Employment Equity Program, 52
Leniency, 485
Levac Supply Limited, 101
Level description method, job evaluation, 557–58
Levi Strauss & Co. (Canada) Inc., 759–60
Liang, Tim, 643
Life insurance, group, 636
Linear programming, 168
Line managers, 16
Living case method (General Electric), 411
Local unions, *see also* Unions
 defined, 723
 directly chartered, 725
 independent, 725
 types of, 723–24
Lockouts, 741
Lump-sum pay, 596

McCormack and Dodge, 455
MacNairn, Jean, 123–24

Mager, R.F., 385, 386
Maintenance, 7
Maintenance action program (MAP), 513
Management by objectives (MBO) programs, 459
 employee development appraisals and, 502–505
Management responses to unionization, 735–40
Management rights, 720–21
Management succession planning, 153
Managers
 attitudes of employees toward, 11
 budgets for, 582
 line, 16
 selecting, 321–22
 self-perception of, 11
Mandatory benefits, 623, 627–32
Mandatory retirement, 75, 94
Manufacturing growth projections, 63
MAP, *see* Maintenance action program (MAP)
Market pricing method, job evaluation, 563–64
Markov analysis, 148
Massed practice, 395
Maternity leave, 118
Maxwell, Ted, 435
Mechanical comprehension test, 312
Mediation, 742
Men, labour force participation rates, 48
Mental Health and the Workplace Program, 685
Mental Measurements Yearbook, 316
Mentoring, 461
Merit pay, 570, 572–74
Micro-motion analysis, 189
Midlife transition training, 460
Midpoint, 568
Miner sentence completion scale, 314
Minimum age for employment, 113
Minimum qualification hiring procedures, 287
Minimum wage rates, 113–14

Minnesota Mining and
  Manufacturing Company
  (3M), 496–97
Minorities, 767
  Native peoples, 52
  recruiting, 244, 248, 249
  training and development and,
    377
  visible, 52
Minors (employment), 92
Mixed standard scales, 490–92
Mixed wage policy, 567
Moonlighters, 246, 247
Morgan Stanley & Co., Inc., 352
Motivation, 58–59
  intrinsic vs. extrinsic, 396
  training programs and, 396
Motor skills, 390
  apprenticeship training, 408
  coaching, 408–409
  job instruction training, 407
  vestibule training, 407–408
  video systems, 409
Muldridge, Harold, 184, 185
Multi-method job design
  questionnaire, 210
Multiple regression equation,
  152

NASA, see National Aeronautics
  and Space Administration
National Aeronautics and Space
  Administration (NASA), 458
National Grocers Co. Ltd.,
  employment equity
  program, 111, 121–22
National Labour Relations Act,
  713
National Union of Provincial
  Government Employees
  (NUPGE), 716, 726
National unions, 726
Native peoples (labour force
  statistics), 52
NDP, see New Democratic Party
Negative learning, 397
Network flow analysis, 148
Neutral learning, 397
New Democratic Party (NDP),
  723
New Faces in the Crowd, 41
Noma Industries, 133
Noranda Inc., 641–42
Northern Telecom, 428–30, 756

NovAtel Communications, 234
  recruiting and, 271–73
NUPGE, see National Union of
  Provincial Government
  Employees (NUPGE)

Observation methods, see Job
  analysis methods
Occupational analyst, 196
Occupational health and safety,
  23
Occupational qualification
  requirements for
  occupational analyst,
  202–203
Old Age Security Plan, 625
O'Malley decision, 96–97
Ontario Hydro, 174–76
  career planning programs, 453
Ontario Occupational Health
  and Safety Act (OHSA)
  employees' responsibilities
    and rights, 669
  employers' responsibilities,
    668
  health and safety
    representatives, 671
  history of, 667
  impact on organizations,
    672–75
  information and record
    keeping, 672
  inspection and enforcement,
    672
  joint health and safety
    committees, 669–71
  provisions of, 667–72
  right to stop work, 671
  supervisors' responsibilities,
    668–69
Ontario Pay Equity Act, 590, 593
Ontario Pension Benefits Act,
  647
Ontario public service (human
  resource planning), 133
Ontario Training Corporation,
  383
Ontario Workers' Health and
  Safety Centre, 683
Operations management jobs, 20
Organizational assessments,
  446–48
Organizational effectiveness, 3,
  136–37

  compensation and, 539–42
Organizational entry, 455, 456
Organized labour, 711
Orientation, 12, 781–82
  anticipatory socialization, 351
  defined, 346
  entry stage, 350–51
  evaluating programs, 363–64
  formal sessions, 359–60
  informal sessions, 360–61
  job analysis and, 191–92
  mutual acceptance stage,
    354–55
  organizational effectiveness
    and, 347–49
  psychological contract,
    354–55
  relation to HRM functions,
    346–47
  Schein's model, 349–56
  as socialization, 346
  socialization stage, 351–54
Ottawa Citizen, The, pay equity
  and, 599–605
Outplacement, 262, 437
Overlap, 57
Overlearning, 397
Overtime, 160

Paired comparison, 493
PAQ, see Position analysis
  questionnaire (PAQ)
Parental leave, 118
Participation rate, 43
  actual vs. projected, 56
  age trends, 48
  defined, 44
  employment/population
    ration, 50
  female, 47
  male, 48
  overall growth, 48–49
  recent trends in, 45–47
Part-time worker(s), 50–52
  defined, 50
  involuntary, 51
  work sharing, 51
Pattern bargaining, 616
Pay, see Compensation
Pay differentials, 539
Pay equity
  vs. equal pay for work of
    equal value, 583

major provisions of in Canada, 584–89
Ontario Pay Equity Act, 590, 593
proportional value method, 593
Royal Bank of Canada and, 591–92
Pay Equity Guide, 590
Pay equity legislation, 5, 23
Pay equity plan, 590–94
Pay for knowledge rewards, 64
Pay for performance, 570–72
Pay for time not worked, 623
Pay grades, 569
Pay policy line, 569
Pay range, 568
Pay structure (pricing), 564–69
Pay surveys, 546–53
　average wage rate, 553
　choosing method, 549
　federal government, 552
　major, 551–53
　questionnaires, 550
　using information from, 553
PC 1003, 714
Peer evaluation, 494–95
Peer nomination, 495
Peer ranking, 494
Peer ratings, 494
Pension Benefits Standards Act, 633
Pension plans, 623, 627–29, *see also* Benefits
　private, 632–34
　vested vs. nonvested, 633
Performance
　analyzing problems, 385–87
　defined, 55
　effort and, 58–61
　relation of to turnover, 73
　skills and, 56–58
Performance appraisal, 6, 13, 783, *see also* Performance appraisal methods; Performance appraisal systems
　administrative purpose, 479
　attribution theory, 512
　defined, 477
　employee development and, 479–80
　evaluator resistance, 509
　formal vs. informal, 477

in human resource planning, 138
interviews, 513–20
job analysis and, 192
monitoring and assessment, 480
purposes of, 478–80
relation to other HRM functions, 481–82
training and development and, 380
using, 484
Performance appraisal data
　discrimination and, 521
　for program assessment, 520
Performance appraisal interviews, 513–20
　developmental action program (DAP), 513
　interviewer behaviour and, 519–20
　maintenance action program (MAP), 513
　preparing for, 513–14
　problem solving approach, 514–16
　remedial action program (RAP), 514
　role of manager, 517
　tell and listen, 514–16
　tell and sell, 514–16
Performance appraisal methods
　behavioural checklist, 496–97
　behaviourally anchored rating scales, 499–502
　essay method, 489
　field review, 495–96
　forced distribution, 494
　graphic rating scales, 489–90
　job results indices, 487–89
　management by objectives (MBO), 502–505
　mixed standard scales, 490–92
　peer evaluation, 494–95
　ranking, 492–94
　team-style peer review, 505–506
Performance appraisal systems, 477
　at CIBC, 477–78
　criteria for evaluation, 483–84
　designing, 482
　fairness, 486
　impact, 486

implementing, 509–513
practicality, 486
raters in, 511
rater training, 511–13
reliability, 484
validity, 485–86
Performance development and review (PD&R) system, 480
Corning, Inc. and, 509
Performance → reward relationship, 61
Perquisites, 639
Personality tests, 314–15
Personnel Association of Ontario, 6
Personnel audit, 170–72
Perspectives on Labour and Income, 41
Pipe, P., 385, 386
Placement, 287
Plant-wide pay systems, 577–80
Point method, job evaluation, 560–63
Policy-capturing method, job evaluation, 564
Porter-Lawler model, 55, 65
Position, 186
Position analysis questionnaire (PAQ), 206–209
　job evaluation and, 556
Positive learning, 397
Positive reinforcers, 392
Posting and bidding, 251–52
Practice
　automaticity, 395
　defined, 393–94
　distributed, 395
　massed, 395
　whole vs. part question, 395
Predictor variables, 152, 290
Pricing the pay structure, 654–69
Private employment agencies, 261–62
Private pension plans, *see* Pension plans, private
Problem solving approach (appraisal interviews), 514–16
Productivity
　defined, 160
　labour shortages and, 160–61
Professional meetings, 260
Professional organizations, 21–22

Profit–sharing plans (rewards), 64, 577
  deferred, 637
  at Ipsco Inc., 579
Programmed instruction, 404
Projections
  human resource supply, 141, 143–48, 156–58
  labour force, 44–45
  Markov analysis, 148
Proportional value method, pay equity, 593
Proprioceptive feedback, 390
P → R relationship, see Performance → reward relationship
PSSRA, see Public Service Staff Relations Act (PSSRA)
Psychological contract, 354–55
  employee relations and, 728
Psychomotor tests, 312, 390
Public employment agencies, 260–61
Public Service Staff Relations Act (PSSRA), 714

Quad Graphics, 788–90
Quality of working life (QWL) programs, 27, 748–50
  absenteeism and, 70
  career planning and, 438
  labour relations and, 747–48
Quebec Pension Plan, 623, 627, 628
Questionnaires
  job analysis and, 205–210
  job satisfaction, 66
  multi-method job design questionnaire, 210
  for pay surveys, 550
  position analysis questionnaires, 206–209
  recent methods, 209–210
  in unit forecasting, 152, 153
  VERJAS, 204, 209
Quinan Stores, 273–74
QWL programs, see Quality of working life (QWL) programs

Rand formula, 725
Ranking
  job evaluation and, 557
  methods of, 492–94

RAP, see Remedial action program (RAP)
Ratio of exchange, 59
  compensation and, 554
  equitable vs. inequitable, 59
RBO, see Relationships by objectives (RBO) programs
RCMP, recruitment plan of, 249
Realistic job previews (RJPs), 349
  defined, 357
Reasonable cause clauses, 99
Records, 92
Recruiting, 12, 63, 781–82
  activities, 240
  advertising, 253–56
  business strategy and, 243
  co-op programs, 259
  cost and time restraints, 248–51
  cost effectiveness, 264
  development-oriented approaches, 264
  effectiveness, 264–66
  effect of employment equity, 244
  employee referral, 252–53
  evaluating the effort, 241–42
  executive search firms, 262–63
  external vs. internal, 236, 242
  human resource planning, 138, 139
  indices for evaluating, 267
  job analysis and, 191
  labour market conditions and, 244–47
  legal requirements, 248
  methods and sources (summary), 265–66
  new methods, 263
  organizational characteristics, 242–43
  outplacement, 262
  plans, 240
  posting and bidding, 251–52
  private employment agencies, 261–62
  professional meetings, 260
  public employment agencies, 260–61
  relation to other HRM functions, 238
  relocation of workers, 245

  role of, 237–38
  secondary labour force, 246–47
  skill inventories, 252
  special events, 256–57
  stage of growth of organization and, 243
  technical and trade schools, 257
  temporary employment agencies, 263, 281
  temporary workers, 247, 263
  type of labour and, 243
  union hiring halls, 253
  universities and colleges, 257–60
  walk-ins, 253
  yield ratios, 264
Recruiting messages, 241
Recruiting plans, 240
Recruitment advertisement, example, 255
Red Maple Foods, 83–85
Redundancy planning, 53
Registered retirement savings plans (RRSPs), 632
Regression analysis, 152, 155
Reinforcement, 392–93
Reinforcement schedules, 392–93
Relationships by objectives (RBO) programs, 748
Reliability coefficients, 292, 294–95
Reliability, of performance appraisals, 484–85
Relocation of workers, 245
Remedial action program (RAP), 514
Repap Enterprises, 372–74
Representation vote, 735
Retirement
  mandatory, 75, 94
  reasons for, 76
Reverse discrimination, 109
Rewards, 59
  absenteeism and, 70
  contingency based, 64
  equity theory, 59
  gain sharing, 64
  intrinsic vs. extrinsic, 55, 63–64
  pay for knowledge, 64
  profit-sharing plans, 64

ratio of exchange, 59
small-group incentives, 64
stock purchasing, 64
Rights arbitration, 745
Right to stop work, 671
RJPs, *see* Realistic job previews (RJPs)
Role perceptions, 61–62
Role play, 409–410
Rorschach inkblot test, 314, 315
Ross, Steve, 302
Royal Bank of Canada, pay equity, 591
RRSPs, *see* Registered retirement savings plans (RRSP)
Rules of thumb, 151–52

Safety programs, *see* Employee health and safety, safety training programs
Saillant, Claude, 133
Salaries, 539
Satisfaction, *see* Job satisfaction
SBUs, *see* Strategic business units (SBUs)
Scenarios, 154–55
Schein's career anchors, 442–43
Schein's socialization model, 349–56
  acceptance events, 355
  entry stage, 350–51
  mutual acceptance stage, 354–56
  socialization stage, 351–54
Secondary labour force, 246–47
Sectoral labour–management co-operation, 753–54
Selection, 12, 781, *see also* Selection instruments
  ability tests, 283
  application form, 283
  aptitude tests, 283
  assessment centres, 322
  background and reference checks, 283, 317–18
  basic rate of success, 286
  construct validity, 297–98
  content validity, 298
  correlation coefficients, 291–92
  criterion measures, 290
  criterion-related validity, 295–97

defined, 281
employment interview, 283
false positive and false negative errors, 288, 289
final interview, 283
high-ability employees, 287
high vs. low hit, 288
in human resource planning, 138, 284–85
interest inventories, 283
job analysis and, 191, 285
job-sample tests, 298
managerial talent, 321–22
minimum qualification hiring procedures, 287
outcomes of decision, 288
personality tests, 283
physical examinations, 284
placement, 287
process, 281–84
rank-ordering candidates, 287
reducing costs and errors, 288–89
relation to HRM functions, 285
reliability coefficients, 294–95
screening, 283
tacit knowledge, 322
team members, 284
utility of, 323–25
validating predictors, 289–90
validation process, 290–95
validity, 290
validity coefficients, 292
Selection instruments, *see also* Employment interviews; Tests
  AIDS testing, 320
  application forms, 299
  background and reference checks, 283, 317–18
  biographical inventory blank, 300
  drug testing, 319–20
  employment interviews, 304–311
  horizontal percent method, 299–301
  inter-rater reliability, 305
  job tryouts, 320–21
  physical examinations, 318–20
  rater errors, 305
  tests, 311–16

weighted application blank, 299
Selection ratio, 323
Self-directed work team (SDWT), 498
Self-paced training programs, 399–400
Self-report personality test, 314
Seminars, 401
Sensitivity method, 411
Severity, 485–86
Sexual harassment, 97–98, 122–24
  as defined in Human Rights Act, 129
  Petro-Canada policy on, 129
  training and development and, 376
Shaping, 392
Shell Canada, salary progression and, 605–608
Shortage, *see* Labour shortage
Simpson, Jane, 344
Situation-determined changes, 212
Skill-based systems (compensation), 542, 596–97
Skill inventories, 252
Skills, 58
Small-group incentives, 64
Smoking, 693
Socialization, 346
  anticipatory, 351
  Schein's model, 349–56
  tasks of, 351–54
Specific vocational preparation (SVP) rating, 201
Staffing, 7
Staffing strategy, 10
Statistics Canada
  definitions of labour force terms, 42–43
  labour force data, 41
Statistics sources, 41
Status quo, planning for, 149–51
Statutory school leaving age, 112–13
Stewards, 725, 743
St. Jude's Hospital, 223
Stochastic models (analysis of human resource flows), 146
Stock options, 639
Stock purchase rewards, 64
Straight ranking, 493

Strategic business units (SBUs), 478
Strategic human resource analysis, 7–10, 137–38
Stress management training, 376
Strictness, 485–86
Strikes, 741
Strong vocational interest blank, 315
Succession planning, 134, 151
Sunnybrook Hospital, 328–29
Superannuation, 623
Supervisor, role of in career planning, 457–59
Supply Unlimited, 538–39
Support jobs, 18
Surplus, *see* Labour surplus
SVP rating, *see* Specific vocational preparation (SVP) rating
Systematic discrimination, 96

Tacit knowledge, 322
Targeted interviewing, 308
Target positions, 442
Task Force on Employment-Related Drug Screening, 694–95
Tasks, 189
TAT, *see* Thematic apperception test (TAT)
TEAM, 478
Team-style peer review, 505–506
Technical conferences, 200
Technical jobs, 18
Technology
 and HRM, 23
 training and development, 376
Tell and listen approach, 514–16
Tell and sell approach, 514–16
Temporary employment agencies, 263, 281
Temporary workers, 247, 263
Term insurance, 636
Tests, 311–16
 cognitive ability, 311–12
 interest inventories, 315–16
 job-sample, 312–13
 job-simulation exercises, 313
 language, 314
 mechanical comprehension, 312

Miner sentence completion scale, 314
personality, 314–15
projection techniques, 314
psychomotor, 312
Rorschach inkblot, 314, 315
selecting and evaluating, 316
self-report personality, 314
thematic apperception test (TAT)
validity generalization, 312
Texas Instruments, 356
T-group method, 411
Thematic apperception test (TAT), 314
Thorndike, E.L., 392
Tibbs, Ruth, 461
Time-and-motion studies, 189
Time-determined changes (validity), 211–12
Total wellness and zero accident program (Mazda), 659–60
Townsend, Robert, 460
Trade unions, *see* Unions
Traditional career paths, 450, 451
Trainee(s)
 ability level, 398–99
 characteristics, 398–400
 number of, 398
Trainers, 414
Training and development, 4, 12–13, 63, 782, *see also* Training programs
 analyzing performance problems, 385–87
 apprenticeship training, 408
 attitude change, 390–91, 409–411
 behaviour modelling, 410
 business games, 412–13
 case method, 411
 coaching method, 398, 408–409
 computer-assisted instruction, 404–405
 Conference Board of Canada study, 382–83
 conference/discussion method, 409
 criterion–referenced approach, 399
 Crosby quality program, 378
 decision making, 391, 411–13

feedback, 391–92
films and videotapes, 404
growth of, 374–77
in human resource planning, 138
identifying needs, 384–85
in-basket technique, 412
information acquisition, 390, 401–405
innovation and, 378
interactive videodisk instruction, 405
internships, 413
interpersonal skills, 390–91, 409–411
job analysis and, 192
job instruction, 407
job rotation, 413
key learning principles, 391–98
lectures, 401
line management and, 383
motivation, 396
motor skills, 390
needless, 383
organizational strategy and, 377–80
performance appraisals and, 380
practice, 393–95
problem solving, 391
programmed instruction, 404
proprioceptive feedback, 390
reinforcement, 392–93
relation to HRM functions, 380–82
responsibilities for, 382–83
role of government in, 376–77
role play method, 409–410
seminars, 401
sensitivity training, 411
specifying objectives, 387–88
T-group method, 411
transfer of learning, 396–98, 404
vestibule training, 407–408
video systems, 409
Training programs, *see also* Training and development
 BC Hydro example, 388
 choosing, 388
 content of, 389–91
 cost factors, 400
 evaluating, 419–21

implementing, 413–14
in-house vs. outside organization, 388
prepackaged, 388
self-paced, 399–400
Training rooms, 414
Training survey, 414–18
Transfer of learning, 396–98
 overlearning, 397
 positive vs. negative, 396
 programmed instruction and, 404
Transition matrix, 147
Turnover
 absenteeism and, 73–74
 benefits of, 72–73
 compensation and, 540
 costs of, 72
 defined, 70
 involuntary, 70
 job satisfaction and, 65
 relation of performance to, 73
 voluntary, 70
Turnover rate, 40, 72
 orientation and, 348

UAW, *see* United Auto Workers (UAW)
UI, *see* Unemployment insurance (UI)
Unemployment, 43
Unemployment Insurance Act, 630
Unemployment insurance (UI), 92, 629–31
 supplementary coverage, 631
Unemployment rate, 40, 41, 43
Union hiring halls, 253
Unionization
 job satisfaction and, 65
 management responses to, 735–40
 reasons for, 728–32
Union organizing process
 bargaining unit, 734–35
 certification, 734
 membership campaign, 732–34
 process initiation, 732
 representation vote, 735
Unions, 4–5, 65, *see also* Collective bargaining; Labour relations
 closed shop agreements, 725
 collective agreements, 710
 collective bargaining, 711
 craft, 726
 defined, 710–11
 employee health and safety, 665
 flexible benefit programs and, 644
 goals of, 722–23
 grievances, 711
 industrial, 726
 international, 726–27
 job analysis and, 193–94
 local, 723–26
 management and, 133
 member dissatisfaction, 746–47
 members' interest in, 725
 national, 726–27
 public sector, 716
 Rand formula, 725
 support of for New Democratic Party, 723
 trade, 710
 union shop agreements, 725
United Auto Workers (UAW), 596
Unit forecasting, 152–53
Universal benefits, 623, 625
Universal factors, 560
Untimely death, 623
Utility
 defined, 323
 of selection, 323–25

Vacation pay, 117, 636, 638–39
Validation, 290
Validity
 background/reference checks and, 318
 concurrent, 297
 construct, 297–98
 content, 298, 485
 criterion-related, 295–97
 differential, 316
 error of central tendency, 485
 face, 313
 halo effect, 485
 job analysis methods, 211–13
 of performance appraisals, 485–86
 predictive, 297
 selection, 290
 severity and, 485–86
Validity coefficients, 291, 292
Validity generalization, 312
Variable ratio reinforcement schedule, 393
VERJAS, *see* Versatile job analysis system (VERJAS)
Versatile job analysis system (VERJAS), 204–210
Vestibule training, 407–408
Video systems (training aid), 409
Vision 2000, 428
Voice system, 746
Voluntary turnover, 70

WAB, *see* Weighted application blank (WAB)
Wages, *see also* Compensation
 average rate, 553
 in Canada, 595–96
 defined, 539
 minimum, 113–14
 recovery of unpaid, 119
Wagner Act, 713
Wagner, Robert, 713
Walker, James W., 132, 133
Walk-ins, 252
Warner-Lambert Canada Inc., 452–53
Weekly rest days, 116
Weighted application blank (WAB), 299–301
Wellness programs, 49, 376
Westfield Construction Company, 466–68
White, Julie, 759
Wiklow, Jan, 365
Williams, Rob, 709–710
Women, *see also* Discrimination; Pay equity
 career blockage, 437–38
 equal pay for, 114–15
 interviews and, 310
 job evaluation and, 566–67
 job satisfaction, 439
 labour force participation rates, 47, 767
Wood, Elaine Ide, 352
Woolco department stores, 122–24
Work behaviour, 55–74
 disciplinary sanctions, 67, 68, 69
 effect of co-workers on, 63
 encouraging desired, 67

Workers' compensation, 629, 675–76, *see also* Employee health and safety
    steps in response to claim, 676
Work hours, 115–16

Worklink, 60
Work methods analysis, 199
Workplace health and safety, *see* Employee health and safety

Work sharing, 51
Wyatt Company, 140

Yield ratio, 264

TO THE OWNER OF THIS BOOK:

We are interested in your reaction to the third edition of *Human Resource Management in Canada*, by Thomas H. Stone and Noah M. Meltz. With your comments, we can improve this book in future editions. Please help us by completing this questionnaire.

1. What was your reason for using this book?
    _____university course
    _____college course
    _____continuing education course
    _____professional development
    _____personal interest
    _____other (please specify)

2. If you are a student, please identify your school and course. If you used this text for a program, what was the name of that program?

3. Approximately how much of the book did you use?
   _____all _____ 3/4 _____ 1/2 _____ 1/4

4. Which chapters or sections were omitted from your course?

5. What is the best aspect of this book?

6. Is there anything that should be added?

7. Was the integrated video package used as part of your course? If yes, did you find the videos current and interesting?

8. Were the HRM in Action feature boxes of interest to you?

9. Was the information in this text presented in an interesting manner?

10. Please add any comments or suggestions.

(fold here and tape shut)

Business Reply Mail

No Postage Stamp
Necessary if Mailed
in Canada

POSTAGE WILL BE PAID BY

Scott Duncan
Editorial Director
DRYDEN CANADA
55 Horner Avenue
Toronto, Ontario
M8Z 9Z9

43652